Invitation to
the Life Span

Invitation to the Life Span

third edition

Kathleen Stassen Berger

Bronx Community College
City University of New York

worth publishers
Macmillan Learning
New York

Publisher: Rachel Losh

Associate Publisher: Jessica Bayne

Developmental Editor: Andrea Musick Page

Editorial Assistant: Melissa Rostek

Executive Marketing Manager: Katherine Nurre

Executive Media Editor: Rachel Comerford

Media Editor: Laura Burden

Media Producer: Joe Tomasso

Director, Content Management Enhancement: Tracey Kuehn

Managing Editor: Lisa Kinne

Project Manager: Betsy Draper, MPS North America LLC

Cover and Interior Design: Blake Logan

Permissions Manager: Jennifer MacMillan

Photo Editor: Sheena Goldstein

Photo Researcher: Rona Tuccillo

Art Manager: Matthew McAdams

Illustrations: Todd Buck Illustrations, MPS Ltd., Evelyn Pence, Charles Yuen

Photographic design motif: Vicky Drosos/Ikon Images/Getty Images

Production Manager: Stacey Alexander

Composition: MPS Ltd.

Printing and Binding: LSC Communications

Cover Photograph: Dan Dalton/Photodisc/Getty Images

Library of Congress Control Number: 2015955511

ISBN-13: 978-1-319-01588-6

ISBN-10: 1-319-01588-3

Printed in the United States of America

Second printing

Worth Publishers

One New York Plaza

Suite 4500

New York, NY 10004-1562

www.worthpublishers.com

Brief Contents

About the Author

Kathleen Stassen Berger received her undergraduate education at Stanford University and Radcliffe College, and then she earned an MAT from Harvard University and an MS and PhD from Yeshiva University. Her broad experience as an educator includes directing a preschool, serving as chair of philosophy at the United Nations International School, and teaching child and adolescent development to graduate students at Fordham University in New York and undergraduates at Montclair State University in New Jersey and Quinnipiac University in Connecticut. She also taught social psychology to inmates at Sing Sing Prison who were earning their paralegal degrees.

Currently, Berger is a professor at Bronx Community College of the City University of New York, as she has been for most of her professional career. She began there as an adjunct in English and for the past decades has been a full professor in the Social Sciences Department, which includes sociology, economics, anthropology, political science, human services, and psychology. She has taught introduction to psychology, child and adolescent development, adulthood and aging, social psychology, abnormal psychology, and human motivation. Her students—who come from many ethnic, economic, and educational backgrounds and who have a wide range of ages and interests— consistently honor her with the highest teaching evaluations.

Berger is also the author of *The Developing Person Through the Life Span* and *The Developing Person Through Childhood and Adolescence*. Her developmental texts are currently being used at more than 700 colleges and universities worldwide and are available in Spanish, French, Italian, and Portuguese, as well as English. Her research interests include adolescent identity, immigration, bullying, and grandparents, and she has published articles on developmental topics in the *Wiley Encyclopedia of Psychology* and in publications of American Association for Higher Education and the National Education Association for Higher Education. She continues teaching and learning from students as well as from her four daughters and three grandsons.

Detailed Contents

© 2016 MACMILLAN

© 2016 MACMILLAN

Part Three: Early Childhood   161

CLAUDIA DEWALD/GETTY IMAGES

Part Four: Middle Childhood   237

WMAY/GETTY IMAGES

© 2016 MACMILLAN

ROBIN SKJOLDBORG/GETTY IMAGES

Part Seven: Late Adulthood 501

© ALENA BROZOVAAGE FOTOSTOCK

NANCY RICA SCHIFF/SUPERSTOCK

Preface

My grandson, Asa, is in early childhood. He sees the world in opposites: male/female, child/grown-up, good guys/bad guys. He considers himself one of the good guys, destroying the bad guys in his active imagination with karate kicks in the air.

Oscar, his father, knows better. He asked me whether Asa really believes there are good guys and bad guys, or is that just an expression. I said that most young children think in simple opposites.

Undeterred, Oscar told Asa that he knows some adults who were once bad guys but became good guys.

"No," Asa insisted. "That never happens."

Asa is mistaken. As he matures, his body will grow taller and become better able to sit with feet on the floor, not kicking. His thoughts will include the idea that people change as they grow older, a theme throughout this book. What Asa says "never happens" occurs every day—not that any of us is always a bad guy or a good guy, but that all of us keep developing, ideally for the better.

Oscar is not alone in his awareness. Many folk sayings affirm development: People "turn over a new leaf," are "born again"; parents are granted a "do-over" when they become grandparents; today is "the first day of the rest of your life." We recognize that the past never disappears and that parents always influence children, as in the saying "The apple does not fall far from the tree." But we also recognize many other genetic, biological, and social influences on each person, as detailed in the best-selling book *Far from the Tree* (Solomon, 2012).

Complexity, twists and turns, dynamic unfolding, and endless variety of the human experience throughout life is fascinating to me, which is why I continue to study development and revise this textbook. The study itself is dynamic: New insights, new phrases, and new topics appear in every edition, and old topics require revision.

We all have echoes of Asa in us: We want life to be simple. Some aspects of development do not change—birth, death, families, attachment—and some old theories and perspectives are still insightful. They are detailed in this text. But life is not simple or stagnant. Learning about human development helps everyone respond to life's variations and influences, not with imaginary kicks but with wisdom.

Education occurs in many ways. This textbook is only one of them, an aid to understanding the complexity of your life, my life, and the lives of all the estimated 20 billion humans who are either alive now or once lived. Nonetheless, although life experiences and thousands of other books add to our education, writing this text is my contribution and studying it is one of yours: Together we might learn how to limit the bad and increase the good in each of us as time goes on.

© 2016 MACMILLAN

Pondering My grandson, Asa, looks thoughtfully at his father, Oscar.

New Material

Every year, scientists discover and explain more concepts and research. The best of these are integrated into the text, with hundreds of new references on many topics, including epigenetics at conception, prenatal protections, infant nutrition,

FUSE/GETTY IMAGES

Healthy? Children have high energy but small stomachs, so they enjoy frequent snacks more than big meals. Yet snacks are typically poor sources of nutrition.

autism spectrum disorder, attachment over the life span, high-stakes testing, drug use and drug addiction, sex education, and diversity of all kinds—ethnic, economic, and cultural. Cognizant of the interdisciplinary nature of human development, I include recent research in biology, sociology, education, anthropology, political science, and more—as well as my home discipline, psychology.

Genetics and social contexts are noted throughout. The interaction of nature and nurture are discussed in many chapters, as neuroscience relates to research on family life. Among the many topics described with new research are the variations, benefits, and hazards of breast-feeding, infant day care, preschool education, single parenthood, exercise, vaccination, same-sex marriage—always noting differences, deficits, and resilience.

Renewed Emphasis on Critical Thinking in the Pedagogical Program

We all need to be critical thinkers. Virtually every page of this book presents not only facts but also questions. A new marginal feature, *Think Critically,* encourages student reflection and analysis. There are no pat answers to these questions: They could be used to start a class discussion or begin a long essay.

Every chapter begins with a few *What Will You Know?* questions, one for every major heading. Of course, much of what readers will learn will be reflected in new attitudes and perspectives—hard to quantify. But these *What Will You Know?* questions are intended to be provocative and to pose issues that the students will remember for decades.

In addition, after every major section, *What Have You Learned?* questions appear. They are designed to help students review what they have just read, a pedagogical technique proven to help retention. Ideally, students will answer the learning objective questions in sentences, with specifics that demonstrate knowledge.

Some items on the new lists are straightforward, requiring only close attention to the chapter content. Others require comparisons, implications, or evaluations. Key terms are indicated with bold print and are defined in the margins as well as the glossary, because expanded vocabulary aids expanded understanding. To help students become better observers, occasional "observation quizzes" accompany a photo or figure. The hope is that students will learn to look closely at life around them.

As a professor myself, I continue to seek ways to deepen knowledge. Cognitive psychology and research on pedagogy finds that vocabulary, specific knowledge, attention to experience, and critical thinking are all part of learning. This book and these features are designed to foster all four.

Updated Features: *Opposing Perspectives,* *A View from Science,* and *A Case to Study*

Special topics and new research abound in life-span development. This edition of *Invitation to the Life Span* includes three boxed features in every chapter. *Opposing Perspectives* focuses on controversial topics—from prenatal sex selection to e-cigarettes. Information and opinions on both sides of each issue are presented, so students can weigh evidence, assess arguments, and reach their own conclusions while appreciating that an opposite conclusion also has merit. *A View from Science* explains recent scientific research in more detail, illustrating the benefits of the scientific method for a specific issue. *A Case to Study* focuses on particular individuals, helping students to identify the personal implications of what they learn.

Visualizing Development

Information is sometimes better understood visually and graphically. Carefully chosen, updated photos and figures appear on almost every page to accomplish this, with, as always, captions that explain and increase knowledge. In addition, every chapter of this new edition includes a full-page illustration of a topic in development.

These infographics explain key concepts, from brain development to marriage rates, often with data that encourage students to think of other nations, other cultures, other times. My three awesome editors and I have worked closely with noted designer Charles Yuen to create these infographics, hoping they reinforce key ideas.

Open Wide Synchrony is evident worldwide. It is not easy for parents—notice this father's neck muscles—but it is a joy for both partners.

New Online Data Connections Activities

Understanding how scientists use data helps students realize that the study of human development is not just a matter of personal experience and common sense, but goes far beyond that—sometimes contradicting old myths and pat conclusions. This edition includes interactive activities to allow students to interpret data on topics ranging from breast-feeding to risk taking.

For example, students discover how rates of smoking differ by gender or age during adolescence, which probably is not what they think. These interactive activities will make students more engaged and active learners, while deepening their understanding of the importance of quantitative data. Instructors can assign these activities in the online LaunchPad that accompanies this book.

New Integration with LaunchPad

Throughout the book, the margins include LaunchPad call-outs to online videos about either people in a particular context or key scientists who might become role models. For example, Susan Beal, the Australian scientist who revolutionized our understanding of SIDS (sudden infant death syndrome) and infant sleep position, saving millions of babies, is shown to be a person with whom many students can identify.

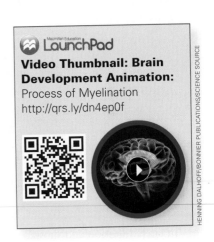

Video Thumbnail: Brain Development Animation: Process of Myelination
http://qrs.ly/dn4ep0f

Child Development and Nursing Career Correlation Guides

Many students taking this course hope to become nurses or early-childhood educators. This book and accompanying testing material are fully correlated to the NAEYC (National Association for the Education of Young Children) career preparation goals and the NCLEX (nursing) licensure exam. These two supplements are available in this book's accompanying online LaunchPad.

New Research Throughout

Life-span development, like all sciences, builds on past learning. Many facts and concepts are scaffolds that continue to foster learning: stages and ages, norms and variations, dangers and diversities, classic theories and fascinating applications. However, discoveries and experiences, current crises, and new research continue to change how developmentalists describe development. No paragraph in this edition is exactly what it was in the first or second edition.

Especially to help professors who taught with the earlier texts, or students who have friends who took the course a few years ago, highlights of updates in the text appear below.

Chapter 1

- New *A View from Science: Are Children Too Overweight?*

- In the section *The Historical Context,* a new discussion of how public perception of marijuana use illustrates the impact of cohort on attitudes and behavior. A new figure shows how support for marijuana legislation has changed over the years.

- New U.S. poverty data in the section *The Socioeconomic Context.*

- New figure on the Gini index, which measures income equality.

- Discussion of gender differences and neurosexism added to illustrate the difference-equals-deficit error.

- New *Visualizing Development: Diverse Complexities,* which shows regional and age differences in ethnicity in the United States.

- New figure depicting neurogenesis added to *Development Is Plastic.*

- The story of David, the author's nephew, is now the subject of *A Case to Study.*

- New two-page infographic: *Highlights of the Science of Human Development.*

- New discussion of how evolutionary theory offers explanations for many human phenomena, such as morning sickness, toddlers' attachment to parents, and adolescent rebellion.

- New example illustrating the experiment: Do summer jobs prevent juvenile delinquency?

- Discussion of e-cigarette use to show how longitudinal research is needed to determine whether certain substances are harmful. Hydrofracking and e-waste are mentioned as well.

- New examples of cross-sequential research: self-esteem in late adulthood and substance use disorder.

- New example of correlation: U.S. counties with more dentists have fewer obese residents.

- The recent Ebola epidemic used to illustrate ethical dilemmas researchers must navigate.

Chapter 2

- New chapter-opening narrative about my daughter giving birth to her second child.

- Ebola as it relates to genetic diversity.

- Additional discussion of how similar the human genetic code is to that of other animals.

- Discussion of HapMap research omitted and replaced with specific examples of how subtle differences in alleles can have both minor and major effects (e.g., apoE2 versus apoE4 and BRAC1 versus BRAC2).

- In the section *Twins,* new mention of older mothers and vanishing twins.

- New discussion of epigenetics, including type 2 diabetes, drug use, and loneliness.

- New mention of IVF and stem cells analyzed for disease.

- Additional discussion of ethical ramifications of resuscitating a non-breathing, extremely preterm infant.

- New photo of fetus at 27 weeks post-conception.

- New discussion of World Health Organization recommendations and statistics regarding c-sections, as well as an updated figure.

- Huntington's disease discussed more thoroughly in *Gene Disorders.*

- Table describing the effects and prevention of teratogens has been omitted and now comprises an interactive Data Connections activity, available in the online LaunchPad.

- The figure *Critical Periods in Human Development* has been heavily revised with more realistic anatomical art.

- New discussion of the importance of careful consultation with doctors about herbal medicine, over-the-counter medications, and psychoactive drug use.

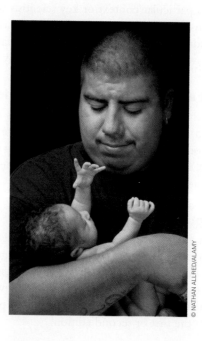

Mutual Joy Ignore this dad's tattoo and earring, and the newborn's head wet with amniotic fluid. Instead recognize that, for thousands of years, hormones and instincts propel fathers and babies to reach out to each other, developing lifelong connections.

© NATHAN ALLRED/ALAMY

- New discussion of how some states are enacting laws that incarcerate pregnant women for using alcohol and drugs while pregnant.
- New *A View from Science: Conflicting Advice.*
- New section *Prenatal Testing* discusses false positives and how early pregnancy testing can cause undue anxiety.
- New *A Case to Study: False Positives and False Negatives.*

Chapter 3
- Failure to thrive discussed as part of explanation of percentile rankings.
- Updated discussion of sleep moved ahead of brain development.
- In the section on the senses, new 3D image of parts of brain where hearing occurs.
- New discussion of infant reflexes.
- New discussion on cross-modal perception and synesthesia in infants.
- New *A Case to Study: Scientist at Work,* on Susan Beal's research on SIDS.
- New *A View from Science: From Breast to Formula and Back* explores historical and cultural trends in breast- and formula-feeding.
- A-not-B error, as well as research of Renee Baillargeon, added to my explanation of Piaget's object permanence experiment.
- fNIRS (functional near infrared spectroscopy) added to the list (and illustration) of techniques used by neuroscientists to understand brain function.
- Revised and expanded discussion of information-processing theory.
- New discussion of mean length of utterance (MLU) as a measure of a child's language progress.
- New research on cultural differences in what sounds infants prefer.
- New coverage of bilingualism in babies.

Chapter 4
- New chapter-opening narrative illustrating caregiver–infant interaction with an exchange between two of my daughters and my newest grandson.
- Expanded discussion of infants' experience of fear.
- Section on brain growth significantly revised; now includes discussion of cultural differences encoded in the brain, developing social awareness, and early caregiving and cortisol.
- New *Opposing Perspectives: Mothers or Genes?,* which explores whether temperament can change.

- Heavily revised *Visualizing Development: Developing Attachment.*
- Discussion of allocare moved to discussion of fathers' role in child-rearing.
- New *A Case to Study: Can We Bear This Commitment?* recounts the dramatic experience of my friend, illustrating attachment between parents and their children.
- New example of how parents can help their young children express emotions in positive ways.
- New sections on humanism and evolutionary theories and infant psychosocial development.
- Section on infant day care now focuses on North America, Norway, and Australia; includes new *A View from Science: The Mixed Realities of Center Day Care.*

Chapter 5
- New chapter-opening narrative, my memory of trying to fly at age 4.
- New research on nutrition, including long-term effects of childhood obesity.
- Condensed section on food allergies; the just-right phenomenon omitted.
- Sections on environmental hazards, injury, and prevention moved to Chapter 6.
- New brain scan image showing myelination.
- New *A Case to Study: Stones in the Belly* illustrates pre-operational cognition.
- Expanded discussion of overimitation.
- New *A View from Science: Witness to a Crime,* regarding children's eyewitness testimony.
- Recent research on the naming explosion and fast-mapping.
- New *Opposing Perspectives: Culture, Child-Centered Versus Teacher-Directed,* comparing child-centered and teacher-directed approaches to early-childhood education.
- New *Visualizing Development: Early-Childhood Schooling.*
- New figure of longitudinal data on the Abecedarian Project.

Chapter 6
- New mention of effortful control.
- Addition of the marshmallow test to illustrate self-control and emotional regulation.
- New discussion on how and when to praise children.
- Elaborated debate about whether play is essential for healthy development.
- New discussion of pretend play versus social play.

Joy Supreme Pretend play in early childhood is thrilling and powerful. For this 7-year-old from Park Slope, Brooklyn, pretend play overwhelms mundane realities, such as an odd scarf or awkward arm.

© 2016 MACMILLAN

- New *Visualizing Development: Less Play, Less Safe?*
- New discussion of screen time and a figure showing daily screen time for U.S. children.
- New *A View from Science: Culture and Parenting Style,* using Mexican American mothers to show that parenting style is more fluid than previously thought.
- Behaviorism, cognitive theory, humanism, and evolutionary theories of gender development now separated into discrete sections.
- Prosocial and antisocial behavior condensed; aggression expanded.
- New discussion of cultural, regional, socioeconomic, and gender differences in spanking among U.S. parents, as well as longitudinal research on children who are physically punished.
- Sections on environmental hazards, injury, and prevention moved from Chapter 5.
- Updated coverage on how maltreatment is noticed and defined.
- New research on long-term impact of child maltreatment on development of social skills.

Chapter 7
- New chapter-opening narrative about my friend's son, illustrating the interaction of genes and environment, asking how much parents are to blame for their children's problems.
- New statistics on illness and death rates in middle childhood, as well as on oral health.
- New research on recess and active play, including a comparison of Texas and Japan.
- New research on childhood obesity, including an updated *Visualizing Development: Childhood Obesity Around the Globe.*
- New research on the reduction of asthma in children of Latino parents and caregivers.

- Significantly reorganized section on cognition.
- New example of hierarchical classification.
- Expanded coverage of connections between lobes and regions in children's brains.
- Expanded discussion of international contexts for social interaction and instruction.
- New research regarding estimating math proficiency and knowledge of fractions.
- Discussion of executive processes within section on control processes.
- New *The Maturing Brain* section discusses reaction time and automatization.
- New research on metaphorical understanding and bilingual children.
- Section on bilingual education expanded and brought forward.
- Recent research about arts education.
- Section on international testing revised and expanded.
- New *A Case to Study: Encouraging Child Learning.*
- New comparison of the United States and Finland in discussion of why U.S. students perform poorly on international tests.
- Added section on the ethnic and economic gap in academic performance in the United States.
- New research on attitudes toward the Common Core.
- New figure showing percent of U.S. students in public, private or parochial, and home schools.
- Second-language learning as an example of how policy affects education.
- New section on ethnic diversity in U.S. schools.
- IQ and intelligence testing now opens the *Developmental Psychopathology* section.
- New *Opposing Perspectives: True Grit.*
- Updated coverage of ADHD, psychopathology, intellectual disability, and special education, including new figure on percentage of U.S. children who are or have been medicated for emotional or behavioral difficulties. (All terminology use updated to DSM-5 classifications.)

Chapter 8
- New chapter-opening narrative illustrating social development in middle childhood.
- Reorganized *The Nature of the Child* section.
- Revised section *Self-Concept* includes focus on the importance of social comparison.
- New *Opposing Perspectives: Protect or Puncture Self-Esteem?*
- New examples in *Cumulative Stress* section—child soldiers in Sierra Leone, U.S. children temporarily living

KIDSTOCK/BLEND IMAGES/GETTY IMAGES

Stay Home, Dad The rate of battle deaths for U.S. soldiers is lower for those deployed in Iraq and Afghanistan than for any previous conflict, thanks to modern medicine and armor. However psychological harm from repeated returns and absences is increasing, especially for children.

in homeless shelters, and children exposed to a wildfire in Australia.

- Expanded discussion of parentification, including children who survived Hurricane Katrina.
- New *A View from Science: "I Always Dressed One in Blue Stuff . . .",* which illustrates how siblings raised in the same households do not necessarily share the same environment.
- Revised section on family structure and divorce.
- New *A Case to Study: How Hard Is It to Be a Kid?*
- Updated *Visualizing Development: A Wedding, or Not? Family Structures Around the World.*
- New research on long-term implications for children who have been bullied.
- Reorganized coverage of moral development.

Chapter 9

- New chapter-opening narrative about one of my former students.
- New research on hormones affecting psychopathology in adolescent girls and boys.
- New *Opposing Perspectives: Algebra at 7 A.M.? Get Real!*
- In discussion of secular trends, new example of the heights of various U.S. presidents.
- New discussion of precocious puberty, including possible environmental causes.
- Updated research about stress and puberty.
- Mention of importance of family dinners to adolescent nutrition.
- New data on nutritional deficiencies.

- Discussion of obesity and rates among teenagers in various U.S. states, which introduces section on eating disorders.
- Addition of binge eating disorder, newly recognized in DSM-5.
- Expanded discussion of how immaturity of the prefrontal cortex leads to risk taking, including new research on texting while driving.
- New *A View from Science: The Pleasures of the Adolescent Brain.*
- Addition of three short problems for students to test themselves on intuitive and analytical reasoning.
- Revised *Visualizing Development: Thinking in Adolescence.*
- New *A Case to Study: "What Were You Thinking?"*
- Major section on technology and cognition reorganized and substantially revised under the heading *Digital Natives.*
- New section on sexting.
- New research on declines in school engagement and performance.
- Updated statistics on enrollment in AP classes and college.
- New figure on U.S. high school dropout rates.

Chapter 10

- New chapter-opening narrative about my parenting during adolescence.
- Updated research on political party identification among U.S. adults and their adolescent children.
- New, separate section on ethnic identity featuring anecdote about racial awareness from a U.S. high school senior.
- Enhanced and revised discussion of gender identity, including an explanation of why the DSM-5 describes gender dysphoria, not gender identity disorder.
- New coverage of parent–child conflict, including updated research on parental monitoring.
- New *A Case to Study: An Ignorant Parent—Me!*
- Updated coverage of peer pressure and influence on adolescent decision making.
- New section on social networking among adolescents.
- Section on sexual interactions now comprises *Human Relationships* section.
- New research on sexual activity among adolescents and the impact of parental involvement.
- Revised section on same-sex relationships.

- New coverage of sex education and teenage pregnancy internationally.
- New *A View from Science: Sex Education in School.*
- New coverage of depression in adolescence, including expanded DSM-5 diagnoses.
- Updated research on suicide, suicidal ideation, and parasuicide.
- Updated research on adolescent crime and incarceration rates.
- Updated coverage of teenage drug use. including e-cigarettes and marijuana.
- New *Opposing Perspectives: E-Cigarettes: Path to Addiction or Healthy Choice?*

Chapter 11

- New chapter-opening narrative about my youngest daughter as an emerging adult.
- New *Opposing Perspectives: A Welcome Stage, or Just WEIRD?*
- Section on body development substantially revised; now includes discussion of organ reserve, homeostasis, and allostasis formerly in Chapter 12.
- New discussion of premarital sex and contraception, and fewer single-sex colleges.
- New *A Case to Study: An Adrenaline Junkie.*
- Expanded coverage of alcohol abuse in emerging adulthood.
- New longitudinal data and research on graduation rates, college debt, and salary differences between college grads and non-grads.
- Revised and expanded section on college contexts, including MOOCs and flipped classes.
- Added discussion and research on college and critical thinking.
- New figures comparing problem-solving abilities in many nations.
- Revised section *Identity Achievement,* including new research and examples of changing identity status, employment patterns, and personality development.
- Extensively updated material on dating, cohabitation, and romance in emerging adults; material on friendships and relationships with parents and peers moved forward.

Chapter 12

- Significantly reorganized chapter: Exercise, drug use (including new material on prescription and over-the-counter drug use), and diet begin the chapter. A new section, *Losses and Gains,* now houses the subsections

Smart Farmer; Smart Teacher This school field trip is not to a museum or a fire station but to a wheat field, where children study grains that will become bread. Like this creative teacher, modern farmers use every kind of intelligence. To succeed, they need to analyze soil, fertilizer, and pests (analytic intelligence); to anticipate market prices and food fads (creative intelligence); and to know what crops and seed varieties grow in each acre of their land as they manage their workers (practical intelligence).

on appearance, disease in adulthood (new), and sex and fertility (including the material on hormone decline).
- New figures showing U.S. rates of cigarette smoking and lung cancer.
- New discussion and research on cancer, including new 3D image of cancer cell.
- New data on adult obesity around the world and new material on reducing obesity.
- New research on in vitro fertilization.
- Revised section *The Aging Brain* now includes material on adult intelligence.
- New *A View from Science: Adult IQ.*
- New research showing how education helps people prepare for and survive disasters.
- Section on stress moved to new section *Selecting and Protecting;* includes new material on posttraumatic growth and weathering.
- Updated coverage of the development of expertise in a new, technologically connected era.
- New *A Case to Study: Jenny, Again.*

Chapter 13

- New updates about marital satisfaction, including cross-cultural data and research.
- New material on same-sex marriages around the globe.
- Updated coverage of parenting joys and challenges—including for foster, step, and adoptive parents.
- New section on culture and caregiving, focusing on elder care internationally, including Japan.

- New *Visualizing Development: Caregiving in Adulthood.*
- Discussion of meta-analysis of job loss and adult happiness.
- New material on the challenges of balancing work and family, particularly for families with "nonstandard" work schedules.
- New *A Case to Study: Having It All.*

Chapter 14

- New chapter-opening narrative about a dinner I attended that challenged my assumptions.
- Updated coverage of stereotype threat and ageism.
- New *A View from Science: I'm Not Like Those Other Old People.*
- New figure on rates of exercise among older adults.
- New *Opposing Perspectives: Stop the Clock?*
- Revised section on demographic shift, including new figures depicting demographic pyramids in India and Japan and percentage of population over age 65 in various countries.
- New example of how statistics about Alzheimer's disease are more frightening than reality.
- Reorganized *Theories of Aging* section.
- New *A Case to Study: Should Older Couples Have More Sex?*
- New subsection within *Selective Optimization with Compensation* called *Medical Compensation: Survival,* which includes discussions of primary and secondary aging, compression of morbidity, and heart disease.
- New research on brain aging comparing humans and other primates.
- New discussion on brain plasticity and neurogenesis in adulthood.

Touch Your Toes? This woman can even put both feet behind her neck. Although everyone loses some flexibility with age, daily practice is crucial. Tao Porchon-Lynch has taught yoga for half a century. At age 92, shown here, she can balance on one leg in tree pose, stretch her hamstrings in downward dog, and then relieve any remaining stress in cobra pose.

- New coverage of "mind wandering" in later life.
- New section on brain diseases, with new research, statistics, and DSM-5 diagnostic criteria.

Chapter 15

- New discussion of experiment showing how elders tend to follow their emotions, not logic.
- Expanded discussion of why compulsive hoarding was not considered a psychological disorder until DSM-5.
- New figure showing life expectancy in various countries.
- New paragraph on how past employment sometimes resulted in poverty for women and ethnic minorities.
- Subsection on age stratification moved to end of *Stratification Theories* section; new subsection critiquing stratification theories.
- New figures showing percentage of elders who are employed and percentage of U.S. labor force over age 65.
- New research and discussion of bridge jobs in subsection on retirement.
- New research findings on how retirees stay active, aging in place.
- Updated material on religious involvement and political activism.
- More discussion of challenges of skipped-generation families.
- Updated material on caregiving for fragile elders.
- New *A View from Science: Leave the Bedroom.*
- New *A Case to Study: Family Encouraging Confusion.*

Epilogue

- New chapter-opening vignette illustrating how people deal with grief differently.
- New example of how the Hmong attitudes about autopsies conflict with Minnesota law.
- New research on how adolescents and emerging adults think about death.
- Added mention of legacy work.
- Updated research on hospice and palliative care.
- Updated data on Death with Dignity.
- New coverage of the DSM-5's treatment of the "bereavement exclusion" for grief-related depression.
- Addition of study on Swedish children that illustrates how bereavement can affect mental health.
- New example of Bali terrorist attack to illustrate cultural differences in mourning practices.
- New example of mass shooting in Charleston, South Carolina, to demonstrate how people find meaning in death.

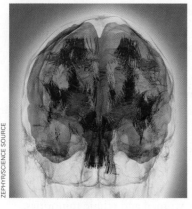

ZEPHYR/SCIENCE SOURCE

Mental Coordination? This brain scan of a 38-year-old depicts areas of myelination (the various colors) within the brain. As you see, the two hemispheres are quite similar, but not identical. For most important skills and concepts, both halves of the brain are activated.

Ongoing Features

Many characteristics of this book have been acclaimed since the first edition and have been retained in this revision.

Writing That Communicates the Excitement and Challenge of the Field

Writing about the science of human development should be lively, just as real people are. Each sentence conveys attitude as well as content. Chapter-opening vignettes describe real-life situations. Examples and clear explanations abound, helping students connect theory, research, and experiences.

Coverage of Brain Research

Inclusion of neuroscience is a familiar feature of this book. Virtually every chapter includes a section on the brain, often enhanced with charts and photos to help students understand the brain's inner workings. The following list highlights some of this material.

Epigenetics and brain function in depressed individuals, p. 7; illustrated (PET scans of brains of a depressed and a nondepressed person), p. 7

Neurological plasticity, pp. 21–22; illustrated, p. 21

Prenatal growth of the brain, pp. 60–61; illustrated, p. 61

Teratogenic effects on brain development, pp. 72–75; illustrated, p. 73

Impact of anoxia on the brain, pp. 75–76

A View from Science: the effects of pesticides and other chemicals on fetal brain development, p. 76

Consequences of low birthweight on brain development, p. 79

Brain development in the first two years, pp. 93–97; illustrated, pp. 94–95

Experience-expectant and experience-dependent brain development, p. 96

Dangers of shaken baby syndrome, p. 97

Parts of the brain in which hearing and language comprehension occur, p. 97

Brain abnormalities as possible cause of SIDS, p. 106

Consequences of stunting for brain growth, p. 111

Limitations of Piaget's theory as revealed by brain scans, p. 117

Brain developments that support social emotions, pp. 132–133

The effect of the stress hormone cortisol on the developing brain, p. 134

Opposing Perspectives: Genetic influences on temperament, especially the combination of DRD4 VNTR and 5-HTTLPR genes, pp. 135–136

Brain maturation and synchrony, pp. 137–138

Brain development in early childhood (prefrontal cortex, myelination, lateralization, the limbic system), pp. 166–173; illustrated, p. 167

Abnormal growth of the corpus callosum and ADHD, p. 171

Maturation of the brain and theory of mind, p. 180

The impact of toxic stress on the developing brain, p. 181

Neuroscience research on bilingualism, as well as its benefits, pp. 185–186

The influence of myelination of the limbic system and growth of the prefrontal cortex in development of emotional regulation, pp. 203–204

Development of the prefrontal cortex and rough-and-tumble play, p. 208

Brain development and the development of empathy and antipathy, p. 219

Decreases in instrumental and reactive aggression as prefrontal cortex matures, p. 220

The effect of lead exposure on brain development, pp. 227–228

The effects of physical exercise on the brain, p. 240

Formation of brain connections during middle childhood, p. 248

Neurological advances and selective attention, p. 249

Neuroscience confirming usefulness of information-processing approach, p. 250

Development of control processes in middle childhood, p. 252

Brain development in middle childhood, pp. 253–254

Coverage of Diversity

Cross-cultural, international, multiethnic, sexual orientation, poverty, age, gender—all these words and ideas are vital to appreciating how people develop. Research uncovers surprising similarities and notable differences: We have much in common, yet each human is unique. From the discussion of social contexts in Chapter 1 to the coverage of cultural differences in death and dying in the Epilogue, each chapter highlights possibilities and variations.

New research on family structures, immigrants, bilingualism, and ethnic differences in health are among the many topics that illustrate human diversity. Listed here is a smattering of the discussions of culture and diversity in this new edition. Respect for human differences is evident throughout. You will note that examples and research findings from many parts of the world are included, not as add-on highlights but as integral parts of the description of each age.

Not Victims An outsider might worry that these two boys would be bullied, one because he is African American and the other because he appears to have a physical disability. But both are well liked for the characteristics shown here: friendship and willingness to help and be helped.

JUSTIN SULLIVAN/GETTY IMAGES

In Every Nation Everywhere, older adolescents are most likely to protest against government authority. Younger adolescents in Alabama celebrate the 50-year anniversary of the historic Selma-to-Montgomery march across the Pettus Bridge. In that historic movement, most of those beaten and killed were under age 25.

Up-to-Date Coverage

My mentors welcomed curiosity, creativity, and skepticism; as a result, I am eager to read and analyze thousands of articles and books on everything from the genes that predispose children to autism spectrum disorder to the complications of zygosity. The recent explosion of research in neuroscience and genetics has challenged me, once again, first to understand and then to explain many complex findings and speculative leaps. My students continue to ask questions and share their experiences, always providing new perspectives and concerns.

Topical Organization Within a Chronological Framework

The book's basic organization remains unchanged. Two chapters begin the book with coverage of definitions, theories, genetics, and prenatal development. These chapters function not only as a developmental foundation but also as the structure for explaining the life-span perspective, plasticity, nature and nurture, multi-cultural awareness, risk analysis, gains and losses, family bonding, and many other concepts that yield insights for all of human development.

The other six parts correspond to the major periods of development. With the exception of a lone chapter on prenatal development and birth, and another lone chapter on emerging adulthood, each age is discussed in two chapters, one for the biological and cognitive, and one for the social world. The topical organization within a chronological framework is a useful scaffold for students' understanding of the interplay between age and domain.

Photographs, Tables, and Graphs That Are Integral to the Text

Students learn a great deal from this book's illustrations because Worth Publishers encourages authors to choose the photographs, tables, and graphs and to write captions that extend the content. *Observation Quizzes* that accompany many of them inspire readers to look more closely at certain photographs, tables, and figures. The online *Data Connections* further this process by presenting numerous charts and tables that contain detailed data for further study.

Girls Can't Do It As Vygotsky recognized, children learn whatever their culture teaches. Fifty years ago, girls were in cooking and sewing classes. No longer. This 2012 photo shows 10-year-olds Kamrin and Caitlin in a Kentucky school, preparing for a future quite different from that of their grandmothers.

MIRANDA PEDERSON/DAILY NEWS/ASSOCIATED PRESS

Supplements

After teaching every semester for many years, I know well that supplements can make or break a class. Students are now media savvy and instructors use tools that did not exist when they themselves were in college. Many supplements are available for both students and professors. I encourage adopters of my textbook to ask their publisher's representative for guidance as to how these might be used. As an instructor who has used books from many publishers, I think you will find that Worth representatives are a cut above the rest, and you will be happy you asked for help.

LaunchPad

A comprehensive Web resource for teaching and learning, Worth Publishers' online course space offers:

- Prebuilt units for each chapter, curated by experienced educators, with relevant media organized and ready to be assigned or customized to suit your course.

- One location for all online resources, including an interactive e-Book, Learning-Curve's adaptive quizzing (see p. xxviii), videos, activities, and more.

- Intuitive and useful analytics, with a gradebook that lets you track how students in the class are performing individually and as a whole.

- A streamlined and intuitive interface that lets you build an entire course in minutes.

The LaunchPad can be previewed at www.macmillanhighered.com/launchpad/bergerinvitels3e.

LearningCurve

The **LearningCurve** quizzing system was designed based on the latest findings from learning and memory research. LearningCurve's adaptive and formative quizzing provides an effective way to get students involved in the coursework. It combines:

- A unique learning path for each student, with quizzes shaped by each individual's correct and incorrect answers.
- A personalized study plan to guide students' preparation for class and for exams.
- Feedback for each question with live links to relevant e-Book pages, guiding students to the resources they need to improve their areas of weakness.

It combines adaptive question selection, immediate feedback, and an interactive interface to engage students in a learning experience that is unique to them. Each LearningCurve quiz is fully integrated with other resources in LaunchPad, so students will be able to review with Worth's extensive library of videos and activities. And state-of-the-art question-analysis reports allow instructors to track the progress of individual students as well as their class as a whole. A team of dedicated instructors—including Diana Riser (Columbus State University), Chrysalis Wright (University of Central Florida), Matthew Isaak (University of Louisiana at Lafayette), and Jason Spiegelman (The Community College of Baltimore County)—has worked closely to develop more than 5,000 quizzing questions specifically for this book.

You will find the following in our LaunchPad:

Human Development Videos

In collaboration with dozens of instructors and researchers, Worth has developed an extensive archive of video clips. This collection covers the full range of the course, from classic experiments (like the Strange Situation and Piaget's conservation tasks) to investigations of children's play to adolescent risk taking. Instructors can assign these videos to students through LaunchPad or choose 1 of 50 popular video activities that combine videos with short-answer and multiple-choice questions. For presentation purposes, our videos are available in a variety of formats to suit your needs.

Instructor's Resources

Now fully integrated with LaunchPad, this collection of resources written by Richard O. Straub (University of Michigan, Dearborn) has been hailed as the richest collection of instructor's resources in developmental psychology. The resources include learning objectives, springboard topics for discussion and debate, handouts for student projects, course-planning suggestions, ideas for term projects, and a guide to audiovisual and online materials.

Interactive Presentation Slides

A new, extraordinary series of "next-generation" interactive presentations gives instructors a dynamic yet easy-to-use way to engage students during lectures on core developmental psychology topics. Each presentation enables lively classroom discussion and interaction with an unprecedented number of embedded video clips and animations from Worth Publishers' library of videos. In addition to these animated presentations, Worth Publishers also offers two other sets of prebuilt slides: one comprised of chapter art and illustrations, and another consisting of comprehensive, book-specific lectures created by Pauline Davey Zeece, PhD. These slides can be used as is, or they can be customized to fit individual needs.

Test Bank and Computerized Test Bank

The test bank, prepared by Diana Riser (Columbus State University), includes at least 100 multiple-choice and 70 fill-in-the-blank, true-false, and essay questions for each chapter. Good test questions are critical to every course, and we have gone through each and every one of these test questions with care. We have added more challenging questions, and questions are keyed to the textbook by topic, page number, and level of difficulty. Questions are also organized by NCLEX, NAEYC, and APA goals and Bloom's taxonomy. We have also written rubrics for grading all of the short-answer and essay questions in the test bank.

The Diploma computerized test bank guides instructors step by step through the process of creating a test. It also allows them to quickly add an unlimited number of questions; edit, scramble, or re-sequence items; format a test; and include pictures, equations, and media links. The accompanying gradebook enables instructors to record students' grades throughout the course and includes the capacity to sort student records, view detailed analyses of test items, curve tests, generate reports, and add weights to grades.

Thanks

I would like to thank the academic reviewers who have read this book in every edition and who have provided suggestions, criticisms, references, and encouragement. They have all made this a better book. I want to mention especially those who have reviewed this edition:

Joshua Becker, *Greenfield Community College*

Kazuko Behrens, *State University of New York Polytechnic Institute*

Maria Bermudez, *University of Georgia*

Charles Mark Brewer, *Tacoma Community College*

Katharine Ann Buck, *University of Saint Joseph*

Andrea R. Cartwright, *Jefferson Community & Technical College*

Patricia Coon, *West Liberty University*

Katherine Demitrakis, *Central New Mexico Community College*

Rebecca D. Foushée, *Fontbonne University*

Carolyn June Grasse-Bachman, *Pennsylvania State University–Harrisburg*

Ginny Harmelink, *Pima County Community College–Desert Vista*

Toni Stepter Harris, *Virginia State University*

August Hoffman, *Metropolitan State University*

David E. Johnson, *John Brown University*

Kevin J. Kelley, *Pennsylvania State University*

Joanna Key, *Gwinnett Technical College*

Don Knox, *Wayland Baptist University*

Becky Kochenderfer-Ladd, *Arizona State University*

Kathy L. Kufskie, *Southwestern Illinois College*

Dawn Kulpanowski, *Florida SouthWestern State College*

Ryan C. Leonard, *Gannon University*

Christopher J. Mazurek, *Columbia College*

Michael McCarty, *Texas Tech University*

Anne Mullis, *Florida State University*

Lisa Murphy, *York County Community College*

Christina Nash, *Drexel University*

Ann Orr, *Eastern Michigan University*

Jennifer Powell-Lunder, *Pace University*

Kimberly Renk, *University of Central Florida*

Laurel Shaler, *Liberty University*

Brooke R. Spangler, *Miami University*

Jeannine Stamatakis, *Lincoln University*

Andrew Supple, *University of North Carolina*

Virginia Tompkins, *Ohio State University–Lima*

Andrea C. Walker, *Oral Roberts University*

Kristine Walker, *Northwest College*

Stacy Walker, *Lone Star College*

Elizabeth A. Ware, *Viterbo University*

Ryan Zayac, *University of North Alabama*

Special thanks to those instructors who took the time to review the infographics in preparation for this new edition. Their insight and care have helped us revise, refine, and revisit much of this visual program, and I hope they will be pleased with the results.

Judith Addelston, *Valencia College—East Campus*

Diana L. Ciesko, *Valencia College—East Campus*

Christie Cunningham, *Pellissippi State Technical Community College—Hardin Valley Campus*

Jessica Herrick, *Colorado Mesa University*

Rosalyn M. King, *Northern Virginia Community College—Loudoun Campus*

Barbara J. Myers, *Virginia Commonwealth University—Monroe Park Campus*

Brian Parry, *Colorado Mesa University*

Dereck Schorsch, *Valencia College—East Campus*

Jillene Grover Seiver, *Bellevue College*

In addition, I wish to thank the instructors who participated in our survey. We have tried to apply the insights gained from their experiences with the last edition to make this new edition even better.

Amanda Grieme Bradley, *Trevecca Nazarene University*

Pamela G. Costa, *Tacoma Community College*

Christie Cunningham, *Pellissippi State Community College*

David B. Daniel, *James Madison University*

Jim Deal, *North Dakota State University*

Nicholas Fernandez, *El Paso Community College*

Roy Fish, *Ohio State University*

Amy Holmes, *Davidson County Community College—Davie Campus*

Rebecca Howell, *Forsyth Technical Community College*

Mark Jackson, *Trinity Lutheran College*

Staci M. Simmelink Johnson, *Walla Walla Community College*

Ariel Hooker Jones, *Maryville University*

Douglas J. Lalama, *Ivy Tech Community College*

Laura Lansing, *Mount Aloysius College*

Todd Lawson, *University of Texas at Tyler*

Brian N. Lee, *Western Kentucky University*

Melinda Leonard, *University of Louisville*

Daniel S. McConnell, *University of Central Florida*

Brian T. McCoy, *Nichols College*

Patrick McCoy, *Mount Aloysius College*

Amanda McPherson, *Pima Community College*

Cristian Meier, *Eastern Iowa Community College*

Stephanie Olsen, *Finger Lakes Community College*

Suyin Phillips, *Kapi'olani Community College*

Bridget Reigstad, *Normandale Community College*

Bruce Reinauer, *Ventura County Community College*

Chandra A. Reynolds, *University of California—Riverside*

Rachel G. Riskind, *Guilford College*
Regina Traficante, *Community College of Rhode Island*
Isabel Trombetti, *Community College of Rhode Island*
Margot Underwood, *Joliet Junior College*

The editorial, production, and marketing people at Worth Publishers are dedicated to meeting the highest standards of excellence. Their devotion of time, effort, and talent to every aspect of publishing is a model for the industry. I particularly would like to thank Andrea Musick Page, Stacey Alexander, Jessica Bayne, Betsy Draper, Laura Burden, Matthew Christensen, Tom Churchill, Sheena Goldstein, Lisa Kinne, William LaDue, Blake Logan, Daria Kaczorowska, Tracey Kuehn, Jennifer MacMillan, Matthew McAdams, Hilary Newman, Katherine Nurre, Chelsea Roden, Melissa Rostek, Rona Tuccillo, Victor Wong, and Charles Yuen.

Kathleen Stassen Berger
New York, September 2015

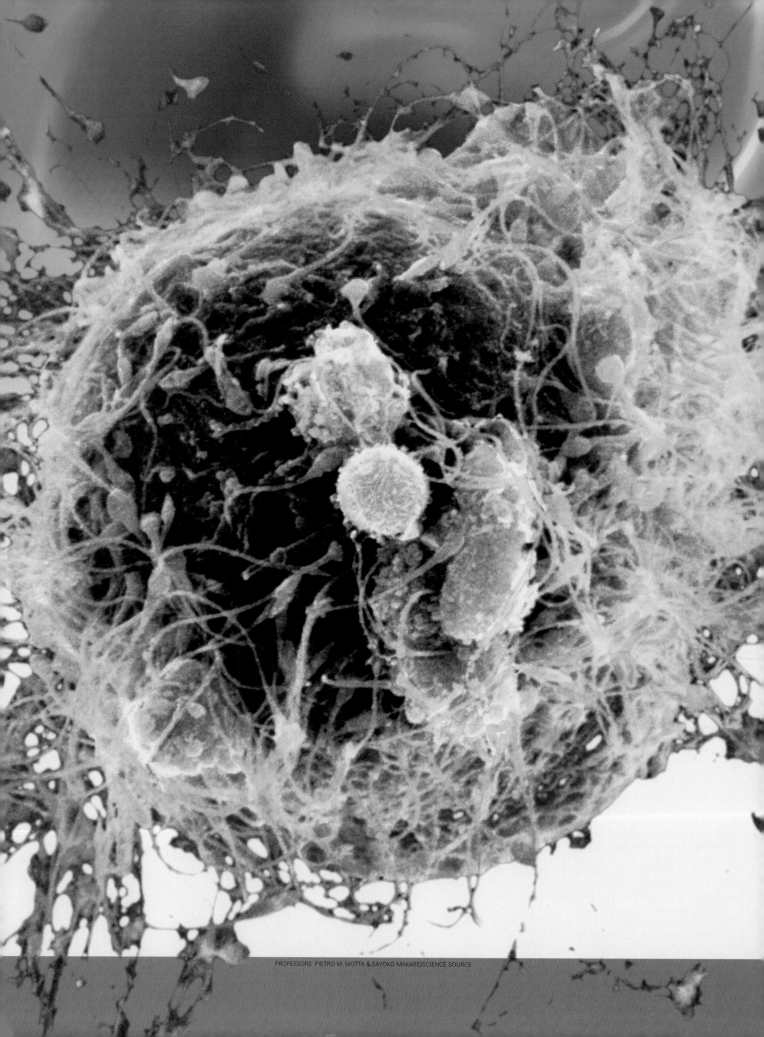

PART ONE

The Beginning

The science of human development has many beginnings. Chapter 1 introduces the science, explaining some theories, strategies, and methods used to understand how people grow and change. Chapter 2 traces early development, from the genetic interactions that produce all inherited characteristics to the newborn's first movements, sounds, and reactions.

Throughout these chapters, the interplay of nature (heredity) and nurture (the environment) is illustrated. For instance, whether or not a person will develop type 2 diabetes at age 60 depends on both nature (genetic vulnerability) and nurture (the mother's diet during pregnancy and the adult's exercise and eating habits). Understanding the interplay of biology and culture is the foundation that allows us to reach *the goal of our study: a happy and meaningful life for all 7 billion people on Earth, of all ages, cultures, and aspirations*.

CHAPTER OUTLINE

THE BEGINNING

The Science of Human Development

CHAPTER 1

WHAT WILL YOU KNOW?

- How can the study of people be considered a science?
- Are people the same, always and everywhere, or is each person unique, changing from day to day?
- Do all the major theories of human development agree with each other?
- What cautions do developmental scientists need to remember?[1]

I am holding my daughter's bent right leg in place with all my strength. A nurse holds her left leg while Bethany pulls on a sheet tied to a metal structure over her bed. The midwife commands, "Push . . . push . . . push." Finally, a head is visible, small and wet, but perfect. In a moment, body and limbs emerge, all 4,139 grams of Caleb, perfect as well. Apgar is 9, and every number on the monitor is good. Bethany, smiling, begins to nurse.

Decades of learning, studying, teaching, praying, and mothering have led me to this miracle at 6:11 A.M., my first-born with her first-born. Celestial music rings in my ears. The ringing grows louder. Suddenly, I am on the floor, looking up at six medical professionals: I have fainted.

"I am fine," I insist, getting back on the couch where I spent the night. They stare at me.

"You need to go to triage."

"No, I am fine. Sorry I fainted."

"Hospital policy."

"No. I belong here."

"We must send you to triage, in a wheelchair."

What should I say to make them ignore me and focus on Caleb?

Another nurse wisely adds, "You can refuse treatment."

Of course. I remember; the law now requires patient consent.

So I am wheeled down the hall, wait for the elevator, go to Admitting, explain that I was with my laboring daughter all night with neither food nor sleep. I fainted, but I am fine. I refuse treatment.

The admitting nurse takes my blood pressure—normal—and checks with her supervisor.

---

[1] "What Will You Know?" questions, one for each major heading, are a preview before each chapter. They are big ideas that you will still know a decade from now, unlike the "What Have You Learned" questions after each major heading, which are more specific.

Born Blissful One of us rests after an arduous journey, and the other rejoices after crying and fainting.

"I refuse treatment," I repeat.

I am approved to leave, so I stand up to walk back.

"Sit down. Someone must wheel you back. Hospital policy."

I am puzzled. Bethany chose me for her birth partner because of my knowledge, experience, and steadiness. I can interpret numbers, jargon, monitors, body language, medical competence, hospital cleanliness, hall noises, and more. I do not panic; I know that Bethany is strong, healthy, and conscientious. I appreciate all the advances of modern medicine, sadly not part of every birth but available to my well-insured, well-educated daughter.

Consequently, I was grateful but not surprised that Caleb was perfect. I told the triage nurse that I had not slept or eaten all night—true, but I had gone without sleep and food before, never fainting. She accepted my explanation, but I do not. What happened this time?

This incident introduces Chapter 1, which begins to explain what we know, what we don't know, and how we learn about human development. Emotions mix with intellect, family bonds with professional competence, contexts with cultures, personal experiences with academic knowledge. Much is known and yet new questions arise, surprises occur. I learned more about physiology, relationships, and cognition because I fainted. I also thought more about family and aging as well as about genetics and prenatal care. This chapter, and those that follow, will help you learn as well. ■

Understanding How and Why

The **science of human development** seeks to understand how and why people—all kinds of people, everywhere, of every age—change over time.

Development over the life span is *multi-directional, multi-contextual, multi-cultural,* and *plastic*—four terms that will be explained soon. First we must emphasize that developmental study is a *science*. It depends on theories, data, analysis, critical thinking, and sound methodology, like every other science. Scientists ask questions and seek answers to ascertain "how and why."

Science is especially necessary when the topic is human development. People disagree about what pregnant women should eat; where babies should sleep; when children should be punished; whether adults should go to college, marry, divorce, and have children; how people in late adulthood should approach aging, caregiving, and dying.

Some parents beat their children; other people put such parents in prison. Some people quit working as soon as they can; other people never retire. Everyone's choices affect everyone else. Scientists seek to progress from personal opinions to proven facts, from wishes to evidence that might affect us all.

The Scientific Method

As you surely realize, facts may be twisted, and applications sometimes spring from false assumptions. To rein in personal biases and avoid misinterpretations, researchers follow the **scientific method** (see Figure 1.1):

1. *Begin with curiosity.* Pose a question, guided by theory, research, or observation.

2. *Develop a hypothesis.* Shape the question into a **hypothesis,** a testable prediction.

3. *Test the hypothesis.* Conduct research to gather **empirical evidence** (data).

---

science of human development
The science that seeks to understand how and why people of all ages and circumstances change or remain the same over time.

THINK CRITICALLY: What are the limitations of a scientific approach to human development?[2]

scientific method
A way to answer questions using empirical research and data-based conclusions.

hypothesis
A specific prediction that can be tested.

empirical evidence
Evidence that is based on observation, experience, or data; not theoretical.

---

[2]*Think Critically* questions occur several times in each chapter. They are intended to provoke thought, not simple responses, and hence have no obvious answers.

1. Curiosity

2. Hypothesis

3. Test

4. Analyze data and draw conclusions

5. Report the results

FIGURE 1.1 Process, Not Proof Built into the scientific method—in questions, hypotheses, tests, and replication—is a passion for possibilities, especially unexpected ones.

4. *Draw conclusions.* Use the evidence to support or refute the hypothesis.
5. *Report the results.* Share data, conclusions, limitations, and alternative explanations.

As you see, developmental scientists begin with curiosity and then seek facts, drawing conclusions after careful research.

Replication—repeating the procedures and methods of a study with different participants—is often a sixth and crucial step (Jasny et al., 2011). Scientists study the reports of other scientists and build on what has gone before. Sometimes they try to duplicate a study exactly; often they follow up with related research (Stroebe & Strack, 2014). Conclusions are revised, refined, rejected, or confirmed after replication.

replication
Repeating a study, usually using different participants, perhaps of another age, location, socioeconomic status (SES), or culture.

This method is not foolproof. Scientists sometimes draw conclusions too hastily, misinterpret data, or ignore alternative perspectives.

Occasionally scientists discover, to their shock and horror, that another scientist has not followed the procedures outlined above. This is one reason that detailed procedures and replication are needed. Asking questions and testing hypotheses by gathering data are the foundation of science.

A VIEW FROM SCIENCE

Are Children Too Overweight?*

Obesity is a serious problem. In every age group, from childhood to age 60, rates of obesity increase. Rates begin to decrease at about age 60, perhaps because some of the heaviest people die of the consequences of a lifetime of overweight—heart disease, diabetes, and strokes.

The connection between overweight and disease was not always known. Since before written history, observers have noted that some children were heavier than others and that underweight children were more likely to die. That led to an assumption, still held by some adults: Heavy children are healthy (Laraway et al., 2010).

Sixty years ago another untested assumption was that heart attacks in older adults could not be prevented, or even predicted. Doctors were "baffled" and decided to study more than 5,000 adults in Framingham, Massachusetts, to see what they could learn (Levy & Brink, 2005).

What Will Become of Her? This happy, beautiful girl in Sweden may become an obese woman . . . or she may not. Research finds that if she slims down by adulthood, she is likely to be healthier than the average woman who was never overweight.

*Every chapter of this text features *A View from Science*, which explains surprising insights from recent scientific research.

The Framingham Heart Study began in 1948, collecting data and drawing conclusions that, by 1990, revolutionized adult behavior—a historic example of the scientific method applied to human behavior. Because of that study, cigarette smoking is down, exercise is up, and doctors now routinely monitor blood pressure, weight, and cholesterol, advising and prescribing accordingly. Millions of premature deaths have been averted.

That research led to a new thought: Since obese adults are likely to die of heart attacks and strokes, childhood obesity might be a health risk, too. That thought (Step 1) led to the hypothesis (Step 2) that childhood overweight impairs adult health.

This hypothesis is now widely assumed to be true. For instance, a poll found that most Californians consider childhood obesity "very serious," with a third of them rating poor eating habits as a worse risk to child health than drug use or violence (Hennessy-Fiske, 2011).

The best way to test that hypothesis (Step 3) is to examine adult health in people who had been weighed and measured in childhood. Several researchers did exactly that. Indeed, four studies measured and weighed children and then assessed the same people as adults. Most (83 percent) of the people in these studies maintained their relative weight (see Figure 1.2a).

From that research, a strong conclusion was reached (Step 4) and published (Step 5): Overweight and obese children are likely to become obese adults, who then are at high risk for cardiovascular disease, diabetes, and early death (Juonala et al., 2011). For instance, in those four studies, 29 percent of those who were overweight from childhood on had high blood pressure as adults, compared to 11 percent of those who were never overweight.

A new question arose (Step 1), building on the earlier findings. What about overweight children who become normal-weight adults? That led to a new hypothesis (Step 2): Childhood obesity predicts heart attacks, strokes, diabetes, and early death in adulthood, even if the person slims down. The research design was the same, measuring health in formerly overweight adults (Step 3). The data (Step 4) (see Figure 1.2b) found that the hypothesis was wrong: As normal-weight adults they were *not* at high risk of disease, a conclusion replicated by four studies with different participants (Juonala et al., 2011).

Many other issues, complications, and conclusions regarding obesity are discussed later in this book. For now, all you need to remember are the steps of the scientific method and that developmentalists are right: Significant "change over time" is possible.

FIGURE 1.2 **Not Yet Obese** You probably know that more than half of all adults in the United States are overweight, so this chart—with only 21 percent of adults obese—may seem wrong. However, three facts explain why the data are accurate: (1) "Obese" is much heavier than overweight; (2) the average adult in this study was 34 years old (middle-aged and older adults are more often obese); and (3) one of the studies that provided much of the longitudinal data was in Finland, where rates of obesity are lower than in the United States.

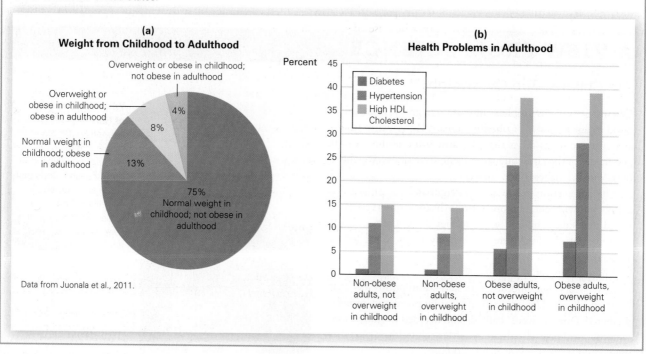

(a) Weight from Childhood to Adulthood

Overweight or obese in childhood; not obese in adulthood — 4%

Overweight or obese in childhood; obese in adulthood — 8%

Normal weight in childhood; obese in adulthood — 13%

75% Normal weight in childhood; not obese in adulthood

Data from Juonala et al., 2011.

(b) Health Problems in Adulthood

Percent

- Diabetes
- Hypertension
- High HDL Cholesterol

Non-obese adults, not overweight in childhood / Non-obese adults, overweight in childhood / Obese adults, not overweight in childhood / Obese adults, overweight in childhood

The Nature–Nurture Controversy

An easy example of the need for science concerns a great issue in development, the *nature–nurture question*. **Nature** refers to the influence of the genes that people inherit. **Nurture** refers to environmental influences, beginning with the health and diet of the embryo's mother and continuing lifelong, including family, school, community, culture, and society.

The nature–nurture issue has many other names, among them *heredity vs. environment* and *maturation vs. learning*. Under whatever name, the basic question is: *How much of any characteristic, behavior, or emotion is the result of genes and how much is the result of experience?*

Some people believe that most traits are inborn, that children are innately good (an "innocent child") or bad ("beat the devil out of them"). Other people stress nurture, crediting or blaming parents, or neighborhoods, or society, or drugs.

Neither extreme is accurate. The question is "how much," not "which," because *both* genes and experience affect every characteristic: Nature always affects nurture, and then nurture affects nature.

Some scientists think that even "how much" is misleading: It implies that nature and nurture each contribute a fixed amount when actually their explosive interaction is crucial (Eagly & Wood, 2013; Lock, 2013).

EPIGENETICS A new discipline related to genetics is called **epigenetics**—it explores the many ways environmental forces alter genetic expression. Neuroscientists have shown that loneliness, for example, can literally change structures in the brain (Cacioppo et al., 2014).

Sometimes protective factors, in either nature or nurture, outweigh liabilities. As one review explains, "there are, indeed, individuals whose genetics indicate exceptionally high risk of disease, yet they never show any signs of the disorder" (Friend & Schadt, 2014, p. 970). Why? Epigenetics.

DANDELIONS AND ORCHIDS There is increasing evidence of **differential susceptibility**—that is, how sensitivity to any particular environmental experience differs from one person to another because of the particular genes each person has inherited.

Some people are like *dandelions*—hardy, growing and thriving in good soil or bad, with or without ample sun and rain. Other people are like *orchids*—quite wonderful, but only when ideal growing conditions are met (Ellis & Boyce, 2008; Laurent, 2014).

For example, in one study, depression in pregnant women was assessed and then the emotional maturity of their children was measured. Those children who had a particular version of the serotonin transporter gene (5-HTTLPR) were likely to be emotionally immature if their mothers were depressed, but *more* mature than average if their mothers were not depressed (Babineau et al., 2015).

The interaction between nature and nurture is apparent for every topic in this book, as you will see, and in every moment of our lives, as I see in myself. In retrospect, I fainted at Caleb's birth because of the interaction of at least eight factors (low blood sugar, lack of sleep, physical exertion, gender, age, joy, memories, relief), all influenced by both nature and nurture, a combination that threw me to the floor.

The Three Domains

Obviously, it is impossible to examine nature and nurture in every aspect of human development at once, especially for any one individual. I do not

nature
In development, nature refers to the traits, capacities, and limitations that each individual inherits genetically from his or her parents at the moment of conception.

nurture
In development, nurture includes all the environmental influences that affect the individual after conception. This includes everything from the mother's nutrition while pregnant to the cultural influences in the nation.

epigenetics
The study of how environmental factors affect genes and genetic expression—enhancing, halting, shaping, or altering the expression of genes.

differential susceptibility
The idea that people vary in how sensitive they are to particular experiences. Often such differences are genetic, which makes some people affected "for better or for worse" by life events. (Also called *differential sensitivity*.)

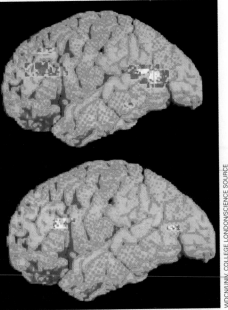

Red Means Stop At top, the red areas on this PET scan show abnormally low metabolic activity and blood flow in a depressed person's brain, in contrast to the normal brain at bottom. Neuroscience confirms that depression is biological, not just psychological.

know how much of my fainting was affected by my genes, nor how much by my past experiences.

A century ago, nature (especially physical development such as tooth eruption or running speed) was the main focus of developmental research. Scientists now realize that social factors affect every aspect of development and that intellect and emotions, not just physical growth, develop throughout the entire life span. All three are always responsive to each other.

Consequently, the traditional emphasis on physical growth has been accompanied by recognition of cognition and social interactions. Development is often divided into three domains—*biological, cognitive,* and *psychosocial* (see Figure 1.3), or body, mind, and social world. As you see in this text, body and mind are separate halves of Chapters 3, 5, 7, 9, 12, and 14, and the other chapters includes the social world—except for Chapter 11, on emerging adulthood, which includes all three. Other books differ, but everyone distinguishes these three.

Each domain includes several academic disciplines: Biological includes physiology, neuroscience, and medicine; cognitive includes psychology, linguistics, and education; and psychosocial includes economics, sociology, and history.

Typically, each scientist pursues a particular thread within one discipline, using clues, research, and conclusions from scientists in other disciplines who have concentrated on that same thread. Yet always remember that the interaction between and among domains—an *interdisciplinary approach*—is essential to understanding the whole developing person.

Since every individual is a tapestry of many-colored threads, every aspect of growth touches on all three domains. For example, babies start speaking when the brain, mouth, and vocal cords mature (*biological*), which allows them to express connections between objects, events, and words (*cognitive*), which depends on people talking to them (*psychosocial*).

From the recognition of the interaction of domains comes a related concept in psychology called *embodied cognition,* the idea that people's thinking and social relationships are affected by their bodies. For instance, walking in a happy, open way makes a person feel happier, and standing arms akimbo makes a person feel confident and makes other people perceive that person as competent. More research is needed, as the evidence for embodied cognition is mixed, but no one doubts that all three domains interact (Marmolejo-Ramos & D'Angiulli, 2014; Shapiro, 2014).

FIGURE 1.3 The Three Domains The division of human development into three domains makes it easier to study, but remember that very few factors belong exclusively to one domain or another. Development is not piecemeal but holistic: Each aspect of development is related to all three domains.

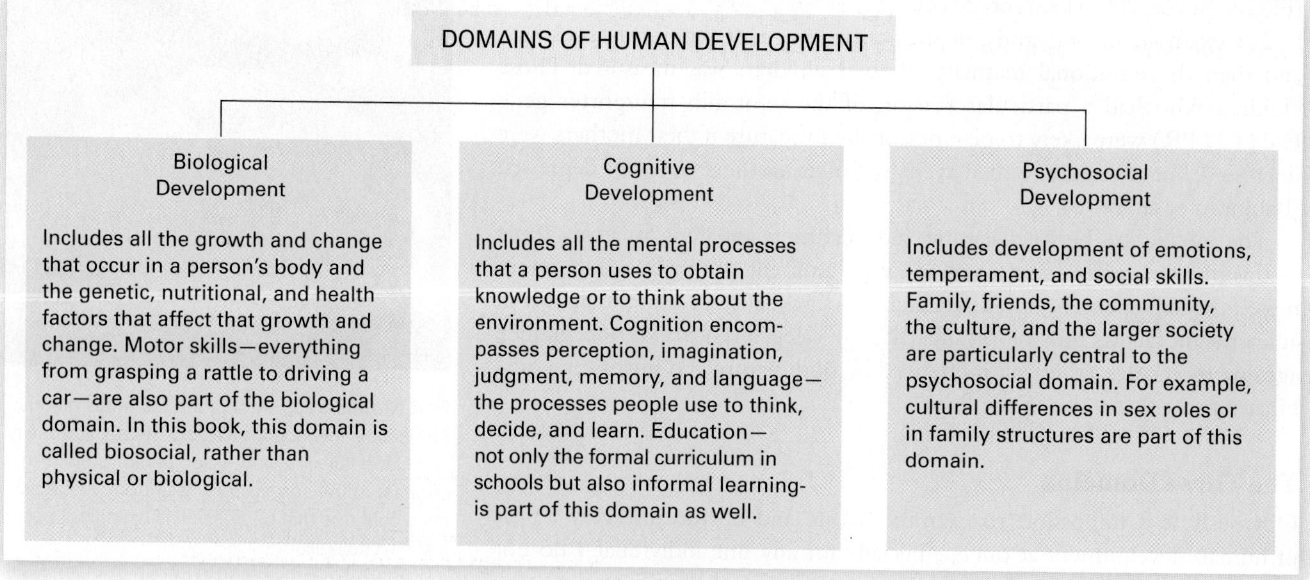

DOMAINS OF HUMAN DEVELOPMENT

Biological Development

Includes all the growth and change that occur in a person's body and the genetic, nutritional, and health factors that affect that growth and change. Motor skills—everything from grasping a rattle to driving a car—are also part of the biological domain. In this book, this domain is called biosocial, rather than physical or biological.

Cognitive Development

Includes all the mental processes that a person uses to obtain knowledge or to think about the environment. Cognition encompasses perception, imagination, judgment, memory, and language—the processes people use to think, decide, and learn. Education—not only the formal curriculum in schools but also informal learning—is part of this domain as well.

Psychosocial Development

Includes development of emotions, temperament, and social skills. Family, friends, the community, the culture, and the larger society are particularly central to the psychosocial domain. For example, cultural differences in sex roles or in family structures are part of this domain.

WHAT HAVE YOU LEARNED?

1. What are the five steps of the scientific method?
2. Why is replication important?
3. What basic question is at the heart of the nature–nurture controversy?
4. What is the difference between "genetics" and "epigenetics"?
5. How might differential susceptibility apply to understanding students' varied responses to a low exam grade?
6. What are the three domains of development?
7. How does multidisciplinary research connect with the three domains?

The Life-Span Perspective

The **life-span perspective** (Baltes et al., 2006; Fingerman et al., 2011; Raz & Lindenberger, 2013) takes into account all phases of life, not just the first two decades (which were once the sole focus of developmental study). By including the entirety of life (see Table 1.1), this perspective has led to the realization that human development is multi-directional, multi-contextual, multi-cultural, and plastic. Now we examine each of these four.

Development Is Multi-Directional

Multiple changes, in every direction, characterize the life span: Development is *multi-directional*. If human traits were all charted over time from birth to death, some traits would appear, others disappear, with increases, decreases, and zigzags (see Figure 1.4). The traditional idea—that all development advances until about age 18, steadies, and then declines—has been refuted by life-span research.

The pace of change varies as well. Sometimes *discontinuity* is evident: Change can occur rapidly and dramatically, as when caterpillars become butterflies. Sometimes *continuity* is found: Growth can be gradual, as when redwoods grow taller over hundreds of years.

Even stability is possible. Some characteristics seem not to change. For instance, chromosomal sex is lifelong: A zygote that is XY or XX (male or female) for life. Of course, the power and meaning of that biological fact change, but the chromosomes themselves stay the same.

TABLE 1.1	Age Ranges for Different Periods of Development
Infancy	0 to 2 years
Early childhood	2 to 6 years
Middle childhood	6 to 11 years
Adolescence	11 to 18 years
Emerging adulthood	18 to 25 years
Adulthood	25 to 65 years
Late adulthood	65 years and older

As you will learn, developmentalists are reluctant to specify chronological ages for any period of development, since time is only one of many variables that affect each person. However, age is a crucial variable, and development can be segmented into periods of study. Approximate ages for each period are given here.

life-span perspective
An approach to the study of human development that takes into account all phases of life, not just childhood or adulthood.

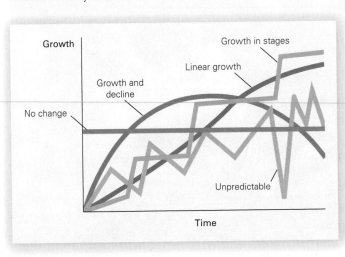

FIGURE 1.4 Patterns of Developmental Growth Many patterns of developmental growth have been discovered by careful research. Although linear (or nonlinear) progress seems most common, scientists now find that almost no aspect of human change follows the linear pattern exactly.

There is simple growth, radical transformation, improvement, and decline as well as stability, stages, and continuity—day to day, year to year, and generation to generation. Life-span theorists see *gains and losses* throughout life (Lang et al., 2011; Villar, 2012). For example, when babies begin to talk, they are less able to distinguish sounds from other languages (a gain and a loss); when adults retire, they may become more creative (a loss and a gain).

CRITICAL PERIODS The speed and timing of impairments or improvements vary as well. Some changes are sudden and profound because of a **critical period,** a time when something *must* occur for normal development or the only time when an abnormality can occur. For instance, the critical period for humans to grow arms and legs, hands and feet, fingers and toes, is between 28 and 54 days after conception.

After day 54, that critical period is over. Unlike some insects, humans never grow replacement limbs or digits.

We know the critical period for limb formation because of a tragic occurrence. Between 1957 and 1961, thousands of newly pregnant women in 30 nations took *thalidomide*, an antinausea drug. This change in nurture (via the mother's bloodstream) disrupted nature (the embryo's genetic program).

If an expectant woman swallowed thalidomide between day 28 and 54, her newborn's arms or legs were malformed or absent (Moore & Persaud, 2007). Whether all four limbs, or just arms, or just hands were missing depended on dose and timing. If thalidomide was ingested only after day 54, the newborn had normal body structures.

SENSITIVE PERIODS Life has few critical periods. Often, however, a particular development occurs more easily—not exclusively—at a certain time. Such a time is called a **sensitive period.**

An example is found in language. If children do not communicate in their first language between ages 1 and 3, they might do so later (hence, these years are not critical), but their grammar is often impaired (hence, these years are sensitive).

Similarly, childhood is a sensitive period for learning to pronounce a second or third language. A new language can be learned in adulthood, but strangers might detect an accent and ask, "Where are you from?"

---

critical period
A time when a particular type of developmental growth (in body or behavior) must happen for normal development to occur.

sensitive period
A time when a certain type of development is most likely, although it may still happen later with more difficulty. For example, early childhood is considered a sensitive period for language learning.

I Love You, Mommy We do not know what words, in what language, her son is using, but we do know that Sobia Akbar speaks English well, a requirement for naturalized U.S. citizens. Here she obtains citizenship for her two children born in Pakistan. Chances are they will speak unaccented American English, unlike Sobia, whose accent might indicate that she learned British English as a second language.

JOHN MOORE/GETTY IMAGES

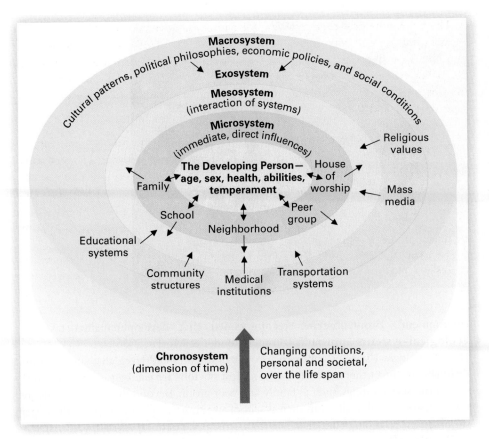

FIGURE 1.5 **The Ecological Model** According to developmental researcher Urie Bronfenbrenner, each person is significantly affected by interactions among a number of overlapping systems, which provide the context of development. *Microsystems*—family, peer groups, classroom, neighborhood, house of worship—intimately and immediately shape human development. Surrounding and supporting the microsystems are the *exosystems*, which include all the external networks, such as community structures and local educational, medical, employment, and communications systems, that influence the microsystems. Influencing both of these systems is the *macrosystem*, which includes cultural patterns, political philosophies, economic policies, and social conditions. *Mesosystems* refer to interactions among systems, as when parents and teachers coordinate to educate a child. Bronfenbrenner eventually added a fifth system, the *chronosystem*, to emphasize the importance of historical time.

Often in development, individual exceptions to general patterns occur. Accent-free speech *usually* must be learned before puberty, but exceptional nature and nurture (an adult with exceptional hearing and then immersion in a new language) can result in flawless second-language pronunciation (Birdsong, 2006; Muñoz & Singleton, 2011).

Because of sensitive periods, however, such exceptions are rare. A study of native Dutch speakers who become fluent in English found only 5 percent had mastered native English (Schmid et al., 2014).

Development Is Multi-Contextual

The second insight from the life-span perspective is that development is *multi-contextual*. It takes place within many contexts, including physical surroundings (climate, noise, population density, etc.) and family configurations (married couple, single parent, cohabiting couple, extended family, etc.). Each context can influence development, sometimes for a moment, sometimes for years.

A student might choose to go to a party instead of to the library. The social context of the party, such as whether drinks are free, the music lively, and friends are there, influences that student's next several decisions. As you can imagine, the context of the party, and the decisions influenced by that context, affect later development: It may be hard to go to class the next day, or, in class, hard to apply math formulas or history facts. Each individual is responsible for his or her actions, of course, but social contexts are powerful.

ECOLOGICAL SYSTEMS A leading developmentalist, Urie Bronfenbrenner (1917–2005), led the way to considering contexts. Just as a naturalist studying an organism examines the ecology (the multifaceted relationship between the organism and its

Breathe, Don't Sink Ben Schwenker is learning "drown-proofing," important for a skinny 8-year-old, since his low body fat (a physiological system) makes floating harder. Ecological systems also make this skill vital, since Ben is in Marietta, a city with thousands of pools, in Georgia, a state bordered by the Atlantic Ocean. Another system is relevant: Ben was diagnosed with autism spectrum disorder at age 1; for him, a sense of body strength and autonomy is particularly important.

© ZUMA PRESS, INC./ALAMY

ecological-systems approach
Bronfenbrenner's perspective on human development that considers all the influences from the various contexts of development. (Later renamed *bioecological theory*.)

environment), Bronfenbrenner recommended that developmentalists take an **ecological-systems approach** (Bronfenbrenner & Morris, 2006).

The ecological-systems approach recognizes three nested levels that surround individuals and affect them (see Figure 1.5). Most obvious are *microsystems,* each person's immediate surroundings, such as family and peer group. Beyond the microsystems are the *exosystems* (local institutions such as school and church) and *macrosystems* (the larger social setting, including cultural values, economic policies, and political processes).

Bronfenbrenner also stressed the role of historical conditions and therefore included the *chronosystem* (literally, "time system"). Further, because he appreciated the dynamic interaction among all the systems, he included a fifth system, the *mesosystem,* consisting of the connections between and among the other systems.

Throughout his life, Bronfenbrenner studied people in natural settings, interacting with each other at home, at school, or at work instead of coming to a scientist's laboratory or answering questionnaires. Before he died, he renamed his approach *bioecological* to highlight the role of biology, recognizing that systems within the body (e.g., the sexual-reproductive system, the cardiovascular system) affect all the external contexts (Bronfenbrenner & Morris, 2006).

As you can see, a contextual approach to development requires simultaneous consideration of many systems. Two contexts—historical and socioeconomic—are crucial in understanding all the systems of life-span development, yet they are often ignored. They merit explanation now.

cohort
People born within the same historical period. They experience historical events (such as wars), technologies (such as the smartphone), and cultural shifts (such as women's liberation) at the same ages.

WILLIAM HAEFELI THE NEW YORKER COLLECTION/ THE CARTOON BANK

"Hey! Elbows off the table."

THE HISTORICAL CONTEXT All persons born within a few years of one another are said to be a **cohort,** a group defined by its members' shared age. Cohorts travel through life together, affected by the interaction of their chronological age with the values, events, technologies, and culture of the era.

Twenty-First-Century Manners If he obeyed his father but kept texting, would Emily Post be pleased?

in those groups, children are encouraged to talk freely, and when they do, the adults listen approvingly. Among other U.S. groups, a prime cultural value is that children respect their parents, and, by extension, every adult: Children should never interrupt an adult conversation.

One of my students remembered:

> My mom was outside on the porch talking to my aunt. I decided to go outside; I guess I was being nosey. While they were talking I jumped into their conversation which was very rude. When I realized what I did it was too late. My mother slapped me in my face so hard that it took a couple of seconds to feel my face again.
>
> [C., personal communication]

Notice how my student reflects her culture; she labels her own behavior "nosey" and "very rude." She later wrote that she expects children to be seen but not heard and that her own son makes her "very angry" when he interrupts. Whether you agree depends on your culture.

DEFICIT OR JUST DIFFERENCE? Whatever a person's culture or cultures may be, humans tend to believe that they, their nation, their group, and their culture are better than others. That belief becomes destructive if it reduces respect and appreciation. Developmentalists recognize the **difference-equals-deficit error,** the assumption that people who are different are thereby deficient, which means lacking in some important ways. Too quickly and without thought, differences are assumed to be problems (Akhtar & Jaswal, 2013).

> **difference-equals-deficit error**
> The mistaken belief that a deviation from some norm is necessarily inferior to behavior or characteristics that are more typical.

Negative judgments are often made about how other people raise children, or worship God, or even eat. Age differences are also stereotyped. Have you heard adults complain about the attitudes, abilities, or actions of teenagers, or of senior citizens? Such age stereotypes are evidence of judging a difference as a deficit.

Gender differences are another easy example. We are amused when young girls say, "Boys stink," or their male classmates say, "Girls are stupid." However, even though the sexes have far more similarities than differences, humans of all ages tend to notice differences and then make sexist judgments.

According to one scholar, even neuroscientists make that mistake. They are susceptible to "neurosexism," seeing and explaining gender differences "in the absence of data" (Fine, 2014, p. 915).

One of the very few proven gender differences is that women are more tenderhearted and men more sexually driven (Hyde, 2014). If you are male, do you think that women are weak because they are too emotional; if you are female, do you think men are too obsessed with sex? If you answer yes, how human of you. And how mistaken.

The difference-equals-deficit error is one reason a multi-cultural approach is crucial. Various ways of thinking or acting are not necessarily wrong or right, better or worse. The scientific method, which requires empirical data, is needed for accurate assessments.

Sometimes a difference is actually an asset (Marschark & Spencer, 2003). For example, cultures that discourage dissent also foster harmony. The opposite is also true—cultures that encourage dissent also value independence. Whatever your personal judgment on this cultural difference, the opposite opinion has some merit. A multi-cultural understanding requires recognition that some differences signify strengths, not weaknesses.

LEARNING WITHIN A CULTURE Russian developmentalist Lev Vygotsky (1896–1934) was a leader in describing the interaction between culture and education

Macmillan Education
LaunchPad
Video: Research of Geoffrey Saxe
http://qrs.ly/9c4eoxh

FOOTAGE BY GEOFFREY SAXE

Attention for Children Vygotsky lived from 1896 to 1934, when war, starvation, and revolution led to the deaths of millions. Throughout this political turmoil, Vygotsky focused on learning. His love of children is suggested by this portrait: He and his daughter have their arms around each other.

DR. JAMES WERTSCH

(Wertsch & Tulviste, 2005). He noticed that adults from the many cultures of the Soviet Union (Asians and Europeans, of many religions) taught their children whatever beliefs and habits they might need as adults within their local community.

Vygotsky (discussed in more detail in Chapter 5) believed that *guided participation* is a universal process used by mentors to teach cultural knowledge, skills, and habits. Guided participation can occur via school instruction but more often happens informally, through "mutual involvement in several widespread cultural practices with great importance for learning: narratives, routines, and play" (Rogoff, 2003, p. 285).

ethnic group
People whose ancestors were born in the same region and who often share a language, culture, and religion.

ETHNIC AND RACIAL GROUPS It is easy to confuse culture, ethnicity, and race because these terms sometimes overlap (see Figure 1.8). People of an **ethnic group** share certain attributes, almost always including ancestral heritage and usually national origin, religion, and language (Whitfield & McClearn, 2005). That means that ethnic groups often share a culture, but this is not a requirement. Some people of a particular ethnicity differ culturally (consider people of Irish descent in Ireland, Australia, and North America), and some cultures include people of several ethnic groups (consider British culture).

Ethnic groups are primarily social constructions, dependent on context. For example, African-born people who live in North America typically consider themselves African, but African-born people living on that continent identify with a more specific ethnic group, Yoruba not Ibo or Hausa (Nigeria), or Kikuyo not Luhya or Luo (Kenya). Although many Americans consider warring participants within distant nations (e.g., Syria, Iraq, Russia) to be of the same ethnicity as their enemies, the rivals themselves do not.

Race is also a social construction—and a misleading one. There are good reasons to abandon the term, and good reasons to keep it, as the following explains.

ANSWER TO OBSERVATION QUIZ
(from page 16) Nine—not counting the standing boy or the possible tenth one whose head is under the blanket. Rumpled blankets suggest that eight more are elsewhere at the moment. Each night hundreds of children sleep in this Border Protection Processing Facility in Brownsville, Texas. They are detained while authorities decide whether to send them back to the countries they fled or to a safe place in the United States. ●

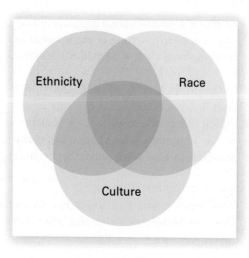

FIGURE 1.8 Overlap—But How Much?
Ethnicity, culture, and race are three distinct concepts, but they often—though not always—overlap.

OPPOSING PERSPECTIVES*

Using the Word *Race*

The term **race** is used to categorize people via physical markers, particularly outward appearance. Historically, most North Americans believed that race was the outward manifestation of inborn biological differences. Fifty years ago, races were categorized by skin color: white, black, red, and yellow (Coon, 1962).

It is obvious now, but was not a few decades ago, that no one's skin is white (like this page) or black (like these letters) or red or yellow. Social scientists consider race a social construction. They contend that color terms were used to exaggerate differences in skin tones.

Genetic analysis confirms that the biological concept of race is inaccurate. Although most genes are identical in every human, those few genetic differences that distinguish one person from another are poorly indexed by appearance (Race, Ethnicity, and Genetics Working Group, 2005).

Skin color is particularly misleading because dark-skinned people with African ancestors have "the highest levels of genetic diversity" (Tishkoff et al., 2009, p. 1035) and dark-skinned people with non-African ancestors (such as indigenous Australians or Maori in New Zealand) share neither culture nor ethnicity with Africans.

Race is more than a flawed concept; it is a destructive one. Slavery, lynching, and segregation were directly connected to the conviction that race was inborn. Racism continues today in less obvious ways (some highlighted later in this book), impeding the goal of our study—to help everyone fulfill their potential.

Since race is a social construction that leads to racism, some social scientists believe that the term should be abandoned (Gilroy, 2000). It is no longer used in many nations. A study of 141 nations found that 85 percent never use the word *race* on their census forms (Morning, 2008). Only in the United States does the census still distinguish between race and ethnicity, stating that Hispanics "may be of any race."

Because of the way human cognition works, such labels encourage stereotyping (Kelly et al., 2010). As one scholar explains:

> The United States' unique conceptual distinction between race and ethnicity may unwittingly support the longstanding belief that race reflects biological difference and ethnicity stems from cultural difference . . . [and] preclude understanding of the ways in which racial categories are also socially constructed.
>
> *[Morning, 2008, p. 255]*

Perhaps to avoid racism, the word *race* should not be used.

But consider the opposite perspective (Bliss, 2012). In a society with a history of racial discrimination, reversing that cultural heritage may *require* recognizing race. Although race is a social construction, not a biological distinction, it is powerful

race
A group of people who are regarded by themselves or by others as distinct from other groups on the basis of physical appearance, typically skin color.

nonetheless. Many medical, educational, and economic conditions—from low birthweight to college graduation, from family income to health insurance—reflect racial disparities.

Furthermore, particularly in adolescence, people who are proud of their racial identity are likely to achieve academically, resist drug addiction, and feel better about themselves (Crosnoe & Johnson, 2011; Zimmerman et al., 2013). To encourage racial pride, race may first need to be recognized.

Indeed, many social scientists argue that pretending that race does not exist allows racism to thrive (e.g., sociologists Marvasti & McKinney, 2011; anthropologist McCabe, 2011). Two political scientists studying criminal justice found that people who claim to be color-blind display "an extraordinary level of naiveté" (Peffley & Hurwitz, 2010, p. 113).

According to some scholars, criticism of President Obama reveals racial prejudice, and uninformed anti-racism actually is a new form of racism (Sullivan, 2014; Hughey & Parks, 2014).

RYUHEI SHINDO/TAXI/GETTY IMAGES

Young Laughter Friendship across ethnic lines is common at every age, when schools, workplaces, and neighborhoods are not segregated. However, past history has an impact: These two girls share so much that they spontaneously laugh together, unaware that this scene in a restaurant could not have happened 50 years ago. Many of the youngest cohorts have trouble understanding lynching, poll taxes, separate swimming pools, or even the historic March on Washington in 1963.

THINK CRITICALLY: To fight racism, must race be named and recognized?

---

*Every page of this text includes information that requires critical thinking and evaluation, and every chapter includes some brief "Think Critically" questions. In addition, once in each chapter you will find an Opposing Perspectives feature in which an issue that has compelling opposite perspectives is highlighted.

Diverse Complexities

It is often repeated that "the United States is becoming more diverse," a phrase that usually refers only to ethnic diversity and not to economic and religious diversity (which are also increasing and merit attention). From a developmental perspective, two other diversities are also important—age and region, as shown below. What are the implications for schools, colleges, employment, health care, and nursing homes in the notable differences in the ages of people of various groups? And are attitudes about immigration, or segregation, or multiracial identity affected by the ethnicity of one's neighbors?

THE ETHNIC MAKE-UP OF THE UNITED STATES IS CHANGING DATA FROM 2000-2009

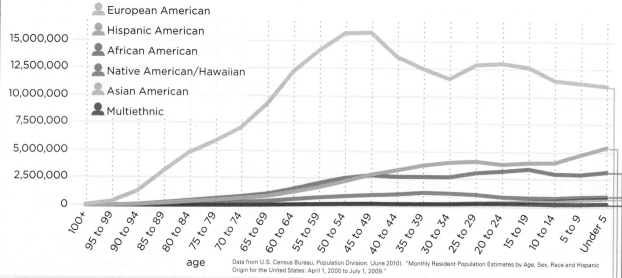

age

Data from U.S. Census Bureau, Population Division. (June 2010). "Monthly Resident Population Estimates by Age, Sex, Race and Hispanic Origin for the United States: April 1, 2000 to July 1, 2009."

REGIONAL DIFFERENCES IN ETHNICITY ACROSS THE UNITED STATES

In the United States, there are regional as well as age differences in ethnicity. This map shows which counties have an ethnic population greater than the national average. Counties where more than one ethnicity or race is greater than the national average are shown as multiethnic. Areas for which data are unavailable are left unshaded.

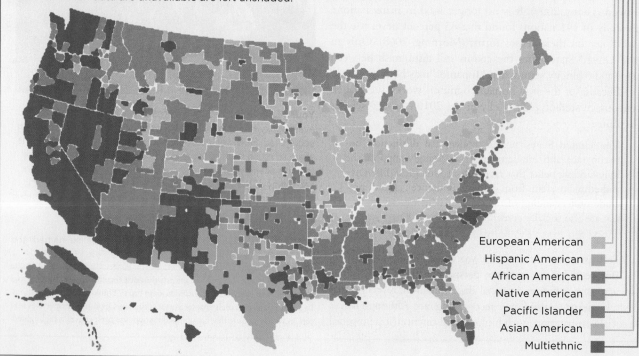

Development Is Plastic

Both brain and behavior are far more plastic than once was thought. The term *plasticity* denotes two complementary aspects of development: Human traits can be molded (as plastic can be), and yet people maintain a certain durability (as plastic does). This provides both hope and realism—hope because change is possible and realism because development builds on what has come before.

Plasticity is basic to our contemporary understanding of human development because it simultaneously incorporates two facts: People can change over time, and new behavior depends partly on what has already happened.

This is evident in the **dynamic-systems approach,** a framework many contemporary developmentalists use. The idea behind this approach is that human development is an ongoing, ever-changing interaction between the individual and all the systems, domains, and cultures.

Note the word *dynamic:* Physical contexts, emotional influences, the passage of time, each person, and every aspect of the ecosystem are always interacting, always in flux, always in motion. For instance, a useful strategy for developing motor skills in children with autism spectrum disorder (described in Chapter 7) is to think of the dynamic systems that undergird movement—the changing physical and social contexts (Lee & Porretta, 2013). Systematically considering contexts helps such children—not to make the autism disappear (past conditions are always influential) but to improve the child's ability to function.

The most surprising example of plasticity in recent years involves the brain. Expansion of neurological structures, networks of communication between one cell and another, and even creation of neurons (brain cells) occurs in adulthood. This neurological plasticity is evident in hundreds of studies mentioned later in this text (see Figure 1.9).

Plasticity is especially useful when anticipating growth of a particular person: Everyone is constrained by past circumstances, but no one is confined by them. Consider David.

AP PHOTO/JIM MONE

Dynamic Interaction A dynamic-systems approach highlights the ever-changing impact that each part of a system has on all the other parts. This classroom scene reflects the eagerness for education felt by many immigrants, the reticence of some boys in an academic context, and a global perspective (as demonstrated by the world map). These facets emerge from various systems—family, gender, and culture—and they have interacted to produce this moment.

OBSERVATION QUIZ
What country is this? (see answer, page 23) ▲

dynamic-systems approach
A view of human development as an ongoing, ever-changing interaction between the physical, cognitive, and psychosocial influences.

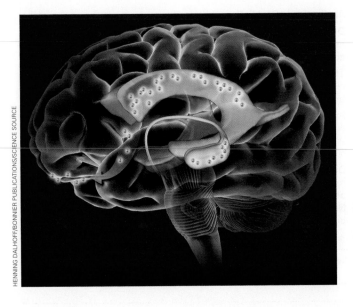

HENNING DALHOFF/BONNIER PUBLICATIONS/SCIENCE SOURCE

FIGURE 1.9 Birth of a Neuron A decade ago neuroscientists thought that adult brains lost neurons, with age or alcohol, but never gained them. Now we know that precursors of neurons arise in the lateral ventricles (bright blue, center) to become functioning neurons in the olfactory bulb (for smell, far left) and the hippocampus (for memory, the brown structure just above the brain stem). Adult neurogenesis is much less prolific than earlier in life, but the fact that it occurs at all is astounding.

A CASE TO STUDY*

My Nephew David

My sister-in-law contracted rubella (also called German measles) early in her third pregnancy, a fact not recognized until David was born, blind and dying. Heart surgery two days after birth saved his life, but surgery at 6 months to remove a cataract destroyed that eye. Malformations of his thumbs, ankles, teeth, feet, spine, and brain became evident. David did not walk or talk or even chew for years. Some people wondered why his parents did not place him in an institution.

Yet dire early predictions—from me as well as many others—have proven false. David is a productive adult, and happy, sometimes surprisingly so. His father died in 2014. In the days after the death, most of us were sad and grieving, but not David. "Dad is in a better place. I miss him, but he is happy," he told me.

He attended regular public school, then the Kentucky School for the Blind, and then the University of Kentucky, earning a college degree. He then studied at an international school in Germany for translators. He relates well to his two older brothers (see photo) and especially to his two sisters-in-law, who call him every week to discuss family and politics.

Remember, plasticity cannot erase a person's genes, childhood, or permanent damage. David's disabilities are always with him (at age 46 he still lives with his mother). But his childhood experiences gave him lifelong strengths. His family loved and nurtured him, sending him to four preschools and then public kindergarten at age 6. By age 10, David had skipped a year of school and was a fifth-grader, reading large print at the eleventh-grade level. He learned to speak a sec-

ond and a third language. In college, after one failing semester (requiring family assistance again), he earned several As.

David works as a translator, which he enjoys because "I like providing a service to scholars, giving them access to something they would otherwise not have." As his aunt, I have seen him repeatedly defy predictions, evidence of plasticity. All four of the characteristics of the life-span perspective are evident in David's life, as summarized in Table 1.3.

My Brother's Children Michael, Bill, and David *(left to right)* are adults now, with quite different personalities, abilities, and offspring (4, 2, and none), and contexts (in Massachusetts, Pennsylvania, and California). Yet despite genes, prenatal life, and contexts, I see the shared influence of Glen and Dot, my brother and sister-in-law—evident here in their similar, friendly smiles.

TABLE 1.3	Four Characteristics of Development	
Characteristic	**Application in David's Story**
Multi-directional. Change occurs in every direction, not always in a straight line. Gains and losses, predictable growth, and unexpected transformations are evident.	David's development seemed static (or even regressive, as when early surgery destroyed one eye) but then accelerated each time he entered a new school or college.
Multi-contextual. Human lives are embedded in many contexts, including historical conditions, economic constraints, and family patterns.	The high SES of David's family made it possible for him to receive good medical and educational care. His two older brothers protected him.
Multi-cultural. Many cultures—not just between nations but also within them—affect how people develop.	Appalachia, where David and his family lived, has a particular culture, including acceptance of people with disabilities and willingness to help families in need. Those aspects of that culture benefited David and his family.
Plasticity. Every individual, and every trait within each individual, can be altered at any point in the life span. Change is ongoing, although neither random nor easy.	David's measured IQ changed from about 40 (severely mentally retarded) to about 130 (far above average), and his physical disabilities became less crippling as he matured. Nonetheless, because of a virus contracted before he was born, his entire life will never be what it might have been.

*Every chapter of this text has A Case to Study. No single case can prove or disprove a hypothesis, but often one example illustrates a general finding or an important concept.

Plasticity emphasizes that people can and do change, that predictions are not always accurate. Three insights already explained have improved predictions: (1) Nature and nurture always interact. (2) Certain ages are sensitive periods for particular kinds of development. (3) Genes predispose people to respond to certain circumstances, in differential susceptibility.

This was apparent for David: His inherited characteristics (from his smart parents) affected his ability to learn, his four preschools in early childhood (a sensitive period for language) helped him lifelong, and his inborn temperament (he is still devastated by criticism but overjoyed by praise) helped him flourish because he was easily influenced by his parents' devoted guidance. If I had known more about human development when he was born with multiple disabilities, I would have predicted a brighter—and more accurate—future for him.

ANSWER TO **OBSERVATION** QUIZ
(from page 21) The three Somali girls wearing headscarves may have thrown you off, but these first-graders attend school in Minneapolis, Minnesota, in the United States. Clues include the children's diversity (this school has students from 17 nations), clothing (obviously Western), and—for the sharp-eyed—the flag near the door. ●

WHAT HAVE YOU LEARNED?

1. How can both continuity and discontinuity be true for human development?
2. What are some of the contexts of your life?
3. How does the exosystem affect children's schooling?
4. What are some cohort differences between your generation and the one of your parents?
5. What factors comprise a person's SES (socioeconomic status)?
6. Can you think of an example (not one in the book) of a social construction?
7. What is the difference between race and ethnicity?
8. How does a culture pass on values to the next generation, according to Vygotsky?
9. In what two contrasting ways is human development plastic?
10. What is implied when human development is described as dynamic?

Theories of Human Development

As you read earlier in this chapter, the scientific method begins with observations, questions, and theories (Step 1). That leads to specific hypotheses that can be tested (Step 2). A *theory* is a comprehensive and organized explanation of many phenomena; a *hypothesis* is more limited and may be proven false. Theories are generalities; hypotheses are specific.

Theories sharpen perceptions and organize the thousands of behaviors we observe every day. Each **developmental theory** is a systematic statement of principles and generalizations, providing a framework for understanding how and why people change over the life span.

Imagine building a house from a heap of lumber, nails, and other materials. Without a plan and workers, the heap cannot become a home. Likewise, observations of human development are raw materials, but theories put them together. Kurt Lewin (1943) once quipped, "Nothing is as practical as a good theory."

Dozens of such theories appear throughout this text. The five theories about to be explained are chosen because each provides a comprehensive, influential, and somewhat distinctive view of human development. Many social scientists are strongly influenced by other theories, as you will see.

Psychoanalytic Theory

Inner drives and motives are the foundation of **psychoanalytic theory.** These basic underlying forces are thought to influence every aspect of thinking and behavior, from the smallest details of daily life to the crucial choices of a lifetime.

developmental theory
A group of ideas, assumptions, and generalizations that interpret and illuminate thousands of observations about human growth. A developmental theory provides a framework for explaining the patterns and problems of development.

psychoanalytic theory
A theory of human development that holds that irrational, unconscious drives and motives, often originating in childhood, underlie human behavior.

AKG/PHOTO RESEARCHERS

Freud at Work In addition to being the world's first psychoanalyst, Sigmund Freud was a prolific writer. His many papers and case histories, primarily descriptions of his patients' symptoms and sexual urges, helped make the psychoanalytic perspective a dominant force for much of the twentieth century.

FREUD'S STAGES Psychoanalytic theory originated with Sigmund Freud (1856–1939), an Austrian physician who treated patients suffering from mental illness. He listened to their dreams and fantasies and constructed an elaborate, multifaceted theory.

According to Freud, development in the first six years occurs in three stages, each characterized by sexual pleasure centered on a particular part of the body. Infants experience the *oral stage* because their erotic body part is the mouth, followed by the *anal stage* in early childhood, with the focus on the anus. In the preschool years (the *phallic stage*), the penis becomes a source of pride and fear for boys and a reason for sadness and envy for girls.

In middle childhood comes *latency,* a quiet period that ends with the *genital stage* at puberty. Freud thought that the genital stage continued throughout adulthood, which makes him the most famous theorist who thought that development stopped after puberty (see Table 1.4). As you remember, this assumption is no longer held by developmentalists.

Freud maintained that at each stage, sensual satisfaction (from the mouth, anus, or genitals) is linked to developmental needs, challenges, and conflicts. How people experience and resolve these conflicts—especially those related to weaning (oral), toilet training (anal), male roles (phallic), and sexual pleasure (genital)—determines personality patterns because "the early stages provide the foundation for adult behavior" (Salkind, 2004, p. 125).

ERIKSON'S STAGES Many of Freud's followers became famous theorists themselves. The most notable for our study of human development was Erik Erikson (1902–1994), who described eight developmental stages, each characterized by a challenging crisis (summarized in Table 1.4). Although Erikson's first five stages build on Freud's theory, he also described three adult stages, perhaps because he saw himself changed with several adult shifts in context. He was a wandering artist in Italy, a teacher in Austria, and a Harvard professor in the United States.

© 2016 MACMILLAN

No Choking During the oral stage, children put everything in their mouths, as Freud recognized and as 12-month-old Harper Vasquez does here. Toy manufacturers and lawyers know this, too, which is why many toy packages say "Choking hazard: small parts, not appropriate for children under age 3."

TABLE 1.4	Comparing Stages: Freud and Erikson	
Approximate Age	**Freud (Psychosexual)**	**Erikson (Psychosocial)**
Birth to 1 year	*Oral Stage* The lips, tongue, and gums are the focus of pleasurable sensations in the baby's body, and sucking and feeding are the most stimulating activities.	*Trust vs. Mistrust* Babies either trust that others will care for their basic needs, including nourishment, warmth, cleanliness, and physical contact, *or* develop mistrust about the care of others.
1–3 years	*Anal Stage* The anus is the focus of pleasurable sensations in the baby's body, and toilet training is the most important activity.	*Autonomy vs. Shame and Doubt* Children either become self-sufficient in many activities, including toileting, feeding, walking, exploring, and talking, *or* doubt their own abilities.
3–6 years	*Phallic Stage* The phallus, or penis, is the most important body part, and pleasure is derived from genital stimulation. Boys are proud of their penises; girls wonder why they don't have one.	*Initiative vs. Guilt* Children either want to undertake many adultlike activities *or* internalize the limits and prohibitions set by parents. They feel either adventurous *or* guilty.
6–11 years	*Latency* Not really a stage, latency is an interlude during which sexual needs are quiet and children put psychic energy into conventional activities like schoolwork and sports.	*Industry vs. Inferiority* Children busily learn to be competent and productive in mastering new skills *or* feel inferior, unable to do anything as well as they wish they could.
Adolescence	*Genital Stage* The genitals are the focus of pleasurable sensations, and the young person seeks sexual stimulation and sexual satisfaction in heterosexual relationships.	*Identity vs. Role Confusion* Adolescents try to figure out "Who am I?" They establish sexual, political, and vocational identities *or* are confused about what roles to play.
Adulthood	Freud believed that the genital stage lasts throughout adulthood. He also said that the goal of a healthy life is "to love and to work."	*Intimacy vs. Isolation* Young adults seek companionship and love *or* become isolated from others, fearing rejection and disappointment. *Generativity vs. Stagnation* Middle-aged adults contribute to the next generation through meaningful work, creative activities, and raising a family, *or* they stagnate. *Integrity vs. Despair* Older adults try to make sense out of their lives, either seeing life as a meaningful whole *or* despairing at goals never reached.

Erikson named two polarities at each stage (which is why the word *versus* is used in each), but he recognized that many outcomes between these opposites are possible (Erikson, 1993). For most people, development at each stage leads to neither extreme.

For instance, the generativity-versus-stagnation stage of adulthood rarely involves a person who is totally stagnant—no children, no work, no creativity. Instead, most adults are somewhat stagnant and somewhat generative. As the dynamic-systems theory would predict, the balance may shift year by year.

Erikson, like Freud, believed that adult problems echo childhood conflicts. For example, an adult who cannot form a secure, close relationship (intimacy

A Legendary Couple In his first 30 years, Erikson never fit into a particular local community, since he frequently changed nations, schools, and professions. Then he met Joan. In their first five decades of marriage, they raised a family and wrote several books. If he had published his theory at age 73 (when this photograph was taken) instead of in his 40s, would he still have described life as a series of crises?

TED STRESHINSKY/THE LIFE IMAGES COLLECTION/GETTY IMAGES

TABLE 1.5 Psychoanalytic Theory vs. Behaviorism

Area of Disagreement	Psychoanalytic Theory	Behaviorism
The unconscious	Emphasizes unconscious wishes and urges, unknown to the person but powerful all the same	Holds that the unconscious not only is unknowable but also may be a destructive fiction that keeps people from changing
Observable behavior	Holds that observable behavior is a symptom, not the cause—the tip of an iceberg, with the bulk of the problem submerged	Looks only at observable behavior—what a person does rather than what a person thinks, feels, or imagines
Importance of childhood	Stresses that early childhood, including infancy, is critical; even if a person does not remember what happened, the early legacy lingers throughout life	Holds that current conditioning is crucial; early habits and patterns can be unlearned, even reversed, if appropriate reinforcements and punishments are used
Scientific status	Holds that most aspects of human development are beyond the reach of scientific experiment; uses ancient myths, the words of disturbed adults, dreams, play, and poetry as raw material	Is proud to be a science, dependent on verifiable data and carefully controlled experiments; discards ideas that sound good but are not proven

behaviorism
A theory of human development that studies observable behavior. Behaviorism is also called *learning theory* because it describes the laws and processes by which behavior is learned.

ARCHIVES OF THE HISTORY OF AMERICAN PSYCHOLOGY/THE UNIVERSITY OF AKRON

An Early Behaviorist John Watson was an early proponent of learning theory. His ideas are still influential and controversial today.

conditioning
According to behaviorism, the processes by which responses become linked to particular stimuli and learning takes place. The word *conditioning* is used to emphasize the importance of repeated practice, as when an athlete *conditions* his or her body by training for a long time.

versus isolation) may not have resolved the crisis of infancy (trust versus mistrust). However, Erikson's stages differ significantly from Freud's in that they emphasize family and culture, not sexual urges. He called his theory *epigenetic,* partly to stress that genes and biological impulses are powerfully influenced by the social environment.

Behaviorism

Another influential theory, **behaviorism,** arose in direct opposition to the psychoanalytic emphasis on unconscious, hidden urges (differences are described in Table 1.5). Behaviorists emphasize nurture, the specific responses from other people and the environment to whatever a developing person does.

WATSON Early in the twentieth century, John B. Watson (1878–1958) argued that scientists should examine only what they could observe and measure. According to Watson, if psychologists focus on behavior, they will realize that anything can be learned. For this reason, behaviorism is also called *learning theory.* Watson wrote:

> Give me a dozen healthy infants, well-formed, and my own specified world to bring them up in and I'll guarantee to take any one at random and train him to become any type of specialist I might select—doctor, lawyer, artist, merchant chief, and yes, even beggar-man and thief, regardless of his talents, penchants, tendencies, abilities, vocations, and race.
>
> *[Watson, 1998, p. 82]*

Many other psychologists, especially in the United States, agreed. They found that the unconscious motives and drives that Freud described were difficult (or impossible) to verify via the scientific method (Uttal, 2000). For instance, researchers discovered that, contrary to Freud's view, the parents' approach to toilet training did *not* determine a child's later personality.

For every individual at every age, from newborn to centenarian, behaviorists have identified laws to describe how environmental responses shape what people do. All behavior—from reading a book to robbing a bank, from saying "Good morning" to a stranger to saying "I love you" to a spouse—follows these laws. Every action is learned, step by step.

PAVLOV The specific laws of learning apply to **conditioning,** the processes by which responses become linked to particular stimuli.

More than a century ago, Ivan Pavlov (1849–1936), a Russian medical doctor born in poverty who won a Nobel Prize for his work on digestion, noticed something in his experimental dogs that awakened his curiosity (Step 1 of the scientific method) (Todes, 2014). The dogs drooled not only when they saw and smelled food but also when they heard the footsteps of the attendants who brought the food. This observation led Pavlov to hypotheses and experiments in which he conditioned dogs to salivate when they heard a specific noise (Steps 2 and 3).

Pavlov began by sounding a tone just before presenting food. After a number of repetitions of the tone-then-food sequence, dogs began salivating at the sound, even when there was no food. This simple experiment demonstrated *classical conditioning*, when a person or animal learns to associate a neutral stimulus (the sound) with a meaningful stimulus (the food), gradually reacting to the neutral stimulus in the same way as to the meaningful one (Step 4). The fact that Pavlov published (Step 5) in Russian is one reason his research took decades to reach the United States (Todes, 2014).

SKINNER One influential North American behaviorist, B. F. Skinner (1904–1990), was inspired by Pavlov (1953). Skinner agreed that classical conditioning explains some behavior. Then he went further, experimenting to demonstrate another type of conditioning, **operant conditioning.**

In operant conditioning (also called *instrumental conditioning*), animals (including humans) perform some action and then a response occurs. If the response is useful or pleasurable, the animal is likely to repeat the action; if the response is painful, the animal is not likely to repeat the action. In both cases, the animal has learned.

Pleasant consequences are sometimes called *rewards,* and unpleasant consequences are sometimes called *punishments.* Behaviorists hesitate to use those words, however, because what people think of as punishment can actually be a reward, and vice versa.

For example, how should a parent punish a child? Withholding dessert? Spanking? Not letting them play? Speaking harshly? If a child hates that dessert, being deprived of it is actually a reward, not a punishment. Another child might not mind a spanking, especially if he or she craves parental attention. For that child, the intended punishment (spanking) is actually a reward (attention).

Any consequence that follows a behavior and makes the person (or animal) likely to repeat that behavior is called a reinforcement, *not* a reward. Once a behavior has been conditioned, humans and other creatures will repeat it even if reinforcement occurs only occasionally. Similarly, an unpleasant response makes a creature less likely to repeat a certain action.

A Contemporary of Freud Ivan Pavlov was a physiologist who received the Nobel Prize in 1904 for his research on digestive processes. It was this line of study that led to his discovery of classical conditioning, when his research on dog saliva led to insight about learning.

OBSERVATION QUIZ

In appearance, how is Pavlov similar to Freud, and how do both look different from the other theorists pictured? (see answer, page 29) ▲

operant conditioning
The learning process by which a particular action is followed by something desired (a reinforcer which makes the person or animal more likely to repeat the action) or by something unwanted (a punishment which makes the action less likely to be repeated). (Also called *instrumental conditioning.*)

Rats, Pigeons, and People
B. F. Skinner is best known for his experiments with rats and pigeons, but he also applied his knowledge to human behavior. For his daughter, he designed a glass-enclosed crib in which controlling temperature, humidity, and perceptual stimulation made her experience enjoyable and educational. He encouraged her first attempts to talk by smiling and responding with words, affection, or other positive reinforcement.

Still Social Learning Even in his 80s, Albert Bandura (shown here in midlife) is on the faculty at Stanford University. One reason, of course, it that he is esteemed by his peers, and another reason is that, as a proponent of social learning, he believes he can still influence many others. Social interaction is central to social learning theory.

Video Activity: Modeling: Learning by Observation features the original footage of Bandura's famous experiment.

social learning theory
An extension of behaviorism that emphasizes the influence that other people have over a person's behavior. Even without specific reinforcement, every individual learns many things through observation and imitation of other people. (Also called *observational learning*.)

cognitive theory
A theory of human development that focuses on changes in how people think over time. According to this theory, thoughts shape attitudes, beliefs, and behaviors.

Would You Talk to This Man? Children loved talking to Jean Piaget, and he learned by listening carefully—especially to their incorrect explanations, which no one had paid much attention to before. All his life, Piaget was absorbed with studying the way children think. He called himself a "genetic epistemologist"—one who studies how children gain knowledge about the world as they grow.

Almost all daily behavior, from combing your hair to joking with friends, is a result of past operant conditioning, according to behaviorists. Likewise, things people fear, from giving a speech to eating raw fish, are avoided because of past punishment.

This insight has many practical applications for human development. Early responses are crucial because children learn habits that endure. For instance, if parents want their child to share, and their baby offers them a gummy, half-eaten cracker, they should take the gift with apparent delight and then return it, smiling.

According to behaviorism, people are never too old to learn. If an adult is afraid of speaking in public (a particular kind of social phobia, very common), then repeated reinforcement for talking (such as a professor praising a student's question) could eventually lead to speeches before an audience.

BANDURA A major extension of behaviorism is **social learning theory,** first described by Albert Bandura (b. 1925). This theory notes that, because humans are social beings, they learn from observing others, even without personally receiving any reinforcement (Bandura, 1977; 2006).

For example, many studies find that most children who witness domestic violence are influenced by it. As differential susceptibility and multi-contextualism would predict, the particular lesson learned depends on each individual's genes and experiences. For instance, if their father often hit their mother, one son might identify with the abuser and another with the victim, perhaps because of how their mother cared for them when they were infants.

Later in adulthood, because of their past social learning, one man might slap his wife and spank his children, while his brother might be fearful and apologetic at home. Social learning taught them opposite lessons. A third brother might be more like a dandelion than an orchid, unaffected by past memories.

Cognitive Theory

In **cognitive theory**, each person's ideas and beliefs are crucial. This theory has dominated psychology since about 1980 and has branched into many versions. The word *cognitive* refers not just to thinking but also to attitudes, beliefs, and assumptions.

The most famous cognitive theorist was Jean Piaget (1896–1980). Unlike other scientists of the early twentieth century, Piaget realized that babies are curious and thoughtful, creating their own interpretations about their world. He began by observing his own three infants; later he studied thousands of older children (Inhelder & Piaget, 1958/2013b).

From this work, Piaget developed the central thesis of cognitive theory: How

TABLE 1.6   Piaget's Periods of Cognitive Development

Age Range	Name of Period	Characteristics of the Period	Major Gains During the Period
Birth to 2 years	Sensorimotor	Infants use senses and motor abilities to understand the world. Learning is active; there is no conceptual or reflective thought.	Infants learn that an object still exists when it is out of sight (object permanence) and begin to think through mental actions.
2–6 years	Preoperational	Children think magically and poetically, using language to understand the world. Thinking is egocentric, causing children to perceive the world from their own perspective.	The imagination flourishes, and language becomes a significant means of self-expression and of influence from others.
6–11 years	Concrete operational	Children understand and apply logical operations, or principles, to interpret experiences objectively and rationally. Their thinking is limited to what they can personally see, hear, touch, and experience.	By applying logical abilities, children learn to understand concepts of conservation, number, classification, and many other scientific ideas.
12 years through adulthood	Formal operational	Adolescents and adults think about abstractions and hypothetical concepts and reason analytically, not just emotionally. They can be logical about things they have never experienced.	Ethics, politics, and social and moral issues become fascinating as adolescents and adults take a broader and more theoretical approach to experience.

people think (not just what they know) changes with time and experience, and then human thinking influences actions. Piaget maintained that cognitive development occurs in four major age-related periods, or stages: *sensorimotor, preoperational, concrete operational,* and *formal operational* (see Table 1.6).

Intellectual advancement occurs lifelong because humans seek *cognitive equilibrium,* that is, a state of mental balance. An easy way (called *assimilation*) to achieve this balance is to interpret new experiences through the lens of preexisting ideas. For example, infants discover that new objects can be grasped in the same way as familiar objects; adolescents explain the day's headlines as evidence that supports their existing worldviews; older adults speak fondly of the good old days as embodying values that should endure.

Sometimes, however, a new experience is jarring and incomprehensible. The resulting experience is one of *cognitive disequilibrium,* an imbalance that initially creates confusion. As Figure 1.10 illustrates, disequilibrium leads to cognitive growth because it forces people to adapt their old concepts (called *accommodation*). Current research supports the idea that learning is more likely to occur if it took some effort to achieve (Brown et al., 2014).

How to Think About Flowers A person's stage of cognitive growth influences how he or she thinks about everything, including flowers. *(a)* To an infant, in the sensorimotor stage, flowers are "known" through pulling, smelling, and even biting. *(b)* At the concrete operational stage, children become more logical. This boy can understand that flowers need sunlight, water, and time to grow. *(c)* At the adult's formal operational stage, flowers can be part of a larger, logical scheme—for instance, to earn money while cultivating beauty. As illustrated by all three photos, thinking is an active process from the beginning of life until the end.

(a) (b) (c)

Highlights of the Science of Human Development

As evident throughout this textbook, much more research and appreciation of the brain, social context, and the non-Western world has expanded our understanding of human development in the twenty-first century. This timeline lists a few highlights of the past.

200,000–50,000 BCE With their large brains, long period of child development, and extensive social and family support, early humans were able to sustain life and raise children more effectively than other primates.

c. 400 BCE In ancient Greece, ideas about children from philosophers like Plato (c. 428–348 BCE) and Aristotle (384–322 BCE) influenced further thoughts about children. Plato believed children were born with knowledge. Aristotle believed children learn from experience.

1650–1800 European philosophers like John Locke (1632–1704) and Jean-Jacques Rousseau (1712–1778) debate whether children are born as "blank slates" and how much control parents should take in raising them.

1797 First European vaccination: Edward Jenner (1749–1823) publicizes smallpox inoculation, building on vaccination against smallpox in Asia, the Middle East, and Africa.

1750–1850 Beginning of Western laws regulating child labor and protecting the rights of children.

1879 First experimental psychology laboratory established in Leipzig, Germany.

1885 Sigmund Freud (1856–1939) publishes *Studies on Hysteria*, one of the first works establishing the importance of the subconscious and marking the beginning of the theories of psychoanalytic theory.

1895 Ivan Pavlov (1849–1936) begins research on dogs' salivation response.

1905 Max Weber (1864–1920), the founder of sociology, writes *The Protestant Work Ethic*, about human values and adult work.

1905 Alfred Binet's (1857–1911) intelligence test published.

1907 Maria Montessori (1870–1952) opens her first school in Rome.

HARVEY WATTS PHOTOGRAPHY/GETTY IMAGES

1913 John B. Watson (1878–1958) publishes *Psychology As the Behaviorist Views It*.

140 BCE In China, imperial examinations are one of the first times cognitive testing is used on young people.

500–1500 During the Middle Ages in Europe, many adults believed that children were miniature adults.

1100–1200 First universities founded in Europe. Young people pay to be educated together.

1837 First kindergarten opens in Germany, part of a movement to teach young children before they entered the primary school system.

1859 Charles Darwin (1809–1882) publishes *On the Origin of Species*, sparking debates about what is genetic and what is environmental.

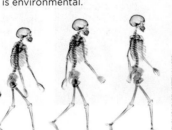

1900 Compulsory schooling for children is established for most children in the United States and Europe.

1903 The term "gerontology," the branch of developmental science devoted to studying aging, first coined.

1920 Lev Vygotsky (1896–1934) develops sociocultural theory in the former Soviet Union.

1923 Jean Piaget (1896–1980) publishes *The Language and Thought of the Child*.

1933 Society for Research on Child Development, the preeminent organization for research on child development, founded.

1939 Mamie (1917–1983) and Kenneth Clark (1914–2005) receive their research grants to study race in early childhood.

JGI/JAMIE GRILL/GETTY IMAGES

1943 Abraham Maslow (1908–1970) publishes *A Theory of Motivation*, establishing the hierarchy of needs.

1950 Erik Erikson (1902–1994) expands on Freud's theory to include social aspects of personality development with the publication of *Childhood and Society*.

©2016 MACMILLAN

1951 John Bowlby (1907–1990) publishes *Maternal Care and Mental Health*, one of his first works on the importance of parent–child attachment.

MONKEY BUSINESS IMAGES/SHUTTERSTOCK

1953 Publication of the first papers describing DNA, our genetic blueprint.

DIGITAL VISION VECTORS/GETTY IMAGES

1957 Harry Harlow (1905–1981) publishes *Love in Infant Monkeys*, describing his research on attachment in rhesus monkeys.

MARTIN ROGERS/GETTY IMAGES

1961 The morning sickness drug thalidomide is banned after children are born with serious birth defects, calling attention to the problem of teratogens during pregnancy.

1961 Alfred Bandura (b. 1925) conducts the Bobo Doll experiments, leading to the development of social learning theory.

1979 Urie Bronfenbrenner (1917–2005) publishes his work on ecological systems theory.

1986 John Gottman (b. 1942) founded the "Love Lab" at the University of Washington to study what makes relationships work.

1987 Carolyn Rovee–Collier (1942–2014) shows that even young infants can remember in her classic mobile experiments.

FOTOSEARCH/FOTOSEARCH/SUPERSTOCK

1990 The United Nations treaty *Convention on the Rights of the Child* in effect, requiring the best interests of children be considered. Children are no longer considered solely the possession of their parents. Currently all UN nations have signed on, except Somalia, South Sudan, and the United States.

TONGRO/GETTY IMAGES

1993 Howard Gardner (b. 1943) publishes *Multiple Intelligences*, a major new understanding of the diversity of human intellectual abilities. Gardner has since revised and expanded his ideas in many ways.

1800 | 1900 | 2000

ANYAIVANOVA/ISTOCK/THINKSTOCK

1953 B.F. Skinner (1904–1990) conducts experiments on rats and establishes operant conditioning.

1955 Emmy Werner (b. 1929) begins her Kauai study, which focuses on the power of resilience.

DONNA DAY/EXACTOSTOCK 1598/SUPERSTOCK

1956 K. Warner Schaie's (b. 1928) Seattle Longitudinal Study of Adult Intelligence begins.

1965 Head Start, an early-childhood-education program, launched in the United States.

1965 Mary Ainsworth (1913–1999) starts using the "Strange Situation" to measure attachment.

©2016 MACMILLAN

1966 Diana Baumrind (b. 1928) publishes her first work on parenting styles.

1972 Beginning of the Dunedin, New Zealand, study—one of the first longitudinal studies to include genetic markers.

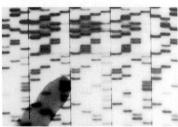

TETRA IMAGES/GETTY IMAGES

1990–Present New brain imaging technology allows pinpointing of brain areas involved in everything from executive function to Alzheimer's disease.

BARIS SIMSEK/GETTY IMAGES

1990 Barbara Rogoff (b. 1950) publishes *Apprenticeship in Thinking*, making developmentalists more aware of the significance of culture and context. Rogoff provided new insights and appreciation of child–rearing in Latin America.

1994 Steven Pinker (b. 1954) publishes *The Language Instinct*, focusing attention on the interaction between neuroscience and behavior, helping developmentalists understand the need for physiological understanding as part of human growth. These themes continue in his later work, such as *How the Mind Works* in 1997.

1995–Present Onward. There are many more discoveries and research chronicled in this book.

BLEND IMAGES/BLEND IMAGES/SUPERSTOCK

FIGURE 1.10 Challenge Me
Most of us, most of the time, prefer the comfort of our conventional conclusions. According to Piaget, however, when new ideas disturb our thinking, we have an opportunity to expand our cognition with a broader and deeper understanding.

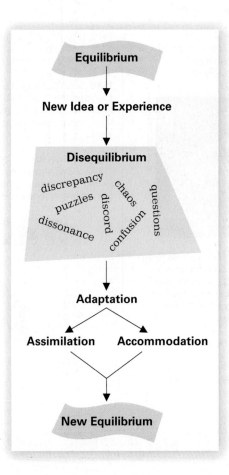

Equilibrium

↓

New Idea or Experience

↓

Disequilibrium

discrepancy
puzzles
dissonance
discord
chaos
confusion
questions

↓

Adaptation

Assimilation ← → **Accommodation**

↓

New Equilibrium

humanism
A theory that stresses the potential of all humans, who have the same basic needs, regardless of culture, gender, or background.

Hope and Laughter Maslow studied law before psychology, and he enjoyed deep discussions with many psychoanalytic theorists who escaped Nazi-dominated Europe. He believed the human spirit could overcome oppression and reach self-actualization, where faith, hope, and humor abound.

Another influential cognitive theory, called *information processing*, is not a stage theory but rather provides a detailed description of the steps of cognition, with attention to perceptual and neurological processes. This theory is especially useful in understanding thinking processes in middle childhood and late adulthood, as you will see in Chapters 7 and 14.

Many researchers, in addition to those influenced by information-processing theory, now think that some of Piaget's conclusions were mistaken. However, every developmentalist appreciates Piaget's basic insight: Thoughts can influence emotions and actions. People of all ages *construct* their understanding of themselves and their world, combining their experiences and their interpretations.

Humanism

Many scientists are convinced that there is something hopeful, unifying, and noble in the human spirit, something often ignored by psychoanalytic theory and by behaviorism. The limits of those two major theories were especially apparent to Abraham Maslow (1908–1970), one of the founders of the psychological theory of **humanism.** Maslow believed that all people—no matter what their culture, gender, or background—have the same basic needs and drives. He arranged these needs in a hierarchy (see Figure 1.11):

1. Physiological: needing food, water, warmth, and air
2. Safety: feeling protected from injury and death
3. Love and belonging: having loving friends, family, and a community
4. Esteem: being respected by the wider community as well as by oneself
5. Self-actualization: becoming truly oneself, fulfilling one's unique potential

At the final level, self-actualization, when all other needs have been met, people can be fully themselves—creative, spiritual, curious, appreciative of nature, able to respect everyone else. The person has "peak experiences" when life is so intensely joyful that time stops and self-seeking disappears (Maslow, 1962/1998).

Maslow contended that everyone must satisfy each lower level before moving higher. A starving man, for instance, may risk his life to secure food (level 1 precedes level 2), or an unloved woman might not care about self-respect because she needs affection (level 3 precedes level 4). People may be destructive and inhumane, not self-actualizing, because of unmet lower needs.

Although humanism does not postulate stages, a developmental application of this theory is that satisfying

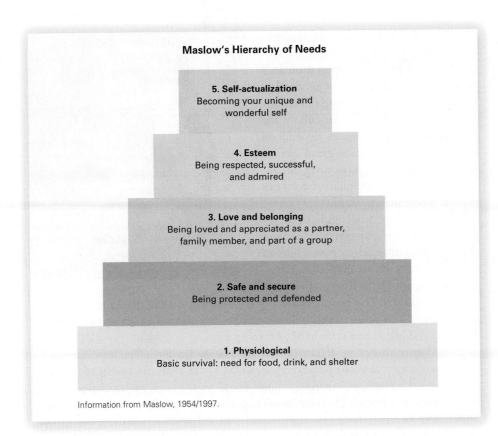

Maslow's Hierarchy of Needs

5. Self-actualization
Becoming your unique and wonderful self

4. Esteem
Being respected, successful, and admired

3. Love and belonging
Being loved and appreciated as a partner, family member, and part of a group

2. Safe and secure
Being protected and defended

1. Physiological
Basic survival: need for food, drink, and shelter

Information from Maslow, 1954/1997.

FIGURE 1.11 Moving Up, Not Looking Back Maslow's hierarchy is like a ladder: Once a person stands firmly on a higher rung, the lower rungs are no longer needed. Thus, someone who has arrived at step 4 might devalue safety (step 2) and be willing to risk personal safety to gain respect.

childhood needs allows later growth. Thus, when babies cry in hunger, someone should feed them because their basic needs (level 1) should be met. People may become thieves or even killers, unable to reach their potential, if they were unsafe (level 2) or unloved (level 3) as children.

This theory is prominent among medical professionals because they realize that pain can be physical (the first two levels) or social (the next two), and they are concerned that their focus on physical health might overlook the person's higher needs (Brown et al., 2014).

A practicing general practitioner writes that Maslow's hierarchy is "a useful reference tool," although he accepts that most of what doctors do is at the lower levels of the pyramid (Dawlatly, 2014). Even the dying need love and belonging (family should be with them) and esteem (the dying need respect).

Evolutionary Theory

Charles Darwin's basic ideas about evolution were first published 150 years ago (Darwin, 1859), but serious research on human development inspired by evolutionary theory is quite recent. According to this theory, nature works to ensure that each species does two things: survive and reproduce. Consequently, many human impulses, needs, and behaviors evolved to help humans survive and thrive over the past 100,000 years (Konner, 2010).

To understand human development, this theory contends, one needs to recognize what was adaptive thousands of years ago. For example, it is irrational that many people are terrified of snakes (which now cause less than one U.S. death in a million), but virtually no one fears automobiles (which cause more than one death in a hundred). Evolutionary theory suggests that the fear instinct evolved to protect life when snakes killed many people, which was true until quite recently in the history of our species. Fears have not caught up to modern life.

Got Milk! Many people in Sweden (like this barefoot preschooler at her summer cottage) drink cow's milk and eat many kinds of cheese. That may be because selective adaptation allowed individuals who could digest lactose to survive in the long Northern winters when no crops grew.

Some of the best human qualities, such as cooperation, spirituality, and self-sacrifice, may have originated thousands of years ago, when groups of people survived because they took care of one another. Childhood itself, particularly the long period when children depend on others while their brains grow, can be explained via evolution (Konner, 2010).

One fact that evolutionary theory can explain is that human mothers welcome child-raising help from fathers, other relatives, and even strangers. Shared child rearing allows women to have children every two years or so, unlike chimpanzees, who space births four or five years apart (Hrdy, 2009). The reason, according to this theory, is the need for survival and reproduction. The result: seven billion humans alive today, but about two hundred thousand chimpanzees, a ratio of 35,000 to one.

Evolutionary theory in developmental psychology has intriguing explanations for many phenomena: women's nausea in pregnancy; 1-year-olds' attachment to their parents; adolescent rebellion; emerging adults' sexual preferences; parents' investment in their children; and late adulthood increases in major neurocognitive disorder and cancer.

All these interpretations are controversial. The influence of nature versus nurture on male/female differences is particularly controversial and provocative (Chapman, 2015). Nonetheless, this theory provides many hypotheses to be explored.

WHAT HAVE YOU LEARNED?

1. What is the role of the unconscious in Freud's theory?
2. What are the stages envisioned by Freud?
3. How do Erikson's stages differ from Freud's?
4. How is behaviorism a reaction to psychoanalytic theory?
5. How do classical and operant conditioning differ?
6. How is social learning connected to behaviorism?
7. What is the basic idea of cognitive theory?
8. How does information processing differ from Piaget's theory?
9. According to Maslow, what are the needs of a person?
10. Why is humanism particularly relevant for the medical professions?
11. How does evolutionary theory apply to human development?

Video Activity: What's Wrong with This Study? explores some of the major pitfalls of the process of designing a research study.

Using the Scientific Method

There are hundreds of ways to design scientific studies and analyze results. Often statistical measures help scientists discover relationships between various aspects of the data. (Some statistical perspectives are presented in Table 1.7.)

Every research design, method, and statistic has strengths as well as weaknesses. Now we describe three basic research designs—observation, the experiment, and the survey—and then three ways developmentalists study change over time.

TABLE 1.7	Statistical Measures Often Used to Analyze Research Results
Measure	**Use**
Effect size	Indicates how much one variable affects another. Effect size ranges from 0 to 1: An effect size of 0.2 is called small, 0.5 moderate, and 0.8 large.
Significance	Indicates whether the results might have occurred by chance. A finding that chance would produce the results only 5 times in 100 is significant at the 0.05 level. A finding that chance would produce the results once in 100 times is significant at 0.01; once in 1,000 times is significant at 0.001.
Cost-benefit analysis	Calculates how much a particular independent variable costs versus how much it saves. This is particularly useful for analyzing public spending, such as whether investment in early education pays off in later years. (It does—see Chapter 5.)
Odds ratio	Indicates how a particular variable compares to a standard, set at 1. For example, one study found that, although less than 1 percent of all child homicides occurred at school, the odds were similar for public and private schools. The odds of such deaths occurring in high schools, however, were 18.47 times that of elementary or middle schools (set at 1.0) (MMWR, January 18, 2008).
Factor analysis	Hundreds of variables could affect any given behavior. In addition, many variables (such as family income and parental education) overlap. To take this into account, analysis reveals variables that can be clustered together to form a factor, which is a composite of many variables. For example, SES might become one factor, child personality another.
Meta-analysis	A "study of studies." Researchers use statistical tools to synthesize the results of previous, separate studies. Then they analyze the accumulated results, using criteria that weight each study fairly. This combines studies that were too small, or too narrow, to lead to solid conclusions.

Research Strategies

Scientific observation requires researchers to record behavior systematically and objectively. Observations often occur in a naturalistic setting (such as a home, school, or public park), where people behave as they usually do and where the observer is ignored or even unnoticed. Observation can also occur in a laboratory, where scientists record human reactions in various situations, often with wall-mounted video cameras and the scientist in another room.

A crucial endeavor in development is to determine the cause and sequence of behavior: Observation does not pin that down. An **experiment** is needed. In the social sciences, experimenters typically impose a particular treatment on a group of participants (formerly called *subjects*) or expose them to a specific condition and then note whether their behavior changes.

In technical terms, the experimenters manipulate an **independent variable,** the imposed treatment or special condition (also called the *experimental variable*). (A *variable* is anything that can vary.) They note whether this independent variable affects

scientific observation
A method of testing a hypothesis by unobtrusively watching and recording participants' behavior in a systematic and objective manner—in a natural setting, in a laboratory, or in archival data.

experiment
A research method in which the researcher tries to determine the cause-and-effect relationship between two variables by manipulating one (called the *independent variable*) and then observing and recording the ensuing changes in the other (called the *dependent variable*).

independent variable
In an experiment, the variable that is introduced to see what effect it has on the dependent variable. (Also called *experimental variable*.)

Friendly Dogs? Dr. Sabrina Schuck is observing children with ADHD (attention-deficit/hyperactive disorder), who are singing as part of a 12-week therapy program. She notes specific disruptions (can you see that child's flailing arm?). Half the children in her study have sessions with therapy dogs that are trained not to bark when the children get too lively. Those children were most likely to calm down.

dependent variable
In an experiment, the variable that may change as a result of whatever new condition or situation the experimenter adds. In other words, the dependent variable *depends* on the independent variable.

whatever they are studying, called the **dependent variable,** which *depends* on the independent variable.

Thus, the independent variable is the new, special treatment; any change in the dependent variable is the result. The purpose of an experiment is to find out whether an independent variable affects the dependent variable. In a typical experiment (as diagrammed in Figure 1.12), two groups of participants are studied. One group, the *experimental group,* gets a particular treatment (the independent variable). The other group, the *comparison group* (also called the *control group*), does not.

For example, many mayors believe that summer jobs prevent juvenile delinquency, a hypothesis that springs from ideology, not science. One scientist (Heller, 2014) reviewed several studies that found no effects of summer work for youth who had already quit school and been arrested for serious crimes. This raises two possibilities: (1) serious delinquents need more than summer work, or (2) summer work itself makes no difference.

To find out, an experiment was needed. Consequently, 1,634 high school students (average age, 17) from high-crime Chicago neighborhoods were divided into a control group (904 students, no job offered) and an experimental group (730 students who were paid minimum wage for 25 hours a week for 8 weeks). As Vygotsky's idea of guided participation would recommend, the students in the experimental group had mentors, each assigned to about ten students to discuss job issues, such as getting along with supervisors and coworkers.

For 16 months after their summer jobs ended, students' police and school records were examined. The students in the experimental group had only half as many arrests for violent crime (assaults, rapes, and so on—usually the result of impulsive, uncontrolled anger).

However, the intervention did not reduce arrests for nonviolent crimes (over 16 months, about 1 in 5 were arrested for drugs, theft, and so on) or improve school attendance (students in both groups were absent from school almost 30 days a year).

That experiment led to an important conclusion: Summer work helps adolescents to be less impulsive, but it does not transform them into conscientious students or

FIGURE 1.12 How to Conduct an Experiment The basic sequence diagrammed here applies to all experiments. Many additional features, especially the statistical measures listed in Table 1.7 and various ways of reducing experimenter bias, affect whether publication occurs. (Scientific journals reject reports of experiments that were not rigorous in method and analysis.)

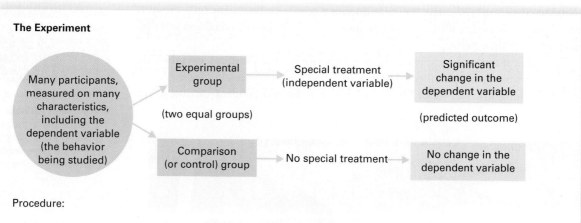

The Experiment

Procedure:

1. Divide participants into two groups that are matched on important characteristics, especially the behavior that is the dependent variable on which this study is focused.

2. Give special treatment, or intervention (the independent variable), to one group (the experimental group).

3. Compare the groups on the dependent variable. If they now differ, the cause of the difference was probably the independent variable.

4. Publish the results.

law-abiding citizens. This lack of comprehensive transformation is not surprising, given the importance of context and culture. However, "this study provides causal evidence . . . The results echo a common conclusion in education and health research: that public programs might do more with less by shifting from remediation to prevention" (Heller, 2014, p. 1222).

Note how crucial the scientific method and the experiment can be. Liberals and conservatives have argued for decades about the value of public programs to help the poor. This study provided some evidence about what might do some good for whom—and what was unlikely to change after a summer's employment. The research came to a sound conclusion, on which people of all political perspectives can agree.

In addition to observation and experimentation, a third research method is the **survey.** Information is collected from a large number of people, usually by simply asking them questions. This is a quick, direct way to obtain data. It is better than assuming that the experiences and attitudes of people we happen to talk with are valid for everyone we do not know.

For example, if you know a 16-year-old who is pregnant, or an adult who hates his job, or an old person who watches television all day, surveys will keep you from jumping to false conclusions. As you will read later, teenage pregnancy is no longer common, most people appreciate their jobs, and older people watch less television than children do.

Unfortunately, although surveys are quick and direct, they are not always accurate. People sometimes lie, and answers are influenced by the wording and the sequence of the questions. For instance, "climate change" and "global warming" are two ways to describe the same phenomenon, according to many scientists, yet many people believe in climate change but not in global warming (McCright & Dunlap, 2011). For that reason, surveys that seem to be about the same issue may reach opposite conclusions.

Survey respondents may even lie to themselves. For instance, every two years since 1991, high school students in the United States have been surveyed confidentially. The most recent survey included 13,633 students from all 50 states and from schools large and small, public and private (MMWR, June 13, 2014).

Students are asked whether they had sexual intercourse *before* age 13. Every year, more ninth-grade than twelfth-grade boys say they had sex before age 13, yet those twelfth-graders were ninth-graders a few years before (see Figure 1.13). Do twelfth-graders forget or do ninth-graders lie? Or do some 14-year-olds brag about the same thing that later makes them ashamed? The survey cannot tell us.

survey
A research method in which information is collected from a large number of people by interviews, written questionnaires, or some other means.

THINK CRITICALLY: If you want to predict who will win the next U.S. presidential race, what survey question would you ask, and who would you ask?

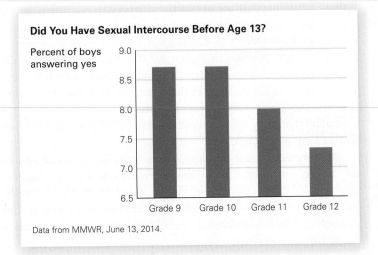

Data from MMWR, June 13, 2014.

FIGURE 1.13 I Forgot? If these were the only data available, you might conclude that ninth-graders have suddenly become more sexually active than twelfth-graders. But we have 20 years of data—many of those who are ninth-graders now will answer differently by twelfth grade.

MARK BOWDEN-+/GETTY IMAGES

SVETIKD/E-+/GETTY IMAGES

Compare These with Those These children seem ideal for cross-sectional research—they are schoolchildren of both sexes and many ethnicities. Their only difference seems to be age, so a study might conclude that 6-year-olds raise their hands but 16-year-olds do not. But any two groups in cross-sectional research may differ in ways that are not obvious—perhaps income, national origin, or culture—and that may be the underlying reason for any differences by age.

cross-sectional research
A research design that compares groups of people who differ in age but are similar in other important characteristics.

longitudinal research
A research design in which the same individuals are followed over time, as their development is repeatedly assessed.

Studying Development over the Life Span

In addition to conducting observations, experiments, and surveys, developmentalists must measure how people *change or remain the same over time,* as our definition stresses. Remember that systems are dynamic, ever-changing. To capture that dynamism, developmental researchers use one of three basic research designs: cross-sectional, longitudinal, or cross-sequential.

CROSS-SECTIONAL VERSUS LONGITUDINAL RESEARCH The quickest and least expensive way to study development over time is with **cross-sectional research,** in which groups of people of one age are compared with people of another age. You saw that at the beginning of the chapter: With every decade of age, the proportion of obese people increases.

Cross-sectional design seems simple. However, it is difficult to ensure that the various groups being compared are similar in every way except age. Because most women now in their 50s gained an average of a pound every year throughout their adulthood, does this mean that women now aged 20 who weigh 140 pounds will, on average, weigh 170 pounds at age 50? Not necessarily.

To help discover whether age itself rather than cohort causes a developmental change, scientists undertake **longitudinal research.** This requires collecting data repeatedly on the same individuals as they age. It is only through longitudinal research that we learned that a third of overweight children become normal weight adults.

However, longitudinal research has several drawbacks. Over time, participants may withdraw, move to an unknown address, or die. These losses can skew the final results if those who disappear are unlike those who stay, as is often the case. Another problem is that participants become increasingly aware of the questions or the goals of the study—knowledge that could affect their behavior over time.

For example, you saw in Figure 1.2 that most overweight children who became normal-weight adults were actually healthier than adults who had never been overweight. How could that be? Perhaps the fact that they knew they had been heavy and that they were now repeatedly measured caused them to eat more fruits and vegetables than they otherwise would have. That is a wonderful result, but it is also a flaw of longitudinal research.

Probably the biggest problem comes from the historical context. Science, popular culture, and politics alter life experiences, and those changes limit the current relevance of data collected on people born decades ago. Results from longitudinal studies of people born in the early twentieth century, as they made their way through childhood, adulthood, and old age, may not be relevant to people born in the twenty-first century.

Six Stages of Life These photos show Sarah-Maria, born in 1980 in Switzerland, at six stages of her life: infancy (age 1), early childhood (age 3), middle childhood (age 8), adolescence (age 15), emerging adulthood (age 19), and adulthood (age 30).

OBSERVATION QUIZ
Longitudinal research best illustrates continuity and discontinuity. For Sarah-Maria, what changed over 30 years and what didn't? (see answer, page 41) ▲

Many recent substances are thought to be harmful by some people but advocated as beneficial by others, among them *phthalates* and *bisphenol A* (BPA) (chemicals used in manufacturing) in plastic baby bottles, *hydrofracking* (a process used to get gas for fuel from rocks), *e-waste* (from old computers and cell phones), and more. Some nations and states ban or regulate each of these; others do not, because verified, longitudinal data are not yet possible.

One example that is directly developmental is *e-cigarettes,* which are less toxic (how much less?) to the heart and lungs than combustible cigarettes. Some (how many?) adult smokers reduce their risk of cancer and heart disease by switching to e-cigs (Bhatnagar et al., 2014). But for some teenagers (how many?) vaping introduces them to using more damaging substances that they otherwise would never use.

Until we know rates of addiction and death for all those e-cig smokers, 10 or 20 years from now, we cannot be sure whether the harm outweighs the benefits (Ramo et al., 2015; Hajek et al., 2014; Dutra & Glantz, 2014). Forty U.S. states have restricted e-cig sales. A spokesman for the Utah Department of Health said, "while we wait for the science on long-term effects . . . thousands of teens in Utah are starting a nicotine addiction via e-cigarettes . . . it's imperative that we get one finger in the dam until we know more" (Bramwell, quoted in McGill, 2015, p. 12).

cross-sequential research
A hybrid research design in which researchers first study several groups of people of different ages (a cross-sectional approach) and then follow those groups over the years (a longitudinal approach). (Also called *cohort-sequential research* or *time-sequential research.*

CROSS-SEQUENTIAL RESEARCH Scientists have discovered a third strategy, combining cross-sectional and longitudinal research. This combination is called **cross-sequential research** (also referred to as *cohort-sequential* or *time-sequential research*). With this design, researchers study several groups of people of different ages (a cross-sectional approach), follow them over the years (a longitudinal approach), and then combine the results.

A cross-sequential design lets researchers compare findings for a group of, say, 16-year-olds with findings for the same individuals at age 1, as well as with

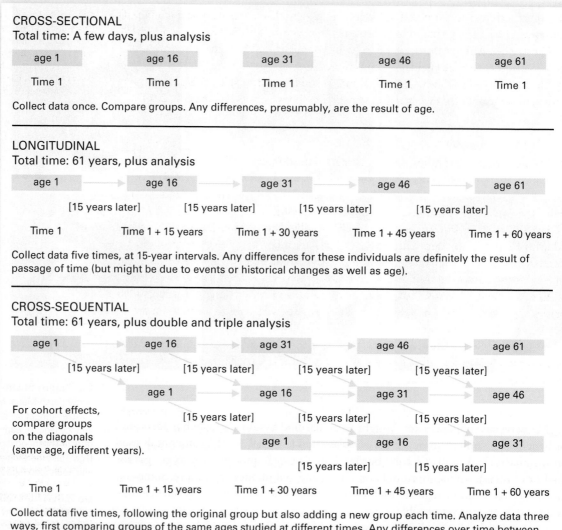

CROSS-SECTIONAL
Total time: A few days, plus analysis

age 1	age 16	age 31	age 46	age 61
Time 1	Time 1	Time 1	Time 1	Time 1

Collect data once. Compare groups. Any differences, presumably, are the result of age.

LONGITUDINAL
Total time: 61 years, plus analysis

age 1	age 16	age 31	age 46	age 61
	[15 years later]	[15 years later]	[15 years later]	[15 years later]
Time 1	Time 1 + 15 years	Time 1 + 30 years	Time 1 + 45 years	Time 1 + 60 years

Collect data five times, at 15-year intervals. Any differences for these individuals are definitely the result of passage of time (but might be due to events or historical changes as well as age).

CROSS-SEQUENTIAL
Total time: 61 years, plus double and triple analysis

age 1 → age 16 → age 31 → age 46 → age 61

[15 years later] [15 years later] [15 years later] [15 years later]

age 1 → age 16 → age 31 → age 46

For cohort effects, compare groups on the diagonals (same age, different years).

[15 years later] [15 years later] [15 years later]

age 1 → age 16 → age 31

[15 years later] [15 years later]

Time 1	Time 1 + 15 years	Time 1 + 30 years	Time 1 + 45 years	Time 1 + 60 years

Collect data five times, following the original group but also adding a new group each time. Analyze data three ways, first comparing groups of the same ages studied at different times. Any differences over time between groups who are the same age are probably cohort effects. Then compare the same group as they grow older. Any differences are the result of time (not only age). In the third analysis, compare differences between the same people as they grow older, *after* the cohort effects (from the first analysis) are taken into account. Any remaining differences are almost certainly the result of age.

FIGURE 1.14 **Which Approach Is Best?** Cross-sequential research is the most time-consuming and complex, but it yields the best information. One reason that hundreds of scientists conduct research on the same topics, replicating one another's work, is to gain some advantages of cohort-sequential research without waiting for decades.

findings for groups who were 16 long ago, and who are now ages 31, 46, and 61(see Figure 1.14). Cross-sequential research is complicated, in recruitment and analysis, but it lets scientists disentangle age from history.

One well-known cross-sequential study (the *Seattle Longitudinal Study*) found that some intellectual abilities (vocabulary) increase even after age 60, whereas others (speed) start to decline at age 30 (Schaie, 2005/2013), confirming that development is multi-directional. This study also discovered that declines in adult math ability are more closely related to education than to age, something neither cross-sectional nor longitudinal research could reveal.

A more recent cross-sequential study looked at self-esteem in late adulthood. The results were surprising: Self-esteem varied markedly from one person to another, but was quite stable over the decades. Elders with high self-esteem were social and self-sufficient, characteristics that often continued from age 70 to 105 (Wagner et al., 2015).

Cross-sequential research is useful for young adults as well. For example, drug addiction (called *substance use disorder, SUD*) is most common in the early 20s and decreases by the late 20s. But one cross-sequential study found that the origins of SUD are much earlier, in adolescent behaviors and in genetic predispositions (McGue et al., 2014).

Cautions and Challenges from Science

The scientific method illuminates and illustrates human development as nothing else does. Facts, consequences, and possibilities have all emerged that would not be known without science—and people of all ages are healthier, happier, and more capable than people of previous generations because of it.

For example, infectious diseases in children, illiteracy in adults, depression in late adulthood, and racism and sexism at every age are much less prevalent today than a century ago. Science deserves credit for all these advances. Even violent death is less likely, with scientific discoveries and education likely reasons (Pinker, 2011).

Developmental scientists have also discovered unexpected sources of harm. Video games, cigarettes, television, shift work, asbestos, and even artificial respiration are all less benign than people first thought.

As these examples attest, the benefits of science are many. However, there are also serious pitfalls. We now discuss three potential hazards: misinterpreting correlation, depending too heavily on numbers, and ignoring ethics.

CORRELATION AND CAUSATION Probably the most common mistake in interpreting research is confusing correlation with causation. A **correlation** exists between two variables if one variable is more (or less) likely to occur when the other does. A correlation is *positive* if both variables tend to increase together or decrease together, *negative* if one variable tends to increase while the other decreases, and *zero* if no connection is evident.

To illustrate: From birth to age 9, there is a positive correlation between age and height (children grow taller as they grow older), a negative correlation between age and amount of sleep (children sleep less as they grow older), and zero correlation between age and number of toes (children do not have more or fewer toes as they grow older).

Expressed in numerical terms, correlations vary from +1.0 (the most positive) to −1.0 (the most negative). Correlations are almost never that extreme; a correlation of +0.3 or −0.3 is noteworthy; a correlation of +0.8 or −0.8 is astonishing.

Many correlations are unexpected. For instance, first-born children are more likely to develop asthma than are later-born children, teenage girls have higher rates of mental health problems than do teenage boys, and counties in the United States with more dentists have fewer obese residents. That later study controlled for the number of medical doctors and the poverty of the community. The authors suggest that dentists provide information about nutrition that improves health (Holzer et al., 2014).

At this point, remember that *correlation is not causation.* Just because two variables are correlated does not mean that one causes the other—even if it seems logical that it does. It proves only that the variables are connected somehow. Many mistaken and even dangerous conclusions are drawn because people misunderstand correlation.

QUANTITY AND QUALITY A second caution concerns how heavily scientists should rely on data produced by **quantitative research** (from the word *quantity*). Quantitative research data can be categorized, ranked, or numbered and thus can be easily translated across cultures and for diverse populations. One example of quantitative

ANSWER TO OBSERVATION QUIZ
(from page 39) Of course, much changed and much did not change, but evident in the photos is continuity in Sarah-Maria's happy smile and discontinuity in her hairstyle (which shows dramatic age and cohort changes). ●

correlation
A number between +1.0 and −1.0 that indicates the degree of relationship between two variables, expressed in terms of the likelihood that one variable will (or will not) occur when the other variable does (or does not). A correlation indicates only that two variables may be somehow related, not that one variable causes the other to occur.

quantitative research
Research that provides data that can be expressed with numbers, such as ranks or scales.

research is the use of children's school achievement scores to compare the effectiveness of education within a school or nation.

Since quantities can be easily summarized, compared, charted, and replicated, many scientists prefer quantitative research. Statistics require numbers. Quantitative data are easier to replicate and less open to bias, although researchers who choose this method have some implicit beliefs about evidence and verification (Creswell, 2009).

However, when data are presented in categories and numbers, some nuances and individual distinctions are lost. Many developmental researchers thus turn to **qualitative research** (from *quality*)—asking open-ended questions, reporting answers in narrative (not numerical) form.

Qualitative researchers are "interested in understanding how people interpret their experiences, how they construct their worlds . . ." (Merriam, 2009, p. 5). Qualitative research reflects cultural and contextual diversity, but it is also more vulnerable to bias and harder to replicate. Both types of research are needed.

ETHICS The most important caution for all scientists, especially for those studying humans, is to uphold ethical standards. Each academic discipline and professional society involved in the study of human development has a *code of ethics* (a set of moral principles) and specific practices within a scientific culture to protect the integrity of research.

Ethical standards and codes are increasingly stringent. Most educational and medical institutions have an *Institutional Review Board* (IRB), a group that permits only research that follows certain guidelines.

Although IRBs often slow down scientific study, some research conducted before they were established was clearly unethical, especially when the participants were children, members of minority groups, prisoners, or animals. Some argue that serious ethical dilemmas remain (Leiter & Herman, 2015).

Researchers must ensure that participation is voluntary, confidential, and harmless. In Western nations, this entails the *informed consent* of the participants—that is, the participants must understand and agree to the research procedures and know what risks are involved. A dilemma occurs when severe consequences might follow either participation or non-participation.

Many ethical dilemmas arose in the Ebola epidemic (Rothstein, 2015; Gillon, 2015). Among them: Is it fair to use vaccines that have not been proven safe, when such proof would take months and the death rate from Ebola would increase? What kind of informed consent is needed to avoid both false hope and false fears? Is it justified to keep relatives away from sick people who might have Ebola, even though

qualitative research Research that consider qualities instead of quantities. Descriptions of particular conditions and participants' expressed ideas are often part of qualitative studies.

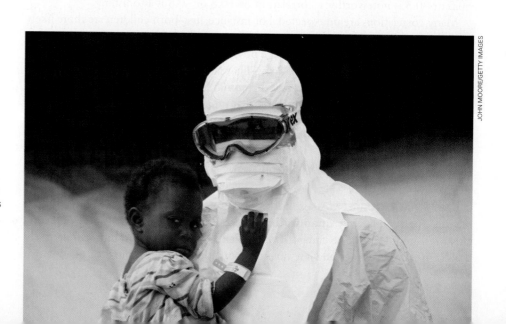

Science and Ebola Ebola halted as much because of social science as medicine, which has not yet found an effective vaccine. Fortunately, social workers taught practices that were contrary to West African culture—no more hugging, touching, or visiting from one neighborhood to another. Psychologists advised health workers, like this one from Doctors Without Borders, to hold, reassure, and comfort children as much as possible. This girl was *not* among the 5,000 Liberians who died.

JOHN MOORE/GETTY IMAGES

social isolation might increase the death rate? Should drugs that researchers are uncertain about be given to Ebola patients?

More broadly, is justice served by a health care system that is inadequate in some countries and high-tech in others? Medicine has tended to focus on individuals, ignoring the customs and systems that make some people more vulnerable. One observer noted:

> When people from the United States and Europe working in West Africa have developed Ebola, time and again the first thing they wanted to take was not an experimental drug. It was an airplane that would cart them home.
> *[Cohen, 2014, p. 911]*

Is that ethical?

IMPLICATIONS OF RESEARCH RESULTS Once a study has been completed, additional issues arise. Scientists are obligated to "promote accuracy, honesty, and truthfulness" (American Psychological Association, 2010).

Deliberate falsification leads to ostracism from the scientific community, dismissal from a teaching or research position, and, sometimes, criminal prosecution. Another obvious breach of ethics is to "cook" the data, or distort one's findings, in order to make a particular conclusion seem to be the only reasonable one.

Some of the benefits (promotion, acclaim) of publishing remarkable, unreplicated findings encourage unethical research, such as slanting conclusions. Further, there is "ferocious . . . pressure from commercial funders to ignore good scientific practice" (Bateson, 2005, p. 645). Pressures from politicians and corporations are part of the problem, but nonprofit research groups and academic institutions also want particular results.

As stressed in the beginning of this chapter, researchers, like all other humans, have strong opinions, which they expect research to confirm. Therefore, they might try (sometimes without even realizing it) to achieve the results they want. As one team explains:

> Our job as scientists is to discover truths about the world. We generate hypotheses, collect data, and examine whether or not the data are consistent with those hypotheses . . . . [but we] often lose sight of this goal, yielding to pressure to do whatever is justifiable to compile a set of studies we can publish. This is not driven by a willingness to deceive but by the self-serving interpretation of ambiguity . . .
> *[Simmons et al., 2011, pp. 1359, 1365]*

Obviously, collaboration, replication, and transparency are essential ethical safeguards for all scientists.

UNKNOWNS AND UNKNOWN UNKNOWNS Hundreds of crucial questions regarding human development need answers, and researchers have yet to find them. For instance:

- Do we know enough about prenatal drug abuse to protect every fetus?
- Do we know enough about poverty to enable everyone to be healthy?
- Do we know enough about same-sex relationships, or polygamy, or single parenthood, or divorce to make sure all people develop well no matter what their family structure?
- Do we know enough about dying to enable everyone to die with dignity?

The answer to all these questions is a resounding *NO*. The reasons are many. Scientists and funders tend to avoid questions that might lead to answers they do not want. People have strong opinions about drugs, income, families, and death that may conflict with scientific findings and conclusions. Religion, politics, and ethics shape scientific research, sometimes stopping investigation before it begins.

THINK CRITICALLY: Is it ethical that the death rate from Ebola in the United States was a fraction of the rate in Liberia?

Video Activity: Eugenics and the Feebleminded: A Shameful History illustrates what can happen when scientists fail to follow a code of ethics.

An even greater question is about the "unknown unknowns," the topics that we assume we understand but do not, hypotheses that have not yet occurred to anyone because our thinking is limited by our cultures and contexts.

The next cohort of developmental scientists will build on what is known, mindful of what needs to be explored, and will raise questions that no one has thought of before. Remember that the goal is to help all 7 billion people on Earth fulfill their potential. Much more needs to be learned. The next 14 chapters are only a beginning.

WHAT HAVE YOU LEARNED?

1. Why do careful observations not prove "what causes what"?

2. Why do experimenters use a control (or comparison) group as well as an experimental group?

3. What are the strengths and weaknesses of the survey method?

4. Why would a scientist conduct a cross-sectional study?

5. What are the advantages and disadvantages of longitudinal research?

6. Why do developmentalists prefer cross-sequential research, even though it takes longer and is more expensive?

7. Why does correlation not prove causation?

8. What are the advantages and disadvantages of quantitative research?

9. What are the advantages and disadvantages of qualitative research?

10. What is the role of the IRB?

11. Why should a study not be done without informed consent and confidentiality?

12. What reasons might a political leader have to not fund developmental research?

13. What is one additional question that you can think of about development that you think should be answered?

SUMMARY

Understanding How and Why

1. The study of human development is a science that seeks to understand how people change or remain the same over time. As a science, it begins with questions and hypotheses and then gathers empirical data. Researchers draw conclusions based on the evidence. Replication confirms, modifies, or refutes the conclusions of a scientific study.

2. Nature (genes) and nurture (environment) always interact, affected by every human characteristic. Neuroscience has discovered differential susceptibility—that certain genes increase or decrease the likelihood that a child will be affected by the environment.

3. Development is divided into three domains—biological, cognitive, and psychosocial, or body, mind, and social world. Every domain is involved in every characteristic, which makes the science of human development always multidisciplinary.

The Life-Span Perspective

4. The assumption that growth is linear and progress is inevitable has been replaced by the idea that both continuity (sameness) and discontinuity (sudden shifts) are part of every life, that gains and losses are apparent at every age. Development is multi-directional.

5. Time is a crucial variable in studying human development. A critical period is a time when something *must* occur to ensure normal development or the only time when an abnormality might occur. Often a particular development can occur more easily—but not exclusively—at a particular time, called a sensitive period.

6. Urie Bronfenbrenner's ecological-systems approach notes that each of us is situated within larger systems of family, school, community, and culture, as well as part of a historical cohort. Changes within a person, or changes in the context, affect all other aspects of the system. Development is multi-contextual.

7. Socioeconomic status (SES) is an important influence on human development, affecting a person's opportunities, health, and even abilities at every stage.

8. Culture includes beliefs and patterns; ethnicity refers to ancestral heritage. These two often overlap, but they are not identical. Race is a social construction, sometimes mistakenly thought to be biological.

9. Developmentalists try to avoid the difference-equals-deficit error. Differences may be alternate ways to think or act, not necessarily less beneficial than the familiar ways. Development is multi-cultural.

10. Throughout life, human development is plastic. *Plasticity* emphasizes that it is possible for brains and behaviors to change over time, although it is also true that early experiences affect later development.

Theories of Human Development

11. Psychoanalytic theories stress the legacy of childhood. According to Freud, conflicts associated with children's erotic impulses have a lasting impact on adult personality. Erikson thought that the resolution of each crisis affects later life and that new crises appear in adulthood.

12. Behaviorists, or learning theorists, believe that scientists should study observable and measurable behavior. Behaviorism emphasizes conditioning, in which one stimulus may be associated with another (classical conditioning) or reinforcement and punishment may guide future behavior (operant conditioning).

13. Cognitive theorists believe that thoughts and beliefs powerfully affect attitudes, actions, and perceptions. Piaget proposed four age-related periods of cognition. Information processing focuses on each aspect of cognitive input, processing, and output.

14. Humanism emphasizes the potential of humankind. For example, Maslow proposed a hierarchy of needs, which could lead to self-actualization.

15. Evolutionary theory contends that genes have fostered survival and reproduction of the human species for tens of thousands of years. Those genes continue to influence human behavior today, in alloparenting, attachment, and male/female behavior.

Using the Scientific Method

16. Commonly used research methods are scientific observation, the experiment, and the survey. Each can provide insight and discoveries that were not apparent before the research, although no method is perfect.

17. A challenge for developmentalists is to study change over time. Methods include cross-sectional, longitudinal, and cross-sequential research.

18. A correlation shows that two variables are related. However, it does not prove that one variable *causes* the other.

19. Ethical behavior is crucial in all the sciences. Not only must participants be protected and data kept confidential (primary concerns of IRBs), but results must be fairly reported and honestly interpreted.

20. The most important ethical question is whether scientists are designing, conducting, analyzing, publishing, and applying the research that is most critically needed. This is a challenge for the next generation of developmentalists.

KEY TERMS

science of human development (p. 4)
scientific method (p. 4)
hypothesis (p. 4)
empirical evidence (p. 4)
replication (p. 5)
nature (p. 7)
nurture (p. 7)
epigenetics (p. 7)
differential susceptibility (p. 7)
life-span perspective (p. 9)
critical period (p. 10)

sensitive period (p. 10)
ecological-systems approach (p. 12)
cohort (p. 12)
socioeconomic status (SES) (p. 14)
culture (p. 15)
social construction (p. 16)
difference-equals-deficit error (p. 17)
ethnic group (p. 18)
race (p. 19)

dynamic-systems approach (p. 21)
developmental theory (p. 23)
psychoanalytic theory (p. 23)
behaviorism (p. 26)
conditioning (p. 26)
operant conditioning (p. 27)
social learning theory (p. 28)
cognitive theory (p. 28)
humanism (p. 32)
scientific observation (p. 35)
experiment (p. 35)

independent variable (p. 35)
dependent variable (p. 36)
survey (p. 37)
cross-sectional research (p. 38)
longitudinal research (p. 38)
cross-sequential research (p. 39)
correlation (p. 41)
quantitative research (p. 41)
qualitative research (p. 42)

APPLICATIONS

1. It is said that culture is pervasive but that people are unaware of it. List 30 things you did *today* that you might have done differently in another culture. Begin with how and where you woke up.

2. How would your life be different if your parents were much higher or lower in SES than they are? Consider all three domains.

3. Design an experiment to answer a question you have about human development. Specify the question and the hypothesis and then describe the experiment. How would you prevent your conclusions from being biased and subjective?

4. A longitudinal case study can be insightful but also limited in application to other people. Describe the life of one of your older relatives, explaining what aspects of their development are unique and what aspects might be relevant for everyone.

ZHANG BO/GETTY IMAGES

CHAPTER OUTLINE

CHAPTER 2

THE BEGINNING

From Conception to Birth

WHAT WILL YOU KNOW?

- How do genes affect each individual?
- Do fathers have any role in pregnancy and birth?
- How can serious birth disorders be avoided?
- Is alcohol use disorder genetic or cultural?

My daughter Elissa recently had her second child. Her husband and midwife were with her in the Labor Room of the Birthing Center; I was with Asa, age 5, in the Family Room. Periodically, Asa ran down the hall to see his parents. Usually the midwife let us enter, and Elissa smiled and asked him how he was doing. Sometimes we had to wait a minute. Then, contraction over, mother and son greeted each other again.

When the baby was born, the nurse came to tell us, "There's a new person who wants to meet you." Asa said, "Let me put this last Lego piece in." He did, and brought his creation to show his parents, who introduced him to his breast-feeding brother, Isaac. Six hours later, the whole family was home.

The contrast between this 2014 birth and Elissa's own arrival is stark. Back then, midwives were banned from my New York City hospital. Fathers were relegated to waiting rooms, as my husband, Martin, had been. The nurses did not let me hold Elissa until she was 24 hours old. Her older sisters were banned from the hospital floor where I stayed for 5 days.

The science of human development is not only about how individuals change over time, it is about how contexts and cultures change, as evident in the contrast between Elissa as newborn and Elissa as new mother. Some things endure: Both births, and indeed every pregnancy and birth, were miraculous.

Further, genes have been passed down for thousands of years. Every baby has the genes from both parents, so my grandson has one-fourth of mine. However, historical change—Bronfenbrenner's chronosystem—is dramatically apparent in conception, in prenatal development and in birth.

This chapter describes the unchanged biology of human genes, conception, prenatal development, and birth, as well as the vast differences in all four from one era, one culture, even one family to another. Possible harm is noted: causes and consequences of diseases, malnutrition, drugs, pollution, stress, and so on. Fathers, particularly, have become more active partners. All of us—professionals, governments, communities, and families—need to know more, because we all shape the beginning of each developing person. ■

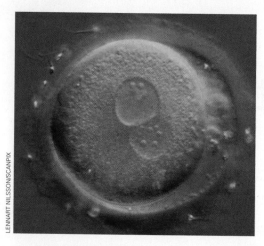

The Moment of Conception This ovum is about to become a zygote. It has been penetrated by a single sperm, whose nucleus now lies next to the nucleus of the ovum. Soon, the two nuclei will fuse, bringing together about 20,000 genes to guide development.

zygote
The single cell that is formed from the fusing of two gametes, a sperm and an ovum.

DNA (deoxyribonucleic acid)
The molecule that contains the chemical instructions for cells to manufacture various proteins.

chromosome
One of the 46 structures made of DNA (in 23 pairs) that almost every cell of the human body contains and that, together, contain all the genes. Other species have more or fewer chromosomes.

gene
A small section of a chromosome; the basic unit for the transmission of heredity. A gene consists of a string of chemicals that provide instructions for the cell to manufacture certain proteins.

gamete
A reproductive cell; that is, a sperm or an ovum that can produce a new individual if it combines with a gamete from the other sex to form a zygote.

allele
Any of the possible forms of a gene. Genes with various alleles are called polymorphic.

Life Begins

Every person starts life as a single cell, called a **zygote.** Each zygote is distinct from any other human cell ever created, yet that cell contains genes that have been passed down for hundreds of thousands of years. The first hours of development are a compelling example of both the universal and the unique characteristics of each human.

Genes and Chromosomes

First, the universal. All living things are composed of cells that promote growth and sustain life according to instructions in their molecules of **DNA (deoxyribonucleic acid)** (see Figure 2.1). Each molecule of DNA is on a **chromosome.** Chromosomes contain units of instructions called **genes,** with each gene located on a particular chromosome.

With one important exception, every cell of a normal human being has a copy of that person's 46 chromosomes, arranged in 23 pairs. That one exception is the reproductive cell, called a **gamete.** Each gamete—*sperm* in a man and *ovum* in a woman—has only 23 chromosomes, one from each of a person's 23 pairs.

At conception, the genes on each of the 22 non-sex chromosomes from the sperm pair up with the genes on the same 22 chromosomes from the ovum. For instance, an eye-color gene from the father on chromosome 15 connects with an eye-color gene from the mother on the zygote's other chromosome 15.

If the match between the two genes is exact (as it usually is since most genes are identical for every human), the person is said to be *homozygous* (literally, "same zygote") for that trait.

However, some genes come in slightly different versions, as is obvious for eye-color genes. Each version is called an **allele.** Genes that have various alleles are called *polymorphic* (literally, "many forms"). If the allele of a particular gene from the father differs from the allele of that gene from the mother, the person is said to be *heterozygous* (literally, "other zygote").

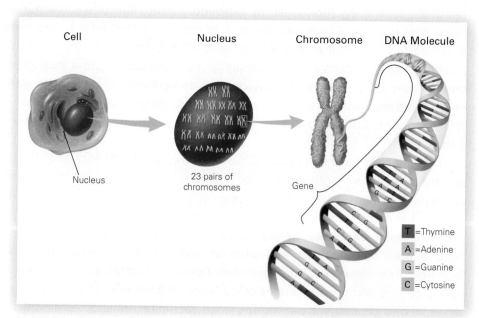

FIGURE 2.1 How Proteins Are Made The genes on the chromosomes in the nucleus of each cell instruct the cell to manufacture the proteins needed to sustain life and development. The code for a protein is the particular combination of four bases, T-A-G-C (thymine, adenine, guanine, and cytosine).

Variations Among People

Now, the unique. Since each gamete has only 23 chromosomes (one from each pair of the parent's 23 pairs), each man or woman can produce 2^{23} different gametes—more than 8 million versions of their chromosomes (actually 8,388,608).

When a sperm and an ovum combine, the zygote they create is a new cell in which the genes on one of 8 million possible sperm from the father interact with the genes on one of the 8 million possible ova from the mother. Your parents could have given you an astronomical number of siblings, each unique.

TRIPLET VARIATIONS More variations occur because the DNA code on those chromosomes contains about 3 billion pairs of chemicals organized in triplets (sets of three pairs), each of which specifies production of one of 20 possible amino acids. Those amino acids combine to produce proteins, and those proteins combine to produce a person. Small variations, mutations, or repetitions (called *copy number variations*) in the base pairs or triplets could make a notable difference in the proteins and thus, eventually, in the person.

And that is what happens. Some genes have triplet transpositions, deletions, or repetitions not found in other versions of the same gene. Not only do alleles affect the person, but also genes "are themselves transmitted to individual cells with large apparent mistakes—somatically acquired deletions, duplications, and other mutations" (Macosko & McCarroll, 2013, p. 564).

NOT JUNK All these variations already make each person unique, but there is more. Additional DNA and RNA (another molecule) surround each gene. In a process called *methylation,* this material enhances, transcribes, connects, empowers, silences, regulates, and alters genes. This material used to be called *junk*—but no longer. As one team explains:

> One of the most important discoveries in genetics in the last 10 years is that the vast majority of trait-associated DNA variations occur in regions of the genome that were once labeled a 'junk DNA' because they do not code for proteins. We now know that these regions harbor genetic elements that control where, when, and to what extent specific genes are expressed.
>
> *[Furey & Sethupathy, 2013, p. 705]*

Pause for a moment to consider how significant this is. Obviously genes are crucial, but even more crucial is whether or not a gene is expressed. RNA turns some genes and alleles off. In other words, a person can have the genetic tendency for a particular trait, disease, or behavior, but that tendency might never appear in that person's life because it was never turned on.

Think of turning on a lamp. Many elements must be in place before the room is illuminated. The lamp needs an unspent bulb screwed into the socket, a cord correctly plugged in, an electric bill paid, and an electricity source from the grid. Yet the room will be dark until the switch is flipped. That's RNA.

Researchers who sought a single gene for, say, schizophrenia, or homosexuality, or even a tiny detail such as memory for chemistry formulas, have been disappointed. No such single genes exist. Instead, almost every trait arises from a combination of genes, each with a small potential impact, each dependent on epigenetic factors that determine whether that gene is expressed or silenced (Ayyanathan, 2014).

GENOTYPE AND PHENOTYPE For each individual, the collection of his or her genes is called the **genotype.** It was once thought that the genotype led directly to facial characteristics, body formation, intelligence, personality, and so on, but this is much too simplistic.

genotype
An organism's entire genetic inheritance, or genetic potential.

phenotype
The observable characteristics of a person, including appearance, personality, intelligence, and all other apparent traits.

The **phenotype,** which is a person's actual appearance and behavior, reflects much more than the genotype. The genotype is the beginning of diversity; the phenotype is the actual manifestation of it, the result of "multiple interactions among numerous genetic and environmental factors" (Nadeau & Dudley, 2011, p. 1015).

Diversity not only distinguishes each person (you can immediately spot a close friend in a crowd) but also allows adaptation. We are the only species that thrives on every continent, from the poles to the equator, eating blubber or locusts as the case may be.

One of the best parts of our adaptive genes is that we teach each other. If you or I suddenly found ourselves in a climate we had never experienced, we would quickly learn how to dress, where to sleep, and what to eat by observing people who had already adapted to that place. If our descendants stayed in the new place, eventually our great-great-grandchildren would have genes slightly changed from ours, to help them thrive.

Thanks to our genetic diversity, even devastating diseases do not kill us all. For instance, a few people have alleles that defend them from HIV/AIDS (Aouizerat et al., 2011). Similarly, genotype differences allowed some of our ancestors to survive tuberculosis, malaria, the Black Death, and other scourges. In the most recent manifestation, a few people may have a genetic defense against Ebola, remaining healthy despite contact with body fluids from someone sick with that highly contagious virus (Rasmussen et al., 2014).

THINK CRITICALLY: You do not have some condition (perhaps addiction or asthma or anxiety) that troubles another member of your family. Do you credit genes or upbringing?

More on Shared and Divergent Genes

The entire packet of instructions that make a living organism is called the **genome.** There is a genome for every species, from *Homo sapiens* to the smallest insect, even for every kind of plant. A worldwide effort to map all the human genes led to the *Human Genome Project,* which was virtually completed in 2003.

SURPRISES FROM THE HUMAN GENOME PROJECT Until 2001, scientists thought humans had about 100,000 genes, but that turned out to be a gross overestimate. The Human Genome Project found only about 20,000 to 23,000 genes.

Genomes from other creatures led to more surprises: Dogs and mice have more genes than humans, and mice have several times more. The precise count is still unknown, partly because of another surprise: It is not always clear where one gene ends and another begins.

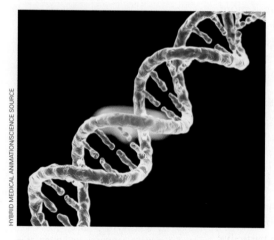

Twelve of Three Billion Pairs This is a computer illustration of a small segment of one gene. Even a small difference in one gene can cause major changes in a person's phenotype.

HYBRID MEDICAL ANIMATION/SCIENCE SOURCE

genome
The full set of genes for a certain species.

Another surprise is that any two men or women, of whatever ethnicity, share 99.5 percent of their genetic codes. Not only are all humans much more alike than some thought, but also humans are much more similar to other mammals than most people imagined.

The genetic codes for humans and chimpanzees are 98 percent the same (although chimp genes are on 48, not 46, chromosomes), and the genomes for every other mammal are at least 90 percent the same as for people. All these shared genes allow scientists to learn about human genetics from other creatures, especially mice, by transposing, deactivating, enhancing, and duplicating their genes.

Although human similarities are astounding, differences that seem minor are significant, too. Some alleles are relatively common, detectable, and understood. For example, the apoE4 allele, unlike apoE2, renders a person more susceptible to AIDS, heart disease, and Alzheimer's disease.

But many alleles have unknown effects, or perhaps no effects. And some polymorphisms are very rare: Each of us probably has one or two alleles that only one person

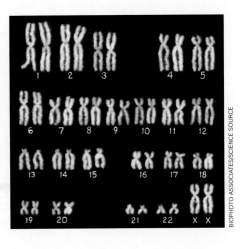

BIOPHOTO ASSOCIATES/SCIENCE SOURCE

Uncertain Sex Every now and then, a baby is born with "ambiguous genitals," meaning that the child's sex is not abundantly clear. When this happens, a quick analysis of the chromosomes is needed, to make sure there are exactly 46 and to see whether the 23rd pair is XY or XX. The karyotypes shown here indicate a normal baby boy *(left)* and girl *(right)*.

in a million has. We have learned a lot about genes, and that makes us realize how much we do not know.

Research on breast cancer, for instance, has found two relatively common genes, named BRCA1 and BRCA2, that make it likely a woman will develop breast cancer if she lives long enough. Less than a fourth of the women who develop breast cancer carry one or the other of those genes. Perhaps another fourth have one of ten other known alleles that increase the risk, although how much and in what way is "ambiguous" (Kean, 2014, p. 1458).

That omits half of the millions (estimated at one woman in eight) who will develop breast cancer. Their disease is caused by a combination of genes, alleles, mutations, diet, and other epigenetic factors—but no one knows what and how. If we knew, millions of lives might be saved.

THE 23RD PAIR The difference between one person and another—and between one species and another—begins with the genes, but it is much more epigenetic than genetic. Consider sex differences, which originate from one gene on one chromosome, the Y, which is half of the 23rd pair.

In females, the 23rd pair is composed of two large X-shaped chromosomes. Accordingly, it is designated **XX.** In males, the 23rd pair has one large X-shaped chromosome with many genes and one quite small chromosome, with only a few genes, which is Y-shaped. That 23rd pair is called **XY.**

Because a female's 23rd pair is XX, every ovum contains one X or the other—but always an X. Because a male's 23rd pair is XY, when his 46 chromosomes divide to make gametes, half of his sperm carry an X chromosome and half carry a Y.

The Y chromosome has a gene (SRY) that directs the developing fetus to make male organs. Thus, the sex of the developing organism depends on which sperm penetrates the ovum—either an X sperm, which creates a girl (XX), or a Y sperm, which creates a boy (XY) (see Figure 2.2).

At conception, there are about 120 males for every 100 females, perhaps because Y sperm swim faster and reach the ovum first (remember, they carry fewer genes, so they are lighter than the X sperm).

However, male embryos are more vulnerable than female ones (because of fewer genes, again?), so they are less likely to survive prenatally: At birth the boy/girl ratio is about 104:100.

The sex ratio seems to be nature, not nurture, but the environment already has an effect. The United Nations reports that the natural sex ratio at birth in most developed nations (such as the United States) is 105:100, but it is lower in the poorest nations, probably because hunger and lack of prenatal care harms more male fetuses

XX
A 23rd chromosome pair that consists of two X-shaped chromosomes, one each from the mother and the father. XX zygotes become females.

XY
A 23rd chromosome pair that consists of an X-shaped chromosome from the mother and a Y-shaped chromosome from the father. XY zygotes become males.

FIGURE 2.2 Determining a Zygote's Sex Any given couple can produce four possible combinations of sex chromosomes; two lead to female children and two, to male. In terms of the future person's sex, it does not matter which of the mother's Xs the zygote inherited. All that matters is whether the father's Y sperm or X sperm fertilized the ovum. However, for X-linked conditions it matters a great deal because typically one, but not both, of the mother's Xs carries the trait.

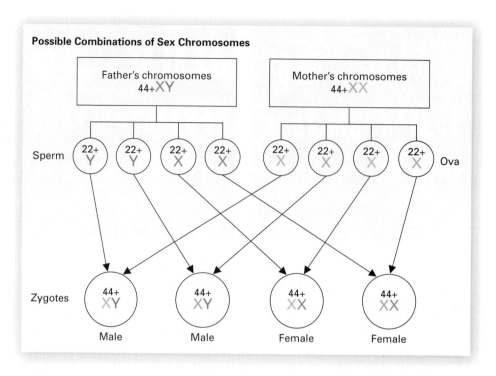

Possible Combinations of Sex Chromosomes

than female. In Angola, the ratio is 103:100 (United Nations, Department of Economic and Social Affairs, 2015).

Biological sex differences become cultural as soon as a newborn is named and wrapped in blue or pink. Indeed, cultural differences can begin before conception. Consider sex selection.

OPPOSING PERSPECTIVES

Too Many Boys?

In past centuries, millions of newborns were killed because they were the wrong sex, a practice that is considered murder today. Now the same goal is achieved in three ways: (1) by inactivating X or Y sperm before conception, (2) by inserting only the male or female zygotes after in vitro conception, or (3) by aborting XX or XY fetuses.

Should sex selection be illegal? It is, in at least 36 nations. It is not in the United States (Murray, 2014).

Why do some nations allow sex selection, and others not? Should governments legislate morals, or choose one culture over another? People disagree (Wilkinson, 2015).

One nation that forbids prenatal sex selection is China. This was not always so. In about 1979, China began a "one-child" policy, urging and sometimes forcing couples to have only one child. That achieved the intended goal: Severe poverty was almost eliminated.

But advances in prenatal testing, and the Chinese tradition that sons, not daughters, must care for aged parents, led many couples to want their only child to be a boy. Among the unanticipated results: (1) since 1980 an estimated 9 million abortions of female fetuses; (2) between 1980 and 2006,

My Strength, My Daughter That's the slogan these girls in New Delhi are shouting at a demonstration against abortion of female fetuses in India. The current sex ratio of children in India suggests that this campaign has not convinced every couple.

MANISH SWARUP/AP PHOTO

adoption of an estimated 200,000 newborn girls by Westerners; (3) in 2010, far more unmarried young men than women.

In 1993, the Chinese government forbade prenatal testing for sex selection. In 2007, China became much less likely to allow adoption, and the number of children from China adopted by Westerners plummeted from 14,496 in 2005 to 4,418 in 2011. In 2013, China rescinded the one-child policy. Yet the infant boy/girl ratio is still about 117:100 (United Nations, Department of Economic and Social Affairs, 2015).

Sex preferences are apparent everywhere. One elderly Indian man said, "We should have at least four children per family, three of them boys" (quoted in Khanna, 2010, p. 66). Couples of Asian ancestry in the United States also have more boys than girls (Puri et al., 2011). In some Western nations, including Germany, girls are preferred—both as newborns and as caregivers of the old (Wilhelm et al., 2013).

The argument in favor of sex selection is freedom from government interference. Some fertility doctors and many individuals believe that each couple should be able to decide how many children to have, and what sex they should be (Murray, 2014).

The argument against sex selection is that society might suffer. For instance, 30 years after the one-child policy began, many more young Chinese men than women die. Why? Developmental psychology suggests an answer. Unmarried young men everywhere take risks to attract women and become depressed if they remain unpartnered. That increases the risk of early death, from accidents, suicide, drug overdoses and poor health practices.

Other problems may occur that affect a society that has many males. Males have higher rates than females of learning disabilities, drug addiction, suicide, homicide (as victims and killers), and heart attacks. They are more likely to vote for wars and advocate long sentences for criminals.

But wait: Genes do not *determine* behavior. Every sex difference is influenced by culture. Even traits that originate with biology, such as the propensity to heart attacks, are affected more by environment (in this case, diet and cigarettes) than by XX or XY chromosomes. Perhaps nurture would change if nature produced more males than females.

Already, medical measures and smoking reductions have reduced heart attacks in men. In the United States in 1950, among people under age 65, four times as many men as women died of heart disease. By 2010, the rate was lower for both sexes, but especially for men, 2:1 not 4:1. Lifelong, cardiovascular deaths are now close to sex-neutral (Centers for Disease Control, 2015). Similarly, every gender difference is influenced by nurture.

Might laws against prenatal sex selection be unnecessary if culture shifted? "Might" . . . "if" . . . Critical thinking is needed; both opposing perspectives make sense.

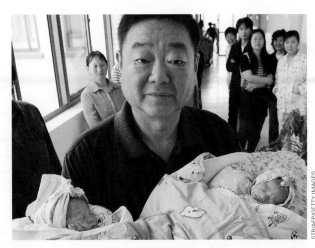

Mama Is 60 Wu Jingzhou holds his newborn twin daughters, born to his 60-year-old wife after in vitro fertilization. Ordinarily, it is illegal in China, as in most other nations, for women to have children after menopause. But an exception was made for this couple since the death of their only child, a young woman named Tingling, was partly the government's fault.

Twins

There is one major exception to genetic diversity. Although every zygote is genetically unique, not every newborn is.

About once in every 250 human conceptions, the zygote not only duplicates but splits apart completely, creating two, or four, or even eight separate zygotes, each genetically identical to that first single cell (see Visualizing Development, page 54). If each separate cell implants and grows, multiple births occur, usually with every newborn genetically identical. This does not seem to be genetic, as the rate is similar—and rare—in every ethnic group.

One separation results in **monozygotic twins,** from one *(mono)* zygote. Two or three separations create monozygotic quadruplets or octuplets. (An incomplete split creates *conjoined twins,* formerly called Siamese twins.)

Because monozygotic multiples originate from the same zygote, they have virtually identical genetic instructions for physical appearance, psychological traits, vulnerability to diseases, and everything else. However, because nurture always affects nature, even before birth, identical twins do not have exactly the same phenotype.

LaunchPad

Video Activity: Identical Twins: Growing Up Apart gives a real-life example of how genes play a significant role in people's physical, emotional, social, and mental development.

monozygotic twins
Twins who originate from one zygote that splits apart very early in development. (Also called *identical twins.*)

VISUALIZING DEVELOPMENT

One Baby or More

Humans usually have one baby at a time, but sometimes twins are born. Most often they are from two ova fertilized by two sperm (*lower left*), resulting in dizygotic twins. Sometimes, however, one zygote splits in two (*lower right*), resulting in monozygotic twins; if each of these zygotes splits again, the result is monozygotic quadruplets.

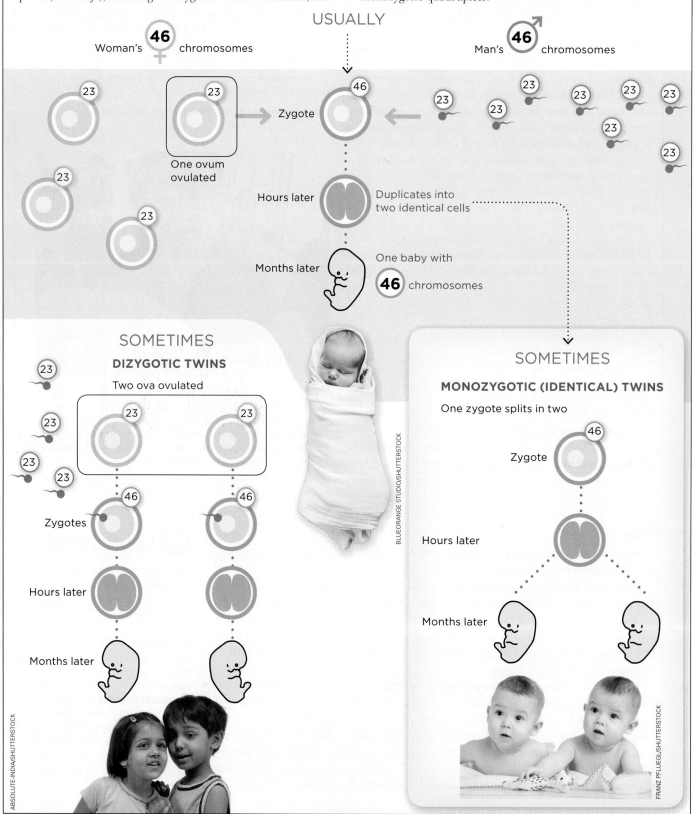

USUALLY

Woman's **46** chromosomes

Man's **46** chromosomes

23

23 — One ovum ovulated

23

23

Zygote — 46

23

23

23

23

23

23

23

23

Hours later — Duplicates into two identical cells

Months later — One baby with **46** chromosomes

SOMETIMES
DIZYGOTIC TWINS
Two ova ovulated

23

23

23

23

23 — 23

Zygotes — 46 — 46

Hours later

Months later

BLUEORANGE STUDIO/SHUTTERSTOCK

SOMETIMES
MONOZYGOTIC (IDENTICAL) TWINS

One zygote splits in two

Zygote — 46

Hours later

Months later

ABSOLUTE-INDIA/SHUTTERSTOCK

FRANZ PFLUEGL/SHUTTERSTOCK

Usually, monozygotic twins develop their own identities while enjoying twinship. They might both have inherited athletic ability, for instance, but one chooses basketball and the other, soccer. One monozygotic twin writes:

> Twins put into high relief *the* central challenge for all of us: self-definition. How do we each plant our stake in the ground, decide how sensitive, callous, ambitious, cautious, or conciliatory we want to be every day? . . . Twins come with a built-in constant comparison, but defining oneself against one's twin is just an amped-up version of every person's life-long challenge: to individuate—to create a distinctive persona in the world.
>
> [Pogrebin, 2010, p. 9]

Dizygotic twins, also called *fraternal twins,* are born three times as often as monozygotic twins. They began life as two zygotes created by two ova fertilized by two sperm. (Usually, the ovaries release only one ovum per month, but sometimes two or more ova are released.) Dizygotic twins, like any offspring from the same two parents, have half their genes in common. Their phenotypes may differ (about half are male–female pairs) or they can look quite similar, again like other siblings.

dizygotic twins
Twins who are formed when two separate ova are fertilized by two separate sperm at roughly the same time. (Also called *fraternal twins.*)

The incidence of multiple ovulation is influenced by genes, and thus is more common in some ethnic groups than others. For example, about 1 in 11 Yorubas in Nigeria is a twin, as are about 1 in 45 European Americans, 1 in 75 Japanese and Koreans, and 1 in 150 Chinese.

Age matters, too: Older women more often double-ovulate. Not all twin conceptions result in twin births. Sometimes an early sonogram reveals two developing organisms, but later only one embryo continues to grow. This *vanishing twin* phenomenon may occur in about 12 percent of pregnancies (Giuffrè et al., 2012).

Because genes endure lifelong, if a woman has one set of twins, she is more likely to have another set (Painter et al., 2010). Her daughters also have a 50/50 chance of inheriting her twin-producing X, and hence they are likely to have twins themselves. Her sons are not likely to have twins because they do not ovulate. But her son's daughters may have twins because their X is from his mother, and half the time it is the multiple-ovulation X.

Genetic Interactions

No gene functions alone. Thus, almost every trait is *polygenic* (affected by many genes) and *multifactorial* (influenced by many factors). Almost daily, researchers describe new complexities in multifactorial interaction. Here we describe some of those complexities.

© 2016 MACMILLAN

Genetic Mix Dizygotic twins Olivia and Harrison have half their genes in common, as do all siblings from the same parents. If the parents are close relatives, who themselves share most alleles, the non shared half is likely to include many similar genes. That is not the case here, as Mother (Nicola) is from Wales and Father (Gleb) is from the nation of Georgia, which includes many people of Asian ancestry. Their phenotypes, and the many family photos on the wall, show many additive genetic influences.

Most genes are **additive genes.** Their effects *add up* to make the phenotype. When genes interact additively, the phenotype may reflect all the genes that are involved. Height, hair curliness, and skin color, for instance, are influenced by additive genes. Indeed, height is probably influenced by 180 genes, each contributing a very small amount (Enserink, 2011).

Less common are *nonadditive* genes, which do not contribute equal shares. In one nonadditive form of heredity, alleles interact in a **dominant–recessive pattern,** in which one allele, the *dominant gene,* is far more influential than the other, the *recessive gene.* When someone inherits a recessive gene that is not expressed in the phenotype, that person is said to be a **carrier** of that gene: The recessive gene is *carried* on the genotype.

Most recessive genes are harmless. For example, blue eyes are determined by a recessive allele and brown eyes by a dominant one, which means that a child conceived by a blue-eyed person and a brown-eyed person will usually have brown eyes.

"Usually" is accurate, because sometimes a brown-eyed person is a carrier of the blue-eye gene. In that case, in a blue-eye/brown-eye couple, every child certainly has a blue-eye gene from the blue-eyed parent and has a 50/50 chance of having another blue-eye gene from the carrier parent. Half the children of this couple will have blue eyes, half brown, on average.

Sometimes both parents are carriers. Then their children have one chance in four of inheriting the recessive gene from both parents. A blue-eyed child can be born to brown-eyed parents. A word to the wise: When a child looks like neither parent, do not question paternity (see Figure 2.3).

A special case of the dominant–recessive pattern occurs with genes that are **X-linked** (located on the X chromosome). If an X-linked gene is recessive—as are the genes for most forms of color blindness, many allergies, several diseases (including hemophilia and Duchenne muscular dystrophy), and some learning disabilities—the fact that it is on the X chromosome is critical (see Table 2.1).

This follows from what you already know. Since the Y chromosome is much smaller than the X, an X-linked recessive gene almost never has a dominant counterpart on the Y. Therefore, recessive traits carried on the X affect the phenotypes of sons more often than those of daughters. The daughters are protected by their other X chromosome, which usually has the dominant gene.

This explains why males with an X-linked disorder inherited it from their mothers, not their fathers. Because of their mothers, 20 times more boys than girls are color-blind (McIntyre, 2002).

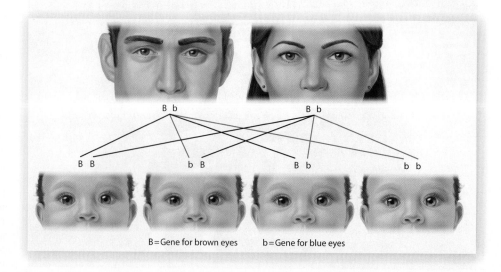

FIGURE 2.3 Changeling? No. If two brown-eyed parents both carry the blue-eye gene, they have one chance in four of having a blue-eyed child. Other recessive genes include the genes for red hair, Rh-negative blood, and many genetic diseases.

B = Gene for brown eyes   b = Gene for blue eyes

TABLE 2.1	The 23rd Pair and X-Linked Color Blindness			

23rd Pair	Phenotype	Genotype	Next Generation
1. XX	Normal woman	Not a carrier	No color blindness from mother
2. XY	Normal man	Normal X from mother	No color blindness from father
3. XX	Normal woman	Carrier from father	Half her children will inherit her X. The girls with that X will be carriers; the boys with her X will be color-blind.
4. XX	Normal woman	Carrier from mother	Half her children will inherit her X. The girls with her X will be carriers; the boys with her X will be color-blind.
5. XY	Color-blind man	Inherited from mother	All his daughters will have his X. None of his sons will have his X. All his children will have normal vision, unless their mother also had an X for color blindness.
6. XX	Color-blind woman (rare)	Inherited from both parents	Every child will have one X from her. Therefore, every son will be color-blind. Daughters will be only carriers, unless they also inherit an X from the father, as their mother did.

Note: On this chart, the red X means that it contains the gene for color blindness.

The final complexity is *epigenetic,* not solely genetic. All important human characteristics are influenced by nurture, including diseases known to be inherited, such as cancer, schizophrenia, and autism (Kundu, 2013; Plomin et al., 2013).

Diabetes is a notable example. People who inherit genes that put them at risk for type 2 (non-juvenile) diabetes do not always become diabetic. However, their lifestyle—especially body fat and exercise—might activate their genetic risk. Then epigenetic changes make diabetes irreversible (Reddy & Natarajan, 2013).

One intervention—bariatric surgery to dramatically reduce weight—leads to remission of the diabetes in most (72 percent) patients, but diet and exercise remain crucial. In more than half of those 72 percent, diabetes returns: Epigenetic changes can be controlled but not erased (Sjöström et al., 2014).

The same may be true for other developmental changes over the life span. Drug use—cocaine, cigarettes, alcohol, and so on—may produce epigenetic changes that make addiction likely, even if a person has stopped using the drug for years (Bannon et al., 2014). The addict can never use the drug again as an unaffected person might.

Some environmental factors that suppress or release genes are cognitive, not biological. For example, if a person feels lonely and rejected, that feeling can affect the RNA, which allows genetic potential for heart disease or social anxiety to be expressed (Slavich & Cole, 2013). Note that it is the *feeling* of loneliness, not the objective number of friends or social contacts, that has significant epigenetic influence.

COURTESY KATE NURRE

Sisters, But Not Twins, In Iowa
From their phenotype, it is obvious that these two girls share many of the same genes, as their blond hair and facial features are strikingly similar. And you can see that they are not twins; Lucy is 7 years old and Ellie is only 4. It may not be obvious that they have the same parents, but they do—and they are both very bright and happy because of it. This photo also shows that their genotypes differ in one crucial way: One of them has a dominant gene for a serious condition.

OBSERVATION QUIZ
Who has that genetic condition?
(see answer, page 58) ▲

WHAT HAVE YOU LEARNED?

1. What is the relationship among DNA, chromosomes, and genes?
2. Why is it said that your parents could have given you millions of different siblings?
3. What surprises came from the Human Genome Project?
4. How is the sex of a zygote determined?
5. How do monozygotic twins, dizygotic twins, and nontwin siblings differ?
6. How could a child inherit a disease neither parent has?
7. How is diabetes both genetic and not genetic?

TABLE 2.2	Timing and Terminology

Popular and professional books use various words to segment pregnancy. The following comments help to clarify the terms used.

- *Beginning of pregnancy:* Pregnancy begins at conception, which is also the starting point of *gestational age.* However, the organism does not become an embryo until about two weeks later, and pregnancy does not affect the woman (and cannot be confirmed by blood or urine testing) until implantation. Paradoxically, many obstetricians date the onset of pregnancy from the date of the woman's last menstrual period (LMP), about 14 days *before* conception.

- *Length of pregnancy:* Full-term pregnancies last 266 days, or 38 weeks, or 9 months. If the LMP is used as the starting time, pregnancy lasts 40 weeks, sometimes referred to as 10 lunar months (a lunar month is 28 days long).

- *Trimesters:* Instead of *germinal period, embryonic period,* and *fetal period,* some writers divide pregnancy into three-month periods called *trimesters.* Months 1, 2, and 3 are called the *first trimester;* months 4, 5, and 6, the *second trimester;* and months 7, 8, and 9, the *third trimester.*

- *Due date:* Although doctors assign a specific due date (based on the woman's LMP), only 5 percent of babies are born on that exact date. Babies born between three weeks before and two weeks after that date are considered "full term" or "on time." Babies born earlier are called *preterm;* babies born later are called *post-term.* The words *preterm* and *post-term* are more accurate than *premature* and *postmature.*

From Zygote to Newborn

Prenatal development is often divided into three main periods: The first two weeks are the **germinal period;** the third through the eighth week is the **embryonic period;** the ninth week until birth is the **fetal period** (see Table 2.2 for alternative terms).

Germinal: The First 14 Days

germinal period
The first two weeks of development after conception, characterized by rapid cell division and the beginning of cell differentiation.

embryonic period
The stage of prenatal development from the end of the second week through the eighth week after conception, during which the basic forms of body structures, including internal organs but not sex organs, develop.

fetal period
The stage of prenatal development from nine weeks after conception until birth, during which the fetus grows in size and matures in functioning.

stem cells
Cells from which any other specialized type of cell can form.

Within hours after conception, the zygote begins *duplication* and *division.* First, the 23 pairs of chromosomes duplicate, forming two complete sets of the genome. The cell divides neatly down the middle into two cells, each containing the original genetic code. These two new cells duplicate and divide, becoming four, which duplicate and divide, becoming eight, and so on.

Those first cells are **stem cells,** able to produce every other cell and thus become a complete person. If conception occurs in vitro, in a laboratory, one stem cell could be removed and analyzed (for instance, if both parents are carriers of a serious disease). If no abnormality is found, the other cells are implanted, to become a normal, complete human being.

After about the eight-cell stage, a third process, *differentiation,* begins. Cells specialize, taking different forms and reproducing at various rates, depending on where they are located. They are no longer omnipotent stem cells.

First Stages of the Germinal Period The original zygote as it divides into *(a)* two cells, *(b)* four cells, and *(c)* eight cells. Occasionally at this early stage, the cells separate completely, forming the beginning of monozygotic twins, quadruplets, or octuplets.

(a)

(b)

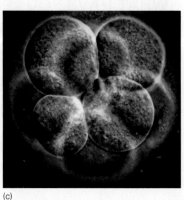

(c)

ANATOMICAL TRAVELOGUE/SCIENCE SOURCE

TABLE 2.3	**Vulnerability During Prenatal Development**

The Germinal Period
An estimated 60 percent of all zygotes do not grow or implant properly and thus do not survive the germinal period. Many of these organisms are abnormal; few women realize they were pregnant.

The Embryonic Period
About 20 percent of all embryos are aborted spontaneously. This is usually called an early *miscarriage*, a term that implies something wrong with the woman, when in fact the most common reason for a spontaneous abortion is a chromosomal abnormality.

The Fetal Period
About 5 percent of all fetuses are aborted spontaneously before viability at 22 weeks or are *stillborn*, defined as born dead after 22 weeks. This is much more common in poor nations.

Birth
Because of all these factors, only about 31 percent of all zygotes grow and survive to become living newborn babies. Age of the mother is crucial. One estimate is that less than 3 percent of all conceptions after age 40 result in live births.

Data from Bentley & Mascie-Taylor, 2000; Corda et al., 2012; Laurino et al., 2005.

Differentiation means that some cells become part of an eye, others part of a finger, still others part of the brain. About a week after conception, the multiplying cells (now numbering more than 100) separate into two distinct masses.

The outer cells form a shell that will become the *placenta* (the organ that surrounds and protects the developing creature), and the inner cells form a nucleus that will, in a few more days, become the embryo. The placenta grows first, because it must convey nourishment, enabling the embryo to grow.

The first task of those outer cells is **implantation**—that is, to embed themselves in the lining of the uterus. This is far from automatic; about 50 percent of natural conceptions and an even larger percentage of in vitro conceptions never implant (see Table 2.3). Most new life ends before an embryo begins (Sadler, 2015).

Embryo: From the Third Through the Eighth Week

The start of the third week after conception initiates the *embryonic period*, during which the formless mass of cells takes shape and merits a new name, **embryo.**

implantation
The process, beginning about 10 days after conception, in which the developing organism burrows into the tissue that lines the uterus, where it will be nourished.

embryo
The name for a developing human organism from two to eight weeks after conception.

The Embryonic Period *(a)* At 4 weeks past conception, the embryo is only about 1/8 inch (3 millimeters) long, but already the head has taken shape. *(b)* By 7 weeks, the organism is somewhat less than an inch (2 centimeters) long. Eyes, nose, the digestive system, and even the first stage of toe formation can be seen.

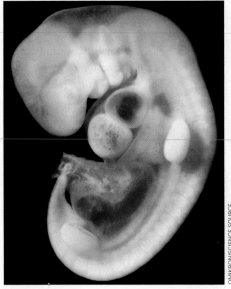

(a)

OMIKRON/SCIENCE SOURCE

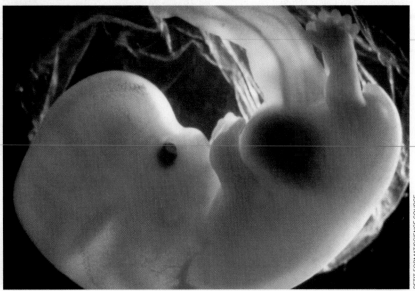

(b)

PETIT FORMAT/SCIENCE SOURCE

The embryonic period begins when a thin line (called the *primitive streak*) appears down the middle of the cell mass. That line becomes the neural tube, eventually becoming the central nervous system, including the brain and spine (Sadler, 2015). The head appears in the fourth week, as eyes, ears, nose, and mouth start to form. Also in the fourth week, a minuscule blood vessel that will become the heart begins to pulsate.

By the fifth week, buds that will become arms and legs emerge. The upper arms and then forearms, palms, and webbed fingers grow. Legs, knees, feet, and webbed toes, in that order, are apparent a few days later. Then, 52 and 54 days after conception, respectively, the fingers and toes separate (Sadler, 2015).

At the end of the eighth week after conception (56 days), the embryo weighs just one-thirtieth of an ounce (1 gram) and is about 1 inch (2½ centimeters) long. It has all the organs and body parts (except sex organs) of a human being, including elbows and knees. It moves frequently, about 150 times per hour, but such movement is random and imperceptible to the woman, who may not yet realize that she is pregnant.

sonogram
An image of a fetus (or an internal organ) produced by using high-frequency sound waves. (Also called *ultrasound*.)

fetus
The name for a developing human organism from the start of the ninth week after conception until birth.

Meet Your Baby This is Elisa Clare McGuinness at 22 weeks postconception. She continued to develop well for the next four months, becoming a healthy, 3,572-gram newborn, finally able to meet her family—two parents and an older brother.

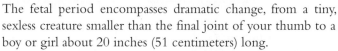

COURTESY OF MANDY MCGUINNESS

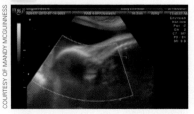

COURTESY OF MANDY MCGUINNESS

Video: Prenatal Period: 3D Ultrasound shows a real-life ultrasound of a developing fetus.

age of viability
The age (about 22 weeks after conception) at which a fetus may survive outside the mother's uterus if specialized medical care is available.

Fetus: From the Ninth Week Until Birth

The fetal period encompasses dramatic change, from a tiny, sexless creature smaller than the final joint of your thumb to a boy or girl about 20 inches (51 centimeters) long.

In the ninth week, sex organs develop, soon visible via a **sonogram** (also called *ultrasound*). The male **fetus** experiences a rush of the hormone testosterone, affecting the brain (Lombardo et al., 2012).

By 3 months, the fetus weighs about 3 ounces (87 grams) and is about 3 inches (7.5 centimeters) long. Those numbers—3 months, 3 ounces, 3 inches—are rounded off for easy recollection, but growth rates vary—some 3-month-old fetuses do not quite weigh 3 ounces and others already weigh 4.

Mid-pregnancy (months 4, 5, and 6) is the period of the greatest brain growth of the entire life span. The brain increases about six times in size and develops many new neurons (*neurogenesis*) and synapses (*synaptogenesis*), as well as divides into hemispheres (O'Rahilly & Müller, 2012). Before this, the cortex had been smooth, but now the brain begins to have the folds and wrinkles that allow a human brain to be far larger and more complex than the brains of other animals.

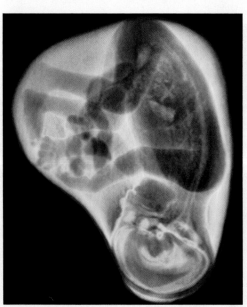

SPL/SCIENCE SOURCE

The entire central nervous system begins to regulate basic body functions such as breathing and sucking (Johnson, 2011). Advances in neurological functioning at the end of this trimester allow the fetus to reach the **age of viability,** the time past gestation when a fetus born far too early can become a baby who is able to survive.

Ready for Birth? We hope not, but this fetus at 27 weeks post-conception is viable, although very small. At full term (38 weeks), weight gain would mean that the limbs are folded close to the body, and the uterus is almost completely full.

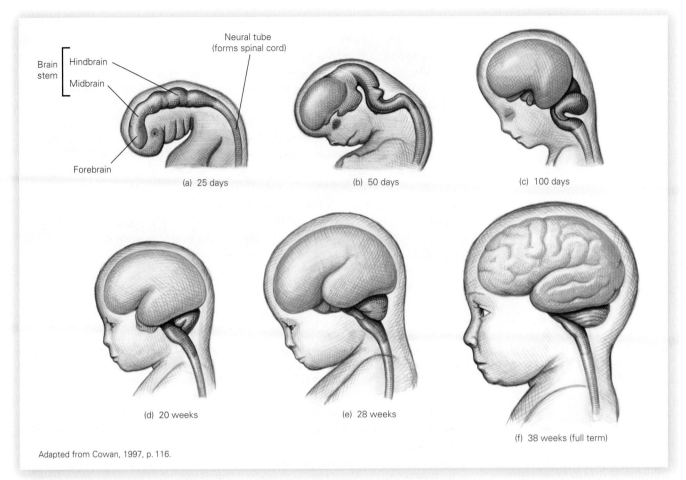

(a) 25 days

(b) 50 days

(c) 100 days

(d) 20 weeks

(e) 28 weeks

(f) 38 weeks (full term)

Adapted from Cowan, 1997, p. 116.

FIGURE 2.4 Prenatal Growth of the Brain Just 25 days after conception *(a)*, the central nervous system is already evident. The brain looks distinctly human by day 100 *(c)*. By the 28th week of gestation *(e)*, when brain activity begins, the various sections of the brain are recognizable. When the fetus is full term *(f)*, all the parts of the brain, including the cortex (the outer layers), are formed, folding over one another and becoming more convoluted, or wrinkled, as the number of brain cells increases.

Thanks to intensive medical care, the age of viability decreased dramatically in the twentieth century, but it now seems stuck at about 22 weeks after conception because even the most advanced technology cannot maintain life without some brain response (see Figure 2.4).

Attaining the age of viability simply means that life outside the womb is *possible*. Whether or not a non-breathing 22- to 25-week-old newborn should be resuscitated is a complex ethical issue for many doctors (Leuthner, 2014). Each day of the final three months improves the odds, not only of survival but also of life without disability.

Usually, by nine months or so, newborns are ready to thrive at home on mother's milk—no expert help, oxygenated air, or special feeding required. The fetus typically gains more than 4½ pounds (2.1 kilograms) in the third trimester, increasing, on average, to almost 7½ pounds (about 3.4 kilograms) at birth (see At About This Time).

Finally, a Baby

About 38 weeks (266 days) after conception, the fetal brain signals the release of hormones to start labor. The average baby is born after about 12 hours of active labor

Macmillan Education
LaunchPad

Video: Brain Development
Animation: Prenatal
http://qrs.ly/j34eoyp

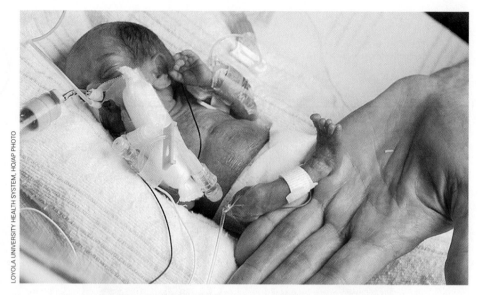

LOYOLA UNIVERSITY HEALTH SYSTEM, HO/AP PHOTO

One of the Tiniest Rumaisa Rahman was born after 26 weeks and 6 days, weighing only 8.6 ounces (244 grams). Nevertheless, she has a good chance of living a full, normal life. Rumaisa gained 5 pounds (2,270 grams) in the hospital and then, 6 months after her birth, went home. Her twin sister, Hiba, who weighed 1.3 pounds (590 grams) at birth, had gone home two months earlier. At their first birthday, the twins seemed normal, with Rumaisa weighing 15 pounds (6,800 grams) and Hiba 17 pounds (7,711 grams) (Nanji, 2005).

for first births and 7 hours for subsequent births, although labor may take twice or half as long. The definition of "active" labor varies, which is one reason some women believe they are in active labor for days and others say 10 minutes.

Women's birthing positions vary—sitting, squatting, lying down. Some women give birth while immersed in warm water, which helps the woman relax (the fetus continues to get oxygen via the umbilical cord).

At About This Time: Average Prenatal Weights*

Period of Development	Weeks Past Conception	Average Weight (nonmetric)	Average Weight (metric)	Notes
End of embryonic period	8	1/30 oz	1 g	Most common time for spontaneous abortion (miscarriage).
End of first trimester	13	3 oz	85 g	
At viability (50/50 chance of survival)	22–25	20–32 oz	565–900 g	A birthweight of less than 2 lb, 3 oz (1,000 g) is extremely low birthweight (ELBW).
End of second trimester	26–28	2–3 lb	900–1,400 g	Less than 3 lb, 5 oz (1,500 g) is very low birthweight (VLBW).
End of preterm period	35	5½ lb	2,500 g	Less than 5½ lb (2,500 g) is low birthweight (LBW).
Full term	38	7½ lb	3,400 g	Between 5½ lb and 9 lb (2,500–4,000 g) is considered normal weight.

*To make them easier to remember, the weights are rounded off (hence the imprecise correspondence between metric and nonmetric). Actual weights vary. For instance, normal full-term infants weigh between 5½ and 9 pounds (2,500 and 4,000 grams); viable preterm newborns, especially twins or triplets, weigh less than shown here.

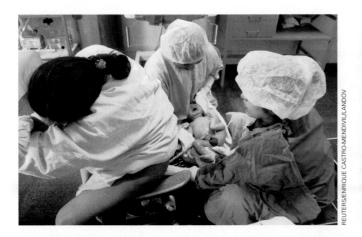

REUTERS/ENRIQUE CASTRO-MENDIVIL/LANDOV

FRANK HERHOLDT/GETTY IMAGES

Preferences and opinions on birthing positions (as on almost every other aspect of prenatal development and birth) are partly cultural and partly personal. In general, physicians find it easier to see the head emerge if the woman lies on her back. However, many women find it easier to push the fetus out if they sit up. (Figure 2.5 shows the stages of birth.)

THE NEWBORN'S FIRST MINUTES Newborns usually breathe and cry on their own. Between spontaneous cries, the first breaths of air bring oxygen to the lungs and

Choice, Culture, or Cohort?
Why do it that way? Both of these women (in Peru, on the *left*, in England, on the *right*) chose methods of labor that are unusual in the United States, where birth stools and birthing pools are uncommon. However, in all three nations, most births occur in hospitals—a rare choice a century ago.

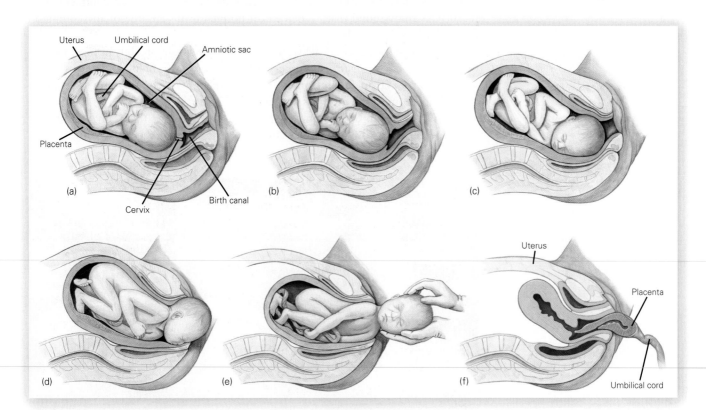

FIGURE 2.5 A Normal, Uncomplicated Birth *(a)* The baby's position as the birth process begins. *(b)* The first stage of labor: The cervix dilates to allow passage of the baby's head. *(c)* Transition: The baby's head moves into the "birth canal," the vagina. *(d)* The second stage of labor: The baby's head moves through the opening of the vagina (the baby's head "crowns") and *(e)* emerges completely. *(f)* The third stage of labor is the expulsion of the placenta. This usually occurs naturally, but the entire placenta must be expelled, so birth attendants check carefully. In some cultures, the placenta is ceremonially buried, to commemorate its life-giving role.

blood, and the infant's color changes from bluish to pinkish. (Pinkish refers to blood color, visible beneath the skin, and applies to newborns of all hues.) Eyes open wide; tiny fingers grab; even tinier toes stretch and retract. The full-term baby is instantly, zestfully, ready for life.

One assessment of newborn health is the **Apgar scale,** first developed by Dr. Virginia Apgar. When she earned her MD in 1933, Apgar wanted to work in a hospital but was told that only men did surgery. Consequently, she became an anesthesiologist.

Apgar saw that "delivery room doctors focused on mothers and paid little attention to babies. Those who were small and struggling were often left to die" (Beck, 2009, p. D1). To save those young lives, Apgar developed a simple rating scale of five vital signs—color, heart rate, cry, muscle tone, and breathing—to alert doctors when a newborn was in crisis.

Since 1950, birth attendants worldwide have used the Apgar (often using the name as an acronym: Appearance, Pulse, Grimace, Activity, and Respiration) at one minute and again at five minutes after birth, assigning each vital sign a score of 0, 1, or 2. If the five-minute Apgar is at least 7, the baby does not need immediate, life-saving care.

MEDICAL ASSISTANCE AT BIRTH The specifics of birth depend on many factors, including the position and size of the fetus, the skill of the birth attendant, and the customs of the culture. In developed nations, births almost always include sterile procedures, electronic monitoring, and drugs to dull pain or speed contractions. A recent U.S. study found that 87 percent of hospital births are free of any complications (Glance et al., 2014).

Midwives are as skilled at delivering babies as physicians are, but in most nations only medical doctors perform surgery. More than one-third of U.S. births occur via **cesarean section (c-section,** or simply *section*), whereby the fetus is removed through incisions in the mother's abdomen.

The World Health Organization suggests that cesareans are medically indicated in 10–15 percent of births. Fifty-four nations have rates of less than 10 percent; 69 have

Apgar scale
A quick assessment of a newborn's health. Heart rate, respiratory effort, muscle tone, color, and reflexes are given a score of 0, 1, or 2, with the total compared with the ideal score of 10 (which is rarely attained).

cesarean section (c-section)
A surgical birth, in which incisions through the mother's abdomen and uterus allow the fetus to be removed quickly, instead of being delivered through the vagina.

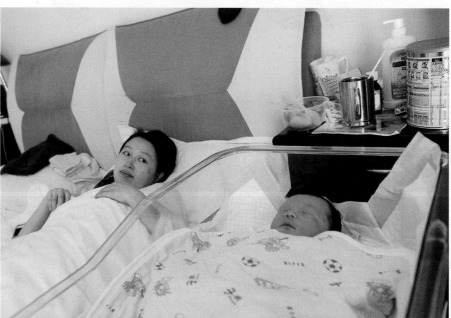

Pick Up Your Baby! Probably she can't. In this maternity ward in Beijing, China, most patients are recovering from cesarean sections, making it difficult to cradle, breast-feed, or carry a newborn until the incision heals.

WANG ZHAO/AFP/GETTY IMAGES

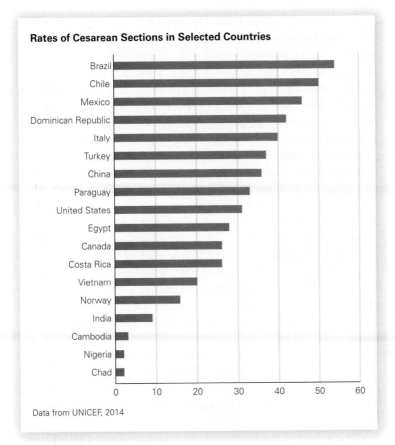

Rates of Cesarean Sections in Selected Countries

Data from UNICEF, 2014

FIGURE 2.6 Too Many
Cesareans or Too Few?
Rates of cesarean deliveries vary
widely from nation to nation. Latin
America has the highest rates in the
world (note that 50 percent of all births
in Chile are by cesarean), and sub-
Saharan Africa has the lowest (the rate
in Chad is 2 percent). The underlying
issue is whether some women who
should have cesareans do not get
them, while other women have
unnecessary cesareans.

more than 15 percent (Gibbons et al., 2012b) (see Figure 2.6). Nations with very low cesarean rates also have high death rates in childbirth.

In the United States, the cesarean rate rose between 1996 and 2008 (from 21 percent to 34 percent) and then stabilized. Variation is dramatic from one hospital to another—from 7 to 70 percent (Kozhimannil et al., 2013).

Cesareans are usually safe for mother and baby, saving lives when the fetal head is too large for the pelvis. Twins may survive more often with c-sections (Roberts et al., 2015). Cesareans also have many advantages for hospitals (easier to schedule, quicker, and more expensive than vaginal deliveries) and for women who want to plan when to give birth.

Disadvantages appear later. C-sections increase medical complications after birth and reduce breast-feeding (Malloy, 2009). By age 3, children born by cesarean have double the rate of childhood obesity: 16 percent compared to 8 percent (Huh et al., 2012). The reason may be that babies delivered vaginally have beneficial bacteria in their gut but those delivered surgically do not (Wallis, 2014).

Less studied is the *epidural*, an injection in the spine that alleviates pain. Epidurals are often used in hospital births, but they increase the rate of cesarean sections, decrease newborn sucking immediately after birth, and increase rates of other complications—at least according to a large study in Pennsylvania (Kjerulff, 2014).

Another medical intervention is *induced labor*, when labor is started, speeded, or strengthened with a drug. The rate of induced labor in developed nations has more than doubled since 1990, up to 20 or 25 percent. Sometimes induction is necessary for the health of the mother or the fetus. However, induced labor itself increases complications (Grivell et al., 2012).

Questions of costs and benefits abound. For instance, c-section and epidural rates vary more by doctor, hospital, day of the week, and region than by medical circumstances.

Complications vary as well. A study of 750,000 births in the United States divided hospitals into three categories—low, average, and high quality—based on obstetric complications for the woman. In low-quality hospitals, cesareans led to five times as many complications (20 percent) and vaginal births twice as many (23 percent) compared to high-quality hospitals (4 and 11 percent) (Glance et al., 2014).

Most U.S. births now take place in hospital labor rooms with high-tech facilities and equipment nearby. Another 5 percent of U.S. births occur in *birthing centers* (not in a hospital), and less than 1 percent occur at home (illegal in some jurisdictions). About half of the home births are planned and half are unexpected because labor happened too quickly. The latter situation is hazardous if no one is nearby to rescue a newborn in distress.

Compared with the United States, *planned* home births are more common in many other developed nations (2 percent in England, 30 percent in the Netherlands) where midwives are paid by the government. In the Netherlands, special ambulances called *flying storks* speed mother and newborn to a hospital if needed. Dutch research finds home births better for mothers and no worse for infants than hospital births (de Jonge et al., 2013).

Many women in the United States and elsewhere have a **doula,** a person trained to support the laboring woman. Doulas time contractions, use massage, provide encouragement, and do whatever else is helpful. The term originally came from ancient Greece, and doulas have been traditional in Latin America for centuries.

Every comparison study finds that the rate of medical intervention is lower when doulas are part of the birth team. Doulas have proven to be particularly helpful for

doula
A woman who helps with the birth process, including massage during birth and help with breast-feeding.

BEA KALLOS/EPA/LANDOV

Mother Laboring, Doula Working In many nations, doulas work to help the birth process, providing massage, timing contractions, and preparing for birth. In the United States, doulas typically help couples decide when to leave home, avoiding long waits between hospital admittance and birth. Here, in Budapest, this expectant mother will have her baby with a licensed midwife at home. Nora Schimcsig is her doula; the two women will be together from this moment in early labor to the first breast-feeding of the newborn.

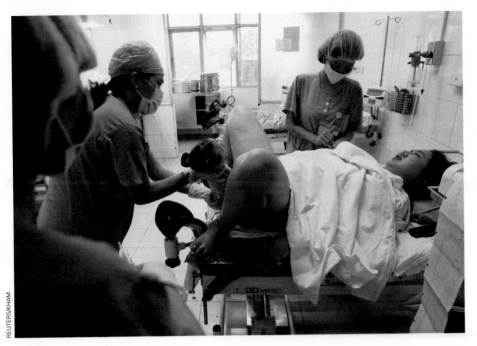

REUTERS/KHAM

Everyone Healthy and Happy A few decades ago in the developing world and a century ago in advanced nations, hospital births were only for birthing women who were near death, and only half of the fetuses survived. That has changed, particularly in Asia, where women prefer to give birth in hospitals. Hospital births themselves are not what they were. Most new mothers participate in the process: Here Le Thi Nga is about to greet her newborn after pulling with all her strength on the belt that helped her push out the head.

OBSERVATION QUIZ
What evidence shows that even in Hanoi, technology is part of this birth? (see answer, page 68) ◄

immigrant, low-income, or unpartnered women who may be intimidated by doctors (Kang, 2014; Vonderheid et al., 2011).

The New Family

Humans are social creatures, seeking interaction with their families and their societies. We have already seen how crucial social support is during pregnancy; social interaction may become even more important for newborns.

THE NEWEST FAMILY MEMBER A newborn's appearance (big hairless head, tiny toes, and so on) stirs the human heart, evident in adults' brain activity and heart rate. Fathers are often enraptured by their scraggly newborn and protective of the exhausted mother, who may appreciate their husband more than before, for hormonal as well as practical reasons.

Newborns are responsive social creatures in the first hours of life (Zeifman, 2013). They listen, stare, cry, stop crying, and cuddle. In the first day or two, a professional might administer the **Brazelton Neonatal Behavioral Assessment Scale (NBAS),** which records 46 behaviors, including 20 reflexes. Parents who watch their baby responding in the NBAS are often amazed—and this fosters early parent–child connection (Hawthorne, 2009).

Technically, a **reflex** is an involuntary response to a particular stimulus. Humans of every age reflexively protect themselves (the eye blink is an example). Reflexes seem automatic. Not quite. The strength and reliability of newborn reflexes varies depending on genes, drugs at birth, and overall health.

Newborns' senses are also responsive: New babies listen more to voices than to traffic, for instance. Thus, in many ways, newborns connect with the people of their world, who are predisposed to respond (Zeifman, 2013). If the baby performing these

INNA ASTAKHOVA/SHUTTERSTOCK

Video: Newborn Reflexes shows several infants displaying the reflexes discussed in this section.

Brazelton Neonatal Behavioral Assessment Scale (NBAS)
A test often administered to newborns that measures responsiveness and records 46 behaviors, including 20 reflexes.

reflex
An unlearned, involuntary action or movement in response to a stimulus. A reflex occurs without conscious thought.

actions on the Brazelton NBAS were your own, you would be proud and amazed; that is part of being human.

NEW MOTHERS Many women experience significant physical problems soon after birth, such as healing from a c-section, painfully sore nipples, or problems with urination. However, worse than physical problems are psychological ones. When the level of birth hormones decreases, between 8 and 15 percent of women experience **postpartum depression,** a sense of inadequacy and sadness (called *baby blues* in the mild version and *postpartum psychosis* in the most severe form).

With postpartum depression, baby care (feeding, diapering, bathing) feels very burdensome. The newborn's cry may not compel the mother to carry and nurse her infant. Instead, the mother may be terrified that she might neglect or abuse her infant.

The first sign that something is amiss may be euphoria after birth. A new mother may be unable to sleep, or to stop talking. After the initial high, severe depression may set in.

Postpartum depression is affected by anesthesia, hormones, pain, financial stress, marital problems, a birth that did not go as planned, surgery, and a baby with feeding or other problems. Successful breast-feeding reduces maternal depression (Figueiredo et al., 2014), but success is elusive for many new mothers. A lactation consultant is an important part of the new mother's support team.

Some researchers believe that postpartum depression is a consequence of modern life, because contemporary women consume less omega-3 fatty acids (especially found in fish), exercise less (especially in the sun), and are far from their mothers and other relatives (Hahn-Holbrook & Haselton, 2014). In any case, a depressed mother needs help, not only for her sake but for the sake of the baby.

NEW FATHERS At birth, the father's presence reduces complications. I observed this when my daughter Elissa birthed Asa (now 5, as noted in the opening of this chapter). Asa's birth took much longer than his younger brother's; Elissa's anxiety rose when the doctor and midwife discussed a possible cesarean for "failure to progress" without consulting her. Her husband told her, "All you need to do is relax between contractions and push when a contraction comes. I will do the rest." She listened. He did. No cesarean.

Whether or not he is present at the birth, the father's legal acceptance of the birth is important to mother and newborn. A study of all live, single births in Milwaukee from 1993 to 2006 (151,869 babies!) found that complications correlated with several expected variables (e.g., maternal cigarette smoking) and one unexpected one—no father listed on the birth record. This connection was especially apparent for European Americans: When no father was listed, rates of long labor, cesarean section, and other complications increased (Ngui et al., 2009).

Currently, about half of all U.S. women are not married when their baby is born (U.S. Census Bureau, 2014), but fathers are usually listed. When fathers acknowledge their role, birth is better for mother and child.

postpartum depression
The deep sadness and inadequacy felt by some new mothers in the days and weeks after giving birth.

ANSWER TO OBSERVATION QUIZ
(from page 67) The computer printout on the far right. Monitors during labor track contractions, fetal heart rate, and sometimes more, printing out the record minute by minute so that medical staff can judge whether to speed up labor or birth. In this case, no medical help was required. ●

Expecting a Girl She is obviously thrilled and ready, and they bought a crib, but he seems somewhat nervous. Perhaps someone should tell him that his newborn will become a happy and accomplished child and adult, a source of paternal pride and joy for the next 40 years or more.

101DALMATIANS/E+/GETTY IMAGES

Fathers may experience pregnancy and birth biologically, not just psychologically. Many fathers experience symptoms, including weight gain and indigestion during pregnancy and pain during labor.

Paternal experiences of pregnancy and birth are called **couvade**—expected in some cultures such as India, normal in many, and considered pathological in others (M. Sloan, 2009; Ganapathy, 2014). In the United States, couvade is unnoticed and unstudied, but many fathers are intensely involved with their future child (Brennan et al., 2007; Raeburn, 2014). Like new mothers, fathers are vulnerable to depression; other people need to help. Indeed, sometimes the father experiences more problems than the mother (Bradley & Slade, 2011).

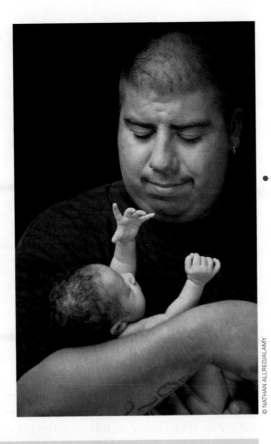

© NATHAN ALLRED/ALAMY

Mutual Joy Ignore this dad's tattoo and earring, and the newborn's head wet with amniotic fluid. Instead recognize that, for thousands of years, hormones and instincts propel fathers and babies to reach out to each other, developing lifelong connections.

couvade
Symptoms of pregnancy and birth experienced by fathers.

WHAT HAVE YOU LEARNED?

1. What major event occurs to end the germinal period?
2. What body parts develop during the embryonic period?
3. What crucial developments occur about halfway through the fetal period?
4. What five vital signs does the Apgar scale measure?
5. What are the advantages and disadvantages of cesarean sections?
6. In what ways do doulas support women before, during, and after labor?
7. What in the newborn's appearance and behavior helps with parental bonding?
8. How do fathers experience pregnancy and birth?
9. What are the signs of postpartum depression?

Problems and Solutions

The early days of prenatal life place the developing person on a path toward health and success—or not. Fortunately, resilience is apparent from the beginning; healthy newborns are the norm, not the exception.

We now look at specific problems that may occur and how to prevent or minimize them. Always remember dynamic systems—every hazard is affected by dozens of factors.

Abnormal Genes and Chromosomes

Perhaps half of all zygotes have serious abnormalities of their chromosomes or genes. Usually they never grow or implant. However, some such zygotes survive, grow, develop, and are born to live a satisfying life.

Macmillan Education
LaunchPad
Video: Genetic Disorders
http://qrs.ly/pg4eoxw

MONKEY BUSINESS IMAGES/SHUTTERSTOCK

Universal Happiness All young children delight in painting brightly colored pictures on a big canvas, but this scene is unusual for two reasons: Daniel has trisomy-21, and this photograph was taken at the only school in Chile where normal and special-needs children share classrooms.

OBSERVATION QUIZ

How many characteristics can you see that indicate that Daniel has Down syndrome? (see answer, page 72) ➤

Down syndrome
A condition in which a person has 47 chromosomes instead of the usual 46, with three rather than two chromosomes at the 21st position. People with Down syndrome often have a distinctive appearance. (Also called *trisomy-21*.)

NOT EXACTLY 46 As you know, each sperm or ovum usually has 23 chromosomes, creating a zygote with 46 chromosomes and eventually a person. However, cells do not always split exactly in half to make gametes, partly because of the age of the parents—particularly the mother. About once in about every 200 births is a baby born with 45, 47, or, rarely, 48 or 49 chromosomes.

If an entire chromosome is missing or added, that leads to a recognizable *syndrome,* a cluster of distinct characteristics that tend to occur together. Usually the cause is three chromosomes at a particular location instead of the usual two (a condition called a *trisomy*).

The most common survivor with 47 chromosomes is a person with **Down syndrome.** This syndrome is also called *trisomy-21* because the person has three copies of chromosome 21. In the United States, 6,000 babies per year are born with Down syndrome.

Some 300 distinct characteristics may result from that third chromosome 21, usually including a thick tongue, round face, slanted eyes, hearing problems, heart abnormalities, muscle weakness, and short stature. Intellectual development is often slow. Family context, educational efforts, and possibly medication can decrease the harm (Kuehn, 2011).

The other common miscount involves the sex chromosomes. Every human has at least 44 autosomes and one X chromosome; an embryo cannot develop without those 45. However, about 1 in every 500 infants is born with only one sex chromosome (no Y) or with three or more (not just two). Having an odd number of sex chromosomes impairs cognition and sexual maturation. Specifics depend on exactly which chromosomes are at that 23rd site (XYY, XXX, XO, and so on) as well as epigenetics (Hong & Reiss, 2014).

GENE DISORDERS Everyone carries alleles that *could* produce serious diseases or handicaps in the next generation. The phenotype is affected only when the inherited gene is dominant or when both parents carry the same recessive gene and the zygote inherits the harmful gene from both, or when a particular combination of genes from both parents triggers a problem.

MARIA PLATT-EVANS/SCIENCE SOURCE

She Laughs Too Much No, not the smiling sister, but the 10-year-old on the right, who has Angelman syndrome. She inherited it from her mother's chromosome 15. Fortunately, her two siblings inherited the mother's other chromosome 15 and are normal. If she had inherited the identical deletion on her father's chromosome 15, she would have developed Prader-Willi syndrome, which would cause her to be overweight as well as always hungry and often angry. With Angelman syndrome, however, laughing, even at someone's pain, is a symptom.

Serious dominant disorders are rare, because those who have them rarely live to become parents. However, a few dominant disorders do not affect the person until adulthood.

Adult onset occurs with *Huntington's disease,* a fatal central nervous system disorder caused by a copy number variation—more than 35 repetitions of a particular set of three base pairs. The symptoms first appear when a person could have had many children, as did the original Mr. Huntington. Half of them inherited his dominant gene.

Recessive diseases are more common, because people are often unaware that they are carriers, and being a carrier may confer some benefit. About 1 in 12 North American men and women carries an allele for cystic fibrosis, thalassemia, or sickle-cell disease.

Consider the most studied example: sickle-cell disease. Carriers die less often from malaria, so the gene protected more people (the carriers) than it killed. If a couple in a malaria prone region were both carriers and had four children, odds are that one would die of sickle-cell disease, one would not be a carrier and might die of malaria, but two would be carriers, protected against a common, fatal disease. They would survive, become parents, and thus the recessive trait would spread.

Almost every genetic disease is more common in one group than in another (Weiss & Koepsell, 2014). About 11 percent of Americans with African ancestors are carriers of the sickle-cell gene; cystic fibrosis is more common among Americans with ancestors from northern Europe because carriers may have been protected from cholera. Dark skin is protective against skin cancer, and light skin allows more vitamin D to be absorbed from the sun—a benefit if sunlight is scarce.

Each nation targets the genetic disorders that are common among its citizens. In the United States, people with cystic fibrosis or sickle-cell anemia can now live normal lives. In Cyprus and southern China, the focus is on thalassemia (Lo, 2015).

Some recessive conditions are X-linked, including **fragile X syndrome,** which is caused by more than 200 repetitions on one gene (Plomin et al., 2013). The cognitive deficits caused by fragile X are the most common form of *inherited* intellectual disability (many other forms, such as trisomy-21, are not usually inherited).

fragile X syndrome
A genetic condition that involves the X chromosome and that causes slow development.

Harm to the Fetus

The early days of life place the developing fetus on the path toward health and success—or not. Most newborns are quite healthy, but if something is amiss, it is often part of a cascade that may become overwhelming (Rossignol et al., 2014).

The cascade may begin before a woman realizes she is pregnant, as many toxins, illnesses, and experiences can cause harm early in pregnancy. Every week, scientists discover an unexpected **teratogen,** which is anything—drugs, viruses, pollutants, malnutrition, stress, and more—that increases the risk of prenatal abnormalities and birth complications.

Many teratogens cause no physical defects but affect the brain, making a child hyperactive, antisocial, or learning-disabled. These are **behavioral teratogens.** One of my students wrote:

> I was nine years old when my mother announced she was pregnant. I was the one who was most excited. . . . My mother was a heavy smoker, Colt 45 beer drinker and a strong caffeine coffee drinker.
>
> One day my mother was sitting at the dining room table smoking cigarettes one after the other. I asked, "Isn't smoking bad for the baby?" She made a face and said, "Yes, so what?"
>
> I asked, "So why are you doing it?"
>
> She said, "I don't know.". . .
>
> During this time I was in the fifth grade and we saw a film about birth defects. My biggest fear was that my mother was going to give birth to a fetal alcohol syndrome (FAS) infant. . . . My baby brother was born right on schedule. The doctors claimed a healthy newborn. . . . Once I heard healthy, I thought everything was going to be fine. I was wrong, then again I was just a child. . . .
>
> My baby brother never showed any interest in toys. . . . [H]e just cannot get the right words out of his mouth. . . . [H]e has no common sense. . . .
>
> Why hurt those who cannot defend themselves?
>
> *[J., personal communication]*

As you remember from Chapter 1, one case proves nothing. J. blames her mother, although genes, postnatal experiences, and lack of preventive information and services may be part of the cascade as well. Nonetheless, J. rightly wonders why her mother took the risk.

teratogen
Any agent or condition, including viruses, drugs, and chemicals, that can impair prenatal development, resulting in birth defects or complications.

behavioral teratogens
Agents and conditions that can harm the prenatal brain, impairing the future child's intellectual and emotional functioning.

ANSWER TO **OBSERVATION** QUIZ
(from page 70) Individuals with Down syndrome vary in many traits, but visible here are five common ones. Compared to most children his age, including his classmate beside him, Daniel has a rounder face, narrower eyes, shorter stature, larger teeth and tongue, and—best of all—a happier temperament. ●

Swing High and Low Adopted by loving parents but born with fetal alcohol syndrome, Philip, shown here at age 11, sometimes threatened to kill his family members. His parents sent him to this residential ranch in Eureka, Montana (non-profit, tuition $3,500 a month) for children like him. This moment during recess is a happy one; it is not known whether he learned to control his fury.

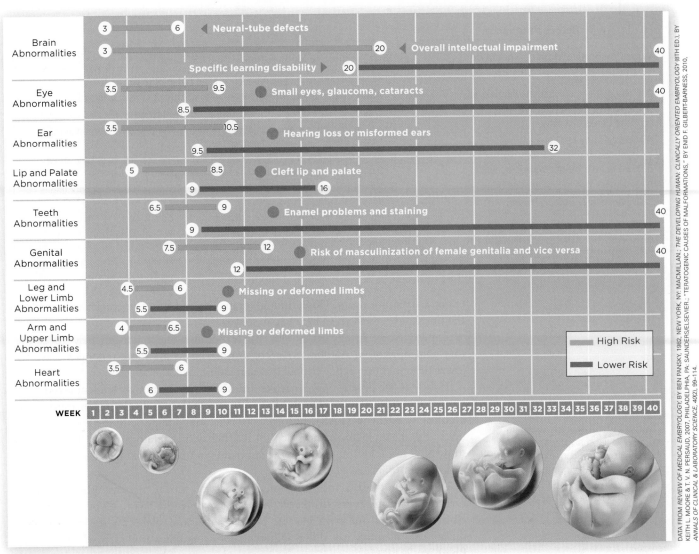

DATA FROM REVIEW OF MEDICAL EMBRYOLOGY, BY BEN PANSKY, 1982, NEW YORK, NY: MACMILLAN.; THE DEVELOPING HUMAN: CLINICALLY ORIENTED EMBRYOLOGY (8TH ED.), BY KEITH L. MOORE & T. V. N. PERSAUD, 2007, PHILADELPHIA, PA: SAUNDERS/ELSEVIER.; "TERATOGENIC CAUSES OF MALFORMATIONS," BY ENID F. GILBERT-BARNESS, 2010, ANNALS OF CLINICAL & LABORATORY SCIENCE, 40(2), 99–114.

FIGURE 2.7 One More Reason to Plan a Pregnancy The embryonic period, before a woman knows she is pregnant, is the most sensitive time for causing structural birth defects. However, at no time during pregnancy is the fetus completely safe from harm.

Individual differences in susceptibility to teratogens may be caused by a fetus's genetic makeup or peculiarities of the mother, including the effectiveness of her placenta or her overall health. The dose and timing of the exposure are also important.

EVALUATING RISKS Risk analysis is crucial in human development (Sheeran et al., 2014). Although all teratogens increase the *risk,* none *always* causes damage. Risk analysis involves probabilities, not certainties (Aven, 2011).

For both risk and protection, timing may be crucial. The first days and weeks after conception (the germinal and embryonic periods) are the *critical period* for body formation, and the final months are important for body weight. Health during the entire fetal period affects the brain (see Figure 2.7).

Obstetricians recommend that *before* pregnancy occurs, women should avoid drugs (especially alcohol), supplement a balanced diet with extra folic acid and iron, update their immunizations, and gain or lose weight if needed. Indeed, preconception health is at least as important as postconception health (see Table 2.4).

A second crucial factor is the dose and/or frequency of exposure. Some teratogens have a **threshold effect;** they are harmless until exposure reaches a certain level, at which point they "cross the threshold" and become damaging. This threshold

threshold effect
A situation in which a certain teratogen is relatively harmless in small doses but becomes harmful once exposure reaches a certain level (the threshold).

TABLE 2.4	Before Pregnancy	
What Prospective Mothers Should Do	**What Prospective Mothers Really Do (U.S. Data)**
1. Plan the pregnancy.	1. At least one-fourth of all pregnancies are not intended.
2. Take a daily multivitamin with folic acid.	2. About 60 percent of women aged 18 to 45 do not take multivitamins.
3. Avoid binge drinking (defined as four or more drinks in a row).	3. One in seven women in their childbearing years binge drink.
4. Update immunizations against all teratogenic viruses, especially rubella.	4. Unlike in many developing nations, relatively few pregnant women in the United States lack basic immunizations.
5. Gain or lose weight, as appropriate.	5. About one-fourth of all U.S. women of childbearing age are obese, and about 5 percent are underweight. Both extremes increase complications.
6. Reassess use of prescription drugs.	6. Ninety percent of pregnant women take prescription drugs (not counting vitamins).
7. Develop daily exercise habits.	7. More than half of women of childbearing age do not exercise regularly.

Data from Bombard et al., 2013; MMWR, July 20, 2012; Brody, 2013; Mosher et al., 2012; U.S. Department of Health and Human Services, December, 2012.

is not a fixed boundary: Dose, timing, frequency, and other teratogens affect when the threshold is crossed (O'Leary et al., 2010).

Experts rarely specify thresholds, partly because one teratogen may affect the threshold of another. Alcohol, tobacco, and marijuana are more teratogenic, with a lower threshold for each, when all three are combined.

Is there a safe dose for psychoactive drugs? Perhaps, but, as my student asked, why risk it? Consider alcohol. During the early weeks, heavy drinking can cause **fetal alcohol syndrome (FAS),** distorting facial features (especially the eyes, ears, and upper lip). Later in pregnancy, alcohol is a behavioral teratogen. One longitudinal study of 7-year-olds found that in the last trimester binge drinking was most harmful to the brain (Niclasen et al., 2014).

Genes are a third factor that influences the effects of teratogens. When a woman carrying dizygotic twins drinks alcohol, for example, the twins' blood alcohol levels are equal; yet one twin may be protected because alleles for the enzyme that metabolizes alcohol may differ. Differential susceptibility is evident (McCarthy & Eberhart, 2014).

The Y chromosome makes male fetuses more vulnerable. They are more likely to be spontaneously aborted or stillborn and more likely to be harmed by teratogens than female fetuses are. This is true overall, but the male/female hazard rate differs from one teratogen to another (Lewis & Kestler, 2012).

Maternal genes may be important during pregnancy. One allele results in low levels of folic acid in a woman's bloodstream. Her deficiency, via the placenta, affects the embryo, which may develop *neural-tube defects*—either *spina bifida*, in which the tail of the spine is not enclosed properly (enclosure normally occurs at about week 7), or *anencephaly*, in which part of the brain is missing.

Neural-tube defects are more common among people from Ireland, England, and Egypt and rare among Asians and sub-Saharan Africans. Rates are down among Americans because folic acid is now a required additive in cereal and bread.

MAKING PREDICTIONS Results of teratogenic exposure cannot be predicted precisely in individual cases, although impact can be measured for the population, as evident with neural-tube defects. Much is also known about how individuals can reduce the risks.

General health is protective. Women who maintain good nutrition and avoid drugs and teratogenic chemicals (often in pesticides, cleaning fluids, and cosmetics) usually have healthy babies. Some medications are necessary (e.g., for women with epilepsy, diabetes, and severe depression), but consultation should begin *before* conception.

fetal alcohol syndrome (FAS)
A cluster of birth defects, including abnormal facial characteristics, slow physical growth, and intellectual disabilities, that may occur in the child of a woman who drinks alcohol while pregnant.

Video Activity: Teratogens explores the factors that enable or prevent teratogens from harming a developing fetus.

Many women assume that herbal medicines or over-the-counter drugs are safe. Not so: One expert explains, "Many over-the-counter drugs were grandfathered in with no studies of their possible effects during pregnancy" (quoted in Brody, 2013, p. D5).

Even doctors are not always careful. Opioids (narcotics) to reduce pain may harm the fetus, and aspirin may cause excessive bleeding during birth. Yet one study found that 23 percent of pregnant women on Medicaid receive a prescription for a narcotic (Desai et al., 2014).

Some doctors do not ask women if they are taking psychoactive drugs. For example, one Maryland study found that almost one-third of pregnant women were not asked if they drank (Cheng et al., 2011). Women over age 35 with college degrees were least likely to be queried. Did their doctors assume they knew the dangers? Wrong. Such women are more likely to drink during pregnancy than are younger women.

SMOKING AFFECTS YOUR PREGNANCY AND YOUR CHILDREN

www.BeTobaccoFree.gov

Smoke-Free Babies Posters such as this one have had an impact. Smoking among adults is only half of what it was 30 years ago. One-third of women smokers quit when they know they are pregnant, while the other two-thirds cut their smoking in half. Unfortunately, the heaviest smokers are least likely to quit—they need more than posters to motivate them to break the habit.

Women of all ages consult the Internet regarding medications in pregnancy. However, a study of 25 Web sites found that only 103 of the 235 medications listed as safe had been evaluated by TERIS (a respected national panel of teratologists). Further, of those 103, only 60 were considered safe. The rest were not *proven* harmful, but the experts said that more evidence was needed (Peters et al., 2013). Sometimes the same drug was on the safe list of one Internet site and the danger list of another.

A CASCADE OF RISK Even when evidence seems clear, the proper response is controversial. Pregnant women can be arrested and jailed for using alcohol or other psychoactive drugs in six states (Minnesota, North Dakota, Oklahoma, South Dakota, Tennessee, and Wisconsin).

Alicia Beltran, 14 weeks pregnant in Wisconsin, told her doctor that she had been addicted to pills but quit before she became pregnant, as confirmed by urine tests. The doctor ordered her to take anti-addiction medication. She thought that might harm her fetus and refused. She was arrested and taken in handcuffs to a holding cell (Eckholm, 2013).

Several women have been jailed when their newborns had illegal substances in their bloodstream (Eckholm, 2013). Such measures may do more harm than good if they make women avoid prenatal care or hospital births.

Every pregnancy and birth has multiple risks, so it is a mistake to blame any problem solely on the mother, or the doctor, or the community.

For instance, **cerebral palsy** (a disease marked by difficulties with movement) was once thought to be caused by birth procedures, such as forceps misused by the doctor. However, we now know that cerebral palsy results from genetic sensitivity, teratogens, and/or maternal infection (Mann et al., 2009), worsened by **anoxia** (insufficient oxygen) to the fetal brain at birth.

cerebral palsy
A disorder that results from damage to the brain's motor centers. People with cerebral palsy have difficulty with muscle control, so their speech and/or body movements are impaired.

anoxia
A lack of oxygen that, if prolonged, can cause brain damage or death.

Anoxia itself is part of a cascade. Normal birth involves moments of low oxygen, as evident from the fetal heart rate. How long anoxia can continue without harming the brain depends on genes, birthweight, gestational age, drugs in the bloodstream (either taken by the mother before birth or given during birth), and much else. Thus, anoxia is part of a cascade that may cause cerebral palsy. Likewise, almost every complication is the result of many factors.

A VIEW FROM SCIENCE

Conflicting Advice

Pregnant women want to know about the thousands of drugs, chemicals, and diseases that cause fetal harm. However, the scientific method is designed to be cautious. It takes years for longitudinal research, testing of alternative hypotheses, and replication before solid conclusions are reached. Only after this process did all scientists agree on such (now obvious) teratogens as rubella and cigarettes.

One current dispute is whether pesticides should be allowed on the large farms that produce most of the fruits and vegetables for consumption in the United States. No biologist doubts that pesticides harm frogs, fish, and bees, but the pesticide industry insists that careful use (e.g., spraying on plants, not workers) does not harm people.

Developmentalists, however, worry that pregnant women who breathe these toxins might have children with brain damage. As one scientist said, "Pesticides were designed to be neurotoxic . . . Why should we be surprised if they cause neurotoxicity?" (Lanbhear, quoted in Mascarelli, 2013, p. 741).

For example, umbilical cord blood proves that many fetuses are exposed to chlorpyrifos, a pesticide. Longitudinal research finds that these children have lower intelligence and more behavior problems than other children (Horton et al., 2012).

However, Dow Chemical Company, which sells the pesticide, argues that the research does not take into account confounding factors, such as the living conditions of farmworkers' children (Mascarelli, 2013). If a child who lives in a shack and attends a different school every few months has learning disabilities, does it matter whether his mother worked in the fields with pesticides when she was pregnant?

The U.S. government has banned chlorpyrifos from household use (it once was commonly used to kill roaches and ants), but it is still used in agriculture and in homes in other nations. In this dispute, developmentalists choose to protect the fetal brain, which is why this chapter advises pregnant women to avoid pesticides. Is that overly cautious?

On many other possible teratogens, developmentalists themselves are conflicted. Fish consumption is an example.

Pregnant women in the United States are told to eat less fish, but those in the United Kingdom are told to eat more fish. The reason for these opposite messages is that fish contains mercury (a teratogen) and DHA (an omega-3 fatty acid needed for fetal brain development). Scientists weigh the benefits and risks, wondering how to teach women to judge each kind of fish and where it swam, choosing benefits while avoiding risks (Lando & Lo, 2014).

To make all this more difficult, pregnant women are, ideally, happy and calm: Stress and anxiety affect the fetus. Pregnancy often increases fear and anxiety (Rubertsson et al., 2014); scientists do not want to add to the worry. Prospective parents want clear, immediate answers, yet scientists cannot always provide them.

Prenatal Testing

Seeing a medical professional in the first trimester has many benefits: Women learn what to eat, what to do, and what to avoid. Some serious conditions, syphilis and HIV among them, can be diagnosed and treated before they harm the fetus. Prenatal tests (of blood, urine, and fetal heart rate as well as ultrasound) reassure parents, facilitating the crucial parent–child bond long before fetal movement is apparent.

In general, early care protects fetal growth, makes birth easier, and renders parents better able to cope. When complications appear (such as twins, gestational diabetes, and infections), early recognition increases the chance of a healthy birth.

Unfortunately, however, about 20 percent of early pregnancy tests *raise* anxiety instead of reducing it. It is now possible to use a simple blood test to indicate many chromosomal and genetic problems. The mother may learn information that she does not want to know (de Jong et al., 2015). Couples may argue about risks that they never discussed before.

One specific example comes from a test in place for decades: alpha-fetoprotein (AFP). If it is too high or too low, it may indicate multiple fetuses, abnormal growth, or Down syndrome. Many such warnings are **false positives;** that is, they falsely suggest a problem that does not exist. Any warning, whether false or true, requires further testing, worry, and soul-searching. Consider the following.

> **false positives**
> The result of a laboratory test (blood, urine or sonogram) that suggests an abnormality that is not present.

A CASE TO STUDY

False Positives and False Negatives

John and Martha, both under age 35, were expecting their second child. Martha's initial prenatal screening revealed low alpha-fetoprotein, which could indicate Down syndrome.

Another blood test was scheduled. . . .

John asked, "What exactly is the problem?" . . .

"We've got a one in eight hundred and ninety-five shot at a retarded baby."

John smiled, "I can live with those odds."

"I'm still a little scared."

He reached across the table for my hand. "Sure," he said, "that's understandable. But even if there is a problem, we've caught it in time. . . . The worst-case scenario is that you might have to have an abortion, and that's a long shot. Everything's going to be fine." . . .

"I might *have to have* an abortion?" The chill inside me was gone. Instead I could feel my face flushing hot with anger. "Since when do you decide what I *have* to do with my body?"

John looked surprised. "I never said I was going to decide anything," he protested. "It's just that if the tests show something wrong with the baby, of course we'll abort. We've talked about this."

"What we've talked about," I told John in a low, dangerous voice, "is that I am pro-choice. That means I decide whether or not I'd abort a baby with a birth defect. . . . I'm not so sure of this."

"You used to be," said John.

"I know I used to be." I rubbed my eyes. I felt terribly confused. "But now . . . look, John, it's not as though we're deciding whether or not to have a baby. We're deciding what *kind* of baby we're willing to accept. If it's perfect in every way, we keep it. If it doesn't fit the right specifications, whoosh! Out it goes.". . .

John was looking more and more confused. "Martha, why are you on this soapbox? What's your point?"

"My point is," I said, "that I'm trying to get you to tell me what you think constitutes a 'defective' baby. What about . . . oh, I don't know, a hyperactive baby? Or an ugly one?"

"They can't test for those things and—"

"Well, what if they could?" I said. "Medicine can do all kinds of magical tricks these days. Pretty soon we're going to be aborting babies because they have the gene for alcoholism, or homosexuality, or manic depression. . . . Did you know that in China they abort a lot of fetuses just because they're female?" I growled. "Is being a girl 'defective' enough for you?"

"Look," he said, "I know I can't always see things from your perspective. And I'm sorry about that. But the way I see it, if a baby is going to be deformed or something, abortion is a way to keep everyone from suffering—*especially* the baby. It's like shooting a horse that's broken its leg. . . . A lame horse dies slowly, you know? . . . It dies in terrible pain. And it can't run anymore. So it can't enjoy life even if it doesn't die. Horses live to run; that's what they do. If a baby is born not being able to do what other people do, I think it's better not to prolong its suffering."

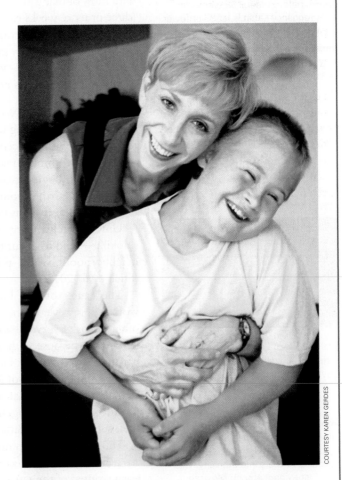

Happy Boy Martha Beck not only loves her son Adam (shown here), but she also writes about the special experiences he has brought into the whole family's life—hers, John's, and their other children's. She is "pro-choice"; he is a chosen child.

". . . And what is it," I said softly, more to myself than to John, "what is it that people do? What do we live to do, the way a horse lives to run?"

[Beck, 2011, pp. 134–136, 138]

The second AFP test was in the normal range, "meaning that there was no reason to fear . . . Down syndrome" (p. 142). John and Martha no longer discussed abortion.

The opposite of a false positive is a *false negative,* a mistaken assurance that all is well. Amniocentesis revealed that the second AFP was a false negative. Their fetus had Down syndrome after all. John and Martha had another angry discussion, and Martha decided to give birth to Adam, who has Down syndrome. Years later they had a third child. When Adam was in early adolescence, Martha and John divorced.

Low Birthweight

low birthweight (LBW)
A body weight at birth of less than 5½ pounds (2,500 grams).

very low birthweight (VLBW)
A body weight at birth of less than 3 pounds, 5 ounces (1,500 grams).

extremely low birthweight (ELBW)
A body weight at birth of less than 2 pounds, 3 ounces (1,000 grams).

preterm birth
A birth that occurs three or more weeks before the full 38 weeks of the pregnancy—that is, at 35 or fewer weeks after conception.

small for gestational age (SGA)
Having a body weight at birth that is significantly lower than expected, given the time since conception. For example, a 5-pound (2,265-gram) newborn is considered SGA if born on time but not SGA if born two months early. (Also called *small-for-dates*.)

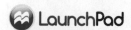

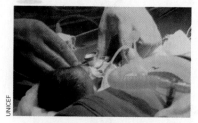

Watch **Video: Low Birthweight in India,** which discusses the causes of LBW among babies in India.

immigrant paradox
The surprising fact that immigrants tend to be healthier than U.S. born residents of the same ethnicity. This was first evident among Mexican Americans.

As you just read, small and immature newborns are more vulnerable to every teratogen and birth complication. The international cutoff for **low birthweight (LBW)** is 2,500 grams (5½ pounds). UNICEF estimated that 22 million low-birthweight babies were born in 2013.

Some LBW babies are **very low birthweight (VLBW),** under 1,500 grams (3 pounds, 5 ounces), and **extremely low birthweight (ELBW),** under 1,000 grams (2 pounds, 3 ounces). It is possible for a newborn to weigh as little as 500 grams. They are the most vulnerable: Half of them die even with excellent care, and none of them live without it (Lau et al., 2013).

Remember that fetal weight normally doubles in the last trimester of pregnancy, with most of that gain occurring in the final three weeks. Thus, a baby born **preterm** (three or more weeks early, no longer called *premature*) is usually, but not always, LBW.

In addition, some fetuses gain weight slowly throughout pregnancy and are *small-for-dates,* or **small for gestational age (SGA).** A full-term baby weighing only 2,600 grams and a 30-week-old fetus weighing only 1,000 grams are both SGA, even though the first is not technically LBW.

CAUSES OF LOW BIRTHWEIGHT Maternal or fetal illness might cause SGA or preterm birth, but maternal drug use is a more common cause. Every psychoactive drug slows fetal growth, with tobacco implicated in 25 percent of all LBW newborns worldwide.

Another common reason for slow growth and preterm birth is malnutrition. Women who begin pregnancy underweight, who eat poorly during pregnancy, or who gain less than 3 pounds (1.3 kilograms) per month in the last six months more often have underweight infants.

Unfortunately, many risk factors—underweight, undereating, underage, and smoking—tend to occur together. To make it worse, many such mothers live in poor neighborhoods, where pollution is high—another risk factor for low birthweight (Stieb et al., 2012).

The causes of low birthweight just mentioned rightly focus on the pregnant woman. However, fathers—and grandmothers, neighbors, and communities—are often crucial. Everyone who affects a pregnant woman also affects the fetus. She may be stressed because of her boss, her mother, her mother-in-law, and especially her partner. Because of the social system, it is not surprising that unintended pregnancies increase the incidence of low birthweight (Shah et al., 2011).

The role of the social network is most apparent in what is called the **immigrant paradox.** Many immigrants have difficulty getting education and well-paid jobs; their socioeconomic status is low. Low SES correlates with low birthweight.

Thus, immigrants should birth more LBW babies. But, paradoxically, their babies are generally healthier in every way, including in weight, than newborns of native-born women of the same gene pool (García Coll & Marks, 2012).

This was first called the *Hispanic paradox* because, although U.S. residents born in Mexico or South America average lower SES than people of Hispanic descent born in the United States, their newborns have fewer problems. The same paradox has been found for immigrants from the Caribbean, Africa, eastern Europe, and Asia. The crucial factor may be fathers and grandmothers, who keep pregnant immigrant women healthy and drug-free, counteracting the stress of poverty (Luecken et al., 2013).

Newborns of Chinese descent born in the United States are an interesting case. If their mothers' socioeconomic status is low, newborns weigh more and are less likely to die *if* their mothers were born in China, not in the United States. However, if the mother is college-educated, then the babies are healthier if their mothers are U.S.-born (Li & Keith, 2011).

This suggests that maternal education, household income, and social support all protect prenatal health. Of the three, social support may be most crucial, but the other two are important as well.

CONSEQUENCES OF LOW BIRTHWEIGHT You have already read that life itself is uncertain for the smallest newborns. Ranking worse than most developed nations—and just behind Cuba and Croatia—the infant mortality rate (death in the first year) of the United States is 34th in the world, about 6 deaths per 1,000 live births. One major reason is that the United States has more ELBW (under 1,000 grams) births (MacDorman et al., 2014).

For survivors born underweight, every developmental accomplishment—smiling, holding a bottle, walking, talking—is late. Low-birthweight babies experience cognitive difficulties as well as visual and hearing impairments. High-risk newborns become infants and children who cry more, pay attention less, disobey, and experience language delays (Aarnoudse-Moens et al., 2009; Stolt et al., 2014).

Longitudinal research from many nations finds that children who were at the extremes of SGA or preterm have many neurological problems in middle childhood, including smaller brain volume, lower IQs, and behavioral difficulties (Clark et al., 2013; Hutchinson et al., 2013; van Soelen et al., 2010). Even in adulthood, risks persist: Adults who were LBW are more likely to develop diabetes and heart disease.

Longitudinal data provide both hope and caution. Remember that risk analysis gives probabilities, not certainties—averages are not true in every case. By age 4, some ELBW infants are normal in brain and body development. Some adults were very small babies and have become happy and successful.

COMPARING NATIONS In some northern European nations, only 4 percent of newborns weigh under 2,500 grams; in several South Asian nations, including India, Pakistan, and the Philippines, more than 20 percent are that small. Worldwide, far fewer low-birthweight babies are born than two decades ago; as a result, neonatal deaths have been reduced by one-third (Rajaratnam et al., 2010).

Some nations, China and Chile among them, have improved markedly (Hellerstein et al., 2015). In many nations, community health programs emphasize prenatal health. That helps, according to a study provocatively titled *Low birth weight outcomes: Why better in Cuba than Alabama?* (Neggers & Crowe, 2013).

In some nations, notably in sub-Saharan Africa, the LBW rate is rising because global warming, HIV, food shortages, wars, and other problems affect pregnant women. Another nation with a troubling rate of LBW is the United States, where the rate fell throughout most of the twentieth century, reaching a low of 7.0 percent in 1990. But then it rose again, with the 2013 rate at 8.02 percent, ranging from under 6 percent in Alaska to over 12 percent in Mississippi (see Figure 2.8).

There are some encouraging data: The U.S. low-birthweight rate was even higher a few years ago, at 8.2 in 2007, and the rate of LBW newborns has fallen, while the medical care of babies born at less than 28 weeks is among the best in the world (MacDorman et al., 2014).

THINK CRÌTICALLY: Food scarcity, drug use, and unmarried parenthood have all been suggested as reasons for the LBW rate in the United States. Which is it—or are there other factors?

FIGURE 2.8 Getting Better Some public health experts consider the rate of low birthweight to indicate of national health, since both reflect the same causes. If that is true, the world is getting healthier, since the LBW world average was 28 percent in 2009 but 16 percent in 2012. When all nations are included, 47 report LBW at 6 per 100 or lower (United States and United Kingdom are not among them).

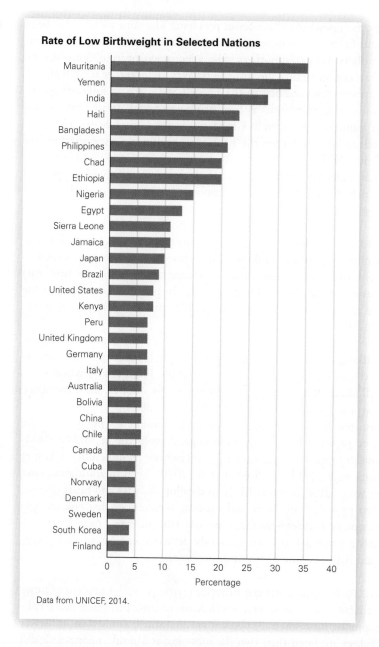

Rate of Low Birthweight in Selected Nations

Data from UNICEF, 2014.

WHAT HAVE YOU LEARNED?

1. What are the consequences if an infant is born with trisomy-21?

2. Why are some recessive traits (such as sickle-cell) quite common?

3. How does the timing of exposure to a teratogen affect the risk of harm to the fetus?

4. How do genes increase or decrease risk to a fetus?

5. What are the potential consequences of drinking alcohol during pregnancy?

6. What are the benefits of prenatal care?

7. What are the differences among LBW, VLBW, and ELBW?

8. What would cause a newborn to be LBW?

9. What are the consequences of low birthweight in childhood and adulthood?

Nature and Nurture

The goal of this chapter is to help every reader grasp the complex interaction between genotype and phenotype. This is not easy. For decades, in many nations, millions of scientists have struggled to understand this complexity. Each year brings advances in statistics and molecular analysis as well as new data to uncover various patterns, all resulting in hypotheses to be explored.

Here we examine only two complex traits: addiction and visual acuity, in two specific manifestations, alcohol use disorder and nearsightedness. These two illustrate a general truth: Every trait is affected by both nature and nurture, and understanding the progression from genotype to phenotype has many practical implications.

Alcohol Use Disorder

People everywhere discovered fermentation thousands of years ago. Alcohol has been declared illegal (as in the United States from 1919 to 1933) or considered sacred (as in many Judeo-Christian rituals). And for thousands of years, people have considered the abuse of alcohol and other drugs to be a moral weakness, a social scourge, or a personality defect. Those with alcohol use disorder have been jailed, jeered, or even burned at the stake.

We now know that inherited biochemistry affects alcohol metabolism. The disorder is as much biological as cultural. Genes create an addictive pull that can be overpowering, extremely weak, or somewhere in between, as each person's biochemistry reacts to alcohol by causing sleep, nausea, aggression, joy, relaxation, forgetfulness, sexual urges, or tears.

There is no "alcoholic gene," but alleles that make alcohol use disorder more likely have been identified on every chromosome except the Y (Epps & Holt, 2011). Although easy availability of alcohol may awaken genetic tendencies, punishing those with the genes does not stop addiction.

Metabolism allows some people to "hold their liquor" and therefore drink too much. Others (including many East Asians) sweat and become red-faced after just a few sips, a physiological response that may lead to a psychological reaction—embarrassment and abstinence. This inherited "flushing" tendency not only makes alcohol addiction rare, but it also improves metabolism (Kuwahara et al., 2014).

Sex (biological—either XX or XY) and gender (cultural) also affect the risk of the disorder. For biological reasons (body size, fat composition, metabolism), women

Welcome Home For many women in the United States, white wine is part of the celebration and joy of a house party, as shown here. Most people can drink alcohol harmlessly; there is no sign that these women are problem drinkers. However, danger lurks. Women get drunk on less alcohol than men, and females with alcohol addiction tend to drink more privately and secretly, often at home, feeling more shame than bravado. All that makes their addiction more difficult to recognize.

© HERO IMAGES INC./ALAMY

become drunk on less alcohol than men, and women who are heavy drinkers double their risk of mortality compared to men (Wang et al., 2014).

Many cultures encourage men to drink but not women (Chartier et al., 2014). For example, in Japan, both sexes have the same genes for metabolizing alcohol, yet women drink only about one-tenth as much as men. When women of Japanese ancestry live in the United States, their alcohol consumption increases.

Apparently, Americans of Asian descent try to adopt the drinking patterns of their new culture (Makimoto, 1998). In this and many other ways, drug addiction is a combination of nature and nurture, biology and culture.

Nearsightedness

All three factors—age, genes, and culture—affect vision as well. The effects of age are easy to notice. Newborns focus only on things within 1 to 3 feet of their eyes; vision improves steadily until about age 10; the eyeball changes shape at puberty, increasing nearsightedness (*myopia*), and again in middle age, decreasing myopia. The effects of genes and culture are more complex than age, as you will see.

HERITABLE? A study of British twins found that the Pax6 gene, which governs eye formation, has many alleles that make people somewhat nearsighted (Hammond et al., 2004). Heritability is almost 90 percent, which means that if one monozygotic British twin was myopic (nearsighted), the other twin is almost always myopic, too.

However, **heritability** indicates only how much of the variation in a particular trait *within a particular population and in a particular context and era* can be traced to genes. For example, the heritability of height is very high (about 95 percent) when children receive good medical care and nutrition, but it is low (about 20 percent) when children are malnourished. Thus, the 90 percent heritability of nearsightedness among the British may not apply elsewhere.

Indeed, it does not. In some African communities, vision heritability is close to zero because severe vitamin A deficiency makes sight depend much more on diet than on genes. If a child has no vitamin A, that child may become blind, even if the genotype is programmed for great vision.

Scientists and public health workers seek to develop and distribute a genetically modified strain of maize (the local staple) that is high in vitamin A. If they succeed, heritability will increase as vision improves (Fiedler et al., 2014).

What about children who are well nourished? Is their vision entirely inherited? Cross-cultural research suggests that it is not (Seppa, 2013).

A NEW EPIDEMIC "We are going down the path of having a myopia epidemic," according to the head of a vision program in Australia (Sankaridurg, quoted in Dolgin, 2015, p. 276). The problem is particularly acute in China, where 90 percent of the teenagers and young adults are nearsighted compared to 10–20 percent 60 years ago (Dolgin, 2015).

The first published research on this phenomenon appeared in 1992, when scholars noticed that, in army-mandated medical exams of all 17-year-old males in Singapore, 26 percent were nearsighted in 1980 but 43 percent were nearsighted in 1990 (Tay et al., 1992). Between the early 1970s and the early 2000s, nearsightedness in the U.S. population increased from 25 to 42 percent (Vitale et al., 2009).

An article in the leading British medical journal suggests that, although genes are to blame for most cases of severe myopia, "any genetic differences may be small" for the common nearsightedness of Asian school children (I. Morgan et al., 2012, p. 1739). Nurture must somehow be involved. But how?

heritability
A statistic that indicates what percentage of the variation in a trait within a population, in a particular context and era, can be traced to genes.

One suggested culprit is indoor study. As Chapter 7 notes, contemporary East Asian children are amazingly proficient in math and science. As their developing eyes focus on their books, those with a genetic vulnerability to myopia may lose acuity for objects far away—which is exactly what nearsightedness means.

However, it does not seem that studying itself is the problem. American children who study less but spend many hours watching television or playing video games also have rising rates of nearsightedness.

Data from the United States on children playing sports have led ophthalmologists to suggest that the underlying cause of myopia among Americans is inadequate time spent in daylight (I. Morgan et al., 2012). An ophthalmologist comments that "we're kind of a dim indoors people nowadays" (Mutti, quoted in Holden, 2010, p. 17).

One suggestion is that even sitting outside and reading could reduce nearsightedness. That seems too simplistic, according to some experts who believe it is not only outdoor light but also the eye adjusting to images at various distances that reduces myopia (Dolgin, 2015).

In any case, evidence from many places finds that in previous decades, genetically vulnerable children did not necessarily become nearsighted, but now they do. Perhaps if children spent more time outside playing, walking, or relaxing, fewer would need glasses.

Applauding Success These eager young men are freshmen at the opening convocation of Shanghai Jiao Tong University. They have studied hard in high school, scoring high on the national college entrance exam. Now their education is heavily subsidized by the government. Although China has more college students than the United States, the proportions are far lower, since the population of China is more than four times that of the United States.

OBSERVATION QUIZ

Name three visible attributes of these young men that differ from a typical group of freshmen in North America. (see answer, page 84) ▲

Practical Applications

Since genes affect every disorder, no one should be blamed or punished for inherited problems. However, knowing that genes never act in isolation allows prevention. For instance, if alcohol use disorder is in the genes, parents can keep alcohol out of their home, hoping their children become cognitively and socially mature before imbibing. If nearsightedness runs in the family, parents can play outdoors with their children every day.

Of course, abstention from alcohol and outdoor play are recommended for all children, as are dozens of other behaviors, such as flossing, saying "please," getting enough sleep, eating vegetables, and writing thank-you notes. No parent can enforce every recommendation, but awareness of genetic risks can guide priorities.

Awareness of genetic risks alerts parents to set priorities and act on them, and it helps professionals advise pregnant women. Some recommendations should be routine (e.g., prenatal vitamins including folic acid) because it is impossible to know who is at risk. Others are tailored to the individual, such as weight gain for underweight women.

Care must be taken to keep pregnancy and birth from being an anxious time, filled with restrictions and fears about diet, diseases, drugs, and other possible dangers. Anxiety itself may reduce sleep, impair digestion, and raise blood pressure—all of which hinder development—which in turn may make birth complicated and postpartum depression likely.

You Take Him Ideally, both parents appreciate each other's caregiving, and each does his or her share—especially when the newborn cries. As you can see, this ideal is hard for either parent to reach.

"Of course I know what he wants when he cries. He wants you."

Indeed, stress reduces the chance of conception, increases the chance of prenatal damage, and slows down the birth process. A conclusion from every page of this chapter is that risks can be minimized if everyone—fathers as well as mothers, professionals as well as community members, grandparents as well as college students—does what is needed to ensure that newborns begin life eager and able to live 80 more healthy years.

WHAT HAVE YOU LEARNED?

1. How has our understanding of alcohol use disorder changed from earlier centuries?

2. What are the sex and gender differences in alcohol use disorder?

3. What is the evidence that vision is inherited?

4. What is the evidence that vision depends on outdoor play?

5. Why do nations in East Asia have lower rates of alcohol use disorder and higher rates of nearsightedness than elsewhere?

6. How does age affect vision?

7. How might an awareness of genetic risks influence parents' behavior before, during, and after pregnancy?

SUMMARY

The Beginning of Life

1. Genes are the foundation for all development. Human conception occurs when two gametes (an ovum and a sperm, each with 23 chromosomes) combine to form a zygote, 46 chromosomes in a single cell.

2. Every cell of every human being has a unique genetic code made up of about 20,000 to 23,000 genes, some in variations called alleles. The environment interacts with the genetic instructions for every trait.

3. The sex of an embryo depends on the sperm: Y sperm create XY (male) embryos; X sperm creates XX (female) embryos. Twins occur if a zygote splits in two (monozygotic, or identical, twins) or if two ova are fertilized by two sperm (dizygotic, or fraternal, twins).

4. Genes interact in various ways: sometimes additively, with multiple genes contributing to a trait, and sometimes in a dominant–recessive pattern. The genotype of each person is set by the genotypes of the parents, but the phenotype (apparent characteristics) may be quite different from the genotype.

From Zygote to Newborn

5. The first two weeks of prenatal growth are the germinal period. The cells differentiate, and the developing organism implants itself in the lining of the uterus.

6. The period from the third through the eighth week after conception is called the embryonic period. The heart begins to beat, and the eyes, ears, nose, and mouth form. By the eighth week, the embryo has the basic organs and features of a human, with the exception of the sex organs.

7. The fetal period extends from the ninth week until birth. By the 12th week, all the organs and body structures have formed. The fetus attains viability at 22 weeks, when the brain is sufficiently mature to regulate basic body functions.

8. The average fetus gains approximately 4½ pounds (2,000 grams) during the last three months of pregnancy. Maturation of the brain, lungs, and heart ensures survival of virtually all full-term babies.

9. Medical intervention can speed contractions, dull pain, measure infant health via the Apgar scale, and save lives.

10. Some women feel unhappy, incompetent, or unwell after giving birth. Postpartum depression gradually disappears with appropriate help. Fathers are affected by pregnancy and birth as well, and are vulnerable to depression after birth.

Problems and Solutions

11. Often a zygote has more or fewer than 46 chromosomes. Such zygotes usually do not develop; the main exceptions are those with three chromosomes at the 21st location (Down syndrome, or trisomy-21) or an odd number of sex chromosomes.

12. Thousands of teratogens, especially drugs and alcohol, have the potential to harm the embryo or fetus. Actual harm occurs because of a cascade: Genes, critical periods, dose, and frequency all have an impact.

13. Birth complications, such as an unusually long and stressful labor that includes anoxia (a lack of oxygen to the fetus), have many causes. Low birthweight (less than 5½ pounds, or 2,500 grams) may result from multiple fetuses, placental problems, maternal illness, genes, malnutrition, smoking, drinking, and drug use.

Nature and Nurture

14. Alcohol use disorder is partly genetic, but not completely. It is particularly crucial that children who are genetically vulnerable avoid early exposure to alcohol.

15. Nearsightedness is also partly genetic, but understanding heritability (the impact of genes within a population, not neces-sarily within an individual) helps show that the relatively recent increase in nearsightedness is affected by outdoor light.

16. Nature and nurture interact to cause virtually all human problems; understanding genes, prenatal development, birth, and childhood increase the odds that a newborn will have a long and healthy life.

KEY TERMS

zygote (p. 48)
DNA (deoxyribonucleic acid) (p. 48)
chromosome (p. 48)
gene (p. 48)
gamete (p. 48)
allele (p. 48)
genotype (p. 49)
phenotype (p. 50)
genome (p. 50)
XX (p. 51)
XY (p. 51)
monozygotic twins (p. 53)
dizygotic twins (p. 55)
additive gene (p. 56)

dominant–recessive pattern (p. 56)
carrier (p. 56)
X-linked (p. 56)
germinal period (p. 58)
embryonic period (p. 58)
fetal period (p. 58)
stem cells (p. 58)
implantation (p. 59)
embryo (p. 59)
sonogram (p. 60)
fetus (p. 60)
age of viability (p. 60)
Apgar scale (p. 64)

cesarean section (c-section) (p. 64)
doula (p. 66)
Brazelton Neonatal Behavioral Assessment Scale (NBAS) (p. 67)
reflex (p. 67)
postpartum depression (p. 68)
couvade (p. 69)
Down syndrome (p. 70)
fragile X syndrome (p. 71)
teratogen (p. 72)
behavioral teratogens (p. 72)
threshold effect (p. 73)

fetal alcohol syndrome (FAS) (p. 74)
cerebral palsy (p. 75)
anoxia (p. 75)
false positives (p. 77)
low birthweight (LBW) (p. 78)
very low birthweight (VLBW) (p. 78)
extremely low birthweight (ELBW) (p. 78)
preterm birth (p. 78)
small for gestational age (SGA) (p. 78)
immigrant paradox (p. 78)
heritability (p. 82)

APPLICATIONS

1. Pick one of your traits, and explain the influences that both nature *and* nurture have on it. For example, if you have a short temper, explain its origins in your genetics, your culture, and your childhood experiences.

2. Draw a genetic chart of your biological relatives, going back as many generations as you can, listing all serious illnesses and causes of death. Include ancestors who died in infancy. Do you see any genetic susceptibility? If so, how can you overcome it?

3. Go to a nearby greeting-card store and analyze the cards about pregnancy and birth. Do you see any cultural attitudes (e.g., variations depending on the sex of the newborn or of the parent)? If possible, compare those cards with cards from a store that caters to another economic or cultural group.

4. Interview three mothers of varied backgrounds about their birth experiences. Make your interviews open-ended—let them choose what to tell you, as long as they give at least a 10-minute description. Then compare and contrast the three accounts, not-ing especially any influences of culture, personality, circumstances, or cohort.

PART TWO

The First Two Years

Adults don't change much in a year or two. They might have longer, grayer, or thinner hair; they might gain or lose weight; they might learn something new. But if you saw friends you hadn't seen for two years, you'd recognize them immediately.

Imagine caring for a newborn 24 hours a day for a month and then leaving for two years. On your return, you might not recognize him or her. The baby would have quadrupled in weight, grown a foot taller, and sprouted a new head of hair. Behavior and emotions change, too—less crying, but new laughter and fear— including fear of you.

A year or two is not much compared with the 80 or so years of the average life. However, in their first two years humans reach half their adult height, learn to talk in sentences, and express almost every emotion—not just joy and fear but also love, jealousy, and shame. The next two chapters describe these radical and awesome changes.

CHAPTER OUTLINE

CHAPTER 3

THE FIRST TWO YEARS
Body and Mind

WHAT WILL YOU KNOW?

- What part of an infant grows most in the first two years?
- Does immunization protect or harm babies?
- If a baby doesn't look for an object that disappears, what does that mean?
- Why do people talk to babies too young to talk back?

Our first child, Bethany, was born when I was in graduate school. I studiously memorized developmental norms, including sitting at 6 months, walking and talking at 12. But at 14 months, Bethany had not yet taken her first step.

Instead of worrying, I told my husband that genes were more influential than anything we did. I had read that babies in Paris are among the latest walkers in the world, and my grandmother was French. My speculation was bolstered when our next two children, Rachel and Elissa, were also slow to walk.

The genetic hypothesis was confirmed by my students, all devoted parents. Those with ancestors from Guatemala and Ghana had infants who walked before a year, unlike those with East Asian or European heritage.

Fourteen years after Bethany, Sarah was born. I could afford a full-time caregiver, Mrs. Todd, from Jamaica. She thought Sarah was the most advanced baby she had ever known, except for her own daughter, Gillian.

I told her that Berger children walk late.

"She'll be walking by a year," Mrs. Todd told me. "Gillian walked at 10 months."

"We'll see," I graciously replied, confident of my genetic explanation.

I underestimated Mrs. Todd. She bounced my delighted baby on her lap, day after day, and spent hours giving her "walking practice." Sarah took her first step at 12 months, late for a Todd, early for a Berger, and a humbling lesson for me.

As a scientist, I know that a single case proves nothing. Sarah shares only half her genes with Bethany. My daughters are only one-eighth French, a fraction I had not considered. It is now obvious to me that caregiving enables babies to grow, move, and learn. Development is not as genetically determined as it once seemed. It is multi-directional and multi-contextual, multi-cultural and plastic. Parents express their devotion in diverse ways, some massaging infant bodies, some talking in response to every burp. No wonder babies vary. ■

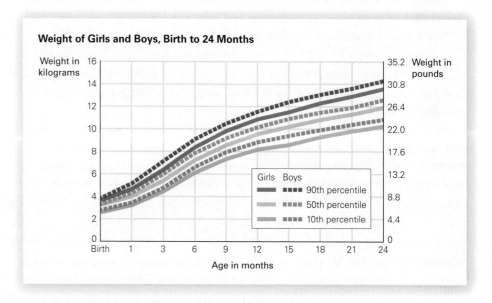

LaunchPad

© 2016 MACMILLAN

Video: Physical Development in Infancy and Childhood offers a quick review of the physical changes that occur in a child's first two years.

norm
An average, or standard, calculated from many individuals within a specific group or population.

percentile
A point on a ranking scale of 0 to 100. The 50th percentile is the midpoint; half the people in the population being studied rank higher and half rank lower.

Growth in Infancy

In infancy, growth is so rapid and the consequences of neglect are so severe that gains are closely monitored. Length, weight, and head circumference should be measured monthly at first, and every organ should be checked to make sure it functions well.

Body Size

Weight gain is dramatic. Newborns lose weight in the first three days and then gain an ounce a day for several months. Birthweight typically doubles by 4 months and triples by a year. An average 7-pound newborn will be 21 pounds at 12 months (9,525 grams, up from 3,175 grams at birth).

Physical growth in the second year is slower but still rapid. By 24 months, most children weigh almost 28 pounds (13 kilograms). They have added more than a foot in height—from about 20 inches at birth to about 34 inches at age 2 (from 51 to 86 centimeters). This makes 2-year-olds about half their adult height and about one-fifth their adult weight, four times heavier than they were at birth (see Figure 3.1).

Each of these numbers is a **norm,** which is a standard, for a particular population. The "particular population" for the norms just cited is North American infants. Remember, however, that genetic diversity means that some perfectly healthy newborns from every continent are smaller or larger than these norms.

At each well-baby checkup, the baby's growth is compared to that baby's previous numbers. Often measurements are expressed as a **percentile,** from 0 to 100, comparing each baby to others the same age. For example, weight at the 30th percentile means that 30 percent of all babies weigh less, and 70 percent weigh more.

For any baby, an early sign of trouble occurs when percentile changes markedly, either up or down. If an average baby moves from, say, the 50th to the 20th percentile, that could be the first sign of *failure to thrive,* which could be caused by dozens of medical conditions. Pediatricians consider it "outmoded" to blame parents for failure to thrive, but in any case the cause should be discovered, and remedied (Jaffe, 2011, p. 100).

Sleep

Throughout life, health and growth correlate with regular and ample sleep (Maski & Kothare, 2013). As with many health habits, sleep patterns begin in the first year.

FIGURE 3.1 Averages and Individuals Norms and percentiles are useful—most 1-month-old girls who weigh 10 pounds should be at least 25 pounds by age 2. But although females weigh less than males on average, lifelong, it is obvious that individuals do not always follow the norms. Do you know a 200-pound woman married to a 150-pound man?

CECILIA VARAS

Same Boy, Much Changed
All three photos show Conor: first at 3 months, then at 12 months, and finally at 24 months. Note the rapid growth in the first two years, especially apparent in the changing proportions of the chin, head, and arms.

Newborns sleep about 15 to 17 hours a day. Every week brings a few more waking minutes. For the first two months the norm for total time asleep is 14¼ hours; for the next 3 months, 13¼ hours; for the next 12 months, 12¾ hours. Remember that norms are averages; individuals vary. Parents report that, among every 20 infants in the United States, one sleeps nine hours or fewer per day and one sleeps 19 hours or more (Sadeh et al., 2009).

National averages vary as well. By age 2, the typical New Zealand toddler sleeps 15 percent more than the typical Japanese one (13⅓ hours compared to 11⅔) (Sadeh et al., 2010).

Infants also vary in how long they sleep at a stretch. Preterm and breast-fed babies wake up often. Part of this depends on an adult's perspective. If a night is thought to be from midnight to 5 A.M., many babies occasionally sleep "through the night" at 3 months. But if night is 10 P.M. to 6 A.M., many 1-year-olds don't sleep all night (C. Russell et al., 2013).

Over the first months, the time spent in each type or stage of sleep changes. Babies born preterm may always seem to be dozing. About half the sleep of full-term newborns is **REM (rapid eye movement) sleep,** with flickering eyelids and rapid brain waves. That indicates dreaming. REM sleep declines over the early weeks, as does "transitional sleep," the half-awake stage. At 3 or 4 months, quiet sleep (also called *slow-wave sleep*) increases markedly.

Sleep varies not only because of biology (age and genes) but also because of culture and caregivers. Babies who are fed formula and cereal sleep longer and more soundly—easier for parents but not necessarily good for the baby. Where babies sleep depends primarily on the baby's age and the culture, with bed-sharing (in the parents' bed) and co-sleeping (in the parents' room) the norm in some cultures, but unusual in others (Esposito et al., 2015).

Parents are soon frustrated if they think their babies will adjust to adult sleep–wake schedules. Infant brain patterns and hunger needs do not allow them to sleep quietly for long stretches. This can create a problem for the entire family: Maternal depression and family dysfunction are more common when infants wake up often at night (Piteo et al., 2013).

Overall, 25 percent of children under age 3 have sleeping problems, according to parents surveyed in an Internet study of more than 5,000 North Americans

REM (rapid eye movement) sleep
A stage of sleep characterized by flickering eyes behind closed lids. REM indicates dreaming.

(Sadeh et al., 2009). Problems are especially common when the baby is the parents' first child.

New parents "are rarely well-prepared for the degree of sleep disruption a newborn infant engenders." As a result many become "desperate" and institute patterns that they may later regret (C. Russell et al., 2013, p. 68). But what patterns should they follow? Experts, strangers, and close relatives give conflicting advice. Co-sleeping is one example.

OPPOSING PERSPECTIVES

Where Should Babies Sleep?

Traditionally, most middle-class U.S. infants slept in cribs in their own rooms; psychiatrists feared that babies would be traumatized if their parents had sex, and many non-professionals thought children would be spoiled if they depended too much on their mothers at night.

By contrast, most infants in Asia, Africa, and Latin America slept near their mothers, a practice called **co-sleeping,** and sometimes in their parents' bed, called **bed-sharing.** In those cultures, nighttime parent–child separation was considered cruel.

Sleeping alone may encourage independence for both child and adult—a quality valued in some cultures, abhorred in others. Since 2000, co-sleeping has been recommended by North Americans who advocate *attachment parenting* (Sears & Sears, 2001). They want babies always near their mothers so that every cry meets a comfort, often with breast milk.

Many companies now sell "co-sleepers" that allow babies to sleep beside their mothers without being on a soft mattress or risking blankets on the face. But bed-sharing itself (not just co-sleeping) is becoming more popular: The rates doubled from 6.5 percent in 1993 to 13.5 percent in 2010 in the United States (Colson et al., 2013).

A 19-nation study found that Asian and African mothers still worry about separation, whereas mothers with European roots worry more about privacy. In the extremes of that study, 82 percent of Vietnamese babies slept with their mothers, as did 6 percent in New Zealand (Mindell et al., 2010) (see Figure 3.2).

North Americans may attribute this international difference to poverty, since few families in poor nations have an extra room. Everywhere, mothers with higher SES are less likely to co-sleep (Colson et al., 2013). But culture trumps SES (Ball & Volpe, 2013), as evident in many wealthy,

co-sleeping
A custom in which parents and their children (usually infants) sleep together in the same room.

bed-sharing
When two or more people sleep in the same bed.

educated, Asian mothers who co-sleep, and many poor U.S. couples who sleep apart from their children.

In the United States the age of the baby is crucial. One study found that even infants in middle-class and upper-class families usually slept in the same room as their parents at 1 month (60 percent, 11 percent of them bed-sharing), but most of them slept in a separate room by 6 months. In that study, mothers who were depressed, and who were unhappy with the father's involvement, were less likely to move the baby out of the parents' room (Teti et al., 2015).

The authors of that study suggest that the correlation between maternal depression and co-sleeping may not be

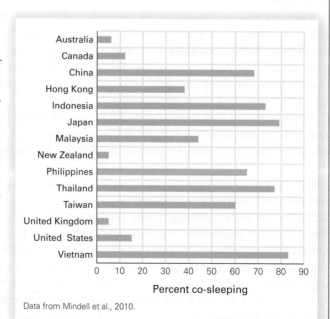

FIGURE 3.2 Awake at Night Why the disparity between Asian and non-Asian rates of co-sleeping? It may be that Western parents use a variety of gadgets and objects—monitors, night lights, pacifiers, cuddle cloths, sound machines—to accomplish the same things Asian parents do by having their infant next to them.

Data from Mindell et al., 2010.

found in other nations, where co-sleeping is the norm. However, even in Japan bed-sharing and marital strain often occur together. For example, one Japanese mother wrote:

> I take care of my baby at night, since my husband would never wake up until morning whatever happens. Babies, who cannot turn over yet, are at risk of suffocation and SIDS because they would not be able to remove a blanket by themselves if it covers over their face. In my case, I sleep with my older child and baby. By the way, my husband sleeps in a separate room because of his bad snoring.
>
> *[Shimizu et al., 2014]*

Contrary to this woman's rationalization, data from the United States find that sudden infant death (SIDS, discussed later) is twice as likely when babies sleep beside their parents. Researchers pinpoint one major reason: Many parents occasionally go to sleep after drinking or drugging. If their baby is beside them, bed-sharing can be fatal (Fleming et al., 2015).

Of course, if the baby is nearby but not beside the parent (co-sleeping but not bed-sharing), no higher SIDS risk occurs. Instead, parents can quickly respond to a hungry or frightened baby, without waiting until cries from another room wake them and then having to get out of bed and walk to the baby. Breast-feeding, often done every hour or two at first, is less exhausting when the mother need not get up to nurse.

As one review explained, "There are clear reasons . . . [for bed-sharing] . . . warmth, comfort, bonding, and cultural tradition, but there are also clear reasons against doing so, such as increased risk of sudden infant death syndrome" (Esposito et al., 2015).

YAGI STUDIO/DIGITAL VISION/GETTY IMAGES

Infant at Risk? Sleeping in the parents' bed is a risk factor for SIDS in the United States, but don't worry about this Japanese girl. In Japan, 97 percent of infants sleep next to their parents, yet infant mortality is only 3 per 1,000—compared with 7 per 1,000 in the United States. Is this bed, or this mother, or this sleeping position protective?

Since both sides have good reasons, why such opposing perspectives? Perhaps past customs are the reason. Adults may be affected, not by logic or data, but by "ghosts in the nursery," decades-old memories and fears—the ghosts of the past—that parents bring into the bedrooms of their children. Those ghosts encourage or discourage co-sleeping.

Developmentalists recognize that this issue is "tricky and complex" (Gettler & McKenna, 2010, p. 77). The physical and psychological needs of many family members must be considered, with many options possible.

THINK CRITICALLY: Should some ghosts be welcomed and others banned?

Brain Development

Prenatal and postnatal brain growth (measured by head circumference) is crucial for later cognition (Gilles & Nelson, 2012). From two weeks after conception to two years after birth, the brain grows more rapidly than any other organ, being about 25 percent of adult weight at birth and almost 75 percent at age 2 (see Figure 3.3). Over the same two years, brain circumference increases from about 14 to 19 inches.

If teething or a stuffed-up nose temporarily slows weight gain, nature protects the brain, a phenomenon called **head-sparing.** Sadly, head-sparing does not last forever: Prolonged malnutrition (discussed later) affects the brain.

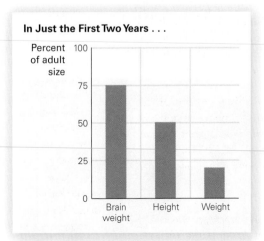

In Just the First Two Years . . .

Percent of adult size

(Bar graph: Brain weight ≈ 75, Height ≈ 50, Weight ≈ 20)

FIGURE 3.3 Growing Up Two-year-olds are totally dependent on adults, but they have already reached half their adult height and three-fourths of their adult brain size.

head-sparing
A biological mechanism that protects the brain when malnutrition disrupts body growth. The brain is the last part of the body to be damaged by malnutrition.

FIGURE 3.4 The Developing Cortex The infant's cortex consists of four to six thin layers of tissue that cover the brain. It contains virtually all the neurons that make conscious thought possible. Some areas of the cortex, such as those devoted to the basic senses, mature relatively early. Others, such as the prefrontal cortex, mature quite late.

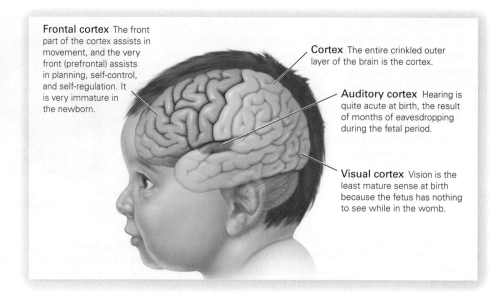

Frontal cortex The front part of the cortex assists in movement, and the very front (prefrontal) assists in planning, self-control, and self-regulation. It is very immature in the newborn.

Cortex The entire crinkled outer layer of the brain is the cortex.

Auditory cortex Hearing is quite acute at birth, the result of months of eavesdropping during the fetal period.

Visual cortex Vision is the least mature sense at birth because the fetus has nothing to see while in the womb.

neurons
Nerve cells in the central nervous system, especially in the brain.

cortex
The outer layers of the brain in humans and other mammals. Most thinking, feeling, and sensing involve the cortex.

prefrontal cortex
The area of the cortex at the very front of the brain that specializes in anticipation, planning, and impulse control.

axons
Fibers that extend from neurons and transmit electrochemical impulses from that neuron to the dendrites of other neurons.

dendrites
Fibers that extend from neurons and receive electrochemical impulses transmitted from other neurons via their axons.

synapses
The intersection between the axon of one neuron and the dendrites of other neurons.

neurotransmitters
Brain chemicals that carry information from the axon of a sending neuron to the dendrites of a receiving neuron.

BRAIN BASICS Findings from neuroscience are discussed in every chapter of this book. We begin here with the basics—neurons, axons, dendrites, neurotransmitters, synapses, and the cortex.

Communication within the central nervous system (CNS)—the brain and spinal cord—begins with nerve cells, called **neurons.** At birth, the human brain has an estimated 86 billion neurons, far more than any other primate. Especially in the **cortex** (the brain's six outer layers (see Figure 3.4) where most thinking, feeling, and sensing occur), humans have more neurons than other mammals (Herculano-Houzel et al., 2014).

The final part of the brain to mature is the **prefrontal cortex,** the area behind the forehead that is crucial for anticipation, planning, and impulse control. The prefrontal cortex is inactive in early infancy and gradually becomes more efficient in childhood, adolescence, and adulthood, with marked variation from one person to another at every age (Walhovd et al., 2014).

Neurons connect to other neurons via intricate networks of nerve fibers called **axons** and **dendrites** (see Visualizing Development, p. 95). Each neuron typically has a single axon and numerous dendrites, which spread out like the branches of a tree. The axon of each neuron reaches toward the dendrites of other neurons at intersections called **synapses,** which are critical communication links within the brain.

Axons and dendrites do not touch at synapses. Instead, the electrical impulses in axons cause the release of chemicals called **neurotransmitters,** which carry information from the axon of the sending neuron to the dendrites of the receiving neuron.

GROWTH AND PRUNING During the first months and years, rapid growth and refinement in axons, dendrites, and synapses occur, especially in the cortex. Dendrite growth is the main reason that brain weight triples from birth to age 2 (Johnson, 2011).

An estimated fivefold increase in dendrites in the cortex occurs in the 24 months after birth, with about 100 trillion synapses present at age 2.

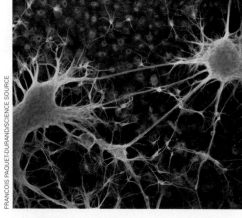

Connecting The color staining on this photo makes it obvious that the two cell bodies of neurons (stained chartreuse) grow axons and dendrites to each other's neurons. This tangle is repeated thousands of times in every human brain. Throughout life, those fragile dendrites will grow or disappear, as the person continues thinking.

FRANCOIS PAQUET-DURAND/SCIENCE SOURCE

Nature, Nurture, and the Brain

The mechanics of neurological functioning are varied and complex; neuroscientists hypothesize, experiment, and discover more each day. Brain development begins with genes and other biological elements, but hundreds of epigenetic factors affect brain development from the first to the final minutes of life. Particularly important in human development are experiences: Plasticity means that dendrites form or atrophy is response to nutrients and events. The effects of early nurturing experiences are lifelong, as proven many times in mice; research on humans suggests similar effects.

NATURE

Human brains are three times as large per body weight and take years longer to mature than the brains of any other creature, but the basics of brains are the same from mouse to elephant. New dendrites form and unused ones die—especially in infancy and adolescence. Brain plasticity is lifelong.

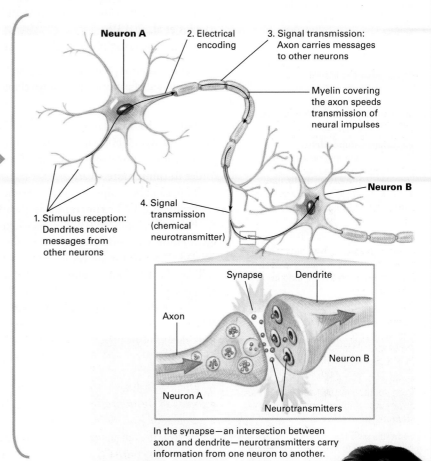

1. Stimulus reception: Dendrites receive messages from other neurons

2. Electrical encoding

3. Signal transmission: Axon carries messages to other neurons

Myelin covering the axon speeds transmission of neural impulses

4. Signal transmission (chemical neurotransmitter)

Neuron A

Neuron B

Synapse

Dendrite

Axon

Neuron B

Neuron A

Neurotransmitters

In the synapse—an intersection between axon and dendrite—neurotransmitters carry information from one neuron to another.

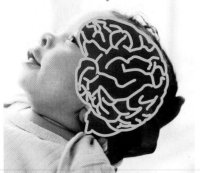

PHOTO: STOCKBYTE/GETTY IMAGES

NURTURE

In the developing brain, connections from axon to dendrite reflect how a baby is treated. In studies of rats, scientists learned that when a mother mouse licks her newborn its methylation of a gene (called Nr3c1) is reduced, allowing increased serotonin to be released by the hypothalamus and reducing stress hormones. Baby mice who were frequently licked and nuzzled by their mothers developed bigger and better brains!

Researchers believe that, just as in rats, the human mothers who cuddle, cradle, and caress their babies shape their brains for decades.

Low Maternal Licking and Grooming	High Maternal Licking and Grooming
• High stress hormone levels • High anxiety	• Low stress hormone levels • Low anxiety

PHOTO: ANYAIVANOVA/ISTOCK/THINKSTOCK

© RUBBERBALL/NICOLE HILL/ALAMY

According to one expert, "40,000 new synapses are formed every second in the infant's brain" (Schore & McIntosh, 2011, p. 502).

Early dendrite growth is called **transient exuberance:** *exuberant* because it is rapid and *transient* because some is temporary. This expansive growth is followed by **pruning.** A gardener might *prune* a rose bush by cutting away some growth to enable more, or more beautiful, roses to bloom. Similarly, unused brain connections atrophy and disappear.

Pruning is beneficial. Indeed, insufficient pruning may be the reason that many toddlers with autism have heads that are larger than average; too many dendrites make them hypersensitive to sights and sounds, unable to tolerate social interaction (Lewis et al., 2013).

As one expert explains it, there is an

> exuberant overproduction of cells and connections, followed by a several-year sculpting of pathways by massive elimination of much of the neural architecture.
>
> *[Insel, 2014, p. 1727]*

Notice the word *sculpting,* as if an artist created an intricate sculpture from raw marble or wood. Human infants are gifted sculptors, designing their brains for whatever family, culture, or society they happen to be born into, discarding the excess in order to think more clearly.

Experiences sculpt the brain. Some sculpting is called **experience-expectant** and some is called **experience-dependent** (Greenough et al., 1987).

Brain development is experience-expectant when it *must* happen for normal brain maturation to occur. Because they are basic to human development, expectant experiences occur for almost every baby. In deserts and in the Arctic, on isolated farms and in crowded cities, almost all babies have things to see, objects to manipulate, and people to love them. Without such expected experiences, dendrites and specific regions within the brain do not grow.

In contrast, certain facets of brain development are experience-dependent: They result from experiences that differ from one infant to another, resulting in brains that also differ. What specific language is heard, whose faces are seen, or how emotions are expressed—from slight pursing of the lips to throwing oneself on the ground—vary from one home to another.

Depending on such variations, infant neurons connect in particular ways; some dendrites grow and others disappear (Stiles & Jernigan, 2010). In other words, every baby needs to develop language—that is expectant, and brains are primed for it. But that language could be Tajik, Tamil, Thai, or Twi. That is experience-dependent. Brains adjust accordingly.

transient exuberance
The great but temporary increase in the number of dendrites that develop in an infant's brain during the first two years of life.

pruning
When applied to brain development, the process by which unused connections in the brain atrophy and die.

experience-expectant
Brain functions that require certain basic common experiences (which an infant can be expected to have) in order to develop normally.

experience-dependent
Brain functions that depend on particular, variable experiences and therefore may or may not develop in a particular person.

Face Lit Up; Brain, Too Thanks to scientists at the University of Washington, this young boy enjoys the EEG of his brain activity. Such research has found that babies respond to language long before they speak. Experiences of all sorts connect neurons and grow dendrites.

AARON MCCOY/PHOTOLIBRARY/GETTY IMAGES

IMPLICATIONS FOR CAREGIVERS Most infants develop well within their culture. Head-sparing usually ensures that brains are nourished, and everywhere adults nurture the young. Even strangers are drawn to babies a few weeks old, talking to them and making faces, holding them if the parents allow it. All that is experience-expectant; babies worldwide expect attention and almost always get it.

Playing with a young baby, allowing varied sensations, and encouraging movement (arm waving in the early months, walking later on) are all fodder for brain connections. Severe lack of stimulation (e.g., no talking at all) stunts the brain.

This does not mean that babies require spinning, buzzing, multitextured, and multicolored toys. In fact, such toys may be a wasted purchase since overstimulated babies may cry to avoid bombardment. Infants are fascinated by simple objects and exaggerated expressions. A mouth opening wide or making smacking sounds captures infant attention.

The slow development of the prefrontal cortex means that infants cannot yet plan, anticipate, or modify their emotions. Unless adults understand this, they might be angry with an infant who does not smile, or stop crying, or sleep when the adult wishes.

If a frustrated caregiver reacts to crying by shaking the baby, that can cause **shaken baby syndrome,** a life-threatening type of abusive head trauma (Nadarasa et al., 2014). Because the brain is still developing, shaking an infant sharply and quickly stops the crying because blood vessels in the brain rupture and fragile neural connections break. Death is possible; lifelong intellectual impairment is likely.

shaken baby syndrome
A life-threatening injury that occurs when an infant is forcefully shaken back and forth, a motion that ruptures blood vessels in the brain and breaks neural connections.

The Senses

Every sense functions at birth. Newborns have open eyes, sensitive ears, and responsive noses, tongues, and skin. Indeed, very young babies use all their senses to attend to everything, especially every person (Zeifman, 2013).

Sensation occurs when a sensory system detects a stimulus, as when the inner ear reverberates with sound or the eye's retina and pupil intercept light. Thus, sensations begin when an outer organ (eye, ear, nose, tongue, or skin) meets anything that can be seen, heard, smelled, tasted, or touched.

sensation
The response of a sensory system (eyes, ears, skin, tongue, nose) when it detects a stimulus.

perception
The mental processing of sensory information when the brain interprets a sensation.

Perception occurs when the brain processes a sensation. This happens in the cortex, usually as the result of a message from one of the sensing organs, such as from the eye to the visual cortex. The sight of a bottle, for instance, is conveyed from the retina to the optic nerve to the visual cortex, but it has no meaning unless the infant has been bottle-fed. Similarly, a scrap of paper means nothing to you unless you are looking for something written on just such a scrap. Perceptions require experience and motivation.

Thus, perception follows sensation, when sensory stimuli are interpreted in the brain. Then cognition follows perception, when people think about what they have perceived. The baby might reach out for the bottle, you might examine the paper. The sequence from sensation to perception to cognition requires first that the sense organs function. No wonder the parts of the cortex dedicated to hearing, seeing, and so on develop rapidly. Now specifics.

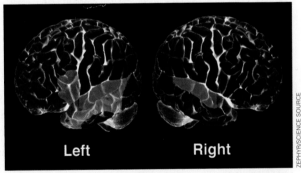

From Sound to Language Hearing occurs in the temporal lobe, in both hemispheres, the green and some of the red parts of the brain. Language comprehension, however, is mostly in the left hemisphere, here shown in the brown region that responds to known words, and Broca's area, the red bulb that produces speech. A person could hear but not understand (a baby) or understand but not speak (if Broca's area is damaged).

HEARING The fetus hears during the last trimester of pregnancy; loud sounds trigger reflexes even without conscious perception. Familiar, rhythmic sounds such as a heartbeat are soothing: Sometimes newborns stop crying if they are held so an ear is on the mother's chest.

Because of early maturation of the language areas of the cortex, even 4-month-olds attend to voices, developing expectations of the rhythm, segmentation, and cadence of spoken words long before comprehension (Minagawa-Kawai et al., 2011). Soon, sensitive hearing combines with the maturing brain to distinguish patterns of sounds and syllables.

Infants become accustomed to the patterns of their native language, such as which syllable is stressed (various dialects differ), whether inflection matters (it is crucial in Chinese), whether certain sound combinations are repeated, and so on. All this is based on very careful listening, including of speech not directed toward them (Buttelmann et al., 2013).

Better are sounds directed to the infant. Thus, a newborn named Emily has no concept that *Emily* is her name, but she has the brain and auditory capacity to hear sounds in the usual speech range (not some sounds that other creatures can hear) and an inborn preference for repeated patterns and human speech.

BLEND IMAGES - MIKE KEMP/BRAND X PICTURES/GETTY IMAGES

Who's This? Newborns don't know much, but they look intensely at faces. Repeated sensations become perceptions, so in about six weeks, this baby will smile at Dad, Mom, a stranger, the dog, and at every other face. If this father in Utah responds like typical fathers everywhere, by 6 months cognition will be apparent: The baby will chortle with joy at seeing him but become wary of unfamiliar faces.

binocular vision
The ability to focus both eyes in a coordinated manner in order to see one image. Depth perception requires it.

THINK CRITICALLY: Which is more important in the first year of life, accurate hearing or seeing?

By about 4 months, when her auditory cortex is rapidly creating dendrites, the repeated word *Emily* is perceived as well as sensed, especially because that sound emanates from interactions with the people she often sees, smells, and touches. Before 6 months, Emily opens her eyes and smiles when her name is called, perhaps babbling in response.

This rapid development of hearing is the reason newborn hearing is tested, and, if necessary, remediation begins in infancy. By age 5, those who got cochlear implants in the early months are much better at understanding and expressing language than those with identical losses but whose implants were added after age 2 (Tobey et al., 2013).

SEEING By contrast, vision is immature at birth. Although in mid-pregnancy the eyes open and are sensitive to bright light (if a pregnant woman is sunbathing in a bikini, for instance), the fetus has nothing much to see. Newborns are legally blind; they focus only on things quite close to their eyes, such as the face of their breast-feeding mother.

Almost immediately, experience combines with maturation of the visual cortex to improve vision. Indeed, vision improves so rapidly that researchers are hard-pressed to describe the day-by-day improvements (Dobson et al., 2009). By 2 months, infants not only stare at faces, but also, with perception and the beginning of cognition, smile. (Smiling can occur earlier but not because of perception.)

As perception builds, visual scanning improves. Thus, 3-month-olds look closely at the eyes and mouth, smiling more at happy faces than at angry or expressionless ones. They pay attention to patterns, colors, and motion—the mobile above the crib, for instance.

Because of this rapid development, babies should be allowed to see many sights. A crying baby might be distracted by being taken outside to watch passing cars. If possible, cataracts (present in about 1 newborn in 2,000) should be surgically removed in the early months (Medsinge & Nischal, 2015).

Binocular vision (coordinating both eyes to see one image) cannot develop in the womb (nothing is far enough away), so many newborns use their two eyes independently, momentarily appearing wall-eyed or cross-eyed. Normally, between 2 and 4 months, experience allows both eyes to focus on a single thing (Wang & Candy, 2010).

Depth perception (which requires binocular vision) is usually present by 3 months, but understanding depth takes experience. Not until toddlers have experienced crawling and walking do they know whether a surface is best traversed upright, sitting, or crawling (Kretch & Adolph, 2013). The senses and motor skills take time to coordinate.

TASTING AND SMELLING As with vision and hearing, smell and taste function at birth and rapidly adapt to the social world. Infants learn to appreciate what their mothers eat, first through breast milk and then through smells and spoonfuls of the family dinner.

The foods of a particular culture may aid survival: For example, bitter foods provide some defense against malaria, hot spices help preserve food and may prevent food poisoning, and so on (Krebs, 2009). Thus, for 1-year-olds, developing a taste for their family cuisine not only helps them join their community, it may save their lives.

Learning About a Lime As with every other normal infant, Jacqueline's curiosity leads to taste and then to a slow reaction, from puzzlement to tongue-out disgust. Jacqueline's responses demonstrate that the sense of taste is acute in infancy and that quick brain perceptions are still to come.

Notice once again how early experiences sculpt the brain. Taste preferences endure when a person migrates to another culture or when a particular food that was once protective is no longer so. Indeed, one reason for the obesity epidemic is that, when starvation was a threat, families sought high-fat foods. Now their descendants enjoy fried foods, whipped cream, and bacon, and their inborn preferences and cultural habits jeopardize their health.

Adaptation also occurs for the sense of smell. When breast-feeding mothers used a chamomile balm to ease cracked nipples, their babies preferred that smell almost two years later, unlike babies whose mothers used an odorless ointment (Delaunay-El Allam et al., 2010).

As babies learn to recognize each person's scent, they prefer to sleep next to their caregivers, and they nuzzle into their caregivers' chests—especially when the adults are shirtless. One way to help infants who are frightened of the bath (some love bathing, some hate it) is for the parent to join the baby in the tub. The smells of the adult's body mixed with the smell of soap and the touch, sight, and voice of the caregiver are pleasant, making the entire experience comforting.

TOUCH AND PAIN Similarly, the sense of touch is acute in infants. Wrapping, rubbing, massaging, and cradling are soothing. Even when their eyes are closed, some infants stop crying and visibly relax when held securely by their caregivers. In the first year of life, the heart rate slows and muscles relax when babies are stroked gently and rhythmically on the arm (Fairhurst et al., 2014).

In every culture, parents cuddle their newborns, rocking, carrying, and so on. Some touch (gentle of course) seems experience-expectant, essential for normal growth. Beyond that, how much a baby is touched is experience-dependent, varying by culture. In some south Asian nations, daily massage begins soon after birth (Trivedi, 2015).

Indeed, in rural India, mothers need to be taught that the newborn's need for warmth is more important than immediate bathing and massage, since both of those practices are common for infants and may, inadvertently, harm a newborn. Mothers are encouraged to wipe their newborns with a dry cloth and breast-feed immediately—practices that keep the baby warm, use the sense of touch, and reduce the risk of early death (Acharya et al., 2015).

Pain, motion, and temperature are not among the traditional five senses, but they are often connected to touch. Some babies cry when being changed, distressed at the sudden coldness on their skin and by having to lie down, not held by their caregivers.

Scientists are not certain about pain. Some experiences that are painful to adults (circumcision, setting of a broken bone) are much less so to newborns, although that

The First Blood Test This baby will cry, but most experts believe the heel prick shown here is well worth it. The drops of blood will reveal the presence of any of several genetic diseases, including sickle-cell disease, cystic fibrosis, and phenylketonuria. Early diagnosis allows early treatment, and the cries subside quickly with a drop of sugar water or a suck of breast milk.

does not prove that newborns are unable to feel pain (Reavey et al., 2014).

Many young infants sometimes cry inconsolably; digestive pain is the usual explanation. Teething is also said to be painful. However, these explanations also are unproven. Certainly for adults, pain and crying do not always occur together.

For many newborn medical procedures, a taste of sugar right before the event is an anesthetic. One example is that newborns typically cry lustily when their heel is pricked (to get a blood sample, routine after birth), but when an experimental group had a drop of sucrose before the heel stick, they were much less likely to cry than babies in a control group who had no sucrose (Harrison et al., 2010).

Some people imagine that even the fetus feels pain; others say that pain receptors in the brain are not activated until months after birth. Physiological measures (stress hormones, erratic heartbeats, and brain waves) are studied to assess pain in preterm infants, who typically undergo many procedures that would be painful to an adult (Holsti et al., 2011). More research is needed.

Motor Skills

THINK CRITICALLY: What political controversy makes objective research on newborn pain difficult?

motor skills
The learned abilities to move some part of the body, in actions ranging from a large leap to a flicker of the eyelid. (The word *motor* here refers to movement of muscles.)

Every basic **motor skill** (any movement ability), from the newborn's head-lifting to the toddler's stair-climbing, develops over the first two years.

REFLEXES The sequence of motor skills begins with reflexes, some of which are listed here in italics. Newborns have even more than the 17 on this list.

- Reflexes that maintain oxygen supply. The *breathing reflex* begins even before the umbilical cord, with its supply of oxygen, is cut. Additional reflexes that maintain oxygen are reflexive *hiccups* and *sneezes,* as well as *thrashing* (moving the arms and legs about) to escape something that covers the face.

- Reflexes that maintain constant body temperature. When infants are cold, they *cry, shiver,* and *tuck their legs* close to their bodies. When they are hot, they try to *push away* blankets and then stay still.

- Reflexes that manage feeding. The *sucking reflex* causes newborns to suck anything that touches their lips—fingers, toes, blankets, and rattles, as well as natural and artificial nipples of various textures and shapes. In the *rooting reflex,* babies turn their mouths toward anything that brushes against their cheeks—a reflexive search for a nipple—and start to suck. *Swallowing* also aids feeding, as does *crying* when the stomach is empty and *spitting up* when too much is swallowed quickly.

Other reflexes are not necessary for survival but signify the state of brain and body functions. Among them are the:

- *Babinski reflex.* When a newborn's feet are stroked, the toes fan upward.
- *Stepping reflex.* When newborns are held upright, feet touching a flat surface, they move their legs as if to walk.
- *Swimming reflex.* When held horizontally on their stomachs, newborns stretch out their arms and legs.

- *Palmar grasping reflex.* When something touches the palms, newborns grip it tightly.
- *Moro reflex.* When someone bangs on the table they are lying on, newborns fling their arms out and then bring them together on their chests, crying with wide-open eyes.

Although the definition of reflexes implies that they are automatic, their strength and duration vary from one baby to another, and cultural responses shape them. Many newborn reflexes disappear by 3 months, but some morph into more advanced motor skills.

Reflexes become skills if they are practiced and encouraged. As you saw in the chapter's beginning, Mrs. Todd set the foundation for my fourth child's walking when Sarah was only a few months old. Similarly, some 1-year-olds can swim—if adults have built on the swimming reflex to teach them to paddle in water from the early weeks.

gross motor skills
Physical abilities involving large body movements, such as walking and jumping. (The word *gross* here means "big.")

OBSERVATION QUIZ

Which of these skills has the greatest variation in age of acquisition? Why? (see answer, page 103) ▼

GROSS MOTOR SKILLS Deliberate actions that use many parts of the body, producing large movements, are called **gross motor skills.** These skills emerge directly from reflexes and proceed in a *cephalocaudal* (head-down) and *proximodistal* (center-out) direction.

Infants first control their heads, lifting them up to look around, an early example of cephalocaudal maturation. Then control moves downward—upper bodies, arms, and finally legs and feet. (See At About This Time, which shows age norms for gross motor skills based on a large, representative, multiethnic sample of U.S. infants.)

Sitting develops gradually. By 3 months, most babies can sit propped up in a lap. By 6 months, they can usually sit unsupported. Babies never propped up (as in some institutions for abandoned infants) sit much later.

Crawling is another example of the head-down and center-out direction of skill mastery. When placed on their stomachs, many newborns reflexively try to lift their heads and move their arms as if they were swimming. As they gain muscle strength, infants wiggle, attempting to move forward by pushing their arms, shoulders, and upper bodies against whatever surface they are lying on.

Usually by 5 months, infants add their legs to this effort, inching forward (or backward) on their bellies. Exactly when this occurs depends partly on how much "tummy time" the infant has had to develop the muscles, and that, of course, is affected by the caregiver's culture (Zachry & Kitzmann, 2011).

Most 8- to 10-month-olds can lift their midsections and crawl (or *creep,* as the British call it) on "all fours," coordinating the movements of their hands and knees. Crawling depends on experience, not just maturation. Some normal babies never do it, especially if the floor is cold, hot, or rough, or if they always lie on their backs. It is not true that babies *must* crawl to develop normally.

All babies find some way to move (inching, bear-walking, scooting, creeping, or crawling) before they can walk, but many resist being

At About This Time: Age Norms (in Months) for Gross Motor Skills

	When 50% of All Babies Master the Skill	When 90% of All Babies Master the Skill
Sit unsupported	6	7.5
Stands holding on	7.4	9.4
Crawls (creeps)	8	10
Stands not holding	10.8	13.4
Walking well	12.0	14.4
Walk backward	15	17
Run	18	20
Jump up	26	29

Note: As the text explains, age norms are affected by culture and cohort. The first five norms are based on babies on five continents [Brazil, Ghana, Norway, United States, Oman, and India] (World Health Organization, 2006). The next three are from a U.S.-only source (Coovadia & Wittenberg, 2004; based on Denver II [Frankenburg et al., 1992]). Mastering skills a few weeks earlier or later does not indicate health or intelligence. Being very late, however, is a cause for concern.

CATHARINA VAN DEN DIKKENBERG/ISTOCKPHOTO

Advancing and Advanced At 8 months, she is already an adept crawler, alternating hands and knees, intent on progress. She will probably be walking before a year.

Bossa Nova Baby? This boy in Brazil demonstrates his joy at acquiring the gross motor skill of walking, which quickly becomes dancing whenever music plays.

RICK GOMEZ/MASTERFILE

placed on their stomachs. Heavier babies master gross motor skills later than leaner ones because practice and balance is harder when the body is heavy (Slining et al., 2010).

As soon as they are able, babies take some independent steps, falling frequently at first, about 32 times per hour. They persevere because walking is much quicker than crawling, and it has other advantages—better sight lines and free hands (Adolph & Tamis-LeMonda, 2014).

Once toddlers take those first unsteady steps, they practice obsessively, barefoot or not, at home or in stores, on sidewalks or streets, on lawns or in mud. They "immediately go more, see more, play more, and interact more" (Adolph & Tamis-LeMonda, 2014, p. 191).

fine motor skills
Physical abilities involving small body movements, especially of the hands and fingers, such as drawing and picking up a coin. (The word *fine* here means "small.")

● **FINE MOTOR SKILLS** Small body movements are called **fine motor skills.** The most valued fine motor skills are finger movements, enabling humans to write, draw, type, tie, and so on. Movements of the tongue, jaw, lips, teeth, and toes are fine movements, too.

Actually, mouth skills precede hand skills by many months (newborns can suck; chewing precedes drawing by a year or more). Since every culture encourages finger dexterity, children practice finger movements, and adults teach how to use spoons, or chopsticks, or markers. By contrast, mouth skills such as spitting or biting are not praised. (Only other children admire blowing bubbles with gum.)

Regarding hand skills, newborns have a strong reflexive grasp but lack control. During their first 2 months, babies excitedly stare and wave their arms at objects dangling within reach. By 3 months, they can usually touch such objects, but because of limited eye–hand coordination, they cannot yet grab and hold on unless an object is placed in their hands.

By 4 months, infants sometimes grab, but their timing is off: They close their hands too early or too late. Finally by 6 months, with a concentrated, deliberate stare, most babies can reach, grab, and grasp almost any object that is of the right size. Some can even transfer an object from one hand to the other.

LaunchPad

Video: Fine Motor Skills in Infancy and Toddlerhood
http://qrs.ly/1h4eozr

AMI PARIKH/SHUTTERSTOCK

Almost all can hold a bottle, shake a rattle, and yank a sister's braids. Toward the end of the first year and throughout the second, finger skills improve as babies master the pincer movement (using thumb and forefinger to pick up tiny objects) and self-feeding (first with hands, then fingers, then utensils) (Ho, 2010). (See At About This Time.)

VAYA VLADIMIR JOVANOVIC/SHUTTERSTOCK

Success At 6 months, this baby is finally able to grab her toes. From a developmental perspective, this achievement is as significant as walking, as it requires coordination of feet and fingers. Note her expression of determination and concentration.

As with gross motor skills, fine motor skills are shaped by culture and opportunity. For example, when given "sticky mittens" (with Velcro) that facilitate grabbing, infants master hand skills sooner than the norm. Their perception advances as well (Libertus & Needham, 2010; Soska et al., 2010). As you remember, experience leads to perception and cognition.

COMBINING SENSES AND SKILLS All senses and motor skills expand the baby's cognitive awareness, with practice advancing both skill and understanding (Leonard & Hill, 2014). In the second year, grasping becomes more selective, as experience sculpts the brain. Toddlers learn when *not* to pull at a sister's braids or an adult's earrings or glasses. (Wise adults, however, remove such accessories before holding a baby.)

The age at which walking occurs is a better predictor than simple chronological age of a child's verbal ability, perhaps because walking children elicit more language from caregivers than crawling ones do (Walle & Campos, 2014). The correlation could go in the opposite direction as well: Walkers see their caregivers more, so they talk more (Adolph & Tamis-LeMonda, 2014, p. 191).

Overall, babies perceive their most important experiences with several senses and skills, in dynamic systems. Breast milk, for instance, is a mild sedative, so the infant literally feels happier at the breast, connecting that pleasure with taste, touch, smell, and sight. But first, a motor skill is needed: The infant must actively suck at the nipple (an inborn reflex, which becomes more efficient with practice).

Because of brain immaturity, *cross-modal perception* (using several senses to understand the same experience) is particularly common in young infants. *Synesthesia* (when a sensation is perceived with more than one sense, as when a sound has a color) is also more common in early infancy, because the various parts of the brain are less distinct (Ozturk et al., 2013).

Remember the dynamic systems of senses and motor skills: If one aspect of the system lags behind, the other parts may be affected as well. On the other hand, young walkers are thrilled to grab dozens of objects they could not explore before—caregivers beware.

At About This Time: Age Norms (in Months) for Fine Motor Skills

	When 50% of All Babies Master the Skill	When 90% of All Babies Master the Skill
Grasps rattle when placed in hand	3	4
Reaches to hold an object	4.5	6
Thumb and finger grasp	8	10
Stacks two blocks	15	21
Imitates vertical line (drawing)	30	39

Data from World Health Organization, 2006.

ANSWER TO OBSERVATION QUIZ (from page 101) Jumping up, with a three-month age range for acquisition. The reason is that the older an infant is, the more impact both nature and nurture have. ●

WHAT HAVE YOU LEARNED?

1. Why is it not a problem if an infant is consistently at the 20th percentile in height and weight?
2. How do sleep patterns change over the first 18 months?
3. What are the reasons for and against co-sleeping?
4. How does the brain change from birth to age 2?
5. How does communication occur within the central nervous system?
6. How can pruning increase brain potential?
7. What is the difference between experience-expectant and experience-dependent brain function?
8. What should caregivers remember about brain development when an infant cries?
9. How does an infant's vision change over the first year?
10. How do infants' senses strengthen their early social interactions?
11. In what two directions do infants' gross motor skills emerge?
12. Which fine motor skills are developed in infancy?

Surviving in Good Health

Although precise worldwide statistics are unavailable, the United Nations estimates that more than 8 billion children were born between 1950 and 2015 and that almost a billion of them died before age 5. Far more would have died without recent public health measures.

In 1950, one young child in five died, but only about one child in twenty died in 2015 (United Nations, 2015). Infant death was worse in earlier centuries, when more than half of all children died in infancy. Those are official statistics; probably millions more died without being counted.

Better Days Ahead

Now almost all newborns who survive the first month live to adulthood. Some nations have seen dramatic improvement. Chile's rate of infant mortality, for instance, was almost four times higher than the rate in the United States in 1970; now both nations have improved and their rates are the same (see Figure 3.5).

As more children survive, parents focus more effort and income on each child, having fewer children overall. That advances the national economy, which allows for better schools and health care.

Infant survival and maternal education are the two main reasons the world's fertility rate in 2010 was half the 1950 rate. This is found in data from numerous nations, especially developing ones, where educated women have far fewer children than those who are uneducated (de la Croix, 2013).

Educated women also have healthier children, in part because they are more aware of research that emphasizes breast-feeding, immunization, and other practices that protect health. You have already read that some cultural practices may benefit infants, and others not. Practices in dispute include co-sleeping, infant massage, and constant mother-care.

In an example reported on the front page of newspapers in the United States and Denmark, a Danish woman, Annette Sorenson, left her 14-month-old daughter asleep in her carriage outside a New York City restaurant where she ate dinner. She said she could see her baby through the window, that babies need fresh air, and that in Copenhagen mothers often leave babies outside when they shop, dine, and so on.

FIGURE 3.5 More Babies Are Surviving Improvements in public health—better nutrition, cleaner water, more widespread immunization—over the past three decades have meant millions of survivors.

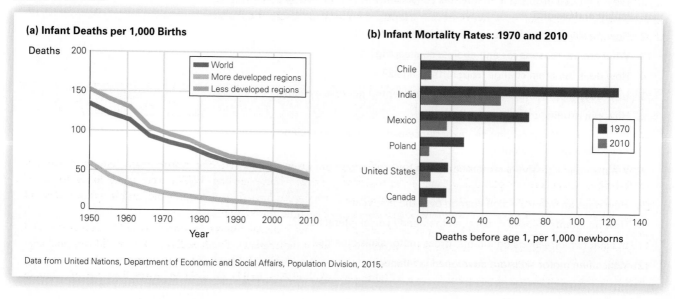

Data from United Nations, Department of Economic and Social Affairs, Population Division, 2015.

Well Protected Disease and early death are common in Africa, where this photo was taken, but neither is likely for 2-year-old Salem. He is protected not only by the nutrition and antibodies in his mother's milk but also by the large blue net that surrounds them. Treated bed nets, like this one provided by the Carter Center and the Ethiopian Health Ministry, are often large enough for families to eat, read, as well as sleep in together, without fear of malaria-infected mosquitoes.

© LOUISE GUBB/CORBIS

Sorenson was arrested for child neglect, her daughter placed in foster care briefly until a judge ordered her returned (Marcano, 1997). The mother sued the city for harming her as well as her child, who was unhurt. The lawsuit was dismissed, but it is obvious that cultures have contrasting assumptions regarding infant care.

Remember, difference is not deficit. Usually variations are simply alternative ways to meet basic infant needs. However, not every cultural practice is equally good. Each practice needs to be considered carefully, especially when cultures differ.

For example, every year until the mid-1990s, tens of thousands of infants died of **sudden infant death syndrome (SIDS),** called *crib death* in North America and *cot death* in England. In every city and village, tiny infants smiled at their caregivers, waved their arms at rattles that small fingers could not yet grasp, went to sleep, and never woke up.

As parents mourned, scientists asked why, testing hypotheses (the cat? the quilt? natural honey? homicide? spoiled milk?) to no avail. Sudden infant death was a mystery. To some extent, it still is, but one risk factor—sleeping on the stomach—is now known worldwide, thanks to the work of one scientist who looked closely at cultural differences. See A Case to Study.

sudden infant death (SIDS)
An infant's unexpected, sudden death; when a seemingly healthy baby, usually between 2 and 6 months old, stops breathing and dies while asleep.

A CASE TO STUDY

Scientist at Work

Susan Beal, a young Australian scientist with four children, studied SIDS. Often she was phoned at dawn, to be told that another baby had died. She drove to the house, sometimes arriving before the police, finding parents who were grateful that someone was trying to discover what had just killed their child.

Parents tended to blame themselves and each other; Beal reassured them that it was not their fault and that scientists shared their bewilderment. Rates were known to be lower in breast-fed babies, one reason many educated women avoided bottle-feeding. Babies were more likely to die if they were boys, 2 to 6 months old, and in winter. Beyond that, little was known.

Beal's detailed notes on dozens of SIDS deaths revealed what didn't matter (birth order) and what did (parental cigarette smoking). She noticed a surprising ethnic variation: Although a sizable minority of Australians are of Chinese

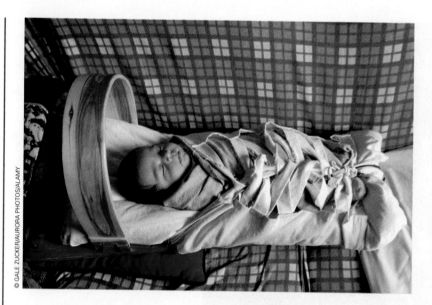

No SIDS Allowed For centuries, Native American babies, such as this boy in Arizona, slept on their backs in cradle boards. Back-sleeping was also customary among the Navajo's genetic ancestors, in Asia, protecting them from SIDS.

descent, their babies almost never died of SIDS. Most experts thought this was genetic, but Beal noted something else. Almost all SIDS babies died when they were sleeping on their stomachs, contrary to the Chinese custom of placing infants on their backs to sleep.

Beal convinced a large group of non-Chinese parents to put their babies to sleep on their backs, contrary to the advice of most pediatricians, including Dr. Benjamin Spock (author of *Baby and Child Care*, purchased more often than any other book except the Bible). Almost no back-sleeping Australian babies died. Beal concluded that back-sleeping protected against SIDS.

Beal's published report in the *Medical Journal of Australia* (Beal, 1988) caught the attention of doctors in the Netherlands. Two Dutch scientists (Engelberts & de Jonge, 1990) recommended back-sleeping. The Netherlands has one of the highest rates of educated women in the world;

thousands of new mothers read the recommendation and followed it. SIDS was reduced in Holland by 40 percent in one year—a stunning replication.

Worldwide, putting babies "Back to Sleep" has now cut the SIDS rate dramatically (Mitchell & Krous, 2015). In 1984 SIDS killed 5,245 babies in the United States; in 1996, 3,050; in 2010, about 1,700 (see Figure 3.6). In the United States alone, 100,000 children and young adults are alive today who would be dead if they had been born before 1990.

Stomach-sleeping is not the only risk. Beyond sleeping position, other risks include low birthweight, exposure to cigarette smoke, soft blankets or pillows, bed-sharing, and abnormalities in the brain stem, heart, mitochondria, or microbiome (Neary & Breckenridge, 2013; Ostfeld et al., 2010). Most SIDS victims experience several risks, a cascade of biological and social circumstances. But thanks to cross-cultural research, one major risk need not occur.

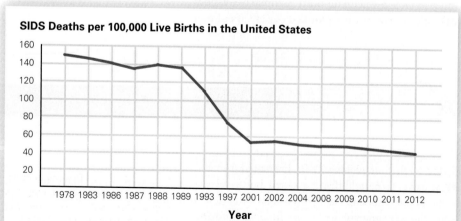

SIDS Deaths per 100,000 Live Births in the United States

Data from National Vital Statistics Reports, Forthcoming; Hoyert & Xu, 2012; Murphy et al., 2012; Kochanek et al., 2011; Miniño et al., 2007; Hoyert et al., 2005; Mathews et al., 2003; Hoyert et al., 1999; Gardner & Hudson, 1996; Macdorman & Rosenberg, 1993; Monthly Vital Statistics Report, 1980.

FIGURE 3.6 Alive Today As more parents learn that a baby should be on his or her "back to sleep," the SIDS rate continues to decrease. Other factors are also responsible for the decline—fewer parents smoke cigarettes in the baby's room.

Immunization

Immunization primes the body's immune system to resist a particular disease. Within the past 50 years, immunization eliminated smallpox and dramatically reduced chicken pox, flu, measles, mumps, pneumonia, polio, rotavirus, tetanus, and whooping cough. Now scientists seek to immunize against HIV/AIDS, malaria, Ebola, and other viral diseases.

Stunning successes include the following:

- Smallpox, the most lethal disease for children in the past, was eradicated worldwide as of 1980. Vaccination against smallpox is no longer needed.

- Polio, a crippling and sometimes fatal disease, is rare. Widespread vaccination, begun in 1955, eliminated polio in the Americas. Currently, the only nation where polio is endemic is Pakistan, where violence prevents public health workers from reaching many children.

- Measles is disappearing, thanks to a vaccine developed in 1963. Prior to that time, 3 to 4 million cases occurred each year in the United States alone (Centers for Disease Control and Prevention, April, 2015). In the United States the lowest year on record was 2012, when only 55 people had measles, most of them born in nations without widespread immunization (MMWR, January 2, 2015).

Immunization protects not only from temporary sickness but also from complications, including deafness, blindness, sterility, and meningitis. Sometimes the damage from illness is not apparent until years later. Having mumps in childhood, for instance, can cause male sterility and doubles the risk of schizophrenia in adulthood (Dalman et al., 2008). Measles weakens the immune system, making later death more likely (Mina et al., 2015).

PROBLEMS WITH IMMUNIZATION Immunization is not safe for newborns or people with impaired immune systems (HIV-positive, aged, or undergoing chemotherapy). To catch the actual disease is much worse for them; they could die of a disease that is quite mild in childhood. Fortunately, each vaccinated child stops transmission of

> **immunization**
> A process that stimulates the body's immune system to defend against attack by a particular contagious disease. Immunization may be accomplished either naturally (by having the disease) or through vaccination (often by having an injection). (Also called *vaccination*.)

SCOTT EELLS/REDUX

True Dedication This young Buddhist monk lives in a remote region of Nepal, where, until recently, measles was a fatal disease. Fortunately, a UNICEF porter carried the vaccine over mountain trails for two days so that this boy—and his whole community—could be immunized.

the disease and thus protects others who are vulnerable, a phenomenon called *herd immunity*. For that reason, proof of immunization is required before children enter school or college.

Some parents refuse to vaccinate their children for medical reasons; every state in the United States allows such exemptions. However, in 19 states, parents can refuse vaccination because of "personal belief" (Blad, 2014). In Colorado, for instance, 15 percent of all kindergartners have never been immunized against measles, mumps, rubella, diphtheria, tetanus, or whooping cough. That is below herd immunity, and an epidemic could occur—with infants most likely to suffer.

Globally, about 20 million cases of measles occur each year, almost all in nations with inadequate public health. If a traveler brings measles back to the United States, unimmunized children and adults may catch the disease. That happened in 2014, when the number of U.S. measles cases was 554, ten times the rate only two years before (MMWR, January 2, 2015).

Infants may react to immunization by being irritable or even feverish for a day or so, to the distress of their parents. However, parents do not notice if their child does *not* get polio, measles, or so on. Before the varicella (chicken pox) vaccine, more than 100 people in the United States died each year from that disease, and 1 million were itchy and feverish for a week. Now almost no one dies of varicella, and only a few get chicken pox.

Many parents worry about the possible side effects of vaccines. This horrifies public health workers, who, taking a longitudinal and society-wide perspective, believe that the risks of the diseases are far greater than the risks from immunization. The 2014 spike in measles cases was the highest since 1994, one result of increasing numbers of parents objecting to vaccination.

As you will see later, the fear that infant immunization leads to autism is unfounded; children who are not immunized are no less likely to have an autism spectrum disorder, but much more likely to become sick. It is easy to understand why parents of such a child would seek to blame something other than genes or teratogens, but in this case a cultural fear is destructive.

Nutrition

As already explained, infant mortality worldwide has plummeted for several reasons: fewer sudden infant deaths, advances in prenatal and newborn care, clean water, and, as you just read, immunization. One more measure is making a huge difference: better nutrition.

COURTESY OF UNICEF

Video: Nutritional Needs of Infants and Children: Breast-Feeding Promotion shows UNICEF's efforts to educate women on the benefits of breast-feeding.

BREAST MILK The World Health Organization now recommends exclusive breast-feeding for the first six months of life. That stunning endorsement of breast milk is based on extensive research from all nations of the world. The specific fats and sugars in breast milk make it more digestible and better for the brain than any substitute (Drover et al., 2009; Wambach & Riordan, 2014).

Breast-feeding mothers should be well nourished and hydrated; then their bodies will make the perfect food for their babies. Formula is preferable only in unusual cases, such as when the mother is HIV-positive or uses toxic or addictive drugs. Even then, however, breast milk without supplementation may be best.

The more research is done, the better breast milk seems. For instance, the composition of breast milk adjusts to the age of the baby, with milk for premature babies distinct from that for older infants. Quantity increases to meet the demand: Twins and even triplets can be exclusively breast-fed for months. Each generation of scientists, and consequently each generation of mothers, knows more about breast milk and formula, as the following explains.

Same Situation, Far Apart: Breast-Feeding Breast-feeding is universal. None of us would exist if our fore-mothers had not successfully breast-fed their babies for millennia. Currently, breast-feeding is practiced world-wide, but it is no longer the only way to feed infants, and each culture has particular practices.

A VIEW FROM SCIENCE

From Breast to Formula and Back

Scientific discovery does not always proceed smoothly in one direction. Research on breast milk shows that. Four generations of women in my family heeded the best evidence known at the time when we fed our children.

A hundred years ago, my grandmother, an immigrant who spoke accented English, breast-fed her 14 children. If women of her generation could not provide adequate breast milk (for instance, if they were sick or seriously malnourished), the alternatives were milk from another woman (called a wet nurse), from a cow, or from a goat. Those alternatives increased the risk of infant malnutrition and death.

Two of Grandma's babies died in infancy. Did insufficient nutrition play a role?

By the middle of the twentieth century, scientists had analyzed breast milk and created *formula*, designed to be far better than cow's milk. Formula solves the problems of breast-feeding, such as insufficient milk and the exhaustion that breast-feeding mothers often experienced. Bottle-fed babies gained more weight than breast-fed ones; in many nations only poor or immigrant women breast-fed.

That is why my mother formula-fed me. She explained that she wanted me to have the best that modern medicine could provide. She recounted an incident meant to convey that my father was less conscientious than she was. He had

volunteered to give me my 2 A.M. feeding (babies were fed on a rigid four-hour schedule). But the next morning, she noticed the full bottle in the refrigerator. She asked what happened. He said I was sound asleep, so he decided I was "fat enough already." I never told her that Dad was right.

Companies that sold formula promoted it in Africa and Latin America as well as North America. They paid local women in developing nations to convince mothers to buy formula.

Then public health workers compiled statistics on infant mortality: In developing nations formula-fed babies were more likely to die. The reason was said to be lack of clean water and proper sterilization. Formula increased the rate of diarrhea (a leading killer of children in poor nations) by a factor of ten (León-Cava et al., 2002). The World Health Organization (WHO) recommended a return to breast-feeding in developing nations.

In sympathy for those dying babies, I was among the thousands of North Americans who boycotted products from the offending manufacturers. I breast-fed my children, to my mother's surprise. But I gladly took my pediatrician's advice to feed my 2-month-olds occasional bottles of formula (carefully sterilized), juice, water, and spoons of baby cereal and bananas.

Longitudinal research continues. The data led to a new conclusion: Even with good sterilization, in every nation breast-fed babies are healthier than other babies, benefiting throughout childhood (see Table 3.1) (Wambach & Riordan, 2014; Drover et al., 2009). The World Health Organization recommends exclusive breast-feeding for four to six months, no juice or baby food until that half-year mark.

International research continues. In Africa, an infant's risk of catching HIV from a breast-feeding, HIV-positive mother is lower than the risk of dying from infections, diarrhea, or malnutrition as a result of bottle-feeding. Fears that medication prescribed for HIV-positive mothers affects the child's later learning are unfounded (Ngoma et al., 2014).

In China, a study of more than a thousand babies in eight cities compared three groups of babies: those exclusively breast-fed (by their own mothers or wet nurses), those fed no breast milk, and those fed a combination of foods, formula, and breast milk. Based on all the data, the researchers suggest that the WHO recommendation for exclusive breast-feeding for the first six months "should be reinforced in China," although some vitamin supplements might be warranted (see Figure 3.7) (Ma et al., 2014, p. 290).

The research has caused a dramatic cohort change in the United States. Currently most (about 80 percent) mothers breast-feed in the beginning (unlike my mother) and 19 percent breast-feed exclusively until 6 months (unlike me). My daughters gave their babies nothing but breast-milk for the first six months of their lives.

Virtually all scientists and pediatricians have reached a conclusion opposite to the one their predecessors held 50 years ago: Infants should be nourished only by breast milk until they are 4 to 6 months old.

As of 2015 about 200 hospitals in the United States and hundreds more worldwide have been designated as

TABLE 3.1	The Benefits of Breast-Feeding

For the Baby

Balance of nutrition (fat, protein, etc.) adjusts to age of baby

Breast milk has micronutrients not found in formula

Less infant illness, including allergies, ear infections, stomach upsets

Less childhood asthma

Better childhood vision

Less adult illness, including diabetes, cancer, heart disease

Protection against many childhood diseases, since breast milk contains antibodies from the mother

Stronger jaws, fewer cavities, advanced breathing reflexes (less SIDS)

Higher IQ, less likely to drop out of school, more likely to attend college

Later puberty, fewer teenage pregnancies

Less likely to become obese or hypertensive by age 12

For the Mother

Easier bonding with baby

Reduced risk of breast cancer and osteoporosis

Natural contraception (with exclusive breast-feeding, for several months)

Pleasure of breast stimulation

Satisfaction of meeting infant's basic need

No formula to prepare; no sterilization

Easier travel with the baby

For the Family

Increased survival of other children (because of spacing of births)

Increased family income (because formula and medical care are expensive)

Less stress on father, especially at night

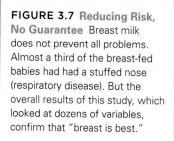

FIGURE 3.7 Reducing Risk, No Guarantee Breast milk does not prevent all problems. Almost a third of the breast-fed babies had had a stuffed nose (respiratory disease). But the overall results of this study, which looked at dozens of variables, confirm that "breast is best."

OBSERVATION QUIZ

In what one way might exclusive breast-feeding be worse than a combination of breast milk and other foods? (see answer, page 113) ➤

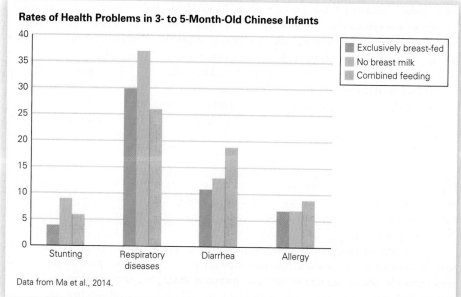

Rates of Health Problems in 3- to 5-Month-Old Chinese Infants

Data from Ma et al., 2014.

"Baby-Friendly," a UNICEF designation that includes putting every baby to the breast within half an hour of birth, and giving newborns nothing but breast milk except in unusual circumstances (such as a very small, fragile baby being tube-fed). My daughters breast-fed in the delivery room; I was not allowed to touch my newborns until 24 hours after birth.

Our knowledge advances with each generation. I wonder what the future will bring when my grandchildren become parents.

THINK CRITICALLY: For new mothers in your community, why do some use formula and others breast-feed exclusively for six months?

MALNUTRITION **Protein-calorie malnutrition** occurs when a person does not consume enough food to sustain normal growth. This form of malnutrition affects roughly one-third of the world's children in developing nations: They suffer from **stunting** (being short for their age), because chronic malnutrition kept them from growing. Stunting is most common in the poorest nations (see Figure 3.8).

Even worse is **wasting,** when children are severely underweight for their age and height (2 or more standard deviations below average). Many nations, especially in East Asia, Latin America, and central Europe, have seen improvement in child nutrition in the past decades, with an accompanying decrease in wasting and stunting.

In other nations, however, primarily in Africa, wasting has increased. And in several nations in South Asia, about one-third of young children are stunted (World Health Organization, 2014). Because of head-sparing, some stunted children may not suffer intellectually. However, adults who were wasted in the first year of life have lower IQs throughout life, even if they are well fed after infancy (Waber et al., 2014).

Some of this is directly related to brain growth, but in addition, the severely malnourished infant has less energy and reduced curiosity. Young children naturally want to do whatever they can: A child with no energy is a child who is not learning.

An added problem is disease. Malnourished children have no body reserves to protect them against common diseases. A decade ago, scientists reported in the

protein-calorie malnutrition
A condition in which a person does not consume sufficient food. This can result in illness, severe weight loss, and even death.

stunting
The failure of children to grow to a normal height for their age due to severe and chronic malnutrition.

wasting
The tendency for children to be severely underweight for their age as a result of malnutrition.

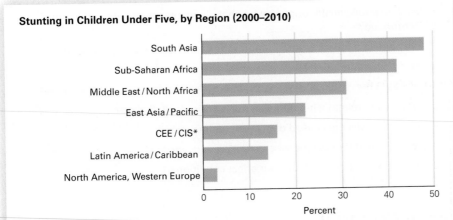

Stunting in Children Under Five, by Region (2000–2010)

*Refer to Central and Eastern Europe (CEE) and Commonwealth of Independent States (CIS), which together comprise the countries of central Europe as well as those of the former Soviet Union.

Data from UNICEF, 2012.

COURTESY OF UNICEF

Video: Malnutrition and Children in Nepal shows the plight of children in Nepal who suffer from protein calorie malnutrition.

FIGURE 3.8 Genetic? The data show that basic nutrition is still unavailable for many children in the developing world. Some critics contend that Asian children are genetically small and therefore that Western norms make it appear as if India and Africa have more stunted children than they really do. However, children of Asian and African descent born and nurtured in North America are as tall as those of European descent. Thus, malnutrition, not genes, accounts for most stunting worldwide.

Same Situation, Far Apart: Children Still Malnourished Infant malnutrition is common in refugees (like this baby now living in Thailand, *right*) or in countries with conflict or crop failure (like Niger, *at left*). Relief programs reach only some of the children in need around the world. The children in these photographs are among the lucky ones who are being fed.

leading medical journal in England that half of all childhood deaths occur because malnutrition makes a childhood disease lethal (Black et al., 2003).

Finally, some diseases result directly from malnutrition—both **marasmus** during the first year, when body tissues waste away, and **kwashiorkor** after age 1, when growth slows down, hair becomes thin, skin becomes splotchy, and the face, legs, and abdomen swell with fluid (edema). Digestive patterns may be impaired lifelong. Giving severely ill children an antibiotic to stop infection saves lives—but always, prevention is best (Gough et al., 2014).

marasmus
A disease of severe protein-calorie malnutrition during early infancy, in which growth stops, body tissues waste away, and the infant eventually dies.

kwashiorkor
A disease of chronic malnutrition in which a protein-calorie deficiency makes a child more vulnerable to other diseases, such as measles, diarrhea, and influenza.

WHAT HAVE YOU LEARNED?

1. Why do public health doctors wish that all infants worldwide would get immunized?
2. Why would a parent blame immunization for autism spectrum disorder?
3. What is herd immunity?
4. What are the reasons for exclusive breast-feeding for the first six months?
5. What is the relationship between malnutrition and disease?
6. What diseases are caused directly by malnutrition?
7. What is the difference between stunting and wasting?
8. In what ways does malnutrition affect cognition?

Infant Cognition

The rapid physical growth of the human infant, just described, is impressive, but intellectual growth during infancy is even more awesome. Concepts, memories, and sentences—nonexistent in newborns—are evident by age 1 and consolidated by age 2.

Sensorimotor Intelligence

sensorimotor intelligence
Piaget's term for the way infants think—by using their senses and motor skills—during the first period of cognitive development.

As you remember from Chapter 1, Piaget called cognition in the first two years **sensorimotor intelligence** because infants learn through their senses and motor skills. He subdivided this period into six stages (see Table 3.2).

TABLE 3.2	The Six Stages of Sensorimotor Intelligence

For an overview of the stages of sensorimotor thought, it helps to group the six stages into pairs.

The first two stages involve the infant's responses to its own body, called **primary circular reactions**.

Stage One (birth to 1 month) *Reflexes:* sucking, grasping, staring, listening

Stage Two (1–4 months) *The first acquired adaptations:* accommodation and coordination of reflexes

Examples: sucking a pacifier differently from a nipple; attempting to hold a bottle to suck it

The next two stages involve the infant's responses to objects and people, called **secondary circular reactions**.

Stage Three (4–8 months) *Making interesting sights last:* responding to people and objects

Example: clapping hands when mother says "patty-cake"

Stage Four (8–12 months) *New adaptation and anticipation:* becoming more deliberate and purposeful in responding to people and objects

Example: putting mother's hands together in order to make her start playing patty-cake

The last two stages are the most creative, first with action and then with ideas, called **tertiary circular reactions**.

Stage Five (12–18 months) *New means through active experimentation:* experimentation and creativity in the actions of the "little scientist"

Example: putting a teddy bear in the toilet and flushing it

Stage Six (18–24 months) *New means through mental combinations:* thinking before doing, new ways of achieving a goal without resorting to trial and error

Example: before flushing the teddy bear, hesitating because of the memory of the toilet overflowing and mother's anger

LaunchPad

Video: Sensorimotor Intelligence in Infancy and Toddlerhood
http://qrs.ly/lj4ep00

© 2016 MACMILLAN

STAGES ONE AND TWO Stage one, called the *stage of reflexes,* lasts only a month. It includes senses as well as motor reflexes, the foundations of infant thought. The newborn's reflexes evoke some brain reactions. Soon sensation leads to perception, which ushers in stage two, *first acquired adaptations* (also called the *stage of first habits*).

Here is one example. In a powerful reflex, full-term newborns suck anything that touches their lips. Their first challenge is to learn to adapt that reflex and thus suck, swallow, and suck again without spitting up too much—a major task that often takes a few days, with the mother learning how to help her baby latch, suck, and breathe.

During the first stage, in the first month, infants adapt their sucking reflex to bottles or breasts, pacifiers or fingers, each requiring specific types of tongue pushing.

ANSWER TO OBSERVATION QUIZ
(from page 110) Combination feeding might provide some protection against the common cold. The advantage is not much (a difference of 5 percent) and may be because exclusively breast-fed infants are fed wherever their mothers are—and that may include outdoors, in polluted air. ●

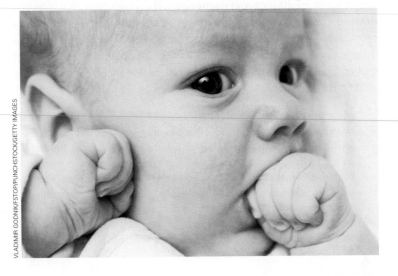

VLADIMIR GODNIK/FSTOP/PUNCHSTOCK/GETTY IMAGES

Time for Adaptation Sucking is a reflex at first, but adaptation begins as soon as an infant differentiates a pacifier from her mother's breast or realizes that her hand has grown too big to fit into her mouth. This infant's expression of concentration suggests that she is about to make that adaptation and suck just her thumb from now on.

"Is this the way you plan to spend your peak learning years?"

Still Wrong Parents used to ignore infant cognition. Now some make the opposite mistake, assuming infants learn via active study.

object permanence
The realization that objects (including people) still exist even if they can no longer be seen, touched, or heard.

This adaptation signifies that infants have begun to interpret sensations; they are using their minds—some would say "thinking."

During stage two, which Piaget pegged from about 1 to 4 months of age, additional adaptation occurs. Infant cognition leads babies to suck in some ways for hunger, in other ways for comfort—and not to suck fuzzy blankets.

STAGES THREE AND FOUR In stages three and four, reactions are no longer confined to the infant's body; they are an *interaction* between the baby and something else. During stage three (4 to 8 months), infants attempt to produce exciting experiences, *making interesting sights last.*

The word *sights* refers to more than what is seen: At this stage, babies try to continue any pleasing event. Realizing that rattles make noise, for example, they wave their arms and laugh whenever someone puts a rattle in their hand. The sight of something delightful—a favorite book, a smiling parent—can trigger active efforts for interaction.

Next comes stage four (8 months to 1 year), *new adaptation and anticipation* (also called the *means to the end*). Babies may ask for help (fussing, pointing, gesturing) to accomplish what they want. An impressive attribute of stage four is that babies work hard to achieve their goals. Babies who are 10 months old, seeing a parent putting on a coat, might drag over their own jackets to signal that they want to go along.

Stage-four babies indicate that they are hungry—and keep their mouths firmly shut if the food on the spoon is something they do not like. If the caregivers have been using sign language, among the first signs learned by 10-month-olds are "eat" and "more." Even without parental signing, babies this age begin displaying some universal signs—pointing, pushing, and reaching up to be held.

With a combination of experience and brain maturation, babies become attuned to the goals of others, an ability much more evident at 10 months than 8 months (Brandone et al., 2014). Personal understanding begins to extend to social understanding.

OBJECT PERMANENCE Piaget thought that, at about 8 months, babies first understand the concept of **object permanence**—the realization that objects or people continue to exist when they are no longer in sight. As Piaget discovered, not until about 8 months do infants search for toys that have fallen from the crib, rolled under a couch, or disappeared under a blanket. Blind babies also acquire object permanence toward the end of their first year, reaching for an object that they hear nearby (Fazzi et al., 2011).

As a recent statement of this phenomenon explains:

> Many parents in our typical American middle-class households have tried out Piaget's experiment in situ: Take an adorable, drooling 7-month-old baby, show her a toy she loves to play with, then cover it with a piece of cloth right in front of her eyes. What do you observe next? The baby does not know what to do to get the toy! She looks around, oblivious to the object's continuing existence under the cloth cover, and turns her attention to something else interesting in her environment. A few months later, the same baby will readily reach out and yank away the cloth cover to retrieve the highly desirable toy. This experiment has been done thousands of times and the phenomenon remains one of the most compelling in all of developmental psychology.
>
> [Xu, 2013, p. 167]

Family Fun Peek-a-boo makes all three happy, each for cognitive reasons. The 9-month-old is discovering object permanence, his sister (at the concrete operational stage) enjoys making brother laugh, and their mother understands more abstract ideas—such as family bonding.

This excerpt describes Piaget's classic experiment to measure object permanence: An adult shows an infant an interesting toy, covers it with a lightweight cloth, and observes the response. The results:

- Infants younger than 8 months do not search for the object by removing the cloth.

- At about 8 months infants search, removing the cloth immediately after the object is covered but not if they have to wait a few seconds.

- At 18 months, they search quite well, even after a wait, but not if they have seen the object put first in one place and then moved to another. They search in the first place, not the second, a mistake called the *A-not-B error*. Thus they search where they remember seeing it put (A), somehow not understanding that they saw it moved (to B). When a healthy, bright toddler exhibits this obvious failing, observers usually agree with Piaget: A-not-B is a sign of immature brain development.

- By 2 years, children fully understand object permanence, progressing through several stages of ever-advanced cognition (Piaget, 1954/2013).

This sequence has intrigued scientists as well as parents for decades.

Renee Baillargeon devised a series of clever experiments in which objects seemed to disappear behind a screen while researchers traced babies' eye movements and brain activity. The data reveal that long before 8 months, infants are surprised if an object vanishes (Baillargeon & DeVos, 1991; Spelke, 1993).

The conclusion that surprise (measured by infant gaze) indicates object permanence is accepted by some scientists, who believe that "infants as young as 2 and 3 months of age can represent fully hidden objects" (Cohen & Cashon, 2006, p. 224). Other scientists are not convinced (Mareschal & Kaufman, 2012).

STAGES FIVE AND SIX In their second year, infants start experimenting in thought and deed—or, rather, in the opposite sequence, deed and thought. They act first (stage five) and think later (stage six). Piaget's stage five (ages 12 to 18 months),

Exploration at 15 Months One of the best ways to investigate food is to squish it in your hands, observe changes in color and texture, and listen for sounds. Taste and smell are primary senses for adults when eating, but it looks as if Jonathan has already had his fill of those.

ARIEL SKELLEY/BLEND IMAGES/AGE FOTOSTOCK

new means through active experimentation, builds on the accomplishments of stage four. Now goal-directed and purposeful activities become more expansive.

Toddlers delight in squeezing all the toothpaste out of the tube, drawing on the wall, or uncovering an anthill—activities they have never seen an adult do. Piaget referred to the stage-five toddler as a "**little scientist**" who "experiments in order to see." Their research method is trial and error. Their devotion to discovery is familiar to every adult scientist—and to every parent.

little scientist
The stage-five toddler (age 12 to 18 months) who experiments without imagining the consequences, using trial and error in active and creative exploration.

Finally, in the sixth stage (ages 18 to 24 months), toddlers use *mental combinations,* intellectual experimentation via imagination that can supersede the active experimentation of stage five. Because they combine ideas, stage-six toddlers think about consequences, hesitating a moment before yanking the cat's tail or dropping a raw egg on the floor.

Thus, the stage-six sequence may begin with thought followed by action. Of course, the urge to explore may overtake caution: Things that are truly dangerous (cleaning fluids, swimming pools, open windows) need to be locked and gated.

The ability to combine ideas allows stage-six toddlers to pretend. For instance, they know that a doll is not a real baby, but they can strap it into a stroller and take it for a walk. At 22 months, my grandson gave me imaginary "shoe ice cream" and laughed when I pretended to eat it.

Piaget describes another stage-six intellectual accomplishment involving both thinking and memory. **Deferred imitation** occurs when infants copy behavior they noticed hours or even days

deferred imitation
A sequence in which an infant first perceives something done by someone else and then performs the same action hours or even days later.

TOOGA PRODUCTIONS, INC/THE IMAGE BANK/GETTY IMAGES

Push Another Button Little scientists "experiment in order to see" as this 14-month-old does. Many parents realize, to their distress, that their infant has deleted a crucial file, or called a distant relative on a cell phone, because the toddler wants to see what happens.

earlier (Piaget, 1962/2013). Piaget described his daughter, Jacqueline, who observed another child

> who got into a terrible temper. He screamed as he tried to get out of a playpen and pushed it backwards, stamping his feet. J. stood watching him in amazement, never having witnessed such a scene before. The next day, she herself screamed in her playpen and tried to move it, stamping her foot lightly several times in succession.
>
> *[Piaget, 1962/2013, p. 63]*

These words from Piaget illustrate his genius: He observed children carefully, noticing how they thought at each stage. However, many researchers find that Piaget underestimated the age at which various accomplishments occurred. You already saw this with object permanence; the same is true for deferred imitation.

Scientists were awed by Piaget's recognition that babies "learn so fast and so well" (Xu & Kushnir, 2013, p. 28). For decades researchers followed Piaget's lead, and they demonstrated that infants master cognition in much the way Piaget described.

However, as brain scans and computerized analysis of heart rate, muscle tension, gaze, and so on made it easier to study infant cognition, Piaget's emphasis on senses and motor abilities seems to have limited his understanding of infant cognition. Piaget missed many early cognitive accomplishments, particularly in memory (Schneider, 2015).

Video: Event-Related Potential (ERP) Research shows a procedure in which the electrical activity of an infant's brain is recorded to see if the brain responds differently to familiar versus unfamiliar words.

PROFESSOR DEBRA L. MILLS, BANGOR UNIVERSITY, UNITED KINGDOM

Information Processing

As explained in Chapter 1, Piaget's sweeping overview of four periods of cognition contrasts with **information-processing theory,** which breaks down cognition into hundreds of small steps between input and output. Computer analysis, gaze-following, and brain scans allow researchers to measure infant cognition long before the baby can demonstrate understanding.

The thinking of young infants is impressive. As one researcher summarizes, "Rather than bumbling babies, they are individuals who . . . can learn surprisingly fast about the patterns of nature" (Keil, 2011, p. 1023). Concepts and categories develop in infants' brains by 6 months or earlier (Mandler & DeLoache, 2012).

MEMORY AT 3 MONTHS We focus now on one specific ability that Piaget underestimated, memory (Schneider, 2015). Within the first weeks after birth, infants recognize their caregivers by face, voice, and smell. Memory improves month by month. In one study, after 6-month-olds had had only two half-hour sessions with a novel puppet, they remembered the experience a month later—an amazing feat for babies who could not talk or even stand up (Giles & Rovee-Collier, 2011).

In studying memory, researchers realize that, instead of noticing children's many "faults or shortcomings relative to an adult standard," we need to appreciate that children remember what they need to remember (Bjorklund & Sellers, 2014, p. 142). Sensory and caregiver memories are apparent in the first month, motor memories by 3 months, and then, at about 9 months, more complex memories including for language (Mullally & Maguire, 2014).

No doubt memory is fragile in the first months of life and improves with age. Repeated sensations and brain maturation are required in order to process and recall whatever happens (Bauer et al., 2010). Everyone's memory fades with time, especially if that memory was never encoded into language, never compared with similar events, never discussed with a friend. No wonder infants forget many things.

That forgetfulness led Piaget, Freud, and other early developmentalists to write about *infant amnesia,* the idea that people forget everything that happened to them before age 3. However, although adults do not remember what happened at age 1, that does not mean that infants have no memory. Infants remember things that

information-processing theory
A perspective that compares human thinking processes, to computer analysis of data, including sensory input, connections, stored memories, and output.

He Remembers! Infants are fascinated by moving objects within a few feet of their eyes—that's why parents buy mobiles for cribs, and why Rovee-Collier tied a string to a mobile and a baby's leg to test memory. Babies not in her experiment, like this one, sometimes flail their limbs to make their cribs shake and thus their mobiles move. Piaget's stage of "making interesting sights last" is evident to every careful observer.

TEK IMAGE/SCIENCE SOURCE

Video: Contingency Learning in Young Infants shows Carolyn Rovee-Collier's procedure for studying instrumental learning in young infants.

happened weeks and even months ago (Mullally & Maguire, 2014), although they are unlikely to remember it decades later.

The most dramatic proof of very early memory comes from a series of innovative experiments in which 3-month-olds learned to move a mobile by kicking their legs (Rovee-Collier, 1987, 1990). The infants lay on their backs connected to a mobile by means of a ribbon tied to one foot (see photo).

Virtually all the babies realized that kicking made the mobile move. They then kicked more vigorously and frequently, sometimes laughing at their accomplishment. So far, this is no surprise—observing self-activated movement is highly reinforcing to infants.

When infants as young as 3 months had the mobile-and-ribbon apparatus reinstalled and reconnected *one week later,* most started to kick immediately, proof that they remembered their previous experience. But when other 3-month-old infants were retested *two weeks later,* they kicked randomly. Had they forgotten? It seemed so.

But then the lead researcher Carolyn Rovee-Collier, *two weeks* after the initial training, allowed some infants to watch the mobile move but did not allow them to kick. The next day, when they were connected to the mobile, they kicked almost immediately.

Apparently, watching the mobile the previous day revived their faded memory. Other research similarly finds that reminders are powerful. In real life, an infant who is reminded, day after day, is likely to remember several weeks later. If Daddy plays with a 3-month-old every day and then goes on a month-long trip, the baby might grin broadly when he reappears.

OLDER INFANTS At 9 months, memory markedly improves. This may partly be the result of new motor ability, since 9-month-olds can usually crawl (Mullally & Maguire, 2014). At 12 months, more improvement is evident. One-year-olds learn

Selective Amnesia As we grow older, we forget about spitting up, nursing, crying, and almost everything else from our early years. However, strong emotions (love, fear, mistrust) may leave lifelong traces.

from parents and strangers, from other babies and older siblings, from picture books and family photographs, from their own walking and talking (Hayne & Simcock, 2009). The dendrites of several areas of the brain grow to reflect remembered experiences.

The crucial insight from information-processing theory is that the brain is a very active organ, changing with each day's events. Therefore, the particulars of early experiences are critically important in determining what a child knows or does not know. Generalization becomes possible as sensations become perceptions, which become expectations (Mullally & Maguire, 2014). Every day of their young lives, infants are processing information and storing conclusions.

WHAT HAVE YOU LEARNED?

1. Why did Piaget call cognition in the first two years "sensorimotor intelligence"?
2. How does stage one of sensorimotor intelligence lead to stage two?
3. In sensorimotor intelligence, what is the difference between stages three and four?
4. Why is the concept of object permanence important to an infant's development?
5. What does the active experimentation of the stage-five toddler suggest for parents?
6. Why did Piaget underestimate infant cognition?
7. What conditions help 3-month-olds remember something?
8. How does the infant brain respond to experiences?

Language

No other species has anything approaching the neurons and networks that support the 6,000 or so human languages. The human ability to communicate, even at age 2, far surpasses that of full-grown adults of every other species. This includes dolphins, ravens, and chimpanzees, all with much better communication mechanisms than was formerly believed.

Here we describe the beginning of language learning, "from burping to grammar" as one scholar put it (Saxton, 2010, p. 2). Before age 1, babies listen intensely, "acquiring much of their native language before they utter their first word" (Aslin, 2012, p. 191).

The Universal Sequence

The timing of language acquisition varies; the most advanced 10 percent of 2-year-olds speak more than 550 words, and the least-advanced 10 percent speak fewer than 100—a fivefold difference (Merriman, 1999). But although timing varies, the sequence is the same.

LISTENING AND RESPONDING Hearing infants begin learning language before birth, via brain connections. Newborns prefer the language their mother speaks over an unheard language; if their mother is bilingual, newborns respond to both languages (Byers-Heinlein et al., 2010).

The ability to distinguish sounds, mouth movements, and gestures in the language (or languages) of caregivers improves over the first year, while the ability to decipher sounds in an unfamiliar language deteriorates (Narayan et al., 2010). By 1 year, babies are more likely to imitate the actions of a stranger speaking their native tongue than those of a person who speaks another language (Buttelmann et al., 2013).

Early language learning is encouraged everywhere by adults who instinctively use higher pitch, simpler words, repetition, varied speeds, and exaggerated emotional tones when they talk to babies (Bryant & Barrett, 2007). This special language form is sometimes called *baby talk* and sometimes called *motherese,* since mothers universally speak it.

Both these terms may be misleading, since people use that form with lovers as well as babies, and since many nonmothers use it as well. Scientists prefer a more formal designation: **child-directed speech.** No matter what term is used, this mode captures infants' attention.

Sounds are preferred over content. Infants like alliteration, rhymes, repetition, rhythm, and varied pitch (Hayes & Slater, 2008; Saxton, 2010; Schön et al., 2008). Think of your favorite lullaby (itself an alliterative word). All infants listen to whatever they can and appreciate the sounds they hear. Even music is culture-specific: 4- to 8-month-olds prefer their own culture's music (Soley & Hannon, 2010).

child-directed speech
The high-pitched, simplified, and repetitive way adults speak to infants. (Also called *baby talk* or *motherese.*)

At About This Time: The Development of Spoken Language in the First Two Years

Age*	Means of Communication
Newborn	Reflexive communication—cries, movements, facial expressions.
2 months	A range of meaningful noises—cooing, fussing, crying, laughing.
3–6 months	New sounds, including squeals, growls, croons, trills, vowel sounds.
6–10 months	Babbling, repeating both consonant and vowel sounds.
10–12 months	Comprehension of simple words; speech-like intonations; specific vocalizations that have meaning to those who know the infant well. Deaf babies express their first signs; hearing babies also use specific gestures (e.g., pointing) to communicate.
12 months	First spoken words that are recognizably part of the native language.
13–18 months	Slow growth of vocabulary, up to about 50 words.
18 months	Naming explosion—three or more words learned per day. Much variation in age and rate.
21 months	First two-word sentence.
24 months	Multiword sentences. Half the toddler's utterances are two or more words long.

*The ages in this table reflect norms. Many healthy, intelligent children attain each linguistic accomplishment earlier or later than indicated here.

The mothers of each type differed, with the engaged mothers matching the infants' actions (bobbing head, opening mouth, and so on) and the negative mothers almost never matching. The researchers suggest that the "distinctive patterns of infants' individual differences" determined the mothers' behavior (Montirosso et al., 2015, p. 67). However, as was already explained, other researchers would do the opposite, with mothers determining the infants' behavior. Either way, a lack of synchrony is a troubling sign.

Attachment

Toward the end of the first year, face-to-face synchrony almost disappears. Once infants can walk, they are no longer content to respond, moment by moment, to adult facial expressions and vocalizations.

Instead **attachment** becomes evident. Actually, as thousands of researchers on every continent have shown, attachment is lifelong, beginning before birth and influencing relationships throughout life (see At About This Time).

Attachment has been studied with atypical populations (e.g., infants with Down syndrome, with autism spectrum disorder, and so on), with teenagers, and with adults (Simpson & Rholes, 2015; K. Grossmann et al., 2014). This field of study was inspired by John Bowlby's theories (1982, 1983) and by Mary Ainsworth, who described mother–infant relationships in central Africa 60 years ago (Ainsworth, 1967).

SIGNS OF ATTACHMENT As Ainsworth noted, infants show their attachment through *proximity-seeking* (such as approaching and following their caregivers) and through *contact-maintaining* (such as touching, snuggling, and holding). Attachment needs are

> **attachment**
> According to Ainsworth, "an affectional tie" that an infant forms with a caregiver—a tie that binds them together in space and endures over time.

At About This Time: Stages of Attachment

Birth to 6 weeks
Preattachment. Newborns signal, via crying and body movements, that they need others. When people respond positively, the newborn is comforted and learns to seek more interaction. Newborns are also primed by brain patterns to recognize familiar voices and faces.

6 weeks to 8 months
Attachment in the making. Infants respond preferentially to familiar people by smiling, laughing, babbling. Their caregivers' voices, touch, expressions, and gestures are comforting, often overriding the infant's impulse to cry. Trust (Erikson) develops.

8 months to 2 years
Classic secure attachment. Infants greet their primary caregivers, play happily when they are present, show separation anxiety when their primary caregivers leave. Both infant and caregiver seek to be close to each other (proximity) and frequently look at each other (contact). In many caregiver–infant pairs, physical touch (patting, holding, caressing) is frequent.

2 to 6 years
Attachment as launching pad. Young children seek their caregivers' praise and reassurance as their social world expands. Interactive conversations and games (hide-and-seek, object play, reading, pretending) are common. Children expect caregivers to comfort and entertain.

6 to 12 years
Mutual attachment. Children seek to make their caregivers proud by learning whatever adults want them to learn, and adults reciprocate. In concrete operational thought (Piaget), specific accomplishments are valued by adults and children.

12 to 18 years
New attachment figures. Teenagers explore and make friendships independent from parents, using their working models of earlier attachments as a base. With formal operational thinking (Piaget), shared ideals and goals become influential.

18 years on
Attachment revisited. Adults develop relationships with others, especially relationships with romantic partners and their own children, influenced by earlier attachment patterns. Past insecure attachments from childhood can be repaired rather than repeated, although this does not always happen.

Data from Grobman, 2008.

secure attachment
A relationship in which an infant obtains both comfort and confidence from the presence of his or her caregiver.

insecure-avoidant attachment
A pattern of attachment in which an infant avoids connection with the caregiver, as when the infant seems not to care about the caregiver's presence, departure, or return.

insecure-resistant/ambivalent attachment
A pattern of attachment in which an infant's anxiety and uncertainty are evident, as when the infant becomes very upset at separation from the caregiver, such infants both resist and seek contact on reunion.

disorganized attachment
A type of attachment that is marked by an infant's inconsistent reactions to the caregiver's departure and return.

evident when a baby cries if the caregiver closes the door when going to the bathroom (lost proximity) or fusses if a back-facing car seat prevents the baby from seeing the parent (lost contact).

Some caregivers take the baby into the bathroom, leading to one mother's complaint that she hadn't been alone in the bathroom for two years (Senior, 2014). Often caregivers sing and talk to the baby when they are out of sight. Maintaining contact need not be physical: Visual or verbal connections can express attachment. Later on, in adulthood, a phone call or a text message may be enough.

Caregivers show many signs that attachment is mutual. They keep a watchful eye on their baby, and they elicit interaction with expressions, gestures, and sounds. Before going to sleep at midnight they might tiptoe to the crib to gaze at their sleeping infant, or, in daytime, absentmindedly smooth their toddler's hair.

Attachment is universal, being part of the inborn social nature of the human species. The particular ways it is expressed depend on culture. For instance, Ainsworth reported that Ugandan mothers never kiss their infants, but they often massage them, contrary to Westerners.

Some adults remain in contact simply by sitting in the same room as each reads quietly. In some cultures, adults often hold hands, hug, or touch each other's faces, shoulders, or buttocks. Some scholars believe that attachment, not only with mothers but also fathers, grandparents, and nonrelatives, is one reason that *Homo sapiens* thrived when other species became extinct (Hrdy, 2009).

SECURE AND INSECURE ATTACHMENT Attachment is classified into four types: A, B, C, and D (see Table 4.1). Infants with **secure attachment** (type B) feel comfortable and confident. The caregiver is a *base for exploration*, providing assurance and enabling discovery. A toddler might, for example, scramble down from the caregiver's lap to play with an intriguing toy but periodically look back and vocalize (contact-maintaining) or bring the toy to the caregiver for inspection (proximity-seeking).

By contrast, insecure attachment (types A and C) is characterized by fear, anxiety, anger, or indifference. Some insecure children play independently without maintaining contact; this is **insecure-avoidant attachment** (type A). The opposite reaction is **insecure-resistant/ambivalent attachment** (type C). Children with this type of attachment cling to the caregiver and are angry at being left.

Ainsworth's original schema differentiated only types A, B, and C. Later researchers discovered a fourth category (type D), **disorganized attachment.** Type D infants may shift suddenly from hitting to kissing their mothers, from staring blankly to crying hysterically, from pinching themselves to freezing in place.

Among the general population, almost two-thirds of infants are secure (type B). Their mothers' presence gives them courage to explore; her departure causes distress;

TABLE 4.1 | Patterns of Infant Attachment

Type	Name of Pattern	In Playroom	Mother Leaves	Mother Returns	Toddlers in Category (%)
A	Insecure-avoidant	Child plays happily.	Child continues playing.	Child ignores her.	10–20
B	Secure	Child plays happily.	Child pauses, is not as happy.	Child welcomes her, returns to play.	50–70
C	Insecure-resistant/ambivalent	Child clings, is preoccupied with mother.	Child is unhappy, may stop playing.	Child is angry; may cry, hit mother, cling.	10–20
D	Disorganized	Child is cautious.	Child may stare or yell; looks scared, confused.	Child acts oddly; may scream, hit self, throw things.	5–10

her return elicits positive social contact (such as smiling or hugging) and then more playing. The infant's balanced reaction—being concerned but not overwhelmed by comings and goings—indicates security. Early research was only on mothers. Later, fathers and other caregivers were included; they also had secure or insecure attachments to their infants.

About one-third of infants are insecure, either indifferent (type A) or unduly anxious (type C). About 5 to 10 percent of infants fit into none of these categories; they are disorganized (type D), with no consistent strategy for social interaction, even avoidance or resistance. Sometimes they become hostile and aggressive, difficult for anyone to relate to (Lyons-Ruth et al., 1999). Unlike the first three types, disorganized infants have elevated levels of cortisol in reaction to stress (Bernard & Dozier, 2010).

MEASURING ATTACHMENT Ainsworth (1973) developed a now-classic laboratory procedure called the **Strange Situation** to measure attachment. In a well-equipped playroom, an infant is observed for eight episodes, each lasting three minutes. First, the child and mother are together. Next, according to a set sequence, the mother and then a stranger come and go. Infants' responses indicate which type of attachment they have formed.

Researchers are trained to distinguish types A, B, C, and D. They focus on the following:

- *Exploration of the toys.* A secure toddler plays happily.
- *Reaction to the caregiver's departure.* A secure toddler shows some sign of dismay when the caregiver leaves.
- *Reaction to the caregiver's return.* A secure toddler welcomes the caregiver's reappearance, usually seeking contact, and then plays again.

Attachment is not always measured via the Strange Situation; surveys and interviews are also used. Sometimes parents answer 90 questions about their children's characteristics, and sometimes adults are interviewed extensively (according to a detailed protocol) about their relationships with their own parents, again with various specific measurements. Attachment can be assessed in middle school children, adolescents who are dating, and with an entire family, via verbal responses or actions (Farnfield & Holmes, 2014).

Research measuring attachment has revealed that some behaviors that might seem normal are, in fact, a sign of insecurity. For instance, an infant who clings to the caregiver and refuses to explore the toys might be type C. Likewise, adults who say their childhood was happy and their mother was a saint, especially if they provide

Strange Situation
A laboratory procedure for measuring attachment by evoking infants' reactions to the stress of various adults' comings and goings in an unfamiliar playroom.

Excited, Troubled, Comforted This sequence is repeated daily for 1-year-olds, which is why the same sequence is replicated to measure attachment. As you see, toys are no substitute for a mother's comfort if the infant or toddler is secure, as this one seems to be. Some, however, cry inconsolably or throw toys angrily when left alone.

few specific memories, might be insecure. And young children who are immediately friendly to strangers may never have formed a secure attachment (Tarullo et al., 2011).

Assessments of attachment that were developed and validated for middle-class North Americans may be less useful in other cultures. Infants who seem dismissive or clingy in the Strange Situation may not necessarily be insecure.

Insecure Attachment and the Social Setting

At first, developmentalists expected secure attachment in infancy to "predict all the outcomes reasonably expected from a well-functioning personality" (Thompson & Raikes, 2003, p. 708). But this expectation turned out to be naive.

Securely attached infants *are* more likely to become secure toddlers, competent preschoolers, high-achieving schoolchildren, and capable parents. Attachment affects early brain development, one reason these later outcomes occur (Diamond & Fagundes, 2010). But insecure infants are not doomed to later failure.

Although attachment patterns form in infancy (see Table 4.2), they are not set in stone; a securely attached infant may become insecure if the family context changes, such as with new abuse or income loss. Poverty increases the likelihood of insecure attachment, and insecure attachment correlates with later learning problems, but a third variable may be the reason for this correlation.

The third variable most often suggested is low SES. Hostile children, fearful adults, delayed language, and low school achievement all correlate with low parental education, as does insecure attachment. The premise—that responsive early parenting leads to secure attachment, which buffers stress and encourages exploration—seems valid, but lack of attachment may be a sign of deeper social problems. Low SES is problematic in many ways, but we should note that both secure and insecure attachment occur at every income level.

Certainly infant responses in the Strange Situation are only one measure of the parent–child relationship. Linking attachment measured by the Strange Situation directly to later problems may not be warranted, especially in cultures with other patterns of mother–child interaction (Keller, 2014).

TABLE 4.2	Predictors of Attachment Type

Secure attachment (type B) is more likely if:
- The parent is usually sensitive and responsive to the infant's needs.
- The infant–parent relationship is high in synchrony.
- The infant's temperament is "easy."
- The parents are not stressed about income, other children, or their marriage.
- The parents have a working model of secure attachment to their own parents.

Insecure attachment is more likely if:
- The parent mistreats the child. (Neglect increases type A; abuse increases types C and D.)
- The mother is mentally ill. (Paranoia increases type D; depression increases type C.)
- The parents are highly stressed about income, other children, or their marriage. (Parental stress increases types A and D.)
- The parents are intrusive and controlling. (Parental domination increases type A.)
- The parents actively abuse alcohol. (Father with alcohol use disorder increases type A; mother with alcohol use disorder increases type D.)
- The child's temperament is "difficult." (Difficult children tend to be type C.)
- The child's temperament is "slow to warm up." (This correlates with type A.)

© JOSEF POLLEROSS/THE IMAGE WORKS

Predict Their Future These three infants, photographed in Romania in 1990, are now young adults, still affected by the deprivation evident here.

OBSERVATION QUIZ
What three possible dangers do you see? (see answer, page 145) ◄

INSIGHTS FROM ROMANIA No scholar doubts that close human relationships should develop in the first year of life and that the lack of such relationships risks dire consequences. Unfortunately, thousands of children born in Romania are proof.

When Romanian dictator Nicolae Ceausescu forbade birth control and abortions in the 1980s, illegal abortions became a leading cause of death for Romanian women aged 15 to 45 (Verona, 2003), and more than 100,000 children were abandoned to crowded, impersonal, state-run orphanages. The children experienced severe deprivation, including virtually no normal interaction, play, or conversation.

In the two years after Ceausescu was ousted and killed in 1989, thousands of those children were adopted by North American, western European, and Australian families. Those who were adopted before 6 months of age fared best; the adoptive parents established synchrony via play and caregiving. Most of them developed normally.

For those adopted after 6 months, and especially after 12 months, early signs were encouraging: Skinny infants gained weight and grew faster than other 1-year-olds, developing motor skills they had lacked (H. Park et al., 2011). However, their early social deprivation soon became evident in their emotions and intellect. Many were overly friendly to strangers throughout childhood, a sign of insecure attachment (Tarullo et al., 2011). At age 11, their average IQ was only 85, which is 15 points below normal (Rutter et al., 2010).

Even those who were well nourished or who caught up to normal growth often became impulsive, angry teenagers. Apparently, the stresses of adolescence and emerging adulthood exacerbated the cognitive and social strains on these young people and their families (Merz & McCall, 2011).

These children are now adults, some with serious emotional or conduct problems. The cause is more social than biological. Research on children adopted nationally and internationally finds that many become normal adults, but every stress—from rejection in infancy to early institutionalization to the circumstances of the adoption process—makes a good outcome more difficult to attain (Grotevant & McDermott, 2014).

Romanian infants are no longer available for international adoption, even though some remain abandoned. Research confirms that early emotional deprivation, not genes or nutrition, is their greatest problem. Romanian infants develop best in their own families, second best in foster families, and worst in institutions (Nelson et al., 2007).

As best we know, this applies to infants everywhere: Families usually nurture their babies better than strangers who care for many infants at once, and the more years children spend in an impersonal institution, the more likely it is they will become socially and intellectually impaired (Julian, 2013).

Developing Attachment

Attachment begins at birth and continues lifelong. Much depends not only on the ways in which parents and babies bond, but also on the quality and consistency of caregiving, the safety and security of the home environment, and individual and family experience. While the patterns set in infancy may echo in later life, they are not determinative.

HOW MANY CHILDREN ARE SECURELY ATTACHED?

The specific percentages of children who are secure and insecure vary by culture, parent responsiveness, and specific temperament and needs of both the child and the caregiver. Generally, about a third of all 1-year-olds seem insecure.

50–70%	10–20%	10–20%	5–10%
Securely Attached (Type B)	Avoidant Attachment (Type A)	Ambivalent Attachment (Type C)	Disorganized Attachment (Type D)

ATTACHMENT IN THE STRANGE SITUATION MAY INFLUENCE RELATIONSHIPS THROUGH THE LIFE SPAN

Attachment patterns formed early affect adults lifelong, but later experiences of love and rejection may change early patterns. Researchers measure attachment by examining children's behaviors in the Strange Situation where they are separated from their parent and play in a room with an unfamiliar caregiver. These early patterns can influence later adult relationships. As life goes on, people become more or less secure, avoidant, or disorganized.

Securely Attached [Type B]

In the Strange Situation, children are able to separate from caregiver but prefer caregiver to strangers.

> Later in life, they tend to have good relationships and good self-esteem.

Avoidant [Type A]

In the Strange Situation, children avoid caregiver.

> Later in life, they tend to be aloof in personal relationships.

Resistant/Ambivalent [Type C]

In the Strange Situation, children appear upset and worried when separated from caregiver; they may hit or cling.

> Later in life, their relationships may be angry, stormy, unpredictable.

Disorganized [Type D]

In the Strange Situation, children appear angry, confused, erratic, or fearful.

> Later in life, they can demonstrate odd behavior—including sudden emotions.

THE CONTINUUM OF ATTACHMENT

Avoidance and anxiety occur along a continuum. Neither genes nor cultural variations were understood when the Strange Situation was first developed (in 1965). Some contemporary researchers believe the link between childhood attachment and adult personality is less straightforward.

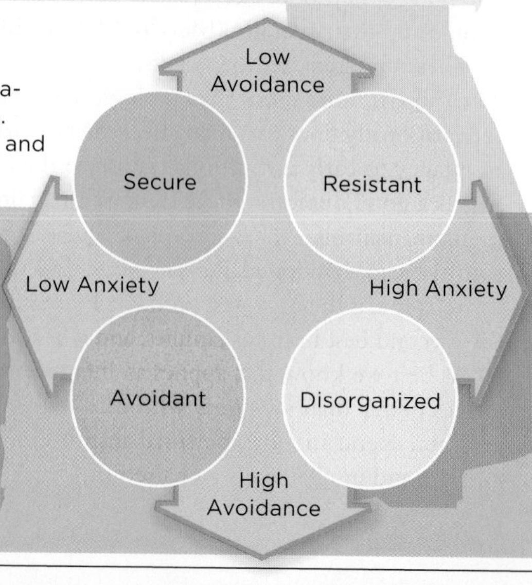

Low Avoidance

Secure | Resistant

Low Anxiety | High Anxiety

Avoidant | Disorganized

High Avoidance

Fortunately, in eastern Europe and elsewhere, institutions have improved or been shuttered; recent international adoptees (often now from Central America or sub-Saharan Africa) are not as impaired as those Romanian orphans (Grotevant & McDermott, 2014). Many nations have severe restrictions on international adoptions, in part because some children were literally snatched from their biological parents to be sent abroad. The number of international adoptees in the United States was 8,668 in 2012, down from 22,884 in 2004.

However, some infants in every nation are deprived of healthy interaction, sometimes within their own families. Ideally, no infant is institutionalized, but if that ideal is not reached, institutions need to change so that psychological health is as important as physical health (McCall, 2013). Children need responsive caregivers, who could be their biological relatives but could be unrelated. When international adoptions become a pawn in international disputes, as in 2014 between the United States and Russia, children suffer.

PREVENTING PROBLEMS All infants need love and stimulation; all seek synchrony and then attachment—secure if possible, insecure if not. Without some adult support, infants become disorganized and adrift, emotionally troubled. Extreme early social deprivation is difficult to overcome.

Since synchrony and attachment develop over the first year, and since more than one-third of all parents have difficulty establishing secure attachments, many developmentalists have sought to discover what particularly impairs these parents and what can be done to improve their parenting. We know that secure attachment is more difficult to achieve when the parents were abused as children, when families are socially isolated, when mothers are young adolescents, or when infants are unusually difficult (Zeanah et al., 2011).

Some birth parents, fearing that they cannot provide responsive parenting, choose adoptive parents. This is best done at birth so that synchrony and attachment can

© PETE STEC/DESIGN PICS/AGEFOTOSTOCK

Doubly Connected Debbie Stec has breast-fed her baby for more than a year while keeping her professional contacts. She is from Jordan, Ontario; her husband has a flexible schedule; and her SES is high—which of these three circumstances promotes breast-feeding? Or, perhaps the strong attachment she and her infant have established is more personal, her choice and her baby's need.

THINK CRITICALLY: Is the Strange Situation a valid way to measure attachment in every culture, or is it biased toward Western idea of the ideal mother–child relationship?

social referencing
Seeking information about how to react to an unfamiliar or ambiguous object or event by observing someone else's expressions and reactions. That other person becomes a social reference.

develop (McCall, 2013). If high-risk birth parents want to provide good care, early support may prevent later problems. Everywhere, parents and infants are attached to each other, and everywhere secure attachment predicts academic success and emotional stability (Erdman & Ng, 2010; Otto & Keller, 2014; Drake et al., 2014).

Social Referencing

Social referencing refers to seeking emotional responses or information from other people, much as a student might consult a dictionary or other reference work. Someone's reassuring glance, cautionary words, or a facial expression of alarm, pleasure, or dismay—those are social references.

Even at 8 months, infants notice where other people are looking and use that information to look in the same direction themselves (Tummeltshammer et al., 2014). After age 1, when infants can walk and are "little scientists," their need to consult others becomes urgent as well as more accurate.

Toddlers search for clues in gazes, faces, and body positions, paying close attention to emotions and intentions. They focus on their familiar caregivers, but they also use relatives, other children, and even strangers to help them assess objects and events. They are remarkably selective, noticing that some strangers are reliable references and others are not (Fusaro & Harris, 2013).

Social referencing has many practical applications. Consider mealtime. Caregivers the world over smack their lips, pretend to taste, and say "yum-yum," encouraging

Rotini Pasta? Look again. Every family teaches their children to relish delicacies that other people avoid. Examples are bacon (not in Arab nations), hamburgers (not in India), and, as shown here, a witchetty grub. This Aboriginal Australian boy is about to swallow an insect larva.

toddlers to eat their first beets, liver, or spinach. For their part, toddlers become astute at reading expressions, insisting on the foods that the adults *really* like. If mother likes it, and presents it on the spoon, then they eat it—otherwise not (Shutts et al., 2013).

Through this process, some children develop a taste for raw fish or curried goat or smelly cheese—foods that children in other cultures refuse, sometimes pretending to gag when presented with delicacies that other children covet. Similarly, toddlers use social cues to understand the difference between real and pretend eating, as well as to learn which objects, emotions, and activities are forbidden.

Fathers as Social Partners

Fathers enhance their children's social and emotional development in many ways (Lamb, 2010). Synchrony, attachment, and social referencing are sometimes more apparent with fathers than with mothers. Fathers typically elicit more smiles and laughter from their infants than mothers do, probably because they play more exciting games, while mothers do more caregiving and comforting (Fletcher et al., 2013).

When asked to play with their baby, mothers typically caress, read, sing, or play traditional games such as peek-a-boo. Fathers are more exciting: They move their infant's limbs in imitation of walking, kicking, or climbing, or they swing the baby through the air, sideways, or even upside down. Mothers might say, "Don't drop him"; fathers and babies laugh with joy. In this way, fathers tend to help children become less fearful.

ETHNIC AND CULTURAL DIFFERENCES Some people still hold the prejudice that African American, Latin American, and Asian American fathers are less nurturing and more strict than other men. In fact, the opposite may be true (Parke, 2013).

Within every ethnic group in the United States, contemporary fathers tend to be more involved with their infants than fathers once were. Fathers are also affected by income (stressed parents are less nurturing) and by where they live. As with humans of all age, social contexts are influential: Fathers are influenced by other fathers (Roopnarine & Hossain, 2013; Qin & Chang, 2013). Thus, fathers of every ethnic group are aware of what other men are doing, and that affects their own behavior.

Close father–infant relationships can teach infants (especially boys) appropriate expressions of emotion, particularly anger. The results may endure: Teenagers are less likely to lash out at friends and authorities if, as infants, they experienced a warm, responsive relationship with their father (Hoeve et al., 2011).

Less rigid gender roles seem to be developing in every nation, allowing a greater caregiving role for fathers (Shwalb et al., 2013). One U.S. example of historical change is the number of married women with children under age 6 who are employed. In 1970, 30 percent of married mothers of young children earned paychecks; in 2012, 60 percent did (U.S. Bureau of Labor Statistics, 2013). These statistics include many mothers of infants, who often rely on the baby's father for child care.

Note the reference to "married" mothers: About half new mothers of infants in the United States are not married, and their employment rates are higher than their married counterparts. Their baby's father—cohabiting or not—may care for their children when mothers are at work.

The fact that father involvement with infants varies by culture, and that fathers tend to be more involved than they were a few decades ago, should not obscure another truth—fathers everywhere and always have cared about their children. To understand this, you need to understand **allocare**—the care of children by people other than the mother (Hrdy, 2009). Allocare is essential for *Homo sapiens'* survival.

Compared with many other species (for instance, mother chimpanzees never let another chimp hold their babies), human mothers have evolved to let other people help with child care, and other people are usually eager to do so (Kachel et al., 2011).

allocare
Literally, "other-care"; the care of children by people other than the biological parents.

Not Manly? Where did that idea come from? Fathers worldwide provide excellent care for their toddlers and enjoy it, evident in the United States *(left)* and India *(right)*, and in every other nation.

Same Situation, Far Apart: Safekeeping Historically, grandmothers were sometimes crucial for child survival. Now, even though medical care has reduced child mortality, grandmothers still do their part to keep children safe, as shown by these two—in the eastern United States *(left)* and Vietnam *(right)*.

Throughout the centuries, the particular person to provide allocare has varied by culture and ecological conditions.

Often fathers helped but not always: Some men were far away, fighting, hunting, or seeking work, while some had several wives and a dozen or more children. In those situations, other women (daughters, grandmothers, sisters, friends) and sometimes other men provided allocare (Hrdy, 2009).

FAMILY COOPERATION Fathers and mothers often work together to raise the children. One researcher reports "mothers and fathers showed patterns of striking similarity: they touched, looked, vocalized, rocked, and kissed their newborns equally" (Parke, 2013, p. 121). Differences were apparent from one couple to another, but not from one gender to another—except for smiling (women did it more).

Children benefit when both parents are caregivers. It is still true, in every culture and ethnic group, that the average father spends much less time with infants than mothers do (Parke, 2013; Tudge, 2008). Some women are gatekeepers, believing that child care is their special domain. They imply that fathers are incompetent (perhaps saying, "You're not holding her right"), laying out the clothes the baby is to wear, as if the father could not find clothes on his own (Pedersen & Kilzer, 2014).

Over the past 20 years, father–infant research has tried to answer three questions:

1. Can men provide care for infants as well as women can?

2. Is father–infant interaction different from mother–infant interaction?

3. How do fathers and mothers cooperate to provide infant care?

Many studies over the past two decades have answered yes to the first two questions. A baby fed, bathed, and diapered by Dad is just as happy and clean as when Mom does it. Gender differences are sometimes found in details, but babies thrive in father-care or mother-care. Fathers' play may be more exciting—they wrestle, chase, and throw more—but they can be as responsive as mothers are.

On the third question, the answer depends on the family (Bretherton, 2010). Usually, mothers are caregivers and fathers are playmates, but not always. Each couple, given their circumstances (perhaps immigrant, low-income, or same-sex), seeks how to complement each other to help their infant thrive (Lamb, 2010). Traditional mother–father roles may be switched with no harm to the baby (Parke, 2013).

A constructive *parental alliance* can take many forms, but it cannot be taken for granted, no matter what the family configuration. Single-parent, same-sex, or grandparent families are not necessarily better or worse than nuclear families; each family can find a way to provide good care.

A CASE TO STUDY

Can We Bear This Commitment?

Parents and children capture my attention, wherever they are. Today I saw one mother ignoring her stroller-bound toddler on a crowded subway (I wanted to tell her to talk to her child) and another mother breast-feed a happy 7-month-old in a public park (which was illegal three decades ago). I look for signs of secure or insecure attachment—the contact-maintaining and proximity-seeking moves that parents do, seemingly unaware that they are responding to primordial depths of human love.

I particularly observe families I know. I am struck by the powerful bond between parent and child, as strong or stronger in adoptive families as in genetic ones.

One adoptive couple is Macky and Nick with their two daughters. I see them echoing my own experiences with my four. Two examples: When Alice was a few days old, I overheard Nick phone another parent, asking which detergent is best for washing baby clothes. Another time, when Macky was engrossed in conversation, Nick interrupted him to insist it was time to get the girls home for their nap.

My appreciation of their attachment was cemented by a third incident. In Macky's words:

I'll never forget the Fourth of July at the spacious home of my mother-in-law's best friend. It was a perfect celebration on a perfect day. Kids frolicked in the pool. Parents socialized nearby, on the sun-drenched lawn or inside the cool house. Many guests had published books on parenting; we imagined they admired our happy, thriving family.

My husband and I have two daughters, Alice who was then 7 and Penelope who was 4. They learned to swim early and are always the first to jump in the pool and the last to leave. Great children, even if their parents have dropped the ball a time or two.

After hours of swimming, the four of us scrambled up to dry land. We walked across the long lawn to join the lunching folk and enjoy hot dogs, relish, mustard, and juicy watermelon.

Suddenly we heard a heart-chilling wail. Panicked, I raced to the pool's edge to see the motionless body of a small child who had gone unnoticed underwater for too long. His blue face was still. Someone was giving CPR. His mother kept wailing, panicked, pleading, destroyed. I had a shameful thought—thank God that is not my child.

He lived. He regained his breath and was whisked away by ambulance. The party came to a quick close.

We four, skin tingling from the summer sun, hearts beating from the near-death of a child who was my kids' playmate an hour before, drove away.

Turning to Nick, I asked: "Can we bear this commitment we have made? Can we raise our children in the face of all hazards—some we try to prevent, others beyond our control?"

That was five years ago. Our children are flourishing. Our confidence is strong and so are our emotions. But it takes only a moment to recognize just how entwined our well-being is with our children and how fragile life is. We are deeply grateful.

A Grateful Family This family photo shows, from left to right, Nick, Penelope, Macky, and Alice with their dog Cooper. When they adopted Alice as a newborn, the parents said, "This is a miracle we feared would never happen."

FIGURE 4.2 Shame on Who? Not on the toddlers, who are naturally curious and careless, but maybe not on the fathers either. Both depression and spanking are affected by financial stress, marital conflict, and cultural norms; who is responsible for those?

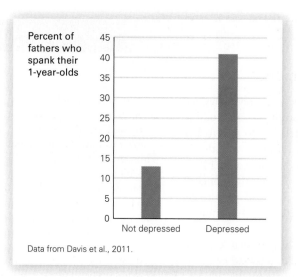

Data from Davis et al., 2011.

Sometimes no one provides good care. One study reported that 7 percent of fathers of 1-year-olds were depressed, and then they were four times as likely to spank as were nondepressed fathers (40 percent versus 10 percent) (Davis et al., 2011) (see Figure 4.2). Thus parental depression, whether it be maternal or paternal, is harmful. We cannot assume that mothers, or fathers, will always be good caregivers.

Family members affect each other. Paternal depression correlates with maternal depression and with sad, angry, disobedient toddlers. Cause and consequence are intertwined. When anyone is depressed or hostile, everyone (mother, father, baby, sibling) needs help.

WHAT HAVE YOU LEARNED?

1. How might synchrony affect early emotional development?
2. What would an infant do to demonstrate attachment?
3. How would a caregiver try to maintain proximity and contact?
4. How would a type B secure adult act in a romantic relationship?
5. How would a type A insecure adult act in a romantic relationship?
6. How would a type C insecure adult act in a romantic relationship?
7. How do negative circumstances (e.g., divorce, abuse, low SES) affect attachment?
8. What can be done to improve the parent–child bond?
9. Whom do infants use as social references?
10. Why is allocare necessary for survival of the human species?
11. How is father-care similar to mother-care?
12. How does father-care differ from mother-care?
13. What ethnic and cohort differences are apparent in father-care?

Video: Theories of Emotional Development in Infancy and Toddlerhood summarizes the theories of personality development described in this section.

Theories of Infant Psychosocial Development

We focus now on ideas regarding infant development from three theories first mentioned in Chapter 1—psychoanalytic, behaviorist, and cognitive. Highlighting these three does not imply that other theories are irrelevant to infancy. In fact, one theory (attachment theory) has just been explained. Another theory, evolutionary theory, has been instrumental in describing allocare, which is crucial for infant development. However, psychoanalytic, behaviorist, and cognitive theories are now explained because each has explicit predictions regarding infant emotions.

Psychoanalytic Theory

Psychoanalytic theory connects biological and social growth. Sigmund Freud and Erik Erikson each described two distinct stages of early development, one in the first year and one beginning in the second.

FREUD: ORAL AND ANAL STAGES According to Freud (1935/1989, 2001), the first year of life is the *oral stage,* so named because the mouth is the young infant's primary source of gratification. In the second year, with the *anal stage,* pleasure comes from the anus—particularly from the sensual satisfaction of bowel movements and, eventually, the psychological pleasure of controlling them.

Freud believed that the oral and anal stages are fraught with potential conflicts. If a mother frustrates her infant's urge to suck—weaning too early, for example, or preventing the baby from sucking a thumb or a pacifier—that may later lead to an *oral fixation.* An adult with an oral fixation is stuck (fixated) at the oral stage, and therefore, eats, drinks, chews, bites, or talks excessively, still seeking the mouthy joys of infancy.

Similarly, if toilet training is overly strict or if it begins too early, then the toddler's refusal—or inability—to comply clashes with the wishes of the adult, who denies the infant normal anal pleasures. That may lead to an anal personality—an adult who seeks control, with a strong need for regularity and cleanliness in all aspects of life.

All Together Now Toddlers in an employees' day-care program at a flower farm in Colombia learn to use the potty on a schedule. Will this experience lead to later personality problems? Probably not.

ERIKSON: TRUST AND AUTONOMY According to Erikson, the first crisis of life is **trust versus mistrust,** when infants learn whether or not the world can be trusted to satisfy basic needs. Babies feel secure when food and comfort are provided with "consistency, continuity, and sameness of experience" (Erikson, 1993, p. 247). If social interaction inspires trust, the child (later the adult) confidently explores the social world.

The second crisis is **autonomy versus shame and doubt,** beginning at about 18 months, when self-awareness emerges. Toddlers want autonomy (self-rule) over their own actions and bodies. Without it, they feel ashamed and doubtful. Like Freud, Erikson believed that problems in early infancy could last a lifetime, creating adults who are suspicious and pessimistic (mistrusting) or easily shamed (lacking autonomy).

Erikson was aware of cultural variations. He knew that mistrust and shame could be destructive or not, depending on local norms and expectations.

For example, Westerners expect toddlers to go through the stubborn and defiant "terrible twos"; that is a sign of the urge for autonomy. Parents in some other places expect toddlers to be obedient. Those parents use shame to control misbehavior.

Cultural pressures are conveyed to children. For example, a study of children found the Japanese highest in shame, the Koreans highest in guilt, and the U.S. children highest in pride (Furukawa et al., 2012). Not surprisingly, U.S. children are less fearful but also less obedient.

trust versus mistrust
Erikson's first crisis of psychosocial development. Infants learn basic trust if the world is a secure place where their basic needs (for food, comfort, attention, and so on) are met.

autonomy versus shame and doubt
Erikson's second crisis of psychosocial development. Toddlers either succeed or fail in gaining a sense of self-rule over their actions and their bodies.

Behaviorism

From the perspective of behaviorism, emotions and personality are molded as parents reinforce or punish a child. Behaviorists believe that parents who respond joyously to every glimmer of a grin will have children with a sunny disposition. The opposite is also true, according to one of the early behaviorists:

> Failure to bring up a happy child, a well-adjusted child—assuming bodily health— falls squarely upon the parents' shoulders. [By the time the child is 3] parents have already determined . . . [whether the child] is to grow into a happy person, wholesome and good-natured, whether he is to be a whining, complaining neurotic, an anger-driven, vindictive, over-bearing slave driver, or one whose every move in life is definitely controlled by fear.
>
> [Watson, 1928, pp. 7, 45]

THINKSTOCK IMAGES/STOCKBYTE/GETTY IMAGES

Only in America Toddlers in every nation of the world sometimes cry when emotions overwhelm them, but in the United States young children are encouraged to express emotions, and Halloween is a national custom, unlike in other nations. Candy, dress-up, ghosts, witches, and ringing doorbells after sunset—no wonder many young children are overwhelmed.

Later behaviorists recognized that infants' behavior also has an element of **social learning,** as infants learn from other people. You already saw an example, social referencing. Social learning occurs throughout life, as Bandura and many others demonstrated. Sensitive parents are able to teach because infants are eager to learn from them, as in this example.

> Kevin is a very active, outgoing person who loves to try new things. Today he takes his 11-month-old daughter, Tyra, to the park for the first time. Tyra is playing alone in the sandbox, when a group of toddlers joins her. At first, Tyra smiles and eagerly watches them play. But as the toddlers become more active and noisy, Tyra's smiles turn quickly to tears. She . . . reaches for Kevin, who picks her up and comforts her. But then Kevin goes a step further. After Tyra calms down, Kevin gently encourages her to play near the other children. He sits at her side, talking and playing with her. Soon Tyra is slowly creeping closer to the group of toddlers, curiously watching their moves.
>
> [Lerner & Dombro, 2004, p. 42]

social learning
The acquisition of behavior patterns by observing the behavior of others.

A more general example of social learning is that toddlers express emotions in various ways—from giggling to cursing—just as their parents or older siblings do. For example, a boy might develop a hot temper if his father's outbursts seem to win his mother's respect; a girl might be coy, or passive-aggressive, if that is what she has seen at home. These examples are deliberately sexist: Gender roles, in particular, are learned, according to social learning theory.

Parents often unwittingly encourage traits in their children. Should parents carry infants most of the time, or will that spoil them? Should babies have many toys, or will that make them too materialistic?

proximal parenting
Caregiving practices that involve being physically close to the baby, with frequent holding and touching.

distal parenting
Caregiving practices that keep some distance from a baby, such as providing toys, food, and face-to-face communication with minimal holding and touching.

Answers to these questions refer to the distinction between **proximal parenting** (being physically close to a baby, often holding and touching) and **distal parenting** (keeping some distance—providing toys, encouraging self-feeding, talking face-to-face instead of communicating by touch). Caregivers tend to behave in proximal or distal ways very early, when infants are only 2 months old (Kärtner et al., 2010).

Every parental action is influenced by whatever assumptions the culture holds. According to behaviorism, each action reinforces a lesson that the baby learns, in this case about people and objects.

The Best Baby Transport Stroller or sling, carriage or carrier, leave babies at home or bring them to work? Such decisions are strongly influenced by culture, with long-lasting implications. Mothers compare particular brands and designs of strollers, trying to decide on the best one, but it rarely occurs to them that taking the baby outside is itself a major decision.

GLENDA POWERS/ISTOCK/360/GETTY IMAGES

Cognitive Theory

Cognitive theory holds that thoughts determine a person's perspective. Early experiences are important because beliefs, perceptions, and memories make them so, not because they are buried in the unconscious (psychoanalytic theory) or burned into the brain's patterns (behaviorism).

According to many cognitive theorists, early experiences help infants develop a **working model,** which is a set of assumptions that becomes a frame of reference for later life (S. Johnson et al., 2010). It is a "model" because early relationships form a prototype, or blueprint; it is "working" because it is a work in progress, not fixed or final.

Ideally, infants develop "a working model of the self as lovable, and competent" because the parents are "emotionally available, loving, and supportive of their mastery efforts" (Harter, 2012, p. 12). However, reality does not always conform to this ideal. A 1-year-old girl might develop a model, based on her parents' inconsistent responses to her, that people are unpredictable. She will continue to apply that model to everyone: Her childhood friendships will be insecure, and her adult relationships will be guarded.

The crucial idea, according to cognitive theory, is that an infant's early experiences themselves are not necessarily pivotal, but the interpretation of those experiences is (Olson & Dweck, 2009). Children may misinterpret their experiences, or parents may offer inaccurate explanations, and these form ideas that affect later thinking and behavior.

In this way, working models formed in childhood echo lifelong. A hopeful message from cognitive theory is that people can rethink and reorganize their thoughts, developing new models. Our mistrustful girl might marry a faithful and loving man and gradually develop a new working model. The form of psychotherapy that seems most successful at the moment is called cognitive-behavioral, in which new thoughts about how to behave are developed. In other words, a new working model is developed.

> **working model**
> In cognitive theory, a set of assumptions that the individual uses to organize perceptions and experiences. For example, a person might assume that other people are trustworthy and be surprised if someone lies, cheats, or betrays a confidence.

WHAT HAVE YOU LEARNED?

1. What might happen if a person is stuck in the oral stage?
2. What might happen if a person is stuck in the anal stage?
3. How might the crisis of "trust versus mistrust" affect later life?
4. How might the crisis of "autonomy versus shame and doubt" affect later life?
5. How do behaviorists explain the development of emotions and personality?
6. What emotional reactions might children learn from watching their parents?
7. How would a child develop a working model about expressing emotions?
8. What would change an adult's working model?

Infant Day Care

Cultural variations in infant care are vast. No theory directly endorses any particular caregiving practice, but each of these theories has been used to justify radically different responses. This is particularly obvious in infant day care, a topic on which developmentalists disagree.

For ideological as well as economic reasons, center-based infant care is common in France, Israel, China, Norway, and Sweden, where it is heavily subsidized by the government. Many families in those nations consider that the government's provision of quality center care is a public obligation, in the same way that people assume that the public fire department will extinguish fires everywhere in the city.

TABLE 4.3	High-Quality Day Care

High-quality day care during infancy has five essential characteristics:

1. *Adequate attention to each infant.* A small group of infants needs two reliable, familiar, loving caregivers. Continuity of care is crucial.

2. *Encouragement of language and sensorimotor development.* Infants need language—songs, conversations, and positive talk—and easily manipulated toys.

3. *Attention to health and safety.* Cleanliness routines (e.g., handwashing), accident prevention (e.g., no small objects), and safe areas to explore are essential.

4. *Professional caregivers.* Caregivers should have experience and degrees/certificates in early-childhood education. Turnover should be low, morale high, and enthusiasm evident.

5. *Warm and responsive caregivers.* Providers should engage the children in active play and guide them in problem solving. Quiet, obedient children may indicate unresponsive care.

Center care is scarce in South Asia, Africa, and Latin America, where many parents believe it would be harmful to infants' well-being. (Table 4.3 lists five essential characteristics of high-quality infant day care, wherever it may be located.)

Many Choices, Many Cultures

It is estimated that about 134 million babies will be born each year from 2010 to 2021 (United Nations, 2013). Most newborns are cared for primarily or exclusively by their mothers. Allocare, especially by the father and grandmother, increases as the baby gets older. Daily care by a nonrelative, trained and paid to provide it, occurs for only about 15 percent of infants worldwide, a statistic that obscures the range from one culture to another.

As discussed above, fathers worldwide increasingly take part in baby care, but some cultures still expect fathers to stay at a distance. Others favor equality (Shwalb et al., 2013). Most nations provide some paid leave for mothers who are in the workforce; some also provide paid leave for fathers; and several nations provide paid family leave that can be taken by either parent or shared between them.

OBSERVATION QUIZ

What three things do you see that suggest good care? (see answer, page 156) ➤

TED RICHARDSON/RALEIGH NEWS & OBSERVER/MCT VIA GETTY IMAGES

Contrast This With That Three infants again, but this infant day care center provides excellent care, as can be seen by comparing this scene with what is depicted in the photo on page 143.

FIGURE 4.3 A Changing World No one was offered maternity leave a century ago because the only jobs that mothers had were unregulated ones. Now, virtually every nation has a maternity leave policy, revised every decade or so. (The data on this chart are from 2011—already outdated.) As of 2014, only Australia, Sweden, Iceland, France, and Canada offered policies reflecting gender equality. That may be the next innovation in many nations.

The length of paid leave varies from a few days to about 15 months (see Figure 4.3). Those variations affect infant care, since an employee who loses money and a job is likely to go back to work as soon as possible after a baby is born.

The other crucial variable is whether day care is free, subsidized, or paid entirely by parents. When most child care is privately funded, quality varies a great deal. That makes it difficult to generalize about the effects of infant day care, since some day care is so much better than others.

NORTH AMERICA Only 20 percent of infants in the United States are cared for *exclusively* by their mothers (i.e., no other relatives or babysitters) throughout their first year. This is in contrast to Canada, which is similar to the United States in ethnic diversity but has far more generous maternal leave and lower rates of maternal employment.

In the first year of life, most Canadians are cared for only by their mothers (Babchishin et al., 2013). Obviously, these differences are affected by culture, economics, and politics more than by any universal needs of babies.

In the United States, some agencies send professional visitors to the homes of new parents, advising them about baby care. Mixed results come from such efforts—some mothers are suspicious, resistant, or overwhelmed (Paulsell et al., 2014). Similarly, grandmother care, informal care, and center care have each sometimes been destructive.

Grandmother care seems particularly complex, as grandmothers vary in personality, competence, and dedication. For example, in most nations and centuries, infants were more likely to survive if their grandmothers were nearby, especially when they were newly weaned (Sear & Mace, 2008). The hypothesis is that grandmothers provided essential nourishment and protection. But in one era (northern Germany, 1720–1874), living with a paternal grandmother (not a maternal one) increased the rate of newborn death (Beise & Voland, 2002).

Mixed evidence can also be found for center care. Although all the research finds that cognitive development benefits from infant day care, several studies have suggested that children in early, extensive center care are somewhat more likely to develop externalizing problems by age 5—hitting, yelling, and disobeying adults. Later development is affected as well. In the United States, adolescents who experienced extensive day care are more impulsive and risk-taking, although maternal sensitivity moderates that tendency (Burchinal et al., 2014). The following further describes some of the research.

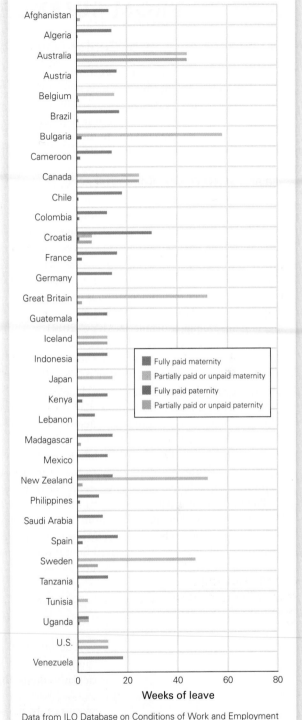

Data from ILO Database on Conditions of Work and Employment Laws, 2011.

Note: In some cases, leave can be shared between parents or other family members. Many nations have increased leave in the past four years.

A VIEW FROM SCIENCE

The Mixed Realities of Center Day Care

A highly respected professional organization, the National Association for the Education of Young Children (NAEYC), recently revised its standards for care of babies from birth to 15 months, based on current research (NAEYC, 2014). Breast-feeding is encouraged (via bottles of breast milk that mothers have pumped), babies are always put to sleep on their backs, group size is small (no more than eight infants), and the ratio of adults to babies is 1:4 or fewer.

Many specific practices are recommended to keep infant minds growing and bodies healthy. For instance, "before walking on surfaces that infants use specifically for play, adults and children remove, replace, or cover with clean foot coverings any shoes they have worn outside that play area. If children or staff are barefoot in such areas, their feet are visibly clean." Another recommendation is to "engage infants in frequent face-to-face social interactions"—including talking, singing, smiling, touching (NAEYC, 2014).

Such responsive care, unfortunately, has not been routine for infants, especially those not cared for by their mothers. A large study in Canada found that infant girls seemed to develop equally well in various care arrangements.

However, Canadian boys from high-income families whose mothers were not exclusive caregivers fared less well than similar boys whose mothers provided all their care. By age 4, high-income boys were slightly more assertive or aggressive, with more emotional problems (e.g., a teacher might note that a kindergarten boy "seems unhappy").

The opposite was true for boys from low-income families: On average, they benefited from nonmaternal care, again according to teacher reports. The researchers insist that no policy implications can be derived from this study, partly because care varied so much in quality, location, and provider (Côté et al., 2008).

Research in the United States has also found that center care benefits children of low-income families (Peng & Robins, 2010). For less impoverished children, questions arise. An ongoing longitudinal study by the Early Child Care Network of the National Institute of Child Health and Human Development (NICHD) has followed the development of more than 1,300 children from birth to age 11. Early day care correlated with many cognitive advances, especially in language.

The social consequences were less stellar, however. Most analyses find that secure attachment to the mother was as common among infants in center care as among infants cared for at home. Like other smaller studies, the NICHD research confirms that the mother–child relationship is pivotal.

Infant day care seemed detrimental when the mother was insensitive *and* the infant spent more than 20 hours a week in a poor-quality program with too many children per group (McCartney et al., 2010). Again, boys in such circumstances had more conflicts with their teachers than did the girls or other boys with a different mix of maternal traits and day-care experiences.

More recent work finds that high-quality care in infancy benefits the cognitive skills of children of both sexes and all income groups, with no evidence of emotional harm, especially when it is followed by good preschool care (W. Li et al., 2013).

This raises another question: Might changing attitudes, female employment, and centers that reflect new research on infant development produce more positive results from center care? Or is there something about the connection between mother and baby that evolved over the millennia, as evolutionary theory might posit, that makes mother-care better in some way than allocare, no matter how expert the provider?

The link between infant day care and later psychosocial problems, although not found in every study, raises concern. For that reason, a large study in Norway is particularly interesting, as is recent research from Australia.

ANSWER TO **OBSERVATION** QUIZ
(from page 154) Remontia Greene is holding the feeding baby in just the right position as she rocks back and forth—no propped-up bottle here. The two observing babies are at an angle and distance that makes them part of the social interaction, and they are strapped in. Finally, look at the cribs— no paint, close slats, and positioned so the babies can see each other. ●

NORWAY In Norway, new mothers are paid at full salary to stay home with their babies for 47 weeks, and high-quality, free center day care is available from age 1 on. Most (62 percent) Norwegian 1-year-olds are in center care, as are 84 percent of 2-year-olds and 93 percent of 3-year-olds. By contrast, in the United States maternal leave is unpaid, and if the mother does not return to work after 3 months, her job may be terminated. Infant care is usually privately financed, which may reduce quality for all but the wealthy.

In the United States, reliable statistics are not kept on center care for infants, but only 42 percent of all U.S. 3-year-olds were in educational programs in 2012, according to the National Center for Education Statistics (Kena et al., 2014). Rates increase slightly as maternal education rises, because mothers with more education are more likely to appreciate and afford early education.

Longitudinal results in Norway find no detrimental results of infant center care that begins at age 1. (Too few children were in center care before their first birthday to find significant longitudinal results.) By kindergarten, Norwegian children in day care had slightly more conflicts with caregivers, but the authors suggest that may be the result of shy children becoming bolder as a result of day care (Solheim et al., 2013).

AUSTRALIA The attitudes of the culture and the mothers may influence the child. An intriguing example comes from Australia, where the government has recently attempted to increase the birth rate. Parents were given $5,000 for each newborn, parental leave is paid, and public subsidies provide child-care centers. The law endorses the concept that young children benefit from interactions with other children and learn from skilled caregivers, yet many Australians contend that babies need exclusive maternal care (Harrison et al., 2014). As you might imagine, each side claims support from psychology: behaviorism versus psychoanalytic theory.

Parents are caught in the middle. For example, one Australian mother of a 12-month-old boy chose center care, but said:

> I spend a lot of time talking with them about his day and what he's been doing and how he's feeling and they just seem to have time to do that, to make the effort to communicate. Yeah they've really bonded with him and he's got close to them. But I still don't like leaving him there. And he doesn't, to be honest . . . Because he's used to sort of having, you know, parents.
>
> *[quoted in Boyd et al., 2013]*

Developmentalists agree that both home quality and national context matter for infants. There is no agreed-upon setting for ideal infant psychosocial development, as long as people provide love, language, and play that are responsive to the baby. As one review explained: "This evidence now indicates that early nonparental care environments sometimes pose risks to young children and sometimes confer benefits" (Phillips et al., 2011, p. 44). The same can be said for parental care: Some provide excellent care; some do not.

Many people believe that the practices of their own family or culture are best and that other patterns harm either the infant or the mother. This is another example of the difference-equals-deficit error. Without evidence, assumptions flourish.

A Stable, Familiar Pattern

No matter what form of care is chosen or what theory is endorsed, individualized care with stable caregivers seems best (Morrissey, 2009). Caregiver change is especially problematic for infants because each simple gesture or sound that a baby makes not only merits an encouraging response but also requires interpretation by someone who knows that particular baby well.

For example, "baba" could mean *bottle, baby, blanket, banana,* or some other word that does not even begin with *b*. This example is an easy one, but similar communication efforts—requiring individualized emotional responses, preferably from a familiar caregiver—are evident even in the first smiles and cries.

A related issue is the growing diversity of baby care providers. Especially when the home language is not the majority language, parents hesitate to let people of another background care for their infants. That is one reason that, in the United States, immigrant parents often prefer care by relatives instead of by professionals (P. Miller et al., 2014). Relationships are crucial, not only between caregiver and infant but also between caregiver and parent (Elicker et al., 2014).

Particularly problematic is instability of nonmaternal care, as when an infant is cared for by a neighbor, a grandmother, a center, and then another grandmother, each for only a month or two. By age 3, children with unstable care histories are likely to be more aggressive than those with stable nonmaternal care, such as being at the same center with the same caregiver for years (Pilarz & Hill, 2014).

As is true of many topics in child development, questions remain. But one fact is without question: Each infant needs personal responsiveness. Someone should serve as a partner in the synchrony duet, a base for secure attachment, and a social reference who encourages exploration. Then infant emotions and experiences—cries and laughter, fears and joys—will ensure that psychosocial development goes well.

WHAT HAVE YOU LEARNED?

1. What are the advantages of nonmaternal day care for the infant?
2. What are the disadvantages of exclusive maternal care for the infant?
3. What might be the problem with infant day care?
4. Why are the effects of center care in Norway different from those in the United States?
5. What are the costs and benefits of infant care by relatives?
6. What do infants need, no matter who cares for them or where care occurs?

SUMMARY

Emotional Development

1. Two emotions, contentment and distress, appear as soon as an infant is born. Smiles and laughter are evident in the early months. Anger emerges in reaction to restriction and frustration, between 4 and 8 months of age, and becomes stronger by age 1.

2. Reflexive fear is apparent in very young infants. Fear of something specific, including fear of strangers and of separation, is typically strong toward the end of the first year.

3. In the second year, social awareness produces more selective fear, anger, and joy. As infants become increasingly self-aware, emotions emerge that encourage an interface between the self and others—specifically, pride, shame, and affection. Self-recognition (on the mirror/rouge test) emerges at about 18 months.

4. Stress impedes early brain and emotional development. Some infants are particularly vulnerable to the effects of early maltreatment.

5. Temperament is a set of genetic traits whose expression is influenced by the context. Inborn temperament is linked to later personality, although plasticity is also evident.

The Development of Social Bonds

6. Often by 2 months, and clearly by 6 months, infants become more responsive and social. Synchrony is evident. Infants are disturbed by a still face because they expect and need social interaction.

7. Attachment, measured by the baby's reaction to the caregiver's presence, departure, and return in the Strange Situation, is crucial. Some infants seem indifferent (type A attachment—insecure-

avoidant) or overly dependent (type C—insecure-resistant/ambivalent) instead of secure (type B). Disorganized attachment (type D) is the most worrisome. Secure attachment provides encouragement for infant exploration.

8. As they play, toddlers engage in social referencing, looking to other people's facial expressions and body language to detect what is safe, frightening, or fun.

9. Infants frequently use fathers as partners in synchrony, as attachment figures, and as social references, developing emotions and exploring their world via father caregiving.

10. Father-care is becoming more common, and it can be as nurturant as mother-care. Generally, father-play is more exciting than mother-play, which is more soothing. Parents vary in their roles; a well-informed functioning *parental alliance* is more important than who does what.

Theories of Infant Psychosocial Development

10. According to all major theories, caregiver behavior is especially influential in the first two years. Freud stressed the mother's impact on oral and anal pleasure; Erikson emphasized trust and autonomy. The impact of these is lifelong.

11. Behaviorists focus on learning; parents teach their babies many things, including when to be fearful or joyful. Reinforcement and repetition are crucial, according to behaviorists. Social learning begins in infancy.

12. Cognitive theory holds that infants develop working models based on their experiences. A person's ideas about life, originating in infancy, can change with later experiences.

Infant Day Care

13. The impact of nonmaternal care depends on many factors; it varies from one nation, one family, and even one child to another. Although center care advances cognition, concerns have been raised in the United States that it may increase the rate of externalizing problems.

14. Nations vary in funding for maternal leave, and for early education, and that affects infants when they enter day care and the quality of that care. In some nations, such as Norway, most 1-year-olds are in public center care; in other nations, no infant is.

15. Although each theory has a somewhat different emphasis, all agree that quality of care (responsive, individualized) is crucial, particularly in infancy, no matter who provides that care.

KEY TERMS

social smile (p. 130)

separation anxiety (p. 130)

stranger wariness (p. 130)

self-awareness (p. 132)

temperament (p. 135)

synchrony (p. 137)

still-face technique (p. 138)

attachment (p. 139)

secure attachment (p. 140)

insecure-avoidant attachment (p. 140)

insecure-resistant/ambivalent attachment (p. 140)

disorganized attachment (p. 140)

Strange Situation (p. 141)

social referencing (p. 146)

allocare (p. 147)

trust versus mistrust (p. 151)

autonomy versus shame and doubt (p. 151)

social learning (p. 152)

proximal parenting (p. 152)

distal parenting (p. 152)

working model (p. 153)

APPLICATIONS

1. One cultural factor influencing infant development is how infants are carried from place to place. Ask four mothers whose infants were born in each of the past four decades how they transported them—front or back carriers, facing out or in, strollers or carriages, in car seats or on mother's laps, and so on. Why did they choose the mode(s) they chose? What are their opinions and yours on how such cultural practices might affect infants' development?

2. Video synchrony for three minutes. Ideally, ask the parent of an infant under 8 months of age to play with the infant. If no infant is available, observe a pair of lovers as they converse. Note the sequence and timing of every facial expression, sound, and gesture of both partners, and analyze what you see.

3. Contact several day-care centers to try to assess the quality of care they provide. Ask about factors such as adult/child ratio, group size, and training for caregivers of children of various ages. Is there a minimum age for infants? For caregivers? Why or why not? Analyze the answers, using Table 4.3 as a guide.

PART THREE

Early Childhood

From ages 2 to 6, young children spend most of their waking hours discovering, creating, laughing, and imagining, as they acquire the skills they need. They chase each other and attempt new challenges (developing their bodies); they play with sounds, words, and ideas (developing their minds); they invent games and dramatize fantasies (learning social skills and morals)—all under the guidance of their families and communities.

These years are sometimes called the *preschool years,* but that term has become a misnomer. Millions of 2- to 6-year-olds go every day to a place where they learn, which is what *school* means, so young children are not necessarily *pre*-schoolers.

Children are active learners from birth on: Ages 2 to 6 are prime time for new ideas, language advances, and education, all while playing and growing. Consequently, this period is best called *early childhood,* a joyful time for young children and for anyone who joins them.

CLAUDIA DEWALD/GETTY IMAGES

CHAPTER OUTLINE

Body and Mind

CHAPTER 5

WHAT WILL YOU KNOW?

- Why are some young children overweight?
- How should adults answer when children ask, "Why?"
- Does it confuse young children if they hear two or more languages?
- What do children learn in early education?

When I was 4, I jumped off the back of our couch again and again, trying to fly. I tried it with and without a cape, with and without flapping my arms. My laughing mother wondered whether she had made a mistake in letting me see *Peter Pan*. An older woman warned that jumping would hurt my uterus. I didn't know what a uterus was, I didn't heed that lady, and I didn't stop until I concluded that I could not fly because I had no pixie dust.

When you were 4, I hope you also wanted to fly and someone laughed while keeping you safe. Protection, appreciation, and fantasy are all needed in early childhood. Do you remember trying to skip, climb a tree, or write your name? Young children try, fail, and try again.

Imagination is strong and wonderful, language explodes, but logic (such the consequences of having no wings) and some words (such as *uterus*) are difficult. Advances in body and mind are themes of this chapter. Amazing growth and remarkable learning are all described. ■

Body Changes

In early childhood, as in infancy, the body and mind develop according to powerful epigenetic forces. This means that nature and nurture continually interact: Growth is biologically driven and socially guided, experience-expectant and experience-dependent.

KATRINA WITTKAMP/GETTY IMAGES

Size and Balance These cousins are only four years apart, but note the doubling in leg length and marked improvement in balance. The 2-year-old needs to plant both legs on the sand, while the 6-year-old cavorts on one foot.

Growth Patterns

Visualize an unsteady 24-month-old and a cartwheeling 6-year-old. Size and shape differences are obvious. Weight and height increase (by about 16 pounds and a foot, almost 8 kilograms and 30 centimeters), and the relation between those two measurements changes. The average body mass index (BMI, a ratio of weight to height) is lower at ages 5 and 6 than at any other time of life.

By the end of early childhood, the infant's protruding belly, round face, short limbs, and large head are distant memories. The center of gravity has moved from the breast to the belly, enabling cartwheels, somersaults, and many other motor skills.

Catching Up, Slimming Down
China has transformed its economy and family life since 1950 with far fewer poor families and malnourished children. Instead, problems and practices of the West are becoming evident, as in these two boys. They are attending a weight-loss camp in Zhengzhou, where the average 8- to 14-year-old child loses 14 pounds in a month.

Mastery of gross and fine motor skills results not only from body growth and maturation but also from extensive, active play. Children take every opportunity to exercise their bodies, and the results are obvious. Many 2-year-olds fall down and bump clumsily into each other. By contrast, some 5-year-olds are skilled and graceful.

Most North American 5-year-olds can ride a tricycle, climb a ladder, and pump a swing, as well as throw, catch, and kick a ball. Some 5-year-olds swim in oceans or climb cliffs. Brain maturation, motivation, and guided practice undergird all these motor skills.

Adults need to make sure children have a safe space to play, with ample time, appropriate equipment, and active playmates. Children learn best from peers who demonstrate whatever the child is ready to try. Of course, culture and locale influence particulars: Some small children learn to ski, others to sail.

"Safe space to play" cannot be taken for granted. A century ago, children with varied skills played together in empty lots or fields without adult supervision, but now more than half the world's children live in cities, often with crowded streets and no open space nearby. Gone are the days when parents told their children to go out and play, to return when hunger, rain, or nightfall brought them home. Now many parents fear strangers and traffic, keeping their 3- to 5-year-olds inside (Rosin, 2014; R. Taylor et al., 2009).

That worries many childhood educators, who believe that children need space and freedom to play in order to develop well. Indeed, many agree that the environment is the third teacher, "because the environment is viewed as another teacher having the power to enhance children's sense of wonder and capacity for learning" (Stremmel, 2012, p. 136). Nature outdoors allows more wonder than four walls inside.

Nutrition

Beyond space to play, another prerequisite for healthy development is good nutrition. Children are sometimes malnourished, even in nations with abundant food. The main reason is that small appetites are often satiated by unhealthy foods, crowding out needed vitamins.

Appetite decreases between ages 2 and 6 because young children naturally grow more slowly than they did as infants. Moreover, if children play less outside, they burn fewer calories. Instead of adjusting to this ecological change, many adults cajole, threaten, and bribe ("Eat all your dinner and you can have ice cream").

Why do adults do that? Because they are still protecting children against famine. For example, 30 years ago in Brazil the most common nutritional problem was lack of food; now it is too much food (Monteiro et al., 2004). Low-income Brazilians are particularly vulnerable, but wealthy Brazilians also consume fewer nutrients, with more calories, than they once did (Monteiro et al., 2011).

There is good news in the United States, however. Obesity among young children has declined markedly, from 14 percent in 2003–2004 to 8 percent in 2011–2012. Rates have not budged for other age groups, but apparently public education combined with parental action has improved diet for the young (Ogden et al., 2014).

"I'm not hungry, I ate with Rover."

Eat Your Veggies On their own, children do not always eat wisely.

NUTRITIONAL DEFICIENCIES Compared with the average child, those who eat more dark-green and orange vegetables and less fried food gain bone mass but not fat. This was demonstrated in a study that controlled for factors that might correlate with body fat, such as gender (girls have more), ethnicity (Chinese children are genetically thinner), and income (poor children have worse diets) (Wosje et al., 2010).

However, it is not easy to get 2- to 6-year-olds to eat well. One complication is that many young children are compulsive about daily routine, which may result in a very limited diet. Fortunately, as a team of experts contends, "Most, if not all, children exhibit normal age-dependent obsessive-compulsive behaviors [that are] usually gone by middle childhood" (March et al., 2004, p. 216). Meanwhile, however, children insist on only certain foods.

Parents need to balance their concern for good nutrition with the child's demand for sameness. This is another reason why toddlers need to be fed a variety of healthy foods, including some that are not the family's usual fare, before the child refuses anything new.

Apples or Oranges? During early childhood, boys and girls love having a choice, so it is the adults' task to offer good options. Which book before bed? Which colored shirt before school? Which healthy snack before going out to play?

FOOD ALLERGIES An added complication is that about 8 percent of U.S. children are allergic to a specific food, often a healthy one. Cow's milk, eggs, peanuts, tree nuts (almonds, walnuts, etc.), soy, wheat, fish, and shellfish are the usual culprits.

For some foods, the allergic reaction is a rash or an upset stomach when too much of the food is consumed, but for others—especially peanuts or shellfish—the reaction is sudden shock and shortness of breath that could be fatal (Dyer et al., 2015).

Some experts advocate total avoidance of the offending food—there are peanut-free schools, where no one may bring a peanut-butter sandwich for lunch. Other experts suggest that tolerance should be gradually increased, such as giving babies a tiny bit of peanut butter under close medical supervision (O'Keefe et al., 2014; Du Toit et al., 2015).

Everyone agrees that when a child has a severe allergic reaction, someone should immediately inject epinephrine to stop the reaction. In 2012, all Chicago schools had EpiPens, which were used in dozens of emergencies (DeSantiago-Cardenas et al., 2015).

ORAL HEALTH Not surprisingly, tooth decay correlates with obesity; both result from too much sugar and too little fiber (Hayden et al., 2013). Sweetened beverages are usually the problem.

"Baby" teeth are replaced naturally from ages 6 to 10. The schedule is genetic, with girls a few months ahead of boys. However, the habit of tooth brushing and a visit to the dentist should begin years before the permanent teeth erupt. Poor oral health in early childhood harms those permanent teeth (forming below the first teeth) and can cause jaw malformation, chewing difficulties, and speech problems.

Teeth are affected by diet and illness, which means that the state of a young child's teeth can alert the doctor or dentist to other health problems. The process works in reverse as well: Infected teeth can affect the rest of the child's body.

Necessary Radiation? We do not know. Every young child should visit a dentist, and those with damaged "baby" teeth (often by too much sugar) need diagnosis and treatment. However, whether 4-year-olds with healthy teeth need routine x-rays is controversial.

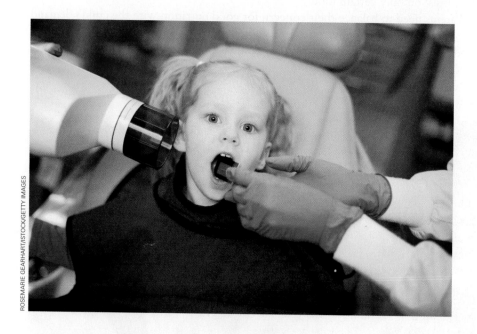

ROSEMARIE GEARHART/ISTOCK/GETTY IMAGES

Brain Development

The 2-year-old's brain already weighs 75 percent of what it will weigh in adulthood; the 6-year-old's brain is 90 percent of adult weight. (The major structures of the brain are diagrammed in Figure 5.1.)

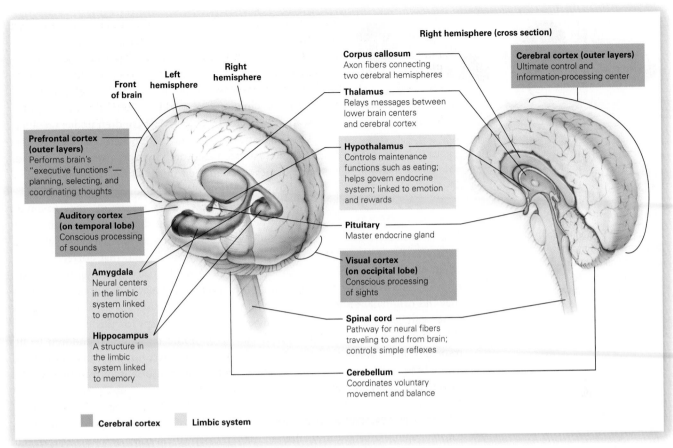

FIGURE 5.1 Brain Complexity Neuroscientists have named and studied literally hundreds of parts of the brain, all of which are connected to other parts. This depiction shows only a few crucial structures.

Although the brains and bodies of other animals are better than humans in some ways (chimpanzees can climb trees earlier and faster, for instance, and dogs can hear and smell better), no other animal has the intellectual capacities that humans do. From an evolutionary perspective, our brains allowed the human species to develop "a mode of living built on social cohesion, cooperation and efficient planning . . . survival of the smartest seems more accurate than survival of the fittest" (Corballis, 2011, p. 194).

MATURATION OF THE PREFRONTAL CORTEX One major difference between human brains and the brains of other animals is a much larger frontal lobe, the site of the prefrontal cortex. That part of the brain supports what is called **executive function,** which is planning, reasoning, and anticipating. Executive function advances throughout childhood, including between ages 2 and 6. As a result:

- Sleep becomes more regular.
- Emotions become more nuanced and responsive.
- Temper tantrums subside.
- Uncontrollable laughter and tears are less common.

A convincing demonstration that something in the brain, not simply in experience, underlies these changes comes from a series of experiments with shapes and colors.

executive function
The cognitive ability to organize and prioritize the many thoughts that arise from the various parts of the brain, allowing the person to anticipate, strategize, and plan behavior.

Matching Should these trucks and flowers be matched by shape or color? Children can do both, but they stick to one way or the other until age 4, when some flexibility is possible.

First, young children are presented with cards that have trucks or flowers, some red and some blue. They are asked to "play the shape game," putting trucks in one pile and flowers in another. Three-year-olds (and even some 2-year-olds) can do this correctly (see figure).

Then children are asked to "play the color game," sorting the cards by color. Most children under age 4 fail. Instead, they sort by shape, as they had done before. This basic test has been replicated in many nations; 3-year-olds usually get stuck in their initial sorting pattern. By age 5 (and sometimes age 4), most children make the switch.

When this result was first obtained, experimenters thought perhaps the children didn't have enough experience to know their colors; so the scientists switched the order, first playing "the color game." Most 3-year-olds did that correctly. Then, when asked to play "the shape game," they still sorted by color! Even with a new set of cards, such as yellow and green or rabbits and boats, 3-year-olds still tend to sort as they did originally, either by color or shape.

Researchers are looking into many possible explanations for this puzzling result (Marcovitch et al., 2010; Ramscar et al., 2013). Some try to teach children to be more advanced in this skill (Perone et al., 2015). All agree, however, that something in the brain matures at about age 4 that enables children to switch from one way of sorting objects to another.

THE BRAIN'S CONNECTED HEMISPHERES One part of the brain that grows and myelinates rapidly during early childhood is the **corpus callosum,** a long, thick band of nerve fibers that connects the left and right sides of the brain. Growth of the corpus callosum makes communication between the hemispheres more efficient, allowing children to coordinate the two sides of their brains and hence, both sides of their bodies.

Each side of the body and brain specializes. This is **lateralization:** literally, "sidedness." The entire human body is lateralized, apparent not only in handedness but also in the feet, the eyes, the ears, and the brain itself. People prefer to kick a ball, wink an eye, or listen on the phone with their preferred foot, eye, or ear. Genes, prenatal hormones, and early experiences all affect which side does what. Lateralization advances with development of the corpus callosum (Kolb & Whishaw, 2013).

Serious disorders result when the corpus callosum fails to develop, which leads to many deficits, including intellectual disability (Cavalari & Donovick, 2014). Undeveloped corpus callosum is one of several possible causes of autism spectrum disorder (Frazier et al., 2012; Floris et al., 2013).

corpus callosum
A long, thick band of nerve fibers that connects the left and right hemispheres of the brain and allows communication between them.

lateralization
Literally, sidedness, referring to the specialization in certain functions by each side of the brain, with one side dominant for each activity.

THE LEFT-HANDED CHILD Lateralization seems to begin with genes. Some newborns already show signs of preferring one side or the other (Ratnarajah et al., 2013), although some infants can switch.

Many cultures try to make every child right-handed, with some success. Left-handed children can be taught to write right-handedly. But their brains are only partly reprogrammed; they may use their left hand to comb their hair, throw a ball, or wield a hammer.

Many cultures imply that being right-handed is best, an example of the *difference-equals-deficit error,* explained in Chapter 1. Consider language: In English, no one wants to have "two left feet" or to be "out in left field." In Latin, *dexter* (as in *dexterity*) means "right" and *sinister* means "left" (and also "evil"). Many languages are written from left to right, which is easier for right-handed people.

The design of doorknobs, scissors, baseball mitts, instrument panels, and other objects favor the right hand. (Some manufacturers have special versions for lefties, but few young children know to ask for them.) In many Asian and African cultures, only the left hand is used for wiping after defecation; it is an insult to give someone anything with that "dirty" hand.

For many reasons, developmentalists advise against switching a child's handedness. A disproportionate number of artists, musicians, political leaders, and sports stars were/are left-handed, including Pele, Babe Ruth, Monica Seles, Bill Gates, Oprah Winfrey, Jimi Hendrix, Lady Gaga, and Justin Bieber. Five of the past six U.S. Presidents were/are lefties: Gerald Ford, Ronald Reagan, George H.W. Bush, Bill Clinton, and Barack Obama. This list does not prove that left-handedness is better, but it implies that adults are foolish to try to change a natural lefty.

Smarter Than Most? Beware of stereotypes. Obviously, this student is a girl, Asian, left-handed, and attending a structured school (note the uniform). Each of these four characteristics leads some to conclude that she is more intelligent than other 7-year-olds. But all children have brains with the potential to learn: Specific teaching, not innate characteristics, is crucial.

STOCKBYTE/GETTY IMAGES

Fortunately, left-handedness is more accepted now than a century ago. Consequently, more adults in Great Britain and the United States claim to be left-handed today (about 10 percent) than in 1900 (about 3 percent) (McManus et al., 2010).

THE WHOLE BRAIN Typically, the brain's left half controls the body's right side as well as areas dedicated to logical reasoning, detailed analysis, and the basics of language. The brain's right half controls the body's left side and areas dedicated to emotional and creative impulses, including appreciation of music, art, and poetry.

This left–right distinction has been exaggerated, especially when broadly applied to people (Hugdahl & Westerhausen, 2010). No one is exclusively left-brained or right-brained (except individuals with severe brain damage). Indeed, especially in the early years, the plasticity of the brain allows a lost function in one hemisphere to be replaced in the other half.

Usually, both sides of the brain are involved in every skill. That is why the maturation of the corpus callosum is crucial. For example, no 2-year-old can hop on one foot, but most 6-year-olds can—an example of brain balancing. At every age, logic (left brain) without emotion (right brain) is a severe impairment, as is the reverse (Damasio, 2012).

FASTER THINKING Another significant brain development in early childhood is increased **myelination,** as the axons of the brain increase in *myelin* (the *white matter* of the brain), a fatty coating that speeds signals between neurons (see Figure 5.2).

Although myelination continues for decades, the effects are especially apparent in early childhood (Silk & Wood, 2011). The areas of the brain that show the greatest early myelination are the motor and sensory areas (Kolb & Whishaw, 2013), so preschoolers react more quickly to sounds and sights with every passing year.

Speed of thought from axon to neuron becomes pivotal when several thoughts must occur in rapid succession. By age 6, most children can see an object and immediately name it, catch a ball and throw it, write their ABCs in proper sequence,

myelination
The process by which axons become coated with myelin, a fatty substance that speeds the transmission of nerve impulses from neuron to neuron.

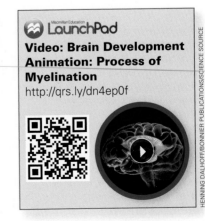

LaunchPad
Video: Brain Development Animation: Process of Myelination
http://qrs.ly/dn4ep0f

HENNING DALHOFF/BONNIER PUBLICATIONS/SCIENCE SOURCE

FIGURE 5.2 Mental Coordination? This brain scan of a 38-year-old depicts areas of myelination (the various colors) within the brain. As you see, the two hemispheres are quite similar, but not identical. For most important skills and concepts, both halves of the brain are activated.

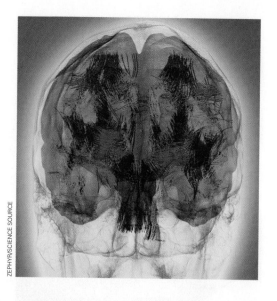

ZEPHYR/SCIENCE SOURCE

and so on. In fact, rapid naming of letters and objects—possible only when myelination is extensive—is a crucial indicator of later reading ability (Shanahan & Lonigan, 2010).

Of course, adults must be patient when listening to young children talk, helping them get dressed, or watching them write each letter of their names. Everything is done more slowly by 6-year-olds than by 16-year-olds because the younger children's brains have less myelination, which slows information processing.

IMPULSIVENESS AND PERSEVERATION Neurons have only two kinds of impulses: on–off or activate–inhibit. Each is signaled by biochemical messages from dendrites to axons to neurons. Both activation and inhibition are necessary for thoughtful adults, who neither leap too quickly nor hesitate too long. A balanced brain is best throughout life: One sign of cognitive loss is when an older person becomes too cautious or too impulsive.

© SKIP O'ROURKE/TAMPA BAY TIMES/ZUMAPRESS.COM

Ashes to Ashes, Dust to Dust Many religious rituals have sustained humans of all ages for centuries, including listening quietly in church on Ash Wednesday—as Nailah Pierre tries to do. Sitting quietly is developmentally difficult for young children, but for three reasons she probably will succeed: (1) gender (girls mature earlier than boys), (2) experience (she has been in church many times), and (3) social context (she is one of 750 students in her school attending a special service at Nativity Catholic church).

"I would share, but I'm not there developmentally."

BARBARA SMALLER/THE NEW YORKER COLLECTION/CARTOONBANK.COM

Good Excuse It is true that emotional control of selfish instincts is difficult for young children because the prefrontal cortex is not yet mature enough to regulate some emotions. However, family practices can advance social understanding.

Many young children are notably unbalanced. They are impulsive, flitting from one activity to another. Some 5-year-olds cannot stay quietly on one task, even in "circle time" in kindergarten, when they are supposed to sit quietly in place, not talking or touching anyone. Poor **impulse control** signifies a personality disorder in adulthood but not in early childhood.

Some preschoolers have the opposite problem: It is hard to get them to switch from one task to another. That tendency is called **perseveration,** when a person perseveres, or sticks to, one thought or action. Perseveration was evident in the card-sorting study just described (Hanania, 2010); it also is evident when a child bursts into tears when it is time to stop playing (a five-minute warning may help).

Perseveration may make a young child repeat one question again and again. A tantrum that occurs when a child is told to put away a toy may itself perseverate, because the crying does not stop even if the reason for it stops. Crying may become uncontrollable because the child is stuck in the emotion. On a happier note, some young children start laughing and then cannot stop!

Impulsiveness and perseveration are opposite manifestations of the same underlying cause: immaturity of the prefrontal cortex. No young child is perfect at regulating attention; impulsiveness and perseveration are evident. A longitudinal study of children from ages 3 to 6 found a steady increase in ability to pay attention, which led to more learning and better emotional control (fewer outbursts or tears) (L. Metcalfe et al., 2013).

Children with attention-deficit/hyperactivity disorder (ADHD) are too impulsive for their age. An imbalance between the left and right sides of the prefrontal cortex and abnormal growth of the corpus callosum seem to underlie ADHD (Gilliam et al., 2011).

EMOTIONS AND THE BRAIN Now we turn to another region of the brain, sometimes called the *limbic system,* the major system for emotions. Emotional expression and regulation advance during early childhood because of three parts of the limbic system—the amygdala, hippocampus, and hypothalamus.

impulse control
The ability to postpone or deny an immediate response to an idea or behavior.

perseveration
The tendency to persevere in, or stick to, one thought or action for a long time.

amygdala
A tiny brain structure that registers emotions, particularly fear and anxiety.

hippocampus
A brain structure that is a central processor of memory.

hypothalamus
A brain area that responds to the amygdala and the hippocampus as well as various experiences to produce hormones that activate the pituitary and other parts of the brain and body.

The **amygdala** is a tiny structure deep in the brain, about the same shape and size as an almond. It registers emotions, both positive and negative, especially fear (Kolb & Whishaw, 2013). Increased amygdala activity is one reason some young children have terrifying nightmares or sudden terrors, overwhelming the prefrontal cortex. A child may refuse to enter an elevator or may be hysterical, half-awake with a bad dream.

Another structure in the emotional network is the **hippocampus,** located next to the amygdala. A central processor of memory, especially memory for locations, the hippocampus responds to the fears from the amygdala by summoning memory. A child can remember, for instance, whether previous elevator riding was scary or fun.

Early memories of location are fragile because the hippocampus is still developing. Even in adulthood, emotional memories from early childhood can interfere with rational thinking: An adult might have a panic attack but not know why.

A third part of the limbic system, the **hypothalamus,** responds to signals from the amygdala (arousing) and from the hippocampus (usually dampening) by producing cortisol, oxytocin, and other hormones that activate the brain and body (see Figure 5.3). Ideally, this occurs in moderation. Both temperament and parental responses affect whether or not the hypothalamus will overreact, making the preschooler overly anxious—as about 20 percent of 4- to 7-year-olds are (Paulus et al., 2014).

As the limbic system develops, young children watch their parents' emotions closely. If a parent looks worried when entering an elevator, the child may cling to the parent when the elevator moves. If this recurs often, the child may become hypersensitive to elevators, as fear from the amygdala joins memories from the hippocampus, increasing cortisol production via the hypothalamus.

If, instead, the parent makes elevator-riding fun (letting the child push the buttons, for instance), initial fears subside. The child's brain will be aroused to enter elevators—even when there is no need to go from floor to floor.

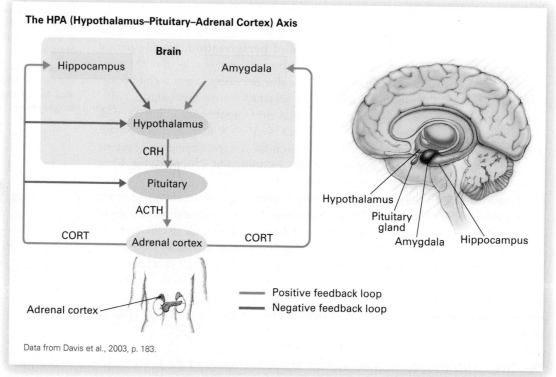

Data from Davis et al., 2003, p. 183.

FIGURE 5.3 From Brain to Body Neuroscientists have traced interaction of several parts of the brain that often work in harmony. As you see from the HPA axis, both on and off (positive and negative) chemical messages from various brain regions contribute to every emotion, thought, and movement.

Knowing the varieties of fears and joys is helpful when an adult takes a group of young children on a trip. To stick with the elevator example, one child might be terrified while another child might rush forward, pushing the "close" button before the teacher enters.

THINK CRITICALLY: How might an understanding of brain development help a teacher who takes 3- to 6-year-olds to visit a fire station?

WHAT HAVE YOU LEARNED?

1. How are growth rates, body proportions, and motor skills related during early childhood?
2. Why do many children in developed nations suffer from malnutrition?
3. What is changing in rates of early childhood obesity and why?
4. When (if ever) and why should a left-handed toddler be changed to a right-handed child?
5. What do children need to learn various motor skills?
6. How does myelination advance skill development?
7. How is the corpus callosum crucial for learning?
8. What do impulse control and perseveration have in common?
9. What is the limbic system?
10. What is the amygdala?
11. What does the hippocampus do?
12. What does the hypothalamus do?

preoperational intelligence
Piaget's term for cognitive development between the ages of about 2 and 6; it includes language and imagination (which involve symbolic thought), but not yet logical, operational thinking.

symbolic thought
In preoperational intelligence, understanding that words can refer to things not seen and that an item, such as a flag, can symbolize something else (in this case, a country).

animism
The belief that natural objects and phenomena are alive in the way that humans are, as in a rock having emotions and a spirit.

Thinking During Early Childhood

You have just learned that every year of early childhood advances motor skills, brain development, and impulse control. That allows impressive, multi-contextual learning, as described by Piaget, Vygotsky, and many others.

Piaget: Preoperational Thought

Preoperational intelligence is the second of Piaget's four periods of cognitive development (described in Table 1.6 on p. 29). He used the prefix *pre-* because children do not yet use logical operations (reasoning processes) (Inhelder & Piaget, 1964/2013a).

Because they are no longer simply sensorimotor, however, young children have language. Knowing words enables **symbolic thought,** when an object or word can stand for something else, including something out of sight or imagined. Words are used to symbolize an object or action; a child can talk about a dog without seeing the actual dog.

Symbolic thought helps explain **animism,** the belief of many young children that natural objects (such as a tree or a cloud) are alive and that nonhuman animals have the same characteristics as the child. Many children's stories include animals or objects that talk and listen (Aesop's fables, *Winnie-the-Pooh, Goodnight Moon, The Day the Crayons Quit*). Childish animism gradually disappears with maturation (Kesselring & Müller, 2011).

Can Fish Talk? Of course they can. As every preschooler who watches *Finding Nemo* knows, some fish talk and help each other, just like egocentric children do.

© WALT DISNEY/COURTESY EVERETT COLLECTION

centration
A characteristic of preoperational thought in which a young child focuses (centers) on one idea, excluding all others.

egocentrism
Piaget's term for children's tendency to think about other people and their own experiences as if everything revolves around them.

focus on appearance
A characteristic of preoperational thought in which a young child assumes that the visible appearance of someone or something is also their essence.

static reasoning
A characteristic of preoperational thought in which a young child thinks that nothing changes. Whatever is now has always been and always will be.

irreversibility
In preoperational thought, the idea that change is permanent, that nothing can be restored to the way it was before a change occurred.

conservation
The principle that the amount of a substance remains the same (i.e., is conserved) even when its appearance changes.

OBSTACLES TO LOGIC Piaget noted four limitations that make logic difficult and thus make children preoperational until about age 6. These four are centration, appearance, static reasoning, and irreversibility.

Centration is the tendency to focus (to center) on only one aspect of a situation. Young children may, for example, insist that Daddy is a father, not a brother, because they center on the role that he fills for them. The daddy example illustrates a particular type of centration that Piaget called **egocentrism**—literally, "self-centeredness." Egocentric children contemplate the world exclusively from their personal perspective.

Egocentrism is not selfishness. I encountered this with my daughter Sarah, when she was 3. We were holding hands and crossing a street.

> **Sarah:** If a car killed one of us, who would you want it to be?
> **Me:** Me.
> **Sarah:** I would want it to be me.

Before I could appreciate what seemed to be her unselfishness, she matter-of-factly gave an egocentric reason.

> **Sarah:** Because if you were dead, I wouldn't know how to get home.

A second characteristic of preoperational thought is a **focus on appearance** to the exclusion of other attributes. For instance, a girl given a short haircut might worry that she has turned into a boy. In preoperational thought, a thing is whatever it appears to be—evident in the joy children have in wearing the shoes of a grown-up, clomping noisily and unsteadily.

Third, preoperational children use **static reasoning.** They believe that the world is stable, unchanging, always in the state in which they currently encounter it. Many children cannot imagine that their own parents were ever children.

If they grasp that their grandmother is their mother's mother because they are repeatedly told, they still cannot imagine how the parent–child relationship changes with age. One young boy told his grandmother to tell his mother to never spank him because "she has to do what her mother says."

The fourth characteristic of preoperational thought is **irreversibility.** Preoperational thinkers fail to recognize that reversing a process sometimes restores whatever existed before. A young girl might cry because her mother put lettuce on her sandwich, rejecting it after the lettuce is removed because she believes that what is done cannot be undone.

CONSERVATION AND LOGIC Piaget demonstrated several ways in which preoperational intelligence disregards logic. A famous set of experiments involved **conservation,** the notion that the amount of something remains the same (is *conserved*) despite changes in its appearance.

Easy Question; Obvious Answer
(below, left) Sadie, age 5, carefully makes sure both glasses contain the same amount. *(below, right)* When one glass of pink lemonade is poured into a wide jar, she triumphantly points to the tall glass as having more. Sadie is like all 5-year-olds; 7-year-olds know better.

The classic test of conservation begins with two identical glasses containing the same amount of liquid. Then the liquid from one glass is poured into a taller, narrower glass. Ask a child whether one glass contains more or both glasses contain the same. Preoperational children insist that the narrow glass (with the higher level) has more. (Figure 5.4 shows other examples.)

All four characteristics of preoperational thought are evident in this mistake. Young children fail to understand conservation because they focus (*center*) on what they see (*appearance*), noticing only the immediate (*static*) condition. It does not occur to them that they could reverse the process and re-create the level of a moment earlier (*irreversibility*).

Piaget's original tests of conservation required children to respond verbally to adult questions. Later research has found that when the tests are simplified or made playful, young children may succeed, perhaps indicating via eye movements or gestures what they know before they put it in words (Goldin-Meadow & Alibali, 2013).

As with sensorimotor intelligence, Piaget underestimated preoperational children. Brain scans, video responses measured in milliseconds, and modern computer analysis were not available to Piaget. Although he was perceptive about children's thinking, recent studies show much more early intellectual activity than Piaget described (Crone & Ridderinkhof, 2011).

Conservation and many more logical ideas are understood bit by bit, with active curiosity. Glimmers of understanding are apparent even at age 4 (Sophian, 2013). But preschoolers' social network is limited. They rely heavily on their own experience, on their parents, and on simple rules governing behavior (Lane & Harris, 2014). Because of their cognitive limits, smart 3-year-olds sometimes are foolish, as Caleb is.

Video Activity: Achieving Conservation focuses on the changes in thinking that make it possible for older children to pass Piaget's conservation-of-liquid task.

Tests of Various Types of Conservation

Type of Conservation	Initial Presentation	Transformation	Question	Preoperational Child's Answer
Volume	Two equal glasses of liquid.	Pour one into a taller, narrower glass.	Which glass contains more?	The taller one.
Number	Two equal lines of checkers.	Increase spacing of checkers in one line.	Which line has more checkers?	The longer one.
Matter	Two equal balls of clay.	Squeeze one ball into a long, thin shape.	Which piece has more clay?	The long one.
Length	Two sticks of equal length.	Move one stick.	Which stick is longer?	The one that is farther to the right.

FIGURE 5.4 One Logical Concept (Conservation), Many Manifestations According to Piaget, until children grasp the concept of conservation at (he believed) about age 6 or 7, they cannot understand that the transformations shown here do not change the total amount of liquid, checkers, clay, and wood.

A CASE TO STUDY

Stones in the Belly

As my grandson and I were reading a book about dinosaurs, 3-year-old Caleb told me that some dinosaurs (*sauropods*) have stones in their bellies. It helps them digest their food and then poop and pee.

I was amazed, never having known this before.

"I didn't know that dinosaurs ate stones," I said.

"They don't eat them."

"Then how do they get the stones in their bellies? They must swallow them."

"They don't eat them."

"Then how do they get in their bellies?"

"They are just there."

"How did they get there?"

"They don't eat them," said Caleb. "Stones are dirty. We don't eat them."

I dropped it, but my question apparently puzzled him. Later he asked his mother, "Do dinosaurs eat stones?"

"Yes, they eat stones so they can grind their food," she answered.

At that, Caleb was quiet.

In all of this, preoperational cognition is evident. Caleb is advanced in symbolic thought: He can name several kinds of dinosaurs. But logic eludes him. He is preoperational, not operational.

It seemed obvious to me that dinosaurs must have swallowed the stones. However, in his static thinking, Caleb said the stones "are just there."

He is egocentric, reasoning from his own experience, and animistic, in that he thinks animals would not eat stones because he does not. He trusts his mother more than me, and she told him never to eat stones, or sand from the sandbox, or food that fell on the floor. He would not trust anyone who, contrary to his mother's prohibition told him to eat those things. Consequently, he did not accept my authority: The implications of my relationship to his mother are beyond his static thinking.

But, like many young children, he is curious, and my question raised his curiosity. He consulted his authority, my daughter.

Should he have told me that I was right? He did not. That would have required far more understanding of reversibility and far less egocentrism than most young children can muster.

Vygotsky: Social Learning

For decades, scientists were understandably awed by Piaget. His description of egocentrism and magical thinking was confirmed daily by anecdotes of young children's behavior. For Western developmentalists, Vygotsky, who wrote in Russian, was unknown until about 1970 when translations began to appear.

Vygotsky emphasized another side of early cognition, the social aspects. He stressed the power of culture, acknowledging that "the culturally specific nature of experience is an integral part of how the person thinks and acts" (Gauvain et al., 2011, pp. 122–123). Learning is not done in isolation; according to many contemporary educators, it depends on joint engagement.

mentor
Someone who teaches or guides someone else, helping a learner master a skill or body of knowledge.

MENTORS AND SCAFFOLDING Vygotsky agreed with Piaget that children are curious and observant. They ask questions—about how machines work, why weather changes, where the sky ends—and seek answers from more knowledgeable sources, called mentors. A **mentor** is anyone who provides guidance—teachers, older siblings, strangers, and, especially, parents. All of them are affected by their culture, and thus culture shapes a child's cognition.

CORBIS RF/AGE FOTOSTOCK

Words Fail Me Could you describe how to tie shoes? The limitations of verbal tests of cognitive understanding are apparent in the explanation of many skills.

OBSERVATION QUIZ

What three sociocultural factors make it likely that the child pictured to the left will learn? (see answer, page 178) ◄

According to Vygotsky, "What children can do with the assistance of others might be in some sense even more indicative of their mental development than what they can do alone" (1980, p. 85). Indeed, mentors:

- Present challenges.
- Offer assistance (without taking over).
- Add crucial information.
- Encourage motivation.

A skilled mentor finds the learner's **zone of proximal development (ZPD),** an intellectual arena in which new ideas and skills can be mastered. *Proximal* means "near," so the ZPD includes whatever ideas children are close to understanding and skills they can almost master. Mentors provide **scaffolding,** or temporary support, to help learners within their zone.

For instance, scaffolding may include telling children to look both ways before crossing the street (while holding the child's hand) or letting them stir the cake batter (while covering the child's hand on the spoon handle, in guided participation). Crucial is joint engagement, with novice and mentor together in the learning zone (Adamson et al., 2014).

As always, culture is crucial. Consider book-reading, for instance, an activity parents worldwide do with their young children, in part because it fosters language, reading, and moral development. Mentors do not merely read the words, they scaffold—explaining, pointing, listening, describing—within the child's zone of development.

Comparative research finds that parents choose books carefully and then teach whatever is important to them. For example, one study found that, compared to European Americans, Chinese American parents were more likely to note how the book's characters created problems by misbehaving and Mexican Americans were more likely to highlight the characters' emotions (Luo et al., 2014).

As good mentors, parents adjust their reading to meet the developmental age of the child, first expanding vocabulary, then focusing on letters, and always listening to the child (Sénéchal & LeFevre, 2014).

Same or Different? Which do you see? Most people focus on differences, such as ethnicity or sex. But a developmental perspective appreciates similarities: book-reading to a preliterate child cradled on a parent's lap.

Count by Tens A large, attractive abacus could be a scaffold. However, in this toy store the position of the balls suggests that no mentor is nearby. Children are unlikely to grasp the number system without a motivating guide.

OBSERVATION QUIZ

Is the girl above right- or left-handed? (see answer, page 179) ▲

zone of proximal development (ZPD)
In sociocultural theory, a metaphorical area, or "zone," surrounding a learner that includes all the skills, knowledge, and concepts that the person is close ("proximal") to acquiring but cannot yet master without help.

scaffolding
Temporary support that is tailored to a learner's needs and abilities and aimed at helping the learner take the next step in learning something.

ANSWER TO OBSERVATION QUIZ
(from page 176): Motivation (this father and son are from Spain, where yellow running shoes are popular), human relationships (note the physical touching of father and son), and materials (the long laces make tying them easier). ●

OVERIMITATION Sometimes scaffolding is inadvertent, as when children observe something said or done that adults wish they had not noticed. Young children may curse and kick because someone else showed them. More benignly, children imitate meaningless habits and customs, a trait called **overimitation.** This stems from the child's eagerness to learn, allowing "rapid, high-fidelity intergenerational transmission of . . . cultural forms" (Nielsen & Tomaselli, 2010, p. 735).

Overimitation was demonstrated in a series of experiments with 3- to 6-year-olds. To understand the role of culture, the researchers studied children from three groups: 64 from San communities (pejoratively called Bushmen) in South Africa and Botswana, 64 from cities in Australia, and 19 from aboriginal communities within Australia (Nielsen & Tomaselli, 2010; Nielsen et al., 2014).

Australian adults often scaffold for children with words and actions, but San adults rarely do. The researchers expected the Australian children to follow adult demonstrations. They were surprised when San children did so also.

In part of the study, one by one some children in each group observed an adult perform irrelevant actions, such as waving a red stick above a box three times and then using that stick to push down a knob to open the box, which could be easily and more efficiently opened by pulling down the same knob by hand. Then children were given the stick and the box. No matter what their cultural background, the children followed the adult example, waving the stick three times and not using their hands directly on the knob.

Other children did not see the demonstration. When they were given the stick and asked to open the box, they simply pulled the knob. Then they observed an adult open the box with stick-waving and they did something odd: They copied those inefficient actions. Apparently, children everywhere learn from others through observation, sometimes contrary to what they know. Across cultures, overimitation is striking.

In this study, the researchers found that the urban and aboriginal Australian children followed the procedures they had just seen when given a new, similar task. The San children did not immediately apply what they had just learned, perhaps because the circumstances of their daily life (which the researchers called "dire and depressing") taught them not to do anything on their own (Nielsen et al., 2014). Or perhaps the power of their culture was so strong that they did not choose to follow the odd new procedures.

Either way, Vygotsky's stress on social context is confirmed.

Children's Theories

Piaget and Vygotsky both recognized that from birth on people strive to understand their world. No contemporary developmental scientist doubts that. How exactly do children acquire their impressive knowledge? Part of the answer is that children do more than master words and ideas; they develop theories to help them understand and remember (Baron-Cohen et al., 2013).

THEORY-THEORY Humans of all ages want explanations. That is one reason traffic slows down when there is an accident on the other side of a divided highway: People want to know what happened and why. **Theory-theory** is the idea that children naturally construct theories to explain whatever they see and hear. In other words, the theory about how children think is that they construct a theory.

> We are perpetually driven to look for deeper explanations of our experience, and broader and more reliable predictions about it. . . . Children seem, quite literally, to be born with . . . the desire to understand the world and the desire to discover how to behave in it.
>
> *[Gopnik, 2001, p. 66]*

New bits of knowledge and observations are used to make sense of experiences. Children revise their theories as new evidence accumulates (Meltzoff & Gopnik, 2013).

In order to develop a theory about what causes what and why, children notice how often a particular event occurs. They follow the same processes that scientists do: asking questions, developing hypotheses, gathering data, and drawing conclusions.

Of course, their methods lack the rigor of scientific experiments, but they explore physics, biology, and the social sciences: "infants and young children not only detect statistical patterns, they use those patterns to test hypotheses about people and things" (Gopnik, 2012, p. 1625).

Some children seem always to ask why, why, why. From the answers they develop theories. This is particularly evident in children's understanding of God. One child thought his grandpa died because God was lonely; another thought thunder occurred because God was rearranging the furniture in heaven.

As you see, a child's conclusions are not always correct. Egocentric young children theorize that everyone operates as they themselves do. Since they see themselves as always the same (static), yet they realize that their behavior changes depending on circumstances, they overestimate the role of context, and underestimate the role of personality, for other people as well.

That explains the results of a series of experiments in which children observe that one puppet refuses to play on a trampoline or ride a bicycle and another puppet does both. Four-year-olds theorize that the playing puppet must know that the trampoline is safe, not that one puppet is brave and the other fearful. By age 6, children are more able to explain behavior based on temperament, not situation (Seiver et al., 2013).

One common theory-theory is that everyone intends to do things correctly. For that reason, when asked to repeat something ungrammatical that an adult says, children often correct the grammar. They theorize that the adult intended to speak grammatically (Over & Gattis, 2010).

This illustrates a general principle: Children theorize about intentions before they imitate what they see. As you have read, when children saw an adult wave a stick before opening a box, the children theorized that, since the adult did it deliberately, stick-waving must somehow be important. If the adult seemed to do it by mistake or thoughtlessly, imitation would not occur.

THEORY OF MIND Mental processes—thoughts, emotions, beliefs, motives, and intentions—are among the most complicated and puzzling phenomena that humans encounter every day.

Adults wonder why people fall in love with the particular persons they do, why they vote for the candidates whose policies would hurt them, or why they make foolish choices—from signing for a huge mortgage to buying an overripe cucumber. Children are likewise puzzled about a playmate's unexpected anger, a sibling's generosity, or an aunt's too-wet kiss.

ANSWER TO OBSERVATION QUIZ
(from page 177): Right-handed. Her dominant hand is engaged in something more comforting than exploring the abacus. ●

Candies in the Crayon Box A classic theory-of-mind experiment begins with a child guessing what is in a box, and then sees something else. The surprise is that once a child sees that candy is inside the crayon box, he expects that everyone else will also know that candies are inside!

WORTH PUBLISHERS

theory of mind
A person's theory of what other people might be thinking. Children gradually realize that other people do not always know and think what they themselves do.

Video: Theory of Mind: False-Belief Tasks

http://qrs.ly/ba4ep0i

To understand what another person thinks, people develop a **theory of mind,** a hypothesis about what other people think and feel. Theory of mind is "essential in communities that rely heavily on the exchange of information, ideas, and points of view" (Lillard & Kavanaugh, 2014, p. 1535). That makes theory of mind crucial for human society in most places.

Theory of mind develops slowly in young children, typically emerging at about age 4 (Carlson et al., 2013). Some aspects of theory of mind develop sooner, and some later. Generally, the preschool years begin with 2-year-olds not realizing that other people think differently than they do and end with 6-year-olds aware that other minds might not know what they know (Wellman et al., 2011).

In one of dozens of false-belief tests that researchers have developed, a child watches a puppet named Max put a toy dog into a red box. Then Max leaves and the child sees the dog taken out of the red box and put in a blue box.

When Max returns, the child is asked, "Where will Max look for the dog?" Most 3-year-olds confidently say, "In the blue box"; most 6-year-olds correctly say, "In the red box," a pattern found in more than a dozen nations. Interestingly, although some cultural differences appear, the most notable differences are neurological, not cultural: Children with autism spectrum disorder are slow to develop theory of mind (Carlson et al., 2013).

The development of theory of mind can be seen when young children try to escape punishment by lying. Their face often betrays them: worried or shifting eyes, pursed lips, and so on. Parents sometimes say, "I know when you are lying," and, to the consternation of most 3-year-olds, parents are usually right.

In one experiment, 247 children, aged 3 to 5, were left alone at a table that had an upside-down cup covering dozens of candies (Evans et al., 2011). The children were told *not* to peek, and the experimenter left the room.

For 142 children (57 percent), curiosity overcame obedience. They peeked, spilling so many candies onto the table that they could not put them back under the cup. The examiner returned, asking how the candies got on the table. Only one-fourth of the participants (more often the younger ones) told the truth.

The rest lied, and their skill increased with their age. The 3-year-olds typically told hopeless lies (e.g., "The candies got out by themselves"); the 4-year-olds told unlikely lies (e.g., "Other children came in and knocked over the cup"). Some of the 5-year-olds, however, told plausible lies (e.g., "My elbow knocked over the cup accidentally").

This particular study was done in Beijing, China, but the results are universal: Older children are better liars. Beyond the age differences, the experimenters found that the more logical liars were also more advanced in theory of mind (Evans et al., 2011).

Many studies have found that a child's ability to develop theories correlates with activity in several areas of the brain (Koster-Hale & Saxe, 2014). A meta-analysis found that executive function in preschoolers led to a better understanding of false belief (as in Max and the boxes) but not vice versa (Devine & Hughes, 2014).

More evidence comes from the same 3- to 5-year-olds whose lying was studied. Researchers asked them to say "day" when they saw a picture of the moon and "night" when they saw a picture of the sun. The children needed to inhibit their automatic reaction.

This is a common measure of executive function. When compared to other children who were the same age, those who failed the day–night tests typically told impossible lies, whereas their age-mates who were high in executive function told plausible lies (Evans et al., 2011).

Of course, many egocentric children convince themselves that something is true when it is not—as do some adults. This does not mean that they are unable to recount what they see and hear, but it does mean that what any witness says may or may not be true.

A VIEW FROM SCIENCE

Witness to a Crime

One application of early cognitive competency has received attention from lawyers and judges. Children may be the only witnesses to crimes, especially of sexual abuse or of serious domestic violence. Can their accounts be trusted? Adults have gone to extremes in answering this question. As one legal discussion begins:

> Perhaps as a result of the collective guilt caused by disbelieving the true victims of abuse, there presently exists an unwavering conviction that a young child is incapable of fabricating a story of abuse, even when the tale of mistreatment is inherently incredible.
>
> *[Shanks, 2011, p. 517]*

As this quote implies, in past years children were never believed, then always believed, but neither extreme is accurate.

The answer to the question, "Can their accounts be trusted?" is: "Sometimes." People of all ages remember and misremember (Frenda et al., 2011; Lyons et al., 2010). Each age group misremembers in particular ways.

Younger children are sometimes more accurate than older witnesses who are influenced by prejudice and stereotypes (Brainerd et al., 2008). However, young children may confuse time, place, person, and action. They want to please adults, and they may lie to do so. With this in mind, developmental psychologists have developed many research-based suggestions to improve the accuracy of child witnesses (Lamb, 2014).

Words and expressions can plant false ideas in young children's minds, either deliberately (as an abuser might) or inadvertently (as a fearful parent might). Children's shaky grasp of reality makes them vulnerable to scaffolding memories that are imagined, not experienced (Bruck et al., 2006). This happened tragically 35 years ago. Some adults leapt to the conclusion that sexual abuse was rampant in preschools, and they set out to prove it.

For instance, biased questioning led 3-year-olds at Wee Care nursery school in New Jersey to convince a judge that a teacher had sexually abused them in bizarre ways (including making them lick peanut butter off her genitals) (Ceci & Bruck, 1995). In retrospect, it is amazing that any adult believed what they said. The accused were finally exonerated. Since that time, much has been learned about witnesses of all ages.

With sexual abuse in particular, a child might believe that some lewd act is OK if an adult says so. Only years later does the victim realize that it was abuse. Research on adult memory finds that adults may reinterpret what happened to them, with genuine memories of experiences that were criminal. However, people of all ages sometimes believe that an event, including abuse, occurred when it did not (Geraerts et al., 2009).

At every age, stress may scramble cognition. There is "extensive evidence of the disruptive impacts of toxic stress" (Shonkoff et al., 2012). Early in life, massive stress hormones may flood the brain and destroy part of the hippocampus, leading to permanent deficits in learning and health, causing major depressive disorder, posttraumatic stress disorder, attention-deficit/hyperactivity disorder, and distorted memories lifelong.

Generally, a balance between arousal and reassurance is needed. For instance, if children are witnesses to a crime (a stressful experience), a child's memory is more accurate when an interviewer is warm and attentive, listening carefully but not suggesting some answers instead of others (Teoh & Lamb, 2013).

When children are witnesses, they should simply be asked to tell what happened, perhaps with eyes closed to reduce their natural attempt to please (Kyriakidou et al., 2014). A stressful experience may be remembered accurately if the child's hippocampus is not damaged. No one, at any age, should be either automatically believed or disbelieved.

WHAT HAVE YOU LEARNED?

1. How does preoperational thought differ from sensorimotor and from concrete operational thought?
2. What barriers to logic exist at the preoperational stage?
3. According to Vygotsky, what should parents and other caregivers do to encourage children's learning?
4. How does scaffolding relate to a child's zone of proximal development?
5. What evidence is there that children overimitate?
6. What aspects of children's thought does theory-theory explain?
7. Before developing theory of mind, what do young children think about other people's knowledge and emotions?
8. How does theory of mind help a child interact with other people?

Video Activity: Language Acquisition in Young Children features video clips of a new sign language created by deaf Nicaraguan children and provides insights into how language evolves.

THINK CRITICALLY: What standard should be used to decide which of these five children knew the vocabulary word?

Language Learning

Brain maturation, myelination, scaffolding, and social interaction make early childhood ideal for learning language. Young children are language sponges; they soak up every verbal drop they encounter, mastering vocabulary and grammar at a rapid pace.

Preoperational thinking—egocentric and illogical—helps with language. One of the valuable (and sometimes frustrating) traits of young children is that they talk nonstop to many people and even to themselves and their toys—unfazed by misuse, mispronunciation, ignorance, stuttering, and so on (Marazita & Merriman, 2010). Egocentrism has advantages; this is one of them.

The Vocabulary Explosion

The average child knows about 500 words at age 2 and more than 10,000 at age 6 (Herschensohn, 2007). That's more than six new words a day. These are averages. Estimates of vocabulary size at age 6 vary from 5,000 to 30,000.

Estimates vary because it is hard to know how many words a child understands, in part because some tests of vocabulary are more stringent than others (Hoffman et al., 2013). For example, after children listened to a book about a raccoon that saw its reflection in the water, they were asked what *reflection* means. Which of these five answers is correct?

1. "It means that your reflection is yourself. It means that there is another person that looks just like you."
2. "Means if you see yourself in stuff and you see your reflection."
3. "Is like when you look in something, like water, you can see yourself."
4. "It mean your face go in the water."
5. "That means if you the same skin as him, you blend in" (Hoffman et al., 2013, pp. 471–472).

At About This Time: Language in Early Childhood

Approximate Age	Characteristic or Achievement in First Language
2 years	*Vocabulary:* 100–2,000 words *Sentence length:* 2–6 words *Grammar:* Plurals; pronouns; many nouns, verbs, adjectives *Questions:* Many "What's that?" questions
3 years	*Vocabulary:* 1,000–5,000 words *Sentence length:* 3–8 words *Grammar:* Conjunctions, adverbs, articles *Questions:* Many "Why?" questions
4 years	*Vocabulary:* 3,000–10,000 words *Sentence length:* 5–20 words *Grammar:* Dependent clauses, tags at sentence end (". . . didn't I?" ". . . won't you?") *Questions:* Peak of "Why?" questions; many "How?" and "When?" questions
6 years	*Vocabulary:* 5,000–30,000 words *Sentence length:* Some seem unending (". . . and . . . who . . . and . . . that . . . and . . .") *Grammar:* Complex, depending on what the child has heard, with some children correctly using the passive voice ("Man bitten by dog") and subjunctive ("If I were . . .") *Questions:* Some about social differences (male–female, old–young, rich–poor) and many other issues

In the same study, when a story included "a chill ran down his spine," children were asked what *chill* meant. One child answered, "When you want to lay down and watch TV—and eat nachos" (Hoffman et al., 2013, p. 473).

FAST-MAPPING After painstakingly learning one word at a time between 12 and 18 months of age, children develop interconnected categories for words, a kind of grid or mental map that makes speedy vocabulary acquisition possible. Learning a word after one exposure is called **fast-mapping** (Woodward & Markman, 1998) because, rather waiting to hear a word in several contexts, children hear a word once and quickly stick it into a category in their mental language grid.

Language mapping is not precise. For example, children rapidly connect new animal names to already-known animal names. Thus, *tiger* is mapped easily if you know *lion*, but a leopard might be called a tiger unless someone introduces the word *leopard*. A trip to the zoo facilitates fast-mapping because zoos scaffold, placing similar animals near each other.

fast-mapping
The speedy and sometimes imprecise way that children learn new words by quickly categorizing them.

© PAUL BROWN/DEMOTIX/CORBIS

I Want a Pet Young children are more fascinated than afraid of snakes, spiders, and—as shown here at the London Pet Show—scorpions. Although some children are temporarily cautious, phobias are learned, not innate. Many children want a pet; many adults say no. Who should prevail?

Picture books offer many opportunities to advance vocabulary through scaffolding and fast-mapping. A mentor might encourage the next steps in the child's zone of proximal development, such as that tigers have stripes and leopards spots, or, for an older child, that calico cats are almost always female and that lions with manes are always male.

This process explains some vocabulary errors. For example, 2-year-olds fast-map color words (K. Wagner et al., 2013). *Red* could be used for orange. Similarly, all women may be called mothers, all cats called kitties. As one team of scientists explains, adult words are the result of slow-mapping (K. Wagner et al., 2013), which is not what young children do.

WORDS AND THE LIMITS OF LOGIC Closely related to fast-mapping is a phenomenon called *logical extension:* After learning a word, children use it to describe other objects in the same category. One child told her father she had seen some "Dalmatian cows" on a school trip to a farm. Instead of criticizing her foolishness, he remembered the Dalmatian dog she had petted the weekend before, and he realized that she saw Holstein cows, not Jersey ones.

Bilingual children who don't know a word in the language they are speaking often insert a word from the other language. That mid-sentence switch may be considered wrong, but actually it is evidence of the child's drive to communicate. When children master theory of mind, they realize who understands which language, and they adjust when speaking to a monolingual person.

Some English words are particularly difficult for any child—*who/whom, have been/had been, here/there, yesterday/tomorrow.* More than one child has awoken on Christmas morning and asked, "Is it tomorrow yet?" A child told to "stay there" or "come here" may not follow instructions because the terms are confusing. Better to say, "Stay there on that bench" or "Come here to hold my hand." Every language has difficult concepts that are expressed in words; children everywhere learn them eventually.

Extensive study of children's language abilities finds that fast-mapping is only one of many techniques that children use to learn language. When a word does not refer to an object on the mental map, children master it in other ways (Carey, 2010). Some words are too abstract; they are ignored. Always action helps. A hole is to dig; love is hugging; hearts beat.

Acquiring Grammar

Remember from Chapter 3 that *grammar* includes structures, techniques, and rules that communicate meaning. That makes grammar essential for speaking, reading, and writing well.

BRAIN AND BASICS As soon as they start speaking, children use basic grammar, first in holophrases and then in combining words. For example, English-speaking toddlers know word order (subject/verb/object), saying, "I eat apple," rather than any of the five other possible sequences of those three words. They use plurals, tenses (past, present, and future), and nominative, objective, and possessive pronouns (*I, me,* and *mine* or *my*).

Children apply rules of grammar as soon as they figure them out. They use their own theories about how language works and use their personal experiences regarding when various rules apply (Meltzoff & Gopnik, 2013).

For example, toddlers learn to add *s* to form the plural, asking for cookies, blocks, and so on. Soon children add an *s* to make the plural of words they have never heard before. If preschoolers are shown a drawing of an abstract shape, told it is called a *wug,* and then shown two of these shapes, they say there are two *wugs* (Berko, 1958).

Children apply the rules of grammar when they should not. This error is called **overregularization.** By age 4, many children overregularize that final *s,* talking about *foots, tooths,* and *mouses.* This signifies knowledge, not ignorance. They are smart enough to apply the rules of grammar (Ramscar & Dye, 2011). The child who says, "I goed to the store" needs to hear, "Oh, you went to the store?" rather than criticism.

More difficult to learn is an aspect of language called **pragmatics**—knowing which words, tones, and grammatical forms to use with whom (Siegal & Surian, 2012). In some languages, it is essential to know which set of words to use when a person is older or not a close friend or family member, or even which grandparents are their fathers' parents and which grandparents are their mothers'.

In English, knowledge of pragmatics is evident when a 4-year-old pretends to be a doctor, a teacher, or a parent. Each role requires different speech, an early sign that theory of mind is beginning (Lillard & Kavanaugh, 2014).

However, pragmatics takes years to develop; adults certainly do not always adjust their communication to their audience. Young children are worse at this. Without an understanding of how other people might think, children often blurt out questions that embarrass their parents ("Why is that lady so fat?" or "I won't kiss grandpa

overregularization
Applying rules of grammar even when exceptions occur, making the language seem more "regular" than it actually is.

pragmatics
The practical use of language, adjusting communication according to audience and context.

because his breath smells."). The pragmatics of polite speech require more understanding than many young children possess.

Learning Two Languages

Language-minority people (those who speak a language that is not their nation's dominant one) suffer if they do not also speak the majority language. In the United States, those who are not proficient in English often have lower school achievement, diminished self-esteem, and inadequate employment, as well as many other problems. Fluency in English can erase these liabilities; fluency in another language then becomes an asset.

In the United States, 15 percent of children entering kindergarten in 2011 spoke a language other than English at home (Mulligan et al., 2014). Some already speak English, and most of them learn English at school, but their achievement tends to be lower unless they are bilingual before age 6. By contrast, in many African, Asian, and European nations, most schoolchildren are bilingual, and some are trilingual, and their fluency advances their intellectual achievement.

Some adults fear that young children who are taught two languages might become semilingual, not bilingual, "at risk for delayed, incomplete, and possibly even impaired language development" (Genesee, 2008, p. 17). Others have used their own experience to argue the opposite, that "there is absolutely no evidence that children get confused if they learn two languages" (Genesee, 2008, p. 18).

This second position has much more research support. Soon after the vocabulary explosion, children who have heard two languages since birth usually master two distinct sets of words and grammar, along with each language's pauses, pronunciations, intonations, and gestures. Proficiency is directly related to how much language they hear (Hoff et al., 2012).

Early childhood is the best time to learn languages. Neuroscience finds that when adults mastered two languages when they were young, both languages are located in the same areas of the brain with no impact on the cortex structure (Klein et al., 2014). Bilingual adults keep the two languages separate, activating one and temporarily inhibiting the other when speaking to a monolingual person. They may be a millisecond slower to respond when they switch languages, but their brains function better overall.

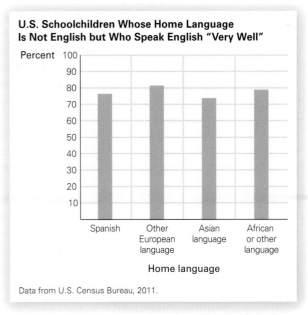

U.S. Schoolchildren Whose Home Language Is Not English but Who Speak English "Very Well"

Data from U.S. Census Bureau, 2011.

FIGURE 5.5 Mastering English: The Younger, the Better Of all the schoolchildren whose home language is not English, this is the proportion who, according to their parents, speak English well. Immigrant children who attend school almost always master English within five years.

Camels Protected, People Confused Why the contrasting signs? Does everyone read English at the international airport in Chicago (O'Hare) but not on the main road in Tunisia?

Far worse is learning no language, as happened to many deaf children in former years when teaching sign language was thought to be detrimental. Instead of learning signs and then learning to read a spoken language as deaf children now do, they were confused and lost. Current evidence suggests that early learning of one language, including sign language, makes it easier to learn other languages (Skotara et al., 2012).

Most published research finds that being bilingual benefits the brain lifelong, further evidence for plasticity. Indeed, the bilingual brain may provide some resistance to Alzheimer's disease in old age (Costa & Sebastián-Gallés, 2014). However, some scholars contend that evidence is mixed on the cognitive advantages of bilingualism, noting that the published research may not represent the complexity of this issue (de Bruin et al., 2015).

In any case, learning a "foreign" language in high school or college, as required of most U.S. children, is too late for fluency. After childhood, the logic of a new language can be understood: Adults can learn the rules of forming the past tense, for instance. However, pronunciation, idioms, and exceptions to the rules are confusing and rarely mastered after puberty. The human brain is designed to learn language best from ages 2 to 6.

Note, however, that many adults who speak the majority language with an accent are nonetheless proficient in comprehension and literacy in that language (difference is not deficit). From infancy on, hearing is more acute than speaking. Almost all young children mispronounce whatever language they speak, blithely unaware of their mistakes. With maturation, pronunciation improves—if a child has heard proper pronunciation in childhood.

LANGUAGE LOSS AND GAINS Schools in all nations stress the dominant language, sometimes exclusively. Consequently, language-minority parents fear that their children will make a *language shift,* becoming fluent in the school language and forgetting their home language. Language shift occurs everywhere if theory-theory leads children to conclude that their first language is inferior to the new one (Bhatia & Ritchie, 2013).

Remember that young children are static thinkers (preoperational). Consequently, they center on the immediate status of their language (not on future usefulness or past glory), on appearance more than substance. No wonder many shift toward the language of the dominant culture.

If a child is to become fluently bilingual, everyone who speaks with the child should show appreciation of both cultures, and children need to hear twice as much talk as usual (Hoff et al., 2012). If the parents do not speak the majority language, their child will benefit if they talk, listen, and play with the child extensively in the

Bilingual Learners These are Chinese children learning a second language.

OBSERVATION QUIZ

Could this be in the United States? (see answer, page 188) ➤

ATTILA KISBENEDEK/AFP/GETTY IMAGES

home language. Ideally, the parents also find someone else to talk, listen, and play in the second language.

A study of English-speaking Canadian children who were schooled in French found that their English stayed strong while they became proficient in French (Sénéchal & LeFevre, 2014). Apparently, learning one language well makes it easier to learn another (Hoff et al., 2014).

LISTENING, TALKING, AND READING Because understanding the printed word is crucial, a meta-analysis of about 300 studies analyzed which activities in early childhood aided reading later on. Both vocabulary and phonics (precise awareness of the sounds of words) predicted literacy (Shanahan & Lonigan, 2010). Five specific strategies and experiences were particularly effective for children of all income levels, languages, and ethnicities.

1. *Code-focused teaching.* In order for children to read, they must "break the code" from spoken to written words. It helps if they learn the letters and sounds of the alphabet (e.g., "*A,* alligators all around" or, conventionally, "*B* is for baby").

2. *Book-reading.* Vocabulary as well as familiarity with pages and print will increase when adults read to children, allowing questions and conversation.

3. *Parent education.* When teachers and other professionals teach parents how to stimulate cognition (as in book-reading), children become better readers. Adults need to use words to expand vocabulary. Unfortunately, too often adults use words primarily to control ("don't touch" or "stop that"), not to teach.

4. *Language enhancement.* Within each child's zone of proximal development, mentors can expand vocabulary and grammar, based on the child's knowledge and experience.

5. *Preschool programs.* Children learn from teachers, songs, excursions, and other children. (We discuss variations of early education next, but every study finds that preschools advance language acquisition, especially if the home language is not the majority language.)

WHAT HAVE YOU LEARNED?

1. What is the evidence that early childhood is a sensitive time for learning language?

2. How does fast-mapping aid the language explosion?

3. How does overregularization signify a cognitive advance?

4. What does the research say about language learning by deaf children?

5. What evidence in language learning shows the limitations of logic in early childhood?

6. Why is early childhood the best time to learn a second (or third) language?

7. What are the advantages of a child learning two languages?

8. How does book-reading to a toddler contribute to later literacy?

Early-Childhood Education

Virtually every nation provides some early-childhood education, sometimes financed by the government, sometimes privately, sometimes only for a privileged few, and sometimes for almost every child (Georgeson & Payler, 2013).

In France, Denmark, Norway, and Sweden, more than 95 percent of all 3- to 5-year-olds are enrolled in government-sponsored schools. Norway also uses public funds to provide education for 1- and 2-year olds, and 80 percent of them attend (Ellingsaeter, 2014). One message from developmental research has reached almost every parent and politician worldwide—young children are amazingly capable and eager to learn.

Homes and Schools

However, beyond the amazing potential of young children to learn, another robust conclusion from research on children's learning seems not yet universally understood: Quality matters (Gambaro et al., 2014). If the home learning environment is poor, a good preschool program aids health, cognition, and social skills. If, instead, a family provides excellent learning, children still benefit from attending a high-quality program, but they do not benefit as much as less fortunate children.

Indeed, it is better for children to be in excellent home care than in a low-quality, overcrowded center. One expert criticizes inadequate subsidies that result in low-quality care: "Parents can find cheap baby-sitting that's bad for their kids on their own. They don't need government help with that" (Barnett, quoted in Samuels & Klein, 2013, p. 21).

A U.S. program to subsidize early child care, with no regard for quality, did not help all the children learn. It was designed to allow low-SES mothers to enter the labor force, and it did increase female employment. For most children, center care had no impact. However, compared to children who stayed home, immigrant children in subsidized center care became better readers, but U.S.-born children became less proficient in math. The researchers suggest that quality—and trained staff—is crucial (Johnson et al., 2014).

Quality cannot be judged by the name of a program or by its sponsorship. Educational institutions for 3- to 5-year-olds are called preschools, nursery schools, day-care centers, pre-primary programs, pre-K classes, and kindergartens. Sponsors can be public (federal, state, or city), private, religious, or corporate. Further, children, parents, and cultures differ, so an excellent program for one child might be less effective for another.

Tricky Indeed Young children are omnivorous learners, picking up habits, curses, and attitudes that adults would rather not transmit. Deciding what to teach—by actions more than words—is essential.

"We teach them that the world can be an unpredictable, dangerous, and sometimes frightening place, while being careful not to spoil their lovely innocence. It's tricky."

Preparing for Life

Several programs designed for children from low-SES families were established in the United States decades ago. Some solid research on the results of these programs is now available.

HEAD START The best known of the intervention programs began in the early 1960s, when millions of young children in the United States were thought to need a "head start" on their formal education to foster better health and cognition before first grade. Consequently, since 1965, the federal government has funded a massive program for 4-year-olds called **Head Start.**

The goals for Head Start have changed over the decades, from lifting families out of poverty to promoting literacy, from providing dental care and immunizations to teaching Standard English. Although initially most Head Start programs were child-centered, they have become increasingly teacher-directed as waves of legislators have approved and shaped them. Children learn whatever their Head Start teachers and curricula emphasize. Not surprisingly, specific results vary by program, home environment, and cohort.

For example, many low-income 3- and 4-year-olds in the United States are not normally exposed to math. After one Head Start program engaged children in a board game with numbers, their mathematical understanding advanced significantly (Siegler, 2009). Especially when parents provide little education at home, Head Start boosts math scores (E. Miller et al., 2014).

Head Start
A federally funded early-childhood intervention program for low-income children in the United States.

Disaster Recovery The success of Head Start led to Early Head Start for children such as this 2-year-old in Biloxi, Mississippi. When Hurricane Katrina destroyed most of the community, it was the first educational program to reopen. Since a family is a system, not just a collection of individuals, this Head Start program helped parents as well as entire families recover.

© JIM WEST/ALAMY

A 2007 congressional reauthorization of funding for Head Start included a requirement for extensive evaluation to answer two questions:

1. What difference does Head Start make to key outcomes of development and learning (in particular, school readiness) for low-income children? How does Head Start affect parental practices?

2. Under what circumstances and for whom does Head Start achieve the greatest impact?

The answers were not as dramatic as either advocates or detractors had hoped (U.S. Department of Health and Human Services, 2010). Most Head Start children advanced in language, math, and social skills, but by elementary school, the comparison children often caught up, with one exception: Head Start children were still ahead in vocabulary.

One explanation for this catch-up is that, unlike when Head Start began, many children in the comparison group were enrolled in other early-childhood programs—sometimes excellent ones, sometimes not. Another explanation is that the elementary schools for low-SES children were of low quality, so the Head Start children sank back to the norm.

The research found that benefits were strongest for children with the lowest family incomes, for those living in rural areas, and for those with disabilities (U.S. Department of Health and Human Services, 2010). These children were least likely to find other sources of early education.

That finding supports what we know about language development. Any good program will introduce children to words they would not learn at home. Children will fast-map those words, gaining a linguistic knowledge base that facilitates vocabulary throughout life.

A recent study of children born in 2001 found that those who went to Head Start were advanced in math and language, but, compared to similar children who had only their mother's care, they had more behavior problems, according to their teachers (R. Lee et al., 2014). Of course, one interpretation of that result is that the teachers reacted negatively to the self-assertion of the Head Start children, rating the children's attitude a problem when really it was the teachers who had the problem.

As already mentioned, Hispanic children are less likely to attend Head Start, even though they are more likely to benefit. This troubles developmentalists, because without preschool education, many Spanish-speaking children begin elementary school behind in English, and their disadvantages increase each year.

Four possible reasons have been suggested. Already mentioned is that parents do not agree with the child-centered emphasis of many teachers. Another possible reason is fear of deportation. Although almost all young Latinos are citizens, their parents might be afraid that enrolling them would jeopardize other members of the family. A third reason is that the parents may be unaware of the educational benefits of preschool education. Finally, since few Head Start teachers speak Spanish, parents and teachers have difficulty communicating, so parents stay away.

LONG-TERM GAINS FROM INTENSIVE PROGRAMS This discussion of philosophies, practices, and programs may give the impression that the research on early-childhood cognition is contradictory. That is not true. Specifics are debatable, but empirical evidence and longitudinal evaluation find that good early education advances learning, especially in language. Ideally, each program has a curriculum that guides practice, all the adults collaborate, and experienced teachers respond to each child.

Early-Childhood Schooling

Preschool can be an academic and social benefit to children. Around the world, increasing numbers of children are enrolled in early-childhood-education programs.

Early-childhood-education programs are described as "teacher-directed" or "child-centered," but in reality, most teachers' styles reflect a combination of both approaches. Some students benefit more from the order and structure of a teacher-directed classroom, while others work better in a more collaborative and creative environment.

TEACHER-DIRECTED APPROACH

Focused on Getting Preschoolers Ready to Learn

Direct instruction

Teacher as formal authority

Students learn by listening

Classroom is orderly and quiet

Teacher fully manages lessons

Fosters autonomy of each individual

Encourages academics

Students learn from teacher

CHILD-CENTERED APPROACH

Focused on Individual Development and Growth

Teacher as facilitator

Teacher as delegator

Students learn actively

Classroom is designed for collaborative work

Students influence content

Fosters collaboration among students

Encourages artistic expression

Students learn from each other

WORTH PUBLISHERS

DIFFERENT STUDENTS, DIFFERENT TEACHERS

There is no "one right way" to teach children. Each approach has potential benefits and pitfalls. A classroom full of creative, self-motivated students can thrive when a gifted teacher acts as a competent facilitator. But students who are distracted or annoyed by noise, or who are shy or intimidated by other children, can blossom under an engaging and encouraging teacher in a more traditional environment.

Done Well

Teacher-Directed	Child-Centered
• engaging teacher	• emphasizes social skills and emotion regulation
• clear, consistent assessment	• encourages critical thinking
• reading and math skills emphasized	• builds communication skills
• quiet, orderly classroom	• fosters individual achievement
• all students treated equally	• encourages creativity and curiosity
• bored students	• chaotic/noisy classrooms
• passive learning	• students may miss/avoid important knowledge and skills
• less independent, critical thinking	• inconclusive assessment of student progress
• teacher may dominate	• some students may dominate classroom

Done Poorly

FIGURE 5.6 And Not in Prison
Longitudinal research on people who attended excellent early-childhood programs finds many cost savings, some shown here and some later—better employment, less disease, and fewer arrests. These data are from one program, the Abecedarian Project in North Carolina, but similar results are found in every intense, high-quality early-education program. Note also that even the best programs do not remedy all problems.

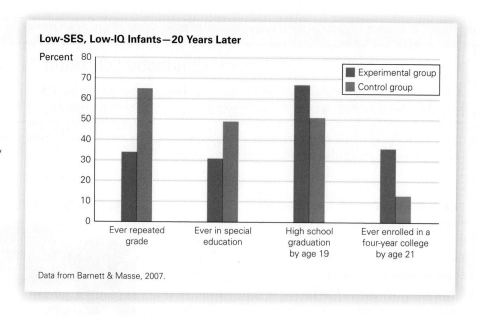

Low-SES, Low-IQ Infants—20 Years Later

Data from Barnett & Masse, 2007.

The best evidence comes from three longitudinal programs that enrolled children for years, sometimes beginning with home visits in infancy, sometimes continuing in after-school programs through first grade. One program, called *Perry* (or *High/Scope*), was spearheaded in Michigan (Schweinhart & Weikart, 1997); another, called *Abecedarian,* got its start in North Carolina (Campbell et al., 2001); a third, called *Child–Parent Centers,* began in Chicago (Reynolds, 2000). Because of the political context that existed when these programs began, all were focused on children from low-SES families.

All three programs compared experimental groups of children with matched control groups, and all reached the same conclusion: Early education has substantial long-term benefits that become most apparent when children reached third grade or higher. By age 10, children who had been enrolled in any of these three programs scored higher on math and reading achievement tests than did other children from the same backgrounds, schools, and neighborhoods. They were less likely to be placed in special classes for children with special needs or to repeat a year of school.

An advantage of decades of longitudinal research is that teenagers and adults who received early education can be compared with those who did not. For all three programs, early investment paid off.

In adolescence, the children who had undergone intensive preschool education had higher aspirations, more pride, and were less likely to have been abused. As young adults, they were more likely to attend college and less likely to go to jail. As middle-aged adults, they were more often employed, paying taxes, healthy, and not needing government subsidies (Reynolds & Ou, 2011; Schweinhart et al., 2005; Campbell et al., 2014).

All three research projects found that providing direct cognitive training, with specific instruction in various school-readiness skills, was useful. Each child's needs and talents were considered—a circumstance made possible because the child/adult ratio was low. This combined child-centered and teacher-directed aspects, with all the teachers trained together and cooperating, so children were not confused. Teachers involved parents in their children's education; each program included strategies to enhance the home–school connection.

These programs were expensive (ranging from $7,000 to $20,000 annually per young child in 2015 dollars). From a developmental perspective, however, the decreased need later for special education and other services made early education a "wise investment" (Duncan & Magnuson, 2013, p. 128). Additional benefits to society, including increased adult employment, more tax revenues, and reduced crime, are worth much more than the cost of the programs.

International research points in the same direction. For instance, Chile now subsidizes early education for 4- to 6-year-olds. Some aspects of the Chilean schools seem teacher-directed (emphasis on whole-group instruction) and some child-centered (responding to individual children).

Overall, researchers found that encouraging teacher–student interaction and promoting classroom organization are effective (Leyva et al., 2015; Yoshikawa et al., 2015). Few student benefits from the intervention are evident so far, but a sleeper effect may appear here as well.

FUTURE POSSIBILITIES The greatest lifetime return from the three intensive U.S. programs came to boys from high-poverty neighborhoods in Chicago: In manhood, the social benefit to society was more than 12 times the initial cost (Reynolds et al., 2011).

Unfortunately, costs are immediate and benefits are long term. Some legislators and voters are unwilling to fund expensive intervention programs that do not pay off until decades later. Further, these programs were small; the United States has about 15 million 2- to 5-year-olds who could benefit from an excellent preschool program, yet few of them are enrolled.

That is slowly changing. In some nations, preschool education is now considered a right, not a privilege: Young children from families of all incomes are educated without cost to the parents. Beyond those nations already mentioned, many others offer everyone some free preschool or give parents a child-care subsidy. For example, England provides 15 free hours per week, New Zealand 20, and Canada pays $100 a month for each child under age 6.

Among developed nations, the United States is an outlier, least likely to support new mothers or young children. However, in the past decade some states (e.g., Oklahoma, Georgia, Florida, New Jersey, and Illinois) and some cities (e.g., New York, Boston, Cleveland, San Antonio, and Los Angeles) have offered preschool to every 4-year-old. Although this investment is likely to result in less need for special education later on, implementation and results are controversial—a topic for further research.

THINK CRITICALLY: Why do educators and taxpayers often disagree about free, early education?

Almost every state in the United States now sponsors some public education for young children—usually only for 4-year-olds, although high-quality education for 2- and 3-year-olds also advances later school achievement (e.g., Li et al., 2013). In 2012–2013 in the United States, over a million children (1,338,737) attended state-sponsored preschools, including Head Start. That is 28 percent of all 4-year olds, twice as many as a decade earlier (Barnett et al., 2013).

Most state programs fund only children living in poverty, but many wealthy families pay for early education, sometimes beginning before age 2. Private schools may be very expensive—as much as $30,000 a year. Not surprisingly, in the United States, families in the highest income quartile are more likely to enroll their 3- and 4-year-olds.

The increases in preschool for 4-year-olds is good news, but developmentalists ask why not start earlier? Children younger than 4 are capable of learning languages, concepts, and much else. Every child benefits from academic stimulation, in school and at home. The amazing potential of young children continues as a theme of the next chapter, where we discuss other kinds of learning—in emotional regulation, social skills, and more.

WHAT HAVE YOU LEARNED?

1. What do most early-education programs provide for children that most homes do not?
2. Why do early-education programs vary in quality and purpose?
3. In child-centered programs, what do the teachers do?
4. Why are Montessori schools still functioning, 100 years after the first such schools opened?
5. How does Reggio Emilia differ from most other early-education programs?
6. What are the advantages and disadvantages of teacher-directed preschools?
7. What are the goals of Head Start?
8. Who benefits most from Head Start?
9. What do the three small intervention programs have in common?
10. What are the long-term results of intervention preschools?

SUMMARY

Body Changes

1. Children continue to gain weight and add height during early childhood. Gross motor skills continue to develop; clumsy 2-year-olds become agile 6-year-olds who move their bodies well, guided by their culture. By playing with other children in safe places, they practice the skills needed for formal education.

2. Many adults overfeed children, not realizing that young children are naturally quite thin. Children often have limited diets due to their compulsiveness with daily routine, and, sometimes, food allergies. Consequently, they may consume too much sugar and too little calcium and other nutrients, which may result in poor oral health.

3. The brain continues to grow in early childhood, reaching 75 percent of its adult weight at age 2 and 90 percent by age 5. Maturation of the prefrontal cortex, known as the executive of the brain, results in better sleep and more predictable behavior.

4. Lateralization is evident in early childhood as the corpus callosum becomes thicker and functions much better. Myelination is substantial, speeding messages from one part of the brain to another and reducing both impulsivity and perseveration.

5. The two hemispheres of the brain work together, but each controls one side of the body. People are naturally left- or right-handed, as their brains dictate.

6. The expression and regulation of emotions are fostered by several brain areas collectively called the limbic system, including the amygdala, the hippocampus, and the hypothalamus. Each brain part has a particular function.

Thinking During Early Childhood

7. Piaget stressed the illogical and egocentric aspects of thought during the play years; he called thinking at this stage preoperational because young children often cannot yet use logical operations. They sometimes focus on only one thing (centration) and see things only from their own viewpoint (egocentrism), remaining stuck on appearances and current reality, unable to understand reversibility.

8. Vygotsky stressed the social aspects of childhood cognition, noting that children learn by participating in various experiences, guided by more knowledgeable adults or peers who scaffold to aid learning. Such guidance assists learning within the zone of proximal development.

9. Children develop theories to explain human actions. One theory about children's thinking is called theory-theory—the hypothesis that children develop theories because people innately seek explanations for everything they observe.

10. In early childhood, children develop a theory of mind—an understanding of what others may be thinking. Advances in theory of mind occur at around age 4. Theory of mind is partly the result of brain maturation, but culture and experiences also have an impact.

Language Learning

11. Language develops rapidly during early childhood. Vocabulary increases dramatically, with thousands of words added between ages 2 and 6. In addition, basic grammar is mastered, although abstractions and exceptions are difficult.

12. Many children learn more than one language, gaining cognitive as well as social advantages. Ideally, children become fluent in two languages, by age 6, avoiding a language shift to exclusively the majority language.

13. Five specific strategies and experiences are known to be particularly effective for children's literacy: code-focused teaching, book-reading, parent education, language enhancement, and preschool programs.

Early-Childhood Education

14. Organized educational programs during early childhood advance cognitive and social skills. Many child-centered programs are inspired by Piaget and Vygotsky; they encourage children to follow their own interests.

15. Teacher-directed early-childhood programs emphasize academics and good behavior. The goal is to prepare children for reading and writing in school.

16. Many types of early education are successful. It is the quality of early education—whether at home or at school—that matters.

17. Intervention programs are targeted for children in poverty. Quality varies, as do results. Three intensive programs—Perry, Abecedarian, and Child–Parent Centers—benefit students lifelong.

KEY TERMS

executive function (p. 167)
corpus callosum (p. 168)
lateralization (p. 168)
myelination (p. 169)
impulse control (p. 171)
perseveration (p. 171)
amygdala (p. 172)
hippocampus (p. 172)

hypothalamus (p. 172)
preoperational intelligence (p. 173)
symbolic thought (p. 173)
animism (p. 173)
centration (p. 174)
egocentrism (p. 174)
focus on appearance (p. 174)

static reasoning (p. 174)
irreversibility (p. 174)
conservation (p. 174)
mentor (p. 176)
zone of proximal development (ZPD) (p. 177)
scaffolding (p. 177)
overimitation (p. 178)

theory-theory (p. 178)
theory of mind (p. 180)
fast-mapping (p. 183)
overregularization (p. 184)
pragmatics (p. 184)
Montessori schools (p. 189)
Reggio Emilia (p. 190)
Head Start (p. 193)

APPLICATIONS

1. Keep a food diary for 24 hours, writing down what you eat, how much, when, how, and why. Then think about nutrition and eating habits in early childhood. Did your food habits originate in early childhood, in adolescence, or at some other time? Explain.

2. Go to a playground or other place where many young children play. Note the motor skills that the children demonstrate, including abilities and inabilities, and keep track of age and sex. What differences do you see among the children?

3. Replicate one of Piaget's conservation experiments. The easiest one is conservation of liquids (illustrated in Figure 5.4). Work with a child under age 5 who tells you that two identically shaped glasses contain the same amount of liquid. Then ask the child to carefully pour one glass of liquid into a taller, narrower glass. Ask the child which glass now contains more or if the glasses contain the same amount.

CHAPTER OUTLINE

EARLY CHILDHOOD
The Social World

CHAPTER 6

WHAT WILL YOU KNOW?

- Why do 2-year-olds have more sudden tempers, tears, and terrors than 6-year-olds?
- What happens if parents let their children do whatever they want?
- What are the long-term effects of spanking children?
- Do maltreated children always become abusive adults?

It was a hot summer afternoon. My thirsty 3- and 4-year-olds were with me in the kitchen, which was in one corner of our living/dining area. The younger one opened the refrigerator and grabbed a bottle of orange juice. The sticky bottle slipped, shattering on the floor. Both daughters stared at me, at the shards, at the spreading juice with extra pulp. I picked them up and plopped them on the couch.

"Stay there until I clean this up," I yelled.

They did, wide-eyed at my fury. As they watched me pick, sweep, and mop, I understood how parents could hit their kids. By the end of the chapter, I hope you also realize how a moment like this—in the heat, with two small children and unexpected and difficult work—can turn a loving, patient adult into something else. It is not easy, day after day, being the guide and model that parents should be. ■

FORTUNATELY, MANY SAFEGUARDS prevented serious maltreatment—the girls stayed on the couch, my beliefs kept me from laying a hand on them, I could afford another bottle of juice. Several aspects of psychosocial development—as children learn to manage their emotions, as parents learn to guide their children, as the macrosystem and microsystem (beliefs and income) influence adult–child interaction—converged at this moment. As this chapter describes, all these affect development of every young child.

Emotional Development

Children gradually learn when and how to express emotions, becoming more capable in every aspect of their lives. Controlling the expression of their feelings, called **emotional regulation,** is the preeminent psychosocial task between ages 2 and 6. Emotional regulation is a lifelong endeavor, with early childhood crucial for its development (Gross, 2014; Lewis, 2013).

emotional regulation
The ability to control when and how emotions are expressed.

By age 6, signs of emotional regulation are evident. Most children can be angry but not explosive, frightened but not terrified, sad but not inconsolable, anxious but not withdrawn, proud but not boastful. Depending on training and temperament, some emotions are easier to control than others, but even temperamentally angry or fearful children learn to regulate their emotions (Moran et al., 2013, Tan et al., 2013).

A Poet and We Know It She is the proud winner of a national poetry contest. Is she as surprised, humbled, and thankful as an adult winner would be?

effortful control
The ability to regulate one's emotions and actions through effort, not simply through natural inclination.

initiative versus guilt
Erikson's third psychosocial crisis, in which young children undertake new skills and activities and feel guilty when they do not succeed at them.

OBSERVATION QUIZ
Does this mother deserve praise? (see answer, page 204) ➤

Genuinely Helpful Children of all ages can be helpful to their families, but their actions depend on family and cohort. Thirty years ago more children gathered freshly laid eggs than re-cycled plastic milk bottles. Indeed, no blue recycling bins existed until tens of thousands of environmentalists advo-cated reducing our carbon footprint.

Cultural differences are apparent: Children may be encouraged to laugh/cry/yell or, the opposite, to hide emotions. Some adults guffaw, slap their knees, and stomp their feet for joy; others use their hands to cover their mouths if a smile spontane-ously appears. No matter what the specifics, parents everywhere teach emotional regulation (Kim & Sasaki, 2014).

Emotional regulation is also called **effortful control** (Eisenberg et al., 2014), a term which highlights that controlling outbursts is not easy, in childhood or later, for reasons that are biological as well as experiential. Effortful control is more difficult when people—of any age—are in pain, tired, or hungry.

I see this in my own life. My 5-year-old grandson burst into tears when he spilled his snack—grapes—on the subway platform. A stranger gave him an orange, and immediately his tears vanished. I worried that he lacked emotional regulation, but then my daughter reminded me that when I am tired and hungry I sometimes snap at her.

Initiative Versus Guilt

Emotional regulation is one of the skills children acquire during Erikson's third de-velopmental stage, **initiative versus guilt.** *Initiative* can mean several things—saying something new, expanding an ability, beginning a project, expressing an emotion. Depending on the outcome (especially reactions from other people), children feel proud or guilty.

Usually, North American parents encourage enthusiasm, effort, and pride in their 2- to 6-year-olds, and they also prevent guilt from becoming self-hatred. If, instead, parents ignore rather than guide those emotions of joy and pride, a child may not learn emotional regulation (Morris et al., 2007).

Guidance, yes; brutal honesty, no. Preschool children are usually proud of them-selves, overestimating their skills. As one team expressed it:

> Compared to older children and adults, young children are the optimists of the world, believing they have greater physical abilities, better memories, are more skilled at imitating models, are smarter, know more about how things work, and rate themselves as stronger, tougher, and of higher social standing than is actually the case.
>
> [Bjorklund & Ellis, 2014, p. 245]

That helps them try new things, which advances learning of all kinds. As Erikson predicted, their optimistic self-concept protects them from guilt and shame.

If young children know the limits of their ability, they will not imagine be-coming an NBA forward, a Grammy winner, a billionaire inventor. But that might discourage them from trying to learn new things (Bjorklund & Ellis, 2014). Initiative is a driving force for young children, and that is as it should be.

PRIDE AND PREJUDICE In the United States, pride quickly includes gender, size, and heritage. Girls are usually happy to be girls; boys to be boys; both are glad they aren't babies. "Crybaby" is an insult; praise for being "a big kid" is welcomed; pride in doing something better than a younger child is expressed, even when it makes the younger child feel sad.

Many young children believe that whatever they are is good. They feel superior to children of the other sex, or of another nationality or religion. This arises because of maturation: Cognition enables children to understand group categories, not only of ethnicity, gender, and nationality, but even categories that are irrelevant. They remember more about cartoon characters whose names begin with the same letter as theirs do (Ross et al., 2011).

One amusing example occurred when preschoolers were asked to explain why one person would steal from another, as occurred in a story about two fictional tribes, the Zaz and the Flurps. As you would expect from theory-theory, they readily found reasons. Their first reason illustrated their understanding of groups. Only when that failed did they consider personality.

> "Why did a Zaz steal a toy from a Flurp?"
> "Because he's a Zaz, but he's a Flurp ... They're not the same kind ..."
> "Why did a Zaz steal a toy from a Zaz?"
> "Because he's a very mean boy."
>
> *[Rhodes, 2013, p. 259]*

THINK CRITICALLY: At what age, if ever, do people understand when pride becomes prejudice?

Brain Maturation

The new initiative that Erikson describes results from myelination of the limbic system, growth of the prefrontal cortex, and a longer attention span—all the result of neurological maturation. Emotional regulation and cognitive maturation develop together, each enabling the other to advance (Bell & Calkins, 2011; Lewis, 2013).

Normally, neurological advances in the prefrontal cortex at about age 4 or 5 make children less likely to throw tantrums, pick fights, or giggle during prayer. Throughout early childhood, violent outbursts, uncontrolled crying, and terrifying *phobias* (irrational, crippling fears) diminish.

The capacity for self-control, such as not opening a present immediately if asked to wait and not expressing disappointment at an undesirable gift, becomes more evident. Consider the most recent time you gave someone a gift. If the receiver was a young child, you probably could tell whether the child liked the present. If the receiver was an adult, you might not know.

In one study, researchers asked children to wait eight minutes while their mothers did some paperwork before opening a wrapped present in front of them (Cole et al., 2010). The children used strategies to help them wait, including distractions and private speech.

Proud Peruvian In rural Peru, a program of early education (Pronoei) encourages community involvement and traditional culture. Preschoolers, like this girl in a holiday parade, are proud to be themselves, and that helps them become healthy and strong.

© MIKE THEISS/NATIONAL GEOGRAPHIC SOCIETY/CORBIS

FADEDINK.NET/SHUTTERSTOCK

Video Activity: Can Young Children Delay Gratification? illustrates how most young children are unable to overcome temptation even when promised an award for doing so.

ANSWER TO OBSERVATION QUIZ (from page 202): Yes—even if you don't consider recycling important. Notice her face and body: She is smiling and kneeling, and her hands are on her legs, all suggesting that she knows how to encourage without interfering. Even more commendable is her boys' behavior: Many brothers would be grabbing, shoving, and throwing, but, at least at this moment, shared cooperation is evident. Kudos to Mom. ●

intrinsic motivation
A drive, or reason to pursue a goal, that comes from inside a person, such as the joy of reading a good book.

extrinsic motivation
A drive, or reason to pursue a goal, that arises from the wish to have external rewards, perhaps by earning money or praise.

imaginary friends
Make-believe friends who exist only in a child's imagination; increasingly common from ages 3 through 7, they combat loneliness and aid emotional regulation.

Keisha was one of the study participants:

"Are you done, Mom?" . . . "I wonder what's in it" . . . "Can I open it now?"
  Each time her mother reminds Keisha to wait, eventually adding, "If you keep interrupting me, I can't finish and if I don't finish . . ." Keisha plops in her chair, frustrated. "I really want it," she laments, aloud but to herself. "I want to talk to mommy so I won't open it. If I talk, Mommy won't finish. If she doesn't finish, I can't have it." She sighs deeply, folds her arms, and scans the room. . . . The research assistant returns. Keisha looks at her mother with excited anticipation. Her mother says, "OK, now." Keisha tears open the gift.

[Cole et al., 2010, p. 59]

This is a more recent example of the famous marshmallow test. Children could eat one marshmallow immediately or get two marshmallows if they waited—sometimes as long as 15 minutes. Children who delayed gobbling up a marshmallow became more successful as teenagers, young adults, and even middle-aged adults—doing well in college, for instance, and having happy marriages (Mischel, 2014).

Of course, this is correlation, not causation: Some preschoolers who did not wait became successful in later life. Many factors influence emotional regulation:

- **Maturation matters.** Three-year-olds are notably poor at impulse control. By age 6 they are better, and effortful control continues to improve throughout childhood.
- **Learning matters.** In the zone of proximal development, children learn from mentors, who offer tactics for delaying gratification.
- **Culture matters.** In the United States many parents tell their children not to be afraid; in Japan they tell them not to be too proud; in the Netherlands, not to be too moody. Children try to do what their culture asks.

Motivation

Motivation is the impulse that propels someone to act. It comes either from a person's own desires or from the social context.

Intrinsic motivation arises from within, when people do something for the joy of doing it: A musician might enjoy making music even if no one else hears it. Intrinsic motivation is thought to advance creativity, innovation, and emotional well-being (Weinstein & DeHaan, 2014). Erikson's psychosocial needs are intrinsic: The young child feels compelled to initiate things, from walking along a ledge to exploring an anthill.

Extrinsic motivation comes from outside the person, when people do something to gain praise or some other reinforcement. A musician might play for applause or money. Social rewards are powerful lifelong: Four-year-olds hold an adult hand crossing the street because they are praised for doing so—and punished if they forget. If an extrinsic reward stops, the behavior stops, unless it has become a habit, continued because it feels right (intrinsic).

Intrinsic motivation is crucial for children. They play, question, and explore for the sheer joy of it. That serves them well. A study found that 3-year-olds who were strong in intrinsic motivation were, two years later, advanced in early math and literacy (Mokrova et al., 2013).

Child-centered preschools, as described in Chapter 5, depend on children's motivation to talk, play, learn, and move. Praise and prizes might be appreciated, but that's not why children work at what they do. When playing a game, few young children keep score; the fun is in the activity (intrinsic), not the winning.

Intrinsic motivation is apparent when children invent dialogues for their toys, concentrate on creating a work of art or architecture, or converse with **imaginary friends.** Such conversations with invisible companions are rarely encouraged by adults (thus no extrinsic motivation), but from about age 2 to 7, imaginary friends are increasingly common. Children know their imaginary friends are invisible and pretend, but conjuring them up meets various intrinsic psychosocial needs (M. Taylor et al., 2009).

The distinction between extrinsic and intrinsic motivation may be crucial in understanding how and when to praise something the child has done. Praise may be effective when it is connected to the particular production, not to a general trait. For example, the adult might say, "You worked hard and did a good drawing," not "You are a great artist." The goal is to help the child feel happy that effort paid off. That motivates future action (Zentall & Morris, 2010).

In a set of experiments which suggest that specific praise for effort is better than generalized statements, some 4- to 7-year-old boys were told that boys are good at a particular game. Knowing this *decreased* their scores on the game. The same thing happened when girls were told that girls were good at the game. The children apparently feared that they would not be as good as most children of their sex. They "felt less happy and less competent, liked the game less, [and] were less persistent" (Cimpian, 2013, p. 272).

By contrast, other children were told that one particular child was good at the game. That led them to believe that personal effort mattered. That belief was motivating; their scores were higher than those told that boys or girls in general were good.

Play

Play is timeless and universal—apparent in every part of the world over thousands of years. Many developmentalists believe that play is the most productive as well as the most enjoyable activity that children undertake (Elkind, 2007; Bateson & Martin, 2013; P. Smith, 2010). Not everyone agrees. Whether play is essential for normal growth or is merely fun is "a controversial topic of study" (Pellegrini, 2011, p. 3).

This controversy underlies many of the disputes regarding preschool education, which increasingly stresses academic skills. One consequence is that "play in school has become an endangered species" (Trawick-Smith, 2012, p. 259). Among the leading theorists of human development, Vygotsky is well known for his respect for child's play, which makes a playing child "a head taller" than his or her actual height (Vygotsky, 1980).

Some educators want children to play less in order to focus on reading and math; others predict emotional and academic problems for children who rarely play. If children are kept quiet for a long time, they tend to play more vigorously when they finally have the chance (Pellegrini, 2013). For people of all ages, taking a break from concentrated intellectual work enhances learning.

PLAYMATES There are two general kinds of play, *pretend play* that often occurs when a child is alone and *social play* that occurs with playmates. One meta-analysis of the research on pretend and social play is careful not to confuse correlation with causation (Lillard et al., 2013). That is an important precaution because imaginative children tend to be intelligent children, not because of their pretend play but simply as a correlation.

The researchers report that evidence is weak or mixed regarding pretend play but that social play has much to commend it. If social play is prevented, children are less happy and less able to learn, which suggests that social play is one way that children develop their minds and social skills.

Young children play best with *peers,* that is, people of about the same age and social status. Although infants are intrigued by other children, most infant play is either

VISUALIZING DEVELOPMENT

Less Play, Less Safe?

Play is universal—all young children do it when they are with each other, if they can. For children, play takes up more time than anything else, whether their family is rich or poor.

WHAT 3-YEAR-OLDS DO WITH THEIR TIME

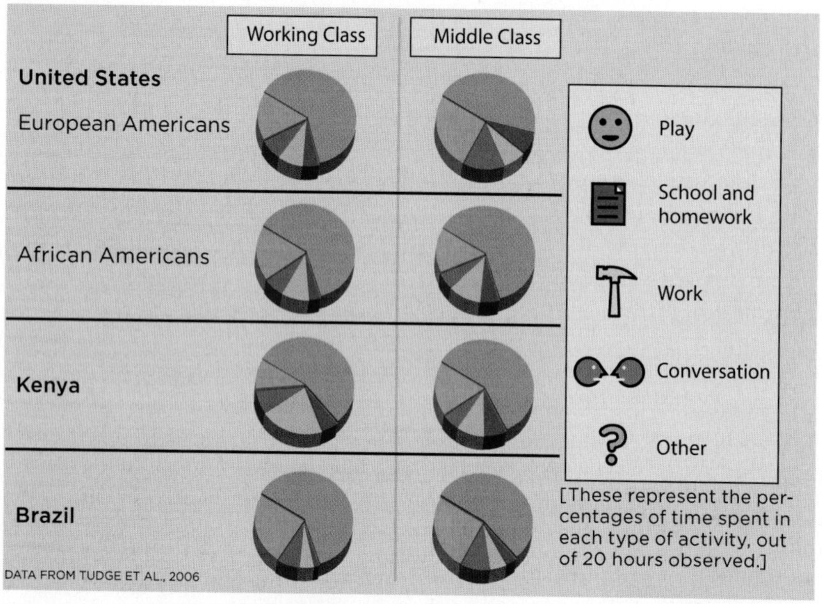

| Working Class | Middle Class |

United States
European Americans

African Americans

Kenya

Brazil

DATA FROM TUDGE ET AL., 2006

😊 Play

📋 School and homework

🔨 Work

Conversation

❓ Other

[These represent the percentages of time spent in each type of activity, out of 20 hours observed.]

However, many developmentalists worry that active play has decreased as screen time has increased, especially in the United States (on average, 2.1 hours per day for 2- to 4-year-olds).

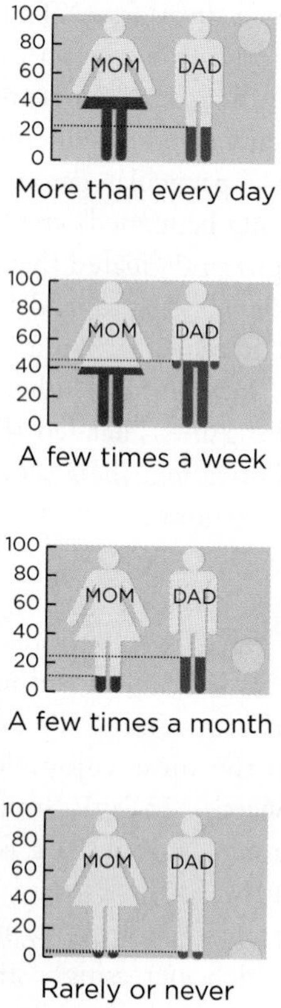

Parents worry that children will be injured if they play outside, but the data suggest the opposite. Only 166 out of every thousand children need to go to the emergency room per year, and almost all of those were injured in the home, or in a car.

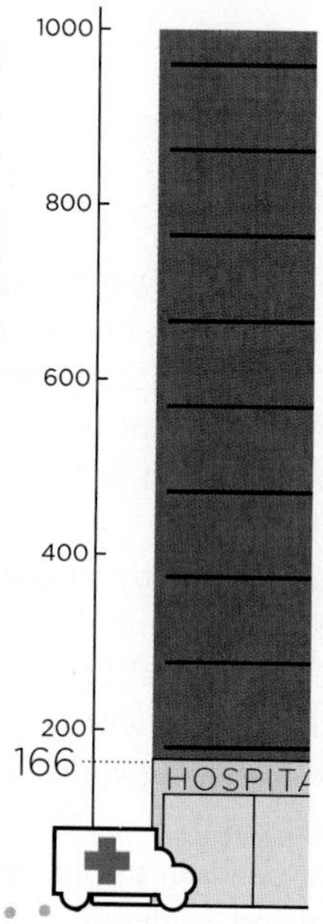

166 ---- HOSPITA

PERCENT OF KIDS WHOSE PARENTS PLAY OUTDOORS WITH THEM

MOM DAD
More than every day

MOM DAD
A few times a week

MOM DAD
A few times a month

MOM DAD
Rarely or never

From what kind of injuries do young children suffer?

Compare 1- to 4-year-olds and 5- to 14-year-olds

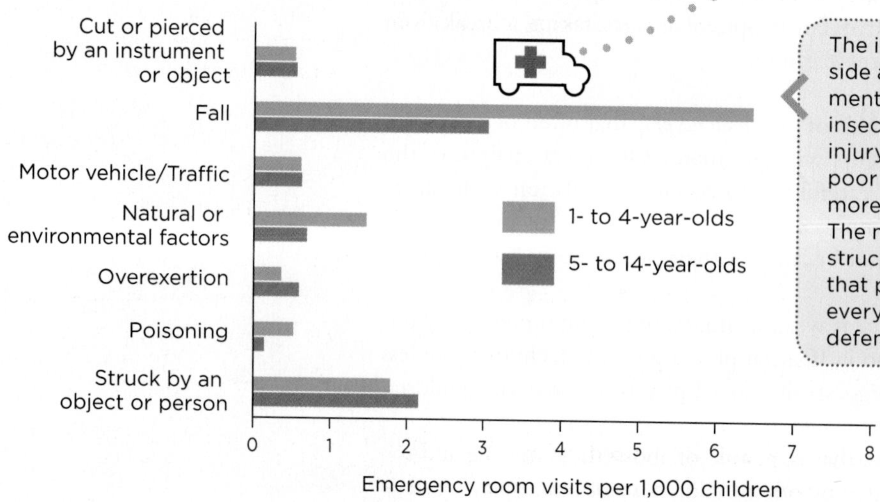

Cut or pierced by an instrument or object

Fall

Motor vehicle/Traffic

Natural or environmental factors

Overexertion

Poisoning

Struck by an object or person

1- to 4-year-olds

5- to 14-year-olds

Emergency room visits per 1,000 children

The injuries most likely to occur outside are lumped together as environmental or natural—usually animal or insect bites. And the most common injury, falls—which may result from poor balance and motor control—is more problematic for inactive children. The next most common injury is being struck by a person—almost always that person is an adult at home. At every age, physical fitness is the best defense against accidental injury.

DATA FROM EMERGENCY ROOM VISITS, 2009–2010, CHILDSTATS.GOV.

solitary or with a parent. Some maturation is required for play with peers (Bateson & Martin, 2013).

Such an advance can be seen over the years of early childhood. Toddlers are too self-absorbed to be good playmates, but they learn quickly. By age 6, most children are quite skilled: Some know how to join a peer group, manage conflict, take turns, find friends, and keep the action going (Şendil & Erden, 2014; Göncü & Gaskins, 2011). As they become better playmates, they learn emotional regulation, empathy, and cultural understanding.

Parents have an obvious task: Find peers and arrange play partners. Of course, some parents play with their children, which benefits both generations. But even the most playful parent is outmatched by another child at negotiating the rules of tag, at play-fighting, at pretending to be sick, at killing dragons, and so on. Specifics vary, but "play with peers is one of the most important areas in which children develop positive social skills" (Xu, 2010, p. 496).

Parents in some cultures consider play important and willingly engage in games and dramas. In other places, sheer survival takes time and energy, and children must help by doing chores. In those places, if children play, it is with each other, not with adults who spend all their energy on basic tasks (Kalliala, 2006; Roopnarine, 2011).

THE HISTORICAL CONTEXT As children grow older, play becomes more social, influenced by brain maturation, playmate availability, and the physical setting. One developmentalist bemoans the twenty-first century's "swift and pervasive rise of electronic media" and adults who lean "more toward control than freedom." He praises children who find places to play independently and "conspire ways to elude adult management" (Chudacoff, 2011, p. 108).

His opinion may be extreme, but it is echoed in more common concerns. As you remember, one dispute in preschool education is the proper balance between unstructured, creative play and teacher-directed learning. Before the electronic age, most families had several children and few mothers worked outside the home. The children played outside with all their neighbors, boys and girls, of several ages.

That was true in the United States a century ago. In 1932, the American sociologist Mildred Parten described the development of five stages of social play, each more advanced than the previous one:

1. *Solitary play:* A child plays alone, unaware of any other children playing nearby.
2. *Onlooker play:* A child watches other children play.
3. *Parallel play:* Children play with similar objects in similar ways but not together.
4. *Associative play:* Children interact, sharing material, but their play is not reciprocal.
5. *Cooperative play:* Children play together, creating dramas or taking turns.

Parten thought that progress in social play was age-related, with 1-year-olds usually playing alone and 6-year-olds usually cooperatively.

Play Ball! In every nation, young children play with balls, but the specific games they play vary with the culture. Soccer is the favorite game in many countries, including Brazil, where these children are practicing their dribbling on Copacabana Beach in Rio de Janeiro.

OBSERVATION QUIZ
Does kicking a soccer ball, as shown above, require fine or gross motor skills? (see answer, page 208) ▲

No Grabbing Maybe the child on the left or the right will soon try to grab. If sharing continues, is it because these children have been raised within Asian families?

THINK CRITICALLY: Is "play" an entirely different experience for adults than for children?

ANSWER TO OBSERVATION QUIZ (from page 207): Although controlling the trajectory of a ball with feet is a fine motor skill, these boys are using gross motor skills—their entire bodies (arms, torsos, even heads)—to run to the ball. ●

rough-and-tumble play
Play that seems to be rough, as in play wrestling or chasing, but in which there is no intent to harm.

sociodramatic play
Pretend play in which children act out various roles and themes in plots or roles that they create.

Joy Supreme Pretend play in early childhood is thrilling and powerful. For this 7-year-old from Brooklyn, New York, pretend play overwhelms mundane realities, such as an odd scarf or awkward arm.

Research on contemporary children finds much more age variation, perhaps because family size is smaller and parents invest heavily in each child. Many Asian parents successfully teach 3-year-olds to take turns, share, and otherwise cooperate (stage 5). Many North American children, encouraged to be individuals, still engage in parallel play at age 6 (stage 3). Given all the social, political, and economic changes over the past century, many forms of social play (not necessarily in Parten's five-step sequence) are normal (Xu, 2010).

ACTIVE PLAY Children need physical activity to develop muscle strength and control. Peers provide an audience, role models, and sometimes competition. For instance, running skills develop best when children chase or race each other, not when a child runs alone. Gross motor play is favored among young children, who enjoy climbing, kicking, and tumbling (Case-Smith & Kuhaneck, 2008).

Active social play—not solitary play—correlates with peer acceptance and a healthy self-concept and may help regulate emotions (Becker et al., 2014; Sutton-Smith, 2011). Adults need to remember this when they want children to sit still and be quiet.

Among nonhuman primates, deprivation of social play warps later life, rendering some monkeys unable to mate, to make friends, or even to survive alongside other monkeys (Herman et al., 2011; Palagi, 2011). Might the same be true for human primates?

The most common form of active play is called **rough-and-tumble play** because it looks quite rough and because the children seem to tumble over one another. The term was coined by British scientists who studied animals in East Africa (Blurton-Jones, 1976). They noticed that monkeys often chased, attacked, rolled over in the dirt, and wrestled quite roughly, but without injuring one another.

If a young male monkey wanted to play, he would simply catch the eye of a peer and then run a few feet away. This invitation to rough-and-tumble play was almost always accepted with a *play face* (smiling, not angry). Puppies, kittens, and young baboons behave similarly.

When these scientists returned to London, they saw that their own children, like baby monkeys, engaged in rough-and-tumble play, signified by the play face. Children chase, wrestle, and grab each other, developing games like tag and cops-and-robbers, with various conventions, expressions, and gestures that children use to signify "just pretend."

Rough-and-tumble play happens everywhere (although cops-and-robbers can be "robots-and-humans" or many other iterations) and has probably been common among children for thousands of years (Fry, 2014). It is much more common among boys than girls and flourishes best in ample space with minimal supervision (Pellegrini, 2013).

Many scientists think that rough-and-tumble play helps the prefrontal cortex develop, as children learn to regulate emotions, practice social skills, and strengthen their bodies (Pellis & Pellis, 2011). Indeed, some believe that play in childhood, especially rough-and-tumble play between father and son, may prevent antisocial behavior (even murder) later on (Fry, 2014; Wenner, 2009).

Another major type of active play is **sociodramatic play,** in which children act out various roles and plots. Through such acting, children:

- Explore and rehearse social roles
- Learn to explain their ideas and persuade playmates

- Practice emotional regulation by pretending to be afraid, angry, brave, and so on
- Develop self-concept in a nonthreatening context

Sociodramatic play builds on pretending, which emerges in toddlerhood. But preschoolers do more than pretend; they combine their imagination with that of their friends, advancing in theory of mind (Kavanaugh, 2011). As they become conscious of gender differences, preschoolers also prefer to play with children of their own sex. Their play differs by gender.

This was evident in a day-care center in Finland, which allowed extensive free play. The boys often enacted dramas of good guys versus bad guys. In this episode, four boys did so, with Joni as the bad guy. Tuomas directed the drama and acted in it.

Good Over Evil or Evil Over Good? Boys everywhere enjoy "strong man" fantasy play, as the continued popularity of Spiderman and Superman attests. These boys follow that script. Both are Afghan refugees now in Pakistan. The taller one has a pretend machine gun.

Tuomas: . . . and now he [Joni] would take me and would hang me. . . . this would be the end of all of me.
Joni: Hands behind!
Tuomas: I can't help it . . . I have to. *[The two other boys follow his example.]*
Joni: I would put fire all around them.
[All three brave boys lie on the floor with hands tied behind their backs. Joni piles mattresses on them, and pretends to light a fire, which crackles closer and closer.]
Tuomas: Everything is lost!
[One boy starts to laugh.]
Petterl: Better not to laugh, soon we will all be dead. . . . I am saying my last words.
Tuomas: Now you can say your last wish. . . . And now I say I wish we can be terribly strong.
[At that point, the three boys suddenly gain extraordinary strength, pushing off the mattresses and extinguishing the fire. Good triumphs over evil, but not until the last moment, because, as one boy explains, "Otherwise this playing is not exciting at all."]

[adapted from Kalliala, 2006, p. 83]

Often boys' sociodramatic play includes danger and then victory over evil. By contrast, girls typically act out domestic scenes, with themselves as the adults. In the same day-care center where Joni piled mattresses on his playmates, preparing to burn them, the girls say their play is "more beautiful and peaceful . . . [but] boys play all kinds of violent games" (Kalliala, 2006, p. 110).

The prevalence of sociodramatic play varies by culture, with parents often following cultural norms. Some cultures find make-believe frivolous and discourage it; in other cultures, parents teach toddlers to be lions, or robots, or ladies drinking tea. Then children elaborate on those themes (Kavanaugh, 2011). Many children are avid television watchers, and they act out superhero themes.

That children copy superheroes and villains from video screens is troubling to many developmentalists, who prefer dramas from a child's imagination. This is not to say that screen time is necessarily bad:

Stopped in Her Tracks The birthday balloon or the tiny horse on the floor are no match for the bright images on the screen, designed to capture every child's attention. Are you critical of the parents who bought, placed, and turned on that large television for their 2-year-old, or the culture that allows such programming? Would you report this as child neglect?

FIGURE 6.1 Learning by Playing
Fifty years ago, the average child spent three hours a day in outdoor play. Video games and television have largely replaced that, especially in cities. Children seem safer if parents can keep an eye on them, but what are they learning? The long-term effects on brain and body may be dangerous.

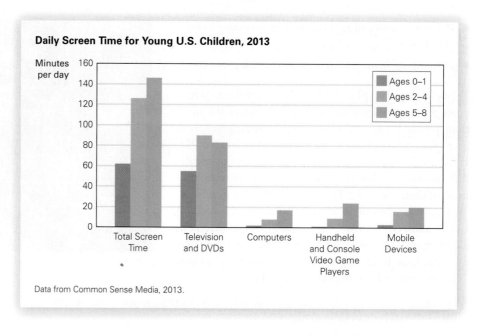

Daily Screen Time for Young U.S. Children, 2013

Data from Common Sense Media, 2013.

Video: The Impact of Media in Early Childhood
http://qrs.ly/on4ep0n

Children learn from videos, especially if adults watch with them. However, children rarely select educational programs over fast-paced cartoons with characters who hit, shoot, and kick. They act out what they have seen.

Canadian as well as U.S. organizations of professionals in child welfare (e.g., pediatricians) suggest zero screen time for children under age 2 and less than an hour a day for 2- to 6-year olds. However, about half of all North American children exceed those limits, with screen time increasing as income falls (Carson et al., 2013; Fletcher et al., 2014).

The data trouble professionals for many reasons. One is simply time—the more children are glued to screens, especially when the screen is their own hand-held device, the less they spend in active, social play (see Figure 6.1). Further, much of the most attractive media teaches aggression, reinforcing gender and ethnic stereotypes.

WHAT HAVE YOU LEARNED?

1. How might protective optimism lead to a child's acquisition of new skills and competencies?

2. How would a child's self-concept affect motivation?

3. What is an example (not in the text) of intrinsic motivation and extrinsic motivation?

4. What are children thought to gain from play?

5. Why might playing with peers help children build muscles and develop self-control?

6. What do children learn from rough-and-tumble play?

7. What do children learn from sociodramatic play?

8. Why do many experts want to limit children's screen time?

Challenges for Caregivers

Limiting screen time is only one of dozens of challenges for caregivers. How caregivers respond depends on the particular temperament of the child, on the culture, and on what the caregiver thinks is best.

Styles of Caregiving

Although thousands of researchers have traced the effects of parenting on child development, the work of one person, 50 years ago, continues to be influential. In her original research, Diana Baumrind (1967, 1971) studied 100 preschool children, all from California, almost all middle-class European Americans.

Baumrind found that parents differed on four important dimensions:

1. *Expressions of warmth.* Some parents are warm and affectionate; others, cold and critical.

2. *Strategies for discipline.* Parents vary in how they explain, criticize, persuade, and punish.

3. *Communication.* Some parents listen patiently; others demand silence.

4. *Expectations for maturity.* Parents vary in expectations for responsibility and self-control.

On the basis of these dimensions, Baumrind identified three parenting styles (summarized in Table 6.1).

> **Authoritarian parenting.** The authoritarian parent's word is law, not to be questioned. Misconduct brings strict punishment, usually physical. Authoritarian parents set down clear rules and hold high standards. They do not expect children to offer opinions; discussion about emotions and expressions of affection are rare. One adult from authoritarian parents said that "How do you feel?" had only two possible answers: "Fine" and "Tired."
>
> **Permissive parenting.** Permissive parents (also called *indulgent*) make few demands, hiding any impatience they feel. Discipline is lax, partly because they have low expectations for maturity. Permissive parents are nurturing and accepting, listening to whatever their offspring say, including cursing at the parent.
>
> **Authoritative parenting.** Authoritative parents set limits, but they are flexible. They encourage maturity, but they usually listen and forgive (not punish) if the child falls short. They consider themselves guides, not authorities (unlike authoritarian parents) and not friends (unlike permissive parents).

Other researchers describe a fourth style, called **neglectful/uninvolved parenting**. Neglectful parents are oblivious to their children's behavior; they seem not to care. Their children do whatever they want, which makes some observers think the

Protect Me from the Water Buffalo
These two are at the Carabao Kneeling Festival. In rural Philippines, hundreds of these large but docile animals kneel on the steps of the church, part of a day of gratitude for the harvest.

© ERIK DE CASTRO/REUTERS/CORBIS

OBSERVATION QUIZ

Is the father above authoritarian, authoritative, or permissive? (see answer, page 212) ▲

authoritarian parenting
An approach to child rearing that is characterized by high behavioral standards, strict punishment of misconduct, and little communication from child to parent.

permissive parenting
An approach to child rearing that is characterized by high nurturance and communication but little discipline, guidance, or control.

authoritative parenting
An approach to child rearing in which the parents set limits and enforce rules but are flexible and listen to their children.

neglectful/uninvolved parenting
An approach to child rearing in which the parents seem indifferent toward their children, not knowing or caring about their children's lives.

TABLE 6.1	Characteristics of Parenting Styles Identified by Baumrind				

				Communication	
Style	**Warmth**	**Discipline**	**Expectations of Maturity**	**Parent to Child**	**Child to Parent**
Authoritarian	Low	Strict, often physical	High	High	Low
Permissive	High	Rare	Low	Low	High
Authoritative	High	Moderate, with much discussion	Moderate	High	High

Pay Attention Children develop best with lots of love and attention. They shouldn't have to ask for it!

"He's just doing that to get attention."

parents are permissive. But permissive parents care very much about their children, unlike neglectful parents.

The following long-term effects of parenting styles have been reported, not only in the United States but in many other nations as well (Baumrind, 2005; Baumrind et al., 2010; Chan & Koo, 2011; Huver et al., 2010; Rothrauff et al., 2009; Deater-Deckard, 2013).

- *Authoritarian* parents raise children who become conscientious, obedient, and quiet but not especially happy. Such children tend to feel guilty or depressed, internalizing their frustrations and blaming themselves when things don't go well. As adolescents, they sometimes rebel, leaving home before age 20.
- *Permissive* parents raise children who lack self-control, especially in the give-and-take of peer relationships. Inadequate emotional regulation makes them immature and impedes friendships, so they are unhappy. They tend to continue to live at home, still dependent on their parents in adulthood.
- *Authoritative* parents raise children who are successful, articulate, happy with themselves, and generous with others. These children are usually liked by teachers and peers, especially in cultures that value individual initiative (e.g., the United States).
- *Neglectful/uninvolved* parents raise children who are immature, sad, lonely, and at risk of injury and abuse, not only in early childhood but also lifelong.

PROBLEMS WITH THE RESEARCH Baumrind's classification schema has been soundly criticized by more recent scientists. You can probably already see some of the ways her research was flawed.

- She did not consider socioeconomic differences.
- She was unaware of cultural differences.
- She focused more on parent attitudes than on parent actions.
- She overlooked children's temperamental differences.
- She did not recognize that some "authoritarian" parents are also affectionate.
- She did not realize that some "permissive" parents provide extensive verbal guidance.

More recent research finds that a child's temperament powerfully affects caregivers. Good caregivers treat each child as an individual who needs personalized care. For example, fearful children require reassurance, while impulsive ones need strong guidelines. Parents of such children may, to outsiders, seem permissive or authoritarian.

Overprotection may be a consequence, not a cause, of childhood anxiety (McShane & Hastings, 2009; Deater-Deckard, 2013). Every child needs some protection and guidance; some more than others. The right balance depends on the particular child, as differential susceptibility makes clear.

A study of parenting at age 2 and children's competence in kindergarten (including emotional regulation and friendships) found "multiple developmental pathways," with the best outcomes dependent on both the child and the adult (Blandon et al., 2010). Such studies suggest that simplistic advice—from a book, a professional, or a neighbor who does not know the child—may be misguided. Longitudinal, careful observation of parent–child interactions is needed before judging that a caregiver is too lax or too rigid.

A VIEW FROM SCIENCE

Culture and Parenting Style

Culture powerfully affects caregiving style. This is obviously internationally. In some nations, parents are expected to beat their children; in other nations, parents are arrested if they punish their children physically. Some cultures advise parents to never praise their children; elsewhere parents often tell their children they are wonderful, even when they are not.

This difference is evident in multiethnic nations including the United States, where parents of Chinese, Caribbean, or African heritage are often stricter than those of European backgrounds. To the surprise of many researchers, the children of some ethnic minority families seem more likely to thrive with strict parents than with easygoing ones (Parke & Buriel, 2006; F. Ng et al., 2014).

A detailed study of Mexican American mothers of 4-year-olds noted 1,477 instances when the mothers tried to change their children's behavior. Most of the time the mothers simply uttered a command and the children complied (Livas-Dlott et al., 2010).

This simple strategy, with the mother asserting authority and the children obeying without question, might be considered authoritarian. Almost never, however, did the mothers use physical punishment or even harsh threats when the children did not immediately do as they were told—which happened 14 percent of the time. For example:

> Hailey [the 4-year-old] decided to look for another doll and started digging through her toys, throwing them behind her as she dug. Maricruz [the mother] told Hailey she should not throw her toys. Hailey continued to throw toys, and Maricruz said her name to remind her to stop. Hailey continued her misbehavior, and her mother repeated "Hailey" once more. When Hailey continued, Maricruz raised her voice but calmly directed, "Hailey, look at me." Hailey continued but then looked at Maricruz as she explained, "You don't throw toys; you could hurt someone." Finally, Hailey complied and stopped.
>
> [Livas-Dlott et al., 2010, p. 572]

Note that the mother's first three efforts failed, and then a look accompanied by an explanation (albeit inaccurate in that setting, as no one could be hurt) succeeded. The researchers explain that these Mexican American families did not fit any of Baumrind's categories; respect for adult authority did not mean an authoritarian relationship. Instead, the relationship shows evident *carino* (caring) (Livas-Dlott et al., 2010).

Although cultural differences are apparent between majority and minority families in the United States, and between African American and Hispanic ethnic groups, we must not exaggerate those differences. Harsh, cold parenting seems harmful in every group, and parents of all groups usually show warmth to their children (Dyer et al., 2014).

Parental affection and warmth allow children to develop self-respect and to become compassionate adults, no matter what the parenting styles or culture (Deater-Deckard, 2013; Eisenberg et al., 2013).

Given a multi-cultural and multi-contextual perspective, developmentalists hesitate to be too specific in recommending any particular parenting style. That does not mean that all families function equally well—far from it. Signs of emotional distress, including a child's anxiety, aggression, and inability to play with others, indicate that the family may not be the safe haven of support and guidance that it should be.

Becoming Boys or Girls: Sex and Gender

Another challenge for caregivers is raising a child with a healthy understanding of sex and gender. Biology determines whether a baby is male or female (except in very rare cases): Those XX or XY chromosomes normally shape organs and produce hormones that differ for males and females.

Many scientists distinguish **sex differences,** which are biological, from **gender differences,** which are culturally prescribed. In theory, this distinction seems straightforward, but, as with every nature–nurture distinction, the interaction between sex and gender makes it hard to separate the two. Scientists need to "treat culture and biology not as separate influences but as interacting components of nature and nurture" (Eagly & Wood, 2013, p. 349).

Although that 23rd pair of chromosomes is crucial, learning is evident, first in the blue or pink caps put on newborn heads, and soon in what the children

sex differences
Biological differences between males and females, in organs, hormones, and body shape.

gender differences
Differences in male and female roles, behaviors, clothes and so on that arise from society, not biology.

Same Situation, Far Apart: Culture Clash? He wears the orange robes of a Buddhist monk, and she wears the hijab of a Muslim girl. Although he is at a week-long spiritual retreat led by the Dalai Lama and she is in an alley in Pakistan, both carry universal toys—a pop gun and a bride doll, identical to those found almost everywhere.

learn. Before age 2, children use gender labels (*Mrs., Mr., lady, man*) consistently. By age 4, children are convinced that certain toys (such as dolls or trucks) and roles (Daddy, Mommy, nurse, teacher, police officer, soldier) are reserved for one sex or the other.

Young children often believe that sex differences are *not* inborn. One little girl said she would grow a penis when she got older, and one little boy offered to buy his mother one. A 3-year-old went with his father to see a neighbor's newborn kittens. Returning home, he told his mother that there were three girl kittens and two boy kittens. "How do you know?" she asked. "Daddy picked them up and read what was written on their tummies," he replied.

Many young children do not realize that their own sex is permanent. In one preschool, the children themselves decided that one wash-up basin was for boys and the other for girls. A girl started to use the boys' basin.

> **Boy:** This is for the boys.
> **Girl:** Stop it. I'm not a girl and a boy, so I'm here.
> **Boy:** What?
> **Girl:** I'm a boy and also a girl.
> **Boy:** You, now, are you today a boy?
> **Girl:** Yes.
> **Boy:** And tomorrow what will you be?
> **Girl:** A girl. Tomorrow I'll be a girl. Today I'll be a boy.
> **Boy:** And after tomorrow?
> **Girl:** I'll be a girl.
>
> *[Ehrlich & Blum-Kulka, 2014, p. 31]*

Although they may not think of sex as biological, many preschoolers are quite rigid about gender roles. Despite their parents' and teachers' wishes, children say, "No girls [or boys] allowed." Most children consider ethnic discrimination immoral, but they accept some sex discrimination (Møller & Tenenbaum, 2011). Why?

Theories about how and why this occurs suggest explanations (Martin & Ruble, 2010; Leaper, 2013). Consider five broad theories.

Test Your Imagination Preschool children have impressive imaginations and strong social impulses. When two friends are together, they launch into amazing fun, drinking tea, crossing swords, wearing special masks and bracelets, or whatever. Adults may be more limited—can you picture these two scenes with genders switched, the boys in the tea party and the girls in the sword fight?

PSYCHOANALYTIC THEORY Freud (1938/1995) called the period from about ages 3 to 6 the **phallic stage,** named after the *phallus,* the Greek word for penis. At age 3 or 4, said Freud, boys become aware of their male sexual organ. They masturbate, fear castration, and develop sexual feelings toward their mother.

These feelings make every young boy jealous of his father—so jealous, according to Freud, that he wants to replace his dad. Freud called this the **Oedipus complex,** after Oedipus, son of a king in Greek mythology. Abandoned as an infant and raised in a distant kingdom, Oedipus returned to his birthplace and, without realizing it, killed his father and married his mother. When he discovered the horror, he blinded himself.

Freud believed that this ancient story dramatizes the overwhelming emotions that all boys feel about their parents—both love and hate. Every male feels guilty about his incestuous and murderous impulses. In self-defense, he develops a powerful conscience called the **superego,** which is quick to judge and punish.

That marks the beginning of morality, according to psychoanalytic theory. This theory contends that a boy's fascination with superheroes, guns, kung fu, and the like arises from his unconscious impulse to kill his father. Further, an adult man's homosexuality, homophobia, or obsession with guns, prostitutes, and hell arises from problems at the phallic stage.

Freud offered several descriptions of the moral development of girls. He thought they also want to eliminate the same-sex parent (her mother) and become intimate with the opposite-sex parent (her father), which explains why they dress in frills to become "daddy's girl."

According to this theory, at about age 5, children cope with guilt and fear about their strong impulses about their parents through **identification;** that is, they try to become like the same-sex parent. Consequently, young boys copy their fathers' mannerisms, opinions, and actions, and girls copy their mothers'. Both sexes exaggerate the male or female role, which is why 5-year-olds have such sexist ideas.

Most psychologists have rejected Freud's theory regarding sex and gender. They favor one or another of many other theories to explain the young child's sex and gender awareness. However, sometimes personal experience seems to confirm Freud.

phallic stage
Freud's third stage of development, when the penis becomes the focus of concern and pleasure.

Oedipus complex
The unconscious desire of young boys to replace their fathers and win their mothers' exclusive love.

superego
In psychoanalytic theory, the judgmental part of the personality that internalizes the moral standards of the parents.

identification
In psychoanalytic theory, considering the behaviors, appearance and attitudes of someone else to be one's own.

A CASE TO STUDY

My Daughters

Freud's theory suggests that parents should encourage children to follow gender roles. Many social scientists disagree. They contend that the psychoanalytic explanation of sexual and moral development "flies in the face of sociological and historical evidence" (David et al., 2004, p. 139).

I learned in graduate school that Freud was unscientific, and I deliberately dressed my baby girls in blue, not pink. However, developmental scientists seek to connect research, theory, and experience. My own experience has made me rethink my assumptions.

My rethinking began with a conversation with my eldest daughter, Bethany, when she was about 4 years old:

Bethany: When I grow up, I'm going to marry Daddy.
Me: But Daddy's married to me.
Bethany: That's all right. When I grow up, you'll probably be dead.
Me: *[Determined to stick up for myself]* Daddy's older than me, so when I'm dead, he'll probably be dead, too.
Bethany: That's OK. I'll marry him when he gets born again.

I was dumbfounded, without a good reply. I had no idea where she had gotten the concept of reincarnation. Bethany saw my face fall, and she took pity on me:

Bethany: Don't worry, Mommy. After you get born again, you can be our baby.

The second episode was a conversation I had with Rachel when she was about 5:

Rachel: When I get married, I'm going to marry Daddy.
Me: Daddy's already married to me.
Rachel: *[With the joy of having discovered a wonderful solution]* Then we can have a double wedding!

The third episode was considerably more graphic. It took the form of a "Valentine" left on my husband's pillow on February 14th by my daughter Elissa (see Figure 6.2).

Finally, when Sarah turned 5, she also said she would marry her father. I told her she couldn't, because he was married to me. Her response revealed one more hazard of watching TV: "Oh, yes, a man can have two wives. I saw it on television."

As you remember from Chapter 1, a single example (or four daughters from one family) does not prove that Freud was correct. I still think Freud was wrong on many counts. But his description of the phallic stage seems less bizarre than I once thought.

FIGURE 6.2 Pillow Talk Elissa placed this artwork on my husband's pillow. My pillow, beside it, had a less colorful, less elaborate note—an afterthought. It read, "Dear Mom, I love you too."

BEHAVIORISM *Behaviorists* believe that virtually all roles, values, and morals are learned. To behaviorists, gender distinctions are the product of ongoing reinforcement and punishment, as well as social learning.

For example, a boy who asks for both a train and a doll for his birthday is likely to get the train. Boys are rewarded for boyish requests, not for girlish ones. Indeed, the parental push toward traditional gender behavior in play and chores is among the most robust findings of decades of research on this topic (Eagly & Wood, 2013).

Gender differentiation may be subtle, with parents unaware that they are reinforcing traditional masculine or feminine behavior. For example, a study of parents talking to young children found that numbers were mentioned more often with the boys (Chang et al., 2011). This may be a precursor to the boys becoming more interested in math and science later on.

Social learning is considered an extension of behaviorism. According to that theory, people model themselves after people they perceive to be nurturing, powerful, and yet similar to themselves. For young children, those people are usually their parents.

As it happens, adults are the most gender-typed of their entire lives when they are raising young children. If an employed woman is ever to leave her job to become a housewife, it is when she has a baby. Fathers behave quite differently than mothers do with their young children. Since children learn gender roles from their parents, it is no surprise that they are quite sexist (Hallers-Haalboom et al., 2014).

Furthermore, although national policies (e.g., subsidizing early education) impact gender roles and many fathers are involved caregivers, women in every nation do much more child care, house cleaning, and meal preparation than do men (Hook, 2010). Children follow those examples, unaware that the behavior they see is caused partly by their very existence: Before children are born, many couples share domestic work equally.

Everywhere young girls and boys are socialized differently. For example, two 4-year-old girls might hug each other and hear "how sweet," but a boy who hugs a boy might be pushed away. Already by age 6, rough-and-tumble play is the only accepted way that boys touch each other. Remember that such play is much more common in boys than girls: Behaviorists would attribute that to gender-based reinforcement.

COGNITIVE THEORY *Cognitive theory* offers an alternative explanation for the strong gender identity that becomes apparent at about age 5 (Kohlberg et al., 1983). Remember that cognitive theorists focus on how children understand various ideas. One idea that children develop is the difference between the sexes. A **gender schema** is the child's understanding of male–female differences (Martin et al., 2011).

As cognitive theorists point out, young children see many gender-related differences, and they tend to perceive the world in simple, egocentric terms, as explained in Chapter 5. Therefore, they categorize male and female as opposites. Nuances, complexities, exceptions, and gradations about gender (and about almost everything else) are beyond them.

During the preoperational stage, appearance trumps logic. One group of researchers who endorse the cognitive interpretation note that "young children pass through a stage of gender appearance rigidity; girls insist on wearing dresses, often pink and frilly, whereas boys refuse to wear anything with a hint of femininity" (Halim et al., 2014, p. 1091).

In research reported by this group, parents discouraged stereotypes, but that did not necessarily sway a preschool girl who wanted a bright pink tutu and a sparkly tiara. The child's gender schema overcame experiences with parents who avoided rigid gender stereotypes.

HUMANISM ~~*Humanism* stresses the hierarchy of needs, beginning with survival, then~~ safety, then love and belonging. The final two needs—respect and self-actualization— are not considered priorities for people until the earlier three have been satisfied.

Ideally, babies have all their basic needs (level one) met, and toddlers learn to feel safe (level two). That makes love and belonging (level three) crucial during early childhood, when children seek acceptance from their peers. Therefore, the girls seek to be one of the girls and the boys to be one of the boys.

In a study of slightly older children, participants wanted to be part of same-sex groups not because they disliked the other sex but because that satisfied their need to

© SWNS/SPLASH NEWS/CORBIS

Banned from Children's Church Club This 5-year-old loves pink, wears princess dresses, and plays with Barbie dolls. Such girlish behavior is not unusual in 5-year-olds, but this child is not welcome because Romeo Clark is a boy.

gender schema
A child's cognitive concept or general belief about male and female differences.

belong (Zosuls et al., 2011). By age 6, they are astute "gender detectives," seeking to belong to the group of boys or girls. Mia is one example:

> On her first day of school, Mia sits at the lunch table eating a peanut butter and jelly sandwich. She notices that a few boys are eating peanut butter and jelly, but not one girl is. When her father picks her up from school, Mia runs up to him and exclaims, "Peanut butter and jelly is for boys! I want a turkey sandwich tomorrow."
>
> *[Quoted in Miller et al., 2013, p. 307]*

Humanism might interpret this as evidence that Mia's need to belong to the girls in her class overruled her earlier basic hunger need, which was satisfied with peanut butter and jelly.

EVOLUTIONARY THEORY *Evolutionary theory* holds that male–female sexual passion is one of humankind's basic drives, because all creatures have a powerful impulse to reproduce. Therefore, males and females try to look attractive to the other sex— walking, talking, and laughing in gendered ways. If girls see their mothers wearing makeup and high heels, they want to do likewise.

Already in early childhood, children have a powerful urge to become like the men, or like the women. This will prepare them, later on, to mate and conceive a new generation, following a deep evolutionary drive.

Thus, according to this theory, over millennia of human history, genes, chromosomes, and hormones have evolved to allow the species to survive. Genes dictate that boys are more active (rough-and-tumble play) and girls more domestic (playing house) because that prepares them for adulthood, when fathers defend against predators and mothers care for the home and children. To deny that is to deny nature.

WHAT IS BEST? Each major developmental theory strives to explain the ideas that young children express and the roles they follow. No consensus has been reached. That challenges caregivers, because they know they should not blindly follow the norms of their culture, yet they also know they need to provide guidance regarding male–female differences and everything else.

Regarding sex or gender, those who contend that nature (sex) is more important than nurture tend to design, cite, and believe studies that endorse their perspective. That has been equally true for those who believe that nurture (gender) is more important than nature. Only recently has a true interactionist perspective, emphasizing how nature affects nurture and vice versa, been endorsed (Eagly & Wood, 2013).

THINK CRITICALLY: Should children be encouraged to combine both male and female characteristics (called androgyny) or is learning male and female roles crucial for becoming a happy man or woman?

Video Activity: The Boy Who Was a Girl presents the case of David/Brenda Reimer as an exploration of what it means to be a boy or a girl.

WHAT HAVE YOU LEARNED?

1. Describe the characteristics of the parenting style that seems to promote the happiest, most successful children.

2. What are the limitations of Baumrind's description of parenting styles?

3. What seems to be the worst parenting style?

4. How does culture affect parenting style?

5. How does a child's temperament interact with parenting style?

6. What does psychoanalytic theory say about the origins of sex differences and gender roles?

7. What do behaviorists say about the origins of sex differences and gender roles?

8. How does preoperational thought lead to sexism?

9. What are the advantages and disadvantages of encouraging children to be unisex?

Teaching Right and Wrong

Parents want their children to develop a morality that is in accord with the parents' understanding of right and wrong. Of course, moral issues arise lifelong. A major discussion of children's moral judgment appears in Chapter 8; drug addiction and sexual activity are covered in Chapters 10 and 11; marriage and divorce are discussed in Chapter 13; choices in dying are explained in the Epilogue. Here we highlight what young children naturally do.

Inborn Impulses

Children have a sense of right and wrong, an outgrowth of bonding, attachment, and cognitive maturation. Children help and defend their parents even when the parents are abusive, and they punish other children who violate moral rules. Even infants may have a moral sense: An experiment found 6-month-olds preferring a puppet who helped another puppet, not an unhelpful one (Hamlin, 2014).

According to evolutionary theory, the survival of our species depended on protection, cooperation, and even sacrifice for one another. Humans needed group defense against harsh conditions and large predators. A moral sense evolved from that essential need to rely on other people (Dunning, 2011). That is why the body produces hormones, specifically oxytocin, to push people toward trust, love, and morality (Zak, 2012).

With the cognitive advances of early childhood, and increased interaction with peers, these innate moral emotions are strengthened. Children develop **empathy,** an understanding of other people's feelings and concerns, and **antipathy,** a feeling of dislike or even hatred.

Empathy leads to compassion and **prosocial behavior**—helpfulness and kindness without any obvious personal benefit. Expressing concern, offering to share, and including a shy child in a game are examples of children's prosocial behavior. The opposite is **antisocial behavior,** hurting other people.

Prosocial behavior seems to result more from emotion than from intellect, more from empathy than from theory (Eggum et al., 2011). The origins of prosocial behavior can be traced to parents who help children understand their own emotions, not from parents who tell children what emotions others might have (Brownell et al., 2013).

The link between empathy and prosocial behavior was traced longitudinally in children from 18 months to 6 years of age. Empathetic preschoolers were more likely to share, help, and play with other children in the first grade (Z. Taylor et al., 2013).

Prosocial reactions may be inborn, but they are not automatic. Some children limit empathy by "avoiding contact with the person in need [which illustrates] . . . the importance of emotion development and regulation in the development of prosocial behavior" and the influence of cultural norms (Trommsdorff & Cole, 2011, p. 136). Feeling distress may be a part of nature, but whether and how a child expresses it is nurture.

Antipathy leads to antisocial actions, which include verbal insults, social exclusion, and physical assaults (Calkins & Keane, 2009). An antisocial 4-year-old might look at another child, scowl, and then kick him or her hard without provocation. This can occur, but generally, children become more prosocial and less antisocial as they mature (Ramani et al., 2010).

Antisocial behavior may be innate as well (Séguin & Tremblay, 2013). Two-year-olds find it hard to share, even to let another child use a crayon that they have already used. Preschool children have a sense of ownership: A teacher's crayon should be shared, but if a child owns it, the other children believe that he or she is allowed to

Video: Interview with Lawrence Walker discusses what parents can do to encourage their children's moral development.

empathy
The ability to understand the emotions and concerns of another person, especially when they differ from one's own.

antipathy
Feelings of dislike or even hatred for another person.

prosocial behavior
Actions that are helpful and kind but that are of no obvious benefit to the person doing them.

antisocial behavior
Actions that are deliberately hurtful or destructive to another person.

MATTHIAS STOLT/GETTY IMAGES

LIZ BANFIELD/GETTY IMAGES

Pinch, Poke, or Pat Antisocial and prosocial responses are actually a sign of maturation: Babies do not recognize the impact of their actions. These children have much more to learn, but they already are quite social.

be selfish (Neary & Friedman, 2014). The rules of ownership are understood by children as young as 3, who apply them quite strictly.

At every age, antisocial behavior indicates less empathy. That may originate in the brain. An allele or gene may have gone awry (Portnoy et al., 2013). But it more directly results from parents who do not discuss or respond to emotions (Z. Taylor et al., 2013; Richards et al., 2014).

Aggression

Not surprisingly, given their moral sensibilities, young children judge whether another child's aggression is justified or not. The focus is on effects, not motives: A child who accidentally spilled water on another's painting may be the target of that child's justified anger.

As with adults, impulsive self-defense is more readily forgiven than is a deliberate, unprovoked attack. As young children gain in social understanding, particularly theory of mind, they gradually become better at understanding someone else's intentions, and that makes them less likely to judge an accidental action as a hostile one (Choe et al., 2013a).

The distinction between impulse and intention is critical in deciding when and how a child's aggression needs to be stopped. Researchers recognize four general types of aggression, each of which is evident in early childhood (see Table 6.2).

Instrumental aggression is common among 2-year-olds, who often want something and try to get it. This is called *instrumental* because it is a tool, or instrument, to get something that is desired. The harm in grabbing a toy, and hitting if someone resists, is not understood.

Because instrumental aggression occurs, **reactive aggression** also is common among young children. Almost every child reacts when hurt, whether or not the hurt was deliberate. The reaction may not be controlled—a child might punch in response to an unwelcome remark—but as the prefrontal cortex matures, the impulse to strike back becomes modified. Both instrumental aggression and reactive aggression are less often physical when children develop emotional regulation and theory of mind (Olson et al., 2011).

Relational aggression (usually verbal) destroys self-esteem and disrupts social networks, becoming more hurtful as children mature. A young child might tell

instrumental aggression
Hurtful behavior that is intended to get something that another person has.

reactive aggression
An impulsive retaliation for another person's intentional or accidental hurtful action.

relational aggression
Nonphysical acts, such as insults or social rejection, aimed at harming the social connection between the victim and other people.

TABLE 6.2	The Four Forms of Aggression	
Type of Aggression	**Definition**	**Comments**
Instrumental aggression	Hurtful behavior that is aimed at gaining something (such as a toy, a place in line, or a turn on the swing) that someone else has	Apparent from age 2 to 6; involves objects more than people; quite normal; more egocentric than antisocial.
Reactive aggression	An impulsive retaliation for a hurt (intentional or accidental) that can be verbal or physical	Indicates a lack of emotional regulation, characteristic of 2-year-olds. A 5-year-old can usually stop and think before reacting.
Relational aggression	Nonphysical acts, such as insults or social rejection, aimed at harming the social connections between the victim and others	Involves a personal attack and thus is directly antisocial; can be very hurtful; more common as children become socially aware.
Bullying aggression	Unprovoked, repeated physical or verbal attack, especially on victims who are unlikely to defend themselves	In both bullies and victims, a sign of poor emotional regulation; adults should intervene before the school years. (Bullying is discussed in Chapter 8.)

another, "You can't be my friend" or "You are fat," hurting another's feelings. Worse, a child might spread rumors, or tell others not to play with so-and-so. These are examples of relational aggression.

The fourth and most ominous type is **bullying aggression,** done to dominate. Bullying aggression occurs among young children but should be stopped before kindergarten, when it becomes more destructive. Not only does it destroy the self-esteem of victims, it impairs the later development of the bullies, who learn behavior habits that harm them lifelong. A 10-year-old bully may be feared and admired; a 50-year-old bully may be hated and lonely. (An in-depth discussion of bullying appears in Chapter 8.)

Aggression usually become less common from ages 2 to 6, as the brain matures and empathy increases. In addition, children learn to use aggression selectively, and that decreases both victimization and aggression (Ostrov et al., 2014). Parents, peers, and preschool teachers are pivotal mentors in this learning process.

It is a mistake to expect children to regulate their emotions on their own. If they are not guided, they may develop destructive patterns. It is also a mistake to punish aggressors too harshly because that may remove them from their zone of proximal development, where they can learn to regulate their anger.

In other words, although there is evidence that preschool children spontaneously judge others who harm people, there also is evidence that prosocial and antisocial behavior are learned (Smetana, 2013). Preschool teachers are often ideally situated to teach prosocial behavior, because aggression often arises in a social setting.

A longitudinal study found that close teacher–student relationships in preschool predicted less aggression and less victimization in elementary school. The probable reason—close relationships led children to want to please the teachers, who guided them toward prosocial, not antisocial, behavior (Runions & Shaw, 2013).

bullying aggression
Unprovoked, repeated physical or verbal attack, especially on victims who are unlikely to defend themselves.

Discipline

Children misbehave. They do not always do what parents want. Sometimes they do not know better, but sometimes they deliberately ignore a parent's request, perhaps doing exactly what they have been told not to do. Since misbehavior is part of growing up, parents must respond, and their responses affect the child's moral development.

PHYSICAL PUNISHMENT In the United States, young children are slapped, spanked, or beaten more often than are infants or older children, and more often than children in Canada or western Europe. Within the United States, frequency varies (MacKenzie et al., 2011; S. Lee et al., 2015; Lee & Altschul, 2015). Spanking is more frequent:

- In the southern United States than in New England
- By mothers than by fathers
- Among conservative Christians than among non-religious families
- Among African Americans than among European Americans
- Among European Americans than among Asian Americans
- Among U.S.-born Hispanics than among immigrant Hispanics
- In low-SES families than in high-SES families

Those differences do not preclude variations from one family to another: Many a secular, European American, immigrant, high-SES father in Boston spanks his child, even though most men who have all those characteristics do not.

Adults usually believe that their upbringing helped them become the person they are. For that reason, most adults tend to think that their past childhood punishment was proper. Moreover, physical punishment (called **corporal punishment** because it hurts the body) usually succeeds momentarily because immediately afterward children are quiet.

However, longitudinal research finds that children who are physically punished are more likely to be disobedient and to become bullies, delinquents, and then abusive adults (Gershoff et al., 2012). They are also less likely to learn quickly in school or to enroll in college (Straus & Paschall, 2009).

In fact, longitudinal research finds that children who are *not* spanked are more likely to develop self-control. As spanking increases, so does misbehavior (Gershoff, 2013). The correlation between spanking and later aggression holds for children of all ethnic groups.

In 33 nations (mostly in Europe), corporal punishment is illegal; in many nations on other continents, it is the norm. In the United States, parents use it often. In schools, teachers may legally paddle children in 19 of the 50 states. Overall, in one recent year, 218,466 children were corporally punished at school, 16 percent of whom had been designated as having an intellectual disability. Further, a disproportionate number of the paddled children are African American boys. These data raise questions about fairness and justice (Morones, 2013; Gershoff et al., 2015).

Although some adults believe that physical punishment will "teach a lesson" of obedience, the lesson that children learn may be that "might makes right." When they become bigger and stronger, children who have been physically disciplined tend to use corporal punishment on others—their classmates, their wives or husbands, their children.

corporal punishment
Discipline techniques that hurt the body (corpus) of someone, from sparking to serious harm, including death.

Smack Will the doll learn never to disobey her mother again?

© URBANZONE/ALAMY

OPPOSING PERSPECTIVES

Is Spanking OK?

Opinions about spanking are influenced by past experience and cultural norms. That makes it hard for opposing perspectives to be understood by people on the other side (Ferguson, 2013). Try to suspend your own assumptions as you read this.

What might be right with spanking? Over the centuries many parents have done it, so it has stood the test of time. Indeed, in the United States, parents who never spank are unusual. Spanking seems less common in the twenty-first century than in the twentieth (Taillieu et al., 2014), but 85 percent of U.S. adolescents who were children at the end of the twentieth century remember being slapped or spanked by their mothers (Bender et al., 2007).

Corporal punishment has decreased worldwide, but it is far from rare. In the first years of the twenty-first century, among low-SES, two-parent families in the United States, 68 percent of parents say they spanked their 3-year-olds within the previous 30 days (S. Lee et al., 2015). Can such a popular method be wrong?

One pro-spanking argument is that the correlations reported by developmentalists (between spanking and later depression, low achievement, aggression, crime, and so on) may be caused by a third variable, not spanking itself. A suggested third variable is child misbehavior: Parents who use corporal punishment think the disobedient child caused the spanking, not vice versa. Perhaps such children are more likely to be delinquent, depressed, and so on, not because they were spanked but in spite of being spanked.

As one team, noting problems with correlational research, explains, "Quite simply, parents do not need to use corrective actions when there are no problems to correct" (Larzelere & Cox, 2013, p. 284). These authors note that every disciplinary technique, if used frequently, correlates with misbehavior, but the punishment may be the result, not the cause.

Another third variable may be poverty. Since people who spank their children tend to have less education than people who use other punishment, SES may be the underlying reason spanked children average lower academic achievement.

The solution may be to eliminate poverty, not to forbid spanking. When researchers try to eliminate the effect of every third variable, especially SES, they find a smaller correlation between spanking and future problems than most other studies do (Ferguson, 2013).

What might be wrong with spanking? One problem is adults' emotions: Angry spankers may become abusive. Children are sometimes seriously injured and even killed by parents who use corporal punishment. One pediatrician who hesitates to argue against all spanking, everywhere, nonetheless notes that physical injury is common and that parents should never spank in anger, cause bruises that last more than 24 hours, use an object, or spank a child under age 2 (Zolotor, 2014).

Another problem is the child's immature cognition. Many children do not understand why they are spanked. Parents assume the transgression is obvious, but children may think the parents' anger, not the child's actions, caused spanking (Harkness et al., 2011).

Almost all the research finds that children who are spanked suffer in many ways. They are more depressed, more antisocial, more likely to hate school, and less likely to have close friends. Many continue to suffer in adulthood. One developmentalist says, "We know enough now to stop hitting our children" (Gershoff, 2013, p. 133).

Yet the evidence does not satisfy everyone. For example, one study of parents who attend conservative Protestant churches found that, as expected, they spanked their children more often than other parents did. However, unexpectedly, children spanked during early (but not middle) childhood did not develop the lower self-esteem and increased aggression that spanked children usually do (Ellison et al., 2011). Indeed, the opposite was more likely.

The authors of the study suggest that, since spanking was the norm among those families, conservative Protestant children do not perceive being spanked as stigmatizing or demeaning. Moreover, religious leaders tell parents to assure children that they are loved and never to spank in anger. As a result, their children may "view mild–to–moderate corporal punishment as legitimate, appropriate, and even an indicator of parental involvement, commitment, and concern" (Ellison et al., 2011, p. 957).

As I write these words, I realize which perspective is mine. As you saw in the opening of this chapter, I believe that children should never be hit. I am one of many developmentalists who are convinced that alternatives to spanking are better for the child and a safeguard against abuse. But a dynamic-systems view considers every form of discipline as part of a complex web, and a multi-cultural perspective suggests that, whenever cultures differ radically about child development, it is wise to reflect before judging.

I do not think children should be spanked. Yet I know that I am influenced by my background and context. So is every researcher; so are you.

She Understands? Children who are spanked remember the pain and anger, but not the reason for the punishment. It is better for parents to explain what the misbehavior was. However, sometimes explanations are not understood.

psychological control
A disciplinary technique that involves threatening to withdraw love and support, using a child's feelings of guilt and gratitude to the parents.

time-out
A disciplinary technique in which a person is separated from other people and activities for a specified time.

Many studies of children from all family constellations and backgrounds find that physical punishment of young children correlates with delayed theory of mind and increased aggression (Olson et al., 2011). To prove cause without a doubt would require parents of monozygotic twins to raise them identically, except that one twin would be spanked often and the other never. Of course, that is unethical as well as impossible.

Nonetheless, most developmentalists wonder why parents would take the chance. The best argument in favor of spanking is that alternative punishments may be worse (Larzelere et al., 2010; Larzelere & Cox, 2013). Let us consider alternatives.

PSYCHOLOGICAL CONTROL Another common method of discipline is called **psychological control,** in which children's shame, guilt, and gratitude are used to control their behavior (Barber, 2002). Psychological control may reduce academic achievement and emotional understanding, just as spanking is thought to do (Alegre, 2011).

Consider Finland, one of the nations where corporal punishment is now forbidden. Parents were asked about psychological control (Aunola et al., 2013). If parents strongly agreed with the following questions, they were considered to use psychological control:

1. "My child should be aware of how much I have done for him/her."
2. "I let my child see how disappointed and shamed I am if he/she misbehaves."
3. "My child should be aware of how much I sacrifice for him/her."
4. "I expect my child to be grateful and appreciate all the advantages he/she has."

The higher the parents scored on these four measures of psychological control, the lower the children's math scores were—and this connection grew stronger over time. Moreover, the children tended to have negative emotions (depression, anger, and so on). Thus, psychological control may have some of the same consequences as corporal punishment.

TIME-OUT AND INDUCTION A disciplinary technique often used with young children in North America is the **time-out,** in which a misbehaving child is required to sit quietly, without toys or playmates, for a short time. Time-out is not to be done in anger, or for too long; it is recommended that parents use a calm voice and that the time-out last only one to five minutes (Morawska & Sanders, 2011). Time-out works as a punishment if the child really enjoys "time-in," when the child is happily engaged with the parents or with peers.

Time-out is favored by many experts. For example, in the large, longitudinal evaluation of the Head Start program highlighted in Chapter 5, an increase in time-outs and a decrease in spankings were considered signs of improved parental discipline (U.S. Department of Health and Human Services, 2010).

However, the same team who criticized the correlation between spanking and misbehavior also criticized the quality of research favoring time-out. They added that time-out did not always work: If "misbehavior is motivated by wanting to escape from the situation . . . time-out reinforces the misbehavior" (Larzelere & Cox, 2013, p. 289).

Often combined with the time-out is another alternative to physical punishment and psychological control—*induction*, in which the parents talk extensively with the offender, helping children understand why their behavior was wrong.

Ideally, time-out allows children to calm down. Then a strong and affectionate parent–child relationship means that children explain their emotions and parents listen carefully. Children can explain what they *might have* done instead of what *was* done, although such hypothetical reasoning is difficult—maybe impossible—for young children.

Bad Boy or Bad Parent? For some children and in some cultures, sitting alone is an effective form of punishment. Sometimes, however, it produces an angry child without changing the child's behavior.

Thus, induction may help children internalize morality, but it takes time and patience. Since 3-year-olds confuse causes with consequences, they cannot answer an angry "Why did you do that?" or appreciate a long explanation.

Simple induction ("Why did he cry?") may be more appropriate, but even that is hard before a child develops theory of mind. Nonetheless, induction seems to pay off over time. Children whose parents used induction when they were 3-year-olds became children with fewer externalizing problems in elementary school (Choe et al., 2013b).

WHAT HAVE YOU LEARNED?

1. What is the nature perspective on how people develop morals?

2. What is the nurture perspective?

3. How might children develop empathy and antipathy as they play with one another?

4. How might children develop antipathy?

5. What is the connection between empathy and prosocial behavior?

6. What are the similarities and differences of the four kinds of aggression?

7. How does moral development relate to discipline?

8. Why have many nations made corporal punishment illegal?

9. What are the arguments for and against psychological control?

10. When is time-out an effective punishment and when is it not?

11. What are the advantages and disadvantages of using induction as punishment?

Harm to Children

We have saved for the end of this chapter the most disturbing topic: child maltreatment. The assumption thus far has been that adults seek the best for young children and that their disagreements (e.g., what to feed, what kind of preschool, how to discipline) arise from contrasting theories about how best to foster happy and healthy children.

However, sometimes parents angrily harm their own offspring and other adults do not protect children. When a child is officially deemed abused or neglected, almost always (90 percent of the time) the perpetrator was the child's biological parent (U.S. Department of Health and Human Services, January 15, 2015).

Parents are not the only ones to blame. The food, air, play space, and medical care that all children need is not always available, in part because communities and governments have other priorities. Often preventive and protective measures that could stop injuries, abuse, or other forms of harm are missing. Far more children die from violence—either accidental or deliberate—than from any specific disease, and almost every child is harmed by hazards that could have been prevented.

Protection for Every Child

Overall, an important change in terminology is needed. Instead of using the term *accident prevention*, public health experts prefer **harm reduction.** *Accident* implies that an injury is random, unpredictable; if anyone is at fault, it's a careless parent or a child. Further, *accident* usually refers to a sudden, unexpected event. Instead, *harm reduction* makes it clear that much can be done long before an injury or illness occurs to reduce the damage from any hazard.

harm reduction
Reducing the potential negative consequences of behavior, such as safety surfaces replacing cement at a playground.

Many community practices and national policies to reduce harm have already been mentioned. Among them are measures to ensure adequate nutrition, oral health, safe play spaces, preventive immunization, and quality preschools.

There is neither time nor space to explore all the other ways young children may be harmed by social neglect of their needs. We present only two examples, motor-vehicle accidents and lead. In both cases, a long process began with research, eventually protecting thousands of young lives.

INJURIES FROM CARS AND TRUCKS Worldwide, motor vehicles cause millions of premature deaths among adults as well as children: Not until age 40 does any specific disease overtake cars and trucks as a cause of mortality. Of all the life years lost worldwide, 14 percent are caused by accidents, with motor-vehicle accidents the most common (World Health Organization, 2010).

In some nations, malnutrition, malaria, and other infectious diseases cause most infant and child deaths, but even in those nations too many children are killed by cars. India, for example, has one of the highest rates worldwide of child motor-vehicle deaths; most children who die in such accidents are pedestrians (Naci et al., 2009). Everywhere, young children are at greater risk than slightly older ones. In the United States, 2- to 5-year-olds are more than twice as likely to be seriously hurt in crashes as 6- to 10-year-olds.

Why are young children so vulnerable? Some reasons have just been explained. Immaturity of the prefrontal cortex makes young children impulsive; they plunge into danger. Unlike infants, their motor skills allow them to run into the street in a flash, before a watching adult can stop them. Their curiosity is boundless; their impulses uninhibited.

Fatal accidents for young passengers and pedestrians are less common than they were a few decades ago, even though more cars are on the road and more miles are driven. In the United States, in 2012, fewer than 3 preschoolers per 100,000 were killed by motor vehicles compared to almost 12 per 100,000 in 1970. How did this victory occur?

A major reason is mandated child-safety seats. In the 1970s, doctors and nurses in a leading hospital in Washington State advised new parents to take their newborn

Same Situation, Far Apart: Keeping Everyone Safe Preventing child accidents requires action by both adults and children. In the United States *(below left)*, adults passed laws and taught children—including this boy who buckles in his stuffed companion. In France *(below right)*, teachers stop cars while children hold hands to cross the street—each child keeping his or her partner moving ahead.

MIDDLE CHILDHOOD
Body and Mind

WHAT WILL YOU KNOW?

- Whose fault is it if a child is obese?
- Why are some math concepts difficult at age 4 but easier at age 8?
- Are schools in the United States better than schools in other nations?
- What causes a child to have autism?

My daughter seemed lonely in first grade. Her teacher suggested she might become friends with Alison, who was also shy and bright. I spoke to Alison's mother, a friendly, big-boned woman named Sharon. We arranged a play date. Soon Bethany and Alison became best friends, as the teacher had predicted.

Unpredicted, however, was that Sharon became my friend. She and her husband, Rick, had one other child, a pudgy boy. All three children thrived in our local public school.

When my daughter and Alison were in fifth grade, I mentioned to Rick my interest in longitudinal research. He recalled a friend, a professional photographer, who took pictures of Alison and her brother every year. The friend wanted them for his portfolio; Rick was happy to oblige. He then retrieved an old album with stunning depictions of sibling relationships and personality development from infancy on. Alison was smiling and coy, even as a baby, and her infant brother was gaunt and serious.

Rick was pleased with my interest; Sharon was not.

"I hate that album," she said, slamming it shut. She explained that her pediatrician insisted she stick to a four-hour breast-feeding schedule and told her to never give her son formula. That's why she hated that album; it was evidence of an inexperienced mother heeding a doctor's advice while starving her son.

Decades later, my daughter and I are still friends with Alison and Sharon, whose adult son is obese. His baby photo haunts me now as well. Did Sharon cause his obesity by underfeeding him in infancy or by overfeeding him later? Or did his genes or culture harm him?

This chapter begins our description of middle childhood, usually a happy time when teachers help children learn, as my daughter's teachers did. This chapter also describes some problems of this period, and the interaction of genes and environment that cause them. Consequences and solutions are complex: Sharon and Rick are not the only aging parents who still wonder what they could have done differently. I wonder, too. ■

CHAPTER 7

A Healthy Time

middle childhood
The period between early childhood and early adolescence, approximately from ages 6 to 11.

Genes and environment usually safeguard **middle childhood,** as the years from about 6 to 11 are called (Konner, 2010). Fatal diseases and accidents are rare; nature and nurture make these the healthiest years of life. In the United States in 2010, the death rate for 5- to 14-year-olds was less than half of the rate for ages 1 to 4, less than one-fifth the rate for ages 15 to 24, and less than one-sixtieth the rate overall (National Center for Health Statistics, 2014).

Genetic diseases are more threatening in early infancy or old age, infectious diseases are kept away via immunization, and fatal accidents—although the most common cause of child death—are relatively uncommon.

The already-low death rate of children this age continues to fall with modern medicine. In the United States in 1950, the death rate per 100,000 for 5- to 14-year-olds was 60; in 2010, it was not quite 13. Minor illnesses—ear infections, tonsils, and flu—have also been reduced (National Center for Health Statistics, 2014).

Oral health has improved, with more brushing and fluoride. A survey found that 75 percent of U.S. children saw a dentist for preventive care in the past year, and for 70 percent of them, the condition of their teeth was very good (Iida & Rozier, 2013).

Expert Eye-Hand Coordination The specifics of motor-skill development in middle childhood depend on the culture. These flute players are carrying on the European Baroque musical tradition that thrives among the poor, remote Guarayo people of Bolivia.

Children's Health Habits

In marked contrast to infancy or adolescence, middle childhood is a time of slow and steady growth, a little more than 2 inches and 5 pounds a year (more than 5 centimeters and 2 kilograms). Children can maintain good health if adults teach them how, providing regular medical care. This is crucial, because those who have inadequate health care in childhood tend to have poor health in adulthood, even if their circumstances improve (Miller & Chen, 2010; Blair & Raver, 2012).

Camps for children with asthma, cancer, diabetes, sickle-cell anemia, and other chronic illnesses are particularly beneficial because the examples of other children and the guidance of knowledgeable adults help children learn self-care. Such care needs to become habitual during these years lest teenage rebellion manifest in resistance to special diets, pills, warning signs, and doctors (Dean et al., 2010; Naughton et al., 2014).

PHYSICAL ACTIVITY Beyond the sheer fun of playing, the benefits of physical activity—especially games with rules, which children now can follow—last a lifetime. Exercise advances physical, emotional, and mental health. Exercise improves academic achievement, with direct benefits of better cerebral blood flow and more neurotransmitters and indirect benefits of better mood and energy (Singh et al., 2012).

A new concept in psychology is *embodied cognition,* the idea that human thoughts are affected by body health, comfort, position, and so on. This suggests that children learn by doing and that an active body promotes learning (Pouw et al., 2014).

Sports are not always beneficial. Organizations have developed guidelines to prevent concussions among 7- and 8-year-olds in football and to halt full-body impact in ice hockey among children under age 12. The fact that regulations are needed to protect children from brain injury is sobering (Toporek, 2012).

Are They Having Fun? Helmets, uniforms, and competition—more appropriate for adults? Children everywhere want to do what the adults do, so probably these ones are proud of their ice hockey team.

WHERE TO EXERCISE Children reap the benefits of exercise in their neighborhoods, schools, and sports leagues. However, finding a place to play is much more difficult than it was.

Neighborhood play was once a daily event. Rules and boundaries were adapted to the context (out of bounds was "past the tree" or "behind the parked truck"). Stickball, touch football, tag, hide-and-seek, and dozens of other running and catching games lasted forever—or at least until dark. The play was active, interactive, and inclusive—ideal for children. It also taught morality. As one scholar notes:

> Children play tag, hide and seek, or pickup basketball. They compete with one another but always according to rules, and rules that they enforce themselves without recourse to an impartial judge. The penalty for not playing by the rules is not playing, that is, social exclusion.
>
> *[Gillespie, 2010, p. 298]*

For school-age children, "social exclusion" is a steep price to pay for insisting on their own way. Peers are crucial for self-esteem.

Unfortunately, modern life undercuts neighborhood play. Vacant lots and empty fields have disappeared, and parents fear "stranger danger"—thinking that a stranger will hurt their child (which is exceedingly rare) and ignoring the many benefits of outside play. As one advocate of unsupervised, creative childhood play sadly notes:

> Actions that would have been considered paranoid in the '70s—walking third-graders to school, forbidding your kid to play ball in the street, going down the slide with your child in your lap—are now routine.
>
> *[Rosin, 2014]*

Indoor activities (homework, screen time) crowd out outdoor play. Parents used to tell their children "go out and play"; now they say "stay inside." Some parents enroll their children in organized sports—tennis, karate, cricket, yoga, rugby, baseball, or soccer. However, few children from poor families or with disabilities are in private sports leagues.

As a result, the children most likely to benefit are least likely to engage, even when enrollment is free. The reasons are many, the consequences sad (Dearing et al., 2009). Another group unlikely to participate are older girls, again a group particularly likely to benefit from athletic activity (Kremer et al., 2014).

"Just remember, son, it doesn't matter whether you win or lose—unless you want Daddy's love."

Idyllic Two 8-year-olds, each with a 6-year-old sister, all four daydreaming or exploring in a very old tree beside a lake in Denmark—what could be better? Ideally, all the world's children would be so fortunate, but most are not.

THINK CRITICALLY: Do you agree with Japan or the United States regarding physical activity in school? Why?

childhood overweight
In a child, having a BMI (body mass index) above the 85th percentile, according to the U.S. Centers for Disease Control's 1980 standards for children of a given age.

childhood obesity
In a child, having a BMI (body mass index) above the 95th percentile, according to the U.S. Centers for Disease Control's 1980 standards for children of a given age.

Active play in school is a logical alternative. However, in the United States, currently schools and teachers are judged by test scores, which shrinks time for physical education and recess. A study of Texas elementary schools found that 24 percent had no recess at all and only 1 percent had recess several times a day (W. Zhu et al., 2010).

Texas is no exception. A survey asking teachers of 10,000 third-graders found that about one-third of the children had less than 15 minutes of recess each day. Children deprived of recess were more often of lower SES, in classes that were "hard to manage," in public schools, and in cities. They also had fewer scheduled gym periods (Barros et al., 2009).

These researchers write that "many children from disadvantaged backgrounds are not free to roam their neighborhoods or even their own yards unless they are accompanied by adults. For many of these children, recess periods may be the only opportunity for them to practice their social skills with other children" (Barros et al., 2009, p. 434).

Even when schools mandate gym, classes may be too full for active play, or requirements may be ignored. For instance, although Alabama requires 30 minutes of physical education daily in primary schools, the average in one district was only 22 minutes. No school in that district had recess or after-school sports (Robinson et al., 2014).

Ironically, schools in Japan, where many children score well on international tests, usually have five or more recess breaks totaling more than an hour each day, in addition to gym classes. Japanese public schools often are well-equipped for physical activity, with outdoor yards, indoor gyms, and pools. The Japanese believe physical activity promotes learning and character development (Webster & Suzuki, 2014).

Health Problems in Middle Childhood

Some chronic health conditions, including Tourette syndrome, stuttering, and allergies, may worsen during the school years. Even minor problems—wearing glasses, repeatedly coughing or blowing one's nose, or having a visible birthmark—can affect children's self-esteem. We will now look at two other examples of physical conditions that can affect learning.

CHILDHOOD OBESITY Body mass index (BMI) reflects the ratio of weight to height. **Childhood overweight** is usually defined as a BMI above the 85th percentile for children at that age, and **childhood obesity** is defined as a BMI above the 95th percentile. Those percentiles were set decades ago, when fewer children were overweight. In 2012, 18 percent of 6- to 11-year-olds in the United States were obese (Ogden et al., 2014). As excessive weight builds, future health risks increase, average achievement decreases, self-esteem falls, and loneliness rises (Harrist et al., 2012).

Childhood obesity has more than doubled since 1980 in all three nations of North America (Ogden et al., 2011). Since 2000, U.S. rates have leveled off, even declining in preschool children, but increases continue in most other nations, including the most populous two, China and India (Gupta et al., 2012; Ji et al., 2013). A group of Chinese scholars concluded: "The prognosis for China's childhood-obesity epidemic is dire" (Ji et al., 2013, p. 1).

There are "hundreds if not thousands of contributing factors" for childhood obesity, from the cells of the body to the norms of the society (Harrison et al., 2011, p. 51). Dozens of genes affect weight by influencing activity level, hunger, food

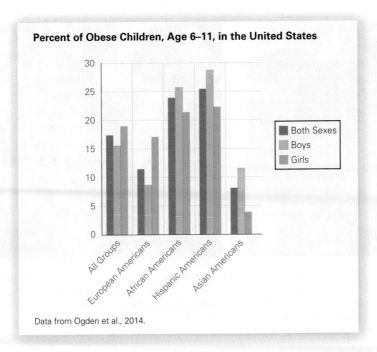

Percent of Obese Children, Age 6–11, in the United States

Data from Ogden et al., 2014.

FIGURE 7.1 Heavier and Heavier The incidence of obesity (defined here as the 95th percentile or above, per the Centers for Disease Control and Prevention 2000 growth charts) increases with age. Infants and preschoolers have lower rates than schoolchildren, which suggests that nurture is more influential than nature.

OBSERVATION QUIZ

Are boys more likely to be overweight than girls? (see answer, page 246) ◄

preferences, body type, and metabolism. New genes and alleles that affect obesity—and that never act alone—are discovered virtually every month (Dunmore, 2013).

Knowing that genes are involved may slow down the impulse to blame people for being overweight. However, genes do not explain the marked increases in obesity, since genes change little over the generations (Harrison et al., 2011).

Look at the figure on obesity among 6- to 11-year-olds in the United States (see Figure 7.1). Are the large ethnic differences genetic?

Before answering, consider gender: European American *girls* are twice as likely to be obese as boys, but in the other groups *boys* are more often obese than girls. Ethnic differences in childhood obesity almost disappeared in a study that controlled for family income and early parenting (Taveras et al., 2013). Therefore, genes are not the primary culprit for overweight children.

What parenting practices make children too heavy? Obesity rates rise if:

● Infants are not breast-fed and if they are fed solid foods before 4 months

● Preschoolers watch TV in their bedrooms and drink soda

● School-age children have insufficient sleep, extensive screen time, and little active play

(Hart et al., 2011; Taveras et al., 2013)

Children themselves have *pester power*—the power to make adults do what they want (Powell et al., 2011). They pester parents to buy foods advertised on television. Attempts to limit sugar and fat clash with the financial goals of many corporations, whose advertising and packaging of calorie-dense foods fuels the epidemic of obesity.

On the plus side, many schools have policies that foster good nutrition. A national survey in the United States found that schools are reducing all types of commercial food advertising. Nonetheless, vending machines are prevalent in high schools, and free fast-food coupons are often used as incentives in elementary schools (Terry-McElrath et al., 2014).

Simply offering healthy food is not enough to convince children to change their habits; context and culture are crucial (Hanks et al., 2013). Communities can build parks, bike paths, and sidewalks, and nations can decrease subsidies for sugar and corn.

Same Situation, Far Apart Children have high energy but small stomachs, so they enjoy frequent snacks more than big meals. Yet snacks are typically poor sources of nutrition. Who is healthier: the Latin American children eating lollypops at a theme park in Florida or the Japanese children eating *takoyaki* (an octopus dumpling) as part of a traditional celebration near Tokyo?

Immigrants who want to "eat American" may not be aware of the correlation between fast food consumption and childhood obesity (Alviola et al., 2013). In North America and Europe, those who immigrated as adults are less often obese than the native-born, yet the opposite is true for their children. A Canadian review of 49 studies on immigrant eating habits suggests that dietary change, itself the product of many factors, is the main reason for obesity increases (Sanou et al., 2014).

ASTHMA **Asthma** is a chronic inflammatory disorder of the airways that makes breathing difficult. Sufferers have periodic attacks, sometimes rushing to the hospital emergency room.

In the United States, childhood asthma rates have tripled since 1980 (see Figure 7.2). Parents report that 15 percent of U.S. 5- to 11-year-olds have been diagnosed with asthma at some time, and almost 11 percent still suffer from it (National Center for Health Statistics, 2014).

Researchers have long sought the causes of asthma. Some alleles are contributors, although none acts alone. Several aspects of modern life—carpets, pollution, house pets, airtight windows, parental smoking, cockroaches, dust mites, less outdoor

asthma
A chronic disease of the respiratory system in which inflammation narrows the airways from the nose and mouth to the lungs, causing difficulty in breathing. Signs and symptoms include wheezing, shortness of breath, chest tightness, and coughing.

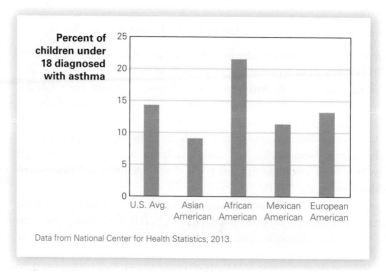

FIGURE 7.2 Not Breathing Easy Of all U.S. children younger than 18, 14 percent have been diagnosed at least once with asthma. Why are African American children more likely to have asthma? Puerto Rican children have even higher rates (not shown). Is that nature or nurture, genetics or pollution?

Data from National Center for Health Statistics, 2013.

VISUALIZING DEVELOPMENT

Childhood Obesity Around the Globe

Obesity now causes more deaths worldwide than malnutrition. Reductions are possible. A multi-faceted prevention effort—including mothers, preschools, pediatricians, grocery stores, and even the White House—has reduced obesity in the United States for 2- to 5-year-olds. It was 13.9 percent in 2002 and was 8.4 percent in 2012. However, obesity rates from age 6 to 60 remain high everywhere.

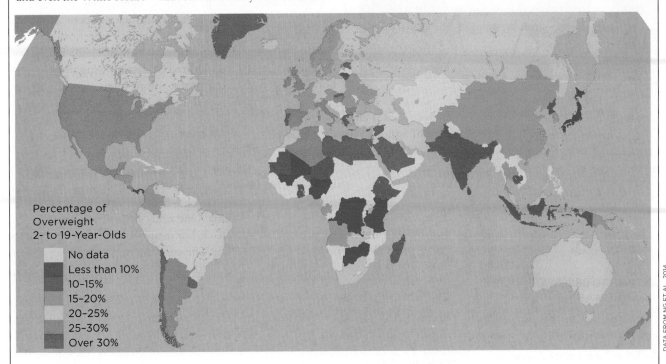

Percentage of Overweight 2- to 19-Year-Olds

- No data
- Less than 10%
- 10–15%
- 15–20%
- 20–25%
- 25–30%
- Over 30%

DATA FROM NG ET AL., 2014.

ADS AND OBESITY

Nations differ in children's exposure to televised ads for unhealthy food. The amount of this advertising continues to correlate with childhood obesity (e.g., Hewer, 2014). Parents can reduce overweight by limiting screen time and playing outside with their children. The community matters as well: When neighborhoods have no safe places to play, rates of obesity soar.

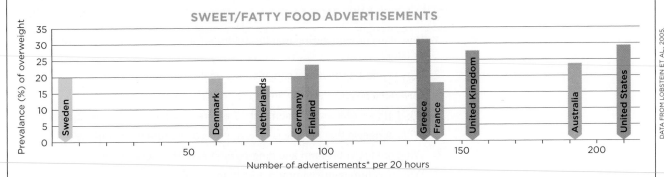

SWEET/FATTY FOOD ADVERTISEMENTS

Prevalance (%) of overweight — *Number of advertisements* per 20 hours*

Sweden, Denmark, Netherlands, Germany, Finland, Greece, France, United Kingdom, Australia, United States

DATA FROM LOBSTEIN ET AL., 2005.

WORLD HEALTH ORGANIZATION (WHO) RECOMMENDATIONS FOR PHYSICAL ACTIVITY FOR CHILDREN

 1 Children ages 5 to 17 should be active for at least an hour a day.

 2 More than an hour of exercise each day brings additional benefits.

 3 Most physical activity should be aerobic. Vigorous activities should occur 3 times per week or more.

WHO also recommends daily exercise for adults of every age—including centenarians.

ADAPTED FROM WORLD HEALTH ORGANIZATION, 2011.

Pride and Prejudice In some city schools, asthma is so common that using an inhaler is a sign of pride, as suggested by the facial expressions of these two boys. The "prejudice" is beyond the walls of this school nurse's room, in a society that allows high rates of childhood asthma.

ANSWER TO OBSERVATION QUIZ (from page 243) Overall, no. But in some groups, yes. Rates of obesity among Asian American boys are almost three times higher than Asian American girls. ●

play—correlate with asthma attacks, but again no single factor is the cause. A combination of sensitivity to allergens, early respiratory infections, and compromised lung function increases wheezing and shortness of breath, making asthma more likely (Mackenzie et al., 2014).

Some experts suggest a *hygiene hypothesis:* that "the immune system needs to tangle with microbes when we are young" (Leslie, 2012, p. 1428). Children may be overprotected from viruses and bacteria. In their concern about hygiene, parents prevent exposure to minor infections, diseases, and family pets that would strengthen their child's immunity.

This hypothesis is supported by data showing that (1) firstborn children develop asthma more often than later-born ones; (2) asthma and allergies are less common among farm children; and (3) children born by cesarean delivery (very sterile) have a greater incidence of asthma. Overall, it may be "that despite what our mothers told us, cleanliness sometimes leads to sickness" (Leslie, 2012, p. 1428).

Perhaps. However, there are "many paths to asthma," with no one cause identified as crucial (H. Kim et al., 2010). As a reviewer of the hygiene hypothesis notes, "the picture can be dishearteningly complicated" (Couzin-Frankel, 2010, p. 1168).

Fortunately, many factors can reduce asthma. One study began by acknowledging that exertion sometimes triggers an asthma attack, but then it examined programs that advance physical fitness in children with asthma. The conclusion: Exercise helps reduce attacks, as long as it is tailored to the particular needs of the child (Wanrooij et al., 2014).

Parents of children with asthma can do their part. In one study, 133 Latino caregivers—all cigarette smokers—agreed to allow a Spanish-speaking counselor who respected Latino culture to come repeatedly to their homes (Borrelli et al., 2010). The counselor placed a smoke monitor in the bedroom of the child with asthma. Each later week she told the caregiver the rate of child exposure to smoke, and she suggested ways to reduce smoking.

Three months later, one-fourth of the caregivers had quit smoking completely, and many of the rest had cut down. The average child's smoke exposure declined by half. Asthma attacks diminished (Borrelli et al., 2010).

WHAT HAVE YOU LEARNED?

1. How does growth during middle childhood compare with growth earlier or later?
2. Why is middle childhood considered a healthy time?
3. How does physical activity affect the child's education?
4. What are several reasons some children are less active than they should be?
5. What suggests that obesity is caused more by culture than genetics?
6. What are the short-term and long-term effects of childhood obesity?
7. Why is asthma more common now than it was?

Cognition

Learning is rapid. Some children, by age 11, beat their elders at chess, play music that adults pay to hear, publish poems, or solve complex math problems. Others survive on the streets or fight in civil wars. Children can learn almost anything. Adults must decide how and what to teach.

Product of Cognition Concrete thinking is specific, such as caring for a lamb until it becomes an award-winning sheep, as this New Jersey 4-H member did.

Piaget in Middle Childhood

Piaget called cognition during these years **concrete operational thought,** characterized by new concepts that enable children to be logical. *Operational* comes from the Latin word *operare,* meaning "to work; to produce." By calling this period operational, Piaget emphasized productive thinking.

The school-age child, no longer limited by egocentrism, performs logical operations on *concrete* experiences and problems, those that are grounded in actual experience, like the concrete of a cement sidewalk. Concrete thinking arises from what is visible, tangible, and real, not abstract and theoretical (as at the next stage, formal operational thought). Children become more systematic, objective, scientific—and educable.

> **concrete operational thought**
> Piaget's term for the ability to reason logically about direct experiences and perceptions.
>
> **classification**
> The logical principle that things can be organized into groups (or categories or classes) according to some characteristic they have in common.
>
> **seriation**
> The concept that things can be arranged in a logical series, such as the number series or the alphabet.

ADVANCES IN LOGIC One logical operation is **classification,** organizing things into groups (or *categories* or *classes*) according to some characteristic. For example, *family* includes parents, siblings, and cousins. Other common classes are animals, toys, and food. Each class includes some elements and excludes others; each is part of a hierarchy.

Food, for instance, is an overarching category, with the next-lower level of the hierarchy being meat, grains, fruits, and so on. Most subclasses can be further divided: Meat includes poultry, beef, and pork, each of which can be divided again. The mental operation of moving up and down the hierarchy (understanding that bacon is always pork, meat, and food, but most food, meat, and pork are not bacon) is beyond preoperational children.

Piaget devised many classification experiments. For example, a child is shown a bunch of nine flowers—seven yellow daisies and two white roses. Then the child is asked, "Are there more daisies or more flowers?"

Until about age 7, most children answer, "More daisies." The youngest children offer no justification, but some 6-year-olds explain that "there are more yellow ones than white ones" or "because daisies are daisies, they aren't flowers" (Piaget et al., 2001). By age 8, most children can classify: "More flowers than daisies," they say.

In addition to classification, two other logical concepts (i.e., conservation and reversibility) were mentioned in Chapter 5. Piaget described a fourth concept, **seriation,** the

Math and Money Third-grader Perry Akootchook understands basic math, so he might beat his mother at "spinning for money," shown here. Compare his concrete operational skills with that of a typical preoperational child, who would not be able to play this game and might give a dime for a nickel.

realization that things can be arranged in a logical *series*. Seriation is crucial for using (not merely memorizing) the alphabet or the number sequence.

By age 5, most children can count up to 100. However, because they do not yet grasp seriation, they may be unable to estimate where any particular two-digit number would be placed on a line that starts at 0 and ends at 100. In many other ways, the advancing logic of the concrete operational child helps with arithmetic—that $12 + 3 = 3 + 12$ and that 15 is always 15 (conservation), that all the numbers from 20 to 29 are in the 20s (classification), that 134 is less than 143 (seriation), and that if $5 \times 3 = 15$, then $15 \div 5$ is 3 (reversibility).

BRAIN CONNECTIONS Brain scans were not available to Piaget, but it is easy to see that his understanding of logic was prescient, reflecting what we now know as brain maturation. As children grow older, connections form between the various lobes and regions of the brain. Such connections are crucial for the complex tasks that children must master, which require "smooth coordination of large numbers of neurons" (P. Stern, 2013, p. 577).

Certain areas of the brain, called *hubs*, are locations where massive numbers of axons meet. Hubs tend to be near the corpus callosum, and damage to them correlates with brain dysfunction, as in dementia (now called neurocognitive disorders) and schizophrenia (Crossley et al., 2014).

Particularly important are links between the hypothalamus and the amygdala, because emotions need to be regulated so that learning can occur. Stress impairs these connections: Slow academic mastery is one more consequence of early maltreatment (Hanson et al., 2015).

On the other hand, the development of many logical concepts, including classification as Piaget described it, depends on neurological pathways from the general (food) to the particular (bacon) and back again. Those paths are not forged until brain maturation allows connective links in the hubs.

One example of the need for brain connections is learning to read, perhaps the most important intellectual accomplishment of middle childhood. Reading is not instinctual: Our ancestors never did it, and until recent centuries, only a few scribes and scholars could make sense of marks on paper. Consequently, the brain has no areas dedicated to reading, the way it does for talking or gesturing (Sousa, 2014).

Instead, reading uses many parts of the brain—one for sounds, another for recognizing letters, another for sequencing, another for comprehension and more. By working together, these parts foster listening, talking, and thinking, and then put it all together (Lewandowski & Lovett, 2014).

Indeed, every skill, every logical idea, every thought suddenly applied from one circumstance to another requires connections between many neurons. As Piaget recognized, a cascade of new intellectual concepts results when connections allow a logical idea to be applied to many specifics.

Vygotsky and the Social Context

Like Piaget, Vygotsky felt that educators should consider children's thought processes, not just the outcomes. He appreciated children as curious, creative learners. He wrote that rote memorization rendered the child "helpless in the face of any sensible attempt to apply any of this acquired knowledge" (Vygotsky, 1994a, pp. 356–357).

THE ROLE OF INSTRUCTION Unlike Piaget, Vygotsky stressed teaching. He thought that learners need a bridge between developmental potential and necessary skills via *guided participation* and *scaffolding,* within the *zone of proximal development* (all concepts already explained).

Confirmation of the role of instruction comes from a U.S. study of children who, because of their school's entry-date cutoff, are either relatively old kindergartners or quite young first-graders. At the end of the school year, achievement scores of the 6-year-old first-graders far exceeded those of kindergarten 6-year-olds who were only one month younger (Lincove & Painter, 2006).

Internationally as well, children who begin school earlier tend to be ahead in academic achievement compared to those who enter later, an effect still evident when the children were in high school. But we shouldn't be too quick to decide that early schooling is necessary. As the author of this study noted, there are many possible explanations, and early schooling did not advance later learning in every nation (Sprietsma, 2010).

Remember that Vygotsky believed that education occurs everywhere, not just at school. He would not be surprised that fifth-grade children from ten U.S. cities who scored high on tests of math and reading had had extensive cognitive stimulation long before fifth grade from three crucial sources:

Girls Can't Do It As Vygotsky recognized, children learn whatever their culture teaches. Fifty years ago, girls were in cooking and sewing classes. No longer. This 2012 photo shows 10-year-olds Kamrin and Caitlin in a Kentucky school, preparing for a future quite different from that of their grandmothers.

1. Families (e.g., parents read to them daily when they were toddlers)

2. Preschools (with a variety of learning activities)

3. First-grade curriculum (e.g., emphasizing literacy, with individualized instruction)

In this study, most children from families of low SES did not experience all three sources of stimulation, but those who did showed more cognitive advances by fifth grade than the average high-SES child (Crosnoe et al., 2010).

Perhaps the most important role of teachers is to help children focus. **Selective attention,** the ability to concentrate on some stimuli while ignoring others, improves markedly at about age 7. For example, many new readers confuse the letters *b, d,* and *p*—which are actually all the same, a small circle connected to a line. An astute mentor is needed to call the child's attention to the placement of that line.

selective attention
The ability to concentrate on some stimuli while ignoring others.

Similar crucial distinctions are present in every script, not just Roman ones—and are confusing to young children and to everyone not guided in that script. (That is why Web sites require decoding of wavy letters and numbers in order to prove that a human, not a robot, wants to access certain information: Humans have learned what to attend to and what to ignore, and it is difficult to program a machine to do so.)

School-age children not only notice various stimuli (one form of attention) but also select appropriate responses when several possibilities conflict (Wendelken et al., 2011). Selective attention improves with guidance and neurological maturation (Stevens & Bavelier, 2012).

For example, children in school listen, take notes, and ignore distractions (all difficult at age 6, easier by age 10). Ignoring the din of the cafeteria, children react quickly to gestures and facial expressions. On the baseball diamond, mentors (coaches and teammates) teach batters to ignore attempts to distract them and teach fielders to move into position as soon as the bat hits the ball. That's selective attention, guided by culture and the brain, as the prefrontal cortex continues to mature.

INTERNATIONAL CONTEXTS Vygotsky's emphasis on sociocultural contexts contrasts with Piaget's maturational, self-discovery approach. Vygotsky believed that cultures educate via customs, structures, objects, and mentors. For example, if a child is surrounded by full bookcases, daily newspapers, street signs, and reading adults, that child will read better than a child who has had little exposure to print, even if both are equally bright and in the same class.

Never Lost These children of Varanasi sleep beside the Ganges in the daytime. At night they use their excellent sense of direction to guide devotees from elsewhere.

THINK CRITICALLY: If some children learn by observation, some by direct instruction, and some by hands-on experience, how should a teacher teach?

Skills of the Street Children In many nations, children sell to visitors, using math and business skills that few North American children know. This boy was offering necklaces to visitors at the Blue Mosque in Afghanistan.

Context affects more than academic learning. A stunning example of knowledge acquired from the social context comes from Varanasi, a city in northeast India. Many Varanasi children have an extraordinary sense of spatial orientation. In one experiment, children were blindfolded, spun around, and led to a second room, yet many still knew which direction was north (Mishra et al., 2009). How did they know? Consider social context.

In Varanasi, everyone refers to direction to locate objects. The English equivalent might be that the dog is sleeping not by the door but southeast. From their early days, children learn north/south/east/west. By middle childhood, they have internalized a sense of direction.

Many studies in the United States validate that the social context shapes what and how children learn. The process is reciprocal: Children are eager to learn, and that drives them to learn in whichever manner their culture presents.

For example, children who are used to learning by observation (as in some American Indian cultures) are better at remembering overheard folktales than children who expect direct instruction (Tsethlikai & Rogoff, 2013). Again, Vygotsky would not be surprised.

Information Processing

Educators and psychologists regard both Piaget and Vygotsky as insightful. International research confirms the merits of their theories.

A third approach to understanding cognition adds crucial insight. The *information-processing perspective* benefits from technology that allows much more detailed data and analysis than was possible for Piaget or Vygotsky.

Thousands of researchers who study cognition benefit from the information-processing approach, although "information processing is not a single theory but, rather, a framework characterizing a large number of research programs" (Miller, 2011, p. 266). The basic assumption of this framework is that, like computers, people can access large amounts of information. They then:

(1) Select relevant units of information (as a search engine does),

(2) Analyze and connect (as software programs do), and

(3) Express their conclusions so that another person can understand (as a networked computer or a printout might do).

By tracing the paths and links of these neurological functions, scientists track learning. The brain's gradual growth, increasingly seen in detailed scans, confirms the usefulness of the information-processing perspective. So do data on children's school achievement: Absences, vacations, new schools, and even new teachers may set back a child's learning because repeated experiences are needed to solidify brain connections.

LEARNING MATH One of the leaders of the information-processing perspective is Robert Siegler, who has studied the details of children's cognition in math (Siegler & Chen, 2008; Siegler & Lortie-Forgues, 2014). Apparently, children do not suddenly grasp the logic of the number system, as Piaget seemed to expect.

Instead, math knowledge accrues gradually. New and better strategies for calculation are tried, ignored, half-used, abandoned, and finally adopted. Siegler compared the acquisition of knowledge to waves on an ocean beach when the tide is rising. There is substantial ebb and flow, although eventually a new level is reached.

One example is the ability to estimate where a number might fall on a line, such as where the number 53 would be placed on a line from 0 to 100. This skill gradually builds from the first grade on, predicting later math skills (Feigenson et al., 2013). Understanding the size of fractions (e.g., that ³⁄₁₆ is smaller than ¼) may also be crucial, as this predicts later math achievement in many nations (Torbeyns et al., 2015). Some other early math achievements (such as counting to 100) do not correlate with math achievement, an interesting finding from information-processing research.

Arithmetic Strategies: The Research of Robert Siegler http://qrs.ly/o84ep10

MEMORY Many scientists who study memory take an information-processing approach. Each of the three major steps in the memory process—sensory memory, working memory, and long-term memory—is affected by both maturation and experience.

Sensory memory (also called the *sensory register*) is the first component of the human information-processing system. It stores incoming stimuli for a split second, with sounds retained slightly longer than sights. To use terms explained in Chapter 3, *sensations* are retained for a moment, and then some become *perceptions*.

Once some sensations become perceptions, the brain selects the meaningful ones and transfers them to working memory for further analysis. It is in **working memory** (formerly called *short-term memory*) that current, conscious mental activity occurs.

Processing, not mere exposure, gets information into working memory. As Siegler's waves metaphor suggests, strategies for processing information do not appear suddenly. Children gradually develop ways to increase working memory (Camos & Barrouillet, 2011). For this reason, working memory improves markedly in middle childhood (Cowan & Alloway, 2009) (see Table 7.1).

sensory memory
The component of the information-processing system in which incoming stimulus information is stored for a split second to allow it to be processed. (Also called the *sensory register*.)

working memory
The component of the information-processing system in which current conscious mental activity occurs. (Formerly called *short-term memory*.)

TABLE 7.1	Advances in Memory from Infancy to Age 11
Child's Age	**Memory Capabilities**
Under 2 years	Infants remember actions and routines that involve them. Memory is implicit, triggered by sights and sounds (an interactive toy, a caregiver's voice).
2–5 years	Words are now used to encode and retrieve memories. Explicit memory begins, although children do not yet use memory strategies. Children remember things by rote (their phone number, nursery rhymes) without truly understanding them.
5–7 years	Children realize that some things should be remembered, and they begin to use simple strategies, primarily rehearsal (repeating an item again and again). This is not a very efficient strategy, but with enough repetition, automatization occurs.
7–9 years	Children use new strategies if they are taught them. Children use visual clues (remembering how a particular spelling word looks) and auditory hints (rhymes, letters), evidence of brain functions called the visual–spatial sketchpad and phonological loop. Children now benefit from the organization of things to be remembered.
9–11 years	Memory becomes more adaptive and strategic as children become able to learn various memory techniques from teachers and other children. They can organize material themselves, developing their own memory aids.

Information from Meadows, 2006.

long-term memory
The component of the information-processing system in which virtually limitless amounts of information can be stored indefinitely.

knowledge base
A body of knowledge that makes it easier to learn new information in a particular area.

control processes
Mechanisms (including selective attention, metacognition, and emotional regulation) that combine memory, processing speed, and knowledge to regulate the analysis and flow of information within the information-processing system. (Also called *executive processes*.)

metacognition
"Thinking about thinking," or the ability to evaluate a cognitive task in order to determine how best to accomplish it and then to monitor and adjust one's performance on that task.

Cultural differences are evident. For example, many Muslim children are taught to memorize all 80,000 words of the Quran, so they learn strategies unknown to non-Muslim children to remember long passages (Hein et al., 2014).

Finally, information from working memory may be transferred to **long-term memory,** to be stored for minutes, hours, days, months, or years. The capacity of long-term memory—how much can be crammed into one brain—is huge by the end of middle childhood. Together with sensory memory and working memory, long-term memory organizes ideas and reactions, fostering more effective learning (Wendelken et al., 2011).

Crucial to long-term memory is not merely *storage* (depositing material into the brain) but also *retrieval* (bringing past learning into working memory). Retrieval is easier for some memories (especially vivid, emotional ones) than for others, but for everyone, long-term memory is imperfect. We all forget and distort memories.

Memory depends on review and repetition, with the learner engaged in practice that involves thought (not mindless review) (Brown et al., 2014). Memories fade unless the information is *processed*. Children might memorize 3 × 9 = 27, but without processing, they might not know how many Valentine's Day candies to buy to give three to each of their nine friends.

THE MORE YOU KNOW . . . Research on information processing finds that the more people know, the more they can learn. Having an extensive **knowledge base,** or a broad body of knowledge, makes it easier to remember and understand related new information.

Three factors affect the knowledge base: past experience, current opportunity, and personal motivation. The last item in this list explains why children's knowledge base is not what their parents or teachers would choose. Some schoolchildren memorize words and rhythms of hit songs, know plots and characters of television programs, or recite the names and histories of basketball players. Yet they do not know whether World War I was in the nineteenth or twentieth century or whether Pakistan is in Asia or Africa.

What Does She See? It depends on her knowledge base and personal experiences. Perhaps this trip to an aquarium in North Carolina is no more than a break from the school routine, with the teachers merely shepherding the children to keep them safe. Or, perhaps she has learned about sharks and dorsal fins, about scales and gills, about warm-blooded mammals and cold-blooded fish, so she is fascinated by the swimming creatures she watches. Or, if her personal emotions shape her perceptions, she feels sad about the fish in their watery cage or finds joy in their serenity and beauty.

CONTROL PROCESSES Memory, processing speed, and the knowledge base come together via **control processes,** which regulate analysis and flow of information. Control processes are related to **metacognition,** which is an understanding of one's own learning. The better a person is at metacognition, the more efficient their control processes become.

According to scholars of cognition, "Middle childhood may be crucial for the development of metacognitive monitoring and study control processes" (Metcalfe & Finn, 2013, p. 19). Metacognition can be considered the ultimate control process because a person can evaluate a learning goal, decide how to accomplish it, monitor performance, and finally adjust effort to make sure it is accomplished.

Control processes require the brain to organize, prioritize, and direct mental operations, much as the CEO (chief executive officer) of a business organizes, prioritizes, and directs business operations. For that reason, control processes are also called *executive processes,* and the ability to use them is called executive function (already mentioned in Chapter 5).

Executive function improves each year of middle childhood (Masten, 2014; Bjorklund et al., 2009). For example, unlike first-graders, fourth-grade students can listen to the teacher talk about the river Nile, ignoring classmates who are chewing gum or passing notes.

Fortunate Child or Too Fortunate?
Mothers everywhere help children with homework, as this mother does. Is it ever true that parents should let their children struggle, and fail, without them?

Older children can decide to do their homework before watching television or to review their spelling words before breakfast, creating mnemonics to remember the tricky parts. They can anticipate what teachers will ask. All these signify executive function.

The Maturing Brain

Recall that emotional regulation, theory of mind, and left–right coordination emerge in early childhood, the outcome of brain maturation. The developing corpus callosum connects the hemispheres, enabling balance and two-handed coordination, while myelination adds speed.

Maturation of the prefrontal cortex—the executive part of the brain—allows better control processes, evident in all three theories—Piaget, Vygotsky, and information-processing. We now describe two additional advances.

THINK QUICK; TOO SLOW Advance planning and impulse control are aided by faster **reaction time,** which is how long it takes to respond to a stimulus. Increasing myelination reduces reaction time every year from birth until about age 16. Skill at games is an obvious example, from scoring on a video game, to swinging at a pitch, to kicking a speeding soccer ball toward a teammate.

Many more complex examples involve social and academic skills. For instance, being able to calculate when to utter a witty remark and when to stay quiet is something few 6-year-olds can do. By age 10, some children have quick reactions, allowing them to (1) realize that a comment could be made and (2) decide what it could be, (3) imagine someone else's response, and in the same split second (4) know when something should *not* be said.

Both quick responses and quick inhibition develop. Children become less likely to blurt out wrong answers but more likely to enjoy games that require speed. Interestingly, children with reading problems are slower as well as more variable in reaction time, and that itself slows down every aspect of reading (Tamm et al., 2014).

AUTOMATIC PROCESSING One final advance in brain function in middle childhood is **automatization,** when a sequence of thoughts and actions is repeated so often that it seems to be automatic. Firing one neuron sets off a chain reaction, just as saying a few words brings to mind an entire phrase.

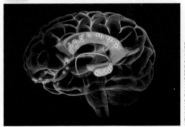

Video Activity: Brain Development: Middle Childhood depicts the changes that occur in a child's brain from age 6 to age 11.

reaction time
The time it takes to respond to a stimulus, either physically (with a reflexive movement such as an eyeblink) or cognitively (with a thought).

automatization
A process in which repetition of a sequence of thoughts and actions makes the sequence routine, so it no longer requires conscious thought.

Consider again learning to read. At first, eyes (sometimes aided by a guiding finger) focus intensely, painstakingly making out letters and sounding out each one. This slowly leads to the perception of syllables and then words. Eventually, the process becomes so routine that people driving along a highway read billboards that they have no interest in reading. Children do the same, gradually learning to read without conscious control.

Automatic reading aids other academic skills. One longitudinal study of second-graders—from the beginning to the end of the school year—found a reciprocal interaction from one type of academic proficiency to another, with automatic processing advancing as learning continued (Lai et al., 2014). Learning to speak a second language, to recite the multiplication tables, and even to write one's name gradually becomes automatic.

WHAT HAVE YOU LEARNED?

1. Why did Piaget call cognition in middle childhood *concrete operational thought*?

2. What might be examples of classification in a category not listed in the text, such as transportation or plants?

3. How do Vygotsky and Piaget differ in their explanation of cognition in middle childhood?

4. How are the children of Varanasi an example of Vygotsky's theory?

5. How does selective attention make it easier for a child to sit in a classroom?

6. What does information processing add to traditional theories of cognitive development?

7. How does Siegler describe the process of learning math concepts?

8. What aspects of memory improve markedly during middle childhood?

9. Why does the knowledge base increase in middle childhood?

10. How might advances in control processes and executive function help a student learn?

11. Why does quicker reaction time improve the ability to learn?

Teaching and Learning

As we have seen, middle childhood is a time of great learning. Children worldwide learn whatever adults in their culture teach, and their brains are ready. Traditionally, they were educated at home, but now more than 95 percent of the world's 7-year-olds are in school, with completion rates for primary education at 92 percent (World Bank, 2015).

A foundation of this is language, with many young children learning two or more languages and almost all mastering several codes. Therefore, to understand education, we begin with language and then focus directly on school.

Language

As you remember, by age 6, children already know the basic vocabulary and grammar of their first language. Many also speak a second language fluently. These linguistic abilities allow the formation of a strong knowledge base, enabling children in middle childhood to learn thousands of new words and to apply complex grammar rules. Here are some specifics.

VOCABULARY As Piaget stressed, in middle childhood thinking becomes more flexible and logical. This allows children to understand prefixes, suffixes, compound words, phrases, and metaphors. For example, 2-year-olds know *jump,* but 10-year-olds also know *jump start, jumpsuit, ski jump,* and both meanings of *jumper.*

Metaphors, jokes, and puns are finally comprehended. Some jokes ("What is black and white and read all over?" "Why did the chicken cross the road?") are funny only during middle childhood. Younger children don't understand why anyone would laugh at them and teenagers find them lame and stale, but 6- to 11-year-olds delight in puns and unexpected answers to normal questions, as well as metaphors and similes.

Indeed, a lack of metaphorical understanding, even if a child has a large vocabulary, signifies cognitive problems (Thomas et al., 2010). Humor is a diagnostic tool; a child who takes a joke too literally may have difficulty with social interaction.

Metaphors are context-specific, building on the knowledge base. For bilingual children, understanding metaphors is difficult—and an important part of language mastery (Heredia & Cieślicka, 2015).

An American who lives in China noted phrases that U.S. children learn but that children in cultures without baseball do not, including "dropped the ball," "on the ball," "play ball," "throw a curve," "strike out" (Davis, 1999). If a teacher says "keep your eyes on the ball," some immigrant children might not pay attention because they are looking for that ball.

CODE-SWITCHING One aspect of language that advances markedly in middle childhood is pragmatics, defined in Chapter 5. This practical knowledge of communication is evident in the contrast between talking formally to teachers and informally with friends. As children master pragmatics, they become more adept at making friends.

Shy 6-year-olds cope far better with the social pressures of school if they use pragmatics well (Coplan & Weeks, 2009). By contrast, children with autism spectrum disorder may learn to talk, but they are still very poor at pragmatics (Klinger et al., 2014).

Mastery of pragmatics allows children to change styles of speech, or "linguistic codes," depending on their audience. Each code includes many aspects of language—tone, pronunciation, gestures, sentence length, idioms, vocabulary, and grammar. Code-switching is part of the social awareness that humans need to function well.

Sometimes the switch is between *formal code* (used in academic contexts) and *informal code* (used with friends); sometimes it is between standard (or proper) speech and dialect or slang (used on the street). Code in texting—numbers (411), abbreviations (LOL), emoticons (:-D), and spelling (r u ok?)—demonstrate pragmatics.

Some children do not know that slang, curses, and even contractions are not used in formal language. Everyone needs some language instruction because the logic of grammar (*who* or *whom*?) and of spelling (*you*) is impossible to deduce. Peers use the informal code; local communities transmit dialect, metaphors, and pronunciation; schools teach the formal code.

BILINGUAL EDUCATION Every nation includes many bilingual children; few of the world's 6,000 languages are school languages. For instance, English is the language of instruction in Australia, but 17 percent of the children speak one of 246 other languages at home (Centre for Community Child Health & Telethon Institute for Child Health Research, 2009).

In the United States, almost 1 school-age child in 4 speaks a language other than English at home. Most of them also speak English well, according to their parents

Typical yet Unusual It's not unusual that these children are texting in French—they live in Bordeaux, and children everywhere text their friends. The oddity is that a girl and a boy are lying head to head, which rarely occurs in middle childhood. The explanation? They are siblings. Like dogs and cats that grow up together, familiarity overtakes hostility.

FIGURE 7.3 Hurray for Teachers? More children in the United States are bilingual and most of them now speak English well, from about 40 percent in 1980 to 82 percent in 2011.

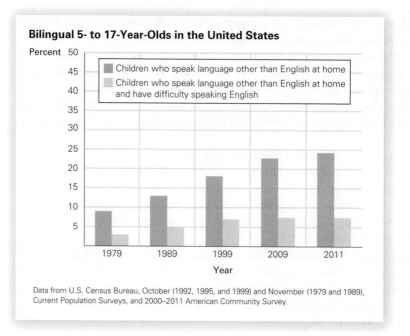

Bilingual 5- to 17-Year-Olds in the United States

Percent

- Children who speak language other than English at home
- Children who speak language other than English at home and have difficulty speaking English

Year: 1979, 1989, 1999, 2009, 2011

Data from U.S. Census Bureau, October (1992, 1995, and 1999) and November (1979 and 1989), Current Population Surveys, and 2000–2011 American Community Survey.

ELLs (English Language Learners)
Children in the United States whose proficiency in English is low—usually below a cutoff score on an oral or written test. Many children who speak a non-English language at home are also capable in English; they are *not* ELLs.

immersion
A strategy in which instruction in all school subjects occurs in the second (usually the majority) language that a child is learning.

bilingual education
A strategy in which school subjects are taught in both the learner's original language and the second (majority) language.

ESL (English as a second language)
An approach to teaching English in which all children who do not speak English are placed together in an intensive course to learn basic English.

Months or Years? ESL classes, like this one in Canada, often use pictures and gestures to foster word learning. How soon will these children be ready for regular instruction?

© IAN TAYLOR/FIRST LIGHT/CORBIS

(see Figure 7.3). In addition, many other children speak a dialect of English that differs from school English. Teachers need to help children master the formal code, without making them feel that their home language is inferior.

If a child learns one language and then masters a second language, the brain adjusts. A study found no brain differences between monolingual children and bilingual children who spoke both languages from the first years of life.

However, from about age 4 through adolescence, the older children are when they learn a second language, the more likely their brains develop more cortical thickness on the left side (the language side) (Klein et al., 2014). This reflects what we know about language: School-age children can master a second language, but they must work at it.

In the United States, some children of every ethnicity are called **ELLs,** or **English Language Learners,** based on their ability to speak, write, and read English. Age, schooling, and SES all have an effect, but even high-SES children of Spanish-speaking homes are, on average, less proficient readers than European American children (Howard et al., 2014). Their learning style may clash with the school's style, and their achievements may not be reflected in the standard tests.

Methods for teaching children the majority language range from **immersion,** in which instruction occurs entirely in the new language, to the opposite, in which children are taught in their first language until the second language can be taught as a "foreign" tongue (a rare strategy in the United States but common elsewhere). Between these extremes in the United States lies **bilingual education,** with instruction in two languages, and **ESL (English as a second language),** with all non-English speakers taught English in one multilingual group.

Each of these methods sometimes succeeds and sometimes fails. The research is not yet clear as to which approach is best at what age, although vast differences are apparent from one nation to another (Mehisto & Genesee, 2015). The success of any method is affected by the literacy of the home environment (frequent reading, writing, and listening in any language helps); the warmth, training, and skill of the teacher; and the national context.

In the United States, in the twenty-first century, many bilingual classes have been eliminated, for reasons less reflective of the minds of children than on the politics of adults (Menken & Solorza, 2014). We turn now to schools. As you will see, political controversies about bilingual education are only one example of many disputed ideas regarding education.

THINK CRITICALLY: Do you think English-speaking children in the United States should learn a second language in elementary school? Why or why not?

International Schooling

Everywhere, children are taught to read, write, and do arithmetic. Because of brain maturation and sequenced learning, 6-year-olds are not expected to multiply three-digit numbers or read paragraphs fluently out loud, but every nation teaches 10-year-olds to do so. [See At About This Time.] International research on economic growth suggests that better-educated adults become more productive workers (Hanushek & Woessmann, 2009).

DIFFERENCES BY NATION Although literacy and numeracy (reading and math, respectively) and educated workers are valued everywhere, curricula vary by nation, by

At About This Time

Math

Age	Norms and Expectations
4–5 years	• Count to 20. • Understand one-to-one correspondence of objects and numbers. • Understand *more* and *less*. • Recognize and name shapes.
6 years	• Count to 100. • Understand *bigger* and *smaller*. • Add and subtract one-digit numbers.
8 years	• Add and subtract two-digit numbers. • Understand simple multiplication and division. • Understand word problems with two variables.
10 years	• Add, subtract, multiply, and divide multidigit numbers. • Understand simple fractions, percentages, area, and perimeter of shapes. • Understand word problems with three variables.
12 years	• Begin to use abstract concepts, such as formulas, algebra.

Math learning depends heavily on direct instruction and repeated practice, which means that some children advance more quickly than others. This list is only a rough guide, meant to illustrate the importance of sequence.

At About This Time

Reading

Age	Norms and Expectations
4–5 years	• Understand basic book concepts. • Understand that books are written from front to back, with print from left to right, and that letters make words that describe pictures. • Recognize letters—name the letters on sight. • Recognize and spell own name.
6–7 years	• Know the sounds of the consonants and vowels, including those that have two sounds (e.g., *c, g, o*). • Use sounds to figure out words. • Read simple words, such as *cat, sit, ball, jump*.
8 years	• Read simple sentences out loud, 50 words per minute, including words of two syllables. • Understand basic punctuation, consonant–vowel blends. • Comprehend what is read.
9–10 years	• Read and understand paragraphs and chapters, including advanced punctuation (e.g., the semicolon). • Answer comprehension questions about concepts as well as facts. • Read polysyllabic words (e.g., *vegetarian, population, multiplication*).
11–12 years	• Demonstrate rapid and fluent oral reading (more than 100 words per minute). • Vocabulary includes words that have specialized meaning in various fields. For example, *liberties, federal, parliament*, and *environment* all have special meanings. • Comprehend paragraphs about unfamiliar topics. • Sound out new words, figuring out meaning using cognates and context. • Read for pleasure.
13+ years	• Continue to build vocabulary, with greater emphasis on comprehension than on speech. Understand textbooks.

Reading is a complex mix of skills, dependent on brain maturation, education, and culture. The sequence given here is approximate; it should not be taken as a standard to measure any particular child.

FIGURE 7.4 Focus on Facts As achievement test scores become the measure of learning, education in art, music, and movement has been squeezed out. Artists worry that creativity and imagination may be lost as well.

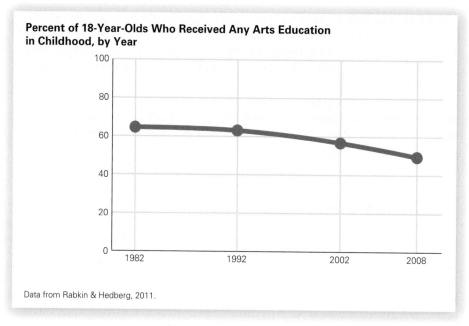

Percent of 18-Year-Olds Who Received Any Arts Education in Childhood, by Year

Data from Rabkin & Hedberg, 2011.

Teacher Technique Some children are riveted by TV but distracted at school. Has this teacher found a solution, or is she making the problem worse?

hidden curriculum
The unofficial, unstated, or implicit rules and priorities that influence the curriculum, organization, and setting in a school.

community, and by school. These variations are evident in the results of international tests, in the mix of school subjects, and in the relative power of parents, educators, and political leaders.

Geography, music, and art are essential in some places, not in others. Half of all U.S. 18- to 24-year-olds say they had no arts education in childhood, either in school or anywhere else (Rabkin & Hedberg, 2011) (see Figure 7.4). By contrast, educators in Finland consider arts education essential in every school, with a positive impact on learning (Nevanen et al., 2014).

Educational practices differ even between nations that are geographically and culturally close, and from one region to another within nations. For example in Canada, children in the province of Quebec study science about half as much as those in Ontario (50 compared to 92 hours per year) (Snyder & Dillow, 2013).

International variations are vast in the **hidden curriculum,** which includes all the implicit values and assumptions evident is course offerings, schedules, tracking, teacher characteristics, discipline, teaching methods, sports competition, student government, extracurricular activities, and so on.

Same Situation, Far Apart: Spot the Hidden Curriculum Literacy is central to the curriculum for schoolchildren everywhere, no matter how far apart they live. However, in the U.S. classroom at the left, boys and girls learn together, clothes are casual, history books are paperback and illustrated, and children of every background read the same stories with the same patriotic—but not religious—themes. The hidden curriculum is quite different for the boy memorizing his holy book on the right.

Having Fun? Not necessarily.

OBSERVATION QUIZ
What three differences do you see between recess in New York City *(left)* and Santa Rosa, California *(right)*? (see answer page 261) ▲

In the United States, the hidden curriculum is thought to be the underlying reason for a disheartening difference in how students respond if teachers offer special assistance. In one study, middle-class children were more likely to ask for help than lower class children, who feared they would be criticized (Calarco, 2014). The researcher concluded that divergent expectations benefited the middle-class students. Teachers need to help low-SES children directly, without criticism, not wait for the children to ask for help.

More generally, if teachers' gender, ethnicity, or economic background is unlike that of the students, children may conclude that education is irrelevant for them. If the school has gifted classes, or if a charter school co-located in the school building has more computers or better lighting, the hidden message is that the rest of the students are less capable.

THINK CRITICALLY: What is the hidden curriculum at your college or university?

INTERNATIONAL TESTING Over the past two decades, more than 50 nations have participated in at least one massive international test of educational achievement. Science and math achievement are measured by **Trends in Math and Science Study (TIMSS).** The main test of reading is the **Progress in International Reading Literacy Study (PIRLS).** These tests have been given every few years since 1995, with East Asian nations ranking at the top.

Elaborate and extensive measures are in place to make the PIRLS and the TIMSS valid. For instance, test items are designed to be fair and culture-free, and participating children represent the diversity (economic, ethnic, etc.) of each nation's children. Consequently, most social scientists respect the data gathered from these tests.

The tests are far from perfect, however. Designing test items that are equally challenging to every student in every nation is impossible. Should fourth-graders be expected to understand fractions, graphs, and simple geometry, or should the test examine only basic operations with whole numbers? Can specific questions be fair to every culture? The following item was used to test fourth-grade math:

> Al wanted to find out how much his cat weighed. He weighed himself and noted that the scale read 57 kg. He then stepped on the scale holding his cat and found that it read 62 kg. What was the weight of the cat in kilograms?

This problem involves simple subtraction, yet 40 percent of U.S. fourth-graders got it wrong. Were they unable to subtract 57 from 62, or did they not understand the example, or did the abbreviation for kilograms confuse them because—unlike children in most nations—they are more familiar with pounds? On this item, children from Yemen were at the bottom, with 95 percent of them failing. Is that because few of them have cats for pets or weigh themselves on a scale? As you see, national and cultural contexts may affect test scores.

Trends in Math and Science Study (TIMSS)
An international assessment of the math and science skills of fourth- and eighth-graders.

Progress in International Reading Literacy Study (PIRLS)
Inaugurated in 2001, a planned five-year cycle of international trend studies in the reading ability.

A CASE TO STUDY

Encouraging Child Learning

Remember that school-age children are ready for intellectual growth (Piaget) and are responsive to mentors (Vygotsky). Everywhere, parents do their best to encourage learning. That much is universal, but cultural differences are notable.

In one study, more than 200 married, middle-class mothers in the United States and Taiwan were asked to recall and then discuss with their 6- to 10-year-olds two learning-related incidents that their child experienced (Li et al., 2014). They were asked to select one in which their child had a "good attitude or behavior in learning" and the other, "not perfect."

The researchers found that the Taiwanese mothers were about 50 percent more likely to mention what the researchers called "learning virtues," such as practice, persistence, and concentration. The American mothers were 25 percent more likely to mention "positive affect," such as happiness and pride.

This distinction is evident in the following two cases:

First, Tim and his American mother discussed a "not perfect" incident.

Mother: I wanted to talk to you about . . . that time when you had that one math paper that . . . mostly everything was wrong and you never bring home papers like that. . . .

Tim: I just had a clumsy day.

Mother: You had a clumsy day. You sure did, but there was, when we finally figured out what it was that you were doing wrong, you were pretty happy about it . . . . and then you were very happy to practice it. Right? . . . Why do you think that was?

Tim: I don't know, because I was frustrated, and then you sat down and went over it with me, and I figured it out right with no distraction and then I got it right.

Mother: So it made you feel good to do well?

Tim: Uh-huh.

Mother: And it's okay to get some wrong sometimes . . .

Tim: And I, I never got that again, didn't I? . . .

In the next excerpt, Ren and his Taiwanese mother discuss a "good attitude or behavior."

Mother: Oh, why does your teacher think that you behave well? . . .

Ren: It's that I concentrate well in class.

Mother: Is your good concentration the concentration to talk to your peer at the next desk?

Ren: I listen to teachers.

Mother: Oh, is it so only for Mr. Chang's class or is it for all classes?

Ren: Almost all classes like that. . . .

Mother: Uh-ha! So you want to behave well because you want to get an . . . honor award. Is that so?

Ren: Yes.

Mother: Or is it also that you yourself want to behave better?

Ren: Yes. I also want to behave better myself.

[Li et al., 2014, p. 1218]

Both Tim and Ren are likely to be good students in their respective schools. When parents support and encourage their child's learning, almost always the child masters the basic skills required of elementary school students. Such children have sufficient strengths to overcome most challenging life experiences (Masten, 2014).

However, the specifics of parental encouragement affect achievement. Some research has found that parents in Asia emphasize the hard work required to learn, whereas parents in North America stress the joy of learning. The result, according to one group of researchers, is that U.S. children are happier but less accomplished than Asian ones (Ng et al., 2014).

"Big deal, an A in math. That would be a D in any other country."

Many educators in the United States have tried to figure out what makes students in some nations do much better than those in others. A recent example is Finland, where scores have improved dramatically in the twenty-first century. Finland reformed their education system, abolishing ability-grouping in 1985 and changing pedagogy in 1994 to foster more cooperation and active learning (Sahlberg, 2011).

Those changes may be crucial, or the teachers themselves may be the pivotal difference. Finnish teachers have more autonomy to decide what to do and when to do it than is typical in other systems. Since the 1990s, they have also had more time and encouragement to work with colleagues than is true elsewhere.

Finland designs school buildings to foster collaboration, with comfortable teacher's lounges (Sparks, 2012). That reflects a hidden curriculum regarding teachers. Many Finns want to be teachers, and teacher colleges are free, but only the top 3 percent of Finland's high school graduates are admitted to them. They must study for five years before they are ready to teach the children.

GENDER DIFFERENCES IN SCHOOL PERFORMANCE In addition to marked national, ethnic, and economic differences, gender differences in international achievement scores are reported. The PIRLS finds girls ahead of boys in verbal skills in every nation by an average of 16 points, almost 4 percent. The female advantage is somewhat less in the United States (10 points), Canada, Germany, and the Netherlands.

Traditionally, boys were ahead of girls in math and science. However, the 2011 TIMSS reported that gender differences among fourth-graders in math have narrowed or disappeared, with the United States showing the greatest male advantage (9 points).

In many nations, girls are ahead in math, sometimes by a great deal, such as 14 points in Thailand. Such results lead to a *gender-similarities hypothesis* that males and females are similar on most test measures, with "trivial" exceptions (Hyde et al., 2008, p. 494).

ANSWER TO OBSERVATION QUIZ
(from page 259) The most obvious is the play equipment, but there are two others that make some New York children eager for recess to end. Did you notice the concrete play surface and the winter jackets? ●

JOSE LUIS PELAEZ INC/GETTY IMAGES

Should They Be Playing? At an age when gifted children may be bored at school, these four are with other high-IQ children, learning advanced math and chemistry.

THINK CRITICALLY: What might have been a biological explanation for gender differences in science achievement?

Classroom performance during elementary school shows more gender differences than tests do. Girls have higher report card grades overall, including in math and science.

Then, at puberty, girls' grades dip, especially in science. In college, fewer women choose STEM (Science, Technology, Engineering, Math) majors, and even fewer pursue STEM careers. For instance, in the United States as in most nations, although women earn more college degrees than men, in 2011 only 22 percent of the doctorates in engineering were awarded to women (Snyder & Dillow, 2013).

Many explanations have been suggested. Analysts once blamed the female brain or body; currently the blame often falls on culture (Kanny et al., 2014).

COURTESY OF UNICEF

Video Activity: Educating the Girls of the World examines the situation of girls' education around the world while stressing the importance of education for all children.

Schools in the United States

Although most national tests indicate improvements in U.S. children's academic performance over the past decade, when U.S. children are compared with children in other nations, they are far from the top. The rank of the United States is below

TABLE 7.2	TIMSS Ranking and Average Scores of Math Achievement for Fourth-Graders, 2011	
Rank*	Country	Score
1.	Singapore	606
2.	Korea	605
3.	Hong Kong	602
4.	Chinese Taipei	591
5.	Japan	585
6.	N. Ireland	562
7.	Belgium	549
8.	Finland	545
9.	England	542
10.	Russia	542
11.	United States	541
12.	Netherlands	540
	Canada (Quebec)	533
	Germany	528
	Canada (Ontario)	518
	Australia	516
	Italy	508
	Sweden	504
	New Zealand	486
	Iran	431
	Yemen	248

*The top 12 groups are listed in order, but after that not all the jurisdictions that took the test are listed. Some nations have improved over the past 15 years (notably, Hong Kong, England) and some have declined (Austria, Netherlands), but most continue about where they have always been.

Data from Provasnik et al., 2012.

TABLE 7.3	PIRLS Distribution of Reading Achievement
Country	Score
Hong Kong	571
Russia	568
Finland	568
Singapore	567
N. Ireland	558
United States	556
Denmark	554
Chinese Taipei	553
Ireland	552
England	552
Canada	548
Italy	541
Germany	541
Israel	541
New Zealand	531
Australia	527
Poland	526
France	520
Spain	513
Iran	457
Colombia	448
Indonesia	428
Morocco	310

Data from Mullis et al., 2012.

Sharing Answers After individually subtracting 269 from 573, these two third-graders check their answers two ways—first by adding and then by showing their work to each other. As you can see, he is not embarrassed at his mistake because students in this class enjoy learning from each other.

several other nations, not only those in East Asia but also some in eastern and western Europe (see Tables 7.2 and 7.3).

THE ETHNIC AND ECONOMIC GAP A particular concern is the gap between children of various ethnic and income households, a gap much wider in the United States than in other nations, including some (e.g., Canada) that have more ethnic groups and immigrants than the United States.

Although many U.S. educators and political leaders (including all the recent presidents) have attempted to eradicate performance disparities linked to a child's background, the gap between fourth-grade European Americans and their Latino and African American peers is as wide as it was 15 years ago (Snyder & Dillow, 2013). The gap between low- and high-SES students is widening, as is the gap between Native Americans and others (Maxwell, 2012).

One reason may be that each state and each school district in the United States determines school policy and funding. Local economic policies and investment in education are thought to be the reason that Massachusetts and Minnesota are consistently at the top of state achievement, and West Virginia, Mississippi, and New Mexico are at the bottom (Pryor, 2014). Similarly within states, the affluent suburbs tend to have smaller classes, bigger playgrounds, and more extracurricular activities than the cities.

NATIONAL STANDARDS International comparisons as well as disparities within the United States led to passage of the **No Child Left Behind Act (NCLB)** of 2001, a federal law promoting high national standards for public schools. One controversial aspect of the law is that it requires frequent testing to measure whether standards are being met. Low-scoring schools lose funding and may be closed; teachers may be dismissed based on student scores.

Most people agree with the NCLB goals (accountability and higher achievement) but not with the consequences (Frey et al., 2012). The NCLB troubles those who value the arts, social studies, or physical education because those subjects are often squeezed out by reading and math (Dee et al., 2013). Teacher evaluation and training has increased, but class size has not decreased. Many parents and educators are critical of tests because they undercut creative teaching and character building.

Since 1990, the **National Assessment of Educational Progress (NAEP)**, a federally sponsored test of fourth-, eighth-, and twelfth-grade students, has measured achievement in reading, mathematics, and other subjects. Note that children are not tested every year by the NAEP. Fewer children are considered proficient on the NAEP than on state tests. For example in one recent year, New York's state tests found 62 percent proficient in math, but the NAEP found only 32 percent (Martin, 2014).

Concern about variability in state tests and standards led the governors of all 50 states to designate a group of experts who developed a *Common Core* of standards, finalized in 2010, for use nationwide. The standards, more rigorous than most state standards, are quite explicit, with half a dozen or more specific expectations for achievement in each subject for each grade. (Table 7.4 provides a sample of the specific standards.)

As of 2013, forty-four states adopted this Common Core for both reading and math. Minnesota is a partial adopter, in reading but not in math, and five states—Texas, Virginia, Alaska, Indiana, and Nebraska—opted out of the Common Core.

Most teachers were initially in favor of the Common Core, but implementation has turned many against it. In 2013, a poll found only 12 percent of teachers were opposed to the Common Core; a year later, 40 percent were (Gewertz, 2014). Likewise, many state legislators as well as the general public have doubts about the

No Child Left Behind Act (NCLB)
A U.S. law enacted in 2001 that was intended to increase accountability in education by requiring states to qualify for federal educational funding by administering standardized tests to measure school achievement.

National Assessment of Educational Progress (NAEP)
An ongoing and nationally representative measure of U.S. children's achievement in reading, mathematics, and other subjects over time; nicknamed "the Nation's Report Card."

TABLE 7.4	The Common Core: Sample Items for Each Grade	
Grade	**Reading and Writing**	**Math**
Kindergarten	Pronounce the primary sound for each consonant	Know number names and the count sequence
First	Decode regularly spelled one-syllable words	Relate counting to addition and subtraction (e.g., by counting 2 more to add 2)
Second	Decode words with common prefixes and suffixes	Measure the length of an object twice, using different units of length for the two measurements; describe how the two measurements relate to the size of the unit chosen
Third	Decode multisyllabic words	Understand division as an unknown-factor problem; for example, find 32 ÷ 8 by finding the number that makes 32 when multiplied by 8
Fourth	Use combined knowledge of all letter–sound correspondences, syllable patterns, and morphology (e.g., roots and affixes) to read accurately unfamiliar multisyllabic words in context and out of context	Apply and extend previous understandings of multiplication to multiply a fraction by a whole number
Fifth	With guidance and support from peers and adults, develop and strengthen writing as needed by planning, revising, editing, rewriting, or trying a new approach	Graph points on the coordinate plane to solve real-world and mathematical problems

Adapted from National Governors Association, 2010.

FIGURE 7.5 Where'd You Go to School? Note that although home schooling is still the least-chosen option, the number of home-schooled children is increasing. Although any child can be home-schooled, more detailed data indicate that the typical home-schooled child is a 7-year-old European American girl living in a rural area of the South with an employed father and a stay-at-home mother.

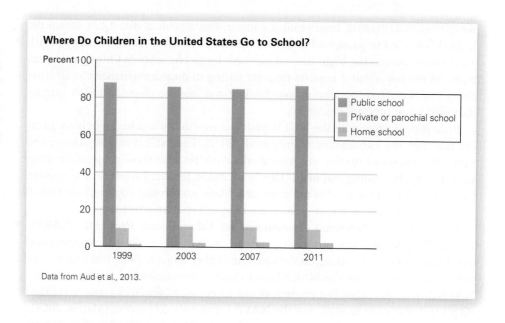

Where Do Children in the United States Go to School?

Data from Aud et al., 2013.

Common Core. This is another example of a general finding: Issues regarding how best to teach children, and what they need to learn, are controversial among teachers, parents, and political leaders.

Choices and Complications

An underlying issue for almost any national or international school is the proper role of parents. In most nations, matters regarding public education—curriculum, funding, teacher training, and so on—are set by the central government. Almost all children attend their local public school, whose resources and standards are similar to those of the other schools in that nation. The parents' job is to support the child's learning, by checking homework and so on.

In the United States, however, local districts provide most of the funds and guidelines, and parents, as voters and volunteers, are often active within their child's school. As part of the trend toward fewer children per family, parents focus more on each child. They evaluate schools, befriend their child's teacher, join parent–teacher associations (PTAs), move to a particular school zone, switch from one school to another, vote for particular policies.

Most U.S. parents send their children to their zoned public school, but almost one-third do not. Other choices include a more distant public school, a public charter school, a private school, or home schooling (see Figure 7.5).

The existence of education options creates a problem for parents. It is hard to judge the quality of a school, partly because neither test scores nor the values a particular school may espouse correlate with the cognitive skills or learning potential that developmentalists recognize in middle childhood (Finn et al., 2014).

charter schools
Public schools with their own set of standards funded and licensed by the state or local district in which they are located.

CHARTER SCHOOLS In the United States, **charter schools** are public schools funded and licensed by states or local districts. Typically, they also have private money and sponsors. They are exempt from some regulations, especially those negotiated by teacher unions (hours, class size, etc.), and they have some control over admissions and expulsions. They tend to be more ethnically and economically segregated and enroll fewer children with special needs (Stern et al., 2015).

On average, charter school teachers are younger and work longer hours than regular public school teachers, and school size is smaller than in traditional public schools. Perhaps 5 percent of U.S. children are in charter schools.

Plagiarism, Piracy, and Public School Charter schools often have special support and unusual curricula, as shown here. These four children are learning about copyright law in a special summer school class at the ReNEW Cultural Arts Academy in New Orleans.

Some charter schools are remarkably successful; others are not (Peyser, 2011). A major criticism is that not every child who enters a charter school stays to graduate; one scholar reports that "the dropout rate for African–American males is really shocking" (Miron, quoted in Zehr, 2011, p. 1).

Overall, children and teachers leave charter schools more often than they leave regular public schools, a disturbing statistic. Substantial variation is evident from state to state and school to school (some schools are sought by many parents; some are avoided for good reasons), which makes it difficult to judge charters as a group.

PRIVATE SCHOOLS **Private schools** are funded by tuition, endowments, and church sponsors. Every nation has private schools. Traditionally in the United States, most private schools were parochial (church-related), organized by the Catholic Church to teach religion and to resist the anti-Catholic rhetoric of many public schools. Recently, many Catholic parochial schools have closed, while some other church-related or independent private schools have opened.

All told, 11 percent of students in the United States attend private schools. Economic factors are a major concern: Since private schools get very limited public funding, tuition costs mean that few private-school children are poor or even middle class.

To solve that disparity, some U.S. jurisdictions issue **vouchers,** which parents can use to pay tuition at a private school, including a church-sponsored one. Advocates say that vouchers increase competition. Vouchers are controversial because they mean less money for public schools and more tax money for religious institutions.

HOME EDUCATION Every child learns more at home than at school, but some parents avoid sending their children to any school. Instead, they choose **home schooling,** educating their children *exclusively* at home. Home schooling is an option in 35 of the 50 states in the United States, and in some—but not all—other nations. In the United States, home-schooled children must learn certain standard subjects (achieving benchmarks in reading, math, and so on), but each family decides specifics of curriculum, schedules, and discipline.

This choice is more common for younger children—6-year-olds more than 16-year-olds. About 2 percent of all U.S. children were home-schooled in 2003, about 3 percent in 2007, and perhaps 4 percent in 2012 (Snyder & Dillow, 2013; Ray, 2013).

Numbers are not expected to increase much more, however, because home schooling requires an adult at home, typically the mother in a two-parent family, who is willing to teach the children. The mother is not paid, so the father typically has a well-paying job. Such families are increasingly uncommon.

private schools
Schools funded by parents and sponsoring institutions. Such schools have control over admissions, hiring, and specifics of curriculum, although some regulations apply.

vouchers
A monetary commitment by the government to pay for the education of a child. Vouchers vary a great deal from place to place, not only in amount and availability, but in who gets them and what schools accept them.

home schooling
Education in which children are taught at home, usually by their parents, instead of attending any school, public or private.

Home-Schooling Opportunity One nation that does not allow home schooling is Germany, which is one reason the Romeike family (shown here) came to the United States. They asked for asylum—do you think their request should be granted?

The major problem with home schooling is not academic (some home-schooled children have high test scores) but social: no classmates. To compensate, many parents plan activities with other home-schooling families. Home schooling is more common in the South and Northwest than in the Northeast or Midwest. Local popularity affects how readily parents can find other home-schooled children.

HOW TO DECIDE? The underlying problem with all these options is that people disagree about what is best and how learning should be measured. For example, many parents consider class size: They may choose private school because fewer students are in each class. Some parents want children to have homework, beginning in the first grade. Yet few developmentalists are convinced that small classes or homework are essential for learning during middle childhood.

Mixed evidence comes from nations where children score high on international tests. Sometimes they have large student–teacher ratios (Korea's average is 28-to-1) and sometimes small (Finland's is 14-to-1). Fourth-graders with no homework sometimes have higher achievement scores than those with homework (Snyder & Dillow, 2010). Many explanations are possible. Perhaps weaker students are assigned to smaller classes with more homework?

Who should decide what children should learn and how? Statistical analysis raises questions about home schooling and about charter schools (Lubienski et al., 2013; Finn et al., 2014), but as our discussion of NAEP, Common Core, TIMSS, and so on makes clear, the evidence allows many interpretations. As one review notes, "the

Loved and Rewarded Marissa Ochoa, a third-grade public school teacher near San Diego, California, is shown moments after she learned that she won $5,000 as a star educator. Which do you think is more rewarding to her, the money or the joy of her students?

OBSERVATION QUIZ

The photo above shows Marissa's students congratulating their teacher. What do you see in the hidden curriculum? (see answer page 268) ➤

modern day, parent-led home-based education movement . . . stirs up many a curious query, negative critique, and firm praise" (Ray, 2013, p. 261). Parents, politicians, and developmental experts agree that school is vital, but disagreement about teachers and curriculum—hidden or overt—abound.

WHAT HAVE YOU LEARNED?

1. How does a child's age affect the understanding of metaphors and jokes?
2. Why would a child's linguistic code be criticized by teachers but admired by friends?
3. What factors in a child's home and school affect language-learning ability?
4. How does the hidden curriculum differ from the stated school curriculum?
5. What are the TIMSS and the PIRLS?
6. What nations score highest on international tests?
7. How do boys and girls differ in school achievement?
8. What problems do the Common Core standards attempt to solve?
9. How do charter schools, private schools, and home schools differ?
10. How do parents choose what school is best for their children?

Developmental Psychopathology

Developmental psychopathology links the study of usual development with the study of children with unusual brain or behavior patterns (Cicchetti, 2013b; Hayden & Mash, 2014). Every topic already described, including "genetics, neuroscience, developmental psychology, . . . must be combined to understand how psychopathology develops and can be prevented" (Dodge, 2009, p. 413).

> **developmental psychopathology**
> The field that uses insights into typical development to understand and remediate developmental disorders.

At the outset, four general principles should be emphasized.

1. *Abnormality is normal.* Most children sometimes act oddly. At the same time, children with serious disorders are, in many respects, like everyone else.

2. *Disability changes year by year.* Most disorders are comorbid, which means that more than one problem is evident in the same person. Which particular disorder is most disabling at a particular time changes, as does the degree of impairment.

3. *Life may get better or worse.* Prognosis is difficult. Many children with severe disabilities (e.g., blindness) become productive, happy adults. Conversely, some conditions (e.g., conduct disorder) may become more disabling.

4. *Diagnosis and treatment reflect the social context.* Each individual interacts with the surrounding setting—including family, school, community, and culture—which modify, worsen, or even create psychopathology.

Measuring the Mind

At every age, people with disorders often have unusual brain patterns, which means that understanding the functioning of their brains might help them thrive among people with more typical neurological development. During middle childhood, school learning is crucial. For that reason, we focus first on intellect.

> **aptitude**
> The potential to master a specific skill or to learn a certain body of knowledge.

APTITUDE, ACHIEVEMENT, AND IQ *In theory,* **aptitude** is the *potential* to master a specific skill or subject, such as the potential to become an accomplished musician, engineer, or student. Learning aptitude is usually measured by answers to a series of questions. The assumption is that there is one general intelligence, called *g* (for *g*eneral). An IQ (intelligence quotient) test consists of questions that, taken together, measure *g*, thought to be learning potential.

© 2016 MACMILLAN

Typical 7-Year-Old? In many ways this boy is typical. He likes video games and school, he usually appreciates his parents, he gets himself dressed every morning. This photo shows him using blocks to construct a design to match a picture, one of the ten kinds of challenges that comprise the WISC, a widely used IQ test. His attention to the task is not unusual for children his age, but his actual performance is more like that of an older child. That makes his IQ score significantly above 100.

achievement test
A measure of mastery or proficiency in reading, mathematics, writing, science, or some other subject.

Flynn effect
The rise in average IQ scores that has occurred over the decades in many nations.

multiple intelligences
The idea that human intelligence is comprised of a varied set of abilities rather than a single, all-encompassing one.

ANSWER TO OBSERVATION QUIZ
(from page 266) All the closest students are girls. What have the boys learned that is not part of the official curriculum? ●

In theory, achievement is what has actually been learned, distinct from aptitude. School **achievement tests** compare scores to norms established for each grade. For example, children of any age who read as well as the average third-grader would be at the third-grade level in reading achievement.

The words *in theory* precede the definitions of aptitude and achievement above because, although potential and accomplishment are supposed to be distinct, the data find substantial overlap. IQ and achievement scores are strongly correlated.

It was once assumed that aptitude was a fixed characteristic, present at birth. Longitudinal data show otherwise. Young children with a low IQ can become above-average or even gifted adults, like my nephew David (discussed in Chapter 1). Indeed, the average IQ scores of entire nations have risen substantially every decade for the past century—a phenomenon called the **Flynn effect,** named after the researcher who first described it (Flynn, 1999, 2012).

Because changes in cohort and education produced intellectual growth in children, IQ tests need to be revised, updated, and renormed to keep the average score at 100—which would have been 115 two generations ago. Both major IQ tests for children, the Stanford-Binet and the Wechsler Intelligence Scale for Children (WISC), are now in fifth editions, with changes to criteria for average scores.

Psychologists now agree that the brain is like a muscle, affected by mental exercise—encouraged or discouraged by the social setting. Brain structures grow or shrink depending on past experience. This is proven in language and music and probably is true in other areas as well (Zatorre, 2013). Both speed and memory are affected by experience, evident in the Flynn effect. During middle childhood, speed of thought is crucial for high IQ, with working memory also influential (Demetriou et al., 2013).

CRITICISMS OF IQ TESTING Since scores change over time, some scientists doubt whether any test can measure the complexities of the human intellect, especially if the test is designed to measure *g*, general aptitude. According to some experts, children inherit many abilities, some high and some low (e.g., Q. Zhu et al., 2010).

A leading developmentalist, Howard Gardner, contends that humans have **multiple intelligences,** not just one. Gardner originally described seven intelligences: linguistic, logical-mathematical, musical, spatial, bodily-kinesthetic (movement), interpersonal (social understanding), and intrapersonal (self-understanding), each associated with a particular brain region (Gardner, 1983). He subsequently added naturalistic (nature, as in biology, zoology, or farming) and spiritual/existential (Gardner, 1999, 2006; Gardner & Moran, 2006).

Although every normal person has some of all nine intelligences, Gardner believes each individual excels in particular ones. For example, someone might be gifted spatially but not linguistically (a visual artist who cannot describe her work) or might have interpersonal but not naturalistic intelligence (an insightful clinical psychologist whose houseplants die).

Gardner's concepts regarding multiple intelligences influence the curriculum in many primary schools. For instance, children might be allowed to demonstrate their understanding of a historical event via a poster with drawings instead of writing a paper with a bibliography.

Many other scholars (including Robert Sternberg, whose ideas are explained in Chapter 12) find that cultures and families dampen or accelerate particular intelligences. What would happen, for instance, if two children were born with equal creative, musical ability but one child's parents were musicians and the other child's parents were tone-deaf? Probably only the first child would develop impressive musical intelligence.

A multi-cultural perspective emphasizes that every test reflects the culture of the people who create, administer, and take it. This is obvious for achievement tests: A child may score low because of home, school, or culture, not because of ability. Indeed, IQ tests are still used partly because achievement tests may be unfair to some bright children.

But IQ tests also are affected by culture. Some experts try to use culture-free aptitude tests, asking children to identify pictures, draw shapes, repeat stories, hop on one foot, name their classmates, sort objects, and so on. To be sensitive to the child's experience, most IQ tests require that a friendly, trained adult ask questions of one child at a time.

Yet culture may still drag IQ scores down. Perhaps a child is told "never talk to strangers." That child might not answer the tester's questions.

Might measuring the brain directly avoid cultural bias? Yes, in theory, but not in practice. Variation is vast in children's brains: Experts are hesitant to judge intelligence via any brain scan (e.g., Goddings & Giedd, 2014). Furthermore, plasticity makes the results of brain scans, like IQ scores, likely to change.

© BROWNIE HARRIS/CORBIS

A Gifted Child Georgie Pocheptsov is an artist, and his family and culture recognized his talent by buying art supplies, giving him time and a place to paint, and selling his creations. Did he lose anything because of his talent, as Picasso did?

OPPOSING PERSPECTIVES

True Grit

Thousands of social scientists—psychologists, educators, sociologists, economists—realize that characteristics beyond IQ scores and test grades are sometimes pivotal for cognitive development. One leading proponent of this idea is Paul Tough, who wrote: "We have been focusing on the wrong skills and abilities in our children, and we have been using the wrong strategies to help nurture and teach those skills" (Tough, 2012, p. xv). Instead of focusing on test scores, we should focus on character, Tough believes.

Many scientists agree that executive control processes with many names (grit, emotional regulation, conscientiousness, resilience, executive function, effortful control) develop over the years of middle childhood and are crucial for cognitive growth. Over the long term, these aspects of character predict achievement in high school, college, and adulthood.

Developmentalists disagree about exactly which qualities are crucial for achievement, with grit considered crucial by some and not others (Ivcevic & Brackett, 2014; Duckworth & Kern, 2011). No one denies that success depends on personality, not just on intellect.

For instance, one of the best longitudinal studies we have (the Dunedin study of an entire cohort of children from New Zealand) found that measures of self-control before age 10 predicted health, happiness, education, and accom-

plishment many years later. That was true even when IQ and SES were already taken into account (Moffitt et al., 2011).

Among the many influences on children, a pivotal one is having at least one adult who encourages accomplishment. For many children, that adult is their mother, although, especially when parents are neglectful or abusive, a teacher, a religious leader, a coach, or someone else can be the mentor and advocate who helps a child overcome adversity (Masten, 2014).

Why is this an opposing perspective rather than a simple fact? Because grit itself may reflect cultural values that work against low-income, non-European American children. The superintendent of schools in one Virginia district said, "We keep [hearing] this narrative that the only way children in poverty are going to succeed is by working harder than their peers who are [in the] middle class. . . . We have to think about our own cultural biases, why Grit appeals to us, and why we want to focus on it in our schools" (Moran, quoted in Herold, 2015, p. 8).

The advocates of grit reply that they know that many social forces—beyond the IQ or personality characteristics of individual children—work against children of color and of low SES. Nonetheless, every measure used to indicate future achievement of children expresses cultural values. People have opposite ideas regarding what those values should be.

Special Needs in Middle Childhood

Developmental psychopathology is relevant lifelong because "[e]ach period of life, from the prenatal period through senescence, ushers in new biological and psychological challenges, strengths, and vulnerabilities" (Cicchetti, 2013b, p. 458). Turning points, opportunities, and past influences are always apparent.

In middle childhood, the challenge for every child is to learn basic skills. Some children find that mastering academic skills is much more difficult than other children do. Fortunately, most learning problems can be mitigated if treatment is early and properly targeted.

Therein lies the crux of the issue: Although early treatment is best, early and accurate diagnosis is difficult, not only because many disorders are comorbid but also because symptoms differ by age. As you learned in Chapter 4, infants have temperamental differences that might or might not become problems, and in Chapter 6, that aggression and shyness are sometimes normal but sometimes ominous. Difference is not necessarily deficit, but some differences signal that intervention is needed. Which is which?

Two basic principles of developmental psychopathology complicate diagnosis and treatment (Hayden & Mash, 2014; Cicchetti, 2013b). First is **multifinality,** which means that one cause can have many (multiple) final manifestations. For example, an infant who has been flooded with cortisol may become quick to cry or rage or the opposite, unusually placid.

The second principle is **equifinality** (equal in final form), which means that one symptom can have many causes. For instance, a nonverbal first-grader may have autism spectrum disorder, a hearing deficit, no experience in the school language, or extreme shyness.

The complexity of diagnosis is evident in the *Diagnostic and Statistical Manual of Mental Disorders,* 5th edition (American Psychiatric Association, 2013), often referred to as DSM-5. A major problem is recognizing the cutoff between normal childish behavior and pathology. Some suggest that childhood psychopathology was under-diagnosed in early editions of the DSM and is over-diagnosed in DSM-5 (Hayden & Mash, 2014).

Perhaps. Both multifinality and equifinality make early diagnosis complex: Some children are considered pathological when really they are not, while other children are not diagnosed when early diagnosis and intervention would help. The following three examples are a beginning, because everyone needs to know something about children with special needs. Teachers, counselors, doctors, and nurses need to know much more.

ATTENTION-DEFICIT/HYPERACTIVITY DISORDER Someone with **attention-deficit/hyperactivity disorder (ADHD)** is often inattentive, unusually active, and impulsive. DSM-5 says symptoms must start before age 12 (in DSM-IV it was age 7) and must impact daily life. (DSM-IV said *impaired,* not just *impacted.*)

Some impulsive, active, and creative actions are quite normal. However, children with ADHD "are so active and impulsive that they cannot sit still, are constantly fidgeting, talk when they should be listening, interrupt people all the time, can't stay on task, . . . accidentally injure themselves." They are "difficult to parent or teach" (Nigg & Barkley, 2014, p. 75).

There is no biological marker for ADHD. Current research, nonetheless, suggests the origin of the disorder is in

multifinality
A basic principle of developmental psychopathology which holds that one cause can have many (multiple) final manifestations.

equifinality
A basic principle of developmental psychopathology that holds that one symptom can have many causes.

attention-deficit/hyperactivity disorder (ADHD)
A condition in which a person not only has difficulty concentrating but also is inattentive, impulsive, and overactive.

A River Is Better Than a School People must be quick and active to avoid capsizing in white-water rafting, but these children are up to the task. They have been diagnosed with ADHD, but they are quite able to respond to fast-changing currents.

brain regulation, because of genes, complications of pregnancy, or toxins (such as lead) (Nigg & Barkley, 2014).

ADHD is often comorbid. Explosive rages, later followed by deep regret, are typical for children with many disorders, including ADHD. One surprising comorbidity is deafness: Children with severe hearing loss often are affected in balance and activity, and that seems to make them prone to developing ADHD (Antoine et al., 2013). In this way, ADHD is an example of equifinality; many causes produce one disorder.

U.S. rates of ADHD among children were about 5 percent in 1980. Currently, rates are 7 percent of 4- to 9-year-olds, 13 percent of 10- to 13-year-olds, and 15 percent of all 14- to 17-year-olds (Schwarz & Cohen, 2013). Rates in other nations are lower than in the United States, but rates are rising everywhere (e.g., Al-Yagon et al., 2013; Hsia & Maclennan, 2009; van den Ban et al., 2010). Increasing incidence worries developmentalists for three reasons:

- *Misdiagnosis.* If ADHD is diagnosed when another disorder is the problem, treatment might make the problem worse, not better (Miklowitz & Cicchetti, 2010). Many psychoactive drugs alter moods, so a child with disruptive mood dysregulation disorder (formerly called childhood-onset bipolar disorder) might be harmed by drugs that help children with ADHD.

- *Drug abuse.* Some adolescents may fake ADHD in order to obtain amphetamines with a doctor's prescription. Are 15 percent of U.S. teenagers really hyperactive?

- *Normal behavior considered pathological.* In young children, high activity, impulsiveness, and curiosity are normal. If a normal child is diagnosed with ADHD, might that harm the child's self-concept? Could normal boy behavior be one reason ADHD is at least twice as common in boys as in girls?

Many adults (71 percent in one study) who were diagnosed with ADHD as children say they no longer have the condition (Barbaresi et al., 2013). Do people overcome or outgrow ADHD, do adults minimize symptoms, or were these adults misdiagnosed? All are possible.

Treatment for ADHD involves: (1) training for the family and child, (2) special education for teachers, and (3) medication. Each of these three is complicated. As equifinality posits, causes vary, so treatment that helps one child may be wrong for another (Mulligan et al., 2013).

SPECIFIC LEARNING DISORDER The DSM-5 diagnosis of **specific learning disorder** now includes disabilities in both perception and processing of information, evident in unexpected low achievement in reading, math, or writing (including spelling) (Lewandowski & Lovett, 2014). Children with specific learning disorders have difficulty mastering skills that most children acquire easily.

Disabilities in reading, writing, and math undercut academic achievement, destroy self-esteem, and qualify a child for special education (according to U.S. law) or formal diagnosis (according to DSM-5). Hopefully, such children find (or are taught) ways to compensate, and other abilities shine. Winston Churchill, Albert Einstein, and Hans Christian Andersen are all said to have had specific learning disorder.

The most common type of specific learning disorder is **dyslexia**—unusual difficulty with reading. Dozens of types and causes of dyslexia have been identified, so no single strategy helps every child (O'Brien et al., 2012).

Early theories hypothesized that visual difficulties—for example, reversals of letters (reading *god* instead of *dog*) and mirror writing (*b* instead of *d*)—caused dyslexia, but experts now believe that the origin is more auditory (in speech and hearing) than visual (Gabrieli, 2009; Swanson, 2013). Traditionally, dyslexia was not diagnosed until a child with normal IQ, vision, and hearing had difficulty reading. Now dyslexia is recognized at age 5 or earlier.

Download the **DSM-5 Appendix** to learn more about the terminology and classification of childhood psychopathology.

specific learning disorder
A marked deficit in a particular area of learning that is not caused by an apparent physical disability, or by an unusually stressful home environment.

dyslexia
A specific learning disorder characterized by unusual difficulty with reading.

Video: Dyslexia: Expert and Children
http://qrs.ly/cg4ep0v

© 2016 MACMILLAN

Happy Reading Those large prism glasses keep the letters from jumping around on the page, a boon for this 8-year-old French boy. Unfortunately, each child with dyslexia needs individualized treatment: These glasses help some, but not most, children who find reading difficult.

 LaunchPad

Video: Current Research into Autism Spectrum Disorder explores why the causes of ASD are still largely unknown.

dyscalculia
A specific learning disorder characterized by unusual difficulty with math.

autism spectrum disorder (ASD)
Any of several conditions characterized by inadequate social skills, impaired communication, and unusual play.

Precious Gifts Many children with autism spectrum disorder are gifted artists. This boy attends a school in Montmoreau, France, that features workshops in which children with ASD develop social, play, and learning skills.

Another specific learning disorder is **dyscalculia**—unusual difficulty with math. For example, when asked to estimate the height of a normal room, second-graders with dyscalculia might answer "200 feet," or, when asked which card is higher, the 5 or the 8 of hearts, a child might use his or her fingers to count each card's hearts (Butterworth et al., 2011).

For specific learning disorders, the problem may originate in the brain, but plasticity allows early remediation to improve brain connections before the young child's eagerness to learn has been crushed by failure. Almost everyone can learn basic skills if they are given extensive and targeted teaching, encouragement, and practice.

AUTISM SPECTRUM DISORDER Of all the children with special needs, those with **autism spectrum disorder (ASD)** are probably the most troubling. Their problems are severe, but both causes and treatments are hotly disputed. As a result, as Thomas Insel, director of the National Institute of Mental Health says, parents and advocates of children with autism spectrum disorder are "the most polarized, fragmented community" (quoted in Solomon, 2012, p. 280).

Many children with ASD show symptoms in the first year of life, but some seem normal and then suddenly regress at about age 2 or 3, perhaps because a certain level of brain development, or a particular medical insult, occurs (Klinger et al., 2014). Most are diagnosed at age 4 or later (MMWR, March 28, 2014), although earlier intervention is best.

Autism spectrum disorder has three characteristics: (1) poor social understanding, (2) impaired language, and (3) unusual play patterns, such as fascination with trains, lights, or spinning objects. In the past, children who developed slowly were usually diagnosed as having a "pervasive developmental disorder" or as "mentally retarded." (The term "mental retardation," used in DSM-IV, has been replaced with "intellectual disability" in DSM-5.)

Much has changed. Far more children are diagnosed with autism spectrum disorder, and far fewer with intellectual disability. In the United States, among 8-year-olds, one child in every 68 is said to have ASD (MMWR, March 28, 2014). Rates are five times higher among boys than girls and about one-third higher among European Americans than Hispanic, Asian, or African Americans.

The DSM-5 autism spectrum disorder diagnosis, formerly reserved for children who were mute or violent, now includes mild, moderate, and severe categories. Mildly impaired children with ASD appear normal at first and may be talented in some specialized area, such as drawing or geometry. Many (46 percent) score in the "normal" or "above normal" range on IQ tests (MMWR, March 28, 2014).

Often children with autism spectrum disorder have a hypersensitive sensory cortex: They are unusually upset by noise, light, and other sensations. Hundreds of genes and dozens of brain abnormalities are more common in people with ASD than in the general population.

Why are far more children diagnosed with ASD in 2015 than in 1990? Has the incidence really increased or are children diagnosed who would not have been earlier (Klinger et al., 2014). Children who once were diagnosed with Asperger syndrome are now said to have "autism spectrum disorder without language or intellectual impairment" (American Psychiatric Association, 2013, p. 32). Is that more accurate?

As more is understood, many people wonder whether ASD is a disorder needing cure or an indication that parents and society foolishly expect everyone to be fluent talkers, gregarious, and flexible—the opposite of autism spectrum disorder. If the latter, children are diagnosed too readily. Advocates of **neurodiversity** suggest that the neurological variations should be accepted, appreciated, celebrated—not patholo-gized (Kapp et al., 2013).

Equifinality certainly applies to ASD: A child can have symptoms for many reasons; no single gene causes the disorder. That makes treatment difficult; an intervention that helps one child is worthless for another.

It is known that biology is crucial (genes, copy number abnormalities, birth complications, prenatal injury, perhaps chemicals during fetal or infant development) and that family nurture does not cause ASD but may modify it. Social and language engagement of the child early in life seems the most promising treatment.

neurodiversity
The idea that people with special needs have diverse brain structures, with each person having neurological strengths and weaknesses that should be appreciated, in much the same way diverse cultures and ethnicities are welcomed.

A VIEW FROM SCIENCE

Drug Treatment for Children

In the United States, more than 2 million people younger than 18 take prescription drugs to regulate their emotions and behavior (see Figure 7.6). The rates are about 14 percent for teenagers (Merikangas et al., 2013), about 10 percent for 6- to 11-year-olds, and less than 1 percent for 2- to 5-year-olds (Olfson et al., 2010).

Drug treatment for children poses a dilemma. Many adults are upset by normal child behavior. Since any physician can prescribe a drug to quiet a child, thousands of children may be overmedicated. But because many parents are suspicious of drugs, refusing to believe that their child needs help (Moldavsky & Sayal, 2013; Rose, 2008), thousands of children may suffer without the drugs they need to learn, make friends, and so on.

Sometimes drugs are helpful, although not a cure. In one careful study, when children with ADHD were given appropriate medication, carefully calibrated, they were more able to concentrate. However, eight years later, many children on and off medication still had learning difficulties (Molina et al., 2009). Many other studies also find that children with ADHD are likely to have academic and vocational difficulties lifelong (Molina et al., 2013).

FIGURE 7.6 One Child in Every Classroom Or maybe two, if the class has more than 20 students or is in Alabama. This figure shows the percent of 6- to 17-year-olds prescribed psychoactive drugs in the previous six months. About half of these children have been diagnosed with ADHD, and the rest have anxiety, mood, and other disorders. These data are averages, gathered from many communities. In fact, some schools, even in the South, have very few medicated children, and others, even in the West, have many in every class. The regional variations evident here are notable, but much more dramatic are rates by school, community, and doctor—some of whom are much quicker to medicate children than others.

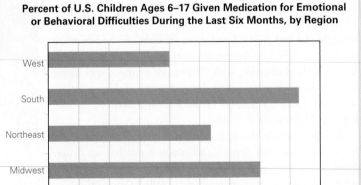

Percent of U.S. Children Ages 6–17 Given Medication for Emotional or Behavioral Difficulties During the Last Six Months, by Region

Data from MMWR, May 2, 2014.

THINK CRITICALLY: What are several possible explanations for the ethnic differences in use of ADHD medication?

Ethnic differences are found in parent responses, teacher responses, and treatment for children. In the United States, it seems that when children are diagnosed with ADHD, African American and Hispanic parents are less likely that European American parents to give them medication (Morgan et al., 2013). Why?

Drugs are also controversial for adults. Medication seems to help adolescents and adults with ADHD (Surman et al., 2013), but most psychologists believe that drugs should never be the first, or the only, treatment for any disorder. In China, psychoactive medication is rarely used. A Chinese child with ADHD symptoms is thought to need correction, not medication (Yang et al., 2013). Wise or cruel?

International comparisons raise many questions. For instance, one study asked 158 child psychologists—half of them from England and half from the United States—to diagnose an 11-year-old girl.

> Parents say Lynda has been hyperactive, with poor boundaries and disinhibited behavior since she was a toddler. . . Lynda has taken several stimulants since age 8. She is behind in her school work, but IQ normal. . . . Psychological testing, age 8, described frequent impulsivity, tendencies to discuss topics unrelated to tasks she was completing, intermittent expression of anger and anxiety, significantly elevated levels of physical activity, difficulties sitting still, and touching everything. Over the past year Lynda has become very angry, irritable, destructive and capricious. She is provocative and can be cruel to pets and small children. She has been sexually inappropriate with peers and families, including expressing interest in lewd material on the Internet, Play Girl magazine, hugging and kissing peers. She appears to be grandiose, telling her family that she will be attending medical school, or will become a record producer, a professional wrestler, or an acrobat. Throughout this period there have been substantial marital difficulties between the parents.
>
> *[Dubicka et al., 2008, appendix p. 3]*

Most (81 percent) of the clinicians diagnosing Lynda thought she had ADHD, and most thought she had another disorder as well. The Americans were likely to suggest a second and third disorder, with 75 percent of them specifying bipolar disorder (now called disruptive mood dysregulation disorder). Only 33 percent of the British psychologists said bipolar (Dubicka et al., 2008).

Lynda's parents thought she had ADHD since toddlerhood; a pediatrician agreed, and at age 8 put her on drugs. Now, at age 11, she seemed to be getting worse, not better, while her parents were increasingly hostile to each other.

Unfortunately, when psychopathology is evident, parental responses vary from irrational hope to deep despair, from blaming doctors and chemical additives to feeling guilty for what they did wrong. Many parents sue schools, or doctors, or the government; many subject their children to drugs and other biological "cures."

Andrew Solomon (2012) writes about one child with autism, medicated with

> Abilify, Topamax, Seroquel, Prozac, Ativan, Depakote, trazodone, Risperdal, Anafranil, Lamictal, Benadryl, melatonin, and the homeopathic remedy, Calms Forté. Every time I saw her, the meds were being adjusted again . . . . [he also describes] physical interventions—putting children in hyperbaric oxygen chambers, putting them in tanks with dolphins, giving them blue-green algae, or megadosing them on vitamins . . . usually neither helpful nor harmful, though they can have dangers, are certainly disorienting, and cost a lot.
>
> *[pp. 229, 270]*

For every problem, from ADHD to specific learning disorder to autism spectrum disorder, developmentalists believe that family interactions and school context are crucial, even though the easiest intervention is to prescribe drugs. Parents are not the cause of child psychopathology, but they may be crucial for treatment.

A Family Learning When Anthony Suppers was diagnosed with ADHD, his mother Michelle (shown here) realized she had it, too. That helps Anthony, because his mother knows how important it is to have him do his homework at his own desk as soon as he comes home from school.

CAITLIN TEAL PRICE/FOR THE WASHINGTON POST VIA GETTY IMAGES

Special Education

The overlap of the biosocial, cognitive, and psychosocial domains means that parents, teachers, therapists, and researchers need to work together to help each child. However, deciding whether or not a child should receive special education, and what that education should be, is complex. Parents and educators often disagree.

LABELS, LAWS, AND LEARNING In the United States, recognition that the distinction between normal and abnormal is not clear-cut (the first principle of developmental psychopathology) led to a series of reforms. According to the 1975 Education of All Handicapped Children Act, children with special needs must be educated in the "least restrictive environment." The law has been revised, but the goal remains that children with special needs should not be segregated unless efforts to remediate problems within the regular classroom have failed.

THE TUSCALOOSA NEWS, DUSTY COMPTON/AP PHOTO

All Together Now Kiemel Lamb *(top center)* leads children with ASD in song, a major accomplishment. For many of these children, music is soothing, words are difficult, and handholding in a group is almost impossible.

Consequently, children with special needs usually learn in regular classes. Sometimes a class is an *inclusion class,* which means that children with special needs are "included" in the general classroom, with "appropriate aids and services" (ideally from a trained teacher who works with the regular teacher).

A more recent educational strategy is called **response to intervention (RTI)** (Fletcher & Vaughn, 2009; Shapiro et al., 2011; Ikeda, 2012). All children are taught specific skills—for instance, learning the sounds that various letters make. Then each child is tested. Those who did not master the skill receive special "intervention"— individualized teaching, usually within the regular class. They are tested again, and, if need be, intervention occurs again.

Only when repeated, focused intervention does not work are children referred for testing and observation to understand why they did not respond to the extra help. Then the school may propose an **individual education plan (IEP),** which is supposed to remedy the problem.

Unfortunately, much is unknown about which remediation is best. The special needs that attract most research are not the more common ones (see Figure 7.7). One example: In the United States, "research funding in 2008–2009 for autistic spectrum disorder was 31 times greater than for dyslexia and 540 times greater than for dyscalculia" (Butterworth & Kovas, 2013, p. 304).

response to intervention (RTI)
An educational strategy that uses early intervention to help children who demonstrate below-average achievement. Only children who are not helped are designated for more intense measures.

individual education plan (IEP)
A document that specifies educational goals and plans for a child with special needs.

FIGURE 7.7 Nature or Nurture Communities have always had some children with special needs, with physical, emotional, and neurological disorders. In some eras, and today in some nations, the education of such children was neglected. Indeed, many children were excluded from normal life even before they quit trying. Now in the United States, every child is entitled to school. Categories have changed, probably because of nurture, not nature. Thus, teratogens and changing parental and community practice probably caused the rise in autism spectrum disorder, the decrease in intellectual disability, and the fluctuation of specific learning disorder apparent here.

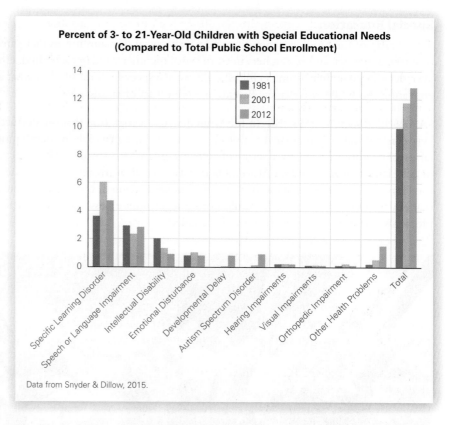

Percent of 3- to 21-Year-Old Children with Special Educational Needs (Compared to Total Public School Enrollment)

Data from Snyder & Dillow, 2015.

Internationally, the connection between special needs and education varies, for cultural and historical reasons more than child-related ones (Rotatori et al., 2014). In many African and Latin American nations, almost no child receives special education in public schools. In the United States, more children are designated with special needs than in any other nation.

GIFTED AND TALENTED Children who are unusually gifted may have special educational needs, but they are not covered by federal laws in the United States. Instead, each U.S. state selects and educates gifted and talented children in a particular way. Educators, political leaders, scientists, and everyone else argue about who is gifted and what should be done about them.

A hundred years ago, the definition was simple: high IQ. A famous longitudinal study followed a thousand "genius" children (Terman, 1925). Even today, some school systems define "gifted" as having an IQ of 130 or above (attained by 1 child in 50). Other children are unusually talented, perhaps recognized by their parents at a young age but not usually by their teachers. Mozart composed music at age 3; Pablo Picasso created works of art at age 4.

A hundred years ago, school placement was simple, too: The gifted were taught with children who were their mental age, not their chronological age. Today that is rarely done because many such children missed social skills and friendship. One woman remembers:

> Nine-year-old little girls are so cruel to younger girls. I was much smaller than them, of course, and would have done anything to have a friend. Although I could cope with the academic work very easily, emotionally I wasn't up to it. Maybe it was my fault and I was asking to be picked on. I was a weed at the edge of the playground.

[Rachel, quoted in Freeman, 2010, p. 27]

Calling herself a weed suggests that she never overcame her conviction that she was less cherished than the other children.

Historically, many famous musicians, artists, and scientists were child prodigies whose fathers recognized their talent (often because the father was talented) and taught them. Often they did not attend regular school. Mozart's father transcribed his earliest pieces and toured Europe with his gifted son. Picasso's father removed him from school in second grade so he could create all day.

That solution also had pitfalls. Although intense early education at home nourishes talent, neither Mozart nor Picasso had happy adult lives or learned basic skills. Picasso said he never learned to read or write, and Mozart had a poor understanding of math and money. Similar problems are evident in gifted young singers, film stars, and athletes.

Neuroscience has recently discovered that children who develop their musical talents with extensive practice in early childhood grow specialized brain structures, as do child athletes and mathematicians. Since plasticity means that children learn whatever their context teaches, special talents may be enhanced with special education, an argument for elementary school classes that are designated for gifted and talented children where their talents can develop while they learn basic social and academic skills.

A related kind of child is the one who is unusually creative (Sternberg et al., 2011). The child may be a *divergent thinker,* finding many solutions and questions for every problem. Such children joke in class, resist drudgery, ignore homework, and bedevil their teachers. They may become innovators, inventors, and creative forces.

They refuse to be *convergent thinkers,* who choose the correct answer on school exams. One divergent thinker was Charles Darwin, whose "school reports complained unendingly that he wasn't interested in studying, only shooting, riding, and beetle-collecting" (Freeman, 2010, p. 283). Other creative geniuses who were poor students were Freud, Newton, Einstein, and more recently, Steve Jobs.

As you can see, all three types of children—high-IQ, unusually talented, and unusually creative—might need to be educated apart from more ordinary children. On the other hand, some nations, and school districts within the United States, believe all children should learn together. Maybe yes, maybe no. As you have read, all children grow well and learn much in middle childhood, yet variations in health, disorders, and abilities are evident. The next chapter continues this theme: Varied family structures further diversify this period of life.

ANDREW H. WALKER/GETTY IMAGES FOR DIFF

Gifted. Then What? Mercan Türkoğlu was awarded a Bambi, the German equivalent of an Oscar, for her star performance in the film *Three Quarter Moon.* She is German of Turkish ancestry, Muslim, and a talented actress. What education will best prepare her for adulthood?

THINK CRITICALLY: If you were the parent of a gifted child, what would you have your child forgo to develop his or her talent?

WHAT HAVE YOU LEARNED?

1. How do aptitude and achievement differ in theory and practice?
2. Why might teachers need to know the theory of multiple intelligences?
3. How might a child's culture affect the results of an IQ test?
4. Why might a child with ADHD have difficulty learning?
5. How should specific learning disorders be recognized and remedied?
6. What are three signs of autism spectrum disorder?
7. How and when should children with special needs have special education?
8. Why might gifted children benefit, or be harmed, by special education?
9. When is it better for children with special needs to be in a regular class?

SUMMARY

A Healthy Time

1. Middle childhood is a time of steady growth and few serious illnesses, thanks to genes and medical advances.

2. Physical activity aids health and joy. However, current social and environmental conditions make informal neighborhood play scarce, school physical education less prevalent, and sports leagues less welcoming.

3. Childhood obesity and asthma are increasing worldwide. Although genes are part of the cause, public policies (e.g., food advertising, pollution standards) and family practices also have an impact.

Cognition

4. According to Piaget, middle childhood is the time of concrete operational thought, when egocentrism diminishes and logical thinking begins. School-age children can understand classification and seriation.

5. Vygotsky stressed the social context of learning, including the specific lessons of school and learning from peers and adults. Culture affects not only what children learn but also how they learn.

6. An information-processing approach examines each step of the thinking process, focusing especially on brain processes, which continue to mature. Siegler took this approach and demonstrated that mathematical knowledge builds gradually rather than emerging at once.

7. Memory begins with information that reaches the brain from the sense organs. Then selection processes allow some information to reach working memory. Finally, long-term memory stores images and ideas indefinitely.

8. A broad knowledge base, logical strategies for retrieval, and speedy processing advance memory and cognition. Control processes, including metacognition, are crucial.

9. Notable advances occur in reaction time and automatization during middle childhood, allowing faster and better coordination of many parts of the brain.

Teaching and Learning

10. Language learning advances during middle childhood, including expansion of vocabulary and understanding of metaphors.

11. Children excel at pragmatics, using one code with their friends and another in school. Many children become fluent in the school language while speaking another language at home.

12. Nations and experts agree that education is critical in middle childhood. Almost all the world's children now attend primary school. Schools differ in what and how they teach, especially with regard to the hidden curriculum.

13. International assessments are useful as comparisons. Reading is assessed with the PIRLS, math and science with the TIMSS.

On both measures, children in East Asia and Finland excel and children in the United States are in the middle.

14. In the United States, the No Child Left Behind Act and the National Assessment of Educational Progress attempt to improve education, with mixed success. The Common Core is a controversial attempt to raise national standards and improve accountability.

15. Unlike almost all other countries, in the United States each state, each district, and sometimes each school retain significant control. Education is a political issue as much or more than a developmental one.

16. Disagreements about the best type of school are frequent. Some parents choose charter schools, others prefer private schools, and still others opt for home schooling. Judging quality is difficult: Parents value class size and homework more than do many educators.

Developmental Psychopathology

17. IQ tests are designed to quantify intellectual aptitude, usually via tests of language and logic. Critics contend that traditional IQ tests assess too narrowly because people have multiple types of intelligence.

18. Achievement tests measure accomplishment, often in specific academic areas. Aptitude and achievement are correlated, both for individuals and for nations.

19. Developmental psychopathology uses knowledge of normal development to inform the study of unusual development. Four lessons have emerged: Abnormality is normal; disability changes over time; a condition may get better or worse; diagnosis depends on context.

20. Children with attention-deficit/hyperactivity disorder (ADHD) are often inattentive, impulsive, and/or overactive. Stimulant medication often helps children with ADHD to learn, but any drug used by children must be carefully monitored.

21. Children diagnosed with specific learning disorders have unusual difficulty in mastering specific skills. The most common disorders that impair achievement in middle childhood are dyslexia (unusual difficulty with reading) and dyscalculia (unusual difficulty with math).

22. Children with autism spectrum disorder typically struggle with social interactions and language. They often exhibit restricted, repetitive patterns of behavior, interests, and activities. Many causes are hypothesized, and treatments are diverse: All are controversial and none is certain to help.

23. About 13 percent of all U.S. school-age children receive special education services, usually in the regular classroom.

24. Some children are unusually intelligent, talented, or creative, and states and nations provide special education for them. Specifics of that education vary and are controversial.

KEY TERMS

middle childhood (p. 240)

childhood overweight (p. 242)

childhood obesity (p. 242)

asthma (p. 244)

concrete operational thought (p. 247)

classification (p. 247)

seriation (p. 247)

selective attention (p. 249)

sensory memory (p. 251)

working memory (p. 251)

long-term memory (p. 252)

knowledge base (p. 252)

control processes (p. 252)

metacognition (p. 252)

reaction time (p. 253)

automatization (p. 253)

ELLs (English Language Learners) (p. 256)

immersion (p. 256)

bilingual education (p. 256)

ESL (English as a second language) (p. 256)

hidden curriculum (p. 258)

Trends in Math and Science Study (TIMSS) (p. 259)

Progress in International Reading Literacy Study (PIRLS) (p. 259)

No Child Left Behind Act (NCLB) (p. 263)

National Assessment of Educational Progress (NAEP) (p. 263)

charter schools (p. 264)

private schools (p. 265)

vouchers (p. 265)

home schooling (p. 265)

developmental psychopathology (p. 267)

aptitude (p. 267)

achievement test (p. 268)

Flynn effect (p. 268)

multiple intelligences (p. 268)

multifinality (p. 270)

equifinality (p. 270)

attention-deficit/hyperactivity disorder (ADHD) (p. 270)

specific learning disorder (p. 271)

dyslexia (p. 271)

dyscalculia (p. 272)

autism spectrum disorder (ASD) (p. 272)

neurodiversity (p. 273)

response to intervention (RTI) (p. 275)

individual education plan (IEP) (p. 275)

APPLICATIONS

1. Developmental psychologists believe that every teacher should be skilled at teaching children with a wide variety of needs. Does teacher training at your college or university reflect this goal? Should some teachers be specialized? Give reasons for your opinions.

2. Internet sources vary in quality on any topic, but this is particularly true of Web sites for parents of children with special needs. Pick one disability or disease and find several Web sources devoted to that condition. How might parents evaluate the information provided?

3. Visit a local elementary school and look for the hidden curriculum. For example, do the children line up? Why or why not, when, and how? Does gender, age, ability, or talent affect the grouping of children or the selection of staff? What is on the walls? Are parents involved? If so, how? For everything you observe, speculate about the underlying assumptions.

4. Interview a 7- to 11-year-old to learn what he or she knows *and understands* about math. Relate both correct and incorrect responses to the logic of concrete operational thought.

CHAPTER OUTLINE

CHAPTER 8

MIDDLE CHILDHOOD
The Social World

WHAT WILL YOU KNOW?

- What helps some children thrive in a difficult family, school, or neighborhood?
- Should parents marry, risking divorce, or not marry, and thus avoid divorce?
- What can be done to stop a bully?
- Why would children lie to adults to protect a friend?

> "But Dad, that's not fair! Why does Keaton get to kill zombies and I can't?"
>
> "Well, because you are too young to kill zombies. Your cousin Keaton is older than you, so that's why he can do it. You'll get nightmares."
>
> "That's soooo not fair."
>
> "Next year, after your birthday, I'll let you kill zombies."
>
> *[adapted from Asma, 2013]*

This conversation between a professor and his 8-year-old illustrates social development in middle childhood, explained in this chapter. Every child wants to do what the bigger children do; parents seek to protect their children, sometimes ineffectively. Throughout middle childhood, issues of parents and peers, fairness and justice, inclusion and exclusion are pervasive. Age takes on new importance, because concrete operational thinking makes chronology more salient, and age-based cutoffs are used by schools, camps, and athletic leagues to decide whether a child is "ready."

I still remember who was the youngest, and the oldest, child in my fourth-grade class—even though we all were born within the same 12 months. In the excerpt above, the professor hoped his son would no longer want to kill zombies when he was 9, but a child's sense of fairness often differs from an adult's. If Keaton is still killing zombies in a year, this boy is likely to remember his father's promise. ■

The Nature of the Child

As explained in the previous chapter, steady growth, brain maturation, and intellectual advances make middle childhood a time for more independence (see At About This Time). One practical result is that between ages 6 and 11, children learn to care for themselves. They not only hold their own spoon but also make their own lunch, not only zip their own pants but also pack their own suitcases, not only walk to school but also organize after-school games with friends.

Over the same years, parent–child interactions shift from primarily physical care (bathing, dressing, and so on) to include more conversation about choices and values, a trend particularly apparent with boys and their fathers (Keown & Palmer, 2014). Children listen to adults but express their own ideas as well. Peers and teachers become more influential than they were for younger children.

Adults Stay Out In middle childhood, children want to do things themselves. What if a parent grabbed each child's hand and wanted to jump in, too? That would spoil the fun.

social comparison
The tendency to assess one's abilities, achievements, social status, and other attributes by measuring them against those of other people, especially one's peers.

industry versus inferiority
The fourth of Erikson's eight psychosocial crises, during which children attempt to master many skills, developing a sense of themselves as either accomplished or a failure, competent or incompetent.

The drive for independence from parents expands the social world. School-age children venture outdoors alone to play with friends, if their parents let them. Some experts think that parents should do just that (Rosin, 2014).

Self-Concept

Throughout the centuries and in every culture, school-age children develop a much more realistic understanding of who they are and what they can do. They busily master whatever skills their culture values. Their physical and cognitive maturation makes such activity possible.

SOCIAL COMPARISON As children mature, they develop their *self-concept,* which is their idea about themselves, including their intelligence, personality, abilities, gender, and ethnic background. Self-concept forms lifelong. As you remember, children discover that they are individuals in toddlerhood (the rouge test), and a positive, global self-concept is typical in early childhood (egocentrism).

Now, in middle childhood, the self-concept becomes more complex and logical, as cognitive development and social awareness increase. Children realize they are not the fastest, smartest, prettiest, best. At some point between ages 6 and 11, when they win a race with their mother, it dawns on them that she could have run faster if she had tried.

Crucial during middle childhood is **social comparison**—comparing oneself to others (Davis-Kean et al., 2009; Dweck, 2013). Ideally, social comparison helps school-age children value themselves and abandon the imaginary, rosy self-evaluation of preschoolers. The self-concept becomes more realistic, incorporating comparison to peers and judgments from society (Davis-Kean et al., 2009).

All children become aware of gender discrimination, with girls complaining that they are not allowed to play some sports and boys complaining that teachers favor the girls (Brown et al., 2011). Some children—especially those from minority ethnic or religious groups—notice social prejudices, and the self-concept must adjust.

Over the years of middle childhood, children who recognize prejudice and react by affirming pride in their gender and background are likely to develop healthy self-esteem (Corenblum, 2014). Parents and teachers can help by noting heroes who were female, African American, Latino, Muslim, Chinese, and so on. Of course, European American boys need heroes, too.

Affirming pride is an important counterbalance, because, for all children, increasing self-understanding and social awareness come at a price. Self-criticism and self-consciousness rise from ages 6 to 11, and "by middle childhood . . . this [earlier] overestimate of their ability or judgments decreases" (Davis-Kean et al., 2009, p. 184). Children's self-concept becomes influenced by the opinions of others, even by other children whom they do not know (Thomaes et al., 2010).

In addition, because children think concretely during middle childhood, materialism increases, and superficial attributes (hair texture, sock patterns) become important, making self-esteem fragile (Chaplin & John, 2007). Insecure 10-year-olds might desperately want the latest jackets, smartphones, and so on. They notice their inadequacies, and they need praise for their actual accomplishments—a spelling worksheet with a gold star, getting up and dressed on time, saving their allowance, hitting a softball, protecting a younger sibling, or whatever.

ERIKSON'S INSIGHTS With regard to his fourth psychosocial crisis, **industry versus inferiority,** Erikson noted that the child "must forget past hopes and wishes, while his exuberant imagination is tamed and harnessed to the laws of impersonal things," becoming "ready to apply himself to given skills and tasks" (Erikson, 1993, pp. 258, 259).

Think of learning to read and add, both pains-taking and boring. (Slowly sounding out "Jane has a dog" or writing "3 + 4 = 7" for the hundredth time is not exciting.) Yet school-age children busily practice reading and math: They are intrinsically motivated to read a page, finish a worksheet, memorize a spelling word, color a map, and so on. Adults can encourage this.

This was apparent in the case in Chapter 7, comparing mothers from Taiwan and New England. When Tim's mother helped him figure out how to do a particular kind of math problem that had him "clumsy" in class, she wrote out a page of problems for him, and then he did "the whole thing lickety split . . . [which made him] very happy" (Li et al., 2014, p. 1218). Similarly, children enjoy collecting, categorizing, and counting whatever they gather—perhaps stamps, stickers, stones, or seashells. That is industry.

> ### At About This Time
>
> Signs of Psychosocial Maturation Developing Between Ages 6 and 11*
>
> Children responsibly perform specific chores.
>
> Children make decisions about a weekly allowance.
>
> Children can tell time, and they adhere to set times for various activities.
>
> Children have homework, including some assignments over several days.
>
> Children are less often punished than when they were younger.
>
> Children try to conform to peers in clothes, language, and so on.
>
> Children express preferences about their after-school care, lessons, and activities.
>
> Children are responsible for younger children, pets, and, in some places, work.
>
> Children strive for independence from parents.
>
> *Of course, culture is crucial. For example, giving a child an allowance is typical for middle-class children in developed nations since about 1960. It was rare, or completely absent, in earlier times and other places.

Overall, children judge themselves as either *industrious* or *inferior*—deciding whether they are competent or incompetent, productive or useless, winners or losers. Self-pride depends not necessarily on actual accomplishments but on how others view those accomplishments. Social rejection is both a cause and a consequence of feeling inferior (Rubin et al., 2013).

Interestingly, the social judgments most valued come from peers of the same sex. Everywhere, children choose to be with other boys or girls. Indeed, boys who write "Girls stay out!" and girls who insist "Boys stink!" are typical. From a developmental perspective, this temporary antipathy (which Freud called *latency*) is a dynamic stage. Children shift away from sexual interests—only to reverse themselves when the hormones of puberty arise (Knight, 2014).

Culture and Self-Esteem

Apparent in many of the examples just mentioned, cultures and families differ in which attitudes and accomplishments they value, and children respond to that. Everywhere, however, academic and social competence benefit from the realistic self-perception that emerges in middle childhood.

Same Situation, Far Apart: Helping at Home Sichuan, in China, and Virginia, in the United States, provide vastly different contexts for child development. For instance, in some American suburbs, laws forbid hanging laundry outside—but not in rural China, where in traditional families, fathers and sons never wash the dishes. Nonetheless, everywhere children help their families with household chores.

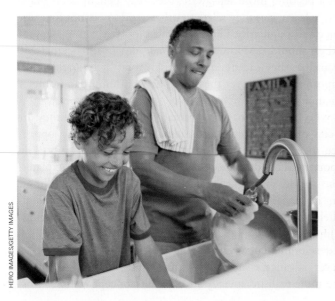

OPPOSING PERSPECTIVES

Protect or Puncture Self-Esteem?

Unrealistically high self-esteem seems to reduce effortful control (described in Chapter 6), which may lead to lower achievement and increased aggression. The same problems appear if self-esteem is unrealistically low. In both cases, however, there are gaps in the research, which makes definitive conclusions difficult (Ostrowsky, 2010). Nonetheless, one leading scholar contends there is no evidence that high self-esteem is beneficial (Baumeister, 2010).

Of course, teachers and parents hope children will have adequate self-esteem, neither too high nor too low. A problem arises, however, in that cultures differ in their definition of "adequate." When are children too self-critical and when not self-critical enough (Robins et al., 2012; Baumeister et al., 2011)?

Many cultures expect children to be humble, not prideful. For example, Australians say that "tall poppies are cut down," the Chinese say "the nail that sticks up is hammered," and the Japanese discourage social comparison aimed at making oneself feel superior. However, that perspective is not held by everyone, even in those cultures.

A trio of researchers, acknowledging that "Whether high or low self-esteem is associated with increased aggression remains a topic of debate" (Teng et al., 2015, p. 45), surveyed 52 studies of self-esteem in Chinese children. They found that low self-esteem correlated with aggression. This was not found in every study, but the researchers believe that Chinese families and schools should not be too quick to criticize children, lest they increase the children's anger.

On the other hand, a study of fourth-grade students in the Netherlands found that "inflated self-esteem" (indicated by agreeing with items such as "I am a great example for other kids to follow") predicted bullying aggression among boys (not girls) (Reijntjes et al., 2015). These researchers were particularly concerned about child narcissism, an exaggerated pride that may be pathological.

Self-esteem is often encouraged in the United States. If 8-year-olds say they want to be President when they grow up, adults usually smile and say, "That would be wonderful." Children's successes and ambitions are praised; teachers hesitate to criticize, especially in middle childhood.

For example, some school report cards are graded from "Excellent" to "Needs improvement," not from A to F. Some schools promote children to the next higher grade each year (called social promotion) whether or not they have learned the work, fearing that children's self-esteem will be damaged if they are told they have failed third grade, for instance.

An opposite perspective is implicit in the No Child Left Behind Act, which closes schools that are rated as failing. Children are tested from the third grade on, and they are held back if they have not achieved third-grade proficiency. Obviously culture, cohort, and age all influence attitudes about self-esteem. That leads to the question: Should children be praised more than criticized or the opposite?

Watch **Video: Interview with Carol Dweck** to learn about how children's mindsets affect their intellectual development.

THINK CRITICALLY: When would a realistic, honest self-assessment be harmful?

One component of self-concept has received considerable research attention (Dweck, 2013). As children become more self-aware, they may benefit from praise for their process, for *how* they learn, *how* they relate to others, and so on, not for static qualities such as intelligence and popularity. This encourages growth.

The hope is that children should develop an *incremental* idea of intellectual and personal traits, which means that they can develop themselves bit by bit, rather than an *entity* concept, which means that whatever they are (smart or dumb, handsome or ugly) is who they are by nature, for life (Dweck, 2013).

For example, children who fail a test may be devastated *if* failure means they are not smart. However, process-oriented children consider failure a "learning opportunity," a time to advance metacognition by planning a better way to study. This becomes increasingly important as children grow older, as the next chapter explains.

Self-conscious emotions (pride, shame, guilt) develop during middle childhood, guiding social interaction. During these years, if those same emotions are uncontrolled, they can overwhelm a healthy self-concept, leading to psychopathology (Muris & Meesters, 2014).

Thus, as with most developmental advances, the potential for psychological growth is evident. However, advance is not automatic—family, culture, and social context affect whether the more realistic, socially attuned self-concept will be a burden or a blessing.

Resilience and Stress

In infancy and early childhood, children depend on their immediate families for food, learning, and life itself. Then "experiences in middle childhood can sustain, magnify, or reverse the advantages or disadvantages that children acquire in the preschool years" (Huston & Ripke, 2006, p. 2). Some children continue to benefit from supportive parents; others escape destructive family influences by finding their own niche in the larger world.

Surprisingly, some children seem unscathed by early experiences. They have been called "resilient" or even "invincible." Current thinking about resilience, with insights from dynamic-systems theory, emphasizes that no one is impervious to past history or current context (see Table 8.1). Many suffer lifelong harm from early maltreatment, but some weather early storms and a few not only survive but also come out stronger (Masten, 2014).

Differential susceptibility is apparent because of genes and also because of early child rearing, preschool education, and culture. As Chapter 1 explains, some children are hardy, more like dandelions than orchids, but all are influenced by their situation (Ellis & Boyce, 2008).

Two leading researchers have similar definitions of **resilience:** "a dynamic process encompassing positive adaptation within the context of significant adversity" (Luthar et al., 2000, p. 543) and "the capacity of a dynamic system to adapt successfully to disturbances that threaten system function, viability, or development" (Masten, 2014, p. 10). Both definitions emphasize that:

resilience
The capacity to adapt well to significant adversity and to overcome serious stress.

- Resilience is *dynamic,* not a stable trait. A given person may be resilient at some periods but not at others. The effects from one period reverberate as time goes on.

- Resilience is a *positive adaptation*. For example, if parental rejection leads a child to a closer relationship with another adult, that is positive adaptation.

- Adversity must be *significant,* a threat to development or even to life itself.

TABLE 8.1	Dominant Ideas About Resilience, 1965 to Present
1965	All children have the same needs for healthy development.
1970	Some conditions or circumstances—such as "absent father," "teenage mother," "working mom," and "day care"—are harmful for every child.
1975	All children are *not* the same. Some children are resilient, coping easily with stressors that cause harm in other children.
1980	Nothing inevitably causes harm. Both maternal employment and preschool education, once thought to be risks, may be helpful.
1985	Factors beyond the family, both in the child (low birthweight, prenatal alcohol exposure, aggressive temperament) and in the community (poverty, violence), are risky for children.
1990	Risk–benefit analysis finds that some children are "invulnerable" to, or even benefit from, circumstances that destroy others.
1995	No child is invincibly resilient. Risks are always harmful—if not to learning, then to emotions; if not immediately, then long term.
2000	Risk–benefit analysis involves the interplay among many biological, cognitive, and social factors, some within the child (genes, disability, temperament), the family (function as well as structure), and the community (including neighborhood, school, church, and culture).
2008	Focus on strengths, not risks. Assets in the child (intelligence, personality), the family (secure attachment, warmth), the community (schools, after-school programs), and the nation (income support, health care) must be nurtured.
2010	Strengths vary by culture and national values. Both universal ideals and local variations must be recognized and respected.
2012	Genes as well as cultural practices can be either strengths or weaknesses; differential susceptibility means identical stressors can benefit one child and harm another.
2015	It is difficult to predict what makes one child resilient and another not, but early intervention—prenatal and infancy—before problems appear, is most effective.

Same Situation, Far Apart: Play Ball! In the war in the Ukraine *(left)* volunteers guard the House of Parliament against a Russian takeover, and in Liberia *(right)* thousands have died from the Ebola epidemic. Nonetheless, one boy practices his soccer kick and four boys celebrate a soccer goal in 2015. Children can ignore national disasters as long as they have familiar caregivers nearby and a chance to play.

OBSERVATION QUIZ

How can you tell that the Liberian boys are celebrating a soccer victory instead of the end of an epidemic? (see answer, page 288) ▲

CUMULATIVE STRESS One important discovery is that stress accumulates over time, with minor disturbances (called "daily hassles") having an impact. A long string of hassles, day after day, is more devastating than an isolated major stress.

Almost every child can withstand one trauma, especially if parents do not add to the fear. Repeated stresses, heightened reactions, daily hassles, and multiple traumatic experiences make resilience difficult (Masten, 2014; Catani et al., 2010).

The social context—especially supportive adults who do not blame the child—is crucial. A chilling example comes from the "child soldiers" in the 1991–2002 civil war in Sierra Leone (Betancourt et al., 2013). Children witnessed and often participated in murder and rape. When the war was over, 529 war-affected youth, then aged 10 to 17, were interviewed. Many were pathologically depressed or anxious.

These war-damaged children were interviewed again two and six years later. Surprisingly, many had overcome their trauma and were functioning normally. Recovery was more likely if they had been in middle childhood, not adolescence, when the war occurred. Furthermore, if at least one caregiver survived, if their communities did not reject them, and if their daily routines were restored, the children usually regained emotional stability.

An example from the United States comes from children temporarily living in a shelter for homeless families (Cutuli et al., 2013; Obradović, 2012). Compared to other children from the same kinds of families (typically high-poverty, often single-parent), on every measure of development they were "significantly behind their low-income, but residentially more stable peers" (Obradović et al., 2009, p. 513).

The probable reasons: Residential disruption, when added to other stresses, is too much. They suffered physiologically, as measured by cortisol levels, blood pressure, and weight, and psychologically, as measured by learning in school and the number of good friends. Again, protective factors buffered the impact: Having a parent with them who provided affection, hope, and stable routines enabled some children living in shelters to be resilient.

Similar results were found in a longitudinal study of children exposed to a sudden, wide-ranging, terrifying wildfire in Australia. Almost all the children suffered stress reactions at the time, but 20 years later, the crucial factor for recovery was not how close they had been to the blaze but whether they had been separated from their mothers (McFarlane & Van Hooff, 2009).

COGNITIVE COPING Obviously, these examples are extreme, but the general finding appears in other research as well. Disasters take a toll, but factors in the child (especially problem-solving ability), in the family (consistency and care), and in the community (good schools and welcoming religious institutions) all increase resilience (Masten, 2014).

A pivotal factor is the child's interpretation of events (Lagattuta, 2014). Cortisol increases in low-income children *if* they interpret circumstances connected to their family's poverty as a personal threat and *if* the family lacks order and routines (thus increasing daily hassles) (E. Chen et al., 2010). When low-SES children do not take things personally and their family is not chaotic, resilience is more likely.

Do you know adults who grew up in low-SES families yet who seem strengthened, not destroyed, by that experience? If so, they probably did not consider themselves poor, perhaps because all their friends had similar circumstances. They may have shared a bed with a sibling, eaten macaroni day after day, dressed in hand-me-downs, and walked to school. However, if their family was not erratic or hostile, and if they did not realize how poor they were, their poverty did not harm them lifelong.

In general, children's interpretation of family circumstances (poverty, divorce, and so on) is crucial. Some consider their situation a temporary hardship; they look forward to leaving childhood behind. If they also have personal strengths, such as creativity and intelligence, they may shine in adulthood—evident in thousands of success stories, from Abraham Lincoln to Oprah Winfrey.

The opposite reaction is called **parentification,** when children feel responsible for the entire family. They become caretakers, including of their actual parents. Here again, interpretation is crucial. If children feel burdened and unable to escape, they are likely to suffer, but if they think they are helpful and their parents and community respect their contribution, they may be resilient. This might explain a curious finding: European American children are more likely to suffer from parentification than African American children are (Khafi et al., 2014).

In one more example, children who endured Hurricane Katrina in 2005 were affected by their thoughts, positive and negative, more than by other expected factors, including their caregivers' distress (Kilmer & Gil-Rivas, 2010). Especially in

COURTESY UNICEF

Video Activity: Child Soldiers and Child Peacemakers examines the state of child soldiers in the world and then explores how adolescent cognition impacts the decisions of five teenage peace activists.

parentification
When a child acts more like a parent than a child. This may occur if the actual parents do not act as caregivers, making a child feel responsible for the family.

JONKMANNS/LAIF/REDUX

NAFTALI HILGER/LAIF/REDUX

Same Situation, Far Apart: Praying Hands Differences are obvious between the Northern Indian girls entering their Hindu school and the West African boy in a Christian church, even in their clothes and hand positions. But underlying similarities are more important. In every culture, many 8-year-olds are more devout than their elders.

THINK CRITICALLY: Is there any harm in having the oldest child take care of the younger ones? Why or why not?

ANSWER TO OBSERVATION QUIZ
(from page 286) They are hugging the ball. ●

OBSERVATION QUIZ

The 12-year-olds are twins. Can you see any differences in their shared environment? (see answer, page 290) ▼

disasters, getting school routines started again quickly is especially helpful because children benefit from routines and preparation for their future. Spiritual faith and religious rituals (prayer, candles, services) also help children cope if they provide hope and meaning (Masten, 2014).

WHAT HAVE YOU LEARNED?

1. How do Erikson's stages of cognition for preschool- and school-age children differ?
2. Why is social comparison particularly powerful during middle childhood?
3. Why do cultures differ in how they value pride and humility?
4. What factors help a child become resilient?
5. Why and when might minor stresses be more harmful than major stresses?
6. How might a child's interpretation affect the ability to cope with repeated stress?
7. What does the evidence say about how children respond to major disasters?

Families and Children

No one doubts that genes affect personality as well as ability, that peers are vital, and that schools and cultures influence what, and how much, children learn. Some experts have gone further, suggesting that genes, peers, and communities are so influential that parenting has little impact—unless it is grossly abusive (Harris, 1998, 2002; McLeod et al., 2007). This suggestion arose from studies about the impact of the environment on child development.

RADIUS IMAGES/MASTERFILE

Shared and Nonshared Environments

Many studies find that children are much less affected by *shared environment* (influences that arise from being in the same environment, such as two siblings living in one home, raised by their parents) than by *nonshared environment* (e.g., the experiences in the school or neighborhood that differ between one child and another).

Almost all personality traits and intellectual characteristics can be traced to the combined influence of genes and nonshared environments, with little left over for the shared influence of being raised together. Even psychopathology, happiness, and sexual orientation (Burt, 2009; Långström et al., 2010; Bartels et al., 2013) arise primarily from genes and nonshared environment.

Since research finds that shared environment has little impact, could it be that parents are merely caretakers? Mothers and fathers need to provide basics (food, shelter) and are harmful when abusive, but might their household restrictions, routines, and responses be irrelevant? If a child

Family Unity Thinking about any family—even a happy, wealthy family like this one—makes it apparent that each child's family experiences differ. For instance, would you expect this 5-year-old boy to be treated the same way as his two older sisters? And how about each child's feelings toward the parents?

becomes a murderer or a hero, could that be genetic and nonshared? Perhaps parents deserve neither blame nor credit!

Recent findings, however, reassert parent power. The analysis of shared and non-shared influences was correct, but the conclusion was based on a false assumption. Siblings raised together do *not* share the same environment.

For example, if relocation, divorce, unemployment, or a new job occurs in a family, the impact on each child depends on his or her age, genes, and gender. Moving to another town upsets a school-age child more than an infant, divorce harms boys more than girls, poverty may hurt preschoolers the most, and so on.

The variations above do not apply for all siblings: Differential susceptibility means that one child is more affected, for better or worse, than another (Pluess & Belsky, 2010). When siblings are raised together, all experiencing the same dysfunctional family, then their genes, age, and gender may lead one child to become antisocial, another to be pathologically anxious, and a third to be resilient, capable, and strong (Beauchaine et al., 2009).

Further, parents do not treat each of their children the same, in part because birth order and gender differ. It is mistaken to assume that family experiences are the same for the eldest and the youngest. Even identical twins might have different family experiences, as in the following.

A VIEW FROM SCIENCE

"I Always Dressed One in Blue Stuff . . ."

To separate the effects of genes and environment, many researchers have studied twins. As you remember from Chapter 2, some twins are dizygotic, with only half of their genes in common, and some are monozygotic, genetically identical.

If monozygotic twins had the same trait as their twin but dizygotic twins did not share that trait, researchers assumed that genes were the reason. However, if monozygotic twins were no more similar than dizygotic twins on a trait, then nonshared environment (i.e., non-family influences) must be the reason. Notice how researchers assumed that, since twins are typically raised together, differences between the two types of twins could not be attributed to the family environment.

Comparing monozygotic and dizygotic twins continues to be a useful research strategy. However, conclusions are now tempered by another finding: Siblings raised in the same households do not necessarily share the same home environment. A seminal study occurred with twins in England.

An expert team of scientists compared 1,000 sets of monozygotic twins reared by their biological parents (Caspi et al., 2004). Of course, the pairs were identical in genes, sex, and age. The researchers asked the mothers to describe each twin. Descriptions ranged from very positive ("my ray of sunshine") to very negative ("I wish I had never had her. . . . She's a cow, I hate her") (quoted in Caspi et al., 2004, p. 153). Many mothers noted personality differences between their twins. For example, one mother said:

> Susan can be very sweet . . . She loves babies . . . she can be insecure . . . she flutters and dances around. . . . There's not much between her ears. . . . She's exceptionally vain, more so than Ann. Ann loves any game involving a ball, very sporty,

climbs trees, very much a tomboy. One is a serious tomboy and one's a serious girlie girl. Even when they were babies I always dressed one in blue stuff and one in pink stuff.

> *[quoted in Caspi et al., 2004, p. 156]*

Some mothers rejected one twin and favored the other:

> He was in the hospital and everyone was all "poor Jeff, poor Jeff" and I started thinking, "Well, what about me? I'm the one's just had twins, I'm the one's going through this, he's a seven-week-old baby and doesn't know a thing about it" . . . I sort of detached and plowed my emotions into Mike. [Jeff's identical twin brother.]

> *[quoted in Caspi et al., 2004, p. 156]*

This same mother later blamed Jeff for favoring his father: "Jeff would do everything for Don but he wouldn't for me, and no matter what I did for either of them [Don or Jeff] it wouldn't be right" (p. 157). She said Mike was much more lovable.

The researchers measured each twin's personality at age 5 (assessing, among other things, antisocial behavior reported by teachers) and again two years later. They found that if a mother was more negative toward one of her twins, that twin *became* more antisocial, more likely to fight, steal, and hurt others at age 7 than at age 5, unlike the favored twin.

These researchers acknowledge that many other nonshared factors—peers, teachers, and so on—are significant. But this personality difference in monozygotic twins confirms that parents matter. This will surprise no one who has a brother or a sister. Children from the same family do not always share the same family experience.

Family Structure and Family Function

family structure
The legal and genetic relationships among family members. Possible structures include nuclear family, extended family, stepfamily, single-parent family, and many others.

family function
The way a family works to meet the physical and psychological needs of its members.

Family structure refers to the legal and genetic connections among related people. Legal connections are via marriage, years of cohabitation, or adoption. Genetic connections are from parent to child, or between siblings, cousins, grandparents and grandchildren, and so on.

Family function refers to how the people in a family work together to care for the family members. Some families function well, others are dysfunctional.

Function is more important than structure, although harder to measure. Some family functions are needed by everyone at every age, such as love and encouragement. Beyond that, what people need from their families differs depending on how old they are: Infants need responsive caregiving, teenagers need guidance, young adults need freedom, the aged need respect.

THE NEEDS OF CHILDREN IN MIDDLE CHILDHOOD What do children need from their families during middle childhood? Ideally, five things:

1. *Physical necessities.* Although 6- to 11-year-olds eat, dress, and go to sleep without help, families provide basic needs, such as for food, clothing, and shelter.

2. *Learning.* Middle childhood covers the prime learning years: Families support, encourage, and guide education.

3. *Self-respect.* Because children from age 6 to 11 become self-critical and socially aware, families provide opportunities for success (in academics, sports, the arts, and so on).

4. *Peer relationships.* Families choose schools and neighborhoods with friendly children and then arrange play dates, group activities, overnight trips, and so on.

5. *Harmony and stability.* Families provide protective, predictable routines within a home that is a safe, peaceful haven.

The final item on the list above is especially crucial in middle childhood: Children cherish safety and stability; they do not like change (Turner et al., 2012). Ironically, many parents move from one neighborhood or school to another during these years. Children who move frequently may be harmed, academically and psychologically (Cutuli et al., 2013).

Stay Home, Dad The rate of battle deaths for U.S. soldiers is lower for those deployed in Iraq and Afghanistan than for any previous conflict, thanks to modern medicine and armor. However psychological harm from repeated returns and absences is increasing, especially for children.

KIDSTOCK/BLEND IMAGES/GETTY IMAGES

The problems arising from instability are evident for U.S. children in military families. Enlisted parents tend to have higher incomes, better health care, and more education than do civilians from the same backgrounds. But they have one major disadvantage: They move. In reviewing earlier research, a scientist reports "military parents are continually leaving, returning, leaving again . . . School work suffers, more for boys than for girls, . . . reports of depression and behavioral problems go up when a parent is deployed" (Hall, 2008, p. 52).

About half the military personnel who are on active duty have children, and many of their children learn to cope with the stresses they experience (Russo & Fallon, 2014). To help them, the U.S. military has instituted special programs. Caregivers are encouraged to avoid changes in the child's life: no new homes, new rules, or new schools (Lester et al., 2011).

DIVERSE STRUCTURES Family diversity should be acknowledged but not exaggerated. More than two-thirds of all U.S. school-age children live with two married adults (see Table 8.2), most often their biological parents. **Nuclear families** are composed of children and their biological parents (married or not) without other

nuclear family
A family that consists of a father, a mother, and their biological children under age 18.

TABLE 8.2	**Family Structures (percent of U.S. 6- to 11-year-olds in each type)***

Two-Parent Families (69%)
1. **Nuclear family (55%).** Named after the nucleus (the tightly connected core particles of an atom), the nuclear family consists of a man and a woman and their biological offspring under 18 years of age. About half of all school-age children live in nuclear families. About 10 percent of such families also include a grandparent, and often an aunt or uncle, living under the same roof. These are extended families.
2. **Stepparent family (10%).** Divorced fathers usually remarry; divorced mothers remarry about half the time. When children from a former relationship live with the new couple, that is a stepparent family. If the stepparent family includes children born to two or more couples (such as children from the spouses' previous marriages and/or children of the new couple), that is called a *blended family.*
3. **Adoptive family (2%).** Although as many as one-third of infertile married couples adopt children, few adoptable children are available and so most adoptive couples have only one or two children. Thus, only 2 percent of children are adopted, although the overall percentage of adoptive families is higher than that.
4. **Grandparents alone (1%).** Grandparents take on parenting for some children when biological parents are absent (dead, imprisoned, sick, addicted, etc.).
5. **Two same-sex parents (1%).** Some two-parent families are headed by a same-sex couple, whose legal status (married, step-, adoptive) varies.

Single-Parent Families (31%)
One-parent families are increasing, but they average fewer children than two-parent families. So in middle childhood, only 31 percent of children have a lone parent.
1. **Single mother—never married (14%).** In 2010, 41 percent of all U.S. births were to unmarried mothers; but when children are school age, many mothers who were unmarried have married or have entrusted their children to their parents' care. So, only about 13 percent of 6- to 11-year-olds, at any given moment, are in single-mother, never married, homes.
2. **Single mother—divorced, separated, or widowed (12%).** Although many marriages end in divorce (almost half in the United States, fewer in other nations), many divorcing couples have no children. Others remarry. Thus, only 12 percent of school-age children currently live with single, formerly married mothers.
3. **Single father (4%).** About 1 father in 25 has physical custody of his children and raises them without their mother or a new wife. This category increased at the start of the twenty-first century but has decreased since 2005.
4. **Grandparent alone (1%).** Sometimes a single grandparent (usually the grandmother) becomes the sole caregiving adult for a child.

More Than Two Adults (10%) [Also listed as two-parent or one-parent family]
1. **Extended family (10%).** Some children live with grandparents or other relatives, as well as with one or both of their parents. This pattern is most common with infants (20 percent) but occurs in middle childhood as well.
2. **Polygamous family (0%).** In some nations (not the United States), men can legally have several wives. This family structure is more favored by adults than children. Everywhere, polyandry (one woman, several husbands) is rare.

*Less than 1 percent of U.S. children live without any caregiving adult; they are not included in this table.

The percentages on this table are estimates, based on data from the U.S. Census Bureau. The category "extended family" in this table is higher than most published statistics, since some families do not tell official authorities about relatives living with them.

relatives in the same home. Other two-parent structures include adoptive, foster, step, same-sex, and grandparents.

single-parent family
A family that consists of only one parent and his or her children.

Single-parent families occur when only one parent is present. The United States has many single-parent families: About 31 percent of all U.S. 6- to 11-year-olds live with a single parent.

Rates of various structures change depending on the age of the child: More than half of all contemporary U.S. children will live in a single-parent family for at least a year before they reach age 18. If the children are young, usually the single parent never married; if the children are teenagers, divorce or separation is the most common reason only one parent is at home.

extended family
A family of three or more generations living in one household.

Extended families consist of relatives residing with parents and children. Usually the additional persons are grandparents; sometimes they are uncles, aunts, or cousins of the child.

The crucial distinction between types of families is based on who lives together in the same household, a distinction that does not necessarily reflect the experience of the child. Many so-called single-parent families actually have two parents involved in the child's life. Likewise, some children see their grandparents every day, even though they do not live with them. The family may function like an extended family, but it is not categorized as such.

polygamous family
A family consisting of one man, more than one wife, and their children.

In many nations, **polygamous families** (one husband with two or more wives) are an acceptable family structure. Family function may suffer in that structure, because often income per child is reduced, and education, especially for the girls, is limited (Omariba & Boyle, 2007). On the other hand, many argue that polygamy is preferable to divorce and remarriage, since most fathers who left one wife and married another are less involved with children from their first marriage than they would have been if they were the head of a polygamous family (Calder & Beaman, 2014).

Related to that is the role of stepsiblings, who are part of many family structures. Living in a family with stepsiblings, even for children who are the biological offspring of the current parents, affects family function. Children in these "complex" family structures are less likely to do well in school and in life (Brown et al., 2015).

DIVORCE Scientists try to provide analysis and insight based on empirical data (of course), but the task goes far beyond reporting facts. Regarding divorce, thousands of studies and several opposing opinions need to be considered, analyzed, and combined—no easy task. One scholar who has attempted this analysis is Andrew Cherlin. He has written 13 books and over 200 articles since 1988.

Among the facts that need analysis are these:

1. The United States leads the world in the rates of marriage, divorce, and remarriage, with almost half of all marriages ending in divorce.

2. Single parents, cohabiting parents, and stepparents sometimes provide good care, but children tend to do best in nuclear families with married parents.

3. Divorce often impairs children's academic achievement and psychosocial development for years, even decades.

Each of these is troubling. Why does this occur? The problem, Cherlin (2009) contends, is that U.S. culture is conflicted: Marriage is idolized, but so is personal freedom. As a result, many people assert their independence by marrying without consulting their parents or community. If such a love-struck couple has a baby, child care becomes overwhelming and family support is lacking. That strains the marriage, precipitating divorce.

However, Cherlin argues, because marriage remains the ideal, divorced adults blame their former mate or their own poor decisions, not the

Didn't Want to Marry This couple was happily cohabiting and strongly committed to each other but didn't wed until they learned that her health insurance would not cover them unless they were legally married.

institution or the society. Consequently, they seek another marriage, which may lead to another divorce. (Divorced people are more likely to remarry than single people their age are to marry). Repeated transitions allow personal freedom for the adults but harm the children.

This leads to a related insight. Cherlin suggests that the main reason children are harmed by divorce—as well as by cohabitation, single parenthood, and stepparenthood—is not the legal status of their parents but the lack of stability.

For example, divorces typically include many disruptions: in residence, in school, in family members, and—this may be crucial—in the relationship between child and parent. Divorced parents often become too strict or too lenient, impose premature responsibility or independence, or tell the child things that relieve the adult's anger or loneliness.

Scholars now describe divorce as a process, with transitions and conflicts before and after the formal event (H. S. Kim, 2011; Putnam, 2011). This process entails repeated changes and ongoing hassles for the children. The child's ability to cope is particularly compromised if the child is experiencing a developmental transition, such as entering first grade or beginning puberty.

Nonetheless, some researchers believe that divorce may be better for the child than an ongoing, destructive family. As one scientist who studied divorced families for decades wrote:

> Although divorce leads to an increase in stressful life events, such as poverty, psychological and health problems in parents, and inept parenting, it also may be associated with escape from conflict, the building of new more harmonious fulfilling relationships, and the opportunity for personal growth and individuation.
>
> [Hetherington, 2006, p. 204]

Not every parent should marry, not every marriage should continue, and not every divorce is harmful. However, every child needs parents to fulfill all five needs of school-age children, and a conflict-filled divorce makes that goal difficult to reach.

Connecting Structure and Function

As obvious with divorce, the fact that family function is more important for children than family structure does not make structure irrelevant. Structure influences function and vice versa. The crucial question is whether the structure makes it more or less likely that the five family functions mentioned earlier (physical necessities, learning, self-respect, friendship, and harmony/stability) will be fulfilled.

NUCLEAR FAMILIES On average, nuclear families function best; children in the nuclear structure tend to achieve better in school with fewer psychological problems. A scholar who summarized dozens of studies concludes: "Children living with two biological married parents experience better educational, social, cognitive, and behavioral outcomes than do other children" (Brown, 2010, p. 1062).

Do the proven benefits of nuclear families mean that everyone should marry before they have a child, and then stay married? Not necessarily. Some benefits are correlates, not causes.

Education, earning potential, and emotional maturity all correlate with getting married and staying married. For example, if women having their first baby are highly educated, they are usually married (78 percent) at conception; but if they are poorly educated, they are rarely married (only 11 percent) (Gibson-Davis & Rackin, 2014). The development of the child correlates with marital status, but obviously the mother's education is the main reason, not whether or not she is wed.

Brides and grooms tend to have personal assets *before* marriage and parenthood, and they bring those assets to their new family. This means that the correlation between child success and married parents occurs partly because of who marries, not

Check out the Data Connections activity **Family Structure in the United States and Around the World.**

Same Situation, Far Apart: Happy Families The boys in both photos are about 4 years old. Roberto *(left)* lives with his single mother in Chicago. She pays $360 a month for her two children to attend a day-care center. The youngest child in the Balmedina family *(right)* lives with his nuclear family—no day care needed—in the Philippines. Which boy has the better life? The answer is not known; family function is more crucial than family structure.

because of the wedding. Indeed, for some very low-SES women, marrying a man who is also a high-school dropout with no steady job would actually undercut their ability to give their baby attention. They are better mothers without marrying!

Income correlates with family structure. Usually, married couples live apart from their parents if everyone can afford it. That means that, at least in the United States, an extended family suggests that someone is financially dependent, not that a child has many loving adults at home.

These two factors—mate selection and income—explain some of the correlation between nuclear families and child well-being, but not all of it (Brown, 2010). The fact that the nuclear family is "not as strong as it appears" does not make marriage irrelevant. Ideally, marriage increases mutual affection and support, making both partners wealthier and healthier than either would have been alone. Further, when both parents live with their children day and night, a *parental alliance* is likely to form. That benefits the child.

Evidence for the benefits of the parental alliance comes from Russia, where recent economic upheaval reduced a man's average life span from age 64 in 1985 to 59 in 2000. Most at risk for an early death are single men, who have high rates of depression and alcoholism. If a Russian man lives with his wife and children, he tends to take better care of himself and his children (Ashwin & Isupova, 2014).

Shared parenting not only decreases rates of depression, in Russia and elsewhere, but it also decreases child maltreatment. Further, having two parents at home makes it more likely that someone will read to the child, check homework, invite friends over, buy new clothes, and save for college. Of course, having two married parents does not guarantee anything. One of my students wrote:

> My mother externalized her feelings with outbursts of rage, lashing out and breaking things, while my father internalized his feelings by withdrawing, being silent and looking the other way. One could say I was being raised by bipolar parents. Growing up, I would describe my mom as the Tasmanian devil and my father as the ostrich, with his head in the sand. . . . My mother disciplined with corporal punishment as well as with psychological control, while my father was permissive. What a pair.

[C., 2013]

OBSERVATION QUIZ
What is unusual about this family?
(see answer, page 296) ◄

Middle American Family This photo seems to show a typical breakfast in Brunswick, Ohio—Cheerios for 1-year-old Carson, pancakes that 7-year-old Carter does not finish eating, and family photos crowded on the far table.

This student never experienced a well-functioning parental alliance. Does that help explain why she is now a single parent, having twice married, given birth, and divorced? For everyone, childhood family experiences echo in adulthood. Especially when children are in middle childhood and adolescence, meaningful father–child relationships are difficult for men who do not live with their children, partly because of the children themselves.

One consequence: When children reach "the age of majority" (usually 18) and fathers are no longer legally responsible, many divorced or unmarried fathers stop child support. Unfortunately, most emerging adults need financial support to attend college or live independently, so a long-ago divorce still hinders their development (Goldfarb, 2014).

This benefit for children in nuclear families is more than financial. When remarried adults have incomes comparable to that of nuclear parents, they contribute less, on average, to children who live with them (Turley & Desmond, 2011). Fathers typically spend less time caring for stepchildren than biological children (Kalil et al., 2014b). As adults, stepchildren tend to live farther from either their biological father or their stepfather than other adult children do (Seltzer et al., 2013). Thus, because divorce weakens the parental alliance in childhood, nuclear families tend to be more cohesive lifelong.

OTHER TWO-PARENT FAMILIES We should not exaggerate the benefits of nuclear families. Adoptive and same-sex parents usually function well for children, not only in middle childhood but lifelong. Stepfamilies may also function well if the biological parent has chosen a partner who will be a good parent. Especially when children are under age 2 and the stepparent and the biological parent develop a strong, healthy relationship, the children who live with them may thrive (Ganong et al., 2011).

No structure is guaranteed to function well, but particular circumstances for all three family types—same-sex, adoptive, and step—can nudge in the right direction. The most difficult family function for stepfamilies to fulfill is the fifth one (harmony and stability).

Don't Judge We know this is a mother and her child, but structure and function could be wonderful or terrible. These two could be half of a nuclear family, or a single mother with one adoptive child, or part of four other family structures. That does not matter as much as family function: If this scene is typical, with both enjoying physical closeness in the great outdoors, this family functions well.

Compared with other two-parent families, stepfamilies more often change residence and community. In addition, family constellations shift: Older stepchildren leave home more often than older biological children, new babies capture parental attention and affection, additional relatives may join the household, and divorce is more common.

Not only is stability more difficult for stepfamilies; harmony is more difficult as well (Martin-Uzzi, & Duval-Tsioles, 2013). Ongoing disputes between the biological parents clash with the child's loyalty to both parents. A solid parental alliance is elusive when it includes three adults—two of whom had such profound differences that they divorced, plus another adult who is a newcomer to a child they did not raise.

Children who gain a stepparent may be angry or sad, so they often act out (e.g., fight with friends, fail in school, disobey adults). That causes arguments for their newly married parents, who may have opposite strategies for managing misbehavior. Further, disputes between half-siblings in blended families are common. Remember, however, that structure affects function but does not determine it. Many stepparent families are difficult for children, but others function well for everyone (van Eeden-Moorefield & Pasley, 2013).

Finally, the grandparent family is often idealized, but reality is much more complex. If a household has grandparents and parents, the grandparents may be care-receivers more than caregivers. Further, the two adult generations often disagree about discipline, diet, and much else.

Sometimes one or two grandparents provide full-time care with no parents present (called a *skipped-generation family*, a common form of foster care). The hope is that their experience and maturity will benefit the grandchildren. But that is not necessarily true. Grandchildren who have been removed from their parents often have health or behavioral problems themselves (Hayslip et al., 2014). They are less likely to succeed in school or have supportive, enduring friendships than other children from the same ethnic and economic backgrounds.

SINGLE-PARENT FAMILIES On average, the single-adult structure functions less well for children than the two-parent home does, primarily because the two-adult family usually has more income, time, and stability. Most single parents fill many roles—wage earner, daughter or son, as well as both mother and father—making it hard for any one adult to provide the steady emotional and academic support a child needs.

Rates of single parenthood and single grandparenthood are far higher among African Americans than other ethnic groups. This makes children from single-parent African American families feel less stigmatized, but it does not lighten the burden on the parents. If a single parent is depressed (and many are), that compounds the problem. The following case is an example.

A CASE TO STUDY

How Hard Is It to Be a Kid?

Neesha's fourth-grade teacher referred her to the school guidance team because Neesha often fell asleep in class, was late 51 days, and was absent 15 days. Although she was only 10 years old and had missed much of the fourth grade, testing found Neesha scoring at the seventh-grade level in reading and writing, and at the fifth-grade level in math. Since ability was not Neesha's problem, something psychosocial must be amiss.

The counselor spoke to Neesha's mother, Tanya, a depressed single parent who was worried about paying rent on the tiny apartment where she had moved when Neesha's father left three years earlier. He lived with his girlfriend, now with a new baby. Tanya said she had no problems with Neesha, who was "more like a little mother than a kid," unlike her 15-year-old son, Tyrone, who suffered from fetal alcohol effects and whose behavior worsened when his father left.

Tyrone was recently beaten up badly as part of a gang initiation, a group he considered "like a family." He was currently in juvenile detention after being arrested for stealing bicycle parts. Note the nonshared environment here: Although the siblings grew up together, 12-year-old Tyrone became rebellious when their father left, whereas 7-year-old Neesha became parentified, "a little mother."

The school counselor spoke with Neesha.

Neesha volunteered that she also worried a lot about things and that sometimes when she worries she has a hard time falling asleep. . . . she got in trouble for being late so many times, but it was hard to wake up. Her mom was sleeping late because she was working more nights cleaning offices. . . . Neesha said she got so far behind that she just gave up. She was also having problems with the other girls in the class, who were starting to tease her about sleeping in class and not doing her work. She said they called her names like "Sleepy" and "Dummy." She said that at first it made her very sad, and then it made her very mad. That's when she started to hit them to make them stop.

[Wilmshurst, 2011, pp. 152–153]

Neesha is coping with poverty, a depressed mother, an absent father, a delinquent brother, and classmate bullying. She seems resilient—her achievement scores are impressive. Shortly after the counselor spoke with her,

The school principal received a call from Neesha's mother, who asked that her daughter not be sent home from school because she was going to kill herself. As she spoke on the telephone, she explained that she was holding a loaded gun in her hand and she had to do it, because she was not going to make this month's rent. She could not take it any longer, but she did not want Neesha to come home and find her dead. . . . While the guidance counselor continued to keep the mother talking, the school contacted the police, who apprehended mom while she was talking on her cell phone. . . . The loaded gun was on her lap. . . . [The] mother . . . was taken to the local psychiatric facility.

[Wilmshurst, 2011, pp. 154–155]

Whether Neesha will be able to cope with her problems depends on whether she can find support beyond her family. Perhaps the school counselor will help:

When asked if she would like to meet with the school psychologist once in a while, just to talk about her worries, Neesha said she would like that very much. After she left the office, she turned and thanked the psychologist for working with her, and added, "You know, sometimes it's hard being a kid."

[Wilmshurst, 2011, p. 154]

Family structure encourages or undercuts healthy function, but many parents and communities overcome structural problems to support their children. Contrary to the averages, thousands single-parent families are wonderful. In some European nations, single parents are given many public resources; in other nations, they are shamed and unsupported. Children benefit or suffer accordingly (Abela & Walker, 2014).

Culture is always influential. In contrast to data from the United States, a study in the slums of Mumbai, India, found rates of psychological disorders among school-age children *higher* in nuclear families than in extended families, presumably because in that culture grandparents, aunts, and uncles provided more care and stability than two parents alone (Patil et al., 2013).

On the other hand, another study found that college students in India who injured themselves (e.g., *cutting*) were more often from extended families than nuclear ones (Kharsati & Bhola, 2014). One explanation is that these two studies had different populations: College students tend to be from wealthier families, unlike the children in Mumbai.

Although these studies from India differed regarding extended families, both studies found that children from single-parent families had more emotional and academic problems than other children. Of course, some nuclear families are dysfunctional, but in general children are likely to thrive when both biological parents provide direct, daily care.

THINK CRITICALLY: Can you describe a situation in which having a single parent would be better for a child than having two parents?

Family Trouble

Two factors impair family function in every structure, ethnic group, and nation: low income and high conflict. Many families experience both: Financial stress increases conflict and vice versa.

A Wedding, or Not? Family Structures Around the World

Children fare best when both parents actively care for them every day. This is most likely to occur if the parents are married, although there are many exceptions. Many developmentalists now focus on the rate of single parenthood, shown on this map. Some single parents raise children well, but the risk of neglect, poverty, and instability in single-parent households increases the chances of child problems.

RATES OF SINGLE PARENTHOOD

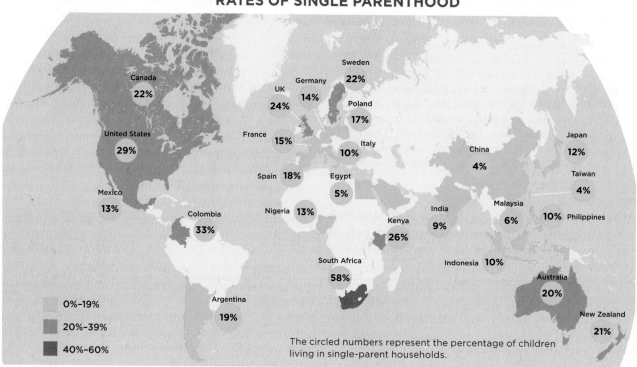

The circled numbers represent the percentage of children living in single-parent households.

A young couple in love and committed to each other—

what next?

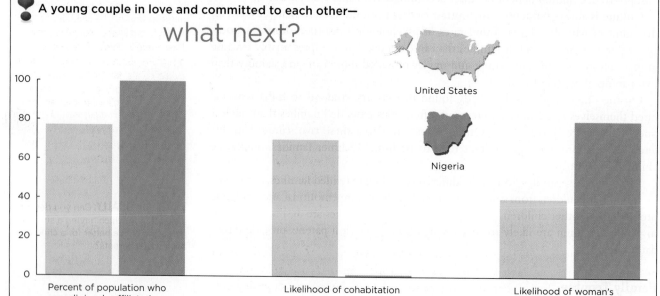

Cohabitation and marriage rates change from year to year and from culture to culture. These two examples are illustrative and approximate. Family-structure statistics like these often focus on marital status and may make it seem as if Nigerian children are more fortunate than American children. However, actual household functioning is more complex than that, and involves many other factors.

DATA FROM: WILCOX, 2011

DATA FROM COPEN ET AL., 2013 AND U.S. CENSUS BUREAU, 2012.

WEALTH AND POVERTY Family income correlates with both function and structure. Marriage rates fall in times of recession, and divorce correlates with unemployment. Low SES increases the rate of many problems; "risk factors . . . pile up in the lives of some children, particularly among the most disadvantaged" (Masten, 2014, p. 95).

Several scholars have developed the *family-stress model,* which holds that any risk factor (such as low income, divorce, single parenthood, or unemployment) damages a family *only if* it increases stress on the parents, who then become impatient and unresponsive with their children.

If economic hardship is ongoing, if uncertainty about the future is high, if education is low—all these factors increase adult hostility and stress. Thus, as many studies have found, although it is easy to understand why worries about food and housing make adults less patient, their reactions are nonetheless crucial (Valdez et al., 2013; Evans & Kim, 2013; D. Lee et al., 2013).

More income correlates with better family functioning. For example, children in single-mother households do much better if their father reliably pays child support (Huang, 2009). Nations that subsidize single parents (e.g., Austria and Iceland) have smaller achievement gaps between low- and middle-SES children on the TIMSS.

Surprisingly, reaction to wealth may also cause difficulty. Children in high-income families have more than their share of developmental problems. Again, parental reaction may be pivotal. If wealthy parents pressure their children to maintain high achievement, stress can lead the children to drug use, delinquency, and poor academic performance (Luthar & Barkin, 2012).

CONFLICT Every researcher agrees that family conflict harms children, especially when adults fight about child rearing. Such fights are more common in stepfamilies, divorced families, and extended families, but nuclear families are not immune. Children suffer if they witness fights between their parents. Fights between siblings can be harmful, too (Turner et al., 2012).

Some researchers hypothesize that children are emotionally troubled in families with feuding parents because of their genes, not because of what they see. The hypothesis is that the parents' genes lead to marital problems. If that is true, and if children inherit those same genes, then genes, not experiences, trouble the children whose parents fight.

This hypothesis was tested in a longitudinal study of 867 adult twins (388 monozygotic pairs and 479 dizygotic pairs), all married with an adolescent child. Each adolescent was compared to his or her cousin, the child of one parent's twin (Schermerhorn et al., 2011). Thus, this study had data from 5,202 individuals—one-third of them adult twins, one-third married to a twin, and one-third adolescents who had half, or a fourth, of the same genes as an adolescent in another family.

The researchers found that, although genes had some influence, witnessing conflict was crucial, causing externalizing problems in boys and internalizing problems in girls. In this study, quiet disagreements did little harm, but open conflict (such as yelling when children could hear) and divorce did (Schermerhorn et al., 2011).

© PHOTOALTO/ALAMY

You Idiot! Ideally, parents never argue in front of the children, as these two do here. However, *how* they argue is crucial. Every couple disagrees about specifics of family life; dysfunctional families call each other names. Hopefully, he said, "I know how to fit this bike into the car" and she answered, "I was just trying to help," rather than either one escalating the fight by saying, "It was your stupid idea to take this trip!"

WHAT HAVE YOU LEARNED?

1. Why do siblings raised together not share the exact same environment?
2. What is the difference between family structure and family function?
3. Why is a harmonious, stable home particularly important during middle childhood?
4. Describe the characteristics of four different family structures.
5. How do children benefit from a nuclear family structure?
6. List three reasons why the single-parent structure might function less well than the two-parent structure for children.
7. In what ways are family structure and family function affected by culture?
8. Using the family-stress model, explain how low family income might affect family function.
9. How can researchers determine whether family conflict affects children directly, not merely through inherited genetic tendencies?

The Peer Group

Peers become increasingly important in middle childhood. With their new awareness of reality (concrete operations), children are painfully aware of their classmates' opinions, judgments, and accomplishments.

The Culture of Children

Children have customs, rules, and rituals that are passed down to younger children from slightly older ones. Jump-rope rhymes, insults, and superstitions are part of peer society. So are clothes: Many children reject clothes that parents buy as too loose, too tight, too long, too short, or wrong in color, style, brand, or decoration.

Communication with peers is vital; children learn the accents and phrases that their friends use. Parents may proudly note how well their children speak a second language but may be distressed when their children spout their peers' curses, accents, and slang.

Independence from adults is acclaimed. Peers pity those (especially boys) whose parents kiss them ("mama's boy"), tease those who please the teachers ("teacher's pet," "suck-up"), and despise those who betray children to adults ("tattletale," "grasser," "snitch," "rat"). Keeping secrets from parents and teachers is a moral mandate (Gillis, 2008).

Because they value independence, children find friends who defy authority, sometimes harmlessly (passing a note in class), sometimes not (shoplifting, smoking). If a bully teases or isolates a child, it is hard for the other children to defend the one who is shunned.

FRIENDSHIPS Teachers often try to separate friends, but developmentalists find that friends teach each other academic and social skills (Bagwell & Schmidt, 2011). Moreover, children learn faster and feel happier when

E. HANAZAKI PHOTOGRAPHY/FLICKR RF/GETTY IMAGES

No Toys Boys in middle childhood are happiest playing outside with equipment designed for work. This wheelbarrow is perfect, especially because at any moment the pusher might tip it.

they have friends. If they had to choose between being friendless but popular (looked up to by many peers) or having close friends but being unpopular (ignored by peers), most would choose to have friends (Bagwell & Schmidt, 2011). A wise choice.

Friendships become more intense and intimate over the years of middle childhood, as social cognition and effortful control advance. Six-year-olds may befriend anyone of the same sex and age who is willing to play with them. By age 10, children demand more. They share confidential secrets and expect loyalty. Compared to younger children, older children change friends less often, become more upset when a friendship breaks up, and find it harder to make new friends.

"Oh yeah? Well, my vocabulary is bigger than your vocabulary!"

JOHNNY HAWKINS/CARTOONSTOCK

Better Than Children of both sexes, all ethnic groups, and every religion, nation, and family, think they are better than children of other groups. They can learn not to blurt out insults, but a deeper understanding of the diversity of human experience and abilities requires maturation.

Older children tend to choose friends whose interests, values, and backgrounds are similar to their own. By the end of middle childhood, close friendships are almost always between children of the same sex, age, ethnicity, and socioeconomic status (Rubin et al., 2013). This occurs not because children naturally become more prejudiced in middle childhood (they do not) but because they seek friends who understand and agree with them.

Gender differences persist in activities (girls converse more whereas boys play more active games), but both boys and girls want best friends. Having no close friends at age 11 predicts depression at age 13 (Brendgen et al., 2010).

THINK CRITICALLY: Do adults also choose friends who agree with them, or whose background is similar to their own?

POPULAR AND UNPOPULAR CHILDREN The particular qualities that make a child liked or disliked depend on culture, cohort, and sometimes the local region or school. For example, shyness is not valued in North America, especially for boys in middle childhood, but this is not true everywhere.

Consider research on shy children in China. A 1990 survey in Shanghai found that shy children were liked and respected (X. Chen et al., 1992). Twelve years later, Chinese culture had shifted and a survey from the same schools found shy children less popular than their shy predecessors had been (X. Chen et al., 2005).

A few years later, a third study in rural China, far from Shanghai, found shyness still valued; it predicted adult adjustment (X. Chen et al., 2009). By contrast, a fourth study from a Chinese city found that shyness in middle childhood predicted unhappiness later on—unless the shy child was also academically superior, in which case shyness was less disabling (X. Chen et al., 2013).

Other traits also vary in how much they are admired. At every age, children who are outgoing, friendly, and cooperative are well liked. In the United States, by the end of middle childhood, a second set of traits also predicts popularity: being dominant and somewhat aggressive (Shi & Xie, 2012).

aggressive-rejected
A child who is not liked by peers because of his or her provocative, confrontational behavior.

withdrawn-rejected
A child who avoids social interaction with peers. Other children do not want to be friends with such a child because of his or her timid, isolative, and anxious behavior.

There are three types of unpopular children. Some are *neglected*, not rejected; they are ignored, but not shunned. The other two types are actively rejected: **aggressive-rejected,** disliked because they are antagonistic and confrontational, and **withdrawn-rejected,** disliked because they are timid and anxious.

Both aggressive-rejected and withdrawn-rejected children misinterpret social situations, lack emotional regulation, and may be mistreated at home, which increases the risk of rejection at school (Stenseng et al., 2015). Unless they are guided toward reciprocal friendship with at least one other child, they may become bullies and victims.

Bullying: Interview with Nicki Crick
http://qrs.ly/nq4ep13

BULLIES AND VICTIMS **Bullying** is defined as repeated, systematic attacks intended to harm those who are unable or unlikely to defend themselves. It occurs in every nation, in every community, and in every kind of school (religious or secular, public or private, progressive or traditional, large or small). Victims are chosen because they are powerless, with many possible characteristics.

As one boy explained:

> You can get bullied because you are weak or annoying or because you are different. Kids with big ears get bullied. Dorks get bullied. You can also get bullied because you think too much of yourself and try to show off. Teacher's pet gets bullied. If you say the right answer too many times in class you can get bullied. There are lots of popular groups who bully each other and other groups, but you can get bullied within your group, too. If you do not want to get bullied, you have to stay under the radar, but then you might feel sad because no one pays attention to you.
>
> [quoted in Guerra et al., 2011, p. 306]

Bullying may be any of four types:

- *Physical* (hitting, pinching, shoving, or kicking)
- *Verbal* (teasing, taunting, or name-calling)
- *Relational* (destroying peer acceptance)
- *Cyber* (bullying that uses cell phones, computers, and other electronic devices)

The first three types are common in primary school and begin even earlier, in preschool. (Cyberbullying is more common later on, and it is discussed in Chapter 10.)

A key word in the definition of bullying is *repeated*. Almost every child experiences an isolated attack or is called a derogatory name at some point. Victims of bullying, however, endure shameful experiences again and again—being forced to hand over lunch money, to laugh at insults, to drink milk mixed with detergent, and so on—with no one defending them. Victims tend to be "cautious, sensitive, quiet . . . lonely and abandoned at school. As a rule, they do not have a single good friend in their class" (Olweus, 1999, p. 15).

Who Suffers More? Physical bullying is typically the target of antibullying laws and policies, because it is easier to spot than relational bullying. Moreover, it is easier to stop—a boy can learn never to put his hands on another boy. But being rejected from the group, especially with gossip and lies, is more devastating to the victim and harder to control. How would the girls respond if the teacher said, "She has to be your friend"?

Although it is often thought that victims are chosen because their appearance or background is odd, this is not usually the case. Victims are chosen because of their emotional vulnerability and social isolation, not how they look. Children new to a school, or who do not know how to make friends, are especially vulnerable.

Remember the three types of unpopular children? Neglected children are not victimized; they are ignored, "under the radar." If their family relationships are good, they suffer less even if they are bullied (which they usually are not) (Bowes et al., 2010).

Withdrawn-rejected children are often victims; they are isolated, feel depressed, and are friendless. Aggressive-rejected children are called **bully-victims** (or *provocative victims*), with neither friends nor sympathizers. They suffer the most because they strike back ineffectively, which increases the bullying (Dukes et al., 2009).

Unlike bully-victims, most bullies are *not* rejected. Although some have low self-esteem, others are proud; they are pleased with themselves and have allies who admire them and classmates who fear them (Guerra et al., 2011). As already mentioned, some are quite popular, with bullying a form of social dominance and authority (Pellegrini et al., 2012). Over the years of middle childhood, bullies become skilled at avoiding adult awareness, picking victims who are rejected by most classmates and who will not resist or tell.

Boy bullies usually physically attack smaller, weaker boys. Girl bullies usually use words to attack shyer, more soft-spoken girls. Young boys may bully girls, although girls ignore rather than bully boys. By puberty (about age 11), cross-sex bullying usually stops, and sexual teasing becomes apparent. Boys who are thought to be gay become targets; suicide attempts are one consequence (Hong & Garbarino, 2012).

bully-victim
Someone who attacks others and who is attacked as well. (Also called *provocative victims* because they do things that elicit bullying.)

CAUSES AND CONSEQUENCES OF BULLYING Bullying may originate with a genetic predisposition or a brain abnormality, but when a toddler is aggressive, parents, teachers, and peers usually teach emotional regulation and effortful control. If home life is stressful, if discipline is ineffectual, if siblings are hostile, or if attachment is insecure, those lessons may not be learned or even taught. Instead, some children develop externalizing and internalizing problems, becoming bullies or victims (Turner et al., 2012).

Peers are crucial. Some peer groups approve of relational bullying, and then children entertain their classmates by mocking and insulting each other (Werner & Hill, 2010). On the other hand, when students themselves disapprove, the incidence of bullying plummets (Guerra & Williams, 2010). Age matters. For most of childhood, bullies are disliked, but a switch occurs at about age 11, when bullying becomes a way to gain social status (Caravita & Cillessen, 2012).

The consequences of bullying can echo for years, worsening with age. Many victims become depressed; many bullies become increasingly cruel. The worst bullies seem unmoved by their victims' distress: Such bullies become more aggressive with age (Willoughby et al., 2014).

Unless bullies are deterred, they and their victims risk impaired social understanding, lower school achievement, and relationship difficulties. Decades later they have higher rates of mental illness (Copeland et al., 2013; Ttofi et al., 2014). Compared to other adults the same age, former bullies are more likely to die young, be jailed, or have destructive marriages.

THINK CRITICALLY: The text says both former bullies and former victims suffer in adulthood. Which would you rather be, and why?

CAN BULLYING BE STOPPED? Most victimized children find ways to halt ongoing bullying—by ignoring, retaliating, defusing, or avoiding. Friends defend each other and restore self-esteem (Bagwell & Schmidt, 2011). Friendships help individual victims, but what can be done to halt a culture of bullying?

"He followed me home — can I punch him?"

Much to Learn Children do not always know when something is hurtful, and adults do not always know when to intervene.

We know what does *not* work: simply increasing students' awareness of bullying, instituting zero tolerance for fighting, or putting bullies together in a therapy group or a classroom (Baldry & Farrington, 2007; Monks & Coyne, 2011). This last measure tends to make daily life easier for some teachers, but it increases aggression.

Another strategy is to talk to the parents of the bully, but this may backfire. Since one cause of bullying is poor parent–child interaction, talking to the parents may "create even more problems for the child, for the parents, and for their relationships" (Rubin et al., 2013, p. 267).

The school community as a whole—teachers and bystanders, parents and aides, bullies and victims and bystanders—needs to change. In fact, the entire school can either increase the rate of bullying or decrease it (Juvonen & Graham, 2014). For example, a Colorado study found that when the overall school climate encouraged learning and cooperation, children with high self-esteem were unlikely to be bullies; when the school climate was hostile, those with high self-esteem were often bullies (Gendron et al., 2011).

Again, peers are crucial: They must do more than simply becoming aware, as some naive adults believe. In fact, some bystanders notice and then disengage from the victims, which increases bullying. Others are sympathetic but feel powerless (Thornberg & Jungert, 2013). However, if children are helped to empathize with victims, feel effective (high in effortful control), and refuse to admire bullies, then classroom aggression is reduced (Salmivalli, 2010).

Efforts to change the entire school are credited with recent successful attempts to decrease bullying in 29 schools in England (Cross et al., 2011), throughout Norway, in Finland (Kärnä et al., 2011), and often in the United States (Allen, 2010; Limber, 2011).

A review of ways to halt bullying (Berger, 2007) finds:

- Everyone in the school must change, not just the identified bullies.
- Intervention is more effective in the earlier grades.
- Evaluation is critical: Programs that seem good might be harmful.

This final point merits emphasis. Longitudinal research on whole-school efforts finds that some programs make a difference and some do not, with variations depending on the age of the children and the indicators (peer report of bullying or victimization, teacher report of incidents reported, and so on).

Objective follow-up efforts suggest that bullying can be reduced but not eliminated. It is foolhardy to blame only the bully and, of course, wrong to blame the victim: The entire school community—including the culture of the school—needs to change. That leads to the final topic of this chapter, the moral development of children.

WHAT HAVE YOU LEARNED?

1. How does what children wear reflect the culture of children?
2. In what ways do friendships change from the beginning to the end of middle childhood?
3. How is a child's popularity affected by culture and cohort?
4. What changes in the criteria for popularity as children mature from early childhood to adolescence?
5. What are the different kinds of bullying?
6. How do boy bullies differ from girl bullies?
7. What school characteristics make bullying more likely?
8. How might bullying be reduced?

Children's Moral Values

Middle childhood is prime time for moral development. Many forces drive children's growing interest in moral issues. Three of them are (1) peer norms, (2) personal experience, and (3) empathy. The culture of children includes moral values, such as loyalty to friends and keeping secrets. Personal experiences also matter.

For all children, empathy increases in middle childhood as children become more socially perceptive. This increasing perception can backfire, however. One example was just described: Bullies become adept at picking victims (Veenstra et al., 2010). An increase in social understanding makes noticing and defending rejected children possible, but in some social contexts, bystanders may decide to be self-protective rather than to intervene (Pozzoli & Gini, 2013).

Children who are slow to develop theory of mind—which, as discussed in Chapter 5, is affected by family and culture—are also slow to develop empathy (Caravita et al., 2010). School-age children *can* think and act morally, but they do not always do so.

The authors of a study of 7-year-olds "conclude that moral *competence* may be a universal human characteristic, but that it takes a situation with specific demand–characteristics to translate this competence into actual prosocial *performance*" (van Ijzendoorn et al., 2010, p. 1).

BOB CHILD/AP PHOTO

Wonderfully Conventional
Krysta Caltabiano displays her poster, "Ways to Be a Good Citizen," which won the Good Citizenship Contest sponsored by the Connecticut Secretary of State.

OBSERVATION QUIZ
Why is Krysta's poster a good example of Erikson's industry versus inferiority stage? (see answer, page 308) ◄

Moral Reasoning

Piaget wrote extensively about the moral development of children, as they developed and enforced their own rules for playing games together (Piaget, 1932/2013). His emphasis on how children think about moral issues led to a famous description of cognitive stages of morality (Kohlberg, 1963).

KOHLBERG'S LEVELS OF MORAL THOUGHT Lawrence Kohlberg described three levels of moral reasoning and two stages at each level (see Table 8.3), with parallels to Piaget's stages of cognition.

- **Preconventional moral reasoning** is similar to preoperational thought in that it is egocentric, with children most interested in their personal pleasure or avoiding punishment.

- **Conventional moral reasoning** parallels concrete operational thought in that it relates to current, observable practices: Children watch what their parents, teachers, and friends do, and they try to follow suit.

- **Postconventional moral reasoning** is similar to formal operational thought because it uses abstractions, going beyond what is concretely observed, willing to question "what is" in order to decide "what should be."

According to Kohlberg, intellectual maturation advances moral thinking. During middle childhood, children's answers shift from being primarily preconventional to being more conventional: Concrete thought and peer experiences help children move past the first two stages (level I) to the next two (level II). Postconventional reasoning (level III) is not usually present until adolescence or adulthood, if then.

Kohlberg posed moral dilemmas to boys (and eventually girls, adolescents, and adults). The most famous of these dilemmas involves a poor man named Heinz,

preconventional moral reasoning
Kohlberg's first level of moral reasoning, emphasizing personal rewards and punishments.

conventional moral reasoning
Kohlberg's second level of moral reasoning, emphasizing social rules and laws.

postconventional moral reasoning
Kohlberg's third level of moral reasoning, emphasizing principles thought to be universal.

TABLE 8.3	Kohlberg's Three Levels and Six Stages of Moral Reasoning

Level I: Preconventional Moral Reasoning

The goal is to get rewards and avoid punishments; this is a self-centered level.

- *Stage one: Might makes right* (a punishment-and-obedience orientation). The most important value is to maintain the appearance of obedience to authority, avoiding punishment while still advancing self-interest. Don't get caught!

- *Stage two: Look out for number one* (an instrumental and relativist orientation). Each person tries to take care of his or her own needs. The reason to be nice to other people is so that they will be nice to you.

Level II: Conventional Moral Reasoning

Emphasis is placed on social rules; this is a parent- and community-centered level.

- *Stage three: Good girl and nice boy.* Proper behavior pleases other people. Social approval is more important than any material reward.

- *Stage four: Law and order.* Proper behavior means being a dutiful citizen and obeying the laws set down by society, even when no police are nearby.

Level III: Postconventional Moral Reasoning

Emphasis is placed on moral principles; this level is centered on ideals.

- *Stage five: Social contract.* Obey social rules because they benefit everyone and are established by mutual agreement. If the rules become destructive or if one party doesn't live up to the agreement, the contract is no longer binding. Under some circumstances, disobeying the law is moral.

- *Stage six: Universal ethical principles.* Universal principles, not individual situations (level I) or community practices (level II), determine right and wrong. Ethical values (such as "life is sacred") are established by individual reflection and may contradict egocentric (level I) or social and community (level II) values.

whose wife was dying. He could not afford the only drug that could save his wife, which the druggist sold for 10 times what it cost to make.

> Heinz went to everyone he knew to borrow the money, but he could only get together about half of what it cost. He told the druggist that his wife was dying and asked him to sell it cheaper or let him pay later. But the druggist said "no." The husband got desperate and broke into the man's store to steal the drug for his wife. Should the husband have done that? Why?
>
> *[Kohlberg, 1963, p. 19]*

The crucial element in Kohlberg's assessment of moral stages is *not* what a person answers but the reasons given. For instance, suppose a child says that Heinz should steal the drug. That itself does not indicate the child's level of moral reasoning. The reason could be that Heinz needs his wife to care for him (preconventional), or that people will blame him if he lets his wife die (conventional), or that a human life is more important than obeying a law (postconventional).

Or suppose another child says Heinz should not steal. The reason could be that he will go to jail (preconventional), or that stealing is against the law (conventional), or that for a community to function, no one should jeopardize another person's livelihood (postconventional).

CRITICISMS OF KOHLBERG Kohlberg has been criticized for not appreciating cultural or gender differences. For example, in some cultures, loyalty to family overrides any other value, so highly moral people might avoid postconventional actions that hurt their family. Also, Kohlberg's original participants were all boys, which may have led him to discount nurturance and relationships, thought to be more valued by females than males (Gilligan, 1982).

Kohlberg seemed to value abstract principles more than individual needs and to prioritize rational thinking. However, critics suggest that emotions may be more influential than logic in moral development (Haidt, 2013). Thus, emotional regulation, empathy, and social understanding, all of which develop throughout childhood, may be more crucial for morality than intellectual development is.

Finally, Kohlberg did not seem to recognize that, although children's morality differs from that of adults, they may be quite moral. If a child questions adult rules that seem unfair, as often occurs in middle childhood (Turiel, 2006, 2008), that may indicate postconventional thinking.

In one respect, however, Kohlberg was undeniably correct. He was right in noting that people use their intellect to justify their morality. In one experiment, children aged 8 to 18 were grouped with two others of about the same age and allotted some money. They were then asked to decide how much to share with another trio of children.

Surprisingly, there were no age trends in the resulting decisions: Some young and some older groups chose to share equally, and other groups of both ages were more selfish. However, the justifications showed age differences. Older children suggested more complex rationalizations for their choices, both selfish and altruistic (Gummerum et al., 2008).

What Children Value

Many lines of research have shown that children develop their own morality, guided by peers, parents, and culture (Killen & Smetana, 2014). Some prosocial values are evident in early childhood. Among these values are caring for close family members, cooperating with other children, and not hurting anyone intentionally. Even very young children think stealing is wrong, and even infants seem to appreciate social support and punish mean behavior (Hamlin, 2014).

As children become more aware of themselves and others in middle childhood, they realize that one person's values may conflict with another's. Concrete operational cognition, which gives children the ability to understand and use logic, propels them to think about moral rules. In the opening anecdote of this chapter, a boy argued that it was "so unfair" that he could not kill zombies. Fairness is a prime moral value in middle childhood.

ADULTS VERSUS PEERS When child culture conflicts with adult morality, children often align themselves with peers. A child might lie to protect a friend, for instance. Friendship itself has a hostile side: Many close friends reject other children who want to join their game or conversation (Rubin et al., 2013). They may also protect a bully if he or she is a friend.

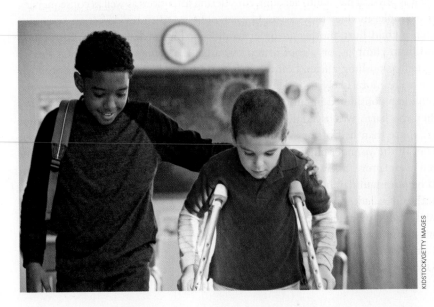

Not Victims An outsider might worry that these two boys would be bullied, one because he is African American and the other because he appears to have a physical disability. But both are well liked for the characteristics shown here: friendship and willingness to help and be helped.

KIDSTOCK/GETTY IMAGES

The conflict between the morality of children and that of adults is evident in the value that children place on education. Adults usually prize school and respect teachers, but children may encourage one another to skip class, cheat on tests, harass a substitute teacher, and so on.

Three common moral imperatives among 6- to 11-year-olds are the following:

● Protect your friends.

● Don't tell adults what is happening.

● Conform to peer standards of dress, talk, and behavior.

These principles can explain both apparent boredom and overt defiance, as well as standards of dress that mystify adults (such as jeans so loose that they fall off or so tight that they impede digestion—both styles worn by my children, who grew up in different cohorts). This may seem like mere social conformity, but children may elevate it to a standard of right and wrong, as adults might do for whether or not a woman wears a head covering, a revealing dress, or even high heels. Given what we know about children, no wonder they do not echo adult morality.

This conflict is evident in one boy who was aware of the moral values of his local church but who also wanted to be part of his peer group. Paul said:

> I think right now about going Christian, right? Just going Christian, trying to do good, you know? Stay away from drugs, everything. And every time it seems like I think about that, I think about the homeboys. And it's a trip because a lot of the homeboys are my family, too, you know?
>
> *[quoted in Nieto, 2000, p. 249]*

Fortunately, peers may help one another act ethically. Children are better at stopping bullying than adults are, because bystanders are pivotal. Since bullies tend to be low on empathy, they need peers to tell them they are mistaken if they think classmates admire their aggression.

None of this means that parents, teachers, and religious institutions are irrelevant. During middle childhood, morality can be scaffolded just as cognitive skills are, with mentors—peers or adults—using moral dilemmas to advance moral understanding and to teach the underlying moral skills of empathy and emotional regulation (Hinnant et al., 2013).

DEVELOPING MORAL VALUES Over the years of middle childhood, moral judgment becomes more comprehensive. Gradually children become better at taking psychological as well as physical harm into account, considering intentions as well as consequences.

For example, in one study 5- to 11-year-olds saw pictures depicting situations in which a child hurt another in order to prevent further harm (such as stopping a friend from climbing on a roof to retrieve a ball), or when one child was simply mean (such as pushing a friend off the swings so the child can swing). The younger children were more likely to judge based on results—if anyone got hurt—but the older children considered intention.

When the harm was psychological, not physical (hurting the child's feelings, not hitting), more than half of the older children considered intentions, but only about 5 percent of the younger children did. Compared to the younger children, the older children were more likely to say justifiable harm was OK but unjustifiable harm should be punished (Jambon & Smetana, 2014).

Another detailed examination of morality began with an update on one of Piaget's moral issues: whether punishment should seek *retribution* (hurting the transgressor) or a more mature punishment called *restitution* (restoring what was lost). Piaget found that children advance from retribution to restitution between ages 8 and 10 (Piaget, 1932/2013).

To learn how this occurs, researchers asked 133 9-year-olds to consider this scenario:

> Late one afternoon there was a boy who was playing with a ball on his own in the garden. His dad saw him playing with it and asked him not to play with it so near the house because it might break a window. The boy didn't really listen to his dad, and carried on playing near the house. Then suddenly, the ball bounced up high and broke the window in the boy's room. His dad heard the noise and came to see what had happened. The father wonders what would be the fairest way to punish the boy. He thinks of two punishments. The first is to say: "Now, you didn't do as I asked. You will have to pay for the window to be mended, and I am going to take the money from your pocket money." The second is to say: "Now, you didn't do as I asked. As a punishment you have to go to your room and stay there for the rest of the evening." Which of these punishments do you think is the fairest?
>
> *[Leman & Björnberg, 2010, p. 962]*

Initially, the children were split almost equally between retribution (stay in your room) and restoration (pay for the window). Then 24 pairs were formed of children who had opposite views. Each pair was asked to discuss the issue, trying to reach agreement. (The other children did not discuss it.) Six pairs were boy–boy, six were boy–girl with the boy favoring restitution, six were boy–girl with the girl favoring restitution, and six were girl–girl.

The conversations typically took only five minutes, and the retribution side was more often chosen. Piaget would consider that a moral backslide, since he thought retribution was less mature. Several weeks later all the children were queried again. At that point, many responses changed toward the more advanced, restitution response (see Figure 8.1). Some of the children who had not discussed it with a peer switched, but children who had discussed it with another child were particularly likely to conclude that restitution was best.

Restore Harm or Hurt the Transgressor? Nine-Year-Olds' Responses

Data from Leman & Björnberg, 2010.

FIGURE 8.1 Benefits of Time and Talking The graph on the left shows that most children, immediately after their initial response, became even more likely to seek punishment rather than to repair damage. However, after some time and reflection, they affirmed the response Piaget would consider more mature. The graph on the right indicates that children who had talked about the broken window example moved toward restorative justice even in examples they had not heard before, which was not true for those who had not talked about the first story.

The researchers wrote, "conversation on a topic may stimulate a process of individual reflection that triggers developmental advances" (Leman & Björnberg, 2010, p. 969). Parents and teachers take note: Raising moral issues, and letting children discuss them, advances morality—not immediately, but soon.

Think again about the opening anecdote for this chapter (killing zombies). The parent used age as a criterion, and the child rejected that argument. A better argument might raise a higher standard, for instance that killing, even in fantasy, is not justified. The child might disagree, but such conversations might help the child think more deeply about moral values. That deeper thought might protect the child during adolescence, when life-changing moral issues arise, as described in the next two chapters.

WHAT HAVE YOU LEARNED?

1. Using your own example, illustrate Kohlberg's three levels of moral reasoning.
2. What are the main criticisms of Kohlberg's theory?
3. When would family values overtake national values?
4. How might children's morality differ from adult morality?
5. How might the morality of children help stop a bully?
6. What kind of punishment did Piaget think was more advanced morally?
7. What seems to advance moral thought during middle childhood?

SUMMARY

The Nature of the Child

1. Children develop their self-concept during middle childhood, basing it on a more realistic assessment of their competence than they had in earlier years.

2. Erikson emphasized industry, when children busily strive to master various tasks. If they are unable to do so, they feel inferior. Freud described a latency period, when psychosexual needs are quiet.

3. Self-respect is always helpful, but high self-esteem may reduce effortful control and is not valued in every culture. Low self-esteem is also harmful.

4. Both daily hassles and major stresses take a toll on children, with accumulated stresses more likely to impair development than any single event on its own. Resilience is aided by the child's interpretation of the situation and the availability of supportive adults, peers, and institutions.

Families and Children

5. Families influence children in many ways, as do genes and peers. Although most siblings share a childhood home and parents, each sibling experiences different (nonshared) circumstances within the family.

6. The five functions of a supportive family are: to satisfy children's physical needs; to encourage learning; to nurture friendships; to foster self-respect; and to provide a safe, stable, and harmonious home.

7. The most common family structure worldwide is the nuclear family, usually with other relatives nearby. Other two-parent families include adoptive, same-sex, grandparent, and stepfamilies, each of which sometimes functions well for children, and sometimes not.

8. On average, children have fewer emotional problems and learn more in school if they live with two parents rather than one, especially if the parents are both caregivers, forming an alliance.

9. Single-parent families are more likely to change where they live and who belongs to the family. That may disrupt the children. Further, such families often have less income and more stress. Nonetheless, some single parents form families that function well for children.

10. Income affects family function. Children from low-SES families may suffer if poverty increases stress and hinders effective parenting. No matter what the family SES, instability and conflict are harmful.

The Peer Group

11. Peers teach crucial social skills during middle childhood. Close friends are wanted and needed. Popular children may be cooperative and easy to get along with, or may be competitive and aggressive.

12. Rejected children may be neglected, aggressive, or withdrawn. Aggressive and withdrawn children have difficulty understanding the normal social interaction of childhood.

Do They See Beauty? Both young women—the Mexican 15-year-old preparing for her Quinceañera and the Malaysian teen applying a rice facial mask—look wistful, even worried. They are typical of teenage girls everywhere, who do not realize how lovely they are.

The pituitary also activates the **gonads,** or sex glands (ovaries in females; testes, or testicles, in males). One hormone in particular, *GnRH* (gonadotropin-releasing hormone), causes the gonads to enlarge and dramatically increase their production of sex hormones, chiefly **estradiol** in girls and **testosterone** in boys.

Estrogens (including estradiol) are female hormones and *androgens* (including testosterone) are male hormones, although both sexes have some of both. The ovaries produce high levels of estrogens and the testes produce dramatic increases in androgens. This "surge of hormones" affects bodies, brains, and behavior before any visible signs of puberty appear, "well before the teens" (Peper & Dahl, 2013, p. 134).

The activated gonads begin to release ova (at menarche) or sperm (at spermarche). Conception is possible, although peak fertility occurs four to six years later. Hormones also awaken interest in sex, as young teenagers fantasize—at first about people who are unlikely to reciprocate (celebrities, teachers) and then about their peers nearby.

Hormones may underlie differences in psychopathology. Compared to the other sex, adolescent males are almost twice as likely to develop schizophrenia and adolescent females more than twice as likely to develop major depression. Of course, hormones are never the sole cause of psychopathology (Tackett et al., 2014; Rudolph, 2014).

Remember that body, brain, and behavior always interact. Sexual thoughts themselves can *cause* physiological and neurological processes, not just result from them. Cortisol (another hormone) levels rise at puberty, and that makes adolescents quicker to become angry or upset (Goddings et al., 2012; Klein & Romeo, 2013).

Then emotions, in turn, increase hormones. For example, when other people react to emerging breasts or beards, that evokes thoughts and frustrations in the adolescent, which raises hormone levels, propels physiological development, and triggers more emotions. Thus the internal and external changes each affect the other.

BODY RHYTHMS The brain of every living creature responds to the environment with natural rhythms that rise and fall by the day and season. For example, in children, height increases more rapidly in summer and weight in winter. Many rhythms

gonads
The sex glands (ovaries in females, testicles in males). The gonads produce hormones and gametes.

estradiol
A sex hormone, considered to be the chief estrogen (female hormone). Females produce much more estradiol than males do.

testosterone
A sex hormone, the best known of the androgens (male hormones); secreted in far greater amounts by males than by females.

THINK CRITICALLY: If a child seems to be unusually short, or unusually slow in reaching puberty, would you give the child hormones? Why or why not?

circadian rhythm
A day–night cycle of biological activity that occurs approximately every 24 hours (*circadian* means "about a day").

PURESTOCK/GETTY IMAGES

I Covered That Teachers everywhere complain that students don't remember what they were taught. Maybe schedules, not daydreaming, are to blame.

are **circadian,** which means they are on a daily cycle. That is why well-rested people tend to wake up at the same time on weekends as during the week, and they also get sleepy at the same time each night.

In addition, some individuals (especially males) are more alert in the evening than in the morning. Other people are the opposite, filled with energy in the morning and then fading as the day wears on. Those differences are genetic.

In addition, at puberty, hormones cause a *phase delay* in the circadian sleep–wake cycles. That compels many teens to be wide awake and hungry at midnight but half asleep, with neither appetite nor energy, all morning. For teens who are already evening people, the phase delay increases the risk of problems: They are up when adults are asleep, but adults still make them get out of bed at dawn. Consequently, in many nations, sleep deprivation increases during adolescence (see Figure 9.1) (Roenneberg et al., 2012).

To make it worse, "the blue spectrum light from TV, computer, and personal-device screens may have particularly strong effects on the human circadian system" (Peper & Dahl, 2013, p. 137). Watching late-night TV, working on the computer, or texting friends at 10 P.M. interferes with normal nighttime sleepiness. Sleeping late on weekends is a sign of deprivation, not compensation.

Sleep deprivation and irregular sleep schedules increase the risk of insomnia, nightmares, mood disorders (depression, conduct disorder, anxiety), and falling asleep while driving. In addition, sleepy people don't learn as well as they do when rested. Many adults ignore these facts, as the following explains.

OBSERVATION QUIZ
As you see, the problems may be worse for girls. Why is that? (see answer, page 320) ➤

FIGURE 9.1 Sleepyheads Three of every four high school seniors are sleep deprived. Even if they go to sleep at midnight, as many do, they must get up before 8 A.M., as almost all do. Then they are tired all day.

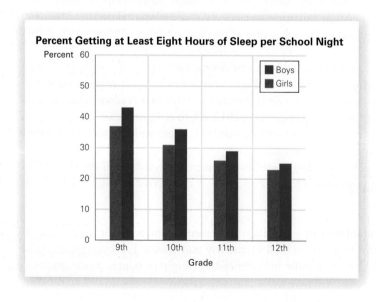

Percent Getting at Least Eight Hours of Sleep per School Night

OPPOSING PERSPECTIVES

Algebra at 7 A.M.? Get Real!

Adults sometimes fight against what is natural to adolescents. This is evident with sexual curiosity ("you're too young to think about boys") and circadian rhythm ("go to sleep, you need to get up for school").

Many adults think adolescents belong at home, just when many adolescents much prefer to be with friends. In 2014, Baltimore implemented a law that required young adolescents (under age 14) to be home by 9 P.M. and older ones (14- to 16-year-olds) off the streets by 10 P.M. on school nights and 11 P.M. on weekends. The idea is that adolescents should be sound asleep in their own beds before midnight.

For many adolescent bodies, early sleep and then early rising are almost impossible. As a result, many sleep-deprived teenagers nod off in class (see Figure 9.2) and take drugs (from caffeine to speed) to stay awake (Mueller et al., 2011; Patrick & Schulenberg, 2011).

Data on the circadian rhythm and the teenage brain convinced social scientists at the University of Minnesota to ask 17 school districts to start high school later. Parents disagreed. Many (42 percent) thought high school should begin before 8:00 A.M. Some (20 percent) wanted their teenagers out of the house by 7:15 A.M. (Wahlstrom, 2002).

Other adults had their own reasons for wanting high school to begin early. Teachers thought that learning was more efficient in the morning; bus drivers hated rush hour; cafeteria workers liked to go home in mid-afternoon; police wanted teenagers off the streets before dusk; coaches needed after-school sports events to end before dark; business owners hired teens for the early evening shift; community groups wanted the school gyms available in the late afternoon.

Initially only one Minnesota school district (Edina) changed the schedule of their high school day, from 7:25–2:05 to 8:30–3:10. After a trial year, most parents (93 percent) and virtually all students approved. One student said, "I have only fallen asleep in school once this whole year, and last year I fell asleep about three times a week" (quoted in Wahlstrom, 2002, p. 190). Fewer students were absent, late, disruptive, or sick (the school nurse became an advocate). Grades rose.

Other school districts noticed. Minneapolis high schools changed their start time from 7:15 to 8:40. Attendance and graduation rates improved. School boards in South Burlington (Vermont), West Des Moines (Iowa), Tulsa (Oklahoma), Arlington (Virginia), Palo Alto (California), and Milwaukee (Wisconsin) voted to start high school later, from an average of 7:45 to an average of 8:30 (Tonn, 2006; Snider, 2012). Unexpected advantages appeared: more efficient energy use, less adolescent depression, and in Tulsa, unprecedented athletic championships.

Many school districts remain stuck to traditional schedules, scheduling school buses to drop off teenagers and then pick up the younger children. Although "the science is there; the will to change is not" (Snider, 2012).

One example comes from Fairfax County (Virginia) where two opposing groups—SLEEP (Start Later for Excellence in Education Proposal) versus WAKE (Worried About Keeping Extra-Curriculars)—argued. One sports reporter wrote:

> The later start would hinder teams without lighted practice fields. Hinder kids who work after-school jobs to save for college or to help support their families. Hinder teachers who work second jobs or take late-afternoon college classes. Hinder commuters who would get stopped behind more buses during peak traffic times. Hinder kids who might otherwise seek after-school academic help, or club or team affiliation. Hinder families that depend on high school children to watch younger siblings after school. Hinder community groups that use school and park facilities in the late afternoons and evenings.
>
> *[Williams, 2009]*

Note that Williams never argued that learning would be reduced, because that would be untrue. He wrote that science was on the side of change but reality was not. To developmentalists, of course, science *is* reality.

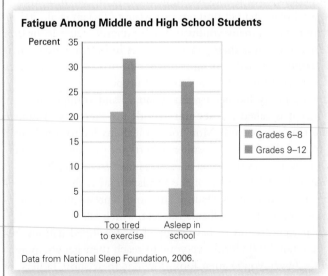

Fatigue Among Middle and High School Students

Data from National Sleep Foundation, 2006.

FIGURE 9.2 Dreaming and Learning? This graph shows the percentage of U.S. students who, once a week or more, fall asleep in class or are too tired to exercise. Not shown are those who say they are usually tired (59 percent of high school students) or who doze in class "almost every day" (8 percent).

In 2009, the Fairfax school board voted to keep the high school start at 7:20 A.M. The SLEEP advocates kept trying. On the eighth try, the Fairfax school board in 2012 finally set a goal: High schools should not start before 8:00 A.M. They hired a team to figure out how to implement that goal. As of 2014, they had not done so.

There is a new reason to change. In August 2014, the American Academy of Pediatrics concluded that high school should not begin until 8:30 or 9:00 A.M., because adolescent sleep deprivation causes intellectual and behavioral problems. They noted that 43 percent of high schools in the United States start *before* 8:00 A.M. The clash between tradition and science, or between adult expectations and adolescent bodies, continues.

ANSWER TO OBSERVATION QUIZ
(from page 318): Girls tend to spend more time studying, talking to friends, and getting ready in the morning. Other data show that many girls get less than seven hours of sleep per night. ●

secular trend
Advances in growth and maturation that result from modern nutrition. For example, improved nutrition and medical care over the past 200 years has led to earlier puberty and taller average height.

Brothers, but Not Twins These brothers are close in age and both exhibit the emotional excitement that accompanies the hormones of puberty. The past year has led to many rapid physical changes, especially for the older boy.

CINDY PRINS/FLICKR/GETTY IMAGES

Many Reasons for Variations

That six-year range in onset of puberty (age 8 to 14) is troubling for parents and preteens who want to be ready but not premature. More precise prediction is possible.

GENES AND GENDER About two-thirds of the variation in age of puberty is genetic, evident not only in families but also in ethnic groups (Dvornyk & Waqar-ul-Haq, 2012; Biro et al., 2013). African Americans reach puberty, on average, about seven months earlier than European or Hispanic Americans; Chinese Americans average several months later.

The other major influence on age of puberty comes from the sex chromosomes. In height, the average girl is two years ahead of the average boy: The female height spurt occurs *before* menarche, whereas for boys the increase in height is relatively late, *after* spermarche. Thus, a sixth-grade boy with sexual fantasies about the taller girls in his class is neither perverted nor precocious; his hormones are simply ahead of his height.

FAT Body fat also affects age of puberty. Heavy girls reach menarche years earlier than malnourished ones do. Most girls weigh at least 100 pounds (45 kilograms) before menarche (Berkey et al., 2000). Although severe malnutrition always delays puberty, body fat may not be as necessary for boys. Indeed, obese boys are often delayed in puberty compared to boys who are neither slim nor overweight (Tackett et al., 2014).

Malnutrition causes many youths to reach puberty at age 15 or later in parts of Africa, whereas their genetic relatives in North America mature much earlier. Similarly, malnutrition is the main reason puberty began at about age 17 in sixteenth-century Europe.

Since then, puberty has occurred at younger and younger ages (an example of what is called the **secular trend,** the increases in human growth as nutrition improved). More food availability led to weight gain in childhood, and that has led to earlier puberty for girls and taller average height for both sexes (Floud et al., 2011; Fogel & Grotte, 2011).

One curious bit of evidence of the secular trend is that U.S. presidents have gotten taller. James Madison, the fourth president, was shortest at 5 feet, 4 inches; Barack Obama is 6 feet, 1 inch tall.

The secular trend seems to have stopped in developed nations, because adequate nutrition allows everyone to reach their genetic potential. Currently, fewer young men look down at their short fathers, or girls at their little mothers, unless their parents were born in Asia or Africa, where the secular trend is still evident.

There is one possible exception in developed nations to the statement "the secular trend has stopped." Very early puberty, before age 8 (called *precocious puberty*), may be increasing, especially in girls, although it is still rare (perhaps 2 percent) (Sørensen et al., 2012). Sometimes precocious puberty is genetic (perhaps 20 percent), but the cause of the increase is largely unknown—perhaps childhood obesity or new chemicals in the environment.

Some research finds that puberty is delayed, not accelerated, in boys who were exposed prenatally to phthalates and bisphenol A (K. Ferguson et al., 2014), or who experienced heavy doses of pesticides in boyhood (T. Lam et al., 2014). Phthalates may delay puberty in girls as well (Wolff et al., 2014).

Caution is needed here. No doubt, heavy doses of many chemicals and pesticides affect fish, frogs, insects, and birds, causing reproductive problems. However, as noted in Chapter 2, experts disagree about the impact on humans.

STRESS Stress hastens the hormonal onset of puberty, especially if a child's parents are sick, drug-addicted, or divorced, or if the neighborhood is violent and impoverished. One study of sexually abused girls found that they began puberty seven months earlier, on average, than did a matched comparison group (Trickett et al., 2011). Particularly for girls who are genetically sensitive, puberty comes early if their family interaction causes high levels of cortisol but late if their family is supportive (Ellis et al., 2011; James et al., 2012).

The link between stress and puberty is one explanation for the fact that children born in one country and adopted in another tend to experience early puberty, especially if their first few years of life were in an institution or a chaotic home. An alternate explanation is that their age at adoption was underestimated, so puberty appears to occur early but actually is at the expected time (Hayes, 2013).

Why would cortisol trigger puberty? An answer comes from evolutionary theory. Thousands of years ago, if harsh conditions threatened survival of the species, adolescents needed to reproduce early and often to increase the chance that at least some children would reach adulthood. By contrast, in peaceful times, puberty could occur later, allowing children to postpone maturity and instead enjoy extra years of childhood nurturance from parents and grandparents.

Of course, this evolutionary rationale no longer applies. Today, early sexual activity and teen parenthood are more likely to harm communities than help the species. However, the genome has been shaped over millennia; if there is a puberty-starting allele that responds to social conditions, it still responds as it did thousands of years ago.

TOO EARLY, TOO LATE For most adolescents, these links between puberty, stress, and hormones are irrelevant. The only timing that matters is their friends' schedules. No one wants to be too early or too late.

Think about the early-maturing girl. If she has visible breasts at age 10, the boys her age tease her; they are unnerved by the sexual creature in their midst. She must fit into a school chair designed for smaller children; she might hide her breasts in large T-shirts and bulky sweaters. Early-maturing girls tend to have lower self-esteem, more depression, and poorer body image than do other girls (Galvao et al., 2014; Compian et al., 2009).

Some early-maturing girls have older boyfriends, who are attracted to their womanly shape and girlish innocence. Having an older boyfriend bestows status, but it also increases problems (including drug and alcohol abuse) that arise from older teens (Mrug et al., 2014).

OBSERVATION QUIZ
Who is least developed and who is most developed? (see answer, page 322) ▼

All the Same? All four girls are 13, and all are from the same community in England. But as you see, each is on her own timetable, and that affects the clothes and expressions. Why is one in a tank top and shorts while another is in a heavy shirt and pants?

© REDSNAPPER/ALAMY

growth spurt
The relatively sudden and rapid physical growth that occurs during puberty. Each body part increases in size on a schedule: Weight usually precedes height, and growth of the limbs precedes growth of the torso.

The effects of early maturation on boys depend on context. In the United States, early-maturing boys who were born around 1930 often became leaders in high school and high wage earners as adults (Jones, 1965; Taga et al., 2006). Since about 1960, however, the risks associated with early male maturation have outweighed the benefits.

In the twenty-first century, early-maturing boys are more aggressive, law-breaking, and drug-abusing than the average boy (Biehl et al., 2007; Lynne et al., 2007; Mendle et al., 2012). This is not surprising: A boy who is experiencing rapid increases in testosterone, and whose body looks more like a man than a child, is likely to cause trouble with parents, peers, schools, and the police.

Late puberty may also be difficult, especially for boys (Benoit et al., 2013). Slow-developing boys tend to be more anxious, depressed, and afraid of sex. Girls are less attracted to them, coaches less often want them on their teams, peers bully or tease them.

Becoming a Grown-Up

Puberty causes two sets of changes. One set is marked by the **growth spurt**—a sudden, uneven jump in the size of almost every body part, turning children into adults. The other set is sexual; turning girls and boys into men and women who could become parents.

THE GROWTH SPURT Growth proceeds from the extremities to the core (the opposite of the earlier proximodistal growth). Thus, fingers and toes lengthen before hands and feet, hands and feet before arms and legs, arms and legs before the torso. This growth is not always symmetrical: One foot, one breast, or even one ear may grow later than the other.

Because the torso is the last body part to grow, many pubescent children are temporarily big-footed, long-legged, and short-waisted. If young teenagers complain that their jeans don't fit, they are probably correct—even if those same jeans fit when their parents paid for them a month earlier. (Advance warning about rapid body growth occurs when parents first have to buy their children's shoes in the adult section.)

As the growth spurt begins, children eat more and gain weight. Exactly when, where, and how much weight they gain depends on heredity, hormones, diet, exercise, and gender. By age 17, the average girl has twice the percentage of body fat as her male classmate, whose increased weight is mostly muscle.

A height spurt follows the weight spurt; then a year or two later a muscle spurt occurs. Thus, the pudginess and clumsiness of early puberty are usually gone by late adolescence. During these years, all the muscles increase in power.

Inner organs grow as well. Lungs triple in weight, allowing adolescents to breathe more deeply and slowly. The heart doubles in size as the heartbeat slows, decreasing the pulse rate while increasing blood pressure. Consequently, endurance improves: Some teenagers can run for miles or dance for hours. Fortunately, red blood cells increase in both sexes, dramatically more in boys, aiding oxygen transport during intense exercise.

One organ system, the lymphoid system (including tonsils and adenoids), *decreases* in size, so teenagers are less susceptible to respiratory ailments. As a result, mild asthma often switches off at puberty—half as many teenagers as children are asthmatic (MMWR, June 8, 2012), and teenagers have fewer colds and allergies than younger children.

When the larynx grows, the voice lowers, especially noticeable in boys. Another organ system, the skin, becomes oilier, sweatier, and more prone to acne. Hair also changes, becoming coarser and darker, with new hair under arms, on faces, and over sex organs. Specifics depend on genes as well as on hormones.

Often teenagers cut, style, or grow their hair in ways their parents do not like, as a sign of independence. To become more attractive, many adolescents spend considerable time, money, and thought on their visible hair—growing, gelling, shaving, curling, straightening, highlighting, brushing, combing, styling, dyeing, wetting, and/or drying. In many ways, hair is far more than a growth characteristic; it is a display of sexuality.

SEXUAL CHARACTERISTICS The body characteristics that are directly involved in conception and pregnancy are called **primary sex characteristics.** During puberty, every primary sex organ (the ovaries, uterus, penis, and testes) increases dramatically in size and matures in function. By the end of the process, reproduction is possible.

At the same time, development occurs in **secondary sex characteristics.** They do not directly affect reproduction (hence they are secondary) but signify gender.

One secondary characteristic is shape. Young boys and girls have similar shapes, but at puberty males widen at the shoulders and grow about 5 inches taller than females, while girls widen at the hips and develop breasts. Those curves are considered signs of womanhood, but neither breasts nor wide hips are required for conception; thus, they are secondary, not primary, sex characteristics.

Secondary sex characteristics are important psychologically, if not biologically. Breasts are an obvious example. Many adolescent girls buy "minimizer," "maximizer," "training," or "shaping" bras, hoping that their breasts will conform to their idealized body image.

During the same years, many overweight boys are horrified to notice a swelling around their nipples—a temporary result of the erratic hormones of early puberty. If a boy's breast growth is very disturbing, tamoxifen or plastic surgery can reduce the swelling, although many doctors prefer to let time deal with the problem (Morcos & Kizy, 2012).

> **primary sex characteristics**
> The parts of the body that are directly involved in reproduction, including the vagina, uterus, ovaries, testicles, and penis.
>
> **secondary sex characteristics**
> Physical traits that are not directly involved in reproduction but that indicate sexual maturity, such as a man's beard and a woman's breasts.

Nutrition

All the changes of puberty depend on adequate nourishment, yet many adolescents do not eat well. They often skip breakfast, binge at midnight, guzzle down unhealthy energy drinks, and munch on salty, processed snacks. Some eat so poorly that their health is damaged lifelong.

NUTRIENTS MISSING Family dinners correlate with healthy adolescent eating and well-being. However, this is tricky: If parents insist on family dinners, clashing directly with the teenager's wish for independence, the benefits of such meals may be undercut by a sullen, angry diner (Meier & Musick, 2014).

Most adolescents consume enough calories, but in 2013 only 16 percent of high school seniors ate the recommended three or more servings of vegetables a day (MMWR, June 13, 2014). Deficiencies of iron, calcium, zinc, and other minerals are common.

Because menstruation depletes iron, anemia is more likely among adolescent girls than among people of any other age or sex. Boys may also be iron-deficient if they engage in physical labor or intensive sports: Muscles need iron for growth and strength.

For the Audience Teenage eating behavior is influenced by other adolescents. Note the evident approval from the slightly older teenager, not from the younger boys. Would the eater have put his head back and mouth wide open if the only onlookers were his parents?

TONY GARCIA/IMAGE SOURCE/GETTY IMAGES

Diet Worldwide, adolescent obesity is increasing. Parental responses differ, from indifference to major concern. For some U.S. parents the response is to spend thousands of dollars trying to change their children, as is the case for the parents of these girls, eating breakfast at Wellspring, a California boarding school for overweight teenagers that costs $6,250 a month. Every day, these girls exercise more than 10,000 steps (tracked with a pedometer) and eat less than 20 grams of fat (normal is more than 60 grams).

STEPHAN GLADIEU/GETTY IMAGES

The cutoff for iron-deficiency anemia is higher for boys than girls because boys require more iron to be healthy (Morón & Viteri, 2009). Yet in developed as well as developing nations, adolescents tend to spurn iron-rich foods (beans, egg yolks, and lean meat) in favor of iron-poor chips, sweets, and fries.

Similarly, although the daily recommended intake of calcium for teenagers is 1,300 milligrams, the average U.S. teen consumes less than 500 milligrams a day. About half of adult bone mass is acquired from ages 10 to 20, which means many contemporary teenagers will eventually develop osteoporosis (fragile bones), a major cause of disability, injury, and death in late adulthood.

One reason for calcium deficiency is that milk drinking has declined. In 1961, most North American children drank at least 24 ounces (about three-fourths of a liter) of milk each day, providing most of their daily calcium requirement. Fifty years later, only 12.5 percent of high school students drank that much milk and 19 percent (more girls than boys) drank no milk at all (MMWR, June 13, 2014).

Fast-food establishments, serving tasty but not healthy food, cluster around high schools, with extra seating that encourages teenagers to hang out. This is especially true for high schools with large Hispanic populations, who are most at risk for obesity (Taber et al., 2011). Forty percent of Hispanic girls in U.S. high schools describe themselves as overweight, as do 27 percent of Hispanic boys (MMWR, June 13, 2014).

body image
A person's idea of how his or her body looks, especially related to size and shape.

BODY DISSATISFACTION One reason for poor nutrition among teenagers is anxiety about **body image**—that is, a person's idea of how his or her body looks. Two-thirds of U.S. high school girls are trying to lose weight, even though only one-fourth are actually overweight or obese (MMWR, June 8, 2012).

Body image dissatisfaction occurs in adolescents of both sexes and every ethnic group, although each adolescent is troubled by particular characteristics that spring from their ancestral genes. Film stars and media models make this worse.

Many adolescents obsess about being too short or too tall, too wide in the hips or too narrow in the face, too hairy or not hairy enough, with fingers too long or legs too fat, and so on. Self-acceptance is difficult at every age, particularly when body changes are new. Indeed, adolescents may become depressed because of some characteristic they wish they had or did not have (Kuzucu et al., 2014).

Video Activity: Eating Disorders introduces the three main types of eating disorders and outlines the signs and symptoms of each.

BENEFITS OF ADOLESCENT BRAIN DEVELOPMENT
It is easy for adults to be critical of adolescent behavior and blame it on hormones, peers, culture, or the latest chosen culprit, brains. Exaggerated metaphors have changed from blaming puberty as the cause of "storm and stress" to blaming brains for "all gas and no brakes" (Payne, 2012).

Yet remember that difference is not always deficit. Gains as well as losses are part of every developmental period, and continuity from one life period to another is evident even as each stage includes specific problems. What might be the benefits of the adolescent brain?

Increasing myelination and slower inhibition allows lightning fast reactions, making adolescent athletes quick and fearless as they steal a base, tackle a fullback, or sprint when their lungs feel about to burst. Ideally, coaches channel such bravery.

DENNIS MACDONALD/PHOTOEDIT

Yes, Not No Diving into cold water with your friends is thrilling if you are a teenage boy and a girl is watching. Adult prohibition increases the joy.

Furthermore, as the brain's reward areas activate positive neurotransmitters, teenagers become happy. A new love, a first job, a college acceptance, or even an A on a term paper can produce a rush of joy, to be remembered and cherished lifelong.

Teenagers need to take risks and learn new things, because "[t]he fundamental task of adolescence—to achieve adult levels of social competence—requires a great deal of learning about the complexities of human social interactions" (Peper & Dahl, 2013, p. 135). That is exactly what their brains enable adolescents to do.

Synaptic growth enhances moral development as well. Adolescents question their elders and forge their own standards. This is an asset if adolescent values are less self-centered and more relevant to current conditions than those of older generations. Values embraced during adolescence are more likely to endure than those acquired later, after brain connections are firmly established.

Thus, the developing prefrontal cortex "confers benefits as well as risks. It helps explain the creativity of adolescence and early adulthood, before the brain becomes set in its ways" (Monastersky, 2007, p. A17). The emotional intensity of adolescents "intertwines with the highest levels of human endeavor: passion for ideas and ideals, passion for beauty, passion to create music and art" (Dahl, 2004, p. 21).

> **formal operational thought**
> In Piaget's theory, the fourth and final stage of cognitive development, characterized by systematic logical thinking and by understanding abstractions.

THINK CRITICALLY: Given the nature of adolescent brain development, how should society respond to adolescent thoughts and actions?

Formal Operational Thought

Adolescents move past concrete operational thinking (discussed in Chapter 7) and consider abstractions. Jean Piaget described a shift to **formal operational thought,** including "assumptions that have no necessary relation to reality" (Piaget, 1950/2010, p. 148).

EGOCENTRISM For many adolescents, the first step toward abstract thought is very personal, although unrealistic, thought. They think deeply about themselves. One reason adolescents spend so much time talking on the phone, e-mailing, and texting is that they like to ruminate about each nuance of whatever they have done, might have done, and could do.

JUPITERIMAGES/STOCKBYTE

Brains and Bodies Can you imagine yourself in their shoes? People of all ages play basketball but these boys display all the signs of adolescence. Note the long, skinny legs and arms, growing before the heads and torsos, and the impulsive brain that provoked the shooter to try the long shot, and the other two to risk injury by jumping so high.

IMAGE SOURCE/GETTY IMAGES

All Eyes on Me Egocentrism and obsession with appearance are hallmarks of adolescence, as shown by these high school cheerleaders. Given teenage thinking, it is not surprising that many boys and girls seek stardom, sometimes with fierce competition within teams and between schools. Cooperation and moderation are more difficult.

adolescent egocentrism
A characteristic of adolescent thinking that leads young people to believe in their own uniqueness, and to imagine that other people are also focused on them.

personal fable
The belief that one's own emotions, experiences, and destiny are unique, more wonderful or awful than anyone else's.

invincibility fable
The fantasy that a person cannot be harmed by anything that might defeat a normal mortal, such as unprotected sex, drug abuse, or high-speed driving.

imaginary audience
The other people who, in an adolescent's egocentric belief, watch his or her appearance, ideas, and behavior.

Duck, Duck, Goose Far more teens are injured in bicycle accidents than hunting ones, because almost all young people ride bicycles and relatively few are hunters. However, especially when no adult is present, young hunters are less likely to wear blaze orange, to attend safety classes, and be licensed to hunt. Most likely these boys will return home safe, without the duck they seek. Nonetheless, guns and off-road vehicles are leading causes of death under age 18, so this scene is not a comforting one.

They also imagine what others—teachers, parents, friends, even classmates who seem to ignore them—think of them. Together these two aspects of thought are called **adolescent egocentrism,** first described by David Elkind (1967).

Egocentrism leads adolescents to interpret everyone else's behavior as if it were a judgment on them. A stranger's frown or a teacher's critique could make a teenager conclude that "No one likes me" and then deduce that "I am unlovable" or even claim that "I can't leave the house."

More positive casual reactions—a smile from a barista or an extra-big hug from a younger brother—could lead to "I am great" or "Everyone loves me" or similarly distorted self-perception. Given the rapid mood changes of adolescence, such conclusions are usually short-lived, susceptible to reversal with another offhand remark.

Several aspects of adolescent egocentrism are named, among them the **personal fable** and the **invincibility fable,** which often appear together (Alberts et al., 2007). The *personal fable* is the belief that one is unique, destined to have a heroic, fabled, legendary life. Some 12-year-olds expect to play in the NBA, or become billionaires, or cure cancer. *Invincible* means impervious to harm.

Some adolescents see no contradiction between the personal fable and invincibility. Some believe that they will not be hurt by fast driving, unprotected sex, or addictive drugs unless fate wills it. If they survive unscathed from a dangerous risk, they may feel invincible, not relieved; special, not unlucky.

Egocentrism creates an **imaginary audience** in the minds of many adolescents. They believe they are at center stage, with all eyes on them, and they imagine how others might react to their appearance and behavior.

MARK JENSEN/GETTY IMAGES

The imaginary audience can cause teenagers to enter a crowded room as if they are the most attractive human beings alive. They might put studs in their lips or blast music for all to hear, calling attention to themselves. The reverse is sometimes evident: Many a 12-year-old refuses to leave the house with a bad haircut or the wrong shoes.

PIAGET'S EXPERIMENTS Egocentrism can coexist with more logical and abstract intelligence. Piaget and his colleagues devised tasks to assess formal operational thought (Inhelder & Piaget, 1958/2013b).

In one experiment (diagrammed in Figure 9.5), children of many ages balance a scale by hooking weights onto the scale's arms. To master this task, they must realize that the weights' heaviness and distance from the center interact reciprocally to affect balance.

The concept of balancing was completely beyond the 3- to 5-year-olds. By age 7, children could balance the scale by putting the same amount of weight on each arm, but they didn't realize that the distance from the center mattered.

By age 10, children thought about location but used trial and error, not logic. Finally, by about age 13 or 14, some children hypothesized and tested the reciprocal relationship between weight and distance and developed the correct formula (Piaget & Inhelder, 1972).

In balancing, as in all of Piaget's experiments, "in contrast to concrete operational children, formal operational adolescents imagine all possible determinants . . . [and] systematically vary the factors one by one, observe the results correctly, keep track of the results, and draw the appropriate conclusions" (P. Miller, 2011, p. 57).

HYPOTHETICAL-DEDUCTIVE REASONING One hallmark of formal operational thought is the capacity to think of possibility, not just reality. "Here and now" is only

A Proud Teacher "Is it possible to train a cockroach?" This hypothetical question, an example of formal operational thought, was posed by 15-year-old Tristan Williams of New Mexico. In his award-winning science project, he succeeded in conditioning Madagascar cockroaches to hiss at the sight of a permanent marker. (His parents' logic about sharing their home with 600 cockroaches is unknown.)

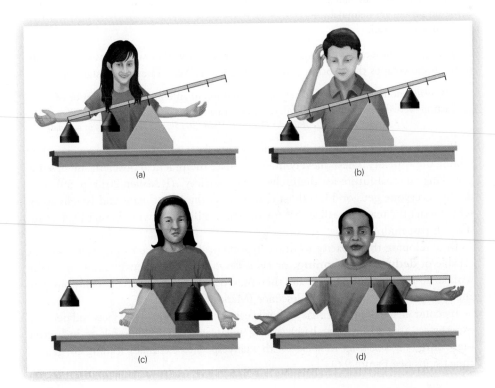

LaunchPad

Video Activity: The Balance Scale Task shows children of various ages completing the task and gives you an opportunity to try it as well.

FIGURE 9.5 How to Balance a Scale Piaget's balance-scale test of formal reasoning, as it is attempted by (a) a 4-year-old, (b) a 7-year-old, (c) a 10-year-old, and (d) a 14-year-old. The key to balancing the scale is to make weight times distance from the center equal on both sides of the center; the realization of that principle requires formal operational thought.

Triple Winners Sharing the scholarship check of $100,000, these high school students are not only high achievers, but they also have learned to collaborate within a comprehensive public school (Hewlett). They learned much more than formal operational logic.

one of many alternatives, including "there and then," "long, long ago," "nowhere," "not yet," and "never." As Piaget said:

> The adolescent . . . thinks beyond the present and forms theories about everything, delighting especially in considerations of that which is not. . . .
>
> *[Piaget, 1950/2010, p. 147]*

hypothetical thought
Reasoning that includes propositions and possibilities that do not reflect reality.

deductive reasoning
Reasoning from a general statement, premise, or principle, through logical steps, to figure out (deduce) specifics. (Also called *top-down reasoning*.)

inductive reasoning
Reasoning from specific experiences or facts to reach (induce) a general conclusion. (Also called *bottom-up reasoning*.)

Adolescents are primed to engage in **hypothetical thought,** reasoning about *if–then* propositions that do not reflect reality. For example, consider this question (adapted from De Neys & Van Gelder, 2009):

> If all mammals can walk,
> And whales are mammals,
> Can whales walk?

Younger adolescents often answer "No!" They know that whales swim, not walk, so the logic escapes them. Some adolescents answer "Yes." They understand *if.*

> *Possibility* no longer appears merely as an extension of an empirical situation or of actions actually performed. Instead, it is *reality* that is now secondary to *possibility.*
>
> *[Inhelder & Piaget, 1958/2013b, p. 251; emphasis in original]*

Because of this new ability, many adolescents sharply criticize their parents, their school, their society. They "naively underestimate the practical problems involved in achieving an ideal future for themselves or for society" (P. Miller, 2011, p. 59). Why doesn't everyone get good health care; why don't the Palestinians and Israelis agree; why doesn't the teacher realize that my question is brilliant; why doesn't Dad let me stay out past midnight?

In developing the capacity to think hypothetically, adolescents gradually become capable of **deductive reasoning,** or *top-down reasoning.* Deductive reasoning begins with an abstract idea or premise and then uses logic to draw specific conclusions. This ability improves during early adolescence (Markovits, 2014).

By contrast, during the primary school years, children accumulate facts and personal experiences (the knowledge base), asking what and why. The result is **inductive reasoning,** or *bottom-up reasoning,* with many specific examples leading to general conclusions (see Figure 9.6).

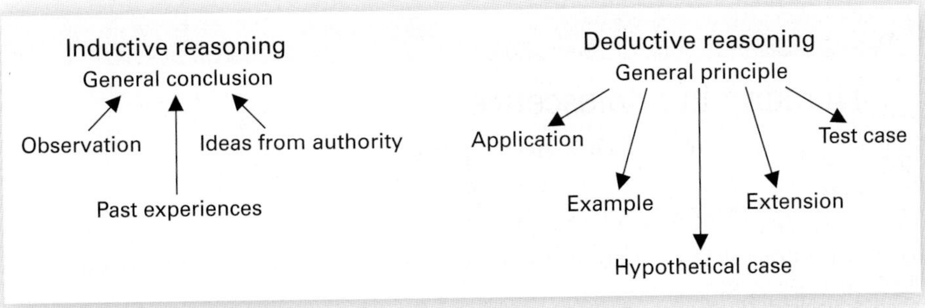

Inductive reasoning
General conclusion
Observation   Ideas from authority
Past experiences

Deductive reasoning
General principle
Application   Test case
Example   Extension
Hypothetical case

FIGURE 9.6 Bottom Up or Top Down? Children, as concrete operational thinkers, are likely to draw conclusions on the basis of their own experiences and what they have been told. This is called inductive, or bottom-up, reasoning. Adolescents can think deductively, from the top down.

One example of moving past personal experience in reasoning ability is the understanding of prejudice. Almost every adolescent knows that racism exists—and opposes it. However, children tend to think the core problem is the attitudes of individuals. Using inductive reasoning, they think that the remedy is to increase tolerance among individuals who are racist.

By contrast, adolescents begin to think, deductively, that policy solutions need to attack racism. That is formal operational thinking.

This interpretation arises from a study of adolescent agreement or disagreement with policies to reduce racial discrimination (Hughes & Bigler, 2011). Not surprisingly, most students in an interracial U.S. high school recognized disparities between African and European Americans and believed that racism was a major cause. What was surprising to the researchers is that age made a difference.

Among those who were aware of marked inequalities, more older adolescents (age 16 to 17) supported systemic solutions (e.g., affirmative action and desegregation) than did younger adolescents (age 14 to 15). The researchers wrote: "during adolescence, cognitive development facilitates the understanding that discrimination exists at the social-systemic level . . . racism awareness begins to inform views of race-conscious policies during middle adolescence" (Hughes & Bigler, 2011, p. 489).

In thinking about race and many other issues, neither adolescents nor adults necessarily reason at the formal operational level. Piaget probably overestimated the prevalence of this fourth period of intelligence. As now discussed, many contemporary scholars believe there are two modes of thinking, and that most people, most of the time, do not use formal operational thought (Barrouillet, 2011).

Two Modes of Thinking

Advanced logic in adolescence is counterbalanced by the increasing power of intuitive thinking. A **dual-process model** of cognition has been formulated (Albert & Steinberg, 2011) (see Visualizing Development, p. 322). This echoes what you have learned about the brain: Sensation seeking temporarily outweighs impulse control (Duckworth & Steinberg, 2015).

dual-process model
The idea that two modes of thinking exist within the human brain, one for intuitive emotional responses and one for analytical reasoning.

INTUITION VERSUS ANALYSIS Cognitive psychologists use various terms for and descriptions of two modes of human cognition (Evans & Stanovich, 2013). The terms include: intuitive/analytic, implicit/explicit, creative/factual, contextualized/decontextualized, unconscious/conscious, gist/quantitative, emotional/intellectual, experiential/rational, personal/impersonal, hot/cold, systems 1 and 2. Although these two modes interact and can overlap, each mode is distinct (Kuhn, 2013).

Thinking in Adolescence

We are able to think both intuitively and analytically, but adolescents tend to rely more on intuitive thinking than do adults.

INDUCTIVE vs. DEDUCTIVE REASONING

INDUCTIVE: Conclusion reached after many of the following. Note that the problem is that the adolescent's nimble mind can rationalize many specifics. Only when the evidence is overwhelming is the conclusion reached.

DEDUCTIVE: The principle is the starting point, not the end point.

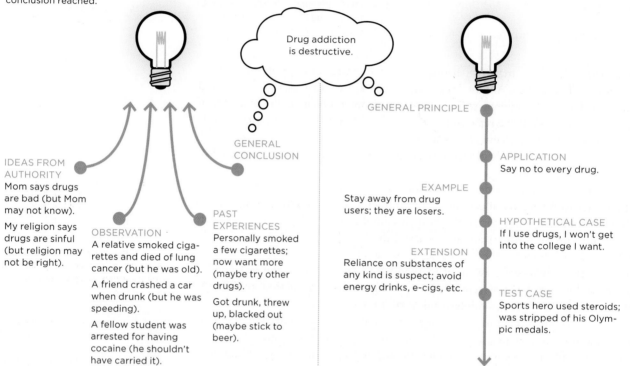

Drug addiction is destructive.

GENERAL CONCLUSION

GENERAL PRINCIPLE

IDEAS FROM AUTHORITY
Mom says drugs are bad (but Mom may not know).

My religion says drugs are sinful (but religion may not be right).

OBSERVATION
A relative smoked cigarettes and died of lung cancer (but he was old).

A friend crashed a car when drunk (but he was speeding).

A fellow student was arrested for having cocaine (he shouldn't have carried it).

PAST EXPERIENCES
Personally smoked a few cigarettes; now want more (maybe try other drugs).

Got drunk, threw up, blacked out (maybe stick to beer).

APPLICATION
Say no to every drug.

EXAMPLE
Stay away from drug users; they are losers.

HYPOTHETICAL CASE
If I use drugs, I won't get into the college I want.

EXTENSION
Reliance on substances of any kind is suspect; avoid energy drinks, e-cigs, etc.

TEST CASE
Sports hero used steroids; was stripped of his Olympic medals.

CHANGES IN AGE

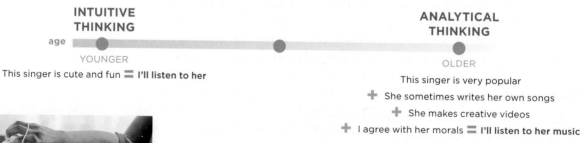

INTUITIVE THINKING

age

YOUNGER

This singer is cute and fun ☰ I'll listen to her

ANALYTICAL THINKING

OLDER

This singer is very popular
➕ She sometimes writes her own songs
➕ She makes creative videos
➕ I agree with her morals ☰ I'll listen to her music

As people age, their thinking tends to move from intuitive processing to more analytic processing. Virtually all cognitive psychologists note these two alternative processes and describe a developmental progression toward more dispassionate logic with maturity. However, the terms used and the boundaries between the two vary. They are roughly analogous to Kahneman's System 1 (which "operates automatically and quickly") and System 2 ("the conscious, reasoning self") (Kahneman, 2011, pp. 20–21), as well as to the traditional distinction between inductive and deductive reasoning, and to Piaget's concrete operational versus formal operational thought. Although experts vary in their descriptions, and individuals vary in when and how they use these two processes, overall adolescents tend to favor intuitive rather than analytic thinking.

Impressive Connections This robot is about to compete in the Robotics Competition in Atlanta, Georgia, but much more impressive are the brains of the Oregon high school team (including Melissa, shown here) who designed the robot.

OBSERVATION QUIZ
Melissa seems to working by herself, but what sign do you see that suggests she is part of a team who built this robot? (see answer, page 336) ◄

In describing adolescent cognition, here we use the terms *intuitive* and *analytic*.

- **Intuitive thought** begins with a belief, assumption, or general rule (called a *heuristic*) rather than logic. Intuition is quick and powerful; it feels "right."

- **Analytic thought** is the formal, logical, hypothetical-deductive thinking described by Piaget. It involves rational analysis of many factors whose interactions must be calculated, as in the scale-balancing problem.

The thinking described by the first half of each pair is easier and quicker, preferred in everyday life. We are all "predictably irrational" at times (Ariely, 2009). Sometimes, however, the second mode is needed, when deeper thought is demanded.

The discrepancy between the maturation of the limbic system and of the prefrontal cortex tilts adolescents toward the more emotional, personal, experiential mode. Adolescents tend to be "fast and furious" intuitive thinkers, unlike their teachers and parents, who prefer slower, more analytic thinking.

Experiences and role models influence choices, not only in deciding what to do but also in choosing which intellectual process to use in making a decision. Conversations, observations, and debate all advance cognition and lead to a deeper consideration of the facts (Kuhn, 2013). As they grow older, adolescents sometimes gain in logic and sometimes regress; the social context and training in statistics are major influences on adolescent cognition (Klaczynski & Felmban, 2014).

To test yourself on intuition and analysis, answer the following three problems:

1. A bat and a ball cost $1.10 in total. The bat costs $1 more than the ball. How much does the ball cost?

2. If it takes 5 minutes for 5 machines to make 5 widgets, how long would it take 100 machines to make 100 widgets?

3. In a lake, there is a patch of lily pads. Every day the patch doubles in size. If it takes 48 days for the patch to cover the entire lake, how long would it take for the patch to cover half the lake?

[From Gervais & Norenzayan, 2012]

Answers are on page 337.

intuitive thought
Thought that arises from an emotion or a hunch, a "gut feeling" influenced by past experiences and cultural assumptions.

analytic thought
Thought that results from analysis, such as a systematic exploration of pros and cons, risks and consequences, possibilities and facts. Analytic thought depends on logic and rationality.

AP PHOTO/GREGORY SMITH

Although many researchers find that logic gradually overcomes biased reasoning during adolescence, whether or not such analysis is used depends on specifics. One instance when being older did not improve logic occurred when adolescents were asked to decide how likely a hypothetical girl named Jennifer, described as lazy and not well liked, was to be obese. Among those teenagers who idealized thinness, the older ones *more* often jumped to the illogical conclusion that Jennifer was probably obese (Klaczynski & Felmban, 2014).

In dozens of studies, being smarter as measured by an intelligence test does not advance logic as much as having more experience, in school and in life. Students can learn to use statistics and to respect expert opinion, and that helps them think more rationally—but not always (Kail, 2013). Many parents of smart adolescents are surprised to realize this, as in the following.

ANSWER TO **OBSERVATION** QUIZ
(from page 335): The flag on the robot matches her T-shirt. Often teenagers wear matching shirts to signify their joint identity. ●

A CASE TO STUDY

"What Were You Thinking?"

Laurence Steinberg is a noted expert on adolescence (e.g., Steinberg, 2014). He is also a father.

> When my son, Benjamin, was 14, he and three of his friends decided to sneak out of the house where they were spending the night and visit one of their girlfriends at around two in the morning. When they arrived at the girl's house, they positioned themselves under her bedroom window, threw pebbles against her window-panes, and tried to scale the side of the house. Modern technology, unfortunately, has made it harder to play Romeo these days. The boys set off the house's burglar alarm, which activated a siren and simultaneously sent a direct notification to the local police station, which dispatched a patrol car. When the siren went off, the boys ran down the street and right smack into the police car, which was heading to the girl's home. Instead of stopping and explaining their activity, Ben and his friends scattered and ran off in different directions through the neighborhood.
>
> . . . After his near brush with the local police, Ben had returned to the house out of which he had snuck, where he slept soundly until I awakened him with an angry telephone call, telling him to gather his clothes and wait for me in front of his friend's house. On our drive home, after delivering a long lecture about what he had done and about the dangers of running from armed police in the dark when they believe they may have interrupted a burglary, I paused.

> "What were you thinking?" I asked.
>
> "That's the problem, Dad," Ben replied, "I wasn't."
>
> *[Steinberg, 2004, pp. 51, 52]*

Steinberg realized that his son was right: When emotions are intense, especially when friends are nearby, the logical part of the brain shuts down. This shutdown is not reflected in questionnaires that require teenagers to respond to paper-and-pencil questions regarding hypothetical dilemmas. In fact, when strong emotions are not activated, teenagers may be more logical than adults (Casey & Caudle, 2013). They remember facts they have learned in biology or health class about sex and drugs. However,

> the prospect of visiting a hypothetical girl from class cannot possibly carry the excitement about the possibility of surprising someone you have a crush on with a visit in the middle of the night. It is easier to put on a hypothetical condom during an act of hypothetical sex than it is to put on a real one when one is in the throes of passion . . . It is easier to just say no to a hypothetical beer than it is to a cold frosty one on a summer night.
>
> *[Steinberg, 2004, p. 53]*

Ben reached adulthood safely. Some other non-thinking teenagers, with less cautious police or less diligent parents, do not.

PREFERRING EMOTIONS Why do high school students, well aware of the logic of the science, sometimes not use formal operational thinking? Dozens of experiments and extensive theorizing have found some answers (Albert & Steinberg, 2011).

Essentially, analysis is more difficult than intuition. It requires questioning ideas that are comforting and familiar. Once people of any age reach an emotional conclusion (sometimes called a "gut feeling"), they resist changing their minds.

Furthermore, weighing alternatives and thinking of possibilities can be paralyzing. The systematic, analytic thought that Piaget called formal operational is slow and costly, not fast and frugal, wasting precious time when a young person wants to act.

One characteristic of adolescents—suspicion of authority—may advance analysis, because teenagers use logic to argue against tradition. But, the same trait may work in the opposite direction. One of my students used logic (quoting the U.S. Constitution) to argue with a police officer who was questioning her young cousin: When the officer grabbed the cousin, she impulsively bit his hand—and spent months in jail.

It is helpful to realize that, even when they are analytical, teenagers might analyze a situation and reach a conclusion other than the one their parents would. A 15-year-old who is offered a cigarette, for example, might rationally choose peer acceptance over the distant risk of cancer. How likely is a teenager who wants to be "cool" or "bad" to say, "No thank you, my mother wouldn't approve"?

More generally, adults want adolescents to take care of their health, which means avoiding cigarettes, junk food, and promiscuity. But emotional thinking pushes in the opposite direction, and some analytic arguments (about the risk of cancer, for instance) are dismissed (Gibbons et al., 2012a). That is why effective messages to halt teen smoking discuss smelly breath, stained fingers, and yellow teeth.

THINK CRITICALLY: When might an emotional response to a problem be better than an analytic one?

Answers	Intuitive	Analytic
1.	10 cents	5 cents
2.	100 minutes	5 minutes
3.	24 days	47 days

Digital Natives

Adults over age 40 grew up without the Internet, instant messaging, Twitter, Snapchat, blogs, cell phones, smartphones, MP3 players, tablets, or digital cameras. In contrast, today's teenagers have been called *digital natives,* although if that term implies that they know everything about digital communication, it is a misnomer (boyd, 2014).

A huge gap between those with and without computers was bemoaned a decade ago; it divided boys from girls and rich from poor (Dijk, 2005; Norris, 2001). Now that *digital divide* is shrinking, and a new one is evident, between the old and the young.

ERIC THAYER/REUTERS/LANDOV

Not All Thumbs After two days of competition among 22 qualified contestants, with tests of texting speed, clarity, and knowledge, 15-year-old Kate Moore of Des Moines, Iowa, was declared champion. She won a trophy and $50,000. She has texted hundreds of friends for years.

As costs tumble, the smartphone has been particularly important among low-SES adolescents of every ethnic group, used primarily to connect with friends (Madden et al., 2013). Connection to peers has always been important to teenagers, and that has always been feared by adults—who in earlier generations feared that the automobile, or the shopping mall, or rock and roll would lead their children astray.

TECHNOLOGY AND COGNITION In general, educators accept, even welcome, students' facility with technology. There are "virtual" schools in which students earn all their credits online, never entering a school building, and in several school districts all the students have tablets.

Remember that research before the technology explosion found that direct instruction, practice, conversation, and experience advance adolescent thought. Social networking via technology may speed up this process, as teens communicate daily with dozens—perhaps hundreds or thousands—of "friends" via texting or instant messaging.

Most secondary students check facts, read explanations, view videos, and thus grasp concepts they would not have understood without technology. For some adolescents, the Internet is their only source of information about health and sex. Almost every high school student in the United States uses the Internet for research, finding it quicker and more extensive than books on library shelves.

Educators claim that the most difficult aspect of technology is teaching students how to evaluate sources, some reputable, some nonsensical. To this end, teachers explain the significance of *.com*, *.org*, *.edu*, and *.gov* (O'Hanlon, 2013).

ABUSE AND ADDICTION? Parents worry about sexual abuse via the Internet. Research is reassuring: Although sexual predators lurk online, most teens never encounter them. Sexual abuse is a serious problem, but if sexual abuse is defined as a perverted older stranger taking advantage of an innocent teenager met online, it is "extremely rare" (Mitchell et al., 2013, p. 1226).

The data show that the percent of teenagers who say that someone online tried to get them to talk about sex declined since 2000 from 10 to 1. Those 1 percent were almost always solicited by another young person whom the teenager already knew—a Facebook friend, for instance (Mitchell et al., 2013).

For some adolescents, chat rooms, video games, and Internet gambling may be considered addictive, taking time from active play, schoolwork, and friendship. Internet addiction is considered a problem in many nations (Tang et al., 2014; Y–H. Lee et al., 2015). For example, among high school students, 15 percent in Turkey and 12 percent in India are said to be addicted to computer use (Şaşmaz et al., 2014; Yadav et al., 2013).

However, some scholars worry that adults tend to pathologize normal teen behavior, particularly in China, where rehabilitation centers are strict—some would say abusive—in keeping teenagers from Internet use (Bax, 2014). Parents may make the same mistake elsewhere (boyd, 2014).

The North American psychiatrists who wrote the new DSM-5 decided against including Internet use as an addiction. Instead, they wrote that further study was needed.

CYBER DANGER When a person is bullied via electronic devices, usually via social media, text messages, or smartphone videos, that is **cyberbullying.** The adolescents involved in cyberbullying are usually already bullies or victims or both, with bully-victims especially likely to engage in, and suffer from, cyberbullying. Technology does not create bullies; it gives them another means to act and a larger audience, which multiplies the harm (Kowalski et al., 2014).

LDPROD/SHUTTERSTOCK

LaunchPad

The Impact of Media on Adolescent Development

http://qrs.ly/zn4ep1c

cyberbullying
Bullying that occurs when one person attacks and harms another via technology (e.g., e-mails, text messages, or cell phones).

DAVID GOLDMAN/AP PHOTO

Fake Face in Georgia Alex stands behind a phony Facebook page that portrays her as a racist, lesbian drug abuser. She is 14, a late developer, which may be one reason she became a cyberbullying target. Also shown are her parents, Amy and Chris Boston, who sued her classmates for libel. The case was dismissed, but then the Court of Appeals of the State of Georgia sent the case back to the local court, suggesting that the parents of the cyberbullies should face trial, since they did not take the site down until a month after the first lawsuit. No matter what happens in court, the worst has already happened: Alex thought the bullies were her friends.

Texted and posted rumors and insults can "go viral," reaching thousands, transmitted day and night. Some adolescents take videos of others drunk, naked, or crying and send them to dozens of others, who may send them to yet others, who may post them on YouTube or Vine. Since young adolescents are impulsive and low on judgment, cyberbullying is particularly prevalent and cruel between ages 11 and 14.

Although the causes of all forms of bullying are similar, each form has its own sting. Cyberbullying is most harmful if the victim believes in the imaginary audience, if sexual impulses are new, and if impulsive thoughts precede analytic ones. All that means that young adolescent victims of cyberbullying are likely to suffer from depression, even suicide (Bonanno & Hymel, 2013).

The vulnerability of adolescence was tragically evident for a California 15-year-old (Sulek, 2013). At a sleepover, Audrie Pott and her friends found alcohol. She got so drunk that she blacked out, or passed out. On the next school day, three boys in her school were bragging that they had had sex with her, showing cell-phone pictures to prove it. The next weekend, Audrie hanged herself. Only then did her parents learn what had happened.

One aspect of this tragedy will come as no surprise to adolescents: *sexting,* as sending sexual photographs is called. As many as 30 percent of adolescents report having received sext photos. Many teens send their own sexy "selfies" and are happy to receive sext messages (Temple et al., 2014). As with Internet addiction, researchers have yet to agree on how to measure sexting or how harmful it is.

There are two dangers: (1) Pictures may be forwarded without the person's knowledge, and (2) those who send erotic self-images risk serious depression if the reaction is negative (Temple et al., 2014). Many teens have distorted self-concepts—no wonder sexting is fraught with trouble.

The danger of all forms of technology lies not in the equipment but in the cognition of the user. That is the conclusion of a national survey which found that 7 percent of all teens willingly sent sext photos of themselves, yet sexting correlated with risky sex, depression, and low self-esteem (Ybarra & Mitchell, 2014).

As is true of many aspects of adolescence (puberty, eating disorders, brain development, egocentric thought, use of contraception, and so on), context, adults, peers, and the adolescent's own personality and temperament "shape, mediate, and/or modify effects" of technology (Oakes, 2009, p. 1142).

Something Worth Sharing But what is it? Is it the same as boys everywhere, or is it something specific to their culture? The four are in England: We do not know if they see a football (soccer) score, a prime minister's proclamation, or a naked female.

ACE STOCK LIMITED/ALAMY

One careful observer claims that instead of being *native* users of technology, many teenagers are *naive* users—believing they have privacy settings that they do not have, trusting sites that are markedly biased, misunderstanding how to search for and verify information (boyd, 2014).

Educators can help with all this—but only if they themselves understand technology and teens. Teens are intuitive, impulsive, and egocentric, often unaware of the impact of what they send or overestimating the validity of what they read. Adults should know better, but this discussion makes it apparent that people of all ages are sometimes illogical and emotional about technology.

THINK CRITICALLY: The older people are, the more likely they are to be critical of social media. Is that wisdom or ignorance? Why?

WHAT HAVE YOU LEARNED?

1. Why does the limbic system develop before the prefrontal cortex?
2. How might seeking sensations lead an adolescent to trouble?
3. What are some of the benefits of adolescent brain function?
4. How does adolescent egocentrism differ from early-childhood egocentrism?
5. What perceptions arise from belief in the imaginary audience?
6. What are the characteristics of formal operational thinking?
7. What is the difference between inductive reasoning and deductive reasoning?
8. When might intuition and analysis lead to opposite conclusions?
9. Why do most people prefer intuitive thinking, not analytic thought?
10. What benefits come from adolescents' use of technology?
11. What problems do adults fear from teenage use of the Internet?
12. Why is cyberbullying particularly harmful during adolescence?
13. Why might sexting be a problem?
14. How is the term *digital native* misleading?

Teaching and Learning

What does our knowledge of adolescents imply about school? As you have read, adolescents are capable of deep and wide-ranging thought, no longer limited by concrete experience, yet they are often egocentric, intuitive, and impulsive.

Education is crucial for later life, but the quality of schooling matters. A year of school can propel thinking forward or can have little impact: What matters is how much learning occurs, not how much time has elapsed (Hanushek & Woessmann, 2015).

Consequently, educators, developmentalists, political leaders, and parents wonder exactly which curricula and school structures are best for 11- to 18-year-olds. There are dozens of options: academic knowledge/vocational skills, single-sex/coed, competitive/cooperative, large/small, public/private, religious/secular, and more.

No single school structure or style of pedagogy seems best for everyone. Various scientists, nations, schools, and teachers try many strategies, some based on opposite but logical hypotheses.

Secondary education—traditionally grades 7 through 12—denotes the school years after elementary or grade school (known as *primary education*) and before college or university (known as *tertiary education*).

Adults are healthier and wealthier if they complete secondary school. This is true within nations and between them, for people of every ethnicity, gender, and SES. Even something seemingly unrelated to education—cigarette smoking by European American adults—is almost three times more common among those with no high school diploma than those with some college (41 to 15 percent) (National Center for Health Statistics, 2014).

secondary education
Education that follows primary education (elementary or grade school) and precedes tertiary education (college). It usually occurs from about age 11 to age 18, although there is some variation by school and by nation.

Middle School

In many nations, two levels of secondary education are provided, once called senior high and junior high. As the average age of puberty declined, **middle schools** were created for grades 6 to 8, and sometimes for grades 5 to 8.

Moving from primary to middle school is stressful, because teachers, classmates, and expectations all change during a developmental period considered especially

middle school
A school for children after elementary school and before high school, usually grades 6 through 8.

MARMADUKE ST. JOHN/ALAMY

IMAGEBROKER/ALAMY

Same Situation, Far Apart: No Romance Here Young adolescents around the globe, such as these in California *(left)* and Pakistan *(right)*, attend middle school, but what they learn depends on the particular curriculum. Many North American schools encourage collaboration and hands-on learning (these girls are dissecting a squid), whereas many south Asian schools stress individual work.

OBSERVATION QUIZ

Although there are many differences in these classrooms, they share one part of the hidden curriculum. What is it? (see answer, page 344) ▲

crucial for learning (McGill et al., 2012). Many developmentalists find middle schools to be "developmentally regressive" (Eccles & Roeser, 2010, p. 13), which means learning goes backward at the very time it could speed up.

For example, a longitudinal study of primarily European American students found a decline in school interests and grades from age 7 to 16, with a notable dip in the transition to middle school (Dotterer et al., 2009). A similar middle school decline in school engagement occurred in research on African American and Latino students (McGill et al., 2012; Hayes et al., 2015).

Indeed, students of every group tend to dislike middle school, for good reason. Bullying increases in middle school, particularly in the first year (Baly et al., 2014), and friendship with either sex is complicated by unfamiliar sexual urges. Students are less likely to have supportive adults, partly because young adolescents seek independence and partly because the school undercuts student–teacher relationships (Meece & Eccles, 2010) and discourages parent involvement.

Parents underestimate the stress of day-to-day social problems of many students in large schools, and they worry instead about rare events. For example, parents tend to fear school shootings, which actually are very rare—an adolescent is far more likely to be hurt at home, on the street, or in an after-school game than in school. Parents also fear that their child will be targeted by another child, but in fact 90 percent of injuries are accidental, usually caused by the student's own impulsiveness (Amanullah et al., 2014).

Unlike primary school, where each classroom has one teacher all year, middle school teachers may have hundreds of students. Teachers become impersonal and distant, opposite to the direct, personal engagement that young adolescents need. Thankfully, some middle schools are organized to allow teachers to have fewer students (such as the same teacher instructing in English and history), but many more keep the old model.

Early signs of a future high-school dropout are visible in middle school, but most prevention measures are absent. For example, low-SES boys from minority ethnic groups are at risk of quitting school, yet few guidance counselors or teachers are African American or Hispanic American men. Given their egocentric and intuitive thinking, some students who see no successful, educated men as role models may decide that school is not for them (Morris & Morris, 2013).

To pinpoint the developmental mismatch between students' needs and the middle school context, note that just when egocentrism leads young people to feelings of shame or fantasies of stardom (the imaginary audience), schools typically require them to change rooms, teachers, and classmates every 40 minutes or so. That makes both public acclaim and supportive new friendships difficult to achieve.

Recognition for academic excellence or for conscientious work is especially elusive because middle school teachers assign marks more harshly than their primary school counterparts. Effort without accomplishment is not recognized, and achievement that earlier was "outstanding" is now only average.

Acclaim from after-school activities is also scarce, because many art, drama, dance, and other programs put adolescents of all ages together, and the younger students are not as skilled as older adolescents. Finally, athletic teams become competitive; those with fragile egos avoid them.

Many middle school students seek acceptance from their peers. Bullying increases, physical appearance becomes more important, status symbols are displayed (from gang colors to trendy sunglasses), expensive clothes are coveted, and sexual conquests are flaunted. Of course, much depends on the cultural context, but almost every middle school student seeks peer approval in ways that adults disapprove (Véronneau & Dishion, 2010).

COPING WITH MIDDLE SCHOOL One way to cope with stress is directly cognitive. Students may blame classmates, teachers, parents, or governments for problems, and that removes some anxiety, as well as some responsibility, from them.

This may explain the surprising results of a Los Angeles study: Students in schools that were *more* ethnically mixed felt safer and *less* lonely. It was not that they had more friends from other groups. Instead, if they felt alone or performed poorly, they could "attribute their plight to the prejudice of other people" rather than blame themselves (Juvonen et al., 2006, p. 398). Furthermore, members of each minority group tended to support and defend each other, giving everyone some ethnic allies.

THINK CRITICALLY: Would there be less bullying if more schools were multiethnic?

Another way middle school students avoid failure is to quit trying. Then they can blame a low grade on their choice ("I didn't study") rather than on their ability. Pivotal is how they think of their potential, according to a series of studies inspired by Carol Dweck's understanding that the interpretation of intellectual achievement is crucial, as already mentioned in Chapter 8.

If students have an **entity theory of intelligence** (i.e., that ability is innate, a fixed quantity present at birth), then they will conclude that nothing can be done to improve their academic skill. Thus, if they think they are innately incompetent at math, or reading, or whatever, they mask the self-assessment by claiming not to study, try, or care. Over the years of middle school, they learn less (Romero et al., 2014).

By contrast, if adolescents adopt the **incremental theory of intelligence** (i.e., that intelligence can increase if they work to master whatever they seek to understand), then they will pay attention, participate in class, study, complete their homework, and learn.

entity theory of intelligence
The idea that intellectual ability is innate, a fixed quantity present at birth. Those who hold this view underrate the role of effort on achievement.

incremental theory of intelligence
The idea that intelligence can be increased by effort, with attention and practice, as in class participation and homework.

This is not hypothetical. In the first year of middle school, students with entity beliefs do not achieve much, whereas those with mastery motivation improve academically. This has been found in many nations, including Norway (Diseth et al., 2014), China (Zhao & Wang, 2014), and the United States (Burnette et al., 2013; Romero et al., 2014).

The contrast between the entity and incremental theories is also apparent for teachers, parents, schools, and cultures. If the hidden curriculum endorses competition

Same Situation, Far Apart: How to Learn Although developmental psychologists find that adolescents learn best when they actively discuss ideas, most teenagers are easier to control when they are taking tests (*left,* Winston-Salem, North Carolina, United States) or reciting scripture (*right,* Kabul, Afghanistan).

ANSWER TO **OBSERVATION QUIZ**

Quiz (from page 342) Both are single-sex. What does that teach these students? ●

among students and if class composition or curriculum conveys the message to some students that they are not "college material," that is entity theory. Then students are less likely to study or help each other (Eccles & Roeser, 2011).

International comparisons reveal that educational systems that track students into higher or lower classes, that expel low-achieving students, and that allow competition between schools for the brightest students (all reflecting entity, not incremental, theory) also show lower average achievement and a larger gap between the students at the highest and lowest score quartiles (OECD, 2011).

Older Adolescents in School

Many of the patterns and problems of middle school continue in high school, although with puberty over, adolescents are better able to cope. As we have seen, adolescents become increasingly able to think abstractly, analytically, hypothetically, and logically (all formal operational thought) as well as subjectively, emotionally, intuitively, and experientially. High school curricula and teaching methods often require the former mode.

THE COLLEGE-BOUND From a developmental perspective, the fact that high schools emphasize formal thinking makes sense, since many older adolescents are capable of abstract logic. Schools need to provide opportunities and encouragement for metacognition so that students can understand how to learn more.

In several nations, adults hope to raise standards so that all high school graduates will be ready for college. For that reason, U.S. schools are increasing the number of students who take classes that are assessed by externally scored exams, either the IB (International Baccalaureate) or the AP (Advanced Placement). Such classes satisfy some college requirements if the student scores well. More and more students take such classes: 33 percent of high school graduates did so in 2013, compared to 19 percent in 2003 (Adams, 2014).

In addition to mandated courses, 24 U.S. states now also require students to pass a **high-stakes test** in order to graduate. (Any exam for which the consequences of failing are severe is called a high-stakes test.) In 2000, no state had such a test as a graduation requirement. Because the more populous states more often have high-stakes tests, 74 percent of U.S. high school students must take exit exams before graduation.

high-stakes test
An evaluation that determines something very important. For example, if a single test determines promotion or graduation, it is a high-stakes test.

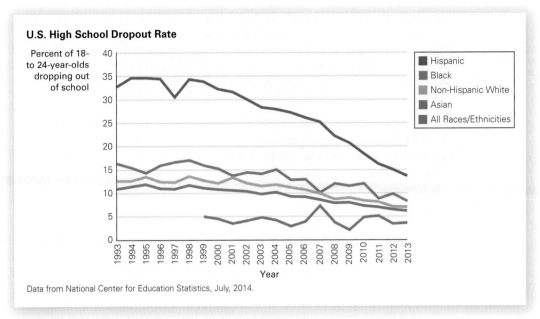

U.S. High School Dropout Rate

Data from National Center for Education Statistics, July, 2014.

FIGURE 9.7 Mostly Good News This depicts improvements in high school graduation rates, especially among Hispanic youth, who drop out less than half as often as they did 20 years ago. However, since high school graduation is increasingly necessary for lifetime success, current rates still lag behind vocational demands. Future health, income, and happiness for anyone who does not complete high school are in jeopardy.

The worry, of course, is that raising standards and requiring a high-stakes test will discourage high school graduation. That does not seem to have happened, as graduation rates are slowly rising in the United States (see Figure 9.7).

COLLEGE FOR EVERYONE? In the United States, some (about 30 percent) high school graduates do not enter college. Moreover, of those who enter public community colleges, most (about three-fourths) do not complete their associate's degree within three years, and almost half of those entering public or private four-year schools do not graduate. Some simply take longer, or they enter the job market first and complete the degree later. But even 10 years after the usual age for high school graduation, only 34 percent of U.S. young adults have earned a bachelor's degree (Snyder & Dillow, 2013).

Internationally, students who do not attend college but instead take courses that explicitly prepare them for employment (combining academic classes and practical experience) get better-paying jobs than those given a general curriculum (Eichhorst et al., 2012). That does not usually happen in the United States: Students who decide to enter the job market typically leave school or college without explicit preparation.

One problem in the United States is that many parents and teachers believe that every student should graduate and then go on to college. Some adolescents resist adult pressure by failing. At the other extreme, many students with high grades and test scores do not enroll for reasons other than ability.

Encouragement and opportunity varies from place to place. That may explain why students who entered ninth grade with high achievement scores in two major cities in neighboring states (Albuquerque, New Mexico and Fort Worth, Texas) had markedly different rates of college enrollment (83 percent compared to 58 percent) (Center for Education Policy, 2012).

THINK CRITICALLY: Is it more important to prepare high school students for jobs or for colleges?

The data present a dilemma. Suggesting that a student should *not* go to college may be racist, classist, sexist, or worse. On the other hand, many students who begin college do not graduate, so they lose time and gain debt when they could have advanced in a vocation. Everyone agrees that adolescents need to be educated for life as well as employment, but it is difficult to decide what that means.

MEASURING PRACTICAL COGNITION Employers usually provide on-the-job training, which is much more specific and current than what high schools provide. They hope their future employees will have learned in secondary school how to think, explain, write, concentrate, and get along with other people.

As one executive of Boeing (which hired 33,000 new employees in two years) wrote:

> We believe that professional success today and in the future is more likely for those who have practical experience, work well with others, build strong relationships, and are able to think and do, not just look things up on the Internet.
>
> *[Stephens & Richey, 2013, p. 314]*

Those skills are hard to measure, especially on national high-stakes tests or on the two international tests explained in Chapter 7, the PIRLS and the TIMSS.

A third set of international tests, the **PISA (Programme for International Student Assessment),** was designed to measure students' ability to apply what they have learned. The PISA is taken by 15-year-olds, an age chosen because some 15-year-olds are close to the end of their formal school career. The questions are written to be practical, measuring knowledge that might apply at home or on the job.

PISA (Programme for International Student Assessment)
An international test taken by 15-year-olds in 50 nations to measure problem solving and cognition in daily life.

For example, among the 2012 math questions on the PISA is this one:

> Chris has just received her car driving license and wants to buy her first car.
> The table below shows the details of four cars she finds at a local car dealer.

Model	Alpha	Bolte	Castel	Dezal
Year	2003	2000	2001	1999
Advertised price (zeds)	4800	4450	4250	3990
Distance travelled (kilometers)	105 000	115 000	128 000	109 000
Engine capacity (liters)	1.79	1.796	1.82	1.783

> What car's engine capacity is the smallest?
>
> A. Alpha   B. Bolte   C. Castel   D. Dezal

For that and the other questions on the PISA, the math is simple—most 10-year-olds can do it; no calculus, calculators, or complex formulas required. However, almost half of the 15-year-olds worldwide, including 20 percent in the top nations of Hong Kong and Singapore, got that question wrong. (The answer is D.)

One problem is decimals: Some students do not remember how to interpret them when a practical question, not an academic one, is asked. Another problem on this question is that distance traveled and price are irrelevant, yet many students are distracted by them.

Overall, the U.S. students perform lower on the PISA compared to many other nations. In the 2012 assessments, U.S. scores are markedly below 27 other educational systems, below the PISA average in science and math, and they are just about average in reading. International analysis finds that the following items correlate with high achievement (OECD, 2010, p. 4):

1. Leaders, parents, and citizens value education overall, with individualized approaches to learning so that all students learn what they need.

2. Standards are high and clear, so every student knows what he or she must do, with a "focus on the acquisition of complex, higher-order thinking skills."

3. Teachers and administrators are valued, and they are given "considerable discretion" in determining content and sufficient salary as well as time for collaboration.

4. Learning is prioritized "across the entire educational system," with high-quality teachers working in the most challenging environments.

The PISA and international comparisons of high-school dropout rates suggest that U.S. secondary education can be improved, especially for those who do not go to college. One complication is that adolescents themselves vary: Some are thoughtful, some are impulsive, some are analytic, some are egocentric. All of them need personal attention.

A study of student emotional and academic engagement from the fifth to the eighth grade found that, as expected, the overall average was a slow and steady decline of engagement, but a distinctive group (about 18 percent) were highly engaged throughout while another distinctive group (about 5 percent) experienced precipitous disengagement year by year (Li & Lerner, 2011). The 18 percent are likely to do well in high school; the 5 percent are likely to drop out. Schools and teachers need many strategies if they hope to reach every adolescent.

Now let us consider a general conclusion for this chapter. The cognitive skills that boost national economic development and personal happiness are creativity, flexibility, relationship building, and analytic ability. Whether or not an adolescent is college-bound, those skills are exactly what the adolescent mind can develop—with proper education and guidance.

Every cognitive theorist and researcher believes that adolescents' logical, social, and creative potential is not always realized, but that it can be. Does that belief end this chapter on a hopeful note?

WHAT HAVE YOU LEARNED?

1. What characteristics of middle schools make them more difficult for students than elementary schools?

2. How does the teacher–student relationship change from primary to secondary school?

3. How does puberty affect a person's ability to learn?

4. How do beliefs about intelligence affect motivation and learning?

5. What evidence is there that standards for high school education are rising?

6. What are the advantages and disadvantages of high-stakes testing?

7. Why do U.S. high schools strive to prepare everyone for college?

8. What do high school students who do not go to college need to learn?

9. How does the PISA differ from other international tests?

10. What characteristics are shared by nations with high PISA scores?

SUMMARY

Puberty

1. Puberty refers to the various changes that transform a child's body into an adult one. A sequence of biochemical signals from the pituitary gland to the hypothalamus to the adrenal glands increases production of testosterone, estradiol, and various other hormones, which in turn cause the body to develop.

2. Hormones regulate daily and seasonal body rhythms. In adolescence, these may result in sleep deprivation because high schools open early and the natural circadian rhythm keeps teenagers wide awake at night.

3. Puberty can begin as early as age 8 and as late as 14, but most often begins between ages 10 and 13. Genes, gender, body fat, and family stress all contribute to this variation in timing, with girls generally beginning puberty before boys.

4. Adolescents who reach puberty earlier or later than their friends experience additional stresses. Early maturation may be especially difficult for girls, whereas culture and cohort influence how early or late maturation affects boys.

5. In the growth spurt, every part of the body grows rapidly. Peak weight usually precedes peak height, which is then followed by peak muscle growth.

6. Males and females develop differently at adolescence, not only in reproductive potential (primary sexual characteristics) but also in body shape, breasts, voice, body hair, and other secondary sexual characteristics.

7. Body image is a concern of many adolescents, who worry about how other people perceive them. They may diet irrationally instead of eating a balanced diet, which can often result in calcium and iron deficiency.

8. Although anorexia, bulimia, and binge eating disorder are not usually diagnosed until early adulthood, their precursors are evident during adolescence. The origins are genetic and familial as well as cultural.

Thinking, Fast and Slow

9. Various parts of the brain develop during adolescence. The regions dedicated to emotional arousal (including the limbic system) mature before those that regulate and rationalize emotion (the prefrontal cortex). Consequently, many adolescents are quick to react and take risks. Depending on specifics, this may be beneficial.

10. Cognition in early adolescence may be egocentric, a kind of self-centered thinking. Adolescent egocentrism gives rise to the personal fable, the invincibility fable, and the imaginary audience.

11. *Formal operational thought* is Piaget's term for the last of his four periods of cognitive development, in which adolescents are no longer earthbound and concrete in their thinking. They prefer to speculate instead of focusing on reality. They develop hypotheses and explore, using deductive reasoning.

12. Intuitive thinking becomes stronger during adolescence, often overwhelming the analytic thinking that also develops. Few teenagers always use logic, although they are capable of doing so. Dual processing is evident.

13. Adolescents use technology, particularly the Internet (via smartphones, laptops, and tablets), more than people of any other age. This advances learning, including access to more information than was available a few decades ago. Stronger friendships and a wider social circle are additional benefits.

14. However, adolescents sometimes use cell phones and instant messaging for cyberbullying or sexting, both of which may be more harmful than senders realize. Adults have two other worries—online predators and Internet addiction—but those concerns are exaggerated.

Teaching and Learning

15. Achievement in secondary education—after primary education (grade school) and before tertiary education (college)—correlates with the health and wealth of individuals and nations.

16. In middle school, many students tend to be bored, difficult to teach, and hurtful to one another. One reason may be that middle schools are not structured to accommodate egocentrism or social learning. Students' beliefs about intelligence may also affect how much they study and pay attention.

17. Education in high school emphasizes formal operational thinking, sometimes to the detriment of applied cognition as measured by the PISA, an international test. In the United States, the demand for high standards has led to high-stakes tests.

18. Student cognitive needs in high school are diverse. Schools that accommodate every student combine personal attention and intellectual challenge.

KEY TERMS

puberty (p. 315)
menarche (p. 316)
spermarche (p. 316)
pituitary (p. 316)
adrenal glands (p. 316)
gonads (p. 317)
estradiol (p. 317)
testosterone (p. 317)
circadian rhythm (p. 318)
secular trend (p. 320)

growth spurt (p. 322)
primary sex characteristics
(p. 323)
secondary sex characteristics
(p. 323)
body image (p. 324)
anorexia nervosa (p. 325)
bulimia nervosa (p. 325)
formal operational thought
(p. 329)

adolescent egocentrism (p. 330)
personal fable (p. 330)
invincibility fable (p. 330)
imaginary audience (p. 330)
hypothetical thought (p. 332)
deductive reasoning (p. 332)
inductive reasoning (p. 332)
dual-process model (p. 333)
intuitive thought (p. 335)
analytic thought (p. 335)

cyberbullying (p. 338)
secondary education (p. 341)
middle school (p. 341)
entity theory of intelligence
(p. 343)
incremental theory of
intelligence (p. 343)
high-stakes test (p. 344)
PISA (Programme for
International Student
Assessment) (p. 346)

APPLICATIONS

1. Visit a fifth-, sixth-, or seventh-grade class. Note variations in the size and maturity of the students. Do you see any patterns related to gender, ethnicity, body fat, or self-confidence?

2. Ask several of your friends about their memories of menarche or spermarche, including their memories of others' reactions. Analyze the connections between body changes and emotional reactions.

3. Talk to a teenager about politics, families, school, religion, or any other topic that might reveal the way that young person thinks. What do you hear that reflects adolescent cognition, such as egocentrism, intuitive thinking, or formal thought?

4. Think of a life-changing decision you have made. How did logic and emotion interact? What might have changed if you had given the matter more thought—or less?

ANNA WEHMEYER · GERMANY/GETTY IMAGES

CHAPTER OUTLINE

ADOLESCENCE
The Social World

CHAPTER 10

WHAT WILL YOU KNOW?

- Why might a teenager be a jock one year and a nerd the next?
- Should parents back off when their teenager disputes every rule, wish, or suggestion they make?
- Which should adults worry about more, teen suicide or juvenile delinquency?
- Why are adolescents forbidden to drink and smoke, but adults are allowed to do so?

It's not easy being a teenager, as the previous chapter makes clear, but neither is it easy being the parent of one. Sometimes I was too lax. For example, once my daughter came home late; I was worried and angry, but I did not think about punishing her until she asked, "How long am I grounded?" And sometimes I was too strict. For years I insisted that my daughters and their friends wash the dinner dishes, until all four daughters said that none of their friends had such mean mothers.

At times, parents like me ricochet from strict to permissive. When our children were infants, my husband and I had discussed how we would react when they became teenagers: We were ready to be firm, united, and consistent regarding illicit drugs, unsafe sex, and serious lawbreaking.

More than a decade later, when our children actually reached that stage, none of those issues appeared. Instead, unanticipated challenges caused us to react, sometimes in ways that surprised us. My husband said, "I knew they would become teenagers. I didn't expect us to become parents of teenagers."

This chapter is about adolescents' behavior and their relationships with friends, parents, and the larger society. It begins with identity and ends with drugs, both of which may seem to be the result of personal choice but actually are strongly affected by other people. I realize now that my children's actions and my reactions were influenced by my personal history (I washed family dishes) and by their current norms (their friends did not). ■

Identity

Psychosocial development during adolescence is often understood as a search for a consistent understanding of oneself. Self-expression and self-concept become increasingly important at puberty. Each young person wants to know, "Who am I?"

According to Erik Erikson, life's fifth psychosocial crisis is **identity versus role confusion:** Working through the complexities of finding one's own identity is the primary task of adolescence (Erikson, 1968/1994). He said this crisis is resolved with **identity achievement,** when adolescents have reconsidered the goals and values of their parents and culture, accepting some and discarding others, forging their own identity.

identity versus role confusion
Erikson's term for his fifth stage of development, in which the person tries to figure out "Who am I?" but is confused as to which of many possible roles to adopt.

identity achievement
Erikson's term for the attainment of identity, or the point at which a person understands who he or she is as a unique individual, in accord with past experiences and future plans. This includes many identities—religions, sexual-gender, political-ethnic, and vocational.

No Role Confusion These are high school students in Junior ROTC training camp. For many youths who cannot afford college, the military offers a temporary identity, complete with haircut, uniform, and comrades.

role confusion
A situation in which people do not seem to know or care about their identity. (Sometimes called *identity diffusion*.)

foreclosure
Erikson's term for premature identity formation, when a person adopts parents' or society's roles and values wholesale, without questioning or analysis.

moratorium
In Erikson's identity stage, a socially acceptable way to postpone achievement. Going to college is a common example.

 LaunchPad

Video Activity: Adolescence Around the World: Rites of Passage presents a comparison of adolescence initiation customs in industrialized and developing societies.

THINK CRITICALLY: Since identity is formed lifelong, has your identity changed in the past five years?

The result is neither wholesale rejection nor unquestioning acceptance of social norms (Côté, 2009). With their new autonomy, teenagers maintain continuity with the past so that they can move to the future.

Each person must achieve his or her own identity. Simply adopting parental norms does not work, because the social context of each generation differs.

Not Yet Achieved

Erikson inspired thousands of researchers. Notable among them was James Marcia, who described and measured four specific ways young people cope with the identity crisis: (1) role confusion, (2) foreclosure, (3) moratorium, and finally (4) identity achievement (Marcia, 1966).

Over the past half-century, major psychosocial shifts have lengthened the duration of adolescence and made identity achievement more complex. However, the above three precursors to identity achievement (confusion, foreclosure, moratorium) still seem evident (Kroger & Marcia, 2011).

Role confusion is the opposite of identity achievement. It is characterized by lack of commitment to any goals or values. Erikson originally called this *identity diffusion* to emphasize that some adolescents seem diffuse, unfocused, and unconcerned about their future. Perhaps worse, adolescents in role confusion see no goals or purpose in their lives, and thus they flounder, unable to move forward (Hill et al., 2013).

Identity **foreclosure** occurs when, in order to avoid the confusion of not knowing who they are, young people accept traditional roles and values (Marcia, 1966; Marcia et al., 1993). They might follow customs transmitted from their parents or culture, never exploring alternatives. Or they might foreclose on an oppositional, *negative identity*—the direct opposite of whatever their parents want—again without thoughtful questioning. Foreclosure is comfortable. For many, it is a temporary shelter, to be followed by more exploration (Meeus, 2011).

A more mature shelter is **moratorium,** a time-out that includes some exploration, either in breadth (trying many things) or in depth (following one path but with a tentative, temporary commitment) (Meeus, 2011). In high school, a student might become focused on playing in a band, not expecting this to be a lifelong career. A few years later, during emerging adulthood, someone might choose a moratorium by signing up for two years in the army. Moratoria are more common after age 18, because some maturity is required to reject some paths while choosing others (Kroger et al., 2010).

Several aspects of the search for identity, especially sexual and vocational identity, take longer and have become more complicated than they were when Erikson described them. Fifty years ago, the drive to become independent and autonomous was thought to be "one of the key normative psychosocial developmental issues of adolescence" (Zimmer-Gembeck & Collins, 2003, p. 177). That task remains and adolescents still seek identity, but "studies among adults revealed that identity is a lifelong process" (Meeus, 2011).

Four Arenas of Identity Formation

Erikson (1968/1994) highlighted four aspects of identity: religious, political, vocational, and sexual. Terminology and emphasis have changed for all four, as has timing. In fact, if an 18-year-old is no longer open to new possibilities in any of these four areas, that may indicate foreclosure, not achievement—and identity might shift again.

None of these four identities occurs in social isolation: Parents and peers are influential, as detailed later in this chapter, and the ever-changing *chronosystem* (historical context) makes identity dynamic. A crucial question is whether the adolescent ponders possibilities and actively makes a choice, thus achieving identity, or whether the adolescent responds to external pressures (Lillevoll et al., 2013), either conforming or rebelling, which signifies foreclosure.

RELIGIOUS IDENTITY For most adolescents, their *religious identity* is similar to that of their parents and community. Few adolescents totally reject religion if they've grown up following a particular faith, especially if they have a good relationship with their parents (Kim-Spoon et al., 2012).

Past parental practices influence adolescent religious identity, although some adolescents express that identity in ways that their parents did not anticipate: A Muslim girl might start to wear a headscarf, a Catholic boy might study for the priesthood, or a Baptist teenager might join a Pentecostal youth group, each surprising their less devout parents.

Such new practices are relatively minor, not a new religious identity. Thus, almost no young Muslim converts to Judaism, and almost no teenage Baptist becomes Hindu—although that might occur in adulthood. Most adolescents question beliefs because cognitive maturation fosters analytic thinking, but few teenagers have a crisis of faith unless unusual circumstances propel it (King & Roeser, 2009).

POLITICAL IDENTITY Parents also influence their children's *political identity*. In the twenty-first century in the United States, party identification is weakening, with more adults saying they are independent rather than Republican, Democrat, or any other party. Their teenage children reflect their lack of party affiliation; some proudly say they do not care about politics, echoing their parents without realizing it.

For everyone, political views are heavily influenced by parents and their culture, with current teenagers somewhat less conservative than their parents (Taylor, 2014). Actually changing one's political identity, if it occurs, is more likely in adulthood

Same Situation, Far Apart: Chosen, Saved, or Just Another Teenager? An Orthodox Jewish boy lighting Hanukkah candles in Israel and an evangelical Christian girl at a religious rally in Michigan are much alike, despite distance and appearance. Many teenagers express such strong religious devotion that outsiders consider them fanatics.

A Person, Not a Stereotype In the United States in 2015, the identity crisis became manifest with massive marches like the one shown here in Madison, Wisconsin, after no charges were filed against police officer Matt Kenny, who killed 19-year-old Tony Robinson.

OBSERVATION QUIZ

Do you see evidence of religious identity? (see answer page 356) ➤

PHOTO BY SCOTT OLSON/GETTY IMAGES

than adolescence. For example, Hillary Clinton's parents were Republican and she was a Young Republican at age 17, not becoming a Democrat until age 21.

Related to political identity is ethnic identity, not a topic discussed by Erikson. Historical changes over the past few decades have made ethnic identity crucial for adolescents in the United States (Rivas-Drake et al., 2014). High school senior Natasha Scott "just realized that my race is something I have to think about." Her mother is Asian and her father is African American, which had not been a concern of hers as she was growing up. However, her college applications required choices regarding ethnic identity (Saulny & Steinberg, 2011).

Natasha is not the only one. In the United States and Canada, about half of all adolescents are of non-European heritage, often with ancestors of more than one ethnic group. Although the census lumps all people of African, or Asian, or Latin American backgrounds together, teenagers forging their personal identity become more specific.

Hispanic American youth must figure out their personal identity in relation to, for example, having grandparents from Mexico, Peru, or Cuba, and/or California, Texas, or New York. Many also have ancestors from both Spain and Africa. Similarly, European American teenagers must decide the significance of having grandparents from, say, Italy, Ireland, or Sweden. No teenager adopts, wholesale, the identity of their ancestors, but all must incorporate, somehow, their family history. Often ethnic identity blends into political identity.

VOCATIONAL IDENTITY *Vocational identity* originally meant envisioning oneself in a particular occupation. Choosing a future career made sense for teenagers a century ago, when most girls became housewives and most boys became farmers, small businessmen, or factory workers. Those few in professions were mostly generalists (doctors practiced family medicine, lawyers handled all kinds of cases, teachers taught all subjects).

Obviously, such early vocational identity is no longer appropriate. No teenager can realistically choose among the tens of thousands of careers available today; most adults change vocations (not just employers) many times.

Vocational identity takes years to establish, with specific skills and knowledge best learned on the job. Currently, vocational identity is dynamic and flexible:

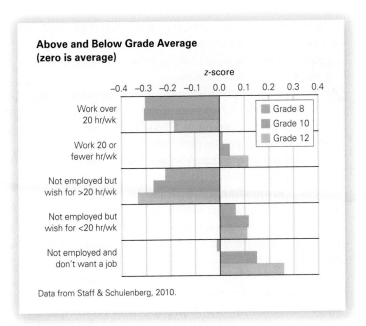

Above and Below Grade Average (zero is average)

z-score

| −0.4 −0.3 −0.2 −0.1 0.0 0.1 0.2 0.3 0.4 |

- Work over 20 hr/wk
- Work 20 or fewer hr/wk
- Not employed but wish for >20 hr/wk
- Not employed but wish for <20 hr/wk
- Not employed and don't want a job

Grade 8
Grade 10
Grade 12

Data from Staff & Schulenberg, 2010.

FIGURE 10.1 Don't Think About It There was a time when high school employment correlated with saving for college and lifetime success. No longer. The surprise is that even wanting a full-time job (and the extra income that would bring) reduces achievement—or is it the other way around? These are *z*-scores, or standard scores, which show the difference from the group average. The effect is not large, but it is significant.

People eventually find a career or, even better, a calling that can lead to several jobs (Skorikov & Vondracek, 2011).

Although some adults hope that having a job will keep teenagers out of trouble as they identify as workers, the opposite may occur (Staff & Schulenberg, 2010). Research that controlled for SES found that adolescents who are employed more than 20 hours a week during the school year tend to quit school, fight with parents, smoke cigarettes, and hate their jobs—not only when they are teenagers but also later on.

Typically, teenagers with a paycheck spend their wages on clothes, cars, drugs, fast food, and music, not on supporting their families or saving for college (Mortimer, 2013). Grades fall: Employment interferes with homework and school attendance (see Figure 10.1).

SEXUAL IDENTITY The fourth type of identity, described by both Erikson and Marcia, is *sexual identity*. As you remember from Chapter 6, for social scientists *sex* and *sexual* refer to biological characteristics, whereas *gender* refers to cultural and social attributes that differentiate males and females. A half-century ago, Erikson and other theorists thought of the two sexes as opposites (Miller & Simon, 1980). They assumed that adolescents who were confused about sexual identity would soon adopt "proper" male or female roles (Erikson, 1968/1994; A. Freud, 1958/2000).

Thus, adolescence was once a time for "gender intensification," when people increasingly identified as male or female (Priess et al., 2009). No longer. Erikson's term *sexual identity* has been replaced by **gender identity** (Denny & Pittman, 2007), which refers primarily to a person's self-definition as male, female, or transgender.

Gender identity often (but not always) begins with the person's biological sex and leads to a gender role, but many adolescents (with the hypothetical reasoning that Piaget described) question aspects of gender roles. This often troubles their parents and grandparents.

Gender roles once meant that only men were employed; they were *breadwinners* (good providers) and women were *housewives* (married to their houses). As women entered the labor market, gender roles expanded but were still strong (nurse/doctor, secretary/businessman, pink collar/blue collar). Even today, women in every nation do far more child care and elder care than men. There is a "slow but steady pace of change in gender divisions of domestic labor . . . combined with a persistence of gender differences and inequalities" (Doucet, 2015, p. 224).

gender identity
A person's acceptance of the roles and behaviors that are associated with the biological categories of male and female.

Now, gender roles are changing everywhere. The speed and specifics of the change vary dramatically by culture and cohort, which makes gender identity complicated for many youth. It is particularly complex for adolescents who feel their sex at birth is not their true gender identity.

Among Western psychiatrists in former decades, people who had "a strong and persistent cross-gender identification" were said to have *gender identity disorder,* a serious diagnosis according to DSM-IV. However, DSM-5 instead describes *gender dysphoria*, when people are distressed at their biological sex.

This is not simply a change in words: A "disorder" means something is amiss with the individual, no matter how he or she feels about it, whereas in dysphoria the problem is in the distress, which can be mitigated by social conditions and/or by perception (Zucker et al., 2013).

No matter what gender identity a young person develops, every teenager experiences a surge of sexual hormones and most adjust to that. As Erikson recognized, although the hormones are universal, many adolescents are confused regarding when, how, and with whom to express their sexuality.

Some foreclose by exaggerating male or female roles; others seek a moratorium by trying to be asexual. Some who feel their gender identity is fragile aspire to a gender-stereotypic career (Sinclair & Carlsson, 2013). Choosing a career to establish gender identity, rather than to follow interests and affirm values, is another reason why settling on a vocational identity during adolescence may be premature.

WHAT HAVE YOU LEARNED?

1. What is Erikson's fifth psychosocial crisis, and how is it resolved?
2. How does identity foreclosure differ from identity moratorium?
3. What has changed over the past decades regarding political identity?
4. What role do parents play as adolescents form religious and political identity?
5. Why is ethnic identity complicated for many young North Americans?
6. Why is it premature for today's adolescents to achieve vocational identity?
7. What assumptions about sexual identity did most adults hold 50 years ago?
8. Why is gender dysphoria, not gender identity disorder, described in the DSM-5?
9. What behaviors might a teenage boy do if he has foreclosed on gender identity?

Human Relationships

The adolescent's search for identity may seem self-absorbed, because each young person works to establish his or her unique self. But that does not occur in isolation.

As at every age, adolescents are social beings, dependent on other people to validate whatever identity they seek. Adults as well as peers have an impact: Relationships at home, in school, or with peers correlate with relationships in the other two areas. Likewise, conflict in one setting increases conflict and affects mood in the other settings (Timmons & Margolin, 2015; Flook & Fuligni, 2008; Chung et al. 2011).

With Adults

Adolescence is often characterized as a time when children distance themselves from their elders. That is only half true. Adult influence is less obvious but no less important.

PARENTS Parent–adolescent relationships are pivotal, not always peaceful (Laursen & Collins, 2009). Disputes are common because the drive for independence, arising from biological as well as psychological impulses and social expectations, clashes with the parents' desire for control.

Conflict peaks in early adolescence, especially with mothers. Typical are repeated, petty arguments (more nagging than fighting) about routine, day-to-day concerns such as cleanliness, clothes, chores, and schedules. Bickering and squabbling is considered normal, even necessary, primarily because adolescents are driven to seek autonomy and parents are programmed to guide and protect (Amsel & Smetana, 2011).

Each generation tends to misjudge the other, which may add to the conflict. Parents think their offspring resent them more than they actually do, and adolescents imagine their parents want to dominate them more than they actually do (Sillars et al., 2010).

Unspoken concerns need to be aired so that both generations better understand each other. Imagine a parent seeing filthy socks on the living room floor. The parent might interpret that as deliberate disrespect and react angrily to the attack, yelling "Put those socks in the hamper right now!" But perhaps the adolescent was merely egocentric and distracted, oblivious to the parent's desire for a neat house. If so, then the parent could merely sigh and put the socks in the child's room.

"So I blame you for everything—whose fault is that?"

Some bickering may indicate a healthy family, since close relationships almost always include conflict. A study of mothers and their adolescents suggested that "although too much anger may be harmful . . . some expression of anger may be adaptive" (Hofer et al., 2013, p. 276).

The parent–child relationship usually improves with time. Over the years, teenagers learn to modify their outbursts and parents increasingly grant autonomy. Parents learn to ignore most adolescent behaviors that bother them (the purple hair, the loud music) and focus on the serious ones (cigarette smoking, anorexia). By age 18, many teenagers appreciate their parents (and put their socks in the hamper) and many parents adjust to their child's independence (suggesting that every family member put his or her clothes away) (Masche, 2010).

You already know that authoritative parenting is best for children and that uninvolved parenting is worst. This continues in adolescence. Neglect is always destructive and authoritarian parenting can boomerang, resulting in teenagers who lie or leave. The effect is reciprocal: Teenagers of authoritarian parents become secretive, which makes the parents even more authoritarian (Kerr et al., 2012).

CLOSENESS WITHIN THE FAMILY More important than conflict may be family closeness, which has four aspects:

1. Communication (Do family members talk openly with one another?)
2. Support (Do they rely on one another?)
3. Connectedness (How emotionally close are they?)
4. Control (Do parents encourage or limit adolescent autonomy?)

No social scientist doubts that the first two, communication and support, are helpful, perhaps essential, for healthy development. Patterns set in place during childhood continue, ideally buffering the turbulence of adolescence (Amsel & Smetana, 2011; Laursen & Collins, 2009).

A Study in Contrasts? These two teenagers appear to be opposites: one yelling at his mother and the other conscientiously helping his father. However, adolescent moods can change in a flash, especially with parents. Later in the day, these two might switch roles.

Regarding the next two, connectedness and control, consequences vary and observers differ in what they see. How do you react to this example, written by one of my students?

> I got pregnant when I was sixteen years old, and if it weren't for the support of my parents, I would probably not have my son. And if they hadn't taken care of him, I wouldn't have been able to finish high school or attend college. My parents also helped me overcome the shame that I felt when . . . my aunts, uncles, and especially my grandparents found out that I was pregnant.
>
> *[I., personal communication]*

My student is grateful to her parents, but did teenage motherhood give her parents too much control, requiring her to depend on them instead of seeking her identity? Indeed, had they unconsciously encouraged pregnancy, by permitting her to be with her boyfriend but not explaining contraception? The child's father was no longer in her life when I knew her; was that an unhealthy disconnection?

An added complexity is that this young woman's parents had emigrated from South America. Cultural expectations affect everyone's responses, so her dependence may have been normative in her culture but not elsewhere. A longitudinal study of nonimmigrant adolescent mothers in the United States found that most (not all) fared best if their parents were supportive but did not take over child care (Borkowski et al., 2007).

Note that family relationships for this young mother, as potentially for everyone, include other relatives. In this case, the parents buffered the relationship between the 16-year-old and her grandparents, but the opposite is sometimes the case, with grandparents supporting a child when the parents do not. For many youths who feel misunderstood at home, the most influential adult advisors are other family members—older siblings, cousins, aunts and uncles, or grandparents.

Sometimes parents ask the adolescent's aunt or uncle to discuss taboo topics, such as sex or delinquency that make parents uncomfortable (Milardo, 2009). Links between teenagers and relatives are especially common in developing nations and among immigrant groups for two reasons: (1) Relatives often live together or nearby, and (2) cultural values make family central.

A related issue that is not as simple as it appears is **parental monitoring**—that is, parental knowledge about each child's whereabouts, activities, and companions.

parental monitoring
Parents' ongoing awareness of what their children are doing, where, and with whom.

Many studies have shown that parental monitoring helps adolescents become confident, well-educated adults, avoiding drugs, depression, and risky sex (Hamza & Willoughby, 2011; Criss et al., 2015).

However, researchers note that monitoring is a mutual process, with adults who care and adolescents who communicate. If the parents are cold, strict, and punitive, demands for information may provoke deception and rebellion.

Note that adolescents participate in their own monitoring: Some happily tell everyone about their activities, whereas others are secretive (Vieno et al., 2009). A "dynamic interplay between parent and child behaviors" (Abar et al., 2014, p. 2177) is particularly apparent in adolescence. Most teenagers disclose only part of the truth to their parents, selectively omitting whatever would meet disapproval (Brown & Bakken, 2011).

Thus, monitoring may signify a mutual, close interaction (Kerr et al., 2010). However, monitoring may be harmful when it derives from suspicion. Especially in early adolescence, if adolescents resist telling their parents much of anything, they are more likely to develop problems such as aggression against peers, lawbreaking, and drug abuse (Laird et al., 2013). But lack of communication may be the symptom, not the cause.

If a parent asks "tell me about that party last night," the adolescent may reply "it was okay" or "nothing happened." Disclosure may occur, instead, when the parent is tired, busy, or distracted—such as at bedtime, or in the middle of making dinner, or while driving to school. Whenever the teenager begins to disclose, good monitors are ready to listen.

Control can backfire. Adolescents expect adults to exert some control, especially over moral issues. However, overly restrictive and controlling parenting correlates with many problems, including severe depression (Brown & Bakken, 2011). Further, adults may restrict the wrong activity. One researcher laments that parents sometimes refuse to let their children use social media, inadvertently limiting supportive friendship (boyd, 2014).

Video: Parenting in Adolescence examines how family structure can help or hinder parent–teen relationships.

THINK CRITICALLY: When do parents forbid an activity they should approve of, or ignore a behavior that should alarm them?

With Peers

Adolescents rely on peers to help them navigate the physical changes of puberty, the intellectual challenges of high school, and the social changes of leaving childhood. Friendships are important at every stage, but during early adolescence popularity (not just friendship) is especially coveted (LaFontana & Cillessen, 2010).

A CASE TO STUDY

An Ignorant Parent—Me!

Adults are sometimes oblivious to adolescents' desire for respect from their contemporaries. My own case is presented here.

- My oldest daughter wore the same pair of jeans in tenth grade, day after day. She washed them each night by hand and asked me to put them in the dryer early each morning. I did. My husband was bewildered. "Is this some weird female ritual?" he asked. Years later, she explained that she was afraid that if she wore different pants each day, her classmates would think she cared about her clothes and then criticize her choices.

- My second daughter, at 16, pierced her ears for the third time. When I asked if this meant she would do drugs, she laughed at my naiveté. I later saw that many of her friends had multiple holes in their earlobes.

- At age 15, my third daughter was diagnosed with Hodgkin's disease, cancer. My husband and I weighed opinions from four physicians, each explaining treatment that would minimize the risk of death. She had other priorities: "I don't care what you choose, as long as I keep my hair." (Now her health is good, and her hair grew back.)

- My youngest, in sixth grade, refused to wear her jacket, even in midwinter. I thought the problem may have been egocentric concern for appearance, so I took her shopping and let her buy exactly the jacket she wanted—not the one I would have chosen. That jacket was almost never worn, despite freezing temperatures. Not until high school did she tell me she did it so that her classmates would think she was tough.

In retrospect, I am amazed that I was unaware of the power of peers.

Sometimes adults conceptualize adolescence as a tug-of-war between peers and parents, with the peers winning. This is not accurate. Relationships with parents are the model for peer relationships, and parental guidelines, examples, and respect make constructive peer relationships likely. The only common tug-of-war regards with whom the teen spends time. On this, peers have the strongest pull.

Parents and peers are often mutually reinforcing, although many adolescents downplay the influence of their parents and many parents are unaware of the influence of peers, as I was. Only when parents are harsh or neglectful does peer influence reign alone (Brown & Bakken, 2011).

Closeness to parents protects adolescent self-esteem. However, if adolescents have a poor relationship with parents, then it is particularly beneficial for the adolescent to have some good friends (Birkeland et al., 2014).

Helpful friends can be of either gender. Although same-sex friends are often preferred, many adolescents have members of the other sex as close friends. Other-sex friends increase the likelihood of drug use and early romance, but much depends on the social context: Parents should not assume that a good friend of the other sex means trouble (C. Lam et al., 2014).

peer pressure
When people of the same age group encourage particular behavior, dress, and attitude. This is usually considered negative, when peers encourage behavior that is contrary to norms or morals, but can also be positive.

PEER PRESSURE Adults worry about **peer pressure;** that is, they fear that peers will push innocent children to use drugs, break laws, and so on. But peers can be more helpful than harmful, especially in early adolescence, if biological and social stresses are overwhelming. Some adolescents are more influenced by peers than

More Familiar Than Foreign? Even in cultures with strong and traditional family influence, teenagers choose to be with peers whenever they can. These boys play at Cherai Beach in India.

OBSERVATION QUIZ
What evidence do you see that traditional norms remain in this culture? (see answer, page 362) ➤

EYESWIDEOPEN/GETTY IMAGES

others, because genes and early experiences differ (Prinstein et al., 2011; Choukas-Bradley et al., 2014). In later adolescence, teenagers are less susceptible to peer pressure, either positive or negative (Monahan et al., 2009).

Peers are particularly needed by adolescents of minority and immigrant groups as they strive to achieve ethnic identity, attaining their own firm self-concept (not confused or foreclosed). They need to accept who they are—glad to be Asian, African, Latino, and so on.

The larger society may promulgate stereotypes and prejudice, and that may make teenagers depressed. Ideally, parents combat that with racial socialization, describing ethnic heroes and reasons to be proud (Umana-Taylor et al., 2010; Priest et

Everyday Danger After cousins Alex and Arthur, ages 16 and 20, followed family wishes to shovel snow around their Denver home, they followed their inner impulses and jumped from the roof. Few adolescents can afford some of the risk-taking sports that emerging adults love, but many leap into risks that few adults would dare.

al., 2014). Then peers of the same group bolster self-esteem, allowing teenagers to withstand discrimination and criticize their parents while maintaining their integrity.

For example, a study of Hispanic adolescents found that, compared to those who did not notice discrimination, those who experienced ethnic prejudice were more likely to abuse drugs. However, their risk of drug abuse was reduced if they proudly identified as Hispanic (Grigsby et al., 2014).

The particular peers who are most influential are those with the adolescent at the moment. This was found in a study in which all the eleventh-graders in several public schools in Los Angeles were offered a free, online SAT prep course (worth $200). They could register for the course on a paper the organizers distributed (Bursztyn & Jensen, 2014). Students were *not* allowed to talk before deciding whether or not to accept the offer, so they did not know that although all the papers had identical, detailed descriptions of the SAT program, one word differed.

The two versions were:

> *Your decision to sign up for the course will be kept completely private from everyone, except the other students in the room.*

or:

> *Your decision to sign up for the course will be kept completely private from everyone, including the other students in the room.*

A marked difference was found if students thought their classmates would learn of their decision, with the honors students more likely to sign up and the non-honors students less likely to sign up if they thought their classmates would know. To make sure this was a peer effect, not just divergent motivation and ability between honors and non-honors students, the researchers compared 107 students who took exactly two honors classes and several non-honors ones.

When the decisions of these 107 were said to be unknown to classmates, acceptance rates were similar (72 and 79 percent) no matter which class they were in at the moment of the sign up. But if they thought their classmates might know their decision, imagined peer pressure affected them. For those students who were

Social or Solitary? Adults have criticized the Internet for allowing teenagers to keep friends at a distance. By contrast, sitting around an outdoor fire is romanticized as a bonding experience. Which is more accurate? Are these two girls about to talk about what they are reading?

PREAPPY/FLICKR RF/GETTY IMAGES

ANSWER TO OBSERVATION QUIZ
(from page 360): The girls are only observers, keeping a respectful distance. ●

enrolled in two honors classes and several non-honors ones, if they registered when they happened to be sitting in an honors class, 97 percent signed up for the SAT program. But if they were in a non-honors class, only 54 percent did so, a 43 percent difference (Bursztyn & Jensen, 2014).

SOCIAL NETWORKING You read in Chapter 9 about the dangers of technology. Remember, however, that technology is a tool. It might exacerbate depression or self-destruction but not cause it (Yom-Tov et al., 2012). "Stranger danger" is more in the adult mind than in the adolescent reality (boyd, 2014).

Indeed, technology usually brings friends together in adolescence (Mesch & Talmud, 2010). This is obvious with texting, instant messaging, and social media, but it also occurs with video games. Many games now pit one player against another or require cooperation among several players (Collins & Freeman, 2013). Technology users, including video game players, are usually at least as extraverted and socially connected as other adolescents.

Although most social networking is between friends who know each other well, the Internet may be a lifeline for teenagers who are isolated because of their sexual orientation, culture, religion, or home language. These teenagers are vulnerable to depression; technology can help.

Technology may also be vital for adolescents with special health needs. During these years, many refuse to follow special diets, take medication, see doctors, do exercises, or whatever. However, among teenagers with diabetes, some monitor their insulin via smart phone, talk to the doctor via Skype, and chat with other young people with diabetes via the Internet (Harris et al., 2012).

deviancy training
When one person shows another how to rebel against authority or social norms.

SELECTING FRIENDS Of course, peers *can* lead one another into trouble. Collectively, they may provide **deviancy training,** when one person shows another how to resist social norms (Dishion et al., 2001).

The same phenomenon occurs for many destructive behaviors. A study found that the suicide of a peer, of an admired celebrity, or of a family member, markedly increased the risk of adolescent suicide (Abrutyn & Mueller, 2014).

Especially during adolescence, the actions of other people are contagious. However, innocent teens are not corrupted by deviant peers. Adolescents choose their friends and models—not always wisely, but never randomly.

A developmental progression can be traced: The combination of "problem behavior, school marginalization, and low academic performance" at age 11 leads to gang involvement two years later, deviancy training two years after that, and violent behavior at age 18 or 19 (Dishion et al., 2010, p. 603). This cascade is not inevitable; adults need to engage marginalized 11-year-olds instead of blaming their friends years later.

To further understand the impact of peers, two concepts are helpful: *selection* and *facilitation*. Teenagers *select* friends whose values and interests they share, abandoning former friends who follow other paths. Then friends *facilitate* destructive or constructive behaviors. It is easier to do wrong ("Let's all skip school on Friday") or right ("Let's study together for the chem exam") with friends. Peer facilitation helps adolescents do things with friends that they might not do alone.

Thus, adolescents select and facilitate, choose and are chosen. Happy, energetic, and successful teens have close friends who themselves are high achievers, with no major emotional problems. The opposite also holds: Those who are drug users, sexually active, and alienated from school choose compatible friends.

A study of identical twins from ages 14 to 17 found that selection typically precedes facilitation, rather than the other way around. Those who *later* rebelled chose more lawbreaking friends at age 14 compared to their more conventional twin (Burt et al., 2009).

Research on teenage cigarette smoking also found that selection precedes peer pressure (Kiuru et al., 2010). Another study found that young adolescents tend to select peers who drink alcohol and then start drinking themselves (Osgood et al., 2013). Finally, a third study, of teenage sexual activity, again found that peer selection was crucial (van de Bongardt et al., 2014). Thus, peers provide opportunity, companions, and encouragement for what adolescents are inclined to do.

THINK CRITICALLY: Why is peer pressure thought to be much more sinister than it actually is?

With Romantic Partners

A half-century ago, Dexter Dunphy (1963) described the sequence of male–female relationships during childhood and adolescence:

1. Groups of friends, exclusively one sex or the other
2. A loose association of girls and boys, with public interactions within a crowd
3. Small mixed-sex groups of the advanced members of the crowd
4. Formation of couples, with private intimacies

Culture affects the timing and manifestation of each step on Dunphy's list, but subsequent research in many nations validates the sequence. Heterosexual youths worldwide (and even the young of other primates) avoid the other sex in childhood and are attracted to them by adulthood. Biology underlies this universal sequence, but the specific types of interaction—dating, dancing, texting, hooking up, or just hanging out—vary by cohort and culture.

The peer group is part of the process. Romantic partners, especially in early adolescence, are selected not for their individual traits as much as for the traits that peers admire. If the leader of a girls' group pairs with the leader of a boys' group, the unattached members of the two cliques tend to pair off as well.

A classic example is football players and cheerleaders: They often socialize together and then pair off with someone from the other group. Which particular football player or cheerleader is chosen depends more on availability than compatibility, which helps explain why adolescent romantic partners tend to have less in

Video: Romantic Relationships in Adolescence explores teens' attitudes and assumptions about romance and sexuality.

common, in personality and attitudes, than adult couples do (Zimmer-Gembeck & Ducat, 2010).

FIRST LOVE Teens' first romances typically occur in high school, with girls having a steady partner more often than boys do. Exclusive commitment is the ideal, but it is hard to maintain: "cheating," flirting, switching, and disloyalty are rife. Breakups are common, as are unreciprocated crushes.

All teen romances are fraught with complications, and emotions zigzag from exhilaration to despair, leading to revenge or depression. In such cases, peer support can be a lifesaver; friends help adolescents cope with romantic ups and downs (Mehta & Strough, 2009).

For adults, satisfaction with a romantic relationship is a powerful antidote to depression. However, teen romances are unlike adult ones. One study of 60 adolescent couples found that "Contrary to expectation, relationship break-up and relationship satisfaction were unrelated to changes in depressive symptoms" over a two-year period (Ha et al., 2014, p. 551). This again suggests that teen romances are less closely connected to the actual interactions and more related to the teen's overall emotional state.

Many teenage romances do not include coitus. In the United States in 2013, even though more than one-third of all tenth-grade students had experienced vaginal intercourse, about another one-third were virgins at high school graduation (see Figure 10.2). Norms vary markedly from group to group, school to school, city to city, and nation to nation.

For instance, more than twice as many high school students in Memphis than in San Francisco say they have had intercourse (60 percent versus 26 percent) (MMWR, June 13, 2014). Within every city are many subgroups, each with its own norms.

Parents have an impact. Thus, when parent–child relationships are good, girls from religious families tend to be romantically involved with boys from religious families. Their shared values typically slow down sexual activity (Kim-Spoon et al., 2012).

SAME-SEX ROMANCES Another slowdown occurs for those adolescents who are attracted to peers of the same sex. **Sexual orientation** refers to the direction of a person's erotic desires. One meaning of *orient* is to "turn toward"; thus, sexual orientation refers to whether a person is romantically attracted to (turned on by) people

Check out the Data Connections activity **Sexual Behaviors of U.S. High School Students**, which examines how sexually active teens really are.

sexual orientation
A person's sexual and romantic attraction to others of the same sex, the other sex, or both sexes.

FIGURE 10.2 Many Virgins For 30 years, the Youth Risk Behavior Survey has asked high school students from all over the United States dozens of confidential questions about their behavior. As you can see, about one-third of all students have already had sex by the ninth grade, and about one-third have not yet had sex by their senior year—a group whose ranks have been increasing. Other research finds that sexual behaviors are influenced by peers, with some groups sexually experienced by age 14 and others still virgins at age 18.

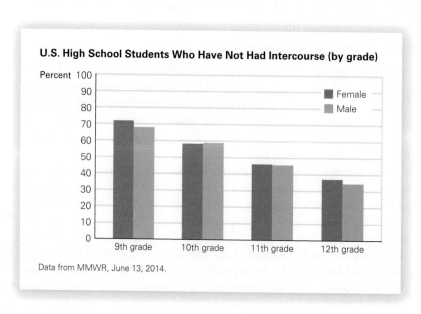

U.S. High School Students Who Have Not Had Intercourse (by grade)

Data from MMWR, June 13, 2014.

JOHNER ROYALTY-FREE/GETTY IMAGES

Girls Together These two girls from Sweden seem comfortable touching one another. Many boys of this age wouldn't want their photograph taken if they were this close together. Around the world, there are cultural and gender norms about what are acceptable expressions of affection among friends during adolescence.

of the other sex, the same sex, or both sexes. Sexual orientation can be strong, weak, overt, secret, or unconscious.

Obviously, culture and cohort are powerful. Some cultures accept youth who are gay, lesbian, bisexual, or transgender (the census in India asks people to identify as male, female, or Hijra [transgender]). Other cultures criminalize them (as do 38 of the 53 African nations), sometimes even killing them (Uganda).

Worldwide, many gay youths date members of the other sex to hide their orientation; deception puts them at risk for binge drinking, suicidal thoughts, and drug use. Those hazards are less common in cultures where same-sex partnerships are accepted (see Figure 10.3), especially when parents affirm their offspring's sexuality.

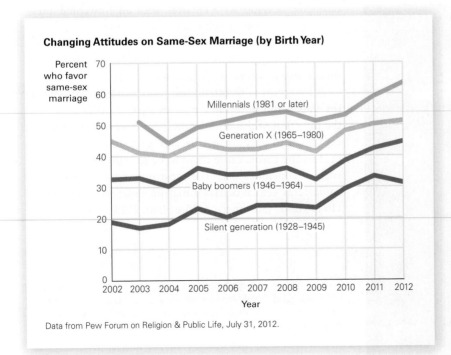

Changing Attitudes on Same-Sex Marriage (by Birth Year)

Percent who favor same-sex marriage

Millennials (1981 or later)

Generation X (1965–1980)

Baby boomers (1946–1964)

Silent generation (1928–1945)

Year

Data from Pew Forum on Religion & Public Life, July 31, 2012.

FIGURE 10.3 Young and Old Everyone knows that attitudes about same-sex relationships are changing. Less well known is that cohort differences are greater than the shift over the first decade of the twenty-first century.

At least in the United States, adolescents have similar difficulties and strengths whether they are gay or straight (Saewyc, 2011). However, lesbian, gay, transsexual, and bisexual youth are at greater risk of depression and anxiety, for reasons from every level of Bronfenbrenner's ecological approach (Mustanski et al., 2014).

Sexual orientation is surprisingly fluid during the teen years. Girls often recognize their orientation only after their first sexual experiences; many adult lesbians had other-sex relationships in adolescence (Saewyc, 2011).

In one detailed study, 10 percent of sexually active teenagers had had same-sex partners, but more than one-third of that 10 percent nonetheless identified themselves as heterosexual (Pathela & Schillinger, 2010). In that study, those most at risk of sexual violence and **sexually transmitted infections (STIs)** were those who had partners of both sexes. This specific finding is confirmed by more general studies (e.g., Russell et al., 2014).

sexually transmitted infection (STI)
An infection spread by sexual contact; includes syphilis, gonorrhea, genital herpes, chlamydia, and HIV.

SEX EDUCATION Many adolescents have strong sexual urges but minimal logic about pregnancy and disease, as might be expected from the ten-year interval between maturation of the body and of the brain. Millions of teenagers worry that they are oversexed, undersexed, or deviant, unaware that thousands, maybe millions, of people are just like them.

As a result, "students seem to waffle their way through sexually relevant encounters driven both by the allure of reward and the fear of negative consequences" (Wagner, 2011, p. 193). They have much to learn. Where do they learn it?

Many adolescents learn about sex from the media. The Internet is a common source. Unfortunately, Web sites are often frightening (featuring pictures of diseased sexual organs) or mesmerizing (containing pornography), and young adolescents are particularly naive. Further, adolescents tend to focus on what is funny or odd, not on what is accurate, because, as one young man explained, "no one wants to get a lecture whilst they are online and trying to be doing their social thing" (quoted in Evers et al., 2013, p. 269).

Media consumption peaks at puberty. The TV shows most watched by teenagers include sexual content almost seven times per hour (Steinberg & Monahan, 2011). That content is alluring: Almost never does a television character develop an STI, deal with an unwanted pregnancy, or mention (much less use) a condom.

Music and magazines may be worse. One study found that men's magazines convince teenage boys that maleness means sexual conquests (Ward et al., 2011).

Adolescents with intense exposure to sexual content on the screen and in music are more often sexually active, but the direction of this correlation is controversial. Are teenagers drawn to sexy images because they are sexually active, or does the media cause them to be sexually involved? One analysis concludes that "the most important influences on adolescents' sexual behavior may be closer to home than to Hollywood" (Sternberg & Monahan, 2011, p. 575).

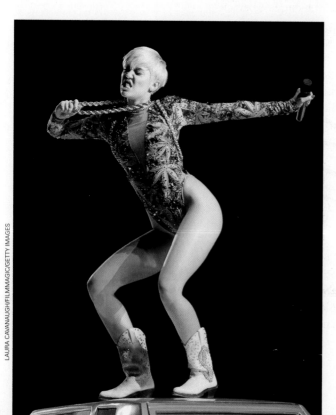

To Be a Woman Here Miley Cyrus performs for thousands of fans in Brooklyn, New York. No wonder teenagers of both sexes have difficulty reconciling their own sexual impulses with the images of their culture.

As that quote implies, sex education begins within the family. Every study finds that parental communication influences adolescents' behavior, and many programs of sex education explicitly require parental participation (Silk & Romero, 2014; J. Grossman et al., 2014). However, some parents wait too long and are uninformed about current STIs and contraception.

Parents often express clichés and generalities, unaware of their adolescents' sexuality, and adolescents conclude that parents know nothing about sex. Embarrassment, silence, and ignorance are common. An attempt to combat that is a program of sex education for parents of adolescents, which increased conversation as well as information (Colarossi et al., 2014).

It is not unusual for parents to think their own child is not sexually active while fearing that the child's social connections are far too sexual (Elliott, 2012). One study makes the point: Parents of 12-year-old girls were asked whether their daughters had hugged or kissed a boy "for a long time" or hung out with older boys (signs that sex information is urgently needed). Only 5 percent of the parents said yes, as did 38 percent of the girls (O'Donnell et al., 2008).

What should parents say? That is the wrong question, according to a longitudinal study of thousands of adolescents. Teens who were most likely to risk an STI had parents who warned them to stay away from sex.

In contrast, adolescents were more likely to remain virgins if their relationship with their parents was good. Specific information was less important than open communication (Deptula et al., 2010). Parents should not avoid talking about sex, but honest conversation provides better protection than specifics (Hicks et al., 2013).

Especially when parents are silent, forbidding, or vague, adolescent sexual behavior is strongly influenced by peers. Boys learn about sex from other boys (Henry et al., 2012), girls from other girls, with the strongest influence being what peers say they have done, not something abstract or moral (Choukas-Bradley et al., 2014).

Partners also teach each other. However, their lessons are more about pleasure than consequences: Most U.S. adolescent couples do not decide together *before* they have sex how they will prevent pregnancy and disease, and what they will do if their prevention efforts fail. Adolescents were asked with whom they discussed sexual issues. Friends were the most common confidants, then parents, and last of all dating partners. Indeed, only half of them had *ever* discussed anything about sex with their romantic partner (Widman et al., 2014).

Most parents of pre-adolescent children would like some sex education in school, a sentiment almost universally held by parents of adolescents. This would not only save the parents from seeming ignorant (contraception and STIs are not what they were two decades ago) but would also protect against misinformation from peers and the media. However, often sex education in schools is very limited. On this an international perspective is useful (Schalet, 2011).

Teachers in most northern European middle schools discuss masturbation, same-sex romance, oral and anal sex, abortion, and various methods of contraception. Although most students in the United States have some sex education, especially on the dire consequences of STIs, topics routinely covered in Scandinavian schools are rarely covered in the United States, even in high school.

Rates of teenage pregnancy in European nations are less than half those in the United States. Perhaps curriculum is the reason, although schools are affected by society, and cultural differences regarding sexual values and behavior are vast. Nonetheless, in non-European nations as well, students who learn about sexual activity in school are less likely to have early, unprotected sex than students in nations without sex education (Fonner et al., 2014).

The Data Connections activity **Major Sexually Transmitted Infections: Some Basics** offers more information about the causes, symptoms, and rates of various STIs.

A VIEW FROM SCIENCE

Sex Education in School

Within the United States, the timing and content of sex education vary by state and community. Among the variations:

- Some middle and high schools provide comprehensive education, free condoms, and medical treatment; others provide nothing.
- The American Academy of Pediatrics, in 2013, recommended condom distribution in school, but many school board members disagree.
- Some schools begin sex education in the sixth grade; others wait until senior year of high school.
- Some middle school sex-education programs successfully increase condom use and delay sexual activity, but other programs have no apparent impact

[Hamilton et al., 2013; Kirby & Laris, 2009]

One controversy has been whether sexual abstinence should be taught as the only acceptable strategy. Of course, abstaining from sex (including oral and anal sex) prevents STIs and pregnancy, but longitudinal data on abstinence-only education, four to six years after the class, are disappointing. For instance, in careful research with matched experimental and control groups, about half the students in both abstinence-only and comprehensive sex education groups experienced intercourse by age 16 (Trenholm et al., 2007).

In that research, students in the abstinence group were found to know slightly less about preventing disease and pregnancy, but every measured sexual activity was similar in both groups. A more recent meta-analysis again found that abstinence-only education was no better, and probably worse, than comprehensive programs at slowing down sexual risk (Goesling et al., 2014)

A developmental concern is that for the past thirty years adolescents in the United States have more STIs and unwanted pregnancies than adolescents in other developed nations. In some European nations, sex education is part of the curriculum even before puberty, although politics sometimes clash with comprehensive, early sex education in every nation (Parker et al., 2009).

The problem may be that sex education does not consider what we know about adolescent thinking and psychology. Teachers present morals and facts, but teens respond to customs, impulses, and emotions. Sexual behavior does not spring from the prefrontal cortex but from deep within the brain. Knowing how and why to use a condom does not guarantee a wise choice when passions run high and the pain of social rejection looms.

Consequently, effective sex education must engage emotions more than logic, and it must include role-playing with other teens and frank discussions with parents (J. Grossman et al., 2014; Suleiman & Brindis, 2014). Apparently, sex education in school may be beneficial, but involvement of peers and parents is pivotal.

GODDARD, CLIVE/CARTOONSTOCK.COM

"Smirking or non-smirking?"

WHAT HAVE YOU LEARNED?

1. How does the influence of peers and parents differ for adolescents?
2. When, and about what, are parents and adolescents most likely to argue?
3. When is parental monitoring of adolescent activity beneficial and when is it not helpful?
4. Why do many adults misunderstand the role of peer pressure?
5. How do parents and society affect an adolescent's development of ethnic identity?
6. How do friends help adolescents?
7. How do adolescents choose romantic partners?
8. How does culture affect sexual orientation?
9. From whom do adolescents usually learn about sex?
10. What are national variations in sex education in schools?

Sadness and Anger

Adolescence is usually a wonderful time, perhaps better for current generations than for any earlier cohort. Nonetheless, serious troubles plague about 20 percent of youths. For instance, one specific survey of over ten thousand 13- to 17-year-olds in the United States using the categories of the DSM-IV found that 23 percent had a psychological disorder in the past month (Kessler et al., 2012). Another review cited a statistic that "one in five adolescents have a mental illness that will persist into adulthood" (F. Lee et al., 2014, p. 547).

Comprehensive surveys have not yet been reported from DSM-5, but changing definitions of disorders within DSM-5 are likely to find more problems rather than fewer. Most disorders are *comorbid,* with several problems occurring at once. Distinguishing between pathology and normal moodiness, between behavior that is seriously troubled versus merely unsettling, is complex, especially in adolescence.

It is typical for an adolescent to be momentarily less happy and more angry than a younger child, but that is not usually a problem because teen emotions often change quickly (Neumann et al., 2011). For a few, however, negative emotions cloud every moment, becoming intense, chronic, even deadly.

Download the **DSM-5 Appendix** to learn more about the terminology and classification of various disorders.

Depression

The general emotional trend from childhood to early adolescence is toward less confidence and more depression, and then, gradually, self-esteem increases. A dip in self-esteem at puberty is found for children of every ethnicity and gender (Fredricks & Eccles, 2002; Greene & Way, 2005; Kutob et al., 2010; Zeiders et al., 2013). Often self-esteem rises after middle school (especially for African American girls and European American boys), but reports vary, and every study finds notable individual differences.

The same seems true for adolescents worldwide. A report from China also finds a dip in self-esteem in seventh grade (when many Chinese children experience puberty) and then a gradual rise. Sociocultural conditions always have an impact, evident in other data from China that find that the self-esteem of Chinese teenagers has decreased in recent years. The authors ascribe this to reduced family connections: Currently, many Chinese youth have no siblings or cousins, divorce rates are rising, and more parents work and live far from their children (Liu & Xin, 2014).

Adolescent self-esteem tends to be higher in boys than girls, in older adolescents than younger ones, in African Americans than European Americans, who themselves are higher than Asian Americans (Bachman et al., 2011). These same trends, in reverse, apply to most disorders, with girls at puberty having high rates of psychological stress (Kessler et al., 2012).

The above are only averages: Every study finds notable variability among individuals as well as evident continuity within each person. Thus, most young Asian American girls are at risk, but few actually are severely depressed. No matter what the age or sex of a depressed person, it may be less severe with age, but it rarely disappears (Huang, 2010).

Context matters. When compared to the high rates of depression among European American girls, the Latina rise in self-esteem is particularly notable (Zeiders et al., 2013). One explanation is **familism**—the cultural belief that family members should care for one another. Latinas become increasingly helpful at home, which makes their parents appreciative and them proud, unlike other U.S. teenage girls.

familism
The belief that family members should support one another, sacrificing individual freedom and success, if necessary, because the family is more important.

clinical depression
Feelings of hopelessness, lethargy, and worthlessness that last two weeks or more.

CLINICAL DEPRESSION Some adolescents sink into **clinical depression,** a deep sadness and hopelessness that disrupts all normal, regular activities. The causes, including genes and early care, predate adolescence. Then the onset of puberty—with

Hanging Out These three adolescents live on the Rosebud Sioux Reservation in South Dakota. Adolescence can be challenging for all teenagers, but the suicide rate among Native American teenagers is more than three times the rate for U.S. adolescents overall. Tribal officials in South Dakota are trying to improve the lives of young people so that they feel are more hopeful about the future.

KEVIN MOLONEY/THE NEW YORK TIMES/REDUX

its myriad physical and emotional ups and downs—pushes some vulnerable children, especially girls, into despair.

The rate of clinical depression more than doubles from childhood to adolescence and continues to increase in adulthood. One study found that the rate of clinical depression in a sample of 13- to 18-year-olds at 7.5 percent (Avenevoli et al., 2015). Every study finds that girls have much higher rates than boys, usually about twice as high.

Hormones are probably part of the reason for gender differences, but girls also experience social pressures from their families, peers, and cultures that boys do not. Women's roles have changed markedly in the past decades, so a 12-year-old girl who is trying to figure out her sexual and vocational identity is confronted with many contradictory options (Naninck et al., 2011). A combination of biological and psychosocial stresses causes some to slide into depression.

Differential susceptibility is apparent. One study found that the short allele of the serotonin transporter promoter gene (5-HTTLPR) increased the rate of depression among girls everywhere but increased depression among boys only if they lived in low-SES communities (Uddin et al., 2010).

It is not surprising that vulnerability to depression is partly genetic, or that girls have higher rates than boys, but why does living in a middle- or upper-class neighborhood protect boys more than girls? Perhaps cultural factors depress females everywhere, but boys may be protected unless jobs, positive male role models, a protective police force, and encouragement within their community are scarce.

A cognitive explanation for gender differences in depression focuses on **rumination**—talking about, brooding, and mentally replaying past experiences. Girls ruminate much more than boys, and rumination often leads to depression (Michl et al., 2013).

Indeed, some research finds that close mother–daughter relationships increase the rate of depression if the pair ruminate about the mother's problems (Waller & Rose, 2010). On the other hand, when rumination occurs with a close friend after a stressful event, the friend's support relieves some shame (Rose et al., 2014). This shows differential susceptibility again, in this case not genetic but social.

A distinction can be made between internalizing and externalizing psychopathology, depending on whether the problem is expressed inward (such as depression

rumination
Repeatedly thinking and talking about past experiences and possibilities.

KEY TERMS

identity versus role confusion (p. 351)

identity achievement (p. 351)

role confusion (p. 352)

foreclosure (p. 352)

moratorium (p. 352)

gender identity (p. 355)

parental monitoring (p. 358)

peer pressure (p. 360)

deviancy training (p. 362)

sexual orientation (p. 364)

sexually transmitted infection (STI) (p. 366)

familism (p. 369)

clinical depression (p. 369)

rumination (p. 370)

suicidal ideation (p. 371)

parasuicide (p. 371)

cluster suicides (p. 372)

adolescence-limited offender (p. 374)

life-course-persistent offender (p. 374)

generational forgetting (p. 383)

APPLICATIONS

1. Teenage cliques and crowds may be more important in large U.S. high schools than elsewhere. Interview people who attended high schools of various sizes in different nations. Describe and discuss any differences in peer relationships.

2. Locate a news article about a teenager who committed suicide. Can you find evidence in the article that there were warning signs that were ignored? Does the report inadvertently encourage cluster suicides?

3. Research suggests that most adolescents have broken the law but that few have been arrested or incarcerated. Ask 10 of your fellow students if they ever broke the law when they were younger than 18 and, if so, how often, in what ways, and with what consequences. (Assure them of confidentiality.) Include minor law-breaking, e.g., texting while driving or buying cigarettes. What hypothesis arises about lawbreaking in your cohort?

4. Cultures vary in standards for drug use among children, adolescents, and adults. Interview three people from different cultures (not necessarily from different nations; each occupation, generation, or religion can be said to have a culture) about drug-use standards. Ask your respondents to explain the reasons behind the cultural standards.

PART SIX

Adulthood

We now begin the sixth part of this text. These three chapters cover 47 years (ages 18 to 65), when bodies mature, minds master new material, and people work productively.

No decade of adulthood is exclusively programmed for any one event: Adults at many ages get stronger and weaker, learn and produce, nurture friendships and marriages, care for children and aging relatives. Some experience hiring and firing, wealth and poverty, births and deaths, weddings and divorces, windfalls and disasters, illness and recovery. Adulthood is a long sweep, punctuated by events, joyful and sorrowful.

There are some chronological norms, noted in these chapters. Early in adulthood, few people are married or settled in a career; later, most people have partners and offspring. Expertise at a particular job is more likely at age 50 than 20.

Past development is always relevant: Adults are guided by their nature and nurture, as they choose partners, activities, communities, and habits. For the most part, these are good years, when each person's goals become more attainable.

The experience of adulthood is not the same everywhere. In some nations and cultures, dominant influences are families, economics, and history; in others, genetic heritage and personal choice predominate. Economic forces are particularly strong when governments provide no safety nets, whereas genes and choice are stronger when governments and cultures help everyone. For example, virtually everyone marries in some nations, but genetic heritage and the ability to make a broader range of personal choices are stronger influences elsewhere. Many adults in such countries are not married.

The following three chapters describe adulthood: the universals, the usual, and the diverse. As this introduction explains, be careful: Generalities are often wrong.

© 2016 MACMILLAN

CHAPTER OUTLINE

CHAPTER 11

ADULTHOOD
Emerging Adulthood

WHAT WILL YOU KNOW?

■ Why do young adults have so few children?

■ Does college change the way people think?

■ Do emerging adults still need and want their parents in their lives?

This chapter is the pivot between childhood and adulthood, between growing up and being "a grown-up," as children call adults. The earlier and later periods of this book are all explained in twin chapters: one for Body and Mind, and one for the Social World. But this period of life blurs the boundaries of development. One chapter is best.

Emerging adulthood is a time when people continue learning and exploring, postponing marriage, parenthood, and career while preparing for the rest of life. This once seemed a luxury stage for those with relatively high SES from developed nations, but now it is apparent worldwide.

In every nation, the average age of marriage and parenthood is later than it was 50 years ago. Millions of young adults are attending college and exploring vocations—unlike the generations preceding them, who were quick to settle down. Emerging adulthood is a dramatic example of a cohort change: Now we see it, then we did not. Readers of this text have probably witnessed this stage in themselves or their friends.

I witnessed it, too. One example is my youngest daughter. My husband and I worried that she was not taking life seriously, not doing what needed to be done, not sticking to any one goal, or friend, or hobby. When she was in high school we thought the problem was too much TV. We hid the television. She was furious; she searched and found it. In desperation, my husband cut the wire (he reconnected it later).

My daughter vowed not to study and to watch her favorite programs elsewhere. Her English teacher said we shouldn't worry; some teenagers take longer to settle down. We knew about identity confusion, so we waited.

We were relieved when she chose a small college in a semirural community; we hoped that context would quiet her down. Wrong.

She still experimented and explored, as emerging adults do. She tutored refugees, got a part-time job at a chain restaurant, and applied to transfer to another college with an essay that began "I miss sidewalks." The following year, at her new urban college, she joined the crew team (which meant rising at dawn), majored in economics (as no one in our family ever had), and spent a semester in a nation none of us had visited (Spain).

emerging adulthood
The period of life between the ages of 18 and 25. Emerging adulthood is now widely thought of as a separate distinct stage.

After graduation, she still did not follow one straight path. She lived in three places within a few years (breaking one lease because the landlord did not get rid of bedbugs), worked as an intern at one company, a temporary employee at another, and was an unemployed job-searcher for a while.

Finally, since age 25, she has had one job, one apartment, one persona. There is much more to her story, as is true for everyone from ages 18 to 25 as they navigate the new complexities of work and relationships. Suffice it to say that, in retrospect, I have seen emerging adulthood in many people I know. You probably have, too. ■

Body Development

Biologically, the years from ages 18 to 25 are prime time for hard physical work and safe reproduction. However, the fact that young adults can carry rocks, plow fields, or produce babies is no longer admired.

If a contemporary young couple dropped out of high school to marry and then had a new baby year after year, their neighbors would be appalled, not approving. Societies, families, and young adults themselves expect more education, later marriage, and fewer offspring than the norm a few decades ago.

By this point in your study, the previous paragraph probably raises questions in your mind, because you are well aware of cultural differences in what societies expect. Might some neighbors in some regions of the world approve of a young, fertile couple? As the following Opposing Perspectives suggests, developmentalists also ask this question.

OPPOSING PERSPECTIVES

A Welcome Stage, or Just WEIRD?

This chapter is about emerging adulthood as a stage of human development, a time for questions, exploration, and experimentation. Careful questioning allows people to choose mates and jobs carefully. But some scholars consider emerging adulthood neither beneficial nor universal. Instead, this new stage may be a cultural phenomenon for privileged youth who can afford to postpone work and family commitments.

The term *emerging adulthood* was coined by Jeffrey Arnett, a college professor in Missouri who listened to his own students and realized they were neither adolescents nor adults. As a good researcher, he also queried young adults of many backgrounds in other regions of the United States, he read published research about "youth" or "late adolescence," and he thought about his own life. He decided that a new stage, requiring a new label, had appeared.

Arnett and others have now studied young adults in many Western European nations, and youth there also meet the criteria for emerging adults. For example, when Danish 20- to 30-year-olds were asked what signified adulthood,

they chose marriage, parenthood, financial self-sufficiency, and independence from parents. Relatively few of those under age 25 thought that they themselves were adults (Arnett & Padilla-Walker, 2015).

But some scientists hold an opposing perspective. They are particularly critical of any faculty member at a U.S. university who studies his or her own students and then draws conclusions about all humankind.

Conclusions based on American college students may apply only to those who are WEIRD—from Western, Educated, Industrialized, Rich, Democracies (Henrich et al., 2010). Most of the world's people are poor (even low-SES North Americans are rich by global measures), never reach college, and live in nations without regular elections. WEIRD people are unusual.

From that perspective, skewed perceptions are apparent. Indeed, referring to "the West" (North America and Western Europe) exposes a bias. Since the earth is round, people in "East Asia" (Japan, Korea, China) should call the United States "the East," and call the Middle East (Israel, Jordan,

Saudi Arabia, and so on) "the Midwest." Arnett himself contended that too much of developmental science focuses on only 5 percent of humanity (Arnett, 2008).

The Canadian professor who developed the acronym WEIRD wrote, "many psychologists . . . tend to think of cross-cultural research as a nuisance, necessary only to confirm the universality of their findings (which are usually based on WEIRD undergraduates)" (Henrich, 2015, p. 86). Another critic reports that his academic colleague felt misguided to study memory among non-literate people; he thought he should have focused exclusively on college students (Cole & Vossoughi, 2015).

If WEIRD people differ in notable ways from others, that calls into question the stage of emerging adulthood that depicts young adults as autonomous and independent, forging a future untethered by parents, partners, children, or work commitments. A contrasting worldview may be especially apparent in Asia, where social interdependence—not dependence—is the ideal (Yeung & Alipio, 2013).

For example, in Thailand youth involvement with parents and community is a bulwark against drug abuse (Wongtongkam et al., 2014). Looking at the data, researchers suggest that Thai youth should be encouraged to stay home until they marry, avoiding the allure of Western independence. Perhaps emerging adulthood is a luxury stage, attained only by U.S. college students.

Some scientists have directly examined the assumption that emerging adulthood is universal. One study of personality development among youth in 62 nations found that this transition time was evident everywhere but also that the age when adulthood began was strongly affected by having a steady job. When work began early (as in Pakistan, Malaysia, and Zimbabwe), personality maturation was rapid; when work began late (as in the Netherlands, Canada, and the United States), emerging adulthood lasted many years (Bleidorn et al., 2013).

Recent research suggests that emerging adulthood is coming to every nation, not just the WEIRD ones. For example, an analysis of Chinese culture over the past 40 years finds that communal values decreased while individual competitiveness increased (Zeng & Greenfield, 2015). Evidence such as this leads most scholars to believe that, although it was first recognized in Missouri, emerging adulthood is now evident worldwide.

Consider statistics on age of first marriage. A century ago, most women married in their teens. Now in sub-Saharan Africa the average marriage age is 21 (women) and 25 (men); in East Asia, 26 and 28; in Western Europe, 31 and 33. The U.S. age of marriage has been rising every decade since 1960 and averaged 27 and 29 in 2014 (American Community Survey, 2015).

Data on childbearing, college attendance, and career commitment show similar worldwide trends. Perhaps those who do not acknowledge a time between adolescence and adulthood are stuck in the past, when economic pressure meant everyone had to become an adult by age 18.

However, consider a new risk. By bestowing a label on this period, does that imply that it is acceptable or even laudable for young people to experiment and explore in their 20s? Should they refuse to settle down, or is that WEIRD? Is a new opposing perspective needed?

Strong and Active Bodies

Health from ages 18 to 25 is one aspect of development that has not changed, except maybe to improve. As has been true for thousands of years, every body system—including the digestive, respiratory, circulatory, and sexual-reproductive systems—functions optimally at the end of adolescence (see Table 11.1).

Serious diseases rarely appear, and some childhood ailments are outgrown. As young people with chronic problems such as diabetes develop their identity, their sense of who they are and what they want in life leads some to incorporate good health habits that sustain them lifelong (Schwartz et al., 2013).

Peak Performance Because this is a soccer match, of course we see skilled feet and strong legs—but also notice the arms, torsos, and feats of balance. Deniz Naki and Luis Gustavo, here in their early 20s, are German soccer team members in better shape than most emerging adults, but imagine these two a decade earlier or later and you will realize why, physiologically, the early 20s are considered the prime of life.

TABLE 11.1	U.S. Deaths from the Top Three Causes (Heart Disease, Stroke, Cancer)
Age Group	**Annual Rate per 100,000**
15–24	7
25–34	17
35–44	55
45–54	207
55–64	560
65–74	1,280
75–84	2,974
85+	7,730

Data from National Center for Health Statistics, 2013.

organ reserve
The extra capacity built into each organ, such as the heart and lungs, that allows a person to cope with extraordinary demands and to withstand organ strain.

homeostasis
The adjustment of all the body's systems to keep physiological functions in equilibrium, moment by moment.

allostasis
A dynamic body adjustment to long-term biological conditions of a person's life.

allostatic load
The stresses of basic body systems that burden overall functioning, such as hypertension.

EXTRA CAPACITY, EXTRA BURDEN To appreciate emerging adult health, it helps to understand three aspects of body functioning: organ reserve, homeostasis, and allostatic load.

Organ reserve refers to the extra power that each organ can employ when needed. Organ reserve shrinks each year of adulthood, so by old age, a strain—shoveling snow, catching the flu, minor surgery—can overwhelm the body.

In the beginning of adulthood, however, organ reserve allows speedy recovery from physical demands. Emerging adults sometimes exercise too long, stay awake all night, or drink too much alcohol. Usually they recover quickly, unlike older adults who might be affected for days.

Closely related to organ reserve is **homeostasis**—a balance between various body reactions that keeps every physical function in sync with every other. For example, if the air temperature rises, people sweat, move slowly, and thirst for cold drinks—three aspects of body functioning that cool them. Homeostasis is quickest in early adulthood, partly because all the organs have power in reserve for sudden demands.

The next time you read about a rash of heat-wave deaths (Australia in 2014 and India and Pakistan in 2015), note the age of the victims. Because homeostasis takes longer, the body dissipates heat less efficiently with age. Sometimes the demands temporarily overwhelm the heart, kidneys, or other organs. Even middle-aged adults are less protected from temperature changes—or any other stress on the body—than emerging adults (Larose et al., 2013).

Related to homeostasis is **allostasis,** a dynamic body adjustment that gradually changes overall physiology. The main difference between homeostasis and allostasis is time: Homeostasis requires an immediate response from body systems, whereas allostasis refers to long-term adjustment.

Allostasis depends on the biological circumstances of every earlier time of life, beginning at conception. The process continues, with early adulthood conditions affecting later life, as evident in a measure called **allostatic load.** Although organ reserve usually protects emerging adults, the effects accumulate because some of that reserve is spent to maintain health, gradually adding to the burden on overall health.

A Moment or a Lifetime These three in New Delhi enjoy free pizza at the opening of the 600th Domino's in India, just one of more than 5,000 outside the United States. Cheese and pepperoni may satisfy homeostatic drive, but they increase the allostatic load in every nation.

Because of the protective effects of homeostasis and allostasis, few emerging adults reach the threshold that results in serious illness. However, already by early adulthood, childhood health affects metabolism, weight, lung capacity, and cholesterol. As allostatic load builds, the risk of chronic disease later in life increases.

EXAMPLES OF LOAD AND BALANCING Consider sleep. One night's poor sleep makes a person tired the next day—that is homeostasis, the body's way to maintain equilibrium. But if poor sleep quality is typical every day in youth, then appetite, mood, and activity adjust (more, down, less) to achieve homeostasis, while allostatic load rises. By mid- and late adulthood, years of inadequate sleep load down overall health (McEwen & Karatsoreos, 2015; Carroll et al., 2015).

Another obvious example is nutrition. If severe malnutrition characterizes fetal or infant development, later on the person might eat too much, becoming obese. Childhood obesity increases the risk of adult obesity—not always, as Chapter 1 explains, but often.

Of course, appetite is affected by much more than fetal development. How much a person eats on a given day is affected by many factors, as the peripheral nervous system sends messages to the brain. An empty stomach triggers hormones, stomach pains, low blood sugar, and so on, all signaling that it is time to eat. If that is occasional, the cascade of homeostatic reactions makes you suddenly realize at 6 P.M. that you haven't eaten since breakfast. Dinner becomes a priority; your body tells you that food is needed.

But if a person begins a serious diet, ignoring hunger messages for days and weeks, rapid weight loss soon triggers new homeostatic reactions, allowing the person to function with reduced calorie intake. That makes it harder to lose more weight (Tremblay & Chaput, 2012).

Over the years, allostasis is evident. If a person overeats or starves day after day, the body adjusts: Appetite increases or decreases accordingly. But that ongoing homeostasis increases allostatic load. Obesity is one cause of diabetes, heart disease, high blood pressure, and so on—all the result of physiological adjustment (allostasis) to daily overeating (Sterling, 2012). At the opposite extreme, allostasis allows people with anorexia to feel energetic, not hungry, but the burden on their body eventually kills them.

A third example comes from exercise. After a few minutes of exercise, the heart beats faster and breathing becomes heavier—these are homeostatic responses. Because of organ reserve, such temporary stresses on the body in early adulthood are no problem. Over time, homeostasis adjusts and allows the person to exercise longer and harder. That decreases allostatic load by reducing the health risks evident in one's blood and weight.

The opposite is also true, as found in an impressive longitudinal study, CARDIA (Coronary Artery Risk Development in Adulthood), which began with thousands of healthy 18- to 30-year-olds, many (3,154) reexamined 7 and 20 years later. Those who were the least fit at the first assessment (more than 400 of them) were four times more likely to have diabetes and high blood pressure in middle age.

In CARDIA, problems for the least fit began but were unnoticed (except in blood work) when participants were in their 20s. Organ reserve allowed them to function quite well. Nonetheless, each year their allostatic load increased, unless their daily habits changed (Camhi et al., 2013). By age 65, a disproportionate number had died.

These ideas help us understand the long-term effects of poverty, neglect, and abuse in childhood. Those problems affect all the functions of the body, impairing health in middle age even if the childhood problems stopped decades ago (Widom et al., 2015).

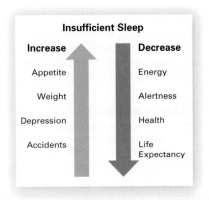

Insufficient Sleep

Increase — Decrease

Increase	Decrease
Appetite	Energy
Weight	Alertness
Depression	Health
Accidents	Life Expectancy

Don't Set the Alarm? Every emerging adult sometimes sleeps too little and is tired the next day—that is homeostasis. But years of poor sleep habits reduce years of life—a bad bargain. That is allostatic load.

Anywhere In some ways, life in China is radically different from life elsewhere, but universals are also apparent. This emerging-adult couple poses in front of the Beijing stadium.

OBSERVATION QUIZ
One detail in the young man's hands suggests that the setting is Asia, not North America. What is it? (see answer, page 396) ➤

© ULANA SWITUCHA/AGE FOTOSTOCK

FERTILITY, THEN AND NOW As already mentioned, the sexual-reproductive system is at its strongest during emerging adulthood: Orgasms are frequent, the sex drive is powerful, erotic responses are joyful, fertility is optimal, miscarriage less common, serious birth complications unusual. Historically, most people married before age 20, had their first child within two years, and often a second and third before age 25.

That has changed dramatically. The bodies of emerging adults still crave sex, but their minds know they are not ready for parenthood. Society deems teenage pregnancy a problem, not a blessing. For emerging adults, modern contraception has provided a solution: sex without pregnancy. The world's 2010 birth rate for 15- to 25-year-olds is half of what it was in 1960 (United Nations, 2013).

Challenges to Health

Modern medicine has prevented most young-adult deaths and many teenage pregnancies. The typical emerging adult is healthier than was true in former times. However, problems are prevalent that were rare earlier.

SEX, NOT MARRIAGE Premarital sex was once forbidden, a taboo enforced with diligent chaperoning, single-sex schools, and even the threat of death. The reason made sense: Premarital sex meant premarital pregnancy, and that was bad for society because children thrive best if both parents are committed to each other as well as to the children. In many cultures, if an unmarried woman became pregnant, the father of her child was obligated to marry her (sometimes called a *shotgun wedding* because her father threatened to kill the man).

However, effective contraception now allows gratification of sexual impulses without the risk of parenthood. The shotgun wedding "is rapidly becoming a relic" of another era (Jayson, 2014), evidence of a cohort change. When unmarried women today become pregnant, if they continue the pregnancy, less than 10 percent of those in the United States marry before the birth.

Society has adjusted to this new reality in many ways. One example is the demise of the single-sex college: A century ago, most private colleges were all male or all female (Miller-Bernal, 2000). In the United States as of 2015, except for religious colleges, only 3 all-male and about 30 all-female colleges continue to exist. The thousands of new colleges opening in other nations are virtually all co-ed.

Some feminists contend that, academically, women's colleges are better, but in terms of protecting women from pregnancy, contraception has replaced segregation. Worldwide, more than 99 percent of college students enroll in co-educational institutions.

NEW DISEASES Fatal diseases are rare during emerging adulthood, and premarital sex without pregnancy seems a good solution to the conflict between physical and psychological maturation. However, that solution creates a new problem.

The rate of sexually transmitted infections (STIs) is rising. Organ reserve and medical treatment almost always prevent death in emerging adulthood, but STIs cause infertility and later adult deaths that seem unrelated, such as from cancer and tuberculosis.

Transportation advances have unanticipated consequences. During the same years that contraception improved, travel became far easier and cheaper. In earlier times, prostitution was local, which kept STIs local as well. Now, with globalization, an STI caught in one place quickly spreads. Sex trafficking adds to the problem: Women and girls from one nation who are sent to another sometimes bring infections and sometimes catch diseases they never would have contracted at home.

This proliferation is particularly tragic with HIV/AIDS, which may have existed occasionally and locally for a hundred years. However, within 30 years, primarily because of travel and the sexual activities of young adults, HIV has become a worldwide epidemic, with more female than male victims (Fan et al., 2014).

Young adults are the prime STI vectors (those who spread disease) as well as the most common new victims. Genetic research finds that the subtypes and recombinations of HIV—once quite localized—are now present in many regions (Tatem et al., 2012).

Indeed, tracing HIV shows that it originally was confined to one city, Kinshasa, in the Democratic Republic of the Congo. Then it spread following the route of the railroads built as part of colonial modernization: Carriers took the disease to other nations of Africa, and later to other continents, where it had not been (Faria et al., 2014).

Now jets and bullet trains allow almost every young adult to wander far from home. Travel expands the mind and develops cultural understanding, but it also spreads diseases.

THINK CRITICALLY: What are the benefits and risks of other innovations, such as the cell phone, bypass surgery, frozen food, or air conditioning?

Taking Risks

Remember that each age group has its own gains and losses, characteristics that can be an asset or a liability. This is apparent with risk taking. Some emerging adults bravely, or foolishly, take risks—a behavior that is gender- and age-related, as well as genetic and hormonal. Those who are genetically impulsive *and* male *and* emerging adults are most likely to be brave and foolish.

In one study, 10- to 30-year-olds judged "how good or bad an idea is it to . . ." do various risky items (from riding a bicycle down the stairs to taking pills at a party) (Shulman & Cauffman, 2014). The participants had only two seconds to make a snap judgment on a sliding scale from 0 to 100. For instance, the bicycle riding could be rated at 70 (somewhat bad idea) and the pills at 99 (very bad idea). There also were eight items that were not risky at all, such as eating a sandwich.

Risky items were rated more favorably (closer to a good idea) every year from age 10 to 20 and then less favorably (closer to a bad idea) every year from age 20 to 30. Experience increased (the average 15- to 17-year-old had done four of the items; the average 20- to 25-year-old had done seven), but that did not affect how good or bad each item was thought to be. Maturation, not experience, affected the assessment of risk.

The emerging adult's willingness to take chances sometimes is beneficial. Enrolling in college, moving to a new state or nation, getting married, having a baby—all risky. So is starting a business, filming a documentary, entering an athletic contest,

FIGURE 11.1 Send Them Home
Accidents, homicides, and suicides occur more frequently during emerging adulthood than later. Note that the age range of more patients falls within the six years of emerging adulthood than within the 20 years of adulthood. If all the data were reported by six-year groups, the chart would be much starker. Fewer young adults *stay* in the hospital, however. They are usually stitched, bandaged, injected, and sent home.

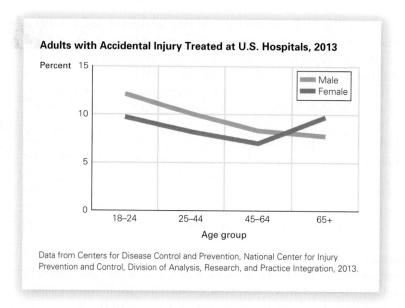

Adults with Accidental Injury Treated at U.S. Hospitals, 2013

Data from Centers for Disease Control and Prevention, National Center for Injury Prevention and Control, Division of Analysis, Research, and Practice Integration, 2013.

ANSWER TO OBSERVATION QUIZ
(from page 394) The cigarette, not the camera. Most young men in Canada and the United States do not smoke, especially publicly and casually, as this man does. ●

enlisting in the military, or joining the Peace Corps. Emerging adults do all these more than older adults, and societies benefit.

DANGEROUS RISKS However, risk taking is often destructive. Although their bodies are strong and their reactions quick, emerging adults nonetheless have more serious accidents than do people of any other age (see Figure 11.1). The low rate of disease between ages 18 and 25 is counterbalanced by a high rate of violent death.

Risks that are more common in emerging adulthood than any other time include unprotected sex with a new partner, driving without a seat belt, carrying a loaded gun, abusing drugs, and addictive gambling—all done partly for a rush of adrenaline (Cosgrave, 2010). In the United States, the peak age for serious crime is 19, for unintended pregnancy, 18–19, for automobile driver death, 21 (Shulman & Cauffman, 2014).

Fatal accidents, homicide, and suicide result in more deaths in emerging adulthood than all other causes combined, even in nations with high rates of infectious diseases and malnutrition. The contrast between sudden, violent deaths and slower, disease-related deaths is most stark in nations with good medical systems.

In the United States, of the 15- to 24-year-olds who died in 2013, about 71 percent came to a sudden, violent end. The leading cause of disease-related deaths was cancer, at about 6 percent. Homicide alone caused 4,481 deaths of 10- to 24-year olds—with rates highest in the early 20s—more than double the rate of cancer mortality (MMWR, February 27, 2015).

RISKY SPORTS Many young adults enjoy challenging recreation: They climb mountains, swim in oceans, run in pain, play past exhaustion, and so on. This has always been true. Marriage and parenthood slow down risk taking, so when adult responsibilities began earlier, risks were less common. But the impulse to seek danger has always been apparent in young men (think of the soldiers of the previous centuries).

Now recreational risks are more popular, including new ones advertised for hundreds of millions of emerging adults. Among such activities are skydiving, bungee jumping, pond swooping, parkour, potholing (in caves), waterfall kayaking, and ziplining. Serious injury is not the goal, but the possibility adds to the thrill.

Competitive **extreme sports** (such as *freestyle motocross*—motorcycle jumping off a ramp into "big air," doing tricks during the fall, and hoping to land upright) are new sports for some emerging adults, who find golf, bowling, and so on too tame (Breivik, 2010).

extreme sports
Forms of recreation that include apparent risk of injury or death and are attractive and thrilling as a result.

A CASE TO STUDY

An Adrenaline Junkie

The fact that extreme sports are age-related is evident in Travis Pastrana, "an extreme sports renaissance man—a pro adrenaline junkie/daredevil/speed demon—whatever you want to call him" (Giblin, 2014). After several accidents that almost killed him, Pastrana won the 2006 X Games freestyle motocross competition at age 22 with a double backflip because, he explained, "The two main things are that I've been healthy and able to train at my fullest, and a lot of guys have had major crashes this year" (quoted in Higgins, 2006, p. D-7).

Four years later, Pastrana set a new record for leaping through big air in an automobile, as he drove over the ocean from a ramp on the California shoreline to a barge more than 250 feet out. He crashed into a barrier on the boat but emerged, seemingly ecstatic and unhurt, to the thunderous cheers of thousands of other young adults on the shore (Roberts, 2010).

In 2011, a broken foot and ankle made him temporarily halt extreme sports—but soon he returned to the acclaim of his cohort, winning races rife with flips and other hazards. In 2013, after some more serious injuries, he said he was "still a couple of surgeries away" from racing on a motorcycle, so he turned to NASCAR auto racing. In 2014, age 30, after

becoming a husband and a father (twice), he quit NASCAR. He says his most hazardous race days are over. He is an icon for the next generation of daredevil young men.

JOHN HARRELSON/GETTY IMAGES

Dangerous Pleasure Here Travis Pastrana prepares to defy death once again as a NASCAR driver. Two days later, his first child was born, and two months later, he declared his race record disappointing. At age 30 he quit, declaring on Facebook that he would devote himself to his wife and family. Is that maturation, fatherhood, or failure?

DRUG ABUSE The same impulses that are admired by the young in extreme sports also lead to actions that are clearly destructive, not only for individuals but for the community. The most studied of these are sexual risks and drug abuse.

Both promiscuity and drug use increase in emerging adulthood, which suggests that one might lead to the other. Many colleges now restrict alcohol on campus, believing this will prevent or reduce sexual assault, which tends to occur only when both parties have been drinking or drugging (Zinzow & Thompson, 2015). However, although they often co-occur, instead of alcohol leading to assault, the origin may be the impulsive and foolish risk taking that are common personality traits in these years. In Chapter 1's terms: They correlate because of a third variable.

By definition, **drug abuse** occurs whenever a drug (legal or illegal, prescribed or not) is used in a harmful way, damaging a person's physical, cognitive, or psychosocial well-being. The interaction between age and drug abuse helps illustrate the nature of the emerging adult, who may be attracted rather than repulsed by the potential for harm and arrest in buying, carrying, and using an illegal drug.

Illegal drug use peaks at about age 20 and declines sharply with age (see Figure 11.2). Addiction to legal drugs (no arrest imminent) may continue in adulthood, but after age 25, most who drink and smoke to excess want to quit.

Quitting an addictive drug is difficult at any age, but as the years go on, adults no longer enjoy the taste, the thrill, or the sensation as they once did. They use drugs to relieve anxiety, or out of habit, not primarily for pleasure. For that reason, abstinence becomes more common, a source of pride not embarrassment, after emerging adulthood (Heyman, 2013).

Drug abuse is more frequent among college students than among emerging adults who are not in college, partly because groups of emerging adults urge each other on. For instance, some hazing rituals for college fraternities involve excessive

> **drug abuse**
> When a drug impairs the user's biological or psychological well-being.

Substance Abuse at Various Ages—United States, 2013

Percent

- Alcohol binge (5 or more drinks on one occasion)
- Current cigarette smoker
- Illegal drug use, past month

Age group

Data from SAMHSA, 2014.

FIGURE 11.2 Too Old for That As you can see, emerging adults are the biggest substance abusers, but illegal drug use drops faster and sooner than does cigarette use or binge drinking.

Video: College Binge Drinking shows college students engaging in (and rationalizing) this risky behavior.

THINK CRITICALLY: Why are wealthier emerging adults more likely to drink too much alcohol than their less wealthy contemporaries?

consumption of alcohol. Such forced drinking is a symptom of a general problem: One study found that 25 percent of young college men consumed 10 or more drinks in a row at least once in the previous two weeks (Johnston et al., 2009).

In the United States, the problem is not confined to men. A nationwide study found that 24 percent of women aged 18–25 had binged on alcohol in the past month (for women a binge is defined as four or more drinks on one occasion). That emerging adult rate was higher than the rate for either younger or older women (MMWR, January 11, 2013). Moreover, those 24 percent *averaged* four binge episodes per month and six drinks per occasion, both more than older female bingers. Rates rose with income.

Many colleges try to reduce alcohol consumption and enforce age restrictions—now 21 in the United States—without success. As one review states, "more students now drink to get drunk, choose hard liquor over beer, and front-load, or drink in advance of social events. For many, the goal is to black out" (McMurtrie, 2014, p. A23). The impulse to abuse alcohol arises from the same drive as extreme sports or other risks—with the same possible consequence: death.

WHAT HAVE YOU LEARNED?

1. Why is maximum physical strength usually attained in emerging adulthood?
2. What has changed, and what has not changed, in the past decades regarding sexual and reproductive development?
3. Why are STIs more common currently than 50 years ago?
4. What are the social benefits of risk taking?
5. Why are some sports more attractive at some ages than others?
6. Why are serious accidents more common in emerging adulthood than later?
7. Why are college students more likely to abuse drugs than those who are not in college?

Cognitive Development

Piaget changed our understanding of cognitive development by recognizing that maturation does not simply add knowledge; it allows a leap forward at each stage, first from sensorimotor to preoperational because of language (symbolic thought),

Crammed Together Students flock to the Titan Student Union at Cal State Fullerton for the biannual All Night Study before final exams, making cramming a social experience. This is contrary to what scientific evidence has shown is the best way to learn—that is, through distributed practice, which means studying consistently throughout the semester, not bunching it all at the end. Is cramming simply the result of poor time management or is it a rational choice?

and then with more advanced logical operations, from preoperational to concrete to formal (analytic).

Many cognitive psychologists find that post–adolescent thinking is also distinct from earlier thought. Adults are more practical and flexible, finding a way to combine intuitive and analytic thought. This advance may begin in emerging adulthood.

Postformal Thought and Brain Development

Some developmentalists propose a fifth stage, called **postformal thought,** a "type of logical, adaptive problem–solving that is a step more complex than scientific formal-level Piagetian tasks" (Sinnott, 2014, p. 3). As one group of scholars explained, in postformal thought "one can conceive of multiple logics, choices, or perceptions . . . in order to better understand the complexities and inherent biases in 'truth'" (Griffin et al., 2009, p. 173).

As you remember from Chapter 9, adolescents use two modes of thought (dual processing) but have difficulty combining them. They use formal analysis to learn science, distill principles, develop arguments, and resolve the world's problems. Alternatively, they think spontaneously and emotionally about personal issues, such as what to wear, whom to befriend, whether to skip class. For personal issues, they prefer quick actions and reactions, only later realizing the consequences.

Postformal thinkers are less impulsive and reactive. They take a more flexible and comprehensive approach, with forethought, noting difficulties and anticipating problems, instead of denying, avoiding, or procrastinating. As a result, postformal thinking is more practical, creative, and imaginative than thinking in previous cognitive stages (Wu & Chiou, 2008). It is particularly useful in human relationships (Sinnott, 2014).

As you have read, some, but certainly not all, developmentalists dispute Piaget's stage theory of childhood cognition. The ranks of dissenters swell regarding this fifth stage. As two scholars writing about emerging adulthood ask, "Who needs stages anyway?" (Hendry & Kloep, 2011).

Piaget himself never used the term *postformal.* If the definition of cognitive *stage* is to attain a new set of intellectual abilities (such as the symbolic use of language that distinguishes sensorimotor from preoperational thought), then adulthood has no stages.

postformal thought
A proposed adult stage of cognitive development. Postformal is more practical, flexible, and dialectical (i.e., more capable of combining contradictory elements into a comprehensive whole) than earlier cognition.

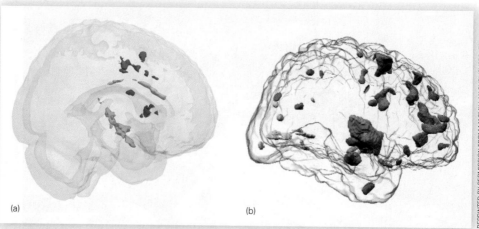

IMAGE COURTESY CRAIG BENNETT & ABIGAIL BAIRD, FROM "ANATOMICAL CHANGES IN THE EMERGING ADULT BRAIN: A VOXEL-BASED MORPHOMETRY STUDY," BY CRAIG M. BENNETT & ABIGAIL A. BAIRD, HUMAN BRAIN MAPPING VOL27, ISSUE 9, PP. 766-777, SEPT. 2006. COPYRIGHT©2006, JOHN WILEY AND SONS.

REPRINTED BY PERMISSION FROM MACMILLAN PUBLISHERS LTD: E.R. SOWELL ET AL., "IN VIVO EVIDENCE FOR POST-ADOLESCENT BRAIN MATURATION IN FRONTAL AND STRIATAL REGIONS," NATURE NEUROSCIENCE 2, 859–861 (1999)

Thinking Away from Home *(a)* Entering a residential college means experiencing new foods, new friends, and new neurons. A longitudinal study of 18-year-old students at the beginning and end of their first year in college (Dartmouth) found increases in the brain areas that integrate emotion and cognition—namely, the cingulate (blue and yellow), caudate (red), and insula (orange). Researchers also studied one-year changes in the brains of students over age 25 at the same college and found no dramatic growth. *(b)* Shown here are the areas of one person's brain changes from age 14 to 25. The frontal cortex (purple) demonstrated many changes in particular parts, as did the areas for processing speech (green and blue)—a crucial aspect of young adult learning. Areas for visual processing (yellow) showed less change.

Researchers now know that brains mature in many ways between adolescence and adulthood; scientists are not yet sure of the cognitive implications.

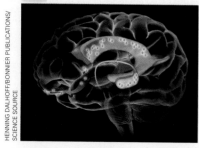

Try **Video Activity: Brain Development: Emerging Adulthood** for a quick look at the changes that occur in a person's brain between ages 18 and 25.

HENNING DALHOFF/BONNIER PUBLICATIONS/ SCIENCE SOURCE

stereotype threat
The thought that one's appearance or behavior might confirm another person's oversimplified, prejudiced attitudes, a thought that causes anxiety even when the stereotype is not held by other people.

However, the prefrontal cortex is not fully mature until the early 20s, and new dendrites connect throughout life. As more is understood about brain development after adolescence, it seems likely that thinking changes as the brain matures. Of course, maturation never works alone. Several studies find that adult cognition benefits from the varied experiences of the social world beyond home and neighborhood that typically occur during emerging adulthood (Sinnott, 2014).

Piaget may have envisioned a fifth stage, according to one scholar:

> we hypothesize that there exists, after the formal thinking stage, a fifth stage of post-formal thinking, as Piaget had already studied its basic forms and would have concluded the same thing, had he the time to do so.
>
> *[Lemieux, 2012, p. 404]*

COUNTERING STEREOTYPES Cognitive flexibility, particularly the ability to change childhood assumptions, helps counter stereotypes. Young adults show many signs of such flexibility. The very fact that emerging adults did marry later than previous generations shows that, couple by couple, thinking is not determined by childhood culture or by traditional norms. Early experiences are influential, but postformal thinkers are not stuck by them.

Research on racial prejudice is another example. Many people are less prejudiced than their parents. This is a cohort change. However, emerging adults may overestimate the change. Tests often reveal implicit discrimination. Thus, many adults have both unconscious prejudice and rational tolerance—a combination that illustrates dual processing.

The wider the gap between explicit and implicit, the stronger the stereotypes (Shoda et al., 2014). Ideally, postformal reasoning allows rational thinking to overcome emotional reactions, with responses dependent on reality, not stereotypes (Sinnott, 2014). A characteristic of adult thinking may be the flexibility that allows recognition and reconciliation of contradictions, thus reducing prejudice.

Unfortunately, many young people do not recognize their own stereotypes, even when false beliefs harm them. One of the most pernicious results is **stereotype threat,**

The Threat of Bias If students fear that others expect them to do poorly in school because of their ethnicity or gender, they might not identify with academic achievement and therefore do worse on exams than they otherwise would have.

arising in people who worry that other people might judge them as stupid, lazy, oversexed, or worse because of their ethnicity, sex, age, or appearance.

The idea is that people have a stereotype that other people have a stereotype. Then the *possibility* of being stereotyped arouses emotions and hijacks memory, disrupting cognition (Schmader, 2010). That is stereotype threat, as further explained below.

A VIEW FROM SCIENCE

Stereotype Threat

One statistic has troubled social scientists for decades: African American men have lower grades in high school and earn only half as many college degrees as African American women (Chronicle of Higher Education, 2014). This cannot be genetic, since the women have the same genes (except one chromosome) as the men.

Most scientists have blamed the historical context as well as current discrimination, which falls particularly hard on men. Even today, African American women have an easier time finding employment, and the unarmed African Americans who are killed are almost always men (recent examples that became nationally known: Martin, Brown, Garner, Gray, Scott).

Another hypothesis focuses on parenting. According to one study, African American mothers in particular grant far more autonomy to their teenage boys and have higher and stricter standards of achievement for their teenage girls (Varner & Mandara, 2014). These researchers suggest that if sons and daughters were treated equally, most gender differences in achievement would disappear.

One African American scholar, Claude Steele, thought of a third possibility, that the problem originated in the mind,

not in the family or society. He labeled it *stereotype threat,* a "threat in the air," not in reality (Steele, 1997). The mere *possibility* of being negatively stereotyped may disrupt cognition and emotional regulation.

Steele suspected that African American males who know the stereotype that they are poor scholars will become anxious in educational settings. Their anxiety may increase stress hormones that reduce their ability to respond to intellectual challenges.

Then, if they score low, they protect their pride by denigrating academics. They come to believe that school doesn't matter, that people who are "book smart" are not "street smart." That belief leads them to disengage from high school and college, which results in lower achievement. The greater the threat, the worse they do (Taylor & Walton, 2011).

Stereotype threat is more than a hypothesis. Hundreds of studies show that anxiety reduces achievement. The threat of a stereotype causes women to underperform in math, older people to be forgetful, bilingual students to stumble with English, and every member of a stigmatized minority in every nation to handicap themselves because of what they imagine others might think (Inzlicht & Schmader, 2012).

Not only academic performance but also athletic prowess and health habits may be impaired if stereotype threat makes people anxious (Aronson et al., 2013). Every sphere of life may be affected. One recent example is that blind people are underemployed if stereotype threat makes them hesitate to learn new skills (Silverman & Cohen, 2014).

The worst part of stereotype threat is that it is self-imposed. People who are alert to the possibility of prejudice are not only hypersensitive when it occurs, but their minds are hijacked, undercutting potential. Their initial reaction may be to try harder to prove the stereotype wrong, and if that extra effort fails, they stop trying (Mangels et al., 2012; Aronson et al., 2013).

The harm from anxiety is familiar to those who study sports psychology. When star athletes unexpectedly under-perform (called "choking"), stereotype threat arising from past team losses may be the cause (Jordet et al., 2012). Many female players imagine they are not expected to play as well as men (e.g., someone told them "you throw like a girl"), and that itself impairs performance (Hively & El-Alayli, 2014).

The next step for many developmentalists is figuring out how stereotype threat can be eliminated, or at least reduced (Inzlicht & Schmader 2012; Sherman et al., 2013; Dennehy et al., 2014). Reminding people of their own potential, and the need to pursue their goals, is one step. The questions for each of us are, what imagined criticisms from other people impair our own achievement, and how do we overcome that?

The Effects of College

A major reason why emerging adulthood has become a new period of development, when people postpone the usual markers of adult life (marriage, a steady job), is that many older adolescents seek further education instead of taking on adult responsibilities.

MASSIFICATION There is no dispute that tertiary education improves health and wealth. The data on virtually every physical condition, and every indicator of material success, show that college graduates are ahead of high school graduates, who themselves are ahead of those without a high school diploma. This is apparent even when the comparisons are between students of equal ability: It's the education, not just the potential, that makes a difference.

Because of that, every nation has increased the number of college students. This is a phenomenon called *massification*, based on the idea that college could benefit almost everyone (the masses) (Altbach et al., 2010).

Culture and Cohort Ideally, college brings together people of many backgrounds who learn from each other. This scene from a college library in the United Arab Emirates would not have happened a few decades ago. The dress of these three suggests that culture still matters, but worldwide education is recognized as benefitting every young person in every nation.

© CELIA PETERSON/ARABIANEYE/CORBIS

The United States was the first major nation to endorse massification, with state-funded universities in all 50 states, often more than one per state (California has 36). That is why, among older adults, the United States leads in the percentage of college graduates.

Recently, however, other nations have increased public funding for college while the United States has decreased it. As a result, eleven other nations have a higher proportion of 25- to 34-year-olds who are college graduates (OECD, 2014). The decline in massification in the United States is the reason for "declining living standards . . . [and] wages for many Americans" according to one analysis (Greenstone & Looney, 2012, p. 32).

U.S. Census data and surveys of individuals find that college education pays off for individuals as well as for societies more than it did 30 years ago. The average college man earns an additional $17,558 per year compared to a high school graduate. Women also benefit, but not as much, earning $10,393 more per year (Autor, 2014). That higher salary is averaged over the years of employment: Most new graduates do not see such a large wage difference; but in a decade or two, the differences are dramatic.

The reasons for the gender gap are many. Some observers blame culture, some blame employers, and others blame the women themselves, who are less likely to demand more pay. Even among contemporary emerging adults, women seem to undervalue their worth (stereotype threat again). This was one conclusion of a series of experiments with college students in which women were more likely to attribute success of a team project to a male partner than to themselves (Haynes & Heilman, 2013).

DEBTS AND DROPOUTS The typical American with a master's degree earns twice as much as the typical one with only a high school diploma (Doubleday, 2013) (see Figure 11.3), but most U.S. adults believe that college is too expensive. According to a survey, 94 percent of parents expect their children to go to college, but 75 percent

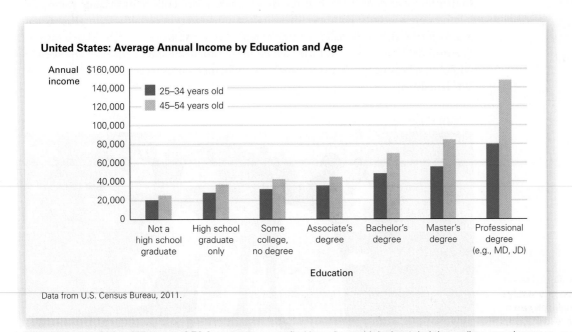

United States: Average Annual Income by Education and Age

Data from U.S. Census Bureau, 2011.

FIGURE 11.3 Older, Wiser, and Richer Adolescents find it easier to think about their immediate experiences (a boring math class) rather than their middle-age income, so some quit high school to take a job that will someday pay $500 a week. But over an average of 40 years of employment, someone who completes a master's degree earns half a million dollars more than someone who leaves school in eleventh grade. That translates into about $90,000 for each year of education from twelfth grade to a master's. The earnings gap is even wider than those numbers indicate because this chart compares adults who have jobs, and finding work is more difficult for those with less education.

of the public (parents or not) believe that college costs are beyond what most parents can afford (Pew Research Center, May 17, 2012).

The longitudinal data make it clear that a college degree is worth the expense and that investing in college education returns the initial expense more than five times. That means if a student spends a nickel now, they get a quarter back in a few years, or if a degree costs $200,000, over a lifetime the return is a million dollars.

However, there is a major problem with that calculation. Although most freshmen expect to graduate, many of them leave college before graduating. Some income benefits come from simply attending college, but most result from earning a degree. Yet the costs come from enrolling, not from graduating, so the benefits may be far less than the million dollars mentioned in the previous paragraph.

Statistics on college graduation are discouraging. Even six years after entering a college designed to award a bachelor's degree after four years of study, less than half the students graduate. Data from 2013 find that only 34 percent of the students at private, for-profit colleges earn a degree; at public institutions, the six-year graduation rate is 50 percent; at private, nonprofit colleges, 58 percent (Chronicle of Higher Education, 2014).

Ironically, schools with the lowest graduation rates are the most popular: 2,352,054 students attend for-profit colleges, 1,111,151 public colleges, and 814,598 private, nonprofit colleges. The reasons may be the marketing efforts of the for-profit schools, which are designed to appeal to the emotional, intuitive thinking of the adolescent, not the logical reflection of the adult.

The sad truth is that many freshmen will be disappointed: Almost all (88 percent) expect to earn a degree in four years, and many (76 percent) expect a master's or professional degree after completing their bachelor's (Chronicle of Higher Education, 2014). Rates of completed advanced degrees are also discouraging.

One effort to improve graduation rates is to make college loans easier to obtain so that fewer students leave because they cannot afford college or because their paid job interferes with study time. However, for some emerging adults, paying back loans is a major burden, especially because interest on those loans is high. Many analysts question the impact of such loans, which may burden students, taxpayers, and society without increasing graduation rates or employment prospects (Best & Best, 2014; Webber, 2015).

Educating Congress Justin Neisler is a medical student, about to testify before Congress. As an openly gay man, he hopes to serve LGBTQ youth, a group with many unmet medical needs. However, he and all his classmates have a major problem: The clash between their idealism and the money they owe for their education—a median of $170,000 for new MDs in 2012.

ANDREW HARRER/BLOOMBERG VIA GETTY IMAGES

Nonetheless, every study over the past several decades reaches the same conclusion: When 18-year-old high school graduates of similar backgrounds and abilities are compared, those who enter the labor market rather than pursuing higher education eventually achieve less and are less satisfied by middle age than those who earned a college degree (Hout, 2012).

The financial benefits of college seem particularly strong for ethnic minorities and low-income families. Ironically, they are least likely to enter college or earn a degree, but most likely to benefit when they do so.

COLLEGE AND COGNITION For developmentalists interested in cognition, the crucial question about college education is not about wealth, health, rates, expense, or even graduation. Instead, developmentalists wonder whether college advances critical thinking and postformal thought. The answer seems to be yes, but some studies dispute that.

Let us begin with the classic work of William Perry (1981, 1970/1998). After repeatedly questioning students at Harvard, Perry described students' thinking through nine levels of complexity over the four years that led to a bachelor's degree (see Table 11.2).

TABLE 11.2		Perry's Scheme of Cognitive and Ethical Development During College
Freshmen	Position 1	Authorities know, and if we work hard, read every word, and learn Right Answers, all will be well.
Dualism modified	Transition	But what about those Others I hear about? And different opinions? And Uncertainties? Some of our own Authorities disagree with each other or don't seem to know, and some give us problems instead of Answers.
	Position 2	True Authorities must be Right; the others are frauds. We remain Right. Others must be different and Wrong. Good Authorities give us problems so we can learn to find the Right Answer by our own independent thought.
	Transition	But even Good Authorities admit they don't know all the answers yet!
	Position 3	Then some uncertainties and different opinions are real and legitimate temporarily, even for Authorities. They're working on them to get to the Truth.
	Transition	But there are so many things they don't know the Answers to! And they won't for a long time.
Relativism discovered	Position 4a	Where Authorities don't know the Right Answers, everyone has a right to his own opinion; no one is wrong!
	Transition	Then what right have They to grade us? About what?
	Position 4b	In certain courses, Authorities are not asking for the Right Answer. They want us to think about things in a certain way, supporting opinion with data. That's what they grade us on.
	Position 5	Then all thinking must be like this, even for Them. Everything is relative but not equally valid. You have to understand how each context works. Theories are not Truth but metaphors to interpret data with. You have to think about your thinking.
	Transition	But if everything is relative, am I relative, too? How can I know I'm making the Right Choice?
	Position 6	I see I'm going to have to make my own decisions in an uncertain world with no one to tell me I'm Right.
	Transition	I'm lost if I don't. When I decide on my career (or marriage or values), everything will straighten out.
Commitments in relativism developed	Position 7	Well, I've made my first Commitment!
	Transition	Why didn't that settle everything?
	Position 8	I've made several commitments. I've got to balance them—how many, how deep? How certain, how tentative?
	Transition	Things are getting contradictory. I can't make logical sense out of life's dilemmas.
Seniors	Position 9	This is how life will be. I must be wholehearted while tentative, fight for my values yet respect others, believe my deepest values are right yet be ready to learn. I see that I shall be retracing this whole journey over and over—but, I hope, more wisely.

Information from Perry, 1981, 1970/1998.

Perry found that freshmen arrived thinking in a simplistic dualism. Most tended to think in absolutes, believing that things were either right or wrong. Answers to questions were yes or no, the future led to success or failure, and the job of the professor (Authorities) was to distinguish between the two and then tell the students.

By the end of college, Perry's subjects believed strongly in relativism, recognizing that many perspectives might be valid and that almost nothing was totally right or wrong. But they were able to overcome that discouraging idea: They had become critical thinkers, realizing that they needed to move forward in their lives by adopting one point of view, yet expecting to change their thinking if new challenges and experiences produced greater insight.

Perry found that the college experience itself caused this progression: Peers, professors, books, and class discussion all stimulated new questions and thoughts. Other research confirmed Perry's conclusions. In general, the more years of higher education a person had, the deeper and more postformal that person's reasoning became (Pascarella & Terenzini, 1991).

CURRENT CONTEXTS But wait. You probably noticed that Perry's study was first published decades ago. Hundreds of other studies in the twentieth century also found that college deepens cognition. Since you know that cohort and culture are influential, you are right to wonder whether those conclusions still hold in the twenty-first century.

Many recent books criticize college education on exactly those grounds. Notably, a twenty-first-century longitudinal study of a cross section of U.S. college students found that students' growth in critical thinking, analysis, and communication over the four years of college was only half as much as among college students two decades ago. This analysis of the first two years of college found that 45 percent of the students made no significant advances at all (Arum & Roksa, 2011).

The reasons were many. Compared to decades ago, students study less, professors expect less, and students avoid classes that require reading at least 40 pages a week or writing 20 pages a semester. Administrators and faculty still hope for intellectual growth, but rigorous classes are canceled, not required, or taken by only a few.

A follow-up study of the same individuals after graduation found that those who spent most of their college time socializing rather than studying were likely to be unemployed or have low-income jobs. What they had gained from college was a sense that things would get better, but not the critical-thinking skills or the self-discipline that is needed for adult success (Arum & Roksa, 2014).

Other observers blame the exosystem for forcing colleges to follow a corporate model with students as customers who need to be satisfied rather than youth who need to be challenged (Deresiewicz, 2014). Customers, apparently, demand dormitories and sports facilities that are costly, and students take out loans to pay for them. The fact that the United States has slipped in massification is not surprising, given the political, economic, and cultural contexts of contemporary college.

A related development is that U.S. young adults are less proficient in various skills, including reading comprehension, problem solving, and especially math, according to international tests (see Figure 11.4). A report highlighting those results is particularly critical of the disparity in education between the rich and the poor, stating "to put it bluntly, we no longer share the growth and prosperity of the nation the way we did in the decades between 1940 and 1980" (Goodman et al., 2015, p. 2).

Two new pedagogical techniques may foster greater learning, or may be evidence of the decline of standards. One is called the *flipped class,* in which students are required to watch videos of a lecture on their computers or other devices before class. They then use class time for discussion, with the professor prodding and encouraging but not lecturing.

The other technique is classes that are totally online, including **massive open online courses (MOOCs).** A student can enroll in such a class and do all the work off campus. Among the advantages of MOOCs is that students can be anywhere.

massive open online courses (MOOCs)
College courses that are offered solely online. Typically, thousands of students enroll.

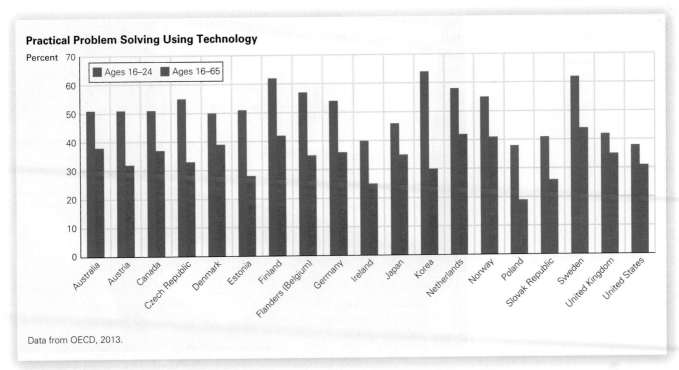

Practical Problem Solving Using Technology

Data from OECD, 2013.

FIGURE 11.4 Blue Is Higher Except . . . Since blue is for emerging adults, and red for adults of all ages (including emerging ones), it is no surprise that massification has produced higher scores among the young adults than the old ones. Trouble appears when young adults score about the same as older ones.

For example, MOOCs have enrolled students who are: in rural areas far from college; unable to leave home because they have young children or mobility problems; serving in the armed forces far from college; living in countries with few rigorous or specialized classes. The first MOOC offered by Massachusetts Institute of Technology (MIT) and Harvard enrolled 155,000 students from 194 nations, including 13,044 from India (Breslow et al., 2013).

Only 4 percent of the students in that first MOOC completed the course. Completion rates have risen in later courses, but almost always the dropout rate is over 80 percent. Researchers agree that "learning is not a spectator sport," that active engagement, not merely clicking on a screen, is needed for education. Although MOOCs are attractive for many reasons, colleges are wary of "knee-jerk reactions and bandwagon-jumping," as one article explained (Kolowich, 2013).

The crucial variable may be the students. MOOCs are most successful if students are highly motivated, adept at computer use, and have the needed prerequisites (Reich, 2015). That first MIT course had many enrollees who did not have the necessary math skills (Breslow et al., 2013).

Students learn best in MOOCs if they have another classmate, or an expert, as a personal guide. This is true for all kinds of college learning: Face-to-face interaction seems to improve motivation and learning. As developmentalists find for every emerging adult, challenging conversations and new experiences advance cognition.

MOTIVATION TO ATTEND COLLEGE Motivation is crucial for every intellectual accomplishment. An underlying problem in the controversy about college education is that people disagree about its purpose, and thus, students who are motivated to accomplish one thing clash with professors who are motivated to teach something else. Parents and governments who subsidize college may have a third goal in mind.

OBSERVATION QUIZ

In what nation do emerging adults excel the most compared to older adults, and in what nation is the contrast smallest? (see answer, page 408) ▲

Video: The Effects of Mentoring on Intellectual Development: The University-Community Links Project shows how an after-school study enhancement program has proven beneficial for both its mentors and the at-risk students who attend it.

Writing on the Wall In Oakland, California, Selina Wong is learning physics online from a MOOC offered by San Jose State University. The most common criticism of online courses is that they are not interactive, but, as you see, this is not always true.

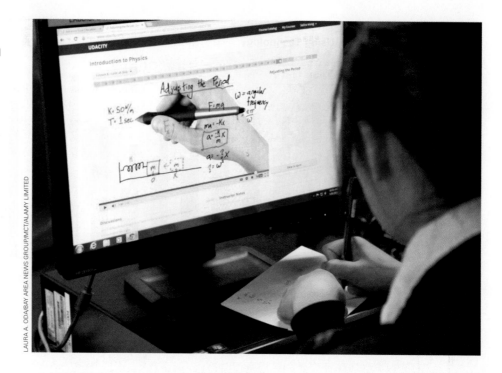

Developmentalists, most professors, and many college graduates believe that the main purpose of higher education is "personal and intellectual growth," which means that professors should focus on fostering critical thinking and analysis. However, adults who have never attended college believe that "acquiring specific skills and knowledge" is more important. For them, success is a high-paying job.

In the Arum and Roksa report (2011), students majoring in business and other career fields were less likely to gain in critical thinking compared to those in the liberal arts (courses that demand more reading and writing). These researchers suggest that colleges, professors, and students themselves who seek easier, more popular courses are short-changing themselves for future maturity and success (Arum & Roksa, 2014).

However, many students attend college primarily for career reasons (see Figure 11.5). They want jobs with good pay; they select majors and institutions accordingly, not for intellectual challenge and advanced communication skills. Business has

FIGURE 11.5 Cohort Shift
Decades before this study was done, students thought new ideas and a philosophy of life were prime reasons to go to college—they were less interested in jobs, careers, and money than were students in 2012. If this thinking causes a conflict between student motivation and professor's goals, who should adjust?

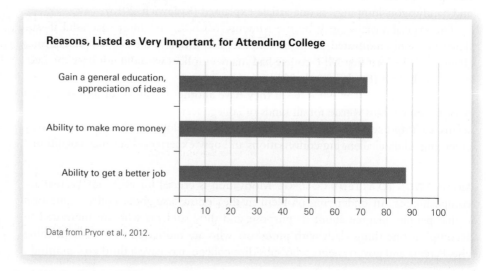

Reasons, Listed as Very Important, for Attending College

Data from Pryor et al., 2012.

VISUALIZING DEVELOPMENT

Why Study?

From a life-span perspective, college graduation is a good investment, for individuals (they become healthier and wealthier) and for nations (national income rises). That long-term perspective is the main reason why nations that control enrollment, such as China, have opened dozens of new colleges in the past two decades. However, when the effort and cost of higher education depend on immediate choices made by students and families, as in the United States, many decide it is not worth it, as illustrated by the number of people who earn bachelor's degrees.

EDUCATION IN THE UNITED STATES

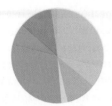  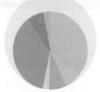 

10-year-olds in school (98.5%) **High school graduates (85%)** **Enrolled in college (66%)** **BA or BS earned (30%)**

- ■ European American males
- ■ European American females
- ■ African American males
- ■ African American females
- ■ Hispanic American males
- ■ Hispanic American females
- ■ Asian American males
- ■ Asian American females

DATA FROM U.S. CENSUS BUREAU, 2012, EDUCATION WEEK, 2013, AND KENA ET AL., 2015.

AMONG ALL ADULTS

The percentage of U.S. residents with high school and college diplomas is increasing as more of the oldest cohort (often without degrees) dies and the youngest cohorts aim for college. However, many people are insufficiently educated and less likely to find good jobs. It is not surprising that in the current recession, college enrollment is increasing. These data can be seen as encouraging or disappointing. The encouraging perspective is that rates are rising for everyone, with the only exception being associate's degrees for Asian Americans, and the reason for that is itself encouraging—more of them are earning bachelor's degrees. The discouraging perspective is that almost two-thirds of all adults and more than four-fifths of all Hispanics Americans have no college degrees. International data find that many European and East Asian nations have higher rates of degree holders than the United States.

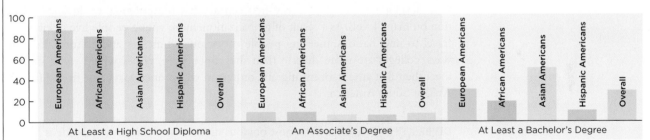

DATA FROM KENA ET AL., 2015 AND U.S. CENSUS BUREAU, 2013 AMERICAN COMMUNITY SURVEY.

INCOME IMPACT

Over an average of 40 years of employment, someone who completes a master's degree earns $500,000 more than someone who leaves school in eleventh grade. That translates into about $90,000 for each year of education from twelfth grade to a master's. The earnings gap is even wider than those numbers indicate because this chart includes only adults who have jobs, yet finding work is more difficult for those with less education.

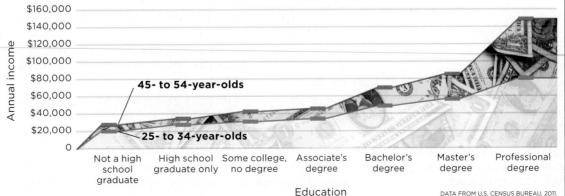

DATA FROM U.S. CENSUS BUREAU, 2011.

PHOTO: JUPITERIMAGES/THINKSTOCK

become a popular major. Professors are critical when college success is measured via the future salaries of graduates, but that metric may be what the public expects. Cohorts clash.

In 1955, most U.S. colleges were four-year institutions, and most students majored in the liberal arts. There were only 275 "junior" colleges. In 2014, there were almost 1,920 such colleges, now often called community colleges. (Some of these also offer four-year degrees, but their primary focus is on two-year associate degrees.) Similarly, for-profit colleges were scarce until about 1980; now the United States has more than 752, far more than two decades ago but nonetheless fewer than four years ago (Chronicle of Higher Education, 2014).

No nation has reached consensus on the purpose of college. For example in China, where the number of college students now exceeds the U.S. number (but remember that the Chinese population is much larger), the central government has fostered thousands of new institutions of higher learning. The main reason is to provide more skilled workers for economic advancement, not to deepen intellectual understanding and critical thinking. However, even in that centralized government, disagreement about the goals and practices of college is evident (Ross & Wang, 2013).

For example, in 2009, a new Chinese university (called South University of Science and Technology of China, or SUSTC) was founded to encourage analysis and critical thinking. SUSTC does not require prospective students to take the national college entry exam (*Gao Kao*); instead, "creativity and passion for learning" are the admission criteria (Stone, 2011, p. 161).

It is not clear whether SUSTC is successful, again because people disagree about how to measure success. The Chinese government praises SUSTC's accomplishments but has not replicated it (Shenzhen Daily, 2014).

THINK CRITICALLY: What is the purpose of college education?

The Effects of Diversity

One development of the twenty-first century has the potential to advance cognition on many levels. As a result of globalization, more young people live in cities and travel to new nations, meeting people of various ethnicities and cultures. In many ways, colleges are more diverse than they once were, places where some students meet their first atheist, or immigrant, or person whose ancestors came from Africa, or Asia, or South America.

DIVERSITY IN COLLEGE The most obvious diversity in colleges worldwide is gender: In 1970, at least two-thirds of college students were male, often educated in exclusively male institutions. Now, in every developed nation (except Germany), more than half the college students are female, with women enrolled in every class, including physics and engineering.

A historic example is Virginia Military Institute (VMI), a state-supported military academy that had never admitted women since its founding in 1839. Administrators at the college said that women could not do the physical tasks required at VMI, and besides, no woman would want to be an army officer. However, in 1997 the U.S. Supreme Court ruled (7-1) that, as a public institution, it could not discriminate based on sex alone. In 2015, 11 percent (about 185) of the VMI students are female.

In addition to gender diversity, students' ethnic, economic, religious, and cultural backgrounds are more varied. Compared to 1970, more students are parents, are older than age 24, are of non-European heritage, attend school part-time, and live and work off campus. This is true not only in North America but also worldwide.

In the United States, when undergraduate and graduate students are tallied by ethnicity, 35 percent are "minorities" of some kind (Black, Hispanic, Asian, Native

Unlike Their Parents Both photos show large urban colleges in the United States, with advantages the older college generations did not have: wireless technology (in use by all three on the left) and classmates from 50 nations (evident in the two on the right).

American, Pacific Islander, two or more races). Faculty members are also more diverse; 19 percent are non-White (Chronicle of Higher Education, 2014).

These numbers overstate diversity: It is not true that most colleges are a third minority. Instead, some colleges are almost exclusively minority (usually only one minority, as with historically African American or Native American colleges). Many other colleges are almost entirely European American, as are most tenured professors. Further, the typical college student is still 18 to 22 years old and attends college full-time. Nonetheless, almost every institution of higher education is more diverse than it was 50 years ago.

DIVERSITY AS THOUGHT-PROVOKING Diversity of any kind *can* advance cognition. Honest conversations among people of different backgrounds and varied perspectives lead to intellectual challenge and deeper thought, with the benefits lasting for years after graduation (Pascarella et al., 2014).

Colleges that make use of their diversity—via curriculum, assignments, discussions, cooperative education, learning communities, and so on—stretch student understanding, not only of other people but also of themselves (Harper & Yeung, 2013).

Such advances are not guaranteed. Emerging adults, like people of every age, tend to feel most comfortable with people who agree with them. Critical thinking develops outside the personal comfort zone, when cognitive dissonance requires deeper thought.

Regarding colleges, some people hypothesize that critical thinking is less likely to develop when students enroll in colleges near home or when they join fraternities or sororities. However, that hypothesis does not seem valid (Martin et al., 2015).

The crucial factor seems to be honest talk with a peer who differs in background and values, and that can happen in many places—a college classroom, a sports event, a work project, or a fraternity dining room. It is less likely to happen with parents in an emerging adult's childhood home. Most young people leave their childhood home to study, work, and travel, and for that reason emerging adulthood often entails intellectual growth.

Again, meeting people who are from various backgrounds is a first step. For cognitive development to occur, the willingness to listen to someone with opinions unlike one's own, and to modify one's own thinking accordingly, is crucial. That openness, and flexibility, is characteristic of postformal thought.

The validity of this conclusion is illustrated by the remarkable acceptance of homosexuality over the past 50 years, not only in recognition of marriage but in everything from bullying in middle school to adoption of children by gay and lesbian parents. Fourteen percent of Americans—including religious believers and African Americans who historically rejected homosexuals—have changed their minds.

The main reason that individuals became more accepting of homosexuality is that people realized that they knew LGBT people personally (Pew Research Center, March 20, 2013). That occurred not only because people were more open about their sexual orientation but also because young adults in particular spoke with their LGBT peers. The research finds that those in the vanguard of this social revolution were emerging adults, for all the reasons just described about cognitive development.

WHAT HAVE YOU LEARNED?

1. Why did scholars choose the term *postformal* to describe the fifth stage of cognition?
2. How does postformal thinking differ from typical adolescent thought?
3. Why might the threat of a stereotype affect cognition?
4. Who is vulnerable to stereotype threat and why?
5. How do current U.S. college enrollment patterns differ from those of 50 years ago?
6. How has college attendance changed internationally in recent decades?
7. Why do people disagree about the goals of a college education?
8. In what way does exposure to diversity affect college students' learning?

Becoming Your Own Person

A theme of all human development is that continuity and change are evident throughout life. In emerging adulthood, the legacy of childhood is apparent amidst new achievements. Erikson recognized this ongoing process in his description of the fifth of his eight stages, *identity versus role confusion*.

Remember that the identity crisis begins in adolescence, when teenagers reexamine the identities their parents imposed on them. However, as you learned, the identity crisis is not usually resolved in adolescence.

Identity Achievement

Erikson believed that the outcome of earlier crises provides the foundation for each new stage. The identity crisis is an example (see Table 11.3).

Certainly the adolescent push for independence from parents is often expressed in a search for self-expression, yet adults of all ages continue to reflect on their identities. This is particularly

Just Like Me Emerging adults of every ethnicity take pride in their culture. In Japan, adulthood begins with a celebration at age 20, to the evident joy of these young women on Coming of Age Day, a national holiday.

true in emerging adulthood, which "is the period of life that offers the most opportunities for identity exploration" (Luyckx et al., 2013, p. 703).

All four identity statuses (achievement, foreclosure, moratorium, diffusion) are evident in emerging adulthood, as the identity crisis continues (Schwartz et al., 2011). At least in developed nations, it seems normative for emerging adults to question who they really are in the four areas that Erikson originally termed—sex, vocation, politics, and religion.

TABLE 11.3	**Erikson's Eight Stages of Development**	
Stage	**Virtue/Pathology**	**Possible in Emerging Adulthood If Not Successfully Resolved**
Trust vs. mistrust	Hope/withdrawal	Suspicious of others, making close relationships difficult
Autonomy vs. shame and doubt	Will/compulsion	Obsessively driven, single-minded, not socially responsive
Initiative vs. guilt	Purpose/inhibition	Fearful, regretful (e.g., very homesick in college)
Industry vs. inferiority	Competence/inertia	Self-critical of any endeavor, procrastinating, perfectionistic
Identity vs. role diffusion	Fidelity/repudiation	Uncertain and negative about values, lifestyle, friendships
Intimacy vs. isolation	Love/exclusivity	Anxious about close relationships, jealous, lonely
Generativity vs. stagnation	Care/rejection	[In the future] Fear of failure
Integrity vs. despair	Wisdom/disdain	[In the future] No "mindfulness," no life plan

Information from Erikson, 1982/1998.

CHANGING STATUS Many young adults change their identity status in the years after age 25. A detailed, longitudinal study in Sweden (Carlsson et al., 2015) found that some (41 percent) had achieved identity by age 25, and some (32 percent) had foreclosed. But many of those changed (most often from foreclosure to achievement) in the next few years. The group who changed most often were in moratorium at age 25. Almost all (94 percent) changed status by age 29, usually to achievement but sometimes to foreclosure.

The main finding of that study, however, was not change in status but in depth; identity often became deeper, more reflective, and meaningful during the 20s, as life experiences require the various aspects of identity to come together. One example was Alice, who at 25 was considering several possible careers. By age 29 she was midway through an advanced degree in archeology, a firm choice. Thus, her vocational identity had been achieved.

Alice's gender identity seemed firm at age 25: She wanted to marry and have a child, and she said this was more important than her career. But by age 29, although she had become a wife and mother, she said, "To me children should never hinder me from doing what I want, and a job should never hinder me from having children. It just can't be like that" (Carlsson et al., 2015, p. 340).

This determination to "have it all" (family and vocation) is part of identity achievement among many contemporary young adults. This is apparent not only in nations at the forefront of emerging adulthood (such as Sweden) but also among younger adults with advanced education in other nations (Montez et al., 2014; Mishra, 2014).

Research on almost 2,000 German emerging adults found that, for men as well as women, commitment to both work and family is the combination most likely to lead to emotional satisfaction. However, in that study only 18 percent of emerging adults had reached firm identity achievement in both domains (Luyckx et al., 2013). (The work/family conflict is discussed in Chapter 13.)

CAREERS Developmental psychologists influenced by Erikson, and emerging adults themselves, consider establishing a vocational identity part of growing up (Arnett, 2004). Emerging adulthood is a "critical stage for the acquisition of

Ordinary Workers Most children and adolescents want to be sports heroes, star entertainers, billionaires, or world leaders—yet fewer than 1 in 1 million succeed in doing so.

resources"—including the education, skills, and experience needed for vocational success (Tanner et al., 2009, p. 34).

Current emerging adults often quit one job and seek another. Between ages 18 and 25, the average U.S. worker changes jobs every year, with the college-educated worker changing jobs more than those who are less educated (U.S. Bureau of Labor Statistics, July 25, 2012). They want interesting work with coworkers who share their values, and they do not want to climb a particular vocational ladder, rung by rung. That is a problem for employers, who must interview, choose, and train new employees (Meister, 2012).

Readiness to seek a new job is less problematic for young workers themselves, since exploration is part of their identity search. However, prolonged unemployment is a problem. The economic recession has been particularly harsh on the current cohort of young adults, as their unemployment rate is close to double that of older job seekers. In Europe as well as North America, unemployment during emerging adulthood is common, leading to anxiety and depression (Arnett et al., 2014).

Emerging adulthood is a crucial time for developing values regarding work, such as whether job security and salary (extrinsic rewards) are more important than joy of doing the work one loves (intrinsic rewards). The particular work values that emerging adults develop are likely to be affected by the current worldwide economic recession, an example of the exosystem shaping this cohort in ways their parents did not experience (Johnson et al., 2012; Chow et al., 2014).

Personality in Emerging Adulthood

Both continuity and change are evident in personality lifelong. Temperament, childhood trauma, and emotional habits endure: If self-doubt, anxiety, depression, and so on are present in childhood and adolescence, they are often still evident years later. Traits strongly present at age 5 or 15 do not disappear by age 25.

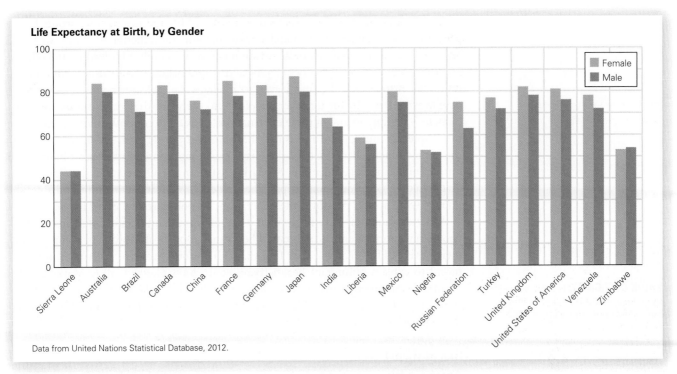

Life Expectancy at Birth, by Gender

Data from United Nations Statistical Database, 2012.

FIGURE 12.4 Not So Many Old Men International comparisons of life expectancy are useful for raising questions (why is the United States more similar to Mexico than to Japan?) and for highlighting universals (females live longer), no matter what their culture.

Using life itself to indicate health, people in the richest nations (e.g., Japan) live 25 years longer than those in the poorest ones (e.g., Sierra Leone) (see Figure 12.4). Or, to pick one non-fatal disease, rheumatoid arthritis (which typically occurs in mid-adulthood, unlike osteoarthritis) is more common internationally as income falls (Putrik et al., 2015).

SES differences are apparent *within* every nation as well. For example, in the United States, adults (age 25) with a college degree live an average of nine years longer than those with no high school diploma (National Center for Health Statistics, 2012). [Level of education is often used as a proxy for income, as it correlates closely.] Recent data find the SES gap widening in the United States, and health disparities follow (Olshansky et al., 2012).

OBSERVATION QUIZ

Young men everywhere play ball, but at least five cultural differences are apparent between these two scenes. What are they? (see answer, page 441) ▼

Playground? Cities that create play space for people of all ages keep the residents active, like these young men in Hong Kong *(left)* and Rio de Janeiro *(right)*.

It is not obvious why the connection between SES and health is so strong. Does education teach better health habits? Does income allow better medical care? Do advantages cascade, such as childhood stimulation and family SES leading to college, and then degrees leading to better jobs and neighborhoods with less pollution and more places to walk, bike, and play? Do intelligent people eat better? Do wealthy people avoid stress by hiring other people to do the work they do not want to do?

Before settling on any of these explanations, consider a conundrum first explained in Chapter 2: Immigrants are usually healthier yet poorer than the native-born of the same ethnicity. Paradoxically, they have less heart disease, drug abuse, obesity, and birth complications (García Coll & Marks, 2012). In the United States, children and grandchildren of immigrants surpass their elders in education, income, and English fluency—but as SES rises over the generations, so does virtually every illness.

Many explanations have been offered for the immigrant paradox. Perhaps healthy people are more likely to emigrate. Then their good health protects them despite their poverty. However, the data find that this "healthy migrant" theory is not sufficient to explain immigrant health (Bates et al., 2008; García Coll & Marks, 2012). From a developmental perspective, the most plausible explanation is social support, often very strong in new immigrant families and proven to protect health from cradle to grave (Priest & Woods, 2015).

Sex and Fertility

Another adult set of gains and losses occur with sexuality. Arousal, orgasm, and fertility are all affected by age.

SEXUAL RESPONSIVENESS Sexual arousal occurs more slowly and orgasm takes longer with senescence. However, some say that sexual responses improve with age. Could that be? Might familiarity with one's own body and with that of one's partner make slower response more often a joy than an anxiety?

A U.S. study of women aged 40 and older found that sexual activity decreased each decade but that sexual satisfaction did not (Trompeter et al., 2012). A British study of more than 2,000 adults in their 50s found that almost all of them were sexually active (94 percent of the men and 76 percent of the women) and, again, that most were quite satisfied with their sex lives (D. Lee et al., 2015).

INFERTILITY Although sexual satisfaction may not decline with age, reproduction certainly does. Rates of **infertility** (often defined as failure to conceive after a year of

THINK CRITICALLY: Is there something toxic about U.S. culture that harms the poor but does not affect new immigrants?

infertility
The failure to conceive a child after trying for at least a year.

Long Lasting Joy In every nation and culture, many couples who have been together for decades continue to delight in their relationship. Talk shows and headline stories tend to focus on bitter divorces, ignoring couples like these who are clearly happy together.

trying) vary from nation to nation, primarily because the rate increases when medical care is scarce (Gurunath et al., 2011).

Age matters as well. In the United States, about 12 percent of all adult couples are infertile, partly because many postpone childbearing. Peak fertility is at about age 18.

If couples in their 40s try to conceive, about half fail and the other half risk various complications. Of course, risk is not reality: In 2011 in the United States, 116,000 babies were born to women age 40 and older, the only age group for whom the birth rate is steadily rising (Hamilton et al., 2012). Most of their babies become healthy, well-loved children.

When couples are infertile, either or both partners may be the problem. A common reason for male infertility is low sperm count. Conception is most likely if a man ejaculates more than 20 million sperm per milliliter of semen, two-thirds of them mobile and viable, because each sperm's journey to the ovum is aided by millions of fellow travelers.

Depending on the man's age, each day about 100 million sperm reach maturity after a developmental process that lasts about 75 days. Anything that impairs body functioning over those 75 days (e.g., fever, radiation, drugs, time in a sauna, stress, environmental toxins, alcohol, cigarettes) reduces sperm number, shape, and motility (activity), making conception less likely. Sedentary behavior, perhaps particularly watching television, also correlates with lower sperm count (Gaskins et al., 2013).

As with men, women's fertility is affected by anything that impairs physical functioning—including disease, smoking, extreme dieting, and obesity. Many infertile women do not realize they have contracted one specific disease that impairs fertility—*pelvic inflammatory disease (PID)*. PID creates scar tissue that may block the fallopian tubes, preventing sperm from reaching an ovum (Brunham et al., 2015).

ASSISTED REPRODUCTION In the past 50 years, medical advances have solved about half of all fertility problems. Surgery repairs reproductive systems, and *assisted reproductive technology (ART)* overcomes obstacles such as a low sperm count and blocked fallopian tubes. ART, especially IVF (in vitro fertilization), has led to an estimated 5 million births (Fisher & Giudice, 2013).

IVF is quite different from the typical conception. The woman must take hormones to increase the number of fully developed ova, and the man must ejaculate into a receptacle. Then surgeons remove several ova from one or both ovaries and technicians combine the ova and sperm in a laboratory dish, often inserting one active sperm into each normal ovum.

Success is evident a few hours later, as several zygotes form and duplicate. Then one or more healthy blastocysts are inserted into the uterus, which is ready for implantation via additional drugs. Everyone waits and hopes.

Even with careful preparation, fewer than half of the inserted blastocysts successfully implant and grow to become newborns. Age of the ova is one crucial factor, so some young women freeze their ova for IVF years later (Mac Dougall et al., 2013). Miscarriages (perhaps one in three implanted embryos) increase with age.

If IVF newborns are normal weight, they do as well or better than other babies, not only in childhood health, intelligence, and school achievement but also in self-reported emotional development as teenagers (Wagenaar et al., 2011). One reason is that their parents tend to be more responsive. A study in Jamaica found that IVF parents are more authoritative, less permissive or authoritarian, than other parents (Pottinger & Palmer, 2013).

IVF children may grow well because they are planned and wanted. Of course, planning itself is cultural and contextual. National policy and culture have an effect, and traditionally, men tend to want more children than women do, although each half of a couple is affected by the fertility hopes of the other (Billingsley & Ferrarini, 2014),

ANSWER TO OBSERVATION QUIZ
(from page 439) Shoes or bare feet, pants or shorts, skyscrapers or smaller buildings, basketball or soccer, large, open space or small, fenced area. ●

IVF to the Rescue In every nation some babies begin life in a laboratory dish, as IVF overcomes blocked fallopian tubes, low sperm count, and other common fertility impediments. IVF now solves uncommon problems as well. In Kentucky, Avery Kennedy *(left)* began life via a donated frozen ovum, fertilized by Jared (shown here) and implanted in Wendy's uterus. In Spain *(right),* a few hours after Roger's conception, one stem cell was removed and tested for the gene for Huntington's disease. Since one of his parents (shown here) has that dominant gene, a zygote had a 50/50 chance of inheriting it. Roger did not.

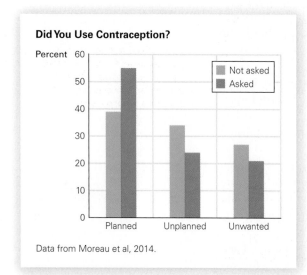

Did You Use Contraception?

Data from Moreau et al, 2014.

FIGURE 12.5 Actions and Intentions Can you say a child of yours was unwanted or unplanned if you didn't use contraception? For about one in every eight couples in this study, remembering their behavior when their children were conceived led them to conclude that the child was wanted and planned after all.

menopause
The time in middle age, usually around age 50, when a woman's menstrual periods cease and the production of estrogen, progesterone, and testosterone drops. Strictly speaking, menopause begins one year after a woman's last menstrual period.

The availability of contraception affects planning, but even when birth control is available and free, estimating how many pregnancies are planned is complex.

For instance, more than 8,000 parents in France were asked whether each pregnancy was planned, unplanned (mistimed), or unwanted. Half of them were asked that simple question. The answers were: 39 percent planned, 34 percent mistimed, and 27 percent unwanted. The other half were first asked whether they had been using contraception at conception. That made 55 percent say they planned the pregnancy: 24 percent said it was mistimed and 21 percent unwanted (Moreau et al., 2014) (see Figure 12.5).

MENOPAUSE During adulthood, the level of sex hormones circulating in the bloodstream declines—suddenly in women, gradually in men. As a result, sexual desire, frequency of intercourse, and odds of reproduction decrease. The specifics differ for women and men.

For women, sometime between ages 42 and 58 (the average age is 51), ovulation and menstruation stop because of a marked drop in production of several hormones. This is **menopause.** The precise age is affected primarily by genes (17 have been identified) (Morris et al., 2011; Stolk et al., 2012) but also by smoking (earlier menopause) and exercise (later).

In the United States, one in four women has a *hysterectomy* (surgical removal of the uterus), which may include removal of her ovaries. If she was premenopausal, removal of ovaries causes vaginal dryness and body temperature disturbance, including hot flashes (feeling hot), hot flushes (looking hot), and cold sweats (feeling chilled).

Natural menopause produces the same symptoms, but not as suddenly and not in everyone. Early menopause, surgical or not, increases the risk of health problems later on (Hunter, 2012).

The psychological consequences of menopause vary more than the physiological ones. Some menopausal women have erratic moods, others are more energetic, and still others become depressed (Judd et al., 2012). Many women are relieved that menstruation and fear of pregnancy have ended. Margaret Mead (famous anthropologist

Pausing, not Stopping During the years of menopause, these two women experienced more than physiological changes: Jane Goodall *(left)* was widowed and Ellen Johnson-Sirleaf *(right)* was imprisoned. Both, however, are proof that post-menopausal women can be productive. After age 50, Goodall (shown visiting a German zoo at age 70) founded and led several organizations that educate children and protect animals, and Johnson-Sirleaf (shown speaking to the International Labor Organization at age 68) became the president of Liberia.

who studied women throughout the world) felt renewed energy after age 50 and called it "post-menopausal zest" (Mark, 1999, p. 51).

Do men undergo anything like menopause? Some say yes, suggesting that the word **andropause** should be used to signify age-related reduction in testosterone, which reduces sexual desire, erections, and muscle mass (Samaras et al., 2012). Even with erection-inducing drugs such as Viagra and Levitra, sexual desire and speed of orgasm decline with age, as do many other physiological and cognitive functions.

But most experts think that the term *andropause* (or *male menopause*) is misleading because it implies a sudden drop in reproductive ability or hormones. Some men produce viable sperm and hence become new fathers at age 80 or older. Sexual inactivity and anxiety can reduce testosterone—superficially similar to menopause but with a psychological, not physiological, cause.

To combat the symptoms of the natural decline in estrogen or testosterone, some adults have turned to hormone replacement. Most physicians are wary, citing correlations between artificial hormones and breast cancer in women and heart disease in men (Zbuk & Anand, 2012; Handelsman, 2011). Nonetheless, hormones are sometimes prescribed (Samaras et al., 2012; Panay et al., 2013; Giannoulis et al., 2013). All physicians agree, however, that adult health depends more on habits than on hormones.

> **andropause**
> A term coined to signify a drop in testosterone levels in older men, which reduces sexual desire, erections, and muscle mass. (Also called *male menopause*.)

WHAT HAVE YOU LEARNED?

1. How are people affected by the visible changes in the skin between ages 25 and 65?
2. How does the ability to move the body change with age?
3. How does the body shape change between ages 25 and 65?
4. What is the relationship between cancer and aging?
5. What is the relationship between income, education, and disease in adulthood?
6. How are couples affected by the changes in sexual responsiveness with age?
7. What are the causes of infertility?
8. How easy or difficult is the process of artificial reproductive technology?
9. What are the sex differences in the decline of sex hormones with age?
10. What are the advantages and disadvantages of menopause?

Video: Brain Development Animation: Middle Adulthood

http://qrs.ly/g94sqlu

The Aging Brain

As just explained, superficial changes in appearance need not be devastating, diseases usually are not fatal until old age, and sex can be satisfying throughout adulthood. However, decline in brain functioning cannot be so easily dismissed. Descartes famously said, "I think, therefore I am." Loss of brain power is equated with loss of self. Is that what adulthood brings?

Pathological Changes

Like every other part of the body, the brain slows down with age. Neurons take longer to fire, and messages sent from the axon of one neuron are not picked up as quickly by the dendrites of other neurons. Reaction time lengthens.

However, *major neurocognitive disorder* (formerly called *dementia*), when thinking is so erratic or memory so impaired that normal life is impossible, rarely occurs until after age 70 or so—if then (Neurocognitive disorders (NCDs) are described in detail in Chapter 14).

For most adults under age 65, brain changes do not correlate with intellectual depth (Greenwood & Parasuraman, 2012). To use a metaphor, adult brains cannot sprint but they can run a marathon—judges, bishops, and world leaders in politics, religion, and industry are usually at least 50, often much older than that. Their thinking has benefited from experience.

A leading researcher on adult intellect wrote, "Decline prior to 60 years of age is almost inevitably a symptom or precursor of pathological age changes" (Schaie, 2005/2013, p. 497). *Pathological* means disease-connected, not the result of normal aging. If severe brain loss occurs before late adulthood, the cause is one of the following:

- *Drug abuse.* All psychoactive drugs harm the brain, especially prolonged, excessive use of alcohol, which can cause Wernicke-Korsakoff syndrome ("wet brain").

- *Poor circulation.* Everything that impairs blood flow—such as hypertension (high blood pressure) and heavy cigarette smoking—also impairs cognition.

- *Viruses.* The blood–brain barrier keeps most viruses away, but a few—including HIV and the prion that causes mad cow disease—can destroy neurons.

- *Genes.* About 1 in 1,000 people inherits a dominant gene for Alzheimer's disease, which destroys memory. Other uncommon genes also affect the brain.

Intelligence in Adulthood

Brains and intelligence vary as much as humans do. Intellectual abilities can rise, fall, zigzag, or stay the same, depending on genes and on the specifics of each life. This again illustrates the life-span perspective: Intelligence is multi-directional, multi-cultural, multi-contextual, and plastic. Generally, brain functioning is maintained: If you think deeply and clearly at age 20, you will probably do so at age 60.

You read in Chapter 7 that IQ correlates with school achievement in childhood. But what about achievement over the years of adulthood?

One leading theoretician, Charles Spearman (1927), proposed that there is a single entity that he called **general intelligence (g),** which each adult has to some degree. Although g cannot be measured directly, it can be inferred from various abilities, such as vocabulary, memory, and reasoning. Measuring those abilities produces an IQ score. That score correlates with health and wealth in adulthood.

Once a person reaches adulthood, an IQ score indicates whether that adult is a genius, average, or slow, no matter what the person's age. As you remember, in childhood, a person's score depends not only on items correct, with different items for

LaunchPad

Video Activity: Research Methods and Cognitive Aging explores how various research methods have been employed to study how intelligence changes with age.

general intelligence (g)
The idea that intelligence is one basic trait, underlying all cognitive abilities. According to this concept, people have varying levels of this general ability.

Smart Enough for the Trenches?
These young men were drafted to fight in World War I. Younger men (about age 17 or 18) did better on the military's intelligence tests than slightly older ones did. Problems with cross-sectional research were not yet recognized.

OBSERVATION QUIZ

In addition to intellectual ability, what two aspects of this test situation might affect older men differently than younger ones? (see answer, page 447) ◄

preschoolers and older children, but also on the child's age. That it not true for adults. The same IQ tests are usually given to people aged 18 to 88, and they are scored the same way.

The belief that *g* exists still influences thinking and testing on intelligence. Many neuroscientists seek genetic underpinnings for the intellect. Efforts to find specific genes or abilities that comprise *g* have not succeeded (Deary et al., 2010; Haier et al., 2009), but some aspects of brain function, particularly in the prefrontal cortex, hold promise (Barbey et al., 2013; Roca et al., 2010). Other scientists believe that *g* may arise from prenatal brain development, experiences in infancy, or physical health.

Still others question whether a single entity, *g*, exists. They emphasize the role of experience, noting that national and ethnic differences in average IQ scores suggest that context is crucial. Some aspects of this controversy were explored by a famous researcher, K. Warner Schaie, as the following explains.

A VIEW FROM SCIENCE

Adult IQ

At the University of Washington in 1956, K. Warner Schaie tested a cross section of 500 adults, aged 20 to 50, on five standard primary mental abilities considered to be the foundation of intelligence: (1) verbal meaning (vocabulary), (2) spatial orientation, (3) inductive reasoning, (4) number ability, and (5) word fluency (rapid verbal associations).

His cross-sectional results showed age-related decline in all five abilities, as others had found before. This suggested that biological changes of aging (nature) determined intel-

ligence and that every aspect of IQ was affected, as proponents of *g* might expect.

As mentioned briefly in Chapter 1, Schaie then had a brilliant idea, to combine longitudinal and cross-sectional methods. Seven years later, he retested his initial participants (longitudinal) and also tested a new group of people who were the same age that his earlier sample had been. Then he could compare people not only to their own earlier scores but also to people currently as old as his original group had been when first tested.

Schaie did so over his entire career, retesting and adding a new group every seven years. Known as the **Seattle Longitudinal Study,** this was the first *cross-sequential* study

Seattle Longitudinal Study
A major cross-sequential study of adult intelligence. This study began in 1956 and has been repeated every 7 years.

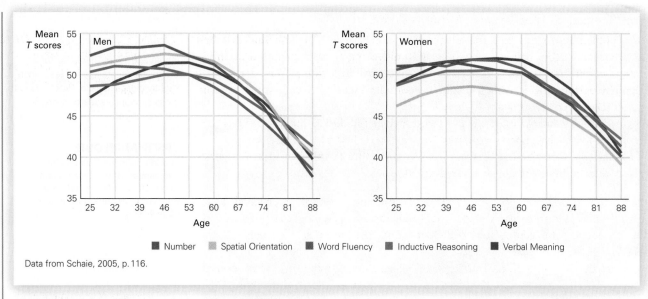

Data from Schaie, 2005, p. 116.

FIGURE 12.6 Age Differences in Intellectual Abilities Cross-sectional data on intellectual abilities at various ages would show much steeper declines. Longitudinal research, in contrast, would show more notable rises. Because Schaie's research is cross-sequential, the trajectories it depicts are more revealing: None of the average scores for the five abilities at any age are above 55 or below 35, which means that most people of every age are able to function intellectually.

of adult intelligence. Schaie confirmed and extended what others had found: Cross-sectional research shows declines, but longitudinal research shows improvement in most mental abilities during adulthood (Schaie, 2005/2013). So *g* varies more than others thought.

As Figure 12.6 shows, Schaie found that each ability at each age has a distinct pattern. Men are initially better at number skills and women at verbal skills, but the two sexes grow closer over time.

You can see that some abilities increase over the years of adulthood. As many other scientists have found, vocabulary is particularly likely to increase. Schaie found that everyone declined by age 60 in at least one of their basic abilities, but not until age 88 did everyone decline from their own earlier scores in all five skills.

Other researchers from many nations find similar trends, although specifics differ (Hunt, 2011). IQ scores typically increase, or are at least maintained, in adulthood. Individuals may show marked intellectual ups or downs year by year. Some people and some abilities fall by middle age, but others not until decades later (W. Johnson et al., 2014; Kremen et al., 2014). Such marked individual variation is one argument against *g*.

Schaie confirmed the Flynn effect (mentioned in Chapter 7): IQ rises when nations improve childhood nutrition and education. He also discovered more detailed cohort changes than had been recognized before.

Each successive cohort (born at seven-year intervals from 1889 to 1973) scored higher in adulthood than did the previous generations in verbal memory and inductive reason-

ing. However, number ability (math) peaked for those born in 1924 and then declined slowly in future cohorts until about 1970 (Schaie, 2005/2013).

School curricula influenced these differences: By the mid-twentieth century, reading, writing, and self-expression were more emphasized than they had been earlier, while memorizing "math facts" and doing long division were less central. Moreover, fewer adults practice their math skills every day: scanners at stores, cash registers, and calculators on smart phones make math skills atrophy.

Other cohort effects are that women have increased in IQ since they entered the labor market, and age-related declines appear for everyone about a decade later than they used to (Schaie, 2005/2013), probably because of better communication, education, and health.

Many studies using sophisticated designs and statistics have supplanted early cross-sectional, longitudinal, and cross-sequential studies. Decades of research confirm that cultures, eras, and individuals vary substantially in which cognitive abilities are nurtured and tested. From about age 20 to 70, national values, specific genes, and education affect IQ scores more than chronological age (W. Johnson et al., 2014).

Schaie found "virtually every possible permutation of individual profiles" (Schaie, 2005/2013, p. 497) of intelligence over adulthood. Although *average* scores on subtests decline, especially on timed tests, overall intellectual ability is usually maintained. Nature and nurture interact—and adults are smarter because of it.

Components of Intelligence: Many and Varied

Developmentalists study patterns of cognitive gain and loss. They contend that, because virtually every pattern is possible, it is misleading to ask whether adult intelligence either increases or decreases; it does not move in lockstep. "Vast domains of cognitive performance . . . may not follow a common, age-linked trajectory of decrement" (Dannefer & Patterson, 2008, p. 116).

Consequently, many researchers focus on specific intellectual abilities, finding that each component has its own pattern. One proposal, Howard Gardner's multiple intelligences, was described in Chapter 7. Here we consider two more: One that posits two distinct abilities and another that posits three.

TWO CLUSTERS OF INTELLIGENCE Broadly speaking, tests of intellectual abilities can be sorted into two clusters, those that measure raw learning potential and those that measure accumulated knowledge. The first group is called *fluid* and the second, *crystallized*.

As its name implies, **fluid intelligence** is like water, flowing to its own level no matter where it happens to be. Fluid intelligence is quick and flexible, enabling people to learn anything, even abstractions that are neither familiar nor connected to what they already know. Curiosity, learning for the joy of it, solving puzzles, and the thrill at discovering something new are marks of fluid intelligence (Silvia & Sanders, 2010).

The kinds of questions that test fluid intelligence among Western adults might be:

What comes next in each of these two series?

4 9 16 2 5 3
V X Z B D*

Puzzles are often used to measure fluid intelligence, with speedy solutions given bonus points (as on many IQ tests). Immediate recall—of nonsense words, of numbers, of a sentence just read—is one indicator of fluid intelligence because working memory is crucial (Chuderski, 2013; Nisbett et al., 2012).

Since fluid intelligence appears to be disconnected from past learning, it may seem impractical. Not so. A study of adults aged 34 to 83 found that people high in fluid intelligence were more exposed to stress but were less likely to suffer from it. They used their intellect to turn stresses into positive experiences (Stawski et al., 2010).

The ability to detoxify stress may be one reason that high fluid intelligence in emerging adulthood leads to longer life and higher IQ later on. Fluid intelligence is associated with openness to new experiences and overall brain health (Batterham et al., 2009; Silvia & Sanders, 2010).

By contrast, facts, information, and knowledge as a result of education and experience comprise **crystallized intelligence**. The size of a person's vocabulary, the knowledge of chemical formulas, and the long-term memory for dates in history might all indicate crystallized intelligence. Tests to measure this intelligence might include questions like these:

What does *eleemosynary* mean?
Who was Descartes?
Explain the difference between a tangent and a triangle.
Why does the city of Peking no longer exist?†

> **fluid intelligence**
> Those aspects of basic intelligence that make learning quick and thorough. Short-term memory, abstract thought, and speed of thinking are usually considered part of fluid intelligence.

> **crystallized intelligence**
> Those aspects of intellectual ability that reflect accumulated learning. Vocabulary and general information are examples.

ANSWER TO **OBSERVATION** QUIZ
(from page 445) Older adults might be more stressed by the proctors, and might find it uncomfortable to sit on the floor while writing. ●

---

* The correct answers are 6 and F. The clue is to think of multiplication (squares) and the alphabet; some series are much more difficult to complete.

† A charitable institution or donation
A 17th-century French philosopher
A triangle is three lines that enclose a shape; a tangent is a line that touches a curve
Peking has been renamed Beijing, the capital city of China

Think Before Acting Both of these adults combine fluid and crystallized intelligence, insight and intuition, logic and experience. One *(left)* is a surgeon, studying X-rays before picking up her scalpel. The other *(right)* is drafting plans for a new building, a task that requires technical skill as well as visual imagination.

Although such questions seem to measure achievement more than aptitude, these two are connected, especially in adulthood. Intelligent adults read widely, think deeply, and remember what they learn, so achievement reflects aptitude. Thus, crystallized intelligence is an outgrowth of fluid intelligence (Nisbett et al., 2012).

Vocabulary, for example, improves with reading. Using the words *joy, ecstasy, bliss,* and *delight*—each appropriately, with distinct nuances (quite apart from the drugs, perfumes, or yogurts that use these names)—is a sign of intelligence. Remember the knowledge base (Chapter 7): As people know more, they learn more. That explains why a person's years of education are considered a rough indicator of adult IQ (Nisbett et al., 2012).

To know the whole of a person's intelligence, both fluid and crystallized intelligence must be measured. Age complicates the IQ calculation because scores on items measuring fluid intelligence decrease with age, whereas scores on crystallized intelligence increase.

Thus total IQ is often fairly steady from ages 30 to 70. Although brain slowdown begins early in adulthood, it is rarely apparent until massive declines in fluid intelligence affect crystallized intelligence. Only then do overall IQ scores fall.

This suggests that it is foolish to try to find *g,* a single omnibus intelligence, because components need to be measured separately. In testing for *g,* real developmental changes will be masked because fluid and crystallized abilities cancel each other out.

THREE FORMS OF INTELLIGENCE: STERNBERG Robert Sternberg (1988, 2003, 2011, 2015) agrees that a single intelligence score is misleading. He believes that successful intelligence is not simply the ability to do well in school (the focus of early IQ tests) but the ability to adapt to various cultural contexts, learning from experience (Sternberg, 2015).

Obviously, the years of adulthood bring many experiences, which provide opportunities for intelligence to grow. Sternberg proposed three fundamental intelligences: analytic, creative, and practical, each of which can be tested (see Table 12.1).

Analytic intelligence includes all the mental processes that foster academic proficiency by making efficient learning, remembering, and thinking possible. Analytic strengths are valuable in emerging adulthood, particularly in college, in graduate school, and in job training. Multiple-choice tests and brief essays that call forth remembered information, with one and only one right answer, indicate analytic intelligence.

Creative intelligence involves intellectual flexibility and innovation. Creative thinking is divergent rather than convergent, valuing the unexpected, imaginative, and unusual rather than standard and conventional answers. Sternberg developed tests of creative intelligence that include writing a short story titled "The Octopus's

analytic intelligence
Intelligence that involves logic, planning, strategy selection, focused attention, and information processing.

creative intelligence
Intelligence that involves the capacity to be flexible and innovative, thinking unusual ideas.

TABLE 12.1	Sternberg's Three Forms of Intelligence		
	Analytic Intelligence	**Creative Intelligence**	**Practical Intelligence**
Mental Processes	• Abstract planning • Strategizing • Focused attention • Verbal skills • Logic	• Imagination • Appreciation of the unexpected or unusual • Originality • Vision	• Adaptive actions • Understanding and assessing daily problems • Applied skills and knowledge
Valued for	• Analyzing • Learning and understanding • Remembering • Thinking	• Intellectual flexibility • Originality • Future hopes	• Adaptability • Concrete knowledge • Real-world experience
Indicated by	• Multiple-choice tests • Brief essays • Recall of information	• Inventiveness • Innovation • Resourcefulness • Ingenuity	• Performance in real situations • "Street smarts"

Based on Sternberg, 1988, 2003, 2011, 2015.

Sneakers" or planning an advertising campaign for a new doorknob. Those with many unusual ideas earn high scores.

Practical intelligence involves adapting to the demands of a given situation, including understanding the expectations and needs of other people. This form of intelligence is particularly needed in adulthood.

Sternberg emphasizes that everyone should deploy the strengths and guard against the limitations of each type of intelligence. Choosing which intelligence to use takes wisdom, which Sternberg considers a fourth ingredient of successful intelligence:

> One needs creativity to generate novel ideas, analytical intelligence to ascertain whether they are good ideas, practical intelligence to implement the ideas and persuade others of their value, and wisdom to ensure that the ideas help reach a common good.
>
> [Sternberg, 2012, p. 21]

practical intelligence
The intellectual skills used in everyday problem solving. (Sometimes called *tacit intelligence*.)

Smart Farmer; Smart Teacher
This school field trip is not to a museum or a fire station but to a wheat field, where children study grains that will become bread. Like this creative teacher, modern farmers use every kind of intelligence. To succeed, they need to analyze soil, fertilizer, and pests (analytic intelligence); to anticipate market prices and food fads (creative intelligence); and to know what crops and seed varieties grow in each acre of their land as they manage their workers (practical intelligence).

© PETER BECK/CORBIS

INTELLIGENCE IN DAILY LIFE Practical intelligence is sometimes called *tacit intelligence* because it is not obvious on tests. Instead it comes from "the school of hard knocks" and may be "street smarts," not "book smarts." Experience advances practical intelligence, and thus adults who are able to learn from their past may gain in practical intelligence every year.

The benefits of practical intelligence in adult life are obvious. Few adults need to define obscure words or deduce the next element in a number sequence (analytic intelligence); and few need to compose new music, restructure local government, or invent a useful gadget (creative intelligence). Ideally, those few have already found a niche for themselves and rely on people with practical intelligence to implement their analytic or creative ideas.

Almost every adult, however, must solve real-world challenges: maintaining a home; advancing a career; managing family finances; sifting information from media, mail, and the Internet; addressing the emotional needs of family members, neighbors, and colleagues (Blanchard-Fields, 2007). Scores on tests of practical intelligence hold steady from age 20 to 70, because these skills are needed throughout life (Schaie, 2005/2013).

Without practical intelligence, analytic intelligence in adulthood is ineffective because people resist academic brilliance as unrealistic and elite, as the term *ivory tower* implies. Similarly, a stunningly creative idea may be rejected as ridiculous and weird rather than seriously considered—if it is not accompanied by practical intelligence.

For example, imagine a business manager, or a school principal, or a political leader, or a parent without practical intelligence trying to change routine practices. Some routines *should* be changed, of course, but that does not mean that they will be.

Perhaps that manager, principal, leader, or parent used analytic intelligence to determine that the old way was destructive and then used creative intelligence to find a better way. But practical intelligence is essential. If innovation does not take into account human views and needs, then the workers, teachers, voters, or family members may resist, misinterpret, and predict failure. The innovator would be frustrated; the people stuck to their old ways.

Same Situation, Far Apart: Men at Work The balloon vendor in Pakistan *(left)* and the construction supervisor in Beijing, China *(right)*, have much in common: They work outdoors, use practical intelligence, and have good jobs in nations where many people do not. Context is crucial. If they were to trade places, each would be lost at first. However, practical intelligence could save the day—each might be able to learn the skills required in a new job.

No abstract test can assess practical intelligence because context is crucial. Instead, adults need to be observed coping with daily life. In hiring a new employee, the interviewer might describe an actual situation and ask how the applicant would handle it. Many companies use such situational tests to hire managers. The prospective employee may be asked:

> *You assign a new project to one of your subordinates, who protests, saying it cannot be done without more resources and time. Rank your possible responses, from best to worst. Explain your reasoning.*
>
> *a. You find someone else to do the job.*
> *b. You ask your subordinate to figure out how it can be done with current constraints.*
> *c. You reallocate work, to give your subordinate more time.*
> *d. You fire the subordinate.*
> *e. You ask your supervisor what to do.*
> *f. You postpone the new task until you find more resources.*
>
> *(from Salter & Highhouse, 2009)*

Situational tests are used so often in the medical professions that review books have been made available for those preparing for such exams (e.g., Varian & Cartwright, 2013). Because practical intelligence is crucial on the job, probationary periods, internships, apprentices, and so on are common.

LEARNING IN NATIONS Difficult as it is to determine which adults are truly intelligent, it is even more difficult to judge nations, in part because each culture has its own concept of intelligence based partly on tradition and partly on current needs. Earl Hunt, a psychologist who studies intelligence, contends that the nations with the most advanced economies and greatest national wealth are those that make the best use of **cognitive** ●
artifacts—that is, ways to amplify and extend general cognitive ability (Hunt, 2012).

Historically, written language, the number system, universities, and the scientific method were cognitive artifacts. Each of these artifacts extended human intellectual abilities by helping people interact to learn more.

Sheer survival (in earlier centuries, more newborns died than lived) and longer life (few people survived past age 65) resulted from cognitive artifacts. One example is the germ theory of disease, a cognitive artifact developed from other artifacts such

cognitive artifacts
Intellectual tools, such as writing, invented by one generation and then passed down from generation to generation to foster learning within societies.

Focus It might seem as if Cindy Fay, shown here, has too many distractions to get anything done, but this scene actually depicts her intense, productive focus. She is a meteorologist for the National Weather Service, predicting the weather in the next 24 hours in Hastings, Nebraska. The monitors, phones, keyboards, and notes on her expansive desk are all carefully selected to optimize her forecasting ability.

as the scientific method that enabled doctors to do research and learn from each other (Hunt, 2011).

In more recent times, universal education, immunization, clean water, electricity, global travel, and the Internet have resulted in advanced societies. According to this idea, smart people are better able to use the cognitive artifacts of their society to advance their own intelligence. Then they develop more cognitive artifacts, and the whole community benefits.

For instance, most developed nations provide free preschool and kindergarten to all children. That increases learning in the young, eventually advancing the nation. By contrast, other nations value fertility more than health, choose profit instead of education, educate one gender more than the other, and forbid some expressions of knowledge. That undercuts intellectual development (Hunt, 2011).

A recent meta-analysis of 167 nations found that disaster deaths decreased when education increased (measured by the proportion of women, aged 20 to 39, with at least an eighth-grade education) (Lutz et al., 2014). The hypothesis was that educated people are better able to support prevention measures and to use various cognitive artifacts (such as safer housing construction, stockpiling supplies, physical and mental health care). Elaborate statistical testing found "female education is indeed strongly associated with a reduction in disaster fatalities" but national wealth was not (Lutz et al., 2014, p. 1061).

THINK CRITICALLY: If an adult lived in another nation, would he or she be smarter? And, because of that, would that adult live longer and healthier?

WHAT HAVE YOU LEARNED?

1. How is the brain affected by aging during adulthood?

2. How successful have neuroscientists been in finding g?

3. What are the age-related differences in fluid and crystallized intelligence?

4. Why would someone want greater crystallized intelligence than fluid intelligence?

5. Why would someone want greater fluid intelligence than crystallized intelligence?

6. When would analytic intelligence be particularly useful?

7. Would you like to be an adult high in one of Sternberg's three intelligences but low in the other two? Why or why not?

8. How might cognitive artifacts affect the economic wealth of a nation?

Selecting and Protecting

Aging neurons, cultural pressures, historical conditions, and past education all affect adult cognition. None of these can be controlled directly by an individual. Nonetheless, many researchers believe that each adult has the power to make crucial choices about his or her intellectual development.

For example, if adults decided to discard their calculators, their math skills might improve. Of course, most adults would consider that strange: Spending more time on math might help number intelligence, but few modern adults want to do double-digit division in their heads.

Similarly, memory would improve if a person never relied on their smart phone or e-mail to reach their friends. Are modern cultural artifacts making us lazy intellectually, or have we merely focused on new challenges? The answer may be both.

A theme of the first half of this chapter is that choices and perceptions affect adult health. That applies to intellectual development as well. As you have seen, adult IQ is variable, sometimes increasing and sometimes falling. We now look at some factors that influence this, a combination of individual choices and social pressures.

Stressors and Thought

Many health decisions that adults make, as seen earlier in this chapter, prioritize immediate comfort over long-term health. Choices of foods, drugs, exercise, and health care affect cognition because anything that slows down blood circulation in the body also slows down the brain. That affects speed of thought and leads to brain shrinkage.

Moreover, harmful choices increase stress, which impairs brain functioning (Prenderville et al., 2015). Stress does not merely correlate with illness of all kinds—it *causes* illness, as hundreds of studies on the immune system and stressors have found.

Sometimes people are told "it's all in your head" when they complain of physical ailments. That is neither fair nor accurate. A recent comparison between stress-free adults and adults who were caring for a family member with brain cancer found that the caregivers had signaling factors in their brains that increased expression of genes for inflammation. Thus, basic immunity is affected when stress is high (G. Miller et al., 2014). As in this case, caregiving may be the expression of basic values. For many people, no other option is possible.

Chronic stress increases depression and other psychological illnesses that impair thinking, and it attacks the brain itself (Marin et al., 2011; McEwen & Gianaros, 2011). The psychological disorder posttraumatic stress disorder (PTSD) is recognized as harming a person long after an initial trauma. Avoiding all stress is impossible, but people can choose to reduce stress, reinterpreting problems that arise, and to care for themselves so that coping is easier.

THE STRESS OF MODERN LIFE All the demands of modern life increase the stress on each adult. Some of those stresses become stressors. A **stressor** is an experience, circumstance, or condition that affects a person. Thus, a stress is external; some stresses are internalized, becoming stressors.

Drug abuse, obesity, lack of exercise, cigarette smoking, high-fat diets, uncontrolled diabetes, avoiding medication to control hypertension—all chosen by many adults—impair thought. Are such choices a reaction to the demands and pace of current life? Was life simpler when it was shorter?

Video Activity: The Effects of Psychological Stress outlines the explanations for and causes of stress, and then it allows you to evaluate the stress in your own life.

stressor
Any situation, event, experience, or other stimulus that causes a person to feel stressed. Many circumstances become stressors for some people but not for others.

Same Situation, Far Apart: Two 2013 Disasters In the Boston Marathon *(left)*, three people were killed and more than 200 injured when two terrorist bombs exploded, and in South Africa *(right)*, 34 striking mine workers were shot dead when police opened fire. Despite the obvious differences, survivors everywhere cope by crying and holding each other.

Perhaps adults must cope with more stressors than was true earlier, although certainly some stresses are reduced. Deaths in war and revenge for crimes are decreasing (Pinker, 2011), so fewer people must cope with a premature death of a parent or child. However, the rate and scope of disasters—caused by human and natural events—is increasing. That causes multiple stresses in survivors (Leaning & Guha-Sapir, 2013).

To be specific, the World Health Organization defines disasters as unexpected events—both from nature (floods, earthquakes, and so on) and from nurture (bombs, epidemics)—that cause at least 10 deaths and 100 serious injuries. The rate in the first decade of the twenty-first century was ten times that of a century ago and three times the rate 20 years earlier (Leaning & Guha-Sapir, 2013).

Moreover, globalization and high-speed communication networks mean that each disaster adds stress to millions far from the event—think of television footage of 9/11, or Hurricane Katrina, or the bombings of Gaza, Yemen, Syria. Research finds that when people watch immediate coverage of disasters, that increases acute stress reactions to later disasters—even for people far from the trauma and personally unaffected (Garfin et al., 2015).

In addition, personal events that are stressful—divorce, intellectual disabilities, relocation, immigration, job loss—are more common than they were, so every adult experiences major stress. Finally, every life has many minor stresses called *hassles*—traffic jams, noise at night, rude strangers, computer breakdowns—that trouble many adults.

COPING Throughout history adults have used various ways to cope with stress. Some of these are effective; others are not.

avoidant coping
Responding to a stressor by ignoring, forgetting, or hiding it.

The worst coping is **avoidant coping,** which averts dealing with the problem. All the bad habits described earlier in the chapter—drug use, overeating, underexercising—temporarily relieve anxiety but eventually make things worse. Ignoring a problem, either literally forgetting it via a drug-induced blackout or hiding it (one person who owed back taxes threw all official letters under his bed, unopened) is the worst response to stress—it increases depression and the risk of suicide.

Avoidant reactions cause yet more stressors. An effective way to gain perspective on stress is to help other people, yet some people in avoidant coping isolate themselves. For instance, parents of disabled children need help from each other and from relatives, but such parents have higher rates of divorce than the average parent. Similarly, some people diagnosed with serious illness do not tell their friends, some LGBTQ (lesbian, gay, bisexual, transgender, questioning) individuals stay "in the closet," some people with serious addictions hide from other people.

problem-focused coping
A strategy to deal with stress by tackling a stressful situation directly.

emotion-focused coping
A strategy to deal with stress by changing feelings and interpretations about the stressor rather than changing the stressor itself.

Psychologists distinguish two positive strategies. In **problem-focused coping,** people attack the stressor directly—for instance, confronting a difficult boss, moving out of a noisy neighborhood, helping community members caught in the same earthquake, donating money, or food, or blood (as millions of Americans did after 9/11). The other way to cope is with **emotion-focused coping,** changing their emotional reactions—for instance, from anger to acceptance, from resentment to understanding. This mode of coping is one form of the cognitive coping, mentioned in Chapter 8, as well as the positivity effect that seems to occur in late adulthood.

Of course, natural disasters, such as earthquakes, and personal tragedies, such as the death of a loved one, are always stressful immediately and cannot be erased. However, reinterpretation may be possible. Instead of dwelling on their misfortune, they emphasize their good fortune—not "why me?" but "it could have been worse." The stresses are seen as a challenge, even when outsiders would consider them threats (Reich et al., 2010).

For example, although Hurricane Katrina occurred years ago, survivors continue to cope with the aftermath, and social scientists continue to study them. One team considered religious beliefs before and after the disaster. Victims who believed in a vengeful and punishing God continued to suffer, but those who believed that God is caring and benevolent coped well, experiencing *posttraumatic growth,* not PTSD (posttraumatic stress disorder) (Chan & Rhodes, 2013).

This study confirms a general trend. Some people use religion to cope with stress, especially when unexpected illness or disaster occurs (in the United States, church attendance was up after 9/11), which may either bring solace or make things worse (Burke et al., 2013; Thuné-Boyle et al., 2013).

Are there gender differences in preferred coping styles? Men may be problem-focused, reacting with "fight or flight." Their sympathetic nervous system (faster heart rate, increased adrenaline) prepares them for attack or escape. Testosterone rises when men confront a problem and decreases if they fail. From childhood, males are encouraged to express anger, use force (fight), or disappear (flight).

Females, however, may be emotion-focused, likely to "tend and befriend"—that is, to seek the company of other people when they are under pressure. Their bodies produce oxytocin, a hormone that leads them to seek confidential and caring interactions (S. Taylor, 2006; S. Taylor et al., 2000). Their first reaction when something goes wrong might be to call a friend. A woman might be troubled if a man won't talk about his problems; a man might get upset if a woman does not take his advice and solve her problems.

This distinction appeared among 634 mothers and fathers who had lost a baby, either stillborn at birth or dying within the first days and months of life (D. Christiansen et al., 2014). The women were more likely to anxiously seek social support from other people (sometimes overprotecting another child), and men were more likely to avoid attachment (sometimes spending hours away from home).

Gender differences should not be exaggerated. Both problem- and emotion-focused coping can be effective; everyone should sometimes fight and sometimes befriend. In the study of bereaved parents, the researchers noted that both parents sometimes suffered from PTSD and suggested that they could help each other (D. Christiansen et al., 2014). A review suggests that gender differences, including fight-or-flight versus tend-and-befriend responses, are much smaller in reality than in popular assumptions (Carothers & Reis, 2013).

CHOOSING METHODS Not only do adults of both sexes need to find the best strategy for each particular problem, but they also need to decide who will help, how and when (Aldwin, 2009). Getting social support is generally a good strategy—other people provide suggestions, lighten a load, and add humor or perspective (Fiori & Denckla, 2012). But sometimes other people criticize, distract, or delay a person's coping.

Related to social support is the overall social context, which may diminish stress or may increase it. A U.S. study of 65,000 adults compared biomedical signs of poor health, such as hypertension and insulin resistance, which collectively are called **weathering.** In this study, weathering happened faster among African Americans—by age 60 their average biological age was 10 years older than that of European Americans.

One explanation is that something within African Americans (their genes? their diet? their personal coping style?) causes faster weathering. However, the authors of this study blame the "chronic stress" of living in a "race-conscious society" (Geronimus et al., 2006, p. 832). Another study of White, Black, and Hispanic adults in Chicago pinpointed the correlation between hypertension and *vigilance,* i.e., being chronically on the alert for discrimination (Hicken et al., 2014).

Ideally, with age and experience adults learn to respond wisely, and social supports are in place so that trauma—from the televised accounts of distant wars to

weathering
The gradual accumulation of stressors over a long period of time, wearing down a person's resilience and resistance.

Nine Were Killed, and Then . . .
Coping with the 2015 murder of nine people at a prayer meeting in Charleston, South Carolina, led some people to depression, others to revenge, others to forgiveness. Most—Black and White—turned their emotions to public mourning (shown here) and then anger at the Confederate flag flying above the State House, where the leaders of the South Carolina government work. The legislators, mostly White, took action, voting 94 to 20 to take the flag down. Both emotional and problem-solving coping were evident.

the daily hassles of living in a crime-ridden neighborhood—does not wear down resilience. Hopefully, maturity reduces stress. As described in Chapter 15, over the years of adulthood, a more positive attitude toward life develops, making it easier to reinterpret stresses so that they do not fester.

Optimization with Compensation

selective optimization with compensation
The theory that people specialize in some abilities and to ameliorate any physical and cognitive losses they may experience.

Paul and Margret Baltes (1990) developed a theory called **selective optimization with compensation** to describe the "general process of systematic functioning" (P. Baltes, 2003, p. 25). They believe that people seek to *optimize* their development, *selecting* the best way to *compensate* for physical and cognitive losses, becoming more proficient at activities they want to perform well and deciding to avoid other tasks.

Selective optimization with compensation applies to every aspect of life, from choosing friends to playing baseball. Each adult seeks to maximize gains and minimize losses, practicing some abilities and ignoring others. Such choices are critical, because any ability can be enhanced or diminished, depending on how, when, and why a person uses it. It is possible to "teach an old dog new tricks," but adults need to choose to learn those new tricks.

Research on adult cognition finds that, when adults are motivated, few age-related deficits are apparent. However, compared with younger adults, older adults are less motivated to put forth their best effort when the task at hand is not particularly engaging (Hess et al., 2009). That works against them if they take an IQ test.

As Baltes and Baltes (1990) explain, selective optimization means that each adult selects certain aspects of intelligence to optimize and neglects the rest. If the ignored aspects happen to be the ones measured on intelligence tests, then IQ scores will fall, even if the adult's selection improves (optimizes) other aspects of intellect. The brain is plastic over the life span, developing new dendrites and activation sequences, adjusting to whatever the person chooses to learn (Karmiloff-Smith, 2010).

For example, suppose someone is highly motivated to learn about a particular area of the world, perhaps East Timor, a tiny independent nation since 2002. That someone goes to the library, selecting key articles and the two dozens books in English about East Timor, ignoring other interesting topics (*selection*).

Then suppose that aging vision makes it hard to read the fine print of some news articles about East Timor. Time for *compensation*—new glasses, a magnifier, increased font size. Some bits of knowledge may be pivotal: Note-taking strategies may include color coding and underlining to emphasize crucial facts. The result: if a local lawmaker or history buff wants to know about genocide, or Indonesia, or the United Nations, then that someone can provide valuable knowledge about East Timor that few others have (*optimization*).

If the expert on East Timor takes an IQ test that includes *tamarind* as a vocabulary word, that person might score high in vocabulary but fail questions of general knowledge. Thus, knowledge increases in depth but decreases in breadth.

Expert Cognition

Another way to describe gains and losses, or selective optimization with compensation, is to say that every adult is an expert in something. Each adult specializes in whatever is personally meaningful, anything from car repair to gourmet cooking, from illness diagnosis to fly fishing. One of my students said she was an expert in makeup; she always looked beautiful.

As people develop expertise in some areas, they pay less attention to others. For example, everyone watches only a few television channels or none at all, ignoring vast realms of experience. Each person has no interest in attending certain events for which others wait in line for hours. I wish my beautiful student had wanted to be an expert in developmental psychology, but adulthood has taught me that my passions are not shared by everyone.

Culture and context guide us in selecting areas of expertise. Many adults born 60 years ago are much better than more recent cohorts at penmanship, which was taught by their teachers in childhood. Those students practiced, became experts, and now maintain expertise.

Today's adults make other choices for children. Reading, for instance, is currently considered crucial, unlike a century ago when adult illiteracy was common. Parents buy blocks with letters on them for babies and read books to toddlers. Teachers and parents are pleased when kindergartners can read, unlike 50 years ago when reading began in first grade. Schools are closed down if too many third-graders are poor

Same Situation, Far Apart: Don't Be Afraid The police officer in Toronto collecting slugs and the violinist in Jakarta collecting donations have both spent years refining their skills. Many adults would fear being that close to a murder victim or that close to thousands of rushing commuters, but both of these men have learned to practice their vocation no matter where they are. They are now experts: The cop discovered that two guns were used, and the musician earns more than $5 a day (the average for street musicians in Indonesia).

LaunchPad

Video: Expertise in Adulthood: An Expert Discusses His Work In this video, Kenneth Davis discusses his research on how the neurotransmitter acetylcholine affects memory.

readers; states brag about their reading proficiency scores—and do not pay attention to penmanship.

Experts, as cognitive scientists define them, are not necessarily people with rare and outstanding proficiency. Nor are they simply people who are competent at a particular skill (Tracey et al., 2014). Although sometimes the term *expert* connotes an extraordinary genius, to researchers it means more—and less—than that. Expertise is not innate, although people with inherited abilities often select those abilities to develop. Experts are more intuitive, automatic, strategic, and flexible in their chosen field, as now explained.

INTUITIVE Novices follow formal procedures and rules. Experts rely more on past experiences and immediate contexts; their actions are therefore more intuitive and less stereotypic than those of the novice. The role of experience and intuition is evident in every vocation, from surgeons to musicians, from teachers to truck drivers.

One study compared psychotherapists, both experienced and new—all with the requisite academic knowledge. The therapists were asked to talk aloud as they analyzed a hypothetical case. The experts did more "forward thinking," using inferences and developing a possible treatment plan. The novices were less likely to think about the social relationships of the person and more likely to stick to describing what is rather than wondering what might be (Eells et al., 2011).

This conclusion needs to be qualified, however. A review of expertise and therapy found that, although they generally improve the lives of their clients, few therapists become genuine experts. Needed is more feedback and readjustment based on the eventual outcomes of their clients—an application of the scientific method (Tracey et al., 2014). Expertise develops best when learning is ongoing; intuition needs to be tempered by data on success.

An experiment involved 486 Dutch college students, asked to predict the winners of four World Cup soccer matches soon to be played. The students who were avid fans (the experts) made *better* predictions when they had two minutes of unconscious thought (when they could not think about soccer because they had to solve a difficult math problem) than when they had time to mull over their choice (see Figure 12.7).

Those who didn't care much about soccer (the nonexperts) did poorly overall, but they did *worse* when they had time to use unconscious intuition (Dijksterhuis et al., 2009). Intuition works for experts, but not for others.

AUTOMATIC This experiment with soccer experts and nonexperts also confirms that many elements of expert performance are automatic; that is, the complex, time-consuming action and thought required by most people have become routine for experts. Experts process incoming information quickly, analyze it efficiently, and then act in well-rehearsed ways that make their efforts appear unconscious. In fact, some automatic actions are no longer accessible to the conscious mind.

This is apparent if you have tried to teach someone to drive. Excellent drivers who are inexperienced instructors do not recognize or verbalize automatic knowledge—such as scanning the far side of the road for pedestrians and cyclists, or feeling the car shift gears as it heads up an incline, or hearing the tires lose traction on a bit of sand. Yet such factors differentiate the expert from the novice.

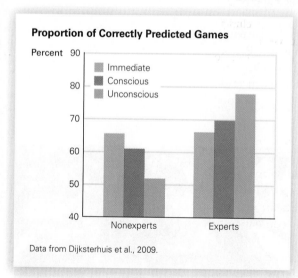

Proportion of Correctly Predicted Games

Data from Dijksterhuis et al., 2009.

FIGURE 12.7 If You Don't Know, Don't Think! Undergraduates at the University of Amsterdam were asked to predict winners of four World Cup soccer matches in one of three conditions: (1) immediate—as soon as they saw the names of the nations that were competing in each of the contests, (2) reflective—after thinking for two minutes about their answers, and (3) unconscious—two minutes after they saw the names, with those two minutes spent solving math tasks. As you can see, the experts were better at predicting winners after unconscious processing, but the nonexperts became less accurate after two minutes of thought, either consciously or unconsciously.

This may explain why, despite powerful motivation, quicker reactions, accurate knowledge of road rules, and better vision, teenagers' rate of fatal car accidents is three times that of adults (Insurance Institute, 2012). Sometimes they take risks (speeding, running a red light, drinking, and so on), but often they simply misjudge and misperceive conditions that a more experienced driver would automatically notice.

The same gap between knowledge and instruction occurs when a computer expert tries to teach a novice what to do, as I know myself when my daughters try to help me with the finer points of Excel. They are unable to verbalize what they know, although they can do it very well on my computer. It is much easier to click the mouse or do the keystroke oneself than to teach someone else what has become automatic.

The fact that such skill is automatic, not the result of increased motivation or practice, was evident in EEGs of the brain activity in musicians and non-musicians when they heard music (Rigoulot et al., 2015). All were instructed to listen for a target sound within the music, and they all tried their best, with some of both groups succeeding. But automaticity was apparent: The brains of the musicians responded more rapidly and robustly as soon as the music started.

Automatic processing is thought to explain why expert chess and Go players are much better than novices. They see a configuration of game pieces and automatically encode it as a whole, rather than analyzing it bit by bit. A study of expert chess players (aged 17 to 81) found minor age-related declines, but expertise was much more important than age (Jastrzembski et al., 2006).

This was particularly apparent for speedy recognition that the king was threatened: Older experts did that in a fraction of a second, almost as quickly as younger adults who knew the game well, despite the elders' steep, age-related declines on standard tests of memory and speed (Jastrzembski et al., 2006).

When something—such as an audience, an unfamiliar place, or too much conscious thought—interferes with automatic processing, the result may be clumsy performance. This is thought to be the problem when some experienced athletes "choke under pressure"—their automatic actions are hijacked (DeCaro et al., 2011).

automatic processing
Thinking that occurs without deliberate, conscious thought. Experts process most tasks automatically, saving conscious thought for unfamiliar challenges.

STRATEGIC Experts have more and better strategies, especially when problems are unexpected. Indeed, strategy may be the most pivotal difference between a skilled and an unskilled person, as the skilled person has sufficient experience to be able to have alternate strategies available when new problems arise.

Determining how people choose strategies is a complex question (Marewski & Schooler, 2011), and it is difficult to compare experts and novices except to note that experience prevents panic. Expert chess players have general strategies for winning and dozens of specific strategies that prevent quitting too readily, or continuing to play when checkmate is inevitable (Bilalić et al., 2009).

Scientists seek to understand the variations and origins of cognitive strategies needed to sort through the many bits of information that are accumulated over the years. Experts use their *cognitive reserve* (a special form of organ reserve) to develop appropriate strategies (Barulli & Stern, 2013).

Expertise has been demonstrated in the following areas: "computer programing, chess playing, teaching . . . playing bridge, solving algebra word problems, solving economic problems, and judicial decision making" (Tracey et al., 2014, p. 220). Considering those, you can see that effective strategies are essential—no one could be proficient at, for example, solving algebra word problems without a good method, far beyond good calculating skills.

Another example, familiar to everyone, is teaching. Think about your most expert professor. He or she institutes routines and policies early in the semester, which are

Many Skills Nurse Rolanda Florence checks the glucose level of a person with diabetes as part of three days of free health screenings in Los Angeles.

OBSERVATION QUIZ
What two sets of skills are needed for this nurse? (see answer, page 461) ➤

DAVID MCNEW/GETTY IMAGES

strategies for avoiding problems later. If a sudden student outburst occurs, the expert calms the student and uses that to teach; the novice professor might be unnerved and make things worse.

FLEXIBLE Finally, perhaps because they are intuitive, automatic, and strategic, experts are also flexible. The expert artist, musician, or scientist is creative and curious, deliberately experimenting and enjoying the challenge when unexpected things occur (Csikszentmihalyi, 2013). Remember Pavlov (Chapter 1). He already had won the Nobel Prize when he noticed his dogs' unexpected reaction to being fed. His expertise made him notice, then investigate, and eventually develop insights that opened a new perspective in psychology.

Experts in all walks of life adapt to individual cases and exceptions—much as an expert chef will adjust ingredients, temperature, technique, and timing as a dish develops, tasting to see whether a little more spice is needed, seldom following a recipe exactly. Standards are high: Some chefs throw food in the garbage rather than present a dish that many nonexperts would happily serve. Expert athletes, mechanics, and musicians are similarly flexible, able to tailor their responses to nuances that escape the novice.

In the field of education, best practices for the educator emphasize flexibility and strategy, as each group of students has distinct and often erroneous assumptions. It is not helpful to simply teach the right answers; flexibility requires matching the instruction to the individual students, discovering what learning is needed (Ford & Yore, 2012).

A review of expertise finds that flexibility includes understanding which particular skills are necessary to become an expert in each profession. For example, repeated practice is needed in typing, sports, and games; collaboration skills are needed for leadership; and task management strategies are needed for aviation (Morrow et al., 2009). Practice is not merely rote repetition; it must be deliberate, allowing learning from experience (Ericsson, 2006).

EXPERTISE AND AGE The relationship between age and expertise is not straightforward. Much depends on the task: The young have an advantage when speed is needed, but they are less adept at vocabulary. Further, they have less experience, which may be crucial for some tasks, and they have had less time to practice—although some teenagers practice day and night at music, or math, or something else and become quite expert in early adulthood.

An interesting example of age and practice comes from perfumers. For that profession, an acute sense of smell is essential as they seek to develop new scents. Usually the sense of smell is reduced with age, but this does not seem true for perfumers. One study found that older experts outdid younger nonexperts at detecting smells, because parts of the professionals' brains were better developed for smell (Delon-Martin et al., 2013).

This illustrates a general conclusion from research on cognitive plasticity: Experienced adults often use selective optimization with compensation, becoming expert. This is apparent in many workplaces. The best employees may be the older, more experienced ones—if they are motivated to do their best.

Complicated work requires more cognitive practice and expertise than routine work; as a result, such work may have intellectual benefits for the workers themselves. In the Seattle Longitudinal Study, the cognitive demands of the occupations of more than 500 workers were measured, including the complexities involved in the interactions with other people, with things, and with data. In all three occupational challenges, older workers maintained their intellectual prowess (Schaie, 2005/2013).

One final example of the relationship between age and job effectiveness comes from an occupation familiar to all of us: driving a taxi. In major cities, taxi drivers must find the best route (factoring in traffic, construction, time of day, and many other details). They also must know where and when new passengers are likely to be and who wants to talk, who wants silence, and how to respond when the passenger has opinions the driver finds narrow and wrong. Expert drivers earn far more in tips than novices; they have learned from experience.

Research in England—where taxi drivers "have to learn the layout of 25,000 streets in London and the locations of thousands of places of interest, and pass stringent examinations" (Woollett et al., 2009, p. 1407)—found not only that the drivers became more expert with time but also that their brains adjusted to the need for particular knowledge. In fact, some regions of their brains (areas dedicated to spatial representation) were far more extensive and active than those of an average person (Woollett et al., 2009). On ordinary IQ tests, the taxi drivers' scores were average, but in navigating London, expertise was apparent.

Other studies also show that people become more expert, and their brains adapt, as they practice various skills (Park & Reuter-Lorenz, 2009). This development occurs not only for motor skills—playing the violin, dancing, driving a taxi—but also for logic and other reasoning skills (Zatorre et al., 2012). The human brain is plastic lifelong, as new learning is always possible and practice is crucial.

Now we return to Jenny, who left my office decades ago. As I wrote, she came to me because I am an expert in human development, but over the years I have realized that her expertise regarding her life contexts was far ahead of mine.

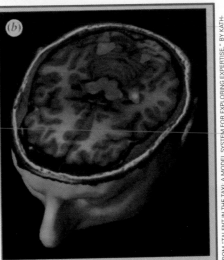

FROM "TALENT IN THE TAXI: A MODEL SYSTEM FOR EXPLORING EXPERTISE," BY KATHERINE WOOLLETT, HUGO J. SPIERS, & ELEANOR A. MAGUIRE, 2009, *PHILOSOPHICAL TRANSACTIONS OF THE ROYAL SOCIETY OF LONDON, 364(1522),* P. 1408. DOI: 10.1098/RSTB.2008.0288. COPYRIGHT 2009 BY THE ROYAL SOCIETY.

Red Means Go! The red shows the activated brain areas in London taxi drivers as they navigated the busy London streets. Not only were these areas more active than the same areas in the average person's brain, but they also had more dendrites. In addition, the longer a cabby had been driving, the more brain growth was evident. This research confirms plasticity, implying that we all could develop new skills, not only by remembering but also by engaging in activities that change the very structures of our brains.

ANSWER TO OBSERVATION QUIZ
(from page 460) Medical expertise and interpersonal skills. Puncturing the finger to draw blood must be automatic, but her response to the patient must be intuitive and flexible—that winning smile sometimes must become a look of serious competence. ●

A CASE TO STUDY

Jenny, Again

A dispassionate analysis of Jenny's situation when she consulted me would conclude that another baby—with no marriage, no job, and an apartment in the south Bronx—would doom her to poor health, poor prospects, and a depressing life. This is not a stereotype: The data show that lifelong poverty is the usual future for low-income mothers who have another child, out-of-wedlock, with a married man.

But those statistics do not reflect Jenny's intelligence, creativity, and practical expertise. She already had a habit of gathering social support, evident by her seeking me out. She was not daunted by her poverty; remember, she found many free activities for her children to enjoy, including sending them on vacation in the country. She was exceptional, but not unique: Some low-SES people overcome the potential stressors of poverty (Chen & Miller, 2012).

Jenny used her knowledge well. She asked Billy to be tested for sickle-cell anemia (negative), and she knew that honest communication is crucial for human relationships. She told Billy she loved him but that she would have the baby, contrary to his advice. She continued to encourage her children in public school, befriending their teachers, who in turn gave special attention to her speech-impaired son.

When she was 8 months pregnant, she interviewed for a city job tutoring children in her home. She hoped to earn money while caring for her newborn (a full-term, healthy girl).

I brought baby clothes to her railroad apartment on the eighth floor of the projects. I noticed that her framed Bronx Community College diploma was not displayed. She explained that she feared that the city investigator, who would come to her house to see whether it was adequate for tutoring, might decide she was overqualified. That was expertise: She got the job.

When her baby was a little older, Jenny headed back to college, earning a BA on a full scholarship. Her peers and professors recognized her intelligence: She gave the student speech at graduation. The two orphaned nephews reached age 18 and moved out.

She then found work as a receptionist in a city hospital, a job that provided day care and health benefits for her and her three children. That allowed her to move to a better neighborhood of the Bronx (Co-op City).

Billy continued to visit Jenny and the daughter he had not wanted. His wife became suspicious and hired a detective to follow him—and then gave him an ultimatum: Stop seeing Jenny or file for divorce.

At that point, I realized that Jenny had some insight into human relations that I did not recognize in my office years earlier: Billy chose divorce and married Jenny. Within a few years, they moved to Florida, where Jenny earned a master's degree (she phoned to say she was assigned my textbook) and then worked as a supervisor in a public school. Their young daughter graduated from high school in Florida.

The last time I saw her, I learned that she bikes, swims, and gardens every day. I met her speech-impaired son: He not only overcame his speech problem, he earned a PhD in psychology. Both her daughters are now college graduates.

Not everyone becomes an expert in human relations; Jenny is exceptional in many ways. But one lesson from this chapter is that health, intelligence, and even wisdom may improve over the years of adulthood. As further explained in Chapter 13, choices and relationships affect how lives unfold, true for Jenny and for us all.

WHAT HAVE YOU LEARNED?

1. In what situations is emotion-focused coping the best?
2. In what situations is problem-focused coping the best?
3. What might a person do to optimize ability in some area *not* discussed in the book, such as playing the flute, or growing tomatoes, or building a cabinet?
4. How does the saying "Can't see the forest for the trees" relate to what you have learned about adult cognition?
5. Explain how intuition might help or diminish ability.
6. How does automatic processing contribute to expertise?
7. In what occupations would age be an asset, and why?

SUMMARY

Growing Older

1. Senescence causes a universal slowdown during adulthood, but aging is often imperceptible because organ reserve maintains capacity. Most adults are quite strong and capable.

2. Probably the most crucial health habit for adults is regular exercise, in part because it makes other good health habits more likely. Sedentary people have more illnesses of almost every kind.

3. Adults in North America smoke fewer cigarettes than they once did, and rates of lung cancer and other diseases are falling, largely for that reason. Gender differences in smoking show cohort effects. For all drugs, national context is crucial; cigarette smoking is increasing in some nations, especially for women.

4. Although illegal drug abuse declines in adulthood, prescription drug overuse and abuse remains a problem. Alcohol use disorder remains a major health problem in North America, with even worse rates worldwide.

5. Nutrition keeps adults healthy and strong, but metabolism slows over adulthood, which may result in weight gain. Research suggests that some diets are better than others.

Losses and Gains

6. Appearance changes with age, especially evident in the skin. Ease of movement decreases as people become less agile. Shape and reaction time change as well.

7. Sexual satisfaction may improve with age, but infertility becomes more common. Sperm count gradually decreases in men, and every step of female reproduction—ovulation, implantation, fetal growth, labor, and birth—slows down.

8. A number of assisted reproductive technology (ART) procedures, including in vitro fertilization (IVF), offer potential answers to infertility.

9. At menopause, ovulation ceases and estrogen is markedly reduced. Hormone production declines more gradually in men. For both sexes, hormone replacement therapy should be used cautiously, if at all.

The Aging Brain

10. The brain slows down and begins a gradual decline. The brain benefits from measures to improve overall health, especially exercise, and is harmed by most psychoactive drugs.

11. It was traditionally assumed that there is one general intelligence (*g*), measurable by IQ tests. That idea is not accepted by all current cognitive scientists.

12. Crystallized intelligence, reflecting accumulated knowledge, increases, but fluid, flexible reasoning declines in adults. That makes IQ, overall, steady over the decades of adulthood until old age.

13. Sternberg proposed three fundamental forms of intelligence: analytic, creative, and practical. Cultural values encourage development of some cognitive abilities more than others. Each person responds to these cultural priorities, which may not be reflected in IQ scores. Practical intelligence is particularly useful in daily life.

Selecting and Protecting

14. The rate of homicide has decreased, but the rate of disasters has increased. In addition, people experience many stresses and hassles over the 40 years of adulthood, which affects their health.

15. People use many methods of coping with stress. Avoidant copying is destructive, but both problem-focused and emotion-focused coping may prevent stresses from becoming stressors.

16. As people grow older, they select certain aspects of their lives to focus on, optimizing development in those areas and compensating for declines in others. Selective optimization with compensation is apparent in many aspects of adult life.

17. In cognition, people become experts in some aspects of knowledge and intellect, allowing others to fade. Expertise is characterized by more intuitive, automatic, strategic, and flexible thinking.

18. Experienced adults may surpass younger adults if they specialize, compensating for any deficits. According to a study of taxi drivers in London, as well as research on musicians, brains grow to support selective expertise.

KEY TERMS

senescence (p. 429)
infertility (p. 440)
menopause (p. 442)
andropause (p. 443)
general intelligence (*g*) (p. 444)

Seattle Longitudinal Study (p. 445)
fluid intelligence (p. 447)
crystallized intelligence (p. 447)
analytic intelligence (p. 448)
creative intelligence (p. 448)

practical intelligence (p. 449)
cognitive artifacts (p. 451)
stressor (p. 453)
avoidant coping (p. 454)
problem-focused coping (p. 454)

emotion-focused coping (p. 454)
weathering (p. 455)
selective optimization with compensation (p. 456)
automatic processing (p. 459)

APPLICATIONS

1. Guess the ages of five people you know and then ask them how old they are. Analyze the clues you used for your guesses and the people's reactions to your question.

2. Find a speaker willing to come to your class who is an expert on weight loss, adult health, smoking, or drinking. Write a one-page proposal explaining why you think this speaker would be good and what topics he or she should address. Give this proposal to your instructor, with contact information for your speaker. The instructor can call the potential speakers, thank them for their willingness, and decide whether to actually invite them to speak.

3. The importance of context and culture is illustrated by the things that people think are basic knowledge. Choose a partner, and each of you write four questions that you think are hard but fair as measures of general intelligence. Then give your test to your partner and answer the four questions that person has prepared for you. What did you learn from the results?

4. Skill at video games is sometimes thought to reflect intelligence. Interview three or four people who play such games. What abilities do they think video games require? What do you think these games reflect in terms of experience, age, and motivation?

CHAPTER OUTLINE

ADULTHOOD
The Social World

CHAPTER 13

WHAT WILL YOU KNOW?

- Does personality change much from childhood to adulthood?
- Are adults happier married or single?
- Is being a parent work or joy?

I broke two small bones in my pelvis—a mishap I caused myself: I was rushing, wearing old smooth-soled shoes, carrying books, in the rain, after dark, stepping up a curb. I fell hard on the sidewalk. That led to a 911 call, an ambulance, five hospital days, five rehab days, heartfelt admiration for the physical therapists who got me walking, and deep appreciation of the chair of my department, who found colleagues to teach my classes for two weeks.

I mention that minor event because it spotlights generativity. My friends and four children, adults now, cared for me far beyond what I thought I needed.

A passerby/friend called the EMS (Emergency Medical Services) and stayed with me until the two nearby daughters, Elissa and Sarah, were at the emergency room within an hour; Rachel flew in from Minnesota and bought me new shoes with slip-proof treads; Bethany drove down from Connecticut with planters, dirt, flowers, and trees to beautify my home.

That was not all. My daughters questioned nurses and doctors; brought me books, mail, and my computer; filled prescriptions; rearranged my bathroom; scheduled taxis; pushed my wheelchair; did laundry, shopping, cooking, cleaning; doggedly pursued insurance companies.

It was hard to accept help. I told my friends, "No visitors." One laughed and said, "You are stuck in bed, I am coming." I hoped to return quickly to the college because I thought my students needed me. But soon I realized I needed them as much as, or more than, they needed me. In retrospect, I am glad my friend visited and grateful that my daughters did all they did.

Again and again I am reminded that generativity is mutual: We receive as well as give.

That is a theme of this chapter, which focuses on the social aspects of adult lives: partnering and parenting, mating and mentoring. Adults have personality traits and values that respond to the personalities and traits of other people of all ages. Adults seek love and work, intimacy and generativity. ■

Personality Development in Adulthood

Remember from Chapter 4 that every infant is born with a unique temperament and from Chapter 6 that parents have diverse parenting styles. That is part of what makes up adult personality, but there is much more. Like a tree adding another ring of growth each year, an ongoing mixture of genes, experiences, and cultures results in each person's unique actions, emotions, and attitudes, a combination called personality.

Continuity is evident: Few adults develop characteristics that are the reverse of their childhood temperament. But one noteworthy finding about adulthood is that people can change, not only in actions but also in personality, usually for the better.

Theories of Adult Personality

Erikson originally described eight stages of development. His first five stages (already explained) each begin in a particular chronological period. But adult stages are less age-based (see Table 13.1).

Chronological age is an imperfect marker in adulthood. The three adult stages—*intimacy versus isolation, generativity versus stagnation,* and *integrity versus despair*—do not always appear in sequence, and the adolescent stage *identity versus role confusion* can linger long past the teenage years.

Further, adult stages disappear and reappear. For example, intimacy needs may seem satisfied in early adulthood with a good marriage, but then they may reappear decades later after an unanticipated divorce.

Maslow's hierarchy of five needs (explained in Chapter 1) is thought to characterize everyone. Unless mired in poverty or war, or suffering from severe early trauma, adults have moved past the two lower stages (safety and basic needs) and seek love and then respect (levels three and four). Only a few reach self-actualization (level five). Again, adults change over the decades.

Not only Maslow and Erikson, but also every well-known theorist of adult personality, echo the same themes. Freud enunciated them first: He said that adults need *lieben und arbeiten* (to love and to work). Sometimes these two needs are called

---

TABLE 13.1 | **Erikson's Stages of Adulthood**

Unlike Freud or other early theorists who thought adults simply worked through the legacy of their childhood, four of Erikson's eight psychosocial stages occur after puberty. His most famous book, *Childhood and Society* (1993), devoted only two pages to each adult stage, but elaborations in later works have led to a much richer depiction (Hoare, 2002).

Identity versus Role Confusion
Although Erikson originally situated the identity crisis during adolescence, he realized that identity concerns could be lifelong. Identity combines values and traditions from childhood with the current social context. Since contexts keep evolving, many adults reassess all four types of identity (sexual/gender, vocational/work, religious/spiritual, and political/ethnic).

Intimacy versus Isolation
Adults seek intimacy—a close, reciprocal connection with another human being. Intimacy is mutual, not self-absorbed, which means that adults need to devote time and energy to one another. This process begins in emerging adulthood and continues lifelong. Isolation is especially likely when divorce or death disrupts established intimate relationships.

Generativity versus Stagnation
Adults need to care for the next generation, either by raising their own children or by mentoring, teaching, and helping others. Erikson's first description of this stage focused on parenthood, but later he included other ways to achieve generativity. Adults extend the legacy of their culture and their generation with ongoing care, creativity, and sacrifice.

Integrity versus Despair
When Erikson himself reached his 70s, he decided that integrity, with the goal of combating prejudice and helping all humanity, was too important to be left to the elderly. He also thought that each person's entire life connects his or her personal journey with human society. The ultimate integrity occurs when the specifics of a person's life, within a particular history and culture, is in harmony with the universal human destiny.

Same Situation, Far Apart: Caution to the Winds Generally, risk taking decreases with age, but modern technology allows older adults to put their bodies on the line. This 80-year-old Israeli woman *(left)* has just skydived, and this man in his 50s *(right)* chases tornados with a "Doppler on Wheels."

affiliation/achievement, or *emotional/instrumental,* or *communion/agency.* We will use Erikson's terms, *intimacy* and *generativity,* as a scaffold. Every theory recognizes both; every adult seeks to love and to work, each in a way that fits his or her personality.

Personality Traits

Some babies are shy, others outgoing; some are frightened, others fearless. Such traits begin with genes, but they are affected by experiences.

Big Five
The five basic clusters of personality traits that remain quite stable throughout adulthood: openness, conscientiousness, extroversion, agreeableness, and neuroticism.

THE BIG FIVE Temperament is partly genetic; genes are lifelong. There are hundreds of examples, some that are surprising. One study found, for instance, that temperament at age 3 predicted gambling addiction at age 32 (Slutske et al., 2012).

Longitudinal, cross-sectional, and multi-cultural research has identified five clusters of personality traits that appear in every culture and era, called the **Big Five.** (To remember the Big Five, the acronym OCEAN is useful.)

- *Openness:* imaginative, curious, artistic, creative, open to new experiences
- *Conscientiousness:* organized, deliberate, conforming, self-disciplined
- *Extroversion:* outgoing, assertive, active
- *Agreeableness:* kind, helpful, easygoing, generous
- *Neuroticism:* anxious, moody, self-punishing, critical

Each person's personality is somewhere between extremely high and extremely low on each of these five. The low end might be described, in the same order as above, with these five adjectives: *closed, careless, introverted, hard to please,* and *placid.*

Adults choose their contexts, selecting vocations, hobbies, health habits, mates, and neighborhoods in part because of their own traits. Personality affects almost everything, including whether an emerging adult develops an eating disorder, an adult becomes an impulsive shopper, or an older adult retires (Sansone & Sansone, 2013; Thompson & Prendergast, 2015; Robinson et al., 2010).

Among the actions and attitudes linked to the Big Five are education (conscientious people are more likely to complete college), cheating on exams (low on agreeableness), marriage (extroverts more often marry), divorce (more likely for neurotics), IQ (higher in openness), verbal fluency (again, openness and extroversion), and even political views (conservatives less open) (Duckworth et al., 2007; Gerber et al., 2011; Silvia & Sanders, 2010; Giluk & Postlethwaite, 2015).

If only I could accept that I can't accept being someone who finds it hard to accept acceptance from those who accept me for the person that I can't accept I really am.

Maybe Next Year Self-acceptance is a gradual process over the years of adulthood, aided by the appreciation of friends and family. At some point in adulthood, people shift from striving to fulfill their potential to accepting their limitations.

Same Situation, Far Apart: Scientists at Work Most scientists are open-minded and conscientious (two of the Big Five personality traits), as both of these women are. Culture and social context are crucial, however. If the woman on the right were in Tanzania, would she be a doctor surrounded by patients in the open air, as the Tanzanian woman on the left is? Or is she so accustomed to her North American laboratory, protected by gloves and a screen, that she could not adjust? The answer depends on personality, not knowledge.

THINK CRITICALLY: Would your personality fit better in another culture?

International research confirms that human personality traits (there are hundreds of them) can be grouped in the Big Five (Carlo et al., 2014), although some scholars believe another list of five or six might be better. Everyone agrees that personality is influenced by many factors beyond temperament. The paragraph above notes tendencies, not always realities. People try to shape their personality to the norms of their culture. As one team wrote, "personality may acculturate" (Güngör et al., 2013, p. 713).

Generally, a study of well-being and self-esteem in 28 nations found that people are happiest if their personality traits match the norms of their social context. For example, extroversion was relatively high in Canada and low in Japan, and both the Canadians and the Japanese had a stronger sense of well-being if their personal ratings on extroversion were consistent with their culture's norms (Fulmer et al., 2010).

AGE AND COHORT Many researchers find that personality shifts slightly with age, but the rank order of various traits stays the same. Thus, 20-year-old extroverts are still extroverts at age 80, more outgoing than most other people their age, although not necessarily more than most 20-year-olds.

The general age trend is positive. People are more likely to grow closer to their cultural norms, as well as to become more stable in their traits. Personality change, if it ever is to occur, is more likely early or late in life, not in the middle (Specht et al., 2011).

Traits that are considered pathological (such as neuroticism) tend to be modified as people mature. By contrast, traits that are valued (such as conscientiousness) increase slightly (L. Clark, 2009; Lehman et al., 2013). Not surprisingly, then, self-esteem rises from early adulthood until about age 50, as people develop whatever personality is most appreciated within their community (Orth et al., 2012).

Both nature and nurture are always relevant, but the power of each may be affected by a person's age. People under the age of 30 "actively try to change their environment," moving away from home and finding new friends, changing their nurture. Later in life, context shapes traits, because once adults have chosen their vocation, family, and neighborhoods, they "change the self to fit the environment" (Kandler, 2012, p. 294).

Cohort is important too, affecting the interaction of personality and behavior. This is evident in one of the most important decisions an adult must make—childbearing.

For both men and women born in 1920, those high in openness had about the same number of children as those low in that trait because the entire culture valued

ADAPTED FROM: "TESTING PREDICTIONS FROM PERSONALITY NEUROSCIENCE," BY COLIN G. DEYOUNG, JACOB B. HIRSH, MATTHEW S. SHANE, XENOPHON PAPADEMETRIS, NALLAKKANDI RAJEEVAN & JEREMY R. GRAY, 2010, *PSYCHOLOGICAL SCIENCE*, 21(6), P. 825. DOI: 10.1177/0956797610370159 COPYRIGHT 2010 BY THE AUTHORS.

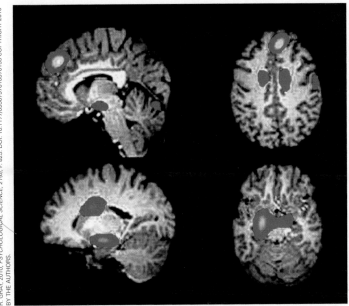

Active Brains, Active Personality The hypothesis that individual personality traits originate in the brain was tested by scientists who sought to find correlations between brain activity (shown in red) and personality traits. People who rated themselves high in four of the Big Five (conscientiousness, extroversion, agreeableness, neuroticism—but not openness) also had more activity in brain regions that are known to relate to those traits. Here are two side views *(left)* and a top and bottom view *(right)* of brains of people high in neuroticism. Their brain regions known to be especially sensitive to stress, depression, threat, and punishment (yellow bullseyes) were more active than the same brain regions in people low in neuroticism (DeYoung et al., 2010).

fertility. Consequently, no matter what an individual's personality, everyone hoped to marry and have several children unless biology made that impossible.

For those born in 1960, biology was less significant but personality traits mattered more. The average person had only two children, a new norm. Those high in openness had fewer than average, sometimes choosing to have one or none, particularly if that open person was a woman high in conscientiousness (Jokela, 2012). Her openness may have encouraged her to consider family planning, overpopulation, and nontraditional roles, and her conscientiousness made her careful to plan each birth. Context matters, always interacting with personality.

WHAT HAVE YOU LEARNED?

1. What are other names for Erikson's intimacy stage?
2. What are the descriptions of what Freud called the need to work?
3. What are thought to be the origins of personality?
4. Why does personality change as people grow older?
5. How might the personality trait of openness affect people's choice of jobs, mates, lifestyle, and neighborhood?
6. How might the personality trait of extraversion affect people's choice of colleges, friends, and community involvement?
7. How might the trait of conscientiousness affect a parent's interactions with his or her children?

Intimacy: Connecting with Others

Humans are not meant to be loners. Every adult seeks to connect with other people, experiencing the crisis Erikson called **intimacy versus isolation,** as already explained in Chapter 11. Decades of research find that physical health and psychological well-being flourish best if both family members and friends are part of an adult's life (Li & Zhang, 2015).

intimacy versus isolation
The sixth of Erikson's stages of development. Every adult seeks close relationships with other people in order to live a happy and healthy life.

Variations are apparent by culture, age, and personality, with some people more connected with their friends, others with their "family of origin" (the family they were born into), and still others with their "family of choice" (mates and children). Intimacy needs can be met by each of these.

Romantic Partners

We begin our discussion of intimacy with romance. However, although sometimes the term "intimacy" implies sexual intimacy, according to Erikson and other personality theorists, intimacy includes far more than romance. Although we start with romance, we will soon discuss friends and other family members.

MARRIAGE Traditionally, the most common way that adults met intimacy needs was through marriage. Every culture and era had some sort of marriage ceremony. Historically, most adults paired off "till death did them part."

Marriage is still a major event. Two sets of families come together, routines and rituals are enacted, the couple wears special clothes, makes public vows blessed by a respected elder, and then perhaps travels on a honeymoon, or crosses a threshold, or changes a name.

Particulars vary of course, but one trend in universal: Marriage is far less common than it once was. Cohort is crucial (see Figure 13.1).

The American Community Survey, which surveys a cross section of U.S. adults each year, reports that almost all U.S. residents born before 1940 married (96 percent). Of those born between 1940 and 1960, fewer (89 percent) did so, and among those born in the 1970s, 62 percent are married, including about 16 percent in a second or third marriage. Another group, about 16 percent, are separated or divorced and not remarried, and about 22 percent have never married. That trend continues: Marriage rates continue to fall.

Similar trends are found worldwide. Consider Japan. In 1950, almost every Japanese adult was married, with many marrying before age 20. Now the Japanese marry later (on average at age 30), and many (an estimated 20 percent) will never marry (Raymo, 2013).

Share My Life Marriage often requires one partner to support the other's aspirations. That is evident in the French couple *(left)*, as Nicole embraces her husband, Alain Maignan, who just completed a six-month solo sail around the world. For 20 years, he spent most of his money and time building his 10-meter boat. Less is known about the Nebraska couple *(right)*, but many farm wives forgo the pleasures of city life in order to support the men they love.

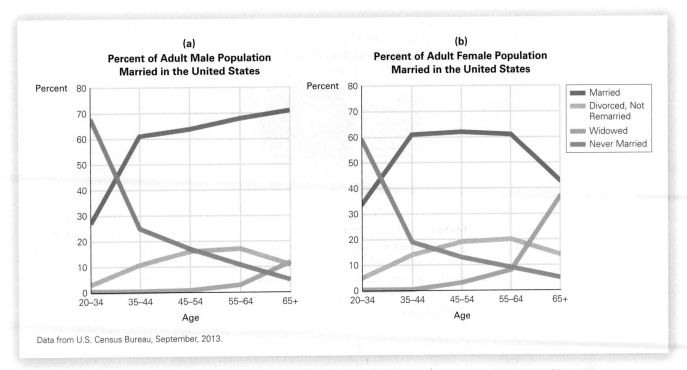

Data from U.S. Census Bureau, September, 2013.

FIGURE 13.1 Not Like Their Parents Each cohort is less likely to marry than the previous one. At first scientists thought that emerging adults were postponing marriage. Now it seems clear that when the unmarried adults under age 35 reach age 65, far more than 5 percent will be "never married."

OBSERVATION QUIZ
What are the most dramatic gender differences in marriage rates?
(see answer, page 474) ▲

Most adults hope to marry eventually, and a majority still do, but increasing numbers do not. Marriage continues to seem desirable in theory, although not in practice. For instance, most divorced people are not disillusioned with marriage: Typically they find another mate within five years. In the United States, 40 percent of new marriages have at least one partner who has been married before (Livingston, 2014).

THINK CRITICALLY: Is marriage a failed institution?

OPPOSING PERSPECTIVES

Marriage and Happiness

Researchers disagree as to whether marriage leads to personal happiness or not. However, regarding the benefits to society, marriage increases the happiness of a community.

To be specific, generally adults benefit if a partner is committed to their well-being; children benefit when both parents are legally and emotionally dedicated to them; societies are stronger if individuals sort themselves into families who care for each other; and elderly people are healthier (with better emotional care) if they have a living spouse.

From the individual's perspective, the consequences of marriage are more complex. A satisfying marriage improves health, wealth, and happiness, but not all marriages are satisfying (Fincham & Beach, 2010; R. Miller et al., 2013). Married people are happier, healthier, and richer on average than never-married ones—but not by much. Divorced people are

less happy, and the only sure way to avoid divorce is not to marry.

It was once thought that men were happier in marriage and women less happy (Bernard, 1982). Suggested reasons were that women had higher expectations for marriage and thus greater disillusionment, or that women did far more housework, child care, and emotional work. However, that is changing by cohort and varies by culture (Stavrova et al., 2012).

It also varies by education, with low-SES women more burdened by marriage. Women who are higher in SES are not only more likely to have happy marriages, they are also more likely "to stay in good marriages and leave bad marriages" (Kreager et al., 2013, p. 580).

A recent meta-analysis found no marked gender differences in marital happiness (Jackson et al., 2014). Early in a marriage, the wives tended to be slightly more satisfied with the relationship than the husbands, but this shifted by about the 15-year mark, with husbands slightly more satisfied. That study found one cultural exception to overall gender neutrality: In Chinese and Japanese marriages, wives were more often dissatisfied than husbands (Jackson et al., 2014).

Research on marriage and happiness comes to opposing conclusions depending on how the researchers account for factors besides the marriage. The complication is that married adults of every age tend to be wealthier, better educated, and more social than those who are not. In order to decide whether marriage itself is beneficial, those factors need to be controlled.

For example, if a married 50-year-old who is financially secure and well educated is happier than an unmarried 50-year-old who is unemployed and dropped out of high school, we cannot conclude that the happi-

LaunchPad
Macmillan Education

Marriage in Adulthood
http://qrs.ly/t24sqml

ness of those two depends on their marital status.

Public opinion is also conflicted. For instance, adults from different cohorts have opposite views on whether children should have married parents. More than a third (36 percent) of those under age 50 think current changes in family structure—including single parents raising children—are not harmful for society. Less than a fifth (19 percent) of those over age 65 agree.

Research controlling for SES finds that children learn more, are sick less, and present fewer emotional problems if their parents are married—but that research is based on children a decade ago. Marriage may be changing; is child rearing changing, too?

THINK CRITICALLY: Are current young adults forgoing happiness by avoiding marriage? Or are they averting the pain of divorce or unhappy marriage?

OTHER FORMS OF ROMANTIC PARTNERSHIP Partnership does not always mean marriage, as already explored in Chapter 11. Cohabitation is particularly common in emerging adulthood. However, for adults over age 25, not only are marriage rates declining but cohabitation rates are increasing. More adults of all ages are living together, often with children. Some plan to marry; some do not.

Cohabiters vary a great deal in their plans and prospects. In general, cohabiters in eastern Europe are more likely to want to marry someday than those in western Europe (Hiekel & Castro-Martín, 2014). Within North America, those who are low in SES are less likely to marry than those high in SES.

Many people now prefer cohabitation to marriage. Several decades ago in 1980, about half (52 percent) of new mothers without a high school education were married. Most of the rest planned to marry someday. Thirty years later, only 17 percent of them were wed (Gibson–Davis & Rackin, 2014), and most of the remaining 83 percent did not seek marriage. Women with more education have always been more likely to be married when their first baby was born, but even for high-SES women, single motherhood is increasing, often by choice.

A sizable number of adults have found a third way (neither marriage nor cohabitation) to meet their intimacy needs with a steady romantic partner. They are *living apart together* (LAT). They have separate residences, but especially when the partners are over age 30, they function as a couple for decades, sexually faithful, vacationing together, and so on (Duncan & Phillips, 2010).

Financial patterns are a particular issue for LAT couples. Most married couples pool their money; many cohabiting couples do not (Hamplová et al., 2014). LAT couples struggle with this aspect of their relationship, with the women particularly wanting to pay their own way (Lyssens-Danneboom & Mortelmans, 2014).

Every couple's decision to marry, cohabit, or LAT is influenced by their families and cultures. Children are influential. Cohabiters who have had children together are more likely to marry than those without, especially when the children start school. Likewise, married couples sometimes stay together for the children, and sometimes one parent leaves a violent mate to protect the children. As for LAT couples, many older parents maintain separate households because they do not want to upset their grown children (de Jong Gierveld & Merz, 2013).

PARTNERSHIPS OVER THE YEARS The four boxes that questionnaires typically provide—married, single, divorced, widowed—do not reflect personal happiness or love, especially cross-culturally or over the decades of adulthood. Love is complex, a matter of relationship function, not structure. This has been described by many psychologists in recent years. Sternberg wrote:

> My whole life I have been searching for love. At a personal level, after a number of false starts, I have found it. In my research—initiated when a love relationship in my personal life was failing—I have tried to come closer to understanding what love is, how it develops, and why it succeeds or fails.
>
> *[Sternberg, 2013a, p. 98]*

Since 1986, Sternberg has studied three aspects of love: *passion, intimacy,* and *commitment.* That triad continues to be explored by many other researchers (Sternberg & Weis, 2006; Sumter et al., 2013; Fletcher et al., 2015). Among twenty-first-century Westerners, passion is usually first, then shared confidences create intimacy, and finally commitment leads to an enduring relationship. When all three are evident, that is *consummate love*—an ideal that is only sometimes attained.

A wealth of research finds that for most adults mutual commitment is the most crucial of the three. A long-term committed partnership correlates with health and happiness throughout life (R. Miller et al., 2013). The reasons for this correlation range from the deep human need for someone who listens, understands, and shares one's goals to the mundane details of a mate who monitors diet, exercise, and medical attention.

The passage of time also makes a difference. In general, the honeymoon period tends to be happy, but frustration with a partnership increases as conflicts—even those not directly between the couple—arise (see At About This Time). Partnerships (including heterosexual married couples, committed cohabiters, same-sex couples, and LAT couples) tend to be less happy when the first child is born and again when children reach puberty (Umberson et al., 2010). Divorce risk rises and then falls.

Remember, however, that averages obscure many differences of age, ethnicity, personality, and circumstances. In the United States, Asian Americans are least likely to divorce and African Americans are most likely to do so. These ethnic differences are partly cultural and partly economic, making any broad effort to encourage marriage for everyone doomed to disappoint the politicians, social workers, and individuals involved (Johnson, 2012).

Education matters too: College-educated couples are less likely to divorce no matter what their ethnic background. Some unhappy couples stay

One Love, Two Homes Their friends and family know that Jonathan and Diana are a couple, happy together day and night, year after year. But one detail distinguishes them from most couples: Each owns a house. They commute 10 miles and are living apart together—LAT.

FRANK BARON/CAMERA PRESS/GUARDIAN/REDUX

At About This Time: Marital Happiness Over the Years

Interval After Wedding	Characterization
First 6 months	Honeymoon period—happiest of all
6 months to 5 years	Happiness dips; divorce is more common now than later in marriage
5 to 10 years	Happiness holds steady
10 to 20 years	Happiness dips as children reach puberty
20 to 30 years	Happiness rises when children leave the nest
30 to 50 years	Happiness is high and steady, barring serious health problems

Not Always These are trends, often masked by more pressing events. For example, some couples stay together because of the children, so unlike most couples, for them the empty nest stage becomes a time of conflict or divorce.

empty nest
The time in the lives of parents when their children have left the family home to pursue their own lives.

married for religious reasons, and the result may be a long-lasting, conflict-filled relationship. Husbands and wives in happy marriages tend to agree that their marriage is a good one, but in unhappy marriages often one spouse is much less content than the other (Brown et al., 2012).

As already noted, the divorce risk falls with age, but older couples are divorcing at increasing rates. In 1990, 8 percent of divorces were of people age 50 and older; in 2010, 25 percent of divorcees were that old, often in marriages that had lasted for decades (Brown & Lin, 2013).

Contrary to outdated impressions, the **empty nest**—when parents are alone again after the children have left—is usually a time for improved relationships. Simply having time for each other, without crying babies, demanding children, or rebellious teenagers, improves intimacy. Partners can focus on their mates, doing together whatever they both enjoy.

Of course, time does not fix every relationship. Economic stress causes marital friction no matter how many years a couple has been together (Conger et al., 2010). Under the weight of major crises—particularly financial (such as a foreclosed home or a stretch of unemployment) or relational (such as demanding in-laws or an extramarital affair)—a long-standing relationship might well crumble.

Remember the concept of *linked lives* from Chapter 11. Couples increasingly link their lives over time, with marital satisfaction connected to what they have achieved together and how happy the other one is (Carr et al., 2014). Children suffer or benefit accordingly.

GAY AND LESBIAN PARTNERS Almost everything just described applies to gay and lesbian partners as well as to heterosexual ones (Biblarz & Savci, 2010; Cherlin, 2013; Herek, 2006). Some same-sex couples are faithful and supportive of each other; their emotional well-being thrives on their intimacy and commitment, which increases over the decades.

Others are conflicted: Problems of finances, communication, and domestic abuse resemble those in heterosexual marriages. As the U.S. Supreme Court recently confirmed, love between partners is the crucial bond. As with every romance, when love fades, problems arise.

The similarity of all partnerships was apparent in a study of alcohol abuse in romantic couples. Researchers expected that the stress of minority status among the gay and lesbian couples would increase the rate of alcohol use disorder. That was *not* what the data revealed. Instead, the crucial variable was whether the couple was married or cohabiting. For both same-sex and other-sex couples, cohabiters drank to excess much more than married people (Reczek et al., 2014).

Another finding is relevant for all partnerships—connections to parents and in-laws. Although legal, moral, and financial arguments (health insurance, child rearing, equal rights, and the like) were frequently cited in the recent public debate about same-sex marriage, often same-sex couples marry not for legal benefits but for psychic well-being. They want recognition for their love from relatives as well as from strangers.

In a study of married gay couples in Iowa, one man decided to marry because of his mother: "I had a partner that I lived with . . . And I think she, as much as she accepted him, it wasn't anything permanent in her eyes" (Ocobock, 2013, p. 196). Another man wrote about his father: "[He] told us how proud of

Why Marry? Because many young people question the need for a wedding, marriage rates are down overall, but a sudden increase in rates is apparent now that same-sex marriage is legal. Miriam Brown and Carol Anastasio were among the 16,046 people to marry in New York City on July 24, 2011, the first day such marriages were legal. Extra judges and courtrooms were pressed into service.

Never Easy These two men both want the best for their children. The affluent German dad *(left)* seems to be more able to provide it than the Afghan dad *(right)*, who has just lost his asylum case and, with his Belgium-born daughter, is about to be deported. However, both fathers seem to have a warm relationship with their children, which may benefit everyone.

Most nonparents underestimate the generative demands of parenthood. Indeed, "having a child is perhaps the most stressful experience in a family's life" (McClain, 2011, p. 889).

In Erikson's view, after establishing intimacy, many adults seek generativity. A couple may choose parenthood, willingly coping with the many stresses that come with that role. Bearing and rearing children are labor-intensive expressions of generativity, "a transformative experience" with more costs than benefits when children are young (Umberson et al., 2010, p. 612).

Parenthood is particularly difficult when intimacy, not generativity, is a person's most urgent psychosocial need. As already noted, marital happiness may dip when a baby arrives, because intimacy needs must sometimes be postponed. Worse yet is having a baby as part of the search for identity (as teenagers may discover too late).

Children reorder adult perspectives. One sign of a good parent is the parent's realization that the infant's cries are communicative, not selfish, and that adults need to care for children more than vice versa (Katz et al., 2011).

Care can be expressed in many ways. The dynamic experience of raising children tests every parent, perhaps increasingly so when most women have jobs before they become mothers. Specifics vary from family to family, but always some adjustment is needed.

For example, a study of men and women who had been in the top 0.01 percent in math ability when they were in high school, and who had gone on to earn graduate degrees and impressive jobs decades later, found that parenthood changed both sexes. The fathers worked harder to achieve more status and income, while the mothers became more communal, focusing on community and family (Ferriman et al., 2009).

Those parents were studied a decade ago, but the same patterns persist. A 16-nation study found that fathers do more child care than they did, and women earn more money than they did; however, the gender division of labor remains (Kan et al., 2011). Fathers and mothers realize that raising a child requires more work for both of them, and they usually follow traditional gender patterns to accomplish that.

Video: Interview with Jay Belsky explores how problematic parenting practices are transmitted (or not) from one generation to the next.

Not always, of course, but even when roles are nontraditional, the old patterns are apparent. For example, one man became the prime caregiver for his infant and 2-year-old but soon found he wanted to earn a paycheck. He found a part-time job that allowed him to bring his children along (as a schoolbus driver). He said:

> In the last generation it's changed so much . . . it's almost like you're on ice that's breaking up. That's how I felt. Like I was on ice that's breaking up. You don't really know what or where the father role is. You kind of have to define it for yourself . . . I think that is what I have learned most from staying home with the kids . . . Does it emasculate me that my wife is making more money?
>
> *[Geoff, quoted in Doucet, 2015, p. 235]*

Another father in the same study decided to open a business as a day-care provider, for his own children and several others.

Both these men were conscious of gender roles, even as they resisted them. Both mothers and fathers realize that raising a child requires much generative work. Social roles have changed, but children still require caregiving. Parenting becomes an ongoing challenge, because just when parents figure out how to care for their infants, or preschoolers, or schoolchildren, those children grow older, presenting new dilemmas. One exasperated mother told her criticizing teenager, "I'm learning on the job, I've never been a mother of an adolescent before."

Over the decades of family life, parents must adjust to babies who disrupt sleep, toddlers who have temper tantrums, preschoolers who want to explore, schoolchildren who need help with homework or friendship or skills, teenagers who are moody, or defiant, or depressed.

Not every child presents every problem, but privacy and income rarely seem adequate, and all children need extra care and attention at some point. The more children a couple has, the more family problems arise, according to a study in many nations (Margolis & Myrskylä, 2011).

Couples usually learn to compromise or set aside their own needs to accommodate a beloved partner, but setting aside one's assumptions is much harder when the welfare of one's child may be affected. Children may cement a relationship, but they also may strain it.

ADOPTIVE PARENTS Roughly one-third of all North American adults become nonbiological parents. Each form provides abundant opportunities for generativity, although each has distinct vulnerabilities. The easiest form of nonbiological parenting may be the adoptive parent, who is legally connected to the child for life. In addition, adoptive children are chosen and wanted, so the parents are ready to sacrifice their own needs to be generative for the child.

Current adoptions are usually "open," which means that the biological parents decided that someone else would be a better parent, but they still want some connection to the child. The child knows about this arrangement, which proves an advantage for all the adults who seek the best for the child.

Strong parent–child attachments are often evident with adoption, especially when children are adopted as infants. Secure bonds can also develop if adoption occurs when the children are older, especially when the adopting mother was strongly attached to her own mother (Pace et al., 2011).

Sadly, some adopted children have spent their early years in an institution, never attached to any caregiver. Although some children are resilient, most are afraid to love anyone (Van IJzendoorn et al., 2011). That obviously makes child rearing more difficult for the

Carry Me Every 3-year-old wants to be carried, but not every father enjoys it as much as this one seems to do, as he marches in a Korean American parade in midtown Manhattan. Many adoptive parents go out of their way to encourage their children to be proud of their heritage.

© EDUARDO MUNOZ/REUTERS/CORBIS

This is the most difficult form of parenting of all, partly because foster children typically have emotional and behavioral needs that require intense involvement. Foster parents need to spend far more time and effort on each child than biological parents do, and yet the social context tends to devalue their efforts (J. Smith et al., 2013).

Contrary to popular prejudice, adults become foster parents more often for psychosocial than financial reasons, part of the adults' need to be needed (Geiger et al., 2013). Official foster parents are paid, but they typically earn far less than a babysitter or than they would in a conventional job.

Most children are in foster care for less than a year, as the goal is often reunification with the birth parent. The children may be moved from one placement to another, or from foster care back to the dysfunctional family, for reasons unrelated to the wishes, competence, or emotions of the foster parents. This makes it doubly hard for the foster parents to develop a generative attachment to their children, and doubly admirable when they do.

The average child entering the foster-care system is 7 years old (Child Welfare Information Gateway, 2013). Many spent their early years with their birth families and are attached to them. Such human bonding is normally beneficial, not only for the children but also for the adults.

However, if birth parents are so neglectful or abusive that foster care is needed, the child's early insecure or disorganized attachment to their birth parents impedes relationships with the foster parent. Most foster children have experienced long-standing maltreatment and have witnessed violence; they are understandably suspicious of any adult (Dorsey et al., 2012).

As a result, adult caregivers of such children, either in foster families or institutions, face the dilemma of "whether to 'love' the children or maintain a cool, aloof posture with minimal sensitive or responsive interactions" (St. Petersburg–USA Orphanage Research Team, 2008, p. 15). Nonetheless, for adolescents who have been with a foster family for some time, about half the children and adults develop a healthy, mutual attachment, a marked contrast to the relationship with their biological parents (Joseph et al., 2014).

For all forms of parenting, generative caring does not occur in the abstract; it involves a particular caregiver and care receiver. That means everything needs to be done to encourage attachment between the foster parent and child, including stable placement and support for foster parents.

GRANDPARENTS As already mentioned, the empty-nest stage of a marriage, when children have finally grown up and started independent lives, is often a happy time for parents. Grown children are more often a source of pride than of stress. A new opportunity for generativity arises if grandchildren arrive. That event once occurred on average at age 40, but now, in developed nations, grandparenthood begins at about age 50 (Leopold & Skopek, 2015).

Especially when the grandchildren's parents are troubled, grandparents worldwide believe their work includes helping their grandchildren (Herlofson & Hagestad, 2012). Specifics depend on policies, customs, gender, past parenting, and income of both adult generations, but for every adult, the generative impulse extends to caring for the youngest generation.

Currently in developed nations, most grandparents try to be easygoing and helpful, partly because all three generations expect them to be companions, not authorities. This requires the older adult to learn a new role: One grandmother said her tongue was scarred because she had to bite it so often (Holmes & Nash, 2015).

The supportive role is not unwanted. Grandparents prefer to provide occasional babysitting and emergency financial help but not advice or discipline (May et al., 2012). Grandparents want to be intensely generative, but they realize that support requires granting independence and autonomy.

Again, do not confuse residence with emotional closeness. Poverty, more than family harmony, is the main reason some grandparents live with their children and grandchildren. In extended families, the mother still provides most of the child care. Of course, much depends on specific needs and abilities: In about a third of three-generation U.S. households, the grandmother is the primary caregiver, with fathers, aunts, older siblings, and other family members also providing care.

About 1 percent of all U.S. households are two-generation families because the middle generation is missing. That is a *skipped-generation* family, with all the parenting work done by the grandparents. Skipped-generation families require every ounce of generativity grandparents can muster, often at the expense of their own health and happiness. This family type is sometimes official kinship care (true for a third of the foster children), and it may include formal adoption by the grandparents.

Even more than grandfathers, many grandmothers prioritize the welfare of their children and grandchildren. In Maslow's hierarchy, they ignore their own basic food and shelter needs, or love and companionship needs, to ensure the success of the younger generations. That may explain why caregiving grandmothers who are surrogate parents for their grandchildren are usually less healthy and less happy than their peers from the same neighborhoods (Chen et al., 2014; Shakya et al., 2012; Muller & Litwin, 2011).

If a grandmother is employed, as many of those under age 65 now are, she is likely to retire early if grandchildren come to live with her. Otherwise, balancing the needs of the youngest generation with the needs of a job reduces her own well-being (Meyer, 2014). If the grandmother is married, grandchild care can harm the marriage. One grandmother reports:

> When my daughter divorced, they nearly lost the house to foreclosure, so I went on the loan and signed for them. But then again they nearly foreclosed, so my husband and I bought it. . . . I have to make the payment on my own house and most of the payment on my daughter's house, and that is hard . . . I am hoping to get that money back from our daughter, to quell my husband's sense that the kids are all just taking and no one is ever giving back. He sometimes feels used and abused.
>
> *[quoted in Meyer, 2014, pp. 5, 6]*

Especially when one of the children or grandchildren is seriously ill or disabled, grandmothers often help despite the grandfather's wishes (Meyer, 2012).

In general, skipped-generation families have several strikes against them. Both the grandparents and the grandchildren are sad about the missing middle generation. In addition, difficult grandchildren (such as drug-affected infants and rebellious school-age boys) are more likely to live with grandparents.

But before concluding that grandparents suffer when they are responsible for grandchildren, consider China, where many grandparents (almost always under age 65) become full-time caregivers because the middle generation is working in the cities, unable to take children with them. The working parents typically make sure the grandparents want to be caregivers, and then they send money and visit when they can. For those grandparents, caring for their grandchildren actually improves their physical and psychological health (Baker & Silverstein, 2012).

This discussion of grandparents who live with their grandchildren should not obscure the general fact that most grandparents enjoy their role, gain generativity from it, and are appreciated by younger family members. Some are even rhapsodic and spiritual about the experience. As one writes:

> Not until my grandson was born did I realize that babies are actually miniature angels assigned to break through our knee-jerk habits of resistance and to remind us that love is the real reason we're here.
>
> *[Golden, 2010, p. 125]*

Caregiving

Parenting is the most common form of generativity for adults, but caregiving can and does occur in many other ways as well. Indeed, "life begins with care and ends with care" (Tally & Montgomery, 2013, p. 3).

Erikson (1993) wrote that a mature adult "needs to be needed" (p. 266). Some caregiving requires meeting physical needs—feeding, cleaning, and so on—but much of it involves fulfilling psychological needs. The receiver could be a child, a spouse, a parent, or someone else. Indeed, as the anecdote that began this chapter shows, everyone needs care at some point. Caregiving is part of generative adulthood.

KINKEEPERS A prime example of caregiving in most multigenerational families is the **kinkeeper,** a person who gathers everyone for holidays; spreads the word about anyone's illness, relocation, or accomplishments; buys gifts for special occasions; and reminds family members of one another's birthdays and anniversaries (Sinardet & Mortelmans, 2009). Guided by their kinkeeper, all the relatives become more generative.

Fifty years ago, kinkeepers were almost always women, usually the mother or grandmother of a large family. Now families are smaller and gender equity is more apparent, so some men or young women are kinkeepers. Generally, however, most kinkeepers are still middle-aged or older mothers with several adult children. This role may seem burdensome, but caregiving provides both satisfaction and power (Mitchell, 2010).

Sometimes one family member is called on to do more than keep the family together. Because of their position in the generational hierarchy, middle-aged adults are expected to help both the older and younger generations.

Middle-aged adults have been called the **sandwich generation,** a term that evokes an image of a layer of filling pressed between two slices of bread. This analogy suggests that the middle generation is squeezed between the needs of younger and older relatives. This sandwich metaphor is vivid, but it is misleading (Gonyea, 2013; Grundy & Henretta, 2006).

Far from being squeezed, middle-aged adults who provide some financial and emotional help to their adult children are *less* likely to be depressed than those adults whose children no longer relate to them. Meanwhile, the young-adult generation, depicted as squeezing their parents, are caregivers as well.

kinkeeper
Someone who becomes the gatherer and communication hub for their family.

sandwich generation
The generation of middle-aged people who are supposedly "squeezed" by the needs of the younger and older members of their families.

Everybody Contributes A large four-generation family such as this one helps meet the human need for love and belonging, the middle level of Maslow's hierarchy. When social scientists trace who contributes what to whom, the results show that everyone does their part but the flow is more down than up: Grandparents give more money and advice to younger generations than vice versa.

JODI COBB/NATIONAL GEOGRAPHIC/GETTY IMAGES

When adult children take care of their adult parents, the manifestation of care is not usually financial, but cultural. They help their parents understand music, media, fashion, and technology—programming their cell phones, sending digital photos, fixing computer glitches. They also are more cognizant of nutritional and medical discoveries and guidelines.

I have often experienced this in my family. For years, one of my adult daughters insisted that my Christmas present to her was for *me* to have a mammogram. Another daughter said that my present to her should be to allow her to take me clothes shopping for *myself*. She told me what to try on and what to buy. All I had to do was to pay for my own new clothes.

As for caregiving in the other direction, from middle-aged adults to their elderly parents, this is not typically the case. Most in the over-60 generation are still quite capable of caring for themselves, and many still help their middle-aged children. If they need extensive daily care, a spouse, another elderly person, or a paid caregiver is more likely to provide it than a daughter or son. Adults are often part of a caregiving team, but they are not often stuck in the middle of a sandwich.

Instead, every adult of a family cares for every other one, each in their own way. The specifics depend on many factors, including childhood attachments, personality patterns, and the financial and practical resources of each generation. Mutual caregiving strengthens family bonds; wise kinkeepers share the work, allowing everyone to be generative.

CULTURE AND CAREGIVING Some cultures assume that elderly parents should live with their adult children and that unmarried adults should live with their parents. National and ethnic variations are evident in how interdependent family members are expected to be. Some families expect to see each other often and share food, money, child care, shelter, and so on. Although people may assume that closeness means affection, such closeness may increase conflict (Voorpostel & Schans, 2011).

Regarding elder care specifically, cultures differ as to which child is responsible. The traditional assumption in Asian nations is that the eldest son and his wife provide for parents, whereas unmarried daughters are the prime caregivers in most Western nations. This varies from one family to another within each culture. For instance, in mainland China, if an elderly person lives with an adult child, it is usually with a son, but in Taiwan it is usually with a daughter (Chu et al., 2011).

The traditional custom of a frail older person living with their eldest son and being cared for by the son's wife was apparent in a survey of elders needing care in one Japanese city (see Figure 13.2). Almost a third (30 percent) were cared for by a daughter-in-law, about a fourth by a daughter (25 percent), about a fifth by a wife (20 percent), and the remaining fourth split between the two men, son (13 percent) and husband (13 percent) (Tsutsui et al., 2014).

The Japanese daughter-in-law role made sense when almost no woman was employed and when the eldest son inherited all the land or business. However, much has changed in Japan—not only more women with jobs, but also many aged people with no daughters-in-law. As a result, in 2000, Japan instituted free physical care for all elderly people who needed it.

One study examined how the law changed Japanese caregivers' sense of filial obligation Tsutsui et al., 2014). Even before the law, more

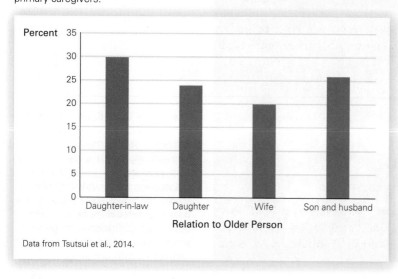

FIGURE 13.2 Caregiving Women In every nation women are much more likely to be the main caregivers for the frail elderly. This chart shows caregiving in Japan, where women provide 75 per cent of the care, and daughters-in-law provide most. In other nations, wives provide the most care, but nowhere are men the primary caregivers.

Data from Tsutsui et al., 2014.

people "slightly agreed" than "agreed" that adult children should provide financial, physical, and emotional care for the elderly. Those least likely to agree were the older women themselves who had seen how that norm had burdened their cohort. Two years after the law, the sense of filial obligation had decreased, especially among the daughters-in-law and especially regarding physical care. Emotional care was still considered important among most Japanese caregivers.

In Japan, as in the United States, the elderly who do not live with their grown children tend to be healthier. Similar changes are found in other Asian nations, including Korea and Taiwan, but not in every Asian nation. For example, most of the elderly in India live with their children and grandchildren and are healthier because of it. The elderly Indians who live alone, or only with a spouse, tend to get sick more often (Samanta et al., 2014).

Further discussion of the care needs of the aged occurs in Chapter 15. Here it is notable that adults tend to be more willing to give care than receive it: Middle-aged adults believe more strongly in filial obligation than older adults, who are more likely to need it (Gans & Silverstein, 2006; Tsutsui et al., 2014).

One last observation on caregiving and care-receiving: Many older adult couples try to take care of each other but resent it when they themselves need care. Further, husbands and wives often have divergent assumptions about elder care, or about support for grown children, or about what each spouse should contribute to finances, or housework, or social obligations. Clashes may result. From a psychological perspective, adults are happier if they care for others, not just themselves, but how, when and for whom such caregiving occurs varies by individual, by family, and by culture.

Employment

Besides parenthood and caregiving, the other major avenue for generativity is employment, a topic neglected by many developmentalists until recently. Some important work has been done regarding job choice, helping people find the right career that fits with their personality. Beyond that, most social science research on jobs has considered economic productivity, which has improved efficiency of workers, markets, and investments.

That is important work, because for optimal human development, a thriving economy helps. Then people are less likely to starve and suffer, and more likely to have everything from clean water to high-speed Internet. Obviously, much more needs to be done in this aspect of social science.

However, productivity is not central to our study of adult development. We focus instead on the psychological costs and benefits of employment for the workers.

GENERATIVITY AND WORK As is evident from many terms that describe healthy adult development—*generativity, success and esteem, instrumental,* and *achievement*—adults have psychosocial needs that work can fill.

Work meets these needs by allowing people to do the following:

- Develop and use their personal skills.
- Express their creative energy.
- Aid and advise coworkers, as mentor or friend.
- Support the education and health of their families.
- Contribute to the community by providing goods or services.

These facts highlight the distinction between the **extrinsic rewards of work** (the tangible benefits such as salary, health insurance, and pension) and the **intrinsic rewards of work** (the intangible gratifications of actually doing the job). Generativity is intrinsic.

extrinsic rewards of work
The tangible benefits, usually in salary, insurance, pension, and status, that come with employment.

intrinsic rewards of work
The personal gratifications, such as pleasure in a job well done or friendship with coworkers, that accompany employment.

Caregiving in Adulthood

Longer life expectancies for elders and a challenging economy means that more adults than ever are meeting the needs of their aging parents, children, and even their grandchildren. While children account for most of the financial strain, caring for adult parents often involves the stresses, and rewards, of hands-on caregiving. Problems arise if caregivers feel isolated, but generally caregiving adults are as happy as those who are not. Perhaps the benefits of close family relationships outweigh the stress of responsibilities.

U.S. HOUSEHOLDS IN 2012

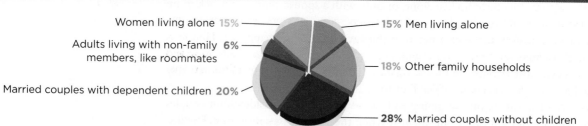

Women living alone 15%

Adults living with non-family 6% members, like roommates

Married couples with dependent children 20%

15% Men living alone

18% Other family households

28% Married couples without children

DATA FROM U.S. CENSUS BUREAU, 2012 AMERICAN COMMUNITY SURVEY.

SUPPORTING FAMILY MEMBERS

Some middle-aged adults are living with their children, grandchildren, and parents.

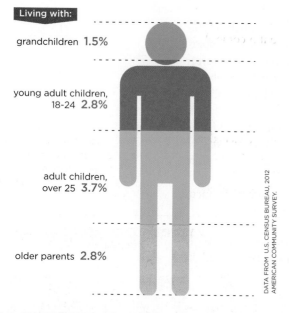

Living with:

grandchildren 1.5%

young adult children, 18-24 2.8%

adult children, over 25 3.7%

older parents 2.8%

DATA FROM U.S. CENSUS BUREAU, 2012 AMERICAN COMMUNITY SURVEY.

Almost half of 40- to 59-year-old adults are either raising a child under age 18 or financially supporting their grown children.

About 15% give financial support to both a child (of any age) and an aging parent.

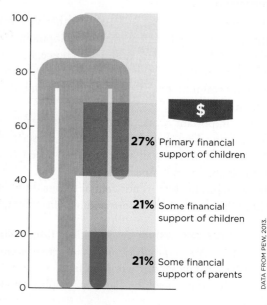

27% Primary financial support of children

21% Some financial support of children

21% Some financial support of parents

DATA FROM PEW, 2013.

Only 16% of adults under 65 are caregivers for someone over 65. Of those adults:

4.3% care for a spouse or partner.

19.1% care for a grandparent.

20.7% care for another relative (aunt, uncle, great-grandparent, etc.).

25% care for a friend.

42.4% care for a parent.

0   10   20   30   40   50

DATA FROM U.S. BUREAU OF LABOR STATISTICS, 2012.

The power of these rewards is affected by age. Extrinsic rewards tend to be more important when young people are first hired (Kooij et al., 2011). After a few years, in a developmental shift, the intrinsic rewards of work, especially relationships with coworkers, become more important (Inceoglu et al., 2012).

The power of intrinsic rewards explains why older employees are, on average, less often absent or late, and more committed to doing a good job, than younger workers are (Rau & Adams, 2014). Because of seniority, they also have more control over what they do, as well as when and how they do it. (Autonomy reduces strain and increases dedication.) Further, experienced workers are more likely to be mentors—people who help new workers navigate the job. Mentors benefit in many ways, gaining status and generativity.

Some people think older workers are less motivated to work. However, the research finds that they are as motivated as younger workers, although specifics may differ (Ng & Feldman, 2012). Especially at older ages, pride in a job well done and the joy at the final product (which might be a satisfied customer or client) are important parts of job satisfaction.

Surprisingly, absolute income (whether a person earns $30,000 or $40,000 or even $100,000 a year, for instance) matters less for job satisfaction than how a person's income compares with others in their profession or neighborhood, or to their own salary a year or two ago. It is a human trait to react more strongly to personal losses than to personal gains, ignoring systemic losses unless they become personal (Kahneman, 2011). Consequently, salary cuts have emotional, not just financial, effects.

The sense of unfairness is innate and universal, encoded in the human brain (Hsu et al., 2008). Awareness of this fact helps explain some of the attitudes of adults about pay. For example, a detailed longitudinal study of nursing assistants who stayed or left their jobs over a one-year period found that respect, coworker relations, and health benefits were significant factors in their decision to stay or to leave, but income alone was not (Rosen et al., 2011).

For adults of any age, unemployment—especially if it lasts more than a few weeks—is destructive of mental and physical health. Psychological needs are unmet, which increases the rate of domestic abuse, substance use disorder, depression, and many other social and mental health problems (Paul & Moser, 2009; Wanberg, 2012).

Some of the specific data are troubling, given that unemployment reached almost 10 percent in the United States in 2009, and 20 percent in several European nations. Adults who can't find work are 60 percent more likely to die than other people their age, especially if they are younger than 40 (Roelfs et al., 2011); twice as likely to be clinically depressed (Wanberg, 2012); and almost twice as likely to be drug-addicted (Compton et al., 2014).

A meta-analysis looking at eight stressful events that might affect adult happiness found that losing a job was the worst. A bout of unemployment caused more stress over the long term than even divorce or bereavement, at least as measured by diminished self-esteem. The stress of unemployment is likely to linger even after finding a job (Luhmann et al., 2012).

Moreover, most Americans are aware that a large gap exists between the rich and the poor. They wish that the income distribution were less skewed. However, relatively few consider this a major problem (Norton & Ariely, 2011). Given that a sense of fairness is innate, many psychologists wonder why. One answer is that people believe that social mobility is possible, that they themselves will be able to earn more (Davidai & Gilovich, 2015).

Lowered Expectations It was once realistic, a "secular trend," for adults to expect to be better off than their parents had been, but hard times have reduced the socioeconomic status of many adults.

NOT AS WELL OFF AS OUR PARENTS WERE AT OUR AGE

Apparently, resentment about work arises not directly from wages and benefits but from how wages are determined and whether or not a person believes that income or status might improve. If workers have a role in setting wages and they perceive those wages are fair, they are more satisfied (Choshen-Hillel & Yaniv, 2011).

OBSERVATION QUIZ

Does this graph indicate that, in 2012, a European American adult was six times more likely to be employed than an African American adult? (see answer, page 495) ▼

THE CHANGING WORKPLACE Obviously, work is changing in many ways that affect adult development. We focus here on only three—diversity among workers, job changes, and alternate schedules. Dramatic shifts have occurred in all three. This is true everywhere: We use statistics for the United States as an example.

Fifty years ago, the U.S. civilian labor force was 74 percent male and 89 percent non-Hispanic White. In 2012, 53 percent were male and 65 percent non-Hispanic White (16 percent were Hispanic, 12 percent African American, 5 percent Asian, and 2 percent multiracial) (see Figure 13.3). The military also has become more diverse, from virtually no women or minorities on active duty in the first half of the twentieth century to 15 percent female and 37 percent minorities in 2011 (U.S. Department of Defense, 2012).

This shift is also notable within occupations. For example, in 1960, male nurses and female police officers were rare, perhaps 1 percent. Now 13 percent of registered nurses are men and 9 percent of police officers are women—still an unbalanced ratio, but a dramatic shift nonetheless. Job discrimination relating to gender and ethnicity obviously still exists—but much less than it did.

Such changes benefit millions of adults who would have been jobless in previous decades, but it also requires workers and employers to be sensitive to differences they did not notice. Younger adults may have an advantage, because they are more likely to accept diversity—a 25-year-old employee is not surprised to have a female boss or a coworker from another ethnic group. Since a goal of human development is for everyone to fill their potential, diversity is welcomed by developmentalists. The next two changes are not as welcome.

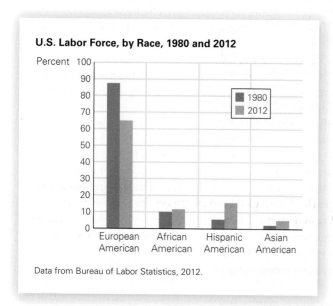

U.S. Labor Force, by Race, 1980 and 2012

Data from Bureau of Labor Statistics, 2012.

FIGURE 13.3 Diversity at Work The U.S. labor force is increasingly non-White, even according to Labor Department statistics (which exclude some low-wage workers). The next challenge is for women and people of all ethnic groups to be more proportionally distributed in various vocations, management positions, and workplaces.

A VIEW FROM SCIENCE

Accommodating Diversity

Accommodating the various sensitivities and needs of a diverse workforce requires far more than reconsidering the cafeteria menu and the holiday schedule. Private rooms for breast-feeding, revised uniform guidelines, new office design, and changing management practices may be necessary. Exactly what is needed depends on the particular culture of the workers: Some are satisfied with conditions that others would reject.

Supervisors of European descent in New Zealand criticize Maori workers (descendent from the dark-skinned people who were in New Zealand when the first Europeans arrived) for "extending the leave they were given for attending a family or tribe *hui* (gathering or meeting) without notifying

them . . . If the reasons behind are not understood, such critical incidents may . . . easily lead to over-generalizations and stereotyping and finally to less employment of people who are labeled as 'unreliable'" (Podsiadlowski & Fox, 2011, p. 8).

What might those "reasons behind" be? For British New Zealanders, a funeral of a cousin might take a day. Employees from that culture resent that a Maori coworker might take not only the allotted day but much longer, appearing back at work a week or more later.

Yet the Maori were expected by their families to stay for several days: It would be disrespectful to leave quickly. The cultural clash regarding work schedules and family obligations led to anger.

Less obvious examples occur daily, at every workplace. Certain words, policies, jokes, or mannerisms seem innocuous to one group but hostile to others.

- Women object to sexy pin-up calendars in construction offices—something male workers once accepted as routine.
- Exchanging Christmas presents may be troubling to those who are Jehovah's Witnesses, or to those who are not Christian.
- Resentment may stir if a man calls a woman "honey," or if a supervisor creates a nickname for an employee with a hard-to-pronounce name.

Researchers have begun to explore *micro-aggressions*—small things unnoticed by one person that seem aggressive to another (Sue, 2010). Comments about "senior moments," or being "color-blind" or the "fairer sex" or "the model minority," can be perceived as aggressive, even though the speaker believes they are benign.

The question "where are you from?" may seem innocent, or even friendly, but it implies that someone is not from the nation in which they live. This question may be micro-aggressive to a Hispanic American born in Puerto Rico or Texas, whose family members have been U.S. citizens for decades (Nadal et al., 2014).

Micro-aggressions can be felt by anyone who feels different because of ethnicity, age, gender, sexual orientation, religion, or anything else. For example, one research group found that older workers were particularly likely to notice ageist micro-aggression at their workplace, but that some young men also noticed micro-aggressions aimed at them (Chou & Choi, 2011).

To create a workplace that respects diversity, mutual effort is needed. Not only must everyone learn about sensitivities and customs, but also everyone must adjust and communicate.

When something insensitive occurs, the offended person should not nurse a resentment but instead should speak up. Then, the listener should not take offense at a prickly misinterpretation but should instead remember how we all react when hot buttons are pushed.

It may help to realize that we all adjust to each other in our close relationships. Romantic partners change personal habits that the other does not like; family members are careful when they discuss politics, or religion, or sex; close friends are chosen because they understand vulnerabilities.

Such awareness is part of flexible adult cognition: Adults learn to how to relate to each other in families; they need to practice the same skills at work. To return to the example in New Zealand, a Maori employee could ask for, and the supervisor could grant, a much longer time to spend with their family and tribe. Then the employee could make it a priority to return on the promised day. Less resentment, more learning, happier workers.

CHANGING LOCATIONS Today's workers change employers more often than did workers decades ago. Hiring and firing are common. Employers constantly downsize, reorganize, relocate, outsource, or merge. Loyalty between employee and employer, once assumed, now seems quaint.

These changes may increase corporate profits, worker benefits, and consumer choice. However, churning employment may harm human development. Every change severs work friendships and adds stress. Workers new to a job experience more stress than joy. One study found that people who frequently changed jobs by age 36 were three times more likely to have health problems by age 42 (Kinnunen et al., 2005). This study controlled for smoking and drinking; if it had not, the health impact would have been greater.

As adults age, losing a job becomes increasingly stressful for several reasons (Rix, 2011):

1. Seniority brings higher salaries, more respect, and greater expertise; workers who leave a job they have had for years lose these advantages.

2. Many skills required for employment were not taught decades ago, so older workers are less likely to be hired or promoted in a new job.

3. Age discrimination is illegal, but workers believe it is widespread. Even if age discrimination is absent, stereotype threat undercuts successful job searching.

4. Relocation reduces long-standing intimacy and generativity.

From a developmental perspective, this last factor is crucial. Imagine that you are a 40-year-old adult who has always lived in Michigan, and your employer goes out of business. You try to find work, but no one hires you, partly because unemployment

If You Had to Choose Which is more important, a high salary or comfortable working conditions? Intrinsic rewards of work are scarce for these workers in Mumbai, India *(left),* who talk to North Americans who phone in confused about their computers, their bills, or their online orders, as well as for the man in eastern Colorado *(right).* His relationships with coworkers and supervisors are not comforting, and he has heard that fracking increases pollution, earthquakes, and cancer (hence the protective gear). Most workers who have few psychosocial benefits at work are much younger than the average employee.

in Michigan is among the highest in the nation. Would you move a thousand miles west to North Dakota, where the unemployment rate is only one-fourth that in Michigan?

If you were unemployed and in debt, and a new job was guaranteed, you might make the move. You would leave your friends and community, but at least you would have a paycheck.

But would your spouse and children quit their jobs, schools, and social networks to move with you? If not, you would be cut off from all your social support, but if they did, their food and housing would be expensive, their schools overcrowded, and their lives lonely (at least initially). For you and anyone who comes with you, moving means losing intimacy—harmful for psychosocial development.

Such difficulties are magnified for immigrants, who make up about 15 percent of the U.S. adult workforce and 22 percent of Canada's. Many of them depend on other immigrants for housing, work, and social connections (García Coll & Marks, 2012). That meets some of their intimacy and generativity needs, but their relationship to their family of origin and childhood friends are strained by distance; the climate, the food, and the language are not comforting.

These developmental needs are ignored by most business owners and by many workers themselves. However, adults' intimacy and generatively needs are best satisfied by a thriving social network, and each particular community and workplace fosters that. When that is disrupted, both psychological and physical health suffers.

No Perfect Job Colin Drummond is an independent photographer who earns a good living. He does most of his work here at home in Virginia, where he lives with his wife and children. Sounds ideal, but no job is perfect: Sometimes he must stand for hours outside in the rain; his profession is highly competitive, so he does not know if he will earn any money next year. He is one of those photographers known as paparazzi.

CHANGING SCHEDULES The standard work week is 9 A.M. to 5 P.M., Monday through Friday—a schedule that is increasingly unusual. In the United States, about a third of all workers have nonstandard schedules. Retail services (virtual and in-store) are increasingly available 24/7, which requires night and weekend employees, and many other parts of the economy need employees with nonstandard schedules.

Work schedules vary by income and age, with the impact on human development rarely considered by employers or recognized by employees. Therefore, that is our focus here.

Most U.S. workers are in the service sector of the economy (80 percent, see Figure 13.4). Younger service workers, particularly in retail sales (15 million jobs) and health (14 million jobs), often have nonstandard shifts. Those segments are also the fastest growing, so increasingly new workers will find jobs with nonstandard shifts (Henderson, 2013).

The estimate in the first paragraph of this discussion (one-third of all workers in nonstandard schedules) is a rough average. Much depends on the definition of "nonstandard" work.

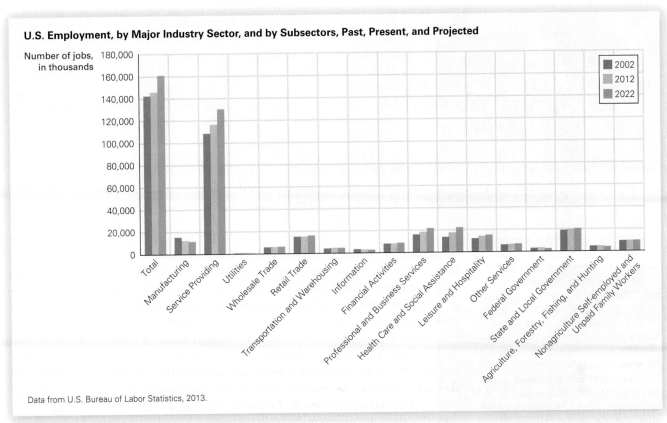

U.S. Employment, by Major Industry Sector, and by Subsectors, Past, Present, and Projected

Data from U.S. Bureau of Labor Statistics, 2013.

FIGURE 13.4 May I Help You? The overall job growth in recent years is almost all in services of one sort or another (seen overall, and then in 12 separate categories). Unfortunately, the manufacturing jobs that are declining were well paid with benefits.

One survey of mothers with relatively low SES found that half of those who were employed had nonstandard schedules (Dunifon et al., 2013). Other research puts the number much lower, perhaps 11 percent.

Uncertainties arise because of definition and participants: Low-SES women are more likely to have nonstandard schedules than high-SES men. On the other hand, people in high status jobs often feel compelled to answer email or travel evenings and weekends, to the detriment of their physical and psychological health (Barber & Jenkins, 2014).

In any case, if parents work nonstandard shifts, their families suffer because of it. Weekend work, especially with mandatory overtime, is difficult for father–child relationships, because "normal rhythms of family life are impinged upon by irregular schedules" (Hook, 2012, p. 631). With nonstandard employment, mothers get less sleep and are more stressed (Kalil et al., 2014b) and couples are more likely to divorce (Maume & Sebastian, 2012).

Negative effects for nonstandard work are not inevitable: Some benefits come from more income and a stronger parental alliance. The main family advantage, of course, is that nonstandard shifts may allow at least one parent to be home all the time. Nonetheless, married parents rarely benefit from nonstandard schedules, and cohabiting parents almost never do. Work requirements undercut the needs of a romantic relationship (Liu et al., 2011).

A different problem more often arises for skilled, higher-income, experienced workers. They may benefit from *flextime* (some choice as to days and hours) or *telecommuting* (working via Internet, phone, and fax, often at home). Employers can see advantages and disadvantages in such arrangements, but employees often appreciate that they have some control over their work hours.

ANSWER TO OBSERVATION QUIZ
(from page 492) No. Remember that the percentage of adults who are African American is about 13 percent. Chance of employment is almost equal for adults of every ethnicity. Inequality is most evident in salary and type of work, not in employment itself. ●

BARTOSZ HADYNIAK/VETTA/GETTY IMAGES

BRIAN CASSELLA/ZUMA PRESS/NEWSCOM

Never Easy Juggling job responsibilities and child care simultaneously is difficult. Which is more complicated, caring for an infant while farming in Southeast Asia or supervising a teenager while conferring with a client? At times these two mothers might want to trade places or wish that men did as much child care as women. At other times, they would have it no other way.

However, with more skills and responsibilities also come more demands: Many such workers find that they work, sometimes "on call," on evenings and weekends. The boundaries between work life and family life are porous, as a text message at home can interrupt family time with an unanticipated deadline, last-minute travel, or other demands.

One crucial variable for job satisfaction for both skilled and unskilled workers is whether employees can choose their own hours and work demands. Workers who volunteer for paid overtime are usually satisfied, but workers who are required to work overtime are not (Beckers et al., 2008). This is true no matter how experienced the workers are, what their occupation is, or where they live (Tuttle & Garr, 2012).

For instance, a nationwide study of 53,851 nurses, ages 20 to 59, found that *required* overtime was one of the few factors that reduced job satisfaction in every cohort (Klaus et al., 2012). Similarly, a study of office workers in China also found that the extent of required overtime correlated with less satisfaction and poorer health (Houdmont et al., 2011). Apparently, although work (paid or unpaid) is satisfying, working too long and not by choice undercuts the psychological and physical benefits.

In theory, part-time work and self-employment might allow adults to balance conflicting demands. But reality does not conform to the theory. In many nations (except the Netherlands, where half the workers are part time), part-time work is underpaid, and typically benefits such as health care or pensions are available only to full-time employees. Thus, workers avoid part-time employment if they can, again making a choice that undercuts emotional well-being and family life.

FINDING THE BALANCE As you see, adulthood is filled with opportunities and challenges. Adults can finally choose their mates, their locations, their lifestyles to express their personality, with the extroverts surrounding themselves with many social activities and the introverts choosing a more quiet, but no less rewarding, life.

Both men and women have intimacy and generativity needs, and both sexes have many ways to meet those needs. Intimacy can occur with partners of the same sex or other sex, marriage or cohabiting, friends and family, parents or siblings or grown children, or, ideally some chosen combination of all that. Similarly, generativity can focus on raising children or employment. Again, modern life often allows men and women to meet their needs in both arenas at once, as more men are active fathers and more women are employed.

In some ways, then, modern life allows adults to "have it all," to combine family and work in such a way that all needs are satisfied at once. However, some very articulate observers suggest that "having it all" is an illusion or, at best, a mistaken ideal achievable only by the very rich and very talented (Slaughter, 2012; Sotomayor, 2014), as the following explains.

A CASE TO STUDY

Having It All

Gender and child care have changed markedly in the past half-century, as has the proportion of women in college. In top professions and at the highest levels of government, industry, and the arts, the successful leaders 50 years ago were all men. Now, hundreds of women have reached the top in many fields. The glass ceiling has broken, although men still predominate. The idea that adult women must choose between work and family seems wrong; women should be able to "have it all." Or is that a fantasy?

In every nation, child care consumes more time and thought from women than men, and males have more power and pay than females. It is not hard to find exceptions to these generalities—this chapter included a comment from one father who was the primary caregiver of his young children while his wife was the primary wage earner. However, the averages from every nation and group show gender differences. For example, for the U.S. Supreme Court, only three of the nine are women, including the two most recently appointed—neither of whom has children.

Many feminists conclude that the "revolution has stalled," that progress toward gender equity in the last decades of the twentieth century has halted in the first decades of the twenty-first (Sandberg, 2013, p. 7). Why?

Are social structures and cultural patterns keeping women from professional success, forcing them to choose between dedication to motherhood and dedication to their jobs? Or are women handicapping themselves by their actions and attitudes? We present two cases, both highly successful women with two children. One concludes that women could "have it all" if only society would change.

Anne-Marie Slaughter wrote:

Eighteen months into my job as the first woman director of policy planning at the State Department, a foreign-policy dream job that traces its origins back to George Kennan, I found myself in New York, at the United Nations' annual assemblage of every foreign minister and head of state in the world. On a Wednesday evening, President and Mrs. Obama hosted a glamorous reception at the American Museum of Natural History. I sipped champagne, greeted foreign dignitaries, and mingled. But I could not stop thinking about my 14-year-old son, who had started eighth grade three weeks earlier and was already resuming what had become his pattern of skipping homework, disrupting classes, failing math, and tuning out any adult who tried to reach him.

[Slaughter, 2012, p. 84]

Slaughter left that "dream job" in Washington, D.C., six months later to be closer to her children in New Jersey. She still believes that men and women can "have it all," with satisfying work and thriving families, but she does not think that possible today. Only if a mother has work where she controls the schedule, a job that requires little travel or evening work, can she be a good mother *and* employee.

The problem as Slaughter sees it is that society is still geared to the old days, when mothers stayed home with the children. What needs to happen is "changing social policies and bending career tracks to accommodate *our* choices" (Slaughter, 2012, p. 102).

Another extremely successful woman, Sheryl Sandberg, the chief operating officer of Facebook, says that "having it all" is a myth, never possible. She says, "I fall very short of doing it all" (Sandberg, 2013, p. 139). When women are less successful in the world of work, she argues that the problem is that women hold themselves back; they lean away from challenges rather than "lean in," because "stereotypes and biases cloud our beliefs and perpetuate the status quo" (Sandberg, 2013, p. 159).

Sandberg thinks it is folly when any man or woman believes they can do everything well all the time. But it is even more destructive for women to believe they are less capable of doing work as well as any man. Misguided belief leads to less ambition and then less success: Women need to believe in themselves, says Sandberg.

As you see, the essential controversy here is whether women are held back by society or by their own stereotypes.

There is a third perspective: that some gender differences are as they should be. The idea is that, since only females can become pregnant and nurse their children, it is natural for women to provide more child care. Men are designed, biologically, to brave the outside, competitive world: Their testosterone leads them to the top of many professions, as it should.

Which of these perspectives seems right to you? What would you like to read in a case study of you?

Compromises, trade-offs, and selective optimization with compensation may be essential to find an appropriate work–family balance. Both halves of the balance can bring joy, but both can bring stress—and often do.

For example, a large study of adult Canadians found that about half of the variation in their distress was related to employment (working conditions, support at work, occupation, job security), but at least as much was related to family issues (having children younger than 5, support at home) and feelings of personal competence (Marchand et al., 2012).

In linked lives, husbands and wives usually adjust to each other's needs, allowing them to function better as a couple than they did as singles (Abele & Volmer, 2011). When they become parents, men spend more hours on the job and women more hours at home. Consequently, five years after their wedding the man's salary is notably higher than it would have been if he were single, while their shared home is notably more accommodating (Kuperberg, 2012). Thus, people help each other with the problems of adulthood, together balancing generativity needs.

Grandparents, too, help with balance. If parents have reliable, nearby grandparents, they are likely to have more children, and the children they have are likely to do better in school and, later on, in college and life.

Do adults fare better or worse with today's economic climate and social norms? As you see, alternatives to marriage, nonbiological parenthood, workplace diversity, job changes, and schedule variation have benefits as well as costs. For example, maternal employment is more likely to benefit families than not, but children still need parental attention—so children suffer if their mothers or fathers have no time for them.

Because personality is enduring and variable, opinions about current adult development reflect personality as well as objective research. Some people are optimists—high in extroversion and agreeableness—and they tend to believe that adulthood is better now than it used to be. Others are pessimists—high in neuroticism and low in openness—and they are likely to conclude that adult life was better before the rise of cohabitation, LAT, divorce, and economic stress, praising the time when almost all couples married and stayed married to raise their children on the man's steady salary from his 9-to-5 job with one employer.

Data could be used to support both perspectives. For instance, in the United States, suicide is less common than it used to be (life is better), but the gap between rich and poor is increasing (life is worse). Fewer people are marrying and fewer children are born: Is that evidence for improved adult lives or the opposite?

From a developmental perspective, personality, intimacy, and generativity continue to be important in every adult life. Further, every adult benefits from friends and family, caregiving responsibilities, and satisfying work. Whether finding a satisfying combination of all of this is easier or more difficult at this historical moment is debatable.

As the next two chapters detail, there are many possible perspectives on life in late adulthood as well. Some view the last years of life with horror, others consider them golden. Neither view is quite accurate, as you will soon see.

WHAT HAVE YOU LEARNED?

1. What is the basic idea of generativity?
2. In what ways does parenthood satisfy an adult's need to be generative?
3. What factors might make it difficult for foster children and foster parents to bond?
4. How might each of the Big Five personality traits make it easier or more difficult to develop positive relationships with stepchildren?
5. What advantages do adoptive parents have over foster parents or stepparents?
6. Is it a blessing or a burden that women are more often kinkeepers and caregivers than are men?
7. Why are middle-aged adults mistakenly called the "sandwich generation"?
8. What are some extrinsic and intrinsic rewards of work?
9. What are the advantages of greater ethnic diversity at work?
10. Why is changing jobs stressful?
11. How have innovations in work scheduling helped and harmed families?
12. Why, overall, might people be happier with current employment patterns than earlier ones?

the population aged 80 and older has doubled, not quadrupled (from 1.6 percent to 3.7 percent, 1965–2015). That does not overwhelm the other 96.3 percent. It is true that the risk of Alzheimer's disease increases with age, so as more people become very old, the total number of Americans with Alzheimer's is increasing. However, the *proportion* of people with Alzheimer's is decreasing (as detailed later). So is the proportion of people in nursing homes—less than 4 percent of those over age 65 on any given day.

Theories of Aging

Underlying our study of aging is a fundamental question: Why do people age? If we could stop senescence, or even slow down the aging process, we could decrease the rate of cancer, heart diseases, strokes, and every frailty that undermines the body and brain.

Hundreds of theories and thousands of scientists have tried to understand the biology of aging, with the hope that understanding will lead to ways to slow the process. To simplify, these theories are grouped in three clusters: wear and tear, genetic adaptation, and cellular aging.

STOP MOVING? STOP EATING? The oldest, most general theory of aging is known as **wear and tear.** The idea is that the body wears out, part by part, after years of use. Organ reserve and repair processes are exhausted as the decades pass (Gavrilov & Gavrilova, 2006).

This theory begins by recognizing that some body parts suffer from overuse. Athletes who put repeated stress on their shoulders or knees may have chronically painful joints by middle age; workers who inhale asbestos and smoke cigarettes damage their lungs; hockey, football, and boxing stars who suffer repeated blows to the head may destroy their brains.

In addition, sometimes the body wears out because of weather, or harmful food, or pollution, or radiation. For instance, skin cancer is caused partly by too much sun, clogged arteries are caused partly by too much animal fat, and some cancer tumors result from too much pollution and radiation.

Every older person's hands and face are wrinkled, often with discolorations known as "age spots." By contrast, the skin on the torso may be smooth and clear, even at age 80. The reason is wear and tear via daily sun, wind, and cold to the face, but almost never to the stomach.

However, most scientists have rejected wear and tear as a general theory of aging, because other body functions benefit from activity. Exercise improves heart and lung functioning; tai chi improves balance; weight training increases muscle mass; sexual activity stimulates the sexual-reproductive system. The slogan "use it or lose it" may apply to cognition, as well.

An astonishing finding from lower animals suggests an application of wear and tear. If an adult reduced wear and tear on digestion, metabolism, and so on by eating 1,800 calories a day instead of the usual 3,000, would that slow all aging processes? **Calorie restriction**—a drastic reduction in calories consumed—increases the life span in many organisms.

The most dramatic evidence comes from fruit flies, which can live three times as long if they eat less. Many other species benefit from calorie restriction, but not all. Some research on monkeys, mice, and other animals reports that calorie restriction extends life, but other research does not (Mattison et al., 2012).

Results may depend on small genetic differences between one species (or strain of mice) and another, or on details of the diet. Some research suggests that a high-nutrient, low-protein diet may be crucial (Bruce et al., 2014). Periodic fasting and scheduled eating may also be relevant (Fontana & Partridge, 2015).

Video: Portrait of Aging: Mary http://qrs.ly/xr4sqmm

wear and tear
A view of aging as a process by which the human body wears out because of the passage of time and exposure to environmental stressors.

calorie restriction
The practice of limiting dietary energy intake (while consuming sufficient quantities of vitamins, minerals, and other important nutrients) in hopes of slowing down the aging process.

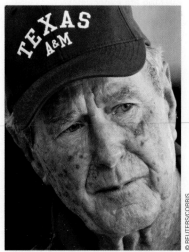

© REUTERS/CORBIS

Skin Deep Those spots on former president Bush's face are signs of an anti-aging treatment, specifically nitrogen to freeze the damaged cells on his skin. For him as well as for everyone else, aging that results from wear and tear can be treated, unlike the aging that is genetic or cellular.

"If you give up alcohol, cigarettes, sex, red meat, cake and chocolate, and don't get too excited, you can enjoy life for a few more years yet."

THINK CRITICALLY: Do people want the comforts of daily life—driving and eating—more than longer lives?

maximum life span
The oldest possible age that members of a species can live under ideal circumstances. For humans, that age seems to be 122 years.

average life expectancy
The number of years the average person in a particular population group is likely to live.

genetic clock
A mechanism in the DNA of cells that regulates the aging process by triggering hormonal changes and cellular death and repair.

Regarding humans, thousands of members of the Calorie Restriction Society voluntarily undereat (Roth & Polotsky, 2012). They give up some things that many people cherish, not just cake and hot dogs but also a strong sex drive and high energy. As a result, they have lower blood pressure, fewer strokes, less cancer, and almost no diabetes. But that does not convince most scientists, in part because they are a self-selective sample.

In several places (e.g., Okinawa, Denmark, and Norway), wartime occupation forced severe calorie reduction for almost everyone. People ate local vegetables, and not much else, and they were often hungry. But they were less likely to die of disease (Fontana et al., 2011).

Similar results were reported from Cuba, already mentioned in Chapter 12. Because the United States led an embargo of Cuban products, that nation experienced food and gas shortages from 1991 to 1995. People ate local fruits and vegetables, walked more, and lost weight. Death, particularly due to heart disease and diabetes, was reduced (Franco et al., 2013).

In all these examples, populations benefited when everyone ate less, particularly less meat; but in all these nations, once more food was available, people eagerly ate more. Disease deaths rose again. Apparently, most humans choose some wear and tear in order to live the life they want.

IT'S ALL GENETIC A second cluster of theories focuses on genes, both genes of the entire species and genes that vary from one person to another (Sutphin & Kaeberlein, 2011). About one-third of longevity can be attributed directly to genes and the other two-thirds to epigenetic and environmental factors. Those proportions vary from person to person, as differential susceptibility would predict (Govindaraju et al., 2015).

Every species has a **maximum life span,** defined as the oldest possible age that members of that species can attain (Wolf, 2010). Genes determine the maximum: for rats, 4 years; rabbits, 13; tigers, 26; house cats, 30; brown bats, 34; brown bears, 37; chimpanzees, 55; Indian elephants, 70; finback whales, 80; humans, 122; lake sturgeon, 150; giant tortoises, 180.

Maximum life span is quite different from **average life expectancy,** which is the average life span of individuals in a particular group. In human groups, average life expectancy varies a great deal, depending on historical, cultural, and socioeconomic factors (Sierra et al., 2009).

The average human life expectancy has more than doubled in the past century and continues to rise. Worldwide, in 2015, the average is about 71 (69 for men, 73 for women). In the United States, in 2015, average life expectancy at birth is 80 (77 for men, 82 for women), eight years more than half a century ago, and projected to be six years longer by 2065 (United Nations, Department of Economic and Social Affairs, Population Division, 2015).

Average life expectancy is increasing primarily because public health measures (clean water, immunization, nutrition, newborn care) prevented many infant and child deaths, and recent medical measures have decreased midlife death from heart disease and cancer.

Eventually, however, a **genetic clock** regulates life, growth, and aging. Just as genes trigger puberty at a certain age, genes may switch on to cause gray hair, slower movement, and, eventually, death. That is true for each species.

In addition, some genes cause unusually fast or slow aging. Children born with Hutchinson-Gilford syndrome (a genetic disease also called *progeria*) stop growing at about age 5 and begin to look old, with wrinkled skin and balding heads, dying in their teens of diseases typically found in people five times their age.

Other genes seem to program a long and healthy life. People who reach age 100 usually have alleles that other people do not (Govindaraju et al., 2015).

Two alleles of the *ApoE* gene prove the point. *ApoE2* is found in 12 percent of men in their 70s and 17 percent of men over age 85. Those numbers make it apparent that *ApoE2* aids survival. However, another allele of the same gene, *ApoE4*, increases the rate of death by heart disease, stroke, neurocognitive disorders, and—if a person is HIV-positive—by AIDS (Kuhlmann et al., 2010).

Almost every disease is partly genetic, so disease rates vary among people with ancestors from particular parts of the world. For instance, many genes for type 2 diabetes are shared across ethnic groups, but some are more common among African Americans than other U.S. groups (Palmer et al., 2012). For genetic reasons, people with Asian ancestors develop diabetes at younger ages and lower weights than Europeans (Chan et al., 2009; Hsu et al., 2015).

CELLS QUIT REPRODUCING The third cluster of theories examines **cellular aging,** focusing on molecules and cells. Remember, cells duplicate many times over the life span, duplicating and reproducing. Minor errors in copying accumulate. Early in life, the immune system repairs such errors, but eventually, the immune system itself becomes less adept.

When the organism can no longer repair every cellular error, senescence occurs. This process is first apparent in the skin, an organ that replaces itself often, particularly if damage occurs (such as peeling skin with sunburn). Cellular aging also occurs inside the body, notably in cancer, as the aging immune system is increasingly unable to control abnormal cells.

Even without specific infections or stresses, healthy cells stop replicating at a certain point. This point is referred to as the **Hayflick limit,** named after the scientist who discovered it. Hayflick believes that aging is caused primarily by a natural loss of molecular fidelity—that is, by inevitable errors in transcription as each cell reproduces itself. He believes that aging is natural, built into our cells (Hayflick, 2004).

One cellular change occurs with **telomeres**—material at the ends of the chromosome that becomes shorter with each duplication. Telomeres are longer in children (except those with progeria) and shorter in older adults. Eventually, at the Hayflick limit, the telomere is gone, duplication stops, and the creature dies (Aviv, 2011).

The length of telomeres is related to both genes and stress. The more stress a person experiences, from childhood on, the shorter their telomeres are in late adulthood and the sooner they will die (J. Lin et al., 2012).

Telomere length is about the same in newborns of both sexes and all ethnic groups, but by late adulthood telomeres are longer in women than in men, and longer in European Americans than in African Americans (Aviv, 2011). There are many possible causes, but cellular-aging theorists focus on the consequences: Women outlive men, and European Americans outlive African Americans, at least until age 80.

THINK CRITICALLY: For the benefit of the species as a whole, why would genes promote aging?

cellular aging
The ways in which molecules and cells are affected by age. Many theories aim to explain how and why aging causes cells to deteriorate.

Hayflick limit
The number of times a human cell is capable of dividing. The limit for most human cells is approximately 50 divisions, an indication that the life span is limited by our genetic program.

telomeres
The area of the tips of each chromosome that is reduced a tiny amount as time passes. By the end of life, the telomeres are very short.

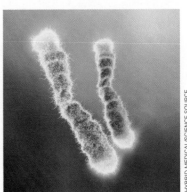

HYBRID MEDICAL/SCIENCE SOURCE

Old Caterpillars? No, these are young chromosomes, stained to show the glowing white telomeres at the ends.

OPPOSING PERSPECTIVES

Stop the Clock?

Many scientists, as well as older people, seek to extend life. Those who restrict their calories may be extreme, but millions eat special foods (blueberries, red wine, fish oil?) or take certain drugs (sirtuins, rapamycin, resveratrol?) to extend life.

All the theories of aging, and all the research on genes, cells, calorie restriction, foods, drugs, antioxidants, and so on, have not yet led to any sure way to postpone death. Scientists are following numerous leads because many are convinced that something will slow aging.

For instance, a team of researchers traces about half of all adult cognitive decline to three specific diseases (Alzheimer's disease, vascular disease, and Lewy body disease—all described soon) but contends that much more research must be done on the unknown yet common causes of cognitive decline (Boyle et al., 2013). Many medical researchers believe that more funding for anti-aging research, and less for specific diseases, would reduce the cost of health care (Goldman et al., 2013).

But the opposing perspective is that anti-aging research is both foolish and unethical. Perhaps now that major causes of premature death have been prevented, further longevity is not possible. In the most advanced nations, the rate of increase in longevity has slowed down. Gerontologists are engaged in a "fiery debate" as to whether the maximum is genetically fixed (Couzin-Frankel, 2011).

For example, the oldest well-documented life ended at age 122, when Jeanne Calment died in southern France in 1997. No one has yet been proven to have outlived her, despite documented birth dates for a billion people who have died since then. Some of the very old from regions of the world without accurate birth records are said to be older (e.g., Benet, 1974), but most researchers believe that is wishful thinking (Thorson, 1995).

Further, is it ethical to strive for increased longevity for wealthy 80-year-olds when many low-SES infants, children, and young adults die? Perhaps training doctors and nurses in the poorest nations and reducing SES disparities in wealthy nations are better goals.

Many worry that by extending life, nations are adding medical costs to society. Currently, the U.S. health benefit for the aged of any income—Medicare—costs three times as much as the elderly themselves pay for the benefit. Thus, the concern is that any lengthening of life will result in less public money for schools, colleges, and health care for those under age 65.

Further, unconscious prejudice may be fueling the efforts to extend life. Compared to the average U.S. resident, older Americans tend to be more often of European than African ancestry, more often native-born than immigrant, more often Protestant Christian than other religions, more often middle class than poor. The effort to extend their life, rather than, say, put research funds into gun violence, or teratogens, or early childhood education, may be selfishly promoted by lawmakers (who know that older people vote), by senior scientists, and by the elderly themselves.

Or is it ageist and prejudiced to suggest such a thing? Opposing perspectives.

THINK CRITICALLY: Are anti-aging measures a selfish endeavor by older people who protect themselves while harming the young?

WHAT HAVE YOU LEARNED?

1. How is ageism similar to racism?
2. How is benevolent ageism harmful?
3. What is elderspeak and how is it used?
4. What is encouraging about the research on calorie restriction?
5. What is discouraging about the research on calorie restriction?
6. Regarding maximum and average life span, should both, neither, or only one be extended?
7. What is the connection between telomeres and the Hayflick limit?
8. Why might a society consider it harmful for people to live past a certain age?

Selective Optimization with Compensation

How does a person cope with senescence without succumbing to ageism? The answer, already mentioned in Chapter 12, is to choose (select) to specialize (optimize), using effective strategies (compensation). Here we stress the varied source of those strategies: from the individual, from the community, or from medicine.

Accordingly, we now provide three examples. In one (sex), personal thinking and behavior is effective; in another (driving), community laws and practices are crucial; and in the third (diseases), medical measures compensate for bodily changes.

Personal Compensation: Sex

Most people are sexually active throughout adulthood. Some continue to have intercourse long past age 65 (Lindau & Gavrilova, 2010) (see Figure 14.5), but generally intercourse becomes less frequent and sometimes stops completely. Nonetheless, sexual satisfaction often increases *after* middle age (Heiman et al., 2011). How can that be?

Respondents in an Intimate Relationship Who Had Sexual Intercourse in Previous Year (%)

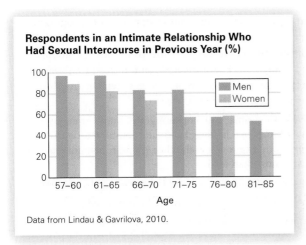

Data from Lindau & Gavrilova, 2010.

FIGURE 14.5 Your Reaction Older adults who consider their health good (most of them) were asked whether they had had sexual intercourse within the past year. If they answered yes, they were considered sexually active. What is your reaction to the data? Some young adults might be surprised that many adults, aged 60 to 80, still experience sexual intercourse. Other people might be saddened that most healthy adults over age 80 do not. However, neither reaction may be appropriate. For many elders, sexual affection is expressed in many more ways than intercourse, and it continues lifelong.

OBSERVATION QUIZ

What are the male–female differences and how can they be explained, since all of these respondents had partners of the other sex? (see answer, page 518) ▲

Compensation for diminished arousal results from both thinking and behavior.

Many older adults reject the idea that intercourse is the only, or best, measure of sexual activity. Instead, cuddling, kissing, caressing, desiring, and fantasizing become more important. To optimize, they do more of these (Chao et al., 2011).

A five-nation study (United States, Germany, Japan, Brazil, Spain) found that kissing and hugging, not intercourse, predicted happiness in long-lasting romances (Heiman et al., 2011). Is that optimization, compensation, or both? Consider the following cases.

To Have and to Hold In McMinnville, Oregon *(top),* and in Montevideo, Uruguay *(bottom),* these married couples, like many other elderly ones, enjoy their physical as well as psychological closeness.

A CASE TO STUDY

Should Older Couples Have More Sex?

Sexual needs and interactions vary extremely from one person to another, so no single case illustrates general trends. Further, questionnaires and physiological measures designed for young bodies may be inappropriate for the aged. Accordingly, two researchers studied elderly sex using a method called *grounded theory.*

They found 34 people (17 couples, aged 50 to 86, married an average of 34 years), interviewing each privately and

extensively. They read and reread all the transcripts, tallying responses and topics by age and gender (that was the grounded part). Then they analyzed common topics, interpreting trends (that was theory).

They concluded that sexual activity is more a social construction than a biological event (Lodge & Umberson, 2012). All their cases said that intercourse was less frequent with age, including four couples for whom intercourse stopped completely because of the husband's health. Nonetheless, more respondents said that their sex life had improved than said it deteriorated (44 percent compared to 30 percent).

Surprisingly, those 44 percent were more likely to be over age 65 than middle-aged. Some midlife men were troubled by difficulty maintaining an erection, and many women worried that they were not sexy.

One woman said:

> All of a sudden, we didn't have sex after I got skinny. And I couldn't figure that out . . . I look really good now and we're not having sex. It turns out that he was going through a major physical thing at that point and just had lost his sex drive . . . I went through years thinking it was my fault.
>
> *[Irene, quoted in Lodge & Umberson, 2012, p. 435]*

The authors theorize that "images of masculine sexuality are premised on high, almost uncontrollable levels of penis-driven sexual desire" (Lodge & Umberson, 2012, p. 430), while the cultural ideals of feminine sexuality emphasize women's passivity and yet "implore women to be both desirable and receptive to men's sexual desires and impulses," deeming "older women and their bodies unattractive" (Lodge & Umberson, 2012, p. 430).

Thus, when middle-aged adults first realize that aging has changed their sexual interaction, both sexes are distressed. By late adulthood they realize that the young idea of good sex (frequent intercourse) was not relevant. Instead they *compensated* for physical changes by *optimizing* their relationship in other ways. As one man over age 70 said:

> I think the intimacy is a lot stronger . . . more often now we do things like holding hands and wanting to be close to each other or touch each other. It's probably more important now than sex is.
>
> *[Jim, quoted in Lodge & Umberson, 2012, p. 438]*

An older woman said her marriage improved because

> We have more opportunities and more motivation. Sex was wonderful. It got thwarted, with . . . the medication he is on. And he hasn't been functional since. The doctors just said that it is going to be this way, so we have learned to accept that. But we have also learned long before that there are more ways than one to share your love.
>
> *[Helen, quoted in Lodge & Umberson, 2012, p. 437]*

The next cohort of older adults may have other attitudes; the male/female and midlife/older differences evident with these 17 couples may not apply. These cases do suggest, however, that selective optimization with compensation is possible.

Social Compensation: Driving

In a life-span perspective "aging is a process, socially constructed as be a problem" (Cruikshank, 2009, p. 7). The process is biological, but the problem arises in the social world. Selective optimization with compensation is needed by societies. One example is driving.

With age, reading road signs takes longer, turning the head becomes harder, reaction time slows, and night vision worsens. The elderly compensate: Many drive slowly and reduce driving in the dark.

However, relying on each older person's judgment as to whether to stop driving is foolhardy, because the culture connects driving a car with pride and independence. Of course, the elderly hate to quit; it destroys their freedom. Consequently, many older drivers contend that their critics are ageist, not that they are accurate (Satariano et al., 2012). A family conflict occurs when adult children take car keys from an elderly parent.

It is no wonder that many elders insist they are good drivers and resent age-based restriction. They are correct that requiring everyone to stop driving at age 70, or 80, or whenever is unfair. Then, if a crash occurs, they blame the other driver, who blames them. Wrong targets, both.

The problem begins with license renewal. Some jurisdictions require only a mailed form and a check. Others require a written test about stop signs and parking and/or reading large letters on a well-lit chart. Anyone who fails should have stopped driving long ago, but passing does not guarantee competence.

And on Icy Curves . . . Everywhere in the world, the elderly want to keep driving. Some nations require extensive training for license renewals. This is a special safety class for elderly drivers in Germany.

AXEL HEIMKEN/PICTURE-ALLIANCE/DPA/AP IMAGES

Social Comparison: Elders Behind the Wheel

Older people often change their driving habits in order to compensate for their slowing reaction time. Many states have initiated restrictions, including requiring older drivers to renew their licenses in person, to make sure they stay safe. Because most older drivers limit themselves (they avoid night, rainy, and distance driving), their crash rate is low overall, but not when measured by the rate per miles driven.

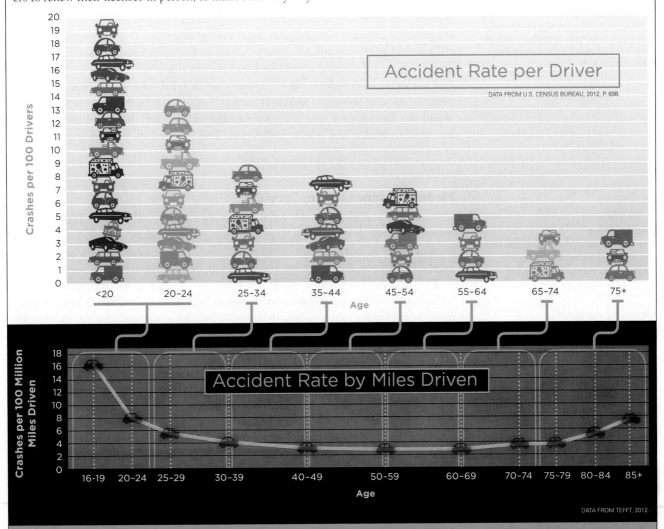

Accident Rate per Driver

DATA FROM U.S. CENSUS BUREAU, 2012, P. 698.

Accident Rate by Miles Driven

DATA FROM TEFFT, 2012.

Self-Check

Humans of all ages tend to overestimate their abilities. As a result, they may cause a kitchen fire, or fall on ice, or ignore a lump or a chest pain until it is too late.

Especially after age 65, adults who want to drive need to answer six questions:

1. **Is your vision fading?** [Ask your optometrist if any visual losses affect driving.]

2. **Do your medications affect reaction time or alertness?** [Ask both doctor and pharmacist.]

3. **Do your physical limitations affect neck-turning, foot-pushing, wheel-turning?**

4. **Do you get lost more easily now than in earlier years?**

5. **Do other drivers honk at you?** [Don't just get angry, consider the reason.]

6. **Have you had any minor accidents?** [Even a scrape or a fender bender signify something.]

If your answers are all no, review them with someone who will be honest with you. Some of the elderly are very safe drivers whereas others can be a risk to themselves and to those around them. Before you step on the accelerator, make sure you are one of the safe ones.

A national panel recommends every renewal include simulated driving, with the applicant seated with a steering wheel, accelerator, and brakes in front of a video (Staplin et al., 2012). The results of this test allow some 80-year-olds to keep driving, some to have their licenses revoked, and many to recognize that they are less proficient than they thought.

Beyond retesting, there is much else that societies can do. Accidents would be reduced for every driver if larger-print signs preceded a freeway exit, if mirrors replaced the need to turn the neck, if side streets and driveways were well lit, if the glare of headlights and hazard flashers were reduced, and if drivers were alerted about upcoming ice, fog, or construction. Selective optimization and compensation by society would allow competent elderly drivers to maintain independence, while dangerous drivers (of all ages) would be kept off the road.

Another society-wide initiative is sorely needed. Efficient and inexpensive public transportation, in suburban and rural areas as well as in cities, would benefit everyone. When the British gave free bus passes to the elderly, they walked more and drove less, and each city had fewer traffic jams and less pollution (Coronini-Cronberg et al., 2012).

Medical Compensation: Survival

primary aging
The universal and irreversible physical changes that occur in all living creatures as they grow older. Primary aging is inevitable, programmed for each species.

secondary aging
The specific physical illnesses or conditions that become more common with aging but are caused by health habits and other influences that vary from person to person.

Gerontologists distinguish between **primary aging,** which involves universal changes that occur with the passage of time, and **secondary aging,** which are the consequences of particular inherited weaknesses, chosen health habits, and environmental conditions. Am I sick because I am old, or because of bad choices?

The benefits of modern medicine, based on science not custom, are obvious. In earlier centuries, people avoided hospitals and doctors. Some medical measures made people sicker, such as blood-letting (bleeding a sick person), germ-spreading (causing fever), and surgery (such as removing the uterus in a hysterectomy to cure hysteria!).

One obvious example is in childbirth. For centuries medical intervention (including blood-letting to make the woman unconscious) was harmful for baby or mother. Childbed fever (when a new mother died because the doctor used unsterilized instruments) was a common cause of death. One review notes, "It is small wonder that a non-intervention approach was preferred" (Halpern & Garg, 2015, p. 285). By contrast, in the past three decades, evidence-based medicine has saved millions, perhaps billions, of newborns and mothers.

Similar, although less dramatic, results occur in late adulthood. Each year in the United States, 16 percent of those age 65 and older are admitted to a hospital. No longer is that usually a death sentence; almost all recover quickly and go back home. The average hospital stay for those age 65 and older is only 6 days (National Center for Health Statistics, 2014).

compression of morbidity
A shortening of the time a person spends ill or infirm before dying, accomplished by postponing illness.

Modern medicine slows down primary aging and prevents secondary aging. That has doubled the life span in the past century. The goal now is **compression of morbidity,** which means fewer years (compression) of disability (morbidity) before death, adding "life to years, not years to life." That goal was highlighted by the United Nations in 2002 and endorsed by every developed nation (Walker, 2015).

Ideally, a person is in good health for decades after age 65, and then, within a few days or months, develops serious illnesses that lead to death. Medical research has discovered which personal habits, drugs, therapies, and/or surgeries reduce frailty for almost every disease and condition until that final episode.

The World Health Organization and many experts recognize that disability is the result of person–environment interaction, so changing the environment limits disability (Phillipson, 2013). This third type of compensation is so vital that we look closely at two specifics, heart disease and osteoporosis.

HEART DISEASE Primary aging causes a slowdown of the heart rate as the vascular network becomes less flexible (blood pressure rises). That increases the risk of stroke and heart attack. Secondary aging—especially as a result of smoking and obesity—makes it worse.

Although medical research, beginning with the Framingham Heart Study, has discovered many aspects of *secondary* aging that harm the heart, adults overall are probably as vulnerable to heart disease as they were 50 years ago. To be specific, although far fewer adults smoke, far more are obese.

However, medical measures have targeted *primary* aging with great success. The heart disease death rate is lower for every age and gender group, dramatically apparent in the elderly. For example, cardiovascular deaths of 64- to 75-year-olds in the United States in 2013 were less than one-fourth (22.4 percent) the rate in 1960 (390 versus 1,749 per 100,000) (National Center for Health Statistics, 2014).

Some of this reduction is in bypass surgery, pacemakers, and in healthier eating and exercising after a heart attack. Further, one medical measure to halt primary aging and heart deaths is the reduction of hypertension (high blood pressure), a problem for more than two-thirds of all U.S. residents over age 64. High blood pressure is called a "silent killer" because it has no symptoms unless it becomes extremely high.

Even doctors did not realize the danger of hypertension 50 years ago. Now, about half of all adults (especially older ones) with hypertension refuse treatment.

Men are less likely to take medication for hypertension than women, with rates of uncontrolled hypertension (age-adjusted, among those with hypertension) at 75 percent for Mexican American men and 69 percent for African American men. Instead, they suffer headaches and shortness of breath, sometimes for years before a fatal heart attack. For them, morbidity is not compressed.

One reason for their "medication non-adherence" is "mistrust of the utility of the medications prescribed by their doctor" (McNeill et al., 2015, p. 48). Their mistrust is understandable, given the Tuskegee (Alabama) syphilis study in which 399 African American men were not cured of that disease. That horrifying study ended in 1972, but it still makes men suspicious of doctors. That is said to be one reason heart disease kills more African American men, at younger ages, than African American women or men of other ethnic groups.

Science continues to find new ways to cure or prevent diseases, discovering age differences in how people respond. Some measures that work for adults are not effective for children, and the very old need particular treatment guidelines. For example, after age 80, medication is not recommended until hypertension reaches 150/90, not 140/90 (Kithas & Supiano, 2015).

OSTEOPOROSIS Compression of morbidity is also dramatic in **osteoporosis** (fragile bones). Primary aging makes bones more porous, as cells that build bone (osteoblasts) are outnumbered by cells that reabsorb bone (osteoclasts) (Rachner et al., 2011). Osteoporosis is especially common in underweight women with European ancestry, although men and people of other ethnic groups experience it.

> **osteoporosis**
> Fragile bones that result from primary aging, which makes bones more porous, especially if a person is at genetic risk.

Because of osteoporosis, a fall that would have merely bruised a young person may result in a broken wrist, hip, or spine, starting a cascade of medical problems. Fractures once led to death for 10 percent of osteoporosis sufferers within a year, with a broken hip "a leading cause of morbidity and excess mortality among older adults" (MMWR, March 31, 2000). Half of those with broken hips never walked again. Immobility causes body systems to deteriorate, spreading, not compressing, morbidity.

Note the 2000 date. A more recent report: "In the 21st century, osteoporosis, a disease once considered an inevitable consequence of aging, is both diagnosable and treatable" (Black et al., 2012, p. 2051). Medical compression of morbidity has occurred.

Early diagnosis via a bone density test (not available a few decades ago) detects bone weakening long before the first fracture. Doctors advise prevention, with

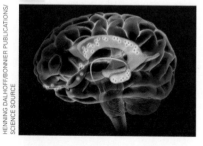

Strike or Washout When college students, including Marcus Drendel shown here, brought Nintendo Wii bowling to a senior residence, this woman (Margaret Roeder) and hundreds of others became enthusiasts. Teams from several senior homes will compete in a championship tournament for the national title. Active sports provide exercise for mind and body at every age—unlike the mind-numbing television that some senior residences keep on day and night in their "recreation" rooms.

weight-bearing and muscle-strengthening exercises, and a lifelong diet with sufficient calcium and vitamin D. In addition, a dozen drugs reduce bone loss. If a hip bone breaks, an artificial hip restores mobility. Morbidity, and mortality, caused by osteoporosis have become unusual.

Because a focus on chronic conditions is relatively new and treatment of osteoporosis is newer yet, scientists do not know the consequences of ingesting preventive drugs over many years. The data suggest caution (Black et al., 2012), because drugs that prevent one problem may eventually cause another. Nonetheless, the 44 million people over age 50 in the United States who have weak bones need not experience the disabling breaks that those with osteoporosis once did. That is compression of morbidity.

Hearts and bones are only two examples. For almost every disease and condition, morbidity can be compressed by all three of the types of measures detailed here—first by medicine, then by society that makes medical care available, and then by individuals who get the care they need or change the habits that harm them.

WHAT HAVE YOU LEARNED?

1. How can couples continue to have satisfying sex lives in old age?
2. What is the age-related relationship between intercourse and sexual satisfaction?
3. How should it be decided whether or not an elderly person can drive?
4. How does heart disease illustrate both primary and secondary aging?
5. What is the continued impact of the Tuskegee study?
6. Why would a broken hip make death more likely?
7. How does osteoporosis illustrate compression of morbidity?

The Aging Brain

Ageism impairs elders in many ways, but the most feared and insidious impairment involves the mind, not the body. As with many stereotypes, the notion of cognitive decline in late adulthood begins with a half-truth: Cognition does change in old age. But the fear is worse than the facts.

Losses and Gains

As at every earlier stage of development, losses and gains are evident. Ageism prevents people from seeing the gains. A realistic view notices both.

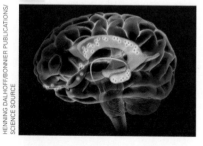

Video: Brain Development Animation: Late Adulthood shows gray matter loss in the normal aging brain.

SLOWDOWN AND SHRINKAGE As humans age, connections between parts of the brain slow down. It takes longer, with age, to understand what is needed in a particular situation and then to respond. For instance, reading, conversation, and reflexes all take more time.

Senescence reduces the production of neurotransmitters—glutamate, acetylcholine, serotonin, and especially dopamine—that allow a nerve impulse to jump quickly across the synaptic gap from one neuron to another. Neural fluid decreases, myelination thins, and cerebral blood circulates more slowly. The result is an overall slowdown of the brain, evident in reaction time, movement, speech, and thought.

Deterioration of cognition correlates with almost every motor slowdown. For example, gait speed predicts many measures of intellect (Hausdorff & Buchman, 2013). Walks slow? Talks slow? Oh no—thinks slow!

Brain size decreases with each passing year—less than 1 percent per year through most of adulthood but accelerating after age 60, such that a typical brain at age 80 is 20 percent smaller than at age 30 (Hedman et al., 2012).

The hippocampus (storing memories) and the prefrontal cortex (deciding and planning) shrink most. Cognitive reserve allows some brains to function well even in late, late adulthood; education is protective lifelong. However, neither of these completely compensates for brain senescence (Stern, 2013). No centenarian thinks as well as he or she did at age 30.

In every part of the brain, the volume of gray matter (crucial for processing new experiences) is reduced, in part because the cortex becomes thinner with every decade (Zhou et al., 2013). White matter generally is reduced as well, slowing the mind. However, white matter also increases in an odd way: Bright white spots appear on MRIs after age 50 or so.

These white matter lesions are thought to result from tiny impairments in blood flow. They increase the time it takes for a thought to be processed (Rodrigue & Kennedy, 2011). With age, transmission of impulses from regions of the brain, especially from parts of the cortex and the cerebellum, is disrupted. This correlates more with cognitive ability than with age (Bernard et al., 2013).

A comparative study finds that brain aging is similar in all primates, but humans experience losses relatively earlier than chimpanzees do—at the beginning of late adulthood instead of right before death (Xu Chen et al., 2013). That study's authors speculate that medical measures have increased the life span, so the human brain survives longer than it was designed to do.

Evidence finds that older adults are as intellectually sharp as they always were on many tasks. However, with multitasking that requires younger adults to use all their cognitive resources, older adults are less proficient, perhaps because they already are using their brains to the max (Cappell et al., 2010). This is a loss but may also be a gain, if older adults no longer make the impulsive mistakes of the young.

New Neurons

Can anything compensate for brain losses in old age, to optimize thinking as people can optimize sex, or driving ability, or health? The answer is *yes, sometimes*. Brain plasticity occurs throughout life (e.g., Ram et al., 2011; Erickson et al., 2013). Medical research has not been able to stop cognitive aging directly, but protecting the body protects the brain. So cognition is aided if people exercise, eat well, and avoid most drugs (including cigarettes).

Furthermore, new neurons form and dendrites grow in adulthood. That surprised many scientists when it was first discovered. Almost everyone thought that humans never developed brain cells after infancy.

We now know that neurons appear in two specific areas, the olfactory region (smelling) and the hippocampus (remembering) (Surget et al., 2011). In addition, old neurons can develop new dendrites, allowing adults to resist depression and anxiety (Mateus-Pinheiro et al., 2013).

Although neurogenesis may occur in many living things, an evolutionary perspective suggests that humans may have had unique reasons to generate new neurons (Kempermann, 2012). When agriculture began (approximately 10,000 years ago), adults required more planning, remembering, and strategizing than before.

Atrophy Ranking

FROM FARRELL C, ET AL. DEVELOPMENT AND INITIAL TESTING OF NORMAL REFERENCE MR IMAGES FOR THE BRAIN AT AGES 65-70 AND 75-80 YEARS. EUROPEAN RADIOLOGY 2009;19: 177-183. COPYRIGHT J.M.WARDLAW.

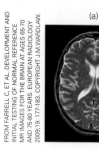 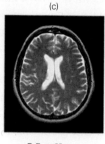 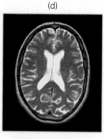 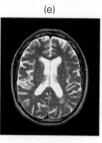

(a) (b) (c) (d) (e)

Lowest   **25th Percentile**   **Median**   **75th Percentile**   **Highest**

Not All Average A team of neuroscientists in Scotland (Farrell et al., 2009) published these images of the brains of healthy 65- to 70-year-olds. The images show normal brain loss (the white areas) from the lowest (5th percentile) to the highest (95th percentile). Some atrophy is inevitable (even younger brains atrophy), but few elders are merely average.

Agriculture meant living in towns, not small nomadic clans, and that made human interaction more complex. Thus, "[m]oving actively in a changing world and dealing with novelty and complexity regulate adult neurogenesis. New neurons might thus provide the cognitive adaptability to conquer ecological niches rich with challenging stimuli" (Kempermann, 2012, p. 727).

As you remember, Flynn found that the intellectual ability of each new cohort is better than that of the previous one. Perhaps the increasing complexity of modern life requires continuing improvement, with urbanization and globalization demanding intellectual expansion. If that is true, older people who continue to cope with challenges will continue to grow neurons.

PET and fMRI scans find that, compared with younger adults, older adults use more parts of their brains, including both hemispheres, to solve problems. This may be compensation: Using only one brain region may no longer be sufficient if that part has shrunk, so the older brain automatically activates more parts.

The positive finding that neurons are created is tempered by another finding—growth of the brain in late adulthood is slow and limited (S. Lee et al., 2012), and treatment for various illnesses, and general anesthesia for surgery, may kill neurons without creating new ones (Monje & Dietrich, 2012; Mashour & Avidan, 2013). The creation and growth of new neurons is less prolific than earlier in life, so it is not sufficient to restore the aging brain to its earlier state.

Health is crucial. Exercise, nutrition, and normal blood pressure are powerful influences on brain health, and these factors predict intelligence in old age. Some experts contend that with good health habits and favorable genes, no intellectual decrement will occur (Greenwood & Parasuraman, 2012).

Particular experiences may be important as well. One team recognizes "considerable heterogeneity in individual trajectories; whereas some persons decline rapidly, others exhibit slower decline, and still others remain stable or even improve as a result of practice and learning" (Boyle et al., 2013, p. 478).

Video: Old Age: Thinking and Moving at the Same Time features a research study demonstrating how older brains are quite adaptable.

Information Processing in Late Adulthood

Given the complexity, variation, and diversity of late-life cognition, we need to examine specifics to combat general stereotypes. For this purpose, the information-processing approach is useful, with details of input (sensing), memory (storage), programming (control), and output.

INPUT The first step in information processing is input, in which the brain receives information from the senses. No sense is as sharp at age 65 as at age 15. Glasses and hearing aids mitigate severe sensory losses, but subtle deficits impair cognition. Information must cross the *sensory threshold*—the divide between what is sensed and what is not—before a person can think about it.

Older adults are less able to decipher the emotional content in speech, even when they hear the words correctly (Dupuis & Pichora-Fuller, 2010). They are also less able to see nuances of facial expression—a momentarily averted gaze, for instance. Further, it is harder to understand speech when vision is impaired (Tye-Murray et al., 2011), probably because watching lips and facial expressions aids understanding. Thus, small sensory losses—unnoticed but inevitable—impair cognition.

I know a father—not elderly but already with fading eyesight—who was scolding his 6-year-old daughter who was standing 10 feet away. Without his glasses, he did not see that her lip had started to quiver. He was startled when she cried; he did not realize how harsh his words seemed to her.

The cognition of almost 2,000 intellectually normal adults, average age 77, was repeatedly tested 5, 8, 10, and 11 years after the initial intake (Lin et al., 2013). At the 5-year retesting, an audiologist assessed their hearing. Between the start of the study and 11 years later, the average cognitive scores of the adults with hearing loss (who were often unaware of it) were down 7 percent, while those with normal hearing lost 5 percent.

That 2-percent difference seems small, but statistically it was highly significant (0.004). Greater hearing losses correlated with greater declines (Lin et al., 2013). Many other researchers likewise find that small input losses have a notable effect on output.

No Quitter When hearing fades, many older people avoid social interaction. Not so for Don Shula, former head coach of the Miami Dolphins, who led his team to two Super Bowl victories. He kept his players fighting, often surging ahead from behind. Here he proudly displays his hearing aid.

MEMORY If older people suspect memory loss, anxiety itself impairs their memory (Ossher et al., 2013). Worse than that, simply knowing that they are taking a memory test makes them feel years older (Hughes et al., 2013). Stereotype threat is powerful.

The more psychologists study memory, the more they realize that memory is not one function but many, each with a specific pattern. Some losses of the elderly are quite normal and others pathological (Markowitsch & Staniloiu, 2012). A person who cannot recall a word or a name is experiencing a normal loss of one aspect of memory; a person who cannot remember their city of birth has a pathological deficit.

Generally, explicit memory (recall of learned material) shows more loss than implicit memory (recognition and habits), which means that names are harder to remember than actions: Grandpa can still swim, ride a bike, and drive a car, even if he cannot name both current U.S. senators from his state. Memory tested individually typically shows declines, but memory as part of social learning is less likely to fade (Derksen et al., 2015).

One specific memory deficit is *source amnesia*—forgetting the origin of a fact, idea, or snippet of conversation. Source amnesia is particularly problematic in the twenty-first century, as video, audio, and print information bombards the mind.

In practical terms, source amnesia means that elders might believe a rumor or political advertisement because they forget the source. Compensation requires deliberate attention to the reason behind a message before accepting a con artist's promises or the politics of a TV ad. However, elders are less likely than younger adults to analyze, or even notice, information surrounding the material they remember (Boywitt et al., 2012).

A hot political debate in the United States is about "dark money," where by financial contributions to political candidates can be anonymous (Dawood, 2015). If dark money is banned, that will help younger voters make informed judgments, but older voters, with fragile source memory, may be less affected.

Another crucial type of memory is called *prospective memory*—remembering to do something in the future (to take a pill, to meet someone for lunch, to buy milk). Prospective memory also fades notably with age (Kliegel et al., 2008). This loss becomes dangerous if, for instance, a person cooking dinner forgets to turn off the stove, or a person driving on the thruway is in the far lane when the exit appears.

One crucial aspect of prospective memory seems to be the ability to shift the mind quickly from one task to another: Older adults get immersed in one thought and have trouble changing gears (Schnitzspahn et al., 2013). For that reason, many elders follow routine sequences (brush teeth, take medicine, get the paper) and set an alarm to remind them to leave for a doctor's appointment. (That is compensation.)

Working memory (remembering information for a moment before evaluating, calculating, and inferring its significance) also declines with age. Speed is critical: Older individuals take longer to perceive and process sensations, and that reduces working memory because some items fade before they can be considered (Stawski et al., 2013). Indeed, some experts think speed is the crucial variable that affects IQ over the years.

For example, a common test of IQ is to ask someone to repeat a string of digits just heard, but a slow-thinking person may be unable to process each number and then hold them all in memory. Speed of processing would explain why memory for vocabulary (especially recognition memory, not recall) is often unaffected by age. For instance, speed is irrelevant in knowing that *chartreuse* is a color, not an animal.

control processes
The part of the information-processing system that regulates the analysis and flow of information. Memory and retrieval strategies, selective attention, and rules or strategies for problem solving are all control processes.

CONTROL PROCESSES Processing of information requires **control processes,** including selective attention, strategic judgment, and then appropriate action. Together these are the *executive function* of the brain, the work of the prefrontal cortex.

Each of these is theorized to slip in late adulthood. Crucial for paying attention is avoiding distractions and mind wandering. However, several studies report that the elderly are *less* likely to find their minds wandering than younger adults (Jackson & Balota, 2012; Frank et al., 2015).

Judgment, on the other hand, might be impaired. Instead of using analysis and forethought, the elderly tend to rely on prior knowledge, general principles, familiarity, and rules of thumb as they make decisions (Peters et al., 2011), basing actions on past experiences and current emotions.

For example, casinos have noticed that elderly gamblers gravitate to slot machines rather than to games requiring analysis. The reason, according to a study of brain scans of young and old slot players, is that the activated parts of older brains are less often the regions in which analysis occurs (McCarrey et al., 2012). When gamblers are able to analyze the odds, as younger players do, they spend less time with the slots.

One particular control process is development of strategies for retrieval. Some developmentalists believe that impaired retrieval is an underlying cause of intellectual lapses in old age because elders have many thoughts and memories that they cannot access. Since deep thinking requires recognizing and comparing the similarities and differences of experiences, if a person cannot retrieve memories of the past, new thinking is shallower than it might be.

Inadequate control processes may also explain why many older adults have extensive vocabularies (measured by written tests) but limited fluency (when they write or talk), why they are much better at recognition than recall, why tip-of-the-tongue forgetfulness is common, and why spelling is poorer than pronunciation.

Many gerontologists think elders would benefit by learning better control strategies. Unfortunately, even though "a high sense of control is associated with being happy, healthy, and wise," many older adults resist suggested strategies because they believe that declines are "inevitable or irreversible" (Lachman et al., 2009, p. 144). Efforts to improve their use of control strategies are successful, but only when the strategy is explicitly taught (Murray et al., 2015; Brom & Kliegel, 2014; McDaniel & Bugg, 2012).

OUTPUT The final step in information processing is output. In daily life, output is usually verbal. If the timbre and speed of a person's speech sounds old, ageism might cause younger adults to dismiss the content without realizing that the substance may be profound. Then, if elders realize that what they say is ignored, they talk less, and output is diminished. Mutual respect is crucial.

Scientists usually measure output through use of standardized tests of mental ability. As already noted, if older adults think their memory is being tested, that alone impairs them (Hughes et al., 2013). Even without stereotype threat, output on cognitive tests may not reflect ability, as you will now see.

Measurement of ability needs to take into account the age and the needs of the person. For example, older adults are at their best in the early morning, when adolescents are half asleep. If both age groups are tested at the same time of day, that would be unfair for either the old or the young.

Similarly, if intellectual ability were to be assessed via a timed test, then faster thinkers (usually young) would score higher than slower thinkers (usually old), even if the slower ones would excel after a few more seconds to think. Further, some places—e.g., a college laboratory—would be more familiar to emerging adults than to older ones, and that might affect results.

These are some reasons that certain age differences in prospective memory appear in laboratory tests but disappear in naturalistic settings, a phenomenon called the "age-prospective memory-paradox" (Schnitzspahn et al., 2011). Motivation seems crucial; elders may remember whatever they believe is important—phoning grandchildren on their birthday, for instance—but not care about repeating a series of disconnected words (a common test of memory).

A focus on what elders actually need and want to remember is called **ecological validity.** Results of research that takes context and circumstances into account finds that elders have far better memories than ageist predictions and measurements find.

Again, good news must be tempered: "There is no objective way to evaluate the degree of ecological validity . . . because ecological validity is a subjective concept" (Salthouse, 2010, p. 77). It is impossible to be totally objective in assessing memory.

The final ecological question is, "What is memory for?" Fear of memory loss is more typical at age 60 than at age 80. Unless they develop a brain condition such as Alzheimer's disease (soon described), elders remember how to live their daily lives. Is that enough?

> **ecological validity**
> The idea that cognition should be measured in natural settings and schedules.

WHAT HAVE YOU LEARNED?

1. What aspects of the brain slow down with age?
2. What does the research find about the development of new neurons with age?
3. How does sensory loss affect cognition?
4. Which kinds of things are harder to remember with age?
5. Why is source memory particularly important in current times?
6. What aspects of memory are least likely to fade?
7. Why do some elderly people resist learning strategies for memory retrieval?
8. Why is ecological validity especially important for measuring prospective memory?

Brain Diseases

Most older people are less sharp than they were, but they still think and remember quite well. Others experience serious decline. They have a **neurocognitive disorder (NCD).**

> **neurocognitive disorder (NCD)**
> Any of a number of brain diseases that affects a person's ability to remember, analyze, plan, or interact with other people.

Download the **DSM-5 Appendix** to learn more about the terminology and classification of brain diseases in late adulthood.

The Ageism of Words

The rate of neurocognitive disorders increases with every decade after age 60. But ageism distorts and exaggerates that fact. To understand and prevent NCDs, we need to begin by using words carefully.

Senile simply means "old." If the word *senility* is used to mean severe mental impairment, that implies that old age always brings intellectual failure—an ageist myth. *Dementia* (used in DSM-IV) was a more precise term than *senility* for irreversible, pathological loss of brain functioning, but *dementia* has the same root as *demon,* and thus it has inaccurate connotations.

The DSM-5 now describes neurocognitive disorders, either *major* (previously called dementia) or *mild* (previously called mild cognitive impairment).

Memory problems occur in every cognitive disorder, although some people with NCDs have other notable symptoms, such as in judgment (they do foolish things) and moods (they are suddenly rageful or tearful). The line between normal age-related changes, mild disorder, and major disorder is not clear, and symptoms vary depending on the specifics of brain loss as well as context. Even when the disorder is major, the individual remains unique.

The former word—*dementia*—and the inaccurate word—*senility*—are both still prevalent, and once a word is used it tends to obscure variations. As two gerontologists explain, the emphasis on a medical diagnosis tends

> to ignore the subjectivity and quality of life of those who are suffering dementia, and to stigmatize, devalue, disempower, banish, objectify, and invalidate them on account of their neuropathological condition.
>
> *[George & Whitehouse, 2010, p. 351]*

In Japanese, the traditional word for neurocognitive disorder was *chihou,* translated as "foolish" or "stupid." As more Japanese reached old age, a new word, *ninchihou,* which means "cognitive syndrome," was chosen (George & Whitehouse, 2010). That is far better, for, as you remember with Down syndrome, a syndrome is a cluster of characteristics, with each person somewhat different.

Many scientists seek biological indicators (called biomarkers, such as in the blood or cerebrospinal fluid) or brain indicators (as on brain scans) that predict major memory loss. However, although abnormal scores on many tests (biological, neurological, or psychological) indicate *possible* problems, an examination of 24 such measures found that no single test, or combination of tests, is 100-percent accurate (Ewers et al., 2012).

One new and promising test, a PET scan that reveals amyloid plaques which indicate Alzheimer's disease, is not reimbursed by Medicaid because the link between presence of amyloid and effective treatment is "insufficient." More research is needed (Centers for Medicare and Medicaid Services, 2014).

Prevalence of NCDs

How many people suffer from neurocognitive disorders in their older years? To answer this question, researchers selected a representative sample of people over age 69 from every part of the United States. Each was interviewed and tested. Then the researchers interviewed someone who knew the elder well (usually an immediate relative). This information was combined with medical records and clinical judgment.

The conclusion was that 14 percent of the elders had some form of neurocognitive disorder (Plassman et al., 2007) (see Figure 14.6). Extrapolated to the overall population, that means that about 4 million U.S. residents have a serious

FIGURE 14.6 Not Everyone Gets It Most elderly people never experience major NCD. Among people in their 70s, only 1 person in 20 does, and most of those who reach 90 or 100 do not suffer significant cognitive decline. Presented another way, the prevalence data sound more dire: Almost 4 million people in the United States have a major NCD.

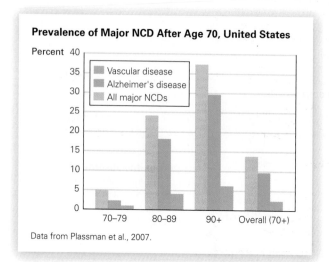

Data from Plassman et al., 2007.

neurocognitive disorder. Another study, this one of people already diagnosed with **major neurocognitive disorder,** found much lower rates, about 8 percent of the aged population (Koller & Bynum, 2014). The discrepancy may be that many people are not diagnosed, or that the rate has decreased.

An estimated 47 million people (again, estimates vary from 35 million to 60 million) are affected worldwide, 60 percent of them in low-income nations (World Health Organization, 2015). The poorest nations have the lowest rates because fewer people reach old age, but as longevity increases rates of major NCD rise as well. This has already occurred in China, where 9 million people had a major NCD in 2010, compared to only 4 million in 1990 (K. Chan et al., 2013).

Eventually, better education and public health will reduce the rate (if not the number) of cognitive impairments everywhere. In England and Wales the rate of major NCD for people over age 65 was 8.3 percent in 1991 but only 6.5 percent in 2011 (Matthews et al., 2013). Sweden had a similar decline (Qiu et al., 2013). In China, rates are much higher in rural areas than in cities, perhaps because rural Chinese have less education or worse health (Jia et al., 2014).

The Many Neurocognitive Disorders

As more is learned, it has become apparent that there are many types of brain disease, with each beginning in a distinct part of the brain and having particular symptoms. Once it was thought that if a person seemed to have a good memory, he or she could not be suffering from a neurocognitive disorder. That mistaken idea prevented diagnosis and treatment. Accordingly, we describe some of the many disorders now.

ALZHEIMER'S DISEASE In the past century, millions of people in every large nation have been diagnosed with **Alzheimer's disease (AD),** (now formally referred to as *major NCD due to Alzheimer's disease*). Severe and worsening memory loss is the main symptom, but the diagnosis is not definitive until an autopsy finds extensive plaques and tangles in the cerebral cortex.

Plaques are clumps of a protein called *beta-amyloid* in tissues surrounding the neurons; **tangles** are twisted masses of threads made of a protein called *tau* within the neurons. A normal brain contains some beta-amyloid and some tau, but in brains with AD these plaques and tangles proliferate, especially in the hippocampus, a brain

major neurocognitive disorder (major NCD)
Irreversible loss of intellectual functioning caused by organic brain damage or disease. Formerly called *dementia*, major NCD becomes more common with age, but it is abnormal and pathological even in the very old.

Alzheimer's disease (AD)
The most common cause of major NCD, characterized by gradual deterioration of memory and personality and marked by the formation of plaques of beta-amyloid protein and tangles of tau in the brain.

plaques
Clumps of a protein called *beta-amyloid*, found in brain tissues surrounding the neurons.

tangles
Twisted masses of threads made of a protein called *tau* within the neurons of the brain.

TABLE 14.2	**Stages of Alzheimer's Disease**

Stage 1. People in the first stage forget recent events or new information, particularly names and places. For example, they might forget the name of a famous film star or how to get home from a familiar place. This first stage is similar to mild cognitive impairment—even experts cannot always tell the difference. In retrospect, it seems clear that President Ronald Reagan had early AD while in office, but no doctor diagnosed it.

Stage 2. Generalized confusion develops, with deficits in concentration and short-term memory. Speech becomes aimless and repetitious, vocabulary is limited, words get mixed up. Personality traits are not curbed by rational thought. For example, suspicious people may decide that others have stolen the things that they themselves have mislaid.

Stage 3. Memory loss becomes dangerous. Although people at stage 3 can care for themselves, they might leave a lit stove or hot iron on or might forget whether they took essential medicine and thus take it twice—or not at all.

Stage 4. At this stage, full-time care is needed. People cannot communicate well. They might not recognize their closest loved ones.

Stage 5. Finally, people with AD become unresponsive. Identity and personality have disappeared. When former president Ronald Reagan was at this stage, a longtime friend who visited him was asked, "Did he recognize you?" The friend answered, "Worse than that—I didn't recognize him." Death comes 10 to 15 years after the first signs appear.

In **Video Activity: Alzheimer's Disease,** experts and family members discuss the progression of the disease.

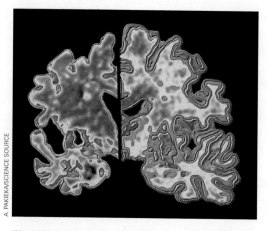

The Alzheimer's Brain This computer graphic shows a vertical slice through a brain ravaged by Alzheimer's disease *(left)* compared with a similar slice of a normal brain *(right)*. The diseased brain is shrunken because neurons have degenerated. The red indicates plaques and tangles.

structure crucial for memory. Forgetfulness is the dominant symptom, from momentary lapses to—after years of progressive disease—forgetting the names and faces of one's own children.

An autopsy that finds massive plaques and tangles proves that a person had Alzheimer's disease. However, between 20 and 30 percent of cognitively normal elders have, at autopsy, extensive plaques in their brains (Jack et al., 2009). One explanation is that cognitive reserve enables some people to bypass the disconnections caused by plaques. Education does seem to prevent, or modify, AD (Langa, 2015).

Alzheimer's disease is partly genetic. If it develops in middle age, the affected person either has trisomy-21 (Down syndrome) or has inherited one of three genes: amyloid precursor protein (APP), presenilin 1, or presenilin 2. For these people, the disease progresses quickly, reaching the last phase within three to five years.

Most cases begin much later, at age 75 or so. Many genes have some impact, including *SORL1* and *ApoE4* (allele 4 of the *ApoE* gene). People who inherit one copy of *ApoE4* (as about one-fifth of all U.S. residents do) have about a 50/50 chance of developing AD. Those who inherit two copies almost always develop the disorder if they live long enough.

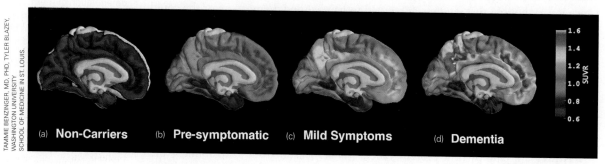

(a) **Non-Carriers** (b) **Pre-symptomatic** (c) **Mild Symptoms** (d) **Dementia**

Hopeful Brains Even the brain without symptoms *(a)* might eventually develop Alzheimer's disease, but people with a certain dominant gene definitely will. They have no symptoms in early adulthood *(b)*, some symptoms in middle adulthood *(c)*, and stage-five Alzheimer's disease *(d)* before old age. Research finds early brain markers (such as those shown here) that predict the disease. This is not always accurate, but may soon lead to early treatment that halts AD, not only in those genetically vulnerable, but in everyone.

VASCULAR DISEASE The second most common cause of neurocognitive disorder is a *stroke* (a temporary obstruction of a blood vessel in the brain) or a series of strokes, called *transient ischemic attacks* (TIAs, or ministrokes). The interruption in blood flow reduces oxygen, destroying part of the brain. Symptoms (blurred vision, weak or paralyzed limbs, slurred speech, and mental confusion) suddenly appear.

In a TIA, symptoms may vanish quickly, unnoticed. However, unless recognized and prevented, another TIA is likely, eventually causing **vascular disease,** commonly referred to as *vascular* or *multi-infarct dementia* (see Figure 14.7).

Vascular disease also correlates with the *ApoE4* allele (Cramer & Procaccio, 2012). For some of the elderly, it is caused by surgery that requires general anesthesia. They suffer a ministroke, which, added to reduced cognitive reserve, damages their brains (Stern, 2013).

FRONTOTEMPORAL NCDS Several types of neurocognitive disorders affect the frontal lobes and thus are called **frontotemporal NCDs,** or *frontotemporal lobar degeneration* (Pick disease is the most common form). These disorders cause perhaps 15 percent

vascular disease
Formerly called *vascular* or *multi-infarct dementia*, vascular disease is characterized by progressive loss of intellectual functioning caused by repeated infarcts (strokes), or temporary obstructions of blood vessels.

frontotemporal NCDs
Brain disorders that occur with serious impairment of the frontal lobes. (Also called *frontotemporal lobar degeneration*.)

of all cases of NCDs in the United States. Frontotemporal NCDs tend to occur under age 70, unlike Alzheimer's or vascular disease (Seelaar et al., 2011).

In frontotemporal NCDs, parts of the brain that regulate emotions and social behavior (especially the amygdala and prefrontal cortex) deteriorate. Emotional and personality changes are the main symptoms (Seelaar et al., 2011). A loving mother with a frontotemporal NCD might reject her children, or a formerly astute businessman might invest in a hare-brained scheme.

Frontal lobe problems may be worse than more obvious types of neurocognitive disorders, in that compassion, self-awareness, and judgment fade in a person who otherwise seems normal. One wife, Ruth French, was furious because her husband

> threw away tax documents, got a ticket for trying to pass an ambulance and bought stock in companies that were obviously in trouble. Once a good cook, he burned every pot in the house. He became withdrawn and silent, and no longer spoke to his wife over dinner. That same failure to communicate got him fired from his job.
>
> [Grady, 2012, p. A1]

Finally, he was diagnosed with a frontotemporal NCD. Ruth asked him to forgive her fury. It is not clear that he understood either her anger or her apology. (See photo.)

Although there are many forms and causes of frontotemporal NCDs—including a dozen or so alleles—they usually progress rapidly, leading to death in about five years.

OTHER DISORDERS Many other brain diseases begin with impaired motor control (shaking when picking up a coffee cup, falling when trying to walk), not with impaired thinking. The most common of these is **Parkinson's disease,** the cause of about 3 percent of all cases of NCDs.

Parkinson's disease starts with rigidity or tremor of the muscles as dopamine-producing neurons degenerate, affecting movement long before cognition. Middle-aged adults with Parkinson's disease usually have sufficient cognitive reserve to avoid major intellectual loss, although about one-third have mild cognitive decline (S. Gao et al., 2014).

Older people with Parkinson's develop cognitive problems sooner (Pfeiffer & Bodis-Wollner, 2012). If people with Parkinson's live 10 years or more, almost always major neurocognitive impairment occurs (Pahwa & Lyons, 2013).

Another 3 percent of people with NCD in the United States suffer from **Lewy body disease:** excessive deposits of a particular kind of protein in their brains. Lewy bodies are also present in Parkinson's disease, but in Lewy body disease they are more numerous and dispersed throughout the brain, interfering with communication between neurons. The main symptom is loss of inhibition: A person might gamble or become hypersexual.

Comorbidity is common with all these disorders. For instance, most people with Alzheimer's disease also show signs of vascular impairment (Doraiswamy, 2012). Parkinson's, Alzheimer's, and Lewy body diseases can occur together: People who have all three experience more rapid and severe cognitive loss (Compta et al., 2011).

Some other types of NCDs begin in middle age or even earlier, caused by Huntington's disease, multiple

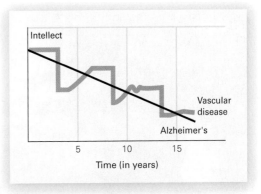

FIGURE 14.7 The Progression of Alzheimer's Disease and Vascular Disease Cognitive decline is apparent in both Alzheimer's disease and vascular disease. However, the pattern of decline for each disease is different. Victims of AD show steady, gradual decline, while those who suffer from vascular disease get suddenly much worse, improve somewhat, and then experience another serious loss.

Parkinson's disease
A chronic, progressive disease that is characterized by muscle tremor and rigidity and sometimes major NCD; caused by reduced dopamine production in the brain.

Lewy body disease
A form of major NCD characterized by an increase in particular abnormal cells in the brain. Symptoms include visual hallucinations, momentary loss of attention, falling, and fainting.

To Have and to Hold Ruth wanted to divorce Michael until she realized he suffered from a frontotemporal NCD. Now she provides body warmth and comfort in his nursing home bed.

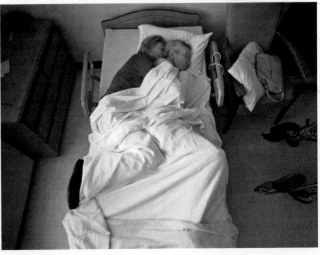

Who Are You? Ralph Wenzel was a football guard for seven years in the National Football League, a handsome catch for his wife, Eleanor, shown here. He lost his memory, did not recognize her, and died two years after this photo. His autopsied brain showed CTE, and Eleanor became an advocate for safer football.

sclerosis, a severe head injury, or the last stages of syphilis, AIDS, or bovine spongiform encephalopathy (BSE, or mad cow disease). Repeated blows to the head, even without concussions, can cause chronic traumatic encephalopathy (CTE), which first causes memory loss and emotional changes (Voosen, 2013).

Although the rate of systemic brain disease increases dramatically with every decade after age 60, brain disease can occur at any age, as revealed by the autopsies of a number of young professional athletes. For them, prevention includes better helmets and fewer body blows. Already, tackling is avoided in football practice.

These changes in athletic practices have come too late for thousands of adults, including Derek Boogaard, a National Hockey League enforcer who died of a drug overdose in 2011 at age 28. His autopsied brain showed traumatic brain injury, now called CTE.

For Boogaard, chronic traumatic encephalopathy may have been a cause of drug addiction and would have become major NCD if he lived longer. The brain disorder probably already occurred, undiagnosed. Another hockey player said of him, "His demeanor, his personality, it just left him . . . He didn't have a personality anymore" (John Scott, quoted in Branch, 2011, p. B13). Obviously, *senility* is not a synonym for *neurocognitive disorder*.

Preventing Impairment

Severe brain damage cannot be reversed, although the rate of decline and some of the symptoms can be treated. However, education, exercise, and good health not only ameliorate mild losses, they may prevent worse ones. That may be happening: "A growing number of studies, at least nine over the past 10 years, have shown a declining risk for dementia incidence or prevalence in high-income countries, including the US, England, The Netherlands, Sweden, and Denmark" (Langa, 2015, p. 34).

Because brain plasticity is lifelong, exercise that improves blood circulation not only prevents cognitive loss but also builds capacity and repairs damage. The benefits of exercise have been repeatedly cited in this text. Now we simply reiterate that physical exercise—even more than good nutrition and mental exercise—prevents,

Selective Optimization When they were younger, they sprinted; when they were middle-aged, they jogged. Now they hike with walking sticks. Exercise is beneficial at every age, but the specifics differ.

OBSERVATION QUIZ

What three things do you see that promote cognitive health? (see answer, page 532) ➤

postpones, and slows cognitive loss of all kinds (Erickson et al., 2012; Gregory et al., 2012; Lövdén et al., 2013).

Medication to prevent stroke also protects against neurocognitive disorders. In a Finnish study, half of a large group of older Finns were given drugs to reduce lipids in their system (primarily cholesterol). Years later, fewer of them had developed NCDs than did a comparable group who were not given the drug (Solomon et al., 2010).

Avoiding specific pathogens is critical. For example, beef can be tested to ensure that it does not have BSE, condoms can protect against HIV/AIDS, and syphilis can be cured with antibiotics.

For most neurocognitive disorders, however, despite the efforts of thousands of scientists and millions of older people, no foolproof prevention or cure has been found. Avoiding toxins (lead, aluminum, copper, and pesticides) or adding supplements (hormones, aspirin, coffee, insulin, antioxidants, red wine, blueberries, and statins) have been tried as preventatives but have not proven effective in controlled, scientific research.

Thousands of scientists have sought to halt the production of beta-amyloid, and they have had some success in mice but not yet in humans. One current goal is to diagnose Alzheimer's disease 10 or 15 years before the first outward signs appear in order to prevent brain damage. That is one reason for the interest in mild NCDs: They often (though not always) progress to major problems. If it were known why some mild losses do not lead to major ones, prevention might be possible.

Early, accurate diagnosis years before obvious symptoms appear leads to more effective treatment. Drugs do not cure NCDs, but some slow progression. Sometimes surgery or stem cell therapy is beneficial. The U.S. Pentagon estimates that more than 200,000 U.S. soldiers who were in Iraq or Afghanistan suffered traumatic brain injury, predisposing them to major NCD before age 60 (G. Miller, 2012). Measures to remedy their brain damage may help the civilian aged as well.

Among professionals, hope is replacing despair. Earlier diagnosis seems possible; many drug and lifestyle treatments are under review. "Measured optimism" (Moye, 2015, p. 331) comes from contemplating the success that has been achieved in combating other diseases. Heart attacks, for instance, were once the leading cause of death for middle-aged men. No longer.

Same Situation, Far Apart: Strong Legs, Long Life As this woman in a Brooklyn, New York, seniors center *(left)* and this man on a Greek beach *(right)* seem to realize, exercise that strengthens the legs is particularly beneficial for body, mind, and spirit in late adulthood.

Reversible Neurocognitive Disorder?

Care improves when everyone knows that a disease is undermining intellectual capacity. Accurate diagnosis is even more crucial when memory problems do *not* arise from a neurocognitive disorder. Brain diseases destroy parts of the brain, but some people are thought to be permanently "losing their minds" when a reversible condition is really at fault.

DEPRESSION The most common reversible condition that is mistaken for major NCD is depression. Normally, older people tend to be quite happy; frequent sadness or anxiety is not normal. Ongoing, untreated depression increases the risk of major NCD (Y. Gao et al., 2013).

Ironically, people with untreated anxiety or depression may exaggerate minor memory losses or refuse to talk. Quite the opposite reaction occurs with early Alzheimer's disease, when victims are often surprised when they cannot answer questions, or with Lewy body disease or frontotemporal NCDs, when people talk too much without thinking.

Specifics provide other clues. People with neurocognitive loss might forget what they just said, heard, or did because current brain activity is impaired, but they might repeatedly describe details of something that happened long ago. The opposite may be true for emotional disorders, when memory of the past is impaired but short-term memory is not.

NUTRITION Malnutrition and dehydration can also cause symptoms that may seem like brain disease. The aging digestive system is less efficient but needs more nutrients and fewer calories. This requires new habits, less fast food, and more grocery money (which many do not have).

Some elderly people deliberately drink less because they want to avoid frequent urination, yet adequate liquid in the body is needed for cell health. Since homeostasis slows with age, older people are less likely to recognize and remedy their hunger and thirst, and thus they may inadvertently impair their cognition.

Beyond the need to drink water and eat vegetables, several specific vitamins have been suggested as decreasing the rate of major NCD. Among the suggested foods to add are those containing antioxidants (C, A, E) and vitamin B-12. Homocysteine (from animal fat) may need to be avoided, since high levels correlate with major NCD (Perez et al., 2012; Whalley et al., 2014).

Obviously, any food that increases the risk of heart disease and stroke also increases the risk of vascular disease. In addition, some prescribed drugs destroy certain nutrients, although specifics require more research (Jyrkkä et al., 2012).

Indeed, well-controlled longitudinal research on the relationship between particular aspects of nutrition and NCD has not been done (Coley et al., 2015). It is known, however, that people who already suffer from NCD tend to forget to eat or tend to choose unhealthy foods, hastening their mental deterioration. It is also known that alcohol abuse interferes with nutrition, directly (reducing eating and hydration) and indirectly (destroying vitamins).

POLYPHARMACY At home as well as in the hospital, most elderly people take numerous drugs—not only prescribed medications, but also over-the-counter preparations and herbal remedies—a situation known as **polypharmacy.** Excessive reliance on drugs can occur on doctor's orders as well as via patient ignorance.

The rate of polypharmacy is increasing in the United States. For instance, in 1988 the number of people over age 65 who took *five* drugs or more was 13 percent; by 2010 that number had tripled to 39 percent (Charlesworth et al., 2015).

Unfortunately, recommended doses of many drugs are determined primarily by clinical trials with younger adults, for whom homeostasis usually eliminates excess medication (Herrera et al., 2010). When homeostasis slows down, excess may linger. In

polypharmacy
Refers to a situation in which people take many medications. The various side effects and interactions of those medications can result in NCD symptoms.

addition, most trials to test the safety of a new drug exclude people who have more than one disease. That means drugs are not tested on the people who will use them most.

The average elderly person in the United States sees a physician eight times a year (National Center for Health Statistics, 2014). Typically, each doctor follows "clinical practice guidelines," which are recommendations for one specific condition. A "prescribing cascade" (when many interacting drugs are prescribed) may occur.

In one disturbing case, a doctor prescribed medication to raise his patient's blood pressure, and another doctor, noting the raised blood pressure, prescribed a drug to lower it (McLendon & Shelton, 2011–2012). Usually, doctors ask patients what medications they are taking and why, which could prevent such an error. However, people who are sick and confused may not give accurate responses.

A related problem is that people of every age forget when to take which drugs (before, during, or after meals? after dinner or at bedtime?) (Bosworth & Ayotte, 2009). Short-term memory loss makes this worse, and poverty cuts down on pill purchases.

Even when medications are taken as prescribed and the right dose reaches the bloodstream, drug interactions can cause confusion and memory loss. Cognitive side effects can occur with almost any drug, but especially with drugs intended to reduce anxiety and depression.

Finally, following recommendations from the radio, friends, and television ads, many of the elderly try supplements, compounds, and herbal preparations that contain mind-altering toxins. Some of the elderly believe that only illegal drugs are harmful to the mind, which makes alcohol and pill addiction harder to recognize in the elderly.

The solution seems simple: Discontinue drugs. However, that may increase both disease and cognitive decline. One expert warns of polypharmacy but adds that "underuse of medications in older adults can have comparable adverse effects on quality of life" (Miller, 2011–2012, p. 21).

For instance, untreated diabetes and hypertension cause cognitive loss. Lack of drug treatment for those conditions may be one reason why low-income elders experience more illness, more cognitive impairment, and earlier death than do high-income elders: They may not be able to afford good medical care or life-saving drugs.

Obviously, money complicates the issue: Prescription drugs are expensive, which increases profits for drug companies, but they can also reduce surgery and hospitalization, thus saving money. As one observer notes, the discussion about spending for prescription drugs is highly polarized, emotionally loaded, with little useful debate. A war is waged over the cost of prescriptions for older people, and it is a "gloves-off, stab-you-in-the-guts, struggle to the death" (Sloan, 2011–2012, p. 56).

THINK CRITICALLY: Who should decide what drugs a person should take—doctor, family, or the person him- or herself?

WHAT HAVE YOU LEARNED?

1. What brain diseases or conditions correlate with loss of cognition?
2. How does changing terminology reflect changing attitudes?
3. How does exercise affect the brain?
4. What changes in the prevalence of neurocognitive disorders have occurred in recent years?
5. What indicates that Alzheimer's disease is partly genetic?
6. How does the progression of Alzheimer's differ from vascular disease?
7. In what ways are frontotemporal NCDs worse than Alzheimer's disease?
8. Why is Lewy body disease sometimes mistaken for Parkinson's disease?
9. How successful are scientists at preventing major NCD?
10. What is the relationship between depression, anxiety, and neurocognitive disorders?
11. Why is polypharmacy particularly common among the elderly?

Older and Wiser?

You have learned that most older adults maintain adequate intellectual power. Only a minority suffer from a major neurocognitive disorder.

The life-span perspective holds that gains as well as losses occur during every period. What might be the cognitive gains in late adulthood? New depth, enhanced creativity, and even wisdom are possible.

Erikson and Maslow

Both Erik Erikson and Abraham Maslow were interested in the elderly, interviewing older people to understand their views. Erikson wrote his final book, *Vital Involvement in Old Age* (Erikson et al., 1986/1994), when he was in his 90s. It was based on responses from other 90-year-olds—the cohort who had been studied since they were babies in Berkeley, California.

Erikson found that in old age many people gained interest in the arts, in children, and in the human experience as a whole. His eighth stage, *integrity versus despair*, marks the time when life comes together in a "re-synthesis of all the resilience and toughness of the basic strengths already developed" (Erikson et al., 1986/1994, p. 40).

Maslow maintained that older adults are more likely than younger people to reach what he originally thought was the highest stage of development, **self-actualization.** Remember that Maslow rejected an age-based sequence of life, refusing to confine self-actualization to the old. However, Maslow also believed that life experience helps people move forward, so more of the old reach the final stage.

The stage of self-actualization is characterized by aesthetic, creative, philosophical, and spiritual understanding (Maslow, 1954/1997). A self-actualized person might have a deeper spirituality than ever; might be especially appreciative of nature; or might find life more amusing, laughing often at himself or herself.

This seems characteristic of many of the elderly. Jeanne Calment, the French woman who lived the maximum (122), was notably happy. She said, "I will die laughing."

> **self-actualization**
> The final stage in Maslow's hierarchy of needs, characterized by aesthetic, creative, philosophical, and spiritual understanding.

Learning Late in Life

Many people have tried to improve the intellectual abilities of older adults by teaching or training them in various tasks (Lustig et al., 2009; Stine-Morrow & Basak, 2011).

Almost all researchers have accepted the conclusion that people younger than 80 can advance in cognition if the educational process is carefully targeted to their motivation and ability.

For instance, in one study in southern Europe elderly people were taught memory strategies and attended motivational discussions to help them understand why and how memory was useful. Their memory improved compared to a control group, and the improvements were still evident 6 months later (Vranić et al., 2013).

How about those over age 80? The older people are, the harder it is for them to master new skills and then apply what they know (Stine-Morrow & Basak, 2011). Older adults sometimes learn cognitive strategies and skills, but they forget new learning if it is not applied (Park & Bischof, 2013). They revert back to familiar, and often inferior, cognitive patterns.

Let's return to the question of cognitive gains in late adulthood. In many nations, education programs have been created for the old, called Universities for the Third Age in Europe and Australia, and Road Scholar (formerly Exploritas) in the United States. Classes for seniors must take into account their needs and motivations: Some want intellectually challenging courses and others want practical skills (Villar & Celdrán, 2012). When motivated, older adults can learn.

AESTHETIC SENSE AND CREATIVITY Robert Butler was a geriatrician responsible for popularizing the study of aging in the United States. He coined the word *ageism* and wrote a book, *Why Survive?: Being Old in America,* first published in 1975. Partly because his grandparents were crucial in his life, Butler understood that the elderly need society to recognize their potential.

Butler explained that "old age can be a time of emotional sensory awareness and enjoyment" (Butler et al., 1998, p. 65). For example, some of the elderly take up gardening, bird-watching, sculpting, painting, or making music, even if they have never done so before.

Many well-known artists continue to work in late adulthood, sometimes producing their best work. Michelangelo painted the awe-inspiring frescoes in the Sistine Chapel at age 75; Verdi composed the opera *Falstaff* when he was 80; Frank Lloyd Wright completed the design of New York City's Guggenheim Museum when he was 91.

In a study of extraordinarily creative people, almost none felt that their ability, their goals, or the quality of their work had been much impaired by age. The leader of that study observed, "Now in their seventies, eighties, and nineties, they may lack the fiery ambition of earlier years, but they are just as focused, efficient, and committed as before" (Csikszentmihalyi, 2013, p. 207).

But an older artist does not need to be extraordinarily talented. Some of the elderly learn to play an instrument, and many enjoy singing. In China people gather spontaneously in public parks to sing together. The groups are intergenerational—but a disproportionate number are elderly (Wei, 2013).

Music and singing are often used to reduce anxiety in those who suffer from neurocognitive impairment, because the ability to appreciate music is preserved in the brain when other functions fail (Ueda et al., 2013). Many experts believe that creative activities—poetry and pottery, jewelry making and quilting, music and sculpture—benefit all the elderly (Flood & Phillips, 2007; Malchiodi, 2012). Artistic expression may aid social skills, resilience, and even brain health (McFadden & Basting, 2010).

It may be that everyone can become a writer or storyteller in old age. In the **life review,** elders provide an account of their personal journey by writing or telling their story. They want others to know their history, not only their personal experiences but also those of their family, cohort, or ethnic group. According to Robert Butler:

> We have been taught that this nostalgia represents living in the past and a preoccupation with self and that it is generally boring, meaningless, and time-consuming. Yet as a natural healing process it represents one of the underlying human capacities on which all psychotherapy depends. The life review should be recognized as a necessary and healthy process in daily life as well as a useful tool in the mental health care of older people.
>
> [Butler et al., 1998, p. 91]

Hundreds of developmentalists, picking up on Butler's suggestions, have guided elderly people in self-review. Sometimes the elderly write down their thoughts, and sometimes they simply tell their story, guided by questions from the listener.

WISDOM It is possible that "older adults . . . understand who they are in a newly emerging stage of life and discovering the wisdom that they have to offer" (Bateson, 2011, p. 9). A massive international survey of 26 nations from every corner of the world found that most people everywhere agree that wisdom is a characteristic of the elderly (Löckenhoff et al., 2009).

PIERRE BESSARD/REA/REDUX

© RODRIGO TORRES/GLOWIMAGES/CORBIS

Exercise and the Mind Creative activity may improve the intellect, especially when it involves social activity. Both the woman in a French ceramics class *(top),* subsidized by the government for residents of Grenoble over age 60, and the man playing the tuba in a band in Cuba *(bottom)* are gaining much more than the obvious finger or lung exercise.

life review
An examination of one's own role in the history of human life, engaged in by many elderly people. This can be written or oral.

Long Past Warring Many of the oldest men in Mali, like this Imam, are revered. Unfortunately, Mali has experienced violent civil wars and two national coups in recent years, perhaps because 75 percent of the male population is under age 30 and less than 2 percent is over age 70.

In **Video Portrait of Aging: Bill, Age 99**, one man shares his secret to longevity.

Contrary to these wishes and opinions, most objective research finds that wisdom does not necessarily increase with age. Starting at age 25 or so, some adults of every age are wise, but most, even at age 80, are not (Staudinger & Glück, 2011).

But what is wisdom? Each culture and each cohort has its own concept, with fools sometimes seeming wise (as in the works of Shakespeare) and those who are supposed to be wise sometimes acting foolishly (provide your own examples). Older and younger adults differ in how they make decisions; one interpretation of such differences is that the older adults are wiser, but not every younger adult would agree (Worthy et al., 2011).

One summary describes wisdom as an "expert knowledge system dealing with the conduct and understanding of life" (Baltes & Smith, 2008, p. 58). Several factors just mentioned, including the ability to put aside one's personal needs (as in self-actualization), self-reflective honesty (as in integrity), and perspective on past living (the life review), are considered part of wisdom.

If this is true, the elderly may have an advantage in developing wisdom, particularly if they have: (1) dedicated their lives to the "understanding of life," (2) learned from their experiences, and (3) become more mature and integrated (Ardelt, 2011, p. 283). That may be why popes and Supreme Court justices are usually quite old.

Similarly, the author of a detailed longitudinal study of 814 people concludes that wisdom is not reserved for the old, and yet humor, perspective, and altruism increase over the decades, gradually making people wiser. He then wrote:

> To be wise about wisdom we need to accept that wisdom does—and wisdom does not—increase with age . . . Winston Churchill, that master of wise simplicity and simple wisdom, reminds us, "We are all happier in many ways when we are old than when we are young. The young sow wild oats. The old grow sage."
>
> *[Vaillant, 2002, p. 256]*

WHAT HAVE YOU LEARNED?

1. How can older people help to improve their own cognitive abilities?
2. Why might older people become more creative, musical, and spiritual than before?
3. What educational opportunities are available for the elderly?
4. What happens with creative ability as people grow older?
5. What is the purpose of the life review?
6. Why are scientists hesitant to say that wisdom comes from age?

SUMMARY

Prejudice and Predictions

1. Contrary to ageist stereotypes, most older adults are happy, quite healthy, and active. Benevolent as well as dismissive ageism reduces health and self-image, as elderspeak illustrates.

2. An increasing percentage of the population is older than 64, but the numbers are sometimes presented in misleading ways. Currently, about 13 percent of people in the U.S. population are elderly, and most of them are self-sufficient and productive.

3. Hundreds of theories address the causes of aging. The most common are theories of wear and tear, of genes, and of cellular change. All seem plausible, but none seems sufficient.

4. One attempt to stop the aging process is calorie restriction. That seems to benefit health and prolong life in many species, but experts are conflicted as to whether it would be useful for people.

Selective Optimization with Compensation

5. Sexual intercourse occurs less often, driving a car becomes more difficult, and diseases become more common with age. However, selective optimization with compensation can mitigate almost any loss. A combination of personal determination, adjustment by society, and medical research is needed.

6. Primary aging happens to everyone, reducing organ reserve in body and brain. Secondary aging depends on the individual's past health habits and genes. Heart disease and osteoporosis are both examples of ways to optimize health, compensate for losses, and achieve compression of morbidity.

The Aging Brain

7. Brain scans and measurements show that the speed of processing slows down, parts of the brain shrink, and more areas of the brain are activated in older people.

8. Memory is affected by aging, but specifics vary. As the senses become dulled, some stimuli never reach the sensory memory. Working memory shows notable declines with age because slower processing means that some thoughts are lost.

9. Control processes are less effective with age, as retrieval strategies become less efficient. Anxiety may prevent older people from using the best strategies for cognitive control. Ecologically valid, real-life measures of cognition are needed.

10. With age, some new neurons and dendrites grow, more parts of the brain are activated at once, and some types of cognition seem preserved. In daily life, many older people seem as cogent as ever.

Brain Diseases

11. Neurocognitive disorders, whether they occur in late adulthood or earlier, are diseases that reduce brain functioning. Most people never suffer from a brain disease, but it is devastating when it occurs.

12. The most common cause of neurocognitive disorder (NCD) in the United States is Alzheimer's disease, an incurable ailment that becomes more prevalent with age and worsens over time. The main symptom is extreme memory loss.

13. Also common worldwide is vascular disease (also called vascular or multi-infarct dementia), which results from a series of ministrokes that occur when impairment of blood circulation destroys portions of brain tissue.

14. Other neurocognitive disorders, including frontotemporal NCDs and Lewy body disease, also become more common with age. Several other types of NCDs can occur in early or middle adulthood. One is Parkinson's disease, which begins with loss of muscle control. Parkinson's disease can also cause significant cognitive decline, particularly in the old.

15. Major NCD (formerly called dementia) is sometimes mistakenly diagnosed when individuals are suffering from a reversible problem, such as anxiety, depression, brain tumors, and polypharmacy. The elderly take many drugs, sometimes with uncertain side effects.

Older and Wiser

16. Many people become more interested and adept in creative endeavors, as well as more philosophical, as they grow older. The life review is a personal reflection that many older people undertake, remembering earlier experiences, putting their entire lives into perspective, and achieving integrity or self-actualization.

17. Wisdom does not necessarily increase as a result of age, but some elderly people are unusually wise or insightful.

KEY TERMS

ageism (p. 503)
elderspeak (p. 506)
universal design (p. 507)
demographic shift (p. 508)
wear and tear (p. 511)
calorie restriction (p. 511)
maximum life span (p. 512)
average life expectancy (p. 512)

genetic clock (p. 512)
cellular aging (p. 513)
Hayflick limit (p. 513)
telomeres (p. 513)
primary aging (p. 518)
secondary aging (p. 518)
compression of morbidity (p. 518)
osteoporosis (p. 519)

control processes (p. 524)
ecological validity (p. 525)
neurocognitive disorder (NCD) (p. 525)
major neurocognitive disorder (major NCD) (p. 527)
Alzheimer's disease (AD) (p. 527)
plaques (p. 527)

tangles (p. 527)
vascular disease (p. 528)
frontotemporal NCDs (p. 528)
Parkinson's disease (p. 529)
Lewy body disease (p. 529)
polypharmacy (p. 532)
self-actualization (p. 534)
life review (p. 535)

APPLICATIONS

1. Analyze Web sites that have information about aging for evidence of ageism, anti-aging measures, and exaggeration of longevity.

2. Ask five people of various ages whether they want to live to age 100, and record their responses. Would they be willing to eat half as much, exercise much more, experience weekly dialysis, or undergo other procedures in order to extend life? Analyze the responses, including any age differences.

3. Visit someone in a hospital. Note all the elements in the environment—such as noise, lights, schedules, and personnel—that might cause an elderly patient to seem disoriented.

NANCY RICA SCHIFF/SUPERSTOCK

CHAPTER OUTLINE

LATE ADULTHOOD
The Social World

CHAPTER 15

WHAT WILL YOU KNOW?

- Do older people become more sad or more hopeful?
- Do the elderly want to move to a distant, warm place?
- What do adult children owe their elderly parents?
- Is home care better than nursing-home care?

Almost every week I walk through a park with my friend Doris, a widow in her 80s, to a meeting we both attend. Many people of all backgrounds greet her by name, including men who play chess on a park table and a woman who owns a nearby hotel. Doris is an icon for street performers, including Colin, who plays his piano (on wheels) outside on sunny days. The police ticketed him for not having a permit.

Doris organized a protest. She got Community Board 2 (she is the oldest member, reappointed by the City Council every two years since 1964) to pass a resolution about free speech. The city withdrew the ticket, and the Parks Department revised their policy.

We walk slowly because Doris greets babies, birds, and other animals. Squirrels scamper up to grab peanuts from her hand, and sometimes pigeons perch on her arm. Doris dresses well, appropriate for each season. One hot August day I was surprised that she wore a long-sleeved blouse. She proudly told me why: Her arm was scratched because two pigeons fought over the same spot. She tells me about her grandmother from Finland, her two marriages, her journalist days as a dance critic, her efforts to style her very white hair.

Often we stop at the mailbox to drop in a timely greeting card: I have become one of hundreds on her list. Colorful envelopes arrive in my box—green for St. Patrick's Day, orange for Halloween, gray for Thanksgiving, red for July 4th, and multicolored for my birthday. Doris sent 426 Christmas cards; she orders stamps from a post office catalog.

Usually friends have much in common, but I am unlike Doris. I never send cards, feed squirrels, or protect pianists (although Doris did get me to help Colin). We belong to opposing political parties. She has no children; I have four.

How did we become friends? Seven years ago, Doris had knee surgery and needed volunteers to wheel her to her many meetings, appointments, and social engagements. Dozens of people offered their services. I did, too. Soon Doris could walk alone with her walker, but I have come to enjoy her anecdotes, her memories, her attitudes. I watch for cars when we cross the street, but I get more from Doris than I give. And I am not referring to Thanksgiving cards.

Not a Puppet One park regular is a puppeteer, Ricky Syers, who entertains hundreds of tourists with an array of puppets. He recently made one of Doris, one more bit of evidence that the real Doris is beloved by many—and not controlled by anyone.

Recently Doris broke her hip. The rehab center soon put her in a private room because her younger roommate complained that Doris had too many visitors all day long. They came because they like her, not because they agree with her. She often is the sole dissenting vote on Community Board resolutions, yet everyone respects her.

Back at home, Doris continues to be active, social, and appreciated by many. Her life defies stereotyping, which makes her an illustration of the theme of this chapter: the variability and complexity of development in later life. Some of the elderly are frail, lonely, and vulnerable because of private circumstances and public failures. For most, however, psychosocial development includes working and socializing, concern for others as well as self-care. Doris does all this admirably. I hope to be like her someday. ■

Theories of Late Adulthood

Some elderly people run marathons and lead nations; others no longer walk or talk. Social scientists theorize about this diversity, yet everyone respects her.

Self Theories

Certain theories of late adulthood can be called **self theories;** they focus on individuals, especially the self-concept and challenges to identity. Self-awareness begins, as you remember, before age 2, and it builds throughout childhood and adolescence. In those early decades, self-image is greatly affected by physical appearance and by other people's perceptions (Harter, 2012). Appearance and external opinions become less crucial with age.

self theories
Theories of late adulthood that emphasize the core self, or the search to maintain one's integrity and identity.

THE SELF AND AGING Perhaps people become more truly themselves with age. That is what Anna Quindlen found:

> It's odd when I think of the arc of my life, from child to young woman to aging adult. First I was who I was. Then I didn't know who I was. Then I invented someone and became her. Then I began to like what I'd invented. And finally I was what I was again. It turned out I wasn't alone in that particular progression.
>
> *[Quindlen, 2012, p. ix]*

Always a Mother In this photo, in Nepal, a volunteer gives food to an elderly woman in an Aama Ghar, a home for elderly mothers. Is such an institution an example of self theory (identity as mother endures decades after children are independent) or of stratification theory (older people segregated from ordinary life)?

Older adults maintain their self-concept despite senescence, which alters appearance and social status in ways that might undercut self-esteem. In late adulthood, the "creation and maintenance of identity" is "a key aspect of healthy living" (Allen et al., 2011, p. 10). Even the oldest-old and those who suffer from neurocognitive disorders preserve their sense of self, although memory, ability, and health fade (Klein, 2012).

A central idea of self theory is that each person ultimately depends on himself or herself. As one woman explained:

> I actually think I value my sense of self more importantly than my family or relationships or health or wealth or wisdom. I do see myself as on my own, ultimately . . . Statistics certainly show that older women are likely to end up being alone, so I really do value my own self when it comes right down to things in the end.
>
> *[quoted in Kroger, 2007, p. 203]*

Self theory is one explanation for an interesting phenomenon: Compared to younger adults, older people rely more on their personal experiences than on objective statistics, or, in dual-processing terms, more on intuition than on analysis.

For example, one research team asked, "What does one do when rational deliberation suggests calling it off with Julie to commit to Jane, but a powerful gut feeling suggests just the opposite?" (Mikels et al., 2012, p. 1). In an experiment, blindfolded participants (aged, on average, 21 or 75) were challenged to pick a red jelly bean from one of two dishes, each with more white beans than red. The odds of success for each dish were clearly labeled. There were 12 trials, each with another pair of dishes and set of odds.

The elders did not always make the logical choice. Thirty-six percent of their choices were against the odds, as were 21 percent of the choices of the younger participants (Mikels et al., 2012). By analogy, the elders sometimes chose Julie, not Jane. The researchers noted, perhaps surprisingly, that the older adults, who sometimes followed their emotions rather than logic, tended to be happier with themselves.

INTEGRITY The most comprehensive self theory came from Erik Erikson. His eighth and final stage of development, **integrity versus despair,** requires adults to integrate their unique experiences with their community concerns (Erikson et al., 1986/1994). The word *integrity* is often used to mean honesty, but it also means a feeling of being whole, not scattered, and comfortable with oneself. The virtue of old age, according to Erikson, is wisdom, which implies a broad perspective.

As an example of integrity, many older people are proud of their personal history. They glorify their past, even boasting about bad experiences such as skipping school, taking drugs, escaping arrest, or being physically abused. Psychologists sometimes call this the "sucker to saint" phenomenon, when people interpret their experiences as signs of their nobility (saintly), not their stupidity (Jordan & Monin, 2008).

As Erikson explained it, such self-glorifying distortions are far better than despair because "time is now short, too short for the attempt to start another life" (Erikson, 1993, p. 269). For every stage, the tension between the two opposing aspects (here integrity versus despair) propels growth. In this final stage,

> life brings many, quite realistic reasons for experiencing despair: aspects of a past we fervently wish had been different; aspects of the present that cause unremitting pain; aspects of a future that are uncertain and frightening. And, of course, there remains inescapable death, that one aspect of the future which is both wholly certain and wholly unknowable. Thus, some despair must be acknowledged and integrated as a component of old age.
>
> *[Erikson et al., 1986/1994, p. 72]*

Integration of death and the self is the crucial accomplishment of this stage. The life review (explained in Chapter 14) and the acceptance of death (explained in the Epilogue) are crucial aspects of the integrity envisioned by Erikson (Zimmerman, 2012).

Self theory may explain why many of the elderly strive to maintain childhood cultural and religious practices. For instance, grandparents may painstakingly teach a grandchild a language that is rarely used, or they may encourage the child to repeat traditional rituals and prayers. In cultures such as the United States that emphasize newness, elders worry that their traditional values will be lost and thus that they themselves will disappear.

As Erikson wrote, the older person

> knows that an individual life is the accidental coincidence of but one life cycle with but one segment of history; and that for him all human integrity stands or falls with the one style of integrity of which he partakes. . . . In such a final consolation, death loses its sting.
>
> *[Erikson, 1968/1994, p. 104]*

integrity versus despair
The final stage of Erik Erikson's developmental sequence, in which older adults seek to integrate their unique experiences with their vision of community.

Trash or Treasure? Tryphona Flood, threatened with eviction, admitted she's a hoarder and got help from Megan Tolen, shown here discussing what in this four-room apartment can be discarded. Flood sits on the only spot of her bed that is not covered with stuff. This photo was taken midway through a three-year effort to clean out the apartment—the clutter was worse a year earlier.

compulsive hoarding
The urge to accumulate and hold on to familiar objects and possessions, sometimes to the point of their becoming health and/or safety hazards. This impulse tends to increase with age.

THINK CRITICALLY: Is hoarding a universal disorder or a cohort problem?

socio-emotional selectivity theory
The theory that older people prioritize regulation of their own emotions and seek familiar social contacts who reinforce generativity, pride, and joy.

HOLDING ON TO THE SELF Most older people consider their personalities and attitudes quite stable over their life span, even as they acknowledge physical changes of their bodies and gaps in their memory (Klein, 2012). One 103-year-old woman, wrinkled, shrunken, and severely crippled by arthritis, displayed a photo of herself as a beautiful young woman. She said, "My core has stayed the same. Everything else has changed" (quoted in Troll & Skaff, 1997, p. 166).

Many older people refuse to move from drafty and dangerous dwellings into smaller, safer apartments because leaving familiar places means abandoning personal history. That is irrational, but it is explained by self theory. Likewise, an older person may avoid surgery or refuse medicine because they fear anything that might distort their thinking or emotions: Their priority is self-protection, even if it shortens life (S. Miller, 2011–2012).

The insistence on protecting the self may explain **compulsive hoarding,** saving reams of old papers, books, mementos . . . anything that might someday be useful. The fifth edition of the DSM recognizes hoarding as a psychological disorder (American Psychiatric Association, 2013, pp. 247–251).

Earlier DSM editions did not consider hoarding a disorder. Why not? Many elderly hoarders grew up in the Great Depression and World War II, when saving scraps and reusing products meant survival and patriotism. That habit is contrary to the current ethos: Expiration dates are now stamped on food and drugs; electronics, from computers to televisions, are quickly obsolete.

A prime motive for elderly hoarders is avoiding waste. Hoarding brings them emotional satisfaction (Frost et al., 2015), which a younger person might get from the opposite action, replacing something old. (My youngest daughter enjoys throwing out everything in my refrigerator that has an expiration date that has passed.)

A contemporary problem is that fewer dwellings have attics and basements, so hoarding occurs within living areas. In cramped apartments, hoarding takes over, becoming not only irrational but sometimes dangerous. Self theory helps explain what social workers and younger relatives do not understand: Possessions are part of self-expression. The elderly seek to protect childhood values, lifelong habits, and past history.

My friend Doris (opening anecdote) hoards old newspaper articles, records, and other things that are precious to her. She lives alone, with her possessions and two cats. She has an answering machine and a fax, but she proudly resists the Internet. She likes it that way.

SOCIO-EMOTIONAL SELECTIVITY THEORY Another self theory is **socio-emotional selectivity theory** (Carstensen, 1993). The idea is that older people select familiar social contacts who reinforce their generativity, pride, and joy. As socio-emotional theory would predict, when people believe that their future time is limited, they think about the meaning of life and then decide that they should be more appreciative of family and friends, thus furthering their happiness (Hicks et al., 2012).

Socio-emotional selectivity could be a specific version of *selective optimization with compensation,* which you read about in Chapters 12 and 14. As senescence changes appearance and status, older adults select the key aspects of their social world to optimize.

Selectivity is central to self theories. Individuals set personal goals, assess their abilities, and figure out how to accomplish their goals despite limitations. When older people are resilient, they maintain their identity despite wrinkles, slowdowns, and losses, and their emotional health is preserved (Resnick et al., 2011).

An outgrowth of both socio-emotional selectivity and selective optimization is known as the **positivity effect.** A meta-analysis of more than 115 comparisons between younger and older adults found that the elderly perceive, prefer, and remember positive images and experiences more than negative ones (Reed et al., 2014). Unpleasant experiences are ignored, forgotten, or reinterpreted.

For that reason, stressful events (economic loss, serious illness, death of friends or relatives) become less central to identity with age. Because elders think of themselves more positively, they protect their emotional health (Boals et al., 2012), becoming more optimistic about themselves and happier because of it. A strong sense of self-efficacy (the idea that a person has the power to control and change a situation) correlates with a happier and longer life (Gerstorf et al., 2014).

The positivity effect may explain why, in every nation and religion, older people tend to be more patriotic and devout than younger ones. They see their national history and religious beliefs in positive terms, and they are proud to be themselves—Canadian, Czech, Chinese, or whatever. Of course, this same trait can keep them mired in their earlier prejudices—racist, sexist, or homophobic, for instance.

Anna Quindlen was quoted on page 540 as glad she "was what I was again." Does this mean that she, and most older people, do not see current world problems? Consider my daughter, my mother, and me.

positivity effect
The tendency for elderly people to perceive, prefer, and remember positive images and experiences more than negative ones.

What Is She Thinking? At her 117th birthday, Misao Okawa was the oldest living person in the world. She died a few weeks later—but not before making a statement indicating the positivity effect. She said that the secret to a long life was to eat delicious things.

UDDHIKA WEERASINGHE/GETTY IMAGES

OPPOSING PERSPECTIVES

Too Sweet or Too Sad?

When I was young, I liked movies that were gritty, dramatic, violent. My mother questioned my choices; I told her I hated sugar-coating. She liked romantic comedies that made her laugh; I told her that was frivolous.

Now my youngest daughter wants me to read dystopian novels. *Hunger Games* is an example. I tell her the world has enough poverty and conflict; I don't need to read about imaginary killing. Have I become my mother?

Many researchers have found that a positive worldview increases with age. The positivity effect correlates with believing that life is meaningful. Elders who are happy, not frustrated or depressed, agree strongly that their life has a purpose (e.g., "I have a system of values that guides my daily activities" and "I am at peace with my past") (Hicks et al.,

2012). Meaningfulness and positivity correlate with a long and healthy life.

The elderly are quicker to let go of disappointments, thinking positively about going forward. As a result, many studies have found "an increase in emotional well-being from middle age onward, whereas the experience of anger declines" (Brassen et al., 2012, p. 614).

Researchers have measured reactions to disappointment, not only in attitudes and actions but also in brain activity and heart rate. One study compared three groups: young adults, healthy older adults, and older adults with late-life depression.

In reaction to disappointment, the healthy older adults recovered quickly, but the other two groups took longer:

The brains, bodies, and behavior of the depressed elders and the younger adults were similar, but the healthy elders had broken free of those destructive forces The conclusion: "emotionally healthy aging is associated with a reduced responsiveness to regretful events" (Brassen et al., 2012, p. 614) (see Figure 15.1).

A pair of researchers asked whether the positivity effect in social interaction occurred because older adults simply avoided unpleasant people (Luong & Charles, 2014). Accordingly, they assigned younger and older adults to work on a task with a disagreeable partner.

In fact, that partner was an actor, trained to be nasty with everyone. For example, the actor never smiled, and said, "I really don't see where you're coming from." True to expectations, compared to the younger participants, the older adults more often reported that they liked the partner and enjoyed the task. They did not try to change their partner or feel resentful; the positivity effect protected them (see Figure 15.2).

One perspective is that anger and frustration are useful emotions. From that viewpoint, too much rosy acceptance may be wrong in a world that needs changing, and that may be annoying to younger people who interpret life differently. My daughter recently apologized for criticizing me. I replied, honestly, that I had forgotten her critique. I do not think that was what she wanted to hear. Do I ignore criticism? Am I stuck in my ways?

Back to the study of the nasty partner. The elders' blood pressure rose less and came down more quickly than did the younger adults' pressure after the disagreeable interaction. The pulse of the older participants hardly changed at all (Luong & Charles, 2014). Having a positive outlook not only makes a person happier, it also makes them healthier.

THINK CRITICALLY: Does the positivity effect avoid reality, or was my mother right?

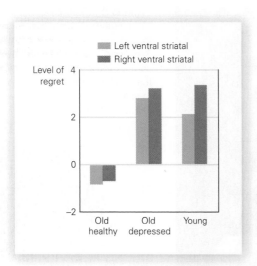

FIGURE 15.1 Let Bygones Be Bygones Areas of the brain (the ventral striatal) are activated when a person feels regret. In this experiment, brain activation correlated with past loss and then unwise choices, with participants repeating behavior that had just failed. Older adults were usually wiser, as evidenced in brain activation as well as actions. However, elders who had been diagnosed as depressed seemed to dwell on past losses. The positivity effect had passed them by.

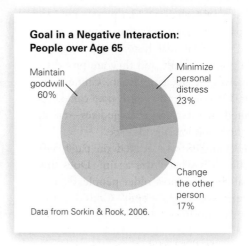

FIGURE 15.2 Keep the Peace When someone does something mean or unpleasant, what is your goal in your interaction with that person? If your goal is to maintain goodwill, as was the case for a majority of studies on older adults, you are likely to be quicker to forgive and forget.

Stratification Theories

A second set of theories, called **stratification theories,** emphasizes social forces that position each person in a social stratum or level. That positioning creates disadvantages for some and advantages for others.

Stratification begins in the womb, as "individuals are born into a society that is already stratified—that is differentiated—along key dimensions, including sex, race, and SES" (Lynch & Brown, 2011, p. 107). Indeed, stratification affects the prenatal environment, so some newborns already suffer from being born to a disadvantaged mother.

Every form of stereotyping makes it more difficult for people to break free from social institutions that assign them to a particular path. The results are cumulative, over the entire life span (Brandt et al., 2012).

stratification theories
Theories that emphasize that social forces, particularly those related to a person's social stratum or social category, limit individual choices and affect a person's ability to function in late adulthood because past stratification continues to limit life in various ways.

For instance, as described in many of the preceding chapters, children who are both African American and poor are more likely to be underweight at birth; less likely to talk at age 1 or read before age 6; more likely to drop out of school and use drugs; less likely to obtain a college degree, find a job, or marry; and finally, more likely to die before age 70 of cancer, diabetes, heart disease, or other serious health problems. Each of these outcomes is more likely because of the previous one.

As you have also read, at each step some individuals break away from the usual path, but stratification theory contends that overcoming the liabilities of the past is increasingly difficult as life unfolds. By old age, people who have experienced poverty and prejudice all their lives almost never overcome their past, becoming healthy and wealthy (see Figure 15.3).

Stratification theory suggests that to help the aged, intervention can begin before birth. The fact that health problems result from a lifetime of stratification "suggests multiple intervention points at which disparities can be reduced" (Haas et al., 2012, p. 238).

Each stereotype adds to stratification and thus adds to the risk of problems, perhaps putting those who are female, non-European American, and poor in triple jeopardy. However, as explained at the end of this section, not everyone agrees with that conclusion (Rosenfield, 2012).

GENDER STRATIFICATION Irrational, gender-based fear may limit female independence, even in old age. For example, adult children are more likely to insist that their widowed mothers live with them than their widowed fathers. In fact, however, men living alone are more likely than women to have a sudden health crisis. For example, although heart disease kills elders of both sexes, men are more likely to have a fatal heart attack and women are more likely to have gradual heart failure, eventually killing them.

Twice Fortunate Ageism takes many forms. Some cultures are youth-oriented, devaluing the old, while others are the opposite. These twin sisters are lucky to be alive: They were born in rural China in 1905, a period when most female twins died. When this photo was taken, they were age 103, and fortunate again, venerated because they have lived so long.

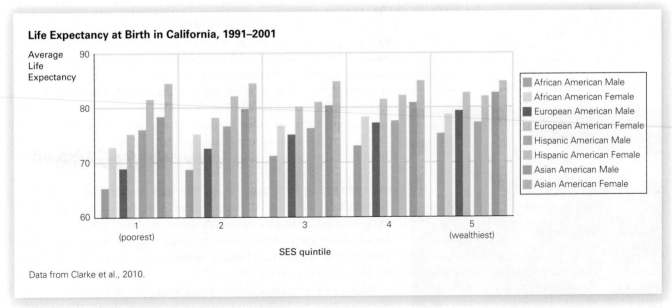

Life Expectancy at Birth in California, 1991–2001

Legend:
- African American Male
- African American Female
- European American Male
- European American Female
- Hispanic American Male
- Hispanic American Female
- Asian American Male
- Asian American Female

(Y-axis: Average Life Expectancy, 60 to 90; X-axis: SES quintile, 1 (poorest) to 5 (wealthiest))

Data from Clarke et al., 2010.

FIGURE 15.3 Gender, Ethnicity, and SES These life-expectancy data provide obvious evidence for ethnic and income stratification, but sex differences are more puzzling. One possibility is that stratification by sex favors women. However, older women are more often disabled and are poorer than men the same age, which supports the original triple jeopardy concept.

Twice-Abandoned Widows Traditionally in India, widows walked into the funeral pyre that cremated their husband's body, a suicide called sati. If they hesitated, the husband's relatives would sometimes push. Currently, sati is outlawed, but many Indian widows experience a social death: They are forbidden to meet men and remarry, except sometimes to the dead man's brother. Hundreds go to the sacred city of Vrindavan, where they are paid a pittance to chant prayers all day, as this woman does.

Memories Older adults often provide links between the past and present. Toni Morrison won a Pulitzer Prize for her novel *Beloved*, published when she was 56. It provided insight into the emotional horror of slavery for women who died long ago. Here, in Paris at age 81, Morrison dedicates a bench commemorating slavery's abolition.

In another example, the United States Bureau of Justice Statistics reported in 2013 that even though more old women live alone than old men, fewer old women are victims of every major type of crime. (Generally, rates of criminal victimization for both sexes fall with age, with less than half a percent of crime victims being over age 65.)

In another example of gender stratification, young women typically marry men a few years older and then outlive them. Especially in former years, many married women relied on their husbands to manage money. Thus, past gender stratification produced many old widows who were lonely, poor, and dependent for decades.

Longevity itself may result from lifelong gender stratification. Boys are taught to be stoic, repressing emotions and avoiding medical attention, which makes old men avoid doctors. In 2012 in the United States, twice as many men as women never saw a doctor (21 percent versus 11 percent) (National Center for Health Statistics, 2014). Thus, gender stratification may make men die too soon and women lonely for too long.

ETHNIC STRATIFICATION Remember that ethnic differences are sometimes codified as racial differences, with racial attitudes and experiences over a lifetime affecting many elders. As you remember from Chapter 12, racism causes weathering in African Americans, increasing allostatic load, shortening healthy life (Thrasher et al., 2012).

Past ethnic discrimination results in poverty for many minority families, itself a result of the quality of education, the health of neighborhoods, the salary of jobs.

Consider one detailed example, home ownership, which is a source of financial security for many seniors. Fifty years ago, stratification prevented most African Americans from buying homes. Laws then reduced housing discrimination, which meant that many African Americans finally bought homes. However, they often had new, and expensive, mortgages, so they suffered more than other groups in the foreclosure crisis that began in 2007. Is this a new example of an old story: stratification causing poverty (Saegert et al., 2011)?

A particular form of ethnic stratification affects immigrant elders. Most immigrants to North America come from non-Western cultures, where younger generations are expected to care for the elderly. However, U.S. homes are designed for nuclear families, and pensions and Social Security are earned by employees who worked for decades "on the books" within established companies, not to older immigrants who came to help their younger family members.

Thus, U.S. practices leave many older immigrants poor, lonely, and dependent on their children, who live in homes and apartments not designed for extended families. That may lead to two harmful family dynamics: unwelcome closeness in crowded, multigenerational homes, or distressing distance between elders and their descendants.

INCOME STRATIFICATION Finally, the most harmful effect of stratification may be financial, directly from poverty and then magnified by gender and ethnicity. As one reviewer explains, "[W]omen . . . are much more likely to live in households that fall below the federal poverty line. Black and Hispanic women are particularly vulnerable" (J. Jackson et al., 2011, p. 93).

Many of the poorest elderly never held jobs that paid into Social Security. Thus, an important source of income is absent. When ethnic discrimination affects employment opportunity, poverty in old age is particularly likely. Further, when money is scarce, that itself undercuts the ability to plan for the future (Haushofer & Fehr, 2014).

Income stratification is more apparent than either gender or ethnic stratification among the very old. Low-SES European American men have less education, worse health, and spottier work history (more unemployment, fewer benefits, no pensions) than men of higher SES. The recent economic crisis in many nations results in less social governmental support for the poor of any age (Phillipson, 2013).

AGE STRATIFICATION Ageism and age segregation affects life in many ways, including income and health. For example, seniority builds in the workplace, increasing income up to a certain point, and then employment stops, perhaps with a pension but never with as much income as before. People who are unskilled or temporary workers are particularly likely to be hurt by current old-age pension structures (Phillipson, 2013).

The most controversial version of age stratification is **disengagement theory** (Cumming & Henry, 1961), which holds that as people age, four significant changes occur: Traditional roles become unavailable; the social circle shrinks; coworkers stop relying on them; and adult children turn away to focus on their own children. Meanwhile, older people become less mobile and less able to engage in social interaction.

> **disengagement theory**
> The view that aging makes a person's social sphere increasingly narrow, resulting in role relinquishment, withdrawal, and passivity.

According to this theory, disengagement is a mutual process, chosen by both adult generations. Thus, younger adult workers and parents disengage from the old, who themselves disengage, withdrawing from life's action.

This theory provoked a storm of protest. Many gerontologists insisted that older people need and want new involvements. An opposing theory, **activity theory,** holds that the elderly seek to remain active with relatives, friends, and community groups. Activity theorists contended that if the elderly disengage, they do so unwillingly and suffer because of it (Kelly, 1993; Rosow, 1985).

> **activity theory**
> The view that elderly people want and need to remain active in a variety of social spheres—with relatives, friends, and community groups.

Extensive research supports activity theory. Being active correlates with happiness, intelligence, and health. This is true at younger ages as well, but the correlation between activity and well-being is particularly strong at older ages (Potočnik & Sonnentag, 2013; Bielak et al., 2012).

Disengagement is more likely among those low in SES, which suggests it is another harmful outcome of past economic stratification (Clarke et al., 2011). Literally being active—bustling around the house, climbing stairs, walking to work—lengthens life and increases satisfaction.

Both disengagement and activity theories need to be applied with caution, however. The positivity effect may mean that an older person disengages from emotional events that cause anger, regret, and sadness while actively enjoying other experiences. Current theories and research emphasize the variations in the lives of the aged, with neither disengagement nor activity theory always accurate (Johnson & Mutchler, 2014).

CRITIQUE OF STRATIFICATION THEORIES Contrary to all the preceding examples, might women, ethnic minorities, and low-income people develop habits and attitudes by old age that protect them from the worst effects of stratification (Rosenfield, 2012)? Evidence is spotty, and low SES and ill health are harmful at every age, but perhaps gender, ethnicity, or SES are less damaging for the very old than they are earlier in life.

Both age-related stratification theories—that all the elderly want to withdraw and that they all should stay active—may arise from cultural stereotypes, not reality. If that is true, an older person could choose to be both active and inactive, whichever is best for them at the moment, instead of sticking to the cultural script.

Contrary to gender stratification, older women live longer and are happier than older men. They usually have closer relationships with friends and families, and grown children pay more attention to their aged mothers than their aged fathers. All this suggests that they might be less disadvantaged in late adulthood than they were as young women.

Similarly, cautionary data come from comparing the aged of various ethnic groups. Although in childhood and adulthood African Americans have poorer health and higher death rates than European Americans, that inequality disappears at about age 80 and then reverses. The average African American centenarian lives seven months longer than does the average European American one. Other minority ethnic groups do even better: Older Asian Americans have a several-year advantage.

One scholar suggests that older African American women in the United States have the best mental health of all the race, age, and gender groups. He does not think "stratification systems such as gender, race and class" result in high risk for older adults. Instead "multiple minority statuses affect mental health in paradoxical ways . . . that refute triple jeopardy approaches" (Rosenfield, 2012, p. 1791).

One explanation for the *race crossover* in longevity is called selective survival—the idea that only extremely healthy non–European Americans reach old age. But perhaps there are social advantages of being a minority. Perhaps past stratification teaches coping strategies such as humor and social connections that become protective in late adulthood.

THINK CRITICALLY: Could years of being at the top of the social hierarchy become a liability in old age?

WHAT HAVE YOU LEARNED?

1. How does Erikson's use of the word *integrity* differ from its usual meaning?
2. How does hoarding relate to self theory?
3. What are the advantages of the positivity effect?
4. What are the disadvantages of the positivity effect?
5. What are the problems with being female, according to stratification theory?
6. What are the problems with being male, according to stratification theory?
7. How does immigrant status impair elderly people, according to stratification theory?
8. Which type of stratification is most burdensome—economic, ethnic, or gender?
9. How can disengagement be mutual?
10. If activity theory is correct, what does that suggest older adults should do?
11. What data support stratification theory, and what data refute it?

FIGURE 15.4 Along with Everyone Else Although younger adults might imagine that older people stop work as soon as they can, this is clearly not true for everyone.

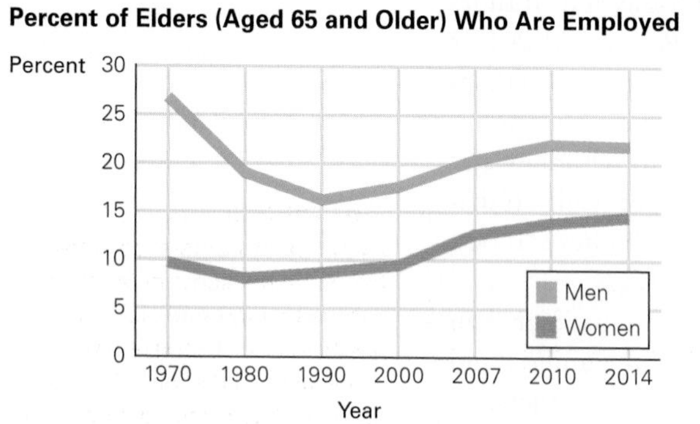

Percent of Elders (Aged 65 and Older) Who Are Employed

Data from U.S. Department of Labor, various publications.

Activities in Late Adulthood

As you read, most of the research finds that active elders live longer and more happily than inactive ones. Elders themselves bear this out. Most of them wish they had more time to do all they want to do, and they enjoy their active, busy lives.

This might surprise young college students, who see few gray hairs at sports events, political rallies, job sites, or midnight concerts. But most of the elderly are far from inactive; it's just that their activities differ from the young. We now present specifics.

Working

A significant proportion of the elderly continue working, because work provides social support and status. Many elders are reluctant to give that up (see Figure 15.4). Others retire from their paid jobs but nonetheless remain productive.

Many government policies affect the elderly, especially those regarding housing, pensions, prescription drugs, and medical costs. However, members of this age group do not necessarily vote their own economic interests or vote as a bloc. Instead, they are divided on most national issues, including global warming, military conflicts, and public education.

Political scientists believe the idea of "gray power" (that the elderly vote as a bloc) is a myth, promulgated to reduce support for programs that benefit the old (Walker, 2012). Given that ageism zigzags from hostile to benign—and is often based on beliefs that are far from reality—it is not surprising that "older persons [are] attacked as too powerful and, at the same time, as a burdensome responsibility" (Schulz & Binstock, 2008, p. 8).

In the United States, the media sometimes stereotypes people who support the Tea Party (about 18 percent of all adults in 2010) as elderly, but that is not accurate. Most Tea Party supporters are middle-aged (40–65), and only a fourth are over age 65. Few of the elderly who identify with that group attend rallies or donate money (The New York Times & CBS News, 2010).

WHAT HAVE YOU LEARNED?

1. Why would a person keep working after age 65?
2. How does retirement affect the health of people who have worked all their lives?
3. Who is more likely to volunteer and why?
4. What are the benefits and liabilities for elders who want to age in place?
5. How does religion affect the well-being of the aged?
6. How does the political activity of older and younger adults differ?

Friends and Relatives

Companions are particularly important in old age. As socio-emotional theory predicts, the size of the social circle shrinks with age, but close relationships are crucial. Negative social relationships are destructive of mind and body (K. Rook, 2014).

For most of the elderly, however, negative relationships have been abandoned, and positive ones remain. Bonds formed over the years allow people to share triumphs and tragedies with others who understand and appreciate. Siblings, old friends, and spouses are ideal convoy members.

Many of the older adults in **Video: Active and Healthy Aging: The Importance of Community** frequent senior centers for continual social contact, and some benefit from volunteering.

(a) (b)

A Lover's Kiss Ralph Young awakens Ruth *(a)* with a kiss each day, as he has for most of the 78 years of their marriage. Here they are both 99, sharing a room in their Indiana residence, "more in love than ever." Half a world away, in Ukraine *(b)*, more kisses occur, with 70 newly married couples and one couple celebrating their golden anniversary. Developmental data suggest that now, several years after these photos, the two old couples are more likely to be happily married than the 70 young ones.

Long-Term Partnerships

For many of the current cohort of elders, their spouse is the central convoy member, a buffer against the problems of old age. Even more than other social contacts, including friends and children, a spouse is protective of health (Wong & Waite, 2015). All the research finds that married older adults are healthier, wealthier, and happier than unmarried people their age.

Mutual interaction is crucial: Each healthy and happy partner improves the other's well-being (Ruthig et al., 2012). Of course, not every marriage is good: About one in every six long-term marriages decreases health and happiness (Waldinger & Schulz, 2010). But that is not the usual pattern.

A lifetime of shared experiences—living together, raising children, and dealing with financial and emotional crises—brings partners closer. Often couples develop "an exceedingly positive portrayal" (O'Rourke et al., 2010) of their mate, seeing their partner's personality as better than their own.

Older couples have learned how to disagree, considering conflicts to be discussions, not fights. I know one example personally.

Irma and Bill are both politically active, proud parents of two adult children, devoted grandparents, and informed about current events. They seem happily married and they cooperate admirably when caring for their 2- and 4-year-old grandsons.

However, they vote for opposing candidates for president. I was puzzled until Irma explained: "We sit together on the fence, seeing both perspectives, and then, when it's time to vote, Bill and I fall on opposite sides." I can predict who will fall on which side, but for them, the discussion is productive. Their long-term affection keeps disagreements from becoming fights.

Outsiders might judge many long-term marriages as unequal, since one or the other spouse usually provides most of the money, or needs most of the care, or does most of the housework. Yet such disparities do not bother most older partners, who accept each other's dependencies, remembering times (perhaps decades ago) when the situation was reversed.

One crucial factor is coping with challenges of child rearing, home ownership, economic crises, and so on. The importance of past sharing, rather than each living independent lives, is suggested by research that finds that older husbands and wives with mutual close friends are more likely to help each other if special needs arise (Cornwell, 2012).

Given the importance of relationship building over the life span, it is not surprising that elders who are disabled (e.g., have difficulty walking, bathing, and so on) are less depressed and anxious if they are in a close marital relationship (Mancini & Bonanno, 2006). A couple together can achieve selective optimization with compensation.

For example, I know a man whose memory is fading. He is married to a woman whose legs are so weak that she has difficulty getting out of bed. If either had been alone, he or she would need extensive care. However, the husband helps the wife move, and she keeps track of what needs to be done—working together they need only minimal outside help.

Relationships with Younger Generations

In past centuries, many adults died before their grandchildren were born. For 10-year-olds in 1900, only one in twenty-five had all four grandparents alive; in 2000 close to half (41 percent) did (Hagestad & Uhlenberg, 2007). In 2010 in China, 50 percent of 18-year-olds had four living grandparents (Jiang & Sanchez-Barricarte, 2011). Some contemporary families span five generations. Most families have intergenerational connections (Szydlik, 2012).

MIKE BALDWIN/CARTOONSTOCK.COM

"They grow old too fast."

Ignorant? Each generation has much to teach as well as much to learn.

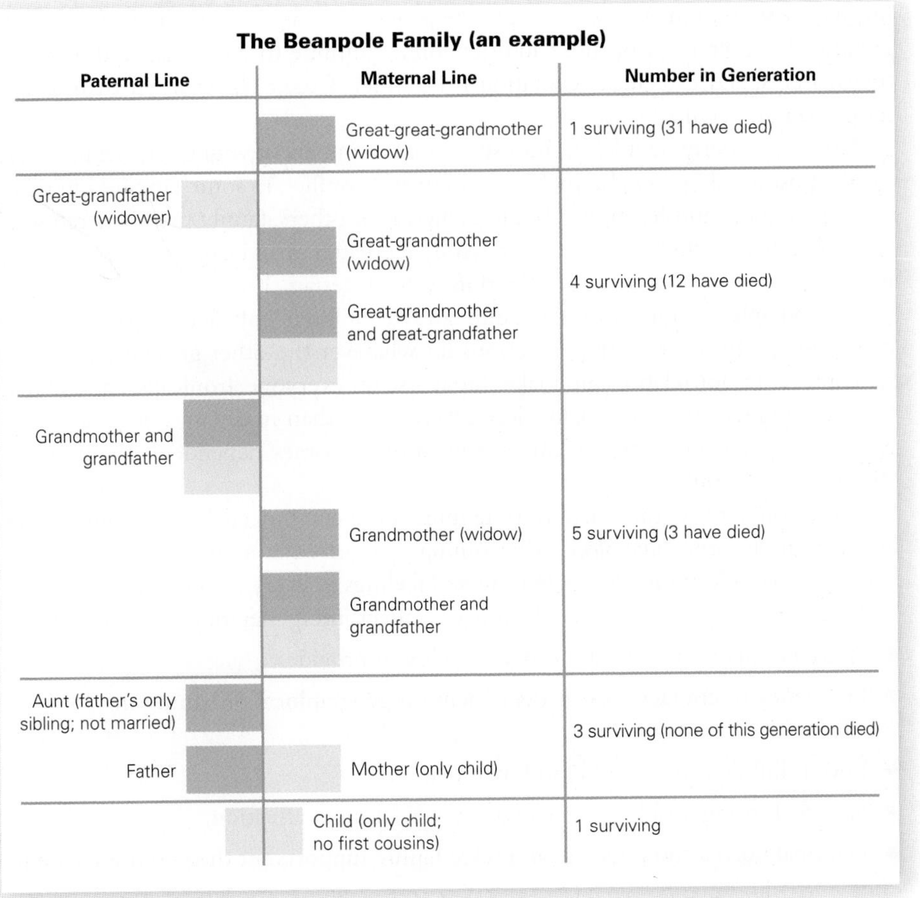

The Beanpole Family (an example)

Paternal Line	Maternal Line	Number in Generation
	Great-great-grandmother (widow)	1 surviving (31 have died)
Great-grandfather (widower)	Great-grandmother (widow)	4 surviving (12 have died)
	Great-grandmother and great-grandfather	
Grandmother and grandfather		
	Grandmother (widow)	5 surviving (3 have died)
	Grandmother and grandfather	
Aunt (father's only sibling; not married)		3 surviving (none of this generation died)
Father	Mother (only child)	
	Child (only child; no first cousins)	1 surviving

FIGURE 15.8 **Many Households, Few Members** The traditional nuclear family consists of two parents and their children living together. Today, as couples have fewer children, the beanpole family is becoming more common. This kind of family has many generations, each typically living in its own household, with few members in each generation.

Since the average couple now has fewer children, the *beanpole family,* with multiple generations but with only a few members at each level, is becoming more common (Murphy, 2011) (see Figure 15.8). Some children have no cousins, brothers, or sisters but a dozen elderly relatives.

INTERGENERATIONAL RELATIONSHIPS   As you remember, *familism* prompts family caregiving among all the relatives. One norm is **filial responsibility,** the obligation of adult children to care for their aging parents. This is a value in every nation, with some variation by culture (Saraceno, 2010).

filial responsibility
The obligation of adult children to care for their aging parents.

As a value, filial responsibility is strongest in Asia, but in practice, some scholars find Asians less likely to care for elderly parents than in Western cultures. For example, a survey in China found that half of adult children saw their parents only once a year or less (Kim et al., 2015).

Familism works down the generations, not just up. Many elders believe the older generations should help the younger ones. Specifics vary by culture. When the government provides more help for the aged (housing, pensions, and so on), the generations are *more* involved with each other, not less (Herlofson & Hagestad, 2012). The reason is that emotional support flows most easily when basic care is less crucial.

As you also remember, older adults do not want to move in with younger generations, doing so only if poverty and frailty require it. Especially in the United States, every generation values independence. That is why, after midlife and especially after the death of their own parents, elders are *less* likely to agree that children should provide substantial care for their parents and more likely to strive to be helpful to their children.

Complications and surprises regarding parent–child relationships appear in many nations. One example comes from Moldova, a new nation that was once part of the former Soviet Union. Many of the middle generation migrated, leaving aged parents behind. However, most of those adult children continue to write, call, and subsidize their parents, and the elder generation is healthier if their children left than if they stayed (Böhme et al., 2015).

Although elderly people's relationships with members of younger generations are usually positive, they can also include tension and conflict. In some families intergenerational respect and harmony abound; whereas in others, family members refuse to see each other. Each culture and each family has patterns and expectations regarding interactions between generations (Herlofson & Hagestad, 2011).

A good relationship with successful grown children enhances a parent's well-being, especially when both generations do whatever the other generation expects. By contrast, a poor relationship makes life worse for everyone. Ironically, conflict may be more frequent in emotionally close relationships than in distant ones (Silverstein et al., 2010), especially when either generation becomes dependent on the other (Birditt et al., 2009).

Some conflict is common, as is some mutual respect. Indeed, both within families and within cultures, *ambivalence* is becoming recognized as a common intergenerational pattern (Connidis, 2015), with mixed feelings in every generation.

Extensive research finds many factors that affect intergenerational relationships:

- Assistance arises from both need and ability to provide.
- Frequency of contact is more dependent on geographical proximity than affection.
- Love is influenced by childhood memories.
- Sons feel stronger obligation; daughters feel stronger affection.
- National norms and policies can nudge family support, but they do not create it.

GRANDPARENTS AND GREAT-GRANDPARENTS Eighty-five percent of U.S. elders currently older than 65 are grandparents. (The rate was lower in previous cohorts because the birth rate fell during the 1930s, and it is expected to be lower again.) Almost all grandparents provide some caregiving and gifts, unless the middle generation does not allow it. In most nations (less so in Asia), grandparents are more involved with their daughters' children than their sons'.

As with parents and children, specifics of the grandparent–grandchild relationship depend partly on personality and partly on the age of both generations. The oldest grandparents tend to be less actively involved in day-to-day activities. Grandparents typically delight in the youngest children, provide material support for the school-age children, and offer advice, encouragement, and a role model for the older grandchildren. One of my college students realized this when she wrote:

> Brian and Brianna are twins and are turning 13 years old this coming June. Over the spring break my family celebrated my grandmother's 80th birthday and I overheard the twins' talking about how important it was for them to still have grandma around because she was the only one who would give them money if they really wanted something their mom wasn't able to give them. . . . I lashed out . . . how lucky we were to have her around and that they were two selfish little brats. . . . Now that I am older, I learned to appreciate her for what she really is. She's the rock of the family and "the bank" is the least important of her attributes now.
>
> *[Giovanna, personal communication]*

Grandparents fill one of four roles:

1. *Remote grandparents* (sometimes called *distant grandparents*) are emotionally distant from their grandchildren. They are esteemed elders who are honored, respected, and obeyed, expecting to get help whenever they need it.

2. *Companionate grandparents* (sometimes called *"fun-loving" grandparents*) entertain and "spoil" their grandchildren—especially in ways that the parents would not.

3. *Involved grandparents* are active in the day-to-day lives of their grandchildren. They live near them and see them often.

4. *Surrogate parents* raise their grandchildren, usually because the parents are unable or unwilling to do so.

Currently, in developed nations, most grandparents are companionate, partly because all three generations expect them to be companions, not authorities. Contemporary elders usually enjoy their own independence. They provide babysitting and financial help but not advice or discipline (May et al., 2012).

As you remember from Chapter 13, in *skipped generation* families, grandparent health and happiness are sometimes sacrificed when the grandparent takes on the stresses and responsibilities of the parent role. Usually such grandparents are relatively young, far more often age 50 than 70. Often full parental responsibility ages them quickly.

A middle ground is best. Just as too much responsibility impairs health and happiness, too little may be harmful as well. One Australian study focused on grandparents whose children prevented contact with the grandchildren.

For example, one reported this conversation with her daughter:

> She said: "You've never been a good mother, only when I was little". I said: "now that is ridiculous and you know that is ridiculous". She said: "you be quiet and listen to what I have to say, what I have to tell you now. . . I never want to see or hear from you the rest of your life" . . . I said: "I have fought hard. I have provided for both of your children. I've done all that I can to help you and [son-in-law]."
>
> *[Sims & Rofail, 2014, p. 3]*

Same Situation, Far Apart: Happy Grandfathers No matter where they are, grandparents and grandchildren often enjoy each other partly because conflict is less likely, as grandparents are usually more relaxed about child-rearing. Indeed, Sam Levinson quipped, "The reason grandparents and grandchild get along so well is that they have a common enemy."

Another grandmother in the same study first was thrilled with her grandchildren and then despondent when she could no longer see them.

> It was so enjoyable and now to think about it brings me to tears . . . this breaks our hearts , , , the consequence of this is that I have had issues of anxiety and depression, none of which I had previously and now I have been diagnosed with a severe heart problem, cardiomyopathy . . . this is more than I can bear—it breaks my heart to think of them.
>
> *[Sims & Rofail, 2014, pp. 4–5]*

Sometimes past parent–child relationships provoke the middle generation to cut off grandparent–grandchild interaction. However, developmental research finds:

1. Adults change over time, even in late adulthood. A grandparent can become less, or more, strict, following parental rules that differ from past practices. As with every human relationship, mutual compromise and explicit communication is essential.

2. Relationships with the younger generation promote the emotional and physical well-being of the older generation. Not only heart problems, high blood pressure, and sleepless nights, but even life itself is affected by social interaction (Paúl, 2014).

One of the realities of human development that appears in study after study is that family connections are pivotal for optimal growth, from pregnancy (when relatives help keep the expectant mother healthy and drug-free) to the end of life (when family members provide essential comfort). That is no less true in late adulthood, as the elderly benefit in many ways from connections to younger generations.

In **Video: Grandparenting,** several individuals discuss their close, positive attachments to their grandchildren.

Same Situation, Far Apart: Partners Whether at the Vietnam Veterans Memorial in Washington, D.C. *(left)* or in the Philippines *(right)*, elderly people support each other in joy and sorrow. These women are dancing together, and these men are tracing the name of one of their buddies who died 40 years earlier.

Los Amigos Some cultures seem to encourage male friendships. These men in Santa Fe de Antioquia, Colombia, are not afraid to show their closeness in the public square.

Friendship

Friendship networks typically are reduced with each decade. Emerging adults tend to have the most friends on average. By late adulthood, the number of people considered friends is notably smaller (Wrzus et al., 2013). Added to this normal shrinkage are two circumstances: Some older friends die, and retirees usually lose contact with work friends.

Family friends tend to be the most loyal. Elders are healthiest if some family friends are among their closest social circle. Yet if the circle includes only relatives, and not several non-family friends, that correlates with worse health (Shiovitz-Ezra & Litwin, 2015). Having at least some family friends is less problematic than it will be in later generations, because the current cohort of elders is the most married, and the most childbearing, in U.S. history, a dramatic contrast to the younger generations.

As explained in Chapters 11 and 13, each younger cohort is more often unmarried. In the United States, the never-married are 5 percent of those aged 65 to 74, 8 percent of those 55 to 64, and 12 percent of those 45 to 54. Rates continue to increase as age falls. The same is true for siblings, as family size decreased throughout the twentieth century.

Further, more middle-aged adults, married or not, have no children, and those with children often have no grandchildren. Accordingly, this next generation of the elderly will have fewer family members. Will they be lonely, lacking social support?

Not necessarily. Recent data find that elders who never married are usually quite content, not lonely. Some of them have partners, of the same sex or other sex, and are cohabiting or living apart together, seemingly just as happy as traditionally married people (Brown & Kawamura, 2010). Further, having a smaller friendship circle is not a problem if a person has at least a few close friends—as most of the aged do (Wrzus et al., 2013).

People who have spent years without a romantic partner usually have close friendships, meaningful activities, and social connections that keep them busy and happy. The crucial factor is having friends—some of whom may also be relatives, but not necessarily (Blieszner, 2014). Grown children who urge their distant parents to move closer to them may make a mistake if they do not appreciate the social networks—including consequential strangers as well as close friends—that surround most older people.

WHAT HAVE YOU LEARNED?

1. What is the usual relationship between older adults who have been partners for decades?
2. Who benefits most from relationships between older adults and their grown children?
3. Which type of grandparenting seems to benefit both generations the most?
4. Why do older people tend to have fewer friends as they age?
5. Why are people who have never married not likely to be lonely and sick?
6. How do demographic changes affect family relationships?

The Frail Elderly

Now that we have dispelled stereotypes by describing most aging adults as active, enjoying supportive friends and family, we can turn to the **frail elderly**—those who are infirm, inactive, seriously disabled, or cognitively impaired. Frailty is not defined by any single disease, no matter how serious, but by an overall loss of energy and strength. It is systemic, often accompanied by weight loss and exhaustion.

frail elderly
Older adults who are severely impaired, usually unable to care for themselves.

The frail are not the majority. Typically, older people are happy and active for decades, but eventually about one-third will become frail before they die. Note that weight loss is one of the signs: At most ages, overweight is far more problematic than underweight, but if an older adult loses weight, that might signify a problem.

Activities of Daily Life

One way to measure frailty, according to insurance standards and medical professionals, is by assessing a person's ability to perform the tasks of self-care. Gerontologists often assess five physical **activities of daily life (ADLs):** eating, bathing, toileting, dressing, and moving (transferring) from a bed to a chair. Some scales to measure ADLs include personal hygiene (combing hair and brushing teeth) and some measure more extensive mobility (walking a certain number of feet).

activities of daily life (ADLs)
Typically identified as five tasks of self-care: eating, bathing, toileting, dressing, and transferring from a bed to a chair. The inability to perform any of these tasks is a sign of frailty.

Equally important may be the **instrumental activities of daily life (IADLs),** which require intellectual competence and forethought. Indeed, difficulty with IADLs often precedes problems with ADLs since planning and problem solving help frail elders maintain self-care.

instrumental activities of daily life (IADLs)
Actions (for example, paying bills and driving a car) that are important to independent living and that require some intellectual competence and forethought.

The five ADL's are fairly standard: People everywhere who cannot do them need help. However, that does not mean they are dependent forever; ADLs are dynamic: Most of the elderly who have difficulty with one of more ADL are able to recover (Ciol et al., 2014).

Recovery is especially likely if someone teaches them how to, for instance, put on shoes without bending down, or get out of bed without risking a fall. Physical therapists may be crucial here, not only in explaining ways to accomplish self-care, and in recommending specialized equipment, but also in teaching exercises that might, for instance, increase the range of motion of the arms so that hair brushing is easier.

IADLs vary from culture to culture, although again targeted help may be beneficial. In developed nations, IADLs may include understanding the labels on

TABLE 15.1	Instrumental Activities of Daily Life
Domain	**Exemplar Task**
Managing medical care	Keeping current on checkups, including teeth and eyes
	Assessing supplements as good, worthless, or harmful
Food preparation	Evaluating nutritional information on food labels
	Preparing and storing food to eliminate spoilage
Transportation	Comparing costs of car, taxi, bus, and train
	Determining quick and safe walking routes
Communication	Knowing when, whether, and how to use landline, cell, texting, mail, e-mail
	Programming speed dial for friends, emergencies
Maintaining household	Following instructions for operating an appliance
	Keeping safety devices (fire extinguishers, carbon monoxide alarms) active
Managing one's finances	Budgeting future expenses (housing, utilities, etc.)
	Completing timely income tax returns
	Avoiding costly scams, unread magazines

medicine bottles, improving nutrition of the daily diet, filing income tax, using modern appliances, making and keeping doctor appointments (see Table 15.1). Even within developed nations, professionals vary in their lists of IADLs (Chan et al., 2012).

In rural areas of developing nations, feeding the chickens, cultivating the garden, mending clothes, getting water from the well, and making dinner might be IADLs. As with ADLs, some assistance might be needed, but taking over the task ("you can't do it, you're too old") may precipitate frailty.

Caregiving may be a crucial IADL. Some caregiving requires quite advanced competence, such as caring for a toddler. Some does not, as in caring for a pet or a plant. For many of the elderly, caregiving maintains dignity as well and cognition—although remember that too much caregiving may precipitate illness, not health.

Whose Responsibility?

There are marked cultural differences in care for the frail elderly. Many African and Asian cultures hold sons responsible for the care of their parents. Some men and their wives take elders into their homes, providing meals, medical care, and conversation.

However, as already mentioned, this is increasingly difficult in modern times in every nation. The governments of China and India have mandated that children care for their parents, a mandate that itself suggests that many parents need care they are not getting.

The problem is that demographics have changed, which impacts filial responsibility. Some people still romanticize elder care, believing that frail older adults should live with their caregiving children. That assumption worked when the demographic pyramid meant that each surviving elder had many descendants, but it may overburden beanpole families.

Some middle-aged couples have a dozen living ancestors. If they are in a nation with excellent health care, high rates of marriage, few divorces, and high rates of childbearing, they may have four elderly parents and eight grandparents, whose care is shared by several siblings. That number is lower if some of those dozen die before age 85, but it may be higher if some of the older generation divorced and remarried, adding a stepparent to the mix, or if a childless aunt or uncle is still alive. Sometimes the couple has no siblings, and then the filial responsibility is theirs alone.

Fortunately, as already mentioned, most elderly people care for themselves. However, typically, at least one of the oldest generation of an average couple is frail and alone, and others need help with money management, or throwing away old food, or the like. If a middle-aged couple has one or more elders living with them, that can create tension for their marriage, or their teenagers—who seek independence, not sharing a home and spending time with a frail grandparent.

Preventing Frailty

The ideal is to prevent frailty and to compress morbidity, as described in Chapter 14. Some elders are healthy and self-sufficient one day and dead the next, but that is increasingly rare. Instead, almost every older person has some chronic conditions that can get worse, causing frailty, but that can be treated, resulting in additional years of capable self-care.

Prevention of frailty depends on everyone considering that disability is dynamic, not static, with self-sufficiency extended if individuals, families, and the larger community all do their part. We focus on two examples: first, an older person whose leg muscles are weakening, and second, medical intervention that focuses on symptoms, not overall health.

Better or Worse? It depends. The advantage of having a mobile wheelchair is that a person can stay engaged in life, even, as shown here, on the streets of Beijing. The disadvantage is the riding may replace walking—but that is up to the person. This man might be on his way to strength-training at the gym, and if he gets there safely and regularly, his electric wheelchair can add years to his life.

MOBILITY Muscles weaken with age, a condition called *sarcopenia*. In fact, muscle mass at age 90 is only half of what it was at age 30, with much of that loss occurring in late adulthood (McLean & Kiel, 2015).

Bones and balance weaken as well. Thus, elderly people are more likely to fall than younger people are, and they are more likely to break a bone when doing so.

As already mentioned, osteoporosis (weak bones) is a common problem, and broken bones—particularly the hip—cause immobility, morbidity, and death. All three—the elder, the family, and the community—could prevent or at least postpone frailty by improving mobility.

A VIEW FROM SCIENCE

Leave the Bedroom

Medical intervention has remedied much of one cause of frailty (osteoporosis) in that prescription drugs and vitamin D strengthen bones. In addition, for many people hip or knee replacement restores mobility (Jenkins et al., 2013). Both require surgery, pain, and rehabilitation exercises, and require an active choice. Unfortunately, sarcopenia and immobility may be accepted, not remediated. Fear of falling may increase the risk.

For some elders, aging in place might mean staying in a home with steep stairs and a kitchen and bathroom far

from the bedroom. Then an overly solicitous caregiver might bring meals, put a portable toilet in their room, and buy a remote control for their large bedroom TV. The community may contribute to the fear of going outside, if sidewalks are lacking and if the TV news highlights violent crime. Note that everyone contributes to frailty in this example.

To prevent frailty, the individual, the family, and the community could change. The person could exercise daily, walking with family members on pathways built to be safe and pleasant. A physical therapist—paid by the individual, the family, or the government—could individualize the exercise and select appropriate equipment (a walker? a cane? special shoes?). The house could be redesigned, or the elder could move to a place where walking is safe and encouraged.

Extensive research has found again and again that lack of exercise leads to lower quality of life, increasing both ADLs and IADLs. On the other hand, exercise improves life and health in the elderly who live in the community (Motl & McAuley, 2010) as well as those already frail in nursing homes (Weening-Dijksterhuis et al., 2011).

For instance, one study randomly assigned nursing-home residents to one of three groups: usual care, cognitive-behavioral intervention designed to increase exercise and reduce fear of falling, and the same cognitive-behavioral therapy plus a physical therapist to prescribe specific exercise. The latter group benefited most, not only in activity and muscle strength but in emotional outlook (Huang et al., 2015).

In general, both attitude change and exercise carefully tailored to the individual is beneficial. However, translating that research into action—the steps of habit change outlined in Chapter 12—remains the problem, and loss of ADLs and IADLs is the result.

Mental Capacity

Problems with IADLs may be worse than problems with ADLs. Here again, the family and community may be crucial.

The social support networks that prevent physical decline also prevent mental decline (Boss et al., 2015). With many types of failing physical and mental health, delay, moderation, and sometimes prevention are possible. Often older individuals, and the people who love them, need to put in place all the safeguards and develop all the habits that will prevent frailty.

A CASE TO STUDY

Family Encouraging Confusion

Consider this case, noting what the family did and did not do.

[A] 70-year-old Hispanic man came to his family doctor for evaluation following a visit to his family in Colombia, where he had appeared to be disoriented (he said he believed he was in the United States and he did not recognize places that were known to be familiar to him) and he was very agitated, especially at night. An interview with the patient and a family member revealed a history that had progressed over the past six years, at least, of gradually worsening cognitive deficit, which the family had interpreted as part of normal aging. Recently, his symptoms had included difficulty operating simple appliances, misplacement of items, and difficulty finding words, with the latter attributed to his having learned English in his late 20s . . . [His] family had been very protective and increasingly had compensated for his cognitive problems.

. . . . He had a lapse of more than five years without proper control of his medical problems [hypertension and diabetes] because of difficulty gaining access to medical care. . . .

Based on the medical history, a cognitive exam . . . and a medical evaluation in which magnetic resonance imaging of the brain . . . the diagnosis of moderate Alzheimer's disease was made. Treatment with ChEI [cholinesterase inhibitors] was started . . . His family noted that his apathy improved and that he was feeling more connected with the environment.

[*Griffith & Lopez, 2009, p. 39*]

Both the community (those five years without treatment for hypertension and diabetes) and the family (making excuses, protecting him) contributed to major neurocognitive disorder that could have been delayed, if not prevented altogether.

Often with IADLs, the elderly person him- or herself needs to understand and prevent problems. In this case, the elderly man did not take care of his health. His trip to Colombia was the worst thing he could have done because disorientation increases in an unfamiliar place. Of course, family members helped him arrange the trip: Why did no one realize how destructive such an excursion could be?

Caring for the Frail Elderly

Prevention is best, but not always sufficient. Some problems, such as major neurocognitive disorder or severe heart failure, can be postponed or slowed, but not eliminated. Caregivers themselves are usually elderly, and they often have poor health, limited strength, and impaired immune systems (Lovell & Wetherell, 2011). Thus an aging parent who cares for the other parent is especially likely to need help.

Caregiving is especially difficult when a person has failing IADLs, because they do not realize what help they need. If people have trouble with an ADL, they know that they cannot walk, for instance. But if a person has trouble with an IADL, they might insist that they can submit tax forms perfectly well and may become angry if the IRS fines them.

After listing the problems and frustrations of caring for someone who is mentally incapacitated but physically strong, the authors of one overview note:

> The effects of these stressors on family caregivers can be catastrophic. Family caregiving has been associated with increased levels of depression and anxiety as well as higher use of psychoactive medications, poorer self-reported physical health, compromised immune function, and increased mortality.
>
> [Gitlin et al., 2003, pp. 361–362]

Not What You Think This photo is a stereotype check: What do you think is happening here? In fact, the hairdresser is a volunteer, the place is a nursing home, and the country is Haiti. Do any of these surprise you?

Remember variability, however. Some caregivers feel they are repaying past caregiving, and sometimes every other family member or friend, including the care receiver, expresses appreciation. That relieves resentment and makes caregiving easier (I-F. Lin et al., 2012). In fact, a longitudinal study found that when caregivers feel supported by their family, with practical help as well as emotional encouragement, stress diminishes as time goes on, even as the frail person's needs increase (Roth et al., 2005).

The designated caregiver of a frail elderly person is chosen less for logical reasons (e.g., the relative with the most patience, time, and skill) than for cultural ones. Currently in the United States, the usual caregiver is the spouse (the wife twice as often as the husband), who often has no prior experience caring for a frail elder.

Grown children may assume that another sibling has fewer responsibilities, or lives closest, and thus should be the caregiver. As you might imagine, resentment is common, particularly in daughters with more education (I-F. Lin et al., 2012). They often have significant work and child-care concerns, and they bristle if their brothers assume they must become caregivers of their elderly parents.

Not only do family assumptions vary; nations, cultures, and ethnic groups vary as well. In northern European nations, most elder care is provided through a social safety net of senior day-care centers, senior homes, and skilled nurses; in African cultures, families are fully responsible for the aged.

In some cultures, an older person who is dying is taken to a hospital; in others, such intervention is seen as interference with the natural order. In the United States, African Americans who enter nursing homes are more likely than European Americans to suffer from major intellectual deficits, perhaps because elderly African Americans with merely physical frailties (ADLs not IADLs) are more often cared for at home. Only when care becomes emotionally crushing are alternatives to home care considered.

Even in ideal circumstances, family members disagree about appropriate nutrition, medical help, and dependence of an older relative. One family member may insist that an elderly person never enter a nursing home, and that insistence may create family conflict.

Public agencies rarely intervene unless a crisis arises. This troubles developmentalists, who study "change over time." From a life-span perspective, caregiver exhaustion and elder abuse are predictable and preventable.

NICOLE BENGIVENO/THE NEW YORK TIMES/REDUX

Sweet but Sad Family support is evident here, as an older sister (Lillian, age 75) escorts the younger sister (Julia, age 71) to the doctor. Unseen is how family support wrecked their lives: The sisters lost their life savings and their childhood home because their nephew was addicted to crack.

integrated care
Cooperative actions by professionals, friends, family members, and the care receiver to achieve optimal caregiving.

If elders need extensive care, ideally skilled people provide it, teaching family members to help. But many elders are terrified of nursing homes and suspicious of strangers; many informal caregivers do not ask for help, and instead experience depression, poor health, and isolation—true in many cultures (Yıkılkan et al., 2014).

The ideal is **integrated care,** in which professionals and family members cooperate to provide good individualized care, whether at a long-term care facility or at someone's home (Lopez-Hartmann et al., 2012). Just as a physical therapist knows specific exercises and movements to improve mobility, a case manager can evaluate an impaired elder and develop a comprehensive plan. Some tasks are best done by a relative, some by the frail person themselves, some by a medical professional.

Integrated care does not erase the burden of caregiving, but it helps. In one study, a year after a professional helped plan and coordinate care, family caregivers improved in their overall attitude and quality of life. Although the total time spent on caregiving was not reduced by integrated care, the tasks performed changed, with more time on household tasks (e.g., meal preparation and cleanup) and less on direct care (Janse et al., 2014). Emotional support—a sympathetic listener—may be the best use of a relative's time.

The idea that a frail person is cared for either exclusively by family or exclusively in a nursing home is not only wrong, it is destructive of health and well-being. Family members want and need to be involved, whether care occurs at home or in an institution. Isolation—either at home or in a nursing home—makes poor care more likely.

ELDER ABUSE When caregiving results in resentment and social isolation, the risk of depression, sickness, and abuse (of either the frail person or the caregiver) escalates (G. Smith et al., 2011; Johannesen & LoGiudice, 2013). Abuse is likely if:

- the *caregiver* suffers from emotional problems or substance abuse
- the *care receiver* is frail, confused, and demanding
- the *care location* is isolated, where visitors are few

Ironically, although relatives are less prepared to cope with difficult patients than professionals are, they often provide round-the-clock care with little outside help or supervision. Ideally, other family members provide respite care, but instead they may avoid visiting.

Often professionals begin their care too late. Most doctors treat a patient in a medical crisis (a fall, heart attack, and so on) but not before. Legal authorities intervene only after repeated and blatant abuse. Preventive care could have forestalled both kinds of problems.

As a result, some caregivers overmedicate, lock doors, and use physical restraints, all of which may be abusive. That may lead to inadequate feeding, medical neglect, or rough treatment. Obvious abuse is less likely in nursing homes and hospitals, not only because laws forbid it but also because workers are not alone, nor expected to work 24/7.

Of course, adequate staffing and supervision are essential in such places as well: Abuse can occur anywhere. One kind of abuse is particularly likely in nursing homes when staff supervision is inadequate, specifically abuse by other residents. Typically the abuser is a man with a history of aggression who is suffering from major neuro-cognitive disorder; obviously such men need to be prevented from harming others (Ferrah et al., 2015).

Extensive public and personal safety nets are needed. Most social workers and medical professionals are suspicious if an elder is unexpectedly quiet, or losing weight, or injured. They are currently "mandated reporters," which means they must alert the authorities if they believe abuse is occurring.

Not all elder abuse is physical. It may instead be financial, yet bankers, lawyers, and investment advisors are not trained to recognize it or obligated to respond and notify anyone (Jackson & Hafemeister, 2011).

A major problem is awareness: Professionals and relatives alike hesitate to spot and then question a family caregiver who spends the Social Security check, disrespects the elder, or does not comply with the elder's demands. At what point is this abuse? Typically, abuse begins gradually and continues for years, unnoticed. Political and legal definitions and remedies are not clear-cut (Dong & Simon, 2011).

The U.S. incidence of elder abuse is estimated at less than 3 percent of the population over age 65 (Bond & Butler, 2013). That percentage seems small, but remember that the vast majority of older people are vital and independent, not vulnerable to abuse. Those 3 percent (about a million individuals per year) are almost always the most vulnerable and impaired.

Accurate incidence data and intervention are complicated by definitions: If an elder feels abused but a caregiver disagrees, who is right? Abused elders are often depressed, ill, and suffering from neurocognitive disorders. Does that prove abuse or absolve abusers (Dong et al., 2011)?

Sometimes caregivers become victims, attacked by a confused elderly person. As with other forms of abuse, the dependency of the victim makes prosecution difficult, especially when secrecy, suspicion, and family pride keep outsiders away. Social isolation makes abuse possible; fear of professionals makes it worse.

LONG-TERM CARE The trend in the United States and elsewhere is away from nursing homes and toward aging in place. Currently, residents of nursing homes tend to be very old—at least age 80—with significant cognitive decline. They also are disproportionately women (because men are usually married and predecease their wives), with few descendants who could provide care.

Fortunately, outright abuse in such institutions is rare. Laws forbid the use of physical restraints except temporarily in specific, extraordinary circumstances. Some nursing homes provide individualized, humane care, allowing residents to decide what to eat, where to walk, whether to have a pet. In the United States, nursing homes are frequently visited by government inspectors to "stop dreadful things from happening" (Baker, 2007).

In North America, good nursing-home care is available for those who can afford it and know what to look for. Some nonprofit homes are run by religious organizations, and these may be excellent. In some European nations, the federal government subsidizes care for anyone (rich or poor) who needs it.

Good care allows independence, individual choice, and privacy. As with day care for young children, continuity of care is crucial: An institution with a high rate of staff turnover is to be avoided. At every age, establishing relationships with other people is crucial: If the residents feel that their caregivers are the same year after year, that improves well-being.

The training and the workload of the staff, especially of the aides who provide frequent, personal care, are crucial: Such simple tasks as helping a frail person out of bed can be done clumsily, painfully, or skillfully. Skill, experience, and patience are all critical, and all are possible with a sufficient number of well-trained and well-paid

Same Situation, Far Apart: Diversity Continues No matter where they live, elders thrive with individualized care and social interaction, as is apparent here. Lenore Walker *(left)* celebrates her 100th birthday in a Florida nursing home with her younger sister nearby, and an elderly chess player in a senior residence in Kosovo *(right)* contemplates protecting his king. Both photos show, in details such as the women's earrings and the men's head coverings, that these elders maintain their individuality.

staff. Currently, however, most front-line workers have little training, low pay, and many patients—and almost half leave each year (Golant, 2011).

Many nursing homes now have dedicated areas and accommodation for people with Alzheimer's disease or other neurocognitive disorders. Among the special characteristics are *memory boxes*, in addition to names on the doors of the rooms. A memory box is open to view and displays photographs and other mementos so that the person knows which room is his or hers.

Many people with major neurocognitive disorder do not understand why they need care and often resist it. Nursing homes may treat such resistance with psychoactive drugs (Kleijer et al., 2014), but other tactics may be better at reducing anxiety (Konno et al., 2014). For instance, music, friendly dogs, and favorite foods can be appreciated by someone whose memory is so impaired that reading and conversing are impossible.

Quality care is much more labor-intensive and expensive than most people realize. Variations are dramatic, primarily because of the cost of personnel. According to John Hancock Life & Health Insurance Company in 2015, the cost of a year in a private room at a nursing home is $200,750 in Alaska and $56,575 in Louisiana. (Most people think that Medicare, Medicaid, or long-term insurance covers the entire cost—an expensive misconception.)

In the United States, the trend over the past 20 years has been toward a lower proportion of those over age 60 residing in nursing homes, and those few are usually over 80 years old, frail and confused, with several medical problems (Moore et al., 2012).

Another trend is toward smaller nursing homes with more individualized care, where nurses and aides work closely together. Some homes are called Eden Alternative or Green, named after exemplars that stress individual autonomy (Sharkey et al., 2011).

Although more than 90 percent of elders are independent and live in the community at any given moment, many of them will someday need nursing-home care. Stays are often for less than a month after a few days in a hospital. However, some need such care for more than a year, and a very few—the oldest and least capable—stay for 10 years or more.

ALTERNATIVE CARE An ageist stereotype is that older people are either completely capable of self-care or completely dependent on others. In actuality, everyone is on a continuum, with some self-care and yet needing some help.

Once that is understood, a range of options can be envisioned. Remember the study cited in Chapter 14 that found that major neurocognitive disorder is less

Many Possibilities This couple in Wyoming *(left)* sold their Georgia house and now live in this RV, and this Cuban woman *(right)* continues to live in her familiar home. Ideally, all the elderly have a range of choices—and when that is true, almost no one needs nursing-home care.

common in England than it used to be? That study also found that the percentage of people with neurocognitive disorders in nursing homes has risen, from 56 percent in 1991 to 65 percent in 2011, primarily because of a rise in the number of oldest-old women in such places (Matthews et al., 2013).

This means that more British elderly who need help with ADLs are now in the community. This is good news for the elderly, for developmentalists, and for the community, because aging in place, assisted living, and other options are less costly and more individualized than institutions.

The number of assisted-living facilities has increased as nursing homes have decreased. Typically, assisted-living residences provide private apartments for each person and allow pets and furnishings as in a traditional home.

The "assisted" aspects vary, often one daily communal meal, special transportation and activities, household cleaning, and medical assistance, such as supervision of pill taking and monitoring of blood pressure or diabetes. Usually, a nurse, doctor, and ambulance are available if needed. In the United States, many of these assistances involve additional expenses.

Assisted-living facilities range from group homes for three or four elderly people to large apartment or townhouse developments for hundreds (Golant, 2011). Almost every state, province, or nation has its own standards for assisted-living facilities, but many such places are unlicensed. Some regions of the world (e.g., northern Europe) have many assisted-living options, while others (e.g., sub-Saharan Africa) have almost none.

Another form of elder care is sometimes called *village care.* Although not really a village, it is so named because of the African proverb, "It takes a whole village to raise a child." In village care, elderly people who live near each other pool their resources, staying in their homes but also getting special assistance when they need it. Village care communities require that the elderly contribute financially and that they be relatively competent, so village care is not suited for everyone. However, for some it is ideal (Scharlach et al., 2012).

Overall, as with many other aspects of aging, the emphasis in living arrangements is on selective optimization with compensation. Elders need settings that allow them to be safe, social, respected, and as independent as possible. Housing solutions vary depending not only on ADLs and IADLs but also the elder's personality and social network of family and friends. One expert explains: "There is no one-size-fits-all set of optimum residential activities, experiences, and situations" (Golant, 2011).

We close with an example of family care and nursing-home care at their best. A young adult named Rob related that his 98-year-old great-grandmother "began to fail. We . . . thought, well, maybe she is growing old" (quoted in Adler, 1995, p. 242). All three younger generations decided that she should move to a nearby nursing home, leaving the place she had lived for decades. She reluctantly agreed.

Fortunately, this nursing home did not assume that decline is always a sign of "final failing" (Rob's phrase). The doctors discovered that her pacemaker was not working properly. Rob tells what happened next:

> We were very concerned to have her undergo surgery at her age, but we finally agreed. . . . Soon she was back to being herself, a strong, spirited, energetic, independent woman. It was the pacemaker that was wearing out, not Great-grandmother.
>
> *[quoted in Adler, 1995, p. 242]*

This story contains a lesson repeated throughout this book. Whenever a toddler does not talk, a preschooler grabs a toy, a teenager gets drunk, an emerging adult takes risks, an adult seeks divorce, or an older person becomes frail, it is easy to conclude that this is normal. Indeed, each of these possible problems is common at the ages mentioned and may be appropriate and acceptable for some individuals.

But none should simply be accepted without question. Each should also alert others to encourage talking, sharing, moderation, caution, communication, or self-care. The life-span perspective holds that, at every age, people can be "strong, spirited, and energetic."

WHAT HAVE YOU LEARNED?

1. What factors make an older person frail?
2. What are the basic differences between ADLs and IADLs?
3. Why might IADLs be more important than ADLs in deciding how much care a person needs?
4. What are the signs of frailty?
5. What can be done to increase mobility in the aged?
6. How is cognitive decline related to prevention of frailty?
7. What three factors increase the likelihood of elder abuse?
8. What are the advantages and disadvantages of assisted living for the elderly?
9. When is a nursing home a good solution for the problems of the frail elderly?
10. What factors distinguish a good nursing home from a bad one?

SUMMARY

Theories of Late Adulthood

1. Self theories hold that adults make personal choices in ways that allow them to become fully themselves. One such theory arises from Erikson's last stage, integrity versus despair, in which individuals seek integrity that connects them to the human community.

2. The positivity effect and a tendency toward self-actualization also can be seen as part of the drive to become more oneself.

3. Compulsive hoarding can be understood as an effort to hold onto the self, keeping objects from the past that others might consider worthless.

4. Stratification theories maintain that social forces—such as ageism, racism, and sexism—limit personal choices throughout the life span, keeping people on a particular level or stratum of society.

5. Age stratification can be blamed for the disengagement of older adults. Activity theory counters disengagement theory, stressing that older people need to be active.

6. Because of earlier discrimination and past experiences—in health, education, and employment—people who are from low-income backgrounds, especially if they are from minority ethnic groups, have a more difficult old age. This does not seem to be true if they reach very old age, 90 and older.

Activities in Late Adulthood

7. At every age, employment can provide social and personal satisfaction as well as needed income. However, retirement may be welcomed by the elderly, if they remain active in other ways.

8. Some elderly people perform volunteer work and are active politically—writing letters, voting, staying informed. These activities enhance health and well-being and benefit the larger society.

9. Common among retirees are an increase in religious activity (but not church attendance) and a wish to age in place. Many of the elderly engage in home improvement or redecoration, preferring to stay in their own homes and attend their local house of worship.

Friends and Relatives

10. A romantic partner is the most important member of a person's social convoy. Older adults in long-standing marriages tend to be satisfied with their relationships and to safeguard each other's health. As a result, married elders tend to live longer, happier, and healthier lives than unmarried ones.

11. Elders who have never married tend to have many friends. Everyone needs someone who is a close confidant.

12. Relationships with adult children and grandchildren are usually mutually supportive, although conflicts arise as well. Financially, elders more often support the younger generations than vice versa.

13. Most of the elderly prefer to maintain their independence, living alone, but some become surrogate parents, raising their grandchildren. This adds stress to the older generation, who typically are more depressed and in worse health than others their age.

The Frail Elderly

14. Most elderly people are self-sufficient, but some eventually become frail. They need help with their activities of daily life, either with physical tasks (such as eating and bathing) or with instrumental ones (such as completing income taxes and comparing transportation options).

15. Care of the frail elderly is usually undertaken by adult children or spouses, who are often elderly themselves. Most families have a strong sense of filial responsibility, although elder abuse may occur when stress is great and social support is lacking.

16. Nursing homes, assisted living, and professional home care are of varying quality and availability. Each of these arrangements can provide necessary and beneficial care, but they do not always do so. Good care for the frail elderly involves a combination of professional and family support, recognizing diversity in needs and personality.

KEY TERMS

self theories (p. 540)

integrity versus despair (p. 541)

compulsive hoarding (p. 542)

socio-emotional selectivity theory (p. 542)

positivity effect (p. 543)

stratification theories (p. 544)

disengagement theory (p. 547)

activity theory (p. 547)

age in place (p. 552)

naturally occurring retirement community (NORC) (p. 552)

filial responsibility (p. 557)

frail elderly (p. 561)

activities of daily life (ADLs) (p. 561)

instrumental activities of daily life (IADLs) (p. 561)

integrated care (p. 566)

APPLICATIONS

1. Attitudes about disabilities are influential. Visit the disability office on your campus, asking both staff and students what they see as the effects of attitude on performance. How do your findings relate to the elderly?

2. People of different ages, cultures, and experiences vary in their values regarding family caregiving, including the need for safety, privacy, independence, and professional help. Find four people whose backgrounds (age, ethnicity, SES) differ. Ask their opinions, and analyze the results.

3. Visit a nursing home or assisted-living residence in your community. Record details about the physical setting, the social interactions of the residents, and the activities of the staff. Would you like to work or live in this place? Why or why not?

CHAPTER OUTLINE

Death and Dying

WHAT WILL YOU KNOW?

■ How can death be a source of hope, not despair?

■ What is the difference between a good death and a bad one?

■ How does mourning help with grief?

A nearby hospital (St. Vincent's) closed two years ago, the victim of budget cuts. Six other hospitals have been shuttered recently in New York City for the same reason. St. Vincent's closure struck my local community hard—emotions are still hot. At a rally at the hospital site, the editor of a local newspaper slapped our state senator, who responded with surprise and compassion.

Why did that slap happen? The editor said that his wife died a few days earlier in a Bronx hospital, and if St. Vincent's were still open, "I could have walked two blocks and spent time with her through the last hours of her life" (Taylor, 2013, p. A16). Of course, that is no excuse for violence, but mourners want to blame someone—a hospital, a senator, a doctor, the dying person. Men tend to get rageful, women depressed (Corr & Corr, 2013a). People say, "It didn't have to happen," even though they know that death, whether two blocks or a long subway ride away, is part of life.

That editor is not the only irrational one. When Joan Didion's husband died, she experienced a "year of magical thinking," including keeping his shoes in the closet because he would need them if he came back (Didion, 2005). Mourners are not always logical.

This chapter acknowledges those emotions and helps us understand dying, death, grief, and bereavement. We can expect powerful feelings to surface; hopefully they can be directed toward help for the living. Tears, yes; slaps, no. There is *hope* in death, *choices* in dying, and *affirmation* in mourning, as the three sections of this chapter describe. ■

Death and Hope

A multi-cultural life-span perspective reveals that reactions to death are filtered through many cultural prisms, affected by historical changes and regional variations as well as by the age of both the dying and the bereaved.

One emotion is constant, however: hope. It appears in many ways: hope for life after death, hope that the world is better because someone lived, hope that death occurred for a reason, hope that survivors rededicate themselves to whatever they deem meaningful in life.

TABLE EP.1	How Death Has Changed in the Past 100 Years

Death occurs later. A century ago, the average life span worldwide was less than 40 years (47 in the rapidly industrializing United States). Half of the world's babies died before age 5. Now newborns are expected to live to age 71 (79 in the United States); in many nations, centenarians are the fastest-growing age group.

Dying takes longer. In the early 1900s, death was usually fast and unstoppable; once the brain, the heart, or any other vital organ failed, the rest of the body quickly followed. Now death can often be postponed through medical technology: Hearts can beat for years after the brain stops functioning, respirators can replace lungs, and dialysis does the work of failing kidneys.

Death often occurs in hospitals. For most of our ancestors, death occurred at home, with family nearby. Now most deaths occur in hospitals or other institutions, with the dying surrounded by medical personnel and machines.

The causes of death have changed. People of all ages once usually died of infectious diseases (tuberculosis, typhoid, smallpox), or, for many women and most infants, in childbirth. Now disease deaths before age 50 are rare, and in developed nations most newborns (99 percent) and their mothers (99.99 percent) live.

And after death . . . People once knew about life after death. Some believed in heaven and hell; others, in reincarnation; others, in the spirit world. Prayers were repeated—some on behalf of the souls of the deceased, some for remembrance, some to the dead asking for protection. Believers were certain that their prayers were heard. People now are aware of cultural and religious diversity; many raise doubts that never occurred to their ancestors.

Cultures, Epochs, and Death

Few people in developed nations have witnessed someone die. This was not always the case (see Table EP.1). If someone reached age 50 in 1900 in the United States and had had 20 high school classmates, at least six of those fellow students would have already died. The survivors would have visited and reassured friends who were dying at home, promising to see them in heaven. Almost everyone believed in life after death.

Now few die before old age, and if a young person dies, most often it occurs too quickly to say goodbye. Ironically, death has become more feared as dying has become less familiar (Carr, 2012). Accordingly, we begin by describing traditional responses when familiarity with death was common.

ANCIENT TIMES Paleontologists believe that 100,000 years ago the Neanderthals buried their dead with tools, bowls, or jewelry, signifying belief in an afterlife (Hayden, 2012). The date is controversial: Burial could have begun 200,000 years ago or more recently—but it is certain that long ago death was an occasion for hope, mourning, and remembrance. Two Western civilizations with written records—Egypt and Greece—had elaborate death rituals.

The ancient Egyptians built magnificent pyramids, refined mummification, and scripted instructions (called the *Book of the Dead*) to aid the soul (*ka*), personality (*ba*), and shadow (*akh*) in reuniting after death so that the dead could bless and protect the living (Taylor, 2010).

The fate of dead Egyptians depended partly on their actions while alive, partly on the circumstances of death, and partly on proper burial. Death was a reason to live morally and to honor the past. If the dead were not appropriately cared for, the living would suffer.

Another set of beliefs comes from the Greeks. Again, continuity between life and death was evident, with hope for this world and the next. The fate of a dead person depended on past deeds. A few would have a blissful afterlife, a few

Conversation Who is talking here? Unless you are an Egyptologist, you would not guess that this depicts a dead man conversing with the gods of the Underworld. Note that the deceased is relatively young, and does not seem afraid—both typical for people in ancient Egypt.

were condemned to torture in Hades, and most would enter a shadow world until they were reincarnated.

Three themes are apparent in all the known ancient societies, not only in Greece and Egypt but also in the Mayan, Chinese, Indian, and African cultures.

- Actions during life were thought to affect destiny after death.
- An afterlife was more than a hope; it was assumed.
- Mourners said particular prayers and made specific offerings, in part to prevent the spirit of the dead from haunting and hurting them.

CONTEMPORARY RELIGIONS Now consider contemporary religions. Each faith seems distinct in its practices surrounding death. One review states, "Rituals in the world's religions, especially those for the major tragic and significant events of bereavement and death, have a bewildering diversity" (Idler, 2006, p. 285).

Some details illustrate this diversity. According to one expert, in Hinduism the casket is always open, in Islam, never (Gilbert, 2013). In many Muslim and Hindu cultures the dead person is bathed by the next of kin; among some Native Americans (e.g., the Navajo) no family member touches the dead person.

Specific rituals vary as much by region as by religion. In North America, Christians of all sects often follow local traditions. Similarly, each of 500 Native American tribes has its own heritage: It is a mistake to assume all have the same customs (Cacciatore, 2009).

According to many branches of Hinduism, a person should die on the floor, surrounded by family, who neither eat nor wash until the funeral pyre is extinguished. By contrast, among some (but not all) Christians, the very sick should be taken to the hospital; if they die, then mourners gather to eat and drink, often with music and dancing.

Diversity is also evident in Buddhism. The First Noble Truth of Buddhism is that life is suffering. Some rituals help believers accept death and detach from grieving in order to decrease the suffering that living without the deceased person entails. Other rituals help people connect to the dead as part of the continuity between life and death (Cuevas & Stone, 2011). Thus, some Buddhists leave the dying alone; other Buddhists hover nearby.

Religious practices change with historical conditions. One example comes from Korea. Koreans traditionally opposed autopsies because the body is a sacred gift. However, Koreans value science education. This created a dilemma, because medical schools need bodies to autopsy in order to teach. The solution was to start a new custom: a special religious service honoring the dead who have given their body for medical education (J-T. Park et al., 2011). The result: a dramatic increase in the number of bodies donated for research.

Autopsies create problems in the United States as well. Autopsies may be legally required and yet considered religious sacrilege. For instance, for the Hmong in Southeast Asia, any mutilation of the dead body has "horrifying meanings" and "dire consequences for . . . the spiritual well-being of surviving family and community" (Rosenblatt, 2013, p. 125). In Minnesota, however, where many Hmong now live, the

COLIN MCCONNELL/TORONTO STAR VIA GETTY IMAGES

Dance for the Dead This woman dances on Dia de los Muertos, wearing a traditional skull headdress. People in many Latin American communities remember death and celebrate life on November 1 (All Saints Day) and November 2 (All Souls Day) each year.

OBSERVATION QUIZ
Is this in Mexico?
(see answer, page 576) ▲

family does not need to be told about, much less give permission for, an autopsy if the coroner has "any question about the cause of death."

Ideas about death are expressed differently in various cultures. Many people believe that the spirits of ancestors visit the living, but how and when that happens varies by culture. Spirits are particularly likely to appear during the Hungry Ghost Festival (in many East Asian nations), on the Day of the Dead (in many Latin American nations), or on All Souls Day (in many European nations). People from none of those traditions sometimes believe that their dead family member came to them in a dream.

Consequently, do not get distracted by death customs or beliefs that may seem odd to you, such as mummies, hungry ghosts, reincarnation, or hell. Instead, notice that death has always inspired strong emotions, often benevolent ones. It is the *denial* of death that leads to despair (Wong & Tomer, 2011). In all faiths and cultures, death is considered a passage, not an endpoint, a reason for families and strangers to come together.

Understanding Death Throughout the Life Span

Thoughts about death—as about everything else—are influenced by each person's cognitive maturation and past experiences. Here are some of the specifics.

DEATH IN CHILDHOOD   Some adults think children are oblivious to death; others believe children should participate in funerals and other rituals, just as adults do (Talwar et al., 2011). You know from your study of childhood cognition that neither view is completely correct.

Very young children have some understanding of death, but their perspective differs from that of older people. They may not understand that the dead cannot come to life again. For that reason, a child might not immediately be sad when someone dies. Later, moments of profound sorrow might occur when reality sinks in, or simply when the child realizes that a dead parent will never again tuck them into bed at night.

Children are affected by the attitudes of others. If a child encounters death, adults should listen with full attention, neither ignoring the child's concerns nor expecting adultlike reactions (Doering, 2010). Because the limbic system matures more rapidly than the prefrontal cortex, children may seem happy one day and morbidly depressed the next.

Young children who themselves are fatally ill typically fear that death means being abandoned (Wolchik et al., 2008). Consequently, parents should stay with a dying child, holding, reading, singing, and sleeping. A frequent and caring presence is more important than logic. By school age, many children seek independence. Parents and professionals can be too solicitous; older children do not want to be babied. Often they want facts and a role in "management of illness and treatment decisions" (Varga & Paletti, 2013, p. 27).

Children who lose a friend, a relative, or a pet might, or might not, seem sad, lonely, or angry. For example, one 7-year-old boy seemed unfazed by the loss of three grandparents and an uncle within two years. However, he was extremely upset when his dog, Twick, died. That boy's parents, each grieving for a dead mother, were taken aback by the depth of his emotions. The boy was angry that he was not taken to the animal hospital before the dog was euthanized, and he refused to go back to school, saying, "I had wanted to see him one more time. . . . You don't understand" (quoted in Kaufman & Kaufman, 2006, pp. 65–66).

Because the loss of a particular companion is a young child's concern, it is not helpful to say that a dog can be replaced. Even a 1-year-old knows that a new puppy is not the same dog. Nor should a child be told that Grandma is sleeping, that God wanted

Sorrow All Around When a 5-day-old baby died in Santa Rosa, Guatemala, the entire neighborhood mourned. Symbols and a procession help with grief: The coffin is white to indicate that the infant was without sin and will therefore be in heaven.

JOHAN ORDÓÑEZ/AFP/GETTY IMAGES

his sister in heaven, or that Grandpa went on a trip. The child may take such explanations literally, wanting to wake up Grandma, complain to God, or phone Grandpa to say "come home."

If a child realizes that adults are afraid to say that death has occurred, the child might decide that death is so horrible that adults cannot talk about it—a terrifying conclusion (Doering, 2010). Even worse is the idea that adults lie to children.

Remember how cognition changes with development. Egocentric preschoolers (discussed in Chapter 5) might fear that they, personally, caused death with their unkind words.

As children become concrete operational thinkers (Chapter 7), they seek facts, such as exactly how a person died and where he or she is now. They want something to do: bring flowers, repeat a prayer, write a letter. The boy whose dog died went back to school after his parents framed and hung a poem he wrote to Twick. Children see no contradiction between biological death and spiritual afterlife, as long as adults neither lie nor disregard the child's concerns (Talwar et al., 2011).

DEATH IN ADOLESCENCE AND EMERGING ADULTHOOD As you learned in Chapter 9, adolescents may be self-absorbed, philosophical, analytic, or distraught—or all four at different moments. Counselors emphasize that adults must listen to teenagers. Self-expression is part of the search for identity; death of a loved one does not stop that search. Some adolescents use the Internet to write to the dead person or to vent their grief—an effective way to express their personal identity concerns (DeGroot, 2012).

"Live fast, die young, and leave a good-looking corpse" is advice often attributed to actor James Dean, who died in a car crash at age 24. At what stage would a person be most likely to agree? Emerging adulthood, of course. Worldwide, older teenagers and emerging adults control their anxiety about death by taking risks (de Bruin et al., 2007; Luxmoore, 2012).

Terror management theory explains some illogical responses to death, including why young people take death-defying risks (Mosher & Danoff-Burg, 2007). By surviving, they manage their terror by proving that death cannot get them. Especially when people aged 15 to 24 have access to guns and cars, this developmental tendency can be deadly (see Figure EP.1). Cluster suicides, foolish dares, fatal gang fights, and drug-impaired driving are more common during those years than later. Three attitudes typical of older adolescents are correlated: ageism, terror management, and risk taking (Popham et al., 2011).

Many studies have found that messages about the deadly consequences of smoking may provoke smokers to *increase* their consumption (Arndt et al., 2013). One study found that college students who were told that binge drinking is sometimes fatal were more willing to binge, not less so (Jessop & Wade, 2008). Thus, teenagers and young adults may protect their pride and self-esteem by defying death and resisting the advice of adults.

Other research in many nations finds that when adolescents and emerging adults think about death, they sometimes become more patriotic and religious but less tolerant of other worldviews and less generous to people of other nations (Ellis & Wahab, 2013; Jonas et al., 2013). Apparently, as people try to manage the terror of death, they try to convince themselves that loyal, conscientious members of their own group (including themselves) are especially worthy of living (Pyszczynski et al., 2015).

terror management theory
The idea that people adopt cultural values and moral principles in order to cope with their fear of death. This system of beliefs protects individuals from anxiety about their mortality and bolsters their self-esteem.

FIGURE EP.1 Typhoid Versus Driving into a Tree In 1905, most young adults in the United States who died were victims of diseases, usually infectious ones like tuberculosis and typhoid. In 2012, four times more died violently (accidents, homicide, suicide) than died of all the diseases combined.

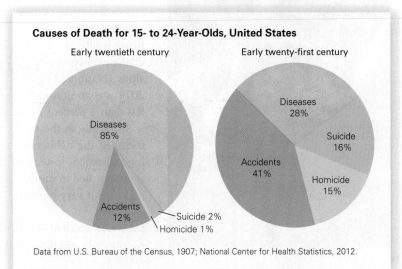

Causes of Death for 15- to 24-Year-Olds, United States

Early twentieth century

Diseases 85%
Accidents 12%
Suicide 2%
Homicide 1%

Early twenty-first century

Diseases 28%
Suicide 16%
Homicide 15%
Accidents 41%

Data from U.S. Bureau of the Census, 1907; National Center for Health Statistics, 2012.

DEATH IN ADULTHOOD When adults become responsible for work and family, attitudes shift. Death is not romanticized. Many adults quit addictive drugs, start wearing seat belts, and adopt other death-avoiding behaviors when they become parents. One of my students eagerly anticipated the thrill of her first skydive, paying in advance. However, the day before the scheduled dive she learned she was pregnant. She forfeited the money and shopped for prenatal vitamins.

To defend against the fear of aging and untimely death, adults do not readily accept the death of others. For instance, when the inspired poet Dylan Thomas was about age 30, he wrote to his dying father: "Do not go gentle into that good night/ Rage, rage against the dying of the light" (Thomas, 2003, p. 239). Nor do adults readily accept their own death. A woman diagnosed at age 42 with a rare and almost always fatal cancer (a sarcoma) wrote:

> I hate stories about people dying of cancer, no matter how graceful, noble, or beautiful. . . . I refuse to accept I am dying; I prefer denial, anger, even desperation.
>
> *[Robson, 2010, pp. 19, 27]*

When adults hear about another's death, their reaction depends on the dead person's age. Death in the prime of life, especially when caused by the person's own actions, is particularly disturbing. Michael Jackson, Whitney Houston, and Robin Williams were mourned by millions, in part because they were not yet old (50, 48, and 63, respectively). Older entertainers who die of natural causes at age 70 or later are less mourned.

Reactions to one's own mortality differ depending on developmental stage as well. In adulthood, from ages 25 to 65, terminally ill people worry about leaving something undone or abandoning family members, especially children.

One dying middle-aged adult was Randy Pausch, a 47-year-old professor and father of three. Ten months before he died of cancer in 2008, he delivered a famous last lecture, detailing his childhood dreams and saluting those who would continue his work. After advising his students to follow their own dreams, he concluded, "This talk is not for you, it's for my kids" (Pausch, 2007). Not surprisingly, that message was embraced by his wife, also in mid-adulthood, who wrote her own book, titled *Dream New Dreams,* which deals with overcoming death by focusing on life (J. Pausch, 2012).

Adult attitudes about death are often irrational. Logically, adults should work to change social factors that increase the risk of mortality—such as air pollution, junk foods, and legal drugs, each of which contributes to millions of deaths in the United States each year. Instead, many people react more strongly to the very rare events that cause death, such as anthrax and avalanches. People particularly fear deaths that seem random.

For example, people fear traveling by plane more than by car, because passengers know they personally have no control over the flight. In fact, flying is safer: In 2013, only 265 people in the entire world died in airplane crashes, compared to 32,719 killed by motor vehicles in the United States alone (National Highway Traffic and Safety Administration, 2014). The year 2014 was an unusually high one for airplane fatalities (1,320), but that was less than 1 percent of the deaths worldwide from cars and trucks.

Ironically, in the weeks after September 11, 2001, when a terrorist attack included the deliberate crash of four planes, many North Americans drove long distances instead of flying. In the next few months, 2,300 more U.S. residents died in motor-vehicle crashes than usual (Blalock et al., 2009). Not logical, but very human.

DEATH IN LATE ADULTHOOD In late adulthood, attitudes shift again. Anxiety decreases; hope rises (De Raedt et al., 2013). Life-threatening illnesses reduce

"For My Kids" Randy Pausch was a brilliant, innovative scientist at Carnegie Mellon University. When he was diagnosed with terminal pancreatic cancer, he gave a talk titled "The Last Lecture: Really Achieving Your Childhood Dreams" that became famous worldwide. He devoted the final 10 months of his life to his family—his wife Jai and their children Chloë, Dylan, and Logan.

life satisfaction more among the middle-aged than the elderly, who often seem untroubled by the prospect of dying (Wurm et al., 2008). Terror-management irrationality diminishes (Maxfield et al., 2007) (see Figure EP.2).

Some older people are quite happy even when they are fatally ill. Indeed, many developmentalists believe that one sign of mental health among older adults is acceptance of mortality, which often increases their concern for others. Some elders engage in *legacy work,* trying to leave something meaningful for later generations (Lattanzi-Licht, 2013).

As evidence of this attitude change, older people seek to reconcile with estranged family members and tie up loose ends that most young adults leave hanging (Kastenbaum, 2012). Some younger adults are troubled if their parents or grandparents allocate heirlooms, discuss end-of-life wishes, or buy a burial plot, but all of those actions are developmentally appropriate.

Acceptance of death does not mean that the elderly give up on living; rather, their priorities shift. In an intriguing series of studies (Carstensen, 2011), people were presented with the following scenario:

> Imagine that in carrying out the activities of everyday life, you find that you have half an hour of free time, with no pressing commitments. You have decided that you'd like to spend this time with another person. Assuming that the following three persons are available to you, with whom would you want to spend that time?
> * A member of your immediate family
> * The author of a book you have just read
> * An acquaintance with whom you seem to have much in common
>
> *[adapted from Carstensen, 2011, p. 113]*

Older adults, more than younger ones, choose the family member. The researchers explain that family becomes more important when death seems near.

This is supported by a study of 329 people of various ages who had recently been diagnosed with cancer and a matched group of 170 people (of the same ages) who had no serious illness (Pinquart & Silbereisen, 2006). The most marked difference was between those with and without cancer, regardless of age (see Figure EP.3). Attitudes change when death becomes more likely.

Near-Death Experiences

Even coming close to death may be an occasion for hope. This is most obvious in what is called a *near-death experience,* in which a person almost dies. Survivors sometimes report having left the body and moving toward a bright light while feeling peace and joy. The following classic report is typical:

> I was in a coma for approximately a week. . . . I felt as though I were lifted right up, just as though I didn't have a physical body at all. A brilliant white light appeared. . . . The most wonderful feelings came over me—feelings of peace, tranquility, a vanishing of all worries.
>
> *[quoted in Moody, 1975, p. 56]*

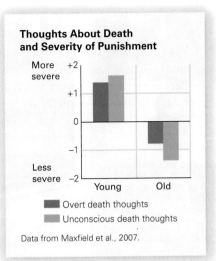

Thoughts About Death and Severity of Punishment

Overt death thoughts
Unconscious death thoughts

Data from Maxfield et al., 2007.

FIGURE EP.2 A Toothache Worse Than Death? A cohort of young adults (average age 21) and old adults (average age 74) were divided into three groups. One group wrote about their death (giving them overt thoughts about dying), another did a puzzle with some words about death (giving them unconscious thoughts about death), and the third wrote about dental pain (they were the control group). Then they all judged how harshly people should be punished for various moral transgressions. Those who wrote about dental pain are represented by the zero point on this graph. Compared with them, older adults were less punitive, but younger adults were more so.

OBSERVATION QUIZ

Which seems more powerful, conscious or unconscious thoughts about death? (see answer, page 582) ▲

FIGURE EP.3 Turning to Family as Death Approaches Both young and old people diagnosed with cancer (one-fourth of whom died within five years) more often preferred to spend a free half-hour with a family member rather than with an interesting person whom they did not know well.

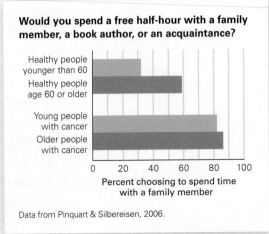

Would you spend a free half-hour with a family member, a book author, or an acquaintance?

Healthy people younger than 60
Healthy people age 60 or older
Young people with cancer
Older people with cancer

Percent choosing to spend time with a family member

Data from Pinquart & Silbereisen, 2006.

Praise Famous Men The funerals of two men, Chris Kelly *(left)*, half of the Kriss Kross rap duo, and Paul Celluci *(right)*, former governor of Massachusetts, show cultural contrasts and underlying universals.

OBSERVATION QUIZ
What three similarities do you see in these funerals? (see answer, page 582) ▲

Near-death experiences often include religious elements (angels seen, celestial music heard). Survivors often become more spiritual, less materialistic. To some, near-death experiences prove that "Heaven is for real" (Burpo & Vincent, 2011). Most scientists are skeptical, claiming that

> there is no evidence that what happens when a person really dies and "stays dead" has any relationship to the experience reported by those who have recovered from a life-threatening episode. In fact, it is difficult to imagine how there could ever be such evidence.
>
> *[Kastenbaum, 2012]*

Nevertheless, a reviewer of near-death experiences is struck by their similarity to religious beliefs about death. In every culture, "all varieties of the dying experience" move people toward the same realizations: (1) limitations of social status, (2) insignificance of material possessions, and (3) narrowness of self-centeredness (Greyson, 2009).

WHAT HAVE YOU LEARNED?

1. Why are people less familiar with death today than they were 100 years ago? What impact might this have?

2. According to the ancient Egyptians and Greeks, what determined a person's fate after death?

3. What is one example of contrasting rituals about death?

4. What should parents remember when talking with children about death?

5. How does terror management theory explain young people's risk taking?

6. How does parenthood affect people's thoughts about their own death?

7. How do attitudes about death shift in late adulthood?

8. In what ways do people change after a near-death experience?

Choices in Dying

Do you recoil at the heading, "Choices in Dying"? If so, you may be living in the wrong century. Every twenty-first-century death involves choices, beginning with risks taken or avoided, habits sustained, and specific measures to postpone or hasten death.

It might seem that war deaths, or bystander gun deaths, or accidents of many kinds are not chosen. But always, decisions by the society, the family, or the individual make life or death more likely. For instance, 15,000 fewer motor-vehicle deaths occurred in the United States in recent years than in 1980, when such deaths reached the highest level ever. The reduction since then resulted from thousands of choices, by legislators, police, car designers, and drivers.

A Good Death

People everywhere hope for a good death (Vogel, 2011), one that is:

- At the end of a long life
- Peaceful
- Quick
- In familiar surroundings
- With family and friends present
- Without pain, confusion, or discomfort

Many would add that *control over circumstances* and *acceptance of the outcome* are also characteristics of a good death, but on this cultures and individuals differ. Some dying individuals willingly cede control to doctors or caregivers, and others fight every sign that death is near. Some cultures praise the dying for non-acceptance.

MODERN MEDICINE In some ways, modern medicine makes a good death more likely. The first item on the list has become the norm: Death usually occurs at the end of a long life.

Younger people still get sick, of course, but surgery, drugs, radiation, and rehabilitation typically mean that, in developed countries, the ill go to the hospital and then return home. If young people die, death is typically quick (before medical intervention could save them) and that makes it a good death for them (if not for their loved ones).

In other ways, however, contemporary medical advances have made a bad death more likely, especially the last items on this list. When a cure is impossible, physical and emotional comfort deteriorate (Kastenbaum, 2012). Instead of acceptance, people submit to surgery and drugs that prolong pain and confusion. Hospitals sometimes exclude visitors from intensive-care units, and patients may become delirious or unconscious, unable to die in peace.

The underlying problem may be medical care itself, which is so focused on life-saving that dying invites "the dangers of well-intentioned over 'medicalization'" (Ashby, 2009, p. 94). Dying involves emotions, values, and a community—not just a heart that might stop beating. As my religious adviser told my brother, who wanted to keep it quiet that he was dying, "Cancer is a family disease." Fortunately, three factors that make a good death more likely have increased: honest conversation, the hospice, and palliative care.

HONEST CONVERSATION In about 1960, researcher Elisabeth Kübler-Ross (1969, 1975) asked the administrator of a large Chicago hospital for permission to speak with dying patients. He told her that no one in the hospital was dying! Eventually, she found a few terminally ill patients who, to everyone's surprise, wanted very much to talk.

Too Late for Her When Brittany Maynard was diagnosed with progressive brain cancer that would render her unable to function before killing her, she moved from her native California to establish residence in Oregon, so she could die with dignity. A year later, the California Senate Health Committee debated a similar law, with Brittany's photo on a desk. They approved the law, 5–2.

Video: End of Life: Interview with Laura Rothenberg
http://qrs.ly/na4sqmv

From ongoing interviews, Kübler-Ross identified emotions experienced by dying people and by their loved ones. She divided these emotions into five sequential stages.

1. Denial ("I am not really dying.")
2. Anger ("I blame my doctors, or my family, or God for my death.")
3. Bargaining ("I will be good from now on if I can live.")
4. Depression ("I don't care about anything; nothing matters anymore.")
5. Acceptance ("I accept my death as part of life.")

Another set of stages of dying is based on Abraham Maslow's hierarchy of needs, first introduced in Chapter 1 (Zalenski & Raspa, 2006).

1. Physiological needs (freedom from pain)
2. Safety (no abandonment)
3. Love and acceptance (from close family and friends)
4. Respect (from caregivers)
5. Self-actualization (appreciating one's unique past and present)

Maslow later suggested a possible sixth stage, *self-transcendence* (Koltko-Rivera, 2006), which emphasizes the acceptance of death.

Other researchers have *not* found these sequential stages. Remember the woman dying of a sarcoma, cited earlier? She said that she would never accept death and that Kübler-Ross should have included desperation as a stage. Kübler-Ross herself later said that her stages have been misunderstood, as "our grief is as individual as our lives. . . . Not everyone goes through all of them or goes in a prescribed order" (Kübler-Ross & Kessler, 2014, p. 7).

Nevertheless, both lists remind caregivers that each dying person has strong emotions and needs that may be unlike that same person's emotions and needs a few days or weeks earlier. Furthermore, those emotions may differ from those of the caregivers, who themselves may have different emotions from each other.

It is vital that everyone—doctors, nurses, family, friends, and the patient—knows that a person is dying; then, appropriate care is more likely (Lundquist et al., 2011). Unfortunately, even if a patient is dying, most doctors never ask about end-of-life care. The result is not longer life but more pain, more procedures, and higher hospital bills. By contrast, patients whose treatment includes discussion of palliative care are happier and live longer (Sher, 2015).

Most dying people want to be with loved ones and to talk honestly with medical and religious professionals. Individual differences continue, of course. Some people do *not* want the whole truth; some want every possible medical intervention to occur; some do *not* want many visitors. In many Asian families, telling people they are dying is thought to destroy hope (Corr & Corr, 2013a).

Better Ways to Die

Several practices have become more prevalent since the contrast between a good death and the traditional hospital death has become clear. The hospice and the palliative care specialty are examples.

hospice
An institution or program in which terminally ill patients receive palliative care to reduce suffering; family and friends of the dying are helped as well.

HOSPICE In 1950s London, Cecily Saunders opened the first modern **hospice,** where terminally ill people could spend their last days in comfort (Saunders, 1978). Thousands of other hospices have opened in many nations, and hundreds of thousands of hospice caregivers now bring medication and care to dying people where they live. In the United States, more than half of all hospice deaths occur at home (NHPCO, 2014).

Hospice professionals relieve discomfort, avoiding measures that merely delay death; their aim is to make dying easier. Comfort can include measures that some hospitals

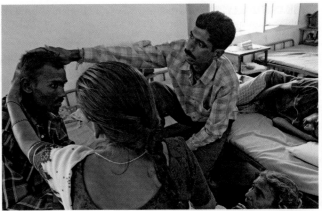

Same Situation, Far Apart: As It Should Be Dying individuals and their families benefit from physical touch and suffer from medical practices (gowns, tubes, isolation) that restrict movement and prevent contact. A good death is likely for these two patients—a husband with his wife in their renovated hotel/hospital room in North Carolina *(left)*, and a man with his family in a Catholic hospice in Andhra Pradesh, India *(right)*.

forbid: acupuncture, special foods, flexible schedules, visitors when the patient wants them (which could be 2 A.M.), massage, aromatic oils, and so on (Doka, 2013).

There are two principles for hospice care:

- Each patient's autonomy and decisions are respected. For example, pain medication is readily available, not on a schedule or minimal dosage. Most hospice patients use less medication than a doctor might prescribe, but they decide when to take it and how much they want.

- Family members and friends are counseled before the death, taught to provide care, and guided in mourning. Their needs are as important as those of the patient. Death is thought to happen to a family, not just to an individual.

In 2013 in the United States, 43 percent of deaths occurred with hospice care, one-third of them within a week after hospice care began (National Center for Health Statistics, 2011). Hospice caregivers wish they had more time to assess and meet the particular medical and emotional needs of the dying person and their loved ones. Dying and mourning are lengthy processes. It is not true that hospice care necessarily means a quick death, although doctors are reluctant to recommend hospice unless they are certain that death is imminent.

Unfortunately, hospice does not reach many dying people (see Table EP.2), even in wealthy nations, much less in developing ones (Kiernan, 2010).

TABLE EP.2	Barriers to Entering Hospice Care

- Hospice patients must be terminally ill, with death anticipated within six months, but predictions are difficult. For example, in one study of noncancer patients, physician predictions were 90 percent accurate for those who died within a week but only 13 percent accurate when death was predicted in three to six weeks (usually the patients died sooner) (Brandt et al., 2006).

- Patients and caregivers must accept death. Traditionally, entering a hospice meant the end of curative treatment (chemotherapy, dialysis, and so on). This is no longer true. Now treatment can continue. Many hospice patients survive for months, and some are discharged alive (Salpeter et al., 2012).

- Hospice care is costly. Skilled workers—doctors, nurses, psychologists, social workers, clergy, music therapists, and so on—provide individualized care day and night.

- Availability varies. Hospice care is more common in England than in mainland Europe and is a luxury in poor nations. In the United States, western states have more hospices than midwestern states do. Even in one region (northern California) and among clients of one insurance company (Kaiser), the likelihood that people with terminal cancer will enter hospice depends on exactly where they live (Keating et al., 2006).

THINK CRITICALLY: What are the possible reasons that fewer people in hospice are from non-European backgrounds?

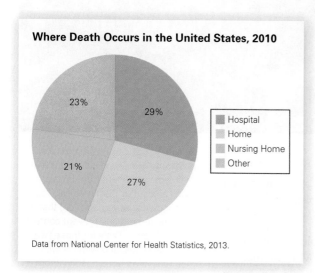

Where Death Occurs in the United States, 2010

- 29% Hospital
- 27% Home
- 21% Nursing Home
- 23% Other

Data from National Center for Health Statistics, 2013.

FIGURE EP.4 Not with Family Almost everyone prefers to die at home, yet most people die in an institution, surrounded by medical personnel and high-tech equipment, not by the soft voices and gentle touch of loved ones. The "other" category is even worse, as it includes most lethal accidents or homicides. But improvement is evident. Twenty years ago the proportion of home deaths was notably lower.

palliative care
Medical treatment designed primarily to provide physical and emotional comfort to the dying patient and guidance to his or her loved ones.

double effect
When an action (such as administering opiates) has two effects, such as relieving pain and suppressing respiration.

THINK CRITICALLY: At what point, if ever, should intervention stop in order to allow death?

There are ethnic differences as well. In the United States, only 6 percent of hospice patients are Latino (NHPCO, 2014). Compared to European Americans, African Americans are more often admitted to hospice from a hospital than from a home and are likely to die relatively quickly (one week, on average), whereas the average hospice death occurs two weeks after admission (K. S. Johnson et al., 2011). The reason is thought to be cultural, not economic, since Medicare now pays most hospice expenses.

Nationally, about 15 percent of hospice patients are discharged alive. Sometimes their health has improved. However, the hospices with the highest "live discharge" rates tend to be recently founded, private, profit-making institutions: Their hospice admissions and discharges may occur for financial, not medical, reasons (Teno et al., 2014). (Originally, hospices were all nonprofit.)

Home hospice care requires family or friends trained by hospice workers to provide care. Although this has led to an increase of "good deaths" at home, not everyone has available caregivers. Most deaths still occur in hospitals, and many others occur in nursing homes (see Figure EP.4).

PALLIATIVE CARE In 2006, the American Medical Association approved a new specialty, **palliative care,** which focuses on relieving pain and suffering, in hospitals, homes, or hospice. Palliative doctors are trained to discuss options with patients and their families. Some interventions (especially surgery) may be refused if people understand the risks and benefits (Mynatt & Mowery, 2013). Palliative doctors also prescribe powerful drugs and procedures that make patients comfortable.

Morphine and other opiates have a **double effect:** They relieve pain (a positive effect), but they also slow down respiration (a negative effect). Painkillers that reduce both pain and breathing are allowed by law, ethics, and medical practice.

In England, for instance, although it is illegal to cause death, even of a terminally ill patient who repeatedly asks to die, it is legal to prescribe drugs that have a double effect. One-third of all English deaths include such drugs. This itself raises the issue of whether some narcotics are used to hasten death more than to relieve pain (Billings, 2011).

Heavy sedation is another method sometimes used to alleviate pain. Concerns have been raised that this may merely delay death rather than prolong meaningful life, since the patient becomes unconscious, unable to think or feel (Raus et al., 2011).

Ethical Issues

As you see, the success of medicine has created new dilemmas. Death is no longer the natural outcome of age and disease; when and how death occurs involves human choices.

DECIDING WHEN DEATH OCCURS No longer does death necessarily occur when a vital organ stops. Breathing continues with respirators; stopped hearts are restarted; stomach tubes provide calories; drugs fight pneumonia.

Almost every life-threatening condition results in treatments started, stopped, or avoided, with death postponed, prevented, or welcomed. This has fostered impassioned arguments about ethics, both between nations (evidenced by radically different laws) and within them.

Religious advisers, doctors, and lawyers disagree with colleagues within their respective professions. Family members disagree with one another. Members of every group disagree with members of their own group and the other groups (Ball, 2012; Engelhardt, 2012; Nelson-Becker et al., 2015).

One physician, a specialist in palliative care, advised his colleagues:

> The highway of aggressive medical treatment runs fast, is heavily travelled, but can lack landmarks and the signage necessary to know when it is time to make for the exit ramp . . . These signs are there and it is your responsibility to communicate them to patients and families.
>
> *[Fins, 2006, p. 73]*

Good advice, hard to follow.

EVIDENCE OF DEATH Historically, death was determined by listening to a person's chest: No heartbeat meant death. To make sure, a feather was put to the person's nose to indicate respiration—a person who had no heartbeat and did not exhale was pronounced dead. Very rarely, but widely publicized when it happened, death was declared but the person was still alive.

Modern medicine has changed that: Hearts and lungs need not function on their own. Many life-support measures and medical interventions circumvent the diseases and organ failures that once caused death. Checking breathing with feathers is a curiosity that, thankfully, is never used today.

But how do we know when death has happened? In the late 1970s, a group of Harvard physicians concluded that death occurred when brain waves ceased, a definition now used worldwide (Wijdicks et al., 2010). However, many doctors believe that death can occur even if primitive brain waves continue (Kellehear, 2008; Truog, 2007) (see Table EP.3).

It is critical to know when people are in a permanent vegetative state (and thus will never regain the ability to think) and when they are merely in a coma but might recover. One crucial factor is whether the person could ever again breathe without a respirator, but that is hard to guarantee if "ever again" includes 10 or 20 years hence.

In 2008, the American Academy of Neurology gathered experts to conduct a meta-analysis of recent studies regarding end-of-life brain functioning. They found 38 empirical articles. Two experts independently read each one, noting measures used to determine death and how much time elapsed between lack of sentient brain function and pronouncement of death. They found no consensus. Only two indicators were confirmed: Dead people no longer breathe spontaneously, and their eyes no longer respond to stimuli.

TABLE EP.3	Dead or Not? Yes, No, and Maybe

Brain death: Prolonged cessation of all brain activity with complete absence of voluntary movements; no spontaneous breathing; no response to pain, noise, and other stimuli. Brain waves have ceased; the electroencephalogram is flat; *the person is dead.*

Locked-in syndrome: The person cannot move, except for the eyes, but normal brain waves are still apparent; *the person is not dead.*

Coma: A state of deep unconsciousness from which the person cannot be aroused. Some people awaken spontaneously from a coma; others enter a vegetative state; *the person is not yet dead.*

Vegetative state: A state of deep unconsciousness in which all cognitive functions are absent, although eyes may open, sounds may be emitted, and breathing may continue; *the person is not yet dead.* The vegetative state can be *transient, persistent,* or *permanent.* No one has ever recovered after two years; most who recover (about 15 percent) improve within three weeks (Preston & Kelly, 2006). After sufficient time has elapsed, the person may, effectively, be dead, although exactly how many days that requires has not yet been determined (Wijdicks et al., 2010).

As this article points out, everyone needs to know when a person is brain-dead, but there is not yet a definitive, instant test because there are "severe limitations in the current evidence base" (Wijdicks et al., 2010, p. 1914). Thus, family members may spend months hoping for life long after medical experts believe no recovery is possible.

Consequently, a person who wanted to donate organs after death is unable to do so because so much time elapsed between death and donation that the organs are no longer usable. A survey of many nations found that there is no international agreement as to brain death, nor does that seem possible in the near future (Wahlster et al., 2015).

EUTHANASIA Euthanasia, sometimes called mercy killing, is common for pets but rare for people. Many people see a major distinction between active and passive euthanasia, although the final result is the same. In **passive euthanasia,** a person near death is allowed to die. They may have a **DNR (do not resuscitate) order,** instructing medical staff not to restore breathing or restart the heart if breathing or pulsating stops.

Passive euthanasia is legal everywhere if the dying person chooses it, but many emergency personnel start artificial respiration and stimulate hearts without asking whether a patient has a DNR. That makes passive euthanasia impossible.

Active euthanasia is deliberately doing something to cause death, such as turning off a respirator or giving a lethal drug. Some physicians condone active euthanasia when three conditions occur: (1) suffering cannot be relieved, (2) incurable illness, and (3) a patient who wants to die. Active euthanasia is legal in the Netherlands, Belgium, Luxembourg, and Switzerland, and illegal (but rarely prosecuted) elsewhere.

Attitudes may be changing. For example, over the past decade in Austria, doctors in training have increasingly valued patients' autonomy, which has led to more acceptance of active euthanasia (Stronegger et al., 2013) (see Figure EP.5). In every nation surveyed, some physicians would never perform active euthanasia and others have done so. Opinions from the public vary as well, although generally nations in eastern Europe are less accepting than those in western Europe (J. Cohen et al., 2013).

THE DOCTOR'S ROLE Between passive and active euthanasia is another option: A doctor may provide the means for patients to end their own lives, typically by prescribing lethal medication. This is called **physician-assisted suicide.**

---

passive euthanasia
When a person is allowed to die naturally, instead of intervening with active attempts to prolong life.

DNR (do not resuscitate) order
A written order from a physician (sometimes initiated by a patient's advance directive or by a health care proxy's request) that no attempt should be made to revive a patient if he or she suffers cardiac or respiratory arrest.

active euthanasia
When someone does something that hastens another person's death, hoping to end that person's suffering.

physician-assisted suicide
A form of active euthanasia in which a doctor provides the means for someone to end his or her own life, usually by prescribing lethal drugs.

FIGURE EP.5 Mercy or Sin?
Most Austrians of every age think euthanasia is sometimes merciful. But almost a third disagree, and some of those think God agrees with them. If those opposite opinions are held by children of a dying parent, who should prevail?

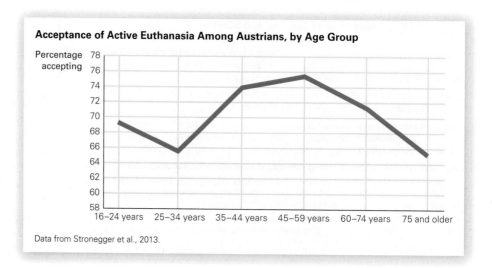

Acceptance of Active Euthanasia Among Austrians, by Age Group

Data from Stronegger et al., 2013.

Physician-assisted suicide poses many controversial ethical issues. Even the name is in dispute: The laws in Oregon, Washington, Vermont, and California assert that such deaths should be called "death with dignity," not suicide. No matter what the name, acceptance varies markedly by culture. Reasons have less to do with people's personal experience than with religion, education, and local values (Verbakel & Jaspers, 2010).

For example, some cultures believe that suicide may be noble, as when Buddhist monks publicly burned themselves to death to advocate Tibetan independence from China, or when people choose to die for the honor of their nation or themselves. However, in the United States, physicians of Asian heritage are *less* likely to condone physician-assisted suicide than are non-Asian physicians (Wolenberg et al., 2013; Curlin et al., 2008).

This reluctance of Asian doctors to speed up death helps explain a practice in Thailand: When it becomes apparent that a hospitalized patient will soon die, an ambulance takes that person back home, where death occurs naturally. Then the person and the family can benefit from a better understanding of life, suffering, and death (Stonington, 2012).

PAIN: PHYSICAL AND PSYCHOLOGICAL The Netherlands has permitted active euthanasia and physician-assisted suicide since 1980 and extended the law in 2002. The patient must be aware, the request must be clearly expressed, and the goal must be to halt "unbearable suffering" (Buiting et al., 2009). Consequently, Dutch physicians first try to make the suffering bearable via better medication.

However, a qualitative analysis found that "fatigue, pain, decline, negative feelings, loss of self, fear of future suffering, dependency, loss of autonomy, being worn out, being a burden, loneliness, loss of all that makes life worth living, hopelessness, pointlessness and being tired of living were constituent elements of unbearable suffering" (Dees et al., 2011, p. 727). Obviously, medication cannot alleviate all that.

Oregon voters approved physician-assisted "death with dignity" (but not other forms of active euthanasia) in 1994 and again in 1997. The first such legal deaths occurred in 1998. The law requires the following:

- The dying person must be an Oregon resident and over age 17.

- The dying person must request the lethal drugs twice orally and once in writing.

- Fifteen days must elapse between the first request and the prescription.

- Two physicians must confirm that the person is terminally ill, has less than six months to live, and is competent (i.e., not mentally impaired or depressed).

The law also requires record-keeping and annual reporting. About one-third of the requests are granted, and about one-third of those who are approved die naturally, never using the drugs. Between 1998 and 2012, about 200,000 people in Oregon died. Only 738 of them died after taking the prescribed lethal drugs.

As Table EP.4 shows, Oregon residents requested the drugs primarily for psychological, not biological, reasons—they were more concerned

Liberté or Death? In many nations, most people approve death with dignity but most legislators do not. This woman's sign says that 94 percent of her fellow citizens approve legalizing euthanasia.

OBSERVATION QUIZ

Where did this rally take place? (see answer, page 589) ▲

TABLE EP.4	Oregon Residents' Reasons for Requesting Physician Assistance in Dying, 1998–2012
Percent of Patients Giving Reason (most had several reasons)	
Loss of autonomy	91.2
Less able to enjoy life	88.8
Loss of dignity	82.0
Loss of control over body	51.6
Burden on others	38.6
Pain	23.5
Financial implications of treatment	2.7

Data from Oregon Public Health Division, 2013.

THINK CRITICALLY: Why would someone take all the steps to obtain a lethal prescription and then not use it?

about their autonomy than their pain. In 2012, some 115 Oregonians obtained lethal prescriptions, and 77 legally used drugs to die. Most of the rest died naturally, but some were alive in January 2013 and expected to use the drug in the future (about 10 percent use their prescriptions the year after obtaining them) (Oregon Public Health Division, 2013).

OPPOSING PERSPECTIVES

The "Right to Die"?

Many people fear that legalizing euthanasia or physician-assisted suicide creates a **slippery slope,** that hastening death for the dying who request it will cause a slide toward killing people who are *not* ready to die—especially those who are disabled, old, poor, or of minority ethnicity. The data refute that concern.

In Oregon and the Netherlands, people from non-white groups are *less* likely to use fatal prescriptions. In fact, in Oregon almost all of those who have done so were European American (97 percent), had health insurance, and were well educated (81 percent had some college). There is no evidence of ageism: Most had lived a long life (average age is 71) (see Figure EP.6). Almost all (97 percent) died at home, with close friends or family nearby.

slippery slope
The argument that a given action will start a chain of events that will culminate in an undesirable outcome.

All these statistics refute both the slippery-slope and the social-abuse arguments because the ones who actually die with physician assistance are not likely to slide anywhere they do not wish to go, nor are they likely to be pushed to die. Nonetheless, even those who believe that people should decide their own medical care do not themselves choose death when they are fatally ill. African Americans are particularly mistrustful of hospices, euthanasia, and physician-assisted suicide (Wicher & Meeker, 2012).

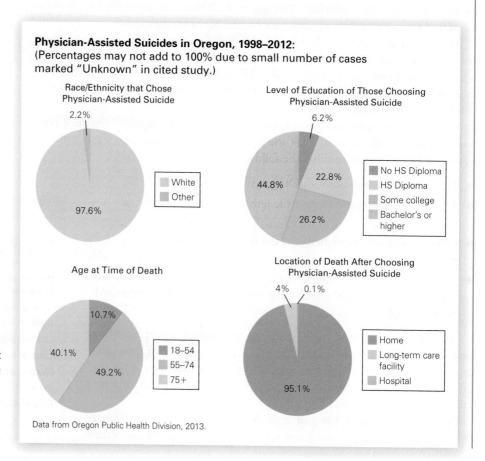

Physician-Assisted Suicides in Oregon, 1998–2012:
(Percentages may not add to 100% due to small number of cases marked "Unknown" in cited study.)

Race/Ethnicity that Chose Physician-Assisted Suicide
2.2%
97.6%
White
Other

Level of Education of Those Choosing Physician-Assisted Suicide
6.2%
22.8%
44.8%
26.2%
No HS Diploma
HS Diploma
Some college
Bachelor's or higher

Age at Time of Death
10.7%
40.1%
49.2%
18–54
55–74
75+

Location of Death After Choosing Physician-Assisted Suicide
4%   0.1%
95.1%
Home
Long-term care facility
Hospital

Data from Oregon Public Health Division, 2013.

FIGURE EP.6 Death with Dignity The data on who chooses death with dignity in Oregon do not suggest that people of low SES are unfairly pushed to die. In fact, it is quite the opposite—people who choose physician-assisted suicide tend to be among the older, better-educated, more affluent citizens.

The 1980 Netherlands law was revised in 2002 to allow euthanasia not only when a person is terminally ill but also when a person is chronically ill and in pain. The number of Dutch people who choose euthanasia is increasing, about 1 in 30 deaths in 2012. Is this a slippery slope? Some people think so, especially those who believe that God alone decides the moment of death and that anyone who interferes is defying God.

Arguing against that perspective, a cancer specialist writes:

> To be forced to continue living a life that one deems intolerable when there are doctors who are willing either to end one's life or to assist one in ending one's own life, is an unspeakable violation of an individual's freedom to live—and to die—as he or she sees fit. Those who would deny patients a legal right to euthanasia or assisted suicide typically appeal to two arguments: a "slippery slope" argument, and an argument about the dangers of abuse. Both are scare tactics, the rhetorical force of which exceeds their logical strength.
>
> [Benatar, 2011, p. 206]

Not everyone agrees with that cancer specialist. Might the decision to die be evidence of depression? If so, no physician should prescribe lethal drugs (Finlay & George, 2011). Declining ability to enjoy life was cited by 89 percent of Oregonians who requested physician-assisted suicide in 2012 (see Table EP.4). Is that a sign of sanity or depression?

Acceptance of death signifies mental health in the aged but not necessarily in the young: Should death with dignity be allowed only after age 54? That would have excluded 11 percent of Oregonians who have used the act thus far. Is the idea that only the old be allowed to choose death an ageist idea, perhaps assuming that the young don't understand what they are choosing or that the old are the ones for whom life is over?

The number of people who die by taking advantage of Oregon's law has increased steadily, from 16 in 1998 (the first year) to 77 in 2012. Some might see that as evidence of a slippery slope. Others consider it proof that the practice is useful though rare—only 1 in 200 Oregon deaths involves physician assistance (Oregon Public Health Division, 2013).

People with disabling, painful, and terminal conditions who die after choosing futile measures to prolong life are eulogized as "fighters" who "never gave up." That indicates social approval of such choices. This same attitude about life and death is held by most voters and lawmakers around the world. The majority oppose laws that allow physician-assisted suicide.

However, that majority is not evident everywhere.

- In November 2008, in the state of Washington, just north of Oregon, 58 percent of voters approved a death with dignity law.
- In 2009, Luxembourg joined the Netherlands and Belgium in allowing active euthanasia.
- In 2011, the Montana senate refused to forbid physician-assisted suicide.
- In 2012, a legal scholar contended that the U.S. Constitution's defense of liberty includes the freedom to decide how to die (Ball, 2012).
- In 2013, Vermont joined Oregon.
- In 2014, New Mexico courts allowed such deaths (but legislators may disallow it in 2015).
- In October 2015, after California's End of Life Option Act passed in the state Senate and Assembly, Governor Jerry Brown signed the bill into law.

All that might seem like a growing trend, but proposals to legalize physician-assisted suicide have been defeated in several other U.S. states and in other nations. Most jurisdictions recognize the dilemma: They do not prosecute doctors who help people die as long as it is done privately and quietly. Opposing perspectives, and opposite choices, are evident.

ADVANCE DIRECTIVES **Advance directives** can describe everything regarding end-of-life care. This may include where the person wants to die and what should happen to their body after death. Typically the focus is on medical measures.

Among the explicit statements in medical directives are: whether artificial feeding, breathing, or heart stimulation should be used; whether antibiotics that might merely prolong life or pain medication that causes coma or hallucinations are desired; whether religious music or clergy are welcome; and so on.

The legality of such directives varies by jurisdiction. Sometimes a lawyer is needed to ensure that documents are legal; sometimes a written request, signed and witnessed, is adequate.

Many people want personal choice about death; thus they approve of advance directives in theory but are uncertain about specifics. For example, few know that restarting the heart may extend life for decades in a healthy young adult but is likely to cause major brain damage, or merely prolong dying, in an elderly person whose health is failing.

Added to the complications are personal factors, such as additional morbidities and exactly what other factors are present. For example, the effect of cardiopulmonary

advance directives
Any description of what a person wants to happen as they die and after they die. This can include medical measures, visitors, funeral arrangements, cremation and so on.

ANSWER TO OBSERVATION QUIZ
(from page 587): Paris, France. Two clues: That is the Eiffel Tower, and François Hollande was elected president of France in 2012. ●

resuscitation depends partly on how long the heart has stopped (Bass, 2011). Data on overall averages are contradictory (Elliot et al., 2011). Furthermore, the data given to family about the consequences may include only the medical consequences for survivors, not the odds of death.

Even talking about choices is controversial. Originally, the U.S. health care bill passed in 2010 allowed doctors to be paid for describing treatment options (e.g., Kettl, 2010). Opponents called those "death panels," an accusation that almost torpedoed the entire package. As a result, that measure was scrapped: Physicians cannot bill for time spent explaining palliative care, options for treatment, or dying.

WILLS AND PROXIES Advance directives often include a living will and/or a health care proxy. Hospitals and hospices strongly recommend both of these. Nonetheless, most people resist: A study of cancer patients in a leading hospital found that only 16 percent had living wills and only 48 percent had designated a proxy (Halpern et al., 2011).

A **living will** indicates what sort of medical intervention a person wants or does not want in the event that they become unable to express their preferences. (If the person is conscious, hospital personnel ask about each specific procedure, often requiring written consent before surgery. Patients who are conscious and lucid can choose to override any instructions they wrote earlier in their living will.)

The reason a person might want to override their own earlier wishes is that living wills include phrases such as "incurable," "reasonable chance of recovery," and "extraordinary measures," and it is difficult to know what those phrases mean until a specific issue arises. Even then, medical judgments vary. Doctors and family members disagree about what is "extraordinary" or "reasonable."

Some people designate a **health care proxy**—another person to make medical decisions for them if they become unable to do so. That seems logical, but unfortunately neither a living will nor a health care proxy guarantees that medical care will be exactly what a person would choose.

For one thing, proxies find it difficult to allow a loved one to die. A larger problem is that few people—experts included—understand the risks, benefits, and alternatives to every medical procedure. It is hard to decide for oneself, much less for a patient or family member, exactly when the risks outweigh the benefits.

Medical professionals advocate advance directives, but they also acknowledge the problems with them. As one couple wrote:

> Working within the reality of mortality, coming to death is then an inevitable part of life, an event to be lived rather than a problem to be solved. Ideally, we would live the end of our life from the same values that have given meaning to the story of our life up to that time. But in a medical crisis, there is little time, language, or ritual to guide patients and their families in conceptualizing or expressing their values and goals.
>
> *[Farber & Farber, 2014, p. 109]*

THE SCHIAVO CASE A famous example of the need for a health care proxy occurred with Theresa (Terri) Schiavo, who was 26 years old when her heart suddenly stopped. Emergency personnel restarted her heart, but she fell into a deep coma. Like almost everyone her age, Terri had no advance directives. A court designated Michael, her husband of six years, as her proxy.

Michael attempted many measures to bring back his wife, but after 11 years he accepted her doctors' repeated diagnosis: Terri was in a persistent vegetative state. He petitioned to have her feeding tube removed. The court agreed, noting the testimony of witnesses who said that Terri had told them that she never wanted to be on

living will
A document that indicates what medical intervention an individual prefers if he or she is not conscious when a decision is to be expressed. For example, some do not want mechanical breathing.

health care proxy
A person chosen to make medical decisions if a patient is unable to do so, as when in a coma.

Glossary

A

absent grief When mourners do not grieve, either because other people do not allow expressions of grief or because the mourners do not allow themselves to feel sadness. (p. 592)

achievement test A measure of mastery or proficiency in reading, mathematics, writing, science, or some other subject. (p. 268)

active euthanasia When someone does something that hastens another person's death, hoping to end that person's suffering. (p. 586)

activities of daily life (ADLs) Typically identified as five tasks of self-care: eating, bathing, toileting, dressing, and transferring from a bed to a chair. (p. 561)

activity theory The view that elderly people want and need to remain active in a variety of social spheres—with relatives, friends, and community groups. (p. 547)

additive gene A gene that contributes to the phenotype, usually with other additive genes. (p. 56)

adolescence-limited offender A person whose criminal activity occurs only during adolescence. (p. 374)

adolescent egocentrism A characteristic of adolescent thinking that leads young people to believe in their own uniqueness, and to imagine that other people are also focused on them. (p. 330)

adrenal glands Two glands, located above the kidneys, that produce hormones in response to signals from the pituitary. (p. 316)

advance directives Any description of what a person wants to happen as they die and after they die. This can include medical measures, visitors, funeral arrangements, cremation and so on. (p. 589)

age in place To remain in the same home and community in later life, adjusting but not leaving when health fades. (p. 552)

age of viability The age (about 22 weeks after conception) when survival is possible if a fetus is born and if specialized medical care is available. (p. 60)

ageism A prejudice whereby people are categorized and judged by their chronological age. (p. 503)

aggressive-rejected A child who is not liked by peers because of his or her provocative, confrontational behavior. (p. 301)

allele Any of the possible forms of a gene. Genes with various alleles are called polymorphic. (p. 48)

allocare Literally, "other-care"; the care of children by people other than the biological parents. (p. 147)

allostasis A dynamic body adjustment to long-term biological conditions of a person's life. (p. 392)

allostatic load The stresses of basic body systems that burden overall functioning, such as hypertension. (p. 392)

Alzheimer's disease (AD) The most common cause of major NCD, characterized by gradual deterioration of memory and personality and marked by the formation of plaques of beta-amyloid protein and tangles of tau in the brain. (p. 527)

amygdala A tiny brain structure that registers emotions, particularly fear and anxiety. (p. 172)

analytic intelligence Intelligence that involves logic, planning, strategy selection, focused attention, and information processing. (p. 448)

analytic thought Thought that results from analysis, such as a systematic exploration of pros and cons, risks and consequences, possibilities and facts. Analytic thought depends on logic and rationality. (p. 335)

andropause A term coined to signify a drop in testosterone levels in older men, which reduces sexual desire, erections, and muscle mass. (Also called *male menopause*.) (p. 443)

animism The belief that natural objects and phenomena are alive in the way that humans are, as in a rock having emotions and a spirit. (p. 173)

anorexia nervosa An eating disorder characterized by self-starvation and obsession with weight. Affected individuals become pathologically thin, depriving their vital organs of nutrition. (p. 325)

anoxia A lack of oxygen that, if prolonged, can cause brain damage or death. (p. 75)

antipathy Feelings of dislike or even hatred for another person. (p. 219)

antisocial behavior Actions that are deliberately hurtful or destructive to another person. (p. 219)

Apgar scale A quick assessment of a newborn's health. Heart rate, respiratory effort, muscle tone, color, and reflexes are given a score of 0, 1, or 2, with the total compared with the ideal score of 10 (which is rarely attained). (p. 64)

aptitude The potential to master a specific skill or to learn a certain body of knowledge. (p. 267)

asthma A chronic disease of the respiratory system in which inflammation narrows the airways from the nose and mouth to the lungs, causing difficulty in breathing. Signs and symptoms include wheezing, shortness of breath, chest tightness, and coughing. (p. 244)

attachment According to Ainsworth, "an affectional tie" that an infant forms with a caregiver—a tie that binds them together in space and endures over time. (p. 139)

attention-deficit/hyperactivity disorder (ADHD) A condition in which a person not only has difficulty concentrating but also is inattentive, impulsive, and overactive. (p. 270)

authoritarian parenting An approach to child rearing that is characterized by high behavioral standards, strict punishment of misconduct, and little communication from child to parent. (p. 211)

authoritative parenting An approach to child rearing in which the parents set limits and enforce rules but are flexible and listen to their children. (p. 211)

autism spectrum disorder (ASD) Any of several conditions characterized by inadequate social skills, impaired communication, and unusual play. (p. 272)

automatic processing Thinking that occurs without deliberate, conscious thought. Experts process most tasks automatically, saving conscious thought for unfamiliar challenges. (p. 459)

automatization A process in which repetition of a sequence of thoughts and actions makes the sequence routine, so it no longer requires conscious thought. (p. 253)

autonomy versus shame and doubt Erikson's second crisis of psychosocial development. Toddlers either succeed or fail in gaining a sense of self-rule over their actions and their bodies. (p. 151)

average life expectancy The number of years the average person in a particular population group is likely to live. (p. 512)

avoidant coping Responding to a stressor by ignoring, forgetting, or hiding it. (p. 454)

axons Fibers that extend from neurons and transmit electrochemical impulses from that neuron to the dendrites of other neurons. (p. 94)

B

babbling The extended repetition of certain syllables, such as *ba-ba-ba,* when babies are between 6 and 9 months old. (p. 121)

bed-sharing When two or more people sleep in the same bed. (p. 92)

behavioral teratogens Agents and conditions that can harm the prenatal brain, impairing the future child's intellectual and emotional functioning. (p. 72)

behaviorism A theory of human development that studies observable behavior. Behaviorism is also called *learning theory* because it describes the laws and processes by which behavior is learned. (p. 26)

Big Five The five basic clusters of personality traits that remain quite stable throughout adulthood: openness, conscientiousness, extroversion, agreeableness, and neuroticism. (p. 467)

bilingual education A strategy in which school subjects are taught in both the learner's original language and the second (majority) language. (p. 256)

binocular vision The ability to focus both eyes in a coordinated manner in order to see one image. Depth perception requires it. (p. 98)

body image A person's idea of how his or her body looks, especially related to size and shape. (p. 324)

Brazelton Neonatal Behavioral Assessment Scale (NBAS) A test often administered to newborns that measures responsiveness and records 46 behaviors, including 20 reflexes. (p. 67)

bulimia nervosa An eating disorder characterized by binge eating and subsequent purging, usually by induced vomiting and/or use of laxatives. (p. 325)

bully-victim Someone who attacks others and who is attacked as well. (Also called *provocative victims* because they do things that elicit bullying.) (p. 303)

bullying aggression Unprovoked, repeated physical or verbal attack, especially on victims who are unlikely to defend themselves. (p. 221)

bullying Repeated, systematic efforts to inflict harm on other people through physical, verbal, or social attack on a weaker person. (p. 302)

C

calorie restriction The practice of limiting dietary energy intake (while consuming sufficient quantities of vitamins, minerals, and other important nutrients) in hopes of slowing down the aging process. (p. 511)

carrier A person whose genotype includes a gene that is not expressed in the phenotype. Such an unexpressed gene occurs in half the carrier's gametes and thus is passed on to half the carrier's children. (p. 56)

cellular aging The ways in which molecules and cells are affected by age. Many theories aim to explain how and why aging causes cells to deteriorate. (p. 513)

centration A characteristic of preoperational thought in which a young child focuses (centers) on one idea, excluding all others. (p. 174)

cerebral palsy A disorder that results from damage to the brain's motor centers. People with cerebral palsy have difficulty with muscle control, so their speech and/or body movements are impaired. (p. 75)

cesarean section (c-section) A surgical birth, in which incisions through the mother's abdomen and uterus allow the fetus to be removed quickly, instead of being delivered through the vagina. (p. 64)

charter schools Public schools with their own set of standards funded and licensed by the state or local district in which they are located. (p. 264)

child maltreatment Intentional harm to or avoidable endangerment of anyone under 18 years of age. (p. 228)

child-directed speech The high-pitched, simplified, and repetitive way adults speak to infants. (Also called *baby talk* or *motherese.*) (p. 120)

childhood obesity In a child, having a BMI (body mass index) above the 95th percentile, according to the U.S. Centers for Disease Control's 1980 standards for children of a given age. (p. 242)

childhood overweight In a child, having a BMI (body mass index) above the 85th percentile, according to the U.S. Centers for Disease Control's 1980 standards for children of a given age. (p. 242)

chromosome One of the 46 structures made of DNA (in 23 pairs) that almost every cell of the human body contains and that, together, contain all the genes. Other species have more or fewer chromosomes. (p. 48)

circadian rhythm A day–night cycle of biological activity that occurs approximately every 24 hours (*circadian* means "about a day"). (p. 318)

classification The logical principle that things can be organized into groups (or categories or classes) according to some characteristic they have in common. (p. 247)

clinical depression Feelings of hopelessness, lethargy, and worthlessness that last two weeks or more. (p. 369)

cluster suicides Several suicides committed by members of a group within a brief period. (p. 372)

co-sleeping A custom in which parents and their children (usually infants) sleep together in the same room. (p. 92)

cognitive artifacts Intellectual tools, such as writing, invented by one generation and then passed down from generation to generation to foster learning within societies. (p. 451)

cognitive theory A theory of human development that focuses on changes in how people think over time. According to this theory, thoughts shape attitudes, beliefs, and behaviors. (p. 28)

cohabitation An arrangement in which a couple live together in a romantic relationship but are not married. (p. 422)

cohort People born within the same historical period. They experience historical events (such as wars), technologies (such as the smartphone), and cultural shifts (such as women's liberation) at the same ages. (p. 12)

complicated grief A type of grief that impedes a person's future life, usually because the person clings to sorrow or is buffeted by contradictory emotions. (p. 592)

compression of morbidity A shortening of the time a person spends ill or infirm before dying, accomplished by postponing illness. (p. 518)

compulsive hoarding The urge to accumulate and hold on to familiar objects and possessions, sometimes to the point of their becoming health and/or safety hazards. This impulse tends to increase with age. (p. 542)

concrete operational thought Piaget's term for the ability to reason logically about direct experiences and perceptions. (p. 247)

conditioning According to behaviorism, the processes by which responses become linked to particular stimuli and learning takes place. The word *conditioning* is used to emphasize the importance of repeated practice, as when an athlete *conditions* his or her body by training for a long time. (p. 26)

consequential strangers People who are not in a person's closest friendship circle but nonetheless have an impact. (p. 477)

conservation The principle that the amount of a substance remains the same (i.e., is conserved) even when its appearance changes. (p. 174)

control processes Mechanisms (including selective attention, metacognition, and emotional regulation) that combine memory, processing speed, and knowledge to regulate the analysis and flow of information within the information-processing system. (Also called *executive processes*.) (p. 252)

control processes The part of the information-processing system that regulates the analysis and flow of information. Memory and retrieval strategies, selective attention, and rules or strategies for problem solving are all control processes. (p. 524)

conventional moral reasoning Kohlberg's second level of moral reasoning, emphasizing social rules and laws. (p. 305)

corporal punishment Discipline techniques that hurt the body (corpus) of someone, from sparking to serious harm, including death. (p. 222)

corpus callosum A long, thick band of nerve fibers that connects the left and right hemispheres of the brain and allows communication between them. (p. 168)

correlation A number between +1.0 and −1.0 that indicates the degree of relationship between two variables, expressed in terms of the likelihood that one variable will (or will not) occur when the other variable does (or does not). A correlation indicates only that two variables may be somehow related, not that one variable causes the other to occur. (p. 41)

cortex The outer layers of the brain in humans and other mammals. Most thinking, feeling, and sensing involve the cortex. (p. 94)

couvade Symptoms of pregnancy and birth experienced by fathers. (p. 69)

creative intelligence Intelligence that involves the capacity to be flexible and innovative, thinking unusual ideas. (p. 448)

critical period A time when a particular type of developmental growth (in body or behavior) must happen for normal development to occur. (p. 10)

cross-sectional research A research design that compares groups of people who differ in age but are similar in other important characteristics. (p. 38)

cross-sequential research A hybrid research design in which researchers first study several groups of people of different ages (a cross-sectional approach) and then follow those groups over the years (a longitudinal approach). (Also called *cohort-sequential research* or *time-sequential research*. (p. 39)

crystallized intelligence Those aspects of intellectual ability that reflect accumulated learning. Vocabulary and general information are examples. (p. 447)

culture A system of shared beliefs, norms, behaviors, and expectations that persist over time and prescribe social behavior and assumptions. (p. 15)

cyberbullying Bullying that occurs when one person attacks and harms another via technology (e.g., e-mails, text messages, or cell phones). (p. 338)

D

deductive reasoning Reasoning from a general statement, premise, or principle, through logical steps, to figure out (deduce) specifics. (Also called *top-down reasoning*.) (p. 332)

deferred imitation A sequence in which an infant first perceives something done by someone else and then performs the same action hours or even days later. (p. 116)

demographic shift A shift in the proportions of the populations of various ages. (p. 508)

dendrites Fibers that extend from neurons and receive electrochemical impulses transmitted from other neurons via their axons. (p. 94)

dependent variable In an experiment, the variable that may change as a result of whatever new condition or situation the experimenter adds. In other words, the dependent variable *depends* on the independent variable. (p. 36)

developmental psychopathology The field that uses insights into typical development to understand and remediate developmental disorders. (p. 267)

developmental theory A group of ideas, assumptions, and generalizations that interpret and illuminate thousands of observations about human growth. A developmental theory provides a framework for explaining the patterns and problems of development. (p. 23)

deviancy training When one person shows another how to rebel against authority or social norms. (p. 362)

difference-equals-deficit error The mistaken belief that a deviation from some norm is necessarily inferior to behavior or characteristics that are more typical. (p. 17)

differential susceptibility The idea that people vary in how sensitive they are to particular experiences. Often such differences are genetic, which makes some people affected "for better or for worse" by life events. (Also called *differential sensitivity*.) (p. 7)

disenfranchised grief A situation in which certain people, although they are bereaved, are prevented from mourning publicly by cultural customs or social restrictions. (p. 593)

disengagement theory The view that aging makes a person's social sphere increasingly narrow, resulting in role relinquishment, withdrawal, and passivity. (p. 547)

disorganized attachment A type of attachment that is marked by an infant's inconsistent reactions to the caregiver's departure and return. (p. 140)

distal parenting Caregiving practices that keep some distance from a baby, such as providing toys, food, and face-to-face communication with minimal holding and touching. (p. 152)

dizygotic twins Twins who are formed when two separate ova are fertilized by two separate sperm at roughly the same time. (Also called *fraternal twins*.) (p. 55)

DNA (deoxyribonucleic acid) The molecule that contains the chemical instructions for cells to manufacture various proteins. (p. 48)

DNR (do not resuscitate) order A written order from a physician (sometimes initiated by a patient's advance directive or by a health care proxy's request) that no attempt should be made to revive a patient if he or she suffers cardiac or respiratory arrest. (p. 586)

dominant–recessive pattern The interaction of a pair of genes in such a way that the phenotype reveals the influence of one (the dominant gene) more than that of the other (the recessive gene). (p. 56)

double effect When an action (such as administering opiates) has two effects, such as relieving pain and suppressing respiration. (p. 584)

doula A woman who helps with the birth process, including massage during birth and help with breast-feeding. (p. 66)

Down syndrome A condition in which a person has 47 chromosomes instead of the usual 46, with three rather than two chromosomes at the 21st position. People with Down syndrome often have a distinctive appearance. (Also called *trisomy-21*.) (p. 70)

drug abuse When the ingestion of a drug impairs the user's biological or psychological well-being. (p. 397)

dual-process model The idea that two modes of thinking exist within the human brain, one for intuitive emotional responses and one for analytical reasoning. (p. 333)

dynamic-systems approach A view of human development as an ongoing, ever-changing interaction between the physical, cognitive, and psychosocial influences. (p. 21)

dyscalculia A specific learning disorder characterized by unusual difficulty with math. (p. 272)

dyslexia A specific learning disorder characterized by unusual difficulty with reading. (p. 271)

E

ecological validity The idea that cognitive or social measurements are most accurate in natural settings. (p. 525)

ecological-systems approach Bronfenbrenner's perspective on human development that considers all the influences from the various contexts of development. (Later renamed *bioecological theory*.) (p. 12)

effortful control The ability to regulate one's emotions and actions through effort, not simply through natural inclination. (p. 202)

egocentrism Piaget's term for children's tendency to think about other people and their own experiences as if everything revolves around them. (p. 174)

elderspeak A condescending way of speaking to older adults that resembles baby talk, with simple and short sentences, exaggerated emphasis, repetition, and a slower rate and a higher pitch than used in normal speech. (p. 506)

ELLs (English Language Learners) Children in the United States whose proficiency in English is low—usually below a cut-off score on an oral or written test. Many children who speak a non-English language at home are also capable in English; they are *not* ELLs. (p. 256)

embryo The name for a developing human organism from two to eight weeks after conception. (p. 59)

embryonic period The stage of prenatal development from the end of the second week through the eighth week after conception, during which the basic forms of body structures, including internal organs but not sex organs, develop. (p. 58)

emerging adulthood The period of life between the ages of 18 and 25. Emerging adulthood is now widely thought of as a distinct developmental stage. (p. 389)

emotion-focused coping A strategy to deal with stress by changing feelings and interpretations about the stressor rather than changing the stressor itself. (p. 454)

emotional regulation The ability to control when and how emotions are expressed. (p. 201)

empathy The ability to understand the emotions and concerns of another person, especially when they differ from one's own. (p. 219)

empirical evidence Evidence that is based on observation, experience, or data; not theoretical. (p. 4)

empty nest The time in the lives of parents when their children have left the family home to pursue their own lives. (p. 474)

entity theory of intelligence The idea that intellectual ability is innate, a fixed quantity present at birth. Those who hold this view underrate the role of effort on achievement. (p. 343)

epigenetics The study of how environmental factors affect genes and genetic expression—enhancing, halting, shaping, or altering the expression of genes. (p. 7)

equifinality A basic principle of developmental psychopathology that holds that one symptom can have many causes. (p. 270)

ESL (English as a second language) An approach to teaching English in which all children who do not speak English are placed together in an intensive course to learn basic English. (p. 256)

estradiol A sex hormone, considered to be the chief estrogen (female hormone). Females produce much more estradiol than males do. (p. 317)

ethnic group People whose ancestors were born in the same region and who often share a language, culture, and religion. (p. 18)

executive function The cognitive ability to organize and prioritize the many thoughts that arise from the various parts of the brain, allowing the person to anticipate, strategize, and plan behavior. (p. 167)

experience-dependent Brain functions that depend on particular, variable experiences and therefore may or may not develop in a particular person. (p. 96)

experience-expectant Brain functions that require certain basic common experiences (which an infant can be expected to have) in order to develop normally. (p. 96)

experiment A research method in which the researcher tries to determine the cause-and-effect relationship between two variables by manipulating one (called the *independent variable*) and then observing and recording the ensuing changes in the other (called the *dependent variable*). (p. 35)

extended family A family of three or more generations living in one household. (p. 292)

extreme sports Forms of recreation that include apparent risk of injury or death and are attractive and thrilling as a result. (p. 396)

extremely low birthweight (ELBW) A body weight at birth of less than 2 pounds, 3 ounces (1,000 grams). (p. 78)

extrinsic motivation A drive, or reason to pursue a goal, that arises from the wish to have external rewards, perhaps by earning money or praise. (p. 204)

extrinsic rewards of work The benefits, usually in salary, insurance, pension, and status, that come with employment. (p. 489)

F

false positives The result of a laboratory test (blood, urine or sonogram) that suggests an abnormality that is not present. (p. 77)

familism The belief that family members should support one another, sacrificing individual freedom and success, if necessary, because the family is more important. (p. 369)

family function The way a family works to meet the physical and psychological needs of its members. (p. 290)

family structure The legal and genetic relationships among family members. Possible structures include nuclear family, extended family, stepfamily, single-parent family, and many others. (p. 290)

fast-mapping The speedy and sometimes imprecise way that children learn new words by quickly categorizing them. (p. 183)

fetal alcohol syndrome (FAS) A cluster of birth defects, including abnormal facial characteristics, slow physical growth, and intellectual disabilities, that may occur in the child of a woman who drinks alcohol while pregnant. (p. 74)

fetal period The stage of prenatal development from nine weeks after conception until birth, during which the fetus grows in size and matures in functioning. (p. 58)

fetus The name for a developing human organism from the start of the ninth week after conception until birth. (p. 60)

fictive kin People who become accepted as part of a family who have no genetic or legal relationship to that family. (p. 480)

filial responsibility The obligation of adult children to care for their aging parents. (p. 557)

fine motor skills Physical abilities involving small body movements, especially of the hands and fingers, such as drawing and picking up a coin. (The word *fine* here means "small.") (p. 102)

fluid intelligence Those aspects of basic intelligence that make learning quick and thorough. Short-term memory, abstract thought, and speed of thinking are usually considered part of fluid intelligence. (p. 447)

Flynn effect The rise in average IQ scores that has occurred over the decades in many nations. (p. 268)

focus on appearance A characteristic of preoperational thought in which a young child assumes that the visible appearance of someone or something is also their essence. (p. 174)

foreclosure Erikson's term for premature identity formation, when a person adopts parents' or society's roles and values wholesale, without questioning or analysis. (p. 352)

formal operational thought In Piaget's theory, the fourth and final stage of cognitive development, characterized by systematic logical thinking and by understanding abstractions. (p. 329)

foster care When a person (usually a child) is cared for by someone other than the parents. (p. 232)

fragile X syndrome A genetic condition that involves the X chromosome and that causes slow development. (p. 71)

frail elderly Older adults who are severely impaired, usually unable to care for themselves. (p. 561)

frontotemporal NCDs Brain disorders that occur with serious impairment of the frontal lobes. (Also called *frontotemporal lobar degeneration*.) (p. 528)

G

gamete A reproductive cell; that is, a sperm or an ovum that can produce a new individual if it combines with a gamete from the other sex to form a zygote. (p. 48)

gender differences Differences in male and female roles, behaviors, clothes and so on that arise from society, not biology. (p. 213)

gender identity A person's acceptance of the roles and behaviors that are associated with the biological categories of male and female. (p. 355)

gender schema A child's cognitive concept or general belief about male and female differences. (p. 217)

gene A small section of a chromosome; the basic unit for the transmission of heredity. A gene consists of a string of chemicals that provide instructions for the cell to manufacture certain proteins. (p. 48)

general intelligence (g) The idea that intelligence is one basic trait, underlying all cognitive abilities. According to this concept, people have varying levels of this general ability. (p. 444)

generational forgetting The idea that each new generation forgets what the previous generation learned. (p. 383)

generativity versus stagnation The seventh of Erikson's eight stages of development. Adults seek to be productive in a caring way, often as parents. Generativity also occurs through art, caregiving, and employment. (p. 480)

genetic clock A mechanism in the DNA of cells that regulates the aging process by triggering hormonal changes and cellular death and repair. (p. 512)

genome The full set of genes for a certain species. (p. 50)

genotype An organism's entire genetic inheritance, or genetic potential. (p. 49)

germinal period The first two weeks of development after conception, characterized by rapid cell division and the beginning of cell differentiation. (p. 58)

gonads The sex glands (ovaries in females, testicles in males). The gonads produce hormones and gametes. (p. 317)

grammar All the methods—word order, verb forms, and so on—that languages use to communicate meaning, apart from the words themselves. (p. 122)

grief The deep sorrow that people feel at the death of another. Grief is personal and unpredictable. (p. 592)

gross motor skills Physical abilities involving large body movements, such as walking and jumping. (The word *gross* here means "big.") (p. 101)

growth spurt The relatively sudden and rapid physical growth that occurs during puberty. Each body part increases in size on a schedule: Weight usually precedes height, and growth of the limbs precedes growth of the torso. (p. 322)

H

harm reduction Reducing the potential negative consequences of behavior, such as safety surfaces replacing cement at a playground. (p. 225)

Hayflick limit The number of times a human cell is capable of dividing. The limit for most human cells is approximately 50 divisions, an indication that the life span is limited by our genetic program. (p. 513)

Head Start A federally funded early-childhood-intervention program for low-income children in the United States. (p. 193)

head-sparing A biological mechanism that protects the brain when malnutrition disrupts body growth. The brain is the last part of the body to be damaged by malnutrition. (p. 93)

health care proxy A person chosen to make medical decisions if a patient is unable to do so, as when in a coma. (p. 590)

helicopter parent The label used for parents who hover (like a helicopter) over their emerging adult children. (p. 417)

heritability A statistic that indicates what percentage of the variation in a trait within a population, in a particular context and era, can be traced to genes. (p. 82)

hidden curriculum The unofficial, unstated, or implicit rules and priorities that influence the curriculum, organization, and setting in a school. (p. 258)

high-stakes test An evaluation that determines something very important. For example, if a single test determines promotion or graduation, it is a high-stakes test. (p. 344)

hippocampus A brain structure that is a central processor of memory. (p. 172)

holophrase A single word that is used to express a complete, meaningful thought. (p. 121)

home schooling Education in which children are taught at home, usually by their parents, instead of attending any school, public or private. (p. 265)

homeostasis The adjustment of all the body's systems to keep physiological functions in equilibrium, moment by moment. (p. 392)

hookup A sexual encounter between two people who are not in a romantic relationship. Neither intimacy nor commitment is expected. (p. 421)

hospice An institution or program in which terminally ill patients receive palliative care to reduce suffering; family and friends of the dying are helped as well. (p. 582)

humanism A theory that stresses the potential of all humans, who have the same basic needs, regardless of culture, gender, or background. (p. 32)

hypothalamus A brain area that responds to the amygdala and the hippocampus as well as various experiences to produce hormones that activate the pituitary and other parts of the brain and body. (p. 172)

hypothesis A specific prediction that can be tested. (p. 4)

hypothetical thought Reasoning that includes propositions and possibilities that do not reflect reality. (p. 332)

I

identification In psychoanalytic theory, considering the behaviors, appearance and attitudes of someone else to be one's own. (p. 215)

identity achievement Erikson's term for the attainment of identity, or the point at which a person understands who he or she is as a unique individual, in accord with past experiences and future plans. This includes many identities—religions, sexual-gender, political-ethnic, and vocational. (p. 351)

identity versus role confusion Erikson's term for his fifth stage of development, in which the person tries to figure out "Who am I?" but is confused as to which of many possible roles to adopt. (p. 351)

imaginary audience The other people who, in an adolescent's egocentric belief, watch his or her appearance, ideas, and behavior. (p. 330)

imaginary friends Make-believe friends who exist only in a child's imagination; increasingly common from ages 3 through 7, they combat loneliness and aid emotional regulation. (p. 204)

immersion A strategy in which instruction in all school subjects occurs in the second (usually the majority) language that a child is learning. (p. 256)

immigrant paradox The surprising fact that immigrants tend to be healthier than U.S.-born residents of the same ethnicity. This was first evident among Mexican Americans. (p. 78)

immunization A process that stimulates the body's immune system to defend against attack by a particular contagious disease. Immunization may be accomplished either naturally (by having the disease) or through vaccination (often by having an injection). (Also called *vaccination.*) (p. 107)

implantation The process, beginning about 10 days after conception, in which the developing organism burrows into the tissue that lines the uterus, where it will be nourished. (p. 59)

impulse control The ability to postpone or deny an immediate response to an idea or behavior. (p. 171)

incomplete grief When circumstances, such as a police investigation or an autopsy, interfere with the process of grieving. (p. 593)

incremental theory of intelligence The idea that intelligence can be increased by effort, with attention and practice, as in class participation and homework. (p. 343)

independent variable In an experiment, the variable that is introduced to see what effect it has on the dependent variable. (Also called *experimental variable.*) (p. 35)

individual education plan (IEP) A document that specifies educational goals and plans for a child with special needs. (p. 275)

inductive reasoning Reasoning from specific experiences or facts to reach (induce) a general conclusion. (Also called *bottom-up reasoning.*) (p. 332)

industry versus inferiority The fourth of Erikson's eight psychosocial crises, during which children attempt to master many skills, developing a sense of themselves as either accomplished or a failure, competent or incompetent. (p. 282)

infertility The failure to conceive a child after trying for at least a year. (p. 440)

information-processing theory A perspective that compares human thinking processes, to computer analysis of data, including sensory input, connections, stored memories, and output. (p. 117)

initiative versus guilt Erikson's third psychosocial crisis, in which young children undertake new skills and activities and feel guilty when they do not succeed at them. (p. 202)

insecure-avoidant attachment A pattern of attachment in which an infant avoids connection with the caregiver, as when the infant seems not to care about the caregiver's presence, departure, or return. (p. 140)

insecure-resistant/ambivalent attachment A pattern of attachment in which an infant's anxiety and uncertainty are evident, as when the infant becomes very upset at separation from the caregiver, such infants both resist and seek contact on reunion. (p. 140)

instrumental activities of daily life (IADLs) Actions (for example, paying bills and driving a car) that are important to independent living and that require some intellectual competence and forethought. (p. 561)

instrumental aggression Hurtful behavior that is intended to get something that another person has. (p. 220)

integrated care Cooperative actions by professionals, friends, family members, and the care receiver to achieve optimal caregiving. (p. 566)

integrity versus despair The final stage of Erik Erikson's developmental sequence, in which older adults seek to integrate their unique experiences with their vision of community. (p. 541)

intimacy versus isolation The sixth of Erikson's eight stages of development. Adults seek someone with whom to share their lives in an enduring and self-sacrificing commitment. Without such commitment, they risk profound loneliness and isolation. (p. 416)

intimacy versus isolation The sixth of Erikson's stages of development. Every adult seeks close relationships with other people in order to live a happy and healthy life. (p. 469)

intrinsic motivation A drive, or reason to pursue a goal, that comes from inside a person, such as the joy of reading a good book. (p. 204)

intrinsic rewards of work The personal gratifications, such as pleasure in a job well done or friendship with coworkers, that accompany employment. (p. 489)

intuitive thought Thought that arises from an emotion or a hunch, a "gut feeling" influenced by past experiences and cultural assumptions. (p. 335)

invincibility fable The fantasy that a person cannot be harmed by anything that might defeat a normal mortal, such as unprotected sex, drug abuse, or high-speed driving. (p. 330)

irreversibility In preoperational thought, the idea that change is permanent, that nothing can be restored to the way it was before a change occurred. (p. 174)

K

kinkeeper Someone who becomes the gatherer and communication hub for their family. (p. 487)

kinship care A form of foster care in which a relative, usually a grandmother, becomes the approved caregiver of a child. (p. 232)

knowledge base A body of knowledge that makes it easier to learn new information in a particular area. (p. 252)

kwashiorkor A disease of chronic malnutrition in which a protein-calorie deficiency makes a child more vulnerable to other diseases, such as measles, diarrhea, and influenza. (p. 112)

L

language acquisition device (LAD) Chomsky's term for a hypothesized mental structure that enables humans to learn language, including the basic aspects of grammar, vocabulary, and intonation. (p. 124)

lateralization Literally, sidedness, referring to the specialization in certain functions by each side of the brain, with one side dominant for each activity. (p. 168)

Lewy body disease A form of major NCD characterized by an increase in particular abnormal cells in the brain. Symptoms include visual hallucinations, momentary loss of attention, falling, and fainting. (p. 529)

life review An examination of one's own role in the history of human life, engaged in by many elderly people. This can be written or oral. (p. 535)

life-course-persistent offender A person whose criminal activity continues throughout life; a career criminal. (p. 374)

life-span perspective An approach to the study of human development that takes into account all phases of life, not just childhood or adulthood. (p. 9)

linked lives When the success, health, and well-being of each family member are connected to those of other members. (p. 417)

little scientist The stage-five toddler (age 12 to 18 months) who experiments without imagining the consequences, using trial and error in active and creative exploration. (p. 116)

living will A document that indicates what medical intervention an individual prefers if he or she is not conscious when a decision is to be expressed. For example, some do not want mechanical breathing. (p. 590)

long-term memory The component of the information-processing system in which virtually limitless amounts of information can be stored indefinitely. (p. 252)

longitudinal research A research design in which the same individuals are followed over time, as their development is repeatedly assessed. (p. 38)

low birthweight (LBW) A body weight at birth of less than 5½ pounds (2,500 grams). (p. 78)

M

major neurocognitive disorder (major NCD) Irreversible loss of intellectual functioning caused by organic brain damage or disease. Formerly called *dementia*, major NCD becomes more common with age, but it is abnormal and pathological even in the very old. (p. 527)

marasmus A disease of severe protein-calorie malnutrition during early infancy, in which growth stops, body tissues waste away, and the infant eventually dies. (p. 112)

massive open online courses (MOOCs) College courses that are offered solely online. Typically, thousands of students enroll. (p. 406)

maximum life span The oldest possible age that members of a species can live under ideal circumstances. For humans, that age seems to be 122 years. (p. 512)

mean length of utterance (MLU) The average number of meaningful sound combination in a typical sentence (called utterance, because children may not use conventional words). MLU is often used to indicate a child's language development. (p. 122)

menarche A girl's first menstrual period, signaling that she has begun ovulation. Pregnancy is biologically possible, but ovulation and menstruation are often irregular for years after menarche. (p. 316)

menopause The time in middle age, usually around age 50, when a woman's menstrual periods cease and the production of estrogen, progesterone, and testosterone drops. Strictly speaking, menopause begins one year after a woman's last menstrual period. (p. 442)

mentor Someone who teaches or guides someone else, helping a learner master a skill or body of knowledge. (p. 176)

metacognition "Thinking about thinking," or the ability to evaluate a cognitive task in order to determine how best to accomplish it and then to monitor and adjust one's performance on that task. (p. 252)

middle childhood The period between early childhood and early adolescence, approximately from ages 6 to 11. (p. 240)

middle school A school for children after elementary school and before high school, usually grades 6 through 8. (p. 341)

monozygotic twins Twins who originate from one zygote that splits apart very early in development. (Also called *identical twins*.) (p. 53)

Montessori schools Schools that offer early-childhood education based on the philosophy of Maria Montessori, which emphasizes careful work and individualized accomplishment. (p. 189)

moratorium In Erikson's identity stage, a socially acceptable way to postpone achievement. Going to college is a common example. (p. 352)

motor skills The learned abilities to move some part of the body, in actions ranging from a large leap to a flicker of the eyelid. (The word *motor* here refers to movement of muscles.) (p. 100)

mourning The ceremonies and behaviors that a religion or culture prescribes for people to express their grief after a death. (p. 593)

multifinality A basic principle of developmental psychopathology which holds that one cause can have many (multiple) final manifestations. (p. 270)

multiple intelligences The idea that human intelligence is comprised of a varied set of abilities rather than a single, all-encompassing one. (p. 268)

myelination The process by which axons become coated with myelin, a fatty substance that speeds the transmission of nerve impulses from neuron to neuron. (p. 169)

naming explosion A sudden increase in an infant's vocabulary, especially in the number of nouns, that begins at about 18 months of age. (p. 121)

N

National Assessment of Educational Progress (NAEP) An ongoing and nationally representative measure of U.S. children's achievement in reading, mathematics, and other subjects over time; nicknamed "the Nation's Report Card." (p. 263)

naturally occurring retirement community (NORC) A neighborhood or apartment complex whose population is mostly retired people who moved to the location as younger adults and never left. (p. 552)

nature In development, nature refers to the traits, capacities, and limitations that each individual inherits genetically from his or her parents at the moment of conception. (p. 7)

neglectful/uninvolved parenting An approach to child rearing in which the parents seem indifferent toward their children, not knowing or caring about their children's lives. (p. 211)

neurocognitive disorder (NCD) Any of a number of brain diseases that affects a person's ability to remember, analyze, plan, or interact with other people. (p. 525)

neurodiversity The idea that people with special needs have diverse brain structures, with each person having neurological strengths and weaknesses that should be appreciated, in much the same way diverse cultures and ethnicities are welcomed. (p. 273)

neurons Nerve cells in the central nervous system, especially in the brain. (p. 94)

neurotransmitters Brain chemicals that carry information from the axon of a sending neuron to the dendrites of a receiving neuron. (p. 94)

No Child Left Behind Act (NCLB) A U.S. law enacted in 2001 that was intended to increase accountability in education by requiring states to qualify for federal educational funding by administering standardized tests to measure school achievement. (p. 263)

norm An average, or standard, calculated from many individuals within a specific group or population. (p. 90)

normal grief The usual response to a loss. Initial sadness and then recovery are normal. (p. 596)

nuclear family A family that consists of a father, a mother, and their biological children under age 18. (p. 291)

nurture In development, nurture includes all the environmental influences that affect the individual after conception. This includes everything from the mother's nutrition while pregnant to the cultural influences in the nation. (p. 7)

O

object permanence The realization that objects (including people) still exist even if they can no longer be seen, touched, or heard. (p. 114)

Oedipus complex The unconscious desire of young boys to replace their fathers and win their mothers' exclusive love. (p. 215)

operant conditioning The learning process by which a particular action is followed by something desired (a reinforcer which makes the person or animal more likely to repeat the action) or by something unwanted (a punishment which makes the action less likely to be repeated). (Also called *instrumental conditioning*.) (p. 27)

organ reserve The extra capacity built into each organ, such as the heart and lungs, that allows a person to cope with extraordinary demands and to withstand organ strain. (p. 392)

osteoporosis Fragile bones that result from primary aging, which makes bones more porous, especially if a person is at genetic risk. (p. 519)

overimitation When a person imitates an action unnecessarily. Overimitation is common among 2- to 6-year-olds when they copy adult actions that are irrelevant and inefficient. (p. 178)

overregularization Applying rules of grammar even when exceptions occur, making the language seem more "regular" than it actually is. (p. 184)

P

palliative care Medical treatment designed primarily to provide physical and emotional comfort to the dying patient and guidance to his or her loved ones. (p. 584)

parasuicide Any potentially lethal action against the self that does not result in death. (Also called *attempted suicide* or *failed suicide*.) (p. 371)

parental monitoring Parents' ongoing awareness of what their children are doing, where, and with whom. (p. 358)

parentification When a child acts more like a parent than a child. This may occur if the actual parents do not act as caregivers, making a child feel responsible for the family. (p. 287)

Parkinson's disease A chronic, progressive disease that is characterized by muscle tremor and rigidity and sometimes major NCD; caused by reduced dopamine production in the brain. (p. 529)

passive euthanasia When a person is allowed to die naturally, instead of intervening with active attempts to prolong life. (p. 586)

peer pressure When people of the same age group encourage particular behavior, dress, and attitude. This is usually considered negative, when peers encourage behavior that is contrary to norms or morals, but can also be positive. (p. 360)

percentile A point on a ranking scale of 0 to 100. The 50th percentile is the midpoint; half the people in the population being studied rank higher and half rank lower. (p. 90)

perception The mental processing of sensory information when the brain interprets a sensation. (p. 97)

permissive parenting An approach to child rearing that is characterized by high nurturance and communication but little discipline, guidance, or control. (p. 211)

perseveration The tendency to persevere in, or stick to, one thought or action for a long time. (p. 171)

personal fable The belief that one's own emotions, experiences, and destiny are unique, more wonderful or awful than anyone else's. (p. 330)

phallic stage Freud's third stage of development, when the penis becomes the focus of concern and pleasure. (p. 215)

phenotype The observable characteristics of a person, including appearance, personality, intelligence, and all other apparent traits. (p. 50)

physician-assisted suicide A form of active euthanasia in which a doctor provides the means for someone to end his or her own life, usually by prescribing lethal drugs. (p. 586)

PISA (Programme for International Student Assessment) An international test taken by 15-year-olds in 50 nations to measure problem solving and cognition in daily life. (p. 346)

pituitary A gland in the brain that produces many hormones, including those that regulate growth and that signal the adrenal and sex glands to produce additional hormones. (p. 316)

plaques Clumps of a protein called *beta-amyloid,* found in brain tissues surrounding the neurons. (p. 527)

polygamous family A family consisting of one man, more than one wife, and their children. (p. 292)

polypharmacy Refers to a situation in which people take many medications. The various side effects and interactions of those medications can result in NCD symptoms. (p. 532)

positivity effect The tendency for elderly people to perceive, prefer, and remember positive images and experiences more than negative ones. (p. 543)

postconventional moral reasoning Kohlberg's third level of moral reasoning, emphasizing principles thought to be universal. (p. 305)

postformal thought A proposed adult stage of cognitive development. Postformal is more practical, flexible, and dialectical (i.e., more capable of combining contradictory elements into a comprehensive whole) than earlier cognition. (p. 399)

postpartum depression The deep sadness and inadequacy felt by some new mothers in the days and weeks after giving birth. (p. 68)

posttraumatic stress disorder (PTSD) An anxiety disorder that develops as a delayed reaction to having experienced or witnessed a shocking or frightening event. Its symptoms may include flashbacks, hypervigilance, anger, nightmares, and sudden terror. (p. 230)

practical intelligence The intellectual skills used in everyday problem solving. (Sometimes called *tacit intelligence.*) (p. 449)

pragmatics The practical use of language, adjusting communication according to audience and context. (p. 184)

preconventional moral reasoning Kohlberg's first level of moral reasoning, emphasizing personal rewards and punishments. (p. 305)

prefrontal cortex The area of the cortex at the very front of the brain that specializes in anticipation, planning, and impulse control. (p. 94)

preoperational intelligence Piaget's term for cognitive development between the ages of about 2 and 6; it includes language and imagination (which involve symbolic thought), but not yet logical, operational thinking. (p. 173)

preterm birth A birth that occurs three or more weeks before the full 38 weeks of the pregnancy—that is, at 35 or fewer weeks after conception. (p. 78)

primary aging The universal and irreversible physical changes that occur in all living creatures as they grow older. Primary aging is inevitable, programmed for each species. (p. 518)

primary prevention Actions that change overall background conditions to prevent some unwanted event or circumstance, such as injury, disease, or abuse. (p. 231)

primary sex characteristics The parts of the body that are directly involved in reproduction, including the vagina, uterus, ovaries, testicles, and penis. (p. 323)

private schools Schools funded by parents and sponsoring institutions. Such schools have control over admissions, hiring, and specifics of curriculum, although some regulations apply. (p. 265)

problem-focused coping A strategy to deal with stress by tackling a stressful situation directly. (p. 454)

Progress in International Reading Literacy Study (PIRLS) Inaugurated in 2001, a planned five-year cycle of international trend studies in the reading ability. (p. 259)

prosocial behavior Actions that are helpful and kind but that are of no obvious benefit to the person doing them. (p. 219)

protein-calorie malnutrition A condition in which a person does not consume sufficient food. This can result in illness, severe weight loss, and even death. (p. 111)

proximal parenting Caregiving practices that involve being physically close to the baby, with frequent holding and touching. (p. 152)

pruning When applied to brain development, the process by which unused connections in the brain atrophy and die. (p. 96)

psychoanalytic theory A theory of human development that holds that irrational, unconscious drives and motives, often originating in childhood, underlie human behavior. (p. 23)

psychological control A disciplinary technique that involves threatening to withdraw love and support, using a child's feelings of guilt and gratitude to the parents. (p. 224)

puberty The time at the end of childhood between the first onrush of growth hormones and full adult size. (p. 315)

Q

qualitative research Research that consider qualities instead of quantities. Descriptions of particular conditions and participants' expressed ideas are often part of qualitative studies. (p. 42)

quantitative research Research that provides data that can be expressed with numbers, such as ranks or scales. (p. 41)

R

race A group of people who are regarded by themselves or by others as distinct from other groups on the basis of physical appearance, typically skin color. (p. 19)

reaction time The time it takes to respond to a stimulus, either physically (with a reflexive movement such as an eyeblink) or cognitively (with a thought). (p. 253)

reactive aggression An impulsive retaliation for another person's intentional or accidental hurtful action. (p. 220)

reflex An unlearned, involuntary action or movement in response to a stimulus. A reflex occurs without conscious thought. (p. 67)

Reggio Emilia A program of early-childhood education that originated in the town of Reggio Emilia, Italy, and that encourages each child's creativity in a carefully designed setting. (p. 190)

relational aggression Nonphysical acts, such as insults or social rejection, aimed at harming the social connection between the victim and other people. (p. 220)

REM (rapid eye movement) sleep A stage of sleep characterized by flickering eyes behind closed lids. REM indicates dreaming. (p. 91)

replication Repeating a study, usually using different participants, perhaps of another age, location, socioeconomic status (SES), or culture. (p. 5)

reported maltreatment Harm or endangerment about which someone has notified the authorities. (p. 228)

resilience The capacity to adapt well to significant adversity and to overcome serious stress. (p. 285)

response to intervention (RTI) An educational strategy that uses early intervention to help children who demonstrate below-average achievement. Only children who are not helped are designated for more intense measures. (p. 275)

role confusion A situation in which people do not seem to know or care about their identity. (Sometimes called *identity diffusion*.) (p. 352)

rough-and-tumble play Play that seems to be rough, as in play wrestling or chasing, but in which there is no intent to harm. (p. 208)

rumination Repeatedly thinking and talking about past experiences and possibilities. (p. 370)

S

sandwich generation The generation of middle-aged people who are supposedly "squeezed" by the needs of the younger and older members of their families. (p. 487)

scaffolding Temporary support that is tailored to a learner's needs and abilities and aimed at helping the learner take the next step in learning something. (p. 177)

science of human development The science that seeks to understand how and why people of all ages and circumstances change or remain the same over time. (p. 4)

scientific method A way to answer questions using empirical research and data-based conclusions. (p. 4)

scientific observation A method of testing a hypothesis by unobtrusively watching and recording participants' behavior in a systematic and objective manner—in a natural setting, in a laboratory, or in archival data. (p. 35)

Seattle Longitudinal Study A major cross-sequential study of adult intelligence. This study began in 1956 and has been repeated every 7 years. (p. 445)

secondary aging The specific physical illnesses or conditions that become more common with aging but are caused by health habits and other influences that vary from person to person. (p. 518)

secondary education Education that follows primary education (elementary or grade school) and precedes tertiary education (college). It usually occurs from about age 11 to age 18, although there is some variation by school and by nation. (p. 341)

secondary prevention Actions that avert harm in a high-risk situation, such as using seat belts in cars. (p. 231)

secondary sex characteristics Physical traits that are not directly involved in reproduction but that indicate sexual maturity, such as a man's beard and a woman's breasts. (p. 323)

secular trend Advances in growth and maturation that result from modern nutrition. For example, improved nutrition and medical care over the past 200 years has led to earlier puberty and taller average height. (p. 320)

secure attachment A relationship in which an infant obtains both comfort and confidence from the presence of his or her caregiver. (p. 140)

selective attention The ability to concentrate on some stimuli while ignoring others. (p. 249)

selective optimization with compensation The theory that people specialize in some abilities and to ameliorate any physical and cognitive losses they may experience. (p. 456)

self theories Theories of late adulthood that emphasize the core self, or the search to maintain one's integrity and identity. (p. 540)

self-actualization The final stage in Maslow's hierarchy of needs, characterized by aesthetic, creative, philosophical, and spiritual understanding. (p. 534)

self-awareness A person's realization that he or she is a distinct individual whose body, mind, and actions are separate from those of other people. (p. 132)

senescence The process of aging. (p. 429)

sensation The response of a sensory system (eyes, ears, skin, tongue, nose) when it detects a stimulus. (p. 97)

sensitive period A time when a certain type of development is most likely, although it may still happen later with more difficulty. For example, early childhood is considered a sensitive period for language learning. (p. 10)

sensorimotor intelligence Piaget's term for the way infants think—by using their senses and motor skills—during the first period of cognitive development. (p. 112)

sensory memory The component of the information-processing system in which incoming stimulus information is stored for a split second to allow it to be processed. (Also called the *sensory register*.) (p. 251)

separation anxiety Distress when a familiar caregiver or loved one leaves; most obvious between 9 and 14 months. (p. 130)

seriation The concept that things can be arranged in a logical series, such as the number series or the alphabet. (p. 247)

sex differences Biological differences between males and females, in organs, hormones, and body shape. (p. 213)

sexual orientation A person's sexual and romantic attraction to others of the same sex, the other sex, or both sexes. (p. 364)

sexually transmitted infection (STI) An infection spread by sexual contact; includes syphilis, gonorrhea, genital herpes, chlamydia, and HIV. (p. 366)

shaken baby syndrome A life-threatening injury that occurs when an infant is forcefully shaken back and forth, a motion that ruptures blood vessels in the brain and breaks neural connections. (p. 97)

single-parent family A family that consists of only one parent and his or her children. (p. 292)

slippery slope The argument that a given action will start a chain of events that will culminate in an undesirable outcome. (p. 588)

small for gestational age (SGA) Having a body weight at birth that is significantly lower than expected, given the time since conception. For example, a 5-pound (2,265-gram) newborn is considered SGA if born on time but not SGA if born two months early. (Also called *small-for-dates*.) (p. 78)

social comparison The tendency to assess one's abilities, achievements, social status, and other attributes by measuring them against those of other people, especially one's peers. (p. 282)

social construction An idea that is built on shared perceptions, not on objective reality. Many age-related terms (such as *childhood, adolescence, yuppie,* and *senior citizen*) are social constructions, strongly influenced by social assumptions. (p. 16)

social convoy Collectively, the family members, friends, acquaintances, and even strangers who move through the years of life with a person, all aging together. (p. 476)

social learning The acquisition of behavior patterns by observing the behavior of others. (p. 152)

social learning theory An extension of behaviorism that emphasizes the influence that other people have over a person's behavior. Even without specific reinforcement, every individual learns many things through observation and imitation of other people. (Also called *observational learning*.) (p. 28)

social referencing Seeking information about how to react to an unfamiliar or ambiguous object or event by observing someone else's expressions and reactions. That other person becomes a social reference. (p. 146)

social smile A smile evoked by a human face, normally first evident in full-term infants about 6 weeks after birth. (p. 130)

socio-emotional selectivity theory The theory that older people prioritize regulation of their own emotions and seek familiar social contacts who reinforce generativity, pride, and joy. (p. 542)

sociodramatic play Pretend play in which children act out various roles and themes in plots or roles that they create. (p. 208)

socioeconomic status (SES) A person's position in society as determined by income, occupation, education, and place of residence. (Sometimes called *social class*.) (p. 14)

sonogram An image of a fetus (or an internal organ) produced by using high-frequency sound waves. (Also called *ultrasound*.) (p. 60)

specific learning disorder A marked deficit in a particular area of learning that is not caused by an apparent physical disability, or by an unusually stressful home environment. (p. 271)

spermarche A boy's first ejaculation of sperm. Erections can occur as early as infancy, but ejaculation signals sperm production. Spermarche may occur during sleep (in a "wet dream") or via direct stimulation. (p. 316)

static reasoning A characteristic of preoperational thought in which a young child thinks that nothing changes. Whatever is now has always been and always will be. (p. 174)

stem cells Cells from which any other specialized type of cell can form. (p. 58)

stereotype threat The thought that one's appearance or behavior might confirm another person's oversimplified, prejudiced attitudes, a thought that causes anxiety even when the stereotype is not held by other people. (p. 400)

still-face technique An experimental practice in which an adult keeps his or her face unmoving and expressionless in face-to-face interaction with an infant. (p. 138)

Strange Situation A laboratory procedure for measuring attachment by evoking infants' reactions to the stress of various adults' comings and goings in an unfamiliar playroom. (p. 141)

stranger wariness An infant's expression of concern—a quiet stare while clinging to a familiar person, or a look of fear—when a stranger appears. (p. 130)

stratification theories Theories that emphasize that social forces, particularly those related to a person's social stratum or social category, limit individual choices and affect a person's ability to function in late adulthood because past stratification continues to limit life in various ways. (p. 544)

stressor Any situation, event, experience, or other stimulus that causes a person to feel stressed. Many circumstances become stressors for some people but not for others. (p. 453)

stunting The failure of children to grow to a normal height for their age due to severe and chronic malnutrition. (p. 111)

substantiated maltreatment Harm or endangerment that has been reported, investigated, and verified. (p. 228)

sudden infant death (SIDS) An infant's unexpected, sudden death; when a seemingly healthy baby, usually between 2 and 6 months old, stops breathing and dies while asleep. (p. 105)

suicidal ideation Thinking about suicide, usually with serious emotional and intellectual impact. (p. 371)

superego In psychoanalytic theory, the judgmental part of the personality that internalizes the moral standards of the parents. (p. 215)

survey A research method in which information is collected from a large number of people by interviews, written questionnaires, or some other means. (p. 37)

symbolic thought In preoperational intelligence, understanding that words can refer to things not seen and that an item, such as a flag, can symbolize something else (in this case, a country). (p. 173)

synapses The intersection between the axon of one neuron and the dendrites of other neurons. (p. 94)

synchrony A coordinated, rapid, and smooth exchange of responses between a caregiver and an infant. (p. 137)

T

tangles Twisted masses of threads made of a protein called *tau* within the neurons of the brain. (p. 527)

telomeres The area of the tips of each chromosome that is reduced a tiny amount as time passes. By the end of life, the telomeres are very short. (p. 513)

temperament Inborn differences between one person and another in emotions, activity, and self-regulation. It is measured by the person's typical responses to the environment. (p. 135)

teratogen Any agent or condition, including viruses, drugs, and chemicals, that can impair prenatal development, resulting in birth defects or complications. (p. 72)

terror management theory The idea that people adopt cultural values and moral principles in order to cope with their fear of death. This system of beliefs protects individuals from anxiety about their mortality and bolsters their self-esteem. (p. 577)

tertiary prevention Actions, such as immediate and effective medical treatment, after an adverse event (such as illness or injury). (p. 231)

testosterone A sex hormone, the best known of the androgens (male hormones); secreted in far greater amounts by males than by females. (p. 317)

theory of mind A person's theory of what other people might be thinking. Children gradually realize that other people do not always know and think what they themselves do. (p. 180)

theory-theory The idea that children attempt to explain everything they see and hear by constructing theories. (p. 178)

threshold effect A situation in which a certain teratogen is relatively harmless in small doses but becomes harmful once exposure reaches a certain level (the threshold). (p. 73)

time-out A disciplinary technique in which a person is separated from other people and activities for a specified time. (p. 224)

transient exuberance The great but temporary increase in the number of dendrites that develop in an infant's brain during the first two years of life. (p. 96)

Trends in Math and Science Study (TIMSS) An international assessment of the math and science skills of fourth- and eighth-graders. (p. 259)

trust versus mistrust Erikson's first crisis of psychosocial development. Infants learn basic trust if the world is a secure place where their basic needs (for food, comfort, attention, and so on) are met. (p. 151)

U

universal design The creation of settings and equipment that can be used by everyone, whether or not they are able-bodied and sensory-acute. (p. 507)

V

vascular disease Formerly called *vascular* or *multi-infarct dementia*, vascular disease is characterized by progressive loss of intellectual functioning caused by repeated infarcts (strokes), or temporary obstructions of blood vessels in the brain. (p. 528)

very low birthweight (VLBW) A body weight at birth of less than 3 pounds, 5 ounces (1,500 grams). (p. 78)

vouchers A monetary commitment by the government to pay for the education of a child. Vouchers vary a great deal from place to place, not only in amount and availability, but in who gets them and what schools accept them. (p. 265)

W

wasting The tendency for children to be severely underweight for their age as a result of malnutrition. (p. 111)

wear and tear A view of aging as a process by which the human body wears out because of the passage of time and exposure to environmental stressors. (p. 511)

weathering The gradual accumulation of stressors over a long period of time, wearing down a person's resilience and resistance. (p. 455)

withdrawn-rejected A child who avoids social interaction with peers. Other children do not want to be friends with such a child because of his or her timid, isolative, and anxious behavior. (p. 301)

working memory The component of the information-processing system in which current conscious mental activity occurs. (Formerly called *short-term memory*.) (p. 251)

working model In cognitive theory, a set of assumptions that the individual uses to organize perceptions and experiences. For example, a person might assume that other people are trustworthy and be surprised if someone lies, cheats, or betrays a confidence. (p. 153)

X

X-linked A gene carried on the X chromosome. If a male inherits an X-linked recessive trait from his mother, he expresses that trait because the Y from his father has no counteracting gene. Females are more likely to be carriers of X-linked traits but are less likely to express them. (p. 56)

XX A 23rd chromosome pair that consists of two X-shaped chromosomes, one each from the mother and the father. XX zygotes become females. (p. 51)

XY A 23rd chromosome pair that consists of an X-shaped chromosome from the mother and a Y-shaped chromosome from the father. XY zygotes become males. (p. 51)

Z

zone of proximal development (ZPD) In sociocultural theory, a metaphorical area, or "zone," surrounding a learner that includes all the skills, knowledge, and concepts that the person is close ("proximal") to acquiring but cannot yet master without help. (p. 177)

zygote The single cell that is formed from the fusing of two gametes, a sperm and an ovum. (p. 48)

References

Aarnoudse-Moens, Cornelieke S. H.; Smidts, Diana P.; Oosterlaan, Jaap; Duivenvoorden, Hugo J. & Weisglas-Kuperus, Nynke. (2009). Executive function in very preterm children at early school age. *Journal of Abnormal Child Psychology*, *37*(7), 981–993. doi: 10.1007/s10802-009-9327-z

Abar, Caitlin C.; Jackson, Kristina M. & Wood, Mark. (2014). Reciprocal relations between perceived parental knowledge and adolescent substance use and delinquency: The moderating role of parent–teen relationship quality. *Developmental Psychology*, *50*(9), 2176–2187. doi: 10.1037/a0037463

Abela, Angela & Walker, Janet (Eds.). (2014). *Contemporary issues in family studies: Global perspectives on partnerships, parenting and support in a changing world*. Malden, MA: Wiley.

Abele, Andrea E. & Volmer, Judith. (2011). Dual-career couples: Specific challenges for work-life integration. In Stephan Kaiser et al. (Eds.), *Creating balance? International perspectives on the work-life integration of professionals* (pp. 173–189). Heidelberg, Germany: Springer. doi: 10.1007/978-3-642-16199-5_10

Abrutyn, Seth & Mueller, Anna S. (2014). Are suicidal behaviors contagious in adolescence? Using longitudinal data to examine suicide suggestion. *American Sociological Review*, *79*(2), 211–227. doi: 10.1177/0003122413519445

Acharya, Arnab; Lalwani, Tanya; Dutta, Rahul; Knoll Rajaratnam, Julie; Ruducha, Jenny; Varkey, Leila Caleb, . . . Bernson, Jeff. (2015). Evaluating a large-scale community-based intervention to improve pregnancy and newborn health among the rural poor in India. *American Journal of Public Health*, *105*(1), 144–152. doi: 10.2105/AJPH.2014.302092

Adams, Caralee. (2014). High school students' participation in advanced placement continues to grow [Web log post]. *Education Week*. Retrieved from http://blogs.edweek.org/edweek/college_bound/2014/02/high_school_students_participating_in_advanced_placement_continues_to_grow.html

Adams, Ted D.; Davidson, Lance E.; Litwin, Sheldon E.; Kolotkin, Ronette L.; LaMonte, Michael J.; Pendleton, Robert C., . . . Hunt, Steven C. (2012). Health benefits of gastric bypass surgery after 6 years. *JAMA*, *308*(11), 1122–1131. doi: 10.1001/2012.jama.11164

Adamson, Lauren B. & Bakeman, Roger. (2006). Development of displaced speech in early mother-child conversations. *Child Development*, *77*(1), 186–200. doi: 10.1111/j.1467-8624.2006.00864.x

Adamson, Lauren B.; Bakeman, Roger; Deckner, Deborah F. & Nelson, P. Brooke. (2014). From interactions to conversations: The development of joint engagement during early childhood. *Child Development*, *85*(3), 941–955. doi: 10.1111/cdev.12189

Adler, Lynn Peters. (1995). *Centenarians: The bonus years*. Santa Fe, NM: Health Press.

Adolph, Karen E. & Tamis-LeMonda, Catherine S. (2014). The costs and benefits of development: The transition from crawling to walking. *Child Development Perspectives*, *8*(4), 187–192. doi: 10.1111/cdep.12085

Ainsworth, Mary D. Salter. (1967). *Infancy in Uganda: Infant care and the growth of love*. Baltimore, MD: Johns Hopkins Press.

Ainsworth, Mary D. Salter. (1973). The development of infant-mother attachment. In Bettye M. Caldwell & Henry N. Ricciuti (Eds.), *Child development and social policy* (pp. 1–94). Chicago, IL: University of Chicago Press.

Aizer, Anna & Currie, Janet. (2014). The intergenerational transmission of inequality: Maternal disadvantage and health at birth. *Science*, *344*(6186), 856–861. doi: 10.1126/science.1251872

Akhtar, Nameera & Jaswal, Vikram K. (2013). Deficit or difference? Interpreting diverse developmental paths: An introduction to the special section. *Developmental Psychology*, *49*(1), 1–3. doi: 10.1037/a0029851

Al-Yagon, Michal; Cavendish, Wendy; Cornoldi, Cesare; Fawcett, Angela J.; Grünke, Matthias; Hung, Li-Yu, . . . Vio, Claudio. (2013). The proposed changes for DSM-5 for SLD and ADHD: International perspectives–Australia, Germany, Greece, India, Israel, Italy, Spain, Taiwan, United Kingdom, and United States. *Journal of Learning Disabilities*, *46*(1), 58–72. doi: 10.1177/0022219412464353

Alasuutari, Pertti; Bickman, Leonard & Brannen, Julia (Eds.). (2008). *The SAGE handbook of social research methods*. Los Angeles, CA: SAGE.

Alavinia, Seyed Mohammad & Burdorf, Alex. (2008). Unemployment and retirement and ill-health: A cross-sectional analysis across European countries. *International Archives of Occupational and Environmental Health*, *82*(1), 39–45. doi: 10.1007/s00420-008-0304-6

Albert, Dustin; Chein, Jason & Steinberg, Laurence. (2013). The teenage brain: Peer influences on adolescent decision making. *Current Directions in Psychological Science*, *22*(2), 114–120. doi: 10.1177/0963721412471347

Albert, Dustin & Steinberg, Laurence. (2011). Judgment and decision making in adolescence. *Journal of Research on Adolescence*, *21*(1), 211–224. doi: 10.1111/j.1532-7795.2010.00724.x

Albert, Steven M. & Freedman, Vicki A. (2010). *Public health and aging: Maximizing function and well-being* (2nd ed.). New York, NY: Springer.

Alberts, Amy; Elkind, David & Ginsberg, Stephen. (2007). The personal fable and risk-taking in early adolescence. *Journal of Youth and Adolescence*, *36*(1), 71–76. doi: 10.1007/s10964-006-9144-4

Aldwin, Carolyn M. (2009). *Stress, coping, and development: An integrative perspective* (2nd ed.). New York, NY: Guilford Press.

Aldwin, Carolyn M. & Gilmer, Diane Fox. (2013). *Health, illness, and optimal aging: Biological and psychosocial perspectives* (2nd ed.). New York, NY: Springer.

Alegre, Alberto. (2011). Parenting styles and children's emotional intelligence: What do we know? *The Family Journal, 19*(1), 56–62. doi: 10.1177/1066480710387486

Allen, Kathleen P. (2010). A bullying intervention system in high school: A two-year school-wide follow-up. *Studies In Educational Evaluation, 36*(3), 83–92. doi: 10.1016/j.stueduc.2011.01.002

Allen, Rebecca S.; Haley, Philip P.; Harris, Grant M.; Fowler, Stevie N. & Pruthi, Roopwinder. (2011). Resilience: Definitions, ambiguities, and applications. In Barbara Resnick et al. (Eds.), *Resilience in aging: Concepts, research, and outcomes* (pp. 1–14). New York, NY: Springer.

Altbach, Philip G.; Reisberg, Liz & Rumbley, Laura E. (2010). Tracking a global academic revolution. *Change: The Magazine of Higher Learning, 42*(2), 30–39. doi: 10.1080/00091381003590845

Alviola, Pedro A.; Nayga, Rodolfo M. & Thomsen, Michael. (2013). Food deserts and childhood obesity. *Applied Economic Perspectives and Policy, 35*(1), 106–124. doi: 10.1093/aepp/pps035

Amanullah, Siraj; Heneghan, Julia A.; Steele, Dale W.; Mello, Michael J. & Linakis, James G. (2014). Emergency department visits resulting from intentional injury in and out of school. *Pediatrics, 133*(2), 254–261. doi: 10.1542/peds.2013-2155

Amato, Michael S.; Magzamen, Sheryl; Imm, Pamela; Havlena, Jeffrey A.; Anderson, Henry A.; Kanarek, Marty S. & Moore, Colleen F. (2013). Early lead exposure (<3 years old) prospectively predicts fourth grade school suspension in Milwaukee, Wisconsin (USA). *Environmental Research, 126*, 60–65. doi: 10.1016/j.envres.2013.07.008

Amato, Paul R. (2010). Research on divorce: Continuing trends and new developments. *Journal of Marriage and Family, 72*(3), 650–666. doi: 10.1111/j.1741-3737.2010.00723.x

Ambady, Nalini & Bharucha, Jamshed. (2009). Culture and the brain. *Current Directions in Psychological Science, 18*(6), 342–345. doi: 10.1111/j.1467-8721.2009.01664.x

American Community Survey. (2014). Washington, DC: U.S. Census Bureau.

American Psychiatric Association. (2013). *Diagnostic and statistical manual of mental disorders: DSM-5* (5th ed.). Washington, DC: American Psychiatric Association.

American Psychological Association. (2010). Ethical principles of psychologists and code of conduct: Including 2010 amendments. http://www.apa.org/ethics/code/index.aspx

Amrock, Stephen M.; Zakhar, Joseph; Zhou, Sherry & Weitzman, Michael. (2015). Perception of e-cigarette harm and its correlation with use among U.S. Adolescents. *Nicotine & Tobacco Research, 17*(3), 330–336. doi: 10.1093/ntr/ntu156

Amsel, Eric & Smetana, Judith (Eds.). (2011). *Adolescent vulnerabilities and opportunities: Developmental and constructivist perspectives.* New York, NY: Cambridge University Press.

Anderson, Michael. (2001). 'You have to get inside the person' or making grief private: Image and metaphor in the therapeutic reconstruction of bereavement. In Jenny Hockey et al. (Eds.), *Grief, mourning, and death ritual* (pp. 135–143). Buckingham, UK: Open University Press.

Ansary, Nadia S. & Luthar, Suniya S. (2009). Distress and academic achievement among adolescents of affluence: A study of externalizing and internalizing problem behaviors and school performance. *Development and Psychopathology, 21*(1), 319–341. doi: 10.1017/S0954579409000182

Antoine, Michelle W.; Hübner, Christian A; Arezzo, Joseph C. & Hébert, Jean M. (2013). A causative link between inner ear defects and long-term striatal dysfunction. *Science, 341*(6150), 1120–1123. doi: 10.1126/science.1240405

Antonucci, Toni C.; Akiyama, Hiroko & Merline, Alicia. (2001). Dynamics of social relationships in midlife. In Margie E. Lachman (Ed.), *Handbook of midlife development* (pp. 571–598). New York, NY: Wiley.

Aouizerat, Bradley; Pearce, C. Leigh & Miaskowski, Christine. (2011). The search for host genetic factors of HIV/AIDS pathogenesis in the post-genome era: Progress to date and new avenues for discovery. *Current HIV/AIDS Reports, 8*(1), 38–44. doi: 10.1007/s11904-010-0065-1

Apgar, Virginia. (1953). A proposal for a new method of evaluation of the newborn infant. *Current Researches in Anesthesia and Analgesia, 32*, 260–267.

Ardelt, Monika. (2011). Wisdom, age, and well-being. In K. Warner Schaie & Sherry L. Willis (Eds.), *Handbook of the psychology of aging* (7th ed., pp. 279–291). San Diego, CA: Academic Press. doi: 10.1016/B978-0-12-380882-0.00018-8

Ariely, Dan. (2009). *Predictably irrational: The hidden forces that shape our decisions.* New York, NY: Harper.

Arndt, Jamie; Vail III, Kenneth E.; Cox, Cathy R.; Goldenberg, Jamie L.; Piasecki, Thomas M. & Gibbons, Frederick X. (2013). The interactive effect of mortality reminders and tobacco craving on smoking topography. *Health Psychology, 32*(5), 525–532. doi: 10.1037/a0029201

Arnett, Jeffrey J. (2004). *Emerging adulthood: The winding road from the late teens through the twenties.* New York, NY: Oxford University Press.

Arnett, Jeffrey J. (2008). The neglected 95%: Why American psychology needs to become less American. *American Psychologist, 63*(7), 602–614. doi: 10.1037/0003-066X.63.7.602

Arnett, Jeffrey J. & Padilla-Walker, Laura M. (2015). Brief report: Danish emerging adults' conceptions of adulthood. *Journal of Adolescence, 38*(1), 39–44. doi: 10.1016/j.adolescence.2014.10.011

Arnett, Jeffrey J.; Žukauskienė, Rita & Sugimura, Kazumi. (2014). The new life stage of emerging adulthood at ages 18–29 years: Implications for mental health. *The Lancet Psychiatry, 1*(7), 569–576. doi: 10.1016/S2215-0366(14)00080-7

Aron, Arthur; Lewandowski, Gary W.; Mashek, Debra & Aron, Elaine N. (2013). The self-expansion model of motivation and cognition in close relationships. In Jeffry A. Simpson & Lorne Campbell (Eds.), *The Oxford handbook of close relationships* (pp. 90–115). New York, NY: Oxford University Press.

Aronson, Joshua; Burgess, Diana; Phelan, Sean M. & Juarez, Lindsay. (2013). Unhealthy interactions: The role of stereotype threat in health disparities. *American Journal of Public Health*, *103*(1), 50–56. doi: 10.2105/AJPH.2012.300828

Aronson, Joshua; Fried, Carrie B. & Good, Catherine. (2002). Reducing the effects of stereotype threat on African American college students by shaping theories of intelligence. *Journal of Experimental Social Psychology*, *38*(2), 113–125. doi: 10.1006/jesp.2001.1491

Arterburn, David E.; Bogart, Andy; Sherwood, Nancy E.; Sidney, Stephen; Coleman, Karen J.; Haneuse, Sebastien, . . . Selby, Joe. (2013). A multisite study of long-term remission and relapse of type 2 diabetes mellitus following gastric bypass. *Obesity Surgery*, *23*(1), 93–102. doi: 10.1007/s11695-012-0802-1

Arum, Richard & Roksa, Josipa. (2011). *Academically adrift: Limited learning on college campuses.* Chicago, IL: University of Chicago Press.

Arum, Richard & Roksa, Josipa. (2014). *Aspiring adults adrift: Tentative transitions of college graduates.* Chicago, IL: University of Chicago Press.

Ashby, Michael. (2009). The dying human: A perspective from palliative medicine. In Allan Kellehear (Ed.), *The study of dying: From autonomy to transformation* (pp. 76–98). New York, NY: Cambridge University Press.

Ashwin, Sarah & Isupova, Olga. (2014). "Behind every great man…": The male marriage wage premium examined qualitatively. *Journal of Marriage and Family*, *76*(1), 37–55. doi: 10.1111/jomf.12082

Aslin, Richard N. (2012). Language development: Revisiting Eimas et al.'s /ba/ and /pa/ study. In Alan M. Slater & Paul C. Quinn (Eds.), *Developmental psychology: Revisiting the classic studies* (pp. 191–203). Thousand Oaks, CA: Sage.

Asma, Stephen T. (2013). *Against fairness.* Chicago, IL: University of Chicago Press.

Atchley, Robert C. (2009). *Spirituality and aging.* Baltimore, MD: Johns Hopkins University Press.

Atzil, Shir; Hendler, Talma & Feldman, Ruth. (2014). The brain basis of social synchrony. *Social Cognitive & Affective Neuroscience*, *9*(8), 1193–1202. doi: 10.1093/scan/nst105

Aud, Susan; Wilkinson-Flicker, Sidney; Kristapovich, Paul; Rathbun, Amy; Wang, Xiaolei & Zhang, Jijun. (2013). *The condition of education 2013.* Washington, DC: U.S. Department of Education, National Center for Education Statistics.

Aunola, Kaisa; Tolvanen, Asko; Viljaranta, Jaana & Nurmi, Jari-Erik. (2013). Psychological control in daily parent–child interactions increases children's negative emotions. *Journal of Family Psychology*, *27*(3), 453–462. doi: 10.1037/a0032891

Autor, David H. (2014). Skills, education, and the rise of earnings inequality among the "other 99 percent". *Science*, *344*(6186), 843–851. doi: 10.1126/science.1251868

Aven, Terje. (2011). On some recent definitions and analysis frameworks for risk, vulnerability, and resilience. *Risk Analysis*, *31*(4), 515–522. doi: 10.1111/j.1539-6924.2010.01528.x

Avenevoli, Shelli; Swendsen, Joel; He, Jian-Ping; Burstein, Marcy & Merikangas, Kathleen Ries. (2015). Major depression in the National Comorbidity Survey–Adolescent Supplement: Prevalence, correlates, and treatment. *Journal of the American Academy of Child & Adolescent Psychiatry*, *54*(1), 37–44.e32. doi: 10.1016/j.jaac.2014.10.010

Aviv, Abraham. (2011). Leukocyte telomere dynamics, human aging and life span. In Edward J. Masoro & Steven N. Austad (Eds.), *Handbook of the biology of aging* (7th ed., pp. 163–176). San Diego, CA: Academic Press. doi: 10.1016/B978-0-12-378638-8.00007-5

Ayalon, Liat & Ancoli-Israel, Sonia. (2009). Normal sleep in aging. In Teofilo L. Lee-Chiong (Ed.), *Sleep medicine essentials* (pp. 173–176). Hoboken, NJ: Wiley-Blackwell.

Ayyanathan, Kasirajan (Ed.). (2014). *Specific gene expression and epigenetics: The interplay between the genome and its environment.* Oakville, Canada: Apple Academic Press.

Babchishin, Lyzon K.; Weegar, Kelly & Romano, Elisa. (2013). Early child care effects on later behavioral outcomes using a Canadian nation-wide sample. *Journal of Educational and Developmental Psychology*, *3*(2), 15–29. doi: 10.5539/jedp.v3n2p15

Babineau, Vanessa; Green, Cathryn Gordon; Jolicoeur-Martineau, Alexis; Minde, Klaus; Sassi, Roberto; St-André, Martin, . . . Wazana, Ashley. (2015). Prenatal depression and 5-HTTLPR interact to predict dysregulation from 3 to 36 months – A differential susceptibility model. *Journal of Child Psychology and Psychiatry*, *56*(1), 21–29. doi: 10.1111/jcpp.12246

Bachman, Jerald G.; O'Malley, Patrick M.; Freedman-Doan, Peter; Trzesniewski, Kali H. & Donnellan, M. Brent. (2011). Adolescent self-esteem: Differences by race/ethnicity, gender, and age. *Self Identity*, *10*(4), 445–473. doi: 10.1080/15298861003794538

Bagwell, Catherine L. & Schmidt, Michelle E. (2011). *Friendships in childhood & adolescence.* New York, NY: Guilford Press.

Baillargeon, Renée & DeVos, Julie. (1991). Object permanence in young infants: Further evidence. *Child Development*, *62*(6), 1227–1246. doi: 10.1111/j.1467-8624.1991.tb01602.x

Baker, Beth. (2007). *Old age in a new age: The promise of transformative nursing homes.* Nashville, TN: Vanderbilt University Press.

Baker, Lindsey A. & Silverstein, Merril. (2012). The well-being of grandparents caring for grandchildren in rural China and the United States. In Sara Arber & Virpi Timonen (Eds.), *Contemporary grandparenting: Changing family relationships in global contexts* (pp. 51–70). Chicago, IL: Policy Press.

Baldry, Anna C. & Farrington, David P. (2007). Effectiveness of programs to prevent school bullying. *Victims & Offenders*, *2*(2), 183–204. doi: 10.1080/15564880701263155

Ball, Howard. (2012). *At liberty to die: The battle for death with dignity in America.* New York, NY: New York University Press.

Ball, Helen L. & Volpe, Lane E. (2013). Sudden Infant Death Syndrome (SIDS) risk reduction and infant sleep location—Moving the discussion forward. *Social Science & Medicine*, *79*(1), 84–91. doi: 10.1016/j.socscimed.2012.03.025

Baltazar, Alina; Hopkins, Gary; McBride, Duane; Vanderwaal, Curt; Pepper, Sara & Mackey, Sarah. (2013). Parental influence on inhalant use. *Journal of Child & Adolescent Substance Abuse*, *22*(1), 25–37. doi: 10.1080/1067828X.2012.729904

Baltes, Paul B. (2003). On the incomplete architecture of human ontogeny: Selection, optimization and compensation as foundation of developmental theory. In Ursula M. Staudinger & Ulman Lindenberger (Eds.), *Understanding human development: Dialogues with lifespan psychology* (pp. 17–43). Boston, MA: Kluwer Academic Publishers.

Baltes, Paul B. & Baltes, Margret M. (1990). Psychological perspectives on successful aging: The model of selective optimization with compensation. In Paul B. Baltes & Margret M. Baltes (Eds.), *Successful aging: Perspectives from the behavioral sciences* (pp. 1–34). New York, NY: Cambridge University Press.

Baltes, Paul B.; Lindenberger, Ulman & Staudinger, Ursula M. (2006). Life span theory in developmental psychology. In William Damon & Richard M. Lerner (Eds.), *Handbook of child psychology* (6th ed., Vol. 1, pp. 569–664). Hoboken, NJ: Wiley.

Baltes, Paul B. & Smith, Jacqui. (2008). The fascination of wisdom: Its nature, ontogeny, and function. *Perspectives on Psychological Science, 3*(1), 56–64. doi: 10.1111/j.1745-6916.2008.00062.x

Baly, Michael W.; Cornell, Dewey G. & Lovegrove, Peter. (2014). A longitudinal investigation of self- and peer reports of bullying victimization across middle school. *Psychology in the Schools, 51*(3), 217–240. doi: 10.1002/pits.21747

Bandini, Julia. (2015). The medicalization of bereavement: (Ab)normal grief in the DSM-5. *Death Studies, 39*(6), 347–352. doi: 10.1080/07481187.2014.951498

Bandura, Albert. (1977). *Social learning theory.* Englewood Cliffs, NJ: Prentice Hall.

Bandura, Albert. (2006). Toward a psychology of human agency. *Perspectives on Psychological Science, 1*(2), 164–180. doi: 10.1111/j.1745-6916.2006.00011.x

Bannon, Michael J.; Johnson, Magen M.; Michelhaugh, Sharon K.; Hartley, Zachary J.; Halter, Steven D.; David, James A., . . . Schmidt, Carl J. (2014). A molecular profile of cocaine abuse includes the differential expression of genes that regulate transcription, chromatin, and dopamine cell phenotype. *Neuropsychopharmacology, 39*(9), 2191–2199. doi: 10.1038/npp.2014.70

Barbaresi, William J.; Colligan, Robert C.; Weaver, Amy L.; Voigt, Robert G.; Killian, Jill M. & Katusic, Slavica K. (2013). Mortality, ADHD, and psychosocial adversity in adults with childhood ADHD: A prospective study. *Pediatrics, 131*(4), 637–644. doi: 10.1542/peds.2012-2354

Barber, Brian K. (Ed.). (2002). *Intrusive parenting: How psychological control affects children and adolescents.* Washington, DC: American Psychological Association.

Barber, Larissa K. & Jenkins, Jade S. (2014). Creating technological boundaries to protect bedtime: Examining work–home boundary management, psychological detachment and sleep. *Stress and Health, 30*(3), 259–264. doi: 10.1002/smi.2536

Barbey, Aron K.; Colom, Roberto; Paul, Erick J. & Grafman, Jordan. (2013). Architecture of fluid intelligence and working memory revealed by lesion mapping. *Brain Structure and Function, 219*(2), 485–494. doi: 10.1007/s00429-013-0512-z

Barnett, W. Steven; Carolan, Megan E.; Squires, James H. & Brown, Kirsty C. (2013). *The state of preschool, 2013: State preschool yearbook.* New Brunswick, NJ: The National Institute for Early Education Research.

Barnett, W. S. & Masse, Leonard N. (2007). Comparative benefit–cost analysis of the Abecedarian program and its policy implications. *Economics of Education Review, 26*(1), 113–125. doi: 10.1016/j.econedurev.2005.10.007

Baron-Cohen, Simon; Tager-Flusberg, Helen & Lombardo, Michael (Eds.). (2013). *Understanding other minds: Perspectives from developmental social neuroscience* (3rd ed.). New York, NY: Oxford University Press.

Barrett, Anne E. (2012). Feeling young—A prescription for growing older? *Aging Today, 33,* 3–4.

Barros, Romina M.; Silver, Ellen J. & Stein, Ruth E. K. (2009). School recess and group classroom behavior. *Pediatrics, 123*(2), 431–436. doi: 10.1542/peds.2007-2825

Barrouillet, Pierre. (2011). Dual-process theories and cognitive development: Advances and challenges. *Developmental Review, 31*(2/3), 79–85. doi: 10.1016/j.dr.2011.07.002

Bartels, Meike; Cacioppo, John T.; van Beijsterveldt, Toos C. E. M. & Boomsma, Dorret I. (2013). Exploring the association between well-being and psychopathology in adolescents. *Behavior Genetics, 43*(3), 177–190. doi: 10.1007/s10519-013-9589-7

Barulli, Daniel & Stern, Yaakov. (2013). Efficiency, capacity, compensation, maintenance, plasticity: Emerging concepts in cognitive reserve. *Trends in Cognitive Sciences, 17*(10), 502–509. doi: 10.1016/j.tics.2013.08.012

Bass, Madeline. (2011). The tough questions: Do not attempt resuscitation discussions. In Keri Thomas & Ben Lobo (Eds.), *Advance care planning in end of life care* (pp. 113–124). New York, NY: Oxford University Press.

Bates, Lisa M.; Acevedo-Garcia, Dolores; Alegria, Margarita & Krieger, Nancy. (2008). Immigration and generational trends in body mass index and obesity in the United States: Results of the National Latino and Asian American Survey, 2002-2003. *American Journal of Public Health, 98*(1), 70–77. doi: 10.2105/ajph.2006.102814

Bateson, Mary Catherine. (2011). *Composing a further life: The age of active wisdom.* New York, NY: Vintage Books.

Bateson, Patrick. (2005). Desirable scientific conduct. *Science, 307*(5710), 645. doi: 10.1126/science.1107915

Bateson, Patrick & Martin, Paul. (2013). *Play, playfulness, creativity and innovation.* New York, NY: Cambridge University Press.

Batterham, Philip J.; Christensen, Helen & Mackinnon, Andrew J. (2009). Fluid intelligence is independently associated with all-cause mortality over 17 years in an elderly community sample: An investigation of potential mechanisms. *Intelligence, 37*(6), 551–560. doi: 10.1016/j.intell.2008.10.004

Bauer, Patricia J.; San Souci, Priscilla & Pathman, Thanujeni. (2010). Infant memory. *Wiley Interdisciplinary Reviews: Cognitive Science, 1*(2), 267–277. doi: 10.1002/wcs.38

Baumeister, Roy F. (2010). The Self. In Roy F. Baumeister & Eli J. Finkel (Eds.), *Advanced social psychology: The state of the science* (pp. 139–175). New York, NY: Oxford University Press.

Baumeister, Roy F. & Tierney, John. (2012). *Willpower: Rediscovering the greatest human strength.* New York, NY: Penguin.

Baumrind, Diana. (1967). Child care practices anteceding three patterns of preschool behavior. *Genetic Psychology Monographs, 75*(1), 43–88.

Baumrind, Diana. (1971). Current patterns of parental authority. *Developmental Psychology, 4*(1, Pt. 2), 1–103. doi: 10.1037/h0030372

Baumrind, Diana. (2005). Patterns of parental authority and adolescent autonomy. *New Directions for Child and Adolescent Development, 2005*(108), 61–69. doi: 10.1002/cd.128

Baumrind, Diana; Larzelere, Robert E. & Owens, Elizabeth B. (2010). Effects of preschool parents' power assertive patterns and practices on adolescent development. *Parenting, 10*(3), 157–201. doi: 10.1080/15295190903290790

Bax, Trent. (2014). *Youth and Internet addiction in China.* New York, NY: Routledge.

Beal, Susan. (1988). Sleeping position and sudden infant death syndrome. *The Medical Journal of Australia, 149*(10), 562.

Beauchaine, Theodore P.; Klein, Daniel N.; Crowell, Sheila E.; Derbidge, Christina & Gatzke-Kopp, Lisa. (2009). Multifinality in the development of personality disorders: A Biology × Sex × Environment interaction model of antisocial and borderline traits. *Development and Psychopathology, 21*(3), 735–770. doi: 10.1017/S0954579409000418

Beck, Melinda. (2009, May 26). How's your baby? Recalling the Apgar score's namesake. *The Wall Street Journal,* p. D1.

Beck, Martha N. (2011). *Expecting Adam: A true story of birth, rebirth, and everyday magic.* New York, NY: Three Rivers Press.

Becker, Derek R.; McClelland, Megan M.; Loprinzi, Paul & Trost, Stewart G. (2014). Physical activity, self-regulation, and early academic achievement in preschool children. *Early Education and Development, 25*(1), 56–70. doi: 10.1080/10409289.2013.780505

Beckers, Debby G. J.; van der Linden, Dimitri; Smulders, Peter G. W.; Kompier, Michiel A. J.; Taris, Toon W. & Geurts, Sabine A. E. (2008). Voluntary or involuntary? Control over overtime and rewards for overtime in relation to fatigue and work satisfaction. *Work & Stress, 22*(1), 33–50. doi: 10.1080/02678370801984927

Beise, Jan & Voland, Eckart. (2002). A multilevel event history analysis of the effects of grandmothers on child mortality in a historical German population: Krummhörn, Ostfriesland, 1720–1874. *Demographic Research, 7*(13), 469–498. doi: 10.4054/DemRes.2002.7.13

Belfield, Clive R.; Nores, Milagros; Barnett, Steve & Schweinhart, Lawrence. (2006). The High/Scope Perry Preschool Program: Cost benefit analysis using data from the age-40 followup. *Journal of Human Resources, 41*(1), 162–190. doi: 10.3368/jhr.XLI.1.162

Belin, David; Belin-Rauscent, Aude; Murray, Jennifer E. & Everitt, Barry J. (2013). Addiction: failure of control over maladaptive incentive habits. *Current Opinion in Neurobiology, 23*(4), 564–572. doi: 10.1016/j.conb.2013.01.025

Bell, Martha Ann & Calkins, Susan D. (2011). Attentional control and emotion regulation in early development. In Michael I. Posner (Ed.), *Cognitive neuroscience of attention* (2nd ed., pp. 322–330). New York, NY: Guilford Press.

Belsky, Daniel W.; Caspi, Avshalom; Houts, Renate; Cohen, Harvey J.; Corcoran, David L.; Danese, Andrea, . . . Moffitt, Terrie E. (2015). Quantification of biological aging in young adults. *Proceedings of the National Academy of Sciences of the United States of America, 112*(30), E4104–E4110. doi: 10.1073/pnas.1506264112

Ben-Zur, Hasida & Zeidner, Moshe. (2009). Threat to life and risk-taking behaviors: A review of empirical findings and explanatory models. *Personality and Social Psychology Review, 13*(2), 109–128. doi: 10.1177/1088868308330104

Benatar, David. (2011). A legal right to die: Responding to slippery slope and abuse arguments. *Current Oncology, 18*(5), 206–207. doi: 10.3747/co.v18i5.923

Bender, Heather L.; Allen, Joseph P.; Mcelhaney, Kathleen Boykin; Antonishak, Jill; Moore, Cynthia M.; Kelly, Heather O'beirne & Davis, Steven M. (2007). Use of harsh physical discipline and developmental outcomes in adolescence. *Development and Psychopathology, 19*(1), 227–242. doi: 10.1017/S0954579407070125

Benet, Sula. (1974). *Abkhasians: The long-living people of the Caucasus.* New York, NY: Holt, Rinehart & Winston.

Bennett, Craig M. & Baird, Abigail A. (2006). Anatomical changes in the emerging adult brain: A voxel-based morphometry study. *Human Brain Mapping, 27*(9), 766–777. doi: 10.1002/hbm.20218

Benoit, Amelie; Lacourse, Eric & Claes, Michel. (2013). Pubertal timing and depressive symptoms in late adolescence: The moderating role of individual, peer, and parental factors. *Development and Psychopathology, 25*(2), 455–471. doi: 10.1017/S0954579412001174

Bentley, Gillian R. & Mascie-Taylor, C. G. Nicholas. (2000). Introduction. In Gillian R. Bentley & C. G. Nicholas Mascie-Taylor (Eds.), *Infertility in the modern world: Present and future prospects* (pp. 1–13). New York, NY: Cambridge University Press.

Berger, Kathleen S. (2007). Update on bullying at school: Science forgotten? *Developmental Review, 27*(1), 90–126. doi: 10.1016/j.dr.2006.08.002

Berk, Michele; Adrian, Molly; McCauley, Elizabeth; Asarnow, Joan; Avina, Claudia & Linehan, Marsha. (2014). Conducting research on adolescent suicide attempters: Dilemmas and decisions. *Behavior Therapist, 37*(3), 65–69.

Berkey, Catherine S.; Gardner, Jane D.; Frazier, A. Lindsay & Colditz, Graham A. (2000). Relation of childhood diet and body size to menarche and adolescent growth in girls. *American Journal of Epidemiology, 152*(5), 446–452. doi: 10.1093/aje/152.5.446

Berkman, Lisa F.; Ertel, Karen A. & Glymour, Maria M. (2011). Aging and social intervention: Life course perspectives. In Robert H. Binstock & Linda K. George (Eds.), *Handbook of aging and the social sciences* (7th ed., pp. 337–351). San Diego, CA: Academic Press. doi: 10.1016/B978-0-12-380880-6.00024-1

Berko, Jean. (1958). The child's learning of English morphology. *Word, 14*, 150–177.

Bernard, Jessica A.; Peltier, Scott J.; Wiggins, Jillian Lee; Jaeggi, Susanne M.; Buschkuehl, Martin; Fling, Brett W., . . . Seidler, Rachael D. (2013). Disrupted cortico-cerebellar connectivity in older adults. *NeuroImage, 83*, 103–119. doi: 10.1016/j.neuroimage.2013.06.042

Bernard, Jessie S. (1982). *The future of marriage* (Revised ed.). New Haven, CT: Yale University Press.

Bernard, Kristin & Dozier, Mary. (2010). Examining infants' cortisol responses to laboratory tasks among children varying in attachment disorganization: Stress reactivity or return to baseline? *Developmental Psychology, 46*(6), 1771–1778. doi: 10.1037/a0020660

Bernard, Kristin; Lind, Teresa & Dozier, Mary. (2014). Neurobiological consequences of neglect and abuse. In Jill E. Korbin & Richard D. Krugman (Eds.), *Handbook of child maltreatment* (pp. 205–223). New York, NY: Springer. doi: 10.1007/978-94-007-7208-3_11

Best, Joel & Best, Eric. (2014). *The student loan mess: How good intentions created a trillion-dollar problem.* Berkeley, CA: University of California Press.

Betancourt, Theresa S.; McBain, Ryan; Newnham, Elizabeth A. & Brennan, Robert T. (2013). Trajectories of internalizing problems in war-affected Sierra Leonean youth: Examining conflict and postconflict factors. *Child Development, 84*(2), 455–470. doi: 10.1111/j.1467-8624.2012.01861.x

Bhatia, Tej K. & Ritchie, William C. (Eds.). (2013). *The handbook of bilingualism and multilingualism* (2nd ed.). Malden, MA: Wiley-Blackwell.

Bhatnagar, Aruni; Whitsel, Laurie P.; Ribisl, Kurt M.; Bullen, Chris; Chaloupka, Frank; Piano, Mariann R., . . . Benowitz, Neal. (2014). Electronic cigarettes: A policy statement from the American Heart Association. *Circulation, 130*(16), 1418–1436. doi: 10.1161/CIR.0000000000000107

Biblarz, Timothy J. & Savci, Evren. (2010). Lesbian, gay, bisexual, and transgender families. *Journal of Marriage and Family, 72*(3), 480–497. doi: 10.1111/j.1741-3737.2010.00714.x

Biblarz, Timothy J. & Stacey, Judith. (2010). How does the gender of parents matter? *Journal of Marriage and Family, 72*(1), 3–22. doi: 10.1111/j.1741-3737.2009.00678.x

Biehl, Michael C.; Natsuaki, Misaki N. & Ge, Xiaojia. (2007). The influence of pubertal timing on alcohol use and heavy drinking trajectories. *Journal of Youth and Adolescence, 36*(2), 153–167. doi: 10.1007/s10964-006-9120-z

Bielak, Allison A. M.; Anstey, Kaarin J.; Christensen, Helen & Windsor, Tim D. (2012). Activity engagement is related to level, but not change in cognitive ability across adulthood. *Psychology and Aging, 27*(1), 219–228. doi: 10.1037/a0024667

Bilalić, Merim; McLeod, Peter & Gobet, Fernand. (2009). Specialization effect and its influence on memory and problem solving in expert chess players. *Cognitive Science, 33*(6), 1117–1143. doi: 10.1111/j.1551-6709.2009.01030.x

Billings, J. Andrew. (2011). Double effect: A useful rule that alone cannot justify hastening death. *Journal of Medical Ethics, 37*(7), 437–440. doi: 10.1136/jme.2010.041160

Billingsley, Sunnee & Ferrarini, Tommy. (2014). Family policy and fertility intentions in 21 European countries. *Journal of Marriage and Family, 76*(2), 428–445. doi: 10.1111/jomf.12097

Birditt, Kira S.; Miller, Laura M.; Fingerman, Karen L. & Lefkowitz, Eva S. (2009). Tensions in the parent and adult child relationship: Links to solidarity and ambivalence. *Psychology and Aging, 24*(2), 287–295. doi: 10.1037/a0015196

Birdsong, David. (2006). Age and second language acquisition and processing: A selective overview. *Language Learning, 56*(Suppl. 1), 9–49. doi: 10.1111/j.1467-9922.2006.00353.x

Birkeland, Marianne S.; Breivik, Kyrre & Wold, Bente. (2014). Peer acceptance protects global self-esteem from negative effects of low closeness to parents during adolescence and early adulthood. *Journal of Youth and Adolescence, 43*(1), 70–80. doi: 10.1007/s10964-013-9929-1

Biro, Frank M.; Greenspan, Louise C.; Galvez, Maida P.; Pinney, Susan M.; Teitelbaum, Susan; Windham, Gayle C., . . . Wolff, Mary S. (2013). Onset of breast development in a longitudinal cohort. *Pediatrics, 132*(6), 1019–1027. doi: 10.1542/peds.2012-3773

Biro, Frank M.; McMahon, Robert P.; Striegel-Moore, Ruth; Crawford, Patricia B.; Obarzanek, Eva; Morrison, John A., . . . Falkner, Frank. (2001). Impact of timing of pubertal maturation on growth in black and white female adolescents: The National Heart, Lung, and Blood Institute Growth and Health Study. *Journal of Pediatrics, 138*(5), 636–643. doi: 10.1067/mpd.2001.114476

Bjorklund, David F.; Dukes, Charles & Brown, Rhonda D. (2009). The development of memory strategies. In Mary L. Courage & Nelson Cowan (Eds.), *The development of memory in infancy and childhood* (2nd ed., pp. 145–175). New York, NY: Psychology Press.

Bjorklund, David F. & Ellis, Bruce J. (2014). Children, childhood, and development in evolutionary perspective. *Developmental Review, 34*(3), 225–264. doi: 10.1016/j.dr.2014.05.005

Bjorklund, David F. & Sellers, Patrick D. (2014). Memory development in evolutionary perspective. In Patricia Bauer & Robyn Fivush (Eds.), *The Wiley handbook on the development of children's memory* (Vol. 1, pp. 126–150). Malden, MA: Wiley.

Black, Dennis M.; Bauer, Douglas C.; Schwartz, Ann V.; Cummings, Steven R. & Rosen, Clifford J. (2012). Continuing bisphosphonate treatment for osteoporosis—for whom and for how long? *New England Journal of Medicine, 366*, 2051–2053. doi: 10.1056/NEJMp1202623

Black, Robert E.; Morris, Saul S. & Bryce, Jennifer. (2003). Where and why are 10 million children dying every year? *The Lancet, 361*(9376), 2226–2234. doi: 10.1016/S0140-6736(03)13779-8

Blad, Evie. (2014). Some states overhauling vaccine laws. *Education Week, 33*(31), 1, 23.

Blair, Clancy & Raver, C. Cybele. (2012). Child development in the context of adversity: Experiential canalization of brain and behavior. *American Psychologist, 67*(4), 309–318. doi: 10.1037/a0027493

Blalock, Garrick; Kadiyali, Vrinda & Simon, Daniel H. (2009). Driving fatalities after 9/11: A hidden cost of terrorism. *Applied Economics, 41*(14), 1717–1729. doi: 10.1080/00036840601069757

Blanchard-Fields, Fredda. (2007). Everyday problem solving and emotion: An adult developmental perspective. *Current Directions in Psychological Science, 16*(1), 26–31. doi: 10.1111/j.1467-8721.2007.00469.x

Blandon, Alysia Y.; Calkins, Susan D. & Keane, Susan P. (2010). Predicting emotional and social competence during early childhood from toddler risk and maternal behavior. *Development and Psychopathology, 22*(1), 119–132. doi: 10.1017/S0954579409990307

Blas, Erik & Kurup, Anand Sivasankara (Eds.). (2010). *Equity, social determinants, and public health programmes.* Geneva, Switzerland: World Health Organization.

Bleidorn, Wiebke; Klimstra, Theo A.; Denissen, Jaap J. A.; Rentfrow, Peter J.; Potter, Jeff & Gosling, Samuel D. (2013). Personality maturation around the world: A cross-cultural examination of social-investment theory. *Psychological Science, 24*(12), 2530–2540. doi: 10.1177/0956797613498396

Bleske-Rechek, April; Somers, Erin; Micke, Cierra; Erickson, Leah; Matteson, Lindsay; Stocco, Corey, . . . Ritchie, Laura. (2012). Benefit or burden? Attraction in cross-sex friendship. *Journal of Social and Personal Relationships, 29*(5), 569–596. doi: 10.1177/0265407512443611

Blieszner, Rosemary. (2014). The worth of friendship: Can friends keep us happy and healthy? *Generations, 38*(1), 24–30.

Bliss, Catherine. (2012). *Race decoded: The genomic fight for social justice.* Stanford, CA: Stanford University Press.

Blonigen, Daniel M.; Carlson, Marie D.; Hicks, Brian M.; Krueger, Robert F. & Iacono, William G. (2008). Stability and change in personality traits from late adolescence to early adulthood: A longitudinal twin study. *Journal of Personality, 76*(2), 229–266. doi: 10.1111/j.1467-6494.2007.00485.x

Bloom, David E. (2011). 7 billion and counting. *Science, 333*(6042), 562–569. doi: 10.1126/science.1209290

Blurton-Jones, Nicholas G. (1976). Rough-and-tumble play among nursery school children. In Jerome S. Bruner et al. (Eds.), *Play: Its role in development and evolution* (pp. 352–363). New York, NY: Basic Books.

Boals, Adriel; Hayslip, Bert; Knowles, Laura R. & Banks, Jonathan B. (2012). Perceiving a negative event as central to one's identity partially mediates age differences in posttraumatic stress disorder symptoms. *Journal of Aging and Health, 24*(3), 459–474. doi: 10.1177/0898264311425089

Boerner, Kathrin; Schulz, Richard & Horowitz, Amy. (2004). Positive aspects of caregiving and adaptation to bereavement. *Psychology and Aging, 19*(4), 668–675. doi: 10.1037/0882-7974.19.4.668

Boerner, Kathrin; Wortman, Camille B. & Bonanno, George A. (2005). Resilient or at risk? A 4-year study of older adults who initially showed high or low distress following conjugal loss. *The Journals of Gerontology: Series B: Psychological Sciences and Social Sciences, 60*(2), 67–73. doi: 10.1093/geronb/60.2.P67

Bögels, Susan M.; Knappe, Susanne & Clark, Lee Anna. (2013). Adult separation anxiety disorder in DSM-5. *Clinical Psychology Review, 33*(5), 663–674. doi: 10.1016/j.cpr.2013.03.006

Bogle, Kathleen A. (2008). *Hooking up: Sex, dating, and relationships on campus.* New York, NY: New York University Press.

Böhme, Marcus H.; Persian, Ruth & Stöhr, Tobias. (2015). Alone but better off? Adult child migration and health of elderly parents in Moldova. *Journal of Health Economics, 39,* 211–227. doi: 10.1016/j.jhealeco.2014.09.001

Bollyky, Thomas J. (2012). Developing symptoms: Noncommunicable diseases go global. *Foreign Affairs, 91*(3), 134–144.

Bombard, Jennifer M.; Robbins, Cheryl L.; Dietz, Patricia M. & Valderrama, Amy L. (2013). Preconception care: The perfect opportunity for health care providers to advise lifestyle changes for hypertensive women. *American Journal of Health Promotion, 27*(3), S43–S49. doi: 10.4278/ajhp.120109-QUAN-6

Bonanno, George A. & Lilienfeld, Scott O. (2008). Let's be realistic: When grief counseling is effective and when it's not. *Professional Psychology: Research and Practice, 39*(3), 377–378. doi: 10.1037/0735-7028.39.3.377

Bonanno, Rina A. & Hymel, Shelley. (2013). Cyber bullying and internalizing difficulties: Above and beyond the impact of traditional forms of bullying. *Journal of Youth and Adolescence, 42*(5), 685–697. doi: 10.1007/s10964-013-9937-1

Bond, Michael C. & Butler, Kenneth H. (2013). Elder abuse and neglect: Definitions, epidemiology, and approaches to emergency department screening. *Clinics in Geriatric Medicine, 29*(1), 257–273. doi: 10.1016/j.cger.2012.09.004

Borkowski, John G.; Farris, Jaelyn Renee; Whitman, Thomas L.; Carothers, Shannon S.; Weed, Keri & Keogh, Deborah A. (Eds.). (2007). *Risk and resilience: Adolescent mothers and their children grow up.* Mahwah, NJ: Lawrence Erlbaum Associates.

Bornstein, Marc H.; Mortimer, Jeylan T.; Lutfey, Karen & Bradley, Robert. (2011). Theories and processes in life-span socialization. In Karen L. Fingerman et al. (Eds.), *Handbook of life-span development* (pp. 27–56). New York, NY: Springer.

Borrelli, Belinda; McQuaid, Elizabeth L.; Novak, Scott P.; Hammond, S. Katharine & Becker, Bruce. (2010). Motivating Latino caregivers of children with asthma to quit smoking: A randomized trial. *Journal of Consulting and Clinical Psychology, 78*(1), 34–43. doi: 10.1037/a0016932

Boss, Lisa; Kang, Duck-Hee & Branson, Sandy. (2015). Loneliness and cognitive function in the older adult: A systematic review. *International Psychogeriatrics, 27*(4), 541–553. doi: 10.1017/S1041610214002749

Bosworth, Hayden B. & Ayotte, Brian J. (2009). The role of cognitive and social function in an applied setting: Medication adherence as an example. In Hayden B. Bosworth & Christopher Hertzog (Eds.), *Aging and cognition: Research methodologies and empirical advances* (pp. 219–239). Washington, DC: American Psychological Association. doi: 10.1037/11882-011

Bowers, Edmond P. & Lerner, Richard M. (2013). Familial and nonfamilial relationships as ecological sources of health and positive development across the life span: A view of the issues. *Research in Human Development, 10*(2), 111–115. doi: 10.1080/15427609.2013.786535

Bowes, Lucy; Maughan, Barbara; Caspi, Avshalom; Moffitt, Terrie E. & Arseneault, Louise. (2010). Families promote emotional and behavioural resilience to bullying: Evidence of an environmental effect. *Journal of Child Psychology and Psychiatry, 51*(7), 809–817. doi: 10.1111/j.1469-7610.2010.02216.x

Bowlby, John. (1982). *Loss: Sadness and depression.* New York, NY: Basic Books.

Bowlby, John. (1983). *Attachment* (2nd ed.). New York, NY: Basic Books.

boyd, danah. (2014). *It's complicated: The social lives of networked teens.* New Haven, CT: Yale University Press.

Boyd, Wendy; Walker, Susan & Thorpe, Karen. (2013). Choosing work and care: Four Australian women negotiating return to paid work in the first year of motherhood. *Contemporary Issues in Early Childhood, 14*(2), 168–178. doi: 10.2304/ciec.2013.14.2.168

Boyle, Patricia A.; Wilson, Robert S.; Yu, Lei; Barr, Alasdair M.; Honer, William G.; Schneider, Julie A. & Bennett, David A. (2013). Much of late life cognitive decline is not due to common neurodegenerative pathologies. *Annals of Neurology, 74*(3), 478–489. doi: 10.1002/ana.23964

Boyraz, Guler; Horne, Sharon G. & Sayger, Thomas V. (2012). Finding meaning in loss: The mediating role of social support between personality and two construals of meaning. *Death Studies, 36*(6), 519–540. doi: 10.1080/07481187.2011.553331

Boywitt, C. Dennis; Kuhlmann, Beatrice G. & Meiser, Thorsten. (2012). The role of source memory in older adults' recollective experience. *Psychology and Aging, 27*(2), 484–497. doi: 10.1037/a0024729

Bracken, Bruce A. & Crawford, Elizabeth. (2010). Basic concepts in early childhood educational standards: A 50-state review. *Early Childhood Education Journal, 37*(5), 421–430. doi: 10.1007/s10643-009-0363-7

Bradley, Rachel & Slade, Pauline. (2011). A review of mental health problems in fathers following the birth of a child. *Journal of Reproductive and Infant Psychology, 29*(1), 19–42. doi: 10.1080/02646838.2010.513047

Brainerd, Charles J.; Reyna, Valerie F. & Ceci, Stephen J. (2008). Developmental reversals in false memory: A review of data and theory. *Psychological Bulletin, 134*(3), 343–382. doi: 10.1037/0033-2909.134.3.343

Brame, Robert; Bushway, Shawn D.; Paternoster, Ray & Turner, Michael G. (2014). Demographic patterns of cumulative arrest prevalence by ages 18 and 23. *Crime & Delinquency, 60*(3), 471–486. doi: 10.1177/0011128713514801

Branch, John. (2011, December 5). Derek Boogaard: A brain 'going bad'. *The New York Times,* p. B13.

Brandone, Amanda C.; Horwitz, Suzanne R.; Aslin, Richard N. & Wellman, Henry M. (2014). Infants' goal anticipation during failed and successful reaching actions. *Developmental Science, 17*(1), 23–34. doi: 10.1111/desc.12095

Brandt, Hella E.; Ooms, Marcel E.; Ribbe, Miel W.; van der Wal, Gerrit & Deliens, Luc. (2006). Predicted survival vs. actual survival in terminally ill noncancer patients in Dutch nursing homes. *Journal of Pain and Symptom Management, 32*(6), 560–566. doi: 10.1016/j.jpainsymman.2006.06.006

Brandt, Martina; Deindl, Christian & Hank, Karsten. (2012). Tracing the origins of successful aging: The role of childhood conditions and social inequality in explaining later life health. *Social Science & Medicine, 74*(9), 1418–1425. doi: 10.1016/j.socscimed.2012.01.004

Brassen, Stefanie; Gamer, Matthias; Peters, Jan; Gluth, Sebastian & Büchel, Christian. (2012). Don't look back in anger! Responsiveness to missed chances in successful and nonsuccessful aging. *Science, 336*(6081), 612–614. doi: 10.1126/science.1217516

Breivik, Gunnar. (2010). Trends in adventure sports in a post-modern society. *Sport in Society: Cultures, Commerce, Media, Politics, 13*(2), 260–273. doi: 10.1080/17430430903522970

Brendgen, Mara; Lamarche, Véronique; Wanner, Brigitte & Vitaro, Frank. (2010). Links between friendship relations and early adolescents' trajectories of depressed mood. *Developmental Psychology, 46*(2), 491–501. doi: 10.1037/a0017413

Brennan, Arthur; Ayers, Susan; Ahmed, Hafez & Marshall-Lucette, Sylvie. (2007). A critical review of the Couvade syndrome: The pregnant male. *Journal of Reproductive and Infant Psychology, 25*(3), 173–189. doi: 10.1080/02646830701467207

Breslow, Lori; Pritchard, David E.; Deboer, Jennifer; Stump, Glenda S.; Ho, Andrew D. & Seaton, Daniel T. (2013). Studying learning in the worldwide classroom research into edX's first MOOC. *Research and Practice in Assessment, 8*(1), 13–25.

Bretherton, Inge. (2010). Fathers in attachment theory and research: A review. *Early Child Development and Care, 180*(1/2), 9–23. doi: 10.1080/03004430903414661

Brody, Jane E. (2013, February 26). Too many pills in pregnancy. *The New York Times,* p. D5.

Brom, Sarah S. & Kliegel, Matthias. (2014). Improving everyday prospective memory performance in older adults: Comparing cognitive process and strategy training. *Psychology and Aging, 29*(3), 744–755. doi: 10.1037/a0037181

Bronfenbrenner, Urie & Morris, Pamela A. (2006). The bioecological model of human development. In William Damon & Richard M. Lerner (Eds.), *Handbook of child psychology* (6th ed., Vol. 1, pp. 793–828). Hoboken, NJ: Wiley.

Brooker, Rebecca J.; Buss, Kristin A.; Lemery-Chalfant, Kathryn; Aksan, Nazan; Davidson, Richard J. & Goldsmith, H. Hill. (2013). The development of stranger fear in infancy and toddlerhood: Normative development, individual differences, antecedents, and outcomes. *Developmental Science, 16*(6), 864–878. doi: 10.1111/desc.12058

Brown, B. Bradford & Bakken, Jeremy P. (2011). Parenting and peer relationships: Reinvigorating research on family–peer linkages in adolescence. *Journal of Research on Adolescence, 21*(1), 153–165. doi: 10.1111/j.1532-7795.2010.00720.x

Brown, Christia Spears; Alabi, Basirat O.; Huynh, Virginia W. & Masten, Carrie L. (2011). Ethnicity and gender in late childhood and early adolescence: Group identity and awareness of bias. *Developmental Psychology, 47*(2), 463–471. doi: 10.1037/a0021819

Brown, Edna; Birditt, Kira S.; Huff, Scott C. & Edwards, Lindsay L. (2012). Marital dissolution and psychological well-being: Race and gender differences in the moderating role of marital relationship quality. *Research in Human Development,* 9(2), 145–164. doi: 10.1080/15427609.2012.681202

Brown, Peter C.; Roediger, Henry L. & McDaniel, Mark A. (2014). *Make it stick: The science of successful learning.* Cambridge, MA: Belknap Press of Harvard University Press.

Brown, Susan L. (2010). Marriage and child well-being: Research and policy perspectives. *Journal of Marriage and Family,* 72(5), 1059–1077. doi: 10.1111/j.1741-3737.2010.00750.x

Brown, Susan L. & Kawamura, Sayaka. (2010). Relationship quality among cohabitors and marrieds in older adulthood. *Social Science Research,* 39(5), 777–786. doi: 10.1016/j.ssresearch.2010.04.010

Brown, Susan L. & Lin, I-Fen. (2013). The gray divorce revolution. *Family Focus, National Council on Family Relations,* (FF57), F4–F5.

Brown, Susan L.; Manning, Wendy D. & Stykes, J. Bart. (2015). Family structure and child well-being: Integrating family complexity. *Journal of Marriage and Family,* 77(1), 177–190. doi: 10.1111/jomf.12145

Brownell, Celia A.; Svetlova, Margarita; Anderson, Ranita; Nichols, Sara R. & Drummond, Jesse. (2013). Socialization of early prosocial behavior: Parents' talk about emotions is associated with sharing and helping in toddlers. *Infancy,* 18(1), 91–119. doi: 10.1111/j.1532-7078.2012.00125.x

Bruce, Kimberley D.; Hoxha, Sany; Carvalho, Gil B.; Yamada, Ryuichi; Wang, Horng-Dar; Karayan, Paul, . . . Ja, William W. (2010). High carbohydrate–low protein consumption maximizes Drosophila lifespan. *Experimental Gerontology,* 48(10), 1129–1135. doi: 10.1016/j.exger.2013.02.003

Bruck, Maggie; Ceci, Stephen J. & Principe, Gabrielle F. (2006). The child and the law. In William Damon & Richard M. Lerner (Eds.), *Handbook of child psychology* (6th ed., Vol. 4, pp. 776–816). Hoboken, NJ: Wiley.

Brunham, Robert C.; Gottlieb, Sami L. & Paavonen, Jorma. (2015). Pelvic inflammatory disease. *New England Journal of Medicine,* 372, 2039–2048. doi: 10.1056/NEJMra1411426

Bryant, Gregory A. & Barrett, H. Clark. (2007). Recognizing intentions in infant-directed speech: Evidence for universals. *Psychological Science,* 18(8), 746–751. doi: 10.1111/j.1467-9280.2007.01970.x

Bucx, Freek; van Wel, Frits & Knijn, Trudie. (2012). Life course status and exchanges of support between young adults and parents. *Journal of Marriage and Family,* 74(1), 101–115. doi: 10.1111/j.1741-3737.2011.00883.x

Buiting, Hilde; van Delden, Johannes; Onwuteaka-Philpsen, Bregje; Rietjens, Judith; Rurup, Mette; van Tol, Donald, . . . van der Heide, Agnes. (2009). Reporting of euthanasia and physician-assisted suicide in the Netherlands: Descriptive study. *BMC Medical Ethics,* 10(18). doi: 10.1186/1472-6939-10-18

Burchinal, Margaret R.; Lowe Vandell, Deborah & Belsky, Jay. (2014). Is the prediction of adolescent outcomes from early child care moderated by later maternal sensitivity? Results from the nichd study of early child care and youth development. *Developmental Psychology,* 50(2), 542–553. doi: 10.1037/a0033709

Burke, Laurie A.; Neimeyer, Robert A.; Holland, Jason M.; Dennard, Sharon; Oliver, Linda & Shear, M. Katherine. (2013). Inventory of Complicated Spiritual Grief: Development and validation of a new measure. *Death Studies,* 38(4), 239–250. doi: 10.1080/07481187.2013.810098

Burnette, Jeni L.; O'Boyle, Ernest H.; VanEpps, Eric M.; Pollack, Jeffrey M. & Finkel, Eli J. (2013). Mind-sets matter: A meta-analytic review of implicit theories and self-regulation. *Psychological Bulletin,* 139(3), 655–701. doi: 10.1037/a0029531

Burpo, Todd & Vincent, Lynn. (2011). *Heaven is for real: A little boy's astounding story of his trip to heaven and back.* Nashville, TN: Thomas Nelson.

Burstein, David D. (2013). *Fast future: How the millennial generation is shaping our world.* Boston, MA: Beacon Press.

Burstyn, Igor. (2014). Peering through the mist: Systematic review of what the chemistry of contaminants in electronic cigarettes tells us about health risks. *BMC Public Health,* 14(1), 18. doi: 10.1186/1471-2458-14-18

Bursztyn, Leonardo & Jensen, Robert. (2014). How does peer pressure affect educational investments? *NBER working paper series,* (Working Paper 20714).

Burt, S. Alexandra. (2009). Rethinking environmental contributions to child and adolescent psychopathology: A meta-analysis of shared environmental influences. *Psychological Bulletin,* 135(4), 608–637. doi: 10.1037/a0015702

Burt, S. Alexandra; McGue, Matt & Iacono, William G. (2009). Nonshared environmental mediation of the association between deviant peer affiliation and adolescent externalizing behaviors over time: Results from a cross-lagged monozygotic twin differences design. *Developmental Psychology,* 45(6), 1752–1760. doi: 10.1037/a0016687

Butler, Robert N.; Lewis, Myrna I. & Sunderland, Trey. (1998). *Aging and mental health: Positive psychosocial and biomedical approaches* (5th ed.). Boston, MA: Allyn & Bacon.

Buttelmann, David; Zmyj, Norbert; Daum, Moritz & Carpenter, Malinda. (2013). Selective imitation of in-group over out-group members in 14-month-old infants. *Child Development,* 84(2), 422–428. doi: 10.1111/j.1467-8624.2012.01860.x

Butterworth, Brian & Kovas, Yulia. (2013). Understanding neurocognitive developmental disorders can improve education for all. *Science,* 340(6130), 300–305. doi: 10.1126/science.1231022

Butterworth, Brian; Varma, Sashank & Laurillard, Diana. (2011). Dyscalculia: From brain to education. *Science,* 332(6033), 1049–1053. doi: 10.1126/science.1201536

Byers-Heinlein, Krista; Burns, Tracey C. & Werker, Janet F. (2010). The roots of bilingualism in newborns. *Psychological Science,* 21(3), 343–348. doi: 10.1177/0956797609360758

Cacciatore, Joanne. (2009). Appropriate bereavement practice after the death of a Native American child. *Families in Society: The Journal of Contemporary Social Services,* 90(1), 46–50. doi: 10.1606/1044-3894.3844

Cacioppo, John T.; Cacioppo, Stephanie; Gonzaga, Gian C.; Ogburn, Elizabeth L. & VanderWeele, Tyler J. (2013). Marital satisfaction and break-ups differ across on-line and off-line meeting venues. *PNAS, 110*(25), 10135–10140. doi: 10.1073/pnas.1222447110

Cacioppo, Stephanie; Capitanio, John P. & Cacioppo, John T. (2014). Toward a neurology of loneliness. *Psychological Bulletin, 140*(6), 1464–1504. doi: 10.1037/a0037618

Calarco, Jessica McCrory. (2014). The inconsistent curriculum: Cultural tool kits and student interpretations of ambiguous expectations. *Social Psychology Quarterly, 77*(2), 185–209. doi: 10.1177/0190272514521438

Calder, Gillian & Beaman, Lori G. (Eds.). (2014). *Polygamy's rights and wrongs: Perspectives on harm, family, and law.* Vancouver, BC: University of British Columbia Press.

Calkins, Susan D. & Keane, Susan P. (2009). Developmental origins of early antisocial behavior. *Development and Psychopathology, 21*(4), 1095–1109. doi: 10.1017/S095457940999006X

Calzo, Jerel P.; Masyn, Katherine E.; Corliss, Heather L.; Scherer, Emily A.; Field, Alison E. & Austin, S. Bryn. (2015). Patterns of body image concerns and disordered weight- and shape-related behaviors in heterosexual and sexual minority adolescent males. *Developmental Psychology, 51*(9), 1216–1225. doi: 10.1037/dev0000027

Camhi, Sarah M.; Katzmarzyk, Peter T.; Broyles, Stephanie; Church, Timothy S.; Hankinson, Arlene L.; Carnethon, Mercedes R., . . . Lewis, Cora E. (2013). Association of metabolic risk with longitudinal physical activity and fitness: Coronary artery risk development in young adults (CARDIA). *Metabolic Syndrome and Related Disorders, 11*(3), 195–204. doi: 10.1089/met.2012.0120

Camos, Valérie & Barrouillet, Pierre. (2011). Developmental change in working memory strategies: From passive maintenance to active refreshing. *Developmental Psychology, 47*(3), 898–904. doi: 10.1037/a0023193

Campbell, Frances; Conti, Gabriella; Heckman, James J.; Moon, Seong H.; Pinto, Rodrigo; Pungello, Elizabeth & Pan, Yi. (2014). Early childhood investments substantially boost adult health. *Science, 343*(6178), 1478–1485. doi: 10.1126/science.1248429

Campbell, Frances A.; Pungello, Elizabeth P.; Miller-Johnson, Shari; Burchinal, Margaret & Ramey, Craig T. (2001). The development of cognitive and academic abilities: Growth curves from an early childhood educational experiment. *Developmental Psychology, 37*(2), 231–242. doi: 10.1037/0012-1649.37.2.231

Camras, Linda A. & Shutter, Jennifer M. (2010). Emotional facial expressions in infancy. *Emotion Review, 2*(2), 120–129. doi: 10.1177/1754073909352529

Cappell, Katherine A.; Gmeindl, Leon & Reuter-Lorenz, Patricia A. (2010). Age differences in prefontal recruitment during verbal working memory maintenance depend on memory load. *Cortex, 46*(4), 462–473. doi: 10.1016/j.cortex.2009.11.009

Caravita, Simona C. S. & Cillessen, Antonius H. N. (2012). Agentic or communal? Associations between interpersonal goals, popularity, and bullying in middle childhood and early adolescence. *Social Development, 21*(2), 376–395. doi: 10.1111/j.1467-9507.2011.00632.x

Caravita, Simona C. S.; Di Blasio, Paola & Salmivalli, Christina. (2010). Early adolescents' participation in bullying: Is ToM involved? *The Journal of Early Adolescence, 30*(1), 138–170. doi: 10.1177/0272431609342983

Carey, Susan. (2010). Beyond fast mapping. *Language Learning and Development, 6*(3), 184–205. doi: 10.1080/15475441.2010.484379

Carlo, Gustavo; Knight, George P.; Roesch, Scott C.; Opal, Deanna & Davis, Alexandra. (2014). Personality across cultures: A critical analysis of Big Five research and current directions. In Frederick T. L. Leong et al. (Eds.), *APA handbook of multicultural psychology* (Vol. 1, pp. 285–298). Washington, DC: American Psychological Association. doi: 10.1037/14189-015

Carlson, Stephanie M.; Koenig, Melissa A. & Harms, Madeline B. (2013). Theory of mind. *Wiley Interdisciplinary Reviews: Cognitive Science, 4*(4), 391–402. doi: 10.1002/wcs.1232

Carlsson, Johanna; Wängqvist, Maria & Frisén, Ann. (2015). Identity development in the late twenties: A never ending story. *Developmental Psychology, 51*(3), 334–345. doi: 10.1037/a0038745

Carothers, Bobbi J. & Reis, Harry T. (2013). Men and women are from Earth: Examining the latent structure of gender. *Journal of Personality and Social Psychology, 104*(2), 385–407. doi: 10.1037/a0030437

Carr, Deborah. (2012). Death and dying in the contemporary United States: What are the psychological implications of anticipated death? *Social and Personality Psychology Compass, 6*(2), 184–195. doi: 10.1111/j.1751-9004.2011.00416.x

Carr, Deborah; Freedman, Vicki A.; Cornman, Jennifer C. & Schwarz, Norbert. (2014). Happy marriage, happy life? Marital quality and subjective well-being in later life. *Journal of Marriage and Family, 76*(5), 930–948. doi: 10.1111/jomf.12133

Carroll, Judith E.; Irwin, Michael R.; Merkin, Sharon Stein & Seeman, Teresa E. (2015). Sleep and multisystem biological risk: A population-based study. *PLoS ONE, 10*(2), e0118467. doi: 10.1371/journal.pone.0118467

Carson, Valerie; Tremblay, Mark S.; Spence, John C.; Timmons, Brian W. & Janssen, Ian. (2013). The Canadian Sedentary Behaviour Guidelines for the Early Years (zero to four years of age) and screen time among children from Kingston, Ontario. *Paediatrics & Child Health, 18*(1), 25–28.

Carstensen, Laura L. (1993). Motivation for social contact across the life span. In Janis E. Jacobs (Ed.), *Developmental perspectives on motivation: Nebraska Symposium on Motivation (1992)* (pp. 209–254). Lincoln, NE: University of Nebraska.

Carstensen, Laura L. (2011). *A long bright future: Happiness, health, and financial security in an age of increased longevity.* New York, NY: PublicAffairs.

Caruso, Federica. (2013). Embedding early childhood education and care in the socio-cultural context: The case of Italy. In Jan Georgeson & Jane Payler (Eds.), *International perspectives on early childhood education and care.* New York, NY: Open University Press.

Case-Smith, Jane & Kuhaneck, Heather M. (2008). Play preferences of typically developing children and children with developmental delays between ages 3 and 7 years.

OTJR: Occupation, Participation and Health, 28(1), 19–29. doi: 10.3928/15394492-20080101-01

Casey, B. J. & Caudle, Kristina. (2013). The teenage brain: Self control. *Current Directions in Psychological Science, 22*(2), 82–87. doi: 10.1177/0963721413480170

Caspi, Avshalom; Moffitt, Terrie E.; Morgan, Julia; Rutter, Michael; Taylor, Alan; Arseneault, Louise, . . . Polo-Tomas, Monica. (2004). Maternal expressed emotion predicts children's antisocial behavior problems: Using monozygotic-twin differences to identify environmental effects on behavioral development. *Developmental Psychology, 40*(2), 149–161. doi: 10.1037/0012-1649.40.2.149

Catani, Claudia; Gewirtz, Abigail H.; Wieling, Elizabeth; Schauer, Elizabeth; Elbert, Thomas & Neuner, Frank. (2010). Tsunami, war, and cumulative risk in the lives of Sri Lankan schoolchildren. *Child Development, 81*(4), 1176–1191. doi: 10.1111/j.1467-8624.2010.01461.x

Cavalari, Rachel N. S. & Donovick, Peter J. (2014). Agenesis of the corpus callosum: Symptoms consistent with developmental disability in two siblings. *Neurocase: The Neural Basis of Cognition, 21*(1), 95–102. doi: 10.1080/13554794.2013.873059

CBS News. (2013, March 27). Drop in hospital death rates may mean more Americans dying at home. *CBS Interactive Inc.*

Ceci, Stephen J. & Bruck, Maggie. (1995). *Jeopardy in the courtroom: A scientific analysis of children's testimony.* Washington, DC: American Psychological Association.

Cecil, Kim M.; Brubaker, Christopher J.; Adler, Caleb M.; Dietrich, Kim N.; Altaye, Mekibib; Egelhoff, John C., . . . Lanphear, Bruce P. (2008). Decreased brain volume in adults with childhood lead exposure. *PloS Medicine, 5*(5), 741–750. doi: 10.1371/journal.pmed.0050112

Center for Education Policy. (2012). *SDP strategic performance indicator: The high school effect on college-going. The SDP College-Going Diagnostic Strategic Performance Indicators.* Cambridge, MA: Harvard University, Center for Education Policy Research.

Centers for Disease Control. (2015). Atlanta, GA: Division for Heart Disease and Stroke Prevention.

Centers for Disease Control and Prevention. (2012, May). *Epidemiology and prevention of vaccine-preventable diseases* (William Atkinson et al. Eds. Revised 12th ed.). Washington DC: Public Health Foundation.

Centers for Disease Control and Prevention. (2015, April). *Epidemiology and prevention of vaccine-preventable diseases* (Jennifer Hamborsky et al. Eds. 13th ed.). Washington, DC: Public Health Foundation.

Centers for Disease Control and Prevention, National Center for Injury Prevention and Control, Division of Analysis, Research, and Practice Integration. (2013). *Fatal Injury Reports, 1999–2013, for National, Regional, and States.* Atlanta, GA: Centers for Disease Control and Prevention.

Centers for Medicare and Medicaid Services. (2014). *Beta amyloid positron tomography in dementia and neurodegenerative disease.* Baltimore, MD: Centers for Medicare and Medicaid Services.

Centre for Community Child Health & Telethon Institute for Child Health Research. (2009). *A snapshot of early childhood development in Australia: Australian Early Development Index (AEDI) national report 2009.* Canberra, Australia: Australian Government Department of Education.

Chan, Christian S. & Rhodes, Jean E. (2013). Religious coping, posttraumatic stress, psychological distress, and posttraumatic growth among female survivors four years after Hurricane Katrina. *Journal of Traumatic Stress, 26*(2), 257–265. doi: 10.1002/jts.21801

Chan, Juliana C. N.; Malik, Vasanti; Jia, Weiping; Kadowaki, Takashi; Yajnik, Chittaranjan S.; Yoon, Kun-Ho & Hu, Frank B. (2009). Diabetes in Asia: Epidemiology, risk factors, and pathophysiology. *JAMA, 301*(20), 2129–2140. doi: 10.1001/jama.2009.726

Chan, Kitty S.; Kasper, Judith D.; Brandt, Jason & Pezzin, Liliana E. (2012). Measurement equivalence in ADL and IADL difficulty across international surveys of aging: findings from the HRS, SHARE, and ELSA. *The Journals of Gerontology Series B: Psychological Sciences and Social Sciences, 67*(1), 121–132. doi: 10.1093/geronb/gbr133

Chan, Kit Yee; Wang, Wei; Wu, Jing Jing; Liu, Li; Theodoratou, Evropi; Car, Josip, . . . Rudan, Igor. (2013). Epidemiology of Alzheimer's disease and other forms of dementia in China, 1990–2010: A systematic review and analysis. *The Lancet, 381*(9882), 2016–2023. doi: 10.1016/S0140-6736(13)60221-4

Chan, Tak Wing & Koo, Anita. (2011). Parenting style and youth outcomes in the UK. *European Sociological Review, 27*(3), 385–399. doi: 10.1093/esr/jcq013

Chang, Alicia; Sandhofer, Catherine M. & Brown, Christia S. (2011). Gender biases in early number exposure to preschool-aged children. *Journal of Language and Social Psychology, 30*(4), 440–450. doi: 10.1177/0261927X11416207

Chao, Jian-Kang; Lin, Yen-Chin; Ma, Mi-Chia; Lai, Chin-Jen; Ku, Yan-Chiou; Kuo, Wu-Hsien & Chao, I. Chen. (2011). Relationship among sexual desire, sexual satisfaction, and quality of life in middle-aged and older adults. *Journal of Sex & Marital Therapy, 37*(5), 386–403. doi: 10.1080/0092623x.2011.607051

Chaplin, Lan Nguyen & John, Deborah Roedder. (2007). Growing up in a material world: Age differences in materialism in children and adolescents. *Journal of Consumer Research, 34*(4), 480–493. doi: 10.1086/518546

Chapman, Tracey. (2015). Sexual conflict and evolutionary psychology: Towards a unified framework. In Todd K. Shackelford & Ranald D. Hansen (Eds.), *The evolution of sexuality* (pp. 1–28). New York, NY: Springer. doi: 10.1007/978-3-319-09384-0_1

Charlesworth, Christina J.; Smit, Ellen; Lee, David S. H.; Alramadhan, Fatimah & Odden, Michelle C. (2015). Polypharmacy among adults aged 65 years and older in the United States: 1988–2010. *The Journals of Gerontology Series A: Biological Sciences & Medical Sciences, 70*(8), 989–995. doi: 10.1093/gerona/glv013

Charnigo, Richard; Noar, Seth M.; Garnett, Christopher; Crosby, Richard; Palmgreen, Philip & Zimmerman, Rick S. (2013). Sensation seeking and impulsivity: Combined associations with risky sexual behavior in a large sample of young adults. *The Journal of Sex Research, 50*(5), 480–488. doi: 10.1080/00224499.2011.652264

Chartier, Karen G.; Scott, Denise M.; Wall, Tamara L.; Covault, Jonathan; Karriker-Jaffe, Katherine J.; Mills, Britain A., . . . Arroyo, Judith A. (2014). Framing ethnic variations in alcohol outcomes from biological pathways to neighborhood context. *Alcoholism: Clinical and Experimental Research, 38*(3), 611–618. doi: 10.1111/acer.12304

Chassin, Laurie; Bountress, Kaitlin; Haller, Moira & Wang, Frances. (2014). Adolescent substance use disorders. In Eric J. Mash & Russell A. Barkley (Eds.), *Child psychopathology* (3rd ed., pp. 180–124). New York, NY: Guilford Press.

Chatters, Linda M.; Taylor, Robert Joseph; Lincoln, Karen D.; Nguyen, Ann & Joe, Sean. (2011). Church-based social support and suicidality among African Americans and Black Caribbeans. *Archives of Suicide Research, 15*(4), 337–353. doi: 10.1080/13811118.2011.615703

Chein, Jason; Albert, Dustin; O'Brien, Lia; Uckert, Kaitlyn & Steinberg, Laurence. (2011). Peers increase adolescent risk taking by enhancing activity in the brain's reward circuitry. *Developmental Science, 14*(2), F1–F10. doi: 10.1111/j.1467-7687.2010.01035.x

Chen, Edith; Cohen, Sheldon & Miller, Gregory E. (2010). How low socioeconomic status affects 2-year hormonal trajectories in children. *Psychological Science, 21*(1), 31–37. doi: 10.1177/0956797609355566

Chen, Edith & Miller, Gregory E. (2012). "Shift-and-persist" strategies: Why low socioeconomic status isn't always bad for health. *Perspectives on Psychological Science, 7*(2), 135–158. doi: 10.1177/1745691612436694

Chen, Feinian; Mair, Christine A.; Bao, Luoman & Yang, Yang Claire. (2014). Race/ethnic differentials in the health consequences of caring for grandchildren for grandparents. *The Journals of Gerontology Series B: Psychological Sciences and Social Sciences, 70*(5), 793–803. doi: 10.1093/geronb/gbu160

Chen, Xinyin; Cen, Guozhen; Li, Dan & He, Yunfeng. (2005). Social functioning and adjustment in Chinese children: The imprint of historical time. *Child Development, 76*(1), 182–195. doi: 10.1111/j.1467-8624.2005.00838.x

Chen, Xu; Errangi, Bhargav; Li, Longchuan; Glasser, Matthew F.; Westlye, Lars T.; Fjell, Anders M., . . . Rilling, James K. (2013). Brain aging in humans, chimpanzees (Pan troglodytes), and rhesus macaques (Macaca mulatta): Magnetic resonance imaging studies of macro- and microstructural changes. *Neurobiology of Aging, 34*(10), 2248–2260. doi: 10.1016/j.neurobiolaging.2013.03.028

Chen, Xinyin; Rubin, Kenneth H. & Sun, Yuerong. (1992). Social reputation and peer relationships in Chinese and Canadian children: A cross-cultural study. *Child Development, 63*(6), 1336–1343. doi: 10.1111/j.1467-8624.1992.tb01698.x

Chen, Xinyin; Wang, Li & Wang, Zhengyan. (2009). Shyness-sensitivity and social, school, and psychological adjustment in rural migrant and urban children in China. *Child Development, 80*(5), 1499–1513. doi: 10.1111/j.1467-8624.2009.01347.x

Chen, Xinyin; Yang, Fan & Wang, Li. (2013). Relations between shyness-sensitivity and internalizing problems in Chinese children: Moderating effects of academic achievement. *Journal of Abnormal Child Psychology, 41*(5), 825–836. doi: 10.1007/s10802-012-9708-6

Cheng, Diana; Kettinger, Laurie; Uduhiri, Kelechi & Hurt, Lee. (2011). Alcohol consumption during pregnancy: Prevalence and provider assessment. *Obstetrics & Gynecology, 117*(2), 212–217. doi: 10.1097/AOG.0b013e3182078569

Cherlin, Andrew J. (2009). *The marriage-go-round: The state of marriage and the family in America today.* New York, NY: Knopf.

Cherlin, Andrew J. (2013). Health, marriage, and same sex partnerships. *Journal of Health and Social Behavior, 54*(1), 64–66. doi: 10.1177/0022146512474430

Chikritzhs, Tanya; Stockwell, Tim; Naimi, Timothy; Andreasson, Sven; Dangardt, Frida & Liang, Wenbin. (2015). Has the leaning tower of presumed health benefits from 'moderate' alcohol use finally collapsed? *Addiction, 110*(5), 726–727. doi: 10.1111/add.12828

Child Welfare Information Gateway. (2013). *Foster care statistics, 2011.* Washington, DC: U.S. Department of Health and Human Services, Children's Bureau.

Choe, Daniel E.; Lane, Jonathan D.; Grabell, Adam S. & Olson, Sheryl L. (2013a). Developmental precursors of young school-age children's hostile attribution bias. *Developmental Psychology, 49*(12), 2245–2256. doi: 10.1037/a0032293

Choe, Daniel E.; Olson, Sheryl L. & Sameroff, Arnold J. (2013b). The interplay of externalizing problems and physical and inductive discipline during childhood. *Developmental Psychology, 49*(11), 2029–2039. doi: 10.1037/a0032054

Chomsky, Noam. (1968). *Language and mind.* New York, NY: Harcourt Brace & World.

Chomsky, Noam. (1980). *Rules and representations.* New York, NY: Columbia University Press.

Choshen-Hillel, Shoham & Yaniv, Ilan. (2011). Agency and the construction of social preference: Between inequality aversion and prosocial behavior. *Journal of Personality and Social Psychology, 101*(6), 1253–1261. doi: 10.1037/a0024557

Chou, Rita Jing-Ann & Choi, Namkee G. (2011). Prevalence and correlates of perceived workplace discrimination among older workers in the United States of America. *Ageing and Society, 31*(6), 1051–1070. doi: 10.1017/S0144686X10001297

Choukas-Bradley, Sophia; Giletta, Matteo; Widman, Laura; Cohen, Geoffrey L. & Prinstein, Mitchell J. (2014). Experimentally measured susceptibility to peer influence and adolescent sexual behavior trajectories: A preliminary study. *Developmental Psychology, 50*(9), 2221–2227. doi: 10.1037/a0037300

Chow, Angela; Krahn, Harvey J. & Galambos, Nancy L. (2014). Developmental trajectories of work values and job entitlement beliefs in the transition to adulthood. *Developmental Psychology, 50*(4), 1102–1115. doi: 10.1037/a0035185

Chow, Chong Man & Ruhl, Holly. (2014). Friendship and romantic stressors and depression in emerging adulthood: Mediating and moderating roles of attachment representations. *Journal of Adult Development, 21*(2), 106–115. doi: 10.1007/s10804-014-9184-z

Christiansen, Dorte M.; Olff, Miranda & Elklit, Ask. (2014). Parents bereaved by infant death: Sex differences and moderation in PTSD, attachment, coping and social support. *General Hospital Psychiatry, 36*(6), 655–661. doi: 10.1016/j.genhosppsych.2014.07.012

Christiansen, Sofie; Axelstad, Marta; Boberg, Julie; Vinggaard, Anne M.; Pedersen, Gitte A. & Hass, Ulla. (2014). Low-dose effects of bisphenol A on early sexual development in male and female rats. *Reproduction, 147*(4), 477–487. doi: 10.1530/REP-13-0377

Chronicle of Higher Education. (2014). Almanac of higher education 2014-15. *The Chronicle Of Higher Education, 60*(45).

Chu, C. Y. Cyrus; Xie, Yu & Yu, Ruoh Rong. (2011). Coresidence with elderly parents: A comparative study of southeast China and Taiwan. *Journal of Marriage and Family, 73*(1), 120–135. doi: 10.1111/j.1741-3737.2010.00793.x

Chudacoff, Howard P. (2011). The history of children's play in the United States. In Anthony D. Pellegrini (Ed.), *The Oxford handbook of the development of play* (pp. 101–109). New York, NY: Oxford University Press. doi: 10.1093/oxfordhb/9780195393002.013.0009

Chuderski, Adam. (2013). When are fluid intelligence and working memory isomorphic and when are they not? *Intelligence, 41*(4), 244–262. doi: 10.1016/j.intell.2013.04.003

Chung, Grace H.; Flook, Lisa & Fuligni, Andrew J. (2011). Reciprocal associations between family and peer conflict in adolescents' daily lives. *Child Development, 82*(5), 1390–1396. doi: 10.1111/j.1467-8624.2011.01625.x

Chung, Joanne M.; Robins, Richard W.; Trzesniewski, Kali H.; Noftle, Erik E.; Roberts, Brent W. & Widaman, Keith F. (2014). Continuity and change in self-esteem during emerging adulthood. *Journal of Personality and Social Psychology, 106*(3), 469–483. doi: 10.1037/a0035135

Cicchetti, Dante. (2013a). Annual Research Review: Resilient functioning in maltreated children – past, present, and future perspectives. *Journal of Child Psychology and Psychiatry, 54*(4), 402–422. doi: 10.1111/j.1469-7610.2012.02608.x

Cicchetti, Dante. (2013b). An overview of developmental psychopathology. In Philip D. Zelazo (Ed.), *The Oxford handbook of developmental psychology* (Vol. 2, pp. 455–480). New York, NY: Oxford University Press. doi: 10.1093/oxfordhb/9780199958474.013.0018

Cimpian, Andrei. (2013). Generic statements, causal attributions, and children's naive theories. In Mahzarin R. Banaji & Susan A. Gelman (Eds.), *Navigating the social world: What infants, children, and other species can teach us* (pp. 269–274). New York, NY: Oxford University Press.

Ciol, Marcia A.; Rasch, Elizabeth K.; Hoffman, Jeanne M.; Huynh, Minh & Chan, Leighton. (2014). Transitions in mobility, ADLs, and IADLs among working-age Medicare beneficiaries. *Disability and Health Journal, 7*(2), 206–215. doi: 10.1016/j.dhjo.2013.10.007

Clark, Caron A. C.; Fang, Hua; Espy, Kimberly A.; Filipek, Pauline A.; Juranek, Jenifer; Bangert, Barbara, . . . Taylor, H. Gerry. (2013). Relation of neural structure to persistently low academic achievement: A longitudinal study of children with differing birth weights. *Neuropsychology, 27*(3), 364–377. doi: 10.1037/a0032273

Clark, Lee Anna. (2009). Stability and change in personality disorder. *Current Directions in Psychological Science, 18*(1), 27–31. doi: 10.1111/j.1467-8721.2009.01600.x

Clark, Shelley; Kabiru, Caroline & Mathur, Rohini. (2010). Relationship transitions among youth in urban Kenya. *Journal of Marriage and Family, 72*(1), 73–88. doi: 10.1111/j.1741-3737.2009.00684.x

Clarke, Christina A.; Miller, Tim; Chang, Ellen T.; Chang, Daixin; Chang, Myles & Gomez, Scarlett L. (2010). Racial and social class gradients in life expectancy in contemporary California. *Social Science & Medicine, 70*(9), 1373–1380. doi: 10.1016/j.socscimed.2010.01.003

Clarke, Philippa; Marshall, Victor; House, James & Lantz, Paula. (2011). The social structuring of mental health over the adult life course: Advancing theory in the sociology of aging. *Social Forces, 89*(4), 1287–1313. doi: 10.1093/sf/89.4.1287

Coe, Norma B. & Zamarro, Gema. (2011). Retirement effects on health in Europe. *Journal of Health Economics, 30*(1), 77–86. doi: 10.1016/j.jhealeco.2010.11.002

Cohen, Jon. (2014). Saving lives without new drugs. *Science, 346*(6212), 911. doi: 10.1126/science.346.6212.911

Cohen, Joachim; Van Landeghem, Paul; Carpentier, Nico & Deliens, Luc. (2013). Public acceptance of euthanasia in Europe: a survey study in 47 countries. *International Journal of Public Health, 59*(1), 143–156. doi: 10.1007/s00038-013-0461-6

Cohen, Leslie B. & Cashon, Cara H. (2006). Infant cognition. In William Damon & Richard M. Lerner (Eds.), *Handbook of child psychology* (6th ed., Vol. 2, pp. 214–251). Hoboken, NJ: Wiley.

Colarossi, Lisa; Silver, Ellen J.; Dean, Randa; Perez, Amanda & River, Angelic. (2014). Adult role models: Feasibility, acceptability, and initial outcomes for sex education. *American Journal of Sexuality Education, 9*(2), 155–175. doi: 10.1080/15546128.2014.903815

Colbert, Linda; Jefferson, Joseph; Gallo, Ralph & Davis, Ronnie. (2009). A study of religiosity and psychological well-being among African Americans: Implications for counseling and psychotherapeutic processes. *Journal of Religion and Health, 48*(3), 278–289. doi: 10.1007/s10943-008-9195-9

Cole, Michael & Vossoughi, Shirin. (2015). Confronting the home-field disadvantage. *Mind, Culture, and Activity, 22*(1), 78–84. doi: 10.1080/10749039.2014.990038

Cole, Pamela M.; Armstrong, Laura Marie & Pemberton, Caroline K. (2010). The role of language in the development of emotion regulation. In Susan D. Calkins & Martha Ann Bell (Eds.), *Child development at the intersection of emotion and cognition* (pp. 59–78). Washington, DC: American Psychological Association.

Coleman, Marilyn; Ganong, Lawrence H. & Warzinik, Kelly. (2007). *Family life in 20th-century America.* Westport, CT: Greenwood Press.

Coley, Nicola; Vaurs, Charlotte & Andrieu, Sandrine. (2015). Nutrition and cognition in aging adults. *Clinics in Geriatric Medicine, 31*(3), 453–464. doi: 10.1016/j.cger.2015.04.008

Collins, Emily & Freeman, Jonathan. (2013). Do problematic and non-problematic video game players differ in extraversion, trait empathy, social capital and prosocial tendencies? *Computers in Human Behavior, 29*(5), 1933–1940. doi: 10.1016/j.chb.2013.03.002

Colson, Eve R.; Willinger, Marian; Rybin, Denis; Heeren, Timothy; Smith, Lauren A.; Lister, George & Corwin, Michael J. (2013). Trends and factors associated with infant bed sharing, 1993–2010: The National Infant Sleep Position study. *JAMA Pediatrics, 167*(11), 1032–1037. doi: 10.1001/jamapediatrics.2013.2560

Common Sense Media. (2013). *Zero to eight: Children's media use in America 2013.* San Francisco, CA: Common Sense Media.

Compian, Laura J.; Gowen, L. Kris & Hayward, Chris. (2009). The interactive effects of puberty and peer victimization on weight concerns and depression symptoms among early adolescent girls. *The Journal of Early Adolescence, 29*(3), 357–375. doi: 10.1177/0272431608323656

Compta, Yaroslau; Parkkinen, Laura; O'Sullivan, Sean S.; Vandrovcova, Jana; Holton, Janice L.; Collins, Catherine, . . . Revesz, Tamas. (2011). Lewy- and Alzheimer-type pathologies in Parkinson's disease dementia: Which is more important? *Brain: A Journal of Neurology, 134*(5), 1493–1505. doi: 10.1093/brain/awr031

Compton, Wilson M.; Gfroerer, Joe; Conway, Kevin P. & Finger, Matthew S. (2014). Unemployment and substance outcomes in the United States 2002–2010. *Drug & Alcohol Dependence, 142,* 350–353. doi: 10.1016/j.drugalcdep.2014.06.012

Conger, Katherine J. & Little, Wendy M. (2010). Sibling relationships during the transition to adulthood. *Child Development Perspectives, 4*(2), 87–94. doi: 10.1111/j.1750-8606.2010.00123.x

Conger, Rand D.; Conger, Katherine J. & Martin, Monica J. (2010). Socioeconomic status, family processes, and individual development. *Journal of Marriage and Family, 72*(3), 685–704. doi: 10.1111/j.1741-3737.2010.00725.x

Connidis, Ingrid Arnet. (2015). Exploring ambivalence in family ties: Progress and prospects. *Journal of Marriage and Family, 77*(1), 77–95. doi: 10.1111/jomf.12150

Coon, Carleton S. (1962). *The origin of races.* New York, NY: Knopf.

Coovadia, Hoosen M. & Wittenberg, Dankwart F. (Eds.). (2004). *Paediatrics and child health: A manual for health professionals in developing countries* (5th ed.). New York, NY: Oxford University Press.

Copeland, William E.; Wolke, Dieter; Angold, Adrian & Costello, E. Jane. (2013). Adult psychiatric outcomes of bullying and being bullied by peers in childhood and adolescence. *JAMA Psychiatry, 70*(4), 419–426. doi: 10.1001/jamapsychiatry.2013.504

Copen, Casey E.; Daniels, Kimberly & Mosher, William D. (2013). *First premarital cohabitation in the United States: 2006–2010 national survey of family growth. National Health Statistics Report.* Hyattsville, MD: U.S. Department of Health and Human Services, Centers for Disease Control and Prevention, National Center for Health Statistics.

Coplan, Robert J. & Weeks, Murray. (2009). Shy and soft-spoken: Shyness, pragmatic language, and socio-emotional adjustment in early childhood. *Infant and Child Development, 18*(3), 238–254. doi: 10.1002/icd.622

Corballis, Michael C. (2011). *The recursive mind: The origins of human language, thought, and civilization.* Princeton, NJ: Princeton University Press.

Corda, Larisa; Khanapure, Amita & Karoshi, Mahantesh. (2012). Biopanic, advanced maternal age and fertility outcomes. In Mahantesh Karoshi et al. (Eds.), *A textbook of preconceptional medicine and management.* London, UK: Sapiens.

Corenblum, Barry. (2014). Relationships between racial–ethnic identity, self-esteem and in-group attitudes among first nation children. *Journal of Youth and Adolescence, 43*(3), 387–404. doi: 10.1007/s10964-013-0081-8

Cornelis, Marilyn C.; Byrne, E. M.; Esko, T.; Nalls, M A.; Ganna, A.; Paynter, N., . . . Wojczynski, M. K. (2015). Genome-wide meta-analysis identifies six novel loci associated with habitual coffee consumption. *Molecular Psychiatry, 20*(5), 647–656. doi: 10.1038/mp.2014.107

Cornwell, Benjamin. (2012). Spousal network overlap as a basis for spousal support. *Journal of Marriage and Family, 74*(2), 229–238. doi: 10.1111/j.1741-3737.2012.00959.x

Coronini-Cronberg, Sophie; Millett, Christopher; Laverty, Anthony A. & Webb, Elizabeth. (2012). The impact of a free older persons' bus pass on active travel and regular walking in England. *American Journal of Public Health, 102*(11), 2141–2148. doi: 10.2105/AJPH.2012.300946

Corr, Charles A. & Corr, Donna M. (2013a). Culture, socialization, and dying. In David K. Meagher & David E. Balk (Eds.), *Handbook of thanatology: The essential body of knowledge for the study of death, dying, and bereavement* (2nd ed., pp. 3–8). New York, NY: Routledge.

Corr, Charles A. & Corr, Donna M. (2013b). Historical and contemporary perspectives on loss, grief, and mourning. In David Meagher & David E. Balk (Eds.), *Handbook of thanatology: The essential body of knowledge for the study of death, dying, and bereavement* (2nd ed., pp. 135–148). New York, NY: Routledge.

Cosgrave, James F. (2010). Embedded addiction: The social production of gambling knowledge and the development of gambling markets. *Canadian Journal of Sociology, 35*(1), 113–134.

Costa, Albert & Sebastián-Gallés, Núria. (2014). How does the bilingual experience sculpt the brain? *Nature Reviews Neuroscience, 15*(5), 336–345. doi: 10.1038/nrn3709

Côté, James E. (2009). Identity formation and self-development in adolescence. In Richard M. Lerner & Laurence Steinberg (Eds.), *Handbook of adolescent psychology* (3rd ed., Vol. 1, pp. 266–304). Hoboken, NJ: Wiley.

Côté, Sylvana M.; Borge, Anne I.; Geoffroy, Marie-Claude; Rutter, Michael & Tremblay, Richard E. (2008). Nonmaternal care in infancy and emotional/behavioral difficulties at 4 years old: Moderation by family risk characteristics. *Developmental Psychology, 44*(1), 155–168. doi: 10.1037/0012-1649.44.1.155

Couzin, Jennifer. (2009). Friendship as a health factor. *Science, 323*(5913), 454–457. doi: 10.1126/science.323.5913.454

Couzin-Frankel, Jennifer. (2010). Bacteria and asthma: Untangling the links. *Science, 330*(6008), 1168–1169. doi: 10.1126/science.330.6008.1168

Couzin-Frankel, Jennifer. (2011). A pitched battle over life span. *Science, 333*(6042), 549–550. doi: 10.1126/science.333.6042.549

Cowan, Nelson (Ed.). (1997). *The development of memory in childhood.* Hove, East Sussex, UK: Psychology Press.

Cowan, Nelson & Alloway, Tracy. (2009). Development of working memory in childhood. In Mary L. Courage & Nelson Cowan (Eds.), *The development of memory in infancy and childhood* (2nd ed., pp. 303–342). New York, NY: Psychology Press.

Cramer, Steven C. & Procaccio, Vincent. (2012). Correlation between genetic polymorphisms and stroke recovery: Analysis of the GAIN Americas and GAIN International Studies. *European Journal of Neurology, 19*(5), 718–724. doi: 10.1111/j.1468-1331.2011.03615.x

Cranwell, Brian. (2010). Care and control: What motivates people's decisions about the disposal of ashes. *Bereavement Care, 29*(2), 10–12. doi: 10.1080/02682621.2010.484929

Crenshaw, David A. (2013). The family, larger systems, and traumatic death. In David K. Meagher & David E. Balk (Eds.), *Handbook of thanatology: The essential body of knowledge for the study of death, dying, and bereavement* (2nd ed., pp. 305–309). New York, NY: Routledge.

Creswell, John W. (2009). *Research design: Qualitative, quantitative, and mixed methods approaches* (3rd ed.). Thousand Oaks, CA: Sage.

Criss, Michael M.; Lee, Tammy K.; Morris, Amanda Sheffield; Cui, Lixian; Bosler, Cara D.; Shreffler, Karina M. & Silk, Jennifer S. (2015). Link between monitoring behavior and adolescent adjustment: An analysis of direct and indirect effects. *Journal of Child and Family Studies, 24*(3), 668–678. doi: 10.1007/s10826-013-9877-0

Crone, Eveline A. & Ridderinkhof, K. Richard. (2011). The developing brain: From theory to neuroimaging and back. *Developmental Cognitive Neuroscience, 1*(2), 101–109. doi: 10.1016/j.dcn.2010.12.001

Crosnoe, Robert & Johnson, Monica Kirkpatrick. (2011). Research on adolescence in the twenty-first century. *Annual Review of Sociology, 37*(1), 439–460. doi: 10.1146/annurev-soc-081309-150008

Crosnoe, Robert; Leventhal, Tama; Wirth, Robert John; Pierce, Kim M. & Pianta, Robert C. (2010). Family socioeconomic status and consistent environmental stimulation in early childhood. *Child Development, 81*(3), 972–987. doi: 10.1111/j.1467-8624.2010.01446.x

Cross, Donna; Monks, Helen; Hall, Marg; Shaw, Thérèse; Pintabona, Yolanda; Erceg, Erin, . . . Lester, Leanne. (2011). Three-year results of the Friendly Schools whole-of-school intervention on children's bullying behaviour. *British Educational Research Journal, 37*(1), 105–129. doi: 10.1080/01411920903420024

Crossley, Nicolas A.; Mechelli, Andrea; Scott, Jessica; Carletti, Francesco; Fox, Peter T.; McGuire, Philip & Bullmore, Edward T. (2014). The hubs of the human connectome are generally implicated in the anatomy of brain disorders. *Brain, 137*(8), 2382–2395. doi: 10.1093/brain/awu132

Cruikshank, Margaret. (2009). *Learning to be old: Gender, culture, and aging* (2nd ed.). Lanham, MD: Rowman & Littlefield.

Csikszentmihalyi, Mihaly. (2013). *Creativity: Flow and the psychology of discovery and invention.* New York, NY: Harper Perennial.

Cuevas, Bryan J. & Stone, Jacqueline Ilyse (Eds.). (2011). *The Buddhist dead: Practices, discourses, representations.* Honolulu, HI: University of Hawaii Press.

Cuijpers, P.; van Straten, A.; van Oppen, P. & Andersson, G. (2010). Welke psychologische behandeling, uitgevoerd door wie, is het meest effectief bij depressie? *Gedragstherapie, 43,* 79–113.

Cumming, Elaine & Henry, William Earl. (1961). *Growing old: The process of disengagement.* New York, NY: Basic Books.

Curlin, Farr A.; Nwodim, Chinyere; Vance, Jennifer L.; Chin, Marshall H. & Lantos, John D. (2008). To die, to sleep: US physicians' religious and other objections to physician-assisted suicide, terminal sedation, and withdrawal of life support. *American Journal of Hospice and Palliative Medicine, 25*(2), 112–120. doi: 10.1177/1049909107310141

Currie, Janet & Widom, Cathy S. (2010). Long-term consequences of child abuse and neglect on adult economic well-being. *Child Maltreatment, 15*(2), 111–120. doi: 10.1177/1077559509355316

Curry, Laurel Erin; Richardson, Amanda; Xiao, Haijun & Niaura, Raymond S. (2013). Nondisclosure of smoking status to health care providers among current and former smokers in the United States. *Health Education and Behavior, 40*(3), 266–273. doi: 10.1177/1090198112454284

Cutler, Stephen J.; Hendricks, Jon & O'Neill, Greg. (2011). Civic engagement and aging. In Robert H. Binstock & Linda K. George (Eds.), *Handbook of aging and the social sciences* (7th ed., pp. 221–233). San Diego, CA: Academic Press. doi: 10.1016/B978-0-12-380880-6.00016-2

Cutuli, J. J.; Desjardins, Christopher David; Herbers, Janette E.; Long, Jeffrey D.; Heistad, David; Chan, Chi-Keung, . . . Masten, Ann S. (2013). Academic achievement trajectories of homeless and highly mobile students: Resilience in the context of chronic and acute risk. *Child Development, 84*(3), 841–857. doi: 10.1111/cdev.12013

Dahl, Ronald E. (2004). Adolescent brain development: A period of vulnerabilities and opportunities, keynote address. *Annals of the New York Academy of Sciences, 1021,* 1–22. doi: 10.1196/annals.1308.001

Dai, David Yun. (2010). *The nature and nurture of giftedness: A new framework for understanding gifted education.* New York, NY: Teachers College Press.

Dalman, Christina; Allebeck, Peter; Gunnell, David; Harrison, Glyn; Kristensson, Krister; Lewis, Glyn, . . . Karlsson, Håkan. (2008). Infections in the CNS during childhood and the risk of subsequent psychotic illness: A cohort study of more than one million Swedish subjects. *American Journal of Psychiatry, 165*(1), 59–65. doi: 10.1176/appi.ajp.2007.07050740

Damasio, Antonio R. (2012). *Self comes to mind: Constructing the conscious brain.* New York, NY: Vintage.

Dannefer, Dale & Patterson, Robin Shura. (2008). The missing person: Some limitations in the contemporary study of cognitive aging. In Scott M. Hofer & Duane F. Alwin (Eds.), *Handbook of cognitive aging: Interdisciplinary perspectives* (pp. 105–119). Thousand Oaks, CA: Sage. doi: 10.4135/9781412976589

Darwin, Charles. (1859). *On the origin of species by means of natural selection.* London, UK: J. Murray.

Daum, Moritz M.; Ulber, Julia & Gredebäck, Gustaf. (2013). The development of pointing perception in infancy: Effects of communicative signals on covert shifts of attention. *Developmental Psychology, 49*(10), 1898–1908. doi: 10.1037/a0031111

David, Barbara; Grace, Diane & Ryan, Michelle K. (2004). The gender wars: A self-categorization perspective on the development of gender identity. In Mark Bennett & Fabio Sani (Eds.), *The development of the social self* (pp. 135–157). New York, NY: Psychology Press.

Davidai, Shai & Gilovich, Thomas. (2015). Building a more mobile America: One income quintile at a time. *Perspectives on Psychological Science, 10*(1), 60–71. doi: 10.1177/1745691614562005

Davis, Elysia Poggi; Parker, Susan W.; Tottenham, Nim & Gunnar, Megan R. (2003). Emotion, cognition, and the hypothalamic-pituitary-adrenocortical axis: A developmental perspective. In Michelle de Haan & Mark H. Johnson (Eds.), *The cognitive neuroscience of development* (pp. 181–206). New York, NY: Psychology Press.

Davis, Linell. (1999). *Doing culture: Cross-cultural communication in action.* Beijing, China: Foreign Language Teaching & Research Press.

Davis, R. Neal; Davis, Matthew M.; Freed, Gary L. & Clark, Sarah J. (2011). Fathers' depression related to positive and negative parenting behaviors with 1-year-old children. *Pediatrics, 127*(4), 612–618. doi: 10.1542/peds.2010-1779

Davis-Kean, Pamela E.; Jager, Justin & Collins, W. Andrew. (2009). The self in action: An emerging link between self-beliefs and behaviors in middle childhood. *Child Development Perspectives, 3*(3), 184–188. doi: 10.1111/j.1750-8606.2009.00104.x

Davison, Glen; Kehaya, Corinna & Jones, Arwel Wyn. (2014). Nutritional and physical activity interventions to improve immunity. *American Journal of Lifestyle Medicine.* doi: 10.1177/1559827614557773

Dawlatly, Samir L. (2014). Do our consultation models meet our patients' needs? *British Journal of General Practice, 64*(622), 245. doi: 10.3399/bjgp14X679787

Dawood, Yasmin. (2015). Campaign finance and American democracy. *Annual Review of Political Science, 18*, 329–348. doi: 10.1146/annurev-polisci-010814-104523

de Bruin, Angela; Treccani, Barbara & Sala, Sergio Della. (2015). Cognitive advantage in bilingualism: An example of publication bias? *Psychological Science, 26*(1), 99–107. doi: 10.1177/0956797614557866

de Bruin, Wändi Bruine; Parker, Andrew M. & Fischhoff, Baruch. (2007). Can adolescents predict significant life events? *The Journal of Adolescent Health, 41*(2), 208–210. doi: 10.1016/j.jadohealth.2007.03.014

de Jong, Antina; Maya, Idit & van Lith, Jan M. M. (2015). Prenatal screening: Current practice, new developments, ethical challenges. *Bioethics, 29*(1), 1–8. doi: 10.1111/bioe.12123

de Jong Gierveld, Jenny & Merz, Eva-Maria. (2013). Parents' partnership decision making after divorce or widowhood: The role of (step)children. *Journal of Marriage and Family, 75*(5), 1098–1113. doi: 10.1111/jomf.12061

de Jonge, Ank; Mesman, Jeanette A. J. M.; Manniën, Judith; Zwart, Joost J.; van Dillen, Jeroen & van Roosmalen, Jos. (2013). Severe adverse maternal outcomes among low risk women with planned home versus hospital births in the Netherlands: Nationwide cohort study. *BMJ, 346*, f3263. doi: 10.1136/bmj.f3263

de Jonge, Huub. (2011). Purification and remembrance: Eastern and Western ways to deal with the Bali bombing. In Peter Jan Margry & Cristina Sánchez-Carretero (Eds.), *Grassroots memorials: The politics of memorializing traumatic death* (pp. 262–284). New York, NY: Berghahn Books.

de la Croix, David. (2013). *Fertility, education, growth, and sustainability.* New York, NY: Cambridge University Press.

De Neys, Wim & Van Gelder, Elke. (2009). Logic and belief across the lifespan: The rise and fall of belief inhibition during syllogistic reasoning. *Developmental Science, 12*(1), 123–130. doi: 10.1111/j.1467-7687.2008.00746.x

De Raedt, Rudi; Koster, Ernst H. W. & Ryckewaert, Ruben. (2013). Aging and attentional bias for death related and general threat-related information: Less avoidance in older as compared with middle-aged adults. *The Journals of Gerontology, Series B: Psychological Sciences and Social Sciences, 68*(1), 41–48. doi: 10.1093/geronb/gbs047

Dean, Angela J.; Walters, Julie & Hall, Anthony. (2010). A systematic review of interventions to enhance medication adherence in children and adolescents with chronic illness. *Archives of Disease in Childhood, 95*(9), 717–723. doi: 10.1136/adc.2009.175125

Dearing, Eric; Wimer, Christopher; Simpkins, Sandra D.; Lund, Terese; Bouffard, Suzanne M.; Caronongan, Pia, . . . Weiss, Heather. (2009). Do neighborhood and home contexts help explain why low-income children miss opportunities to participate in activities outside of school? *Developmental Psychology, 45*(6), 1545–1562. doi: 10.1037/a0017359

Deary, Ian J.; Penke, Lars & Johnson, Wendy. (2010). The neuroscience of human intelligence differences. *Nature Reviews Neuroscience, 11*(3), 201–211. doi: 10.1038/nrn2793

Deater-Deckard, Kirby. (2013). The social environment and the development of psychopathology. In Philip D. Zelazo (Ed.), *The Oxford handbook of developmental psychology* (Vol. 2, pp. 527–548). New York, NY: Oxford University Press. doi: 10.1093/oxfordhb/9780199958474.013.0021

DeCaro, Marci S.; Thomas, Robin D.; Albert, Neil B. & Beilock, Sian L. (2011). Choking under pressure: Multiple routes to skill failure. *Journal of Experimental Psychology, 140*(3), 390–406. doi: 10.1037/a0023466

Dee, Thomas; Jacob, Brian A. & Schwartz, Nathaniel. (2013). The effects of NCLB on school resources and practices. *Educational Evaluation and Policy Analysis, 35*(2), 252–279. doi: 10.3102/0162373712467080

Dees, Marianne K.; Vernooij-Dassen, Myrra. J.; Dekkers, Wim. J.; Vissers, Kris. C. & van Weel, Chris. (2011). 'Unbearable suffering': A qualitative study on the perspectives of patients who request assistance in dying. *Journal of Medical Ethics, 37*(12), 727–734. doi: 10.1136/jme.2011.045492

Degnan, Kathryn A.; Hane, Amie Ashley; Henderson, Heather A.; Moas, Olga Lydia; Reeb-Sutherland, Bethany C. & Fox, Nathan A. (2011). Longitudinal stability of temperamental exuberance and social–emotional outcomes in early childhood. *Developmental Psychology, 47*(3), 765–780. doi: 10.1037/a0021316

DeGroot, Jocelyn M. (2012). Maintaining relational continuity with the deceased on Facebook. *Omega: Journal of Death & Dying, 65*(3), 195–212. doi: 10.2190/OM.65.3.c

Delaunay-El Allam, Maryse; Soussignan, Robert; Patris, Bruno; Marlier, Luc & Schaal, Benoist. (2010). Long-lasting memory for an odor acquired at the mother's breast. *Developmental Science, 13*(6), 849–863. doi: 10.1111/j.1467-7687.2009.00941.x

Delon-Martin, Chantal; Plailly, Jane; Fonlupt, Pierre; Veyrac, Alexandra & Roye, Jean-Pierre. (2013). Perfumers' expertise induces structural reorganization in olfactory brain regions. *NeuroImage, 68*, 55–62. doi: 10.1016/j.neuroimage.2012.11.044

Demetriou, Andreas; Spanoudis, George; Shayer, Michael; Mouyi, Antigoni; Kazi, Smaragda & Platsidou, Maria. (2013). Cycles in speed-working memory-G relations: Towards a developmental–differential theory of the mind. *Intelligence, 41*(1), 34–50. doi: 10.1016/j.intell.2012.10.010

Dennehy, Tara C.; Ben-Zeev, Avi & Tanigawa, Noriko. (2014). 'Be prepared': An implemental mindset for alleviating social-identity threat. *British Journal of Social Psychology, 53*(3), 585–594. doi: 10.1111/bjso.12071

Denny, Dallas & Pittman, Cathy. (2007). Gender identity: From dualism to diversity. In Mitchell Tepper & Annette Fuglsang Owens (Eds.), *Sexual Health* (Vol. 1, pp. 205–229). Westport, CT: Praeger.

Deptula, Daneen P.; Henry, David B. & Schoeny, Michael E. (2010). How can parents make a difference? Longitudinal associations with adolescent sexual behavior. *Journal of Family Psychology, 24*(6), 731–739. doi: 10.1037/a0021760

Deresiewicz, William. (2014). *Excellent sheep: The miseducation of the American elite and the way to a meaningful life.* New York, NY: Free Press.

Derksen, B. J.; Duffa, M. C.; Weldon, K.; Zhang, J.; Zambac, K. D.; Tranel, D. & Denburg, N. L. (2015). Older adults catch up to younger adults on a learning and memory task that involves collaborative social interaction. *Memory, 23*(4), 612–624. doi: 10.1080/09658211.2014.915974

Desai, Rishi J.; Hernandez-Diaz, Sonia; Bateman, Brian T. & Huybrechts, Krista F. (2014). Increase in prescription opioid use during pregnancy among medicaid-enrolled women. *Obstetrics & Gynecology, 123*(5), 997–1002. doi: 10.1097/AOG.0000000000000208

DeSantiago-Cardenas, Lilliana; Rivkina, Victoria; Whyte, Stephanie A.; Harvey-Gintoft, Blair C.; Bunning, Bryan J. & Gupta, Ruchi S. (2015). Emergency epinephrine use for food allergy reactions in Chicago public schools. *American Journal of Preventive Medicine, 48*(2), 170–173. doi: 10.1016/j.amepre.2014.09.005

Devine, Rory T. & Hughes, Claire. (2014). Relations between false belief understanding and executive function in early childhood: A meta-analysis. *Child Development, 85*(5), 1777–1794. doi: 10.1111/cdev.12237

DeYoung, Colin G.; Hirsh, Jacob B.; Shane, Matthew S.; Papademetris, Xenophon; Rajeevan, Nallakkandi & Gray, Jeremy R. (2010). Testing predictions from personality neuroscience. *Psychological Science, 21*(6), 820–828. doi: 10.1177/0956797610370159

Diamond, Lisa M. & Fagundes, Christopher P. (2010). Psychobiological research on attachment. *Journal of Social and Personal Relationships, 27*(2), 218–225. doi: 10.1177/0265407509360906

Dickinson, George E. & Hoffmann, Heath C. (2010). Roadside memorial policies in the United States. *Mortality: Promoting the interdisciplinary study of death and dying, 15*(2), 154–167. doi: 10.1080/13576275.2010.482775

Didion, Joan. (2005). *The year of magical thinking.* New York, NY: Knopf.

Dijk, Jan A. G. M. van. (2005). *The deepening divide: Inequality in the information society.* Thousand Oaks, CA: Sage.

Dijksterhuis, Ap; Bos, Maarten W.; van der Leij, Andries & van Baaren, Rick B. (2009). Predicting soccer matches after unconscious and conscious thought as a function of expertise. *Psychological Science, 20*(11), 1381–1387. doi: 10.1111/j.1467-9280.2009.02451.x

Dijksterhuis, Ap & Nordgren, Loran F. (2006). A theory of unconscious thought. *Perspectives on Psychological Science, 1*(2), 95–109. doi: 10.1111/j.1745-6916.2006.00007.x

Dingemans, Ellen; Henkens, Kène & Solinge, Hanna van. (2015). Access to bridge employment: Who finds and who does not find work after retirement? *The Gerontologist.* doi: 10.1093/geront/gnu182

Diseth, Åge; Meland, Eivind & Breidablik, Hans J. (2014). Self-beliefs among students: Grade level and gender differences in self-esteem, self-efficacy and implicit theories of intelligence. *Learning and Individual Differences, 35*, 1–8. doi: 10.1016/j.lindif.2014.06.003

Dishion, Thomas J.; Poulin, François & Burraston, Bert. (2001). Peer group dynamics associated with iatrogenic effects in group interventions with high-risk young adolescents. In Douglas W. Nangle & Cynthia A. Erdley (Eds.), *The role of friendship in psychological adjustment* (pp. 79–92). San Francisco, CA: Jossey-Bass.

Dishion, Thomas J.; Véronneau, Marie-Hélène & Myers, Michael W. (2010). Cascading peer dynamics underlying the progression from problem behavior to violence in early to late adolescence. *Development and Psychopathology, 22*(3), 603–619. doi: 10.1017/S0954579410000313

Dix, Theodore & Yan, Ni. (2014). Mothers' depressive symptoms and infant negative emotionality in the prediction of child adjustment at age 3: Testing the maternal reactivity and child vulnerability hypotheses. *Development and Psychopathology, 26*(1), 111–124. doi: 10.1017/S0954579413000898

Dobler, Robert Thomas. (2011). Ghost bikes: Memorialization and protest on city streets. In Peter Jan Margry & Cristina Sanchez-Carretero (Eds.), *Grassroots memorials: The politics of memorializing traumatic death* (pp. 169–187). New York, NY: Berghahn Books.

Dobson, Velma; Candy, T. Rowan; Hartmann, E. Eugenie; Mayer, D. Luisa; Miller, Joseph M. & Quinn, Graham E. (2009). Infant and child vision research: Present status and future directions. *Optometry & Vision Science, 86*(6), 559–560. doi: 10.1097/OPX.0b013e3181aa06d5

Dodge, Elizabeth & Simic, Mima. (2015). Anorexia runs in families: Does this make the families responsible? A commentary on 'Anorexia runs in families: Is this due to genes or the family environment?' (Dring, 2014). *Journal of Family Therapy, 37*(1), 93–102. doi: 10.1111/1467-6427.12065

Dodge, Kenneth A. (2009). Mechanisms of gene-environment interaction effects in the development of conduct disorder. *Perspectives on Psychological Science, 4*(4), 408–414. doi: 10.1111/j.1745-6924.2009.01147.x

Doering, Katie. (2010). Death: The unwritten curriculum. *Encounter: Education for Meaning and Social Justice, 23*(4), 57–62.

Doka, Kenneth J. (2013). Historical and contemporary perspectives on dying. In David K. Meagher & David E. Balk (Eds.), *Handbook of thanatology: The essential body of knowledge for the study of death, dying, and bereavement* (2nd ed., pp. 17–23). New York, NY: Routledge.

Dolgin, Elie. (2015). The myopia boom. *Nature, 519,* 276–278. doi: 10.1038/519276a

Dominguez-Folgueras, Marta & Castro-Martin, Teresa. (2013). Cohabitation in Spain: No longer a marginal path to family formation. *Journal of Marriage and Family, 75*(2), 422–437. doi: 10.1111/jomf.12013

Dong, XinQi & Simon, Melissa A. (2011). Enhancing national policy and programs to address elder abuse. *JAMA, 305*(23), 2460–2461. doi: 10.1001/jama.2011.835

Dong, XinQi; Simon, Melissa A.; Beck, T. T.; Farran, Carol; McCann, Judith J.; Mendes de Leon, Carlos F., . . . Evans, Denis A. (2011). Elder abuse and mortality: The role of psychological and social wellbeing. *Gerontology, 57*(6), 549–558. doi: 10.1159/000321881

Doraiswamy, P. Murali. (2012). Silent cerebrovascular events and Alzheimer's disease: An overlooked opportunity for prevention? *American Journal of Psychiatry, 169*(3), 251–254. doi: 10.1176/appi.ajp.2011.11121830

Dorsey, Shannon; Burns, Barbara J.; Southerland, Dannia G.; Cox, Julia Revillion; Wagner, H. Ryan & Farmer, Elizabeth M. Z. (2012). Prior trauma exposure for youth in treatment foster care. *Journal of Child and Family Studies, 21*(5), 816–824. doi: 10.1007/s10826-011-9542-4

Dotterer, Aryn M.; McHale, Susan M. & Crouter, Ann C. (2009). The development and correlates of academic interests from childhood through adolescence. *Journal of Educational Psychology, 101*(2), 509–519. doi: 10.1037/a0013987

Doubleday, Justin. (2013). Earnings gap narrows, but college education still pays, report says. *The Chronicle Of Higher Education,* A14.

Doucet, Andrea. (2015). Parental responsibilities: Dilemmas of measurement and gender equality. *Journal of Marriage and Family, 77*(1), 224–242. doi: 10.1111/jomf.12148

Downs, Danielle S. & Hausenblas, Heather A. (2007). Pregnant women's third trimester exercise behaviors, body mass index, and pregnancy outcomes. *Psychology & Health, 22*(5), 545–559. doi: 10.1080/14768320701372018

Drabant, Emily M.; Ramel, Wiveka; Edge, Michael D.; Hyde, Luke W.; Kuo, Janice R.; Goldin, Philippe R., . . . Gross, James J. (2012). Neural mechanisms underlying 5-HTTLPR-related sensitivity to acute stress. *PsychiatryOnline, 169*(4), 397–405. doi: 10.1176/appi.ajp.2011.10111699

Drake, Kim; Belsky, Jay & Fearon, R. M. Pasco. (2014). From early attachment to engagement with learning in school: The role of self-regulation and persistence. *Developmental Psychology, 50*(5), 1350–1361. doi: 10.1037/a0032779

Dring, Greg. (2015). Anorexia runs in families: Is this due to genes or the family environment? *Journal of Family Therapy, 37*(1), 79–92. doi: 10.1111/1467-6427.12048

Drover, James; Hoffman, Dennis R.; Castañeda, Yolanda S.; Morale, Sarah E. & Birch, Eileen E. (2009). Three randomized controlled trials of early long-chain polyunsaturated fatty acid supplementation on means-end problem solving in 9-month-olds. *Child Development, 80*(5), 1376–1384. doi: 10.1111/j.1467-8624.2009.01339.x

Du Toit, George; Roberts, Graham; Sayre, Peter H.; Bahnson, Henry T.; Radulovic, Suzana; Santos, Alexandra F., . . . Lack, Gideon. (2015). Randomized trial of peanut consumption in infants at risk for peanut allergy. *New England Journal of Medicine, 372,* 803–813. doi: 10.1056/NEJMoa1414850

Dubicka, Bernadka; Carlson, Gabrielle A.; Vail, Andy & Harrington, Richard. (2008). Prepubertal mania: Diagnostic differences between US and UK clinicians. *European Child & Adolescent Psychiatry, 17*(3), 153–161. doi: 10.1007/s00787-007-0649-5

Duckworth, Angela Lee & Kern, Margaret L. (2011). A meta-analysis of the convergent validity of self-control measures. *Journal of Research in Personality, 45*(3), 259–268. doi: 10.1016/j.jrp.2011.02.004

Duckworth, Angela L.; Peterson, Christopher; Matthews, Michael D. & Kelly, Dennis R. (2007). Grit: Perseverance and passion for long-term goals. *Journal of Personality and Social Psychology, 92*(6), 1087–1101. doi: 10.1037/0022-3514.92.6.1087

Duckworth, Angela L. & Steinberg, Laurence. (2015). Unpacking self-control. *Child Development Perspectives, 9*(1), 32–37. doi: 10.1111/cdep.12107

Dukes, Richard L.; Stein, Judith A. & Zane, Jazmin I. (2009). Effect of relational bullying on attitudes, behavior and injury among adolescent bullies, victims and bully-victims. *The Social Science Journal, 46*(4), 671–688. doi: 10.1016/j.soscij.2009.05.006

Duncan, Greg J. & Magnuson, Katherine. (2013). Investing in preschool programs. *Journal of Economic Perspectives, 27*(2), 109–132. doi: 10.1257/jep.27.2.109

Duncan, Simon & Phillips, Miranda. (2010). People who live apart together (LATs)–How different are they? *The Sociological Review, 58*(1), 112–134. doi: 10.1111/j.1467-954X.2009.01874.x

Dunifon, Rachel; Kalil, Ariel; Crosby, Danielle A.; Su, Jessica H. & DeLeire, Thomas. (2013). Measuring maternal nonstandard work in survey data. *Journal of Marriage and Family, 75*(3), 523–532. doi: 10.1111/jomf.12017

Dunmore, Simon J. (2013). Of fat mice and men: The rise of the adipokines. *Journal of Endocrinology, 216*(1), E1–E2. doi: 10.1530/JOE-12-0513

Dunning, David. (2011). *Social motivation.* New York, NY: Psychology Press.

Dunphy, Dexter C. (1963). The social structure of urban adolescent peer groups. *Sociometry, 26*(2), 230–246. doi: 10.2307/2785909

Dupuis, Kate & Pichora-Fuller, M. Kathleen. (2010). Use of affective prosody by young and older adults. *Psychology and Aging, 25*(1), 16–29. doi: 10.1037/a0018777

Dutra, Lauren M. & Glantz, Stanton A. (2014). Electronic cigarettes and conventional cigarette use among US adolescents: A cross-sectional study. *JAMA Pediatrics, 168*(7), 610–617. doi: 10.1001/jamapediatrics.2013.5488

Dvornyk, Volodymyr & Waqar-ul-Haq. (2012). Genetics of age at menarche: A systematic review. *Human Reproduction Update, 18*(2), 198–210. doi: 10.1093/humupd/dmr050

Dweck, Carol S. (2013). Social Development. In Philip D. Zelazo (Ed.), *The Oxford handbook of developmental psychology* (Vol. 2, pp. 167–190). New York, NY: Oxford University Press. doi: 10.1093/oxfordhb/9780199958474.013.0008

Dyer, Ashley A.; Rivkina, Victoria; Perumal, Dhivya; Smeltzer, Brandon M.; Smith, Bridget M. & Gupta, Ruchi S. (2015). Epidemiology of childhood peanut allergy. *Allergy and Asthma Proceedings, 36*(1), 58–64. doi: 10.2500/aap.2015.36.3819

Dyer, Nazly; Owen, Margaret T. & Caughy, Margaret O'Brien. (2014). Ethnic differences in profiles of mother–child interactions and relations to emerging school readiness in African American and Latin American children. *Parenting, 14*(3/4), 175–194. doi: 10.1080/15295192.2014.972756

Eagly, Alice H. & Wood, Wendy. (2013). The nature–nurture debates: 25 years of challenges in understanding the psychology of gender. *Perspectives on Psychological Science, 8*(3), 340–357. doi: 10.1177/1745691613484767

Ebaugh, Helen Rose & Curry, Mary. (2000). Fictive kin as social capital in new immigrant communities. *Sociological Perspectives, 43*(2), 189–209. doi: 10.2307/1389793

Eccles, Jacquelynne S. & Roeser, Robert W. (2010). An ecological view of schools and development. In Judith L. Meece & Jacquelynne S. Eccles (Eds.), *Handbook of research on schools, schooling, and human development* (pp. 6–22). New York, NY: Routledge.

Eccles, Jacquelynne S. & Roeser, Robert W. (2011). Schools as developmental contexts during adolescence. *Journal of Research on Adolescence, 21*(1), 225–241. doi: 10.1111/j.1532-7795.2010.00725.x

Eckholm, Erik. (2013, October 24). Case explores rights of fetus versus mother. *The New York Times,* pp. A1, A16.

Eells, Tracy D.; Lombart, Kenneth G.; Salsman, Nicholas; Kendjelic, Edward M.; Schneiderman, Carolyn T. & Lucas, Cynthia P. (2011). Expert reasoning in psychotherapy case formulation. *Psychotherapy Research, 21*(4), 385–399. doi: 10.1080/10503307.2010.539284

Eggum, Natalie D.; Eisenberg, Nancy; Kao, Karen; Spinrad, Tracy L.; Bolnick, Rebecca; Hofer, Claire, . . . Fabricius, William V. (2011). Emotion understanding, theory of mind, and prosocial orientation: Relations over time in early childhood. *The Journal of Positive Psychology, 6*(1), 4–16. doi: 10.1080/17439760.2010.536776

Ehrlich, Sara Z. & Blum-Kulka, Shoshana. (2014). 'Now I said that Danny becomes Danny again': A multifaceted view of kindergarten children's peer argumentative discourse. In Asta Cekaite et al. (Eds.), *Children's peer talk: Learning from each other* (pp. 23–41). New York, NY: Cambridge University Press.

Eichhorst, Werner; Rodríguez-Planas, Núria; Schmidl, Ricarda & Zimmermann, Klaus F. (2012). *A roadmap to vocational education and training systems around the world.* Bonn, Germany: Institute for the Study of Labor.

Eisenberg, Nancy; Hofer, Claire; Sulik, Michael J. & Liew, Jeffrey. (2013). The development of prosocial moral reasoning and a prosocial orientation in young adulthood: Concurrent and longitudinal correlates. *Developmental Psychology, 50*(1), 58–70. doi: 10.1037/a0032990

Eisenberg, Nancy; Hofer, Claire; Sulik, Michael J. & Spinrad, Tracy L. (2014). Self-regulation, effortful control, and their socioemotional correlates. In James J. Gross (Ed.), *Handbook of emotion regulation* (2nd ed., pp. 157–172). New York, NY: Guilford Press.

Elder, Glen H. (1998). The life course as developmental theory. *Child Development, 69*(1), 1–12. doi: 10.1111/j.1467-8624.1998.tb06128.x

Elicker, James; Ruprecht, Karen M. & Anderson, Treshawn. (2014). Observing infants' and toddlers' relationships and interactions in group care. In Linda J. Harrison & Jennifer Sumsion (Eds.), *Lived spaces of infant-toddler education and care: Exploring diverse perspectives on theory, research and practice* (pp. 131–145). Dordrecht, Netherlands: Springer. doi: 10.1007/978-94-017-8838-0_10

Elkind, David. (1967). Egocentrism in adolescence. *Child Development, 38*(4), 1025–1034.

Elkind, David. (2007). *The power of play: How spontaneous, imaginative activities lead to happier, healthier children.* Cambridge, MA: Da Capo Press.

Ellingsaeter, Anne L. (2014). Towards universal quality early childhood education and care: The Norwegian model. In Ludovica Gambaro et al. (Eds.), *An equal start?: Providing quality early education and care for disadvantaged children* (pp. 53–76). Chicago, IL: Policy Press.

Elliott, Sinikka. (2012). *Not my kid: What parents believe about the sex lives of their teenagers.* New York, NY: New York University Press.

Elliott, Vanessa J.; Rodgers, David L. & Brett, Stephen J. (2011). Systematic review of quality of life and other patient-centred outcomes after cardiac arrest survival. *Resuscitation, 82*(3), 247–256. doi: 10.1016/j.resuscitation.2010.10.030

Ellis, Bruce J. & Boyce, W. Thomas. (2008). Biological sensitivity to context. *Current Directions in Psychological Science, 17*(3), 183–187. doi: 10.1111/j.1467-8721.2008.00571.x

Ellis, Bruce J.; Shirtcliff, Elizabeth A.; Boyce, W. Thomas; Deardorff, Julianna & Essex, Marilyn J. (2011). Quality of early family relationships and the timing and tempo of puberty: Effects depend on biological sensitivity to context. *Development and Psychopathology, 23*(1), 85–99. doi: 10.1017/S0954579410000660

Ellis, Lee & Wahab, Eshah A. (2013). Religiosity and fear of death: A theory-oriented review of the empirical literature. *Review of Religious Research, 55*(1), 149–189. doi: 10.1007/s13644-012-0064-3

Ellison, Christopher G.; Musick, Marc A. & Holden, George W. (2011). Does conservative Protestantism moderate the association between corporal punishment and child outcomes? *Journal of Marriage and Family, 73*(5), 946–961. doi: 10.1111/j.1741-3737.2011.00854.x

Engelberts, Adèle C. & de Jonge, Guustaaf Adolf. (1990). Choice of sleeping position for infants: Possible association with cot death. *Archives of Disease in Childhood, 65*(4), 462–467. doi: 10.1136/adc.65.4.462

Engelhardt, H. Tristram. (2012). Why clinical bioethics so rarely gives morally normative guidance. In H. Tristram Engelhardt (Ed.), *Bioethics critically reconsidered: Having second thoughts* (pp. 151–174). New York, NY: Springer. doi: 10.1007/978-94-007-2244-6_8

English, Tammy & Carstensen, Laura L. (2014). Selective narrowing of social networks across adulthood is associated with improved emotional experience in daily life. *International Journal of Behavioral Development, 38*(2), 195–202. doi: 10.1177/0165025413515404

Enlow, Michelle B.; King, Lucy; Schreier, Hannah M. C.; Howard, Jamie M.; Rosenfield, David; Ritz, Thomas & Wright, Rosalind J. (2014). Maternal sensitivity and infant autonomic and endocrine stress responses. *Early Human Development, 90*(7), 377–385. doi: 10.1016/j.earlhumdev.2014.04.007

Enserink, Martin. (2011). Can this DNA sleuth help catch criminals? *Science, 331*(6019), 838–840. doi: 10.1126/science.331.6019.838

Epps, Chad & Holt, Lynn. (2011). The genetic basis of addiction and relevant cellular mechanisms. *International Anesthesiology Clinics, 49*(1), 3–14. doi: 10.1097/AIA.0b013e3181f2bb66

Erdbrink, Thomas. (2013, June 3). Seven die in Iran after drinking homemade alcohol. *The New York Times*, p. A3.

Erdman, Phyllis & Ng, Kok-Mun (Eds.). (2010). *Attachment: Expanding the cultural connections.* New York, NY: Routledge.

Erickson, Kirk I.; Gildengers, Ariel G. & Butters, Meryl A. (2013). Physical activity and brain plasticity in late adulthood. *Dialogues in Clinical Neuroscience, 15*(1), 99–108.

Erickson, Kirk I.; Miller, Destiny L.; Weinstein, Andrea M.; Akl, Stephanie L. & Banducci, Sarah. (2012). Physical activity and brain plasticity in late adulthood: A conceptual and comprehensive review. *Ageing Research, 3*(1). doi: 10.4081/ar.2012.e6

Ericsson, K. Anders. (2006). The influence of experience and deliberate practice on the development of superior expert performance. In K. Anders Ericsson et al. (Eds.), *The Cambridge handbook of expertise and expert performance* (pp. 683–703). New York, NY: Cambridge University Press.

Erikson, Erik H. (1968). *Identity: Youth and crisis.* New York, NY: Norton.

Erikson, Erik H. (1982). *The life cycle completed: A review.* New York, NY: Norton.

Erikson, Erik H. (1993). *Childhood and society* (2nd ed.). New York, NY: Norton.

Erikson, Erik H. (1994). *Identity: Youth and crisis.* New York, NY: Norton.

Erikson, Erik H. (1998). *The life cycle completed.* New York, NY: Norton.

Erikson, Erik H.; Erikson, Joan M. & Kivnick, Helen Q. (1986). *Vital involvement in old age.* New York, NY: Norton.

Erikson, Erik H.; Erikson, Joan M. & Kivnick, Helen Q. (1994). *Vital involvement in old age.* New York, NY: Norton.

Ersche, Karen D.; Jones, P. Simon; Williams, Guy B.; Turton, Abigail J.; Robbins, Trevor W. & Bullmore, Edward T. (2012). Abnormal brain structure implicated in stimulant drug addiction. *Science, 335*(6068), 601–604. doi: 10.1126/science.1214463

Esposito, Gianluca; Setoh, Peipei & Bornstein, Marc H. (2015). Beyond practices and values: Toward a physio-bioecological analysis of sleeping arrangements in early infancy. *Frontiers in Psychology, 6*, 264. doi: 10.3389/fpsyg.2015.00264

Estruch, Ramón; Ros, Emilio; Salas-Salvadó, Jordi; Covas, Maria-Isabel; Corella, Dolores; Arós, Fernando,... Martínez-González, Angel Miguel. (2013). Primary prevention of cardiovascular disease with a Mediterranean diet. *New England Journal of Medicine, 368*(14), 1279–1290. doi: 10.1056/NEJMoa1200303

Evans, Angela D.; Xu, Fen & Lee, Kang. (2011). When all signs point to you: Lies told in the face of evidence. *Developmental Psychology, 47*(1), 39–49. doi: 10.1037/a0020787

Evans, Gary W. & Kim, Pilyoung. (2013). Childhood poverty, chronic stress, self-regulation, and coping. *Child Development Perspectives, 7*(1), 43–48. doi: 10.1111/cdep.12013

Evans, Jonathan St. B. T. & Stanovich, Keith E. (2013). Dual-process theories of higher cognition: Advancing the debate. *Perspectives on Psychological Science, 8*(3), 223–241. doi: 10.1177/1745691612460685

Evers, Clifton Westly; Albury, Kath; Byron, Paul & Crawford, Kate. (2013). Young people, social media, social network sites and sexual health communication in Australia: "This is funny, you should watch it". *International Journal of Communication, 7*, 263–280.

Ewers, Michael; Walsh, Cathal; Trojanowski, John Q.; Shaw, Leslie M.; Petersen, Ronald C.; Jack, Clifford R., . . . Hampel, Harald. (2012). Prediction of conversion from mild cognitive impairment to Alzheimer's disease dementia based upon biomarkers and neuropsychological test performance. *Neurobiology of Aging, 33*(7), 1203–1214. doi: 10.1016/j.neurobiolaging.2010.10.019

Ezzati, Majid & Riboli, Elio. (2012). Can noncommunicable diseases be prevented? Lessons from studies of populations and individuals. *Science, 337*(6101), 1482–1487. doi: 10.1126/science.1227001

Fairchild, Amy L. & Bayer, Ronald. (2015). Smoke and fire over e-cigarettes. *Science, 347*(6220), 375–376. doi: 10.1126/science.1260761

Fairhurst, Merle T.; Löken, Line & Grossmann, Tobias. (2014). Physiological and behavioral responses reveal 9-month-old infants' sensitivity to pleasant touch. *Psychological Science, 25*(5), 1124–1131. doi: 10.1177/0956797614527114

Fan, Hung; Conner, Ross F. & Villarreal, Luis P. (2014). *AIDS: Science and society* (7th ed.). Burlington, MA: Jones & Bartlett Learning.

Farber, Stu & Farber, Annalu. (2014). It ain't easy: Making life and death decisions before the crisis. In Leah Rogne & Susana Lauraine McCune (Eds.), *Advance care planning: Communicating about matters of life and death* (pp. 109–122). New York, NY: Springer.

Faria, Nuno R.; Rambaut, Andrew; Suchard, Marc A.; Baele, Guy; Bedford, Trevor; Ward, Melissa J., . . . Lemey, Philippe. (2014). The early spread and epidemic ignition of HIV-1 in human populations. *Science, 346*(6205), 56–61. doi: 10.1126/science.1256739

Farnfield, Steve & Holmes, Paul (Eds.). (2014). *The Routledge handbook of attachment: Assessment.* New York, NY: Routledge.

Farrell, C.; Chappell, F.; Armitage, P. A.; Keston, P.; MacLullich, A.; Shenkin, S. & Wardlaw, J. M. (2009). Development and initial testing of normal reference MR images for the brain at ages 65-70 and 75-80 years. *European Radiology, 19*(1), 177–183. doi: 10.1007/s00330-008-1119-2

Fazzi, Elisa; Signorini, Sabrina G.; Bomba, Monica; Luparia, Antonella; Lanners, Josée & Balottin, Umberto. (2011). Reach on sound: A key to object permanence in visually impaired children. *Early Human Development, 87*(4), 289–296. doi: 10.1016/j.earlhumdev.2011.01.032

FBI. (2013). *Crime in the United States, 2012.* Clarksburg, WV: U.S. Department of Justice, Federal Bureau of Investigation, Criminal Justice Information Services Division.

Feigenson, Lisa; Libertus, Melissa E. & Halberda, Justin. (2013). Links between the intuitive sense of number and formal mathematics ability. *Child Development Perspectives, 7*(2), 74–79. doi: 10.1111/cdep.12019

Feld, Barry C. (2013). *Kids, cops, and confessions: Inside the interrogation room.* New York, NY: New York University Press.

Feldman, Ruth. (2007). Parent-infant synchrony and the construction of shared timing; physiological precursors, developmental outcomes, and risk conditions. *Journal of Child Psychology and Psychiatry, 48*(3/4), 329–354. doi: 10.1111/j.1469-7610.2006.01701.x

Fentiman, Linda C. (2009). Pursuing the perfect mother: Why America's criminalization of maternal substance abuse is not the answer—A comparative legal analysis. *Michigan Journal of Gender & Law, 15*(2), 389–465.

Ferguson, Christopher J. (2013). Spanking, corporal punishment and negative long-term outcomes: A meta-analytic review of longitudinal studies. *Clinical Psychology Review, 33*(1), 196–208. doi: 10.1016/j.cpr.2012.11.002

Ferguson, Gail M.; Iturbide, Maria I. & Gordon, Beverly P. (2014). Tridimensional (3D) acculturation: Ethnic identity and psychological functioning of tricultural Jamaican immigrants. *International Perspectives in Psychology: Research, Practice, Consultation, 3*(4), 238–251. doi: 10.1037/ipp0000019

Ferguson, Kelly K.; Peterson, Karen E.; Lee, Joyce M.; Mercado-García, Adriana; Blank-Goldenberg, Clara; Téllez-Rojo, Martha M. & Meeker, John D. (2014). Prenatal and peripubertal phthalates and bisphenol A in relation to sex hormones and puberty in boys. *Reproductive Toxicology, 47*, 70–76. doi: 10.1016/j.reprotox.2014.06.002

Ferrah, Noha; Murphy, Briony J.; Ibrahim, Joseph E.; Bugeja, Lyndal C.; Winbolt, Margaret; LoGiudice, Dina, . . . Ranson, David L. (2015). Resident-to-resident physical aggression leading to injury in nursing homes: A systematic review. *Age and Ageing, 44*(3), 356–364. doi: 10.1093/ageing/afv004

Ferriman, Kimberley; Lubinski, David & Benbow, Camilla P. (2009). Work preferences, life values, and personal views of top math/science graduate students and the profoundly gifted: Developmental changes and gender differences during emerging adulthood and parenthood. *Journal of Personality and Social Psychology, 97*(3), 517–532. doi: 10.1037/a0016030

Fiedler, John L.; Afidra, Ronald; Mugambi, Gladys; Tehinse, John; Kabaghe, Gladys; Zulu, Rodah, . . . Bermudez, Odilia. (2014). Maize flour fortification in Africa: Markets, feasibility, coverage, and costs. *Annals of the New York Academy of Sciences, 1312*, 26–39. doi: 10.1111/nyas.12266

Field, Nigel P. & Filanosky, Charles. (2010). Continuing bonds, risk factors for complicated grief, and adjustment to bereavement. *Death Studies, 34*(1), 1–29. doi: 10.1080/07481180903372269

Figueiredo, B.; Canário, C. & Field, T. (2014). Breastfeeding is negatively affected by prenatal depression and reduces postpartum depression. *Psychological Medicine, 44*(5), 927–936. doi: 10.1017/S0033291713001530

Fincham, Frank D. & Beach, Steven R. H. (2010). Of memes and marriage: Toward a positive relationship science. *Journal of Family Theory & Review, 2*(1), 4–24. doi: 10.1111/j.1756-2589.2010.00033.x

Fine, Cordelia. (2014). His brain, her brain? *Science, 346*(6212), 915–916. doi: 10.1126/science.1262061

Fingerman, Karen L. (2009). Consequential strangers and peripheral ties: The importance of unimportant relationships. *Journal of Family Theory & Review, 1*(2), 69–86. doi: 10.1111/j.1756-2589.2009.00010.x

Fingerman, Karen L.; Berg, Cynthia; Smith, Jacqui & Antonucci, Toni C. (2011). *Handbook of lifespan development.* New York, NY: Springer.

Fingerman, Karen L.; Cheng, Yen-Pi; Birditt, Kira & Zarit, Steven. (2012a). Only as happy as the least happy child: Multiple grown children's problems and successes and middle-aged parents' well-being. *The Journals of Gerontology Series B: Psychological Sciences and Social Sciences, 67B*(2), 184–193. doi: 10.1093/geronb/gbr086

Fingerman, Karen L.; Cheng, Yen-Pi; Tighe, Lauren; Birditt, Kira S. & Zarit, Steve. (2012b). Relationships between young adults and their parents. In Alan Booth et al. (Eds.), *Early adulthood in family context* (pp. 59–85). New York, NY: Springer. doi: 10.1007/978-1-4614-1436-0_5

Fingerman, Karen L. & Furstenberg, Frank F. (2012, May 30). You can go home again. *The New York Times*, p. A29.

Finkelhor, David & Jones, Lisa. (2012). *Have sexual abuse and physical abuse declined since the 1990s?* Durham, NH: Crimes Against Children Research Center, University of New Hampshire.

Finlay, Ilora G. & George, R. (2011). Legal physician-assisted suicide in Oregon and The Netherlands: Evidence concerning the impact on patients in vulnerable groups—Another perspective on Oregon's data. *Journal of Medical Ethics*, *37*(3), 171–174. doi: 10.1136/jme.2010.037044

Finn, Amy S.; Kraft, Matthew A.; West, Martin R.; Leonard, Julia A.; Bish, Crystal E.; Martin, Rebecca E., . . . Gabrieli, John D. E. (2014). Cognitive skills, student achievement tests, and schools. *Psychological Science*, *25*(3), 736–744. doi: 10.1177/0956797613516008

Fins, Joseph. (2006). *A palliative ethic of care: Clinical wisdom at life's end*. Sudbury, MA: Jones and Bartlett.

Fiori, Katherine L. & Denckla, Christy A. (2012). Social support and mental health in middle-aged men and women: A multidimensional approach. *Journal of Aging and Health*, *24*(3), 407–438. doi: 10.1177/0898264311425087

Fisher, Susan J. & Giudice, Linda C. (2013). Robert G. Edwards (1925–2013). *Science*, *340*(6134), 825. doi: 10.1126/science.1239644

Fleming, Peter; Pease, Anna & Blair, Peter. (2015). Bed-sharing and unexpected infant deaths: What is the relationship? *Paediatric Respiratory Reviews*, *16*(1), 62–67. doi: 10.1016/j.prrv.2014.10.008

Fletcher, Erica N.; Whitaker, Robert C.; Marino, Alexis J. & Anderson, Sarah E. (2014). Screen time at home and school among low-income children attending Head Start. *Child Indicators Research*, *7*(2), 421–436. doi: 10.1007/s12187-013-9212-8

Fletcher, Garth J. O.; Simpson, Jeffry A.; Campbell, Lorne & Overall, Nickola C. (2015). Pair-bonding, romantic love, and evolution: The curious case of *Homo sapiens*. *Perspectives on Psychological Science*, *10*(1), 20–36. doi: 10.1177/1745691614561683

Fletcher, Jack M. & Vaughn, Sharon. (2009). Response to intervention: Preventing and remediating academic difficulties. *Child Development Perspectives*, *3*(1), 30–37. doi: 10.1111/j.1750-8606.2008.00072.x

Fletcher, Richard; St. George, Jennifer & Freeman, Emily. (2013). Rough and tumble play quality: Theoretical foundations for a new measure of father–child interaction. *Early Child Development and Care*, *183*(6), 746–759. doi: 10.1080/03004430.2012.723439

Flood, Meredith & Phillips, Kenneth D. (2007). Creativity in older adults: A plethora of possibilities. *Issues in Mental Health Nursing*, *28*(4), 389–411. doi: 10.1080/01612840701252956

Flook, Lisa & Fuligni, Andrew J. (2008). Family and school spillover in adolescents' daily lives. *Child Development*, *79*(3), 776–787. doi: 10.1111/j.1467-8624.2008.01157.x

Floris, Dorothea L.; Chura, Lindsay R.; Holt, Rosemary J.; Suckling, John; Bullmore, Edward T.; Baron-Cohen, Simon & Spencer, Michael D. (2013). Psychological correlates of handedness and corpus callosum asymmetry in autism: The left hemisphere dysfunction theory revisited. *Journal of Autism and Developmental Disorders*, *4*(8), 1758–1772. doi: 10.1007/s10803-012-1720-8

Floud, Roderick; Fogel, Robert W.; Harris, Bernard & Hong, Sok Chul. (2011). *The changing body: Health, nutrition, and human development in the Western world since 1700*. New York, NY: Cambridge University Press.

Flynn, James R. (1999). Searching for justice: The discovery of IQ gains over time. *American Psychologist*, *54*(1), 5–20. doi: 10.1037/0003-066X.54.1.5

Flynn, James R. (2012). *Are we getting smarter?: Rising IQ in the twenty-first century*. New York, NY: Cambridge University Press.

Fogel, Robert W. & Grotte, Nathaniel. (2011). *An overview of the changing body: Health, nutrition, and human development in the Western world since 1700. NBER working paper series*. Cambridge, MA: National Bureau Of Economic Research.

Fonner, Virginia A.; Armstrong, Kevin S.; Kennedy, Caitlin E.; O'Reilly, Kevin R. & Sweat, Michael D. (2014). School based sex education and HIV prevention in low- and middle-income countries: A systematic review and meta-analysis. *PLoS ONE*, *9*(3), e89692. doi: 10.1371/journal.pone.0089692

Fontana, Luigi; Colman, Ricki J.; Holloszy, John O. & Weindruch, Richard. (2011). Calorie restriction in nonhuman and human primates. In J. Masoro Edward & N. Austad Steven (Eds.), *Handbook of the biology of aging* (7th ed., pp. 447–461). San Diego, CA: Academic Press. doi: 10.1016/B978-0-12-378638-8.00021-X

Fontana, Luigi & Partridge, Linda. (2015). Promoting health and longevity through diet: From model organisms to humans. *Cell*, *161*(1), 106–118. doi: 10.1016/j.cell.2015.02.020

Forbes, Deborah. (2012). The global influence of the Reggio Emilia Inspiration. In Robert Kelly (Ed.), *Educating for creativity: A global conversation* (pp. 161–172). Calgary, Canada: Brush Education.

Ford, Carole L. & Yore, Larry D. (2012). Toward convergence of critical thinking, metacognition, and reflection: Illustrations from natural and social sciences, teacher education, and classroom practice. In Anat Zohar & Yehudit Judy Dori (Eds.), *Metacognition in Science Education* (pp. 251–271). New York, NY: Springer. doi: 10.1007/978-94-007-2132-6_11

Forrest, Walter. (2014). Cohabitation, relationship quality, and desistance from crime. *Journal of Marriage and Family*, *76*(3), 539–556. doi: 10.1111/jomf.12105

Fox, Nathan A.; Henderson, Heather A.; Marshall, Peter J.; Nichols, Kate E. & Ghera, Melissa M. (2005). Behavioral inhibition: Linking biology and behavior within a developmental framework. *Annual Review of Psychology*, *56*, 235–262. doi: 10.1146/annurev.psych.55.090902.141532

Fox, Nathan A.; Henderson, Heather A.; Rubin, Kenneth H.; Calkins, Susan D. & Schmidt, Louis A. (2001). Continuity and discontinuity of behavioral inhibition and exuberance:

Psychophysiological and behavioral influences across the first four years of life. *Child Development, 72*(1), 1–21. doi: 10.1111/1467-8624.00262

Fox, Nathan A.; Reeb-Sutherland, Bethany C. & Degnan, Kathryn A. (2013). Personality and emotional development. In Philip D. Zelazo (Ed.), *The Oxford handbook of developmental psychology* (Vol. 2, pp. 15–44). New York, NY: Oxford University Press. doi: 10.1093/oxfordhb/9780199958474.013.0002

Fraley, R. Chris; Roisman, Glenn I.; Booth-LaForce, Cathryn; Owen, Margaret Tresch & Holland, Ashley S. (2013). Interpersonal and genetic origins of adult attachment styles: A longitudinal study from infancy to early adulthood. *Journal of Personality and Social Psychology, 104*(5), 817–838. doi: 10.1037/a0031435

Franck, Caroline; Budlovsky, Talia; Windle, Sarah B.; Filion, Kristian B. & Eisenberg, Mark J. (2014). Electronic cigarettes in North America: History, use, and implications for smoking cessation. *Circulation, 129*(19), 1945–1952. doi: 10.1161/CIRCULATIONAHA.113.006416

Franco, Manuel; Bilal, Usama; Orduñez, Pedro; Benet, Mikhail; Alain, Morejón; Benjamín, Caballero, . . . Cooper, Richard S. (2013). Population-wide weight loss and regain in relation to diabetes burden and cardiovascular mortality in Cuba 1980–2010: Repeated cross sectional surveys and ecological comparison of secular trends. *BMJ, 346*(7903), f1515. doi: 10.1136/bmj.f1515

Frank, David J.; Nara, Brent; Zavagnin, Michela; Touron, Dayna R. & Kane, Michael J. (2015). Validating older adults' reports of less mind-wandering: An examination of eye movements and dispositional influences. *Psychology and Aging, 30*(2), 266–278. doi: 10.1037/pag0000031

Frankenburg, William K.; Dodds, Josiah; Archer, Philip; Shapiro, Howard & Bresnick, Beverly. (1992). The Denver II: A major revision and restandardization of the Denver Developmental Screening Test. *Pediatrics, 89*(1), 91–97.

Frazier, Thomas W.; Keshavan, Matcheri S.; Minshew, Nancy J. & Hardan, Antonio Y. (2012). A two-year longitudinal MRI study of the corpus callosum in autism. *Journal of Autism and Developmental Disorders, 42*(11), 2312–2322. doi: 10.1007/s10803-012-1478-z

Fredricks, Jennifer A. & Eccles, Jacquelynne S. (2002). Children's competence and value beliefs from childhood through adolescence: Growth trajectories in two male-sex-typed domains. *Developmental Psychology, 38*(4), 519–533. doi: 10.1037/0012-1649.38.4.519

Freeman, Joan. (2010). *Gifted lives: What happens when gifted children grow up?* New York, NY: Routledge.

Frenda, Steven J.; Nichols, Rebecca M. & Loftus, Elizabeth F. (2011). Current issues and advances in misinformation research. *Current Directions in Psychological Science, 20*(1), 20–23. doi: 10.1177/0963721410396620

Freud, Anna. (1958). Adolescence. *Psychoanalytic Study of the Child, 13*, 255–278.

Freud, Anna. (2000). Adolescence. In James B. McCarthy (Ed.), *Adolescent development and psychopathology* (pp. 29–52). Lanham, MD: University Press of America.

Freud, Sigmund. (1935). *A general introduction to psychoanalysis.* New York, NY: Liveright.

Freud, Sigmund. (1938). *The basic writings of Sigmund Freud.* New York, NY: Modern Library.

Freud, Sigmund. (1989). *Introductory lectures on psycho-analysis.* New York, NY: Liveright.

Freud, Sigmund. (1995). *The basic writings of Sigmund Freud.* New York, NY: Modern Library.

Freud, Sigmund. (2001). An outline of psycho-analysis. *The standard edition of the complete psychological works of Sigmund Freud* (Vol. 23). London, UK: Vintage.

Frey, Andy J.; Mandlawitz, Myrna & Alvarez, Michelle. (2012). Leaving NCLB behind. *Children and Schools, 34*(2), 67–69. doi: 10.1093/cs/cds021

Friend, Stephen H. & Schadt, Eric E. (2014). Clues from the resilient. *Science, 344*(6187), 970–972. doi: 10.1126/science.1255648

Fries, Alison B. Wismer & Pollak, Seth D. (2007). Emotion processing and the developing brain. In Donna Coch et al. (Eds.), *Human behavior, learning, and the developing brain: Atypical development* (pp. 329–361). New York, NY: Guilford Press.

Frost, Randy O.; Steketee, Gail; Tolin, David F.; Sinopoli, Nicole & Ruby, Dylan. (2015). Motives for acquiring and saving in hoarding disorder, OCD, and community controls. *Journal of Obsessive-Compulsive and Related Disorders, 4*, 54–59. doi: 10.1016/j.jocrd.2014.12.006

Fry, Douglas P. (2014). Environment of evolutionary adaptedness, rough-and-tumble play, and the selection of restraint in human aggression. In Darcia Narvaez et al. (Eds.), *Ancestral landscapes in human evolution: Culture, childrearing and social wellbeing* (pp. 169–188). New York, NY: Oxford University Press.

Fuligni, Allison Sidle; Howes, Carollee; Huang, Yiching; Hong, Sandra Soliday & Lara-Cinisomo, Sandraluz. (2012). Activity settings and daily routines in preschool classrooms: Diverse experiences in early learning settings for low-income children. *Early Childhood Research Quarterly, 27*(2), 198–209. doi: 10.1016/j.ecresq.2011.10.001

Fuller-Iglesias, Heather R.; Webster, Noah J. & Antonucci, Toni C. (2013). Adult family relationships in the context of friendship. *Research in Human Development, 10*(2), 184–203. doi: 10.1080/15427609.2013.786562

Fulmer, C. Ashley; Gelfand, Micheke J.; Kruglanski, Arie W.; Kim-Prieto, Chu; Diener, Ed; Pierro, Antonio & Higgins, E. Tory. (2010). On "feeling right" in cultural contexts: How person-culture match affects self-esteem and subjective well-being. *Psychological Science, 21*(11), 1563–1569. doi: 10.1177/0956797610384742

Furey, Terrence S. & Sethupathy, Praveen. (2013). Genetics driving epigenetics. *Science, 342*(6159), 705–706. doi: 10.1126/science.1246755

Furman, Wyndol & Shaffer, Laura. (2011). Romantic partners, friends, friends with benefits, and casual acquaintances as sexual partners. *Journal of Sex Research, 48*(6), 554–564. doi: 10.1080/00224499.2010.535623

Furstenberg, Frank F. (2010). On a new schedule: Transitions to adulthood and family change. *Future of Children, 20*(1), 67–87. doi: 10.1353/foc.0.0038

Furukawa, Emi; Tangney, June & Higashibara, Fumiko. (2012). Cross-cultural continuities and discontinuities in shame, guilt, and pride: A study of children residing in Japan, Korea and the USA. *Self and Identity, 11*(1), 90–113. doi: 10.1080/15298868.2010.512748

Fusaro, Maria & Harris, Paul L. (2013). Dax gets the nod: Toddlers detect and use social cues to evaluate testimony. *Developmental Psychology, 49*(3), 514–522. doi: 10.1037/a0030580

Gabrieli, John D. E. (2009). Dyslexia: A new synergy between education and cognitive neuroscience. *Science, 325*(5938), 280–283. doi: 10.1126/science.1171999

Galatzer-Levy, Isaac R. & Bonanno, George A. (2012). Beyond normality in the study of bereavement: Heterogeneity in depression outcomes following loss in older adults. *Social Science & Medicine, 74*(12), 1987–1994. doi: 10.1016/j.socscimed.2012.02.022

Galván, Adriana. (2013). The teenage brain: Sensitivity to rewards. *Current Directions in Psychological Science, 22*(2), 88–93. doi: 10.1177/0963721413480859

Galvao, Tais F.; Silva, Marcus T.; Zimmermann, Ivan R.; Souza, Kathiaja M.; Martins, Silvia S. & Pereira, Mauricio G. (2014). Pubertal timing in girls and depression: A systematic review. *Journal of Affective Disorders, 155*, 13–19. doi: 10.1016/j.jad.2013.10.034

Gambaro, Ludovica; Stewart, Kitty & Waldfogel, Jane (Eds.). (2014). *An equal start?: Providing quality early education and care for disadvantaged children.* Chicago, IL: Policy Press.

Ganapathy, Thilagavathy. (2014). Couvade syndrome among 1st time expectant fathers. *Muller Journal of Medical Science Research, 5*(1), 43–47. doi: 10.4103/0975-9727.128944

Gandini, Leila; Hill, Lynn; Cadwell, Louise & Schwall, Charles (Eds.). (2005). *In the spirit of the studio: Learning from the atelier of Reggio Emilia.* New York, NY: Teachers College Press.

Ganong, Lawrence H.; Coleman, Marilyn & Jamison, Tyler. (2011). Patterns of stepchild–stepparent relationship development. *Journal of Marriage and Family, 73*(2), 396–413. doi: 10.1111/j.1741-3737.2010.00814.x

Gans, Daphna & Silverstein, Merril. (2006). Norms of filial responsibility for aging parents across time and generations. *Journal of Marriage and Family, 68*(4), 961–976. doi: 10.1111/j.1741-3737.2006.00307.x

Gao, Sujuan; Unverzagt, Frederick W.; Hall, Kathleen S.; Lane, Kathleen A.; Murrell, Jill R.; Hake, Ann M.,... Hendrie, Hugh C. (2014). Mild cognitive impairment, incidence, progression, and reversion: Findings from a community-based cohort of elderly African Americans. *The American Journal of Geriatric Psychiatry, 22*(7), 670–681. doi: 10.1016/j.jagp.2013.02.015

Gao, Yuan; Huang, Changquan; Zhao, Kexiang; Ma, Louyan; Qiu, Xuan; Zhang, Lei, . . . Xiao, Qian. (2013). Depression as a risk factor for dementia and mild cognitive impairment: A meta-analysis of longitudinal studies. *International Journal of Geriatric Psychiatry, 28*(5), 441–449. doi: 10.1002/gps.3845

García Coll, Cynthia T. & Marks, Amy K. (2012). *The immigrant paradox in children and adolescents: Is becoming American a developmental risk?* Washington, DC: American Psychological Association.

Gardner, Howard. (1983). *Frames of mind: The theory of multiple intelligences.* New York, NY: Basic Books.

Gardner, Howard. (1999). Are there additional intelligences? The case for naturalist, spiritual, and existential intelligences. In Jeffrey Kane (Ed.), *Education, information, and transformation: Essays on learning and thinking* (pp. 111–131). Upper Saddle River, NJ: Merrill.

Gardner, Howard. (2006). *Multiple intelligences: New horizons in theory and practice.* New York, NY: Basic Books.

Gardner, Howard & Moran, Seana. (2006). The science of multiple intelligences theory: A response to Lynn Waterhouse. *Educational Psychologist, 41*(4), 227–232. doi: 10.1207/s15326985ep4104_2

Gardner, Margo & Steinberg, Laurence. (2005). Peer influence on risk taking, risk preference, and risky decision making in adolescence and adulthood: An experimental study. *Developmental Psychology, 41*(4), 625–635. doi: 10.1037/0012-1649.41.4.625

Gardner, Paula & Hudson, Bettie L. (1996). *Advance report of final mortality statistics, 1993. Monthly Vital Statistics Report, 44*(7, Suppl.). Hyattsville, MD: National Center for Health Statistics.

Garfin, Dana R.; Holman, E. Alison & Silver, Roxane C. (2015). Cumulative exposure to prior collective trauma and acute stress responses to the Boston Marathon bombings. *Psychological Science, 26*(6), 675–683. doi: 10.1177/0956797614561043

Gaskins, Audrey Jane; Mendiola, Jaime; Afeiche, Myriam; Jørgensen, Niels; Swan, Shanna H. & Chavarro, Jorge E. (2013). Physical activity and television watching in relation to semen quality in young men. *British Journal of Sports Medicine, 49*(4), 265–270. doi: 10.1136/bjsports-2012-091644

Gaskins, Suzanne. (1999). Children's daily lives in a Mayan village: A case study of culturally constructed roles and activities. In Artin Göncü (Ed.), *Children's engagement in the world: Sociocultural perspectives* (pp. 25–60). New York, NY: Cambridge University Press.

Gauvain, Mary; Beebe, Heidi & Zhao, Shuheng. (2011). Applying the cultural approach to cognitive development. *Journal of Cognition and Development, 12*(2), 121–133. doi: 10.1080/15248372.2011.563481

Gavrilov, Leonid A. & Gavrilova, Natalia S. (2006). Reliability theory of aging and longevity. In Edward J. Masoro & Steven N. Austad (Eds.), *Handbook of the biology of aging* (6th ed., pp. 3–42). Boston, MA: Academic Press.

Geiger, Jennifer Mullins; Hayes, Megan J. & Lietz, Cynthia A. (2013). Should I stay or should I go? A mixed methods study examining the factors influencing foster parents' decisions to continue or discontinue providing foster care. *Children and Youth Services Review, 35*(9), 1356–1365. doi: 10.1016/j.childyouth.2013.05.003

Gendron, Brian P.; Williams, Kirk R. & Guerra, Nancy G. (2011). An analysis of bullying among students within schools: Estimating the effects of individual normative beliefs, self-esteem, and school climate. *Journal of School Violence, 10*(2), 150–164. doi: 10.1080/15388220.2010.539166

Genesee, Fred. (2008). Early dual language learning. *Zero to Three, 29*(1), 17–23.

George, Danny & Whitehouse, Peter. (2010). Dementia and mild cognitive impairment in social and cultural context. In Dale Dannefer & Chris Phillipson (Eds.), *The SAGE handbook of social gerontology* (pp. 343–356). Los Angeles, CA: Sage.

Georgeson, Jan & Payler, Jane (Eds.). (2013). *International perspectives on early childhood education and care.* New York, NY: Open University Press.

Geraerts, Elke; Lindsay, D. Stephen; Merckelbach, Harald; Jelicic, Marko; Raymaekers, Linsey; Arnold, Michelle M. & Schooler, Jonathan W. (2009). Cognitive mechanisms underlying recovered-memory experiences of childhood sexual abuse. *Psychological Science, 20*(1), 92–98. doi: 10.1111/j.1467-9280.2008.02247.x

Gerber, Alan S.; Huber, Gregory A.; Doherty, David & Dowling, Conor M. (2011). The Big Five personality traits in the political arena. *Annual Review of Political Science, 14,* 265–287. doi: 10.1146/annurev-polisci-051010-111659

Geronimus, Arline T.; Hicken, Margaret; Keene, Danya & Bound, John. (2006). "Weathering" and age patterns of allostatic load scores among Blacks and Whites in the United States. *American Journal of Public Health, 96*(5), 826–833. doi: 10.2105/AJPH.2004.060749

Gershoff, Elizabeth T. (2013). Spanking and child development: We know enough now to stop hitting our children. *Child Development Perspectives, 7*(3), 133–137. doi: 10.1111/cdep.12038

Gershoff, Elizabeth T.; Lansford, Jennifer E.; Sexton, Holly R.; Davis-Kean, Pamela & Sameroff, Arnold J. (2012). Longitudinal links between spanking and children's externalizing behaviors in a national sample of White, Black, Hispanic, and Asian American families. *Child Development, 83*(3), 838–843. doi: 10.1111/j.1467-8624.2011.01732.x

Gershoff, Elizabeth T.; Purtell, Kelly M. & Holas, Igor. (2015). *Corporal punishment in U.S. public schools: Legal precedents, current practices, and future policy.* New York, NY: Springer. doi: 10.1007/978-3-319-14818-2

Gerstorf, Denis; Heckhausen, Jutta; Ram, Nilam; Infurna, Frank J.; Schupp, Jürgen & Wagner, Gert G. (2014). Perceived personal control buffers terminal decline in well-being. *Psychology and Aging, 29*(3), 612–625. doi: 10.1037/a0037227

Gervais, Will M. & Norenzayan, Ara. (2012). Analytic thinking promotes religious disbelief. *Science, 336*(6080), 493–496. doi: 10.1126/science.1215647

Gettler, Lee T. & McKenna, James J. (2010). Never sleep with baby? Or keep me close but keep me safe: Eliminating inappropriate safe infant sleep rhetoric in the United States. *Current Pediatric Reviews, 6*(1), 71–77. doi: 10.2174/157339610791317250

Gewertz, Catherine. (2014, August 19). Support slipping for Common Core, especially among teachers, poll finds [Web log post]. *Education week: Curriculum matters.* Retrieved from http://blogs.edweek.org/edweek/curriculum/2014/08/education_next_poll_shows_comm.html

Giannoulis, Manthos G.; Martin, Finbarr C.; Nair, K. Sreekumaran; Umpleby, A. Margot & Sonksen, Peter. (2013). Hormone replacement therapy and physical function in healthy older men: Time to talk hormones? *Endocrine Reviews, 33*(3), 314–377. doi: 10.1210/er.2012-1002

Gibbons, Frederick X.; Kingsbury, John H. & Gerrard, Meg. (2012a). Social-psychological theories and adolescent health risk behavior. *Social and Personality Psychology Compass, 6*(2), 70–183. doi: 10.1111/j.1751-9004.2011.00412.x

Gibbons, Luz; Belizan, José M.; Lauer, Jeremy A.; Betran, Ana P.; Merialdi, Mario & Althabe, Fernando. (2012b). Inequities in the use of cesarean section deliveries in the world. *American Journal of Obstetrics and Gynecology, 206*(4), 331.e331–331.e319. doi: 10.1016/j.ajog.2012.02.026

Giblin, Chris. (2014). Travis Pastrana makes comeback for Red Bull's inaugural straight rhythm competition. *Men's Fitness.*

Gibson-Davis, Christina & Rackin, Heather. (2014). Marriage or carriage? Trends in union context and birth type by education. *Journal of Marriage and Family, 76*(3), 506–519. doi: 10.1111/jomf.12109

Gilbert, Richard B. (2013). Religion, spirituality, and end-of-life decision making. In David K. Meagher & David E. Balk (Eds.), *Handbook of thanatology: The essential body of knowledge for the study of death, dying, and bereavement* (2nd ed., pp. 63–71). New York, NY: Routledge.

Gilbert-Barness, Enid F. (2010). Teratogenic causes of malformations. *Annals of Clinical & Laboratory Science, 40*(2), 99–114.

Giles, Amy & Rovee-Collier, Carolyn. (2011). Infant long-term memory for associations formed during mere exposure. *Infant Behavior and Development, 34*(2), 327–338. doi: 10.1016/j.infbeh.2011.02.004

Gilles, Floyd H. & Nelson, Marvin D. (2012). *The developing human brain: Growth and adversities.* London, UK: Mac Keith Press.

Gillespie, Michael A. (2010). Players and spectators: Sports and ethical training in the American university. In Elizabeth Kiss & J. Peter Euben (Eds.), *Debating moral education: Rethinking the role of the modern university* (pp. 293–316). Durham, NC: Duke University Press.

Gilliam, Mary; Stockman, Michael; Malek, Meaghan; Sharp, Wendy; Greenstein, Deanna; Lalonde, Francois, . . . Shaw, Philip. (2011). Developmental trajectories of the corpus callosum in Attention-deficit/hyperactivity disorder. *Biological Psychiatry, 69*(9), 839–846. doi: 10.1016/j.biopsych.2010.11.024

Gilligan, Carol. (1982). *In a different voice: Psychological theory and women's development.* Cambridge, MA: Harvard University Press.

Gillis, John R. (2008). The islanding of children: Reshaping the mythical landscapes of childhood. In Marta Gutman & Ning de Coninck-Smith (Eds.), *Designing modern childhoods: History, space, and the material culture of children* (pp. 316–329). New Brunswick, NJ: Rutgers University Press.

Gillon, Raanan. (2015). Defending the four principles approach as a good basis for good medical practice and therefore for good medical ethics. *Journal of Medical Ethics, 41*(1), 111–116. doi: 10.1136/medethics-2014-102282

Gilroy, Paul. (2000). *Against race: Imagining political culture beyond the color line.* Cambridge, MA: Belknap Press of Harvard University Press.

Giluk, Tamara L. & Postlethwaite, Bennett E. (2015). Big Five personality and academic dishonesty: A meta-analytic review. *Personality and Individual Differences, 72*(5), 59–67. doi: 10.1016/j.paid.2014.08.027

Giovino, Gary A.; Mirza, Sara A.; Samet, Jonathan M.; Gupta, Prakash C.; Jarvis, Martin J.; Bhala, Neeraj, . . . Asma, Samira. (2012). Tobacco use in 3 billion individuals from 16 countries: An analysis of nationally representative cross-sectional household surveys. *The Lancet, 380*(9842), 668–679. doi: 10.1016/S0140-6736(12)61085-X

Gitlin, Laura N.; Belle, Steven H.; Burgio, Louis D.; Czaja, Sara J.; Mahoney, Diane; Gallagher-Thompson, Dolores, . . . Ory, Marcia G. (2003). Effect of multicomponent interventions on caregiver burden and depression: The REACH multisite initiative at 6-month follow-up. *Psychology and Aging, 18*(3), 361–374. doi: 10.1037/0882-7974.18.3.361

Giuffrè, Mario; Piro, Ettore & Corsello, Giovanni. (2012). Prematurity and twinning. *Journal of Maternal-Fetal and Neonatal Medicine, 25*(3), 6–10. doi: 10.3109/14767058.2012.712350

Glance, Laurent G.; Dick, Andrew W.; Glantz, Christopher; Wissler, Richard N.; Qian, Feng; Marroquin, Bridget M., . . . Kellermann, Arthur L. (2014). Rates of major obstetrical complications vary almost fivefold among US hospitals. *Health Affairs, 33*(8), 1330–1336. doi: 10.1377/hlthaff.2013.1359

Goddings, Anne-Lise & Giedd, Jay N. (2014). Structural brain development during childhood and adolescence. In Michael S. Gazzaniga & George R. Mangun (Eds.), *The cognitive neurosciences* (5th ed., pp. 15–22). Cambridge, MA: MIT Press.

Goddings, Anne-Lise; Heyes, Stephanie Burnett; Bird, Geoffrey; Viner, Russell M. & Blakemore, Sarah-Jayne. (2012). The relationship between puberty and social emotion processing. *Developmental Science, 15*(6), 801–811. doi: 10.1111/j.1467-7687.2012.01174.x

Godinet, Meripa T.; Li, Fenfang & Berg, Teresa. (2014). Early childhood maltreatment and trajectories of behavioral problems: Exploring gender and racial differences. *Child Abuse & Neglect, 38*(3), 544–556. doi: 10.1016/j.chiabu.2013.07.018

Goesling, Brian; Colman, Silvie; Trenholm, Christopher; Terzian, Mary & Moore, Kristin. (2014). Programs to reduce teen pregnancy, sexually transmitted infections, and associated sexual risk behaviors: A systematic review. *Journal of Adolescent Health, 54*(5), 499–507. doi: 10.1016/j.jadohealth.2013.12.004

Gogtay, Nitin; Giedd, Jay N.; Lusk, Leslie; Hayashi, Kiralee M.; Greenstein, Deanna; Vaituzis, A. Catherine, . . . Ungerleider, Leslie G. (2004). Dynamic mapping of human cortical development during childhood through early adulthood. *Proceedings of the National Academy of Sciences of the United States of America, 101*(21), 8174–8179. doi: 10.1073/pnas.0402680101

Gökbayrak, N. Simay; Paiva, Andrea L.; Blissmer, Bryan J. & Prochaska, James O. (2015). Predictors of relapse among smokers: Transtheoretical effort variables, demographics, and smoking severity. *Addictive Behaviors, 42*, 176–179. doi: 10.1016/j.addbeh.2014.11.022

Golant, Stephen M. (2011). The changing residential environments of older people. In Robert H. Binstock & Linda K. George (Eds.), *Handbook of aging and the social sciences* (7th ed., pp. 207–220). San Diego, CA: Academic Press. doi: 10.1016/B978-0-12-380880-6.00015-0

Golden, Marita. (2010). Angel baby. In Barbara Graham (Ed.), *Eye of my heart: 27 writers reveal the hidden pleasures and perils of being a grandmother* (pp. 125–133). New York, NY: HarperCollins.

Goldfarb, Sally F. (2014). Who pays for the 'boomerang generation'?: A legal perspective on financial support for young adults. *Harvard Journal of Law and Gender, 37*, 46–106.

Goldin-Meadow, Susan & Alibali, Martha W. (2013). Gesture's role in speaking, learning, and creating language. *Annual Review of Psychology, 64*, 257–283. doi: 10.1146/annurev-psych-113011-143802

Goldman, Dana P.; Cutler, David; Rowe, John W.; Michaud, Pierre-Carl; Sullivan, Jeffrey; Peneva, Desi & Olshansky, S. Jay. (2013). Substantial health and economic returns from delayed aging may warrant a new focus for medical research. *Health Affairs, 32*(10), 1698–1705. doi: 10.1377/hlthaff.2013.0052

Goldstein, Michael H.; Schwade, Jennifer A. & Bornstein, Marc H. (2009). The value of vocalizing: Five-month-old infants associate their own noncry vocalizations with responses from caregivers. *Child Development, 80*(3), 636–644. doi: 10.1111/j.1467-8624.2009.01287.x

Golinkoff, Roberta M. & Hirsh-Pasek, Kathy. (2008). How toddlers begin to learn verbs. *Trends in Cognitive Sciences, 12*(10), 397–403. doi: 10.1016/j.tics.2008.07.003

Göncü, Artin & Gaskins, Suzanne. (2011). Comparing and extending Piaget's and Vygotsky's understandings of play: Symbolic play as individual, sociocultural, and educational interpretation. In Anthony D. Pellegrini (Ed.), *The Oxford handbook of the development of play* (pp. 48–57). New York, NY: Oxford University Press. doi: 10.1093/oxfordhb/9780195393002.013.0005

Gonyea, Judith G. (2013). Midlife, multigenerational bonds, and caregiving. In Ronda C. Talley & Rhonda J. V. Montgomery (Eds.), *Caregiving across the lifespan: Research, practice, policy* (pp. 105–130). New York, NY: Springer.

Goodlad, James K.; Marcus, David K. & Fulton, Jessica J. (2013). Lead and Attention-deficit/hyperactivity disorder (ADHD) symptoms: A meta-analysis. *Clinical Psychology Review, 33*(3), 417–425. doi: 10.1016/j.cpr.2013.01.009

Goodman, Madeline J.; Sands, Anita M. & Coley, Richard J. (2015). *America's skills challenge: Millennials and the future.* Princeton, NJ: Educational Testing Service.

Goodman, Sherryl H. & Gotlib, Ian H. (Eds.). (2002). *Children of depressed parents: Mechanisms of risk and implications for treatment.* Washington, DC: American Psychological Association.

Goodnight, Jackson A.; D'Onofrio, Brian M.; Cherlin, Andrew J.; Emery, Robert E.; Van Hulle, Carol A. & Lahey, Benjamin B. (2013). Effects of multiple maternal relationship transitions on offspring antisocial behavior in childhood and adolescence: A cousin-comparison analysis. *Journal of Abnormal Child Psychology, 41*(2), 185–198. doi: 10.1007/s10802-012-9667-y

Gopnik, Alison. (2001). Theories, language, and culture: Whorf without wincing. In Melissa Bowerman & Stephen C. Levinson (Eds.), *Language acquisition and conceptual development* (pp. 45–69). New York, NY: Cambridge University Press.

Gopnik, Alison. (2012). Scientific thinking in young children: Theoretical advances, empirical research, and policy implications. *Science, 337*(6102), 1623–1627. doi: 10.1126/science.1223416

Gough, Ethan K.; Moodie, Erica E. M.; Prendergast, Andrew J.; Johnson, Sarasa M. A.; Humphrey, Jean H.; Stoltzfus, Rebecca J., . . . Manges, Amee R. (2014). The impact of antibiotics on growth in children in low and middle income countries: Systematic review and meta-analysis of randomised controlled trials. *BMJ, 348*, g2267. doi: 10.1136/bmj.g2267

Government of India, Ministry of Home Affairs. Population in five year age-group by residence and sex. Retrieved, from Office of the Registrar General & Census Commissioner

Govindaraju, Diddahally; Atzmon, Gil & Barzilai, Nir. (2015). Genetics, lifestyle and longevity: Lessons from centenarians. *Applied & Translational Genomics, 4*(Suppl. 1), 23–32. doi: 10.1016/j.atg.2015.01.001

Grady, Denise. (2012, May 5). When illness makes a spouse a stranger. *The New York Times*, p. A1

Green, James A.; Whitney, Pamela G. & Potegal, Michael. (2011). Screaming, yelling, whining, and crying: Categorical and intensity differences in vocal expressions of anger and sadness in children's tantrums. *Emotion, 11*(5), 1124–1133. doi: 10.1037/a0024173

Green, Lorraine & Grant, Victoria. (2008). "Gagged grief and beleaguered bereavements?" An analysis of multidisciplinary theory and research relating to same sex partnership bereavement. *Sexualities, 11*(3), 275–300. doi: 10.1177/1363460708089421

Green McDonald, Paige; O'Connell, Mary & Suls, Jerry. (2015). Cancer control falls squarely within the province of the psychological sciences. *American Psychologist, 70*(2), 61–74. doi: 10.1037/a0038873

Greene, Melissa L. & Way, Niobe. (2005). Self-esteem trajectories among ethnic minority adolescents: A growth curve analysis of the patterns and predictors of change. *Journal of Research on Adolescence, 15*(2), 151–178. doi: 10.1111/j.1532-7795.2005.00090.x

Greenfield, Emily A. & Reyes, Laurent. (2015). Continuity and change in relationships with neighbors: Implications for psychological well-being in middle and later life. *The Journal of Gerontology Series B, 70*(4), 607–618. doi: 10.1093/geronb/gbu084

Greenfield, Emily A.; Scharlach, Andrew; Lehning, Amanda J. & Davitt, Joan K. (2012). A conceptual framework for examining the promise of the NORC program and Village models to promote aging in place. *Journal of Aging Studies, 26*(3), 273–284. doi: 10.1016/j.jaging.2012.01.003

Greenough, William T.; Black, James E. & Wallace, Christopher S. (1987). Experience and brain development. *Child Development, 58*(3), 539–559. doi: 10.1111/j.1467-8624.1987.tb01400.x

Greenstone, Michael & Looney, Adam. (2012). The importance of education: An economics view. *Education Week, 32*(11), 32.

Greenwood, Pamela M. & Parasuraman, R. (2012). *Nurturing the older brain and mind.* Cambridge, MA: MIT Press.

Gregory, Sara M.; Parker, Beth & Thompson, Paul D. (2012). Physical activity, cognitive function, and brain health: What is the role of exercise training in the prevention of dementia? *Brain Sciences, 2*(4), 684–708. doi: 10.3390/brainsci2040684

Greyson, Bruce. (2009). Near-death experiences and deathbed visions. In Allan Kellehear (Ed.), *The study of dying: From autonomy to transformation* (pp. 253–275). New York, NY: Cambridge University Press.

Griffin, James; Gooding, Sarah; Semesky, Michael; Farmer, Brittany; Mannchen, Garrett & Sinnott, Jan D. (2009). Four brief studies of relations between postformal thought and non-cognitive factors: Personality, concepts of god, political opinions, and social attitudes. *Journal of Adult Development, 16*(3), 173–182. doi: 10.1007/s10804-009-9056-0

Griffith, Patrick & Lopez, Oscar. (2009). Disparities in the diagnosis and treatment of Alzheimer's disease in African American and Hispanic patients: A call to action. *Generations, 33*(1), 37–46.

Grigsby, Timothy J. H.; Forster, Myriam; Soto, Daniel W.; Baezconde-Garbanati, Lourdes & Unger, Jennifer B. (2014). Problematic substance use among Hispanic adolescents and young adults: Implications for prevention efforts. *Substance Use & Misuse, 49*(8), 1025–1038. doi: 10.3109/10826084.2013.852585

Grivell, Rosalie M.; Reilly, Aimee J.; Oakey, Helena; Chan, Annabelle & Dodd, Jodie M. (2012). Maternal and neonatal outcomes following induction of labor: A cohort study. *Acta Obstetricia et Gynecologica Scandinavica, 91*(2), 198–203. doi: 10.1111/j.1600-0412.2011.01298.x

Grobman, Kevin H. (2008). Learning & teaching developmental psychology: Attachment theory, infancy, & infant memory development. http://www.devpsy.org/questions/attachment_theory_memory.html

Gross, James J. (Ed.). (2014). *Handbook of emotion regulation* (2nd ed.). New York, NY: Guilford Press.

Grossman, Jennifer M.; Tracy, Allison J.; Charmaraman, Linda & Erkut, Sumru. (2014). Protective effects of middle school comprehensive sex education with family involvement. *Journal of School Health, 84*(11), 739–747. doi: 10.1111/josh.12199

Grossmann, Klaus E.; Bretherton, Inge; Waters, Everett & Grossmann, Karin (Eds.). (2014). *Mary Ainsworth's enduring influence on attachment theory, research, and clinical applications.* New York, NY: Routledge.

Grotevant, Harold D. & McDermott, Jennifer M. (2014). Adoption: Biological and social processes linked to adaptation. *Annual Review of Psychology, 65*, 235–265. doi: 10.1146/annurev-psych-010213-115020

Grundy, Emily & Henretta, John C. (2006). Between elderly parents and adult children: A new look at the intergenerational care provided by the 'sandwich generation'. *Ageing & Society, 26*(5), 707–722. doi: 10.1017/S0144686X06004934

Guerra, Nancy G. & Williams, Kirk R. (2010). Implementing bullying prevention in diverse settings: Geographic, economic, and cultural influences. In Eric M. Vernberg & Bridget K. Biggs (Eds.), *Preventing and treating bullying and victimization* (pp. 319–336). New York, NY: Oxford University Press.

Guerra, Nancy G.; Williams, Kirk R. & Sadek, Shelly. (2011). Understanding bullying and victimization during childhood and adolescence: A mixed methods study. *Child Development, 82*(1), 295–310. doi: 10.1111/j.1467-8624.2010.01556.x

Guerri, Consuelo & Pascual, María. (2010). Mechanisms involved in the neurotoxic, cognitive, and neurobehavioral effects of alcohol consumption during adolescence. *Alcohol, 44*(1), 15–26. doi: 10.1016/j.alcohol.2009.10.003

Gummerum, Michaela; Keller, Monika; Takezawa, Masanori & Mata, Jutta. (2008). To give or not to give: Children's and adolescents' sharing and moral negotiations in economic decision situations. *Child Development, 79*(3), 562–576. doi: 10.1111/j.1467-8624.2008.01143.x

Güngör, Derya; Bornstein, Marc H.; De Leersnyder, Jozefien; Cote, Linda; Ceulemans, Eva & Mesquita, Batja. (2013). Acculturation of personality: A three-culture study of Japanese, Japanese Americans, and European Americans. *Journal of Cross-Cultural Psychology, 44*(5), 701–718. doi: 10.1177/0022022112470749

Gupta, Nidhi; Goel, Kashish; Shah, Priyali & Misra, Anoop. (2012). Childhood obesity in developing countries: Epidemiology, determinants, and prevention. *Endocrine Reviews, 33*(1), 48–70. doi: 10.1210/er.2010-0028

Gupta, Ramesh C. (2011). *Reproductive and developmental toxicology.* Boston, MA: Elsevier/Academic Press.

Gurunath, Sumana; Pandian, Z.; Anderson, Richard A. & Bhattacharya, Siladitya. (2011). Defining infertility—A systematic review of prevalence studies. *Human Reproduction Update, 17*(5), 575–588. doi: 10.1093/humupd/dmr015

Guzzo, Karen Benjamin. (2014). Trends in cohabitation outcomes: Compositional changes and engagement among never-married young adults. *Journal of Marriage and Family, 76*(4), 826–842. doi: 10.1111/jomf.12123

Ha, Thao; Dishion, Thomas; Overbeek, Geertjan; Burk, William & Engels, Rutger. (2014). The blues of adolescent romance: Observed affective interactions in adolescent romantic relationships associated with depressive symptoms. *Journal of Abnormal Child Psychology, 42*(4), 551–562. doi: 10.1007/s10802-013-9808-y

Haas, Steven A.; Krueger, Patrick M. & Rohlfsen, Leah. (2012). Race/ethnic and nativity disparities in later life physical performance: The role of health and socioeconomic status over the life course. *The Journals of Gerontology Series B: Psychological Sciences and Social Sciences, 67B*(2), 238–248. doi: 10.1093/geronb/gbr155

Haase, Claudia M.; Heckhausen, Jutta & Wrosch, Carsten. (2013). Developmental regulation across the life span: Toward a new synthesis. *Developmental Psychology, 49*(5), 964–972. doi: 10.1037/a0029231

Hagestad, Gunhild O. & Uhlenberg, Peter. (2007). The impact of demographic changes on relations between age groups and generations: A comparative perspective. In K. Warner Schaie & Peter Uhlenberg (Eds.), *Social structures: Demographic changes and the well-being of older persons* (pp. 239–261). New York, NY: Springer.

Hahn-Holbrook, Jennifer & Haselton, Martie. (2014). Is postpartum depression a disease of modern civilization? *Current Directions in Psychological Science, 23*(6), 395–400. doi: 10.1177/0963721414547736

Haidt, Jonathan. (2013). *The righteous mind: Why good people are divided by politics and religion.* New York, NY: Vintage Books.

Haier, Richard J.; Colom, Roberto; Schroeder, David H.; Condon, Christopher A.; Tang, Cheuk; Eaves, Emily & Head, Kevin. (2009). Gray matter and intelligence factors: Is there a neuro-g? *Intelligence, 37*(2), 136–144. doi: 10.1016/j.intell.2008.10.011

Hajek, Peter; Etter, Jean-François; Benowitz, Neal; Eissenberg, Thomas & McRobbie, Hayden. (2014). Electronic cigarettes: Review of use, content, safety, effects on smokers and potential for harm and benefit. *Addiction, 109*(11), 1801–1810. doi: 10.1111/add.12659

Halim, May Ling; Ruble, Diane N.; Tamis-LeMonda, Catherine S.; Zosuls, Kristina M.; Lurye, Leah E. & Greulich, Faith K. (2014). Pink frilly dresses and the avoidance of all things "girly": Children's appearance rigidity and cognitive theories of gender development. *Developmental Psychology, 50*(4), 1091–1101. doi: 10.1037/a0034906

Hall, Jeffrey A. (2011). Sex differences in friendship expectations: A meta-analysis. *Journal of Social and Personal Relationships, 28*(6), 723–747. doi: 10.1177/0265407510386192

Hall, Lynn K. (2008). *Counseling military families: What mental health professionals need to know.* New York, NY: Taylor & Francis.

Hallers-Haalboom, Elizabeth T.; Mesman, Judi; Groeneveld, Marleen G.; Endendijk, Joyce J.; van Berkel, Sheila R.; van der Pol, Lotte D. & Bakermans-Kranenburg, Marian J. (2014). Mothers, fathers, sons and daughters: Parental sensitivity in families with two children. *Journal of Family Psychology, 28*(2), 138–147. doi: 10.1037/a0036004

Halpern, Neil A.; Pastores, Stephen M.; Chou, Joanne F.; Chawla, Sanjay & Thaler, Howard T. (2011). Advance directives in an oncologic intensive care unit: A contemporary analysis of their frequency, type, and impact. *Journal of Palliative Medicine, 14*(4), 483–489. doi: 10.1089/jpm.2010.0397

Halpern, Stephen H. & Garg, Rahul. (2015). Evidence-based medicine and labor analgesia. In Giorgio Capogna (Ed.), *Epidural Labor Analgesia* (pp. 285–295). New York, NY: Springer. doi: 10.1007/978-3-319-13890-9_21

Halpern-Meekin, Sarah; Manning, Wendy D.; Giordano, Peggy C. & Longmore, Monica A. (2013). Relationship churning: Physical violence, and verbal abuse in young adult relationships. *Journal of Marriage and Family, 75*(1), 2–12. doi: 10.1111/j.1741-3737.2012.01029.x

Hamilton, Alice. (1914). Lead poisoning in the United States. *American Journal of Public Health, 4*(6), 477–480. doi: 10.2105/AJPH.4.6.477-a

Hamilton, Brady E.; Martin, Joyce A. & Ventura, Stephanie J. (2012). *Births: Preliminary data for 2011. National Vital*

Statistics Reports 61(5). Hyattsville, MD: National Center for Health Statistics.

Hamilton, Rashea; Sanders, Megan & Anderman, Eric M. (2013). The multiple choices of sex education. *Phi Delta Kappan, 94*(5), 34–39.

Hamlin, J. Kiley. (2014). The origins of human morality: Complex socio-moral evaluations by preverbal infants. In Jean Decety & Yves Christen (Eds.), *New frontiers in social neuroscience* (pp. 165–188). New York, NY: Springer. doi: 10.1007/978-3-319-02904-7_10

Hammond, Christopher J.; Andrew, Toby; Mak, Ying Tat & Spector, Tim D. (2004). A susceptibility locus for myopia in the normal population is linked to the PAX6 gene region on chromosome 11: A genomewide scan of dizygotic twins. *American Journal of Human Genetics, 75*(2), 294–304. doi: 10.1086/423148

Hampel, Harald; Lista, Simone & Khachaturian, Zaven S. (2012). Development of biomarkers to chart all Alzheimer's disease stages: The royal road to cutting the therapeutic Gordian Knot. *Alzheimer's & Dementia, 8*(4), 312–336. doi: 10.1016/j.jalz.2012.05.2116

Hamplová, Dana; Le Bourdais, Céline & Lapierre-Adamcyk, Évelyne. (2014). Is the cohabitation–marriage gap in money pooling universal? *Journal of Marriage and Family, 76*(5), 983–997. doi: 10.1111/jomf.12138

Hamza, Chloe A. & Willoughby, Teena. (2011). Perceived parental monitoring, adolescent disclosure, and adolescent depressive symptoms: A longitudinal examination. *Journal of Youth and Adolescence, 40*(7), 902–915. doi: 10.1007/s10964-010-9604-8

Hanania, Rima. (2010). Two types of perseveration in the dimension change card sort task. *Journal of Experimental Child Psychology, 107*(3), 325–336. doi: 10.1016/j.jecp.2010.05.002

Handelsman, David J. (2011). Androgen misuse and abuse. *Best Practice & Research Clinical Endocrinology & Metabolism, 25*(2), 377–389. doi: 10.1016/j.beem.2010.09.005

Hane, Amie Ashley; Cheah, Charissa; Rubin, Kenneth H. & Fox, Nathan A. (2008). The role of maternal behavior in the relation between shyness and social reticence in early childhood and social withdrawal in middle childhood. *Social Development, 17*(4), 795–811. doi: 10.1111/j.1467-9507.2008.00481.x

Hank, Karsten & Korbmacher, Julie M. (2013). Parenthood and retirement: Gender, cohort, and welfare regime differences. *European Societies, 15*(3), 446–461. doi: 10.1080/14616696.2012.750731

Hanks, Andrew S.; Just, David R. & Wansink, Brian. (2013). Smarter lunchrooms can address new school lunchroom guidelines and childhood obesity. *The Journal of Pediatrics, 162*(4), 867–869. doi: 10.1016/j.jpeds.2012.12.031

Hanson, Jamie L.; Nacewicz, Brendon M.; Sutterer, Matthew J.; Cayo, Amelia A.; Schaefer, Stacey M.; Rudolph, Karen D., . . . Davidson, Richard J. (2015). Behavioral problems after early life stress: Contributions of the hippocampus and amygdala. *Biological Psychiatry, 77*(4), 314–323. doi: 10.1016/j.biopsych.2014.04.020

Hanushek, Eric A. & Woessmann, Ludger. (2009). Do better schools lead to more growth? Cognitive skills, economic outcomes, and causation. *Journal of Economic Growth, 17*(4), 267–321. doi: 10.1007/s10887-012-9081-x

Hanushek, Eric A. & Woessmann, Ludger. (2015). *The knowledge capital of nations: Education and the economics of growth.* Cambridge, MA: MIT Press.

Harden, K. Paige & Tucker-Drob, Elliot M. (2011). Individual differences in the development of sensation seeking and impulsivity during adolescence: Further evidence for a dual systems model. *Developmental Psychology, 47*(3), 739–746. doi: 10.1037/a0023279

Harkness, Geoff & Khaled, Rana. (2014). Modern traditionalism: Consanguineous marriage in Qatar. *Journal of Marriage & Family, 76*(3), 587–603. doi: 10.1111/jomf.12106

Harkness, Sara; Super, Charles M. & Mavridis, Caroline J. (2011). Parental ethnotheories about children's socioemotional development. In Xinyin Chen & Kenneth H. Rubin (Eds.), *Socioemotional development in cultural context* (pp. 73–98). New York, NY: Guilford Press.

Harlow, Ilana. (2005). Shaping sorrow: Creative aspects of public and private mourning. In Samuel C. Heilman (Ed.), *Death, bereavement, and mourning* (pp. 33–52). New Brunswick, NJ: Transaction.

Harper, Casandra E. & Yeung, Fanny. (2013). Perceptions of institutional commitment to diversity as a predictor of college students' openness to diverse perspectives. *The Review of Higher Education, 37*(1), 25–44. doi: 10.1353/rhe.2013.0065

Harris, Judith R. (1998). *The nurture assumption: Why children turn out the way they do.* New York, NY: Free Press.

Harris, Judith R. (2002). Beyond the nurture assumption: Testing hypotheses about the child's environment. In John G. Borkowski et al. (Eds.), *Parenting and the child's world: Influences on academic, intellectual, and social-emotional development* (pp. 3–20). Mahwah, NJ: Erlbaum.

Harris, Michael A.; Hood, Korey K. & Mulvaney, Shelagh A. (2012). Pumpers, skypers, surfers and texters: Technology to improve the management of diabetes in teenagers. *Diabetes, Obesity and Metabolism, 14*(11), 967–972. doi: 10.1111/j.1463-1326.2012.01599.x

Harris, Peter R.; Brearley, Irina; Sheeran, Paschal; Barker, Margo; Klein, William M. P.; Creswell, J. David, . . . Bond, Rod. (2014). Combining self-affirmation with implementation intentions to promote fruit and vegetable consumption. *Health Psychology, 33*(7), 729–736. doi: 10.1037/hea0000065

Harrison, Denise; Bueno, Mariana; Yamada, Janet; Adams-Webber, Thomasin & Stevens, Bonnie. (2010). Analgesic effects of sweet-tasting solutions for infants: Current state of equipoise. *Pediatrics, 126*(5), 894–902. doi: 10.1542/peds.2010-1593

Harrison, Kristen; Bost, Kelly K.; McBride, Brent A.; Donovan, Sharon M.; Grigsby-Toussaint, Diana S.; Kim, Juhee, . . . Jacobsohn, Gwen Costa. (2011). Toward a developmental conceptualization of contributors to overweight and obesity in childhood: The Six-Cs model. *Child Development Perspectives, 5*(1), 50–58. doi: 10.1111/j.1750-8606.2010.00150.x

Harrison, Linda J.; Elwick, Sheena; Vallotton, Claire D. & Kappler, Gregor. (2014). Spending time with others:

A time-use diary for infant-toddler child care. In Linda J. Harrison & Jennifer Sumsion (Eds.), *Lived spaces of infant-toddler education and care: Exploring diverse perspectives on theory, research and practice* (pp. 59–74). Dordrecht, Netherlands: Springer. doi: 10.1007/978-94-017-8838-0_5

Harrist, Amanda W.; Topham, Glade L.; Hubbs-Tait, Laura; Page, Melanie C.; Kennedy, Tay S. & Shriver, Lenka H. (2012). What developmental science can contribute to a transdisciplinary understanding of childhood obesity: An interpersonal and intrapersonal risk model. *Child Development Perspectives, 6*(4), 445–455. doi: 10.1111/cdep.12004

Hart, Chantelle N.; Cairns, Alyssa & Jelalian, Elissa. (2011). Sleep and obesity in children and adolescents. *Pediatric Clinics of North America, 58*(3), 715–733. doi: 10.1016/j.pcl.2011.03.007

Harter, Susan. (2012). *The construction of the self: Developmental and sociocultural foundations* (2nd ed.). New York, NY: Guilford Press.

Hausdorff, Jeffrey M. & Buchman, Aron S. (2013). What links gait speed and MCI with dementia? A fresh look at the association between motor and cognitive function. *Journals of Gerontology: Series A: Biological Sciences and Medical Sciences, 68*(4), 409–411. doi: 10.1093/gerona/glt002

Haushofer, Johannes & Fehr, Ernst. (2014). On the psychology of poverty. *Science, 344*(6186), 862–867. doi: 10.1126/science.1232491

Hawthorne, Joanna. (2009). Promoting development of the early parent-infant relationship using the Neonatal Behavioural Assessment Scale. In Jane Barlow & P. O. Svanberg (Eds.), *Keeping the baby in mind: Infant mental health in practice* (pp. 39–51). New York, NY: Routledge.

Hayden, Brian. (2012). Neandertal social structure? *Oxford Journal of Archaeology, 31*(1), 1–26. doi: 10.1111/j.1468-0092.2011.00376.x

Hayden, Ceara; Bowler, Jennifer O.; Chambers, Stephanie; Freeman, Ruth; Humphris, Gerald; Richards, Derek & Cecil, Joanne E. (2013). Obesity and dental caries in children: A systematic review and meta-analysis. *Community Dentistry and Oral Epidemiology, 41*(4), 289–308. doi: 10.1111/cdoe.12014

Hayden, Elizabeth P. & Mash, Eric J. (2014). Child psychopathology: A developmental-systems perspective. In Eric J. Mash & Russell A. Barkley (Eds.), *Child psychopathology* (3rd ed., pp. 3–72). New York, NY: Guilford Press.

Hayes, DeMarquis; Blake, Jamilia J.; Darensbourg, Alicia & Castillo, Linda G. (2015). Examining the academic achievement of Latino adolescents: The role of parent and peer beliefs and behaviors. *The Journal of Early Adolescence, 35*(2), 141–161. doi: 10.1177/0272431614530806

Hayes, Peter. (2013). International adoption, "early" puberty, and underrecorded age. *Pediatrics, 131*(6), 1029–1031. doi: 10.1542/peds.2013-0232

Hayes, Rachel A. & Slater, Alan. (2008). Three-month-olds' detection of alliteration in syllables. *Infant Behavior and Development, 31*(1), 153–156. doi: 10.1016/j.infbeh.2007.07.009

Hayflick, Leonard. (2004). "Anti-aging" is an oxymoron. *Journals of Gerontology: Series A: Biological Sciences and Medical Sciences, 59A*(6), 573–578. doi: 10.1093/gerona/59.6.B573

Hayne, Harlene & Simcock, Gabrielle. (2009). Memory development in toddlers. In Mary L. Courage & Nelson Cowan (Eds.), *The development of memory in infancy and childhood* (2nd ed., pp. 43–68). New York, NY: Psychology Press.

Haynes, Michelle C. & Heilman, Madeline E. (2013). It had to be you (not me)!: Women's attributional rationalization of their contribution to successful joint work outcomes. *Personality and Social Psychology Bulletin, 39*(7), 956–969. doi: 10.1177/0146167213486358

Hayslip, Bert; Blumenthal, Heidemarie & Garner, Ashley. (2014). Health and grandparent–grandchild well-being: One-year longitudinal findings for custodial grandfamilies. *Journal of Aging and Health, 26*(4), 559–582. doi: 10.1177/0898264314525664

Hazan, Cindy & Campa, Mary I. (Eds.). (2013). *Human bonding: The science of affectional ties.* New York, NY: Guilford Press.

Hedman, Anna M.; van Haren, Neeltje E. M.; Schnack, Hugo G.; Kahn, René S. & Hulshoff Pol, Hilleke E. (2012). Human brain changes across the life span: A review of 56 longitudinal magnetic resonance imaging studies. *Human Brain Mapping, 33*(8), 1987–2002. doi: 10.1002/hbm.21334

Heflick, Nathan A. & Goldenberg, Jamie L. (2012). No atheists in foxholes: Arguments for (but not against) afterlife belief buffers mortality salience effects for atheists. *British Journal of Social Psychology, 51*(2), 385–392. doi: 10.1111/j.2044-8309.2011.02058.x

Heiman, Julia R.; Long, J. Scott; Smith, Shawna N.; Fisher, William A.; Sand, Michael S. & Rosen, Raymond C. (2011). Sexual satisfaction and relationship happiness in midlife and older couples in five countries. *Archives of Sexual Behavior, 40*(4), 741–753. doi: 10.1007/s10508-010-9703-3

Hein, Sascha; Tan, Mei; Aljughaiman, Abdullah & Grigorenko, Elena L. (2014). Characteristics of the home context for the nurturing of gifted children in Saudi Arabia. *High Ability Studies, 25*(1), 23–33. doi: 10.1080/13598139.2014.906970

Heller, Sara B. (2014). Summer jobs reduce violence among disadvantaged youth. *Science, 346*(6214), 1219–1223. doi: 10.1126/science.1257809

Hellerstein, S.; Feldman, S. & Duan, T. (2015). China's 50% caesarean delivery rate: Is it too high? *BJOG: An International Journal of Obstetrics & Gynaecology, 122*(2), 160–164. doi: 10.1111/1471-0528.12971

Henderson, Richard. (2013). Industry employment and output projections to 2022. *Monthly Labor Review.*

Hendry, Leo B. & Kloep, Marion. (2011). Lifestyles in emerging adulthood: Who needs stages anyway? In Jeffrey Jensen Arnett et al. (Eds.), *Debating emerging adulthood: Stage or process?* (pp. 77–104). New York, NY: Oxford University Press. doi: 10.1093/acprof:oso/9780199757176.003.0005

Hennessy-Fiske, Molly. (2011, February 8). California; Concern about child obesity grows, poll finds; Many Californians support restricting unhealthful food and drink in schools. *Los Angeles Times,* p. AA 3.

Henrich, Joseph. (2015). Culture and social behavior. *Current Opinion in Behavioral Sciences, 3*(84–89). doi: 10.1016/j.cobeha.2015.02.001

Henrich, Joseph; Heine, Steven J. & Norenzayan, Ara. (2010). The weirdest people in the world? *Behavioral and Brain Sciences, 33*(2/3), 61–83. doi: 10.1017/S0140525X0999152X

Henry, David B.; Deptula, Daneen P. & Schoeny, Michael E. (2012). Sexually transmitted infections and unintended pregnancy: A longitudinal analysis of risk transmission through friends and attitudes. *Social Development, 21*(1), 195–214. doi: 10.1111/j.1467-9507.2011.00626.x

Herculano-Houzel, Suzana; Manger, Paul R. & Kaas, Jon H. (2014). Brain scaling in mammalian evolution as a consequence of concerted and mosaic changes in numbers of neurons and average neuronal cell size. *Frontiers in Neuroanatomy, 8,* 77. doi: 10.3389/fnana.2014.00077

Heredia, Roberto R. & Cies licka, Anna B. (Eds.). (2015). *Bilingual figurative language processing.* New York, NY: Cambridge University Press.

Herek, Gregory M. (2006). Legal recognition of same-sex relationships in the United States: A social science perspective. *American Psychologist, 61*(6), 607–621. doi: 10.1037/0003-066X.61.6.607

Herlofson, Katharina & Hagestad, Gunhild. (2011). Challenges in moving from macro to micro: Population and family structures in ageing societies. *Demographic Research, 25*(10), 337–370. doi: 10.4054/DemRes.2011.25.10

Herlofson, Katharina & Hagestad, Gunhild. (2012). Transformations in the role of grandparents across welfare states. In Sara Arber & Virpi Timonen (Eds.), *Contemporary grandparenting: Changing family relationships in global contexts* (pp. 27–49). Chicago, IL: Policy Press.

Herman, Khalisa N.; Paukner, Annika & Suomi, Stephen J. (2011). Gene × environment interactions and social play: Contributions from rhesus macaques. In Anthony D. Pellegrini (Ed.), *The Oxford handbook of the development of play* (pp. 58–69). New York, NY: Oxford University Press. doi: 10.1093/oxfordhb/9780195393002.013.0006

Herman-Giddens, Marcia E. (2013). The enigmatic pursuit of puberty in girls. *Pediatrics, 132*(6), 1125–1126. doi: 10.1542/peds.2013-3058

Herman-Giddens, Marcia E.; Steffes, Jennifer; Harris, Donna; Slora, Eric; Hussey, Michael; Dowshen, Steven A., . . . Reiter, Edward O. (2012). Secondary sexual characteristics in boys: Data from the pediatric research in office settings network. *Pediatrics, 130*(5), e1058–e1068. doi: 10.1542/peds.2011-3291

Herold, Benjamin. (2015). Some educators are calling the concept of 'grit' racist. *Education Week, 34*(20), 8.

Herrera, Angelica P.; Snipes, Shedra A.; King, Denae W.; Torres-Vigil, Isabel; Goldberg, Daniel S. & Weinberg, Armin D. (2010). Disparate inclusion of older adults in clinical trials: Priorities and opportunities for policy and practice change. *American Journal of Public Health, 100*(51), S105–S112. doi: 10.2105/ajph.2009.162982

Herschensohn, Julia R. (2007). *Language development and age.* New York, NY: Cambridge University Press.

Heslin, Kevin C.; Hamilton, Alison B.; Singzon, Trudy K.; Smith, James L.; Lois, Nancy & Anderson, Ruth. (2011). Alternative families in recovery: Fictive kin relationships among residents of sober living homes. *Qualitative Health Research, 21*(4), 477–488. doi: 10.1177/1049732310385826

Hess, Thomas M.; Leclerc, Christina M.; Swaim, Elizabeth & Weatherbee, Sarah R. (2009). Aging and everyday judgments: The impact of motivational and processing resource factors. *Psychology and Aging, 24*(3), 735–740. doi: 10.1037/a0016340

Hetherington, E. Mavis. (2006). The influence of conflict, marital problem solving and parenting on children's adjustment in nondivorced, divorced and remarried families. In Alison Clarke-Stewart & Judy Dunn (Eds.), *Families count: Effects on child and adolescent development* (pp. 203–237). New York, NY: Cambridge University Press.

Heyman, Gene M. (2013). Quitting drugs: Quantitative and qualitative features. *Annual Review of Clinical Psychology, 9,* 29–59. doi: 10.1146/annurev-clinpsy-032511-143041

Heymann, Jody; Raub, Amy & Earle, Alison. (2013). Breastfeeding policy: A globally comparative analysis. *Bulletin of the World Health Organization, 91,* 398–406. doi: 10.2471/BLT.12.109363

Hicken, Margaret T.; Lee, Hedwig; Morenoff, Jeffrey; House, James S. & Williams, David R. (2014). Racial/ethnic disparities in hypertension prevalence: Reconsidering the role of chronic stress. *American Journal of Public Health, 104*(1), 117–123. doi: 10.2105/AJPH.2013.301395

Hicks, Joshua A.; Trent, Jason; Davis, William E. & King, Laura A. (2012). Positive affect, meaning in life, and future time perspective: An application of socioemotional selectivity theory. *Psychology and Aging, 27*(1), 181–189. doi: 10.1037/a0023965

Hicks, Meredith S.; McRee, Annie-Laurie & Eisenberg, Marla E. (2013). Teens talking with their partners about sex: The role of parent communication. *American Journal of Sexuality Education, 8*(1/2), 1–17. doi: 10.1080/15546128.2013.790219

Hiekel, Nicole & Castro-Martín, Teresa. (2014). Grasping the diversity of cohabitation: Fertility intentions among cohabiters across Europe. *Journal of Marriage and Family, 76*(3), 489–505. doi: 10.1111/jomf.12112

Higgins, Matt. (2006, August 7). A series of flips creates some serious buzz. *The New York Times,* p. D7.

Hill, Patrick L.; Burrow, Anthony L. & Sumner, Rachel. (2013). Addressing important questions in the field of adolescent purpose. *Child Development Perspectives, 7*(4), 232–236. doi: 10.1111/cdep.12048

Hinnant, J. Benjamin; Nelson, Jackie A.; O'Brien, Marion; Keane, Susan P. & Calkins, Susan D. (2013). The interactive roles of parenting, emotion regulation and executive functioning in moral reasoning during middle childhood. *Cognition and Emotion, 27*(8), 1460–1468. doi: 10.1080/02699931.2013.789792

Hirvonen, Riikka; Aunola, Kaisa; Alatupa, Saija; Viljaranta, Jaana & Nurmi, Jari-Erik. (2013). The role of temperament in children's affective and behavioral responses in achievement situations. *Learning and Instruction, 27,* 21–30. doi: 10.1016/j.learninstruc.2013.02.005

Hively, Kimberly & El-Alayli, Amani. (2014). "You throw like a girl:" The effect of stereotype threat on women's athletic performance and gender stereotypes. *Psychology of Sport and Exercise, 15*(1), 48–55. doi: 10.1016/j.psychsport.2013.09.001

Ho, Emily S. (2010). Measuring hand function in the young child. *Journal of Hand Therapy, 23*(3), 323–328. doi: 10.1016/j.jht.2009.11.002

Hoare, Carol Hren. (2002). *Erikson on development in adulthood: New insights from the unpublished papers.* New York, NY: Oxford University Press.

Hochman, Oshrat & Lewin-Epstein, Noah. (2013). Determinants of early retirement preferences in Europe: The role of grandparenthood. *International Journal of Comparative Sociology, 54*(1), 29–47. doi: 10.1177/0020715213480977

Hoeve, Machteld; Dubas, Judith S.; Gerris, Jan R. M.; van der Laan, Peter H. & Smeenk, Wilma. (2011). Maternal and paternal parenting styles: Unique and combined links to adolescent and early adult delinquency. *Journal of Adolescence, 34*(5), 813–827. doi: 10.1016/j.adolescence.2011.02.004

Hofer, Claire; Eisenberg, Nancy; Spinrad, Tracy L.; Morris, Amanda S.; Gershoff, Elizabeth; Valiente, Carlos, . . . Eggum, Natalie D. (2013). Mother-adolescent conflict: Stability, change, and relations with externalizing and internalizing behavior problems. *Social Development, 22*(2), 259–279. doi: 10.1111/sode.12012

Hoff, Erika; Core, Cynthia; Place, Silvia; Rumiche, Rosario; Señor, Melissa & Parra, Marisol. (2012). Dual language exposure and early bilingual development. *Journal of Child Language, 39*(1), 1–27. doi: 10.1017/S0305000910000759

Hoff, Erika; Rumiche, Rosario; Burridge, Andrea; Ribota, Krystal M. & Welsh, Stephanie N. (2014). Expressive vocabulary development in children from bilingual and monolingual homes: A longitudinal study from two to four years. *Early Childhood Research Quarterly, 29*(4), 433–444. doi: 10.1016/j.ecresq.2014.04.012

Hoffman, Jessica L.; Teale, William H. & Paciga, Kathleen A. (2013). Assessing vocabulary learning in early childhood. *Journal of Early Childhood Literacy, 14*(4), 459–481. doi: 10.1177/1468798413501184

Holden, Constance. (2010). Myopia out of control. *Science, 327*(5961), 17. doi: 10.1126/science.327.5961.17-c

Hollenstein, Tom & Lougheed, Jessica P. (2013). Beyond storm and stress: Typicality, transactions, timing, and temperament to account for adolescent change. *American Psychologist, 68*(6), 444–454. doi: 10.1037/a0033586

Holmboe, K.; Nemoda, Z.; Fearon, R. M. P.; Sasvari-Szekely, M. & Johnson, M. H. (2011). Dopamine D4 receptor and serotonin transporter gene effects on the longitudinal development of infant temperament. *Genes, Brain and Behavior, 10*(5), 513–522. doi: 10.1111/j.1601-183X.2010.00669.x

Holmes, Tabitha R. & Nash, Alison. (2015). Rules of engagement: Grandmothers, daughters and the mothering of mothers. In Margueite Guzman Bouvard (Ed.), *Mothers of adult children* (pp. 153–164). Lanham, MA: Lexington Books.

Holsti, Liisa; Grunau, Ruth E. & Shany, Eilon. (2011). Assessing pain in preterm infants in the neonatal intensive care unit: Moving to a brain-oriented approach. *Pain Management, 1*(2), 171–179. doi: 10.2217/pmt.10.19

Holt, Raymond. (2013). Design for the ages: Universal design as a rehabilitation strategy (Book Review). *Disability & Society, 28*(1), 142–144. doi: 10.1080/09687599.2012.739364

Holt-Lunstad, Julianne; Smith, Timothy B.; Baker, Mark; Harris, Tyler & Stephenson, David. (2015). Loneliness and social isolation as risk factors for mortality: A meta-analytic review. *Perspectives on Psychological Science, 10*(2), 227–237. doi: 10.1177/1745691614568352

Holzer, Jessica; Canavan, Maureen & Bradley, Elizabeth. (2014). County-level correlation between adult obesity rates and prevalence of dentists. *JADA, 145*(9), 932–939. doi: 10.14219/jada.2014.48

Hong, David S. & Reiss, Allan L. (2014). Cognitive and neurological aspects of sex chromosome aneuploidies. *The Lancet Neurology, 13*(3), 306–318. doi: 10.1016/S1474-4422(13)70302-8

Hong, Jun Sung; Algood, Carl L.; Chiu, Yu-Ling & Lee, Stephanie Ai-Ping. (2011). An ecological understanding of kinship foster care in the United States. *Journal of Child and Family Studies, 20*(6), 863–872. doi: 10.1007/s10826-011-9454-3

Hong, Jun Sung & Garbarino, James. (2012). Risk and protective factors for homophobic bullying in schools: An application of the social–ecological framework. *Educational Psychology Review, 24*(2), 271–285. doi: 10.1007/s10648-012-9194-y

Hook, Jennifer L. (2010). Gender inequality in the welfare state: Sex segregation in housework, 1965-2003. *American Journal of Sociology, 115*(5), 1480–1523. doi: 10.1086/651384

Hook, Jennifer L. (2012). Working on the weekend: Fathers' time with family in the United Kingdom. *Journal of Marriage and Family, 74*(4), 631–642. doi: 10.1111/j.1741-3737.2012.00986.x

Horton, Megan K.; Kahn, Linda G.; Perera, Frederica; Barr, Dana B. & Rauh, Virginia. (2012). Does the home environment and the sex of the child modify the adverse effects of prenatal exposure to chlorpyrifos on child working memory? *Neurotoxicology and Teratology, 34*(5), 534–541. doi: 10.1016/j.ntt.2012.07.004

Houdmont, Jonathan; Zhou, Jieming & Hassard, Juliet. (2011). Overtime and psychological well-being among Chinese office workers. *Occupational Medicine, 61*(4), 270–273. doi: 10.1093/occmed/kqr029

Hout, Michael. (2012). Social and economic returns to college education in the United States. *Annual Review of Sociology, 39,* 379–400. doi: 10.1146/annurev.soc.012809.102503

Howard, Elizabeth R.; Páez, Mariela M.; August, Diane L.; Barr, Christopher D.; Kenyon, Dorry & Malabonga, Valerie. (2014). The importance of SES, home and school language and literacy practices, and oral vocabulary in bilingual children's English reading development. *Bilingual Research Journal, 37*(2), 120–141. doi: 10.1080/15235882.2014.934485

Hoyert, Donna L.; Kochanek, Kenneth D. & Murphy, Sherry L. (1999). *Deaths: Final data for 1997. National Vital Statistics Reports 47*(19). Hyattsville, MD: National Center for Health Statistics.

Hoyert, Donna L.; Kung, Hsiang-Ching & Smith, Betty L. (2005). *Deaths: Preliminary data for 2003. National Vital Statistics Reports 53*(15). Hyattsville, MD: National Center for Health Statistics.

Hoyert, Donna L. & Xu, Jiaquan. (2012). *Deaths: Preliminary data for 2011. National Vital Statistics Reports 61*(6). Hyattsville, MD: National Center for Health Statistics.

Hrdy, Sarah B. (2009). *Mothers and others: The evolutionary origins of mutual understanding.* Cambridge, MA: Harvard University Press.

Hsia, Yingfen & Maclennan, Karyn. (2009). Rise in psychotropic drug prescribing in children and adolescents during 1992–2001: A population-based study in the UK. *European Journal of Epidemiology, 24*(4), 211–216. doi: 10.1007/s10654-009-9321-3

Hsu, Ming; Anen, Cedric & Quartz, Steven R. (2008). The right and the good: Distributive justice and neural encoding of equity and efficiency. *Science, 320*(5879), 1092–1095. doi: 10.1126/science.1153651

Hsu, William C.; Araneta, Maria Rosario G.; Kanaya, Alka M.; Chiang, Jane L. & Fujimoto, Wilfred. (2015). BMI cut points to identify at-risk Asian Americans for type 2 diabetes screening. *Diabetes Care, 38*(1), 150–158. doi: 10.2337/dc14-2391

Hu, Frank B. (2011). Globalization of diabetes: The role of diet, lifestyle, and genes. *Diabetes Care, 34*(6), 1249–1257. doi: 10.2337/dc11-0442

Huang, Chiungjung. (2010). Mean-level change in self-esteem from childhood through adulthood: Meta-analysis of longitudinal studies. *Review of General Psychology, 14*(3), 251–260. doi: 10.1037/a0020543

Huang, Chien-Chung. (2009). Mothers' reports of nonresident fathers' involvement with their children: Revisiting the relationship between child support payment and visitation. *Family Relations, 58*(1), 54–64. doi: 10.1111/j.1741-3729.2008.00534.x

Huang, Tzu-Ting; Chung, Meng-Ling; Chen, Fan-Ru; Chin, Yen-Fan & Wang, Bi-Hwa. (2015). Evaluation of a combined cognitive-behavioural and exercise intervention to manage fear of falling among elderly residents in nursing homes. *Aging & Mental Health,* 1–11. doi: 10.1080/13607863.2015.1020411

Hugdahl, Kenneth & Westerhausen, René (Eds.). (2010). *The two halves of the brain: Information processing in the cerebral hemispheres.* Cambridge, MA: MIT Press.

Hughes, Julie M. & Bigler, Rebecca S. (2011). Predictors of African American and European American adolescents' endorsement of race-conscious social policies. *Developmental Psychology, 47*(2), 479–492. doi: 10.1037/a0021309

Hughes, Matthew L.; Geraci, Lisa & De Forrest, Ross L. (2013). Aging 5 years in 5 minutes: The effect of taking a memory test on older adults' subjective age. *Psychological Science, 24*(12), 2481–2488. doi: 10.1177/0956797613494853

Hughey, Matthew W. & Parks, Gregory. (2014). *The wrongs of the right: Language, race, and the Republican Party in the age of Obama.* New York, NY: New York University Press.

Huh, Susanna Y.; Rifas-Shiman, Sheryl L.; Zera, Chloe A.; Edwards, Janet W. Rich; Oken, Emily; Weiss, Scott T. & Gillman, Matthew W. (2012). Delivery by caesarean section and risk of obesity in preschool age children: A prospective cohort study. *Archives of the Diseases of Childhood, 97*(7), 610–616. doi: 10.1136/archdischild-2011-301141

Hunt, Earl B. (2011). *Human intelligence.* New York, NY: Cambridge University Press.

Hunt, Earl B. (2012). What makes nations intelligent? *Perspectives on Psychological Science, 7*(3), 284–306. doi: 10.1177/1745691612442905

Hunter, Myra Sally. (2012). Long-term impacts of early and surgical menopause. *Menopause, 19*(3), 253–254. doi: 10.1097/gme.0b013e31823e9b2e

Hussain, Amjad; Case, Keith; Marshall, Russell & Summerskill, Steve J. (2013). An inclusive design method for addressing human variability and work performance issues. *International Journal of Engineering and Technology Innovation, 3*(3), 144–155.

Huston, Aletha C. & Ripke, Marika N. (2006). Middle childhood: Contexts of development. In Aletha C. Huston & Marika N. Ripke (Eds.), *Developmental contexts in middle childhood: Bridges to adolescence and adulthood* (pp. 1–22). New York, NY: Cambridge University Press.

Hutchinson, Esther A.; De Luca, Cinzia R.; Doyle, Lex W.; Roberts, Gehan & Anderson, Peter J. (2013). School-age outcomes of extremely preterm or extremely low birth weight children. *Pediatrics, 131*(4), e1053–e1061. doi: 10.1542/peds.2012-2311

Huver, Rose M. E.; Otten, Roy; de Vries, Hein & Engels, Rutger C. M. E. (2010). Personality and parenting style in parents of adolescents. *Journal of Adolescence, 33*(3), 395–402. doi: 10.1016/j.adolescence.2009.07.012

Hvistendahl, Mara. (2014). While emerging economies boom, equality goes bust. *Science, 344*(6186), 832–835. doi: 10.1126/science.344.6186.832

Hyde, Janet S. (2014). Gender similarities and differences. *Annual Review of Psychology, 65,* 373–398. doi: 10.1146/annurev-psych-010213-115057

Hyde, Janet S.; Lindberg, Sara M.; Linn, Marcia C.; Ellis, Amy B. & Williams, Caroline C. (2008). Gender similarities characterize math performance. *Science, 321*(5888), 494–495. doi: 10.1126/science.1160364

Idler, Ellen. (2006). Religion and aging. In Robert H. Binstock & Linda K. George (Eds.), *Handbook of aging and the social sciences* (6th ed., pp. 277–300). Amsterdam, The Netherlands: Elsevier.

Iida, Hiroko & Rozier, R. Gary. (2013). Mother-perceived social capital and children's oral health and use of dental care in the United States. *American Journal of Public Health, 103*(3), 480–487. doi: 10.2105/AJPH.2012.300845

Ikeda, Martin J. (2012). Policy and practice considerations for response to intervention: Reflections and commentary. *Journal of Learning Disabilities, 45*(3), 274–277. doi: 10.1177/0022219412442170

ILO. (2011). Database of conditions of work and employment laws. Retrieved, from International Labour Organization http://www.ilo.org/dyn/travail/travmain.home

Imai, Mutsumi; Kita, Sotaro; Nagumo, Miho & Okada, Hiroyuki. (2008). Sound symbolism facilitates early verb learning. *Cognition, 109*(1), 54–65. doi: 10.1016/j.cognition.2008.07.015

Inan, Hatice Z.; Trundle, Kathy C. & Kantor, Rebecca. (2010). Understanding natural sciences education in a Reggio Emilia-inspired preschool. *Journal of Research in Science Teaching,* 47(10), 1186–1208. doi: 10.1002/tea.20375

Inceoglu, Ilke; Segers, Jesse & Bartram, Dave. (2012). Age-related differences in work motivation. *Journal of Occupational and Organizational Psychology,* 75(2), 300–329. doi: 10.1111/j.2044-8325.2011.02035.x

Inhelder, Bärbel & Piaget, Jean. (1958). *The growth of logical thinking from childhood to adolescence: An essay on the construction of formal operational structures.* New York, NY: Basic Books.

Inhelder, Bärbel & Piaget, Jean. (1964). *The early growth of logic in the child: Classification and seriation.* New York, NY: Harper & Row.

Inhelder, Bärbel & Piaget, Jean. (2013a). *The early growth of logic in the child: Classification and seriation.* New York, NY: Routledge.

Inhelder, Bärbel & Piaget, Jean. (2013b). *The growth of logical thinking from childhood to adolescence: An essay on the construction of formal operational structures.* New York, NY: Routledge.

Insel, Thomas R. (2014). Mental disorders in childhood: Shifting the focus from behavioral symptoms to neurodevelopmental trajectories. *JAMA,* 311(17), 1727–1728. doi: 10.1001/jama.2014.1193

Insurance Institute for Highway Safety. (2012). Fatality facts: Teenagers 2010. http://www.iihs.org/iihs/topics/t/teenagers/fatalityfacts/teenagers/2010

Insurance Institute for Highway Safety. (2013). Older drivers. http://www.iihs.org/iihs/topics/t/older-drivers/fatalityfacts/older-people

Inzlicht, Michael & Schmader, Toni. (2012). *Stereotype threat: Theory, process, and application.* New York, NY: Oxford University Press.

Ivcevic, Zorana & Brackett, Marc. (2014). Predicting school success: Comparing conscientiousness, grit, and emotion regulation ability. *Journal of Research in Personality,* 52, 29–36. doi: 10.1016/j.jrp.2014.06.005

Iyengar, Sheena S. & Lepper, Mark R. (2000). When choice is demotivating: Can one desire too much of a good thing? *Journal of Personality and Social Psychology,* 79(6), 995–1006. doi: 10.1037//0022-3514.79.6.995

Izard, Carroll E. (2009). Emotion theory and research: Highlights, unanswered questions, and emerging issues. *Annual Review of Psychology,* 60, 1–25. doi: 10.1146/annurev.psych.60.110707.163539

Jack, Clifford R.; Lowe, Val J.; Weigand, Stephen D.; Wiste, Heather J.; Senjem, Matthew L.; Knopman, David S.,...Petersen, Ronald C. (2009). Serial PIB and MRI in normal, mild cognitive impairment and Alzheimer's disease: Implications for sequence of pathological events in Alzheimer's disease. *Brain,* 132(5), 1355–1365. doi: 10.1093/brain/awp062

Jackson, Jeffrey B.; Miller, Richard B.; Oka, Megan & Henry, Ryan G. (2014). Gender differences in marital satisfaction: A meta-analysis. *Journal of Marriage and Family,* 76(1), 105–129. doi: 10.1111/jomf.12077

Jackson, James C.; Santoro, Michael J.; Ely, Taylor M.; Boehm, Leanne; Kiehl, Amy L.; Anderson, Lindsay S. & Ely, E. Wesley. (2014). Improving patient care through the prism of psychology: Application of Maslow's hierarchy to sedation, delirium, and early mobility in the intensive care unit. *Journal of Critical Care,* 29(3), 438–444. doi: 10.1016/j.jcrc.2014.01.009

Jackson, Jonathan D. & Balota, David A. (2012). Mind-wandering in younger and older adults: Converging evidence from the sustained attention to response task and reading for comprehension. *Psychology and Aging,* 27(1), 106–119. doi: 10.1037/a0023933

Jackson, James S.; Govia, Ishtar O. & Sellers, Sherrill L. (2011). Racial and ethnic influences over the life course. In Robert H. Binstock & Linda K. George (Eds.), *Handbook of aging and the social sciences* (7th ed., pp. 91–103). San Diego, CA: Academic Press. doi: 10.1016/B978-0-12-380880-6.00007-1

Jackson, Shelly L. & Hafemeister, Thomas L. (2011). Risk factors associated with elder abuse: The importance of differentiating by type of elder maltreatment. *Violence and Victims,* 26(6), 738–757. doi: 10.1891/0886-6708.26.6.738

Jaffe, Arthur C. (2011). Failure to thrive: Current clinical concepts. *Pediatrics in Review,* 32(3), 100–108. doi: 10.1542/pir.32-3-100

Jaiswal, Tulika. (2014). *Indian arranged marriages: A social psychological perspective.* New York, NY: Routledge.

Jambon, Marc & Smetana, Judith G. (2014). Moral complexity in middle childhood: Children's evaluations of necessary harm. *Developmental Psychology,* 50(1), 22–33. doi: 10.1037/a0032992

James, Jenée; Ellis, Bruce J.; Schlomer, Gabriel L. & Garber, Judy. (2012). Sex-specific pathways to early puberty, sexual debut, and sexual risk taking: Tests of an integrated evolutionary–developmental model. *Developmental Psychology,* 48(3), 687–702. doi: 10.1037/a0026427

James, Jacquelyn B.; McKechnie, Sharon & Swanberg, Jennifer. (2011). Predicting employee engagement in an age-diverse retail workforce. *Journal of Organizational Behavior,* 32(2), 173–196. doi: 10.1002/job.681

James, Will. (2012, May 25). Report faults doctors: Long Island grand jury blames physicians, pharmacists for epidemic of abuse. *The Wall Street Journal,* p. A15.

Janse, Benjamin; Huijsman, Robbert; de Kuyper, Ruben Dennis Maurice & Fabbricotti, Isabelle Natalina. (2014). The effects of an integrated care intervention for the frail elderly on informal caregivers: A quasi-experimental study. *BMC Geriatrics,* 14(1). doi: 10.1186/1471-2318-14-58

Jarcho, Johanna M.; Fox, Nathan A.; Pine, Daniel S.; Etkin, Amit; Leibenluft, Ellen; Shechner, Tomer & Ernst, Monique. (2013). The neural correlates of emotion-based cognitive control in adults with early childhood behavioral inhibition. *Biological Psychology,* 92(2), 306–314. doi: 10.1016/j.biopsycho.2012.09.008

Jasny, Barbara R.; Chin, Gilbert; Chong, Lisa & Vignieri, Sacha. (2011). Again, and again, and again... *Science,* 334(6060), 1225. doi: 10.1126/science.334.6060.1225

Jastrzembski, Tiffany S.; Charness, Neil & Vasyukova, Catherine. (2006). Expertise and age effects on knowledge activation in chess. *Psychology and Aging*, *21*(2), 401–405. doi: 10.1037/0882-7974.21.2.401

Jayson, Sharon. (2014, April 26). Shotgun weddings becoming relics of another time. *USA Today*.

Jenkins, Paul J.; Clement, Nick D.; Hamilton, David F.; Gaston, Paul; Patton, James T. & Howie, Colin R. (2013). Predicting the cost-effectiveness of total hip and knee replacement: A health economic analysis. *The Bone & Joint Journal*, *95B*(1), 115–121. doi: 10.1302/0301-620X.95B1.29835

Jensen, Alexander C.; Whiteman, Shawn D.; Fingerman, Karen L. & Birditt, Kira S. (2013). "Life still isn't fair": Parental differential treatment of young adult siblings. *Journal of Marriage and Family*, *75*(2), 438–452. doi: 10.1111/jomf.12002

Jessop, Donna C. & Wade, Jennifer. (2008). Fear appeals and binge drinking: A terror management theory perspective. *British Journal of Health Psychology*, *13*(4), 773–788. doi: 10.1348/135910707X272790

Ji, Cheng Ye; Chen, Tian Jiao & Working Group on Obesity in China (WGOC). (2013). Empirical changes in the prevalence of overweight and obesity among Chinese students from 1985 to 2010 and corresponding preventive strategies. *Biomedical and Environmental Sciences*, *26*(1), 1–12. doi: 10.3967/0895-3988.2013.01.001

Jia, Jianping; Wang, Fen; Wei, Cuibai; Zhou, Aihong; Jia, Xiangfei; Li, Fang, . . . Dong, Xiumin. (2014). The prevalence of dementia in urban and rural areas of China. *Alzheimers and Dementia*, *10*(1), 1–9. doi: 10.1016/j.jalz.2013.01.012

Jiang, Quanbao & Sánchez-Barricarte, Jesús J. (2011). The 4-2-1 family structure in China: A survival analysis based on life tables. *European Journal of Ageing*, *8*(2), 119–127. doi: 10.1007/s10433-011-0189-1

Johannesen, Mark & LoGiudice, Dina. (2013). Elder abuse: A systematic review of risk factors in community-dwelling elders. *Age and Ageing*, *42*(3), 292–298. doi: 10.1093/ageing/afs195

Johnson, Anna D.; Han, Wen-Jui; Ruhm, Christopher J. & Waldfogel, Jane. (2014). Child care subsidies and the school readiness of children of immigrants. *Child Development*, *85*(6), 2140–2150. doi: 10.1111/cdev.12285

Johnson, Kimberly J. & Mutchler, Jan E. (2014). The emergence of a positive gerontology: From disengagement to social involvement. *The Gerontologist*, *54*(1), 93–100. doi: 10.1093/geront/gnt099

Johnson, Kimberly S.; Kuchibhatla, Maragatha & Tulsky, James A. (2011). Racial differences in location before hospice enrollment and association with hospice length of stay. *Journal of the American Geriatrics Society*, *59*(4), 732–737. doi: 10.1111/j.1532-5415.2011.03326.x

Johnson, Matthew D. (2012). Healthy marriage initiatives: On the need for empiricism in policy implementation. *American Psychologist*, *67*(4), 296–308. doi: 10.1037/a0027743

Johnson, Mark H. (2011). *Developmental cognitive neuroscience: An introduction* (3rd ed.). Malden, MA: Wiley-Blackwell.

Johnson, Mark H. & Fearon, R. M. Pasco. (2011). Commentary: Disengaging the infant mind: Genetic dissociation of attention and cognitive skills in infants—reflections on Leppänen

et al. (2011). *Journal of Child Psychology and Psychiatry*, *52*(11), 1153–1154. doi: 10.1111/j.1469-7610.2011.02433.x

Johnson, Monica K. (2013). Parental financial assistance and young adults' relationship with parents and well-being. *Journal of Marriage and Family*, *75*(3), 713–733. doi: 10.1111/jomf.12029

Johnson, Monica K.; Sage, Rayna A. & Mortimer, Jeylan T. (2012). Work values, early career difficulties, and the U.S. economic recession. *Social Psychology Quarterly*, *75*(3), 242–267. doi: 10.1177/0190272512451754

Johnson, Susan C.; Dweck, Carol S.; Chen, Frances S.; Stern, Hilarie L.; Ok, Su-Jeong & Barth, Maria. (2010). At the intersection of social and cognitive development: Internal working models of attachment in infancy. *Cognitive Science*, *34*(5), 807–825. doi: 10.1111/j.1551-6709.2010.01112.x

Johnson, Wendy; McGue, Matt & Deary, Ian J. (2014). Normative cognitive aging. In Deborah Finkel & Chandra A. Reynolds (Eds.), *Behavior genetics of cognition across the lifespan: Advances in behavior genetics* (Vol. 1, pp. 135–167). New York, NY: Springer. doi: 10.1007/978-1-4614-7447-0_5

Johnston, Lloyd D.; O'Malley, Patrick M.; Bachman, Jerald G. & Schulenberg, John E. (2009). *Monitoring the future, national survey results on drug use, 1975-2008: College students and adults ages 19-50.* Bethesda, MD: National Institute on Drug Abuse.

Johnston, Lloyd D.; O'Malley, Patrick M.; Bachman, Jerald G. & Schulenberg, John E. (2012). *Monitoring the future, national survey results on drug use, 1975-2011, Volume I: Secondary school students.* Ann Arbor, MI: Institute for Social Research, The University of Michigan.

Johnston, Lloyd D.; O'Malley, Patrick M.; Bachman, Jerald G.; Schulenberg, John E. & Miech, Richard A. (2014). *Monitoring the future, national survey results on drug use, 1975-2013: Volume I, Secondary school students.* Ann Arbor, MI: Institute for Social Research, The University of Michigan.

Jokela, Markus. (2012). Birth-cohort effects in the association between personality and fertility. *Psychological Science*, *23*(8), 835–841. doi: 10.1177/0956797612439067

Jonas, Eva; Sullivan, Daniel & Greenberg, Jeff. (2013). Generosity, greed, norms, and death—Differential effects of mortality salience on charitable behavior. *Journal of Economic Psychology*, *35*, 47–57. doi: 10.1016/j.joep.2012.12.005

Jones, Mary C. (1965). Psychological correlates of somatic development. *Child Development*, *36*(4), 899–911. doi: 10.2307/1126932

Jong, Jyh-Tsorng; Kao, Tsair; Lee, Liang-Yi; Huang, Hung-Hsuan; Lo, Po-Tsung & Wang, Hui-Chung. (2010). Can temperament be understood at birth? The relationship between neonatal pain cry and their temperament: A preliminary study. *Infant Behavior and Development*, *33*(3), 266–272. doi: 10.1016/j.infbeh.2010.02.001

Jordan, Alexander H. & Monin, Benoît. (2008). From sucker to saint: Moralization in response to self-threat. *Psychological Science*, *19*(8), 809–815. doi: 10.1111/j.1467-9280.2008.02161.x

Jordet, Geir; Hartman, Esther & Vuijk, Pieter J. (2012). Team history and choking under pressure in major soccer penalty shootouts. *British Journal of Psychology*, *103*(2), 268–283. doi: 10.1111/j.2044-8295.2011.02071.x

Jose, Anita; Daniel O'Leary, K. & Moyer, Anne. (2010). Does premarital cohabitation predict subsequent marital stability and marital quality? A meta-analysis. *Journal of Marriage and Family, 72*(1), 105–116. doi: 10.1111/j.1741-3737.2009.00686.x

Joseph, Michelle A.; O'Connor, Thomas G.; Briskman, Jacqueline A.; Maughan, Barbara & Scott, Stephen. (2014). The formation of secure new attachments by children who were maltreated: An observational study of adolescents in foster care. *Development and Psychopathology, 26*(1), 67–80. doi: 10.1017/S0954579413000540

Judd, Fiona K.; Hickey, Martha & Bryant, Christina. (2012). Depression and midlife: Are we overpathologising the menopause? *Journal of Affective Disorders, 136*(3), 199–211. doi: 10.1016/j.jad.2010.12.010

Julian, Megan M. (2013). Age at adoption from institutional care as a window into the lasting effects of early experiences. *Clinical Child and Family Psychology Review, 16*(2), 101–145. doi: 10.1007/s10567-013-0130-6

Juonala, Markus; Magnussen, Costan G.; Berenson, Gerald S.; Venn, Alison; Burns, Trudy L.; Sabin, Matthew A., . . . Raitakari, Olli T. (2011). Childhood adiposity, adult adiposity, and cardiovascular risk factors. *The New England Journal of Medicine, 365*(20), 1876–1885. doi: 10.1056/NEJMoa1010112

Juvonen, Jaana & Graham, Sandra. (2014). Bullying in schools: The power of bullies and the plight of victims. *Annual Review of Psychology, 65*, 159–185. doi: 10.1146/annurev-psych-010213-115030

Juvonen, Jaana; Nishina, Adrienne & Graham, Sandra. (2006). Ethnic diversity and perceptions of safety in urban middle schools. *Psychological Science, 17*(5), 393–400. doi: 10.1111/j.1467-9280.2006.01718.x

Jyrkkä, Johanna; Mursu, Jaakko; Enlund, Hannes & Lönnroos, Eija. (2012). Polypharmacy and nutritional status in elderly people. *Current Opinion in Clinical Nutrition & Metabolic Care, 15*(1), 1–6. doi: 10.1097/MCO.0b013e32834d155a

Kachel, A. Friederike; Premo, Luke S. & Hublin, Jean-Jacques. (2011). Modeling the effects of weaning age on length of female reproductive period: Implications for the evolution of human life history. *American Journal of Human Biology, 23*(4), 479–487. doi: 10.1002/ajhb.21157

Kahana, Eva; Bhatta, Tirth; Lovegreen, Loren D.; Kahana, Boaz & Midlarsky, Elizabeth. (2013). Altruism, helping, and volunteering: Pathways to well-being in late life. *Journal of Aging and Health, 25*(1), 159–187. doi: 10.1177/0898264312469665

Kahneman, Daniel. (2011). *Thinking, fast and slow.* New York, NY: Farrar, Straus and Giroux.

Kail, Robert V. (2013). Influences of credibility of testimony and strength of statistical evidence on children's and adolescents' reasoning. *Journal of Experimental Child Psychology, 116*(3), 747–754. doi: 10.1016/j.jecp.2013.04.004

Kaiser, Jocelyn. (2014). Ambitious children's study meets disappointing end. *Science, 346*(6216), 1441. doi: 10.1126/science.346.6216.1441

Kalil, Ariel; Dunifon, Rachel; Crosby, Danielle & Su, Jessica Houston. (2014a). Work hours, schedules, and insufficient sleep among mothers and their young children. *Journal of Marriage and Family, 76*(5), 891–904. doi: 10.1111/jomf.12142

Kalil, Ariel; Ryan, Rebecca & Chor, Elise. (2014b). Time investments in children across family structures. *The ANNALS of the American Academy of Political and Social Science, 654*(1), 50–168. doi: 10.1177/0002716214528276

Kalliala, Marjatta. (2006). *Play culture in a changing world.* Maidenhead, UK: Open University Press.

Kalmijn, Matthijs. (2010). Country differences in the effects of divorce on well-being: The role of norms, support, and selectivity. *European Sociological Review, 26*(4), 475–490. doi: 10.1093/esr/jcp035

Kan, Man Yee; Sullivan, Oriel & Gershuny, Jonathan. (2011). Gender convergence in domestic work: Discerning the effects of interactional and institutional barriers from large-scale data. *Sociology, 45*(2), 234–251. doi: 10.1177/0038038510394014

Kandel, Denise B. (Ed.). (2002). *Stages and pathways of drug involvement: Examining the gateway hypothesis.* New York, NY: Cambridge University Press.

Kandler, Christian. (2012). Nature and nurture in personality development: The case of neuroticism and extraversion. *Current Directions in Psychological Science, 21*(5), 290–296. doi: 10.1177/0963721412452557

Kang, Hye-Kyung. (2014). Influence of culture and community perceptions on birth and perinatal care of immigrant women: Doulas' perspective. *The Journal of Perinatal Education, 23*(1), 25–32. doi: 10.1891/1058-1243.23.1.25

Kanny, Mary A.; Sax, Linda J. & Riggers-Piehl, Tiffani A. (2014). Investigating forty years of STEM research: How explanations for the gender gap have evolved over time. *Journal of Women and Minorities in Science and Engineering, 20*(2), 127–148. doi: 10.1615/JWomenMinorScienEng.2014007246

Kapp, Steven K.; Gillespie-Lynch, Kristen; Sherman, Lauren E. & Hutman, Ted. (2013). Deficit, difference, or both? Autism and neurodiversity. *Developmental Psychology, 49*(1), 59–71. doi: 10.1037/a0028353

Karmiloff-Smith, Annette. (2010). A developmental perspective on modularity. In Britt Glatzeder et al. (Eds.), *Towards a theory of thinking* (pp. 179–187). Heidelberg, Germany: Springer. doi: 10.1007/978-3-642-03129-8_12

Kärnä, Antti; Voeten, Marinus; Little, Todd D.; Poskiparta, Elisa; Kaljonen, Anne & Salmivalli, Christina. (2011). A large-scale evaluation of the KiVa antibullying program: Grades 4–6. *Child Development, 82*(1), 311–330. doi: 10.1111/j.1467-8624.2010.01557.x

Kärtner, Joscha; Keller, Heidi & Yovsi, Relindis D. (2010). Mother–infant interaction during the first 3 months: The emergence of culture-specific contingency patterns. *Child Development, 81*(2), 540–554. doi: 10.1111/j.1467-8624.2009.01414.x

Kastenbaum, Robert J. (2012). *Death, society, and human experience* (11th ed.). Boston, MA: Pearson.

Katz, Kathy S.; Jarrett, Marian H.; El-Mohandes, Ayman A. E.; Schneider, Susan; McNeely-Johnson, Doris & Kiely, Michele. (2011). Effectiveness of a combined home visiting and group intervention for low income African American mothers: The Pride in Parenting program. *Maternal and Child Health Journal, 15*(Suppl. 1), 75–84. doi: 10.1007/s10995-011-0858-x

Kauffman, Jeffery. (2013). Culture, socialization, and traumatic death. In David K. Meagher & David E. Balk (Eds.), *Handbook of thanatology: The essential body of knowledge for the study of death, dying, and bereavement* (2nd ed.). New York, NY: Routledge.

Kaufman, Kenneth R. & Kaufman, Nathaniel D. (2006). And then the dog died. *Death Studies, 30*(1), 61–76. doi: 10.1080/07481180500348811

Kavanaugh, Robert D. (2011). Origins and consequences of social pretend play. In Anthony D. Pellegrini (Ed.), *The Oxford handbook of the development of play* (pp. 296–307). New York, NY: Oxford University Press. doi: 10.1093/oxfordhb/9780195393002.013.0022

Kean, Sam. (2014). The 'other' breast cancer genes. *Science, 343*(6178), 1457–1459. doi: 10.1126/science.343.6178.1457

Keating, Nancy L.; Herrinton, Lisa J.; Zaslavsky, Alan M.; Liu, Liyan & Ayanian, John Z. (2006). Variations in hospice use among cancer patients. *Journal of the National Cancer Institute, 98*(15), 1053–1059. doi: 10.1093/jnci/djj298

Keil, Frank C. (2011). Science starts early. *Science, 331*(6020), 1022–1023. doi: 10.1126/science.1195221

Kellehear, Allan. (2008). Dying as a social relationship: A sociological review of debates on the determination of death. *Social Science & Medicine, 66*(7), 1533–1544. doi: 10.1016/j.socscimed.2007.12.023

Keller, Heidi. (2014). Introduction: Understanding relationships. In Hiltrud Otto & Heidi Keller (Eds.), *Different faces of attachment: Cultural variations on a universal human need* (pp. 3–25). New York, NY: Cambridge University Press.

Kelly, Daniel; Faucher, Luc & Machery, Edouard. (2010). Getting rid of racism: Assessing three proposals in light of psychological evidence. *Journal of Social Philosophy, 41*(3), 293–322. doi: 10.1111/j.1467-9833.2010.01495.x

Kelly, John R. (1993). *Activity and aging: Staying involved in later life.* Newbury Park, CA: Sage.

Kemp, Candace L. (2005). Dimensions of grandparent-adult grandchild relationships: From family ties to intergenerational friendships. *Canadian Journal on Aging, 24*(2), 161–177. doi: 10.1353/cja.2005.0066

Kempermann, Gerd. (2012). New neurons for 'survival of the fittest'. *Nature Reviews Neuroscience, 13*(10), 727–736. doi: 10.1038/nrn3319

Kena, Grace; Aud, Susan; Johnson, Frank; Wang, Xiaolei; Zhang, Jijun; Rathbun, Amy, . . . Kristapovich, Paul. (2014, May). *The condition of education 2014.* Washington, DC: U.S. Department of Education, National Center for Education Statistics.

Kena, Grace; Musu-Gillette, Lauren; Robinson, Jennifer; Wang, Xiaolei; Rathbun, Amy; Zhang, Jijun, . . . Dunlop Velez, Erin. (2015). *The condition of education 2015.* Washington, DC: Department of Education, National Center for Education Statistics.

Keown, Louise J. & Palmer, Melanie. (2014). Comparisons between paternal and maternal involvement with sons: Early to middle childhood. *Early Child Development and Care, 184*(1), 99–117. doi: 10.1080/03004430.2013.773510

Kerr, Margaret; Stattin, Håkan & Burk, William J. (2010). A reinterpretation of parental monitoring in longitudinal perspective. *Journal of Research on Adolescence, 20*(1), 39–64. doi: 10.1111/j.1532-7795.2009.00623.x

Kerr, Margaret; Stattin, Håkan & Özdemir, Metin. (2012). Perceived parenting style and adolescent adjustment: Revisiting directions of effects and the role of parental knowledge. *Developmental Psychology, 48*(6), 1540–1553. doi: 10.1037/a0027720

Kesselring, Thomas & Müller, Ulrich. (2011). The concept of egocentrism in the context of Piaget's theory. *New Ideas in Psychology, 29*(3), 327–345. doi: 10.1016/j.newideapsych.2010.03.008

Kessler, Ronald C.; Avenevoli, Shelli; Costello, E. Jane; Georgiades, Katholiki; Green, Jennifer G.; Gruber, Michael J., . . . Merikangas, Kathleen R. (2012). Prevalence, persistence, and sociodemographic correlates of DSM-IV disorders in the National Comorbidity Survey Replication Adolescent Supplement. *Archives of General Psychiatry, 69*(4), 372–380. doi: 10.1001/archgenpsychiatry.2011.160

Kettl, Paul. (2010). One vote for death panels. *JAMA, 303*(13), 1234–1235. doi: 10.1001/jama.2010.376

Khafi, Tamar Y.; Yates, Tuppett M. & Luthar, Suniya S. (2014). Ethnic differences in the developmental significance of parentification. *Family Process, 53*(2), 267–287. doi: 10.1111/famp.12072

Khanna, Sunil K. (2010). *Fetal/fatal knowledge: New reproductive technologies and family-building strategies in India.* Belmont, CA: Wadsworth/Cengage Learning.

Kharsati, Naphisabet & Bhola, Poornima. (2014). Patterns of non-suicidal self-injurious behaviours among college students in India. *International Journal of Social Psychiatry.* doi: 10.1177/0020764014535755

Kiernan, Stephen P. (2010). The transformation of death in America. In Nan Bauer Maglin & Donna Marie Perry (Eds.), *Final acts: Death, dying, and the choices we make* (pp. 163–182). New Brunswick, NJ: Rutgers University Press.

Killen, Melanie & Smetana, Judith G. (Eds.). (2014). *Handbook of moral development* (2nd ed.). New York, NY: Psychology Press.

Kilmer, Ryan P. & Gil-Rivas, Virginia. (2010). Exploring posttraumatic growth in children impacted by Hurricane Katrina: Correlates of the phenomenon and developmental considerations. *Child Development, 81*(4), 1211–1227. doi: 10.1111/j.1467-8624.2010.01463.x

Kim, Esther C. (2009). "Mama's family": Fictive kinship and undocumented immigrant restaurant workers. *Ethnography, 10*(4), 497–513. doi: 10.1177/1466138109347000

Kim, Hojin I. & Johnson, Scott P. (2013). Do young infants prefer an infant-directed face or a happy face? *International Journal of Behavioral Development, 37*(2), 125–130. doi: 10.1177/0165025413475972

Kim, Hyun Sik. (2011). Consequences of parental divorce for child development. *American Sociological Review, 76*(3), 487–511. doi: 10.1177/0003122411407748

Kim, Heejung S. & Sasaki, Joni Y. (2014). Cultural neuroscience: Biology of the mind in cultural contexts. *Annual Review of Psychology, 65,* 487–514. doi: 10.1146/annurev-psych-010213-115040

Kim, Hye Young; DeKruyff, Rosemarie H. & Umetsu, Dale T. (2010). The many paths to asthma: Phenotype shaped by innate and adaptive immunity. *Nature Immunology, 11*(7), 577–584. doi: 10.1038/ni.1892

Kim, Joon Sik. (2011). Excessive crying: Behavioral and emotional regulation disorder in infancy. *Korean Journal of Pediatrics, 54*(6), 229–233. doi: 10.3345/kjp.2011.54.6.229

Kim, Kyungmin; Cheng, Yen-Pi; Zarit, Steven H. & Fingerman, Karen L. (2015). Relationships between adults and parents in Asia. In Sheung-Tak Cheng et al. (Eds.), *Successful Aging* (pp. 101–122). Dordrecht, Netherlands: Springer. doi: 10.1007/978-94-017-9331-5_7

Kim-Spoon, Jungmeen; Longo, Gregory S. & McCullough, Michael E. (2012). Parent-adolescent relationship quality as a moderator for the influences of parents' religiousness on adolescents' religiousness and adjustment. *Journal of Youth and Adolescence, 41*(12), 1576–1587. doi: 10.1007/s10964-012-9796-1

Kimmel, Michael S. (2008). *Guyland: The perilous world where boys become men.* New York, NY: HarperCollins.

King, Pamela E. & Roeser, Robert W. (2009). Religion and spirituality in adolescent development. In Richard M. Lerner & Laurence Steinberg (Eds.), *Handbook of adolescent psychology* (3rd ed., Vol. 1, pp. 435–478). Hoboken, NJ: Wiley.

King, Valarie; Thorsen, Maggie L. & Amato, Paul R. (2014). Factors associated with positive relationships between stepfathers and adolescent stepchildren. *Social Science Research, 47,* 16–29. doi: 10.1016/j.ssresearch.2014.03.010

Kinnunen, Marja-Liisa; Kaprio, Jaakko & Pulkkinen, Lea. (2005). Allostatic load of men and women in early middle age. *Journal of Individual Differences, 26*(1), 20–28. doi: 10.1027/1614-0001.26.1.20

Kirby, Douglas & Laris, B. A. (2009). Effective curriculum-based sex and STD/HIV education programs for adolescents. *Child Development Perspectives, 3*(1), 21–29. doi: 10.1111/j.1750-8606.2008.00071.x

Kithas, Philip A. & Supiano, Mark A. (2015). Hypertension in the geriatric population: A patient-centered approach. *Medical Clinics of North America, 99*(2), 379–389. doi: 10.1016/j.mcna.2014.11.009

Kiuru, Noona; Burk, William J.; Laursen, Brett; Salmela-Aro, Katariina & Nurmi, Jari-Erik. (2010). Pressure to drink but not to smoke: Disentangling selection and socialization in adolescent peer networks and peer groups. *Journal of Adolescence, 33*(6), 801–812. doi: 10.1016/j.adolescence.2010.07.006

Kjerulff, Kristen. (2014, November 18). *Epidural analgesia use during labor and adverse maternal and neonatal outcomes: A large-scale observational study.* Paper presented at the Improving Pregnancy Outcomes: Psychosocial Influences on Birth Outcomes, New Orleans, LA.

Klaczynski, Paul A. & Felmban, Wejdan S. (2014). Heuristics and biases during adolescence: Developmental reversals and individual differences. In Henry Markovits (Ed.), *The developmental psychology of reasoning and decision-making* (pp. 84–111). New York, NY: Psychology Press.

Klahr, Ashlea M.; McGue, Matt; Iacono, William G. & Burt, S. Alexandra. (2011). The association between parent-child conflict and adolescent conduct problems over time: Results from a longitudinal adoption study. *Journal of Abnormal Psychology, 120*(1), 46–56. doi: 10.1037/a0021350

Klaus, Susan F.; Ekerdt, David J. & Gajewski, Byron. (2012). Job satisfaction in birth cohorts of nurses. *Journal of Nursing Management, 20*(4), 461–471. doi: 10.1111/j.1365-2834.2011.01283.x

Kleijer, Bart C.; van Marum, Rob J.; Frijter, Dinnus H. M.; Jansen, Paul A. F.; Ribbe, Miel W.; Egberts, Antoine C. G. & Heerdink, Eibert R. (2014). Variability between nursing homes in prevalence of antipsychotic use in patients with dementia. *International Psychogeriatrics, 26*(3), 363–371. doi: 10.1017/S1041610213002019

Klein, Denise; Mok, Kelvin; Chen, Jen-Kai & Watkins, Kate E. (2014). Age of language learning shapes brain structure: A cortical thickness study of bilingual and monolingual individuals. *Brain and Language, 131,* 20–24. doi: 10.1016/j.bandl.2013.05.014

Klein, Hilary. (1991). Couvade syndrome: Male counterpart to pregnancy. *International Journal of Psychiatry in Medicine, 21*(1), 57–69. doi: 10.2190/FLE0-92JM-C4CN-J83T

Klein, Stanley B. (2012). The two selves: The self of conscious experience and its brain. In Mark R. Leary & June Price Tangney (Eds.), *Handbook of self and identity* (pp. 617–637). New York, NY: Guilford Press.

Klein, Zoe A. & Romeo, Russell D. (2013). Changes in hypothalamic–pituitary–adrenal stress responsiveness before and after puberty in rats. *Hormones and Behavior, 64*(2), 357–363. doi: 10.1016/j.yhbeh.2013.01.012

Kliegel, Matthias; Jäger, Theodor & Phillips, Louise H. (2008). Adult age differences in event-based prospective memory: A meta-analysis on the role of focal versus nonfocal cues. *Psychology and Aging, 23*(1), 203–208. doi: 10.1037/0882-7974.23.1.203

Klinger, Laura G.; Dawson, Geraldine; Burner, Karen & Crisler, Megan. (2014). Autism spectrum disorder. In Eric J. Mash & Russell A. Barkley (Eds.), *Child psychopathology* (3rd ed., pp. 531–572). New York, NY: Guilford Press.

Knight, Rona. (2014). A hundred years of latency: From Freudian psychosexual theory to dynamic systems nonlinear development in middle childhood. *Journal of the American Psychoanalytic Association, 62*(2), 203–235. doi: 10.1177/0003065114531044

Knott, Craig S.; Coombs, Ngaire; Stamatakis, Emmanuel & Biddulph, Jane P. (2015). All cause mortality and the case for age specific alcohol consumption guidelines: Pooled analyses of up to 10 population based cohorts. *BMJ, 350,* h384. doi: 10.1136/bmj.h384

Kochanek, Kenneth D.; Xu, Jiaquan; Murphy, Sherry L.; Miniño, Arialdi M. & Kung, Hsiang-Ching. (2011). *Deaths: Preliminary data for 2009. National Vital Statistics Reports 59*(4). Hyattsville, MD: National Center for Health Statistics.

Kohlberg, Lawrence. (1963). The development of children's orientations toward a moral order: I. Sequence in the development of moral thought. *Vita Humana*, *6*(1/2), 11–33. doi: 10.1159/000269667

Kohlberg, Lawrence; Levine, Charles & Hewer, Alexandra. (1983). *Moral stages: A current formulation and a response to critics.* New York, NY: Karger.

Kolb, Bryan & Whishaw, Ian Q. (2013). *An introduction to brain and behavior* (4th ed.). New York, NY: Worth.

Koller, Daniela & Bynum, Julie P. W. (2014). Dementia in the USA: state variation in prevalence. *Journal of Public Health.* doi: 10.1093/pubmed/fdu080

Kolowich, Steve. (2013). Why some colleges are saying no to MOOC deals, at least for now. *Chronicle of Higher Education.*

Koltko-Rivera, Mark E. (2006). Rediscovering the later version of Maslow's hierarchy of needs: Self-transcendence and opportunities for theory, research, and unification. *Review of General Psychology*, *10*(4), 302–317. doi: 10.1037/1089-2680 .10.4.302

Komp, Kathrin; van Tilburg, Theo & van Groenou, Marjolein Broese. (2010). Paid work between age 60 and 70 years in Europe: A matter of socio-economic status? *International Journal of Ageing and Later Life*, *5*(1), 45–75. doi: 10.3384 /ijal.1652-8670.105145

Konner, Melvin. (2007). Evolutionary foundations of cultural psychology. In Shinobu Kitayama & Dov Cohen (Eds.), *Handbook of cultural psychology* (pp. 77–105). New York, NY: Guilford Press.

Konner, Melvin. (2010). *The evolution of childhood: Relationships, emotion, mind.* Cambridge, MA: Harvard University Press.

Konno, Rie; Kang, Hee Sun & Makimoto, Kiyoko. (2014). A best-evidence review of intervention studies for minimizing resistance-to-care behaviours for older adults with dementia in nursing homes. *Journal of Advanced Nursing*, *70*(10), 2167–2180. doi: 10.1111/jan.12432

Kooij, Dorien T. A. M.; Annet, H. D. E. Lange; Jansen, Paul G. W.; Kanfer, Ruth & Dikkers, Josje S. E. (2011). Age and work-related motives: Results of a meta-analysis. *Journal of Organizational Behavior*, *32*(2), 197–225. doi: 10.1002/job.665

Kopp, Claire B. (2011). Development in the early years: Socialization, motor development, and consciousness. *Annual Review of Psychology*, *62*, 165–187. doi: 10.1146/annurev. psych.121208.131625

Korhonen, Tellervo; Latvala, Antti; Dick, Danielle M.; Pulkkinen, Lea; Rose, Richard J.; Kaprio, Jaakko & Huizink, Anja C. (2012). Genetic and environmental influences underlying externalizing behaviors, cigarette smoking and illicit drug use across adolescence. *Behavior Genetics*, *42*(4), 614–625. doi: 10.1007/s10519-012-9528-z

Koster-Hale, Jorie & Saxe, Rebecca. (2013). Functional neuroimaging of theory of mind. In Simon Baron-Cohen et al. (Eds.), *Understanding other minds: Perspectives from developmental social neuroscience* (3rd ed., pp. 132–163). New York, NY: Oxford University Press.

Kowalski, Robin M.; Giumetti, Gary W.; Schroeder, Amber N. & Lattanner, Micah R. (2014). Bullying in the digital age: A critical review and meta-analysis of cyberbullying research among youth. *Psychological Bulletin*, *140*(4), 1073–1137. doi: 10.1037/a0035618

Kozhimannil, Katy B.; Law, Michael R. & Virnig, Beth A. (2013). Cesarean delivery rates vary tenfold among US hospitals; Reducing variation may address quality and cost issues. *Health Affairs*, *32*(3), 527–535. doi: 10.1377/hlthaff.2012.1030

Kozo, Justine; Sallis, James F.; Conway, Terry L.; Kerr, Jacqueline; Cain, Kelli; Saelens, Brian E., . . . Owen, Neville. (2012). Sedentary behaviors of adults in relation to neighborhood walkability and income. *Health Psychology*, *31*(6), 704–713. doi: 10.1037/a0027874

Kreager, Derek; Felson, Richard B.; Warner, Cody & Wenger, Marin R. (2013). Women's education, marital violence, and divorce: A social exchange perspective. *Journal of Marriage and Family*, *75*(3), 565–581. doi: 10.1111/jomf.12018

Krebs, John R. (2009). The gourmet ape: Evolution and human food preferences. *American Journal of Clinical Nutrition*, *90*(3), 707S–711S. doi: 10.3945/ajcn.2009.27462B

Kremen, William S.; Moore, Caitlin S.; Franz, Carol E.; Panizzon, Matthew S. & Lyons, Michael J. (2014). Cognition in middle adulthood. In Deborah Finkel & Chandra A. Reynolds (Eds.), *Behavior genetics of cognition across the lifespan: Advances in behavior genetics* (Vol. 1, pp. 105–134). New York, NY: Springer. doi: 10.1007/978-1-4614-7447-0_4

Kremer, Peter; Elshaug, Christine; Leslie, Eva; Toumbourou, John W.; Patton, George C. & Williams, Joanne. (2014). Physical activity, leisure-time screen use and depression among children and young adolescents. *Journal of Science and Medicine in Sport*, *17*(2), 183–187. doi: 10.1016/j.jsams.2013.03.012

Kretch, Kari S. & Adolph, Karen E. (2013). No bridge too high: Infants decide whether to cross based on the probability of falling not the severity of the potential fall. *Developmental Science*, *16*(3), 336–351. doi: 10.1111/desc.12045

Krisberg, Kim. (2014). Public health messaging: How it is said can influence behaviors: Beyond the facts. *The Nation's Health*, *44*(6), 1–20.

Kroger, Jane. (2007). *Identity development: Adolescence through adulthood* (2nd ed.). Thousand Oaks, CA: Sage.

Kroger, Jane & Marcia, James E. (2011). The identity statuses: Origins, meanings, and interpretations. In Seth J. Schwartz et al. (Eds.), *Handbook of identity theory and research* (pp. 31–53). New York, NY: Springer. doi: 10.1007/978-1-4419-7988-9_2

Kroger, Jane; Martinussen, Monica & Marcia, James E. (2010). Identity status change during adolescence and young adulthood: A meta-analysis. *Journal of Adolescence*, *33*(5), 683–698. doi: 10.1016/j.adolescence.2009.11.002

Kübler-Ross, Elisabeth. (1969). *On death and dying.* New York, NY: Macmillan.

Kübler-Ross, Elisabeth. (1975). *Death: The final stage of growth.* Englewood Cliffs, NJ: Prentice-Hall.

Kübler-Ross, Elisabeth & Kessler, David. (2014). *On grief and grieving: Finding the meaning of grief through the five stages of loss.* New York, NY: Scribner.

Kuehn, Bridget M. (2011). Scientists find promising therapies for fragile X and Down syndromes. *JAMA*, *305*(4), 344–346. doi: 10.1001/jama.2010.1960

Kuhlmann, Inga; Minihane, Anne; Huebbe, Patricia; Nebel, Almut & Rimbach, Gerald. (2010). Apolipoprotein E genotype and hepatitis C, HIV and herpes simplex disease risk: A literature review. *Lipids in Health and Disease, 9*(1), 8. doi: 10.1186/1476-511X-9-8

Kuhn, Deanna. (2013). Reasoning. In Philip D. Zelazo (Ed.), *The Oxford handbook of developmental psychology* (Vol. 1, pp. 744–764). New York, NY: Oxford University Press. doi: 10.1093/oxfordhb/9780199958450.013.0026

Kumar, Santosh; Calvo, Rocio; Avendano, Mauricio; Sivaramakrishnan, Kavita & Berkman, Lisa F. (2012). Social support, volunteering and health around the world: Cross-national evidence from 139 countries. *Social Science & Medicine, 74*(5), 696–706. doi: 10.1016/j.socscimed.2011.11.017

Kundu, Tapas K. (Ed.). (2013). *Epigenetics: Development and disease.* New York, NY: Springer. doi: 10.1007/978-94-007-4525-4

Kuperberg, Arielle. (2012). Reassessing differences in work and income in cohabitation and marriage. *Journal of Marriage and Family, 74*(4), 688–707. doi: 10.1111/j.1741-3737.2012.00993.x

Kuperberg, Arielle. (2014). Age at coresidence, premarital cohabitation, and marriage dissolution: 1985–2009. *Journal of Marriage and Family, 76*(2), 352–369. doi: 10.1111/jomf.12092

Kutob, Randa M.; Senf, Janet H.; Crago, Marjorie & Shisslak, Catherine M. (2010). Concurrent and longitudinal predictors of self-esteem in elementary and middle school girls. *Journal of School Health, 80*(5), 240–248. doi: 10.1111/j.1746-1561.2010.00496.x

Kuwahara, Keisuke; Kochi, Takeshi; Nanri, Akiko; Tsuruoka, Hiroko; Kurotani, Kayo; Pham, Ngoc Minh, . . . Mizoue, Tetsuya. (2014). Flushing response modifies the association of alcohol consumption with markers of glucose metabolism in Japanese men and women. *Alcoholism: Clinical and Experimental Research, 38*(4), 1042–1048. doi: 10.1111/acer.12323

Kuzucu, Ya ar; Bontempo, Daniel E.; Hofer, Scott M.; Stallings, Michael C. & Piccinin, Andrea M. (2014). Developmental change and time-specific variation in global and specific aspects of self-concept in adolescence and association with depressive symptoms. *The Journal of Early Adolescence, 34*(5), 638–666. doi: 10.1177/0272431613507498

Kypri, Kypros; Davie, Gabrielle; McElduff, Patrick; Connor, Jennie & Langley, John. (2014). Effects of lowering the minimum alcohol purchasing age on weekend assaults resulting in hospitalization in New Zealand. *American Journal of Public Health, 104*(8), 1396–1401. doi: 10.2105/AJPH.2014.301889

Kypri, Kypros; Voas, Robert B.; Langley, John D.; Stephenson, Shaun C. R.; Begg, Dorothy J.; Tippetts, A. Scott & Davie, Gabrielle S. (2006). Minimum purchasing age for alcohol and traffic crash injuries among 15- to 19-year-olds in New Zealand. *American Journal of Public Health, 96*(1), 126–131. doi: 10.2105/AJPH.2005.073122

Kyriakidou, Marilena; Blades, Mark & Carroll, Dan. (2014). Inconsistent findings for the eyes closed effect in children: The implications for interviewing child witnesses. *Frontiers in Psychology, 5*, 488. doi: 10.3389/fpsyg.2014.00448

Lachman, Margie E.; Neupert, Shevaun D. & Agrigoro-aei, Stefan. (2011). The relevance of control beliefs for health and aging. In K. Warner Schaie & Sherry L. Willis (Eds.), *Handbook of the psychology of aging* (7th ed., pp. 175–190). San Diego, CA: Academic Press.

Lachman, Margie E.; Rosnick, Christopher B. & Röcke, Christina. (2009). The rise and fall of control beliefs and life satisfaction in adulthood: Trajectories of stability and change over ten years. In Hayden B. Bosworth & Christopher Hertzog (Eds.), *Aging and cognition: Research methodologies and empirical advances* (pp. 143–160). Washington, DC: American Psychological Association. doi: 10.1037/11882-007

LaCour, Michael J. & Green, Donald P. (2014). When contact changes minds: An experiment on transmission of support for gay equality. *Science, 346*(6215), 1366–1369. doi: 10.1126/science.1256151

LaFontana, Kathryn M. & Cillessen, Antonius H. N. (2010). Developmental changes in the priority of perceived status in childhood and adolescence. *Social Development, 19*(1), 130–147. doi: 10.1111/j.1467-9507.2008.00522.x

Lagattuta, Kristin H. (2014). Linking past, present, and future: Children's ability to connect mental states and emotions across time. *Child Development Perspectives, 8*(2), 90–95. doi: 10.1111/cdep.12065

Lai, Stephanie A.; Benjamin, Rebekah G.; Schwanenflugel, Paula J. & Kuhn, Melanie R. (2014). The longitudinal relationship between reading fluency and reading comprehension skills in second-grade children. *Reading & Writing Quarterly: Overcoming Learning Difficulties, 30*(2), 116–138. doi: 10.1080/10573569.2013.789785

Laird, Robert D.; Marrero, Matthew D.; Melching, Jessica A. & Kuhn, Emily S. (2013). Information management strategies in early adolescence: Developmental change in use and transactional associations with psychological adjustment. *Developmental Psychology, 49*(5), 928–937. doi: 10.1037/a0028845

Lalande, Kathleen M. & Bonanno, George A. (2006). Culture and continuing bonds: A prospective comparison of bereavement in the United States and the People's Republic of China. *Death Studies, 30*(4), 303–324. doi: 10.1080/07481180500544708

Lam, Chun Bun; McHale, Susan M. & Crouter, Ann C. (2014). Time with peers from middle childhood to late adolescence: Developmental course and adjustment correlates. *Child Development, 85*(4), 1677–1693. doi: 10.1111/cdev.12235

Lam, Thuy; Williams, Paige L.; Lee, Mary M.; Korrick, Susan A.; Birnbaum, Linda S.; Burns, Jane S., . . . Hauser, Russ. (2014). Prepubertal organochlorine pesticide concentrations and age of pubertal onset among Russian boys. *Environment International, 73*, 135–142. doi: 10.1016/j.envint.2014.06.020

Lamb, Michael E. (Ed.). (2010). *The role of the father in child development* (5th ed.). Hoboken, NJ: Wiley.

Lamb, Michael E. (2014). How I got started: Drawn into the life of crime: Learning from, by, and for child victims and witnesses. *Applied Cognitive Psychology, 28*(4), 607–611. doi: 10.1002/acp.3031

Lamont, Ruth A.; Swift, Hannah J. & Abrams, Dominic. (2015). A review and meta-analysis of age-based stereotype threat: Negative stereotypes, not facts, do the damage. *Psychology and Aging, 30*(1), 180–193. doi: 10.1037/a0038586

Landgren, Kajsa; Lundqvist, Anita & Hallström, Inger. (2012). Remembering the chaos—But life went on and the wound healed: A four year follow up with parents having had a baby with infantile colic. *The Open Nursing Journal, 6,* 53–61. doi: 10.2174/1874434601206010053

Lando, Amy M. & Lo, Serena C. (2014). Consumer understanding of the benefits and risks of fish consumption during pregnancy. *American Journal of Lifestyle Medicine, 8*(2), 88–92. doi: 10.1177/1559827613514704

Lane, Jonathan D. & Harris, Paul L. (2014). Confronting, representing, and believing counterintuitive concepts: Navigating the natural and the supernatural. *Perspectives on Psychological Science, 9*(2), 144–160. doi: 10.1177/1745691613518078

Lane, Rachel F.; Shineman, Diana W. & Fillit, Howard M. (2011). Beyond amyloid: A diverse portfolio of novel drug discovery programs for Alzheimer's disease and related dementias. *Alzheimer's Research & Therapy, 3*(36), 36. doi: 10.1186/alzrt99

Lang, Frieder R.; Rohr, Margund K. & Williger, Bettina. (2011). Modeling success in life-span psychology: The principles of selection, optimization, and compensation. In Karen L. Fingerman et al. (Eds.), *Handbook of lifespan development* (pp. 57–86). New York, NY: Springer.

Langa, Kenneth M. (2015). Is the risk of Alzheimer's disease and dementia declining? *Alzheimer's Research & Therapy, 7*(1), 34. doi: 10.1186/s13195-015-0118-1

Lange, Rense; Houran, James & Li, Song. (2015). Dyadic relationship values in Chinese online daters: Love American style? *Sexuality & Culture, 19*(1), 190–215. doi: 10.1007/s12119-014-9255-0

Långström, Niklas; Rahman, Qazi; Carlström, Eva & Lichtenstein, Paul. (2010). Genetic and environmental effects on same-sex sexual behavior: A population study of twins in Sweden. *Archives of Sexual Behavior, 39*(1), 75–80. doi: 10.1007/s10508-008-9386-1

Lara-Cinisomo, Sandraluz; Fuligni, Allison Sidle & Karoly, Lynn A. (2011). Preparing preschoolers for kindergarten. In DeAnna M. Laverick & Mary Renck Jalongo (Eds.), *Transitions to early care and education* (Vol. 4, pp. 93–105). New York, NY: Springer. doi: 10.1007/978-94-007-0573-9_9

Laraway, Kelly A.; Birch, Leann L.; Shaffer, Michele L. & Paul, Ian M. (2010). Parent perception of healthy infant and toddler growth. *Clinical Pediatrics, 49*(4), 343–349. doi: 10.1177/0009922809343717

Larose, Joanie; Boulay, Pierre; Sigal, Ronald J.; Wright, Heather E. & Kenny, Glen P. (2013). Age-related decrements in heat dissipation during physical activity occur as early as the age of 40. *PLoS ONE, 8*(12), e83148. doi: 10.1371/journal.pone.0083148

Larzelere, Robert; Cox, Ronald & Smith, Gail. (2010). Do nonphysical punishments reduce antisocial behavior more than spanking? A comparison using the strongest previous causal evidence against spanking. *BMC Pediatrics, 10*(10). doi: 10.1186/1471-2431-10-10

Larzelere, Robert E. & Cox, Ronald B. (2013). Making valid causal inferences about corrective actions by parents from longitudinal data. *Journal of Family Theory & Review, 5*(4), 282–299. doi: 10.1111/jftr.12020

Lattanzi-Licht, Marcia. (2013). Religion, spirituality, and dying. In David K. Meagher & David E. Balk (Eds.), *Handbook of thanatology: The essential body of knowledge for the study of death, dying, and bereavement* (2nd ed., pp. 9–16). New York, NY: Routledge.

Lau, Carissa; Ambalavanan, Namasivayam; Chakraborty, Hrishikesh; Wingate, Martha S. & Carlo, Waldemar A. (2013). Extremely low birth weight and infant mortality rates in the United States. *Pediatrics, 131*(5), 855–860. doi: 10.1542/peds.2012-2471

Laurent, Heidemarie K. (2014). Clarifying the contours of emotion regulation: Insights from parent–child stress research. *Child Development Perspectives, 8*(1), 30–35. doi: 10.1111/cdep.12058

Laurino, Mercy Y.; Bennett, Robin L.; Saraiya, Devki S.; Baumeister, Lisa; Doyle, Debra L.; Leppig, Kathleen, . . . Raskind, Wendy H. (2005). Genetic evaluation and counseling of couples with recurrent miscarriage: Recommendations of the National Society of Genetic Counselors. *Journal of Genetic Counseling, 14*(3), 165–181. doi: 10.1007/s10897-005-3241-5

Laursen, Brett & Collins, W. Andrew. (2009). Parent-child relationships during adolescence. In Richard M. Lerner & Laurence Steinberg (Eds.), *Handbook of adolescent psychology* (3rd ed., Vol. 2, pp. 3–42). Hoboken, NJ: Wiley.

Le Grange, Daniel & Lock, James (Eds.). (2011). *Eating disorders in children and adolescents: A clinical handbook.* New York, NY: Guilford Press.

Leach , Penelope. (2011). The EYFS and the real foundations of children's early years. In Richard House (Ed.), *Too much, too soon?: Early learning and the erosion of childhood.* Stroud, UK: Hawthorn.

Leaning, Jennifer & Guha-Sapir, Debarati. (2013). Natural disasters, armed conflict, and public health. *New England Journal of Medicine, 369*(19), 1836–1842. doi: 10.1056/NEJMra1109877

Leaper, Campbell. (2013). Gender development during childhood. In Philip D. Zelazo (Ed.), *The Oxford handbook of developmental psychology* (Vol. 2, pp. 326–377). New York, NY: Oxford University Press. doi: 10.1093/oxfordhb/9780199958474.013.0014

Lee, Dohoon; Brooks-Gunn, Jeanne; McLanahan, Sara S.; Notterman, Daniel & Garfinkel, Irwin. (2013). The Great Recession, genetic sensitivity, and maternal harsh parenting. *Proceedings of the National Academy of Sciences, 110*(34), 13780–13784. doi: 10.1073/pnas.1312398110

Lee, David M.; Nazroo, James; O'Connor, Daryl B.; Blake, Margaret & Pendleton, Neil. (2015). Sexual health and well-being among older men and women in England: Findings from the English longitudinal study of ageing. *Archives of Sexual Behavior.* doi: 10.1007/s10508-014-0465-1

Lee, Francis S.; Heimer, Hakon; Giedd, Jay N.; Lein, Edward S.; Šestan, Nenad; Weinberger, Daniel R. & Casey, B. J. (2014). Adolescent mental health: Opportunity and obligation. *Science, 346*(6209), 547–549. doi: 10.1126/science.1260497

Lee, Jihyun & Porretta, David L. (2013). Enhancing the motor skills of children with autism spectrum disorders: A pool-based approach. *JOPERD: The Journal of Physical Education, Recreation & Dance, 84*(1), 41–45. doi: 10.1080/07303084.2013.746154

Lee, RaeHyuck; Zhai, Fuhua; Brooks-Gunn, Jeanne; Han, Wen-Jui & Waldfogel, Jane. (2014). Head Start participation and school readiness: Evidence from the early childhood longitudinal study–birth cohort. *Developmental Psychology, 50*(1), 202–215. doi: 10.1037/a0032280

Lee, Shawna J. & Altschul, Inna. (2015). Spanking of young children: Do immigrant and U.S.-born Hispanic parents differ? *Journal of Interpersonal Violence, 30*(3), 475–498. doi: 10.1177/0886260514535098

Lee, Shawna J.; Altschul, Inna & Gershoff, Elizabeth T. (2015). Wait until your father gets home? Mother's and fathers' spanking and development of child aggression. *Children and Youth Services Review, 52*, 158–166. doi: 10.1016/j.childyouth.2014.11.006

Lee, Star W.; Clemenson, Gregory D. & Gage, Fred H. (2012). New neurons in an aged brain. *Behavioural Brain Research, 227*(2), 497–507. doi: 10.1016/j.bbr.2011.10.009

Lee, Yuan-Hsuan; Ko, Chih-Hung & Chou, Chien. (2015). Re-visiting Internet addiction among Taiwanese students: A cross-sectional comparison of students' expectations, online gaming, and online social interaction. *Journal of Abnormal Child Psychology, 43*(3), 589–599. doi: 10.1007/s10802-014-9915-4

Lee, Youn Ok; Hebert, Christine J.; Nonnemaker, James M. & Kim, Annice E. (2015). Youth tobacco product use in the United States. *Pediatrics, 135*(3), 409–415. doi: 10.1542/peds.2014-3202

Lehmann, Regula; Denissen, Jaap J. A.; Allemand, Mathias & Penke, Lars. (2013). Age and gender differences in motivational manifestations of the Big Five from age 16 to 60. *Developmental Psychology, 49*(2), 365–383. doi: 10.1037/a0028277

Leiter, Valerie & Herman, Sarah. (2015). Guinea pig kids: Myths or modern Tuskegees? *Sociological Spectrum, 35*(1), 26–45. doi: 10.1080/02732173.2014.978429

Leman, Patrick J. & Björnberg, Marina. (2010). Conversation, development, and gender: A study of changes in children's concepts of punishment. *Child Development, 81*(3), 958–971. doi: 10.1111/j.1467-8624.2010.01445.x

Lemieux, André. (2012). Post-formal thought in gerontagogy or beyond Piage. *Journal of Behavioral and Brain Science, 2*(3), 399–406. doi: 10.4236/jbbs.2012.23046

León-Cava, Natalia; Lutter, Chessa; Ross, Jay & Martin, Luann. (2002). *Quantifying the benefits of breastfeeding: A summary of the evidence*. Washington, DC: Pan American Health Organization.

Leonard, Hayley C. & Hill, Elisabeth L. (2014). Review: The impact of motor development on typical and atypical social cognition and language: A systematic review. *Child and Adolescent Mental Health, 19*(3), 163–170. doi: 10.1111/camh.12055

Leopold, Thomas & Skopek, Jan. (2015). The delay of grandparenthood: A cohort comparison in East and West Germany. *Journal of Marriage and Family, 77*(2), 441–460. doi: 10.1111/jomf.12169

Lerner, Claire & Dombro, Amy Laura. (2004). Finding your fit: Some temperament tips for parents. *Zero to Three, 24*(4), 42–45.

Leslie, Leigh A.; Smith, Jocelyn R.; Hrapczynski, Katie M. & Riley, Debbie. (2013). Racial socialization in transracial adoptive families: Does it help adolescents deal with discriminative stress? *Family Relations, 62*(1), 72–81. doi: 10.1111/j.1741-3729.2012.00744.x

Leslie, Mitch. (2012). Gut microbes keep rare immune cells in line. *Science, 335*(6075), 1428. doi: 10.1126/science.335.6075.1428

Lester, Patricia; Leskin, Gregory; Woodward, Kirsten; Saltzman, William; Nash, William; Mogil, Catherine, . . . Beardslee, William. (2011). Wartime deployment and military children: Applying prevention science to enhance family resilience. In Shelley MacDermid Wadsworth & David Riggs (Eds.), *Risk and resilience in U.S. military families* (pp. 149–173). New York, NY: Springer. doi: 10.1007/978-1-4419-7064-0_8

Leuthner, Steven R. (2014). Borderline viability: Controversies in caring for the extremely premature infant. *Clinics in Perinatology, 41*(4), 799–814. doi: 10.1016/j.clp.2014.08.005

Levy, Becca R.; Slade, Martin D.; Murphy, Terrence E. & Gill, Thomas M. (2012). Association between positive age stereotypes and recovery from disability in older persons. *JAMA, 308*(19), 1972–1973. doi: 10.1001/jama.2012.14541

Levy, Daniel & Brink, Susan. (2005). *A change of heart: How the Framingham Heart Study helped unravel the mysteries of cardiovascular disease*. New York, NY: Knopf.

Lewandowski, Lawrence J. & Lovett, Benjamin J. (2014). Learning disabilities. In Eric J. Mash & Russell A. Barkley (Eds.), *Child psychopathology* (3rd ed., pp. 625–669). New York, NY: Guilford Press.

Lewin, Kurt. (1943). Psychology and the process of group living. *Journal of Social Psychology, 17*(1), 113–131. doi: 10.1080/00224545.1943.9712269

Lewis, John D.; Theilmann, Rebecca J.; Townsend, Jeanne & Evans, Alan C. (2013). Network efficiency in autism spectrum disorder and its relation to brain overgrowth. *Frontiers in Human Neuroscience, 7*, 845. doi: 10.3389/fnhum.2013.00845

Lewis, Michael. (2010). The emergence of human emotions. In Michael Lewis et al. (Eds.), *Handbook of emotions* (3rd ed.). New York, NY: Guilford Press.

Lewis, Michael & Brooks, Jeanne. (1978). Self-knowledge and emotional development. In Michael Lewis & L. A. Rosenblum (Eds.), *Genesis of behavior* (Vol. 1, pp. 205–226). New York, NY: Plenum Press.

Lewis, Michael & Kestler, Lisa (Eds.). (2012). *Gender differences in prenatal substance exposure*. Washington, DC: American Psychological Association.

Lewis, Marc D. (2013). The development of emotional regulation: Integrating normative and individual differences through developmental neuroscience. In Philip D. Zelazo (Ed.), *The Oxford handbook of developmental psychology* (Vol. 2, pp. 81–97). New York, NY: Oxford University Press. doi: 10.1093/oxfordhb/9780199958474.013.0004

Leyva, Diana; Weiland, Christina; Barata, M.; Yoshikawa, Hirokazu; Snow, Catherine; Treviño, Ernesto & Rolla, Andrea. (2015). Teacher—child interactions in Chile and their associations with prekindergarten outcomes. *Child Development*, *86*(3), 781–799. doi: 10.1111/cdev.12342

Li, Jin; Fung, Heidi; Bakeman, Roger; Rae, Katharine & Wei, Wanchun. (2014). How European American and Taiwanese mothers talk to their children about learning. *Child Development*, *85*(3), 1206–1221. doi: 10.1111/cdev.12172

Li, Qing & Keith, Louis G. (2011). The differential association between education and infant mortality by nativity status of Chinese American mothers: A life-course perspective. *American Journal of Public Health*, *101*(5), 899-908. doi: 10.2105/ajph.2009.186916

Li, Ting & Zhang, Yanlong. (2015). Social network types and the health of older adults: Exploring reciprocal associations. *Social Science & Medicine*, *130*(2), 59–68. doi: 10.1016/j.socscimed.2015.02.007

Li, Weilin; Farkas, George; Duncan, Greg J.; Burchinal, Margaret R. & Vandell, Deborah Lowe. (2013). Timing of high-quality child care and cognitive, language, and preacademic development. *Developmental Psychology*, *49*(8), 1440–1451. doi: 10.1037/a0030613

Li, Yibing & Lerner, Richard M. (2011). Trajectories of school engagement during adolescence: Implications for grades, depression, delinquency, and substance use. *Developmental Psychology*, *47*(1), 233–247. doi: 10.1037/a0021307

Libertus, Klaus & Needham, Amy. (2010). Teach to reach: The effects of active vs. passive reaching experiences on action and perception. *Vision Research*, *50*(24), 2750–2757. doi: 10.1016/j.visres.2010.09.001

Lillard, Angeline S. (2013). Playful learning and Montessori education. *American Journal of Play*, *5*(2), 157–186.

Lillard, Angeline S. & Else-Quest, Nicole. (2006). Evaluating Montessori education. *Science*, *313*(5795), 1893–1894. doi: 10.1126/science.1132362

Lillard, Angeline S. & Kavanaugh, Robert D. (2014). The contribution of symbolic skills to the development of an explicit theory of mind. *Child Development*, *85*(4), 1535–1551. doi: 10.1111/cdev.12227

Lillard, Angeline S.; Lerner, Matthew D.; Hopkins, Emily J.; Dore, Rebecca A.; Smith, Eric D. & Palmquist, Carolyn M. (2013). The impact of pretend play on children's development: A review of the evidence. *Psychological Bulletin*, *139*(1), 1–34. doi: 10.1037/a0029321

Lillevoll, Kjersti R.; Kroger, Jane & Martinussen, Monica. (2013). Identity status and locus of control: A meta-analysis. *Identity: An International Journal of Theory and Research*, *13*(3), 253–265. doi: 10.1080/15283488.2013.799471

Lim, Chaeyoon & Putnam, Robert D. (2010). Religion, social networks, and life satisfaction. *American Sociological Review*, *75*(6), 914–933. doi: 10.1177/0003122410386686

Limber, Susan P. (2011). Development, evaluation, and future directions of the Olweus Bullying Prevention Program. *Journal of School Violence*, *10*(1), 71–87. doi: 10.1080/15388220.2010.519375

Lin, Frank R.; Yaffe, Kristine; Xia, Jin; Xue, Qian-Li; Harris, Tamara B.; Purchase-Helzner, Elizabeth, . . . Simonsick, Eleanor M. (2013). Hearing loss and cognitive decline in older adults. *JAMA Internal Medicine*, *173*(4), 293–299. doi: 10.1001/jamainternmed.2013.1868

Lin, I-Fen; Fee, Holly R. & Wu, Hsueh-Sheng. (2012). Negative and positive caregiving experiences: A closer look at the intersection of gender and relationship. *Family Relations*, *61*(2), 343–358. doi: 10.1111/j.1741-3729.2011.00692.x

Lin, Jue; Epel, Elissa & Blackburn, Elizabeth. (2012). Telomeres and lifestyle factors: Roles in cellular aging. *Mutation Research/Fundamental and Molecular Mechanisms of Mutagenesis*, *730*(1/2), 85–89. doi: 10.1016/j.mrfmmm.2011.08.003

Lincove, Jane A. & Painter, Gary. (2006). Does the age that children start kindergarten matter? Evidence of long-term educational and social outcomes. *Educational Evaluation and Policy Analysis*, *28*(2), 153–179 doi: 10.3102/01623737028002153

Lindau, Stacy T. & Gavrilova, Natalia. (2010). Sex, health, and years of sexually active life gained due to good health: Evidence from two US population based cross sectional surveys of ageing. *BMJ*, *340*(7746), c810. doi: 10.1136/bmj.c810

Liu, Dong & Xin, Ziqiang. (2014). Birth cohort and age changes in the self-esteem of Chinese adolescents: A cross-temporal meta-analysis, 1996–2009. *Journal of Research on Adolescence*. doi: 10.1111/jora.12134

Liu, Hui; Wang, Qiu; Keesler, Venessa & Schneider, Barbara. (2011). Non—standard work schedules, work—family conflict and parental well-being: A comparison of married and cohabiting unions. *Social Science Research*, *40*(2), 473–484. doi: 10.1016/j.ssresearch.2010.10.008

Livas-Dlott, Alejandra; Fuller, Bruce; Stein, Gabriela L.; Bridges, Margaret; Mangual Figueroa, Ariana & Mireles, Laurie. (2010). Commands, competence, and *cariño*: Maternal socialization practices in Mexican American families. *Developmental Psychology*, *46*(3), 566–578. doi: 10.1037/a0018016

Livingston, Gretchen. (2014). *Four-in-ten couples are saying 'I do,' again*. Washington, DC: Pew Research Center.

Lloyd-Fox, Sarah; Blasi, Anna; Volein, Agnes; Everdell, Nick; Elwell, Claire E. & Johnson, Mark H. (2009). Social perception in infancy: A near infrared spectroscopy study. *Child Development*, *80*(4), 986–999. doi: 10.1111/j.1467-8624.2009.01312.x

Lo, Y. M. Dennis. (2015). Noninvasive prenatal diagnosis: From dream to reality. *Clinical Chemistry*, *61*(1), 32–37. doi: 10.1373/clinchem.2014.223024

Lobstein, Tim & Dibb, Sue. (2005). Evidence of a possible link between obesogenic food advertising and child overweight. *Obesity Reviews*, *6*(3), 203–208. doi: 10.1111/j.1467-789X.2005.00191.x

Lock, Margaret. (2013). The lure of the epigenome. *The Lancet*, *381*(9881), 1896–1897. doi: 10.1016/S0140-6736(13)61149-6

Löckenhoff, Corinna E.; De Fruyt, Filip; Terracciano, Antonio; McCrae, Robert R.; De Bolle, Marleen; Costa, Paul T., . . . Yik, Michelle. (2009). Perceptions of aging across 26 cultures and their culture-level associates. *Psychology and Aging*, *24*(4), 941–954. doi: 10.1037/a0016901

Lodge, Amy C. & Umberson, Debra. (2012). All shook up: Sexuality of mid- to later life married couples. *Journal of Marriage and Family*, 74(3), 428–443. doi: 10.1111/j.1741-3737.2012.00969.x

Loeber, Rolf & Burke, Jeffrey D. (2011). Developmental pathways in juvenile externalizing and internalizing problems. *Journal of Research on Adolescence*, 21(1), 34–46. doi: 10.1111/j.1532-7795.2010.00713.x

Loeber, Rolf; Capaldi, Deborah M. & Costello, Elizabeth. (2013). Gender and the development of aggression, disruptive behavior, and delinquency from childhood to early adulthood. In Patrick H. Tolan & Bennett L. Leventh (Eds.), *Disruptive behavior disorders* (pp. 137–160). New York, NY: Springer. doi: 10.1007/978-1-4614-7557-6_6

Lombardi, Nathaniel J.; Buchanan, Jeffrey A.; Afflerbach, Shelby; Campana, Kristie & Sattler, Adam. (2014). Is elderspeak appropriate? A survey of certified nursing assistants. *Journal of Gerontological Nursing*, 40(11), 44–52. doi: 10.3928/00989134-20140407-02

Lombardo, Michael V.; Ashwin, Emma; Auyeung, Bonnie; Chakrabarti, Bhismadev; Taylor, Kevin; Hackett, Gerald, . . . Baron-Cohen, Simon. (2012). Fetal testosterone influences sexually dimorphic gray matter in the human brain. *The Journal of Neuroscience*, 32(2), 674–680. doi: 10.1523/JNEUROSCI.4389-11.2012

Lopez-Hartmann, Maja; Wens, Johan; Verhoeven, Veronique & Remmen, Roy. (2012). The effect of caregiver support interventions for informal caregivers of community-dwelling frail elderly: A systematic review. *International Journal of Integrated Care*, 12, 1–16.

Lorber, Michael F. & Egeland, Byron. (2011). Parenting and infant difficulty: Testing a mutual exacerbation hypothesis to predict early onset conduct problems. *Child Development*, 82(6), 2006–2020. doi: 10.1111/j.1467-8624.2011.01652.x

Lortet-Tieulent, Joannie; Soerjomataram, Isabelle; Ferlay, Jacques; Rutherford, Mark; Weiderpass, Elisabete & Bray, Freddie. (2014). International trends in lung cancer incidence by histological subtype: Adenocarcinoma stabilizing in men but still increasing in women. *Lung Cancer*, 84(1), 13–22. doi: 10.1016/j.lungcan.2014.01.009

Lövdén, Martin; Xu, Weili & Wang, Hui-Xin. (2013). Lifestyle change and the prevention of cognitive decline and dementia: What is the evidence? *Current Opinion in Psychiatry*, 26(3), 239–243. doi: 10.1097/YCO.0b013e32835f4135

Lovell, Brian & Wetherell, Mark A. (2011). The cost of caregiving: Endocrine and immune implications in elderly and non elderly caregivers. *Neuroscience & Biobehavioral Reviews*, 35(6), 1342–1352. doi: 10.1016/j.neubiorev.2011.02.007

Lowell, Darcy I.; Carter, Alice S.; Godoy, Leandra; Paulicin, Belinda & Briggs-Gowan, Margaret J. (2011). A randomized controlled trial of Child FIRST: A comprehensive home-based intervention translating research into early childhood practice. *Child Development*, 82(1), 193–208. doi: 10.1111/j.1467-8624.2010.01550.x

Lowrey, Annie. (2014, March 16). Income gap, meet the longevity gap. *The New York Times*, p. BU1.

Lubienski, Christopher; Puckett, Tiffany & Brewer, T. Jameson. (2013). Does homeschooling "work"? A critique of the empirical claims and agenda of advocacy organizations. *Peabody Journal of Education*, 88(3), 378–392. doi: 10.1080/0161956X.2013.798516

Luecken, Linda J.; Lin, Betty; Coburn, Shayna S.; MacKinnon, David P.; Gonzales, Nancy A. & Crnic, Keith A. (2013). Prenatal stress, partner support, and infant cortisol reactivity in low-income Mexican American families. *Psychoneuroendocrinology*, 38(12), 3092–3101. doi: 10.1016/j.psyneuen.2013.09.006

Luengo-Prado, María J. & Sevilla, Almudena. (2012). Time to cook: Expenditure at retirement in Spain. *The Economic Journal*, 123(569), 764–789. doi: 10.1111/j.1468-0297.2012.02546.x

Luhmann, Maike; Hofmann, Wilhelm; Eid, Michael & Lucas, Richard E. (2012). Subjective well-being and adaptation to life events: A meta-analysis. *Journal of Personality and Social Psychology*, 102(3), 592–615. doi: 10.1037/a0025948

Luna, Beatriz; Paulsen, David J.; Padmanabhan, Aarthi & Geier, Charles. (2013). The teenage brain: Cognitive control and motivation. *Current Directions in Psychological Science*, 22(2), 94–100. doi: 10.1177/0963721413478416

Lundquist, Gunilla; Rasmussen, Birgit H. & Axelsson, Bertil. (2011). Information of imminent death or not: Does it make a difference? *Journal of Clinical Oncology*, 29(29), 3927–3931. doi: 10.1200/JCO.2011.34.6247

Luo, Rufan; Tamis-LeMonda, Catherine S.; Kuchirko, Yana; Ng, Florrie F. & Liang, Eva. (2014). Mother–child book-sharing and children's storytelling skills in ethnically diverse, low-income families. *Infant and Child Development*, 23(4), 402–425. doi: 10.1002/icd.1841

Luong, Gloria & Charles, Susan T. (2014). Age differences in affective and cardiovascular responses to a negative social interaction: The role of goals, appraisals, and emotion regulation. *Developmental Psychology*, 50(7), 1919–1930. doi: 10.1037/a0036621

Lustig, Cindy; Shah, Priti; Seidler, Rachael & Reuter-Lorenz, Patricia A. (2009). Aging, training, and the brain: A review and future directions. *Neuropsychology Review*, 19(4), 504–522. doi: 10.1007/s11065-009-9119-9

Luthar, Suniya S. & Barkin, Samuel H. (2012). Are affluent youth truly "at risk"? Vulnerability and resilience across three diverse samples. *Development and Psychopathology*, 24(2), 429–449. doi: 10.1017/S0954579412000089

Luthar, Suniya S.; Cicchetti, Dante & Becker, Bronwyn. (2000). The construct of resilience: A critical evaluation and guidelines for future work. *Child Development*, 71(3), 543–562. doi: 10.1111/1467-8624.00164

Lutz, Wolfgang; Muttarak, Raya & Striessnig, Erich. (2014). Universal education is key to enhanced climate adaptation. *Science*, 346(6213), 1061–1062. doi: 10.1126/science.1257975

Luu, Hung N.; Blot, William J.; Xiang, Yong-Bing; Cai, Hui; Hargreaves, Margaret K.; Li, Honglan, . . . Shu, Xiao-Ou. (2015). Prospective evaluation of the association of nut/peanut consumption with total and cause-specific mortality. *JAMA Internal Medicine*, 175(5), 755–766. doi: 10.1001/jamainternmed.2014.8347

Luxmoore, Nick. (2012). *Young people, death, and the unfairness of everything*. Philadelphia, PA: Jessica Kingsley.

Luyckx, Koen; Klimstra, Theo A.; Duriez, Bart; Van Petegem, Stijn & Beyers, Wim. (2013). Personal identity processes from adolescence through the late 20s: Age trends, functionality, and depressive symptoms. *Social Development*, 22(4), 701–721. doi: 10.1111/sode.12027

Lynch, Scott M. & Brown, J. Scott. (2011). Stratification and inequality over the life course. In Robert H. Binstock & Linda K. George (Eds.), *Handbook of aging and the social sciences* (7th ed., pp. 105–117). San Diego, CA: Academic Press. doi: 10.1016/B978-0-12-380880-6.00008-3

Lynne, Sarah D.; Graber, Julia A.; Nichols, Tracy R.; Brooks-Gunn, Jeanne & Botvin, Gilbert J. (2007). Links between pubertal timing, peer influences, and externalizing behaviors among urban students followed through middle school. *Journal of Adolescent Health*, 40(2), 181.e187–181.e113. doi: 10.1016/j.jadohealth.2006.09.008

Lynskey, Michael T.; Agrawal, Arpana; Henders, Anjali; Nelson, Elliot C.; Madden, Pamela A. F. & Martin, Nicholas G. (2012). An Australian twin study of cannabis and other illicit drug use and misuse, and other psychopathology. *Twin Research and Human Genetics*, 15(5), 631–641. doi: 10.1017/thg.2012.41

Lyons, Kristen E.; Ghetti, Simona & Cornoldi, Cesare. (2010). Age differences in the contribution of recollection and familiarity to false-memory formation: A new paradigm to examine developmental reversals. *Developmental Science*, 13(2), 355–362. doi: 10.1111/j.1467-7687.2009.00889.x

Lyons-Ruth, Karlen; Bronfman, Elisa & Parsons, Elizabeth. (1999). Maternal frightened, frightening, or atypical behavior and disorganized infant attachment patterns. *Monographs of the Society for Research in Child Development*, 64(3), 67–96. doi: 10.1111/1540-5834.00034

Lyssens-Danneboom, Vicky & Mortelmans, Dimitri. (2014). Living apart together and money: New partnerships, traditional gender roles. *Journal of Marriage and Family*, 76(5), 949–966. doi: 10.1111/jomf.12136

Ma, Defu; Ning, Yibing; Gao, Hongchong; Li, Wenjun; Wang, Junkuan; Zheng, Yingdong, . . . Wang, Peiyu. (2014). Nutritional status of breast-fed and non-exclusively breast-fed infants from birth to age 5 months in 8 Chinese cities. *Asia Pacific Journal of Clinical Nutrition*, 23(2), 282–292. doi: 10.6133/apjcn.2014.23.2.16

Mac Dougall, K.; Beyene, Y. & Nachtigall, R.D. (2013). Age shock: Misperceptions of the impact of age on fertility before and after IVF in women who conceived after age 40. *Human Reproduction*, 28(2), 350–356. doi: 10.1093/humrep/des409

MacDorman, Marian F.; Mathews, T. J.; Mohangoo, Ashna D. & Zeitlin, Jennifer. (2014). *International comparisons of infant mortality and related factors: United States and Europe, 2010.* National Vital Statistics Reports 63(5). Hyattsville, MD: National Center for Health Statistics.

MacDorman, Marian F. & Rosenberg, Harry M. (1993). *Trends in infant mortality by cause of death and other characteristics, 1960–88. Vital and Health Statistic 20*(20). Hyattsville, MD: National Center for Health Statistics.

Macgregor, Stuart; Lind, Penelope A.; Bucholz, Kathleen K.; Hansell, Narelle K.; Madden, Pamela A. F.; Richter, **Melinda M., . . . Whitfield, John B.** (2009). Associations of ADH and ALDH2 gene variation with self report alcohol reactions, consumption and dependence: An integrated analysis. *Human Molecular Genetics*, 18(3), 580–593. doi: 10.1093/hmg/ddn372

Mackenzie, Karen J.; Anderton, Stephen M. & Schwarze, Jürgen. (2014). Viral respiratory tract infections and asthma in early life: Cause and effect? *Clinical & Experimental Allergy*, 44(1), 9–19. doi: 10.1111/cea.12139

MacKenzie, Michael J.; Nicklas, Eric; Brooks-Gunn, Jeanne & Waldfogel, Jane. (2011). Who spanks infants and toddlers? Evidence from the fragile families and child well-being study. *Children and Youth Services Review*, 33(8), 1364–1373. doi: 10.1016/j.childyouth.2011.04.007

Macmillan, Ross & Copher, Ronda. (2005). Families in the life course: Interdependency of roles, role configurations, and pathways. *Journal of Marriage and Family*, 67(4), 858–879. doi: 10.1111/j.1741-3737.2005.00180.x

Macosko, Evan Z. & McCarroll, Steven A. (2013). Our fallen genomes. *Science*, 342(6158), 564–565. doi: 10.1126/science.1246942

Madden, Mary; Lenhart, Amanda; Duggan, Maeve; Cortesi, Sandra & Gasser, Urs. (2013). *Teens and technology 2013.* Washington, DC: Pew Research Center, Pew Internet & American Life Project.

Maddi, Salvatore R. (2013). *Hardiness: Turning stressful circumstances into resilient growth.* New York, NY: Springer.

Magill, Molly; Gaume, Jacques; Apodaca, Timothy R.; Walthers, Justin; Mastroleo, Nadine R.; Borsari, Brian & Longabaugh, Richard. (2014). The technical hypothesis of motivational interviewing: A meta-analysis of MI's key causal model. *Journal of Consulting and Clinical Psychology*, 82(6), 973–983. doi: 10.1037/a0036833

Magnuson, Katherine & Waldfogel, Jane. (2014). Delivering high-quality early childhood education and care to low-income children: How well is the US doing? In Ludovica Gambaro et al. (Eds.), *An equal start?: Providing quality early education and care for disadvantaged children* (pp. 193–218). Chicago, IL: Policy Press.

Majdandži , Mirjana; Möller, Eline L.; de Vente, Wieke; Bögels, Susan M. & van den Boom, Dymphna C. (2013). Fathers' challenging parenting behavior prevents social anxiety development in their 4-year-old children: A longitudinal observational study. *Journal of Abnormal Child Psychology*, 42(2), 301–310. doi: 10.1007/s10802-013-9774-4

Makimoto, Kiyoko. (1998). Drinking patterns and drinking problems among Asian-Americans and Pacific Islanders. *Alcohol Health and Research World*, 22(4), 270–275.

Malchiodi, Cathy A. (2012). Creativity and aging: An art therapy perspective. In Cathy A. Malchiodi (Ed.), *Handbook of art therapy* (2nd ed., pp. 275–287). New York, NY: Guilford Press.

Malloy, Michael H. (2009). Impact of cesarean section on intermediate and late preterm births: United States, 2000-2003. *Birth*, 36(1), 26–33. doi: 10.1111/j.1523-536X.2008.00292.x

Mancini, Anthony D. & Bonanno, George A. (2006). Marital closeness, functional disability, and adjustment in late life. *Psychology and Aging*, 21(3), 600–610. doi: 10.1037/0882-7974.21.3.600

Mancini, Anthony D.; Prati, Gabriele & Bonanno, George A. (2011). Do shattered worldviews lead to complicated grief? Prospective and longitudinal analyses. *Journal of Social and Clinical Psychology, 30*(2), 184–215. doi: 10.1521/jscp.2011.30.2.184

Mandler, Jean M. & DeLoache, Judy. (2012). The beginnings of conceptual development. In Sabina M. Pauen (Ed.), *Early childhood development and later outcome.* New York, NY: Cambridge University Press.

Mangels, Jennifer A.; Good, Catherine; Whiteman, Ronald C.; Maniscalco, Brian & Dweck, Carol S. (2012). Emotion blocks the path to learning under stereotype threat. *Social Cognitive Affective Neuroscience, 7*(2), 230–241. doi: 10.1093/scan/nsq100

Mann, Joshua R.; McDermott, Suzanne; Bao, Haikun & Bersabe, Adrian. (2009). Maternal genitourinary infection and risk of cerebral palsy. *Developmental Medicine & Child Neurology, 51*(4), 282–288. doi: 10.1111/j.1469-8749.2008.03226.x

Mann, Ronald D. & Andrews, Elizabeth B. (Eds.). (2007). *Pharmacovigilance* (2nd ed.). Hoboken, NJ: Wiley.

Manning, Wendy D.; Brown, Susan L. & Payne, Krista K. (2014). Two decades of stability and change in age at first union formation. *Journal of Marriage and Family, 76*(2), 247–260. doi: 10.1111/jomf.12090

Marazita, John M. & Merriman, William E. (2010). Verifying one's knowledge of a name without retrieving it: A U-shaped relation to vocabulary size in early childhood. *Language Learning and Development, 7*(1), 40–54. doi: 10.1080/15475441.2010.496099

Marcano, Tony. (1997, May 14). Toddler, left outside restaurant, is returned to her mother. *The New York Times,* p. B3.

March, John S.; Franklin, Martin E.; Leonard, Henrietta L. & Foa, Edna B. (2004). Obsessive-compulsive disorder. In Tracy L. Morris & John S. March (Eds.), *Anxiety disorders in children and adolescents* (2nd ed., pp. 212–240). New York, NY: Guilford Press.

Marchand, Alain; Drapeau, Aline & Beaulieu-Prévost, Dominic. (2012). Psychological distress in Canada: The role of employment and reasons for non-employment. *International Journal of Social Psychiatry, 58*(6), 596–604. doi: 10.1177/0020764011418404

Marcia, James E. (1966). Development and validation of ego-identity status. *Journal of Personality and Social Psychology, 3*(5), 551–558. doi: 10.1037/h0023281

Marcia, James E.; Waterman, Alan S.; Matteson, David R.; Archer, Sally L. & Orlofsky, Jacob L. (1993). *Ego identity: A handbook for psychosocial research.* New York, NY: Springer-Verlag.

Marcovitch, Stuart; Boseovski, Janet J.; Knapp, Robin J. & Kane, Michael J. (2010). Goal neglect and working memory capacity in 4- to 6-year-old children. *Child Development, 81*(6), 1687–1695. doi: 10.1111/j.1467-8624.2010.01503.x

Marcus, Gary F. & Rabagliati, Hugh. (2009). Language acquisition, domain specificity, and descent with modification. In John Colombo et al. (Eds.), *Infant pathways to language: Methods, models, and research disorders* (pp. 267–285). New York, NY: Psychology Press.

Mareschal, Denis & Kaufman, Jordy. (2012). Object permanence in infancy: Revisiting Baillargeon's drawbridge study. In Alan M. Slater & Paul C. Quinn (Eds.), *Developmental psychology: Revisiting the classic studies.* Thousand Oaks, CA: Sage.

Marewski, Julian N. & Schooler, Lael J. (2011). Cognitive niches: An ecological model of strategy selection. *Psychological Review, 118*(3), 393–437. doi: 10.1037/a0024143

Margolis, Rachel & Myrskylä, Mikko. (2011). A global perspective on happiness and fertility. *Population and Development Review, 37*(1), 29–56. doi: 10.1111/j.1728-4457.2011.00389.x

Marin, Marie-France; Lord, Catherine; Andrews, Julie; Juster, Robert-Paul; Sindi, Shireen; Arsenault-Lapierre, Geneviève, . . . Lupien, Sonia J. (2011). Chronic stress, cognitive functioning and mental health. *Neurobiology of Learning and Memory, 96*(4), 583–595. doi: 10.1016/j.nlm.2011.02.016

Mark, Joan T. (1999). *Margaret Mead: Coming of age in America.* New York, NY: Oxford University Press.

Mark, Van Ryzin. & Pellegrini, Anthony D. (2013). Socially competent and incompetent aggressors in middle school: The non-linear relation between bullying and dominance in middle school. *BJEP Monograph Series II, 9,* 123–138.

Markovits, Henry. (2014). On the road toward formal reasoning: Reasoning with factual causal and contrary-to-fact causal premises during early adolescence. *Journal of Experimental Child Psychology, 128,* 37–51. doi: 10.1016/j.jecp.2014.07.001

Markowitsch, Hans J. & Staniloiu, Angelica. (2012). Amnesic disorders. *The Lancet, 380*(9851), 1429–1440. doi: 10.1016/S0140-6736(11)61304-4

Marmolejo-Ramos, Fernando & D'Angiulli, Amedeo. (2014). Current research topics in embodied social cognition. *Cognitive Processing, 15*(3), 235–236. doi: 10.1007/s10339-014-0624-2

Marschark, Marc & Spencer, Patricia E. (2003). What we know, what we don't know, and what we should know. In Marc Marschark & Patricia E. Spencer (Eds.), *Oxford handbook of deaf studies, language, and education* (pp. 491–494). New York, NY: Oxford University Press.

Martin, Carmel. (2014). *Common Core implementation best practices. New York State Office of the Governor Common Core Implementation Panel.* Washington, DC: Center for American Progress.

Martin, Carol L.; Fabes, Richard; Hanish, Laura; Leonard, Stacie & Dinella, Lisa. (2011). Experienced and expected similarity to same-gender peers: Moving toward a comprehensive model of gender segregation. *Sex Roles, 65*(5/6), 421–434. doi: 10.1007/s11199-011-0029-y

Martin, Carol L. & Ruble, Diane N. (2010). Patterns of gender development. *Annual Review of Psychology, 61,* 353–381. doi: 10.1146/annurev.psych.093008.100511

Martin, Georgianna L.; Parker, Gene; Pascarella, Ernest T. & Blechschmidt, Sally. (2015). Do fraternities and sororities inhibit intercultural competence? *Journal of College Student Development, 56*(1), 66–72. doi: 10.1353/csd.2015.0010

Martin, Leslie R.; Haskard-Zolnierek, Kelly B. & DiMatteo, M. Robin. (2010). *Health behavior change and treatment adherence: Evidence-based guidelines for improving healthcare.* New York, NY: Oxford University Press.

Martin-Uzzi, Michele & Duval-Tsioles, Denise. (2013). The experience of remarried couples in blended families. *Journal of Divorce & Remarriage, 54*(1), 43–57. doi: 10.1080/10502556.2012.743828

Marvasti, Amir B. & McKinney, Karyn D. (2011). Does diversity mean assimilation? *Critical Sociology, 37*(5), 631–650. doi: 10.1177/0896920510380071

Mascarelli, Amanda. (2013). Growing up with pesticides. *Science, 341*(6147), 740–741. doi: 10.1126/science.341.6147.740

Masche, J. Gowert. (2010). Explanation of normative declines in parents' knowledge about their adolescent children. *Journal of Adolescence, 33*(2), 271–284. doi: 10.1016/j.adolescence.2009.08.002

Mashour, George A. & Avidan, Michael (Eds.). (2013). *Neurologic outcomes of surgery and anesthesia.* New York, NY: Oxford University Press.

Maski, Kiran P. & Kothare, Sanjeev V. (2013). Sleep deprivation and neurobehavioral functioning in children. *International Journal of Psychophysiology, 89*(2), 259–264. doi: 10.1016/j.ijpsycho.2013.06.019

Maslow, Abraham H. (1954). *Motivation and personality* (1st ed.). New York, NY: Harper & Row.

Maslow, Abraham H. (1962). *Toward a psychology of being* (1st ed.). Princeton, NJ: D. Van Nostrand.

Maslow, Abraham H. (1997). *Motivation and personality* (3rd ed.). New York, NY: Pearson.

Maslow, Abraham H. (1998). *Toward a psychology of being* (3rd ed.). New York, NY: Wiley.

Maslowsky, Julie; Schulenberg, John E. & Zucker, Robert A. (2014). Influence of conduct problems and depressive symptomatology on adolescent substance use: Developmentally proximal versus distal effects. *Developmental Psychology, 50*(4), 1179–1189. doi: 10.1037/a0035085

Masten, Ann S. (2014). *Ordinary magic: Resilience in development.* New York, NY: Guilford Press.

Mateus-Pinheiro, A.; Patrício, P.; Bessa, J. M.; Sousa, N. & Pinto, L. (2013). Cell genesis and dendritic plasticity: A neuroplastic pas de deux in the onset and remission from depression. *Molecular Psychiatry, 18*(7), 748–750. doi: 10.1038/mp.2013.56

Mathews, T. J.; Menacker, Fay & MacDorman, Marian F. (2003). *Infant mortality statistics from the 2001 period linked birth/infant death data set. National Vital Statistics Reports 52*(2). Hyattsville, MD: National Center for Health Statistics.

Matthews, Fiona E.; Arthur, Antony; Barnes, Linda E.; Bond, John; Jagger, Carol; Robinson, Louise & Brayne, Carol. (2013). A two-decade comparison of prevalence of dementia in individuals aged 65 years and older from three geographical areas of England: Results of the Cognitive Function and Ageing Study I and II. *The Lancet, 382*(9902), 1405–1412. doi: 10.1016/S0140-6736(13)61570-6

Mattison, Julie A.; Roth, George S.; Beasley, T. Mark; Tilmont, Edward M.; Handy, April M.; Herbert, Richard L., . . . de Cabo, Rafael. (2012). Impact of caloric restriction on health and survival in rhesus monkeys from the NIA study. *Nature, 489*(7415), 318–321. doi: 10.1038/nature11432

Maume, David J. & Sebastian, Rachel A. (2012). Gender, nonstandard work schedules, and marital quality. *Journal of Family and Economic Issues, 33*(4), 477–490. doi: 10.1007/s10834-012-9308-1

Maxfield, Molly; John, Samantha & Pyszczynski, Tom. (2014). A terror management perspective on the role of death-related anxiety in psychological dysfunction. *The Humanistic Psychologist, 42*(1), 35–53. doi: 10.1080/08873267.2012.732155

Maxfield, Molly; Pyszczynski, Tom; Kluck, Benjamin; Cox, Cathy R.; Greenberg, Jeff; Solomon, Sheldon & Weise, David. (2007). Age-related differences in responses to thoughts of one's own death: Mortality salience and judgments of moral transgressions. *Psychology and Aging, 22*(2), 341–353. doi: 10.1037/0882-7974.22.2.341

Maxwell, Lesli A. (2012). Achievement gaps tied to income found widening. *Education Week, 31*(23), 1, 22–23.

May, Vanessa; Mason, Jennifer & Clarke, Lynda. (2012). Being there, yet not interfering: The paradoxes of grandparenting. In Sara Arber & Virpi Timonen (Eds.), *Contemporary grandparenting: Changing family relationships in global contexts* (pp. 139–158). Chicago, IL: Policy Press.

Mazzonnaa, Fabrizio & Peracchi, Franco. (2012). Ageing, cognitive abilities and retirement. *European Economic Review, 56*(4), 691–710. doi: 10.1016/j.euroecorev.2012.03.004

McAdams, Dan P. & Olson, Bradley D. (2010). Personality development: Continuity and change over the life course. *Annual Review of Psychology, 61*, 517–542. doi: 10.1146/annurev.psych.093008.100507

McCabe, Janice. (2011). Doing multiculturalism: An interactionist analysis of the practices of a multicultural sorority. *Journal of Contemporary Ethnography, 40*(5), 521–549. doi: 10.1177/0891241611403588

McCall, Robert B. (2013). The consequences of early institutionalization: Can institutions be improved?—Should they? *Child and Adolescent Mental Health, 18*(4), 193–201. doi: 10.1111/camh.12025

McCarrey, Anna C.; Henry, Julie D.; von Hippel, William; Weidemann, Gabrielle; Sachdev, Perminder S.; Wohl, Michael J. A. & Williams, Mark. (2012). Age differences in neural activity during slot machine gambling: An fMRI study. *PLoS ONE, 7*(11), e49787. doi: 10.1371/journal.pone.0049787

McCarthy, Kathleen M.; Mahon, Merle; Rosen, Stuart & Evans, Bronwen G. (2014). Speech perception and production by sequential bilingual children: A longitudinal study of voice onset time acquisition. *Child Development, 85*(5), 1965–1980. doi: 10.1111/cdev.12275

McCarthy, Neil & Eberhart, Johann K. (2014). Gene—ethanol interactions underlying fetal alcohol spectrum disorders. *Cellular and Molecular Life Sciences, 71*(14), 2699–2706. doi: 10.1007/s00018-014-1578-3

McCartney, Kathleen; Burchinal, Margaret; Clarke-Stewart, Alison; Bub, Kristen L.; Owen, Margaret T. & Belsky, Jay. (2010). Testing a series of causal propositions relating time in child care to children's externalizing behavior. *Developmental Psychology, 46*(1), 1–17. doi: 10.1037/a0017886

McClain, Lauren Rinelli. (2011). Better parents, more stable partners: Union transitions among cohabiting parents. *Journal of Marriage and Family*, 73(5), 889–901. doi: 10.1111/j.1741-3737.2011.00859.x

McCright, Aaron M. & Dunlap, Riley E. (2011). The politicization of climate change and polarization in the American public's views of global warming, 2001–2010. *Sociological Quarterly*, 52(2), 155–194. doi: 10.1111/j.1533-8525.2011.01198.x

McDaniel, Mark A. & Bugg, Julie M. (2012). Memory training interventions: What has been forgotten? *Journal of Applied Research in Memory and Cognition*, 1(1), 45–50. doi: 10.1016/j.jarmac.2011.11.002

McEwen, Bruce S. & Gianaros, Peter J. (2011). Stress- and allostasis-induced brain plasticity. *Annual Review of Medicine*, 62, 431–445. doi: 10.1146/annurev-med-052209-100430

McEwen, Bruce S. & Karatsoreos, Ilia N. (2015). Sleep deprivation and circadian disruption: Stress, allostasis, and allostatic load. *Sleep Medicine Clinics*, 10(1), 1–10. doi: 10.1016/j.jsmc.2014.11.007

McFadden, Susan H. & Basting, Anne D. (2010). Healthy aging persons and their brains: Promoting resilience through creative engagement. *Clinics in Geriatric Medicine*, 26(1), 149–161. doi: 10.1016/j.cger.2009.11.004

McFarlane, Alexander C. & Van Hooff, Miranda. (2009). Impact of childhood exposure to a natural disaster on adult mental health: 20-year longitudinal follow-up study. *The British Journal of Psychiatry*, 195(2), 142–148. doi: 10.1192/bjp.bp.108.054270

McGill, Natalie. (2015). States taking action to regulate e-cigarettes: FDA working to gain authority as science on products grows. *The Nation's Health*, 45(4), 1–12.

McGill, Rebecca K.; Hughes, Diane; Alicea, Stacey & Way, Niobe. (2012). Academic adjustment across middle school: The role of public regard and parenting. *Developmental Psychology*, 48(4), 1003–1018. doi: 10.1037/a0026006

McGue, Matt; Irons, Dan & Iacono, William G. (2014). The adolescent origins of substance use disorders: A behavioral genetic perspective. In Scott F. Stoltenberg (Ed.), *Genes and the motivation to use substances* (pp. 31–50). New York, NY: Springer. doi: 10.1007/978-1-4939-0653-6_3

McIntyre, Donald A. (2002). *Colour blindness: Causes and effects.* Chester, UK: Dalton Publishing.

McLaren, Paul J.; Fellay, Jacques & Telenti, Amalio. (2013). European genetic diversity and susceptibility to pathogens. *Human Heredity*, 76(3/4), 187–193. doi: 10.1159/000357758

McLean, Robert R. & Kiel, Douglas P. (2015). Developing consensus criteria for sarcopenia: An update. *Journal of Bone and Mineral Research*, 30(4), 588–592. doi: 10.1002/jbmr.2492

McLendon, Amber N. & Shelton, Penny S. (2011–2012). New symptoms in older adults: Disease or drug? *Generations*, 35(4), 25–30.

McLeod, Bryce D.; Wood, Jeffrey J. & Weisz, John R. (2007). Examining the association between parenting and childhood anxiety: A meta-analysis. *Clinical Psychology Review*, 27(2), 155–172. doi: 10.1016/j.cpr.2006.09.002

McManus, I. Chris; Moore, James; Freegard, Matthew & Rawles, Richard. (2010). Science in the making: Right Hand, Left Hand. III: Estimating historical rates of left-handedness. *Laterality: Asymmetries of Body, Brain and Cognition*, 15(1/2), 186–208. doi: 10.1080/13576500802565313

McMurtrie, Beth. (2014). Why colleges haven't stopped students from binge drinking. *Chronicle of Higher Education*, 61(14), A23–A26.

McNamee, Catherine & Raley, Kelly. (2011). A note on race, ethnicity and nativity differentials in remarriage in the United States. *Demographic Research*, 24(13), 293–312. doi: 10.4054/DemRes.2011.24.13

McNeill, Timothy P.; Hayes, Sandra C. & Harley, Jacqueline. (2015). Addressing health disparities through recommendations from the Jackson Heart Study. *Generations*, 38(4), 46–51.

McShane, Kelly E. & Hastings, Paul D. (2009). The New Friends Vignettes: Measuring parental psychological control that confers risk for anxious adjustment in preschoolers. *International Journal of Behavioral Development*, 33(6), 481–495. doi: 10.1177/0165025409103874

Meadows, Sara. (2006). *The child as thinker: The development and acquisition of cognition in childhood* (2nd ed.). New York, NY: Routledge.

Meagher, David K. (2013). Ethical and legal issues and loss, grief, and mourning. In David K. Meagher & David E. Balk (Eds.), *Handbook of thanatology: The essential body of knowledge for the study of death, dying, and bereavement* (2nd ed.). New York, NY: Routledge.

Medsinge, Anagha & Nischal, Ken K. (2015). Pediatric cataract: Challenges and future directions. *Clinical Ophthalmology*, 9, 77–90. doi: 10.2147/OPTH.S59009

Meece, Judith L. & Eccles, Jacquelynne S. (Eds.). (2010). *Handbook of research on schools, schooling, and human development.* New York, NY: Routledge.

Meeus, Wim. (2011). The study of adolescent identity formation 2000–2010: A review of longitudinal research. *Journal of Research on Adolescence*, 21(1), 75–94. doi: 10.1111/j.1532-7795.2010.00716.x

Mehisto, Peeter & Genesee, Fred (Eds.). (2015). *Building bilingual education systems: Forces, mechanisms and counterweights.* New York, NY: Cambridge University Press.

Mehta, Clare M. & Strough, JoNell. (2009). Sex segregation in friendships and normative contexts across the life span. *Developmental Review*, 29(3), 201–220. doi: 10.1016/j.dr.2009.06.001

Meier, Ann; Hull, Kathleen E. & Ortyl, Timothy A. (2009). Young adult relationship values at the intersection of gender and sexuality. *Journal of Marriage and Family*, 71(3), 510–525. doi: 10.1111/j.1741-3737.2009.00616.x

Meier, Ann & Musick, Kelly. (2014). Variation in associations between family dinners and adolescent well-being. *Journal of Marriage and Family*, 76(1), 13–23. doi: 10.1111/jomf.12079

Meier, Barry. (2012, November 16). F.D.A. posts injury data for 3 drinks. *The New York Times*, p. B1.

Meister, Jeanne. (2012). Job hopping is the 'new normal' for millennials: Three ways to prevent a human resource nightmare. *Forbes.*

Meltzoff, Andrew N. & Gopnik, Alison. (2013). Learning about the mind from evidence: Children's development of intuitive theories of perception and personality. In Simon Baron-Cohen et al. (Eds.), *Understanding other minds: Perspectives from developmental social neuroscience* (3rd ed., pp. 19–34). New York, NY: Oxford University Press. doi: 10.1093/acprof:oso /9780199692972.001.0001

Mendle, Jane; Harden, K. Paige; Brooks-Gunn, Jeanne & Graber, Julia A. (2012). Peer relationships and depressive symptomatology in boys at puberty. *Developmental Psychology, 48*(2), 429–435. doi: 10.1037/a0026425

Menken, Kate & Solorza, Cristian. (2014). No child left bilingual: Accountability and the elimination of bilingual education programs in New York City schools. *Educational Policy, 28*(1), 96–125. doi: 10.1177/0895904812468228

Mennis, Jeremy & Mason, Michael J. (2012). Social and geographic contexts of adolescent substance use: The moderating effects of age and gender. *Social Networks, 34*(1), 150–157. doi: 10.1016/j.socnet.2010.10.003

Merikangas, Kathleen R.; He, Jian-ping; Rapoport, Judith; Vitiello, Benedetto & Olfson, Mark. (2013). Medication use in US youth with mental disorders. *JAMA Pediatrics, 167*(2), 141–148. doi: 10.1001/jamapediatrics.2013.431

Merikangas, Kathleen R. & McClair, Vetisha L. (2012). Epidemiology of substance use disorders. *Human Genetics, 131*(6), 779–789. doi: 10.1007/s00439-012-1168-0

Merriam, Sharan B. (2009). *Qualitative research: A guide to design and implementation.* San Francisco, CA: Jossey-Bass.

Merriman, William E. (1999). Competition, attention, and young children's lexical processing. In Brian MacWhinney (Ed.), *The emergence of language* (pp. 331–358). Mahwah, NJ: Erlbaum.

Mersky, Joshua P.; Topitzes, James & Reynolds, Arthur J. (2013). Impacts of adverse childhood experiences on health, mental health, and substance use in early adulthood: A cohort study of an urban, minority sample in the U.S. *Child Abuse & Neglect, 37*(11), 917–925. doi: 10.1016/j.chiabu.2013.07.011

Merz, Emily C. & McCall, Robert B. (2011). Parent ratings of executive functioning in children adopted from psychosocially depriving institutions. *Journal of Child Psychology and Psychiatry, 52*(5), 537–546. doi: 10.1111/j.1469-7610.2010.02335.x

Mesch, Gustavo S. & Talmud, Ilan. (2010). *Wired youth: The social world of adolescence in the information age.* New York, NY: Routledge.

Messinger, Daniel M.; Ruvolo, Paul; Ekas, Naomi V. & Fogel, Alan. (2010). Applying machine learning to infant interaction: The development is in the details. *Neural Networks, 23*(8/9), 1004–1016. doi: 10.1016/j.neunet.2010.08.008

Metcalfe, Janet & Finn, Bridgid. (2013). Metacognition and control of study choice in children. *Metacognition and Learning, 8*(1), 19–46. doi: 10.1007/s11409-013-9094-7

Metcalfe, Lindsay A.; Harvey, Elizabeth A. & Laws, Holly B. (2013). The longitudinal relation between academic/cognitive skills and externalizing behavior problems in preschool children. *Journal of Educational Psychology, 105*(3), 881–894. doi: 10.1037/a0032624

Meyer, Madonna Harrington. (2012). Grandmothers juggling work and grandchildren in the United States. In Sara Arber & Virpi Timonen (Eds.), *Contemporary grandparenting: Changing family relationships in global contexts* (pp. 71–90). Chicago, IL: Policy Press.

Meyer, Madonna Harrington. (2014). *Grandmothers at work: Juggling families and jobs.* New York, NY: New York University Press.

Michl, Louisa C.; McLaughlin, Katie A.; Shepherd, Kathrine & Nolen-Hoeksema, Susan. (2013). Rumination as a mechanism linking stressful life events to symptoms of depression and anxiety: Longitudinal evidence in early adolescents and adults. *Journal of Abnormal Psychology, 122*(2), 339–352. doi: 10.1037/a0031994

Mikels, Joseph A.; Cheung, Elaine; Cone, Jeremy & Gilovich, Thomas. (2013). The dark side of intuition: Aging and increases in nonoptimal intuitive decisions. *Emotion, 13*(2), 189–195. doi: 10.1037/a0030441

Miklowitz, David J. & Cicchetti, Dante (Eds.). (2010). *Understanding bipolar disorder: A developmental psychopathology perspective.* New York, NY: Guilford Press.

Milardo, Robert M. (2010). *The forgotten kin: Aunts and uncles.* New York, NY: Cambridge University Press.

Miller, Alec L.; Rathus, Jill H. & Linehan, Marsha M. (2007). *Dialectical behavior therapy with suicidal adolescents.* New York, NY: Guilford Press.

Miller, Cindy F.; Martin, Carol Lynn; Fabes, Richard A. & Hanish, Laura D. (2013). Bringing the cognitive and the social together: How gender detectives and gender enforcers shape children's gender development. In Mahzarin R. Banaji & Susan A. Gelman (Eds.), *Navigating the social world: What infants, children, and other species can teach us* (pp. 306–313). New York, NY: Oxford University Press.

Miller, Evone; Buys, Laurie & Woodbridge, Sandra. (2012). Impact of disability on families: Grandparents' perspectives. *Journal of Intellectual Disability Research, 56*(1), 102–110. doi: 10.1111/j.1365-2788.2011.01403.x

Miller, Elizabeth B.; Farkas, George; Vandell, Deborah Lowe & Duncan, Greg J. (2014). Do the effects of Head Start vary by parental preacademic stimulation? *Child Development, 85*(4), 1385–1400. doi: 10.1111/cdev.12233

Miller, Greg. (2012). Engineering a new line of attack on a signature war injury. *Science, 335*(6064), 33–35. doi: 10.1126 /science.335.6064.33

Miller, Gregory E. & Chen, Edith. (2010). Harsh family climate in early life: Presages the emergence of a proinflammatory phenotype in adolescence. *Psychological Science, 21*(6), 848–856. doi: 10.1177/0956797610370161

Miller, Gregory E.; Murphy, Michael L. M.; Cashman, Rosemary; Ma, Roy; Ma, Jeffrey; Arevalo, Jesusa M. G., . . . Cole, Steve W. (2014). Greater inflammatory activity and blunted glucocorticoid signaling in monocytes of chronically stressed caregivers. *Brain, Behavior, and Immunity, 41*, 191–199. doi: 10.1016/j.bbi.2014.05.016

Miller, Portia; Votruba-Drzal, Elizabeth; Coley, Rebekah Levine & Koury, Amanda S. (2014). Immigrant families' use of early childcare: Predictors of care type. *Early Childhood Research Quarterly, 29*(4), 484–498. doi: 10.1016/j.ecresq.2014.05.011

Miller, Patricia H. (2011). *Theories of developmental psychology* (5th ed.). New York, NY: Worth Publishers.

Miller, Patricia Y. & Simon, William. (1980). The development of sexuality in adolescence. In Joseph Adelson (Ed.), *Handbook of adolescent psychology* (pp. 383–407). New York, NY: Wiley.

Miller, Richard B.; Hollist, Cody S.; Olsen, Joseph & Law, David. (2013). Marital quality and health over 20 years: A growth curve analysis. *Journal of Marriage and Family, 75*(3), 667–680. doi: 10.1111/jomf.12025

Miller, Susan W. (2011-2012). Medications and elders: Quality of care or quality of life? *Generations, 35*(4), 19–24.

Miller-Bernal, Leslie. (2000). *Separate by degree: Women students' experiences in single-sex and coeducational colleges.* New York, NY: Peter Lang.

Mina, Michael J.; Metcalf, Jessica E.; de Swart, Rik L.; Osterhaus, A. D. M. E. & Grenfell, Bryan T. (2015). Long-term measles-induced immunomodulation increases overall childhood infectious disease mortality. *Science, 348*(6235), 694–699. doi: 10.1126/science.aaa3662

Minagawa-Kawai, Yasuyo; van der Lely, Heather; Ramus, Franck; Sato, Yutaka; Mazuka, Reiko & Dupoux, Emmanuel. (2011). Optical brain imaging reveals general auditory and language-specific processing in early infant development. *Cerebral Cortex, 21*(2), 254–261. doi: 10.1093/cercor/bhq082

Mindell, Jodi A.; Sadeh, Avi; Wiegand, Benjamin; How, Ti Hwei & Goh, Daniel Y. T. (2010). Cross-cultural differences in infant and toddler sleep. *Sleep Medicine, 11*(3), 274–280. doi: 10.1016/j.sleep.2009.04.012

Miniño, Arialdi M.; Heron, Melonie P.; Murphy, Sherry L. & Kochanek, Kenneth D. (2007). *Deaths: Final data for 2004. National Vital Statistics Reports 55*(19). Hyattsville, MD: National Center for Health Statistics.

Mischel, Walter. (2014). *The marshmallow test: Mastering self-control.* New York, NY: Little, Brown and Company.

Mishra, Jyoti. (2014). Having it all. *Science, 345*(6200), 1090. doi: 10.1126/science.345.6200.1090

Mishra, Ramesh C.; Singh, Sunita & Dasen, Pierre R. (2009). Geocentric dead reckoning in Sanskrit- and Hindi-medium school children. *Culture & Psychology, 15*(3), 386–408. doi: 10.1177/1354067x09343330

Missana, Manuela; Rajhans, Purva; Atkinson, Anthony P. & Grossmann, Tobias. (2014). Discrimination of fearful and happy body postures in 8-month-old infants: An event-related potential study. *Frontiers in Human Neuroscience, 8,* 531. doi: 10.3389/fnhum.2014.00531

Mitchell, Barbara A. (2010). Happiness in midlife parental roles: A contextual mixed methods analysis. *Family Relations, 59*(3), 326–339. doi: 10.1111/j.1741-3729.2010.00605.x

Mitchell, Edwin A. & Krous, Henry F. (2015). Sudden unexpected death in infancy: A historical perspective. *Journal of Paediatrics and Child Health, 51*(1), 108–112. doi: 10.1111/jpc.12818

Mitchell, Kimberly J.; Jones, Lisa M.; Finkelhor, David & Wolak, Janis. (2013). Understanding the decline in unwanted online sexual solicitations for U.S. youth 2000–2010: Findings from three Youth Internet Safety Surveys. *Child Abuse & Neglect, 37*(12), 1225–1236. doi: 10.1016/j.chiabu.2013.07.002

Mitchell, Ross E. (2006). How many deaf people are there in the United States? Estimates from the survey of income and program participation. *Journal of Deaf Studies and Deaf Education, 11*(1), 112–119. doi: 10.1093/deafed/enj004

Miyata, Susanne; MacWhinney, Brian; Otomo, Kiyoshi; Sirai, Hidetosi; Oshima-Takane, Yuriko; Hirakawa, Makiko, . . . Itoh, Keiko. (2013). Developmental sentence scoring for Japanese. *First Language, 33*(2), 200–216. doi: 10.1177/0142723713479436

Mize, Krystal D.; Pineda, Melannie; Blau, Alexis K.; Marsh, Kathryn & Jones, Nancy A. (2014). Infant physiological and behavioral responses to a jealousy provoking condition. *Infancy, 19*(3), 338–348. doi: 10.1111/infa.12046

MMWR. (2000, March 31). *Reducing falls and resulting hip fractures among older women. Morbidity and Mortality Weekly Report 49*(RR02), 1–12. Atlanta, GA: U.S. Department of Health and Human Services, Centers for Disease Control and Prevention.

MMWR. (2008, January 18). *School-associated student homicides—United States, 1992–2006. Morbidity and Mortality Weekly Report 57*(2), 33–36. Atlanta, GA: U.S. Department of Health and Human Services, Centers for Disease Control and Prevention.

MMWR. (2012, July 20). *Alcohol Use and Binge Drinking Among Women of Childbearing Age–United States, 2006-2010. Morbidity and Mortality Weekly Report 61*(28), 534–538. Atlanta, GA: U.S. Department of Health and Human Services, Centers for Disease Control and Prevention.

MMWR. (2012, June 8). *Youth risk behavior surveillance—United States, 2011. Morbidity and Mortality Weekly Report 61*(4). Atlanta, GA: U.S. Department of Health and Human Services, Centers for Disease Control and Prevention.

MMWR. (2013, April 5). *Blood lead levels in children aged 1–5 Years—United States, 1999–2010. Morbidity and Mortality Weekly Report 62*(13), 245–248. Atlanta, GA: U.S. Department of Health and Human Services, Centers for Disease Control and Prevention.

MMWR. (2013, January 11). *Vital signs: Binge drinking among women and high school girls—United States, 2011. Morbidity and Mortality Weekly Report 62,* 9–13. Atlanta, GA: Department of Health and Human Services, Centers for Disease Control and Prevention.

MMWR. (2014, June 13). *Youth risk behavior surveillance—United States, 2013. Morbidity and Mortality Weekly Report 63*(4). Atlanta, GA: U.S. Department of Health and Human Services, Centers for Disease Control and Prevention.

MMWR. (2014, March 28). *Prevalence of autism spectrum disorder among children aged 8 years—Autism and Developmental Disabilities Monitoring Network, 11 sites, United States, 2010. Morbidity and Mortality Weekly Report 63*(2). Atlanta, GA: U.S. Department of Health and Human Services, Centers for Disease Control and Prevention.

MMWR. (2014, May 2). *QuickStats: Percentage of children aged 6–17 years prescribed medication during the preceding 6 months for*

emotional or behavioral difficulties, by census region—*National Health Interview Survey, United States, 2011–2012. Morbidity and Mortality Weekly Report 63*(17), 389–389. Atlanta, GA: Centers for Disease Control and Prevention.

MMWR. (2014, September 5). *Prevalence of smokefree home rules—United States, 1992–1993 and 2010–2011. Morbidity and Mortality Weekly Report 63*(35), 765–769. Atlanta, GA: Department of Health and Human Services, Centers for Disease Control and Prevention.

MMWR. (2015, February 27). *CDC grand rounds: Preventing youth violence. Morbidity and Mortality Weekly Report 64*(7), 171–174. Atlanta, GA: Department of Health and Human Services, Centers for Disease Control and Prevention.

MMWR. (2015, January 2). *Notifiable diseases and mortality tables. Morbidity and Mortality Weekly Report 63*(51/52). Atlanta, GA: Department of Health and Human Services, Centers for Disease Control and Prevention.

Moffitt, Terrie E. (2003). Life-course-persistent and adolescence-limited antisocial behavior: A 10-year research review and a research agenda. In Benjamin B. Lahey et al. (Eds.), *Causes of conduct disorder and juvenile delinquency* (pp. 49–75). New York, NY: Guilford Press.

Moffitt, Terrie E.; Arseneault, Louise; Belsky, Daniel; Dickson, Nigel; Hancox, Robert J.; Harrington, HonaLee, . . . Casp, Avshalom. (2011). A gradient of childhood self-control predicts health, wealth, and public safety. *Proceedings of the National Academy of Sciences of the United States of America, 108*(7), 2693–2698. doi: 10.1073/pnas.1010076108

Moffitt, Terrie E.; Caspi, Avshalom; Rutter, Michael & Silva, Phil A. (2001). *Sex differences in antisocial behaviour: Conduct disorder, delinquency, and violence in the Dunedin Longitudinal Study.* New York, NY: Cambridge University Press.

Mokrova, Irina L.; O'Brien, Marion; Calkins, Susan D.; Leerkes, Esther M. & Marcovitch, Stuart. (2013). The role of persistence at preschool age in academic skills at kindergarten. *European Journal of Psychology of Education, 28*(4), 1495–1503. doi: 10.1007/s10212-013-0177-2

Moldavsky, Maria & Sayal, Kapil. (2013). Knowledge and attitudes about Attention-deficit/hyperactivity disorder (ADHD) and its treatment: The views of children, adolescents, parents, teachers and healthcare professionals. *Current Psychiatry Reports, 15*, 377. doi: 10.1007/s11920-013-0377-0

Molina, Brooke S. G.; Hinshaw, Stephen P.; Arnold, L. Eugene; Swanson, James M.; Pelham, William E.; Hechtman, Lily, . . . Marcus, Sue. (2013). Adolescent substance use in the Multimodal Treatment Study of Attention-deficit/hyperactivity disorder (ADHD) (MTA) as a function of childhood ADHD, random assignment to childhood treatments, and subsequent medication. *Journal of the American Academy of Child & Adolescent Psychiatry, 52*(3), 250–263. doi: 10.1016/j.jaac.2012.12.014

Molina, Brooke S. G.; Hinshaw, Stephen P.; Swanson, James W.; Arnold, L. Eugene; Vitiello, Benedetto; Jensen, Peter S., . . . Houck, Patricia R. (2009). The MTA at 8 years: Prospective follow-up of children treated for combined-type ADHD in a multisite study. *Journal of the American Academy of Child and Adolescent Psychiatry, 48*(5), 484–500. doi: 10.1097/CHI.0b013e31819c23d0

Møller, Signe J. & Tenenbaum, Harriet R. (2011). Danish majority children's reasoning about exclusion based on gender and ethnicity. *Child Development, 82*(2), 520–532. doi: 10.1111/j.1467-8624.2010.01568.x

Monahan, Kathryn C.; Steinberg, Laurence & Cauffman, Elizabeth. (2009). Affiliation with antisocial peers, susceptibility to peer influence, and antisocial behavior during the transition to adulthood. *Developmental Psychology, 45*(6), 1520–1530. doi: 10.1037/a0017417

Monahan, Kathryn C.; Steinberg, Laurence; Cauffman, Elizabeth & Mulvey, Edward P. (2013). Psychosocial (im)maturity from adolescence to early adulthood: Distinguishing between adolescence-limited and persisting antisocial behavior. *Development and Psychopathology, 25*(4), 1093–1105. doi: 10.1017/S0954579413000394

Monastersky, Richard. (2007). Who's minding the teenage brain? *Chronicle of Higher Education, 53*(19), A14–A18.

Monje, Michelle & Dietrich, Jörg. (2012). Cognitive side effects of cancer therapy demonstrate a functional role for adult neurogenesis. *Behavioural Brain Research, 227*(2), 376–379. doi: 10.1016/j.bbr.2011.05.012

Monks, Claire P. & Coyne, Iain (Eds.). (2011). *Bullying in different contexts.* New York, NY: Cambridge University Press.

Monteiro, Carlos A.; Conde, Wolney L. & Popkin, Barry M. (2004). The burden of disease from undernutrition and overnutrition in countries undergoing rapid nutrition transition: A view from Brazil. *American Journal of Public Health, 94*(3), 433–434. doi: 10.2105/AJPH.94.3.433

Monteiro, Carlos A.; Levy, Renata B.; Claro, Rafael M.; Ribeiro de Castro, Inês Rugani & Cannon, Geoffrey. (2011). Increasing consumption of ultra-processed foods and likely impact on human health: Evidence from Brazil. *Public Health Nutrition, 14*(1), 5–13. doi: 10.1017/S1368980010003241

Montez, Jennifer Karas; Sabbath, Erika; Glymour, M. Maria & Berkman, Lisa F. (2014). Trends in work–family context among U.S. women by education level, 1976 to 2011. *Population Research and Policy Review, 33*(5), 629–648. doi: 10.1007/s11113-013-9315-4

Monthly Vital Statistics Report. (1980). *Final mortality statistics, 1978: Advance report. Monthly Vital Statistics Report, 29*(6, Suppl. 2). Hyattsville, MD: National Center for Health Statistics.

Montirosso, Rosario; Casini, Erica; Provenzi, Livio; Putnam, Samuel P.; Morandi, Francesco; Fedeli, Claudia & Borgatti, Renato. (2015). A categorical approach to infants' individual differences during the Still-Face paradigm. *Infant Behavior and Development, 38*, 67–76. doi: 10.1016/j.infbeh.2014.12.015

Moody, Raymond A. (1975). *Life after life: The investigation of a phenomenon—Survival of bodily death.* Atlanta, GA: Mockingbird Books.

Moore, Kelly L.; Boscardin, W. John; Steinman, Michael A. & Schwartz, Janice B. (2012). Age and sex variation in prevalence of chronic medical conditions in older residents of U.S. nursing homes. *Journal of the American Geriatrics Society, 60*(4), 756–764. doi: 10.1111/j.1532-5415.2012.03909.x

Moore, Keith L. & Persaud, T. V. N. (2007). *The developing human: Clinically oriented embryology* (8th ed.). Philadelphia, PA: Saunders/Elsevier.

Moran, Lyndsey R.; Lengua, Liliana J. & Zalewski, Maureen. (2013). The interaction between negative emotionality and effortful control in early social-emotional development. *Social Development, 22*(2), 340–362. doi: 10.1111/sode.12025

Morawska, Alina & Sanders, Matthew. (2011). Parental use of time out revisited: A useful or harmful parenting strategy? *Journal of Child and Family Studies, 20*(1), 1–8. doi: 10.1007/s10826-010-9371-x

Morcos, Roy N. & Kizy, Thomas. (2012). Gynecomastia: When is treatment indicated? *Journal of Family Practice, 61*(12), 719–725.

Moreau, Caroline; Bohet, Aline; Le Guen, Mireille; Loilier, Arnaud Régnier & Bajos, Nathalie. (2014). Unplanned or unwanted? A randomized study of national estimates of pregnancy intentions. *Fertility and Sterility, 102*(6), 1663–1670. doi: 10.1016/j.fertnstert.2014.08.011

Morgan, Ian G.; Ohno-Matsui, Kyoko & Saw, Seang-Mei. (2012). Myopia. *The Lancet, 379*(9827), 1739–1748. doi: 10.1016/S0140-6736(12)60272-4

Morgan, Kevin; Gregory, Pamela; Tomeny, Maureen; David, Beverley M. & Gascoigne, Claire. (2012). Self-help treatment for insomnia symptoms associated with chronic conditions in older adults: A randomized controlled trial. *Journal of the American Geriatrics Society, 60*(10), 1803–1810. doi: 10.1111/j.1532-5415.2012.04175.x

Morgan, Paul L.; Staff, Jeremy; Hillemeier, Marianne M.; Farkas, George & Maczuga, Steven. (2013). Racial and ethnic disparities in ADHD diagnosis from kindergarten to eighth grade. *Pediatrics, 132*(1), 85–93. doi: 10.1542/peds.2012-2390

Morin, Rich. (2011). *The public renders a split verdict on changes in family structure.* Washington, DC: Pew Research Center.

Morin, Rich & Fry, Richard. (2012, October 22). More Americans worry about financing retirement: Adults in their late 30s most concerned. *Pew Research, Social and Demographic Trends.*

Morning, Ann. (2008). Ethnic classification in global perspective: A cross-national survey of the 2000 census round. *Population Research and Policy Review, 27*(2), 239–272. doi: 10.1007/s11113-007-9062-5

Morón, Cecilio & Viteri, Fernando E. (2009). Update on common indicators of nutritional status: Food access, food consumption, and biochemical measures of iron and anemia. *Nutrition Reviews, 67*(Suppl. 1), S31–S35. doi: 10.1111/j.1753-4887.2009.00156.x

Morones, Alyssa. (2013). Paddling persists in U.S. schools. *Education Week, 33*(9), 1, 10–11.

Morris, Amanda S.; Silk, Jennifer S.; Steinberg, Laurence; Myers, Sonya S. & Robinson, Lara R. (2007). The role of the family context in the development of emotion regulation. *Social Development, 16*(2), 361–388. doi: 10.1111/j.1467-9507.2007.00389.x

Morris, Danielle H.; Jones, Michael E.; Schoemaker, Minouk J.; Ashworth, Alan & Swerdlow, Anthony J.

(2011). Familial concordance for age at natural menopause: Results from the Breakthrough Generations Study. *Menopause, 18*(9), 956–961. doi: 10.1097/gme.0b013e31820ed6d2

Morris, Vivian G. & Morris, Curtis L. (2013). A call for African American male teachers: The supermen expected to solve the problems of low-performing schools. In Chance W. Lewis & Ivory A. Toldson (Eds.), *Black male teachers: Diversifying the United States' teacher workforce* (pp. 151–165). Bingley, UK: Emerald Group.

Morrissey, Taryn. (2009). Multiple child-care arrangements and young children's behavioral outcomes. *Child Development, 80*(1), 59–76. doi: 10.1111/j.1467-8624.2008.01246.x

Morrow, Daniel G.; Miller, Lisa M. Soederberg; Ridolfo, Heather E.; Magnor, Clifford; Fischer, Ute M.; Kokayeff, Nina K. & Stine-Morrow, Elizabeth A. L. (2009). Expertise and age differences in pilot decision making. *Aging, Neuropsychology, and Cognition, 16*(1), 33–55. doi: 10.1080/13825580802195641

Mortimer, Jeylan. (2013). Work and its positive and negative effects on youth's psychosocial development. In Carol W. Runyan et al. (Eds.), *Health and safety of young workers: Proceedings of a U.S. and Canadian series of symposia* (pp. 66–79). Washington, DC: U.S. Department of Health and Human Services, Centers for Disease Control and Prevention, National Institute for Occupational Safety and Health.

Mosher, Catherine E. & Danoff-Burg, Sharon. (2007). Death anxiety and cancer-related stigma: A terror management analysis. *Death Studies, 31*(10), 885–907. doi: 10.1080/07481180701603360

Mosher, William D.; Jones, Jo & Abma, Joyce C. (2012). *Intended and unintended births in the United States: 1982–2010. National Health Statistics Reports 55*, 1–27. Hyattsville, MD: U.S. Department of Health and Human Services, Centers for Disease Control and Prevention, National Center for Health Statistics.

Moss, Howard B.; Chen, Chiung M. & Yi, Hsiao-ye. (2014). Early adolescent patterns of alcohol, cigarettes, and marijuana polysubstance use and young adult substance use outcomes in a nationally representative sample. *Drug & Alcohol Dependence, 136*(Suppl. 1), 51–62. doi: 10.1016/j.drugalcdep.2013.12.011

Motel, Seth. (2014). *6 facts about marijuana.* Washington, DC: Pew Research Center.

Motl, Robert W. & McAuley, Edward. (2010). Physical activity, disability, and quality of life in older adults. *Physical Medicine and Rehabilitation Clinics of North America, 21*(2), 299–308. doi: 10.1016/j.pmr.2009.12.006

Moye, Jennifer. (2015). Evidence-based treatment of neurocognitive disorders: Measured optimism about select outcomes. *The American Journal of Geriatric Psychiatry, 23*(4), 331–334. doi: 10.1016/j.jagp.2015.01.002

Mrug, Sylvie; Elliott, Marc N.; Davies, Susan; Tortolero, Susan R.; Cuccaro, Paula & Schuster, Mark A. (2014). Early puberty, negative peer influence, and problem behaviors in adolescent girls. *Pediatrics, 133*(1), 7–14. doi: 10.1542/peds.2013-0628

Mueller, Christian E.; Bridges, Sara K. & Goddard, Michelle S. (2011). Sleep and parent-family connectedness: Links, relationships and implications for adolescent depression. *Journal of Family Studies, 17*(1), 9–23.

Mullally, Sinéad L. & Maguire, Eleanor A. (2014). Learning to remember: The early ontogeny of episodic memory. *Developmental Cognitive Neuroscience, 9*(13), 12–29. doi: 10.1016/j.dcn.2013.12.006

Muller, Ziva & Litwin, Howard. (2011). Grandparenting and psychological well-being: How important is grandparent role centrality? *European Journal of Ageing, 8*(2), 109–118. doi: 10.1007/s10433-011-0185-5

Mulligan, Aisling; Anney, Richard; Butler, L.; O'Regan, M.; Richardson, T.; Tulewicz, E. M., . . . Gill, Michael. (2013). Home environment: Association with hyperactivity/impulsivity in children with ADHD and their non-ADHD siblings. *Child: Care, Health & Development, 39*(2), 202–212. doi: 10.1111/j.1365-2214.2011.01345.x

Mulligan, Gail M.; McCarroll, Jill C.; Flanagan, Kristin D. & Potter, Daniel. (2014). *Findings from the first-grade rounds of The Early Childhood Longitudinal Study, Kindergarten Class of 2010–11 (ECLS-K:2011): First look.* Washington, DC: National Center for Education Statistics, Institute of Education Sciences, U.S. Department of Education.

Mullis, Ina V. S.; Martin, Michael O.; Foy, Pierre & Drucker, Kathleen T. (2012). *PIRLS 2011 international results in reading.* Chestnut Hill, MA: TIMSS & PIRLS International Study Center, Boston College.

Muñoz, Carmen & Singleton, David. (2011). A critical review of age-related research on L2 ultimate attainment. *Language Teaching, 44*(1), 1–35. doi: 10.1017/S0261444810000327

Muraco, Anna. (2006). Intentional families: Fictive kin ties between cross-gender, different sexual orientation friends. *Journal of Marriage and Family, 68*(5), 1313–1325. doi: 10.1111/j.1741-3737.2006.00330.x

Muris, Peter & Meesters, Cor. (2014). Small or big in the eyes of the other: On the developmental psychopathology of self-conscious emotions as shame, guilt, and pride. *Clinical Child and Family Psychology Review, 17*(1), 19–40. doi: 10.1007/s10567-013-0137-z

Murphy, Michael. (2011). Long-term effects of the demographic transition on family and kinship networks in Britain. *Population and Development Review, 37*(Suppl. 1), 55–80. doi: 10.1111/j.1728-4457.2011.00378.x

Murphy, Sherry L.; Xu, Jiaquan & Kochanek, Kenneth D. (2012). *Deaths: Preliminary data for 2010. National Vital Statistics Reports 60*(4). Hyattsville, MD: National Center for Health Statistics.

Murray, Brendan D.; Anderson, Michael C. & Kensinger, Elizabeth A. (2015). Older adults can suppress unwanted memories when given an appropriate strategy. *Psychology and Aging, 30*(1), 9–25. doi: 10.1037/a0038611

Murray, Joseph; Farrington, David P. & Sekol, Ivana. (2012). Children's antisocial behavior, mental health, drug use, and educational performance after parental incarceration: A systematic review and meta-analysis. *Psychological Bulletin, 138*(2), 175–210. doi: 10.1037/a0026407

Murray, Thomas H. (2014). Stirring the simmering "designer baby" pot. *Science, 343*(6176), 1208–1210. doi: 10.1126/science.1248080

Mustanski, Brian; Birkett, Michelle; Greene, George J.; Hatzenbuehler, Mark L. & Newcomb, Michael E. (2014). Envisioning an America without sexual orientation inequities in adolescent health. *American Journal of Public Health, 104*(2), 218–225. doi: 10.2105/AJPH.2013.301625

Mustonen, Ulla; Huurre, Taina; Kiviruusu, Olli; Haukkala, Ari & Aro, Hillevi. (2011). Long-term impact of parental divorce on intimate relationship quality in adulthood and the mediating role of psychosocial resources. *Journal of Family Psychology, 25*(4), 615–619. doi: 10.1037/a0023996

Mynatt, Blair Sumner & Mowery, Robyn L. (2013). The family, larger systems, and end-of-life decision making. In David K. Meagher & David E. Balk (Eds.), *Handbook of thanatology: The essential body of knowledge for the study of death, dying, and bereavement* (2nd ed., pp. 91–99). New York, NY: Routledge.

Naci, Huseyin; Chisholm, Dan & Baker, T. D. (2009). Distribution of road traffic deaths by road user group: A global comparison. *Injury Prevention, 15*(1), 55–59. doi: 10.1136/ip.2008.018721

Nadal, Kevin L.; Mazzula, Silvia L.; Rivera, David P. & Fujii-Doe, Whitney. (2014). Microaggressions and Latina/o Americans: An analysis of nativity, gender, and ethnicity. *Journal of Latina/o Psychology, 2*(2), 67–78. doi: 10.1037/lat0000013

Nadarasa, Jeyendran; Deck, Caroline; Meyer, Franck; Willinger, Rémy & Raul, Jean-Sébastien. (2014). Update on injury mechanisms in abusive head trauma - shaken baby syndrome. *Pediatric Radiology, 44*(4, Suppl.), 565–570. doi: 10.1007/s00247-014-3168-9

Nadeau, Joseph H. & Dudley, Aimée M. (2011). Systems genetics. *Science, 331*(6020), 1015–1016. doi: 10.1126/science.1203869

NAEYC. (2014). *NAEYC Early Childhood Program Standards and Accreditation Criteria & Guidance for Assessment.* Washington, DC: National Association for the Education of Young Children.

Nagata, Chisato; Nakamura, Kozue; Wada, Keiko; Oba, Shino; Hayashi, Makoto; Takeda, Noriyuki & Yasuda, Keigo. (2010). Association of dietary fat, vegetables and antioxidant micronutrients with skin ageing in Japanese women. *British Journal of Nutrition, 103*(10), 1493–1498. doi: 10.1017/S0007114509993461

Naninck, Eva F. G.; Lucassen, Paul J. & Bakker, Julie. (2011). Sex differences in adolescent depression: Do sex hormones determine vulnerability? *Journal of Neuroendocrinology, 23*(5), 383–392. doi: 10.1111/j.1365-2826.2011.02125.x

Nanji, Ayaz. (2005, February 8). World's smallest baby goes home. *CBS News.* http://www.cbsnews.com/stories/2005/02/08/health/main672488.shtml

Narayan, Chandan R.; Werker, Janet F. & Beddor, Patrice Speeter. (2010). The interaction between acoustic salience and language experience in developmental speech perception: Evidence from nasal place discrimination. *Developmental Science, 13*(3), 407–420. doi: 10.1111/j.1467-7687.2009.00898.x

National Center for Education Statistics. (2013). *Annual diploma counts and the Averaged Freshmen Graduation Rate (AFGR) in the United States by race/ethnicity: School years 2007–08 through 2011-12. Common Core Data.* Washington, DC: U.S. Department of Education, Institute of Education Sciences, National Center for Education Statistics.

National Center for Education Statistics. (2014, July). *Table 219.70: Percentage of high school dropouts among persons 16 through 24 years old (status dropout rate), by sex and race/ethnicity: Selected years, 1960 through 2013.* Washington, DC: U.S. Department of Education, Institute of Education Sciences, National Center for Education Statistics, The World of Statistics.

National Center for Environmental Health. (2012). *Tested and confirmed elevated blood lead levels by state, year and blood lead level group for children <72 months.* Atlanta, GA: Centers for Disease Control and Prevention.

National Center for Health Statistics. (2011). *Health, United States, 2010: With special feature on death and dying.* Hyattsville, MD: U.S. Department of Health and Human Services, Centers for Disease Control and Prevention.

National Center for Health Statistics. (2012). *Health, United States, 2011: With special feature on socioeconomic status and health.* Hyattsville, MD: U.S. Department of Health and Human Services, Centers for Disease Control and Prevention.

National Center for Health Statistics. (2013). *Health, United States, 2012: With special feature on emergency care.* Hyattsville, MD: U.S. Department of Health and Human Services, Centers for Disease Control and Prevention.

National Center for Health Statistics. (2014). *Health, United States, 2013: With special feature on prescription drugs.* Hyattsville, MD: U.S. Department of Health and Human Services, Centers for Disease Control and Prevention.

National Governors Association Center for Best Practices (NGA Center) and the Council of Chief State School Officers (CCSSO). (2010, October 25). *Common Core state standards initiative.* Washington, DC: National Governors Association.

National Highway Traffic Safety Administration. (1993). *Figure 2. Total miles of travel by age group. Addressing the safety issues related to younger and older drivers: A Report to Congress January 19, 1993 on the research agenda of the National Highway Traffic Safety Administration.* Washington, DC: U.S. Department of Transportation.

National Highway Traffic Safety Administration. (2014, December 19). *U.S. Department of Transportation announces decline in traffic fatalities in 2013.* Washington, DC: U.S. Department of Transportation.

National Vital Statistics Reports. (2013, May 8). *Deaths: Final data for 2010, 61*(4). Hyattsville, MD: National Center for Health Statistics.

National Vital Statistics Reports. (Forthcoming). *Deaths: Final data for 2012. National Vital Statistics Reports 63*(9). Hyattsville, MD: National Center for Health Statistics.

Natsuaki, Misaki N.; Leve, Leslie D.; Neiderhiser, Jenae M.; Shaw, Daniel S.; Scaramella, Laura V.; Ge, Xiaojia & Reiss, David. (2013). Intergenerational transmission of risk for social inhibition: The interplay between parental responsiveness and genetic influences. *Development and Psychopathology, 25*(1), 261–274. doi: 10.1017/S0954579412001010

Naughton, Michelle J.; Yi-Frazier, Joyce P.; Morgan, Timothy M.; Seid, Michael; Lawrence, Jean M.; Klingensmith, Georgeanna J., . . . Loots, Beth. (2014). Longitudinal associations between sex, diabetes self-care, and health-related quality of life among youth with type 1 or type 2 diabetes mellitus. *The Journal of Pediatrics, 164*(6), 1376–1383. e1371. doi: 10.1016/j.jpeds.2014.01.027

Neary, Karen R. & Friedman, Ori. (2014). Young children give priority to ownership when judging who should use an object. *Child Development, 85*(1), 326–337. doi: 10.1111/cdev.12120

Neary, Marianne T. & Breckenridge, Ross A. (2013). Hypoxia at the heart of sudden infant death syndrome? *Pediatric Research, 74*(4), 375–379. doi: 10.1038/pr.2013.122

Needleman, Herbert L. & Gatsonis, Constantine A. (1990). Low-level lead exposure and the IQ of children: A meta-analysis of modern studies. *JAMA, 263*(5), 673–678. doi: 10.1001/jama.1990.03440050067035

Needleman, Herbert L.; Schell, Alan; Bellinger, David; Leviton, Alan & Allred, Elizabeth N. (1990). The long-term effects of exposure to low doses of lead in childhood. *New England Journal of Medicine, 322*(2), 83–88. doi: 10.1056/NEJM199001113220203

Neggers, Yasmin & Crowe, Kristi. (2013). Low birth weight outcomes: Why better in Cuba than Alabama? *Journal of the American Board of Family Medicine, 26*(2), 187–195. doi: 10.3122/jabfm.2013.02.120227

Neigh, Gretchen N.; Gillespie, Charles F. & Nemeroff, Charles B. (2009). The neurobiological toll of child abuse and neglect. *Trauma, Violence, & Abuse, 10*(4), 389–410. doi: 10.1177/1524838009339758

Neimeyer, Robert A. & Holland, Jason M. (2015). Bereavement in later life: Theory, assessment, and intervention. In Peter A. Lichtenberg et al. (Eds.), *APA handbook of clinical geropsychology* (Vol. 2). Washington, DC: American Psychological Association. doi: 10.1037/14459-025

Neimeyer, Robert A. & Jordan, John R. (2013). Historical and contemporary perspectives on assessment and intervention. In David K. Meagher & David E. Balk (Eds.), *Handbook of thanatology: The essential body of knowledge for the study of death, dying, and bereavement* (2nd ed., pp. 219–237). New York, NY: Routledge.

Nelson, Charles A.; Zeanah, Charles H.; Fox, Nathan A.; Marshall, Peter J.; Smyke, Anna T. & Guthrie, Donald. (2007). Cognitive recovery in socially deprived young children: The Bucharest Early Intervention Project. *Science, 318*(5858), 1937–1940. doi: 10.1126/science.1143921

Nelson, Eric E.; Lau, Jennifer Y. F. & Jarcho, Johanna M. (2014). Growing pains and pleasures: How emotional learning guides development. *Trends in Cognitive Sciences, 18*(2), 99–108. doi: 10.1016/j.tics.2013.11.003

Nelson, Geoffrey & Caplan, Rachel. (2014). The prevention of child physical abuse and neglect: An update. *Journal of Applied Research on Children: Informing Policy for Children at Risk, 5*(1).

Nelson, Todd D. (2011). Ageism: The strange case of prejudice against the older you. In Richard L. Wiener & Steven L. Willborn (Eds.), *Disability and aging discrimination: Perspectives in law and psychology* (pp. 37–47). New York, NY: Springer. doi: 10.1007/978-1-4419-6293-5_2

Nelson-Becker, Holly; Ai, Amy L.; Hopp, Faith P.; McCormick, Thomas R.; Schlueter, Judith O. & Camp, Jessica K. (2015). Spirituality and religion in end-of-life care ethics: The challenge of interfaith and cross-generational matters. *British Journal of Social Work, 45*(1), 104–119. doi: 10.1093/bjsw/bct110

Neumann, Anna; van Lier, Pol; Frijns, Tom; Meeus, Wim & Koot, Hans. (2011). Emotional dynamics in the development of early adolescent psychopathology: A one-year longitudinal study. *Journal of Abnormal Child Psychology, 39*(5), 657–669. doi: 10.1007/s10802-011-9509-3

Nevanen, Saila; Juvonen, Antti & Ruismäki, Heikki. (2014). Does arts education develop school readiness? Teachers' and artists' points of view on an art education project. *Arts Education Policy Review, 115*(3), 72–81. doi: 10.1080/10632913.2014.913970

Nevin, Rick. (2007). Understanding international crime trends: The legacy of preschool lead exposure. *Environmental Research, 104*(3), 315–336. doi: 10.1016/j.envres.2007.02.008

Newnham, Carol A.; Milgrom, Jeannette & Skouteris, Helen. (2009). Effectiveness of a modified mother-infant transaction program on outcomes for preterm infants from 3 to 24 months of age. *Infant Behavior and Development, 32*(1), 17–26. doi: 10.1016/j.infbeh.2008.09.004

Ng, Florrie Fei-Yin; Pomerantz, Eva M. & Deng, Ciping. (2014). Why are Chinese mothers more controlling than American mothers? "My child is my report card". *Child Development, 85*(1), 355–369. doi: 10.1111/cdev.12102

Ng, Nawi; Weinehall, Lars & Öhman, Ann. (2007). 'If I don't smoke, I'm not a real man'—Indonesian teenage boys' views about smoking. *Health Education Research, 22*(6), 794–804. doi: 10.1093/her/cyl104

Ng, Thomas W. H. & Feldman, Daniel C. (2012). Evaluating six common stereotypes about older workers with meta-analytical data. *Personnel Psychology, 65*(4), 821–858. doi: 10.1111/peps.12003

Ngoma, Mary S.; Hunter, Jennifer A.; Harper, Jessica A.; Church, Paige T.; Mumba, Scholastica; Chandwe, Mulapati, . . . Silverman, Michael S. (2014). Cognitive and language outcomes in HIV-uninfected infants exposed to combined antiretroviral therapy in utero and through extended breast-feeding. *AIDS, 28*, S323–S330. doi: 10.1097/QAD.0000000000000357

Ngui, Emmanuel; Cortright, Alicia & Blair, Kathleen. (2009). An investigation of paternity status and other factors associated with racial and ethnic disparities in birth outcomes in Milwaukee, Wisconsin. *Maternal and Child Health Journal, 13*(4), 467–478. doi: 10.1007/s10995-008-0383-8

NHPCO. (2014). *NHPCO's facts and figures: Hospice care in America.* Alexandria, VA: National Hospice and Palliative Care Organization.

Niclasen, Janni; Andersen, Anne-Marie N.; Strandberg-Larsen, Katrine & Teasdale, Thomas W. (2014). Is alcohol binge drinking in early and late pregnancy associated with behavioural and emotional development at age 7 years? *European Child & Adolescent Psychiatry.* doi: 10.1007/s00787-013-0511-x

Niedzwiedz, Claire; Haw, Camilla; Hawton, Keith & Platt, Stephen. (2014). The definition and epidemiology of clusters of suicidal behavior: A systematic review. *Suicide and Life-Threatening Behavior, 44*(5), 569–581. doi: 10.1111/sltb.12091

Nielsen, Mark & Tomaselli, Keyan. (2010). Overimitation in Kalahari Bushman children and the origins of human cultural cognition. *Psychological Science, 21*(5), 729–736. doi: 10.1177/0956797610368808

Nielsen, Mark; Tomaselli, Keyan; Mushin, Ilana & Whiten, Andrew. (2014). Exploring tool innovation: A comparison of Western and Bushman children. *Journal of Experimental Child Psychology, 126*, 384–394. doi: 10.1016/j.jecp.2014.05.008

Nieto, Sonia. (2000). *Affirming diversity: The sociopolitical context of multicultural education* (3rd ed.). New York, NY: Longman.

Nigg, Joel T. & Barkley, Russell A. (2014). Attention-deficit/hyperactivity disorder. In Eric J. Mash & Russell A. Barkley (Eds.), *Child psychopathology* (3rd ed., pp. 75–144). New York, NY: Guilford Press.

Nisbett, Richard E.; Aronson, Joshua; Blair, Clancy; Dickens, William; Flynn, James; Halpern, Diane F. & Turkheimer, Eric. (2012). Intelligence: New findings and theoretical developments. *American Psychologist, 67*(2), 130–159. doi: 10.1037/a0026699

Noël-Miller, Claire M. (2013a). Repartnering following divorce: implications for older fathers' relations with their adult children. *Journal of Marriage and Family, 75*(3), 697–712. doi: 10.1111/jomf.12034

Noël-Miller, Claire M. (2013b). Former stepparents' contact with their stepchildren after midlife. *The Journals of Gerontology Series B: Psychological Sciences and Social Sciences, 68*(3), 409–419. doi: 10.1093/geronb/gbt021

Norcross, John C.; Krebs, Paul M. & Prochaska, James O. (2011). Stages of change. *Journal of Clinical Psychology, 67*(2), 143–154. doi: 10.1002/jclp.20758

Nordgren, Loran F.; Harreveld, Frenk van & Pligt, Joop van der. (2009). The restraint bias: How the illusion of self-restraint promotes impulsive behavior. *Psychological Science, 20*(12), 1523–1528. doi: 10.1111/j.1467-9280.2009.02468.x

Noronha, Konrad J. (2015). Impact of religion and spirituality on older adulthood. *Journal of Religion, Spirituality & Aging, 27*(1), 16–33. doi: 10.1080/15528030.2014.963907

Norris, Pippa. (2001). *Digital divide: Civic engagement, information poverty, and the Internet worldwide.* New York, NY: Cambridge University Press.

Norton, Michael I. & Ariely, Dan. (2011). Building a better America: One wealth quintile at a time. *Perspectives on Psychological Science, 6*(1), 9–12. doi: 10.1177/1745691610393524

O'Brien, Beth A.; Wolf, Maryanne & Lovett, Maureen W. (2012). A taxometric investigation of developmental dyslexia subtypes. *Dyslexia, 18*(1), 16–39. doi: 10.1002/dys.1431

O'Donnell, Lydia; Stueve, Ann; Duran, Richard; Myint-U, Athi; Agronick, Gail; Doval, Alexi San & Wilson-Simmons, Renée. (2008). Parenting practices, parents' underestimation of daughters' risks, and alcohol and sexual behaviors of urban girls. *Journal of Adolescent Health, 42*(5), 496–502. doi: 10.1016/j.jadohealth.2007.10.008

O'Hanlon, Leslie H. (2013). Teaching students the skills to be savvy researchers. *Education Week, 32*(32), s12, s15, s16.

O'Keefe, Andrew W.; De Schryver, Sarah; Mill, Jennifer; Mill, Christopher; Dery, Alizee & Ben-Shoshan, Moshe. (2014). Diagnosis and management of food allergies: New and emerging options: A systematic review. *Journal of Asthma and Allergy, 7*, 141–164. doi: 10.2147/JAA.S49277

O'Leary, Colleen M.; Nassar, Natasha; Zubrick, Stephen R.; Kurinczuk, Jennifer J.; Stanley, Fiona & Bower, Carol. (2010). Evidence of a complex association between dose, pattern and timing of prenatal alcohol exposure and child behaviour problems. *Addiction, 105*(1), 74–86. doi: 10.1111/j.1360-0443.2009.02756.x

O'Malley, A. James & Christakis, Nicholas A. (2011). Longitudinal analysis of large social networks: Estimating the effect of health traits on changes in friendship ties. *Statistics in Medicine, 30*(9), 950–964. doi: 10.1002/sim.4190

O'Rahilly, Ronan & Müller, Fabiola. (2001). *Human embryology & teratology* (3rd ed.). New York, NY: Wiley-Liss.

O'Rourke, Norm; Neufeld, Eva; Claxton, Amy & Smith, JuliAnna Z. (2010). Knowing me-knowing you: Reported personality and trait discrepancies as predictors of marital idealization between long-wed spouses. *Psychology and Aging, 25*(2), 412–421. doi: 10.1037/a0017873

O'Rahilly, Ronan & Müller, Fabiola. (2012). Prenatal development of the brain. In Ilan Timor-Tritsch et al. (Eds.), *Ultrasonography of the prenatal brain* (3rd ed., pp. 1–14). New York, NY: McGraw-Hill.

Oakes, J. Michael. (2009). The effect of media on children: A methodological assessment from a social epidemiologist. *American Behavioral Scientist, 52*(8), 1136–1151. doi: 10.1177/0002764209331538

Obradovi , Jelena. (2012). How can the study of physiological reactivity contribute to our understanding of adversity and resilience processes in development? *Development and Psychopathology, 24*(2), 371–387. doi: 10.1017/S0954579412000053

Obradovi , Jelena; Long, Jeffrey D.; Cutuli, J. J.; Chan, Chi-Keung; Hinz, Elizabeth; Heistad, David & Masten, Ann S. (2009). Academic achievement of homeless and highly mobile children in an urban school district: Longitudinal evidence on risk, growth, and resilience. *Development and Psychopathology, 21*(2), 493–518. doi: 10.1017/S0954579409000273

Ocobock, Abigail. (2013). The power and limits of marriage: Married gay men's family relationships. *Journal of Marriage and Family, 75*(1), 191–205. doi: 10.1111/j.1741-3737.2012.01032.x

OECD. (2010). *PISA 2009 results: Learning to learn: Student engagement, strategies and practices* (Vol. 3): PISA, OECD Publishing. doi: 10.1787/9789264083943-en

OECD. (2011). *Education at a glance 2011: OECD indicators.* Paris, France: Organisation for Economic Cooperation and Development. doi: 10.1787/eag-2011-en

OECD. (2013). *Education at a glance 2013: OECD indicators.* Paris, France: Organisation for Economic Cooperation and Development. doi: 10.1787/19991487

OECD. (2014). *Education at a glance 2014: OECD Indicators.* Paris, France: Organisation for Economic Cooperation and Development. doi: 10.1787/eag-2014-en

Ogden, Cynthia L.; Carroll, Margaret D.; Kit, Brian K. & Flegal, Katherine M. (2014). Prevalence of childhood and adult obesity in the United States, 2011–2012. *JAMA, 311*(8), 806–814. doi: 10.1001/jama.2014.732

Ogden, Cynthia L.; Gorber, Sarah C.; Dommarco, Juan A. Rivera; Carroll, Margaret; Shields, Margot & Flegal, Katherine. (2011). The epidemiology of childhood obesity in Canada, Mexico and the United States. In Luis A. Moreno et al. (Eds.), *Epidemiology of obesity in children and adolescents* (Vol. 2, pp. 69–93). New York, NY: Springer. doi: 10.1007/978-1-4419-6039-9_5

Okun, Morris A.; Yeung, Ellen WanHeung & Brown, Stephanie. (2013). Volunteering by older adults and risk of mortality: A meta-analysis. *Psychology and Aging, 28*(2), 564–577. doi: 10.1037/a0031519

Olds, David L. (2006). The nurse–family partnership: An evidence-based preventive intervention. *Infant Mental Health Journal, 27*(1), 5–25. doi: 10.1002/imhj.20077

Olds, David L.; Kitzman, Harriet; Knudtson, Michael D.; Anson, Elizabeth; Smith, Joyce A. & Cole, Robert. (2014). Effect of home visiting by nurses on maternal and child mortality: Results of a 2-decade follow-up of a randomized clinical trial. *JAMA Pediatrics, 168*(9), 800–806. doi: 10.1001/jamapediatrics.2014.472

Olfson, Mark; Crystal, Stephen; Huang, Cecilia & Gerhard, Tobias. (2010). Trends in antipsychotic drug use by very young, privately insured children. *Journal of the American Academy of Child and Adolescent Psychiatry, 49*(1), 13–23. doi: 10.1016/j.jaac.2009.09.003

Olshansky, S. Jay; Antonucci, Toni; Berkman, Lisa; Binstock, Robert H.; Boersch-Supan, Axel; Cacioppo, John T., . . . Rowe, John. (2012). Differences in life expectancy due to race and educational differences are widening, and many may not catch up. *Health Affairs, 31*(8), 1803–1813. doi: 10.1377/hlthaff.2011.0746

Olson, Kristina R. & Dweck, Carol S. (2009). Social cognitive development: A new look. *Child Development Perspectives, 3*(1), 60–65. doi: 10.1111/j.1750-8606.2008.00078.x

Olson, Sheryl L.; Lopez-Duran, Nestor; Lunkenheimer, Erika S.; Chang, Hyein & Sameroff, Arnold J. (2011). Individual differences in the development of early peer aggression: Integrating contributions of self-regulation, theory of mind, and parenting. *Development and Psychopathology, 23*(1), 253–266. doi: 10.1017/S0954579410000775

Olweus, Dan. (1999). Sweden. In Peter K. Smith et al. (Eds.), *The nature of school bullying: A cross-national perspective* (pp. 7–27). New York, NY: Routledge.

Omariba, D. Walter Rasugu & Boyle, Michael H. (2007). Family structure and child mortality in sub-Saharan Africa: Cross-national effects of polygyny. *Journal of Marriage and Family, 69*(2), 528–543. doi: 10.1111/j.1741-3737.2007.00381.x

Oregon Public Health Division. (2013). *Oregon's Death with Dignity Act—2012.* Portland, OR: Oregon Health Authority, Public Health Division.

Orth, Ulrich; Robins, Richard W. & Widaman, Keith F. (2012). Life-span development of self-esteem and its effects on important life outcomes. *Journal of Personality and Social Psychology, 102*(6), 1271–1288. doi: 10.1037/a0025558

Osgood, D. Wayne; Ragan, Daniel T.; Wallace, Lacey; Gest, Scott D.; Feinberg, Mark E. & Moody, James. (2013). Peers and the emergence of alcohol use: Influence and selection processes in adolescent friendship networks. *Journal of Research on Adolescence, 23*(3), 500–512. doi: 10.1111/jora.12059

Ossher, Lynn; Flegal, Kristin E. & Lustig, Cindy. (2013). Everyday memory errors in older adults. *Aging, Neuropsychology, and Cognition: A Journal on Normal and Dysfunctional Development, 20*(2), 220–242. doi: 10.1080/13825585.2012.690365

Ostfeld, Barbara M.; Esposito, Linda; Perl, Harold & Hegyi, Thomas. (2010). Concurrent risks in sudden infant death syndrome. *Pediatrics, 125*(3), 447–453. doi: 10.1542/peds.2009-0038

Ostrov, Jamie M.; Kamper, Kimberly E.; Hart, Emily J.; Godleski, Stephanie A. & Blakely-McClure, Sarah J. (2014). A gender-balanced approach to the study of peer victimization and aggression subtypes in early childhood. *Development and Psychopathology, 26*(3), 575–587. doi: 10.1017/S0954579414000248

Ostrowsky, Michael K. (2010). Are violent people more likely to have low self-esteem or high self-esteem? *Aggression and Violent Behavior, 15*(1), 69–75. doi: 10.1016/j.avb.2009.08.004

Otto, Hiltrud & Keller, Heidi (Eds.). (2014). *Different faces of attachment: Cultural variations on a universal human need.* New York, NY: Cambridge University Press.

Over, Harriet & Gattis, Merideth. (2010). Verbal imitation is based on intention understanding. *Cognitive Development, 25*(1), 46–55. doi: 10.1016/j.cogdev.2009.06.004

Owen, Jesse; Fincham, Frank D. & Moore, Jon. (2011). Short-term prospective study of hooking up among college students. *Archives of Sexual Behavior, 40*(2), 331–341. doi: 10.1007/s10508-010-9697-x

Ozturk, Ozge; Krehm, Madelaine & Vouloumanos, Athena. (2013). Sound symbolism in infancy: Evidence for sound–shape cross-modal correspondences in 4-month-olds. *Journal of Experimental Child Psychology, 114*(2), 173–186. doi: 10.1016/j.jecp.2012.05.004

Pace, Cecilia Serena; Zavattini, Giulio Cesare & D'Alessio, Maria. (2011). Continuity and discontinuity of attachment patterns: A short-term longitudinal pilot study using a sample of late-adopted children and their adoptive mothers. *Attachment & Human Development, 14*(1), 45–61. doi: 10.1080/14616734.2012.636658

Pagán-Rodríguez, Ricardo. (2011). Self-employment and job satisfaction: Evidence for older people with disabilities in Europe. *European Journal of Ageing, 8*(3), 177–187. doi: 10.1007/s10433-011-0194-4

Pahwa, Rajesh & Lyons, Kelly E. (Eds.). (2013). *Handbook of Parkinson's disease* (5th ed.). Boca Raton, FL: CRC Press.

Painter, Jodie N.; Willemsen, Gonneke; Nyholt, Dale; Hoekstra, Chantal; Duffy, David L.; Henders, Anjali K., . . . Montgomery, Grant W. (2010). A genome wide linkage scan for dizygotic twinning in 525 families of mothers of dizygotic twins. *Human Reproduction, 25*(6), 1569–1580. doi: 10.1093/humrep/deq084

Palagi, Elisabetta. (2011). Playing at every age: Modalities and potential functions in non-human primates. In Anthony D.

Pellegrini (Ed.), *The Oxford handbook of the development of play* (pp. 70–82). New York, NY: Oxford University Press. doi: 10.1093/oxfordhb/9780195393002.013.0007

Palatini, Paolo. (2015). Coffee consumption and risk of type 2 diabetes. *Diabetologia, 58*(1), 199–200. doi: 10.1007/s00125-014-3425-3

Palmer, Nicholette D.; McDonough, Caitrin W.; Hicks, Pamela J.; Roh, Bong H.; Wing, Maria R.; An, S. Sandy, . . . Bowden, Donald W. (2012). A genome-wide association search for type 2 diabetes genes in African Americans. *PLoS ONE, 7*(1), e29202. doi: 10.1371/journal.pone.0029202

Palmore, Erdman. (2005). Three decades of research on ageism. *Generations, 29*(3), 87–90.

Panay, Nick; Hamoda, Haitham; Arya, Roopen & Savvas, Michael. (2013). The 2013 British Menopause Society & Women's Health Concern recommendations on hormone replacement therapy. *Post Reprod Health, 19*(2), 59–68. doi: 10.1177/1754045313489645

Panksepp, Jaak & Watt, Douglas. (2011). What is basic about basic emotions? Lasting lessons from affective neuroscience. *Emotion Review, 3*(4), 387–396. doi: 10.1177/1754073911410741

Pansky, Ben. (1982). *Review of medical embryology.* New York, NY: Macmillan.

Park, Denise C. & Bischof, Gérard N. (2013). The aging mind: Neuroplasticity in response to cognitive training. *Dialogues in Clinical Neuroscience, 15*(1), 109–119.

Park, Denise C. & Reuter-Lorenz, Patricia. (2009). The adaptive brain: Aging and neurocognitive scaffolding. *Annual Review of Psychology, 60*, 173–196. doi: 10.1146/annurev.psych.59.103006.093656

Park, D. J. & Congdon, Nathan G. (2004). Evidence for an "epidemic" of myopia. *Annals Academy of Medicine Singapore, 33*(1), 21–26.

Park, Hyun; Bothe, Denise; Holsinger, Eva; Kirchner, H. Lester; Olness, Karen & Mandalakas, Anna. (2011). The impact of nutritional status and longitudinal recovery of motor and cognitive milestones in internationally adopted children. *International Journal of Environmental Research and Public Health, 8*(1), 105–116. doi: 10.3390/ijerph8010105

Park, Jong-Tae; Jang, Yoonsun; Park, Min Sun; Pae, Calvin; Park, Jinyi; Hu, Kyung-Seok, . . . Kim, Hee-Jin. (2011). The trend of body donation for education based on Korean social and religious culture. *Anatomical Sciences Education, 4*(1), 33–38. doi: 10.1002/ase.198

Parke, Ross D. (2013). Gender differences and similarities in parental behavior. In Bradford Wilcox & Kathleen K. Kline (Eds.), *Gender and parenthood: Biological and social scientific perspectives* (pp. 120–163). New York, NY: Columbia University Press.

Parke, Ross D. & Buriel, Raymond. (2006). Socialization in the family: Ethnic and ecological perspectives. In William Damon & Richard M. Lerner (Eds.), *Handbook of child psychology* (6th ed., Vol. 3, pp. 429–504). Hoboken, NJ: Wiley.

Parker, Kim. (2012). *The boomerang generation: Feeling OK about living with Mom and Dad. Pew social and demographic trends.* Washington, DC: Pew Research Center.

Parker, Rachael; Wellings, Kaye & Lazarus, Jeffrey V. (2009). Sexuality education in Europe: An overview of current policies. *Sex Education: Sexuality, Society and Learning, 9*(3), 227–242. doi: 10.1080/14681810903059060

Parks, Sharyn E.; Johnson, Linda L.; McDaniel, Dawn D. & Gladden, Matthew. (2014, January 17). *Surveillance for violent deaths—National Violent Death Reporting System, 16 states, 2010. Morbidity and Mortality Weekly Report 63*(SS01), 1–33. Atlanta, GA: U.S. Department of Health and Human Services, Centers for Disease Control and Prevention, Morbidity and Mortality Weekly Report.

Parladé, Meaghan V. & Iverson, Jana M. (2011). The interplay between language, gesture, and affect during communicative transition: A dynamic systems approach. *Developmental Psychology, 47*(3), 820–833. doi: 10.1037/a0021811

Parten, Mildred B. (1932). Social participation among preschool children. *The Journal of Abnormal and Social Psychology, 27*(3), 243–269. doi: 10.1037/h0074524

Pascarella, Ernest T.; Martin, Georgianna L.; Hanson, Jana M.; Trolian, Teniell L.; Gillig, Benjamin & Blaich, Charles. (2014). Effects of diversity experiences on critical thinking skills over 4 years of college. *Journal of College Student Development, 55*(1), 86–92. doi: 10.1353/csd.2014.0009

Pascarella, Ernest T. & Terenzini, Patrick T. (1991). *How college affects students: Findings and insights from twenty years of research.* San Francisco, CA: Jossey-Bass.

Pathela, Preeti & Schillinger, Julia A. (2010). Sexual behaviors and sexual violence: Adolescents with opposite-, same-, or both-sex partners. *Pediatrics, 126*(5), 879–886. doi: 10.1542/peds.2010-0396

Patil, Rakesh N.; Nagaonkar, Shashikant N.; Shah, Nilesh B. & Bhat, Tushar S. (2013). A cross-sectional study of common psychiatric morbidity in children aged 5 to 14 years in an urban slum. *Journal of Family Medicine and Primary Care, 2*(2), 164–168. doi: 10.4103/2249-4863.117413

Patrick, Megan E. & Schulenberg, John E. (2011). How trajectories of reasons for alcohol use relate to trajectories of binge drinking: National panel data spanning late adolescence to early adulthood. *Developmental Psychology, 47*(2), 311–317. doi: 10.1037/a0021939

Paúl, Constança. (2014). Loneliness and health in later life. In Nancy A. Pachana & Ken Laidlaw (Eds.), *The Oxford handbook of clinical geropsychology.* New York, NY: Oxford University Press. doi: 10.1093/oxfordhb/9780199663170.013.012

Paul, Karsten I. & Moser, Klaus. (2009). Unemployment impairs mental health: Meta-analyses. *Journal of Vocational Behavior, 74*(3), 264–282. doi: 10.1016/j.jvb.2009.01.001

Paulsell, Diane; Del Grosso, Patricia & Supplee, Lauren. (2014). Supporting replication and scale-up of evidence-based home visiting programs: Assessing the implementation knowledge base. *American Journal of Public Health, 104*(9), 1624–1632. doi: 10.2105/AJPH.2014.301962

Paulus, Frank W.; Backes, Aline; Sander, Charlotte S.; Weber, Monika & von Gontard, Alexander. (2014). Anxiety disorders and behavioral inhibition in preschool children: A population-based study. *Child Psychiatry & Human Development, 46*(1), 150–157. doi: 10.1007/s10578-014-0460-8

Pausch, Jai. (2012). *Dream new dreams: Reimagining my life after loss.* New York, NY: Crown Archetype.

Pausch, Randy (Producer). (2007). Randy Pausch last lecture: Really achieving your childhood dreams. [Video] Retrieved from http://www.youtube.com/watch?v=ji5_MqicxSo

Pausch, Randy & Zaslow, Jeffrey. (2008). *The last lecture.* New York, NY: Hyperion.

Payne, Monica A. (2012). "All gas and no brakes!": Helpful metaphor or harmful stereotype? *Journal of Adolescent Research, 27*(1), 3–17. doi: 10.1177/0743558411412956

Pedersen, Daphne E. & Kilzer, Gabe. (2014). Work-to-family conflict and the maternal gatekeeping of dual-earner mothers with young children. *Journal of Family and Economic Issues, 35*(2), 251–262. doi: 10.1007/s10834-013-9370-3

Peffley, Mark & Hurwitz, Jon. (2010). *Justice in America: The separate realities of blacks and whites.* New York, NY: Cambridge University Press.

Pellegrini, Anthony D. (2011). Introduction. In Anthony D. Pellegrini (Ed.), *The Oxford handbook of the development of play* (pp. 3–6). New York, NY: Oxford University Press. doi: 10.1093/oxfordhb/9780195393002.013.0001

Pellegrini, Anthony D. (2013). Play. In Philip D. Zelazo (Ed.), *The Oxford handbook of developmental psychology* (Vol. 2, pp. 276–299). New York, NY: Oxford University Press. doi: 10.1093/oxfordhb/9780199958474.013.0012

Pellis, Sergio M. & Pellis, Vivien C. (2011). Rough-and-tumble play: Training and using the social brain. In Anthony D. Pellegrini (Ed.), *The Oxford handbook of the development of play* (pp. 245–259). New York, NY: Oxford University Press. doi: 10.1093/oxfordhb/9780195393002.013.0019

Peng, Duan & Robins, Philip K. (2010). Who should care for our kids? The effects of infant child care on early child development. *Journal of Children and Poverty, 16*(1), 1–45. doi: 10.1080/10796120903575085

Peper, Jiska S. & Dahl, Ronald E. (2013). The teenage brain: Surging hormones—brain-behavior interactions during puberty. *Current Directions in Psychological Science, 22*(2), 134–139. doi: 10.1177/0963721412473755

Pereira, Vera; Faísca, Luís & de Sá-Saraiva, Rodrigo. (2012). Immortality of the soul as an intuitive idea: Towards a psychological explanation of the origins of afterlife beliefs. *Journal of Cognition and Culture, 12*(1/2), 101–127. doi: 10.1163/156853712X633956

Perez, L.; Helm, L.; Sherzai, A. Dean; Jaceldo-Siegl, K. & Sherzai, A. (2012). Nutrition and vascular dementia. *The Journal Of Nutrition, Health & Aging, 16*(4), 319–324. doi: 10.1007/s12603-012-0042-z

Perone, Sammy; Molitor, Stephen J.; Buss, Aaron T.; Spencer, John P. & Samuelson, Larissa K. (2015). Enhancing the executive functions of 3-year-olds in the dimensional change card sort task. *Child Development, 86*(3), 812–827. doi: 10.1111/cdev.12330

Perry, William G. (1970). *Forms of intellectual and ethical development in the college years: A scheme.* New York, NY: Holt, Rinehart and Winston.

Perry, William G. (1981). Cognitive and ethical growth: The making of meaning. In Arthur Chickering (Ed.), *The modern American college: Responding to the new realities of diverse students and a changing society* (pp. 76–116). San Francisco, CA: Jossey-Bass.

Perry, William G. (1998). *Forms of intellectual and ethical development in the college years: A scheme.* San Francisco, CA: Jossey-Bass.

Peters, Ellen; Dieckmann, Nathan F. & Weller, Joshua. (2011). Age differences in complex decision making. In K. Warner Schaie & Sherry L. Willis (Eds.), *Handbook of the psychology of aging* (7th ed., pp. 133–151). San Diego, CA: Academic Press. doi: 10.1016/B978-0-12-380882-0.00009-7

Peters, Stacey L.; Lind, Jennifer N.; Humphrey, Jasmine R.; Friedman, Jan M.; Honein, Margaret A.; Tassinari, Melissa S., . . . Broussard, Cheryl S. (2013). Safe lists for medications in pregnancy: Inadequate evidence base and inconsistent guidance from Web-based information, 2011. *Pharmacoepidemiology and Drug Safety, 22*(3), 324–328. doi: 10.1002/pds.3410

Petersen, Inge; Martinussen, Torben; McGue, Matthew; Bingley, Paul & Christensen, Kaare. (2011). Lower marriage and divorce rates among twins than among singletons in Danish birth cohorts 1940-1964. *Twin Research and Human Genetics, 14*(2), 150–157. doi: 10.1375/twin.14.2.150

Pew Forum on Religion & Public Life. (2012, July 31). *Two-thirds of democrats now support gay marriage.* Washington, DC: Pew Research Center.

Pew Research Center. (2009, June 29). *Growing old in America: Expectations vs. reality.* Washington, DC: Pew Research Center.

Pew Research Center. (2012, April 11). *What the public knows about the political parties. U.S. Politics & Policy.* Washington, DC: Pew Research Center.

Pew Research Center. (2012, May 17). *College graduation: Weighing the cost . . . and the payoff.* Washington, DC: Pew Research Center.

Pew Research Center. (2013, March 20). *Growing support for gay marriage: Changed minds and changing demographics.* Washington, DC: Pew Research Center.

Pew Research Center. (2014, April 2). *America's new drug policy landscape: Two-thirds favor treatment, not jail, for use of heroin, cocaine.* Washington, DC: Pew Research Center.

Pew Research Center. (2015, May 12). *America's changing religious landscape: Christians decline sharply as share of population; unaffiliated and other faiths continue to grow. Religion & Public Life.* Washington, DC: Pew Research Center.

Peyser, James A. (2011). Unlocking the secrets of high-performing charters. *Education Next, 11*(4), 36–43.

Pfeiffer, Ronald E. & Bodis-Wollner, Ivan (Eds.). (2012). *Parkinson's disease and nonmotor dysfunction.* New York, NY: Springer.

Phillips, Deborah A.; Fox, Nathan A. & Gunnar, Megan R. (2011). Same place, different experiences: Bringing individual differences to research in child care. *Child Development Perspectives, 5*(1), 44–49. doi: 10.1111/j.1750-8606.2010.00155.x

Phillips, Tommy M.; Wilmoth, Joe D.; Wall, Sterling K.; Peterson, Donna J.; Buckley, Rhonda & Phillips,

Laura E. (2013). Recollected parental care and fear of intimacy in emerging adults. *The Family Journal, 21*(3), 335–341. doi: 10.1177/1066480713476848

Phillipson, Chris. (2013). *Ageing.* Cambridge, UK: Polity Press.

Piaget, Jean. (1932). *The moral judgment of the child.* London, UK: K. Paul, Trench, Trubner & Co.

Piaget, Jean. (1950). *The psychology of intelligence.* London, UK: Routledge & Paul.

Piaget, Jean. (1954). *The construction of reality in the child.* New York, NY: Basic Books.

Piaget, Jean. (1962). *Play, dreams and imitation in childhood.* New York, NY: Norton.

Piaget, Jean. (2010). *The psychology of intelligence.* New York, NY: Routledge.

Piaget, Jean. (2013). *The construction of reality in the child.* New York, NY: Routledge.

Piaget, Jean. (2013). *The moral judgment of the child.* New York, NY: Routledge.

Piaget, Jean. (2013). *Play, dreams and imitation in childhood.* New York, NY: Routledge.

Piaget, Jean & Inhelder, Bärbel. (1972). *The psychology of the child.* New York, NY: Basic Books.

Piaget, Jean; Voelin-Liambey, Daphne & Berthoud-Papandropoulou, Ioanna. (2001). Problems of class inclusion and logical implication. In Robert L. Campbell (Ed.), *Studies in reflecting abstraction* (pp. 105–137). Hove, UK: Psychology Press.

Pickles, Andrew; Hill, Jonathan; Breen, Gerome; Quinn, John; Abbott, Kate; Jones, Helen & Sharp, Helen. (2013). Evidence for interplay between genes and parenting on infant temperament in the first year of life: Monoamine oxidase A polymorphism moderates effects of maternal sensitivity on infant anger proneness. *Journal of Child Psychology and Psychiatry, 54*(12), 1308–1317. doi: 10.1111/jcpp.12081

Pietrantonio, Anna Marie; Wright, Elise; Gibson, Kathleen N.; Alldred, Tracy; Jacobson, Dustin & Niec, Anne. (2013). Mandatory reporting of child abuse and neglect: Crafting a positive process for health professionals and caregivers. *Child Abuse & Neglect, 37*(2/3), 102–109. doi: 10.1016/j.chiabu.2012.12.007

Pilarz, Alejandra Ros & Hill, Heather D. (2014). Unstable and multiple child care arrangements and young children's behavior. *Early Childhood Research Quarterly, 29*(4), 471–483. doi: 10.1016/j.ecresq.2014.05.007

Pilkington, Pamela D.; Windsor, Tim D. & Crisp, Dimity A. (2012). Volunteering and subjective well-being in midlife and older adults: The role of supportive social networks. *The Journals of Gerontology Series B: Psychological Sciences and Social Sciences, 67B*(2), 249–260. doi: 10.1093/geronb/gbr154

Pinker, Steven. (2007). *The stuff of thought: Language as a window into human nature.* New York, NY: Viking.

Pinker, Steven. (2011). *The better angels of our nature: Why violence has declined.* New York, NY: Viking.

Pinquart, Martin & Silbereisen, Rainer K. (2006). Socio-emotional selectivity in cancer patients. *Psychology and Aging*, *21*(2), 419–423. doi: 10.1037/0882-7974.21.2.419

Piteo, A. M.; Roberts, R. M.; Nettelbeck, T.; Burns, N.; Lushington, K.; Martin, A. J. & Kennedy, J. D. (2013). Postnatal depression mediates the relationship between infant and maternal sleep disruption and family dysfunction. *Early Human Development*, *89*(2), 69–74. doi: 10.1016/j.earlhumdev.2012.07.017

Plassman, Brenda L.; Langa, Kenneth M.; Fisher, Gwenith G.; Heeringa, Steven G.; Weir, David R.; Ofstedal, Mary Beth, . . . Wallace, Robert B. (2007). Prevalence of dementia in the United States: The aging, demographics, and memory study. *Neuroepidemiology*, *29*(1–2), 125–132. doi: 10.1159/000109998

Plomin, Robert; DeFries, John C.; Knopik, Valerie S. & Neiderhiser, Jenae M. (2013). *Behavioral genetics*. New York, NY: Worth Publishers.

Pluess, Michael & Belsky, Jay. (2010). Differential susceptibility to parenting and quality child care. *Developmental Psychology*, *46*(2), 379–390. doi: 10.1037/a0015203

Podsiadlowski, Astrid & Fox, Stephen. (2011). Collectivist value orientations among four ethnic groups: Collectivism in the New Zealand context. *New Zealand Journal of Psychology*, *40*(1), 5–18.

Pogrebin, Abigail. (2010). *One and the same: My life as an identical twin and what I've learned about everyone's struggle to be singular.* New York, NY: Anchor.

Pollet, Susan L. (2010). Still a patchwork quilt: A nationwide survey of state laws regarding stepparent rights and obligations. *Family Court Review*, *48*(3), 528–540. doi: 10.1111/j.1744-1617.2010.01327.x

Popham, Lauren E.; Kennison, Shelia M. & Bradley, Kristopher I. (2011). Ageism, sensation-seeking, and risk-taking behavior in young adults. *Current Psychology*, *30*(2), 184–193. doi: 10.1007/s12144-011-9107-0

Portnoy, Jill; Gao, Yu; Glenn, Andrea L.; Niv, Sharon; Peskin, Melissa; Rudo-Hutt, Anna, . . . Raine, Adrian. (2013). The biology of childhood crime and antisocial behavior. In Chris L. Gibson & Marvin D. Krohn (Eds.), *Handbook of life-course criminology: Emerging trends and directions for future research* (pp. 21–42). New York, NY: Springer. doi: 10.1007/978-1-4614-5113-6_2

Potočnik, Kristina & Sonnentag, Sabine. (2013). A longitudinal study of well-being in older workers and retirees: The role of engaging in different types of activities. *Journal of Occupational and Organizational Psychology*, *86*(4), 497–521. doi: 10.1111/joop.12003

Pottinger, Audrey M. & Palmer, Tiffany. (2013). Whither IVF assisted birth or spontaneous conception? Parenting anxiety, styles and child development in Jamaican families. *Journal of Reproductive and Infant Psychology*, *31*(2), 148–159. doi: 10.1080/02646838.2012.762085

Pouw, Wim T. J. L.; van Gog, Tamara & Paas, Fred. (2014). An embedded and embodied cognition review of instructional manipulatives. *Educational Psychology Review*, *26*(1), 51–72. doi: 10.1007/s10648-014-9255-5

Powell, Kendall. (2006). Neurodevelopment: How does the teenage brain work? *Nature*, *442*(7105), 865–867. doi: 10.1038/442865a

Powell, Shaun; Langlands, Stephanie & Dodd, Chris. (2011). Feeding children's desires? Child and parental perceptions of food promotion to the "under 8s". *Young Consumers: Insight and Ideas for Responsible Marketers*, *12*(2), 96–109. doi: 10.1108/17473611111141560

Pozzoli, Tiziana & Gini, Gianluca. (2013). Why do bystanders of bullying help or not? A multidimensional model. *The Journal of Early Adolescence*, *33*(3), 315–340. doi: 10.1177/0272431612440172

Prado, Carlos G. (2008). *Choosing to die: Elective death and multiculturalism.* New York, NY: Cambridge University Press.

Prenderville, Jack A.; Kennedy, Paul J.; Dinan, Timothy G. & Cryan, John F. (2015). Adding fuel to the fire: The impact of stress on the ageing brain. *Trends in Neurosciences*, *38*(1), 13–25. doi: 10.1016/j.tins.2014.11.001

Preston, Tom & Kelly, Michael. (2006). A medical ethics assessment of the case of Terri Schiavo. *Death Studies*, *30*(2), 121–133. doi: 10.1080/07481180500455608

Priess, Heather A.; Lindberg, Sara M. & Hyde, Janet Shibley. (2009). Adolescent gender-role identity and mental health: Gender intensification revisited. *Child Development*, *80*(5), 1531–1544. doi: 10.1111/j.1467-8624.2009.01349.x

Priest, Jacob B. & Woods, Sarah B. (2015). The role of close relationships in the mental and physical health of Latino Americans. *Family Relations*, *64*(2), 319–331. doi: 10.1111/fare.12110

Priest, Naomi; Walton, Jessica; White, Fiona; Kowal, Emma; Baker, Alison & Paradies, Yin. (2014). Understanding the complexities of ethnic-racial socialization processes for both minority and majority groups: A 30-year systematic review. *International Journal of Intercultural Relations*, *43*(Part B), 139–155. doi: 10.1016/j.ijintrel.2014.08.003

Prinstein, Mitchell J.; Brechwald, Whitney A. & Cohen, Geoffrey L. (2011). Susceptibility to peer influence: Using a performance-based measure to identify adolescent males at heightened risk for deviant peer socialization. *Developmental Psychology*, *47*(4), 1167–1172. doi: 10.1037/a0023274

Proctor, Laura J. & Dubowitz, Howard. (2014). Child neglect: Challenges and controversies. In Jill E. Korbin & Richard D. Krugman (Eds.), *Handbook of child maltreatment* (pp. 27–61). New York, NY: Springer. doi: 10.1007/978-94-007-7208-3_2

Provasnik, Stephen; Kastberg, David; Ferraro, David; Lemanski, Nita; Roey, Stephen & Jenkins, Frank. (2012). *Highlights from TIMSS 2011: Mathematics and science achievement of U.S. fourth- and eighth-grade students in an international context.* Washington, DC: National Center for Education Statistics, Institute of Education Sciences, U.S. Department of Education.

Pryor, Frederic L. (2014). A note on the determinants of recent pupil achievement. *Scientific Research*, *5*, 1265–1268. doi: 10.4236/ce.2014.514143

Pryor, John H.; Eagan, Kevin; Palucki Blake, Laura; Hurtado, Sylvia; Berdan, Jennifer & Case, Matthew H.

Stevens, Courtney & Bavelier, Daphne. (2012). The role of selective attention on academic foundations: A cognitive neuroscience perspective. *Developmental Cognitive Neuroscience, 2*(Suppl. 1), S30–S48. doi: 10.1016/j.dcn.2011.11.001

Stevenson, Richard J.; Oaten, Megan J.; Case, Trevor I.; Repacholi, Betty M. & Wagland, Paul. (2010). Children's response to adult disgust elicitors: Development and acquisition. *Developmental Psychology, 46*(1), 165–177. doi: 10.1037/a0016692

Stieb, David M.; Chen, Li; Eshoul, Maysoon & Judek, Stan. (2012). Ambient air pollution, birth weight and preterm birth: A systematic review and meta-analysis. *Environmental Research, 117*, 100–111. doi: 10.1016/j.envres.2012.05.007

Stiles, Joan & Jernigan, Terry. (2010). The basics of brain development. *Neuropsychology Review, 20*(4), 327–348. doi: 10.1007/s11065-010-9148-4

Stine-Morrow, Elizabeth A. L. & Basak, Chandramallika. (2011). Cognitive interventions. In K. Warner Schaie & Sherry L. Willis (Eds.), *Handbook of the psychology of aging* (7th ed., pp. 153–171). San Diego, CA: Academic Press. doi: 10.1016/B978-0-12-380882-0.00010-3

Stipek, Deborah. (2013). Mathematics in early childhood education: Revolution or evolution? *Early Education & Development, 24*(4), 431–435. doi: 10.1080/10409289.2013.777285

Stolk, Lisette; Perry, John R. B.; Chasman, Daniel I.; He, Chunyan; Mangino, Massimo; Sulem, Patrick, . . . Lunetta, Kathryn L. (2012). Meta-analyses identify 13 loci associated with age at menopause and highlight DNA repair and immune pathways. *Nature Genetics, 44*, 260–268. doi: 10.1038/ng.1051

Stolt, Suvi; Matomäki, Jaakko; Lind, Annika; Lapinleimu, Helena; Haataja, Leena & Lehtonen, Liisa. (2014). The prevalence and predictive value of weak language skills in children with very low birth weight – A longitudinal study. *Acta Paediatrica, 103*(6), 651–658. doi: 10.1111/apa.12607

Stone, Richard. (2011). Daring experiment in higher education opens its doors. *Science, 332*(6026), 161. doi: 10.1126/science.332.6026.161

Stonington, Scott D. (2012). On ethical locations: The good death in Thailand, where ethics sit in places. *Social Science & Medicine, 75*(5), 836–844. doi: 10.1016/j.socscimed.2012.03.045

Strasburger, Victor C.; Wilson, Barbara J. & Jordan, Amy B. (2009). *Children, adolescents, and the media* (2nd ed.). Los Angeles, CA: Sage.

Straus, Murray A. & Paschall, Mallie J. (2009). Corporal punishment by mothers and development of children's cognitive ability: A longitudinal study of two nationally representative age cohorts. *Journal of Aggression, Maltreatment & Trauma, 18*(5), 459–483. doi: 10.1080/10926770903035168

Stremmel, Andrew J. (2012). A situated framework: The Reggio experience. In Nancy File et al. (Eds.), *Curriculum in early childhood education: Re-examined, rediscovered, renewed* (pp. 133–145). New York, NY: Routledge.

Stroebe, Margaret S.; Abakoumkin, Georgios; Stroebe, Wolfgang & Schut, Henk. (2012). Continuing bonds in adjustment to bereavement: Impact of abrupt versus gradual separation. *Personal Relationships, 19*(2), 255–266. doi: 10.1111/j.1475-6811.2011.01352.x

Stroebe, Margaret S.; Schut, Henk & Boerner, Kathrin. (2010). Continuing bonds in adaptation to bereavement: Toward theoretical integration. *Clinical Psychology Review, 30*(2), 259–268. doi: 10.1016/j.cpr.2009.11.007

Stroebe, Wolfgang & Strack, Fritz. (2014). The alleged crisis and the illusion of exact replication. *Perspectives on Psychological Science, 9*(1), 59–71. doi: 10.1177/1745691613514450

Stronegger, Willibald J.; Burkert, Nathalie T.; Grossschädl, Franziska & Freidl, Wolfgang. (2013). Factors associated with the rejection of active euthanasia: A survey among the general public in Austria. *BMC Medical Ethics, 14*, 26. doi: 10.1186/1472-6939-14-26

Stronegger, Willibald J.; Schmölzer, Christin; Rásky, Éva & Freidl, Wolfgang. (2011). Changing attitudes towards euthanasia among medical students in Austria. *Journal of Medical Ethics, 37*(4), 227–229. doi: 10.1136/jme.2010.039792

Sue, Derald Wing (Ed.). (2010). *Microaggressions and marginality: Manifestation, dynamics, and impact.* Hoboken, NJ: Wiley.

Suellentrop, Katherine; Morrow, Brian; Williams, Letitia & D'Angelo, Denise. (2006). *Monitoring progress toward achieving maternal and infant Healthy People 2010 objectives—19 states, Pregnancy Risk Assessment Monitoring System (PRAMS), 2000–2003. MMWR Surveillance Summaries 55*(SS09), 1–11. Atlanta, GA: Centers for Disease Control and Prevention.

Suleiman, Ahna B. & Brindis, Claire D. (2014). Adolescent school-based sex education: Using developmental neuroscience to guide new directions for policy and practice. *Sexuality Research and Social Policy, 11*(2), 137–152. doi: 10.1007/s13178-014-0147-8

Sulek, Julia P. (2013, April 30). Audrie Pott suicide: Parents share grief, quest for justice in exclusive interview. *San Jose Mercury News.*

Sullivan, Shannon. (2014). *Good white people: The problem with middle-class white anti-racism.* Albany, NY: State University of New York Press.

Sumter, Sindy R.; Valkenburg, Patti M. & Peter, Jochen. (2013). Perceptions of love across the lifespan: Differences in passion, intimacy, and commitment. *International Journal of Behavioral Development, 37*(5), 417–427. doi: 10.1177/0165025413492486

Sung, imin; Beijers, Roseriet; Gartstein, Maria A.; de Weerth, Carolina & Putnam, Samuel P. (2015). Exploring temperamental differences in infants from the USA and the Netherlands. *European Journal of Developmental Psychology, 12*(1), 15–28. doi: 10.1080/17405629.2014.937700

Surget, A.; Tanti, A.; Leonardo, E. D.; Laugeray, A.; Rainer.Q.; Touma, C., . . . Belzung, C. (2011). Antidepressants recruit new neurons to improve stress response regulation. *Molecular Psychiatry, 16*(12), 1177–1188. doi: 10.1038/mp.2011.48

Surman, Craig B. H.; Hammerness, Paul G.; Pion, Katie & Faraone, Stephen V. (2013). Do stimulants improve functioning in adults with ADHD?: A review of the literature. *European Neuropsychopharmacology, 23*(6), 528–533. doi: 10.1016/j.euroneuro.2012.02.010

Susman, Elizabeth J.; Houts, Renate M.; Steinberg, Laurence; Belsky, Jay; Cauffman, Elizabeth; DeHart, Ganie, . . . Halpern-Felsher, Bonnie L. (2010). Longitudinal development of secondary sexual characteristics in girls and boys between ages 9-1/2 and 15-1/2 years. *Archives of Pediatrics & Adolescent Medicine, 164*(2), 166–173. doi: 10.1001/archpediatrics .2009.261

Sutphin, George L. & Kaeberlein, Matt. (2011). Comparative genetics of aging. In Edward J. Masoro & Steven N. Austad (Eds.), *Handbook of the biology of aging* (7th ed., pp. 215–242). San Diego, CA: Academic Press. doi: 10.1016/B978-0-12-378638-8.00010-5

Sutton-Smith, Brian. (2011). The antipathies of play. In Anthony D. Pellegrini (Ed.), *The Oxford handbook of the development of play* (pp. 110–115). New York, NY: Oxford University Press. doi: 10.1093/oxfordhb/9780195393002.013.0010

Swanson, Christopher B. (2014). Graduation rate breaks 80 percent. *Education Week, 33*(33, Suppl. 1), 24–26.

Swanson, H. Lee. (2013). Meta-analysis of research on children with learning disabilities. In H. Lee Swanson et al. (Eds.), *Handbook of learning disabilities* (2nd ed., pp. 627–642). New York, NY: Guilford Press.

Sweeney, Kathryn A. (2013). Race-conscious adoption choices, multiraciality and color-blind racial ideology. *Family Relations, 62*(1), 42–57. doi: 10.1111/j.1741-3729.2012.00757.x

Sweeney, Megan M. (2010). Remarriage and stepfamilies: Strategic sites for family scholarship in the 21st century. *Journal of Marriage and Family, 72*(3), 667–684. doi: 10.1111/j.1741-3737.2010.00724.x

Sweet, Stephen & Moen, Phyllis. (2012). Dual earners preparing for job loss: Agency, linked lives, and resilience. *Work and Occupations, 39*(1), 35–70. doi: 10.1177/0730888411415601

Szanton, Sarah L.; Wolff, Jennifer L.; Leff, Bruce; Roberts, Laken; Thorpe, Roland J.; Tanner, Elizabeth K., . . . Gitlin, Laura N. (2015). Preliminary data from Community Aging In Place, advancing better living for elders, a patient-directed, team-based intervention to improve physical function and decrease nursing home utilization: The first 100 individuals to complete a Centers For Medicare And Medicaid Services innovation project. *Journal of the American Geriatrics Society, 63*(2), 371–374. doi: 10.1111/jgs.13245

Szydlik, Marc. (2012). Generations: Connections across the life course. *Advances in Life Course Research, 17*(3), 100–111. doi: 10.1016/j.alcr.2012.03.002

Taber, Daniel R.; Stevens, June; Evenson, Kelly R.; Ward, Dianne S.; Poole, Charles; Maciejewski, Matthew L., . . . Brownson, Ross C. (2011). State policies targeting junk food in schools: Racial/ethnic differences in the effect of policy change on soda consumption. *American Journal of Public Health, 101*(9), 1769–1775. doi: 10.2105/ajph .2011.300221

Tacken, Mart & van Lamoen, Ellemieke. (2005). Transport behaviour and realised journeys and trips. In Heidrun Mollenkopf et al. (Eds.), *Enhancing mobility in later life: Personal coping, environmental resources and technical support: The out-of-home mobility of older adults in urban and rural regions of five European countries* (pp. 105–139). Amsterdam, The Netherlands: IOS Press.

Tackett, Jennifer L.; Herzhoff, Kathrin; Harden, K. Paige; Page-Gould, Elizabeth & Josephs, Robert A. (2014). Personality × hormone interactions in adolescent externalizing psychopathology. *Personality Disorders: Theory, Research, and Treatment, 5*(3), 235–246. doi: 10.1037/per0000075

Taga, Keiko A.; Markey, Charlotte N. & Friedman, Howard S. (2006). A longitudinal investigation of associations between boys' pubertal timing and adult behavioral health and well-being. *Journal of Youth and Adolescence, 35*(3), 380–390. doi: 10.1007/s10964-006-9039-4

Taillieu, Tamara L.; Afifi, Tracie O.; Mota, Natalie; Keyes, Katherine M. & Sareen, Jitender. (2014). Age, sex, and racial differences in harsh physical punishment: Results from a nationally representative United States sample. *Child Abuse & Neglect, 38*(12), 1885–1894. doi: 10.1016/j.chiabu.2014.10.020

Talley, Ronda C. & Montgomery, Rhonda J. V. (2013). Caregiving: A developmental lifelong perspective. In Ronda C. Talley & Rhonda J. V. Montgomery (Eds.), *Caregiving across the lifespan: Research, practice, policy* (pp. 3–10). New York, NY: Springer.

Talwar, Victoria; Harris, Paul L. & Schleifer, Michael (Eds.). (2011). *Children's understanding of death: From biological to religious conceptions.* New York, NY: Cambridge University Press.

Tamis-LeMonda, Catherine S.; Kuchirko, Yana & Song, Lulu. (2014). Why is infant language learning facilitated by parental responsiveness? *Current Directions in Psychological Science, 23*(2), 121–126. doi: 10.1177/0963721414522813

Tamm, Leanne; Epstein, Jeffery N.; Denton, Carolyn A.; Vaughn, Aaron J.; Peugh, James & Willcutt, Erik G. (2014). Reaction time variability associated with reading skills in poor readers with ADHD. *Journal of the International Neuropsychological Society, 20*(3), 292–301. doi: 10.1017/S1355617713001495

Tan, Patricia Z.; Armstrong, Laura M. & Cole, Pamela M. (2013). Relations between temperament and anger regulation over early childhood. *Social Development, 22*(4), 755–772. doi: 10.1111/j.1467-9507.2012.00674.x

Tang, Jie; Yu, Yizhen; Du, Yukai; Ma, Ying; Zhang, Dongying & Wang, Jiaji. (2014). Prevalence of Internet addiction and its association with stressful life events and psychological symptoms among adolescent Internet users. *Addictive Behaviors, 39*(3), 744–747. doi: 10.1016/j.addbeh .2013.12.010

Tanner, Jennifer L. & Arnett, Jeffrey Jensen. (2011). Presenting emerging adulthood: What makes emerging adulthood developmentally distinctive. In Jeffrey Jensen Arnett et al. (Eds.), *Debating emerging adulthood: Stage or process?* (pp. 13–30). New York, NY: Oxford University Press. doi: 10.1093/acprof: oso/9780199757176.003.0002

Tanner, Jennifer L.; Arnett, Jeffrey J. & Leis, Julie A. (2009). Emerging adulthood: Learning and development during the first stage of adulthood. In M. Cecil Smith & Nancy DeFrates-Densch (Eds.), *Handbook of research on adult learning and development* (pp. 34–67). New York, NY: Routledge.

Tarullo, Amanda R.; Garvin, Melissa C. & Gunnar, Megan R. (2011). Atypical EEG power correlates with indiscriminately friendly behavior in internationally adopted children. *Developmental Psychology, 47*(2), 417–431. doi: 10.1037/a0021363

Tatem, Andrew J.; Hemelaar, Joris; Gray, Rebecca & Salemi, Marco. (2012). Spatial accessibility and the spread of HIV-1 subtypes and recombinants. *AIDS, 26*(18), 2351–2360. doi: 10.1097/QAD.0b013e328359a904

Taveras, Elsie M.; Gillman, Matthew W.; Kleinman, Ken P.; Rich-Edwards, Janet W. & Rifas-Shiman, Sheryl L. (2013). Reducing racial/ethnic disparities in childhood obesity: The role of early life risk factors. *JAMA Pediatrics, 167*(8), 731–738. doi: 10.1001/jamapediatrics.2013.85

Tay, Marc Tze-Hsin; Au Eong, Kah Guan; Ng, C. Y. & Lim, M. K. (1992). Myopia and educational attainment in 421,116 young Singaporean males. *Annals Academy of Medicine Singapore, 21*(6), 785–791.

Taylor, John H. (Ed.). (2010). *Journey through the afterlife: Ancient Egyptian Book of the Dead.* Cambridge, MA: Harvard University Press.

Taylor, Kate. (2013, August 20). Man slaps two supporters at Quinn event. *The New York Times,* p. A16.

Taylor, Marjorie; Shawber, Alison B. & Mannering, Anne M. (2009). Children's imaginary companions: What is it like to have an invisible friend? In Keith D. Markman et al. (Eds.), *Handbook of imagination and mental simulation* (pp. 211–224). New York, NY: Psychology Press.

Taylor, Paul. (2014). *The next America: Boomers, millennials, and the looming generational showdown.* New York, NY: PublicAffairs.

Taylor, Rachael W.; Murdoch, Linda; Carter, Philippa; Gerrard, David F.; Williams, Sheila M. & Taylor, Barry J. (2009). Longitudinal study of physical activity and inactivity in preschoolers: The FLAME study. *Medicine & Science in Sports & Exercise, 41*(1), 96–102. doi: 10.1249/MSS.0b013e3181849d81

Taylor, Shelley E. (2006). Tend and befriend: Biobehavioral bases of affiliation under stress. *Current Directions in Psychological Science, 15*(6), 273–277. doi: 10.1111/j.1467-8721.2006.00451.x

Taylor, Shelley E.; Klein, Laura Cousino; Lewis, Brian P.; Gruenewald, Tara L.; Gurung, Regan A. R. & Updegraff, John A. (2000). Biobehavioral responses to stress in females: Tend-and-befriend, not fight-or-flight. *Psychological Review, 107*(3), 411–429. doi: 10.1037//0033-295X.107.3.411

Taylor, Valerie J. & Walton, Gregory M. (2011). Stereotype threat undermines academic learning. *Personality and Social Psychology Bulletin, 37*(8), 1055–1067. doi: 10.1177/0146167211406506

Taylor, Zoe E.; Eisenberg, Nancy; Spinrad, Tracy L.; Eggum, Natalie D. & Sulik, Michael J. (2013). The relations of ego-resiliency and emotion socialization to the development of empathy and prosocial behavior across early childhood. *Emotion, 13*(5), 822–831. doi: 10.1037/a0032894

Tefft, Brian C. (2012). *Motor vehicle crashes, injuries, and deaths in relation to driver age: United States, 1995–2010.* Washington, DC: AAA Foundation for Traffic Safety.

Telem, Dana A.; Talamini, Mark; Shroyer, A. Laurie; Yang, Jie; Altieri, Maria; Zhang, Qiao, . . . Pryor, Aurora D. (2015). Long-term mortality rates (>8-year) improve as compared to the general and obese population following bariatric surgery. *Surgical Endoscopy, 29*(3), 529–536. doi: 10.1007/s00464-014-3714-4

Temple, Jeff R.; Le, Vi Donna; van den Berg, Patricia; Ling, Yan; Paul, Jonathan A. & Temple, Brian W. (2014). Brief report: Teen sexting and psychosocial health. *Journal of Adolescence, 37*(1), 33–36. doi: 10.1016/j.adolescence.2013.10.008

Teng, Zhaojun; Liu, Yanling & Guo, Cheng. (2015). A meta-analysis of the relationship between self-esteem and aggression among Chinese students. *Aggression and Violent Behavior, 21*(6), 45–54. doi: 10.1016/j.avb.2015.01.005

Teno, Joan M.; Plotzke, Michael; Gozalo, Pedro & Mor, Vincent. (2014). A national study of live discharges from hospice. *Journal of Palliative Medicine, 17*(10), 1121–1127. doi: 10.1089/jpm.2013.0595

Teoh, Yee San & Lamb, Michael E. (2013). Interviewer demeanor in forensic interviews of children. *Psychology, Crime & Law, 19*(2), 145–159. doi: 10.1080/1068316X.2011.614610

Terman, Lewis M. (1925). *Genetic studies of genius.* Stanford, CA: Stanford University Press.

Terry-McElrath, Yvonne M.; Turner, Lindsey; Sandoval, Anna; Johnston, Lloyd D. & Chaloupka, Frank J. (2014). Commercialism in US elementary and secondary school nutrition environments: Trends from 2007 to 2012. *JAMA Pediatrics, 168*(3), 234–242. doi: 10.1001/jamapediatrics.2013.4521

Teti, Douglas M.; Crosby, Brian; McDaniel, Brandon T.; Shimizu, Mina & Whitesell, Corey J. (2015). Marital and emotional adjustment in mothers and infant sleep arrangements during the first six months. *Monographs of the Society for Research in Child Development, 80*(1), 160–176. doi: 10.1111/mono.12150

Tetzlaff, Anne & Hilbert, Anja. (2014). The role of the family in childhood and adolescent binge eating. A systematic review. *Appetite, 76*(1), 208. doi: 10.1016/j.appet.2014.01.050

The New York Times & CBS News. (2010). Poll: National survey of Tea Party supporters, April 5–10, 2010. *The New York Times.*

Thiele, Dianne M. & Whelan, Thomas A. (2008). The relationship between grandparent satisfaction, meaning, and generativity. *International Journal of Aging and Human Development, 66*(1), 21–48. doi: 10.2190/AG.66.1.b

Thomaes, Sander; Reijntjes, Albert; Orobio de Castro, Bram; Bushman, Brad J.; Poorthuis, Astrid & Telch, Michael J. (2010). I like me if you like me: On the interpersonal modulation and regulation of preadolescents' state self-esteem. *Child Development, 81*(3), 811–825. doi: 10.1111/j.1467-8624.2010.01435.x

Thomas, Dylan. (2003). *The poems of Dylan Thomas* (Rev. ed.). New York, NY: New Directions.

Thomas, Michael S. C.; Van Duuren, Mike; Purser, Harry R. M.; Mareschal, Denis; Ansari, Daniel & Karmiloff-Smith, Annette. (2010). The development of metaphorical language comprehension in typical development and in Williams syndrome. *Journal of Experimental Child Psychology, 106*(2/3), 99–114. doi: 10.1016/j.jecp.2009.12.007

Thompson, Edmund R. & Prendergast, Gerard P. (2015). The influence of trait affect and the five-factor personality model on impulse buying. *Personality and Individual Differences, 76*(2), 216–221. doi: 10.1016/j.paid.2014.12.025

Thompson, Ross A. & Raikes, H. Abigail. (2003). Toward the next quarter-century: Conceptual and methodological challenges for attachment theory. *Development and Psychopathology, 15*(3), 691–718. doi: 10.1017/S0954579403000348

Thomson, Samuel; Marriott, Michael; Telford, Katherine; Law, Hou; McLaughlin, Jo & Sayal, Kapil. (2014). Adolescents with a diagnosis of anorexia nervosa: Parents' experience of recognition and deciding to seek help. *Clinical Child Psychology Psychiatry, 19*(1), 43–57. doi: 10.1177/1359104512465741

Thornberg, Robert & Jungert, Tomas. (2013). Bystander behavior in bullying situations: Basic moral sensitivity, moral disengagement and defender self-efficacy. *Journal of Adolescence, 36*(3), 475–483. doi: 10.1016/j.adolescence.2013.02.003

Thorson, James A. (1995). *Aging in a changing society.* Belmont, CA: Wadsworth.

Thrasher, Angela D.; Clay, Olivio J.; Ford, Chandra L. & Stewart, Anita L. (2012). Theory-guided selection of discrimination measures for racial/ethnic health disparities research among older adults. *Journal of Aging and Health, 24*(6), 1018–1043. doi: 10.1177/0898264312440322

Thuné-Boyle, Ingela C. V.; Stygall, Jan; Keshtgar, Mohammed R. S.; Davidson, Tim I. & Newman, Stanton P. (2013). Religious/spiritual coping resources and their relationship with adjustment in patients newly diagnosed with breast cancer in the UK. *Psycho-Oncology, 22*(3), 646–658. doi: 10.1002/pon.3048

Timmons, Adela C. & Margolin, Gayla. (2015). Family conflict, mood, and adolescents' daily school problems: Moderating roles of internalizing and externalizing symptoms. *Child Development, 86*(1), 241–258. doi: 10.1111/cdev.12300

Tishkoff, Sarah A.; Reed, Floyd A.; Friedlaender, Françoise R.; Ehret, Christopher; Ranciaro, Alessia; Froment, Alain, . . . Williams, Scott M. (2009). The genetic structure and history of Africans and African Americans. *Science, 324*(5930), 1035–1044. doi: 10.1126/science.1172257

Tobey, Emily A.; Thal, Donna; Niparko, John K.; Eisenberg, Laurie S.; Quittner, Alexandra L. & Wang, Nae-Yuh. (2013). Influence of implantation age on school-age language performance in pediatric cochlear implant users. *International Journal of Audiology, 52*(4), 219–229. doi: 10.3109/14992027.2012.759666

Todes, Daniel P. (2014). *Ivan Pavlov: A Russian life in science.* New York, NY: Oxford University Press.

Tomasello, Michael. (2006). Acquiring linguistic constructions. In William Damon & Richard M. Lerner (Eds.), *Handbook of child psychology* (6th ed., Vol. 2, pp. 255–298). Hoboken, NJ: Wiley.

Tomasello, Michael & Herrmann, Esther. (2010). Ape and human cognition. *Current Directions in Psychological Science, 19*(1), 3–8. doi: 10.1177/0963721409359300

Tonn, Jessica L. (2006). Later high school start times a reaction to research. *Education Week, 25*(28), 5, 17.

Tonyan, Holli A.; Mamikonian-Zarpas, Ani & Chien, Dorothy. (2013). Do they practice what they preach? An eco-cultural, multidimensional, group-based examination of the relationship between beliefs and behaviours among child care providers. *Early Child Development and Care, 183*(12), 1853–1877. doi: 10.1080/03004430.2012.759949

Toporek, Bryan. (2012). Sports rules revised as research mounts on head injuries. *Education Week, 31*(22), 8.

Torbeyns, Joke; Schneider, Michael; Xin, Ziqiang & Siegler, Robert S. (2015). Bridging the gap: Fraction understanding is central to mathematics achievement in students from three different continents. *Learning and Instruction, 37,* 5–13. doi: 10.1016/j.learninstruc.2014.03.002

Tottenham, Nim. (2014). The importance of early experiences for neuro-affective development. In Susan L. Andersen & Daniel S. Pine (Eds.), *The neurobiology of childhood* (pp. 109–129). Berlin, Germany: Springer. doi: 10.1007/7854_2013_254

Tough, Paul. (2012). *How children succeed: Grit, curiosity, and the hidden power of character.* Boston, MA: Houghton Mifflin Harcourt.

Tracey, Terence J. G.; Wampold, Bruce E.; Lichtenberg, James W. & Goodyear, Rodney K. (2014). Expertise in psychotherapy: An elusive goal? *American Psychologist, 69*(3), 218–229. doi: 10.1037/a0035099

Trawick-Smith, Jeffrey. (2012). Teacher–child play interactions to achieve learning outcomes: Risks and opportunities. In Robert C. Pianta (Ed.), *Handbook of early childhood education* (pp. 259–277). New York, NY: Guilford Press.

Treas, Judith & Gubernskaya, Zoya. (2012). Farewell to moms? Maternal contact for seven countries in 1986 and 2001. *Journal of Marriage and Family, 74*(2), 297–311. doi: 10.1111/j.1741-3737.2012.00956.x

Tremblay, Angelo & Chaput, Jean-Philippe. (2012). Obesity: The allostatic load of weight loss dieting. *Physiology & Behavior, 106*(1), 16–21. doi: 10.1016/j.physbeh.2011.05.020

Trenholm, Christopher; Devaney, Barbara; Fortson, Ken; Quay, Lisa; Wheeler, Justin & Clark, Melissa. (2007). *Impacts of four Title V, Section 510 abstinence education programs final report.* Washington, DC: U.S. Department of Health and Human Services, Mathematica Policy Research, Inc.

Trickett, Penelope K.; Noll, Jennie G. & Putnam, Frank W. (2011). The impact of sexual abuse on female development: Lessons from a multigenerational, longitudinal research study. *Development and Psychopathology, 23*(2), 453–476. doi: 10.1017/S0954579411000174

Trivedi, Daksha. (2015). Cochrane Review Summary: Massage for promoting mental and physical health in typically developing infants under the age of six months. *Primary Health Care Research & Development, 16*(1), 3–4. doi: 10.1017/S1463423614000462

Troll, Lillian E. & Skaff, Marilyn McKean. (1997). Perceived continuity of self in very old age. *Psychology and Aging, 12*(1), 162–169. doi: 10.1037/0882-7974.12.1.162

Trommsdorff, Gisela & Cole, Pamela M. (2011). Emotion, self-regulation, and social behavior in cultural contexts. In Xinyin Chen & Kenneth H. Rubin (Eds.), *Socioemotional development in cultural context* (pp. 131–163). New York, NY: Guilford Press.

Trompeter, Susan E.; Bettencourt, Ricki & Barrett-Connor, Elizabeth. (2012). Sexual activity and satisfaction in healthy community-dwelling older women. *The American Journal of Medicine, 125*(1), 37–43.e31. doi: 10.1016/j.amjmed.2011.07.036

Tronick, Edward. (1989). Emotions and emotional communication in infants. *American Psychologist, 44*(2), 112–119. doi: 10.1037//0003-066X.44.2.112

Tronick, Edward & Weinberg, M. Katherine. (1997). Depressed mothers and infants: Failure to form dyadic states of consciousness. In Lynne Murray & Peter J. Cooper (Eds.), *Postpartum depression and child development* (pp. 54–81). New York, NY: Guilford Press.

Truog, Robert D. (2007). Brain death: Too flawed to endure, too ingrained to abandon. *The Journal of Law, Medicine & Ethics, 35*(2), 273–281. doi: 10.1111/j.1748-720X.2007.00136.x

Tsai, James; Floyd, R. Louise & Bertrand, Jacquelyn. (2007). Tracking binge drinking among U.S. childbearing-age women. *Preventive Medicine, 44*(4), 298–302. doi: 10.1016/j.ypmed.2006.10.002

Tsethlikai, Monica & Rogoff, Barbara. (2013). Involvement in traditional cultural practices and American Indian children's incidental recall of a folktale. *Developmental Psychology, 49*(3), 568–578. doi: 10.1037/a0031308

Tsutsui, Takako; Muramatsu, Naoko & Higashino, Sadanori. (2014). Changes in perceived filial obligation norms among coresident family caregivers in Japan. *The Gerontologist, 54*(5), 797–807. doi: 10.1093/geront/gnt093

Ttofi, Maria M.; Bowes, Lucy; Farrington, David P. & Lösel, Friedrich. (2014). Protective factors interrupting the continuity from school bullying to later internalizing and externalizing problems: A systematic review of prospective longitudinal studies. *Journal of School Violence, 13*(1), 5–38. doi: 10.1080/15388220.2013.857345

Tudge, Jonathan. (2008). *The everyday lives of young children: Culture, class, and child rearing in diverse societies.* New York, NY: Cambridge University Press.

Tudge, Jonathan R. H.; Doucet, Fabienne; Odero, Dolphine; Sperb, Tania M.; Piccinini, Cesar A. & Lopes, Rita S. (2006). A window into different cultural worlds: Young children's everyday activities in the United States, Brazil, and Kenya. *Child Development, 77*(5), 1446–1469. doi: 10.1111/j.1467-8624.2006.00947.x

Tummeltshammer, Kristen S.; Wu, Rachel; Sobel, David M. & Kirkham, Natasha Z. (2014). Infants track the reliability of potential informants. *Psychological Science, 25*(9), 1730–1738. doi: 10.1177/0956797614540178

Turiel, Elliot. (2006). The development of morality. In William Damon & Richard M. Lerner (Eds.), *Handbook of child psychology* (6th ed., Vol. 3, pp. 789–857). Hoboken, NJ: Wiley.

Turiel, Elliot. (2008). Thought about actions in social domains: Morality, social conventions, and social interactions. *Cognitive Development, 23*(1), 136–154. doi: 10.1016/j.cogdev.2007.04.001

Turley, Ruth N. López & Desmond, Matthew. (2011). Contributions to college costs by married, divorced, and remarried parents. *Journal of Family Issues, 32*(6), 767–790. doi: 10.1177/0192513x10388013

Turner, Heather A.; Finkelhor, David; Ormrod, Richard; Hamby, Sherry; Leeb, Rebecca T.; Mercy, James A. & Holt, Melissa. (2012). Family context, victimization, and child trauma symptoms: Variations in safe, stable, and nurturing relationships during early and middle childhood. *American Journal of Orthopsychiatry, 82*(2), 209–219. doi: 10.1111/j.1939-0025.2012.01147.x

Turney, Kristin. (2015). Hopelessly devoted? Relationship quality during and after incarceration. *Journal of Marriage and Family, 77*(2), 480–495. doi: 10.1111/jomf.12174

Tuttle, Robert & Garr, Michael. (2012). Shift work and work to family fit: Does schedule control matter? *Journal of Family and Economic Issues, 33*(3), 261–271. doi: 10.1007/s10834-012-9283-6

Tye-Murray, Nancy; Spehar, Brent; Myerson, Joel; Sommers, Mitchell S. & Hale, Sandra. (2011). Cross-modal enhancement of speech detection in young and older adults: Does signal content matter? *Ear and Hearing, 32*(5), 650–655. doi: 10.1097/AUD.0b013e31821a4578

U.S. Bureau of Democracy, Human Rights and Labor. (2013). *International Religious Freedom Report for 2013: Nigeria.* Washington, DC: United States Department of State.

U.S. Bureau of Labor Statistics. (2012, February 22). *Volunteering in The United States, 2011.* Washington, DC: U.S. Department of Labor.

U.S. Bureau of Labor Statistics. (2012, July 25). *Number of jobs held, labor market activity, and earnings growth among the youngest baby boomers: Results from a longitudinal survey summary.* Washington, DC: U.S. Department of Labor.

U.S. Bureau of Labor Statistics. (2013). *Employment Projections program, Table 2.1 Employment by Major Industry Sector.* Washington, DC: U.S. Department of Labor.

U.S. Bureau of Labor Statistics. (2013, April 30). *Employment characteristics of families, 2012. TED: The editor's desk.* Washington, DC: U.S. Department of Labor.

U.S. Bureau of Labor Statistics. (2014, February 25). *Volunteering in The United States–2013.* Washington, DC: U.S. Department of Labor.

U.S. Bureau of Labor Statistics. (2015). *The employment situation—July 2015.* Washington, DC: U.S. Department of Labor.

U.S. Census Bureau. (2013, September). *Current population Survey: 2013 Annual Social and Economic (ASEC) Supplement.* Washington, DC.

U.S. Census Bureau. (2015). Mid-year population by five year age groups and sex - custom region - Japan. Retrieved, from U.S. Census Bureau, International Data Base.

U.S. Census Bureau. (2015). Mid-year population by five year age groups and sex - custom region - Germany. Retrieved, from U.S. Census Bureau, International Data Base.

U.S. Census Bureau. (1907). *Statistical Abstract of the United States 1906.* Washington, DC: U.S. Department of Commerce.

U.S. Census Bureau. (1981). *Current population survey: November, 1979.* Ann Arbor, MI: U.S. Department of Commerce, Bureau of the Census.

U.S. Census Bureau. (1989). *Current population survey: November, 1989.* Ann Arbor, MI: U.S. Department of Commerce, Bureau of the Census.

U.S. Census Bureau. (1992). *Current population survey: October, 1992.* Washington, DC: U.S. Department of Commerce, Economic and Statistics Administration, U.S. Census Bureau.

U.S. Census Bureau. (1995). *Current population survey: October, 1995.* Washington, DC: U.S. Department of Commerce, Economic and Statistics Administration, U.S. Census Bureau.

U.S. Census Bureau. (1999). *Current population survey: October, 1999.* Washington, DC: U.S. Department of Commerce, Economic and Statistics Administration, U.S. Census Bureau.

U.S. Census Bureau. (2008). *Statistical abstract of The United States: 2009.* Washington, DC: U.S. Department of Commerce.

U.S. Census Bureau. (2010). *America's families and living arrangements: 2009*: U.S. Department of Commerce, Economics and Statistics Administration, U.S. Census Bureau.

U.S. Census Bureau. (2010). *Annual estimates of the resident population by sex, race, and Hispanic origin for the United States: April 1, 2000 to July 1, 2009.* Washington, DC: U.S. Census Bureau.

U.S. Census Bureau. (2011). *America's families and living arrangements: 2011*: U.S. Department of Commerce, Economics and Statistics Administration, U.S. Census Bureau.

U.S. Census Bureau. (2012). *Statistical abstract of the United States: 2012.* Washington, DC: U.S. Department of Commerce.

U.S. Census Bureau. (2014). *America's families and living arrangements: 2014.* Washington, DC: U.S. Department of Commerce, Economics and Statistics Administration, U.S. Census Bureau.

U.S. Department of Defense. (2012). *Suicide event report.* Washington, DC: U.S. Department of Defense.

U.S. Department of Education. *NCES Common Core of Data State Dropout and Graduation Rate Data File, School Year 2011–12, Preliminary Version 1a.* Washington, DC: U.S. Department of Education, Institute of Education Sciences, National Center for Education Statistics, Common Core of Data (CCD).

U.S. Department of Health and Human Services. (2003). *Child maltreatment 2001.* Washington, DC: Administration for Children and Families, Administration on Children Youth and Families, Children's Bureau.

U.S. Department of Health and Human Services. (2008). *Child maltreatment 2006.* Washington, DC: Administration for Children and Families, Administration on Children Youth and Families, Children's Bureau.

U.S. Department of Health and Human Services. (2010). *Head Start impact study: Final report.* Washington, DC: Administration for Children and Families.

U.S. Department of Health and Human Services. (2011, December 31). *Child maltreatment 2010.* Washington, DC: Administration for Children and Families, Administration on Children Youth and Families, Children's Bureau.

U.S. Department of Health and Human Services. (2012, December 12). *Child maltreatment 2011.* Washington, DC: Administration for Children and Families, Administration on Children Youth and Families, Children's Bureau.

U.S. Department of Health and Human Services. (2015, January 15). *Child maltreatment 2013.* Washington, DC: Administration for Children and Families, Administration on Children, Youth and Families, Children's Bureau.

Uddin, Monica; Koenen, Karestan C.; de los Santos, Regina; Bakshis, Erin; Aiello, Allison E. & Galea, Sandro. (2010). Gender differences in the genetic and environmental determinants of adolescent depression. *Depression and Anxiety, 27*(7), 658–666. doi: 10.1002/da.20692

Ueda, Tomomi; Suzukamo, Yoshimi; Sato, Mai & Izumi, Shin-Ichi. (2013). Effects of music therapy on behavioral and psychological symptoms of dementia: A systematic review and meta-analysis. *Ageing Research Reviews, 12*(2), 628–641. doi: 10.1016/j.arr.2013.02.003

Umana-Taylor, Adriana J. & Guimond, Amy B. (2010). A longitudinal examination of parenting behaviors and perceived discrimination predicting Latino adolescents' ethnic identity. *Developmental Psychology, 46*(3), 636–650. doi: 10.1037/a0019376

Umberson, Debra; Pudrovska, Tetyana & Reczek, Corinne. (2010). Parenthood, childlessness, and well-being: A life course perspective. *Journal of Marriage and Family, 72*(3), 612–629. doi: 10.1111/j.1741-3737.2010.00721.x

Underwood, Emily. (2015). A new drug war. *Science, 347*(6221), 469–473. doi: 10.1126/science.347.6221.469

UNESCO. (2011). Institute for statistics database. Retrieved from: http://www.uis.unesco.org/Pages/default.aspx

UNICEF. (2012). *The state of the world's children 2012: Children in an urban world.* New York, NY: United Nations.

UNICEF. (2014, July). *Education: Secondary net attendance ration—Percentage.* UNICEF Global Databases. Retrieved from: http://data.unicef.org

UNICEF. (2014, October). *Low birthweight: Percentage of infants weighing less than 2,500 grams at birth.* UNICEF global databases, based on DHS, MICS, other national household surveys, data from routine reporting systems, UNICEF and WHO. Retrieved from: http://data.unicef.org/nutrition/low-birthweight

United Nations. (2013). *World population prospects: The 2012 revision, Volume 1: Comprehensive tables.* New York, NY: Department of Economic and Social Affairs, Population Division.

United Nations, Department of Economic and Social Affairs, Population Division. (2015). *World population prospects: The 2015 revision.* New York, NY.

Ursache, Alexandra; Blair, Clancy; Stifter, Cynthia & Voegtline, Kristin. (2013). Emotional reactivity and regulation in infancy interact to predict executive functioning in early childhood. *Developmental Psychology, 49*(1), 127–137. doi: 10.1037/a0027728

Uttal, William R. (2000). *The war between mentalism and behaviorism: On the accessibility of mental processes.* Mahwah, NJ: Erlbaum.

Vaillant, George E. (2002). *Aging well: Surprising guideposts to a happier life from the landmark Harvard Study of Adult Development.* Boston, MA: Little Brown.

Vaillant, George E. (2008). *Spiritual evolution: A scientific defense of faith.* New York, NY: Broadway Books.

Valdez, Carmen R.; Chavez, Tom & Woulfe, Julie. (2013). Emerging adults' lived experience of formative family stress: The family's lasting influence. *Qualitative Health Research, 23*(8), 1089–1102. doi: 10.1177/1049732313494271

Valls-Pedret, Cinta; Sala-Vila, Aleix; Serra-Mir, Mercè; Corella, Dolores; de la Torre, Rafael; Martínez-González, Miguel Ángel, . . . Ros, Emilio. (2015). Mediterranean diet and age-related cognitive decline: A randomized clinical trial. *JAMA Internal Medicine, 175*(7), 1094–1103. doi: 10.1001/jamainternmed.2015.1668

van Batenburg-Eddes, Tamara; Butte, Dick & van de Looij-Jansen, Petra. (2012). Measuring juvenile delinquency: How do self-reports compare with official police statistics? *European Journal of Criminology, 9*(1), 23–37. doi: 10.1177/1477370811421644

van de Bongardt, Daphne; Reitz, Ellen; Sandfort, Theo & Deković, Maja. (2014). A meta-analysis of the relations between three types of peer norms and adolescent sexual behavior. *Personality and Social Psychology Review.* doi: 10.1177/1088868314544223

van den Akker, Alithe; Deković, Maja; Prinzie, Peter & Asscher, Jessica. (2010). Toddlers' temperament profiles: Stability and relations to negative and positive parenting. *Journal of Abnormal Child Psychology, 38*(4), 485–495. doi: 10.1007/s10802-009-9379-0

van den Ban, Els; Souverein, Patrick; Swaab, Hanna; van Engeland, Herman; Heerdink, Rob & Egberts, Toine. (2010). Trends in incidence and characteristics of children, adolescents, and adults initiating immediate- or extended-release methylphenidate or atomoxetine in the Netherlands during 2001-2006. *Journal of Child and Adolescent Psychopharmacology, 20*(1), 55–61. doi: 10.1089/cap.2008.0153

van der Houwen, Karolijne; Stroebe, Margaret; Schut, Henk; Stroebe, Wolfgang & van den Bout, Jan. (2010). Mediating processes in bereavement: The role of rumination, threatening grief interpretations, and deliberate grief avoidance. *Social Science & Medicine, 71*(9), 1669–1676. doi: 10.1016/j.socscimed.2010.06.047

van Eeden-Moorefield, Brad & Pasley, Kay. (2013). Remarriage and stepfamily life. In Gary W. Peterson & Kevin R. Bush (Eds.), *Handbook of marriage and the family* (pp. 517–546). New York, NY: Springer. doi: 10.1007/978-1-4614-3987-5_22

van IJzendoorn, Marinus H.; Bakermans-Kranenburg, Marian J.; Pannebakker, Fieke & Out, Dorothée. (2010). In defence of situational morality: Genetic, dispositional and situational determinants of children's donating to charity. *Journal of Moral Education, 39*(1), 1–20. doi: 10.1080/03057240903528535

van IJzendoorn, Marinus H.; Palacios, Jesús; Sonuga-Barke, Edmund J. S.; Gunnar, Megan R.; Vorria, Panayiota; McCall, Robert B., . . . Juffer, Femmie. (2011). Children in institutional care: Delayed development and resilience. *Monographs of the Society for Research in Child Development, 76*(4), 8–30. doi: 10.1111/j.1540-5834.2011.00626.x

Van Petegem, Stijn; Soenens, Bart; Vansteenkiste, Maarten & Beyers, Wim. (2015). Rebels with a cause? Adolescent defiance from the perspective of reactance theory and self-determination theory. *Child Development, 86*(3), 903–918. doi: 10.1111/cdev.12355

Van Puyvelde, Martine; Vanfleteren, Pol; Loots, Gerrit; Deschuyffeleer, Sara; Vinck, Bart; Jacquet, Wolfgang & Verhelst, Werner. (2010). Tonal synchrony in mother-infant interaction based on harmonic and pentatonic series. *Infant Behavior and Development, 33*(4), 387–400. doi: 10.1016/j.infbeh.2010.04.003

van Soelen, Inge L. C.; Brouwer, Rachel M.; Peper, Jiska S.; van Beijsterveldt, Toos C. E. M.; van Leeuwen, Marieke; de Vries, Linda S., . . . Boomsma, Dorret I. (2010). Effects of gestational age and birth weight on brain volumes in healthy 9 year-old children. *The Journal of Pediatrics, 156*(6), 896–901. doi: 10.1016/j.jpeds.2009.12.052

van Tilburg, Theo G.; Aartsen, Marja J. & van der Pas, Suzan. (2015). Loneliness after divorce: A cohort comparison among Dutch young-old adults. *European Sociological Review, 31*(3), 243–252. doi: 10.1093/esr/jcu086

Varga, Mary Alice & Paletti, Robin. (2013). Life span issues and dying. In David K. Meagher & David E. Balk (Eds.), *Handbook of thanatology: The essential body of knowledge for the study of death, dying, and bereavement* (2nd ed., pp. 25–31). New York, NY: Routledge.

Vargas Lascano, Dayuma I.; Galambos, Nancy L.; Krahn, Harvey J. & Lachman, Margie E. (2015). Growth in perceived control across 25 years from the late teens to midlife: The role of personal and parents' education. *Developmental Psychology, 51*(1), 124–135. doi: 10.1037/a0038433

Varian, Frances & Cartwright, Lara. (2013). *The situational judgement test at a glance.* Hoboken, NJ: Wiley-Blackwell.

Varner, Fatima & Mandara, Jelani. (2014). Differential parenting of African American adolescents as an explanation for gender disparities in achievement. *Journal of Research on Adolescence, 24*(4), 667–680. doi: 10.1111/jora.12063

Veenstra, René; Lindenberg, Siegwart; Munniksma, Anke & Dijkstra, Jan Kornelis. (2010). The complex relation between bullying, victimization, acceptance, and rejection: Giving special attention to status, affection, and sex differences. *Child Development, 81*(2), 480–486. doi: 10.1111/j.1467-8624.2009.01411.x

Vélez, Clorinda E.; Wolchik, Sharlene A.; Tein, Jenn-Yun & Sandler, Irwin. (2011). Protecting children from the consequences of divorce: A longitudinal study of the effects of parenting on children's coping processes. *Child Development, 82*(1), 244–257. doi: 10.1111/j.1467-8624.2010.01553.x

Verbakel, Ellen & Jaspers, Eva. (2010). A comparative study on permissiveness toward euthanasia: Religiosity, slippery slope, autonomy, and death with dignity. *Public Opinion Quarterly, 74*(1), 109–139. doi: 10.1093/poq/nfp074

Verona, Sergiu. (2003). Romanian policy regarding adoptions. In Victor Littel (Ed.), *Adoption update* (pp. 5–10). New York, NY: Nova Science.

Véronneau, Marie-Hélène & Dishion, Thomas. (2010). Predicting change in early adolescent problem behavior in the middle school years: A mesosystemic perspective on parenting and peer experiences. *Journal of Abnormal Child Psychology, 38*(8), 1125–1137. doi: 10.1007/s10802-010-9431-0

Vieno, Alessio; Nation, Maury; Pastore, Massimiliano & Santinello, Massimo. (2009). Parenting and antisocial behavior: A model of the relationship between adolescent self-disclosure, parental closeness, parental control, and adolescent antisocial behavior. *Developmental Psychology, 45*(6), 1509–1519. doi: 10.1037/a0016929

Villar, Feliciano. (2012). Successful ageing and development: The contribution of generativity in older age. *Ageing and Society, 32*(7), 1087–1105. doi: 10.1017/S0144686X11000973

Villar, Feliciano & Celdrán, Montserrat. (2012). Generativity in older age: A challenge for Universities of the Third Age (U3A). *Educational Gerontology, 38*(10), 666–677. doi: 10.1080/03601277.2011.595347

Vitale, Susan; Sperduto, Robert D. & Ferris, Frederick L. (2009). Increased prevalence of myopia in the United States between 1971–1972 and 1999–2004. *Archives of Ophthalmology, 127*(12), 1632–1639. doi: 10.1001/archophthalmol.2009.303

Vladeck, Fredda & Altman, Anita. (2015). The future of the NORC-supportive service program model. *Public Policy Aging Report, 25*(1), 20–22. doi: 10.1093/ppar/pru050

Vogel, Lauren. (2011). Dying a "good death". *Canadian Medical Association Journal, 183*(18), 2089–2090. doi: 10.1503/cmaj.109-4059

Voigt, Kevin & Brown, Sophie. (2013, September 17). International adoptions in decline as number of orphans grows. *CNN.*

Volkow, Nora D. & Baler, Ruben D. (2012). To stop or not to stop? *Science, 335*(6068), 546–548. doi: 10.1126/science.1218170

Vonderheid, Susan C.; Kishi, Rieko; Norr, Kathleen F. & Klima, Carrie. (2011). Group prenatal care and doula care for pregnant women. In Arden Handler et al. (Eds.), *Reducing racial/ethnic disparities in reproductive and perinatal outcomes: The evidence from population-based interventions* (pp. 369–400). New York, NY: Springer. doi: 10.1007/978-1-4419-1499-6_15

Vong, Keang-Ieng. (2013). China: Pedagogy today and the move towards creativity. In Jan Georgeson & Jane Payler (Eds.), *International perspectives on early childhood education and care.* New York, NY: Open University Press.

Voorpostel, Marieke & Schans, Djamila. (2011). Sibling relationships in Dutch and immigrant families. *Ethnic and Racial Studies, 34*(12), 2027–2047. doi: 10.1080/01419870.2010.496490

Voosen, Paul. (2013, July 15). A brain gone bad: Researchers clear the fog of chronic head trauma. *The Chronicle Review,* B6–B10.

Vouloumanos, Athena & Werker, Janet F. (2007). Listening to language at birth: Evidence for a bias for speech in neonates. *Developmental Science, 10*(2), 159–164. doi: 10.1111/j.1467-7687.2007.00549.x

Vranić, Andrea; Španić, Ana Marija; Carretti, Barbara & Borella, Erika. (2013). The efficacy of a multifactorial memory training in older adults living in residential care settings. *International Psychogeriatrics, 25*(11), 1885–1897. doi: 10.1017/S1041610213001154

Vygotsky, Lev S. (1980). *Mind in society: The development of higher psychological processes.* Cambridge, MA: Harvard University Press.

Vygotsky, Lev S. (1994). The development of academic concepts in school aged children. In René van der Veer & Jaan Valsiner (Eds.), *The Vygotsky reader* (pp. 355–370). Cambridge, MA: Blackwell.

Waber, Deborah P.; Bryce, Cyralene P.; Fitzmaurice, Garrett M.; Zichlin, Miriam L.; McGaughy, Jill; Girard, Jonathan M. & Galler, Janina R. (2014). Neuropsychological outcomes at midlife following moderate to severe malnutrition in infancy. *Neuropsychology, 28*(4), 530–540. doi: 10.1037/neu0000058

Wagenaar, Karin; van Weissenbruch, Mirjam M.; van Leeuwen, Flora E.; Cohen-Kettenis, Peggy T.; Delemarre-van de Waal, Henriette A.; Schats, Roel & Huisman, Jaap. (2011). Self-reported behavioral and socioemotional functioning of 11- to 18-year-old adolescents conceived by in vitro fertilization. *Fertility and Sterility, 95*(2), 611–616. doi: 10.1016/j.fertnstert.2010.04.076

Wagner, Jenny; Hoppmann, Christiane; Ram, Nilam & Gerstorf, Denis. (2015). Self-esteem is relatively stable late in life: The role of resources in the health, self-regulation, and social domains. *Developmental Psychology, 51*(1), 136–149. doi: 10.1037/a0038338

Wagner, Katie; Dobkins, Karen & Barner, David. (2013). Slow mapping: Color word learning as a gradual inductive process. *Cognition, 127*(3), 307–317. doi: 10.1016/j.cognition.2013.01.010

Wagner, Laura & Lakusta, Laura. (2009). Using language to navigate the infant mind. *Perspectives on Psychological Science, 4*(2), 177–184. doi: 10.1111/j.1745-6924.2009.01117.x

Wagner, Paul A. (2011). Socio-sexual education: A practical study in formal thinking and teachable moments. *Sex Education: Sexuality, Society and Learning, 11*(2), 193–211. doi: 10.1080/14681811.2011.558427

Wahlster, Sarah; Wijdicks, Eelco F. M.; Patel, Pratik V.; Greer, David M.; Hemphill, J. Claude; Carone, Marco & Mateen, Farrah J. (2015). Brain death declaration: Practices and perceptions worldwide. *Neurology, 84*(18), 1870–1879. doi: 10.1212/WNL.0000000000001540

Wahlstrom, Kyla L. (2002). Accommodating the sleep patterns of adolescents within current educational structures: An uncharted path. In Mary A. Carskadon (Ed.), *Adolescent sleep patterns: Biological, social, and psychological influences* (pp. 172–197). New York, NY: Cambridge University Press.

Wahrendorf, Morten; Blane, David; Bartley, Mel; Dragano, Nico & Siegrist, Johannes. (2013). Working conditions in mid-life and mental health in older ages. *Advances in Life Course Research, 18*(1), 16–25. doi: 10.1016/j.alcr.2012.10.004

Waldinger, Robert J. & Schulz, Marc S. (2010). What's love got to do with it? Social functioning, perceived health, and daily happiness in married octogenarians. *Psychology and Aging, 25*(2), 422–431. doi: 10.1037/a0019087

Walhovd, Kristine B.; Tamnes, Christian K. & Fjell, Anders M. (2014). Brain structural maturation and the foundations of cognitive behavioral development. *Current Opinion in Neurology, 27*(2), 176–184. doi: 10.1097/WCO.0000000000000074

Walker, Alan. (2012). The new ageism. *The Political Quarterly, 83*(4), 812–819. doi: 10.1111/j.1467-923X.2012.02360.x

Walker, Alan. (2015). Active ageing: Realising its potential. *Australasian Journal on Ageing, 34*(1), 2–8. doi: 10.1111/ajag.12219

Walle, Eric A. & Campos, Joseph J. (2014). Infant language development is related to the acquisition of walking. *Developmental Psychology, 50*(2), 336–348. doi: 10.1037/a0033238

Waller, Erika M. & Rose, Amanda J. (2010). Adjustment trade-offs of co-rumination in mother-adolescent relationships. *Journal of Adolescence, 33*(3), 487–497. doi: 10.1016/j.adolescence.2009.06.002

Wallis, Claudia. (2014). Gut reactions: Intestinal bacteria may help determine whether we are lean or obese. *Scientific American, 310*(6), 30–33. doi: 10.1038/scientificamerican0614-30

Wambach, Karen & Riordan, Jan. (2014). *Breastfeeding and human lactation* (5th ed.). Burlington, MA: Jones & Bartlett Publishers.

Wanberg, Connie R. (2012). The individual experience of unemployment. *Annual Review of Psychology, 63,* 369–396. doi: 10.1146/annurev-psych-120710-100500

Wang, Chao; Xue, Haifeng; Wang, Qianqian; Hao, Yongchen; Li, Dianjiang; Gu, Dongfeng & Huang, Jianfeng. (2014). Effect of drinking on all-cause mortality in women compared with men: A meta-analysis. *Journal of Women's Health, 23*(5). doi: 10.1089/jwh.2013.4414

Wang, Hua & Wellman, Barry. (2010). Social connectivity in America: Changes in adult friendship network size from 2002 to 2007. *American Behavioral Scientist, 53*(8), 1148–1169. doi: 10.1177/0002764209356247

Wang, Jingyun & Candy, T. Rowan. (2010). The sensitivity of the 2- to 4-month-old human infant accommodation system. *Investigative Ophthalmology and Visual Science, 51*(6), 3309–3317. doi: 10.1167/iovs.09-4667

Wanrooij, Vera H. M.; Willeboordse, Maartje; Dompeling, Edward & van de Kant, Kim D. G. (2014). Exercise training in children with asthma: A systematic review. *British Journal of Sports Medicine, 48*(13), 1024–1031. doi: 10.1136/bjsports-2012-091347

Ward, L. Monique; Epstein, Marina; Caruthers, Allison & Merriwether, Ann. (2011). Men's media use, sexual cognitions, and sexual risk behavior: Testing a mediational model. *Developmental Psychology, 47*(2), 592–602. doi: 10.1037/a0022669

Warner, Lisa M.; Wolff, Julia K.; Ziegelmann, Jochen P. & Wurm, Susanne. (2014). A randomized controlled trial to promote volunteering in older adults. *Psychology and Aging, 29*(4), 757–763. doi: 10.1037/a0036486

Watson, John B. (1928). *Psychological care of infant and child.* New York, NY: Norton.

Watson, John B. (1998). *Behaviorism.* New Brunswick, NJ: Transaction.

Webber, Douglas A. (2015). *Are college costs worth it?: How individual ability, major choice, and debt affect optimal schooling decisions.* Bonn, Germany: Institute for the Study of Labor.

Webster, Collin A. & Suzuki, Naoki. (2014). Land of the rising pulse: A social ecological perspective of physical activity opportunities for schoolchildren in Japan. *Journal of Teaching in Physical Education, 33*(3), 304–325. doi: 10.1123/jtpe.2014-0003

Weening-Dijksterhuis, Elizabeth & de Greef, Mathieu H. G. (2011). Frail institutionalized older persons: A comprehensive review on physical exercise, physical fitness, activities of daily living, and quality-of-life. *American Journal of Physical Medicine & Rehabilitation, 90*(2), 156–168. doi: 10.1097/PHM.0b013e3181f703ef

Wei, Si. (2013). A multitude of people singing together. *International Journal of Community Music, 6*(2), 183–188. doi: 10.1386/ijcm.6.2.183_1

Weinstein, Netta & DeHaan, Cody. (2014). On the mutuality of human motivation and relationships. In Netta Weinstein (Ed.), *Human motivation and interpersonal relationships: Theory, research, and applications* (pp. 3–25). New York, NY: Springer. doi: 10.1007/978-94-017-8542-6_1

Weintraub, Daniel; Raskin, Allen; Ruskin, Paul E.; Gruber-Baldini, Ann L.; Zimmerman, Sheryl Itkin; Hebel, J. Richard, . . . Magaziner, Jay. (2000). Racial differences in the prevalence of dementia among patients admitted to nursing homes. *Psychiatric Services, 51*(10), 1259–1264. doi: 10.1176/appi.ps.51.10.1259

Weiss, Nicole H.; Tull, Matthew T.; Lavender, Jason & Gratz, Kim L. (2013). Role of emotion dysregulation in the relationship between childhood abuse and probable PTSD in a sample of substance abusers. *Child Abuse & Neglect, 37*(11), 944–954. doi: 10.1016/j.chiabu.2013.03.014

Weiss, Noel S. & Koepsell, Thomas D. (2014). *Epidemiologic methods: Studying the occurrence of illness* (2nd ed.). New York, NY: Oxford University Press.

Wellman, Henry M.; Fang, Fuxi & Peterson, Candida C. (2011). Sequential progressions in a theory-of-mind scale: Longitudinal perspectives. *Child Development, 82*(3), 780–792. doi: 10.1111/j.1467-8624.2011.01583.x

Wen, Xiaoli; Elicker, James G. & McMullen, Mary B. (2011). Early childhood teachers' curriculum beliefs: Are they consistent with observed classroom practices? *Early Education & Development, 22*(6), 945–969. doi: 10.1080/10409289.2010.507495

Wendelken, Carter; Baym, Carol L.; Gazzaley, Adam & Bunge, Silvia A. (2011). Neural indices of improved attentional modulation over middle childhood. *Developmental Cognitive Neuroscience, 1*(2), 175–186. doi: 10.1016/j.dcn.2010.11.001

Wenner, Melinda. (2009). The serious need for play. *Scientific American Mind, 20*(1), 22–29. doi: 10.1038/scientificamerican-mind0209-22

Werner, Nicole E. & Hill, Laura G. (2010). Individual and peer group normative beliefs about relational aggression. *Child Development, 81*(3), 826–836. doi: 10.1111/j.1467-8624.2010.01436.x

Wertsch, James V. & Tulviste, Peeter. (2005). L. S. Vygotsky and contemporary developmental psychology. In Harry Daniels (Ed.), *An introduction to Vygotsky.* New York, NY: Routledge.

Westphal, Sarah Katharina; Poortman, Anne-Rigt & Van der Lippe, Tanja. (2015). What about the grandparents? Children's postdivorce residence arrangements and contact with grandparents. *Journal of Marriage and Family, 77*(2), 424–440. doi: 10.1111/jomf.12173

Whalley, Lawrence J.; Duthie, Susan J.; Collins, Andrew R.; Starr, John M.; Deary, Ian J.; Lemmon, Helen, . . . Staff, Roger T. (2014). Homocysteine, antioxidant micronutrients and late onset dementia. *European Journal of Nutrition, 53*(1), 277–285. doi: 10.1007/s00394-013-0526-6

Whitbourne, Susan K. & Whitbourne, Stacey B. (2011). *Adult development and aging: Biopsychosocial perspectives* (4th ed.). Hoboken, NJ: Wiley.

Whitfield, Keith E. & McClearn, Gerald. (2005). Genes, environment, and race: Quantitative genetic approaches. *American Psychologist, 60*(1), 104–114. doi: 10.1037/0003-066X.60.1.104

Wicher, Camille P. & Meeker, Mary Ann. (2012). What influences African American end-of-life preferences? *Journal of Health Care for the Poor and Underserved, 23*(1), 28–58. doi: 10.1353/hpu.2012.0027

Wickrama, K. A. S.; O'Neal, Catherine Walker & Lorenz, Fred O. (2013). Marital functioning from middle to later years: A life course–stress process framework. *Journal of Family Theory & Review, 5*(1), 15–34. doi: 10.1111/jftr.12000

Widman, Laura; Choukas-Bradley, Sophia; Helms, Sarah W.; Golin, Carol E. & Prinstein, Mitchell J. (2014). Sexual communication between early adolescents and their dating partners, parents, and best friends. *The Journal of Sex Research, 51*(7), 731–741. doi: 10.1080/00224499.2013.843148

Widom, Cathy S.; Horan, Jacqueline & Brzustowicz, Linda. (2015). Childhood maltreatment predicts allostatic load in adulthood. *Child Abuse & Neglect, (47),* 59–69. doi: 10.1016/j.chiabu.2015.01.016

Wiik, Kenneth Aarskaug; Keizer, Renske & Lappegård, Trude. (2012). Relationship quality in marital and cohabiting unions across Europe. *Journal of Marriage and Family, 74*(3), 389–398. doi: 10.1111/j.1741-3737.2012.00967.x

Wijdicks, Eelco F. M.; Varelas, Panayiotis N.; Gronseth, Gary S. & Greer, David M. (2010). Evidence-based guideline update: Determining brain death in adults; Report of the quality standards subcommittee of the American Academy of Neurology. *Neurology, 74*(23), 1911–1918. doi: 10.1212/WNL.0b013e3181e242a8

Wilcox, W. Bradford (Ed.). (2011). *The sustainable demographic dividend: What do marriage and fertility have to do with the economy?* New York, NY: Social Trends Institute.

Wilhelm, Miriam; Dahl, Edgar; Alexander, Henry; Brähler, Elmar & Stöbel-Richter, Yve. (2013). Ethical attitudes of German specialists in reproductive medicine and legal regulation of preimplantation sex selection in Germany. *PloS, 8*(2), e56390. doi: 10.1371/journal.pone.0056390

Wilkinson, Stephen. (2015). Prenatal screening, reproductive choice, and public health. *Bioethics, 29*(1), 26–35. doi: 10.1111/bioe.12121

Williams, Kristine N.; Herman, Ruth; Gajewski, Byron & Wilson, Kristel. (2009). Elderspeak communication: Impact on dementia care. *American Journal of Alzheimer's Disease and Other Dementias, 24*(1), 11–20. doi: 10.1177/1533317508318472

Williams, Lela Rankin; Fox, Nathan A.; Lejuez, C. W.; Reynolds, Elizabeth K.; Henderson, Heather A.; Perez-Edgar, Koraly E., . . . Pine, Daniel S. (2010). Early temperament, propensity for risk-taking and adolescent substance-related problems: A prospective multi-method investigation. *Addictive Behaviors, 35*(2), 1148–1151. doi: 10.1016/j.addbeh.2010.07.005

Williams, Preston. (2009, March 5). Teens might need to sleep more, but schools have to work efficiently. *The Washington Post,* p. LZ10.

Willoughby, Michael T.; Mills-Koonce, W. Roger; Gottfredson, Nisha C. & Wagner, Nicholas J. (2014). Measuring callous unemotional behaviors in early childhood: Factor structure and the prediction of stable aggression in middle childhood. *Journal of Psychopathology and Behavioral Assessment, 36*(1), 30–42. doi: 10.1007/s10862-013-9379-9

Wilmshurst, Linda. (2011). *Child and adolescent psychopathology: A casebook* (2nd ed.). Thousand Oaks, CA: Sage.

Windhorst, Dafna A.; Mileva-Seitz, Viara R.; Linting, Mariëlle; Hofman, Albert; Jaddoe, Vincent W. V.; Verhulst, Frank C., . . . Bakermans-Kranenburg, Marian J. (2015). Differential susceptibility in a developmental perspective: DRD4 and maternal sensitivity predicting externalizing behavior. *Developmental Psychobiology, 57*(1), 35–49. doi: 10.1002/dev.21257

Winter, Suzanne M. (2011). Culture, health, and school readiness. In DeAnna M. Laverick & Mary Renck Jalongo (Eds.), *Transitions to early care and education* (Vol. 4, pp. 117–133). New York, NY: Springer. doi: 10.1007/978-94-007-0573-9_11

Wolchik, Sharlene A.; Ma, Yue; Tein, Jenn-Yun; Sandler, Irwin N. & Ayers, Tim S. (2008). Parentally bereaved children's grief: Self-system beliefs as mediators of the relations between grief and stressors and caregiver-child relationship quality. *Death Studies, 32*(7), 597–620. doi: 10.1080/07481180802215551

Wolenberg, Kelly M.; Yoon, John D.; Rasinski, Kenneth A. & Curlin, Farr A. (2013). Religion and United States physicians' opinions and self-predicted practices concerning artificial nutrition and hydration. *Journal of Religion and Health, 52*(4), 1051–1065. doi: 10.1007/s10943-013-9740-z

Wolf, Norman S. (Ed.). (2010). *Comparative biology of aging.* New York, NY: Springer.

Wolfe, Christy D.; Zhang, Jing; Kim-Spoon, Jungmeen & Bell, Martha Ann. (2014). A longitudinal perspective on the association between cognition and temperamental shyness. *International Journal of Behavioral Development, 38*(3), 266–276. doi: 10.1177/0165025413516257

Wolff, Mary S.; Teitelbaum, Susan; McGovern, K.; Windham, Gayle C.; Pinney, Susan M.; Galvez, Maida P., . . . Biro, Frank M. (2014). Phthalate exposure and pubertal development in a longitudinal study of US girls. *Human Reproduction, 29*(7), 1558–1566. doi: 10.1093/humrep/deu081

Wong, Jaclyn S. & Waite, Linda J. (2015). Marriage, social networks, and health at older ages. *Journal of Population Ageing, 8*(1/2), 7–25. doi: 10.1007/s12062-014-9110-y

Wong, Paul T. P. & Tomer, Adrian. (2011). Beyond terror and denial: The positive psychology of death acceptance. *Death Studies, 35*(2), 99–106. doi: 10.1080/07481187.2011.535377

Wongtongkam, Nualnong; Ward, Paul R.; Day, Andrew & Winefield, Anthony H. (2015). Exploring family and community involvement to protect Thai youths from alcohol and illegal drug abuse. *Journal of Addictive Diseases, 34*(1), 112–121. doi: 10.1080/10550887.2014.975616

Woodward, Amanda L. & Markman, Ellen M. (1998). Early word learning. In Deanna Kuhn & Robert S. Siegler (Eds.), *Handbook of child psychology* (5th ed., Vol. 2, pp. 371–420). Hoboken, NJ: Wiley.

Woollett, Katherine; Spiers, Hugo J. & Maguire, Eleanor A. (2009). Talent in the taxi: A model system for exploring expertise. *Philosophical Transactions of the Royal Society of London, 364*(1522), 1407–1416. doi: 10.1098/rstb.2008.0288

Woolley, Jacqueline D. & Ghossainy, Maliki E. (2013). Revisiting the fantasy–reality distinction: Children as naïve skeptics. *Child Development, 84*(5), 1496–1510. doi: 10.1111/cdev.12081

World Bank. (2015). *Population estimates and projections: Fertility and mortality by country.* Retrieved from: http://datatopics.worldbank.org/hnp/popestimates#

World Health Organization. (2006). WHO Motor Development Study: Windows of achievement for six gross motor development milestones. *Acta Paediatrica, 95*(Suppl. 450), 86–95. doi: 10.1111/j.1651-2227.2006.tb02379.x

World Health Organization. (2010). WHO global infobase: NCD indicators. https://apps.who.int/infobase/Indicators.aspx

World Health Organization. (2011). *Global recommendations on physical activity for health: Information sheet: global recommendations on physical activity for health 5—17 years old.* Geneva, Switzerland: World Health Organization.

World Health Organization. (2013). *World health statistics 2013.* Geneva, Switzerland: World Health Organization.

World Health Organization. (2014). *Infant and young child feeding data by country.* Retrieved from: http://www.who.int/nutrition/databases/infantfeeding/countries/en/

World Health Organization. (2015). *First WHO ministerial conference on global action against dementia.* Geneva, Switzerland: World Health Organization.

Worthy, Darrell A.; Gorlick, Marissa A.; Pacheco, Jennifer L.; Schnyer, David M. & Maddox, W. Todd. (2011). With age comes wisdom: Decision making in younger and older adults. *Psychological Science, 22*(11), 1375–1380. doi: 10.1177/0956797611420301

Wosje, Karen S.; Khoury, Philip R.; Claytor, Randal P.; Copeland, Kristen A.; Hornung, Richard W.; Daniels, Stephen R. & Kalkwarf, Heidi J. (2010). Dietary patterns associated with fat and bone mass in young children. *American Journal of Clinical Nutrition, 92*(2), 294–303. doi: 10.3945/ajcn.2009.28925

Wrzus, Cornelia; Hänel, Martha; Wagner, Jenny & Neyer, Franz J. (2013). Social network changes and life events across the life span: A meta-analysis. *Psychological Bulletin, 139*(1), 53–80. doi: 10.1037/a0028601

Wu, Pai-Lu & Chiou, Wen-Bin. (2008). Postformal thinking and creativity among late adolescents: A post-Piagetian approach. *Adolescence, 43*(170), 237–251.

Wurm, Susanne; Tomasik, Martin & Tesch-Römer, Clemens. (2008). Serious health events and their impact on changes in subjective health and life satisfaction: The role of age and a positive view on ageing. *European Journal of Ageing, 5*(2), 117–127. doi: 10.1007/s10433-008-0077-5

Xu, Fei. (2013). The object concept in human infants: Commentary on Fields. *Human Development, 56*(3), 167–170. doi: 10.1159/000351279

Xu, Fei & Kushnir, Tamar. (2013). Infants are rational constructivist learners. *Current Directions in Psychological Science, 22*(1), 28–32. doi: 10.1177/0963721412469396

Xu, Yaoying. (2010). Children's social play sequence: Parten's classic theory revisited. *Early Child Development and Care, 180*(4), 489–498. doi: 10.1080/03004430802090430

Yadav, Priyanka; Banwari, Girish; Parmar, Chirag & Maniar, Rajesh. (2013). Internet addiction and its correlates among high school students: A preliminary study from Ahmedabad, India. *Asian Journal of Psychiatry, 6*(6), 500–505. doi: 10.1016/j.ajp.2013.06.004

Yang, Rongwang; Zhang, Suhan; Li, Rong & Zhao, Zhengyan. (2013). Parents' attitudes toward stimulants use in China. *Journal of Developmental & Behavioral Pediatrics, 34*(3), 225. doi: 10.1097/DBP.0b013e318287cc27

Ybarra, Michele L. & Mitchell, Kimberly J. (2014). "Sexting" and its relation to sexual activity and sexual risk behavior in a national survey of adolescents. *Journal of Adolescent Health, 55*(6), 757–764. doi: 10.1016/j.jadohealth.2014.07.012

Yeung, Wei-Jun Jean & Alipio, Cheryll. (2013). Transitioning to adulthood in Asia: School, work, and family life. *The ANNALS of the American Academy of Political and Social Science, 646*(1), 6–27. doi: 10.1177/0002716212470794

Yıkılkan, Hülya; Aypak, Cenk & Görpelioğlu, Süleyman. (2014). Depression, anxiety and quality of life in caregivers of long-term home care patients. *Archives of Psychiatric Nursing, 28*(3), 193–196. doi: 10.1016/j.apnu.2014.01.001

Yom-Tov, Elad; Fernandez-Luque, Luis; Weber, Ingmar & Crain, Steven P. (2012). Pro-anorexia and pro-recovery photo sharing: A tale of two warring tribes. *Journal of Medical Internet Research, 14*(6), e151. doi: 10.2196/jmir.2239

Yoshikawa, Hirokazu; Leyva, Diana; Snow, Catherine E.; Treviño, Ernesto; Barata, M. Clara; Weiland, Christina, . . . Arbour, Mary Catherine. (2015). Experimental impacts of a teacher professional development program in Chile on preschool classroom quality and child outcomes. *Developmental Psychology, 51*(3), 309–322. doi: 10.1037/a0038785

Yurovsky, Daniel; Fricker, Damian C.; Yu, Chen & Smith, Linda B. (2014). The role of partial knowledge in statistical word learning. *Psychonomic Bulletin & Review, 21*(1), 1–22. doi: 10.3758/s13423-013-0443-y

Zachry, Anne H. & Kitzmann, Katherine M. (2011). Caregiver awareness of prone play recommendations. *American Journal of Occupational Therapy, 65*(1), 101–105. doi: 10.5014/ajot.2011.09100

Zagheni, Emilio; Zannella, Marina; Movsesyan, Gabriel & Wagner, Brittney. (2015). Time is economically valuable: Production, consumption and transfers of time by age and sex. In Emilio Zagheni et al. (Eds.), *A comparative analysis of European time transfers between generations and genders* (pp. 19–33). New York, NY: Springer. doi: 10.1007/978-94-017-9591-3_2

Zak, Paul J. (2012). *The moral molecule: The source of love and prosperity.* New York, NY: Dutton.

Zalenski, Robert J. & Raspa, Richard. (2006). Maslow's hierarchy of needs: A framework for achieving human potential in hospice. *Journal of Palliative Medicine, 9*(5), 1120–1127. doi: 10.1089/jpm.2006.9.1120

Zatorre, Robert J. (2013). Predispositions and plasticity in music and speech learning: Neural correlates and implications. *Science, 342*(6158), 585–589. doi: 10.1126/science.1238414

Zatorre, Robert J.; Fields, R. Douglas & Johansen-Berg, Heidi. (2012). Plasticity in gray and white: Neuroimaging changes in brain structure during learning. *Nature Neuroscience, 15,* 528–536. doi: 10.1038/nn.3045

Zavos, Helena M. S.; Gregory, Alice M. & Eley, Thalia C. (2012). Longitudinal genetic analysis of anxiety sensitivity. *Developmental Psychology, 48*(1), 204–212. doi: 10.1037/a0024996

Zayas, Vivian; Mischel, Walter; Shoda, Yuichi & Aber, J. Lawrence. (2011). Roots of adult attachment: Maternal caregiving at 18 months predicts adult peer and partner attachment. *Social Psychological and Personality Science, 2*(3), 289–297. doi: 10.1177/1948550610389822

Zbuk, Kevin & Anand, Sonia S. (2012). Declining incidence of breast cancer after decreased use of hormone-replacement therapy: Magnitude and time lags in different countries. *Journal of Epidemiol Community Health, 66*(1), 1–7. doi: 10.1136/jech.2008.083774

Zeanah, Charles H.; Berlin, Lisa J. & Boris, Neil W. (2011). Practitioner review: Clinical applications of attachment theory and research for infants and young children. *Journal of Child Psychology and Psychiatry, 52*(8), 819–833. doi: 10.1111/j.1469-7610.2011.02399.x

Zehr, Mary Ann. (2011). Study stings KIPP on attrition rates. *Education Week, 30*(27), 1, 24–25.

Zeiders, Katharine H.; Umaña-Taylor, Adriana J. & Derlan, Chelsea L. (2013). Trajectories of depressive symptoms and self-esteem in Latino youths: Examining the role of gender and perceived discrimination. *Developmental Psychology, 49*(5), 951–963. doi: 10.1037/a0028866

Zeifman, Debra M. (2013). Built to bond: Coevolution, coregulation, and plasticity in parent-infant bonds. In Cindy Hazan & Mary I. Campa (Eds.), *Human bonding: The science of affectional ties* (pp. 41–73). New York, NY: Guilford Press.

Zeng, Rong & Greenfield, Patricia M. (2015). Cultural evolution over the last 40 years in China: Using the Google Ngram Viewer to study implications of social and political change for cultural values. *International Journal of Psychology, 50*(1), 47–55. doi: 10.1002/ijop.12125

Zentall, Shannon R. & Morris, Bradley J. (2010). "Good job, you're so smart": The effects of inconsistency of praise type on young children's motivation. *Journal of Experimental Child Psychology, 107*(2), 155–163. doi: 10.1016/j.jecp.2010.04.015

Zhang, Baohui; Wright, Alexi A.; Huskamp, Haiden A.; Nilsson, Matthew E.; Maciejewski, Matthew L.; Earle, Craig C., . . . Prigerson, Holly G. (2009). Health care costs in the last week of life: Associations with end-of-life conversations. *Archives of Internal Medicine, 169*(5), 480–488. doi: 10.1001/archinternmed.2008.587

Zhang, Xin; Yeung, Dannii Y.; Fung, Helene H. & Lang, Frieder R. (2011). Changes in peripheral social partners and loneliness over time: The moderating role of interdependence. *Psychology and Aging, 26*(4), 823–829. doi: 10.1037/a0023674

Zhao, Jinxia & Wang, Meifang. (2014). Mothers' academic involvement and children's achievement: Children's theory of intelligence as a mediator. *Learning and Individual Differences, 35,* 130–136. doi: 10.1016/j.lindif.2014.06.006

Zhou, Dongming; Lebel, Catherine; Evans, Alan & Beaulieu, Christian. (2013). Cortical thickness asymmetry from childhood to older adulthood. *NeuroImage, 83,* 66–74. doi: 10.1016/j.neuroimage.2013.06.073

Zhu, Qi; Song, Yiying; Hu, Siyuan; Li, Xiaobai; Tian, Moqian; Zhen, Zonglei, . . . Liu, Jia. (2010). Heritability of the specific cognitive ability of face perception. *Current Biology, 20*(2), 137–142. doi: 10.1016/j.cub.2009.11.067

Zhu, Weimo; Boiarskaia, Elena A.; Welk, Gregory J. & Meredith, Marilu D. (2010). Physical education and school contextual factors relating to students' achievement and cross-grade differences in aerobic fitness and obesity. *Research Quarterly for Exercise and Sport, 81*(Suppl. 3), S53–S64. doi: 10.5641/027013610X13100547898194

Zhu, Ying; Zhang, Li; Fan, Jin & Han, Shihui. (2007). Neural basis of cultural influence on self-representation. *NeuroImage, 34*(3), 1310–1316. doi: 10.1016/j.neuroimage.2006.08.047

Zimmer-Gembeck, Melanie J. & Collins, W. Andrew. (2003). Autonomy development during adolescence. In Gerald R. Adams & Michael D. Berzonsky (Eds.), *Blackwell handbook of adolescence* (pp. 175–204). Malden, MA: Blackwell.

Zimmer-Gembeck, Melanie J. & Ducat, Wendy. (2010). Positive and negative romantic relationship quality: Age, familiarity, attachment and well-being as correlates of couple agreement and projection. *Journal of Adolescence, 33*(6), 879–890. doi: 10.1016/j.adolescence.2010.07.008

Zimmerman, Marc A.; Stoddard, Sarah A.; Eisman, Andria B.; Caldwell, Cleopatra H.; Aiyer, Sophie M. & Miller, Alison. (2013). Adolescent resilience: Promotive factors that inform prevention. *Child Development Perspectives, 7*(4), 215–220. doi: 10.1111/cdep.12042

Zimmermann, Camilla. (2012). Acceptance of dying: A discourse analysis of palliative care literature. *Social Science & Medicine, 75*(1), 217–224. doi: 10.1016/j.socscimed.2012.02.047

Zinzow, Heidi M. & Thompson, Martie. (2015). Factors associated with use of verbally coercive, incapacitated, and forcible sexual assault tactics in a longitudinal study of college men. *Aggressive Behavior,* (In Press). doi: 10.1002/AB.21567

Zolotor, Adam J. (2014). Corporal punishment. *Pediatric Clinics of North America, 61*(5), 971–978. doi: 10.1016/j.pcl.2014.06.003

Zosuls, Kristina M.; Martin, Carol Lynn; Ruble, Diane N.; Miller, Cindy F.; Gaertner, Bridget M.; England, Dawn E. & Hill, Alison P. (2011). "It's not that we hate you": Understanding children's gender attitudes and expectancies about peer relationships. *British Journal of Developmental Psychology, 29*(2), 288–304. doi: 10.1111/j.2044-835X.2010.02023.x

Zucker, Kenneth J.; Cohen-Kettenis, Peggy T.; Drescher, Jack; Meyer-Bahlburg, Heino F. L.; Pfäfflin, Friedemann & Womack, William M. (2013). Memo outlining evidence for change for Gender Identity Disorder in the DSM-5. *Archives of Sexual Behavior, 42*(5), 901–914. doi: 10.1007/s10508-013-0139-4

Subject Index